EDUCATION LAW, POLICY, AND PRACTICE

ASPEN PUBLISHERS

EDUCATION LAW, POLICY, AND PRACTICE

Cases and Materials

Second Edition

Michael J. Kaufman, *J.D.*

Dean for Academic Affairs, Director of Childlaw and Education Institute and Professor of Law

Loyola University of Chicago School of Law

With

Sherelyn R. Kaufman, *J.D, M.A., in Teaching, C.A.S. in Early Childhood Administration*

Wolters Kluwer
Law & Business

AUSTIN BOSTON CHICAGO NEW YORK THE NETHERLANDS

Aspen Publishers
Attn: Permissions Department
76 Ninth Avenue, 7th Floor
New York, NY 10011-5201

To contact Customer Care, e-mail customer.care@aspenpublishers.com, call 1-800-234-1660, fax 1-800-901-9075, or mail correspondence to:

Aspen Publishers
Attn: Order Department
PO Box 990
Frederick, MD 21705

Printed in the United States of America.

1 2 3 4 5 6 7 8 9 0

ISBN 978-07355-7807-4

Library of Congress Cataloging-in-Publication Data

Kaufman, Michael J., 1958-
Education law, policy, and practice : cases and materials / Michael J. Kaufman with Sherelyn R. Kaufman. — 2nd ed.
p. cm.
ISBN 978-0-7355-7807-4 (alk. paper)
1. Educational law and legislation—United States. I. Kaufman, Sherelyn R., 1957- II. Title.

KF4118.K38 2009
344.73′071—dc22

2008055700

About Wolters Kluwer Law & Business

Wolters Kluwer Law & Business is a leading provider of research information and workflow solutions in key specialty areas. The strengths of the individual brands of Aspen Publishers, CCH, Kluwer Law International and Loislaw are aligned within Wolters Kluwer Law & Business to provide comprehensive, in-depth solutions and expert-authored content for the legal, professional and education markets.

CCH was founded in 1913 and has served more than four generations of business professionals and their clients. The CCH products in the Wolters Kluwer Law & Business group are highly regarded electronic and print resources for legal, securities, antitrust and trade regulation, government contracting, banking, pension, payroll, employment and labor, and healthcare reimbursement and compliance professionals.

Aspen Publishers is a leading information provider for attorneys, business professionals and law students. Written by preeminent authorities, Aspen products offer analytical and practical information in a range of specialty practice areas from securities law and intellectual property to mergers and acquisitions and pension/ benefits. Aspen's trusted legal education resources provide professors and students with high-quality, up-to-date and effective resources for successful instruction and study in all areas of the law.

Kluwer Law International supplies the global business community with comprehensive English-language international legal information. Legal practitioners, corporate counsel and business executives around the world rely on the Kluwer Law International journals, loose-leafs, books and electronic products for authoritative information in many areas of international legal practice.

Loislaw is a premier provider of digitized legal content to small law firm practitioners of various specializations. Loislaw provides attorneys with the ability to quickly and efficiently find the necessary legal information they need, when and where they need it, by facilitating access to primary law as well as state-specific law, records, forms and treatises.

Wolters Kluwer Law & Business, a unit of Wolters Kluwer, is headquartered in New York and Riverwoods, Illinois. Wolters Kluwer is a leading multinational publisher and information services company.

To our parents and for our children

SUMMARY OF CONTENTS

CONTENTS

SECTION VI THE RIGHTS AND RESPONSIBILITIES OF TEACHERS 855

17 The Constitutional and Statutory Rights of Teachers 857

PREFACE TO THE SECOND EDITION

What makes a "good" education law class? The class should engage students on at least three interdependent levels. First, the students should be exposed to the meaningful constitutional, statutory, and judicial authorities that shape basic education law doctrine. Second, the students should develop practical skills and professional judgment that will enable them to apply the legal doctrine to situations presented to them by persons trusting in their counsel. Third, the students should be encouraged to examine and reexamine the fundamental political and philosophic assumptions underlying education law. Educational best practices also indicate that a good law school or graduate school class is one in which students are allowed to participate in shaping their own learning, to experiment with alternative instructional methods that reflect their multiple learning styles and intelligences and to have the comfort and freedom to analyze critically the values underlying commonly accepted procedures and standards.

This book is designed to facilitate a "good" education law class. Its objective is to empower, engage, and inspire students to integrate education law, policy, and practice. The Second Edition includes carefully edited versions of the latest and most significant Supreme Court, lower federal court, and state court decisions interpreting the constitutional and statutory provisions governing American education. The cases have been organized to permit students to track the evolution of legal standards in each area of education law. Significant and provocative dissenting opinions are included as well. Students are encouraged to analyze these authorities critically and to reconcile and evaluate competing judicial perspectives.

The text also raises "real world" questions, hypotheticals, and practicums designed to push the students into applying the settled law in difficult, unsettled situations. Each chapter places the student into the various roles assumed by stakeholders in the education process, including students, taxpayers, legislators, educators, administrators, school board members, financial planners, union representatives and, of course, lawyers. The practical situations created by the book require students to balance the interests of these stakeholders in an environment invariably characterized by scarce educational resources. They also invite the students to hone their counseling, drafting, negotiating, litigating and even strategic planning skills.

Throughout its chapters, the book cajoles its readers to return to first principles. The book begins by asking whether the legal and political structure governing American education facilitates or inhibits "good" schools. That question never goes away. The opening sections are devoted to educational philosophy so that the students will be able to examine the philosophic assumptions underlying education law and policy throughout the entire book and throughout an entire education law course. This Edition also provides an international and comparative law perspective on the major legal and political questions facing American education. The materials in the text give students the tools to understand the moral authority supporting principles of American education law, but they also challenge students to develop the intellectual autonomy to question that authority.

The topic of education law certainly lends itself to such fundamental questions. The subject is always current. This Second Edition thus includes authorities addressing controversial issues such as racial desegregation, the Pledge of Allegiance, vouchers, school choice, school prayer, affirmative action, gender discrimination, inadequate and inequitable school funding, access to preschool, teacher rights and responsibilities, student rights and responsibilities, student harassment and speech codes, federalism, local control, school governance, special education, and the No Child Left Behind legislation.

Yet, the book also raises issues that resonate in the heart and soul of every student. Law students and graduate students inevitably arrive at their education law course with a wealth of personal experience. They understand what makes a "good" school from their own lives. The materials in the text are designed to encourage the students to draw on their own diverse experiences to create a lively debate about the legal and political structure of American schools.

As American education moves well beyond the fiftieth anniversary of *Brown v. Board of Education,* 347 U.S. 483 (1954), we should be ever-mindful of the Supreme Court's recognition that:

> education is perhaps the most important function of state and local governments. . . . It is required in the performance of our most basic public responsibilities, even service in the armed forces. It is the very foundation of good citizenship. Today it is the principal instrument in awakening the child to cultural values, in preparing

> him for later professional training, and in helping him to adjust normally to his environment. In these days, it is doubtful that any child may reasonably be expected to succeed in life, if he is denied the opportunity of an education.

347 U.S. at 493.

If education is perhaps the most important governmental function, then the law governing education is perhaps the most important legal subject. This book was born out of our profound respect for the subject of education law and for the students who will explore its materials. We sincerely hope that the book will help to awaken students to the task of shaping a legal and political structure conducive to the development of a nation of "good" schools.

Michael J. Kaufman
Sherelyn R. Kaufman

2009

ACKNOWLEDGMENTS

The authors first thank the extraordinary educators who inspired them to write this book, particularly Cindy McPherson, Jean Piaget, Patricia Polacco, Norman Amaker, Judge Nathaniel R. Jones, Francis Allen, George Anastaplo, Nina S. Appel, James P. Carey, Diane Geraghty, Alan Raphael, Lowell Sachnoff, Jack Block, Richard Conviser, William Shapiro, Harry Clor, Ronald Sharp, Peter Rutkoff, Jeffrey Gilbert, Brian Roche, Barry Rosen, Sarah Wolff, Penny Spencer, James Hayes, Kathleen McGrath, Cathy Tough Tamarri, Lisa Makoul, Dolores Kohl, Svetlana Budilovsky, Lella Gandini, Rebekah F. Kaufman, Cathy Fishbain Brown, and Barbara F. Rubin.

We thank as well for their wisdom and guidance regarding education law and policy: United States Department of Education, Office for Civil Rights, directors and attorneys, especially Kenneth A. Mines and John Fry; elected school board members and public servants, Rebecca Baim, Joan Herczeg, Debbie Hymen, Michael Lipsitz, Jerrold Marks, and Terri Olian; school superintendents, Dr. Maureen Hager and Dr. JoAnn Desmond; school district administrators, Gregory M. Kurr, Dr. Michael Lubelfeld, Dr. Guy Schumacher, Lauren Macintyre, and Gary Ofisher; and school lawyers, Nancy Krent, Mike Loizzi, Bob Kohn, Heather Brickman, John A. Relias, and James C. Franczek, Jr.

Thanks also to the caring and dedicated colleagues we have encountered from preschool to law and graduate school: the Ravinia Nursery School staff, including Marilyn Straus, Ginger Uhlmann, Ginger Scott, Rosalie Edelstein, Midge Hechtman, and Roberta Wexler; the elementary school professionals and middle school educators who opened our eyes to what a "good" school could be; the "facilitators" at National-Louis University and Baker Demonstration School in Evanston, Illinois, especially Kathleen McKenna, Dr. Marge Leon, Dr. Cynthia Mee and Alan Rossman; the wonderful teachers, board members and parents of Winnetka Public School Nursery, and the visionary early childhood education experts of Family Network and the Community

Family Center, particularly Ruth Stern, Rosalie Weinfeld, Barbara Haley, Herbert S. Wander, and William S. Kaufman.

For their invaluable research, editorial assistance and feedback on early drafts of the book, we also are grateful to an outstanding group of Loyola University of Chicago law students, including Adam Betzen, Traci Copple, Katherine A. Buchanan, Leah G. Feldhendler, Megan L. Ferkel, Sarah Giauque, Amy S. Hammerman, Anne M. Graber, Elizabeth H. Greer, Anuradha Gupta, Gretchen M. Harris, Alison L. Helin, Erin Hickey, Caroline Hosman, Nicole Williams Koviak, Alisha J. Massie, Shannon Reeves-Rich, Beatriz Rendon, Laura R. Rojas, Sarah Smith, Helaine N. Tiglias, Nicole Torrado, Christina L. Wascher, Beth Miller-Rosenberg, and John Wunderlich.

In addition, the authors wish to thank the outstanding team at Aspen Publishers for their tremendous assistance throughout this project, particularly Carol McGeehan, John Devins, Katy Thompson, Elizabeth Kenny, Sandra Doherty and Mei Wang. We thank as well the scores of anonymous outside reviewers whose expert advice and suggestions greatly improved the final text.

For their incredible support, patience and talent, the authors also wish to thank Christine Heaton, Bella Munari, Kathryn Lindner, Enza Soby, Rita Martinez, Patricia Hrej, Angela Chrusciel, Judy Stevenson, Christopher Gilliam and Elaine Gist.

Finally, we thank the Loyola University of Chicago and the Loyola University of Chicago School of Law for providing financial and administrative support for this project.

EDUCATION LAW, POLICY, AND PRACTICE

SECTION

INTRODUCTION

CHAPTER 1

AN OVERVIEW OF THE BOOK: THE INTEGRATION OF EDUCATION LAW, POLICY AND PRACTICE

Is American education law designed to facilitate the creation of good schools? The serious student of American education law, policy and practice must confront this fundamental question. The first step in attempting to answer that question is to identify the essential attributes of a "good school." The issue of what makes a good school has been debated for centuries, and is extremely difficult to resolve. Contemporary American theorists and researchers continue to struggle with the issue. While the current research is far from conclusive, there is nonetheless significant support for the view that students generally learn best in an educational environment characterized by:

(1) a qualified, skilled and effective faculty; *see, e.g.*, Linda Darling-Hammond, *Enhancing Teaching*, in *Best Practices, Best Thinking, and Emerging Issues in School Leadership*, 77 (William A. Owings & Leslie S. Kaplan, eds. 2003); Comfort O. Okpala et al., *A Clear Link Between School and Teacher Characteristics, Student Demographics, and Student Achievement*, 20 Educ. 491 (2000); Carey Jenkins, *What Is a Good Teacher?*, in *Best Practices for High School Classrooms* 4 (Randi Stone ed. 2002);

(2) relatively small classes in relatively small schools; David Alan Gilman & Susan Kiger, *Should We Try to Keep Class Sizes Small?* 60 Educ. Leadership 80 (2003); Jeremy D. Finn, *Small Classes in American Schools: Research, Practice, and Politics*, 83 Phi Delta Kappan 551 (2002); Mary Anne Raywid, *Small Schools: A Reform That Works*, 55 Educ. Leadership 35 (1998); Del Stover, *Urban Districts Embrace Small Schools Movement*, School Board News, 7 (Natl. School Bds. Assn., Nov. 25, 2003) ("The push to replace large, comprehensive high schools—and some of the nation's larger middle schools—is based on a growing body of research showing that small schools generally have lower dropout rates, better attendance, less violence, and in many cases, higher levels of student achievement"); Tracy Dell'Angela, *Schools Think Small, Win Big*, Chicago Trib. Sept. 14, 2003, at 1, 20 (citing the Burke County North

Carolina Public School Study and the Tennessee Project STAR Report as evidence that class sizes of 15 students or fewer dramatically increases the level of student achievement in the primary grades, particularly in districts with a significant number of low-income or English-language deficient students);

(3) a diverse student population; Patricia Gurin, *New Research on the Benefits of Diversity in College and Beyond: An Empirical Analysis, www.umich.edu/~urel/admissions/legal/expert/gurintoc.html* ("A racially and ethnically diverse student body has far-ranging and significant benefits for all students. . . ."); *Grutter v. Bollinger*, 539 U.S. 306 (2003) (relying on "numerous expert studies and reports showing that . . . diversity promotes learning outcomes. . . ."); Bruce D. Perry, *We're all Different (WE'RE ALL THE SAME)*, 111 Instructor 6 (2002); and

(4) an actively involved parent community. James Griffith, "Relation of Parental Involvement, Empowerment, and School Traits to Student Academic Performance," 90 J. Educ. Res. 33 (1996).

Assuming that this research indicates that a "good" American school is one in which qualified educators teach a small and diverse group of students in a small setting with active parental participation, to what extent does American education law facilitate these "best" educational institutions and practices? How can such institutions and practices be financed? What political hurdles would have to be overcome in fully realizing such an educational vision, and what role would lawyers have to play?

Any serious student of education law must also confront these issues. They provide a consistent theme running throughout each legal doctrine in education law, and hence throughout this book. In each chapter, the student must examine: (1) the cases and statutes establishing education law doctrine; (2) the educational policy implications (political, financial and philosophical) of that legal doctrine; and (3) the skills required of lawyers in their practical application of education law and policy. After examining these materials in each part of the book, the student is encouraged to determine whether it is possible to reconcile education law, policy and practice.

The book's introductory sections explore the legal and financial structure of education in America, as well as the traditional and contemporary perspectives informing American educational policy. With that foundation, the student will be prepared to consider seriously the first major substantive area in the book: the boundaries between public and private education and the related issue of the boundaries between church and state. As the materials in that section indicate, every state requires its children to attend school and endeavors to provide the type of free public education it believes is necessary for participatory citizenship in a democracy. Nonetheless, the law permits students to be home schooled, particularly where public education might interfere with a genuinely held religious belief. Although the states generally may require school attendance, students have no fundamental, constitutional right to an education. In fact, in its seminal *San Antonio Independent School District v. Rodriguez*, 411 U.S. 1 (1973), decision, the Supreme Court declined to find a fundamental constitutional right to education, a right that would have served to invalidate the disparities in per pupil education funding within each state—from preschool to secondary school.

In that same section of the book, students must address and reconcile the significant Supreme Court cases interpreting the First Amendment's limitations on the establishment of religion and the denial of the free exercise of religion within educational institutions. These cases evolve toward the Supreme Court's decision in *Zelman v. Simmons-Harris*, 536 U.S. 639 (2002), allowing the redirection of public funds to private and religious educational purposes in the form of vouchers.

In the third section of the book, the issue of school governance is raised. That section enables students to analyze the power of Congress to regulate education under the Constitution's commerce clause and spending clause. How do these constitutional provisions preclude Congress from regulating the use of handguns on school grounds, but grant Congress the power to influence curriculum in the classroom through legislation, such as the recently enacted No Child Left Behind Act? In addition, the student must consider the concept of "local control" in its various forms. Judges and lawmakers generally defer to the wisdom of local officials and educational professionals regarding the establishment of a school's instructional practices. Suppose, however, local politicians enact practices that disserve student learning. What objective does local control advance in that situation? When should local control be supplanted by federal legislation? This section also develops the practical aspects of school board and administrative governance. The student experiences the various roles played by both nonprofessional, elected officials and professional educators in managing the school district.

In Section IV, the book focuses on the constitutional and statutory rights of students. That section tracks the evolution of the legal treatment of racial segregation and discrimination in education. In *Brown v. Board of Education*, 347 U.S. 483 (1954), the Supreme Court rejected racial segregation in public education, and in its recent University of Michigan affirmative action cases, the Court has recognized the compelling interest in a diverse student body. Nonetheless, the Court has also permitted school districts to allow resegregation based on race, and most recently has limited race-conscious school programs designed to achieve the educational benefits of diversity.

Similarly, while educational experts generally believe that educating students with educational disabilities may require both early and extraordinary interventions and services, the law may not require such interventions or services for all students. Rather, although federal statutes require school districts to meet some of the educational needs of some students with educational disabilities, the case law in this section demonstrates that school districts need only provide to these students a so-called floor of opportunity. The section also considers the social consequences of the potential lack of effective special education services for individual children.

The theme of reconciling the law of education with best educational practices recurs in Section V in the context of a study of the educational environment. Although a physically and emotionally safe environment is vital to learning, the law of torts protects school districts from liability for some types of harm to students in that environment. Nor has tort law generally recognized an enforceable standard of care in the delivery of teaching, or any independent duty to maintain an emotionally secure environment. What competing interests outweigh the interest in encouraging the fulfillment of a standard of care in instructional practices and the provision of an emotionally safe learning environment?

Finally, as reflected in Section VI, the unique constitutional and statutory rights of teachers allow them to exercise academic freedom and to use their professional expertise about best educational practices in their classrooms. Those same protections, however, may in some situations preclude educational institutions from compelling teachers to implement a consistent, district-wide curriculum plan. Tenure and collective bargaining rights help insure that teachers have the freedom to engage their students in a robust exchange of ideas in the classroom. Yet such rights also may make it difficult to remove those teachers who are unsatisfactory.

As this introduction suggests, the law governing education reflects important rights, values or interests that may sometimes outweigh the desired objective of student learning. The student of education law should attempt to identify those countervailing values, and to determine whether they can be reconciled with the value of insuring that all of America's students receive the best educational practices. At times, financial or practical constraints may simply block the development of a truly effective educational system. Those practical impediments may make it extremely difficult to reconcile the law of education with education finance and education policy. Nonetheless, that reconciliation is vital to the future of American education.

CHAPTER 2

THE STRUCTURE OF AMERICAN EDUCATION LAW, FINANCE, PRACTICE AND POLICY

A. THE STRUCTURE OF AMERICAN EDUCATION LAW

The law governing education derives from three primary sources: (1) the federal Constitution and federal statutes and regulations, (2) state constitutions and state statutes, and (3) and the common law of property, torts and contracts.

The ultimate authority for education law is the United States Constitution. The Constitution's First Amendment limits the power of Congress to enact laws "respecting an establishment of religion, or prohibiting the free exercise thereof. . . ." This prohibition, which has been applied to the states through the Fourteenth Amendment, precludes legislation that has the purpose or effect of advancing or inhibiting religious instruction, religious educational institutions, religious uses of open school facilities and religious expression in the public school. The First Amendment also grants teachers and students freedom of speech and association. These constitutional rights limit the power of public school districts to regulate the content of a teacher's expression and the style of a teacher's instructional practices. The right of association generally also allows teachers to unionize and to engage in collective bargaining. Students as well must be permitted freedom to form groups regardless of the groups' political or religious affiliation and to engage in nondisruptive forms of verbal and nonverbal expression.

The Fourth Amendment's prohibition on "unreasonable searches and seizures" similarly grants to students and teachers rights that cabin the ability of public districts to conduct indiscriminate and arbitrary invasions of privacy. The Constitution's Fifth and Fourteenth Amendment due process clauses preclude public schools from depriving teachers of a protectable property interest in a legitimate expectation of continuing employment without notice and hearing procedures. The due process clauses also insure that school districts will afford similar process protections to students before students are suspended or expelled from the educational environment. The Fourteenth Amendment's equal protection clause prohibits states and school districts from purposefully discriminating against teachers or students based on characteristics like race and gender, and thus requires districts to take affirmative steps to desegregate and allows educational institutions to take race into account as part of an individualized assessment of applicants.

The Constitution, of course, also limits the power of Congress in enacting legislation that affects state schools. The Tenth Amendment's reservation of nondelegated powers to the states and the Eleventh Amendment's protection of the states from liability make clear that states in the American regime generally retain sovereignty over affairs such as the education of their own citizens. Nonetheless, Congress, acting primarily pursuant to its "spending" power or its power to regulate interstate commerce, has passed an array of federal statutes that regulate school affairs, including the employment of teachers: *see, e.g.,* 42 U.S.C. §2000e-2 et seq. (Title VII); 29 U.S.C. §206 (Equal Pay Act); the treatment of female students, see, e.g., 20 U.S.C. §1681 = 1688 (Title IX); the education of children with learning disabilities, *see, e.g.,* The Individuals with Disabilities Education Act Amendments of 1997, 20 U.S.C. §§1400-1405; the privacy rights of teachers and students, *see, e.g.,* Family Educational Rights and Privacy Act, 20 U.S.C. §1232; the rights of teachers to take family and medical leave, *see, e.g.,* the Family and Medical Leave Act, 29 U.S.C. §§2601, 2611, 2612; the access of public and private groups to educational facilities, *see, e.g.,* Equal Access Act, 20 U.S.C. §§4071-4072; and even the qualifications of teachers, the content of curriculum and the standards for student achievement. *See, e.g.,* The No Child Left Behind Act (NCLB), 20 U.S.C. §6301 et seq.

Although the parameters established by these federal mandates are significant, the education of students is still primarily a state and local matter. So long as they do not run afoul of constitutional or federal statutory prohibitions, state and local governments have virtually unlimited power to regulate the education of their children. As a rule, the states may require their citizens to attend school and to be exposed to a defined curriculum. They also may, and often do, establish standards for teacher certification, competence, retention, tenure and renewal. Through their own labor relations statutes, the states also regulate the process for teacher unionization and collective bargaining.

In exerting their control over education, the states typically delegate their power to local educational agencies or school boards. School boards set policies that incorporate legal requirements for the school district. Boards also establish specific rules governing district administration, personnel, community relations, student rights, dispute resolution, curriculum and instructional practices. The school board also is empowered to establish a school district's mission, belief statement, strategic objectives and annual goals. School boards typically are composed of elected, volunteer public servants. The publicly elected officials, in turn, often delegate their managerial authority to an educational professional such as a chief administrator or superintendent.

Within the educational environment itself, interactions between administrators, teachers, students and even parents are largely governed by the same common law principals of torts, contracts and property that govern the rights and obligations of all state citizens. State statutes, however, often protect school officials and teachers from liability in the public educational environment. These statutes have created limits on the nature and extent of common law liability that are specific to the education setting.

B. THE STRUCTURE OF AMERICAN EDUCATION FINANCE

Like private corporations, school districts endeavor to maintain a budget that balances their revenues against their expenses.

1. Revenue

The sources of a school district's revenue include federal appropriations, state appropriations, and local taxes. State and local taxes generally make up more than 90 percent of a school district's revenue. *See* National Center for Educational Statistics (2004-2005) (calculating that most school districts rely on federal funding for less than 10 percent of their revenue). Most states produce that local revenue through property taxes, while some states employ income taxes, sales taxes, "sin" taxes, or a combination of taxes.

Property taxes are usually based primarily on a percentage of the assessed valuation of the residential property in a district. Some states redistribute property taxes from property-rich districts to property-poor districts, spread property tax revenue throughout the state, or create a "foundation" level for all districts. The foundation level represents a legislative judgment about the amount of money that must be allocated for each student for that student to receive a minimal education. Where a district's local taxes do not reach that level, some states will allocate statewide funds to make up the difference.

In most states, however, school districts receive local revenue in direct proportion to the value of the residential property in the district. As a result, significant disparities occur in the per-pupil revenue allotted to different school districts within the same state. These disparities have a racial component as well; districts with mostly white students spend on average approximately $900 more per student than do other districts. Moreover, wide disparities exist in the average per-pupil expenditures between different states. For example, while the national average per-pupil expenditure is $5,652, New Jersey spends $9,310 per student, and Utah only spends $3,670 per student. *See* Meglis, *Let's Talk School Business*, at 17 (Assn. School Bus. Officials Intl. 1998) (citing National Education Association Research). This disparity in revenue is further exacerbated because districts also rely on interest earned on their revenue for additional funds. Districts and states that attract less revenue, of course, also garner less interest income from that revenue.

Some states have enacted property tax extension limitation laws, commonly referred to as "tax caps." Under such a law, a school district is barred from increasing its property tax extension by an amount greater than the consumer price index or a predetermined statutory amount (i.e., 5 percent).

Because tax caps are independent of a school district's real expenses, those caps typically reduce the amount of a district's real revenues which are required to keep up with its expenses.

2. Expenses

School districts and local educational agencies incur educational expenses, operational and maintenance expenses, transportation expenses, life-safety expenses and construction expenses. Many of the district's expenses are mandated by law, leaving school district administrators with little discretion in their use of scarce resources. *See Unfunded Mandates Frustrate Superintendents and Principals*, School Board News, at 3 (Natl. School Bds. Assn., Nov. 25, 2003). Some federal statutes require school districts to allocate funds to maintain a safe and healthy environment for students. The Federal Occupational Safety and Health Administration (OSHA), for example, regulates the school environment and requires districts to rid their schools of, inter alia, blood-borne pathogens, asbestos, unclean air, lead paint, hazardous waste and radon. *See, e.g.*, 29 C.F.R. §1910 *et seq.* While such requirements are crucial to the creation of a safe environment for children, they also create a series of fixed costs for a school district.

The resources that a school must devote to "educational" purposes also are largely mandated by law. Educational expenditures include teacher salaries and teacher benefits (i.e., health, dental, life insurance and retirement), special education services (i.e., assistive technology, teaching assistants, therapists, related services, transportation and alternative placements), purchased services (i.e., liability insurance and workers' compensation insurance), supplies (i.e., textbooks) and equipment (i.e., computers).

In the typical school district, more than 90 percent of these expenses are dictated by law. Teacher salaries and benefits, which often constitute 75 percent of an education fund budget, are usually established by a multiyear collective bargaining agreement. Absent extraordinary circumstances, the terms of that agreement bind the district to make the required expenditures, regardless of evolving economic conditions or other pressing needs for the money. Federal law also has created a web of mandates requiring districts to fund needed services to students with educational disabilities without regard to cost. *See, e.g.*, IDEA, 20 U.S.C. §§1400-1405. The provision of effective special education services typically requires a district to allocate far more than its average perpupil amount for a special needs student. Although Congress appropriates federal funding for services required by IDEA, it has failed to provide full funding for these services. *See Center for Special Education Finance Report*, available at *www.ncsl.org/standcomm/scbudg/budgmandates03.htm* (calculating that full funding of IDEA would require an additional $25 billion).

The No Child Left Behind Act itself establishes minimum funding levels that are not sufficient to allow the full implementation of its requirements. Yet not even those minimum funding levels have been achieved. From 2002-2004, the amounts budgeted to meet NCLB mandates fell more than $35 billion short of even the minimum amounts established by the statute. *See* Budget of the

United States Government, Fiscal Years 2002, 2003, 2004, *www.whitehouse.gov. omb/budget. See also Unfunded Mandates Frustrate Superintendents and Principals,* School Board News, at 3 (Natl. School Bds. Assn., Nov. 25, 2003) ("Eighty-nine percent of superintendents . . . call NCLB an 'unfunded mandate' "). These "unfunded mandates" necessarily tax a school district's non-federal revenue, and require districts to make up the inherent shortfall by reducing other educational programs and expenses, or by creatively finding external revenue sources.

C. THE STRUCTURE OF THE PRACTICE OF EDUCATION LAW

Education law is practiced by both private attorneys and public sector governmental lawyers. Private attorneys typically represent either "management" (i.e., a university or a number of school districts) or "labor" (i.e., teachers unions and students).

On the management side, attorneys engaged in school law may act as in-house counsel to a single large school district or a single university. More often, private school lawyers work as "outside" counsel for a number of different school districts. Private attorneys who represent many school districts or a single university engage in work that transcends the traditional boundaries between compliance, transactional and litigation practice. They provide advice about ongoing compliance with legal requirements, but they also negotiate deals, draft transaction documents, conduct compliance investigations, represent the district in collective bargaining sessions, draft employment agreements, and litigate matters before mediators, arbitrators and judges.

Private sector school lawyers often communicate directly with the district's chief executive officer or superintendent and with the school board and its president. The attorney establishes a relationship with individual members of a school district's administration and hence tends to be responsive to their "management" perspective. Truly skilled school lawyers, however, recognize that they represent the school district's organization as a whole. Well-functioning school boards, as well, understand that they serve the interests of the entire district, rather than those of "management." Accordingly, the best private-sector school attorneys are able to help their school board clients to reconcile the interests presented by various stakeholders in a district.

Some private education law practitioners have developed an active practice representing persons who may be adversely affected by a school district's actions. These so-called labor side attorneys represent unions and teacher groups in the context of collective bargaining negotiations. The most experienced school lawyers in this arena are able to lead their diverse teacher groups toward educationally and fiscally responsible negotiating positions, and then to educate the school district's representatives about the merits of those positions. These attorneys also litigate grievances on behalf of teachers whenever a school district acts in a manner that appears to be inconsistent with the rights assigned to teachers by law or contract. Those initial grievance settings are adversarial, but they lack the formality of litigation. When the grievance cannot be resolved or statutory rights have been violated, the attorney proceeds to represent teachers or teacher groups in federal or state litigation. These private sector school lawyers also tend to represent students in their disputes with a school district. Most often, these conflicts involve a district's perceived failure to provide the required special education services to a student with educational disabilities. Occasionally, these matters may involve issues of student discipline, expulsion or the infringement of a student's constitutional rights. These disputes require the attorney to begin a process of informal representation, leading in some cases to more formal hearings and litigation.

Public sector school lawyers serve the government or its educational agencies. In 1978, the federal Department of Education was created. Together with its Office for Civil Rights, the Department of Education is charged with enforcing federal civil rights legislation in schools receiving federal funds. The Department's attorneys may be called upon to draft for the Secretary of Education or Deputy Secretary of Education position papers on the education law emanating from a new statute or key case. For instance, attorneys for the Department of Education were instrumental in drafting guidelines on religion in schools under the No Child Left Behind Act. More often, attorneys working for federal education agencies focus on whether school districts comply with federal law. They work closely with federal investigators to develop a record of compliance or noncompliance with federally funded programs. For example, the attorney may accompany an investigator to perform a field study of a school district to insure that the district's bilingual education programs satisfy the requirements for the receipt of federal funds. If the evidence shows that the district has failed to comply with the statutory preconditions to the receipt of federal funds, the ultimate remedy is to withdraw funds. As experienced school attorneys in this area understand, however, that remedy is often counterproductive; the withdrawal of needed funds may make a noncompliant program even more noncompliant. As such, the attorney's task is to negotiate with the school district toward creating a plan for future compliance so that the funds can be directed to more valuable uses. Therefore, the best public sector school attorneys are skilled in factual investigation, legal analysis, negotiation and dispute resolution.

In both the public sector and private sector, the practice of school law is driven by the financial pressure placed on school districts from unfunded legal mandates. Private attorneys are asked whether a district can satisfy a legal mandate in a novel, inexpensive way. They are sometimes called upon to weigh the costs of failing to comply with such mandates against the costs of compliance. Similarly, attorneys representing teachers, teacher unions and students are called upon to make legitimate demands for compensation or services in an environment of scarce resources. Finally, governmental school lawyers also work daily with the tension created by their responsibility to enforce mandates they know are virtually impossible to satisfy with limited funds.

The finest education lawyers — and the most astute students of education law — therefore, must, in a legally appropriate and fiscally responsible way, reconcile the rights and responsibilities that education law assigns to school districts, board members, administrators, teachers, students, parents and community members. Each of these groups has a role to play in the education of the community's children. The ultimate goal of education law is to help bring these groups together to achieve a shared vision of educational excellence for all students.

D. THE STRUCTURE OF AMERICAN EDUCATION POLICY

What is the fundamental purpose of education? This is not merely an academic question. The philosophic choice a society makes regarding its objectives for education has important implications for the kind of educational institutions it actually creates. The American law governing education is based upon a tradition of philosophic thought about the proper place of education in American life. America's choice of educational goals determines who should be educated, how they should be educated, and who should finance their education. These goals also inform decisions about the type of rules that should govern educational institutions.

The serious student of education law must be able to discern the educational philosophy underlying education law. That philosophy often is vital to understanding the law itself. Moreover, an understanding of the traditions of educational thought that inform America's educational institutions is indispensable to formulating persuasive arguments for the growth of those institutions and the law itself. The following overview of the history of the philosophy of education culminating in current American policy should suffice to raise profound questions about the assumptions supporting the law governing American education today.

1. Classical Philosophies of Education: Education Must Be a Public Concern Because It Has the Power to Shape Character and Support the Particular Political Regime[1]

Plato's *Republic* is arguably the greatest text regarding the philosophy of education.[2] The regime displayed in the *Republic* is built upon critical assumptions about the educational process. First, the goal of education is to create relatively stagnant and stratified role-players for the good of the state; it is a purely public concern. Second, education is extremely powerful; it is capable of altering a person's natural instincts, including the instinct of love of one's own, and of shaping character.[3]

---

[1] *See* S. Cahn, *Classic and Contemporary Readings in the Philosophy of Education* (1997) (hereinafter "Cahn").

[2] *See* Plato's *Republic*, reprinted in Cahn, at 39-109.

[3] The question about whether educators can, and should, shape character arises in the contemporary debates about the merits of character education in public school. In Plato's *Protagoras* dialogue, Socrates appears to concur in Protagoras' argument that virtue can indeed be

In Book VIII of the Politics, Aristotle expressly shares Plato's assumption that "education should be regulated by law and should be an affair of the state. . . ."[4] Aristotle declares that the "citizen should be molded to suit the form of government under which he lives"; each type of government has a "peculiar" character and its education should strive to replicate the character required in its citizens to preserve its peculiar form.[5] Since the whole regime has one end, "it is manifest that education should be one and the same for all, and that it should be public, and not private."[6] In the Politics, Aristotle also concludes that the type of "education of citizens" in a regime must depend on the political structure of that regime. Education in a democracy, for example, must train all citizens in the political skills necessary to participate in both ruling the regime and in being ruled by popular choice.[7] As classical educational theorists, both Aristotle and Plato share a belief in the supreme importance of public education for the health of the regime.

2. Modern Educational Philosophy: Secular Education Is Vital to Moral Freedom and Self-Government

In *Some Thoughts Concerning Education* (1693), John Locke emphasizes the significance of rationality and reason in the education of each individual. Most people, Locke writes, are "good or evil, useful or not, by their education."[8] Like the ancients, therefore, Locke understands the power of education. Yet, education is designed to teach the student to comprehend reason so that there is no need for external politically or religiously imposed forms of discipline.[9] Locke believes that reason, if rightly understood and taught, can be the instrument of political freedom and self-governance.

In 1748, in *The Spirit of the Laws*, Montesquieu also argues that public education is particularly necessary in democracies. In a democratic society that values freedom and self-government, public education is critical to social cohesion. Only public education can inspire that civic virtue requisite to democratic government, which includes the "love of the laws" and a preference for public over private life.

Rousseau, as well, shares Locke's emphasis on individual educational development, declaring that the "supreme good is not authority, but freedom."[10] In the *Emile*, he expressly links that declaration with a proper education: "This is my fundamental maxim. Apply it to childhood and all the rules of education follow."[11] Rousseau associates freedom with mankind's natural state and authority with mankind's unnatural, social condition.

---

taught, agreeing after his arguments that, "human care can make men good." *See* Plato's *Protagoras*, reprinted in Cahn, at 35-39.

[4] *See* Aristotle, *Politics*, Book VIII, reprinted in Cahn, at 137.

[5] *Id.*

[6] *See* Aristotle, *Nicomachean Ethics*, reprinted in Cahn, at 111-118.

[7] *See* Aristotle, *Politics*, Book VII, reprinted in Cahn, at 134.

[8] *See* Locke, *Some Thoughts Concerning Education*, reprinted in part in Cahn, at 145.

[9] *Id.* at 147 ("Every man must some time or other be trusted to himself. . . . ")

[10] *See* Rousseau, *Emile*, Book II, reprinted in Cahn, at 167.

[11] *Id.*

The rules of education, if they are to serve the supreme good of moral freedom, must proceed according to nature. Rousseau believes that children should be educated according to their natural, developmental stages,[12] and that educators must understand the "distinctive genius" of each child. Each child's virtuous "character" is shaped by educators who allow the child "full liberty" to grow.[13] Hence, Rousseau creates the foundation for contemporary arguments against a standardized curriculum, and in favor of a child-centered education. He suggests that any educational process that fails to "differentiate"—to take into account the unique developmental needs of each child—will fail.

In their distinct calls for an education that promotes moral freedom and self-government, Rousseau, Locke, and Montesquieu also share a fundamental distrust of religion in the educational process. Locke's belief in the power of reason suggests the subordination of religious faith to individual, rational thought. Slavish adherence to religious doctrine or received dogma is inimical to self-governance and self-determination. As such, a true education for self-government would stress the freedom to pursue reason toward truth and would eliminate the passive acceptance of religious teaching. For Montesquieu, public education was necessary to replace private religious zeal with a uniform national allegiance to law and country. Rousseau, as well, believes that a proper education is the antidote to politically imposed moral and religious doctrines. If allowed to develop their own interests free from such artificial constraints, students will naturally seek to form socially useful alliances and boundaries, and they will naturally avoid socially destructive behavior.

3. The Foundation of American Educational Philosophy: Democratic Education Must Develop Non-sectarian Bonds Between All Individuals and the Community

(a) Private Sectarian Education Before the Constitution

The history of American education typically begins with the story of the importation of the English educational system to Colonial America.[14]

---

[12] *Id.* at 170 ("Let childhood ripen in children").

[13] *Id.* at 171.

[14] *See, e.g.*, Alexander & Alexander, *American Public School Law* 21-23 (2001). Well before the colonists brought to America their notions of schools, however, Native Americans had developed their own approach to education, an approach that was purposefully discarded by the settling Europeans. For two excellent and thorough discussions of the history of Native American education, *see* Urban & Wagoner, *American Education: A History,* ch. 1 (2000); M. Szasz, *Indian Education in the American Colonies, 1607-1783* (1988). Despite variations among Native American tribes, pre-colonial education had common objectives. The primary goal of education was the development of skills essential to survival. Education in these skills was closely joined with spiritual education. The European missions first attempted to replace Native American spiritual teachings with Catholicism. The elimination of Native American culture and educational practices continued in earnest throughout the late 1800s and early 1900s in the form of boarding school programs designed to "rid" Native American children of their culture through "assimilation." *See* D. Adams, *Education for Extinction: American Indians and the Boarding School Experience, 1875-1928* (1995); A. Peshkin, *Places of Memory: Whiteman's Schools and Native American Communities* (1997); J. Spring, *Deculturalization and the Struggle for Equality: A Brief History of Education of Dominated Cultures in the United States* (2000); B. Sheehan, *Seeds of Extinction: Jeffersonian Philanthropy and the American Indian* (1973).

Contrary to common understanding, the educational tradition brought by the European settlers who conquered and colonized America was not based on a singular New England mode of educational hierarchy and religious conformity. Rather, education in the colonial period was diffuse, localized, haphazard and heterogeneous. There were significant differences between the educational practices in the northern, southern and middle colonies and significant differences within each colony as well.[15] Nonetheless, it is fair to say that American colonists attempted for the most part to recreate the heavily religious educational institutions with which they were most familiar from their European experience.[16]

In 1647, for instance, the Massachusetts General Court enacted the "Old Deluder Satan Act." The Act declared that because Satan was keeping people in the colony from understanding scripture, every town with at least 50 families must provide for reading and writing instruction. If a town had 100 or more families, the town also had to provide grammar schools that would prepare boys for higher education at Harvard. The law threatened the town with a fine if it did not comply. Despite this somewhat modest initial movement toward community-based education, those families with educated adults continued to rely primarily on the home as the institution of learning. Children who did not have the advantage of a learned adult in the home were sent to other homes occupied by adults who offered to teach groups of children together. These private schools were run by men and women who typically instructed their own children and, for a fee, instructed the neighborhood children as well.

These private schools soon developed a shared curriculum with a strong religious flavor. Children were taught to read by first memorizing the Bible. As was true in England, the lessons were often presented on hornbooks—pieces of parchment placed on a wooden paddle, covered with a strip of clear horn to protect them from being smudged. The lesson typically included a prayer, Biblical passage, religious maxim or psalm. The hornbooks were coupled with primers, such that religion and literacy were literally tied together. For example, the *New England Primer* contained the letters of the alphabet arranged so that each letter began a Biblical verse. A series of illustrated rhymes taught children both the alphabet and the doctrine of original sin. The primary goal of these lessons was to teach children to read, but the lessons employed religious doctrine as the setting for language.

A variety of church affiliated or sponsored schools sprang up together with the officially established religious institutions. The various religious sects in America developed a variety of private schools. Moreover, splinters that developed in the Protestant church led to competing schools even within the same religion. The various sects soon competed vigorously for the scarce public resources devoted to education.

---

[15] Urban & Wagoner, *American Education: A History* 15 (2000) (hereinafter "Urban & Wagoner").

[16] Kenneth A. Lockridge, *Literacy in Colonial New England: An Inquiry into the Social Context of Literacy in the Early Modern West* (1974) (hereinafter "Lockridge").

(b) The Founders' Educational Philosophy: Toward a Public, Common and Secular Education

Although the founders of the American regime and the drafters of the Constitution were generally religious people infused with this sectarian educational tradition, they were determined to create a markedly different education system in the new regime.[17] After independence and before the Constitution was drafted, the nation's founders were well aware that the nation was not yet a union. The founders grew to believe that one of the most effective ways to overcome religious differences and to achieve common values was to create a shared system of education. As Urban and Wagoner have observed, "[e]ducation, then, emerged as an essential consideration in the minds of those who faced the momentous task of establishing the new nation."[18] The political structure of the new regime became dependent on the educational structure of the regime, and therefore the "architects of the American nation clearly and deliberately fused educational theory with political theory."[19]

Benjamin Franklin, for example, developed a consistent argument for the education of each individual in practical skills, useful in the world.[20] For Franklin, learned treatises and other established texts were important, but only insofar as they generated ideas that could be put into practice. Ultimately, Franklin wrote *Poor Richard's Almanack* between 1732 and 1757 for the purpose of "conveying instruction among the common people, who bought scarce any other books."[21] In order to create collections of books that could be used by more than a wealthy few, Franklin and his colleagues created the first colonial library by donating their most precious books to a common collection called the "Library Company of Philadelphia." The collection contained classic works such as *Plutarch's Lives*, as well as history books and maps. The library, however, did not contain a single religious text.[22] In 1749, in his *Proposals Relating to the Education of Youth in Pennsylvania*, Franklin designed the "Philadelphia Academy," whose mission was not to create a generation of select scholars, but a generation of common men able to perform practical skills and community service.[23] Although Franklin's success in implementing his ideas was limited, he did succeed in generating a vital discourse regarding the type of education that would serve the new nation and its people.

Thomas Jefferson attempted to advance the ideal of a public, nonsectarian education in his "Bill for the More General Diffusion of Knowledge," which he

---

[17] *See, e.g.*, Frank Lambert, *The Founding Fathers and the Place of Religion in America* 188 (2003).

[18] Urban & Wagoner, at 70.

[19] *Id.*

[20] *See* Leonard W. Larabee et al., *The Autobiography of Benjamin Franklin* (1964); Leonard W. Larabee & Whitfield J. Bell, *The Papers of Benjamin Franklin* (1959); John Hardin Best, *Benjamin Franklin on Education* (1962).

[21] *See* Poor Richard's Almanack, in Larabee & Bell, *The Papers of Benjamin Franklin* (1959).

[22] *See* Urban & Wagoner at 58 (citing Cremin, *American Education: The Colonial Experience 1607-1703*, at 399 (1970)).

[23] *See Proposals*, in Best, *Benjamin Franklin on Education* (1962).

placed before the Virginia legislature in 1779.[24] Rooted in his philosophy that public education was necessary to support the new republic and its democratic government, Jefferson proposed a system of free elementary-level education administered by separate counties or divisions. Each of these so-called little republics would provide citizens with basic literacy skills and with knowledge of history. Jefferson's vision was that American children would have at least three years of education to prepare them to participate as citizens in a democracy, and the brightest students would proceed beyond elementary school to attend one of 20 publicly subsidized secondary schools. He believed that the benefits of education should not be reserved solely for the established aristocracy or for any religious group.[25]

Jefferson also made it clear that the public's interest in, and its funding responsibility for, education did not extend to religious institutions or religious instruction. The public's interest was in providing opportunity for young Americans to gain skills needed for democratic citizenship. In fact, Jefferson believed that a public education was vital to the preservation of liberty. He wrote that a publicly supported educational system would raise the "morals" of citizens to the "high ground of moral respectability necessary to their own safety, and to orderly government.[26] The "most certain and the most legitimate end of government," according to Jefferson, was the provision of a free, public education to its citizens.[27]

The framers' educational philosophy thus is inextricably bound up with their understanding of the proper relationship between church and state. That understanding has its roots in the political philosophy of Locke, Montesquieu and Rousseau. Jefferson's conception of a free, public education itself suggests a dividing line between the existing family- and religious-based educational practices and the very different educational system needed in the new nation. Jefferson's system of public education is not hostile to religious education; rather, it simply understands private religious education to be inadequate to accomplish the political objective of educating all citizens for participation in their own government. To the extent that religious education depletes resources from the public education system, which is indispensable

---

[24] Thomas Jefferson, *Bill for the More General Diffusion of Knowledge, The Educational Work of Thomas Jefferson* 199-204 (1964); *see also* Thomas Jefferson, *Writings* (1984); John Adams, *The Adams-Jefferson Letters* (1971).

[25] *See Act Establishing Religious Freedom* (1779) in Adrienne Koch & William Pedren, *The Life and Selected Writings of Thomas Jefferson* 289-291 (1998) (hereinafter "Koch & Pedren").

[26] Urban & Wagoner, at 73-74 (citing Thomas Jefferson to John Adams, Oct. 28, 1813).

[27] *Id.* As Urban & Wagoner put it: ". . . equal educational opportunity was to allow the identification and proper education of those capable of leadership and worthy of public trust. Jefferson placed himself in opposition to those of his own social background, many of whom constituted the 'artificial aristocracy.' Content with private education for their own children, they were willing to leave the education of others to random local initiative, church benevolence, or perhaps to the well-meaning charity of a concerned citizen-benefactor. To Jefferson, however, the education required for participation and leadership in the new American social order was far too important to be left to chance, parental whim, or restricted to a traditional elite." *Id.*, at 74. One of the tragic ironies of Jefferson's efforts to spread the benefits of education among American citizens, of course, is that his system completely excluded all Native Americans, all African-Americans and virtually all women. *See Notes on the State of Virginia* (1781), in Koch & Pedren at 243-244; E.M. Halliday, *Understanding Thomas Jefferson* 234 (2001) (describing Jefferson's exclusion of African-Americans and Native Americans as an "obvious travesty").

for the survival of democracy, religious education is inimical to the democratic ideal. Accordingly, in 1802, Jefferson wrote that the First Amendment's religion clauses, if properly interpreted, would limit state involvement with religion:

> I contemplate with sovereign reverence that act of the whole American people which declared that their legislature should make "no law respecting the establishment of religion, or prohibiting free exercise thereof," thus, building a wall of separation between church and state.[28]

(c) The Growth of the Founders' Conception of Public Education Through Common Schools and Public Universities

Benjamin Rush, who had signed the Declaration of Independence and served as Surgeon General of the revolutionary army, was instrumental in advancing a free and uniform system of public education.[29] In particular, Rush argued that a general tax should be used to finance a system of American public education, asserting that such a system would in the long-run lessen taxes for all. In arguments that foreshadow contemporary debates about public education, Rush even claimed that all citizens benefit from public education because criminal activity and the expenses of the criminal justice system would be reduced in a nation of educated, law-abiding citizens. Moreover, a national system of education culminating in a public university would bring diverse people together through a shared patriotic love of country that would allow them to internalize prudential restraints on their own freedom.

The founders' idea of a uniform, free, public and publicly funded educational system was further realized in the "common school" movement of the early 1800s. Horace Mann, a Massachusetts legislator and Secretary of the Massachusetts Board of Education, was a leading advocate for common schools. Mann believed that the public, common school could bring diverse peoples and cultures into a common bond. Although Mann's own values were aligned with Protestant beliefs, he advocated broad, unifying principles of morality. Division in religion and class could be overcome by a common education in a common morality.

Like Rush, Mann argued that publicly financed education for the masses was good for society as a whole. In particular, he convinced the wealthy property owners that proper education would give to the working class a respect for the property and wealth of others that would help to preserve the existing power structure.[30] He argued that property landowners had a special

---

[28] *See* Letter from Jefferson to Danbury Baptist Association, Jan. 1, 1802. *www.loc.gov/loc/lcib/9806/danpost.html*. Recently, a prior draft of Jefferson's letter was discovered, which is available through the Library of Congress, *www.loc.gov/loc/lcib/9806/danpre.html*. In his carefully composed letter, Jefferson initially wrote that the First Amendment created a wall of "eternal" separation between church and state.

[29] *See* Rush, *Plan for the Establishment of Public Schools and the Diffusion of Knowledge in Pennsylvania; to which are Added, Thoughts upon the Mode of Education, Proper in a Republic* (1786). *See also* Urban & Wagoner, at 79-85.

[30] *See* Urban & Wagoner, at 102-103.

obligation to fund public education in proportion to their ownership. Yet, Mann also believed that property was a national asset that had been entrusted to individual owners for their use in ways that served the common wealth. Hence, the state had the right to tax personal property for public uses such as the education of all citizens in an integrated, state controlled system of common or "normal" schools.[31]

In 1852, Massachusetts became the first state to erect a compulsory attendance law, thereby exercising the type of power Mann argued states should employ in regulating the education of their citizens.[32] By 1918, every state had passed some form of compulsory school attendance statute.[33] As public school attendance significantly increased in the late 1800s and early 1900s, the illiteracy rate among Americans significantly declined.[34]

The founding ideal of a system of public education, which was advanced by Rush and Mann, eventually spread beyond compulsory elementary and secondary schools, to American colleges and universities. Virtually all of the major institutions of higher learning in this country began as religious institutions. In 1869, however, the Virginia legislature finally answered Jefferson's call for the creation of a publicly supported university.[35] By the mid-1800s, a system of colleges had spread from the east coast to the south and mid-west.[36] American colleges shared a focus on science, liberal arts and classical studies.[37] Beginning in 1868 with the creation of Cornell University, many of these colleges evolved into universities. The states began to develop relatively large public institutions of higher learning. These universities were designed to realize both Franklin's goal of teaching practical skills and Jefferson's goal of facilitating intellectual autonomy and the expansion of knowledge.[38] In particular, the undergraduate programs within universities maintained their liberal arts orientation, while the graduate programs allowed students to elect a specialized field of study or professional training.[39]

---

[31] *See* Urban & Wagoner, at 108-109. Urban and Wagoner also trace the rise of women in the teaching profession to Mann's "common" or "normal" school movement.

[32] *See* Urban & Wagoner, at 173.

[33] *Id.* at 172.

[34] *Id.* at 174 (attendance increased at the turn of the century from 49 percent to 64 percent, while illiteracy declined from 20 percent to 13 percent). In *Brown v. Board of Education*, 347 U.S. 483 at n.4 (1954), the Supreme Court traces the development of public schools and compulsory school attendance laws, both of which grew dramatically after the adoption of the Fourteenth Amendment in 1868.

[35] *See* Urban & Wagoner, at 75.

[36] *Id.* at 182.

[37] *Id.*

[38] *Id.* at 183.

[39] *Id.* at 183. For a compelling argument on behalf of the critical role played by public colleges and universities in America, *see* Clark Kerr's Inaugural Address as President of the University of California at Berkeley in 1958 (available at *www.higher-ed.org/history.htm*). For thorough and insightful studies of the history of colleges and universities in America, *see* Harold S. Wechsler & Lester F. Goodchild, *History of Higher Education* (1997); Christopher J. Lucas, *American Higher Education: A History* (1994); Frederick Rudolph, *The American College and University: A History* (1962); John Brubacher & Willis Rudy, *Higher Education in Transition: A History of American Colleges and Universities, 1636-1976* (1976).

(d) John Dewey and American Democratic Education

The uniquely American educational philosophy of John Dewey approaches Plato in its depth and influence. Indeed, Dewey's educational philosophy has had a profound impact upon the law and practice of education in America. Writing in the early 1900s, Dewey creates a comprehensive educational philosophy built upon democratic principles of equality and individuality. In *Democracy and Education,* Dewey argues that because "a democratic society repudiates the principle of external authority, it must find a substitute in voluntary disposition and interest; these can be created only by education." Education serves democratic institutions where it facilitates the "breaking down of those barriers of class, race, and national territory which kept men from perceiving the full import of their activity."[40]

Dewey then traces the development of educational philosophy from the social constructs of Plato to the individualist ideal of the enlightenment of Locke and Rousseau. He advances a specific "democratic ideal" of education that makes educational resources available in America regardless of class or status and uses those resources to encourage American students to reach beyond their borders and discover things that unite mankind: "The emphasis must be put upon whatever bind people together in cooperative human pursuits and results, apart from geographical limitations."[41] Dewey understands democratic education as a "freeing of individual capacity in a progressive growth directed to social aims."[42]

In Experience and Education, Dewey declares that the educator must understand that learning is "a continuous process of reconstruction of experience."[43] Dewey is often credited with the fundamental belief that students learn by "doing." Dewey believed that the "scientific method" was "the only authentic means at our command for getting at the significance of our everyday experiences of the world in which we live."[44] Only with the help of the scientific method adapted to various degrees of student maturity can students freely construct for themselves patterns discernable in everyday experience. That method, and the "constructivist" learning process that results, includes "the formation of ideas, acting upon ideas, observation of the conditions which result, and the organization of facts and ideas for future use."[45]

4. Contemporary Debates in American Educational Policy

Many of the insights developed by the classical, modern and American educational philosophers are now the foundation for contemporary ideas about education in the American regime. In the current debates about the proper direction of education in America, the following principles are

[40] *See* Dewey, *Democracy and Education,* reprinted in Cahn, at 288-293.
[41] *Id.*
[42] *Id.*
[43] *See* Dewey, *Experience and Education,* reprinted in Cahn, at 362.
[44] *Id.*
[45] *Id.*

generally well accepted: (1) Plato's view that education is a public, political matter that plays a vital role in shaping the character of citizens and the nature of a regime; (2) Aristotle's understanding that a democratic regime requires for its health a unique democratic form of education that trains all citizens both to rule and to be ruled; (3) Locke's view that society must educate its citizens in the "reason" and self-restraint necessary for self government; (4) Montesquieu's view that citizens can be free to govern themselves only if given through education a love of their laws and of their country; (5) Rousseau's perception that education must be attuned to the natural, developmental needs of each child so that each citizen can come naturally to understand their connection with the community; (6) the founders' belief that the general diffusion of knowledge to all citizens through a public nonsectarian educational system was vital to creating a unified American regime; (7) Mann's insight that such an education should be accomplished by the creation of uniform, comprehensive, state-centralized "common" schools, funded by property owners for the good of society; (8) Dewey's doctrine that American education must be designed to allow students the freedom to "construct" their own experience and to find the common human bonds that link all persons, regardless of race, class or religion; and (9) the remarkably consistent view expressed by the greatest education philosophers that a country's public educational system must be separated from religion.

Although there may be a philosophic consensus that a secular, public education is particularly necessary in a liberal democracy, the tension between individual freedom and collective authority inherent in such a regime drives the current debates about the proper role of education in America. In Democratic Education,[46] Amy Gutmann gleans from Dewey and other educational philosophers the necessity in America for a unique type of authoritarian education which "recognizes that educational authority must be shared among parents, citizens and professional educators." According to Gutmann, a "democratic state recognizes the value of professional authority in enabling children to appreciate and to evaluate ways of life other than those favored by their families. . . . a democratic state recognizes the value of political education in predisposing children to accept those ways of life that are consistent with sharing the rights and responsibilities of citizenship in a democratic society. . . ."

In *Moral Education and the Democratic Ideal,*[47] however, Israel Scheffler argues that a more *progressive* democratic education is indispensable to the democratic "ideal." He contends that education must create an environment in which students are free to question authority. Democratic education must support "a society that sustains itself not by the indoctrination of myth, but by the reasoned choices of its citizens, who continue to favor it in the light of a critical scrutiny both of it and its alternatives." Scheffler observes that democratic education is much more difficult than filling students with facts;

---

[46] *See* Gutmann, *Democratic Education,* reprinted in Cahn, 411-434. (Professor Gutmann teaches at Princeton University and wrote this insightful piece for the Princeton University Press in 1987).

[47] *See* Scheffler, *Moral Education and the Democratic Ideal,* reprinted in Cahn, at 436-442.

it requires developing a habit of reasonableness that accompanies free inquiry.[48]

In *The Schools Our Children Deserve* (1999), Alfie Kohn explicitly describes the current division in American educational thought as a conflict between the "authoritarian" and "progressive" educational approaches. The desire to inculcate young people with a core set of properly held national beliefs often leads to an "authoritarian" approach to educational institutions and ultimately to the "standards" movement reflected in the No Child Left Behind Act of 2001.[49] This educational approach is designed to deliver to students the facts and values deemed important by the national or local community. As relatively passive recipients of orthodox wisdom, students can be taught to behave like patriotic citizens and disciplined workers. Proponents of this view of American education may even rely on the Aristotelian notion that democratic citizens must be taught how to be ruled. Education in this form prepares Americans to be consumers.

By this "authoritarian" perspective, learning can be measured by objective standards. If the memorization of accepted facts is the goal of education, then tests can be devised to assess whether or not students have memorized such facts. When students fail to recall facts on these tests, the school has failed in its mission to prepare students to recount such facts on command. Students who fail to demonstrate appropriate external behavior can be made to do so with negative reinforcements like being held back in school. Schools that fail to train their students to perform also will suffer negative reinforcements such as the withdrawal of funds.

This prominent contemporary view of education also has the advantage of the perception that it is cost effective. If the goal of education is to give the same information to classrooms full of students so that they can all recall that information in a testing environment, then there is little apparent need to spend the money required to foster meaningful teacher-student relationships. The "standards" movement accepts the idea that a single teacher can impart a single set of facts to a large group of students at the same time. As such, this type of education for the masses seems cost efficient.

The contrary "progressive" strand in contemporary American education policy originates in the educational philosophy of the founders of the Constitution, as well as Rousseau and Dewey. By this perspective, the overriding goal of a uniquely American education is to prepare American youth to participate in citizenship by allowing them freedom to create the thinking, processing and communication skills necessary to lead, rather than to follow. This "child-centered" or "learner-centered" approach understands that each child learns in a different way and at a different developmental rate. Genuine learning requires "differentiation" in the sense that a teacher must respond to the unique needs and learning styles of each child, one at a time. As such,

[48] The vibrancy of the ongoing debate can be seen in the recent attempt by New York's School Chancellor, Joel Klein to change the City's schools from a traditional model of standards-based instruction to a "progressive," student-centered model that encourages meaningful teacher-student relationships and allows students to construct their own understanding. *See* J. Traub, *New York's New Approach*, N.Y. Times, Education Life, Aug. 3, 2003, at 20-21.

[49] 20 U.S.C. §6301 *et seq.*

education cannot be given by an authoritarian figure to many students in the same way and at the same time. Rather, education is built upon close teacher-student relationships, which allow teachers to recognize and to respond to the different needs and abilities of each child.

Accordingly, educational systems pursuing this approach may have to hire significantly more adult professionals than those pursuing a more authoritarian approach. The desire to meet each child's unique needs also will lead to additional special education services and expenses. This progressive, student-centered approach, therefore, appears to be far more expensive than the authoritarian, standards-based approach. As Benjamin Rush and Horace Mann argued long ago, however, the public funds expended on educational excellence are an invaluable social investment. Proponents of the progressive approach, like Rush and Mann before them, argue that the cost of genuine educational excellence is far less than the health care, crime and welfare costs created by its absence.

Finally, in his book, *The End of Education: Redefining the Value of School*, Neil Postman suggests that the current debates between the "authoritarian, standards" movement and the "progressive, child-centered" movement miss the point.[50] These debates disregard the most important question of all: what is the goal of American education and the law that supports it? Postman declares: "there is no surer way to bring an end to schooling than for it to have no end."[51] In recent decades, the legal and political debates surrounding education have been largely devoted to processes and methods. Ignored in those discussions has been a serious reconsideration of the fundamental *purpose* of education in the American regime. Postman proposes the redevelopment of a shared vision of the goals of American education. Relying on Jefferson, Mann and Dewey, Postman observes that in America, "public education does not serve a public. It *creates* a public." What kind of public does the current education system create, and what kind should it create?

E. IS THE INTEGRATION OF EDUCATION LAW, POLICY AND PRACTICE POSSIBLE?

The issues raised by educational philosophers from Plato to Postman are still very much alive in contemporary policy debates about American education precisely because the values these philosophers advanced are often in tension with each other. These tensions permeate the law of education in America, and can therefore be perceived in each section of this book. For example, the very next section of this book asks: in an American regime that values both personal freedom and common education, what are the boundaries between the liberty of individual families to conduct their own private education and the power of the state to compel attendance in common schools? Similarly, in a constitutional order that guarantees both the freedom to exercise religion and the

[50] Postman, *The End of Education: Redefining the Value of School* 5, 17 (1995).

[51] *Id.*

freedom from a state-established religious education system, what are the appropriate borders between education and religion? What type of "morality" can be advanced in a public school in a country where the founders remonstrated against the teaching of religion in public institutions? Assuming that the "general" diffusion of knowledge through "public" or "common" schools is a valued objective, should these schools be funded unequally by property taxes in a regime that also values equality and private property? Does the value of education rise to the level of a protected, fundamental constitutional right to educational opportunity that would justify the redistribution of private property for the common good? Furthermore, in a democratic nation that prizes both Dewey's national bonds and also state sovereignty and local differences, what are the limits of the national government's power to impose on localities a uniform curriculum? Should the governance of schooling be entrusted to a professional elite or to popularly elected public officials?

The law governing the rights and responsibilities of students raises profound philosophical questions as well. If, as Rousseau suggests, students must be free to discover their world naturally, what are the appropriate limits on student conduct in the educational environment? Moreover, in a regime that values individual differences but also strives for educational equality, should each student receive the exact same education, or is it appropriate to differentiate based on special needs or abilities? How are we to reconcile the value of an education that breaks down racial and economic barriers in a society that also values the freedom of its citizens to live in neighborhoods of their choosing? Finally, how will an American democratic regime that wants all of its children to receive an excellent education draw the line between legitimate state control over education and illegitimate governmental interference with the freedom to teach and to learn? As you analyze those issues, which are raised in the case law and statutes that follow, consider also whether education law has successfully answered Postman's overarching questions: what is the proper end of American education, and does the law serve that end?

SECTION II

THE PARAMETERS OF PUBLIC EDUCATION: PUBLIC AND PRIVATE, CHURCH AND STATE

CHAPTER 3

THE LIMITS OF PUBLIC EDUCATION

Is education a public or private matter? If government is to have a significant role in the education of its citizens, should public school attendance be mandatory, or should parents have the right to educate their children in their own home without governmental regulation? Moreover, if education serves compelling governmental interests, should a right to public education be recognized under the federal and state constitutions? These legal, political and philosophical issues are raised in this chapter.

The answer to the legal questions begins with the leading Supreme Court cases governing the right of a parent to teach a child within the home: *Meyer v. Nebraska,* 262 U.S. 390 (1923), *Pierce v. Society of Sisters,* 268 U.S. 510 (1925), and *Wisconsin v. Yoder,* 406 U.S. 205 (1972). These cases focus on the parental right to control the education of a child and the related issue of religious freedom.

In *Meyer,* the Supreme Court recognizes the state's power to compel its citizens to attend "some school" and to enact reasonable regulations for all schools. Yet the Court also affirms the competing "liberty" interest teachers have in pursuing their teaching profession and the right of parents to engage teachers of their choosing to instruct their children.

The Supreme Court in *Pierce* rejects an Oregon statute requiring parents to send their children to "public" school. The Court's primary rationale for striking down the state's compulsory education statute is that the statute deprives private and parochial educational institutions of a "property" interest in the maintenance of a "remunerative" business. In addition, however, the *Pierce* opinion relies on *Meyer* for its argument that the Oregon statute "unreasonably interferes with the liberty of parents and guardians to direct the upbringing and education of children under their control."

The law governing the right of parents and guardians to direct the education of their children also is influenced by the protection of religious freedom under the First Amendment's free exercise clause. In *Yoder,* the Supreme Court holds that the state of Wisconsin violates the religious freedom of Amish families by forcing them to require their children to attend a state sanctioned school beyond the eighth grade. Yet the Court's holding is narrowly tailored to the unique circumstances surrounding the Amish, reaffirming the validity of compulsory education in most circumstances. Since *Yoder,* the courts generally have upheld state efforts to regulate non-public schools and even home schooling through various devices, including teacher certification, student testing, curriculum standards and home monitoring.

The court decisions in this chapter reflect a consistent appreciation for the importance of education in public life, such that the government can compel its citizens to engage in educational practices and can to a large degree dictate the quality of the educators and the curriculum. Nonetheless, and perhaps paradoxically, the next chapter presents key Supreme Court decisions rejecting a fundamental constitutional right to an education. Can the government force its citizens to be educated and yet not provide its citizens with a right to that education?

A. THE BOUNDARIES BETWEEN PUBLIC EDUCATION AND HOME SCHOOLING

MEYER v. NEBRASKA

262 U.S. 390 (1923)

Justice MCREYNOLDS delivered the opinion of the Court.

Plaintiff in error was tried and convicted in the district court for Hamilton county, Nebraska, under an information which charged that on May 25, 1920, while an instructor in Zion Parochial School he unlawfully taught the subject of reading in the German language to Raymond Parpart, a child of 10 years, who had not attained and successfully passed the eighth grade. The information is based upon 'An act relating to the teaching of foreign languages in the state of Nebraska,' approved April 9, 1919, which follows:

"Section 1. No person, individually or as a teacher, shall, in any private, denominational, parochial or public school, teach any subject to any person in any language than the English language. . . ."

The problem for our determination is whether the statute as construed and applied unreasonably infringes the liberty guaranteed to the plaintiff in error by the Fourteenth Amendment: "No state shall deprive any person of life, liberty or property without due process of law."

While this court has not attempted to define with exactness the liberty thus guaranteed, the term has received much consideration and some of the included things have been definitely stated. Without doubt, it denotes not merely freedom from bodily restraint but also the right of the individual to contract, to engage in any of the common occupations of life, to acquire useful knowledge, to marry, establish a home and bring up children, to worship God according to the dictates of his own conscience, and generally to enjoy those privileges long recognized at common law as essential to the orderly pursuit of happiness by free men. The established doctrine is that this liberty may not be interfered with, under the guise of protecting the public interest, by legislative action which is arbitrary or without reasonable relation to some purpose within the competency of the state to effect. Determination by the Legislature of what constitutes proper exercise of police power is not final or conclusive but is subject to supervision by the courts.

The American people have always regarded education and acquisition of knowledge as matters of supreme importance which should be diligently promoted. The Ordinance of 1787 declares: "Religion, morality and knowledge being necessary to good government and the happiness of mankind, schools and the means of education shall forever be encouraged."

Corresponding to the right of control, it is the natural duty of the parent to give his children education suitable to their station in life; and nearly all the states, including Nebraska, enforce this obligation by compulsory laws.

Practically, education of the young is only possible in schools conducted by especially qualified persons who devote themselves thereto. The calling always has been regarded as useful and honorable, essential, indeed, to the public welfare. Mere knowledge of the German language cannot reasonably be regarded as harmful. Heretofore it has been commonly looked upon as helpful and desirable. Plaintiff in error taught this language in school as part of his occupation. His right thus to teach and the right of parents to engage him so to instruct their children, we think, are within the liberty of the amendment.

The challenged statute forbids the teaching in school of any subject except in English; also the teaching of any other language until the pupil has attained and successfully passed the eighth grade, which is not usually accomplished before the age of twelve. The Supreme Court of the state has held that "the so-called ancient or dead languages" are not "within the spirit or the purpose of the act."

Latin, Greek, Hebrew are not prescribed; but German, French, Spanish, Italian, and every other alien speech are within the ban. Evidently the Legislature has attempted materially to interfere with the calling of modern language teachers, with the opportunities of pupils to acquire knowledge, and with the power of parents to control the education of their own.

It is said the purpose of the legislation was to promote civic development by inhibiting training and education of the immature in foreign tongues and ideals before they could learn English and acquire American ideals, and "that the English language should be and become the mother tongue of all children reared in this state." It is also affirmed that the foreign born population is very large, that certain communities commonly use foreign words, follow foreign leaders, move in a foreign atmosphere, and that the children are thereby hindered from becoming citizens of the most useful type and the public safety is imperiled.

That the state may do much, go very far, indeed, in order to improve the quality of its citizens, physically, mentally and morally, is clear; but the individual has certain fundamental rights which must be respected. The protection of the Constitution extends to all, to those who speak other languages as well as to those born with English on the tongue. Perhaps it would be highly advantageous if all had ready understanding of our ordinary speech, but this cannot be coerced by methods which conflict with the Constitution—a desirable end cannot be promoted by prohibited means.

For the welfare of his Ideal Commonwealth, Plato suggested a law which should provide: "That the wives of our guardians are to be common, and their children are to be common, and no parent is to know his own child, nor any child his parent. . . . The proper officers will take the offspring of the good parents to the pen or fold, and there they will deposit them with certain nurses who dwell in a separate quarter; but the offspring of the inferior, or of the better when they chance to be deformed, will be put away in some mysterious, unknown place, as they should be."

In order to submerge the individual and develop ideal citizens, Sparta assembled the males at seven into barracks and entrusted their subsequent education and training to official guardians. Although such measures have been deliberately approved by men of great genius, their ideas touching the relation between individual and state were wholly different from those upon which our institutions rest; and it hardly will be affirmed that any legislature could impose such restrictions upon the people of a state without doing violence to both letter and spirit of the Constitution.

The desire of the legislature to foster a homogeneous people with American ideals prepared readily to understand current discussions of civic matters is easy to appreciate. Unfortunate experiences during the late war and aversion toward every character of truculent adversaries were certainly enough to quicken that aspiration. But the means adopted, we think, exceed the limitations upon the power of the state and conflict with rights assured to plaintiff in error. The interference is plain enough and no adequate reason therefore in time of peace and domestic tranquility has been shown.

The power of the state to compel attendance at some school and to make reasonable regulation for all schools, including a requirement that they shall give instructions in English, is not questioned. Nor has challenge been made of the state's power to prescribe a curriculum for institutions which it supports. Those matters are not within the present controversy. No emergency has arisen which renders knowledge by a child of some language other than English so clearly harmful as to justify its inhibition with the consequent infringement of rights long freely enjoyed. We are constrained to conclude that the statute as applied is arbitrary and without reasonable relation to any end within the competency of the state.

As the statute undertakes to interfere only with teaching which involves a modern language, leaving complete freedom as to other matters, there seems no adequate foundation for the suggestion that the purpose was to protect the child's health by limiting his mental activities. It is well known that proficiency in a foreign language seldom comes to one not instructed at an early age, and experience shows that this is not injurious to the health, morals or understanding of the ordinary child.

The judgment of the court below must be reversed and the cause remanded for further proceedings not inconsistent with this opinion.

Reversed.

NOTES AND QUESTIONS

1. The Court indicates that the Platonic philosophy of education, while written by a man of "great genius," is incompatible with the United States

Constitution. Where does the Constitution prescribe any particular educational system or practice? What is the "great genius" of the educational system envisioned by the Constitution?

2. The Court declares that the liberty guaranteed by the Fourteenth Amendment to the Constitution includes the freedom to "acquire useful knowledge" and the freedom to "establish a home and bring up children." The Court further alludes to the "natural duty of the parent" to educate a child, the "right" to teach, and the "right of parents to engage" a teacher to instruct their children. What is the origin of these rights and duties?
3. The Supreme Court relies on Article III of The Northwest Ordinance of 1787 as evidence that the "American people have always regarded education and acquisition of knowledge as matters of Supreme importance." What connection is made in the ordinance between religion and education? Is that connection important to the Court?
4. Under the reasoning in *Meyer*, could a state enact legislation that requires all subjects other than foreign language instruction to be delivered in English? For example, Illinois requires that its non-public schools teach the "branches of education taught to children of corresponding age and grade in the public schools . . . in the English language." 105 ILCS 5/26-1(1).

Pierce v. Society of Sisters

268 U.S. 510 (1925)

Justice McReynolds delivered the opinion of the Court.

The challenged Act, effective September 1, 1926, requires every parent, guardian or other person having control or charge or custody of a child between eight and sixteen years to send him "to a public school for the period of time a public school shall be held during the current year" in the district where the child resides; and failure so to do is declared a misdemeanor. There are exemptions — not especially important here — for children who are not normal, or who have completed the eighth grade, or who reside at considerable distances from any public school, or whose parents or guardians hold special permits from the County Superintendent. The manifest purpose is to compel general attendance at public schools by normal children, between eight and sixteen, who have not completed the eighth grade. And without doubt enforcement of the statute would seriously impair, perhaps destroy, the profitable features of appellees' business and greatly diminish the value of their property.

Appellee, the Society of Sisters, is an Oregon corporation, organized in 1880, with power to care for orphans, educate and instruct the youth, establish and maintain academies or schools, and acquire necessary real and personal property. It has long devoted its property and effort to the secular and religious education and care of children, and has acquired the valuable good will of many parents and guardians. It conducts interdependent primary and high schools and junior colleges, and maintains orphanages for the custody and control of children between eight and sixteen. In its primary schools many children between those ages are taught the subjects usually pursued in Oregon public schools during the first eight years. Systematic religious instruction and moral training according to the tenets of the Roman Catholic Church are also regularly provided. All courses of study, both temporal and religious, contemplate continuity of training under appellee's charge; the primary schools are essential to the system and the most profitable. It owns valuable buildings, especially constructed and equipped for school purposes. The business is remunerative—the annual income from primary schools exceeds thirty thousand dollars—and the successful conduct of this requires long time contracts with teachers and parents. The Compulsory Education Act of 1922 has already caused the withdrawal from its schools of children who would otherwise continue, and their income has steadily declined.

. . . The inevitable practical result of enforcing the Act under consideration would be destruction of appellees' primary schools, and perhaps all other private primary schools for normal children within the State of Oregon. These parties are engaged in a kind of undertaking not inherently harmful, but long regarded as useful and meritorious. Certainly there is nothing in the present records to indicate that they have failed to discharge their obligations to patrons, students or the State. And there are no peculiar circumstances or present emergencies which demand extraordinary measures relative to primary education.

Under the doctrine of *Meyer v. Nebraska* . . . we think it entirely plain that the Act of 1922 unreasonably interferes with the liberty of parents and guardians to direct the upbringing and education of children under their control. As often heretofore pointed out, rights guaranteed by the Constitution may not be abridged by legislation which has no reasonable relation to some purpose within the competency of the State. The fundamental theory of liberty upon which all governments in this Union repose excludes any general power of the State to standardize its children by forcing them to accept instruction from public teachers only. The child is not the mere creature of the State; those who nurture him and direct his destiny have the right, coupled with the high duty, to recognize and prepare him for additional obligations.

NOTES AND QUESTIONS

1. What is the *Pierce* Court's fundamental rationale for declaring unconstitutional Oregon's law mandating public school attendance? The Court argues that the Oregon law would "greatly diminish the value of the [Society's] property." Yet, the Court also mentions that the statute interferes with the liberty of parents and guardians to direct the education of their children. Does the Oregon statute deprive the Society of a property interest, or the parents of a liberty interest, or both? Which argument is most compelling?
2. The Court initially concentrates on the property rights of the Society of Sisters. Is the law unconstitutional because it represents an unacceptable taking of that property?
3. In its last substantive paragraph, the Court declares that the Oregon law "unreasonably interferes with the liberty of parents and guardians to direct

the upbringing and education of children under their control." Is that the basis for the Court's holding, elaborate dicta or merely a rhetorical flourish? Where does the "liberty of parents and guardians" relied upon by the Court originate?

4. For its declaration of the "liberty of parents and guardians," the Court cites the "doctrine" in *Meyer v. Nebraska*. What precisely is that doctrine, and where does it appear in *Meyer*?
5. The Court declares that the state has no power to "standardize" its children through the means of requiring them to accept instruction from "public teachers only." What does the Court mean by the power to "standardize" children? Does the state have the power to standardize its children by means other than requiring public school attendance? Should it have such a power?

WISCONSIN v. YODER

406 U.S. 205 (1972)

Mr. Chief Justice BURGER delivered the opinion of the Court.

On petition of the State of Wisconsin, we granted the writ of certiorari in this case to review a decision of the Wisconsin Supreme Court holding that respondents' convictions for violating the State's compulsory school-attendance law were invalid under the Free Exercise Clause of the First Amendment to the United States Constitution made applicable to the States by the Fourteenth Amendment. For the reasons hereafter stated we affirm the judgment of the Supreme Court of Wisconsin.

Respondents Jonas Yoder and Wallace Miller are members of the Old Order Amish religion, and respondent Adin Yutzy is a member of the conservative Amish Mennonite Church. They and their families are residents of Green County, Wisconsin. Wisconsin's compulsory school-attendance law required them to cause their children to attend public or private school until reaching age 16 but the respondents declined to send their children, ages 14 and 15, to public school after they complete the eighth grade. The children were not enrolled in any private school, or within any recognized exception to the compulsory-attendance law, and they are conceded to be subject to the Wisconsin statute.

On complaint of the school district administrator for the public schools, respondents were charged, tried, and convicted of violating the compulsory-attendance law in Green County Court and were fined the sum of $5 each. Respondents defended on the ground that the application of the compulsory-attendance law violated their rights under the First and Fourteenth Amendments. The trial testimony showed that respondents believed, in accordance with the tenets of Old Order Amish communities generally, that their children's attendance at high school, public or private, was contrary to the Amish religion and way of life. They believed that by sending their children to high school, they would not only expose themselves to the danger of the censure of the church community, but, as found by the county court, also endanger their own salvation and that of their children. The State stipulated that respondents' religious beliefs were sincere.

In support of their position, respondents presented as expert witnesses scholars on religion and education whose testimony is uncontradicted. They expressed their opinions on the relationship of the Amish belief concerning school attendance to the more general tenets of their religion, and described the impact that compulsory high school attendance could have on the continued survival of Amish communities as they exist in the United States today. . . . As a result of their common heritage, Old Order Amish communities today are characterized by a fundamental belief that salvation requires life in a church community separate and apart from the world and worldly influence. This concept of life aloof from the world and its values is central to their faith.

A related feature of Old Order Amish communities is their devotion to a life in harmony with nature and the soil, as exemplified by the simple life of the early Christian era that continued in America during much of our early national life. Amish beliefs require members of the community to make their living by farming or closely related activities. . . .

Amish objection to formal education beyond the eighth grade is firmly grounded in these central religious concepts. They object to the high school, and higher education generally, because the values they teach are in marked variance with Amish values and the Amish way of life; they view secondary school education as an impermissible exposure of their children to a "worldly" influence in conflict with their beliefs. The high school tends to emphasize intellectual and scientific accomplishments, self-distinction, competitiveness, worldly success, and social life with other students. Amish society emphasizes informal learning-through-doing; a life of "goodness," rather than a life of intellect; wisdom, rather than technical knowledge, community welfare, rather than competition; and separation from, rather than integration with, contemporary worldly society.

Formal high school education beyond the eighth grade is contrary to Amish beliefs, not only because it places Amish children in an environment hostile to Amish beliefs with increasing emphasis on competition in class work and sports and with pressure to conform to the styles, manners, and ways of the peer group, but also because it takes them away from their community, physically and emotionally, during the crucial and formative adolescent period of life. During this period, the children must acquire Amish attitudes favoring manual work and self-reliance and the specific skills needed to perform the adult role of an Amish farmer or housewife. They must learn to enjoy physical labor. Once a child has learned basic reading, writing, and elementary mathematics, these traits, skills, and attitudes admittedly fall within the category of those best learned through example and "doing" rather than in a classroom. And, at this time in life, the Amish child must also grow in his faith and his relationship to the Amish community if he is to be prepared to accept the heavy obligations imposed by adult baptism. In short, high school attendance with teachers who are not of the Amish faith—and may even be hostile to it—interposes a serious barrier to the integration of the Amish child into the Amish religious community. Dr. John Hostetler, one of the experts on Amish society, testified that the modern high school is not equipped, in curriculum or social environment, to impart the values promoted by Amish society.

The Amish do not object to elementary education through the first eight grades as a general proposition because they agree that their children must have basic skills in the "three R's" in order to read the bible, to be good farmers and citizens, and to be able to deal with non-Amish people when necessary in the course of daily affairs. They view such a basic education as acceptable because it does not significantly expose their children to worldly values or interfere with their development in the Amish community during the crucial adolescent period. While Amish accept compulsory elementary education generally, wherever possible they have established their own elementary schools in many respects like the small local schools of the past. In the Amish belief higher learning tends to develop values they reject as influences that alienate man from God.

On the basis of such considerations, Dr. Hostetler testified that compulsory high school attendance could not only result in great psychological harm to Amish children, because of the conflicts it would produce, but would also, in his opinion, ultimately result in the destruction of the Old Order Amish church community as it exists in the United States today. The testimony of Dr. Donald A. Erickson, an expert witness on education, also showed that the Amish succeed in preparing their high school age children to be productive members of the Amish community. He described their system of learning through doing the skills directly relevant to their adult roles in the Amish community as "ideal" and perhaps superior to ordinary high school education. The evidence also showed that the Amish have an excellent record as law-abiding and generally self-sufficient members of society. . . .

I

There is no doubt as to the power of a State, having a high responsibility for education of its citizens, to impose reasonable regulations for the control and duration of basic education. *See, e.g., Pierce v. Society of Sisters.* Providing public schools ranks at the very apex of the function of a State. Yet even this paramount responsibility was, in *Pierce,* made to yield to the right of parents to provide an equivalent education in a privately operated system. There the Court held that Oregon's statute compelling attendance in a public school from age eight to age 16 unreasonably interfered with the interest of parents in directing the rearing of their off-spring, including their education in church-operated schools. As that case suggests, the values of parental direction of the religious upbringing and education of their children in their early and formative years have a high place in our society . . . thus, a State's interest in universal education, however highly we rank it, is not totally free from a balancing process when it impinges on fundamental rights and interests, such as those specifically protected by the Free Exercise clause of the First Amendment, and the traditional interest of parents with respect to the religious upbringing of their children so long as they, in the words of Pierce, "prepare (them) for additional obligations."

It follows that in order for Wisconsin to compel school attendance beyond the eighth grade against a claim that such attendance interferes with the practice of a legitimate religious belief, it must appear either that the State does not deny the free exercise of religious belief by its requirement, or that there is a state interest of sufficient magnitude to override the interest claiming protection under the Free Exercise Clause. Long before there was general acknowledgment of the need for universal formal education, the Religion Clauses had specifically and firmly fixed the right to free exercise of religious beliefs, and buttressing this fundamental right was an equally firm, even if less explicit, prohibition against the establishment of any religion by government. The values underlying these two provisions relating to religion have been zealously protected, sometimes even at the expense of other interests of admittedly high social importance. . . .

The essence of all that has been said and written on the subject is that only those interests of the highest order and those not otherwise served can overbalance legitimate claims to the free exercise of religion. We can accept it as settled, therefore, that, however strong the State's interest in universal compulsory education, it is by no means absolute to the exclusion or subordination of all other interests.

II

We come then to the quality of the claims of the respondents concerning the alleged encroachment of Wisconsin's compulsory school-attendance statute on their rights and the rights of their children to the free exercise of the religious beliefs they and their forbears have adhered to for almost three centuries. In evaluating those claims we must be careful to determine whether the Amish religious faith and their mode of life are, as they claim, inseparable and interdependent. A way of life, however virtuous and admirable, may not be interposed as a barrier to reasonable state regulation of education if it is based on purely secular considerations; to have the protection of the Religion Clauses, the claims must be rooted in religious belief. Although a determination of what is a "religious" belief or practice entitled to constitutional protection may present a most delicate question, the very concept of ordered liberty precludes allowing every person to make his own standards on matters of conduct in which society as a whole has important interests. Thus, if the Amish asserted their claims because of their subjective evaluation and rejection of the contemporary secular values accepted by the majority, much as Thoreau rejected the social values of his time and isolated himself at Walden Pond, their claims would not rest on a religious basis. Thoreau's choice was philosophical and personal rather than religious, and such belief does not rise to the demands of the Religion Clauses.

Giving no weight to such secular considerations, however, we see that the record in this case abundantly supports the claim that the traditional way of life of the Amish is not merely a matter of personal preference, but one of deep religious conviction, shared by an organized group, and intimately related to daily living. . . .

The record shows that the respondents' religious beliefs and attitude toward life, family, and home have remained constant—perhaps some would say static—in a period of unparalleled progress in human knowledge generally and great changes in education. The respondents freely concede, and indeed assert as an article of faith, that their religious beliefs and what we would today call "life style" have not altered in fundamentals for centuries.

Their way of life in a church-oriented community, separated from the outside world and "worldly" influences, their attachment to nature and the soil, is a way inherently simple and uncomplicated, albeit difficult to preserve against the pressure to conform. Their rejection of telephones, automobiles, radios, and television, their mode of dress, of speech, their habits of manual work do indeed set them apart from much of contemporary society; these customs are both symbolic and practical.

As the society around the Amish has become more populous, urban, industrialized, and complex, particularly in this century, government regulation of human affairs has correspondingly become more detailed and pervasive. The Amish mode of life has thus come into conflict increasingly with requirements of contemporary society exerting a hydraulic insistence on conformity to majoritarian standards. So long as compulsory education laws were confined to eight grades of elementary basic education imparted in a nearby rural schoolhouse, with a large proportion of students of the Amish faith, the Old Order Amish had little basis to fear that school attendance would expose their children to the worldly influence they reject. But modern compulsory secondary education in rural areas is now largely carried on in a consolidated school, often remote from the student's home and alien to his daily home life. As the record so strongly shows, the values and programs of the modern secondary school are in sharp conflict with the fundamental mode of life mandated by the Amish religion; modern laws requiring compulsory secondary education have accordingly engendered great concern and conflict. The conclusion is inescapable that secondary schooling, by exposing Amish children to worldly influences in terms of attitudes, goals, and values contrary to beliefs, and by substantially interfering with the religious development of the Amish child and his integration into the way of life of the Amish faith community at the crucial adolescent stage of development, contravenes the basic religious tenets and practice of the Amish faith, both as to the parent and the child.

The impact of the compulsory-attendance law on respondents' practice of the Amish religion is not only severe, but inescapable, for the Wisconsin law affirmatively compels them, under threat of criminal sanction, to perform acts undeniably at odds with fundamental tenets of their religious beliefs. Nor is the impact of the compulsory-attendance law confined to grave interference with important Amish religious tenets from a subjective point of view. It carries with it precisely the kind of objective danger to the free exercise of religion that the First Amendment was designed to prevent. As the record shows, compulsory school attendance to age 16 for Amish children carries with it a very real threat of undermining the Amish community and religious practice as they exist today; they must either abandon belief and be assimilated into society at large, or be forced to migrate to some other and more tolerant region.[1]

---

[1] Some states have developed working arrangements with the Amish regarding high school attendance. . . . However, the danger to the continued existence of an ancient religious faith cannot be ignored simply because of the assumption that its adherents will continue to be able, at considerable sacrifice, to relocate in some more tolerant State or country or work out accommodations under threat of criminal prosecution. Forced migration of religious minorities was an evil that lay at the heart of the Religion Clauses. *See, e.g.,* Everson v. Board of Education, 330 U.S. 1, 9-10, 67 S. Ct. 504, 508-509, 91 L. Ed. 711 (1947); Madison, Memorial and Remonstrance Against Religious Assessments, 2 Writings of James Madison 183 (G. Hunt ed. 1901).

In sum, the unchallenged testimony of acknowledged experts in education and religious history, almost 300 years of consistent practice, and strong evidence of a sustained faith pervading and regulating respondents' entire mode of life support the claim that enforcement of the State's requirement of compulsory formal education after the eighth grade would gravely endanger if not destroy the free exercise of respondents' religious beliefs.

III

Neither the findings of the trial court nor the Amish claims as to the nature of their faith are challenged in this Court by the State of Wisconsin. Its position is that the State's interest in universal compulsory formal secondary education to age 16 is so great that it is paramount to the undisputed claims of respondents that their mode of preparing their youth for Amish life, after the traditional elementary education, is an essential part of their religious belief and practice. Nor does the State undertake to meet the claim that the Amish mode of life and education is inseparable from and a part of the basic tenets of their religion—indeed, as much a part of their religious belief and practices as baptism, the confessional, or a Sabbath may be for others.

Wisconsin concedes that under the Religion Clauses religious beliefs are absolutely free from the State's control, but it argues that "actions," even though religiously grounded, are outside the protection of the First Amendment. But our decisions have rejected the idea that religiously grounded conduct is always outside the protection of the Free Exercise Clause. It is true that activities of individuals, even when religiously based, are often subject to regulation by the States in the exercise of their undoubted power to promote the health, safety, and general welfare, or the Federal Government in the exercise of its delegated powers. . . . But to agree that religiously grounded conduct must often be subject to the broad police power of the State is not to deny that there are areas of conduct protected by the Free Exercise Clause of the First Amendment and thus beyond the power of the State to control, even under regulations of general applicability. . . . This case, therefore, does not become easier because respondents were convicted for their "actions" in refusing to send their children to the public high school; in this context belief and action cannot be neatly confined in logic-tight compartments. . . .

Nor can this case be disposed of on the grounds that Wisconsin's requirement for school attendance to age 16 applies uniformly to all citizens of the State and does not, on its face, discriminate against religions or a particular religion, or that it is motivated by legitimate secular concerns. A regulation neutral on its face may, in its application, nonetheless offend the constitutional requirement for governmental neutrality if it unduly burdens the free exercise of religion. The Court must not ignore the danger that an exception from a general obligation of citizenship on religious grounds may run afoul of the Establishment Clause, but that danger cannot be allowed to prevent any exception no matter how vital it may be to the protection of values promoted by the right of free exercise. By preserving doctrinal flexibility and recognizing the need for a sensible and realistic application of the Religion Clauses we have been able to chart a course that preserved the autonomy and freedom of religious bodies while avoiding any semblance of established religion. This is a "tight rope" and one we have successfully traversed. . . .

We turn, then, to the State's broader contention that its interest in its system of compulsory education is so compelling that even the established religious practices of the Amish must give way. Where fundamental claims of religious freedom are at stake, however, we cannot accept such a sweeping claim; despite its admitted validity in the generality of cases, we must searchingly examine the interests that the State seeks to promote by its requirement for compulsory education to age 16, and the impediment to those objectives that would flow from recognizing the claimed Amish exemption.

The State advances two primary arguments in support of its system of compulsory education. It notes, as Thomas Jefferson pointed out early in our history, that some degree of education is necessary to prepare citizens to participate effectively and intelligently in our open political system if we are to preserve freedom and independence. Further, education prepares individuals to be self-reliant and self-sufficient participants in society. We accept these propositions.

However, the evidence adduced by the Amish in this case is persuasively to the effect that an additional one or two years of formal high school for Amish children in place of their long-established program of informal vocational education would do little to serve those interests. Respondents' experts testified at trial, without challenge, that the value of all education must be assessed in terms of its capacity to prepare the child for life. It is one thing to say that compulsory education for a year or two beyond the eighth grade may be necessary when its goal is the preparation of the child for life in modern society as the majority live, but it is quite another if the goal of education be viewed as the preparation of the child for life in the separated agrarian community that is the keystone of the Amish faith. *See Meyer v. Nebraska.*

The State attacks respondents' position as one fostering "ignorance" from which the child must be protected by the State. No one can question the State's duty to protect children from ignorance but this argument does not square with the facts disclosed in the record. Whatever their idiosyncrasies as seen by the majority, this record strongly shows that the Amish community has been a highly successful social unit within our society, even if apart from the conventional "mainstream." Its members are productive and very law-abiding members of society; they reject public welfare in any of its usual modern forms. The Congress itself recognized their self-sufficiency by authorizing exemption of such groups as the Amish from the obligation to pay social security taxes.

It is neither fair nor correct to suggest that the Amish are opposed to education beyond the eighth grade level. What this record shows is that they are opposed to conventional formal education of the type provided by a certified high school because it comes at the child's crucial adolescent period of religious development. . . .

We must not forget that in the Middle Ages important values of the civilization of the Western World were preserved by members of religious orders who isolated themselves from all worldly influences against great obstacles. There can be no assumption that today's majority is "right" and the

Amish and others like them are "wrong." A way of life that is odd or even erratic but interferes with no rights or interests of others is not to be condemned because it is different.

The State, however, supports its interest in providing an additional one or two years of compulsory high school education to Amish children because of the possibility that some such children will choose to leave the Amish community, and that if this occurs they will be ill-equipped for life. The State argues that if Amish children leave their church they should not be in the position of making their way in the world without the education available in the one or two additional years the State requires. However, on this record, that argument is highly speculative. . . .

There is nothing in this record to suggest that the Amish qualities of reliability, self-reliance, and dedication to work would fail to find ready markets in today's society. Absent some contrary evidence supporting the State's position, we are unwilling to assume that persons possessing such valuable vocational skills and habits are doomed to become burdens on society should they determine to leave the Amish faith, nor is there any basis in the record to warrant a finding that an additional one or two years of formal school education beyond the eighth grade would serve to eliminate any such problem that might exist.

Insofar as the State's claim rests on the view that a brief additional period of formal education is imperative to enable the Amish to participate effectively and intelligently in our democratic process, it must fall. The Amish alternative to formal secondary school education has enabled them to function effectively in their day-to-day life under self-imposed limitations on relations with the world, and to survive and prosper in contemporary society as a separate, sharply identifiable and highly self-sufficient community for more than 200 years in this country. In itself this is strong evidence that they are capable of fulfilling the social and political responsibilities of citizenship without compelled attendance beyond the eighth grade at the price of jeopardizing their free exercise of religious belief. When Thomas Jefferson emphasized the need for education as a bulwark of a free people against tyranny, there is nothing to indicate he had in mind compulsory education through any fixed age beyond a basic education. Indeed, the Amish communities singularly parallel and reflect many of the virtues of Jefferson's ideal of the "sturdy yeoman" who would form the basis of what he considered as the ideal of a democratic society. Even their idiosyncratic separateness exemplifies the diversity we profess to admire and encourage.

The requirement for compulsory education beyond the eighth grade is a relatively recent development in our history. Less than 60 years ago, the educational requirements of almost all of the States were satisfied by completion of the elementary grades, at least where the child was regularly and lawfully employed. The independence and successful social functioning of the Amish community for a period approaching almost three centuries and more than 200 years in this country are strong evidence that there is at best a speculative gain, in terms of meeting the duties of citizenship, from an additional one or two years of compulsory formal education. Against this background it would require a more particularized showing from the State on this point to justify the severe interference with religious freedom such additional compulsory attendance would entail.

We should also note that compulsory education and child labor laws find their historical origin in common humanitarian instincts, and that the age limits of both laws have been coordinated to achieve their related objectives. In the context of this case, such considerations, if anything, support rather than detract from respondents' position. The origins of the requirement for school attendance to age 16, an age falling after the completion of elementary school but before completion of high school, are not entirely clear. But to some extent such laws reflected the movement to prohibit more child labor under age 16 that culminated in the provisions of the Federal Fair Labor Standards Act of 1938. It is true, then that the 16-year child labor age limit may to some degree derive from a contemporary impression that children should be in school until that age. But at the same time, it cannot be denied that, conversely, the 16-year education limit reflects, in substantial measure, the concern that children under that age should not be employed under conditions hazardous to their health, or in work that should be performed by adults.

The requirement of compulsory schooling to age 16 must therefore be viewed as aimed not merely at providing educational opportunities for children, but as an alternative to the equally undesirable consequence of unhealthful child labor displacing adult workers, or, on the other hand, forced idleness. . . .

In these terms, Wisconsin's interest in compelling the school attendance of Amish children to age 16 emerges as somewhat less substantial than requiring such attendance for children generally. For, while agricultural employment is not totally outside the legitimate concerns of the child labor laws, employment of children under parental guidance and on the family farm from age 14 to age 16 is an ancient tradition that lies at the periphery of the objectives of such laws. There is no intimation that the Amish employment of their children on family farms is in any way deleterious to their health or that Amish parents exploit children at tender years. Any such inference would be contrary to the record before us. Moreover, employment of Amish children on the family farm does not present the undesirable economic aspects of eliminating jobs that might otherwise be held by adults.

IV

Finally, the State, . . . argues that a decision exempting Amish children from the State's requirement fails to recognize the substantive right of the Amish child to a secondary education, and fails to give due regard to the power of the State as parens patriae to extend the benefit of secondary education to children regardless of the wishes of their parents.

. . . Contrary to the suggestion of the dissenting opinion of Mr. Justice DOUGLAS, our holding today in no degree depends on the assertion of the religious interest of the child as contrasted with that of the parents. It is the parents who are subject to prosecution here for failing to cause their children to attend school, and it is their right of free exercise, not that of their children, that must determine Wisconsin's power to impose criminal penalties on the parent. . . . [T]his case involves the fundamental interest of parents, as contrasted with that of the State, to guide the religious future and education of their children. The history and culture of Western civilization reflect a strong tradition of parental concern for the nurture and upbringing of their children. . . . This primary role of the parents in the upbringing of their children is now established beyond debate as an enduring American tradition. . . .

The duty to prepare a child for the "additional obligations," referred to by the Court, must be read to include the inculcation of moral standards, religious beliefs, and elements of good citizenship. *Pierce*, of course, recognized that where nothing more than the general interest of the parent in the nurture and education of his children is involved, it is beyond dispute that the State acts "reasonably" and constitutionally in requiring education to age 16 in some public or private school meeting the standards prescribed by the State.

However read, the Court's holding in *Pierce* stands as a charter of the rights of parents to direct the religious upbringing of their children. And, when the interests of parenthood are combined with a free exercise claim of the nature revealed by this record, more than merely a "reasonable relation to some purpose within the competency of the State" is required to sustain the validity of the State's requirement under the First Amendment. To be sure, the power of the parent, even when linked to a free exercise claim, may be subject to limitation . . . if it appears that parental decisions will jeopardize the health or safety of the child, or have a potential for significant social burdens. But in this case, the Amish have introduced persuasive evidence undermining the arguments the State has advanced to support its claims in terms of the welfare of the child and society as a whole. . . .

In the face of our consistent emphasis on the central values underlying the Religion Clauses in our constitutional scheme of government, we cannot accept a parens patriae claim of such all-encompassing scope and with such sweeping potential for broad and unforeseeable application as that urged by the State.

V

For the reasons stated we hold, with the Supreme Court of Wisconsin, that the First and Fourteenth Amendments prevent the State from compelling respondents to cause their children to attend formal high school to age 16.

Aided by a history of three centuries as an identifiable religious sect and a long history as a successful and self-sufficient segment of American society, the Amish in this case have convincingly demonstrated the sincerity of their religious beliefs, the interrelationship of belief with their mode of life, the vital role that belief and daily conduct play in the continued survival of Old Order Amish communities and their religious organization, and the hazards presented by the State's enforcement of a statute generally valid as to others. Beyond this, they have carried the even more difficult burden of demonstrating the adequacy of their alternative mode of continuing informal vocational education in terms of precisely those overall interests that the State advances in support of its program of compulsory high school education. In light of this convincing showing, one that probably few other religious groups or sects could make, and weighing the minimal difference between what the State would require and what the Amish already accept, it was incumbent on the State to show with more particularity how its admittedly strong interest in compulsory education would be adversely affected by granting an exception to the Amish.

Nothing we hold is intended to undermine the general applicability of the State's compulsory school-attendance statutes or to limit the power of the State to promulgate reasonable standards that, while not impairing the free exercise of religion, provide for continuing agricultural vocational education under parental and church guidance by the Old Order Amish or others similarly situated. The States have had a long history of amicable and effective relationships with church-sponsored schools, and there is no basis for assuming that, in this related context, reasonable standards cannot be established concerning the content of the continuing vocational education of Amish children under parental guidance, provided always that state regulations are not inconsistent with what we have said in this opinion.

NOTES AND QUESTIONS

1. The Court's holding can be characterized as an extremely narrow one. What is that precise holding? The Court's decision has given rise to a term of art in post-*Yoder* home schooling regulation: "the Amish exemption" from compulsory school attendance. Are there facts underlying the Amish exemption that can be analogized to other religious groups?
2. Courts have been extremely reluctant to exempt non-Amish religious groups from compulsory education statutes. The *Yoder* case has been narrowly construed and is limited strictly to the Amish and their way of life. Although advocates of home schooling have tried to use *Yoder*'s reasoning, most courts strike down attempts that have been made by other religious sects. For example, in *Duro v. District Attorney*, 712 F.2d 96 (4th Cir. 1983), *cert. denied*, 465 U.S. 1006 (1984), the Fourth Circuit held that North Carolina's interest in enforcing its compulsory education law overrode the religious interests advanced by Pentacostalist children in being free from the corrupting influence of "secular humanism" in the public schools. The Court distinguished *Yoder*, reasoning:

> The Duros, unlike their Amish counterparts, are not members of a community which has existed for three centuries and has a long history of being a successful, self-sufficient segment of American society. Furthermore, in *Yoder*, the Amish children attended public school through eighth grade and then obtained informal vocational training to enable them to assimilate into the self-contained Amish community. However, in the present case, Duro refuses to enroll his children in any public or non-public school for any length of time, but still expects them to be fully integrated and live normally in the modern world upon reaching the age of 18. . . . Duro has not demonstrated that home instruction will prepare his children to be self-sufficient participants in our modern society or enable them to participate intelligently in our political system, which, as the Supreme Court states, is a compelling interest of the state. Therefore, based on all the regulations

> imposed on religious and non-public schools, we find that North Carolina has maintained a compelling interest in compulsory education for the children of the state.

See e.g., Johnson v. Prince William County School Board, 241 Va. 383, 404 S.E.2d 209 (Va. 1991) (the sole test for determining whether parents are entitled to an exemption from compulsory attendance law on religious grounds is the bonafides of the parents' religious beliefs); *Texas Ed. Agency v. Leeper,* 893 S.W.2d 432 (Texas 1994) (home school can be private school to qualify for exemption to public school attendance law). *See also Fellowship Baptist Church v. Benton,* 815 F.2d 485 (8th Cir. 1987); *State v. Patzer,* 382 N.W.2d 631 (N.D. 1986); *Johnson v. Charles City Community Schools Board of Education,* 368 N.W.2d 74 (Iowa 1985).

3. In cases determining whether a parent or child's religious freedom will prevail or whether the state will prevail, the courts employ a four part test: (1) is the person's mode of life inseparable from the person's sincerely held religious beliefs? (2) does the educational structure sharply conflict with, or unduly burden the exercise of, those beliefs? (3) is the government's action necessary to fulfill a compelling state interest?, and (4) is the government employing the least restrictive means of achieving its interest? In a majority of state supreme court cases, the burden often shifts to the state to prove that the state has an interest in education and that the state is using the least restrictive means of monitoring home schooling. Courts have upheld most forms of regulating home schooling, including mandating that home school teachers be state certified, requiring that home-schooled children be subjected to standardized testing, and requiring notification and approval of curriculum by school district superintendents. *See Grigg v. Commonwealth,* 297 S.E.2d 799 (Va. 1982); *State v. Schmidt,* 505 N.E.2d 627 (Ohio 1987); *State v. Melin,* 428 N.W.2d 227 (N.D. 1988); *Murphy v. Arkansas,* 852 F.2d 1039 (8th Cir. 1988).
4. In *Battles v. Anne Arundel County Board of Education,* 904 F. Supp. 471 (D. Md. 1995), the court upheld the constitutionality of Maryland's compulsory education law and home schooling requirements. Maryland requires children to attend public schools "unless the child is otherwise receiving regular, thorough instruction during the school year in the studies usually taught in the public schools to children of the same age." The state retains a supervisory role over home education, requiring instruction in English, mathematics, science, social studies, art, music, health and physical education. Parents are required to maintain a portfolio of instructional materials and examples of the child's work to demonstrate that the child is receiving regular and thorough instruction in these areas. Parents also must permit a representative to observe the teaching provided and review the portfolio at a mutually agreeable time and place not more than three times a year. To insure compliance with these regulations, parents who educate their children at home are required to sign a consent form allowing the local school system to monitor private education.

   Battles argued that Maryland's compulsory and home education requirements infringed upon the free exercise of her religious beliefs as guaranteed by the First Amendment. The court rejected that claim, however, reasoning:

> In *Employment Div., Dep't of Human Resources of Oregon v. Smith,* 494 U.S. 872 (1990), the Supreme Court held that the Free Exercise Clause permits a state to include religiously inspired use of peyote within the reach of a state's general criminal prohibition of that drug. The Court reached this holding by distinguishing *Sherbert v. Verner,* 374 U.S. 398 (1963), and other cases that used a "compelling interest" test in free exercise cases and announcing a two-part test for determining whether a law is constitutional. First, it must be a valid and generally applicable law. *Smith,* 494 U.S. at 878. Second, the burden on religion must be incidental and not the purpose of the law. *Id.* The second prong of this test was refined in *Church of the Lukumi Babalu Aye, Inc. v. City of Hialeah,* 508 U.S. 520 (1993), which struck down a law banning animal sacrifices because the Court found that it was specifically adopted to suppress a central element of the Santeria religion.
>
> The Maryland education law at issue applies to all children in the state; indeed, this is the crux of Battles' Complaint, for she desires a special exemption for her child. Furthermore, Battles does not claim that the education laws were passed with the purpose of suppressing religion. Her conclusions that the public schools indoctrinate children in an atheistic or antichristian worldview are not sufficient factual allegations to show that the education laws are designed to suppress her religion. Thus, Battles has failed to state a claim under the First Amendment as interpreted in *Smith.*
>
> . . . Battles attempts to escape this conclusion by relying on dictum in *Smith* where the Court stated:
>
>> The only decisions in which we have held that the First Amendment bars application of a neutral, generally applicable law to religiously motivated action have involved . . . the Free Exercise Clause in conjunction with other constitutional protections, such as . . . the right of parents, acknowledged in *Pierce v. Society of Sisters,* to direct the education of their children, *see Wisconsin v. Yoder,* (invalidating compulsory school-attendance laws as applied to Amish parents who refused on religious grounds to send their children to school).
>
> *Smith,* 494 U.S. at 881. Applying this language to her situation, Battles claims that Maryland education law infringes upon her religious beliefs in conjunction with an amalgam of rights she calls the "fundamental right against standardization of education." Her reliance on these cases is misplaced, as they are readily distinguishable.
>
> *Pierce v. Society of Sisters,* 268 U.S. 510 (1925), held that Oregon could not force children to attend state primary schools and thereby limit education to one forum. Unlike the statute at issue in *Pierce,* the Maryland education laws liberally permit private or home education as long as certain educational standards are met. The Court's reasoning emphasized that private schools would be put out of business and that parents would be required to choose instruction from public teachers; the Maryland education laws do not mandate either outcome. Moreover, *Pierce* does not support Battles' proposition that a state cannot oversee non-public education, stating:
>
>> No question is raised concerning the power of the State reasonably to regulate all schools, to inspect, supervise and examine them, their

> teachers and pupils; to require that all children of proper age attend some school, that teachers shall be of good moral character and patriotic disposition, that certain studies plainly essential to good citizenship must be taught, and that nothing be taught which is manifestly inimical to the public welfare.

Pierce, 268 U.S. at 534. This language limits the holding of *Pierce* and prevents undue interference with state education systems.

In *Wisconsin v. Yoder,* 406 U.S. 205 (1972), the Court held that the State could not charge members of the Old Amish religion for violating the compulsory school-attendance law when they refused to send their children to school after the eighth grade. In reaching this holding the Court emphasized that it was a central tenet of the Amish belief that members disassociate themselves from modern society, that education after the eighth grade would greatly endanger their religious beliefs, and that their alternative mode of continuing informal vocational education was adequate preparation for membership in their rural, self-sufficient society. These factors, balanced against the State's interest in basic universal education, dictated relief from compulsory education beyond the eighth grade. The factual allegations in Battles' complaint are quite different, claiming that her daughter received the equivalent of a first or second grade education, which is not comparable to the education level held sufficient to satisfy Wisconsin's interest in *Yoder*. More importantly, Battles does not allege that separation from modern society is a central tenet of her religion or that she lives in a separate, self-sufficient community. *See Duro v. Dist. Atty., Second Jud. Dist. of N.C.,* 712 F.2d 96 (4th Cir. 1983), *cert. denied,* 465 U.S. 1006 (1984) (distinguishing *Yoder* in similar circumstances). Consequently, the Maryland education laws do not pose a grave threat to Battles' religious belief and do not violate the First Amendment.

B. THE REGULATION OF HOME SCHOOLING: REPORTING, CERTIFICATION, ASSESSMENT AND EQUIVALENCY REQUIREMENTS

1. The Landscape of Home Schooling

The number of children who are home schooled in America has grown over the past decade. According to the National Center for Education Statistics, at least 1.1 million children are home schooled, an increase of 29% from 1999. *http://nces.ed.gov/pubs2006/homeschool/*. The 1.1 million home-schooled children represent 2.2% of the school-age population. *Id.* Parents of home-schooled children were surveyed about the most important reason for home-schooling their children and reported as follows: - 31% indicated that concerns about the school environment, including peer pressure, safety and drugs, led them to home schooling; 30% reported that the desire to provide religious or moral instruction led them to home schooling; and 16% replied that dissatisfaction with the academic instruction available at school led them to home schooling. *Id.* Most of the home-schooled children are white and live in two-parent households with three or more children in which only one parent works outside the home. *Id.*

In *State of West Virginia v. Riddle,* 168 W. Va. 429, 285 S.E.2d 359 (W. Va. 2001), the court reviewed the regulations governing home and private schooling in every state and found as follows:

> As would be expected, all fifty States allow for home education of children as an alternative to their attendance at a public or other day school. Thirty-four States (and the District of Columbia) have statutes or regulations that specifically acknowledge home education as a distinct category of private education.[2] The remaining sixteen States either include home schooling under a statute designed for church and private schools,[3] or, as in the case in Massachusetts, permit home education under their more general statutory schemes governing public education.[4] W.M. Gordon, Home Schooling 29 (1994).
>
> An examination of the statutes and regulations throughout the country discloses that the States have concluded that their interests can be satisfied if the home education plan under examination complies with a list of requirements . . . , including periodic assessment of the child's progress by means of standardized testing or other alternatives that measure aptitude and learning.[5] Only one State law that we can find requires home schoolers to submit to home visits by school officials, as a condition to approval of home education plans. That law is designed to regulate private, denominational, and parochial schools, and approval is based in part on "health and safety factors in buildings and grounds." Neb. Rev. Stat. §§79-1601(2), 79-1605(1996). Ohio's guidelines prohibit school officials from conducting home visitations, Rhode Island does not allow school officials to require home visits as a precondition of home education plan approval, and North Carolina and New York have

---

[2] *See, e.g.,* Me. Rev. State. Ann. tit. 20-A §§5001-A(3)(A)(3), 5021, 5022, 5023 (West 1993 & 1998 Supp.) (compulsory attendance in public schools required between the ages of seven and seventeen years; home instruction specifically recognized as an "equivalent instruction alternative"; approval of local school board and State commissioner required, opportunities for part-time enrollment in public school); N.H. Rev. Stat. Ann. c. 193-A (Michie Supp. 1997) (parents have the right to home educate their own children, must notify local or State official, and comply with minimum educational requirements; State has home education program and home education advisory council).

[3] *See, e.g.,* Ill. Ann. Stat. Ch. 105 §5/26-1(1) (West 1993 & Supp. 1998) (children attending private or parochial schools "where children are taught the branches of education taught to children of corresponding age and grade in the public schools, and where the instruction of the child in the branches of education is in the English language" not required to attend public school); Neb. Rev. Stat. §§79-1601–79-1606 (1996) (children attending private, denominational, or parochial schools who have courses of study for each grade that are "substantially the same" as public school offerings are exempt from public school compulsory attendance law).

[4] *See, e.g.,* Conn. Gen. Stat. §10-184 (1997) (parents with children between the ages of seven and sixteen years must send the child to local public school "unless the parent . . . is able to show that the child is elsewhere receiving equivalent instruction"); N.J. State. Ann. §18A:38-25 (West 1989 & Supp. 1998) (same).

[5] Thirty-nine States require parents to notify the State or the school district of their intent to home school their children. *See* W.M. Gordon, Home Schooling 29 (1994). Only six States require advance approval of education plans in addition to notification, and many require compliance with State time and curriculum mandates. *See id.*; Comment, The Constitutionality of State Home Schooling Statutes, 39 Vill. L. Rev. 1309, 1346 (1994). Many States focus on teacher qualifications, and those that group home schools with other private schools require teacher certification. *See id.* Almost all States require periodic assessment of home schooled students' academic progress. *Id.*

eliminated home visitations as conditions of approval. *See* W.M. Gordon, Home Schooling, *supra* at 34-35 & n.122; Kindstedt v. East Greenwich School Comm., R.I. Comm'r of Educ. (Aug. 7, 1986); N.C. Gen. Stat. §155C-564 (Michie 1997); N.Y. Comp. Codes R. & Regs. Tit. 8, §100.10(i)(3) (1995). In 1998, the New York State board of regents promulgated new regulations governing home instruction. These regulations eliminated home visits as a matter of course, . . . instead "authoriz[ing] such visits only after a family's home-schooling program has been placed on probation and the local superintendent has 'reasonable grounds' to believe that the program is not in compliance with state requirements." *Blackwelder v. Safnauer,* 866 F.2d 548, 551-552 (2d Cir. 1989).

In *Homeschooling and Racism*, 20 *Journal of Black Studies* 1 (2007), Professor Tal Levy performed an event history analysis to determine which state characteristics are more likely to provide legislation that facilitates home schooling. The evidence demonstrates that such legislation is more likely to be enacted in states that: (1) are more rural; (2) have a significant Christian fundamentalist presence; and (3) have higher levels of racial integration in public schools.

In light of the prominence of home schooling and its state regulation, consider the judicial treatment of the common governmental monitoring mechanisms in the following cases.

2. Governmental Monitoring Mechanisms for Home Schooling

Fellowship Baptist Church v. Benton

815 F.2d 485 (8th Cir. 1987)

We have reviewed the record carefully, and find that the evidence presented to the district court supports the court's findings and conclusions regarding the reporting and teacher certification requirements. We also find the evidence supports the district court's holding that the denial to plaintiffs of the "Amish exemption" does not violate the equal protection clause or any other constitutional guarantee. Since the district court's ruling on the term "equivalent instruction," the state has promulgated regulations further defining this term, and we remand this aspect of the case to the district court for further consideration. . . .

In this appeal, the Court is presented with a broad attack on Iowa's compulsory school laws. Plaintiffs are two fundamentalist Baptist church schools, the churches' pastors and principals, and several of the schools' teachers, parents and students. . . .

I. Plaintiffs' Religious Beliefs

An understanding of plaintiffs' religious beliefs and practices is essential to the proper evaluation of plaintiffs' claims. The evidence presented by plaintiffs to the district court unquestionably revealed that their religious beliefs stem from the Bible. They view Christ as the Head of their church and all of its ministries, and adhere to the doctrine of separation of church and state. Their schools were created in response to these beliefs. Neither church has a doctrine which requires members to send their children to the church school, however, and parents are not subject to discipline for removing their children from the church schools. Enrollment in the schools is not limited to those who belong to the church, and both schools have enrolled pupils whose parents are not members of the church. Moreover, several members send some of their children to the church school, while others attend the public schools. . . .

Plaintiffs believe themselves to be "in the world but not of the world," but they do not segregate themselves from modern communities. They live in ordinary residential neighborhoods and they interact with their neighbors and others not of their faith. They believe they are called by God to perform certain occupations in life, but these include ordinary occupations such as nurse, lawyer, engineer and accountant, and there is no evidence that they object to the licensing of these occupations. They own and use radios, televisions, motor vehicles and other modern conveniences and advancements. Their dress and lifestyle, while conservative, is not distinctive.

Plaintiffs do, however, object to certain state regulation of their churches' ministries, including the reporting, teacher certification and "equivalent instruction" requirements of Iowa's compulsory school laws. Neither principal has ever filed an annual report as required by Iowa Code, although both stated at trial that they had been aware for several years that the law placed this obligation on them. Officials of Calvary Baptist Christian Academy initially had requested information on becoming an approved school,[6] and had assured the Keokuk School District Superintendent that certified teachers would be employed, but the majority of teachers in both schools currently are not certified. In addition to the reporting and certification requirements, plaintiffs object to the term "equivalent instruction" as unconstitutionally vague and assert that any review of their curriculum by the state would necessarily be "far-reaching" and anti-religious.

With this background we turn to the specific provisions of Iowa law to which plaintiffs object.

II. Reporting Requirements

Iowa's reporting requirements are very straightforward. Each year, the principal of any private school in Iowa must, upon request from the secretary of the local school district, furnish the names, ages and number of days of attendance of each pupil in grades one through eight, the texts used, and the names of the teachers during the preceding year. The district court found the reporting requirements did not impinge on plaintiffs' constitutional rights, and we agree.

[6] Iowa does not require private schools to be approved. Private schools may chose to become approved, as for example the Catholic schools in the Keokuk School District have, or they are free to operate as nonapproved private schools. Parents may satisfy the compulsory school laws by sending their children to nonapproved private schools so long as they provide "equivalent instruction by a certified teacher." Iowa Code §299.1.

Administrators from other private schools confirmed that the intrusion by the state. . . . , is extremely limited. Once each year, the local school district sends each principal a form, which can be completed by a secretary under the principal's supervision in less than one day. The forms require nothing more of plaintiffs than that they provide the minimal information requested, and plaintiff principals admitted that the information was readily available them. Clearly, [the law] does not in any way infringe upon the content, approach or structure of plaintiffs' schools. Plaintiff principals nonetheless argue on appeal, as they did before the district court, that the submission of the form violates their beliefs in the "Headship of Christ" and the separation of church and state. They urge that parental reporting would adequately serve the state's admittedly compelling interest in ensuring its children are receiving an adequate education, and submit that the state should be required to adopt this "least restrictive means." Plaintiff parents and children also assert that the reporting requirements violate their freedom of association, again proposing parental reporting as a "least restrictive means" of obtaining the information sought.

As the district court recognized, free exercise claims in the context of educational requirements have a long history. The Supreme Court's recognition of the state's compelling interest in the education of its children is equally longstanding. . . . In *Brown v. Board of Education,* 347 U.S. 483, 493, 74 S. Ct. 686, 691, 98 L. Ed. 873 (1954), the Court found education to be "perhaps the most important function of state and local governments." The Court continued:

> Compulsory school attendance laws and the great expenditures for education both demonstrate our recognition of the importance of education to our democratic society. In these days, it is doubtful that any child may reasonably be expected to succeed in life if he is denied the opportunity of an education. *Id.*

As the Iowa Supreme Court has recently noted, Iowa's interest in assuring that each child receive a quality education is no less compelling. . . . [That] Court also recognized the "clear authority, even a duty" for some state intervention into private religious schools to ensure the state's interests are being met. In fact, Iowa has enjoyed "a long tradition of friendly coexistence between private and public schools," dating from the first years of its statehood.

The minimal reporting requirements to which plaintiff principals object unquestionably serve the state's interest in knowing whether its children are attending school and receiving an education. Plaintiffs agree that the state's interest is compelling, but urge that Iowa be required to accommodate their religious objections to the method it has chosen to effectuate its interest by allowing parents, rather than principals, to supply the requested information.

The Supreme Court has stated that a state's interest in education "is not totally free from a balancing process when it impinges on fundamental rights and interests," and "it must appear either that the State does not deny the free exercise of religious belief by its requirement, or that there is a state interest of sufficient magnitude to override the interest claiming protection under the Free Exercise Clause." *Wisconsin v. Yoder*. "The essence of all that has been said and written on the subject is that only those interests of the highest order and those not otherwise served can overbalance legitimate claims to the free exercise of religion." *Id.*

While there may be some debate over the precise language to be used in defining the standard of review in free exercise cases, we have no difficulty upholding the reporting requirements in this case. As the district court determined, the burden on plaintiff principals' religious beliefs—if one exists at all—is very minimal and is clearly outweighed by the state's interest in receiving reliable information about where children are being educated and by whom.

Moreover, the record amply supports the district court's finding that the alternative means proposed by plaintiffs would not adequately serve the state's purposes. The district court stated:

> Reports submitted by individual parents or an elected representative would not provide a means by which the information could be verified and there is no guarantee all present or future parents would agree to such proceedings. Thus, a substantial impediment to the State's objective would still result.

We agree with the district court that the reporting requirements contained in Iowa Code do not unconstitutionally infringe upon plaintiff principals' right to the free exercise of religion.

Plaintiffs also advance the argument that the reporting requirements violate their freedom of association. Plaintiffs apparently do not object to the disclosure of the requested information, however, since they propose that parents be allowed to supply it. Thus, plaintiffs are not seeking to maintain privacy in their associations, an essential element of their freedom of association claim. In any event, we . . . find that the state's interest in compulsory education which is served by the reporting requirements justifies any alleged burden on the plaintiffs' freedom of association.

Plaintiffs' constitutional challenge to the state's reporting requirements thus must fail, and the district court's decision upholding Iowa Code is affirmed.

III. Teacher Certification

Plaintiffs also challenge the requirement in Iowa Code that parents of children ages 7 to 16 must send their children to public school or to a private school that utilizes certified teachers until the children complete the eighth grade. Plaintiffs allege the certification requirement violates the free exercise clause, the establishment clause, the due process clause and plaintiff teachers' freedom of expression. Plaintiffs allege these violations stem primarily from the certification requirement's interference with a teacher's calling by God to teach, the supervision of certified teachers by the Iowa Professional Teaching Practices Commission, and the "human relations" course required to obtain or maintain certification. . . .

After hearing all the evidence in the case, the district court found that certification was the "best method now available to satisfy the state's prime interest in seeing that its children are taught by capable persons." The court stated:

> The importance [of the certificate] lies, not in the piece of paper itself, but in the education a person must receive to become eligible for the certificate. Courses in child psychology, how children learn, various methods of conveying information and developing the learning process and knowledge of the subject matter will prepare a person to be a better teacher. This kind of knowledge is essential if one is to become a good teacher. The record amply supports the district court's findings in this regard.

Plaintiffs argue strenuously on appeal that their religious beliefs cannot be reconciled with the state having any role in the certification or approval of teachers in their schools. They urge that standardized testing be substituted for certification, asserting that many other states do not require certification.

We recognize the sincerity of plaintiffs' beliefs and the burden which they believe the certification requirement imposes upon them. We agree with the Supreme Court of Iowa, however, that plaintiffs' position is "not altogether consistent" on this matter. Plaintiffs believe that licensure wrongfully interferes with a teacher's calling by God to teach, yet they apparently do not object to the licensure of those in their church called by God to other occupations, such as doctor or lawyer, nor do they object to obtaining a driver's license for those serving in their bus ministry, even though Pastor Jaspers testified that none of the churches' ministries could properly be regulated by government.

Moreover, while plaintiffs attempt to analogize their situation to that of the Amish in the Yoder case, the burden the certification requirement imposes upon the plaintiffs is not nearly as great as the burden placed upon the plaintiff in *Yoder*. . . .

Unlike the Old Order Amish in *Yoder*, plaintiffs expect and encourage their children to attend college, and have no objection to college-educated teachers per se. The certification requirement applies only to teachers in grades one through eight, and plaintiff schools in fact each employ a teacher who is certified. Iowa's certification process does not prevent teachers in plaintiff schools from teaching from a Biblical perspective nor does it prevent plaintiff schools from hiring only those teachers who meet their religious criteria. Dr. Nearhoof, the State's Director of Teacher Certification, testified that many church-affiliated schools produce certified teachers, and teachers from non-recognized institutions may become certified by taking a few additional courses.

Under these circumstances, the *Yoder* Court's admonition that courts "move with great circumspection in performing the sensitive and delicate task of weighing a State's legitimate social concern when faced with religious claims for exemption from generally applicable education requirements" is particularly instructive. "[C]ourts are not school boards or legislatures, and are ill-equipped to determine the 'necessity' of discrete aspects of a State's program of compulsory education."

In evaluating plaintiffs' claims, we must determine whether, in light of the importance of the state's interest in the education of its children and the nature of the burden the certification requirement places on the plaintiffs' religious beliefs, plaintiffs' proposed testing alternative would adequately serve the state's interest. After carefully considering all of the evidence presented, the district court found it would not.

Plaintiffs object because the certificate requirement relies upon the process (education of the teacher) rather than the product (Is the child learning?). Historically, the emphasis has been on the process. Iowa has required some sort of certificate since 1863. It has been assumed that if the process is followed the children will learn. Recently there has been more interest in attempting to determine if the children are learning. While testing is a valuable tool, it is not sufficient in and of itself to determine whether a student is receiving an adequate education. Tests primarily determine knowledge of content of the subject matter. They do not test other aspects of education necessary to prepare a student for life in today's society.

The court also approved of the Iowa Supreme Court's observations that mere testing would be wholly inadequate to protect the state's rightful interests. A test looks only backward. It can, to a limited extent, measure whether a child has been receiving an education. The state is entitled to the assurance that the child is receiving an education.

These findings concerning the limited effectiveness of testing are well supported by the testimony of [experts]. These individuals expressed their concerns about the reliability and validity of testing as the sole measure of a quality education, concerns which are shared by others in the educational profession. *See, e.g.,* Comment, *Regulation of Fundamentalist Christian Schools: Free Exercise of Religion v. The State's Interest in Quality Education,* 67 Kentucky L.J. 415, 427-29 (1978-1979).

We agree on the basis of the record in this case that the state has met its burden of demonstrating that testing would not adequately serve its interests. Not only do certified teachers receive training in child development and methods of instruction, but they are also mandatory child abuse reporters and take courses on identifying those children with special needs. All of these qualities, as plaintiffs' own expert witnesses conceded, are desirable characteristics for a good teacher. Admittedly, there is a lack of empirical evidence concerning the relationship between certified teachers and a quality education, due to the difficulty of research on this issue, but there is a similar lack of empirical verification concerning plaintiffs' proposed alternative, and we do not believe such evidence is required in this case. For all of these reasons, we agree with the district court that the state's choice of certification as the best means available today to satisfy its interest in the education of its children does not violate plaintiffs' right to the free exercise of their religion.

Plaintiffs also challenge the certification requirement under the establishment clause, but we hold that section 299.1 of the Iowa Code does not violate this clause. Plaintiffs concede the statute has a secular purpose, and we find, contrary to plaintiffs' allegations, that its effect neither advances nor inhibits religion, nor does it foster an excessive entanglement with religion. *See Lemon v. Kurtzman. . . .*

. . . Nothing we have said herein is intended to diminish plaintiffs' religious views or to suggest that the State of Iowa could not legislatively choose to accommodate their beliefs. We hold simply that based on the record before us, the district court properly held that the constitution does not compel the accommodation regarding the state's certification requirement which the plaintiff's have requested.

IV. Equivalent Instruction

[The Iowa statute] also provides that the instruction children receive from a certified teacher must be "equivalent" to that offered by the public schools. At the time of trial, the term "equivalent instruction" was not specifically defined anywhere in the Iowa Code or regulations, although the state was in the process of promulgating such regulations. Plaintiff's challenged the "equivalent instruction" requirement on vagueness grounds, and the state argued to the district court, as it does here, that other statutes sufficiently define the term. The district court rejected the state's contention, based upon statements by the Iowa Supreme Court indicating that Court's rejection of them as well. We agree with the district court's conclusion that the other statutes cited by the state do not cure the vagueness problem inherent in the otherwise undefined term "equivalent instruction."

V. The Amish Exemption

Plaintiffs' final constitutional challenge involves the state's denial of plaintiff parents' request to be exempted from the above requirements through the "Amish exemption," Iowa Code §299.24.[7] As the district court noted, this exemption has been granted only to parents of children attending Amish schools and one conservative Mennonite school, all of which are located in distinct geographical areas of the state and which follow the style of life and religious tenets described by the Supreme Court in *Yoder*. In *Johnson v. Charles City Community Schools Board of Education*, the Iowa Supreme Court specifically ruled that plaintiff parents were not entitled to the exemption because they failed to prove that their church "professes principles or tenets that differ substantially from the 'objectives, goals, and philosophy of education' embodied in the areas of study listed in subsections (3) and (4) of section 257.25," which must be taught in grades one through eight. The Court found that no tenet of plaintiffs' church was in conflict with teaching subjects such as English language arts, social studies, mathematics and science; plaintiffs sought only to teach those subjects in their own way, and nothing in section 257.25 prevented plaintiffs from doing so. Holding that plaintiffs had not established any substantial dissimilarity between their educational goals and those embodied in section 257.25, "certainly none which sets them apart from all the many other parochial schools in the state," the

---

[7] Iowa Code §299.24 provides in relevant part: When members or representatives of a local congregation of a recognized church or religious denomination established for ten years or more within the state of Iowa prior to July 1, 1967, which professes principles or tenets that differ substantially from the objectives, goals, and philosophy of education embodied in standards set forth in section 257.25, and rules adopted in implementation thereof, file with the state superintendent of public instruction proof of the existence of such conflicting tenets or principles, together with a list of the names, ages, and post-office addresses of all persons of compulsory school age desiring to be exempted from the compulsory education law and the educational standards law, whose parents or guardians are members of the congregation or religious denomination, the state superintendent, subject to the approval of the state board of public instruction, may exempt the members of the congregation or religious denomination from compliance with any or all requirements of the compulsory education law and the educational standards law.

Charles City Court approved the administrative denial of plaintiffs' request for an exemption. *Id.*

Plaintiffs argue before this Court, as they did before the district court and before the Iowa Supreme Court, that this denial violates the equal protection clause. They further contend that granting the exemption to the Amish but not to them violates the establishment clause because the effect is to advance the Amish religion and to inhibit the plaintiffs' [religious practices].

Because religion is a fundamental right, any classification of religious groups is subject to strict scrutiny. . . . That is, the state must show the classification has been precisely tailored to serve a compelling state interest. *Plyler v. Doe*, 457 U.S. 202, 216-27 (1982). Of course, this standard is substantially equivalent to the free exercise standards we have already applied to Iowa's reporting and teacher certification requirements.

The equal protection clause directs that "all persons similarly circumstanced shall be treated alike." . . . "But so too, '[t]he Constitution does not require things which are different in fact or opinion to be treated in law as though they were the same.'" Id. In creating an exemption to its compulsory school laws based upon religious beliefs, Iowa treads the fine line between the free exercise clause and the establishment clause noted by the Supreme Court in *Yoder*: The Court must not ignore the danger that an exception from a general obligation of citizenship on religious grounds may run afoul of the Establishment Clause, but that danger cannot be allowed to prevent any exception.

The Court found an exception for the Amish warranted based upon what can only be described as their very unique circumstances and their centuries old insulated, isolated lifestyle. As the Court itself noted, the Amish had made a convincing showing, "one that probably few other religious groups or sects could make," concerning the nature of their religious beliefs, the severe burden placed upon those beliefs by the state's requirements and the adequacy of the continuing informal vocational education which they preferred to serve the state's interest in the education of their children. . . .

We have previously addressed the factual dissimilarities between the plaintiffs and the Amish, and they will not be repeated here. The record in this case contains additional specific evidence of the beliefs and lifestyles of those who have been granted the exemption in Iowa, and we find more dissimilarities than similarities between these individuals and the plaintiffs. Accordingly, we agree with the district court that the denial of the section 299.24 exemption to the plaintiffs does not violate their right to equal protection of the laws.

We also find no establishment clause violation on the facts of this case. As the *Yoder* Court stated, narrow exemptions such as Iowa has adopted successfully traverse the "tight rope" created by the tension between the free exercise clause and the establishment clause. This narrowly drawn accommodation to one religious view does not require the state, under the establishment clause, to accommodate all others. The *Yoder* Court cited the need for "preserving doctrinal flexibility and recognizing the need for a sensible and realistic application of the Religion Clauses," and we believe that such an approach in this case supports to the conclusion that the "Amish exemption" as interpreted by the Iowa Supreme Court is constitutional. . . .

NOTES AND QUESTIONS

1. The Eighth Circuit's decision in *Benton* is typical in its rejection of an Amish exception for a non-Amish religious practice, and in its validation of clearly articulated state mandated reporting, certification, assessment and equivalency requirements for home education. *See also Hansen v. Cushman*, 490 F. Supp. 109 (W.D. Mich. 1980); *Delcante v. State*, 313 N.C. 384, 329 S.E.2d 636 (N.C. 1985); *Murphy v. Arkansas*, 852 F.2d 1039 (8th Cir. 1988).
2. How does *Benton* reconcile the state's interest in public education with the right of parents to education their children?
3. The *Benton* court alludes to several assumptions regarding educational quality, including: (1) the education required to receive a teaching certificate is "essential if one is to become a good teacher" and (2) "[w]hile testing is a valuable tool, it is not sufficient in and of itself to determine whether a student is receiving an adequate education." What is the basis for the Court's validation of the state's belief that the quality of a teacher is more indicative of educational quality than the test scores of a teacher's students? Do you agree?
4. What does the state of Iowa's home schooling legislation suggest about the state's view of standardized testing? If the state were consistent in its view of standardized testing, how would you expect it to legislate in the area of annual testing for its public school students? Compare the Arkansas regime of standardized testing to monitor its home schooling at issue in the *Murphy* case, which follows.

MURPHY V. ARKANSAS

852 F.2d 1039 (8th Cir. 1988)

Appellants challenge the decision of the district court upholding the constitutionality of the Arkansas Home School Act. We affirm the decision of the district court.

I. Facts

Doty and Phyllis Murphy are evangelical Christians who believe that "Christian Scriptures require parents to take personal responsibility for every aspect of their children's training and education." They have six children, ages four through eighteen. The Murphys educate their children at home, providing an "education that is pervasively religious in nature and which does not conflict with the religious beliefs they hold, based upon their understanding of the scriptures."

Under Arkansas law, a parent must educate her children through the age of sixteen. This requirement may be satisfied by sending the child to public, private, or parochial school or by educating the child at home. The Arkansas Home School Act requires parents intending to school their children at home to notify in writing the superintendent of their local school district prior to the commencement of each school year. The notice must provide information concerning the name, age, and grade of each student, the core curriculum to be offered, the schedule of instruction and the qualifications of the person teaching. The parent must also agree to submit the children to standardized achievement tests each year and, when the children reach the age of fourteen, to a minimum performance test. All of these tests are administered, interpreted, and acted upon by the Arkansas Department of Education. Finally, the parent must provide any information to the superintendent which might indicate the need for special educational services for the children.

The achievement test administered to a student schooled at home is chosen by the parent from a list of nationally recognized tests provided by the director of the State Department of Education or the director's designee. The parent may be present when the standardized test is administered, but both parent and student are under the supervision of a test administrator. The results of the standardized tests are used for several purposes. Most significantly, if a home school student does not achieve a composite score within eight months of grade level in designated subjects, the student must be placed in a public, private, or parochial school. No such annual testing is required for students in public, private, or parochial schools. If children not schooled at home are, for some reason, tested, no remedial placement is required for those who do not achieve certain scores. . . .

II. Discussion

A. The Free Exercise Clause

The Murphys assert that Ark. Code Ann. §6-15-504, requiring that a standardized test be given to their children under the supervision of a test administrator, deprives them of the right to free exercise of religion as guaranteed by the first amendment. They argue that their religious beliefs require they must be *completely* responsible for *every* aspect of their children's education. In contrast, the Arkansas Home School Act places responsibility for testing and interpreting test results with the State of Arkansas, rather than with the parents.

To determine whether governmental conduct infringes upon an individual's first amendment free exercise rights, a court must first inquire whether the challenged governmental action interferes with the claimant's "sincerely held religious beliefs." Second, if such a belief is interfered with, the court must determine whether the governmental action is the least restrictive means of achieving some compelling governmental interest. *Wisconsin v. Yoder* . . . .

In the case before us, the parties have stipulated that the testing requirements of the Arkansas law interfere with the Murphys' sincerely held religious beliefs. Thus, we will go no further in examining the subtleties of the Murphys' beliefs. Consequently, the resolution of the free exercise claim involves answering two related questions: First, does the state have a compelling interest in the education of all children? Second, if so, is the Arkansas statutory scheme the least restrictive means of achieving that objective? We believe that the answer to both of these questions is yes.

The government has a compelling interest in educating all of its citizens. Education of the citizenry is and always has been a preeminent goal of

American society. Reaching back through the collective memory of the Republic, the fundamental importance of education in the design of our system of government rapidly becomes clear. Article III of the Northwest Ordinance states in part: "Religion, morality, and knowledge being necessary to good government and the happiness of mankind, schools and the means of education shall forever be encouraged." In *Yoder,* the Supreme Court adopted Thomas Jefferson's often expressed belief that education was a "bulwark" against tyranny. . . .

Following from these recognized concerns, the Supreme Court has observed that a substantial body of case law has confirmed the power of the States to insist that attendance at private schools, if it is to satisfy state compulsory-attendance laws, be at institutions which provide minimum hours of instruction, employ teachers of specified training, and cover prescribed subjects of instruction. . . .

Thus, as the district court correctly noted, it is "settled beyond dispute, as a legal matter, that the state has a compelling interest in ensuring that all its citizens are being adequately educated."

Given the existence of a compelling governmental interest, we must next inquire whether Arkansas' home testing system is the least restrictive means to achieve that purpose. In doing so, we recognize that the state must have a mechanism by which it can confidently and objectively be assured that its citizens are being adequately educated.

Upon examination, it would appear that Arkansas has created the least restrictive system possible to assure its goal. By providing the option of home schooling, Arkansas allows parents vast responsibility and accountability in terms of their children's education—control far in excess of limitations on religious rights that have been previously upheld. For example, in *Fellowship Baptist Church v. Benton,* 815 F.2d 485 (8th Cir. 1987), this Court upheld the power of the State of Iowa to require teachers in "church schools" to be certified by the state for basic competence. On remand, the district court upheld regulations prescribing curriculum in such schools. *Fellowship Baptist Church v. Benton,* 678 F. Supp. 213 (S.D. Iowa 1988). In contrast, Arkansas requires neither that the parent instructing the home-schooled child be a certified teacher nor that the parent follow a mandated curriculum. The state's only safeguard to ensure adequate training of the home-schooled student is the standardized achievement test. Even regarding this test, the state allows wide latitude to the parents. The parent may choose a test administered from a list of nationally recognized standard achievement tests and may be present while the test is administered.

Finally, the Murphys make no showing, as made by the Amish in *Yoder,* that the state can be assured its interest will be attained if appellants' religious beliefs are accommodated. We reject the Murphys' argument that parental "testing" of children provides a sufficient safeguard to assure the state's interest in education is protected. Likewise, parental affidavits concerning the children's progress would also be insufficient. In the end, we believe that the state has no means less restrictive than its administration of achievement tests to ensure that its citizens are being properly educated.

B. Equal Protection

The Murphys argue that the Arkansas Home School Act violates the equal protection clause of the fourteenth amendment. Specifically, they claim that those who school their children at home for religious reasons are a suspect class or that parental control over a child's education involves a fundamental right. Further, they argue that, because the Home School Act discriminates against this class or burdens this right, it fails the strict scrutiny test of the equal protection clause. Alternatively, the Murphys assert that the Home School Act requires various filings with the local superintendent, testing by the state, and remedial action for unsatisfactory test results, while no such requirements are imposed on persons who educate their children in public or private schools. Moreover, although the public schools are subject to pervasive regulation, the Murphys point out that private schools are virtually free of any such supervision. Thus, the Murphys contend that the state appears irrationally to allow parents to educate their children in religious private schools without any state regulatory supervision but subjects children schooled at home to the various requirements of the Home School Act.

While home school families impelled by deep-seated religious convictions might be the type of "discrete and insular minorit[y]" to which Justice Stone referred in footnote four of *United States v. Carolene Products Co.,* 304 U.S. 144, 58 S. Ct. 778, 82 L. Ed. 1234 (1938), the broad secular category of individuals who prefer to school their children at home is not. Clearly, the statute is aimed at this second category of individuals.

It could be argued that the statute, while superficially neutral, has a discriminatory impact on the category of deeply religious individuals impelled by their convictions to school their children at home. Yet, even if such discriminatory impact were shown—which it has not been—this would not be sufficient to invoke strict scrutiny. The Murphys would still bear the burden of proving discriminatory purpose or intent. *Washington v. Davis,* 426 U.S. 229, 96 S. Ct. 2040, 48 L. Ed. 2d 597 (1976). Because no such showing of either discriminatory impact or discriminatory intent has been made, strict scrutiny analysis is inappropriate here.

Second, we find no persuasive arguments advanced that there is a fundamental right of parents to supervise their children's education to the extent that the Murphys contend. The recognition of such a right would fly directly in the face of those cases in which the Supreme Court has recognized the broad power of the state to compel school attendance and regulate curriculum and teacher certification. . . . Thus, again, strict scrutiny cannot be invoked in this case.

Given that strict scrutiny analysis does not apply, we move to the question of whether Arkansas has a rational reason to subject home schooling to regulatory requirements, while at the same time freeing private schools from virtually any regulation. This step by the legislature in Arkansas may at first glance offend common sense, and, sitting as a legislature, we might not have made this same decision. However, our job is *not* to sit as a legislature and the constitutional standard of rationality under the equal protection clause is a relaxed one. In this area of the law, the Supreme Court has declared its willingness to uphold any classification based "upon [any] state of facts that reasonably can be conceived to constitute a distinction, or difference in state policy. . . ."

We believe that such a state of facts exists here. First, it could be argued that the notion of an actual independent school, away from home, implies more formality and structure than a home school. This could lead the state to believe that more serious instruction would be occurring there than in the relaxed atmosphere of a child and parents in their own home. Second, the notion that more than one family is likely to be sending their children to the private school may provide an additional objective indication of the private school's quality that is not present in the context of individual home schools. Finally, unlike a home school, parents sending a child to a private school have to pay money for education and, hence, would be more likely to demand their money's worth of instructional quality from the private school. All these possibilities together could provide Arkansas with a passable reason for the challenged distinction under the minimum rationality standards of the equal protection clause.

C. Right of Privacy

The Murphys argue that the right of privacy should be extended to protect parental decisions concerning the direction of a child's education from state interference.

In *Runyon v. McCrary,* 427 U.S. 160 (1976), the Supreme Court specifically rejected this contention, stating:

> A person's decision whether to bear a child and a parent's decision concerning the manner in which his child is to be educated may fairly be characterized as exercises of familial rights and responsibilities. But it does not follow that because the government is largely or even entirely precluded from regulating the childbearing decision, it is similarly restricted by the Constitution from regulating the implementation of parental decisions concerning a child's education. The Court has repeatedly stressed that while parents have a constitutional right to send their children to private schools and a constitutional right to select private schools that offer specialized instruction, they have no constitutional right to provide their children with private school education unfettered by reasonable government regulation. . . .Indeed, the Court in *Pierce* expressly acknowledged "the power of the State reasonably to regulate all schools, to inspect, supervise and examine them, their teachers and pupils."

The Supreme Court has spoken clearly on this issue, and we are bound by its decision. Moreover, we agree with the Court's reasoning and its conclusion. We thus decline to extend the right of privacy to this situation. . . .

NOTES AND QUESTIONS

1. The federal and state courts generally have upheld equivalency standards for home schooling and certification requirements. *See, e.g., Vandiver v. Hardin County Board of Education,* 925 F.2d 927 (6th Cir. 1991) (upholding Kentucky state law allowing public schools to require students to pass examinations before receiving public school credit for home study

courses); *People v. Bennett,* 442 Mich. 316, 501 N.W.2d 106 (Mich. 1993) (certification requirements for home school educators upheld are reasonable); *Blackwelder v. Safnauer,* 689 F. Supp. 106 (N.D.N.Y. 1988) (New York statute imposing minimum standards of instruction upon school-aged children taught outside of public school not unconstitutional). *But see Ohio v. Whisner,* 47 Ohio St. 2d 181, 351 N.E.2d 750 (Ohio 1976) (declaring unconstitutional Ohio's comprehensive "minimum standard requirements," which, among other things, required all educational practices to "conform to policies adopted by the Board of Education"); *Lawrence v. South Carolina State Board of Education,* 306 S.D. 368, 412 S.E.2d 394 (S.C. 1991) (requirements for certification of home school teachers, which included test of basic skills given to public school teachers, not reasonable since home schooling is fundamentally different from public school).

2. In *Null v. Board of Education of County of Jackson,* 815 F. Supp. 937 (S.D. W. Va. 1993), the court addressed the constitutionality of West Virginia's home schooling "exemption," which provides:

> If the child's composite test results for any single year for English, grammar, reading, social studies, science and mathematics fall below the fortieth percentile on the selected tests, the person or persons providing home instruction shall initiate a remedial program to foster achievement above that level. If, after one year, the child's composite test results are not above the fortieth percentile level, home instruction shall no longer satisfy the compulsory school attendance requirement exemption.

In that case, the plaintiffs' son, Brent Anderson, was removed from public school and began home schooling after second grade. Because Brent failed to achieve the fortieth percentile at the end of the second "remedial" year of home schooling, the plaintiffs were informed that Brent was no longer eligible for home instruction.

The plaintiffs claimed that the West Virginia exemption is unconstitutional on its face and as applied. The plaintiffs argued that it was a violation of due process and equal protection under the Fourteenth Amendment "to deny parents the right to continue to give their children home education when the students achieve test scores which are in average ranges." The equal protection claim was based on alleged unequal treatment in the testing scores required of public school students versus home-schooled students. The due process claim rested on the parents' Fourteenth Amendment liberty interest in directing the education of their children. The Court denied the plaintiffs' request for relief, reasoning:

> states have a strong interest in educating their citizens; providing public schools is one of the most important functions of the State. *Wisconsin v. Yoder.* Correspondingly, parents have a Fourteenth Amendment liberty interest in "direct[ing] the upbringing and education of children under their control." *Pierce v. Society of Sisters.*
>
> The state's interest in education is subject to a balancing process when it impinges on fundamental rights and interests, such as those specifically protected by the Free Exercise Clause of the First Amendment. *Wisconsin v. Yoder.* When no specific fundamental right is involved, and only a general,

> Fourteenth Amendment liberty interest is at stake, then the parents' liberty interest is subject to reasonable state regulation.
>
> The Plaintiffs' amended complaint asserts that [the Exemption] constitutes "a violation of the fundamental right of parents to direct the education of their children," and "a violation of the liberty interest protected by the Due Process Clause." The Plaintiffs' claims therefore involve a general liberty interest subject to reasonable state regulation.
>
> Based on a "reasonableness" standard, this Court concludes that [the] Exemption is reasonable and that Plaintiffs' due process claim is meritless. State statutes are presumed valid and constitutional. . . .
>
> Assuming Brent's test results were "average," as alleged by the Plaintiffs, the state statute's 40 percent cutoff reasonably may be intended to promote above average scores. The Plaintiffs have failed to overcome the presumption favoring the statute's validity. The Court also notes that at least two other states — Virginia and New Hampshire — have laws requiring a composite score of 40 percent or higher.

3. In *Brunelle v. Lynn Public Schools,* 428 Mass. 512, 702 N.E.2d 1182 (Mass. 1998), the court struck down a Massachusetts law allowing a public school superintendent to conduct home visits to monitor the education taking place within the home.
4. In *In re T.M.,* 171 Vt. 1, 756 A.2d 793 (Vt. 2000), the court interpreted the notice-enrollment provisions of Vermont's law to permit automatic enrollment in a home study program without prior notice to the state, thereby shifting the burden to the state to demonstrate nonenrollment in school. The court observed:

> Finally, we note that the notice-enrollment provisions of the Vermont home-study statute are consistent with similar home-study laws across the country. Indeed, adoption of §166b was part of a national trend among the states toward adoption of home-schooling statutes or regulations. *See* N. Devins, *Fundamentalist Christian Educators v. State: An Inevitable Compromise,* 60 Geo. Wash. L. Rev. 818, 819 (1992); Comment, *The Constitutionality of State Home Schooling Statutes,* 39 Vill. L. Rev. 1309, 1336-39 (1994). Although provisions vary, roughly thirty-nine states require home schoolers to provide the state with notice of their intent to home school, and most require various information regarding the children, teachers, and curriculum. *See* Comment, *supra,* at 1341-43 n.204 (listing state statutes and requirements); *Brunelle v. Lynn Public Schools,* 428 Mass. 512, 702 N.E.2d 1182, 1185, n.7 (1998) (noting that thirty-nine states require parents to notify the state or school of their intent to home school). Only six states require advance approval as well as notification, *see Brunelle,* 702 N.E.2d at 1185, largely because of the burden and potential free exercise problems such requirements pose for parents. *See* Comment, *supra,* at 1343. Thus, the enrollment process set forth in the Vermont home-study statute reflects a careful balance between the interests of the state in ensuring that students receive an adequate education, and the right of parents to direct the education of their children.

5. Home schooling regulations generally do not require "homes" to comply with municipal and state health, fire and safety laws applicable to private or public school buildings. *See, e.g., Birst v. Sanstead,* 493 N.W.2d 690 (N.D. 1992) (where the home is used primarily as a residence, and only

incidentally as an educational institution, the home need not comply with regulations applicable to educational buildings). The courts also have recognized the difference between the school year and the school day in the context of home schooling. *In the Interest of J.B.,* 58 S.W.3d 575. (Mo. Ct. App. 2001) (parents engaged in home schooling should be allowed 12 months, not just 10, to satisfy home schooling instructional standards.)

6. In concluding that the government has a compelling interest in educating all of its citizens, the *Murphy* court relies in part on an article by Phillip Kurland, in which Professor Kurland writes: "It has long been an American dream that education affords a means for upward mobility in an open society. The Supreme Court . . . has framed much of the country's constitutional law on the unstated premise that formal education is the means by which American society remains fluid yet cohesive, pluralistic yet unitary, aspiring to be a democracy while being governed by a meritocracy." P. Kurland, *The Supreme Court, Compulsory Education, and the First Amendment Religion Clauses,* 75 W. Va. L. Rev. 213 (1973). Has American education in fact facilitated "upward mobility" for all Americans?
7. In *Board of Education v. Allen,* 392 U.S. 236, 245-246 (1968), the Supreme Court declared: "Indeed, the State's interest in assuring that these standards are being met has been considered a sufficient reason for refusing to accept instruction at home as compliance with compulsory education statutes. These cases were a sensible corollary of *Pierce v. Society of Sisters*: if the State must satisfy its interest in secular education through the instrument of private schools, it has a proper interest in the manner in which those schools perform their secular function." Is governmental regulation of instructional practices in the home merely a "corollary" of *Pierce,* or is it a significantly greater intrusion on parental privacy? Consider the *Murphy* court's rejection of the "right to privacy" argument, and its reliance on the Supreme Court's decision in *Runyon v. McCrary,* 427 U.S. 160 (1976). Where does a parent's constitutionally protected right to educate a child in the privacy of the home stop and the state's right to monitor and regulate that in-home instruction begin?
8. Reconsider the philosophical positions and themes touched upon in Section I. What does the issue of home schooling and its governmental regulation suggest about the private and public spheres of education in the American regime? Is it possible to draw upon those philosophical themes when giving the kind of practical legal and political advice called for in resolving the mandatory education and home schooling issues addressed in the following section?

C. THE PRACTICAL SIDE OF COMPULSORY EDUCATION

The legal boundary between governmental regulation of education and a parent's right to educate a child in the home presents difficult political and practical problems.

1. Truancy

On the political level, the mandatory school attendance issue is raised in the context of a legislature's choice of language in a truancy statute. Every state has a statute that penalizes truancy. A truant is typically defined as a child who is absent from school without a valid excuse. Yet does a religious objection to school or the content of a lesson constitute a valid excuse? Consider how Illinois hedges the limits of state power. "A 'truant' is defined as a child subject to compulsory school attendance and who is absent without valid cause. . . ." 105 ILCS 5/26-2a. The statute is a hedge because it does not define children who are in fact "subject to compulsory school attendance. . . ."

The statute has the advantages of constitutionality and flexibility. On the other hand, the legislation provides little guidance for school district administrators in deciding how and whether to enforce compulsory school attendance.

All mandatory school attendance statutes, even those that expressly define "truancy," present school districts with a practical problem. The enforcement of a state's criminal truancy statute is within the authority of the local police department. In reality, however, the school district's administrators begin the enforcement process by deciding to relay information about suspected truancy to the police. Accordingly, school districts often will create an internal process for detecting truancy. School districts typically require parents or guardians to report a child's absence and provide a legitimate excuse. Where a child is absent from school without a reported legitimate excuse, schools often will notify the parent or guardian of the child's absence. A truly unexcused absence will then be placed on the child's school record. Theoretically, in states such as Illinois, a child's single unexcused absence from one school day or even a part of the school day could result in criminal prosecution of the parents for truancy. More realistically, however, school districts tend to wait until there is a pattern of truancy and until alternative supportive interventions have failed before reporting truancy to the police.

Some school districts have detailed policies and procedures defining truancy and establishing parameters for initiating enforcement. Other districts, however, believe that any definition at odds with the definition of truancy in the state's criminal statute will expose the district to state review and sanction. The challenge for school districts is to draft policy language that allows flexibility to enforce truancy laws on a case-by-case basis, but also complies with state statutes and protects against selective or discriminatory enforcement.

What policy language would you suggest for a school district in a state with statutory language like that in Illinois?

2. Home Schooling and Compulsory Education Practicum

As the mandatory education case law indicates, enforcement of truancy laws takes on an entirely different dimension when the "excuse" for non-attendance touches upon religion. Analyze the following scenario in light of the law and practice surrounding home schooling:

In an effort to counterbalance the increasing federal emphasis on standardized testing, the state has enacted legislation mandating that the curriculum of local school districts includes "character education." In particular, local districts must instruct their children in pillars of good character, including trustworthiness, respect, responsibility, fairness, caring and citizenship. The state also requires that semiannual assessments be given to students to insure that they are acquiring these traits of character.

The Homer family has two children, ages 7 and 10 years old. They have been educated at home since birth. The Homers are members of a religious sect that has at its core the fundamental belief in service to nature and the Earth. Their belief system forbids service to country in the form of citizenship. Accordingly, the Homers have refused to instruct their children in the value of "citizenship." Their children have readily taken all of the standardized tests required by the state as part of its home-schooling regulations. The Homers have passed all portions of the tests with flying colors, with one exception. The parents have refused to permit their children to take that portion of the state's semiannual "character" assessment dealing with the acquisition of the trait of "citizenship." When the local school district's superintendent visited the Homer children for the purpose of administering the character assessment (as the superintendent is allowed to do under the state's home schooling legislation), the children cooperated fully with the testing, until they reached the "citizenship" portion. At that point, the children put their writing instruments down and stared into space. With the support of their parents, the Homer children politely declined to take the "citizenship" assessment.

The school district's superintendent has been authorized to consult the school district's attorney for legal and practical advice. How should the school district's attorney advise the district to proceed?

D. AN INTERNATIONAL AND COMPARATIVE LAW PERSPECTIVE ON COMPULSORY EDUCATION AND HOME SCHOOLING

The discipline of "comparative education" is an invaluable tool for challenging settled assumptions and shaping future developments regarding educational law and policy. For an outstanding analysis of comparative education and its benefits, *see* E.H. Epstein, "Comparative and International Education: Overview and Historical Development," in T. Husen and T.N. Postlethwaite, eds., *International Encyclopedia of Education* (Elsevier, 1994). In addition, for a comprehensive discussion of comparative approaches to the most significant questions confronting American education law and policy, *see* N.F. McGinn and E.H. Epstein, eds., *Comparative Perspectives on the Role of Education in Democratization,* Transitional States and States in Transition (Verlag Peter Lang, 1999); E.H. Epstein and N.F. McGinn, eds., *Comparative*

Perspectives on the Role of Education in Democratization, Socialization, Identity, and the Politics of Control (Verlag Peter Lang, 2000).

The United Nations Convention on the Rights of the Child, adopted in 1989, directs that states that are parties to the Convention "[m]ake primary education compulsory and available free to all." Article 28(1)(a). The Convention also mandates that "secondary education be available and accessible to every child." A "child" is defined as any human being "below the age of eighteen." Article 1. The Convention therefore directs that states require all their children to attend primary school, presumably from kindergarten thru fifth grade. The Convention does not speak to prekindergarten education, but it does mandate that countries ensure the development of "institutions, facilities and services for the care of children." Article 18(2). Those "institutions, facilities and services" are designed to render appropriate assistance to parents and guardians in the performance of their "child-rearing responsibilities." *Id.* Preschool clearly is among them. Accordingly, the Convention dictates that countries (1) require that every child undergo primary education; (2) make secondary education available to every child; and (3) ensure the development of prekindergarten educational programs for every child. The critical importance of free and compulsory education is also recognized in the following key treaty provisions:

> *Universal Declaration of Human Rights* (1948): Education shall be free, at least in the elementary and fundamental stages. Education shall be compulsory. *European Convention on Human Rights, Protocol 1* (1952): No person shall be denied the right to education. *UNESCO Convention against Discrimination in Education* (1960): The States Parties to this Convention undertake to formulate, develop and apply a national policy which, . . . will tend to promote equality of opportunity and of treatment . . . and in particular: (a) To make primary education free and compulsory. *International Covenant on Economic, Social and Cultural Rights* (1966): Primary education shall be compulsory and available free for all. *Protocol of San Salvador the American Convention on Human Rights* (1988): The States Parties to this Protocol recognize that in order to achieve the full exercise of the right to education: (a) Primary education should be compulsory and accessible to all without cost. *Charter on the Rights and Welfare of the African Child* (1990): States Parties to the present Charter shall take all appropriate measures with a view to achieving the full realization of [the right to education] and shall in particular: (a) provide free and compulsory basic education. *(Revised) European Social Charter* (1996): With a view to ensuring the effective exercise of the right of children and young persons to grow up in an environment which encourages the full development of their personality and of their physical and mental capacities, the Parties undertake, either directly or in co-operation with public and private organizations, to take all appropriate and necessary measures designed . . . to provide to children and young persons a free primary and secondary education as well as to encourage regular attendance at schools.

According to UNESCO's *Education for All Global Monitoring Report* (2008), compulsory primary education now exists in 95% of the countries in the world. *See* Report Summary 2. In fact, twenty-three new countries have enacted compulsory education provisions since 2000. *Id.* As a result, the ratio of actually enrolled children to potentially enrolled children rose to 87% in 2005, and the number of out-of-school children dropped by 24 million. *Id.* Nonetheless, the Report concludes:

> subnational disparities in school participation persist between regions, provinces or states and between urban and rural areas. Children from poor, indigenous and disabled populations are also at a systematic disadvantage, as are those living in slums. On current trends, fifty-eight out of eighty-six countries that have not yet reached universal primary enrollment will not achieve it by 2015.

Report at 2.

Similarly, there has been some progress in the number of children enrolled in preschool programs, but the progress is uneven. *See* Report, at 1. The Report finds that 132 million children are enrolled in pre-K educational programs, an increase of 20 million since 2000. *Id.* Yet only 40% of the children in the world attend preschool. *Id.* The participation ranges from 83% in Caribbean countries to only 14% in sub-Saharan Africa. *Id.* Children from poorer and rural backgrounds have the least access to pre-kindergarten programs. *Id.*

CHAPTER 4

THE RIGHT TO A PUBLIC EDUCATION AND THE EQUITABLE DISTRIBUTION OF PUBLIC EDUCATIONAL RESOURCES

As the materials in the previous chapter indicate, the states have been afforded broad power to require that their citizens receive an education. Pursuant to that authority, every state has made education compulsory up to a certain age or grade level. Moreover, virtually every state guarantees to its citizens a free, public education. Each state bears the responsibility of creating a mechanism for funding the education of its students from at least kindergarten through high school. Most states have created local school districts or educational agencies and have delegated to them, among other things, the responsibility to manage their own finances.

A state's education system is funded almost entirely by revenues generated at the state and local level. Less than 10 percent of educational resources come from the federal government, despite the fact that many of the fiscal pressures placed on local school districts are created by expensive federal mandates. As such, the states are left to create revenue streams from state and local taxes. At the statewide level, income and sales taxes are available to provide some resources to local school districts. Yet, the great bulk of funding for education typically is derived from local property taxes. It would not be unusual for a school district to derive more than 90 percent of its revenue from local property taxes. Although the taxing formulas vary from state to state, all local property taxes are necessarily related to property values. Accordingly, the greater the property wealth in a district, the greater the revenue stream to that district from local property taxes.

Because the level of property wealth throughout a state is invariably uneven, the level of educational resources available to students throughout the state is necessarily uneven as well. Most states have adopted mechanisms to mitigate the harsh effects of this funding imbalance. Some shift funds from property-rich districts, while others create a "foundation" level to guarantee that each child would receive at least some minimal level of per-student support. Yet these efforts have not remedied the disparity in educational funding that exists in every state. *See* K. Carey, *The Funding Gap: Low-income and Minority Students Still Receive Fewer Dollars in Many States* (2003); *School Finance: State Efforts to Reduce Funding Gaps Between Poor and Wealthy Districts* (U.S. Office of General Accounting 1997). In a very real sense, the resources devoted to a child's education are dependent on the property wealth of that child's neighbors.

The inequity in resources devoted to education within each state raises significant political and legal concerns. If a state can mandate that all of its citizens receive an education, how can that same state offer blatantly different levels of resources for the education of those citizens? If education is so important to American democracy that the states have the power to impose it on its citizens, do these same citizens have a fundamental right to an education? Could the undeniable inequalities in the provision of educational resources within a state survive a challenge based on the equal protection clause in the Fourteenth Amendment to the United States Constitution?

In *Cumming v. Board of Education*, 175 U.S. 528 (1899), the Supreme Court infamously answered some of these questions by upholding a local school board's decision to eliminate an all-black high school and to require those students to attend private schools. The Court reasoned that so long as citizens shared equitably in the financial burden of educating children, the federal courts had no power to interfere with the purely local educational judgments of the states. In *Brown v. Board of Education*, 374 U.S. 483 (1954), however, the Supreme Court not only declared unconstitutional racial segregation in public schools, it also suggested the basis for arguments supporting a fundamental constitutional right to educational opportunity:

> Today, education is perhaps the most important function of state and local government . . . such an opportunity is a right which must be made available to all on equal terms.

The issue whether the United States Constitution creates a fundamental right to education, however, was not fully addressed until the *Rodriguez* case. As you study the reasoning in *Rodriguez* and its progeny, consider whether that reasoning can be reconciled with the reasoning in the mandatory school attendance cases in the previous chapter. Is there a consistent legal or philosophical principle that links the Supreme Court's understanding of the place of education in the American democracy?

A. THE RIGHT TO A PUBLIC EDUCATION AND EQUITABLE FUNDING UNDER THE UNITED STATES CONSTITUTION

SAN ANTONIO INDEPENDENT SCHOOL DISTRICT v. RODRIGUEZ

411 U.S. 1 (1973)

Mr. Justice POWELL delivered the opinion of the Court. This suit attacking the Texas system of financing public education was initiated by Mexican-American parents whose children attend the elementary and secondary schools in the Edgewood Independent School District, an urban school district in San Antonio, Texas. They brought a class action on behalf of school children throughout the State who are members of minority groups or who are poor and reside in school districts having a low property tax base. . . .

I

The first Texas State Constitution, promulgated upon Texas' entry into the Union in 1845, provided for the establishment of a system of free schools.[6] Early in its history, Texas adopted a dual approach to the financing of its schools, relying on mutual participation by the local school districts and the State. As early as 1883, the state constitution was amended to provide for the creation of local school districts empowered to levy ad valorem taxes with the consent of local taxpayers for the "erection . . . of school buildings" and for the "further maintenance of public free schools." Such local funds as were raised were supplemented by funds distributed to each district from the State's Permanent and Available School Funds. The Permanent School Fund, its predecessor established in 1854 with $2,000,000 realized from an annexation settlement, was thereafter endowed with millions of acres of public land set aside to assure a continued source of income for school support. The Available School Fund, which received income from the Permanent School Fund as well as from a state ad valorem property tax and other designated taxes, served as the disbursing arm for most state educational funds throughout the late 1800's and first half of this century. Additionally, in 1918 an increase in state property taxes was used to finance a program providing free textbooks throughout the State.

Until recent times, Texas was a predominantly rural State and its population and property wealth were spread relatively evenly across the State. Sizable differences in the value of assessable property between local school districts became increasingly evident as the State became more industrialized and as rural-to-urban population shifts became more pronounced. The location of commercial and industrial property began to play a significant role in determining the amount of tax resources available to each school district. These growing disparities in population and taxable property between districts were responsible in part for increasingly notable differences in levels of local expenditure for education.

In due time it became apparent to those concerned with financing public education that contributions from the Available School Fund were not sufficient to ameliorate these disparities. Prior to 1939, the Available School Fund contributed money to every school district at a rate of $17.50 per

---

[6] Tex. Const., Art. X, §1 (1845):

> A general diffusion of knowledge being essential to the preservation of the rights and liberties of the people, it shall be the duty of the Legislature of this State to make suitable provision for the support and maintenance of public schools.
>
> Id., §2:
>
> The Legislature shall as early as practicable establish free schools throughout the State, and shall furnish means for their support, by taxation on property. . . .

school-age child. Although the amount was increased several times in the early 1940's, the Fund was providing only $46 per student by 1945.

Recognizing the need for increased state funding to help offset disparities in local spending and to meet Texas' changing educational requirements, the state legislature in the late 1940's undertook a thorough evaluation of public education with an eye toward major reform. In 1947, an 18-member committee, composed of educators and legislators, was appointed to explore alternative systems in other States and to propose a funding scheme that would guarantee a minimum or basic educational offering to each child and that would help overcome interdistrict disparities in taxable resources. The Committee's efforts led to the passage of the . . . Texas Minimum Foundation School Program. Today, this Program accounts for approximately half of the total educational expenditures in Texas.

The Program calls for state and local contributions to a fund earmarked specifically for teacher salaries, operating expenses, and transportation costs. The State, supplying funds from its general revenues, finances approximately 80% of the Program, and the school districts are responsible—as a unit—for providing the remaining 20%. The districts' share, known as the Local Fund Assignment, is apportioned among the school districts under a formula designed to reflect each district's relative taxpaying ability. The Assignment is first divided among Texas' 254 counties pursuant to a complicated economic index that takes into account the relative value of each county's contribution to the State's total income from manufacturing, mining, and agricultural activities. It also considers each county's relative share of all payrolls paid within the State and, to a lesser extent, considers each county's share of all property in the State. Each county's assignment is then divided among its school districts on the basis of each district's share of assessable property within the county. The district, in turn, finances its share of the Assignment out of revenues from local property taxation.

The design of this complex system was twofold. First, it was an attempt to assure that the Foundation Program would have an equalizing influence on expenditure levels between school districts by placing the heaviest burden on the school districts most capable of paying. Second, the Program's architects sought to establish a Local Fund Assignment that would force every school district to contribute to the education of its children but that would not by itself exhaust any district's resources. Today every school district does impose a property tax from which it derives locally expendable funds in excess of the amount necessary to satisfy its Local Fund Assignment under the Foundation Program.

The school district in which appellees reside, the Edgewood Independent School District, has been compared throughout this litigation with the Alamo Heights Independent School District. This comparison between the least and most affluent districts in the San Antonio area serves to illustrate the manner in which the dual system of finance operates and to indicate the extent to which substantial disparities exist despite the State's impressive progress in recent years. Edgewood is one of seven public school districts in the metropolitan area. Approximately 22,000 students are enrolled in its 25 elementary and secondary schools. The district is situated in the core-city sector of San Antonio in a residential neighborhood that has little commercial or industrial property. The residents are predominantly of Mexican-American descent: approximately 90% of the student population is Mexican-American and over 6% is Negro. The average assessed property value per pupil is $5,960—the lowest in the metropolitan area—and the median family income ($4,686) is also the lowest. At an equalized tax rate of $1.05 per $100 of assessed property—the highest in the metropolitan area—the district contributed $26 to the education of each child for the 1967-1968 school year above its Local Fund Assignment for the Minimum Foundation Program. The Foundation Program contributed $222 per pupil for a state-local total of $248. Federal funds added another $108 for a total of $356 per pupil.

Alamo Heights is the most affluent school district in San Antonio. Its six schools, housing approximately 5,000 students, are situated in a residential community quite unlike the Edgewood District. The school population is predominantly "Anglo," having only 18% Mexican-Americans and less than 1% Negroes. The assessed property value per pupil exceeds $49,000, and the median family income is $8,001. In 1967-1968 the local tax rate of $.85 per $100 of valuation yielded $333 per pupil over $225 provided from that Program [sic], the district was able to supply $558 per student. Supplemented by a $36 per-pupil grant from federal sources, Alamo Heights spent $594 per pupil.

Although the 1967-1968 school year figures provide the only complete statistical breakdown for each category of aid, more recent partial statistics indicate that the previously noted trend of increasing state aid has been significant. For the 1970-1971 school year, the Foundation School Program allotment for Edgewood was $356 per pupil, a 62% increase over the 1967-1968 school year. Indeed, state aid alone in 1970-1971 equaled Edgewood's entire 1967-1968 school budget from local, state, and federal sources. Alamo Heights enjoyed a similar increase under the Foundation Program, netting $491 per pupil in 1970-1971. These recent figures also reveal the extent to which these two districts' allotments were funded from their own required contributions to the Local Fund Assignment. Alamo Heights, because of its relative wealth, was required to contribute out of its local property tax collections approximately $100 per pupil, or about 20% of its Foundation grant. Edgewood, on the other hand, paid only $8.46 per pupil, which is about 2.4% of its grant. It appears then that, at least as to these two districts, the Local Fund Assignment does reflect a rough approximation of the relative taxpaying potential of each.

Despite these recent increases, substantial interdistrict disparities in school expenditures found by the District Court to prevail in San Antonio and in varying degrees throughout the State still exist. And it was these disparities, largely attributable to differences in the amounts of money collected through local property taxation, that led the District Court to conclude that Texas' dual system of public school financing violated the Equal Protection Clause. . . .

Texas virtually concedes that its historically rooted dual system of financing education could not withstand the strict judicial scrutiny that this Court has found appropriate in reviewing legislative judgments that interfere with fundamental constitutional rights or that involve suspect classifications. If, as previous decisions have indicated, strict scrutiny means that the State's system is not entitled to the usual presumption of validity, that the State rather than the complainants must carry a "heavy burden of justification," that the State must demonstrate that its educational system has been structured with "precision," and is "tailored" narrowly to serve legitimate objectives and that it has selected the "less drastic means" for effectuating its objectives, the Texas financing system and its counterpart in virtually every other State will not pass muster. The State candidly admits that "[n]o one familiar with the Texas system would contend that it has yet achieved perfection." Apart from its concession that educational financing in Texas has "defects" and "imperfections," the State defends the system's rationality with vigor and disputes the District Court's finding that it lacks a "reasonable basis."

This, then, establishes the framework for our analysis. We must decide, first, whether the Texas system of financing public education operates to the disadvantage of some suspect class or impinges upon a fundamental right explicitly or implicitly protected by the Constitution, thereby requiring strict judicial scrutiny. If so, the judgment of the District Court should be affirmed. If not, the Texas scheme must still be examined to determine whether it rationally furthers some legitimate, articulated state purpose and therefore does not constitute an invidious discrimination in violation of the Equal Protection Clause of the Fourteenth Amendment.

II

The District Court's opinion does not reflect the novelty and complexity of the constitutional questions posed by appellees' challenge to Texas' system of school financing. In concluding that strict judicial scrutiny was required, that court relied on decisions dealing with the rights of indigents to equal treatment in the criminal trial and appellate processes, and on cases disapproving wealth restrictions on the right to vote. Those cases, the District Court concluded, established wealth as a suspect classification. Finding that the local property tax system discriminated on the basis of wealth, it regarded those precedents as controlling. It then reasoned, based on decisions of this Court affirming the undeniable importance of education, that there is a fundamental right to education and that, absent some compelling state justification, the Texas system could not stand.

We are unable to agree that this case, which in significant aspects is sui generis, may be so neatly fitted into the conventional mosaic of constitutional analysis under the Equal Protection Clause. Indeed, for the several reasons that follow, we find neither the suspect-classification nor the fundamental interest analysis persuasive.

A

The wealth discrimination discovered by the District Court in this case, and by several other courts that have recently struck down school-financing laws in other States, is quite unlike any of the forms of wealth discrimination heretofore reviewed by this Court.

. . . The case comes to us with no definitive description of the classifying facts or delineation of the disfavored class. Examination of the District Court's opinion and of appellees' complaint, briefs, and contentions at oral argument suggests, however, at least three ways in which the discrimination claimed here might be described. The Texas system of school financing might be regarded as discriminating (1) against "poor" persons whose incomes fall below some identifiable level of poverty or who might be characterized as functionally "indigent," or (2) against those who are relatively poorer than others, or (3) against all those who, irrespective of their personal incomes, happen to reside in relatively poorer school districts. Our task must be to ascertain whether, in fact, the Texas system has been shown to discriminate on any of these possible bases and, if so, whether the resulting classification may be regarded as suspect.

The precedents of this Court provide the proper starting point. The individuals, or groups of individuals, who constituted the class discriminated against in our prior cases shared two distinguishing characteristics: because of their impecunity they were completely unable to pay for some desired benefit, and as a consequence, they sustained an absolute deprivation of a meaningful opportunity to enjoy that benefit. . . .

Only appellees' first possible basis for describing the class disadvantaged by the Texas school-financing system—discrimination against a class of definably "poor" persons—might arguably meet the criteria established in these prior cases. Even a cursory examination, however, demonstrates that neither of the two distinguishing characteristics of wealth classifications can be found here. First, in support of their charge that the system discriminates against the "poor," appellees have made no effort to demonstrate that it operates to the peculiar disadvantage of any class fairly definable as indigent, or as composed of persons whose incomes are beneath any designated poverty level. Indeed, there is reason to believe that the poorest families are not necessarily clustered in the poorest property districts. A recent and exhaustive study of school districts in Connecticut concluded that "[i]t is clearly incorrect . . . to contend that the 'poor' live in 'poor' districts . . . Thus, the major factual assumption of Serrano—that the educational financing system discriminates against the 'poor'—is simply false in Connecticut." Defining "poor" families as those below the Bureau of the Census "poverty level," the Connecticut study found, not surprisingly, that the poor were clustered around commercial and industrial areas—those same areas that provide the most attractive sources of property tax income for school districts. Whether a similar pattern would be discovered in Texas is not known, but there is no basis on the record in this case for assuming that the poorest people—defined by reference to any level of absolute impecunity—are concentrated in the poorest districts.

Second, neither appellees nor the District Court addressed the fact that, unlike each of the foregoing cases, lack of personal resources has not occasioned an absolute deprivation of the desired benefit. The argument here is not that the children in districts having relatively low assessable property values are receiving no public education; rather, it is that they are receiving a poorer quality education than that available to children in districts having more assessable wealth. Apart from the unsettled and disputed question whether the quality of education may be determined by the amount of money expended for it, a sufficient answer to appellees' argument is that, at least where wealth is involved, the Equal Protection Clause does not require absolute equality or precisely equal advantages. Nor, indeed, in view of the infinite variables affecting the educational process, can any system assure equal quality of education except in the most relative sense. Texas asserts that the Minimum Foundation Program provides an "adequate" education for all children in the State. By providing 12 years of free public-school education, and by assuring teachers, books, transportation, and operating funds, the Texas Legislature has endeavored to "guarantee, for the welfare of the state as a whole, that all people shall have at least an adequate program of education. This is what is meant by 'A Minimum Foundation Program of Education.'" The State repeatedly asserted in its briefs in this Court that it has fulfilled this desire and that it now assures "every child in every school district an adequate education." No proof was offered at trial persuasively discrediting or refuting the State's assertion. For these two reasons—the absence of any evidence that the financing system discriminates against any definable category of "poor" people or that it results in the absolute deprivation of education—the disadvantaged class is not susceptible of identification in traditional terms.

As suggested above, appellees and the District Court may have embraced a second or third approach, the second of which might be characterized as a theory of relative or comparative discrimination based on family income. Appellees sought to prove that a direct correlation exists between the wealth of families within each district and the expenditures therein for education. That is, along a continuum, the poorer the family the lower the dollar amount of education received by the family's children. . . .

If, in fact, these correlations could be sustained, then it might be argued that expenditures on education—equated by appellees to the quality of education—are dependent on personal wealth. Appellees' comparative-discrimination theory would still face serious unanswered questions, including whether a bare positive correlation or some higher degree of correlation is necessary to provide a basis for concluding that the financing system is designed to operate to the peculiar disadvantage of the comparatively poor, and whether a class of this size and diversity could ever claim the special protection accorded "suspect" classes. These questions need not be addressed in this case, however, since appellees' proof fails to support their allegations or the District Court's conclusions.

. . . This brings us, then, to the third way in which the classification scheme might be defined—district wealth discrimination. Since the only correlation indicated by the evidence is between district property wealth and expenditures, it may be argued that discrimination might be found without regard to the individual income characteristics of district residents. Assuming a perfect correlation between district property wealth and expenditures from top to bottom, the disadvantaged class might be viewed as encompassing every child in every district except the district that has the most assessable wealth and spends the most on education. Alternatively, as suggested in Mr. Justice Marshall's dissenting opinion, the class might be defined more restrictively to include children in districts with assessable property which falls below the statewide average, or median, or below some other artificially defined level.

However described, it is clear that appellees' suit asks this Court to extend its most exacting scrutiny to review a system that allegedly discriminates against a large, diverse, and amorphous class, unified only by the common factor of residence in districts that happen to have less taxable wealth than other districts. The system of alleged discrimination and the class it defines have none of the traditional indicia of suspectness: the class is not saddled with such disabilities, or subjected to such a history of purposeful unequal treatment, or relegated to such a position of political powerlessness as to command extraordinary protection from the majoritarian political process.

We thus conclude that the Texas system does not operate to the peculiar disadvantage of any suspect class. But in recognition of the fact that this Court has never heretofore held that wealth discrimination alone provides an adequate basis for invoking strict scrutiny, appellees have not relied solely on this contention. They also assert that the State's system impermissibly interferes with the exercise of a "fundamental" right and that accordingly the prior decisions of this Court require the application of the strict standard of judicial review. . . . It is this question—whether education is a fundamental right, in the sense that it is among the rights and liberties protected by the Constitution—which has so consumed the attention of courts and commentators in recent years.

B

In *Brown v. Board of Education*, 347 U.S. 483 (1954), a unanimous Court recognized that "education is perhaps the most important function of state and local governments." What was said there in the context of racial discrimination has lost none of its vitality with the passage of time:

> Compulsory school attendance laws and the great expenditures for education both demonstrate our recognition of the importance of education to our democratic society. It is required in the performance of our most basic public responsibilities, even service in the armed forces. It is the very foundation of good citizenship. Today it is a principal instrument in awakening the child to cultural values, in preparing him for later professional training, and in helping him to adjust normally to his environment. In these days, it is doubtful that any child may reasonably be expected to succeed in life if he is denied the opportunity of an education. Such an opportunity, where the state has undertaken to provide it, is a right which must be made available to all on equal terms.

This theme, expressing an abiding respect for the vital role of education in a free society, may be found in numerous opinions of Justices of this Court writing both before and after *Brown* was decided. *Wisconsin v. Yoder*, 406 U.S. 205, 213 (Burger, C.J.), 237, 238-239 (White, J.), (1972); *Abington School Dist. v. Schempp*, 374 U.S. 203, 230 (1963) (Brennan, J.); *McCollum v. Board of Education*, 333 U.S. 203, 212 (1948) (Mr. Justice Frankfurter); *Pierce v. Society of Sisters*, 268 U.S. 510 (1925); *Meyer v. Nebraska*, 262 U.S. 390 (1923); *Interstate Consolidated Street R. Co. v. Massachusetts*, 207 U.S. 79 (1907).

Nothing this Court holds today in any way detracts from our historic dedication to public education. We are in complete agreement with the conclusion of the three-judge panel below that "the grave significance of education both to the individual and to our society" cannot be doubted. But the importance of a service performed by the State does not determine whether it must be regarded as fundamental for purposes of examination under the Equal Protection Clause. . . .

It is not the province of this Court to create substantive constitutional rights in the name of guaranteeing equal protection of the laws. Thus, the key to discovering whether education is "fundamental" is not to be found in comparisons of the relative societal significance of education as opposed to subsistence or housing. Nor is it to be found by weighing whether education is as important as the right to travel. Rather, the answer lies in assessing whether there is a right to education explicitly or implicitly guaranteed by the Constitution.

Education, of course, is not among the rights afforded explicit protection under our Federal Constitution. Nor do we find any basis for saying it is implicitly so protected. As we have said, the undisputed importance of education will not alone cause this Court to depart from the usual standard for reviewing a State's social and economic legislation. It is appellees' contention, however, that education is distinguishable from other services and benefits provided by the State because it bears a peculiarly close relationship to other rights and liberties accorded protection under the Constitution. Specifically, they insist that education is itself a fundamental personal right because it is essential to the effective exercise of First Amendment freedoms and to intelligent utilization of the right to vote. In asserting a nexus between speech and education, appellees urge that the right to speak is meaningless unless the speaker is capable of articulating his thoughts intelligently and persuasively. The "marketplace of ideas" is an empty forum for those lacking basic communicative tools. Likewise, they argue that the corollary right to receive information becomes little more than a hollow privilege when the recipient has not been taught to read, assimilate, and utilize available knowledge.

A similar line of reasoning is pursued with respect to the right to vote. Exercise of the franchise, it is contended, cannot be divorced from the educational foundation of the voter. The electoral process, if reality is to conform to the democratic ideal, depends on an informed electorate: a voter cannot cast his ballot intelligently unless his reading skills and thought processes have been adequately developed.

We need not dispute any of these propositions. The Court has long afforded zealous protection against unjustifiable governmental interference with the individual's rights to speak and to vote. Yet we have never presumed to possess either the ability or the authority to guarantee to the citizenry the most effective speech or the most informed electoral choice. That these may be desirable goals of a system of freedom of expression and of a representative form of government is not to be doubted. These are indeed goals to be pursued by a people whose thoughts and beliefs are freed from governmental interference. But they are not values to be implemented by judicial intrusion into otherwise legitimate state activities.

Even if it were conceded that some identifiable quantum of education is a constitutionally protected prerequisite to the meaningful exercise of either right, we have no indication that the present levels of educational expenditure in Texas provide an education that falls short. Whatever merit appellees' argument might have if a State's financing system occasioned an absolute denial of educational opportunities to any of its children, that argument provides no basis for finding an interference with fundamental rights where only relative differences in spending levels are involved and where—as is true in the present case—no charge fairly could be made that the system fails to provide each child with an opportunity to acquire the basic minimal skills necessary for the enjoyment of the rights of speech and of full participation in the political process.

Furthermore, the logical limitations on appellees' nexus theory are difficult to perceive. How, for instance, is education to be distinguished from the significant personal interests in the basics of decent food and shelter? Empirical examination might well buttress an assumption that the ill fed, ill clothed, and ill housed are among the most ineffective participants in the political process, and that they derive the least enjoyment from the benefits of the First Amendment.

. . . We have carefully considered each of the arguments supportive of the District Court's finding that education is a fundamental right or liberty and have found those arguments unpersuasive. In one further respect we find this a particularly inappropriate case in which to subject state action to strict judicial scrutiny. The present case, in another basic sense, is significantly different from any of the cases in which the Court has applied strict scrutiny to state or federal legislation touching upon constitutionally protected rights. Each of our prior cases involved legislation which "deprived," "infringed," or "interfered" with the free exercise of some such fundamental personal right or liberty. A critical distinction between those cases and the one now before us lies in what Texas is endeavoring to do with respect to education.

. . . Every step leading to the establishment of the system Texas utilizes today—including the decisions permitting localities to tax and expend locally, and creating and continuously expanding state aid—was implemented in an effort to extend public education and to improve its quality. Of course, every reform that benefits some more than others may be criticized for what it fails to accomplish. But we think it plain that, in substance, the thrust of the Texas system is affirmative and reformatory and, therefore, should be scrutinized under judicial principles sensitive to the nature of the State's efforts and to the rights reserved to the States under the Constitution.

It should be clear, for the reasons stated above and in accord with the prior decisions of this Court, that this is not a case in which the challenged state action must be subjected to the searching judicial scrutiny reserved for laws that create suspect classifications or impinge upon constitutionally protected rights.

We need not rest our decision, however, solely on the inappropriateness of the strict-scrutiny test. A century of Supreme Court adjudication under the Equal Protection Clause affirmatively supports the application of the traditional standard of review, which requires only that the State's system be shown to bear some rational relationship to legitimate state purposes. This case represents far more than a challenge to the manner in which Texas provides for the education of its children. We have here nothing less than a direct attack on the way in which Texas has chosen to raise and disburse state and local tax revenues. We are asked to condemn the State's judgment in conferring on political subdivisions the power to tax local property to supply revenues for local interests. In so doing, appellees would have the Court intrude in an area in which it has traditionally deferred to state legislatures. This Court has often admonished against such interferences with the State's fiscal policies under the Equal Protection Clause:

> The broad discretion as to classification possessed by a legislature in the field of taxation has long been recognized. . . . [The] passage of time has only served to underscore the wisdom of that recognition of the large area of discretion which is needed by a legislature in formulating sound tax policies. . . . It has . . . been pointed out that in taxation, even more than in other fields, legislatures possess the greatest freedom in classification. Since the members of a legislature necessarily enjoy a familiarity with local conditions which this Court cannot have, the presumption of constitutionality can be overcome only by the most explicit demonstration that a classification is a hostile and oppressive discrimination against particular persons and classes. . . . *Madden v. Kentucky*, 309 U.S. 83, 87-88 (1940).

Thus, we stand on familiar ground when we continue to acknowledge that the Justices of this Court lack both the expertise and the familiarity with local problems so necessary to the making of wise decisions with respect to the raising and disposition of public revenues. Yet, we are urged to direct the States either to alter drastically the present system or to throw out the property tax altogether in favor of some other form of taxation. No scheme of taxation, whether the tax is imposed on property, income, or purchases of goods and services, has yet been devised which is free of all discriminatory impact. In such a complex arena in which no perfect alternatives exist, the Court does well not to impose too rigorous a standard of scrutiny lest all local fiscal schemes become subjects of criticism under the Equal Protection Clause.

In addition to matters of fiscal policy, this case also involves the most persistent and difficult questions of educational policy, another area in which this Court's lack of specialized knowledge and experience counsels against premature interference with the informed judgments made at the state and local levels. Education, perhaps even more than welfare assistance, presents a myriad of "intractable economic, social, and even philosophical problems. . . ." The very complexity of the problems of financing and managing a statewide public school system suggests that "there will be more than one constitutionally permissible method of solving them," and that, within the limits of rationality, "the legislature's efforts to tackle the problems" should be entitled to respect. On even the most basic questions in this area the scholars and educational experts are divided. Indeed, one of the major sources of controversy concerns the extent to which there is a demonstrable correlation between educational expenditures and the quality of education—an assumed correlation underlying virtually every legal conclusion drawn by the District Court in this case. Related to the questioned relationship between cost and quality is the equally unsettled controversy as to the proper goals of a system of public education. And the question regarding the most effective relationship between state boards of education and local school boards, in terms of their respective responsibilities and degrees of control, is now undergoing searching re-examination. The ultimate wisdom as to these and related problems of education is not likely to be divined for all time even by the scholars who now so earnestly debate the issues. In such circumstances, the judiciary is well advised to refrain from imposing on the States inflexible constitutional restraints that could circumscribe or handicap the continued research and experimentation so vital to finding even partial solutions to educational problems and to keeping abreast of ever-changing conditions.

It must be remembered, also, that every claim arising under the Equal Protection Clause has implications for the relationship between national and state power under our federal system. Questions of federalism are always inherent in the process of determining whether a State's laws are to be accorded the traditional presumption of constitutionality, or are to be subjected instead to rigorous judicial scrutiny. While "[t]he maintenance of the principles of federalism is a foremost consideration in interpreting any of the pertinent constitutional provisions under which this Court examines state action," it would be difficult to imagine a case having a greater potential impact on our federal system than the one now before us, in which we are urged to abrogate systems of financing public education presently in existence in virtually every State.

The foregoing considerations buttress our conclusion that Texas' system of public school finance is an inappropriate candidate for strict judicial scrutiny. These same considerations are relevant to the determination whether that system, with its conceded imperfections, nevertheless bears some rational relationship to a legitimate state purpose. It is to this question that we next turn our attention.

III

. . . Because of differences in expenditure levels occasioned by disparities in property tax income, appellees claim that children in less affluent districts have been made the subject of invidious discrimination. The District Court found that the State had failed even "to establish a reasonable basis" for a system that results in different levels of per-pupil expenditure. We disagree.

In its reliance on state as well as local resources, the Texas system is comparable to the systems employed in virtually every other State. The power to tax local property for educational purposes has been recognized in Texas at least since 1883. When the growth of commercial and industrial centers and accompanying shifts in population began to create disparities in local resources, Texas undertook a program calling for a considerable investment of state funds.

. . . The history of education since the industrial revolution shows a continual struggle between two forces: the desire by members of society to have educational opportunity for all children, and the desire of each family to provide the best education it can afford for its own children.

The Texas system of school finance is responsive to these two forces. While assuring a basic education for every child in the State, it permits and encourages a large measure of participation in and control of each district's schools at the local level. In an era that has witnessed a consistent trend toward centralization of the functions of government, local sharing of responsibility for public education has survived. . . .

The persistence of attachment to government at the lowest level where education is concerned reflects the depth of commitment of its supporters. In part, local control means . . . the freedom to devote more money to the education of one's children. Equally important, however, is the opportunity it offers for participation in the decision making process that determines how those local tax dollars will be spent. Each locality is free to tailor local programs to local needs. Pluralism also affords some opportunity for experimentation, innovation, and a healthy competition for educational excellence. An analogy to the Nation-State relationship in our federal system seems uniquely appropriate. Mr. Justice Brandeis identified as one of the peculiar strengths of our form of government each State's freedom to "serve as a laboratory; and try novel social and economic experiments." No area of social concern stands to profit more from a multiplicity of viewpoints and from a diversity of approaches than does public education.

Appellees do not question the propriety of Texas' dedication to local control of education. To the contrary, they attack the school-financing system precisely because, in their view, it does not provide the same level of local control and fiscal flexibility in all districts. Appellees suggest that local control could be preserved and promoted under other financing systems that resulted in more equality in educational expenditures. While it is no doubt true that reliance on local property taxation for school revenues provides less freedom of choice with respect to expenditures for some districts than for others the existence of "some inequality" in the manner in which the State's rationale is achieved is not alone a sufficient basis for striking down the entire system. It may not be condemned simply because it imperfectly effectuates the State's goals. Nor must the financing system fail because, as appellees suggest, other methods of satisfying the State's interest, which occasion "less drastic" disparities in expenditures, might be conceived. Only where state action impinges on the exercise of fundamental constitutional rights or liberties must it be found to have chosen the least restrictive alternative. It is also well to remember that even those districts that have reduced ability to make free decisions with respect to how much they spend on education still retain under the present system a large measure of authority as to how available funds will be allocated. They further enjoy the power to make numerous other decisions with respect to the operation of the schools. The people of Texas may be justified in believing that other systems of school financing, which place more of the financial responsibility in the hands of the State, will result in a comparable lessening of desired local autonomy. That is, they may believe that along with increased control of the purse strings at the state level will go increased control over local policies.

Appellees further urge that the Texas system is unconstitutionally arbitrary because it allows the availability of local taxable resources to turn on "happenstance." They see no justification for a system that allows, as they contend, the quality of education to fluctuate on the basis of the fortuitous positioning of the boundary lines of political subdivisions and the location of valuable commercial and industrial property. But any scheme of local taxation—indeed the very existence of identifiable local governmental units—requires the establishment of jurisdictional boundaries that are inevitably arbitrary. It is equally inevitable that some localities are going to be blessed with more taxable assets than others. Nor is local wealth a static quantity. Changes in the level of taxable wealth within any district may result from any number of events, some of which local residents can and do influence. For instance, commercial and industrial enterprises may be encouraged to locate within a district by various actions—public and private.

Moreover, if local taxation for local expenditures were an unconstitutional method of providing for education then it might be an equally impermissible means of providing other necessary services customarily financed largely from local property taxes, including local police and fire protection, public health and hospitals, and public utility facilities of various kinds. We perceive no justification for such a severe denigration of local property taxation and control as would follow from appellees' contentions. It has simply never been within the constitutional prerogative of this Court to nullify statewide measures for financing public services merely because the burdens or benefits thereof fall unevenly depending upon the relative wealth of the political subdivisions in which citizens live.

In sum, to the extent that the Texas system of school financing results in unequal expenditures between children who happen to reside in different districts, we cannot say that such disparities are the product of a system that is so irrational as to be invidiously discriminatory. Texas has acknowledged its shortcomings and has persistently endeavored—not without some success—to ameliorate the differences in levels of expenditures without sacrificing the benefits of local participation. The Texas plan is not the result of hurried, ill conceived legislation. It certainly is not the product of purposeful discrimination against any group or class. On the contrary, it is rooted in decades of experience in Texas and elsewhere, and in major part is the product of responsible studies by qualified people. In giving substance to the presumption of validity to which the Texas system is entitled, it is important to remember that at every stage of its development it has constituted a "rough accommodation" of interests in an effort to arrive at practical and workable solutions. One also must remember that the system here challenged is not peculiar to Texas or to any other State. In its essential characteristics, the Texas plan for financing public education reflects what many educators for a half century have thought was an enlightened approach to a problem for which there is no perfect solution. We are unwilling to assume for ourselves a level of wisdom superior to that of legislators, scholars, and educational authorities in 50 States, especially where the alternatives proposed are only recently conceived and nowhere yet tested. The constitutional standard under the Equal Protection Clause is whether the challenged state action rationally furthers a legitimate state purpose or interest. We hold that the Texas plan abundantly satisfies this standard.

IV

In light of the considerable attention that has focused on the District Court opinion in this case . . . a cautionary postscript seems appropriate. It cannot be questioned that the constitutional judgment reached by the District Court and approved by our dissenting Brothers today would occasion in Texas and elsewhere an unprecedented upheaval in public education. Some commentators have concluded that, whatever the contours of the alternative financing programs that might be devised and approved, the result could not avoid being a beneficial one. But, just as there is nothing simple about the constitutional issues involved in these cases, there is nothing simple or certain about predicting the consequences of massive change in the financing and control of public education. Those who have devoted the most thoughtful attention to the practical ramifications of these cases have found no clear or dependable answers and their scholarship reflects no such unqualified confidence in the desirability of completely uprooting the existing system.

The complexity of these problems is demonstrated by the lack of consensus with respect to whether it may be said with any assurance that the poor, the racial minorities, or the children in overburdened core-city school districts would be benefited by abrogation of traditional modes of financing education. Unless there is to be a substantial increase in state expenditures on education across the board—an event the likelihood of which is open to considerable question—these groups stand to realize gains in terms of increased per-pupil expenditures only if they reside in districts that presently spend at relatively low levels, i.e., in those districts that would benefit from the redistribution of existing resources. Yet, recent studies have indicated that the poorest families are not invariably clustered in the most impecunious school districts. Nor does it now appear that there is any more than a random chance that racial minorities are concentrated in property-poor districts. Additionally, several research projects have concluded that any financing alternative designed to achieve a greater equality of expenditures is likely to lead to higher taxation and lower educational expenditures in the major urban centers, a result that would exacerbate rather than ameliorate existing conditions in those areas.

These practical considerations, of course, play no role in the adjudication of the constitutional issues presented here. But they serve to highlight the wisdom of the traditional limitations on this Court's function. The consideration and initiation of fundamental reforms with respect to state taxation and education are matters reserved for the legislative processes of the various States, and we do no violence to the values of federalism and separation of powers by staying our hand. We hardly need add that this Court's action today is not to be viewed as placing its judicial imprimatur on the status quo. The need is apparent for reform in tax systems which may well have relied too long and too heavily on the local property tax. And certainly innovative thinking as to public education, its methods, and its funding is necessary to assure both a higher level of quality and greater uniformity of opportunity. These matters merit the continued attention of the scholars who already have contributed much by their challenges. But the ultimate solutions must come from the lawmakers and from the democratic pressures of those who elect them.

Reversed.

Mr. Justice MARSHALL, with whom Mr. Justice DOUGLAS concurs, dissenting.

The Court today decides, in effect, that a State may constitutionally vary the quality of education which it offers its children in accordance with the amount of taxable wealth located in the school districts within which they reside. The majority's decision represents an abrupt departure from the mainstream of recent state and federal court decisions concerning the unconstitutionality of state educational financing schemes dependent upon taxable local wealth. More unfortunately, though, the majority's holding can only be seen as a retreat from our historic commitment to equality of educational opportunity and as unsupportable acquiescence in a system which deprives children in their earliest years of the chance to reach their full potential as citizens. The Court does this despite the absence of any substantial justification for a scheme which arbitrarily channels educational resources in accordance with the fortuity of the amount of taxable wealth within each district.

In my judgment, the right of every American to an equal start in life, so far as the provision of a state service as important as education is concerned, is far too vital to permit state discrimination on grounds as tenuous as those presented by this record. Nor can I accept the notion that it is sufficient to remit these appellees to the vagaries of the political process which, contrary to the majority's suggestion, has proved singularly unsuited to the task of providing a remedy for this discrimination. I, for one, am unsatisfied with the hope of an ultimate "political" solution sometime in the indefinite future while, in the meantime, countless children unjustifiably receive inferior educations that "may affect their hearts and minds in a way unlikely ever to be undone." *Brown v. Board of Education,* 347 U.S. 483, 494 (1954). I must therefore respectfully dissent.

I

The Court acknowledges that "substantial interdistrict disparities in school expenditures" exist in Texas, and that these disparities are "largely attributable to differences in the amounts of money collected through local property taxation." But instead of closely examining the seriousness of these disparities and the invidiousness of the Texas financing scheme, the Court undertakes an elaborate exploration of the efforts Texas has purportedly made to close the gaps between its districts in terms of levels of district wealth and resulting educational funding. Yet, however praiseworthy Texas' equalizing efforts, the issue in this case is not whether Texas is doing its best to ameliorate the worst features of a discriminatory scheme but, rather, whether the scheme itself is in fact unconstitutionally discriminatory in the face of the Fourteenth Amendment's guarantee of equal protection of the laws. When the Texas financing scheme is taken as a whole, I do not think it can be doubted that it produces a discriminatory impact on substantial numbers of the school age children of the State of Texas. . . .

The appellants do not deny the disparities in educational funding caused by variations in taxable district property wealth. They do contend, however, that whatever the differences in per-pupil spending among Texas districts, there are no discriminatory consequences for the children of the disadvantaged districts. They recognize that what is at stake in this case is the quality of the public education provided Texas children in the districts in which they live. But appellants reject the suggestion that the quality of education in any particular district is determined by money—beyond some minimal level of funding which they believe to be assured every Texas district by the Minimum Foundation School Program. In their view, there is simply no denial of equal educational opportunity to any Texas schoolchildren as a result of the widely varying per-pupil spending power provided districts under the current financing scheme.

In my view, though, even an unadorned restatement of this contention is sufficient to reveal its absurdity. Authorities concerned with educational quality no doubt disagree as to the significance of variations in per-pupil spending. Indeed, conflicting expert testimony was presented to the District Court in this case concerning the effect of spending variations on educational achievement. We sit, however, not to resolve disputes over educational theory but to enforce our Constitution. It is an inescapable fact that if one district has more funds available per pupil than another district, the former will have greater choice in educational planning than will the latter. In this regard, I believe the question of discrimination in educational quality must be deemed to be an objective one that looks to what the State provides its children, not to what the children are able to do with what they receive. That a child forced to attend an underfunded school with poorer physical facilities, less experienced teachers, larger classes, and a narrower range of courses than a school with substantially more funds—and thus with greater choice in educational planning—may nevertheless excel is to the credit of the child, not the *State*. . . . Indeed, who can ever measure for such a child the opportunities lost and the talents wasted for want of a broader, more enriched education? Discrimination in the opportunity to learn that is afforded a child must be our standard.

Hence, even before this Court recognized its duty to tear down the barriers of state-enforced racial segregation in public education, it acknowledged that inequality in the educational facilities provided to students may be discriminatory state action as contemplated by the Equal Protection Clause. As a basis for striking down state-enforced segregation of a law school, the Court in *Sweatt v. Painter*, 339 U.S. 629, 633-634 (1950), stated:

> [W]e cannot find substantial equality in the educational opportunities offered white and Negro law students by the State. In terms of number of the faculty, variety of courses and opportunity for specialization, size of the student body, scope of the library, availability of law review and similar activities, the [whites-only] Law School is superior. . . . It is difficult to believe that one who had a free choice between these law schools would consider the question close.

See also *McLaurin v. Oklahoma State Regents for Higher Education*, 339 U.S. 637 (1950). Likewise, it is difficult to believe that if the children of Texas had a free choice, they would choose to be educated in districts with fewer resources, and hence with more antiquated plants, less experienced teachers, and a less diversified curriculum. In fact, if financing variations are so insignificant to educational quality, it is difficult to understand why a number of our country's wealthiest school districts, which have no legal obligation to argue in support of the constitutionality of the Texas legislation, have nevertheless zealously pursued its cause before this Court.

The consequences, in terms of objective educational input, of the variations in district funding caused by the Texas financing scheme are apparent from the data introduced before the District Court. For example, in 1968-1969, 100% of the teachers in the property-rich Alamo Heights School District had college degrees. By contrast, during the same school year only 80.02% of the teachers had college degrees in the property poor Edgewood Independent School District. Also, in 1968-1969, approximately 47% of the teachers in the Edgewood District were on emergency teaching permits, whereas only 11% of the teachers in Alamo Heights were on such permits. This is undoubtedly a reflection of the fact that the top of Edgewood's teacher salary scale was approximately 80% of Alamo Heights. And, not surprisingly, the teacher-student ratio varies significantly between the two districts. In other words, as might be expected, a difference in the funds available to districts results in a difference in educational inputs available for a child's public education in Texas. For constitutional purposes, I believe this situation, which is directly attributable to the Texas financing scheme, raises a grave question of state-created discrimination in the provision of public education.

. . . The suggestion may be that the state aid received via the Foundation Program sufficiently improves the position of property-poor districts vis-à-vis property-rich districts—in terms of educational funds—to eliminate any claim of interdistrict discrimination in available educational resources which might otherwise exist if educational funding were dependent solely upon local property taxation. Certainly the Court has recognized that to demand precise equality of treatment is normally unrealistic, and thus minor differences inherent in any practical context usually will not make out a substantial equal protection claim. . . . But, as has already been seen, we are hardly presented here with some de minimis claim of discrimination resulting from the play necessary in any functioning system; to the contrary, it is clear that the Foundation Program utterly fails to ameliorate the seriously discriminatory effects of the local property tax.

Alternatively, the appellants and the majority may believe that the Equal Protection Clause cannot be offended by substantially unequal state treatment of persons who are similarly situated so long as the State provides everyone with some unspecified amount of education which evidently is "enough." The basis for such a novel view is far from clear. It is, of course, true that the Constitution does not require precise equality in the treatment of all persons. As Mr. Justice Frankfurter explained: "The equality at which the 'equal protection' clause aims is not a disembodied equality. The Fourteenth Amendment enjoins 'the equal protection of the laws,' and laws are not abstract propositions. . . . The Constitution does not require things which are different in fact or opinion to be treated in law as though they were the same." *Tigner v. Texas,* 310 U.S. 141, 147 (1940).

. . . But this Court has never suggested that because some "adequate" level of benefits is provided to all, discrimination in the provision of services is therefore constitutionally excusable. The Equal Protection Clause is not addressed to the minimal sufficiency but rather to the unjustifiable inequalities of state action. It mandates nothing less than that "all persons similarly circumstanced shall be treated alike."

. . . Even if the Equal Protection Clause encompassed some theory of constitutional adequacy, discrimination in the provision of educational opportunity would certainly seem to be a poor candidate for its application. Neither the majority nor appellants inform us how judicially manageable standards are to be derived for determining how much education is "enough" to excuse constitutional discrimination.

. . . In my view, then, it is inequality—not some notion of gross inadequacy—of educational opportunity that raises a question of denial of equal protection of the laws. I find any other approach to the issue unintelligible and without directing principle. Here appellees have made a substantial showing of wide variations in educational funding and the resulting educational opportunity afforded to the school children of Texas. This discrimination is, in large measure, attributable to significant disparities in the taxable wealth of local Texas school districts. This is a sufficient showing to raise a substantial question of discriminatory state action in violation of the Equal Protection Clause. . . .

Since the Court now suggests that only interests guaranteed by the Constitution are fundamental for purposes of equal protection analysis, and since it rejects the contention that public education is fundamental, it follows that the Court concludes that public education is not constitutionally guaranteed. It is true that this Court has never deemed the provision of free public education to be required by the Constitution. Indeed, it has on occasion suggested that state supported education is a privilege bestowed by a State on its citizens. Nevertheless, the fundamental importance of education is amply indicated by the prior decisions of this Court, by the unique status accorded public education by our society, and by the close relationship between education and some of our most basic constitutional values.

The special concern of this Court with the educational process of our country is a matter of common knowledge. Undoubtedly, this Court's most famous statement on the subject is that contained in *Brown v. Board of Education,* 347 U.S., at 493:

> Today, education is perhaps the most important function of state and local governments. Compulsory school attendance laws and the great expenditures for education both demonstrate our recognition of the importance of education to our democratic society. It is required in the performance of our most basic public responsibilities, even service in the armed forces. It is the very foundation of good citizenship. Today it is a principal instrument in awakening the child to cultural values, in preparing him for later professional training, and in helping him to adjust normally to his environment. . . .

Only last Term, the Court recognized that "[p]roviding public schools ranks at the very apex of the function of a State." *Wisconsin v. Yoder,* 406 U.S. 205, 213 (1972). This is clearly borne out by the fact that in 48 of our 50 States the provision of public education is mandated by the state Constitution. No other state function is so uniformly recognized as an essential element of our society's well being. In large measure, the explanation for the special importance attached to education must rest, as the Court recognized in *Yoder,* on the facts that "some degree of education is necessary to prepare citizens to participate effectively and intelligently in our open political system . . . ," and that "education prepares individuals to be self-reliant and self-sufficient participants in society." Both facets of this observation are suggestive of the substantial relationship which education bears to guarantees of our Constitution.

Education directly affects the ability of a child to exercise his First Amendment rights, both as a source and as a receiver of information and ideas, whatever interests he may pursue in life. This Court's decision in *Sweezy v. New Hampshire,* 354 U.S. 234, 250 (1957), speaks of the right of students "to inquire, to study and to evaluate, to gain new maturity and understanding . . ." Thus, we have not casually described the classroom as the "marketplace of ideas." *Keyishian v. Board of Regents,* 385 U.S. 589, 603 (1967). The opportunity for formal education may not necessarily be the essential determinant of an individual's ability to enjoy throughout his life the rights of free speech and association guaranteed to him by the First Amendment. But such an opportunity may enhance the individual's enjoyment of those rights, not only during but also following school attendance. Thus, in the final analysis, "the pivotal position of education to success in American society and its essential role in opening up to the individual the central experiences of our culture lend it an importance that is undeniable."

Of particular importance is the relationship between education and the political process. "Americans regard the public schools as a most vital civic institution for the preservation of a democratic system of government." *Abington School Dist. v. Schempp,* 374 U.S. 203, 230 (1963) (Brennan, J., concurring). Education serves the essential function of instilling in our young an understanding of and appreciation for the principles and operation of our governmental processes. Education may instill the interest and provide the tools necessary for political discourse and debate. Indeed, it has frequently been suggested that education is the dominant factor affecting political consciousness and participation. A system of "[c]ompetition in ideas and governmental policies is at the core of our electoral process and of the First Amendment freedoms." *Williams v. Rhodes,* 393 U.S. 23, 32 (1968). But of most immediate and direct concern must be the demonstrated effect of education on the exercise of the franchise by the electorate. The right to vote in federal elections is conferred by Art. I, §2, and the Seventeenth Amendment of the Constitution, and access to the state franchise has been afforded special protection because it is "preservative of other basic civil and political rights," . . . Data from the Presidential Election of 1968 clearly demonstrates a direct relationship between participation in the electoral process and level of educational attainment; and, as this Court recognized in *Gaston County v. United States,* 395 U.S. 285, 296 (1969), the quality of education offered may influence a child's decision to "enter or remain in school." It is this very sort of intimate relationship between a particular personal interest and specific constitutional guarantees that has heretofore caused the Court to attach special significance, for purposes of equal protection analysis, to individual interests such as procreation and the exercise of the state franchise.

While ultimately disputing little of this, the majority seeks refuge in the fact that the Court has "never presumed to possess either the ability or the authority to guarantee to the citizenry the most effective speech or the most informed electoral choice." This serves only to blur what is in fact at stake. With due respect, the issue is neither provision of the most effective speech nor of the most informed vote. Appellees do not now seek the best education Texas might provide. They do seek, however, an end to state discrimination resulting from the unequal distribution of taxable district property wealth that directly impairs the ability of some districts to provide the same educational opportunity that other districts can provide with the same or even substantially less tax effort. The issue is, in other words, one of discrimination that affects the quality of the education which Texas has chosen to provide its children; and, the precise question here is what importance should attach to education for purposes of equal protection analysis of that discrimination. As this Court held in *Brown v. Board of Education,* 347 U.S. at 493, the opportunity of education, "where the state has undertaken to provide it, is a right which must be made available to all on equal terms." The factors just considered, including the relationship between education and the social and political interests enshrined within the Constitution, compel us to recognize the fundamentality of education and to scrutinize with appropriate care the bases for state discrimination affecting equality of educational opportunity in Texas' school districts—a conclusion which is only strengthened when we consider the character of the classification in this case.

. . . In my judgment, any substantial degree of scrutiny of the operation of the Texas financing scheme reveals that the State has selected means wholly inappropriate to secure its purported interest in assuring its school districts local fiscal control. At the same time, appellees have pointed out a variety of alternative financing schemes which may serve the State's purported interest in local control as well as, if not better than, the present scheme without the current impairment of the educational opportunity of vast numbers of Texas schoolchildren. I see no need, however, to explore the practical or constitutional merits of those suggested alternatives at this time for, whatever their positive or negative features, experience with the present financing scheme impugns any suggestion that it constitutes a serious effort to provide local fiscal control. If, for the sake of local education control, this Court is to sustain interdistrict discrimination in the educational opportunity afforded Texas school children, it should require that the State present something more than the mere sham now before us. . . .

III

In conclusion, it is essential to recognize that an end to the wide variations in taxable district property wealth inherent in the Texas financing scheme would entail none of the untoward consequences suggested by the Court or by the appellants.

First, affirmance of the District Court's decisions would hardly sound the death knell for local control of education. It would mean neither centralized decision making nor federal court intervention in the operation of public schools. Clearly, this suit has nothing to do with local decision making with respect to educational policy or even educational spending. It involves only a narrow aspect of local control—namely, local control over the raising of educational funds. In fact, in striking down interdistrict disparities in taxable local wealth, the District Court took the course which is most likely to make true local control over educational decision making a reality for all Texas school districts.

Nor does the District Court's decision even necessarily eliminate local control of educational funding. The District Court struck down nothing more than the continued interdistrict wealth discrimination inherent in the present property tax. Both centralized and decentralized plans for educational funding not involving such interdistrict discrimination have been put forward. The choice among these or other alternatives would remain with the State, not with the federal courts. In this regard, it should be evident that the degree of federal intervention in matters of local concern would be substantially less in this context than in previous decisions in which we have been asked effectively to impose a particular scheme upon the States under the guise of the Equal Protection Clause.

. . . Yet no one in the course of this entire litigation has ever questioned the constitutionality of the local property tax as a device for raising educational funds. The District Court's decision, at most, restricts the power of the State to make educational funding dependent exclusively upon local property taxation so long as there exists interdistrict disparities in taxable property wealth. But it hardly eliminates the local property tax as a source of educational funding or as a means of providing local fiscal control.

The Court seeks solace for its action today in the possibility of legislative reform. The Court's suggestions of legislative redress and experimentation will doubtless be of great comfort to the schoolchildren of Texas' disadvantaged districts, but considering the vested interests of wealthy school districts in the preservation of the status quo, they are worth little more. The possibility of legislative action is, in all events, no answer to this Court's duty under the Constitution to eliminate unjustified state discrimination. In this case we have been presented with an instance of such discrimination, in a particularly invidious form, against an individual interest of large constitutional and practical importance. To support the demonstrated discrimination in the provision of educational opportunity the State has offered a justification which, on analysis, takes on at best an ephemeral character. Thus, I believe that the wide disparities in taxable district property wealth inherent in the local property tax element of the Texas financing scheme render that scheme violative of the Equal Protection Clause.

NOTES AND QUESTIONS

1. As the Supreme Court recognizes, Texas concedes that its dual system of financing public education results in grossly unequal allocations of resources to different school districts. If that disparity in educational resources would be unconstitutional if it operated to disadvantage a "suspect class" or if it "impinge[d] upon a fundamental right," why should the constitutionality of an admittedly unequal educational system depend on the nature of the "class" harmed or the "right" impinged upon?
2. The Court concludes that the individuals adversely affected by the Texas system are not a "suspect class" because: (1) the system does not operate to the "peculiar" disadvantage of a class defined as "indigent"; (2) the individuals affected are not absolutely deprived of the benefit of education; and (3) the class of individuals who have low taxable wealth do not share the characteristics of insularity, political powerlessness or a history of unequal treatment which have typically defined "suspect classes." Analyze each of these three claims. What support does the court muster for these arguments? Are the arguments persuasive?
3. The Court ultimately must address the question whether "education is a fundamental right, in the sense that it is among the rights and liberties protected by the Constitution. . . ." After acknowledging the grave significance of education in the lives of Americans, the Court refocuses the inquiry as whether "there is a right to education explicitly or implicitly guaranteed by the Constitution." The Court then finds no explicit or implicit protection for the right to education in the Constitution. Yet, the Court hints that the Constitution may implicitly protect against the "absolute denial of educational opportunities" to children. Is there a fundamental constitutional right to some minimal level of educational opportunity? If so, how does the Constitution implicitly provide for that right? How would you define the minimal level of educational opportunity deserving constitutional protection?
4. The Court considers, but ultimately rejects, the notion that the right to education is fundamental because it is indispensable to other constitutionally protected rights, such as the First Amendment right to speech and the intelligent utilization of the right to vote. The Court nowhere mentions the *Pierce* or *Meyer* cases in this context. Recall that in *Pierce* and *Meyer*, the Supreme Court recognized the fundamental right of parents to educate their children according to their own conscience. Is there a fundamental constitutional right to a private education, but no fundamental constitutional right to a public education?
5. The Court states that education presents a "myriad of intractable economic, social, and even philosophical problems." 411 U.S. at 42. These "problems" are then used by the Court as a justification for its decision to refrain from entering an arena traditionally relegated to local, legislative prerogative. Is the Court generally reluctant to avoid ruling on such difficult issues, or is its decision to avoid doing so here particularly well suited to the issue of education?

6. In his dissent, Justice Marshall extols the virtues of a fundamental constitutional guarantee of public education. Do you find Justice Marshall's dissenting opinion more or less persuasive than the majority's opinion?
7. What are the alternatives to the educational financing scheme upheld in *San Antonio*? In footnote 85 of its opinion, the majority mentions the alternative of creating a basic foundation level of funding for each district in the state that would be the same in every district, and the alternative of transferring wealth from districts with higher property values to districts with lower property values. The Court suggests that these alternatives would present their own economic and political issues that are best resolved by the political branch of government. Do you agree? In addition, the Court indicates that a funding system that transfers wealth from one district to another may present significant equal protection problems. What are those equal protection problems?
8. The Court declares that, "the history of education since the industrial revolution shows a continual struggle between two forces: the desire by members of society to have educational opportunity for all children, and the desire of each family to provide the best education it can afford for its own children." To what extent does this "struggle" predate the industrial revolution? Is this struggle inevitable in a democratic society? Is the struggle inevitable in any society? Is the Supreme Court correct that Texas's system of financing education is responsive to these two competing "forces"? Is it possible to envision an educational system that reconciles the interests of family with that of society? How would such a system be funded?
9. *International and Comparative Law Perspectives on the Right to an Education.* The Supreme Court's conclusion in *Rodriguez* invites a comparative analysis of global approaches to the existence of a right to an education. The American Constitution, as interpreted in *Rodriguez*, is inconsistent with the overwhelming international consensus that education is a fundamental right. Since World War II, the United Nations has promulgated three significant documents declaring education a fundamental right. In 1948, the U.N. adopted the Universal Declaration of Human Rights (UDHR). Created to articulate the inalienable rights and freedoms of all people, the UDHR purports to use education as a means of promoting respect for and recognition of these rights. Universal Declaration of Human Rights G.G. Res. 217A, at 71-72, U.N. GAOR, 3d Sess., 1st plen. mtg., U.N. Doc. A/810 (Dec. 12, 1948). Article 26 of the UDHR declares:

> Everyone has the right to education. Education shall be free, at least in the elementary and fundamental stages. Elementary education shall be compulsory. Technical and professional education shall be made generally available and higher education shall be equally accessible to all on the basis of merit. . . . Education shall be directed to the full development of the human personality and to the strengthening of respect for human rights and fundamental freedoms. It shall promote understanding, tolerance and friendship among racial or religious groups. . . .

The UDHR mandates elementary education be compulsory, and higher education be readily available to all. *Id.* at 76. Moreover, it declares education should encourage in students a respect for human rights, and should promote tolerance without regard to nationality, race, ethnicity, or creed. *Id.*

Although the document itself is not law in the member-states of the U.N., there is significant evidence that the UDHR is recognized as customary international law. Hurst Hannum, *The Status of the Universal Declaration of Human Rights in National and International Law*, 25 *Ga. J. Int'l & Com. L.* 287, 322 (1996). As such, the UDHR is influential in shaping how countries govern their citizens. *Id.* Support for the proposition that the UDHR constitutes customary international law is further garnered from the fact that many provisions of the UDHR have been codified in the constitutions and laws of foreign nations. *Id. See also* Connie de la Vega, *The Right to Equal Education: Merely a Guiding Principle or Customary International Legal Right?*, 11 *Harvard BlackLetter L.J.* 37, 41-44 (1994). While not binding authority, the UDHR is significant in that it was the catalyst for the creation of a similar document, the International Convention on Economic, Social, and Cultural Rights (CESCR). Angela Avis Holland, *Resolving the Dissonance of Rodriquez and the Right to Education: International Human Rights Instruments as a Source of Repose for the United States*, 41 Vand. J. Transnat'l L. 229, 247. While the UDHR is not law, CESCR is a binding treaty for the countries that have ratified it. International Convention on Economic, Social and Cultural Rights, G.A. Res. 2200A(XXI), at 52, U.N. Doc. A/6316 (December 16, 1996).

The CESCR was adopted by the U.N. in 1966 as a recognition and protection of the rights catalogued in the UDHR. *Id.* at 49. UDHR article 13 clearly declares the "Parties to the present Covenant recognize the right of everyone to education." *Id.* at 51. Like the UDHR, the CESCR demands that education promote recognition of human rights for all, and that primary education be compulsory. *Id.*

In 1989, the U.N. adopted the Convention on the Rights of the Child (CRC). Like the UDHR and the CESCR, the CRC mandates that primary education be free and compulsory. Convention on the Rights of the Child, G.A. Res. 44/25, Annex, at 170, U.N. Doc. A/RES/44/25/Annex (Nov. 20, 1989). Moreover, the CRC requires that higher education be accessible to all, and that measures such as free education and financial assistance be instituted when needed. *Id.* More countries have ratified the CRC than any other human rights treaty. U.N. High Commissioner for Human Rights, *Status of Ratifications of the Principal International Human Rights Treaties*, at 12 (2004), http://www.unhcr.ch/pdf/report.pdf. The United States and Somalia are the only two U.N. member-states that have yet to ratify the CRC. *Id.* at 10-11.

While the United States does not recognize a fundamental right to education, it is nevertheless a signatory of the CESCR and the CRC. *Id.* at 11. For what reasons might the United States have signed onto these treaties for adoption by the U.N., but opted not to ratify them?

In *Free and Compulsory Education for All Children: The Gap Between Promise and Performance*, (2001) Katarina Tomasevski graphically demonstrates that, unlike the United States, most countries have recognized a constitutional right to an education:

> **Free and compulsory education for all constitutionally guaranteed:** Albania, Algeria, Argentina, Australia, Austria, Azerbaijan, Barbados, Belgium, Belize, Bolivia, Bosnia and Herzegovina, Brazil, Bulgaria, Canada, Cape Verde, Chile, China, Colombia, Congo/Brazzaville, Costa Rica, Croatia, Cuba, Denmark, Ecuador, Egypt, Estonia, Finland, France, Gambia, Georgia, Germany, Ghana, Haiti, Honduras, Iceland, Ireland, Italy, Japan, Korea (North), Latvia, Liechtenstein, Lithuania, Macedonia, Madagascar, Malta, Mauritius, Mexico, Moldova, Netherlands, Norway, Palau, Panama, Paraguay, Peru, Poland, Portugal, Romania, Russia, Rwanda, Saudi Arabia, South Africa, Spain, Sri Lanka, Suriname, Sweden, Switzerland, Tajikistan, Thailand, Trinidad and Tobago, Tunisia, Ukraine, United Arab Emirates, United Kingdom, Uruguay, Venezuela, Yugoslavia.
>
> **Progressive realization or partial guarantees:** Bangladesh, Belarus, Benin, Bhutan, Burma, Cameroon, Comoros, Guinea, Guinea-Bissau, India, Iran, Iraq, Israel, Maldives, Micronesia, Monaco, Mongolia, Namibia, Nepal, Nigeria, Pakistan, St. Kitts and Nevis, Sierra Leone, Sudan, Tanzania, Togo, Uganda, Uzbekistan, Zimbabwe.
>
> **Guarantees restricted to citizens or residents:** Armenia, Bahrain, Cambodia, Chad, Cyprus, Czech Rep., Dominican Rep., El Salvador, Equatorial Guinea, Greece, Grenada, Guatemala, Guyana, Hungary, Jordan, Kazakhstan, Korea (South), Kuwait, Kyrgystan, Libya, Luxembourg, Malawi, Mali, Morocco, New Zealand, Nicaragua, Philippines, Qatar, Sao Tome, Seychelles, Slovakia, Slovenia, Syria, Turkey, Turkmenistan, Vietnam, Yemen.
>
> **No constitutional guarantee:** Angola, Antigua and Barbuda, Bahamas, Botswana, Brunei, Burkina Faso, Burundi, Central African Rep., Côte d'Ivoire, Djibouti, Dominica, Eritrea, Ethiopia, Fiji, Gabon, Indonesia, Jamaica, Kenya, Kiribati, Laos, Lebanon, Lesotho, Liberia, Malaysia, Marshall Islands, Mauritania, Mozambique, Nauru, Niger, Oman, Papua New Guinea, St. Lucia, St. Vincent, Samoa, San Marino, Senegal, Singapore, Solomon Islands, Swaziland, Tonga, Tuvalu, USA, Vanuatu, Zambia.
>
> *See* K. Tomasevski, *Right to Education Primers* No. 2 at 18 (2001).

PLYLER v. DOE

457 U.S. 202 (1982)

Justice BRENNAN delivered the opinion of the Court.

The question presented by these cases is whether, consistent with the Equal Protection Clause of the Fourteenth Amendment, Texas may deny to undocumented school-age children the free public education that it provides to children who are citizens of the United States or legally admitted aliens.

I

Since the late 19th century, the United States has restricted immigration into this country. Unsanctioned entry into the United States is a crime, . . .

and those who have entered unlawfully are subject to deportation. But despite the existence of these legal restrictions, a substantial number of persons have succeeded in unlawfully entering the United States, and now live within various States, including the State of Texas.

In May 1975, the Texas Legislature revised its education laws to withhold from local school districts any state funds for the education of children who were not "legally admitted" into the United States. The 1975 revision also authorized local school districts to deny enrollment in their public schools to children not "legally admitted" to the country. . . . These cases involve constitutional challenges to those provisions. . . .

II

The Fourteenth Amendment provides that "[no] State shall . . . deprive any person of life, liberty, or property, without due process of law; nor deny to *any person within its jurisdiction* the equal protection of the laws." (Emphasis added.) Appellants argue at the outset that undocumented aliens, because of their immigration status, are not "persons within the jurisdiction" of the State of Texas, and that they therefore have no right to the equal protection of Texas law. We reject this argument.

. . . Appellants seek to distinguish our prior cases, emphasizing that the Equal Protection Clause directs a State to afford its protection to persons *within its jurisdiction* while the Due Process Clauses of the Fifth and Fourteenth Amendments contain no such assertedly limiting phrase. In appellants' view, persons who have entered the United States illegally are not "within the jurisdiction" of a State even if they are present within a State's boundaries and subject to its laws. Neither our cases nor the logic of the Fourteenth Amendment supports that constricting construction of the phrase "within its jurisdiction." We have never suggested that the class of persons who might avail themselves of the equal protection guarantee is less than coextensive with that entitled to due process. To the contrary, we have recognized that both provisions were fashioned to protect an identical class of persons, and to reach every exercise of state authority.

The Fourteenth Amendment to the Constitution is not confined to the protection of citizens. It says: "Nor shall any state deprive any person of life, liberty, or property without due process of law; nor deny to any person within its jurisdiction the equal protection of the laws." *These provisions are universal in their application, to all persons within the territorial jurisdiction,* without regard to any differences of race, of color, or of nationality; and the protection of the laws is a pledge of the protection of equal laws.

. . . Our conclusion that the illegal aliens who are plaintiffs in these cases may claim the benefit of the Fourteenth Amendment's guarantee of equal protection only begins the inquiry. The more difficult question is whether the Equal Protection Clause has been violated by the refusal of the State of Texas to reimburse local school boards for the education of children who cannot demonstrate that their presence within the United States is lawful, or by the imposition by those school boards of the burden of tuition on those children. It is to this question that we now turn.

III

The Equal Protection Clause directs that "all persons similarly circumstanced shall be treated alike." *F.S. Royster Guano Co. v. Virginia*, 253 U.S. 412, 415 (1920). But so too, "[the] Constitution does not require things which are different in fact or opinion to be treated in law as though they were the same." *Tigner v. Texas*, 310 U.S. 141, 147 (1940). The initial discretion to determine what is "different" and what is "the same" resides in the legislatures of the States. A legislature must have substantial latitude to establish classifications that roughly approximate the nature of the problem perceived, that accommodate competing concerns both public and private, and that account for limitations on the practical ability of the State to remedy every ill. In applying the Equal Protection Clause to most forms of state action, we thus seek only the assurance that the classification at issue bears some fair relationship to a legitimate public purpose.

But we would not be faithful to our obligations under the Fourteenth Amendment if we applied so deferential a standard to every classification. The Equal Protection Clause was intended as a restriction on state legislative action inconsistent with elemental constitutional premises. Thus we have treated as presumptively invidious those classifications that disadvantage a "suspect class," or that impinge upon the exercise of a "fundamental right." With respect to such classifications, it is appropriate to enforce the mandate of equal protection by requiring the State to demonstrate that its classification has been precisely tailored to serve a compelling governmental interest. In addition, we have recognized that certain forms of legislative classification, while not facially invidious, nonetheless give rise to recurring constitutional difficulties; in these limited circumstances we have sought the assurance that the classification reflects a reasoned judgment consistent with the ideal of equal protection by inquiring whether it may fairly be viewed as furthering a substantial interest of the State.

. . . We reject the claim that "illegal aliens" are a "suspect class." No case in which we have attempted to define a suspect class, has addressed the status of persons unlawfully in our country. Unlike most of the classifications that we have recognized as suspect, entry into this class, by virtue of entry into this country, is the product of voluntary action. Indeed, entry into the class is itself a crime.

. . . The children who are plaintiffs in these cases are special members of this underclass. Persuasive arguments support the view that a State may withhold its beneficence from those whose very presence within the United States is the product of their own unlawful conduct. These arguments do not apply with the same force to classifications imposing disabilities on the minor *children* of such illegal entrants. At the least, those who elect to enter our territory by stealth and in violation of our law should be prepared to bear the consequences, including, but not limited to, deportation. But the children of those illegal entrants are not comparably situated. Their "parents have the ability to conform their conduct to societal norms," and presumably the ability to remove themselves from the State's jurisdiction; but the children who are plaintiffs in these cases "can affect neither their parents' conduct nor their own status." *Trimble v. Gordon*, 430 U.S. 762, 770 (1977). Even if the State found it expedient to control the conduct of adults by acting against their children, legislation directing the onus of a parent's misconduct against his children does not comport with fundamental conceptions of justice.

> [Visiting] . . . condemnation on the head of an infant is illogical and unjust. Moreover, imposing disabilities on the . . . child is contrary to the basic concept of our system that legal burdens should bear some relationship to individual responsibility or wrongdoing. Obviously, no child is responsible for his birth and penalizing the . . . child is an ineffectual—as well as unjust—way of deterring the parent. *Weber v. Aetna Casualty & Surety Co.*, 406 U.S. 164, 175 (1972) (footnote omitted).

Of course, undocumented status is not irrelevant to any proper legislative goal. Nor is undocumented status an absolutely immutable characteristic since it is the product of conscious, indeed unlawful, action. But [the Texas law] is directed against children, and imposes its discriminatory burden on the basis of a legal characteristic over which children can have little control. It is thus difficult to conceive of a rational justification for penalizing these children for their presence within the United States.

. . . Public education is not a "right" granted to individuals by the Constitution. *San Antonio Independent School Dist. v. Rodriguez*, 411 U.S. 1, 35 (1973). But neither is it merely some governmental "benefit" indistinguishable from other forms of social welfare legislation. Both the importance of education in maintaining our basic institutions, and the lasting impact of its deprivation on the life of the child, mark the distinction. The "American people have always regarded education and [the] acquisition of knowledge as matters of supreme importance." *Meyer v. Nebraska*, 262 U.S. 390, 400 (1923). We have recognized "the public schools as a most vital civic institution for the preservation of a democratic system of government," *Abington School District v. Schempp*, 374 U.S. 203, 230 (1963) (Brennan, J., concurring), and as the primary vehicle for transmitting "the values on which our society rests." *Ambach v. Norwick*, 441 U.S. 68, 76 (1979). "[As] . . . pointed out early in our history, . . . some degree of education is necessary to prepare citizens to participate effectively and intelligently in our open political system if we are to preserve freedom and independence." *Wisconsin v. Yoder*, 406 U.S. 205, 221 (1972). And these historic "perceptions of the public schools as inculcating fundamental values necessary to the maintenance of a democratic political system have been confirmed by the observations of social scientists." . . . In addition, education provides the basic tools by which individuals might lead economically productive lives to the benefit of us all. In sum, education has a fundamental role in maintaining the fabric of our society. We cannot ignore the significant social costs borne by our Nation when select groups are denied the means to absorb the values and skills upon which our social order rests.

In addition to the pivotal role of education in sustaining our political and cultural heritage, denial of education to some isolated group of children poses an affront to one of the goals of the Equal Protection Clause: the abolition of governmental barriers presenting unreasonable obstacles to advancement on the basis of individual merit. Paradoxically, by depriving the children of any disfavored group of an education, we foreclose the means by which that group might raise the level of esteem in which it is held by the majority. But more directly, "education prepares individuals to be self-reliant and self-sufficient participants in society." *Wisconsin v. Yoder*. Illiteracy is an enduring disability. The inability to read and write will handicap the individual deprived of a basic education each and every day of his life. The inestimable toll of that deprivation on the social, economic, intellectual, and psychological well being of the individual, and the obstacle it poses to individual achievement, make it most difficult to reconcile the cost or the principle of a status-based denial of basic education with the framework of equality embodied in the Equal Protection Clause. What we said 28 years ago in *Brown v. Board of Education,* 347 U.S. 483 (1954), still holds true:

> Today, education is perhaps the most important function of state and local governments. Compulsory school attendance laws and the great expenditures for education both demonstrate our recognition of the importance of education to our democratic society. It is required in the performance of our most basic public responsibilities, even service in the armed forces. It is the very foundation of good citizenship. Today it is a principal instrument in awakening the child to cultural values, in preparing him for later professional training, and in helping him to adjust normally to his environment. In these days, it is doubtful that any child may reasonably be expected to succeed in life if he is denied the opportunity of an education. Such an opportunity, where the state has undertaken to provide it, is a right which must be made available to all on equal terms. *Id.*, at 493.

. . . These well-settled principles allow us to determine the proper level of deference to be afforded. . . . Undocumented aliens cannot be treated as a suspect class because their presence in this country in violation of federal law is not a "constitutional irrelevancy." Nor is education a fundamental right; a State need not justify by compelling necessity every variation in the manner in which education is provided to its population. *See San Antonio Independent School Dist. v. Rodriguez*. But more is involved in these cases than the abstract question whether [the law] discriminates against a suspect class, or whether education is a fundamental right.

[The Texas law] imposes a lifetime hardship on a discrete class of children not accountable for their disabling status. The stigma of illiteracy will mark them for the rest of their lives. By denying these children a basic education, we deny them the ability to live within the structure of our civic institutions, and foreclose any realistic possibility that they will contribute in even the smallest way to the progress of our Nation. In determining the rationality of [a law], we may appropriately take into account its costs to the Nation and to the innocent children who are its victims. In light of these countervailing costs, the discrimination contained in [the Texas statute] can hardly be considered rational unless it furthers some substantial goal of the State.

IV

It is the State's principal argument, and apparently the view of the dissenting Justices, that the undocumented status of these children *vel non* establishes a sufficient rational basis for denying them benefits that a State might choose to afford other residents. . . . Indeed, in the State's view, Congress' apparent disapproval of the presence of these children within the United States, and the evasion of the federal regulatory program that is the mark of undocumented status, provides authority for its decision to impose upon them special disabilities. Faced with an equal protection challenge respecting the treatment of aliens, we agree that the courts must be attentive to congressional policy; the exercise of congressional power might well affect the State's prerogatives to afford differential treatment to a particular class of aliens. But we are unable to find in the congressional immigration scheme any statement of policy that might weigh significantly in arriving at an equal protection balance concerning the State's authority to deprive these children of an education.

V

Appellants argue that the classification at issue furthers an interest in the "preservation of the state's limited resources for the education of its lawful residents." Of course, a concern for the preservation of resources standing alone can hardly justify the classification used in allocating those resources. *Graham v. Richardson,* 403 U.S. 365, 374-375 (1971). The State must do more than justify its classification with a concise expression of an intention to discriminate. *Examining Board v. Flores de Otero,* 426 U.S. 572, 605 (1976).

. . . [W]hile it is apparent that a State may "not . . . reduce expenditures for education by barring [some arbitrarily chosen class of] children from its schools," *Shapiro v. Thompson,* 394 U.S. 618, 633 (1969), appellants suggest that undocumented children are appropriately singled out for exclusion because of the special burdens they impose on the State's ability to provide high-quality public education. But the record in no way supports the claim that exclusion of undocumented children is likely to improve the overall quality of education in the State. As the District Court . . . noted, the State failed to offer any "credible supporting evidence that a proportionately small diminution of the funds spent on each child [which might result from devoting some state funds to the education of the excluded group] will have a grave impact on the quality of education." And, after reviewing the State's school financing mechanism, the District Court . . . concluded that barring undocumented children from local schools would not necessarily improve the quality of education provided in those schools. Of course, even if improvement in the quality of education were a likely result of barring some *number* of children from the schools of the State, the State must support its selection of *this* group as the appropriate target for exclusion. In terms of educational cost and need, however, undocumented children are "basically indistinguishable" from legally resident alien children.

Finally, appellants suggest that undocumented children are appropriately singled out because their unlawful presence within the United States renders them less likely than other children to remain within the boundaries of the State, and to put their education to productive social or political use within the State. Even assuming that such an interest is legitimate, it is an interest that is most difficult to quantify. The State has no assurance that any child, citizen or not, will employ the education provided by the State within the confines of the State's borders. In any event, the record is clear that many of the undocumented children disabled by this classification will remain in this country indefinitely, and that some will become lawful residents or citizens of the United States. It is difficult to understand precisely what the State hopes to achieve by promoting the creation and perpetuation of a subclass of illiterates within our boundaries, surely adding to the problems and costs of unemployment, welfare, and crime. It is thus clear that whatever savings might be achieved by denying these children an education, they are wholly insubstantial in light of the costs involved to these children, the State, and the Nation.

VI

If the State is to deny a discrete group of innocent children the free public education that it offers to other children residing within its borders, that denial must be justified by a showing that it furthers some substantial state interest. No such showing was made here. Accordingly, the judgment of the Court of Appeals in each of these cases is *Affirmed*.

NOTES AND QUESTIONS

1. The Court in *Plyler* indicates that education is neither a fundamental right secured by the Constitution nor a typical governmental benefit. Rather, the Court affirms that "education has a fundamental role in maintaining the fabric of our society." That conclusion leads the Court to apply an intermediate level of scrutiny in analyzing the rationality of the state's regime: the regime cannot be "considered rational unless it furthers some substantial goal of the State." Do you find the Court's approach to the place of education in our constitutional structure persuasive?
2. In concluding that education has a "fundamental role" in American life, the Court argues that public education:
    1. is important to "maintaining our basic institutions";
    2. is a most "vital civil institution";
    3. preserves a "democratic system of government";
    4. is the primary vehicle for transmitting the values on which society rests;
    5. is necessary to prepare citizens to participate effectively and intelligently in our open political system";
    6. is necessary to "preserve freedom and independence";
    7. inculcates fundamental values necessary for the maintenance of a democratic political system;
    8. provides the basic tools by which individuals might lead economically productive lives to the benefit of us all;
    9. plays a "pivotal role" in "sustaining our political and social heritage";

10. prepares individuals to be self-reliant and self-sufficient participants in society;
11. is required for the performance of our most basic public responsibilities, even service in the armed forces;
12. is the "very foundation of good citizenship";
13. is the principal instrument in awakening a child to cultural values;
14. prepares a child for later professional training; and
15. helps a child to adjust normally to his or her environment.

Consider each of these arguments for the significance of public education. First, do you agree with each of them as a general proposition? Second, are these arguments consistent with your own educational experience?

3. To what extent are the Court's arguments supporting the value of education limited to "public education"? Can the benefits of education be secured either in a private school or at home?
4. Is it significant that this case involves children who are immigrants to this country? Recall that educational thinkers from the founders to Dewey believed that public education had a particular role to play in educating diverse groups of immigrants.
5. In *Plyler* and *Rodriguez*, the Supreme Court left open the issue whether the Constitution guarantees a minimally adequate education. In the next case, the Court returns to the issue.

PAPASAN v. ALLAIN

478 U.S. 265 (1986)

Justice WHITE delivered the opinion of the Court.

In this case, we consider the claims of school officials and schoolchildren in 23 northern Mississippi counties that they are being unlawfully denied the economic benefits of public school lands granted by the United States to the State of Mississippi well over 100 years ago. . . .

I

The history of public school lands in the United States stretches back over 200 years. Even before the ratification of the Constitution, the Congress of the Confederation initiated a practice with regard to the Northwest Territory which was followed with most other public lands that eventually became States and were admitted to the Union. In particular, the Land Ordinance of 1785, which provided for the survey and sale of the Northwest Territory, "reserved the lot No. 16, of every township, for the maintenance of public schools within the said township . . ." 1 Laws of the United States 565 (1815). In 1802, when the eastern portion of the Northwest Territory became what is now the State of Ohio, Congress granted Ohio the lands that had been previously reserved under the 1785 Ordinance for the use of public schools in the State. 2 Stat. 175.

Following the Ohio example of reserving lands for the maintenance of public schools, "grants were made for common school purposes to each of the public-land States admitted to the Union. . . ." Thus, the basic Ohio example has been followed with respect to all but a few of the States admitted since then. . . . In addition to the school lands designated in this manner, Congress made provision for townships in which the pertinent section or sections were not available for one reason or another. Thus, Congress generally indemnified States for the missing designated sections, allowing the States to select lands in an amount equal to and in lieu of the designated but unavailable lands. . . . Although the basic pattern of school lands grants was generally consistent from State to State in terms of the reservation and grant of the lands, the specific provisions of the grants varied by State and over time.

. . . From these historical circumstances, the current practice in Mississippi with regard to Sixteenth Section lands has evolved directly. Under state law, these lands, which are still apparently held in large part by the State, "constitute property held in trust for the benefit of the public schools and must be treated as such." Miss. Code Ann. §29-3-1(1) (Supp. 1985). In providing for the operation of these trusts, the legislature has retained the historical tie of these lands to particular townships in terms of both trust administration and beneficiary status. Thus, the State has delegated the management of this property to local school boards throughout the State: Where Sixteenth Section lands lie within a school district or where Lieu Lands were originally appropriated for a township that lies within a school district, the board of education of that district has "control and jurisdiction of said school trust lands and of all funds arising from any disposition thereof heretofore or hereafter made." *Ibid.* In this respect, the board of education is "under the general supervision of the state land commissioner." *Ibid.* Further, the State has, by statute, set forth certain prescriptions for the management of these lands. Most important for purposes of this case, however, is Miss. Code Ann. §29-3-109 (Supp. 1985), which provides:

> All expendable funds derived from sixteenth section or lieu lands shall be credited to the school districts of the township in which such sixteenth section lands may be located, or to which any sixteenth sections lieu lands may belong. Such funds shall not be expended except for the purpose of education of the educable children of the school district to which they belong, or as otherwise may be provided by law.

Consequently, all proceeds from Sixteenth Section and Lieu Lands are allocated directly to the specific township in which these lands are located or to which those lands apply. With respect to the Chickasaw Cession counties, to which no lands now belong, the state legislature has for over 100 years paid "interest" on the lost principal acquired from the sale of those lands in the form of annual appropriations to the Chickasaw Cession schools. . . . The result of this dual treatment has for many years been a disparity in the level of school funds from Sixteenth Section lands that are available to the Chickasaw Cession schools as compared to the schools in the remainder of the State.

In 1981, the petitioners, local school officials and schoolchildren from the Chickasaw Cession, filed suit in the United States District Court for the Northern District of Mississippi against the respondents, an assortment of state officials, challenging the disparity in Sixteenth Section funds. The petitioners' complaint traced the history of public school lands in Mississippi, characterizing as illegal several of the actions that resulted in there being now no Sixteenth Section lands in the Chickasaw Cession area. The result of these actions, said the petitioners, was the disparity between the financial support available to the Chickasaw Cession schools and other schools in the State, which disparity in turn allegedly deprived the Chickasaw Cession schoolchildren of a minimally adequate level of education and of the equal protection of the laws.

Based on these allegations, the petitioners sought various forms of relief for breach of the trust regarding the Chickasaw Cession Sixteenth Section lands and for denial of equal protection. . . .

A

In *Rodriguez,* the Court upheld against an equal protection challenge Texas' system of financing its public schools, under which funds for the public schools were derived from two main sources. Approximately half of the funds came from the Texas Minimum Foundation School Program, a state program aimed at guaranteeing a certain level of minimum education for all children in the State. Most of the remainder of the funds came from local sources—in particular local property taxes. As a result of this dual funding system, most specifically as a result of differences in amounts collected from local property taxes, "substantial interdistrict disparities in school expenditures [were] found . . . in varying degrees throughout the State."

In examining the equal protection status of these disparities, the Court declined to apply any heightened scrutiny based either on wealth as a suspect classification or on education as a fundamental right. As to the latter, the Court recognized the importance of public education but noted that education "is not among the rights afforded explicit protection under our Federal Constitution." The Court did not, however, foreclose the possibility "that some identifiable quantum of education is a constitutionally protected prerequisite to the meaningful exercise of either [the right to speak or the right to vote]." Given the absence of such radical denial of educational opportunity, it was concluded that the State's school financing scheme would be constitutional if it bore "some rational relationship to a legitimate state purpose." . . .

Given this rational basis, the Court concluded that the mere "happenstance" that the quality of education might vary from district to district because of varying property values within the districts did not render the system "so irrational as to be invidiously discriminatory." In particular, the Court found that "any scheme of local taxation—indeed the very existence of identifiable local governmental units—requires the establishment of jurisdictional boundaries that are inevitably arbitrary."

Almost 10 years later, the Court again considered the equal protection status of the administration of the Texas public schools—this time in relation to the State's decision not to expend any state funds on the education of children who were not "legally admitted" to the United States. *Plyler v. Doe,* 457 U.S. 202 (1982). The Court did not, however, measurably change the approach articulated in *Rodriguez.* It reiterated that education is not a fundamental right and concluded that undocumented aliens were not a suspect class. Nevertheless, it concluded that the justifications for the discrimination offered by the State were "wholly insubstantial in light of the costs involved to these children, the State, and the Nation."

B

The complaint in this case asserted not simply that the petitioners had been denied their right to a minimally adequate education but also that such a right was fundamental and that because that right had been infringed the State's action here should be reviewed under strict scrutiny. As *Rodriguez* and *Plyler* indicate, this Court has not yet definitively settled the questions whether a minimally adequate education is a fundamental right and whether a statute alleged to discriminatorily infringe that right should be accorded heightened equal protection review.

Nor does this case require resolution of these issues. . . . The petitioners' allegation that, by reason of the funding disparities relating to the Sixteenth Section lands, they have been deprived of a minimally adequate education is just such an allegation. The petitioners do not allege that schoolchildren in the Chickasaw Counties are not taught to read or write; they do not allege that they receive no instruction on even the educational basics; they allege no actual facts in support of their assertion that they have been deprived of a minimally adequate education. As we see it, we are not bound to credit and may disregard the allegation that the petitioners have been denied a minimally adequate education.

Concentrating instead on the disparities in terms of Sixteenth Section lands benefits that the complaint in fact alleged and that are documented in the public record, we are persuaded that the Court of Appeals properly determined that *Rodriguez* dictates the applicable standard of review. The different treatment alleged here constitutes an equal protection violation only if it is not rationally related to a legitimate state interest. . . . As we read their complaint, the petitioners do not challenge the overall organization of the Mississippi public school financing program. Instead, their challenge is restricted to one aspect of that program: The Sixteenth Section and Lieu Lands funding. All of the allegations in the complaint center around disparities in the distribution of these particular benefits, and no allegations concerning disparities in other public school funding programs are included.

Consequently, this is a very different claim than the claim made in *Rodriguez*. In *Rodriguez*, the contention was that the State's overall system of funding was unconstitutionally discriminatory. There, the Court examined the basic structure of that system and concluded that it was rationally related to a legitimate state purpose. In reaching that conclusion, the Court necessarily found that funding disparities resulting from differences in local taxes were acceptable because related to the state goal of allowing a measure of effective local control over school funding levels. *Rodriguez* did not, however, purport to validate all funding variations that might result from a State's public school funding decisions. It held merely that the variations that resulted from allowing local control over local property tax funding of the public schools were constitutionally permissible in that case.

Here, the petitioners' claim goes neither to the overall funding system nor to the local ad valorem component of that system. Instead, it goes solely to the Sixteenth Section and Lieu Lands portion of the State's public school funding. And, as to this claim, we are unpersuaded that *Rodriguez* resolves the equal protection question in favor of the State. The allegations of the complaint are that the State is distributing the income from Sixteenth Section lands or from Lieu Lands or funds unequally among the school districts, to the detriment of the Chickasaw Cession schools and their students. The Sixteenth Section and Lieu Lands in Mississippi were granted to and held by the State itself. Under state law, these lands "constitute property held in trust for the benefit of the public schools and must be treated as such," . . . but in carrying out the trust, the State has vested the management of these lands in the local school boards throughout the State, under the supervision of the Secretary of State, and has credited the income from these lands to the "school districts of the township in which such sixteenth section lands may be located, or to which any sixteenth section lieu lands may belong," such income to be used for the purpose of educating the children of the school district or as otherwise may be provided by law. . . . This case is therefore very different from *Rodriguez*, where the differential financing available to school districts was traceable to school district funds available from local real estate taxation, not to a state decision to divide state resources unequally among school districts. The rationality of the disparity in *Rodriguez*, therefore, which rested on the fact that funding disparities based on differing local wealth were a necessary adjunct of allowing meaningful local control over school funding, does not settle the constitutionality of disparities alleged in this case, and we differ with the Court of Appeals in this respect.

Nevertheless, the question remains whether the variations in the benefits received by school districts from Sixteenth Section or Lieu Lands are, on the allegations in the complaint and as a matter of law, rationally related to a legitimate state interest. We believe, however, that we should not pursue this issue here but should instead remand the case for further proceedings. Neither the Court of Appeals nor the parties have addressed the equal protection issue as we think it is posed by this case: Given that the State has title to assets granted to it by the Federal Government for the use of the State's schools, does the Equal Protection Clause permit it to distribute the benefit of these assets unequally among the school districts as it now does?

A crucial consideration in resolving this issue is whether the federal law requires the State to allocate the economic benefits of school lands to schools in the townships in which those lands are located. If, as a matter of federal law, the State has no choice in the matter, whether the complaint states an equal protection claim depends on whether the federal policy is itself violative of the Clause. If it is, the State may properly be enjoined from implementing such policy. Contrariwise, if the federal law is valid and the State is bound by it, then it provides a rational reason for the funding disparity. Neither the courts below nor the parties have addressed the equal protection issue in these terms. Another possible consideration in resolving the equal protection issue is that school lands require management and that the State has assigned this task to the individual districts in which the lands are located, subject to supervision by the State. The significance, if any, in equal protection terms of this allocation of duties in justifying assigning the income exclusively to those who perform the management function and none of it to those districts that have no lands to manage is a matter that is best addressed by the lower courts in the first instance. . . .

NOTES AND QUESTIONS

1. The Supreme Court in *Papasan* ultimately remands the action to the lower federal courts for a determination of whether the equal protection clause permits the state to distribute the resources given to the state unequally among school districts. On remand, the federal district court entered a consent judgment in which the parties stipulated that the state's "discriminatory" treatment of the Chickasaw plaintiffs was without a rational basis and . . . in violation of the plaintiffs' equal protection rights. . . ." *Papasan v. United States*, 1989 US. Dist. LEXIS 17535 at *3-4. (N.D. Miss. 1989.) The court also entered a "stipulated" remedy requiring the state legislature to appropriate to the Chickasaw area an amount of resources "tied to the average expendable school lands income for the rest of the State." *Papasan*, 1989 U.S. Dist. LEXIS 17535 at of *4. That remedy does not seek to bring the Chickasaw area within the "system that pertains in the rest of the state"; rather, the remedy is designed to give to the Chickasaw plaintiffs "an equivalent substitute." *Id.* What are the advantages and disadvantages of the court's remedy?
2. As the *Papasan* Court declares, the Supreme Court has yet to determine "whether a minimally adequate education is a fundamental right." The Court states that it need not resolve that issue in the *Papasan* case. Why not? How does the Court avoid addressing that question? *See also Kadrmas v. Dickinson Public Schools*, 487 U.S. 450, 466 n.1 (1988) (observing that the issue of the existence of a fundamental constitutional right to a minimal level of education "remains open").
3. Construct arguments favoring and opposing the assertion that a "minimally adequate education" is a fundamental right guaranteed by the United States Constitution. How would you define a "minimally adequate education"? Could it be defined by grade level, *see Wisconsin v. Yoder*, 406 U.S. 205 (1972), or perhaps achievement?
4. The Court stresses that *Rodriguez* did not "purport to validate all funding variations that might result from a State's public school funding decision." Which "funding variations" were validated? Which "funding variations" remain constitutionally suspect?
5. In his separate opinion joined by Justice Rehnquist, Justice Powell reviews the Mississippi public school financing data of record and finds a lack of any significant disparity in overall per student funding across the state. In addition, Justice Powell notes that the State has established a uniform statewide minimal standard for teacher training and compensation and declares that "Mississippi has taken numerous steps to ensure the adequacy of the most important single factor in education: the quality of the teachers." Assuming that Mississippi had taken such steps to ensure the

quality of teachers, do you agree that teacher quality is the "most important single factor in education"? How is teacher quality measured? Recall that in *Rodriguez* the teachers in the affluent Alamo Heights district reached a level of education far superior to that in impoverished districts like Edgewood.

6. Can a state provide excellent schools for all students, but refuse to provide transportation? In *Kadrmas v. Dickinson Public Schools,* 487 U.S. 450 (1988), the Supreme Court upheld North Dakota's law allowing local school districts to charge fees for bus service, even where those fees prohibit some indigent students from using the service at all.

B. THE RIGHT TO A PUBLIC EDUCATION AND EQUITABLE FUNDING UNDER STATE CONSTITUTIONS

The United States Supreme Court's educational funding decisions leave many unanswered questions. Nonetheless, the overriding import of those cases seems clear. The United States Constitution does not expressly or implicitly create a fundamental right to public education. As such, the federal constitution does not prohibit rational disparities in educational funding. In the wake of the Supreme Court's cases erecting a deferential approach to disparities in funding and in light of the unmistakable reality of such disparities in virtually every state, the focus of legal challenges to educational funding regimes has shifted from the federal constitution to state constitutions.

Even before *Rodriguez,* the California Supreme Court had declared education to be a "fundamental interest" warranting a strict scrutiny equal protection standard. *Serrano v. Priest,* 5 Cal. 3d 584, 487 P.2d 1241 (Cal. 1971) ("*Serrano I*"). Under that standard, the state of California failed to establish that its school financing system, which resulted in disparate per-pupil allocations of resources, was necessary to achieve the interest of local control over education. Accordingly, the *Serrano* court found the California system to be invalid under the equal protection clause, but did not specify whether its decision was based on the federal or state constitution.

After the U.S. Supreme Court's rejection of the challenge to inequitable educational funding under the federal equal protection clause in *Rodriguez,* however, the California Supreme Court made clear that its prior decision in *Serrano I* was based on the California state Constitution. In *Serrano II,* 18 Cal. 3d 728, 764, 557 P.2d 929, 950 (Cal. 1976), the court declared that although the language of the equal protection clause in the California state constitution was "substantially the equivalent" of the federal Constitution's equal protection clause, those provisions should not be interpreted in lock step. To the contrary, the two clauses "are possessed of an independent vitality which, in a given case, may demand an analysis different from that which would obtain if only federal standards were applicable." Similarly, in Wyoming, *see*

Washakie County School District No. v. Herschler, 606 P.2d 310 (Wy. 1980); Connecticut, *see Horton v. Meskill*, 376 A.2d 359 (Conn. 1977), and North Dakota, *see In the Interest of G.H.*, 218 N.W. 2d 441 (N.D. 1974), as well, the courts invalidated inequitable educational funding regimes under the equal protection clause in the state constitution.

In addition to revisiting the school-funding question under the equal protection clause of their state constitutions, state courts also faced that issue under local constitutional provisions mandating an "efficient" system of public education. *In Edgewood Independent School District v. Kirby*, 777 S.W.2d 391 (Tex. 1989), in fact, the Texas Supreme Court explicitly reconsidered the Edgewood School District at issue in *Rodriguez*. The court concluded that Texas's statewide system for funding education based on local property taxes, which produced a disparity of resources per student of 700 to one, was contrary to the constitutional requirement that the legislature support and maintain an "efficient system of public free schools." 777 S.W.2d at 394.

In *Campaign for Fiscal Equity, Inc. v. State of New York*, 801 N.E.2d 326 (N.Y. Ct. App. 2003), the New York Court of Appeals concluded that the New York City schools failed to satisfy the state constitution's requirement of a "system of free common schools, wherein all the children of the state may be educated." N.Y. Const., Art. XI, §1. After defining a "sound basic education" as one that affords students the skills and knowledge for "meaningful participation in contemporary society," the court found a "systematic failure" to provide New York City high school students with that constitutionally mandated standard of education. In fact, the court concluded that there was a "mismatch" between the disproportionately higher needs of the city's students and the disproportionately lower level of statewide funding allocated to meet those needs. The court ordered the governor and the legislature to "ascertain the actual cost" of constitutional compliance and then to revise the state's funding formula to insure necessary resources to provide a "sound basic education" for all public school students in New York City. *See also Rose v. The Council for Better Education, Inc.*, 790 S.W.2d 186 (Ky. 1989) (finding that Kentucky's constitutional requirement of an "efficient system of common schools" was violated by maintenance of an underfunded and unequally funded system).

As the next two cases demonstrate, however, the state courts have reached dramatically different conclusions regarding the legitimacy of inequalities in educational funding, even while interpreting virtually identical state constitutional language guaranteeing an "efficient" system of public education.

Committee for Educational Rights v. Edgar

174 Ill. 2d 1, 672 N.E.2d 1178, 220 Ill. Dec. 166 (1996)

Justice Nickels delivered the opinion of the court:

. . . We begin with a general and vastly simplified description of those aspects of public school finance in Illinois that are germane to this appeal. Public schools receive funds from various federal, State and local sources. The controversy in the present case hinges on the relationship between funding derived from local property taxes and funds supplied by the State. Under the School Code school districts are authorized to levy property taxes for various school purposes up to specified maximum rates. The voters of a school district may authorize higher property tax rates by referendum, but even with such voter approval the School Code places an upper limit on school property tax rates. Obviously, the amount which a school district is able to raise through property taxes is determined by the taxable property wealth within the district. Wealthy districts—those with substantial taxable property wealth per pupil—are able to raise more revenue per pupil at a given tax rate than poor districts.

There are principally two categories of State financial assistance which supplement local property tax revenues and other local sources of funding. First, the State provides assistance to school districts in the form of categorical grants for a variety of specific purposes. . . . School districts also receive distributions of general state aid from the State's common school fund pursuant to the formula set forth in section 18-8 of the School Code.

General state aid is distributed based on a weighted average daily attendance (ADA) at schools within a particular district and on the equalized assessed valuation (EAV) of property in the district. The general state aid formula is designed to enable districts with modest property tax bases to achieve a certain minimum level of funding per pupil. This minimum funding level, commonly known as the "foundation level," is computed by the State Board of Education based on the amount available for distribution from the common school fund. The foundation level represents a hypothetical "guaranteed" dollar amount of taxable property wealth per pupil (hereinafter, guaranteed EAV). The amount of general state aid per pupil that a particular district receives is calculated by subtracting the district's EAV per weighted ADA pupil from the guaranteed EAV and multiplying the difference by the foundation rate. The formula may be expressed as follows: general state aid per weighted ADA pupil (guaranteed EAV district EAV per weighted ADA pupil) foundation rate. This formula is structured to provide that if a district levies property taxes at exactly the foundation rate, the sum of local revenues and general state aid will equal the foundation level. In order to receive full state aid under this formula, the district's local tax rates must equal or exceed a specified minimum "qualifying" rate (which is lower than the foundation rate) but the amount of aid received does not otherwise depend on the actual local tax rates applied. Thus, to receive the full amount of general state aid the district must tax at or above the "qualifying" rate. To achieve foundation level funding, the district must tax at the foundation rate. Where a district's local tax rate exceeds the foundation rate, the sum of local revenues and general state aid will exceed the foundation level.

The above method of distributing general state aid only applies in districts where the EAV per weighted ADA pupil is less than 87% of the guaranteed EAV. In wealthier districts, an alternative formula applies. The minimum amount of general state aid under the alternative formula is fixed at 7% of the foundation level.

In their five-count complaint, plaintiffs allege that under the present financing scheme, vast differences in educational resources and opportunities exist among the State's school districts as a result of differences in local taxable property wealth. During the 1989-90 school year, the average tax base in the wealthiest 10% of elementary schools was over 13 times the average tax base in the poorest 10%. For high school and unit school districts, the ratios of the average tax bases in the wealthiest and poorest districts were 8.1 to 1 and 7 to 1, respectively, during the 1989-90 school year.

Plaintiffs allege in their complaint that the general state aid formula does not effectively equalize funding among wealthy and poor districts. While the general State aid formula ensures minimum funding at the foundation level, the wealthiest districts are able to raise funds through property taxes considerably in excess of the foundation level. Moreover, the provision of a minimum grant—equal to 7% of the foundation level—to even the wealthiest school districts is counterequalizing.

Plaintiffs allege that disparities among wealthy and poor districts are reflected in various measures of educational funding; in several "key indicators" of educational quality (such as the percentage of teachers with master's degrees, teacher experience, teacher salaries, administrator salaries and pupil/administrator ratios); and in a comparison of the facilities, resources and course offerings in two neighboring school districts with dramatically disparate tax bases. According to the complaint, these disparities are attributable to variations in property wealth rather than tax effort; on average, the poorest school districts tax at higher rates than the wealthiest.

Based on these allegations, in counts I through III plaintiffs seek a declaratory judgment that to the extent that the statutory school finance scheme "fails to correct differences in spending and educational services resulting from differences in [local taxable property wealth]" the scheme violates our state constitution's equal protection clause (count I), prohibition against special legislation (count II) and education article (count III). Ill. Const. 1970, art. I, §2; art. IV, §13; art. X, §1. . . .

I

We first consider the dismissal of plaintiffs' claims that the statutory system for financing public schools violates the education article of our state constitution. Section 1 of article X of the Illinois Constitution of 1970 provides:

> A fundamental goal of the People of the State is the educational development of all persons to the limits of their capacities. The State shall provide for an efficient system of high quality public educational institutions and services. Education in public schools through the secondary level shall be free. There may be such other free education as the General Assembly provides by law. The State has the primary responsibility for financing the system of public education. Ill. Const. 1970, art. X, §1.

Plaintiffs' challenge to the statutory system for financing public schools is based on the emphasized language above. First, plaintiffs contend that because the system produces vast disparities in the level of funding and educational resources available to various school districts based on differences in local taxable property wealth, it is not "efficient" within the meaning of the constitution. Second, plaintiffs argue that school districts with low property tax bases are unable to provide a "high quality" education to their students due to inadequate funding. Third, plaintiffs contend that under the financing scheme, funding is insufficient to provide a "high quality" education to at-risk children.

A

We first consider plaintiffs' argument that the present school funding system is not "efficient" within the meaning of the constitution because it produces disparities in educational resources and services based on differences in local taxable property wealth. In plaintiffs' view, the efficiency requirement guarantees some measure of equality in educational funding and opportunity. Plaintiffs deny that they seek absolute uniformity in educational offerings or precisely equal spending for each pupil in the State. Plaintiffs would apparently approve variations in educational spending from district to district based on criteria such as local differences in the costs of resources and special educational needs in particular districts. However, plaintiffs maintain that a school district's property wealth is "educationally irrelevant" and is not a proper factor upon which to set the level of resources available to the district.

The trial and appellate courts rejected plaintiffs' argument that the efficiency requirement guarantees parity of educational funding and opportunity. The trial court emphasized that the framers of the 1970 Constitution had considered and rejected specific proposals for a constitutional provision designed to reduce funding disparities among districts by limiting the amount of funds that could be raised by local property taxes. The appellate court concluded that article X of the constitution "does not mandate equal educational benefits and opportunities among the State's school districts as the constitutionally required means of establishing and maintaining an 'efficient' system of free public schools."

"Efficient" has been defined as follows:

> 1: serving as or characteristic of an efficient cause: causally productive: OPERANT . . . 2: marked by ability to choose and use the most effective and least wasteful means of doing a task or accomplishing a purpose. . . . *Webster's Third New International Dictionary* 725 (1981).

This definition does not inherently compel the conclusion that an "efficient system" of public schools necessarily involves statewide parity of educational opportunity and resources. However, we do not believe that the precise meaning of the word "efficient" as used in section 1 of the education article is entirely clear and free from doubt, or that "efficient" could not conceivably be interpreted in the manner that plaintiffs claim. We note that the Court of Appeals of Maryland determined that Maryland's constitutional requirement that the General Assembly establish a "thorough and efficient" system of free public schools was "on its face . . . plainly susceptible of more than one meaning." *Hornbeck v. Somerset County Board of Education,* 295 Md. 597, 619, 458 A.2d 758, 770 (1983). In determining whether the "thorough and efficient" provision required exact equality in per pupil funding and expenditures among Maryland's school districts, the *Hornbeck* court deemed it essential to consider the history underlying the enactment of the provision. . . . Courts in other jurisdictions with similar constitutional efficiency provisions have also looked to sources beyond the language of the constitution to determine the meaning of those provisions. *See Rose v. Counsel for Better Education, Inc.,* 790 S.W.2d 186, 205-06 (Ky. 1989); *Edgewood Independent School District v. Kirby,* 777 S.W.2d 391, 394-96 (Tex. 1989); *Pauley v. Kelly,* 162 W. Va. 672, 681-89, 255 S.E.2d 859, 866-69 (1979); *see also Rose,* 790 S.W.2d at 221 (Vance J., dissenting) ("It is because of [the] universal concern expressed by the delegates to the convention that I conclude that the word 'efficient' as used by them must include not only its dictionary definition but must also be construed to include the requirement of substantial equality of educational opportunity"). We shall likewise consider the history underlying the adoption of section 1 of the education article.

The education article of the 1970 Constitution originated as a proposal submitted by the education committee of the Sixth Illinois Constitutional Convention. 6 Record of Proceedings, Sixth Illinois Constitutional Convention 227 (hereinafter cited as Proceedings). At the outset, we note that an introductory passage in the education committee's report on the proposed education article states, "the opportunity for an education, where the state has undertaken to provide it, is a right which must be made available to all on equal terms." 6 Proceedings 231. Considered in isolation, this statement might lend some credence to plaintiffs' position. However, this general statement of principle was not made in reference to the efficiency requirement or any other specific language in the proposed education article. Instead, as authority for this proposition the education committee report cites the landmark decision in *Brown v. Board of Education,* 347 U.S. 483 (1954), which was, of course, based on the equal protection clause of the fourteenth amendment of the United States Constitution. As explained below, specific references in the convention record to the efficiency requirement place the concept in a significantly different light.

The constitutional requirement that the State provide for an efficient system of high quality educational institutions and services corresponds to section 1 of article VIII of the 1870 Constitution, which stated, "The general assembly shall provide a thorough and efficient system of free schools, whereby all children of this state may receive a good common school education." . . . Under the 1870 Constitution, this court consistently held that the question of the efficiency and thoroughness of the school system was one solely for the legislature to answer, and that the courts lacked the power to intrude. . . . However, under a limited exception to this principle it was held that pursuant to the "thorough and efficient" requirement school district boundaries must be established so that the districts are compact and contiguous. As explained in *People ex rel. Leighty v. Young,* 301 Ill. 67, 71, 133 N.E. 693 (1921), "it cannot be said that a system which places the school house at a point so remote that the children of school age cannot reach it conveniently is either thorough or efficient." School districts organized in contravention of the requirements of compactness and contiguity have been held invalid.

The framers of the 1970 Constitution embraced this limited construction that the constitutional efficiency requirement authorized judicial review of school district boundaries, but they did not intend to otherwise limit legislative discretion. . . . Careful review of the remainder of the debates on section 1 of the education article and other relevant materials in the convention record discloses no persuasive evidence to support the view that section 1's efficiency requirement was intended by the framers to function more broadly as a substantive guarantee of parity in educational opportunity or funding.

Disparity in educational funding was a highly charged and controversial subject during the constitutional convention, but it was not touched upon to any significant degree in connection with section 1's efficiency requirement. Instead, the debate over unequal opportunities and resources ultimately led to the incorporation of section 1's final sentence, which provides that "the State has the primary responsibility for financing the system of public education." Ill. Const. 1970, art. X, §1.

. . . In our view, the foregoing persuasively suggests that the framers of the 1970 Constitution viewed educational equality and "efficiency" to be separate and distinct subjects. The framers of the 1970 Constitution grappled with the issue of unequal educational funding and opportunity, and chose to address the problem with a purely hortatory statement of principle. To ignore this careful and deliberate choice by interpreting the efficiency requirement as an enforceable guarantee of equality would do violence to the framers' understanding of the education article.

. . . Finally, plaintiffs contend that several decisions from other states interpreting similar constitutional language have concluded that "efficiency" dictates fairness and parity in educational funding. *See Abbott v. Burke,* 119 N.J. 287, 575 A.2d 359 (1990); *Rose v. Council for Better Education, Inc.,* 790 S.W.2d 186 (Ky. 1989); *Edgewood Independent School District v. Kirby,* 777 S.W.2d 391 (Tex. 1989); *Pauley v. Kelly,* 162 W. Va. 672, 255 S.E.2d 859 (1979). For various reasons, these decisions provide no persuasive support for plaintiffs' argument.

. . . While plaintiffs place major emphasis on *Kirby,* the historical basis for the court's analysis stands in sharp contrast to the history of our Constitution. In *Kirby,* the court noted that in 1876, when the Texas constitution was written, economic conditions and educational funding were fairly uniform throughout the state, and the framers never contemplated the gross funding disparities that were later to develop as wealth grew at different rates in different districts. . . . In contrast, as discussed above, the framers of the Illinois Constitution of 1970 were well aware of disparities produced under the local property tax based funding system. Indeed, inequality was a recognized feature of education in Illinois when the 1870 Constitution—which introduced the efficiency concept in Illinois—was adopted. As stated in *Richards v. Raymond,* 92 Ill. 612, 617-18 (1879):

> It is a part of the history of the State when the Constitution was framed, that there was a great want of uniformity in the course of study prescribed and taught in the common schools of the State. In the larger and more wealthy counties the free schools were well graded and the course of instruction of a

> high order, while in the thinly settled and poorer counties the old district system was still retained and the course of instruction prescribed was of a lower order.

In view of all of the foregoing considerations, we agree with the courts below that disparities in educational funding resulting from differences in local property wealth do not offend section 1's efficiency requirement.

The remaining question under section 1 of the education article pertains to its guarantee of a system of "high quality" educational institutions and services. There is no dispute as to the nature of this guarantee in the abstract. Instead, the central issue is whether the quality of education is capable of or properly subject to measurement by the courts. Plaintiffs maintain that it is the courts' duty to construe the constitution and determine whether schoolfunding legislation conforms with its requirements and cite a number of decisions from other jurisdictions in which courts have concluded that similar constitutional challenges are capable of judicial resolution. As explained below, however, we conclude that questions relating to the quality of education are solely for the legislative branch to answer.

Historically, this court has assumed only an exceedingly limited role in matters relating to public education, recognizing that educational policy is almost exclusively within the province of the legislative branch. Section 1 of article VIII of the 1870 Constitution provided that "the general assembly shall provide a thorough and efficient system of free schools, whereby all children of this state may receive a good common school education." Ill. Const. 1870, art. VIII, §1. As discussed earlier, except in matters relating to school district boundaries, this court consistently held that questions relating to the efficiency and thoroughness of the school system were left to the wisdom of the legislative branch. This principle has likewise been applied with respect to the efficiency requirement in the 1970 Constitution. . . . More generally, it has been stated that section 1 of article VIII of the 1870 Constitution was both "a mandate to the legislature and a limitation on the exercise of the [legislative] power. [Citation.] The mandate is to provide a thorough and efficient system of schools, and the limitations are that they shall be free to all children of the State and such that all children may receive a good common school education." Yet, while the requirement that schools provide a "good common school education" was explicitly recognized to be a limitation on the legislature's power to enact public school laws, that limitation was not among those held generally capable of *judicial* enforcement.

. . . Our constitutional jurisprudence in the field of public education has been guided by considerations of separation of powers. . . . What constitutes a "high quality" education, and how it may best be provided, cannot be ascertained by any judicially discoverable or manageable standards. The constitution provides no principled basis for a judicial definition of high quality. It would be a transparent conceit to suggest that whatever standards of quality courts might develop would actually be derived from the constitution in any meaningful sense. Nor is education a subject within the judiciary's field of expertise, such that a judicial role in giving content to the education guarantee might be warranted. Rather, the question of educational quality is inherently one of policy involving philosophical and practical considerations that call for the exercise of legislative and administrative discretion.

To hold that the question of educational quality is subject to judicial determination would largely deprive the members of the general public of a voice in a matter which is close to the hearts of all individuals in Illinois. Judicial determination of the type of education children should receive and how it can best be provided would depend on the opinions of whatever expert witnesses the litigants might call to testify and whatever other evidence they might choose to present. Members of the general public, however, would be obliged to listen in respectful silence. We certainly do not mean to trivialize the views of educators, school administrators and others who have studied the problems which public schools confront. But nonexperts—students, parents, employers and other—also have important views and experiences to contribute which are not easily reckoned through formal judicial fact-finding. In contrast, an open and robust public debate is the lifeblood of the political process in our system of representative democracy. Solutions to problems of educational quality should emerge from a spirited dialogue between the people of the State and their elected representatives.

. . . We are well aware that courts in other jurisdictions have seen fit to define the contours of a constitutionally guaranteed education and to establish judicial standards of educational quality reflecting varying degrees of specificity and deference to the other branches of government. *See, e.g., Campbell County School District v. State,* 907 P.2d 1238, 1265 (Wyo. 1995); *Campaign for Fiscal Equity, Inc. v. State,* 86 N.Y.2d 307, 317-19, 655 N.E.2d 661, 666-76, 631 N.Y.S.2d 565, 570-71 (1995); *Claremont School District v. Governor,* 138 N.H. 183, 192, 635 A.2d 1375, 1381 (1993); *McDuffy v. Secretary of the Executive Office of Education,* 415 Mass. 545, 606, 615 N.E.2d 516, 548 (1993); *Tennessee Small School Systems v. McWherter,* 851 S.W.2d 139, 147-48 (Tenn. 1993) (dicta); *Abbott v. Burke,* 119 N.J. 287, 303-04, 575 A.2d 359, 367 (1990); *Rose v. Counsel for Better Education, Inc.,* 790 S.W.2d 186, 208-09 (Ky. 1989); *Pauley v. Kelly,* 162 W. Va. 672, 705-06, 255 S.E.2d 859, 874 (1979); *Seattle School District No. 1 v. State,* 90 Wash. 2d 476, 502, 585 P.2d 71, 86-87 (1978); *see also Idaho Schools for Equal Educational Opportunity v. Evans,* 123 Idaho 573, 583-84, 850 P.2d 724, 734 (1993) (holding that it was court's duty to interpret constitutional "thoroughness" requirement, but adopting standards promulgated by the executive branch); *Unified School District No. 229 v. State,* 256 Kan. 232, 275, 885 P.2d 1170, 1186 (1994) (court would not substitute its judgment as to what type of education was "suitable" within the meaning of the constitution for the standards developed by the legislature and state department of education; where all schools were able to meet those standards, the school finance statute was upheld); *McDaniel v. Thomas,* 248 Ga. 632, 633, 643-44, 285 S.E.2d 156, 157, 165 (1981) (while holding that the question of whether financing system deprived children of constitutionally guaranteed "adequate education" was justiciable court would only inquire whether system met a lower standard of providing a minimum or basic education; because of the inherent difficulty in establishing a judicially manageable standard for determining whether or not pupils are being provided an "adequate education," legislative branch must give content to the term "adequate"). By and large these courts have viewed the process of formulating educational standards as merely an exercise in constitutional interpretation or construction. For the reasons already stated, we disagree; we will not "under the guise of constitutional interpretation, presume to lay down guidelines or ultimatums for [the legislature]."

. . . We conclude that the question of whether the educational institutions and services in Illinois are "high quality" is outside the sphere of the judicial function. To the extent plaintiffs' claim that the system for financing public schools is unconstitutional rests on perceived deficiencies in the quality of education in public schools, the claim was properly dismissed. For the foregoing reasons, we affirm the dismissal of plaintiffs' claims under the education article of our state constitution.

II

We next consider whether the alleged disparities in educational funding and opportunity due to variations in local property wealth give rise to a cause of action under the equal protection clause of our state constitution (Ill. Const. 1970, art. I, §2). This court has recently offered the following description of the analytical framework for evaluating equal protection claims:

"The analysis applied by this court in assessing equal protection claims is the same under both the United States and Illinois Constitutions." . . . While plaintiffs and *amici* perceptively characterize the relationship between education and certain basic aspects of citizenship, we disagree with their conclusion that this relationship justifies treating education as *itself* a fundamental right for equal protection purposes. Generally speaking, the fundamental right analysis is concerned with laws that somehow *restrain* the exercise of a fundamental right. . . . Recognition that rights of expression and participation in the political process are fundamental—and thus safeguarded against unjustified governmental interference—does not necessarily translate into an affirmative governmental obligation to enrich each individual's personal capacity or ability to exercise these rights. In this regard it is significant that while the framers of the 1970 Constitution recognized the importance of "the educational development of all persons to the limits of their capacities," they stopped short of declaring such educational development to be a "right," choosing instead to identify it as a "fundamental *goal*." (Emphasis added.)

. . . While education is certainly a vitally important governmental function it is not a fundamental individual right for equal protection purposes, and thus the appropriate standard of review is the rational basis test. Under the rational basis test, judicial review of a legislative classification is limited and generally deferential. The challenged classification need only be rationally related to a legitimate state goal and if any state of facts can reasonably be conceived to justify the classification, it must be upheld.

The rationality of Illinois' school funding scheme is best gauged in light of the basic philosophical considerations that have defined the policy debate in the area of public education finance. As noted in *Rodriguez:* " 'The history of education since the industrial revolution shows a continual struggle between two forces: the desire by members of society to have educational opportunity for all children, and the desire of each family to provide the best education it can afford for its own children.' "

Similarly, one commentator has observed:

> The character of a public education system can be evaluated in terms of three often competing principles: quality, equality, and liberty. The quality of a school system is high when good educational opportunities are available to the least advantaged children in the state. In a school system featuring a high degree of equality every student has access to the same educational resources as any other student. Liberty is enhanced when localities or families have the autonomy to determine what proportion of their resources they wish to devote to the education of their youth. . . .
>
> A guarantee of equal educational funding does not secure any particular level of quality. It does ensure a high level of equality and a low level of liberty. Liberty is curtailed because equalization of educational funding requires redistribution of resources from wealthy districts to poor ones, which can only be achieved through greater centralization of control over the public schools. Centralization reduces the freedom of localities and families to choose their own levels of educational spending. R. Stark, *Education Reform: Judicial Interpretation of State Constitutions' Education Finance Provisions—Adequacy vs. Equality*, 1991 Annual Survey of American Law 609, 665-66.

The concept of "local control" in public education connotes not only the opportunity for local participation in decision-making but also "the freedom to devote more money to the education of one's children." . . . The general structure of the State's system of funding public schools through State and local resources—and the particular amounts allocated for distribution as general state aid—represent legislative efforts to strike a balance between the competing considerations of educational equality and local control. Certainly reasonable people might differ as to which consideration should be dominant. However, the highly deferential rational basis test does not permit us to substitute our judgment in this regard for that of the General Assembly, and we have no basis to conclude that the manner in which the General Assembly has struck the balance between equality and local control is so irrational as to offend the guarantee of equal protection. We also note that although reliance on local wealth to fund public education produces variations in resources which do not necessarily correspond to differences in educational need, the same may be said for a variety of important governmental services, such as police and fire protection, which have traditionally been funded at the local level. Consequently, the logical implications of declaring Illinois' system of financing public education to be "irrational" might be far reaching indeed. While the present school funding scheme might be thought unwise, undesirable or unenlightened from the standpoint of contemporary notions of social justice, these objections must be presented to the General Assembly.

While some decisions in other jurisdictions have concluded that there is no rational basis for funding disparities based on local wealth (*see, e.g., Tennessee Small School Systems v. McWherter*, 851 S.W.2d 139, 153-56 (Tenn. 1993); *Dupree v. Alma School District No. 30*, 279 Ark. 340, 345, 651 S.W.2d 90, 93 (1983)), financing schemes similar to ours have been upheld by a majority of those courts that have applied the rational basis standard (*see, e.g., City of Pawtucket v. Sundlun*,

662 A.2d 40, 62 (R.I. 1995); *Kukor v. Grover*, 148 Wis. 2d 469, 497-510, 436 N.W.2d 568, 580-85 (1989); *Fair School Finance Counsel of Oklahoma, Inc. v. State*, 746 P.2d 1135, 1150 (Okla. 1987); *Hornbeck v. Somerset County Board of Education*, 295 Md. 597, 651, 458 A.2d 758, 788-90 (1983); *Board of Education, Levittown Union Free School District v. Nyquist*, 57 N.Y.2d 27, 43-46, 439 N.E.2d 359, 366-68, 453 N.Y.S.2d 643, 650-52 (1982); *Lujan v. Colorado State Board of Education*, 649 P.2d 1005, 1022-23 (Colo. 1982); *McDaniel v. Thomas*, 248 Ga. 632, 648, 285 S.E.2d 156, 167-68 (1981); *Board of Education v. Walter*, 58 Ohio St. 2d 368, 377, 390 N.E.2d 813, 820 (1979); *Thompson v. Engelking*, 96 Idaho 793, 537 P.2d 635, 645 (Idaho 1975)). In accordance with *Rodriguez* and the majority of state court decisions, and for all the reasons set forth above, we conclude that the State's system of funding public education is rationally related to the legitimate State goal of promoting local control. Plaintiffs' claims under the equal protection clause of Illinois Constitution were properly dismissed.

Conclusion

In closing, it bears emphasis that our decision in no way represents an endorsement of the present system of financing public schools in Illinois, nor do we mean to discourage plaintiffs' efforts to reform the system. However, for the reasons explained above, the process of reform must be undertaken in a legislative forum rather than in the courts. Plaintiffs' complaint was properly dismissed, and we therefore affirm the judgment of the appellate court.

Affirmed.

DeRolph v. Ohio

78 Ohio St. 3d 193, 1997 Ohio 84, 677 N.E.2d 733 (1997)

Francis E. Sweeney, Sr., J. In 1802, when our forefathers convened to write our state Constitution, they carried within them a deep-seated belief that liberty and individual opportunity could be preserved only by educating Ohio's citizens. These ideals, which spurred the War of Independence, were so important that education was made part of our first Bill of Rights. Section 3, Article VIII of the Ohio Constitution of 1802. Beginning in 1851, our Constitution has required the General Assembly to provide enough funding to secure a "thorough and efficient system of common schools throughout the State."

Over the last two centuries, the education of our citizenry has been deemed vital to our democratic society and to our progress as a state. Education is essential to preparing our youth to be productive members of our society, with the skills and knowledge necessary to compete in the modern world. In fact, the mission statement of defendant, Ohio State Board of Education, echoes these concerns:

> The mission of education is to prepare students of all ages to meet, to the best of their abilities, the academic, social, civic, and employment needs of the twenty-first century, by providing high-quality programs that emphasize the lifelong skills necessary to continue learning, communicate clearly, solve problems, use information and technology effectively, and enjoy productive employment. . . .

Today, Ohio stands at a crossroads. We must decide whether the promise of providing to our youth a free, public elementary and secondary education in a "thorough and efficient system" has been fulfilled. The importance of this case cannot be overestimated. It involves a wholesale constitutional attack on Ohio's system of funding public elementary and secondary education. Practically every Ohioan will be affected by our decision: the 1.8 million children in public schools and every taxpayer in the state. For the 1.8 million children involved, this case is about the opportunity to compete and succeed.

Upon a full consideration of the record and in analyzing the pertinent constitutional provision, we can reach but one conclusion: the current legislation fails to provide for a thorough and efficient system of common schools, in violation of Section 2, Article VI of the Ohio Constitution.

In reaching this conclusion, we dismiss as unfounded any suggestion that the problems presented by this case should be left for the General Assembly to resolve. This case involves questions of public or great general interest over which this court has jurisdiction. . . .

Under the long-standing doctrine of judicial review, it is our sworn duty to determine whether the General Assembly has enacted legislation that is constitutional. *Marbury v. Madison* (1803), 5 U.S. (1 Cranch) 137, 2 L. Ed. 60. We are aware that the General Assembly has the responsibility to enact legislation and that such legislation is presumptively valid. . . .However, this does not mean that we may turn a deaf ear to any challenge to laws passed by the General Assembly. The presumption that laws are constitutional is rebuttable. The judiciary was created as part of a system of checks and balances. We will not dodge our responsibility by asserting that this case involves a nonjusticiable political question. To do so is unthinkable. We refuse to undermine our role as judicial arbiters and to pass our responsibilities onto the lap of the General Assembly. . . .Therefore, we are clearly within our constitutional authority in reviewing this matter and in declaring Ohio's school financing system unconstitutional. We turn now to a review of the record.

Ohio's System of Public School Financing

Ohio's statutory scheme for financing public education is complex. At the heart of the present controversy is the School Foundation Program (R.C. Chapter 3317) for allocation of state basic aid and the manner in which the allocation formula and other school funding factors have caused or permitted to continue vast wealth-based disparities among Ohio's schools, depriving many of Ohio's public school students of high quality educational opportunities.

According to statute, the revenue available to a school district comes from two primary sources: state revenue, most of which is provided through the School Foundation Program, and local revenue, which consists primarily of locally voted school district property tax levies. Federal funds play a minor role in the financing scheme. Ohio relies more on local revenue than state revenue, contrary to the national trend.

Under the foundation program, state basic aid is available for school districts that levy at least twenty mills of local property tax revenue for current operating expenses. State basic aid for qualifying school districts is calculated each biennium as part of the General Assembly's budget. . . . The "formula amount" has no real relation to what it actually costs to educate a pupil. . . . Thus, the foundation level reflects political and budgetary considerations at least as much as it reflects a judgment as to how much money *should* be spent on K-12 education.

The foundation formula amount, which was set at $2,817 per pupil in the 1992-1993 school year, 144 Ohio Laws, Part III, 4122, is adjusted by a school district equalization factor, now called the "cost of doing business" factor. R.C. 3317.02(E). These rates of adjustment vary from county to county and apply equally to all districts within the county without regard to the actual costs of operations within the individual school districts. The cost-of-doing-business factor assumes that costs are lower in rural districts than in urban districts.

A target amount of combined local and state aid per district is reached by multiplying the formula amount, the cost-of-doing-business factor and the average daily membership. R.C. 3317.022(A). However, subtracted or "charged off" from that figure is the total taxable value of real and tangible personal property in the district times a certain percentage. *Id.* Subtracting the applicable charge-off results in a figure constituting basic state aid for the district in question. The effect of an increase in this percentage would be to decrease the amount of basic state aid, resulting in an even greater burden for local schools to fund education through local property and/or income taxes.

The financing scheme is further complicated when special factors are taken into account. For instance, additional appropriations may be made for categorical programs, such as vocational education, special education and transportation. R.C. 3317.024. However, no adjustment is made for the relative wealth of the receiving district. Moreover, children in funded handicapped "units" are not included in the state basic aid formula. R.C. 3317.02(A). Thus, funds for handicapped students, for instance, whose education costs are substantially higher (due to state mandates of small class size and because of related extra services) are disbursed in a flat amount per unit (*see* R.C. 3317.05). If the actual cost exceeds the funds received, wealthier districts are in a better position to make up the difference. . . .

. . . The School Foundation Program contains no aid expressly for capital improvements for Ohio's public schools. Aid for that purpose is provided by the Classroom Facilities Act, R.C. Chapter 3318. However, the evidence showed, and the trial court found, that the Act is insufficiently funded to meet the needs of districts that are poor in real property value.

A "Thorough and Efficient System of Common Schools"

In urging this court to strike the statutory provisions relating to Ohio's school financing system, appellants argue that the state has failed in its constitutional responsibility to provide a thorough and efficient system of public schools. We agree. Section 2, Article VI of the Ohio Constitution requires the state to provide and fund a system of public education and includes an explicit directive to the General Assembly:

> The general assembly shall make such provisions, by taxation, or otherwise, as, with the income arising from the school trust fund, will secure a thorough and efficient system of common schools throughout the State. . . .

The delegates to the 1850-1851 Constitutional Convention recognized that it was the state's duty to both present and future generations of Ohioans to establish a framework for a "full, complete and efficient system of public education." II Report of the Debates and Proceedings of the Convention for the Revision of the Constitution of the State of Ohio, 1850-51 (1851) ("Debates"). Thus, throughout their discussions, the delegates stressed the importance of education and reaffirmed the policy that education shall be afforded to every child in the state regardless of race or economic standing. Debates at 11, 13. Furthermore, the delegates were concerned that the education to be provided to our youth not be mediocre but be as perfect as could humanly be devised. Debates at 698-699. These debates reveal the delegates' strong belief that it is the state's obligation, through the General Assembly, to provide for the full education of all children within the state.

Dr. Samuel Kern Alexander, a leading professor in the area of school law and school finance, testified that, in the context of the historical development of the phrase "thorough and efficient," it is the state's duty to provide a system which allows its citizens to fully develop their human potential. In such a system, rich and poor people alike are given the opportunity to become educated so that they may flourish and our society may progress. It was believed by the leading statesmen of the time that only in this way could there be an efficient educational system throughout the state.

This court has construed the words "thorough and efficient" in light of the constitutional debates and history surrounding them. In *Miller v. Korns* (1923), 107 Ohio St. 287, 297-298, 140 N.E. 773, 776, this court defined what is meant by a "thorough and efficient" system of common schools throughout the state:

> This declaration is made by the people of the state. It calls for the upbuilding of a system of schools throughout the state, and the attainment of efficiency and thoroughness in that system is thus expressly made a purpose, not local, not municipal, but state-wide.
>
> With this very purpose in view, regarding the problem as a statewide problem, the sovereign people made it mandatory upon the General Assembly to secure not merely a system of common schools, but a system thorough and efficient throughout the state.
>
> A thorough system could not mean one in which part or any number of the school districts of the state were starved for funds. An efficient system could not mean one in which part or any number of the school districts of the state lacked teachers, buildings, or equipment.

Cincinnati School Dist. Bd. of Edn. v. Walter (1979), 58 Ohio St. 2d 368, 387, 12 Ohio Op. 3d 327, 338, 390 N.E.2d 813, 825, cited *Miller* with approval. Additionally, *Walter* recognized that while the General Assembly has wide discretion in meeting the mandate of Section 2, Article VI, this discretion is not without limits. *Id. Walter* found that a school system would not be thorough and efficient if "a school district was receiving so little local and state revenue that the students were effectively being deprived of educational opportunity." *Id.*

Other states, in declaring their state funding systems unconstitutional,[6] have also addressed the issue of what constitutes a "thorough and efficient" or a "general or uniform" system of public schools. We recognize that some of these decisions were decided on different grounds or involved different education provisions. Despite these differences, we still are persuaded by the basic principles underlying these decisions.

For instance, in *Edgewood Indep. School Dist. v. Kirby*, the Texas Supreme Court invalidated its state funding structure, in which annual per-student expenditures varied from $2,112 in the poorest districts to $19,333 in the wealthiest districts. The court noted:

> Property-poor districts are trapped in a cycle of poverty from which there is no opportunity to free themselves. Because of their inadequate tax base, they must tax at significantly higher rates in order to meet minimum requirements for accreditation; yet their educational programs are typically inferior. The location of new industry and development is strongly influenced by tax rates and the quality of local schools. Thus, the property-poor districts with their high tax rates and inferior schools are unable to attract new industry or development and so have little opportunity to improve their tax base.

The plaintiffs in *Edgewood* presented compelling evidence of how fiscal inequities produced inadequate educational opportunities. The court in *Edgewood* stated that the inequalities resulting from Texas's school funding system violated the constitutional requirement of efficiency. Thus, the court declared that the legislature must provide for an efficient system in which funds are distributed more equitably. As the court noted to correct the deficiencies, "[a] band-aid will not suffice; the system itself must be changed."

The dissent believes that we rely too heavily upon anecdotal evidence to support our holding that the current system is unconstitutional. Glaringly absent from the dissenting opinion, however, is any consideration of the massive evidence presented to us. There is one simple reason for this noticeable omission. The facts are fatal to the dissent. The dissent wisely recognizes that it could not, in good conscience, address these facts and then conclude that Ohio is providing the opportunity for a basic education. Therefore, it does the only thing that it could do, it ignores them. Instead, it turns to facts outside the record and to laws passed by the General Assembly after this lawsuit was filed as a means of justifying its position. We, however, know that it is imperative to consider the record as presented to us. In doing so, we find that exhaustive evidence was presented to establish that the

---

[6] The following states have declared their school funding statutes unconstitutional: *Roosevelt Elementary School Dist. v. Bishop* (1994), 179 Ariz. 233, 877 P.2d 806; *DuPree v. Alma School Dist. No. 30* (1983), 279 Ark. 340, 651 S.W.2d 90; *Serrano v. Priest* (1976), 18 Cal. 3d 728, 135 Cal. Rptr. 345, 557 P.2d 929; *Horton v. Meskill* (1977), 172 Conn. 615, 376 A.2d 359; *Rose v. Council for Better Edn.* (Ky. 1989), 790 S.W.2d 186; *McDuffy v. Secy., Executive Office of Edn.* (1993), 415 Mass. 545, 615 N.E.2d 516; *Helena Elementary School Dist. No. 1 v. State* (1989), 236 Mont. 44, 769 P.2d 684; *Abbott v. Burke* (1990), 119 N.J. 287, 575 A.2d 359; *Tennessee Small School Sys. v. McWherter* (Tenn. 1993), 851 S.W.2d 139; *Edgewood Indep. School Dist. v. Kirby* (Tex. 1989), 777 S.W.2d 391; *Brigham v. State* (Vt. 1997), 692 A.2d 384, 1997 WL 51794; *Seattle School Dist. No. 1 of King Cty. v. State* (1978), 90 Wash. 2d 476, 585 P.2d 71; *Pauley v. Kelly* (1979), 162 W. Va. 672, 255 S.E.2d 859; *Washakie Cty. School Dist. One v. Herschler* (Wyo. 1980), 606 P.2d 310.

appellant school districts were starved for funds, lacked teachers, buildings, and equipment, and had inferior educational programs, and that their pupils were being deprived of educational opportunity.

In 1989, the General Assembly directed the Superintendent of Public Instruction to conduct a survey of Ohio's public school buildings. . . . The survey identified a need for $10.2 billion in facility repair and construction.

Among its findings, the survey determined that one-half of Ohio's school buildings were fifty years old or older, and fifteen percent were seventy years old or older. A little over half of these buildings contained satisfactory electrical systems; however, only seventeen percent of the heating systems and thirty-one percent of the roofs were deemed to be satisfactory. Nineteen percent of the windows and twenty-five percent of the plumbing and fixtures were found to be adequate. Only twenty percent of the buildings had satisfactory handicapped access. A scant thirty percent of the school facilities had adequate fire alarm systems and exterior doors.

Over three years after the 1990 survey was published, the current Superintendent of Public Instruction, John Theodore Sanders, averred that his visits to Ohio school buildings demonstrated that some students were "making do in a decayed carcass from an era long passed," and others were educated in "dirty, depressing places." . . . Additionally, many districts lack sufficient funds to comply with the state law requiring a district-wide average of no more than twenty-five students for each classroom teacher. Ohio Adm. Code 3301-35-03(A)(3). Indeed, some schools have more than thirty students per classroom teacher, with one school having as many as thirty-nine students in one sixth grade class. As the testimony of educators established, it is virtually impossible for students to receive an adequate education with a student-teacher ratio of this magnitude.

The curricula in the appellant school districts are severely limited compared to other school districts and compared to what might be expected of a system designed to educate Ohio's youth and to prepare them for a bright and prosperous future. . . . None of the appellant school districts is financially able to keep up with the technological training needs of the students in the districts. The districts lack sufficient computers, computer labs, hands-on computer training, software, and related supplies to properly serve the students' needs. In this regard, it does not appear likely that the children in the appellant school districts will be able to compete in the job market against those students with sufficient technological training. . . . Poor performance on the ninth grade proficiency tests is further evidence that these schools lack sufficient funds with which to educate their students.

. . . All the facts documented in the record lead to one inescapable conclusion—Ohio's elementary and secondary public schools are neither thorough nor efficient. The operation of the appellant school districts conflicts with the historical notion that the education of our youth is of utmost concern and that Ohio children should be educated adequately so that they are able to participate fully in society. Our state Constitution was drafted with the importance of education in mind. In contrast, education under the legislation being reviewed ranks miserably low in the state's priorities. In fact, the formula amount is established after the legislature determines the total dollars to be allocated to primary and secondary education in each biennial budget. Consequently, the present school financing system contravenes the clear wording of our Constitution and the framers' intent.

Furthermore, rather than following the constitutional dictate that it is the state's obligation to fund education (as this opinion has repeatedly underscored), the legislature has thrust the majority of responsibility upon local school districts. This, too, is contrary to the clear wording of our Constitution. The responsibility for maintaining a thorough and efficient school system falls upon the state. When a district falls short of the constitutional requirement that the system be thorough and efficient, it is the state's obligation to rectify it.

. . . Also, when we apply the tests of *Miller* and *Walter* as to what is meant by the words "thorough and efficient," the evidence is overwhelming that many districts are "starved for funds," and lack teachers, buildings, or equipment. These school districts, plagued with deteriorating buildings, insufficient supplies, inadequate curricula and technology, and large student-teacher ratios, desperately lack the resources necessary to provide students with a minimally adequate education. Thus, according to the tests of *Miller* and *Walter*, it is painfully obvious that the General Assembly, in structuring school financing, has failed in its constitutional obligation to ensure a thorough and efficient system of common schools. Clearly, the current school financing scheme is a far cry from thorough and efficient. Instead, the system has failed to educate our youth to their fullest potential.

. . . We recognize that disparities between school districts will always exist. By our decision today, we are not stating that a new financing system must provide equal educational opportunities for all. In a Utopian society, this lofty goal would be realized. We, however, appreciate the limitations imposed upon us. Nor do we advocate a "Robin Hood" approach to school financing reform. We are not suggesting that funds be diverted from wealthy districts and given to the less fortunate. There is no "leveling down" component in our decision today.

Moreover, in no way should our decision be construed as imposing spending ceilings on more affluent school districts. School districts are still free to augment their programs if they choose to do so. However, it is futile to lay the entire blame for the inadequacies of the present system on the taxpayers and the local boards of education. Although some districts have the luxury of deciding where to allocate extra dollars, many others have the burden of deciding which educational programs to cut or what financial institution to contact to obtain yet another emergency loan. Our state Constitution makes the state responsible for educating our youth. Thus, the state should not shirk its obligation by espousing clichés about "local control."

We recognize that money alone is not the panacea that will transform Ohio's school system into a model of excellence. Although a student's success depends upon numerous factors besides money, we must ensure that there is enough money that students have the chance to succeed because of the educational opportunity provided, not in spite of it. Such an opportunity requires, at the very least, that all of Ohio's children attend schools which are safe and conducive to learning. At the present, Ohio does not provide many of its students with even the most basic of educational needs.

. . . School funding has been, and continues to be, a Herculean task. As thirty-seven lawmakers concede in their *amicus curiae* brief, despite their recent efforts, the General Assembly has not funded our public schools properly. They assert that unless this court rules in favor of the appellants, the urgency of resolving public school funding will quickly fade. We find that this brief eloquently expresses the helplessness felt even by many of our state legislators.

Conclusion

We know that few issues have the potential to stir such passion as school financing. In many districts in this great state of ours, students and teachers must fight a demoralizing uphill battle to make the system work. All parties concede that the current system needs to be reformed.

By our decision today, we send a clear message to lawmakers: the time has come to fix the system. Let there be no misunderstanding. Ohio's public school financing scheme must undergo a complete systematic overhaul. The factors which contribute to the unworkability of the system and which must be eliminated are (1) the operation of the School Foundation Program, (2) the emphasis of Ohio's school funding system on local property tax, (3) the requirement of school district borrowing through the spending reserve and emergency school assistance loan programs, and (4) the lack of sufficient funding in the General Assembly's biennium budget for the construction and maintenance of public school buildings. The funding laws reviewed today are inherently incapable of achieving their constitutional purpose.

We therefore hold that Ohio's elementary and secondary public school financing system violates Section 2, Article VI of the Ohio Constitution, which mandates a thorough and efficient system of common schools throughout the state. . . .

Remedy

Although we have found the school financing system to be unconstitutional, we do not instruct the General Assembly as to the specifics of the legislation it should enact. However, we admonish the General Assembly that it must create an entirely new school financing system. In establishing such a system, the General Assembly shall recognize that there is but one system of public education in Ohio. It is a statewide system, expressly created by the state's highest governing document, the Constitution. Thus, the establishment, organization and maintenance of public education are the state's responsibility. Because of its importance, education should be placed high in the state's budgetary priorities. A thorough and efficient system of common schools includes facilities in good repair and the supplies, materials, and funds necessary to maintain these facilities in a safe manner, in compliance with all local, state, and federal mandates.

We recognize that a new funding system will require time for adequate study, drafting of the appropriate legislation and transition from the present scheme of financing to one in conformity with this decision. Therefore, we stay the effect of this decision for twelve months. . . .

NOTES AND QUESTIONS

1. In *Edgar*, the Illinois Supreme Court first concludes that admitted disparities in educational funding based on local property wealth do not render Illinois's educational system "inefficient." Rather, the court reaffirms its precedent that an efficient educational system is one with contiguous and compact boundaries. Compare the court's definition of "efficient" in *Edgar* with the court's definition of "thorough and efficient" in *DeRolph*. Is there a principled distinction between the two opinions, or are the apparently different outcomes attributable to the political sensibilities of the justices?
2. How are contiguous and compact boundaries "efficient"? Could it be argued that a patchwork of compact districts may balkanize a state educational system and prevent the efficient pooling of resources among many districts? If the Illinois constitution's efficiency language requires contiguous and compact school district boundaries, does that language also require "neighborhood" schools? Would an educational system that operates magnet schools or transports students across compact neighborhood boundaries violate the Illinois constitution as "inefficient"?
3. In *Edgar*, the Illinois Supreme Court contends that the Illinois constitution's declaration that education is a "fundamental goal" is not the same as a constitutional declaration that education is a fundamental "right." What is the difference, if any, between a "goal" and a "right" in this context?
4. Finally, *Edgar* and *DeRolph* display different views about the role of the judiciary in these matters. The Ohio Supreme Court begins by asserting that the judiciary must perform its "sworn duty" to interpret and apply the state's constitution. The court rejects as "unfounded" the argument that issues of educational governance must be left to the legislature. In *Edgar*, of course, the Illinois Supreme Court relies heavily on its argument that the judiciary is particularly unable to resolve issues of educational quality, and leaves to the legislature such matters. Which court has the better argument? Should the judiciary defer to the state legislature on matters of educational governance, or should the judiciary become involved in that issue as part of its province to test the constitutionality of state legislation?

C. THE POLITICAL ASPECTS OF THE RIGHT TO PUBLIC EDUCATION

1. The Degree of Funding Inequality in the States

The following charts show the persistence of dramatic disparities between the highest and lowest per pupil expenditures in school districts serving kindergarten through twelfth grade students within each state.

ALABAMA		CALIFORNIA	
Mountain Brook City	$5,036	Indian Springs Elementary	$16,343
Roanoke City	$2,776	Pacific Union Elementary	$2,713
ALASKA		COLORADO	
Aleutian	$32,217	Lone Star #101	$8,667
Anchorage	$6,170	Lewis-Palmer #38	$3,757
ARIZONA		CONNECTICUT	
Mobile #86	$18,313	Regional HS District #01	$11,418
Bullhead City #15	$2,947	Chester School District	$5,680
ARKANSAS		DELAWARE	
Witts Springs	$7,045	Kent County Voc/Tech	$11,592
Dardanelle	$2,962	Appoqionimink	$4,999
DISTRICT OF COLUMBIA, D.C.		NEBRASKA	
Public Schools	$8,690	Lewellen Rural H.S.	$14,686
		Whiteclay	$1,769
FLORIDA		NEVADA	
Washington County Seminole	$6,690	Eureka County	$11,546
County	$3,974	Washoe County	$4,137
GEORGIA		NEW HAMPSHIRE	
Atlantic City	$6,498	Nelson	$12,308
Jones County	$3,236	Franklin	$3,535
HAWAII		NEW JERSEY	
Hawaii Dept. of Ed.	$5,332	Union County Regional	$18,116
		Prospect Park Borough	$5,144
IDAHO		NEW MEXICO	
Avery #394	$10,000	Quemado Independent	$6,774
Preston Joint School Dist. 201	$2,805	Hobbs Municipal	$3,196
ILLINOIS		NEW YORK	
Community Consolidated	$16,700	Greenburgh Eleven	$38,752
#211 Aviston #21	$2,276	Allegany	$5,423
INDIANA		NORTH CAROLINA	
Gibson-Pike-Warrick Coop	$8,482	Asheville	$6,118
Beech Grove City	$2,759	Onslow County	$3,196
IOWA		NORTH DAKOTA	
Lost Nation Community	$10,416	Twin Buttes #37	$18,957
ColoNesco Community	$3,131	Salund #10	$2,571
KANSAS		OHIO	
Nes Tre Go	$10,013	Butler County	$14,331
Mulvane	$3,173	Fayetteville Perry	$3,187
KENTUCKY		OKLAHOMA	
Owsley County	$5,856	Frontier	$9,222
Meade County	$3,374	Stroud	$2,614
LOUSIANA		OREGON	
Cameron Parish	$6,012	Pistol River	$14,769
Livingston Parish	$3,001	Central Howell	$2,986
MAINE		PENNSYLVANIA	
Mohegan PLT	$14,750	Bucks County	$16,984
Otis	$2,558	Luzeme	$3,867
MARYLAND		RHODE ISLAND	
Montgomery County Caroline	$7,484	New Shoreham	$10,944
County	$5,101	Smithfield	$5,269

MASSACHUSETTS		SOUTH CAROLINA	
Norfolk County Agricultural	$16,179	Spartanburg	$5,495
Groveland	$3,224	Orangeburg	$3,569
MICHIGAN		SOUTH DAKOTA	
Bois Blanc TWP Bloomfield	$15,750	Wood 47-2	$10,278
Township 7F	$1,942	Yankton 63-3	$3,272
MINNESOTA		TENNESSEE	
Nett Lake	$12,353	Oak Ridge City	$5,142
Sacred Heart	$2,740	Tipton County	$2,469
MISSISIPPI		TEXAS	
Calhoun County	$5,376	Laureles	$42,000
Itawamba Jr. College & AHS	$1,992	Harts Bluff	$3,098
MISSOURI		UTAH	
Clayton	$8,521	Daggett	$7,482
Republic R-III	$2,469	Washington	$2,636
MONTANA		VERMONT	
Ross Elementary	$25,000	Addison Northeast	$16,127
Smith Valley Elementary	$2,276	Richmond	$3,182
VIRGINIA		WISCONSIN	
Falls Church City	$8,533	Paris J1	$10,308
Halifax County	$2,897	Washington-Caldwell	$3,871
WASHINGTON		WYOMING	
Benge	$36,200	Fremont County #09	$17,558
Ridgefield	$3,780	Park County #06	$4,482
WEST VIRGINIA			
Pleasants County	$6,571		
Hardy County	$4,060		

Source: Common Core of Data, School Years 1988-89 through 2004-05, National Center for Education Statistics. *See also* Funding for Justice: Money, Equity and the Future of Public Education, 9 (1997).

Table 4. Current Expenditures Per Student for Public Elementary and Secondary Education, by State

	Expenditures per student					
State	10th percentile	Median	90th percentile	90/10 Ratio	Number of districts	Number of students
United States	$5,560	$6,942	$10,536	1.9	14,028	46,538,723
Alabama	5,435	5,842	6,615	1.2	128	728,532
Alaska	8,316	13,843	21,155	2.5	53	131,985
Arizona	4,740	6,060	10,476	2.2	216	834,377
Arkansas	5,053	5,616	6,778	1.3	310	449,693
California	5,870	6,596	9,077	1.5	975	5,973,228
Colorado	5,572	6,674	10,000	1.8	176	723,696
Connecticut	8,226	9,184	11,427	1.4	166	537,521
Delaware	7,448	8,151	9,373	1.3	16	106,545
District of Columbia	†	12,046	†	†	1	68,925
Florida	5,543	6,055	6,690	1.2	67	2,431,884
Georgia	5,922	6,552	7,869	1.3	179	1,441,297
Hawaii	†	6,599	†	†	1	184,360
Idaho	4,982	6,111	8,916	1.8	113	245,009
Illinois	5,479	6,669	9,449	1.7	892	2,025,249
Indiana	6,049	6,655	7,720	1.3	292	987,854
Iowa	5,776	6,374	7,325	1.3	373	495,080

†Not applicable.

(cont. on following page)

Table 4. (*cont.*)

State	Expenditures per student 10th percentile	Median	90th percentile	90/10 Ratio	Number of districts	Number of students
Kansas	5,618	6,810	8,741	1.6	304	468,347
Kentucky	5,466	6,120	7,209	1.3	176	643,730
Louisiana	5,311	5,954	6,819	1.3	66	737,223
Maine	7,005	8,363	12,438	1.8	225	206,750
Maryland	7,004	7,658	8,760	1.3	24	852,920
Massachusetts	7,307	8,596	12,015	1.6	302	941,080
Michigan	6,269	6,930	8,879	1.4	556	1,648,807
Minnesota	6,012	6,911	8,256	1.4	342	836,386
Mississippi	4,666	5,209	6,145	1.3	152	496,513
Missouri	5,217	6,095	7,850	1.5	522	904,242
Montana	5,000	7,258	13,444	2.7	447	154,700
Nebraska	5,378	7,170	11,162	2.1	544	284,924
Nevada	5,751	7,140	12,168	2.1	17	340,706
New Hampshire	6,246	7,539	9,792	1.6	162	204,721
New Jersey	8,650	10,317	13,256	1.5	552	1,276,094
New Mexico	5,703	7,529	11,256	2.0	89	320,303
New York	8,865	10,598	14,878	1.7	687	2,856,425
North Carolina	5,899	6,600	7,707	1.3	117	1,277,013
North Dakota	5,095	6,850	10,306	2.0	226	108,739
Ohio	5,583	6,281	7,933	1.4	611	1,821,544
Oklahoma	5,115	6,217	8,246	1.6	543	623,098
Oregon	6,501	7,307	13,400	2.1	197	544,756
Pennsylvania	6,224	7,180	8,790	1.4	500	1,771,473
Rhode Island	7,986	8,925	10,513	1.3	36	156,275
South Carolina	5,754	6,504	7,930	1.4	86	676,681
South Dakota	5,499	6,552	8,711	1.6	173	127,986
Tennessee	4,666	5,280	6,326	1.4	137	895,839
Texas	5,864	6,912	9,695	1.7	1,040	4,021,403
Utah	4,388	5,261	7,402	1.7	40	477,380
Vermont	6,629	8,204	11,172	1.7	240	97,715
Virginia	6,179	6,852	8,260	1.3	132	1,143,807
Washington	6,072	6,756	11,811	1.9	296	1,004,843
West Virginia	6,793	7,328	8,050	1.2	55	285,785
Wisconsin	6,933	7,922	9,130	1.3	426	875,569
Wyoming	7,173	8,671	11,836	1.7	48	89,711
Independent charter school districts	4,177	6,213	9,900	2.4	700	179,473

Note: The District of Columbia and Hawaii consist of one school district each.

Source: Data reported by states to U.S. Department of Education, National Center for Education Statistics, Common Core of Data (CCD), School District Finance Survey (F-33), FY 2001.

In its comparisons of the dollar gap between districts at the tenth and ninetieth percentile of per-pupil spending within each state, these figures reveal that the *median* disparity in per-pupil spending between the wealthiest and poorest school districts throughout the United States is nearly $5,000 per student, and that there is almost a 2 : 1 ratio in expenditures. *See also Quality Counts '98: Resources Data Table: Comparisons of Per Pupil Expenditures, http://www.edweek.org/sreports/qc98/states/indicators/res-t3.htm*; *National Center for Educational Statistics* (2002-2003); K. Carey, *The Funding Gap: Low-income and Minority Students Still Receive Fewer Dollars in Many States*, The Education

Trust (2003) (reporting that in 2003, the highest poverty school districts received significantly less funding than the lowest poverty districts). Do these disparities support Jonathan Kozol's argument that "savage inequalities" exist in American education? *See* J. Kozol, *Savage Inequalities* (1991).

Moreover, in 2003, the Education Trust reported that, "[s]chool districts that educate the greatest number of low-income and minority students receive substantially less state and local money per student than districts with the fewest such students." *See* School Board News, at 7 (Natl. Assn. School Bds., Nov. 11, 2003). *See also* K. Carey, *The Funding Gap, Low-income and Minority Students Still Receive Fewer Dollars in Many States,* at 6, The Education Trust (2003) ("The troubling pattern of funding shortfalls repeats itself for school districts educating large numbers of minority students"). In *No Excuses: Closing the Racial Gap in Learning* (2003) (hereinafter *No Excuses*), however, Abigail and Stephan Thernstrom present evidence which shows that school "districts with more minority students did have a little less money, but the differences were surprisingly small." *No Excuses,* at 155. Nonetheless, the authors did find a "substantial" disparity between resources devoted to education in districts with parents of different economic status. *Id.* at 155.

2. The Relationship Between Funding and Quality

The school funding decisions raise the fundamental political issue of the relationship between resources and the quality of education. In *Rodriguez,* the Supreme Court stated that "one of the major sources of controversy concerns the extent to which there is a demonstrable correlation between educational expenditures and the quality of education." The *Rodriguez* Court assumed that quality was to be measured in student outcome, presumably by standardized achievement test results. Alternatively, quality could be measured by inputs: the educational opportunities given to each child to reach their own potential. *See, e.g.,* Coleman, *The Concept of Equality of Educational Opportunity,* 38 Harv. Educ. Rev. 7 (1968).

Despite Justice Powell's suggestion that there is a split among experts regarding the connection between educational funding and educational quality, the weight of authority clearly supports the connection. In fact, the studies that Justice Powell cites as authority for his perceived dispute among scholars are virtually uniform in their conclusion that the *appropriate* allocation of resources has a marked impact on the quality of education, under any legitimate definition of "quality." *See* C. Jencks, *Inequality* (1972); C. Silverman, *Crisis in the Classroom* (1970); *The Coleman Report, Office of Education, Equality of Educational Opportunity* (1966) (hereinafter *Coleman Report*); Moynihan & Mosteller, *On Equality of Educational Opportunity (*1972). *See also* A. Wise, *Rich Schools, Poor Schools: The Promise of Equal Educational Opportunity* (1968); Coons, Clune, Sugarman, *Private Wealth and Public Education* (1970). More recent studies confirm the relationship between funds and quality. *See, e.g., Funding for Justice: Money, Equity, and the Future of Public Education* (1997) (hereinafter *Funding for Justice*); Picus, *Student-Level Finance Data: Wave of the Future* (The Clearing House, Nov./Dec. 2000); R.F. Ferguson, *Paying for Public*

Education: New Evidence on How and Why Money Matters, 28 Harv. J. Legis. 465 (1991).

Where there is a disagreement among scholars regarding the connection between money and quality, that disagreement relates to the method of measuring quality or, more significantly, the role of factors *other* than resources in the quality of education. The *Coleman Report*, for example, offered the controversial finding that "schools bring little influence to bear on a child's achievement that is independent of his background and general social context." As such, the *Report* observed, "inequalities imposed on children by their home, neighborhood, and peer environment are carried along to become the inequalities with which they confront adult life. . . ." *Coleman Report* at 325. Although one of the authors of the *Coleman Report* has since come to accept the idea that educational resources can influence a child's achievement and mobility, *see* Jencks & Phillips, *The Black-White Test Score Gap* (1998), the fundamental questions raised by the *Report* have not gone away. *See, e.g., No Excuses*, at 5-6, 14, 22, 155 and 157. To what extent do educational resources have an "effect" on a child's academic development that is "independent" of that child's "background and social context"?

Assuming that there is no definite answer to the question of whether educational quality is related to resources, what is the consequence of that uncertainty for constitutional jurisprudence? In other words, who bears the burden of proving or disproving the link between funding and quality? In *Abbott v. Burke*, 575 A.2d 359 (1990), the Supreme Court of New Jersey considered the state's claim that "money is not a critical factor in the quality of education." The court concluded that unless the state had met its burden of proving that its claimed lack of a link between money and quality was "clearly right," the state's disparate property tax funding regime could not satisfy the requirement of constitutional equality. The court squarely placed upon the state the burden of disproving any connection between resources and quality.

The New Jersey Supreme Court's view may simply reflect that court's sense of the obvious. Does it simply strain credulity to argue that there is no connection between resources and quality?

3. The Practical Problems with Remedying Constitutional Violations in School Finance Cases

In *Rodriguez*, the Supreme Court suggests that alternatives to the current methods of educational funding may be both ineffective and inequitable. The Court mentions the establishment of a minimum foundation level and the reallocation of resources within a state as two proposed, but unproven alternative methods of educational finance. In addressing the questions of alternatives to an inequitable system of educational funding, however, the starting point must be to define the precise objective of educational funding.

In *Abbott v. Burke*, 575 A.2d 359 (1990), the New Jersey Supreme Court crafted a remedy commensurate with its finding that the "poorer urban districts" in the state failed both on the "absolute level" and in "comparison" with affluent districts. The court first determined that the statewide funding disparities had directly caused the following inadequacies in "poor" districts:

1. No computers and therefore no computer education instruction courses;
2. No science labs and therefore no science lab instruction;
3. No foreign language instruction;
4. No space, instruments or personnel for music instruction;
5. No facilities for art instruction;
6. No facilities or equipment for industrial arts instruction;
7. No physical education facilities;
8. Facilities that are unsafe, unclean and aged;
9. Large class size;
10. Relatively few adult educational professionals per pupil, and
11. Teachers with relatively little experience and training.

The *Abbott* court then found that the "needs of students in poorer districts vastly exceed those of others, especially those from richer districts." The ultimate perversion of Ohio's funding regime—and that of virtually every state—is that it allocates the greatest amount of funds to the students who need them the least. Accordingly, a remedy that genuinely strives for equal educational opportunities, the court concluded, must require that students who are at an educational disadvantage be afforded "more" (not less) resources than other students. The court therefore ordered the state to "assure that their educational expenditures per pupil are substantially equivalent to those of the more affluent suburban districts, and that, in addition, their special disadvantages must be addressed." The court did not preclude the state from continuing its allocation of local property taxes to the local district. Yet, the court made clear that to the extent that the property tax allocation increased the disparities in per-pupil expenditures across the state, the state must make up the difference: "To the extent that the State allows the richer suburban districts to continue to increase that disparity, it will, by our remedy, be required to increase the funding of the poorer urban districts."

Not surprisingly, the political branches in New Jersey responded to the court's directive by imposing a statewide tax (based on income) to fund the required remedies. The tax was politically unpopular and thus modified. The legislature then attempted to meet the court's mandate by passing the Comprehensive Educational Improvement Act of 1996, which purported to link funding to student performance, measured by standardized testing. The New Jersey Supreme Court, however, found that law unconstitutional, indicating that legislation that makes funding contingent on standardized test scores is particularly offensive to the equal protection clause. Such a system punishes poorer schools twice: first by failing to provide adequate funds to allow any measure of achievement, and second by withdrawing funds when the standard of achievement (not surprisingly) is not realized. *See also DeRolph v. Ohio*, 728 N.E.2d 993 (2000) (rejecting a similar attempt by the Ohio legislature to remedy its unconstitutional system of education funding by further punishing poor districts for their students' "failure" to meet unfunded and unattainable standardized testing goals); *DeRolph v. Ohio*, 97 Ohio St. 3d 434, 2002 Ohio 6750 (2002) (reaffirming its directive to the Ohio legislature that it enact a "complete systemic overhaul" of the state's school-funding system).

Ultimately, the New Jersey Supreme Court was forced by legislative backtracking into mandating a clear and detailed remedial plan that, among other things, required the state to create preschool programs, extended day kindergarten programs, integrated health care and social service support, safe and secure schools, effective technology instruction and adequate facilities. When the state still failed to implement these remedial measures, the New Jersey Supreme Court again found the state to be in violation of its constitutional mandate. *Abbott VI*, 748 A.2d 82 (2002).

Why is the legislature in New Jersey and elsewhere so resistant to implementing court-ordered remedial measures? In an era of scarce resources, educational funding legislation that distributes, or is perceived to distribute, wealth to relatively poor districts is rarely politically popular. As the history of the *Abbott* case indicates, legislators who advance such equalizing funding plans tend to meet stiff political resistance. Yet, ironically, those legislators may gain tremendous political "cover" when their initiatives are *ordered* by the courts. The lack of choice created by a firm judicial decree, therefore, may be helpful to enlightened legislators who might otherwise cower from their genuine interest in assisting poor schools for fear of a perceived political backlash.

That backlash may be unavoidable. In 1998, the Vermont Supreme Court declared unconstitutional the state's system of funding education based on local property taxes because it disadvantaged the property-poor districts. In response to the court's ruling, the Vermont legislature passed Act 60. That Act provided that each district must receive a minimal block grant of $5,600 per student. If a district wants to spend more, it can still raise local property taxes. Yet the statute imposes a "luxury" tax on those local property tax revenues.

The district must contribute half of the amount that it raises for itself in local property taxes to a "sharing pool" for poor districts, effectively requiring the district to share its local property taxes with those "poor" districts. Local districts, however, soon devised creative ways to avoid this revenue-sharing system. In relatively affluent Manchester, Vermont, for example, the 4,000 residents decided that they would not raise any extra money through property taxes, but would instead create a "voluntary" school fund. The amount of the "voluntary" contribution can be less than the amount of the property taxes that would have been paid because all of that contribution stays in the district. The district relies entirely on the persuasive power of neighborhood, social pressure to exact compliance with its "voluntary" regime. *See* M. Winerip, *Arm-Twister's Guide to School Finance*, N.Y. Times, A 21 (Feb. 26, 2003).

The social dynamic present in Manchester, Vermont is common even *within* a relatively affluent school district. Where each school in a district has its own parent-teacher organization (PTO) or parent-teacher association (PTA), that organization typically is able to raise thousands of dollars for "enrichment" in that particular school. These "enrichment" funds are over and above the district's per-pupil expenditures. Because such funds are dependent on the wealth of the school's families, gross disparities in the amount of those funds often exist, even within the most affluent districts.

In a microcosm of statewide school funding debates, the parents who are able to generate great sums of PTO/PTA contributions for their own school generally oppose district-wide initiatives to increase funding, such as student fees or tax referendums. Following the Vermont regime by analogy, should a school district impose an internal "luxury tax" on contributions to any particular school, requiring that school to contribute a percentage of its contributions to a district-wide fund? What are the advantages and disadvantages of the "luxury tax" at the intradistrict and statewide levels?

4. The Effective Use of Scarce Resources

The overriding research indicates that the quality of education is related to the money allocated to education, so long as that money is effectively employed. The research also indicates that school districts should direct scarce resources toward specific purposes to achieve the greatest degree of improvement in the quality of education. Robert Slavin, co-director of the Center for Research on the Education of Students Placed at Risk, at John Hopkins University, argues:

> Any funding equity remedy should address two kinds of issues. One is improving base funding for low-wealth districts and improving basic requirements for education: bringing facilities, teachers' salaries, class sizes, electives, and other features that most schools take for granted, up to adequate levels (as defined by levels typical in the region or state). However, improving the general quality of life in historically underfunded schools is by no means an adequate plan. Expenditures also must be earmarked for programs likely to make a substantial difference in student achievement in a relatively short period of time. Given our current state of knowledge, what programs and practices are likely to have the greatest payoff in higher achievements, especially for disadvantaged students likely to have suffered most from inequitable funding policies? Granted, some educators are too quick to point out the "disadvantages" of their students, and fail to build on their students' strengths. It is important that we recognize that schools should adapt their programs to students and not the other way around. In the best of all worlds, class sizes would be small enough to allow for more individualized attention and teachers would have the training and support needed to ensure academic success for all students.

See R. Slavin, *Where Should the Money Go?* in *Funding for Justice*, at 32-33 (1997). As Slavin suggests, the evidence seems to support the proposition that small class size significantly corresponds to student performance on standardized tests and authentic curriculum-based assessments. *See also* B. Miner, *The Benefits of Smaller Classes*, in *Funding for Justice*, at 34-35 (1997).

Moreover, there is a substantial body of empirical evidence demonstrating that one of the most effective ways to reduce the costs of education is through the provision of effective early childhood education programs. According to a recent longitudinal study conducted by Professor Arthur Reynolds of the University of Wisconsin, every dollar spent on high-quality early education programs saves local school districts, the states and federal government (and their taxpayers) $7.00 in future costs in special education, crime, health and delinquency. Professor Reynolds's longitudinal study is available at *www.waisman.wisc.edu/cls/. See also* Arthur J. Reynolds, *Success in Early Intervention: The Chicago Child-Parent Centers* (2000).

Unfortunately, however, the pressure to reduce expenses sometimes leads a district to cut the very type of educational programs that save society money in the long run. For example, if, as is required by the No Child Left Behind Act of 2001, a school district must demonstrate annual progress in its students' standardized test scores in math and language arts, a district will be tempted to prioritize testing skills in math and language arts over other nontested areas of the curriculum. In such an environment, fine arts programs typically suffer. Ironically, the evidence indicates that eliminating fine arts programs to reduce costs is actually counterproductive, because programs incorporating the arts have "proven" to be "cost-effective ways to provide students with the skills they need. . . ." *See* M. Blakeslee, *Art in the Schools*, Vol. 33, National Education Policy Network (Aug. 2002).

In light of these findings, how should a school district prioritize its educational expenditures from limited funds? Would the priorities be different in a district with greater property wealth and therefore greater per-pupil expenditures?

D. THE PRACTICAL SIDE OF THE RIGHT TO PUBLIC EDUCATION

1. Equitable Funding Practicum

In light of the legal and academic debate regarding inequalities in school finance, consider the practical problems raised in an actual school district ("the District").

As is typical, the District reported in 2000-2001 that it received 77.4 percent of its total revenue from local property taxes and another 9.2 percent from other local funding. The District received a mere 2.8 percent of its revenue from the federal government, and 10.6 percent of its revenue from general state funding. By virtue of the fact that the District has a relatively wealthy property base, its local property tax allocation far exceeded the state average on a per-pupil basis. The District's equalized assessed valuation of its property was $355,355 per pupil, compared to a state average for districts of similar size of $100,416 per pupil. As a consequence, the District received revenues of $6,405 per pupil for instruction and $10,867 per pupil for operating expenses. The state average, by contrast, was $4,305 per pupil for instruction and $7,400 per pupil for operating expenses. Hence, the District spent $5,567 more per student than even the state average. The disparity in resources per student between this District and the districts with property wealth lower than the state average would obviously be even greater. Assume that you represent a parent in the affluent district. What arguments would you raise in favor of maintaining the current funding scheme? Assume instead that your client is a school district, a parent or a student adversely affected by the funding regime. What challenges would you raise? Is the inequality created by the regime a violation of equal protection? Is the regime thorough and efficient?

The next issue raised by the cases and commentators, however, is whether a blatant disparity in spending makes a difference in the actual education of a child. As is typical, teachers in this relatively affluent District have reached a more advanced level of training than the state average (75 percent have a Master's degree, as opposed to the 48.3 percent state average). The student-teacher ratio in the affluent District averages at 15:1, as compared with the state average of 19:1. Teachers are paid more ($56,032 to $48,586), and administrators are paid quite a bit more ($104,426 to $92,392). The affluent District clearly has better trained and better paid teachers and administrators.

But, the question remains whether these expenditures make a difference. In the state, each district is mandated to administer standardized achievement tests on a regular basis. The State's Standards Achievement Test (SSAT) measures, among other things, achievement in the areas of reading and math for all third graders. Leaving aside the intense debate about the validity and legitimacy of such standardized testing, the SSAT results provide at least some comparative data. Across the state, 37.8 percent of all third grade students failed to meet state standards in reading and 25.8 percent failed to meet standards in math. In the affluent District, by contrast, only 11.9 percent of third graders failed to meet state reading standards and only 5.9 percent failed to meet math standards. The results and the disparities are virtually identical among fifth graders. Does this data confirm the correlation between money and academic achievement, or does it merely raise additional questions?

To complicate matters further, consider one more data point. In that same affluent District, a significant number of students qualify by virtue of their distressed economic condition for free or reduced lunch. Of the third graders who qualify for free or reduced lunch in the affluent district, 58.3 percent failed to meet state standards in reading and 33.3 percent failed to meet math standards. The number of "free and reduced lunch" students who failed to meet reading standards across the state was 59.7 percent, while the number of such students across the state who failed to meet math standards was 45.7 percent. What do these figures reveal, if anything, about the relationship between socioeconomic status and academic achievement, as measured by standardized tests? Do these numbers support or refute the notion that education funding is less important to educational "quality" than entrenched socioeconomic conditions? Do they support educational philosopher, Alfie Kohn's assertion that, "every empirical investigation . . . has found that socioeconomic status in all its particulars accounts for an overwhelming proportion of the variance in test scores when different schools' towns, or states are compared"? Kohn, *Fighting the Tests: A Practical Guide to Rescuing Our Schools*, Phi Delta Kappan (Jan. 2001). *See also No Excuses*, at 155.

Finally, within this relatively affluent district, there are several different neighborhood schools with uneven property wealth surrounding each school. One school's parent-teacher organization, through creative fund-raising initiatives, has raised $120,000 to be used by that school as the organization, the teachers and the administrators see fit. Another school in the same district is unable to raise any money from neighborhood fund-raising events. The families that attend that particular school do not have the same amount of disposable income as the parents on the other side of town. As a consequence, the more affluent school in the district is able to supplement state and local funds with its own money. It purchases computer monitors, software, playground equipment and even physical education equipment not available to the other, less affluent school in the same district. What, if anything, should that district's school board do about the blatant disparities in resources available to schools within the same district? What are the advantages and disadvantages of "revenue sharing," or pooling the funds raised by one school into a common fund for all district schools? What policy language, if any, should the district adopt regarding this "equity" issue?

2. Student Residence Requirements

As addressed in Chapter 3, the "practical side" of the state's power to require students to attend school is a local school district's responsibility to enforce school attendance and truancy laws. The "practical side" of a state's constitutional or political responsibility to educate its residents coupled with the disparate level of resources available within a state is often manifest in a school district's enforcement of its residency requirements.

A school district must provide a free public education to students who reside within the district, but not to students who do not reside in the district. As a consequence, districts are strongly encouraged to adopt student-residence policies. The policies often begin by proclaiming that a student may attend a district school on a "tuition-free basis" if the student's legal custodian is a resident of the district. Such policies necessarily require some process for determining the residency of a student's legal custodian. What procedures would you suggest a school district use to insure that its students are in the legal custody of a resident of the district?

Some districts require students to present an affidavit or certificate of residence, coupled with evidence of residence in the form of a driver's license, home ownership title or deed, apartment lease, voter registration, utility bills or perhaps automobile insurance. This procedure invariably raises many questions for the district's attorneys.

First, what are the consequences of a false certification? In districts that employ an affidavit requirement, the form is often accompanied by language such as: "falsification of information on this form or otherwise submitted to the District may result in the child's expulsion from school and may expose you to monetary liability for payment of tuition for such time as the child illegally attended school." The form also might warn of the possibility of criminal prosecution under state law for submitting false information to a public body. What are the advantages and disadvantages of such language?

Second, and related, what should a district do when it suspects that a false statement of residency in fact has been submitted? The district has two basic alternatives. It may simply ignore the false submission and permit the suspected nonresident to attend its schools on a tuition-free basis. Alternatively, the district may conduct a thorough investigation, either with the help of local law enforcement or on its own, to determine whether the information submitted is accurate. Each alternative has its pros and cons. What are they?

Third, suppose that the district is an extremely affluent one, and suspects that a significant number of its students are not actually residents of the district. The district believes that some of its students reside in a far less affluent surrounding area. The parents of these students apparently have been driving their children into the district early each morning and dropping them off at a district bus stop near the residence of a friend or relative who does reside in the district. The address of the friend or relative was submitted as the residence of the legal custodian of the student. In other words, the district suspects that nonresident students are being transported into the district to take advantage of the greater educational opportunities afforded by the affluent district. What, if anything, should be done?

Fourth, assume that the affluent district's school board decides that it should allow these nonresidents to attend the district's schools on a tuition-free basis in order to "correct" the blatant disparities in resources available to the state's citizens. The school board wishes to engage in its own social engineering by allowing students in less affluent districts with fewer resources to enjoy the resources otherwise available only to its own affluent families. The school board further claims that allowing these nonresidents access to its schools will have two long-term benefits for its own resident children: (1) it will reduce the costs of crime, poverty and health care that would otherwise have been created if these children had not received the benefits of an excellent education, and (2) it would expose the affluent students to a more diverse population. As the lawyer for the district, how would you advise the school board to proceed? What are the political consequences to the school board of allowing nonresidents to attend district schools?

Fifth, what would happen if district parents began conducting their own investigations by means of videotape and otherwise to demonstrate that nonresidents are being improperly transported into the school district?

Finally, suppose that the district decides to address its "residency" problem by conducting thorough investigations into the veracity of the residence information being submitted. As the district's attorney, what procedures would you recommend the district establish for such investigations? Would they include due process protections like a hearing before a neutral examiner, the opportunity for cross-examination and an appeals process? Can the district authorize a private investigator to conduct surprise inspections at the address submitted on the affidavit of residence to verify that the children actually reside there? What level of suspicion would justify that approach?

3. Homeless Students

The issue of student residency takes on an even more complex dimension when the student is homeless. School districts must afford their residents a free public education, but where does a homeless student reside? The question is not just an academic one. An alarming percentage of homeless people in America are school age children. U.S. Conference of Mayors, *A Status Report on Hunger and Homelessness in America's Cities* (1994) (finding 43 percent of the homeless in shelters to be homeless families). In 1987, Congress passed the McKinney Homeless Assistance Act, 42 U.S.C. §11431 *et. seq.*, which requires each state to "ensure that homeless children and youth are afforded the same free, appropriate public education as provided to other children and youth. . . ." The federal law also prohibits a state and a school district from defining a "compulsory residency requirement" in such a way as to deny a homeless student access to a free public education. *Id.* In 2001, in Title X, Chapter C, §1031 of the No Child Left Behind Act, Congress reinforced the McKinney Act by requiring that children who lack a fixed, regular and adequate nighttime residence receive the same public education as children who have such a residence. See also McKinney-Vento Homeless Education Assistance Improvement Act of 2001, 42 U.S.C. §1031 *et. seq.* In fact, these federal statutes now require districts to transport homeless children to a school located where the child last had a home. How would you advise a school district to meet the unique needs of a homeless child?

4. Lingering Questions

There is no federal constitutional right to an education, but states have the constitutional power to require virtually all of their citizens to attend school. Within each state, districts are given vastly different amounts of educational resources, yet those disparities are justified in part by the need for local control. No district can exercise its local control, however, to permit impoverished *nonresidents* to take advantage of its resources. On the other hand, each district must open its schools and its resources to some nonresidents who are homeless.

What, if anything, do these apparent contradictions indicate about the educational priorities in America? Can these apparent contradictions be reconciled by a consistent legal or political theory about education? Finally, what does the law suggest about the fundamental objective of public education in this country?

CHAPTER 5

THE LAW AND POLICY OF EARLY CHILDHOOD EDUCATION

Preschool is the new frontier of education law and policy. The evidence is unassailable that high-quality pre-kindergarten programs produce dramatic short-term and long-term educational, social, emotional and economic benefits. *See* W. Steven Barnett, "Benefits and Costs of Quality Early Childhood Education," 27 Child. Leg. R.J. 7 (Spring 2007). The evidence also demonstrates that there are tremendous racial and socioeconomic disparities in the level of pre-kindergarten programs available to the nation's three- and four-year-old children. This disparity results in a significant discrepancy in school readiness, and it also results in a virtually insurmountable "achievement" gap as early as kindergarten.

The evidence showing the importance of pre-K education and the inequity in access to that education raises several familiar, but particularly acute, legal questions. First, if there is a federal or state constitutional right to at least a "minimally adequate education," is there a right to a minimally adequate pre-kindergarten educational program? Second, if the state does provide pre-kindergarten programs to some of its children, must it also provide those programs to all of its children on equitable terms? Third, would additional state involvement in pre-kindergarten educational programs represent an intrusion into the interest of parents to direct the upbringing of their young children? Finally, if expansion of access to high-quality preschool programs is desirable, should that expansion be the result of judicial remedies or legislation?

A. THE LEGAL LANDSCAPE OF PRESCHOOL

Each of these questions is at play in the following two cases. In *Abbott v. Burke* (*Abbott V*), 153 N.J. 480 (1998), the New Jersey Supreme Court ordered the state to remedy its unconstitutional failure to give every child a "thorough and efficient" education by providing a high-quality preschool program to all three- and four-year-olds in thirty high-poverty school districts. In *Hoke County Board of Education v. State,* 599 S.E.2d 365 (2004), however, the North Carolina Supreme Court reversed the trial court's order requiring the state to provide preschool education to low-income students who were "at risk" of school failure. Although the *Hoke* court found that the state's failure to provide assistance to "at risk" children was unconstitutional, it concluded that the legislature, and not the courts, should design a comprehensive preschool remedy.

RAYMOND ABBOTT, ET AL. V. BURKE (ABBOTT V)

153 N.J. 480 (1998)

Our Constitution mandates that the "Legislature shall provide for the maintenance and support of a thorough and efficient system of free public schools for the instruction of all the children in the State between the ages of five and eighteen years." *N.J. Const.* art. VIII, §4, ¶ 1. This decision explains the remedial measures that must be implemented in order to ensure that public school children from the poorest urban communities receive the educational entitlements that the Constitution guarantees them.

The required remedial measures incorporate many of the recommendations made by Judge Michael Patrick King pursuant to the remand ordered by this Court in *Abbott v. Burke,* 149 N.J. 145 (1997) (*Abbott* IV). These measures are based on a solid evidentiary record that was fully informed by the views and recommendations of the Commissioner of the Department of Education, expert and knowledgeable witnesses offered by both parties, and the Special Master. Most important, the educational programs to be implemented through these remedial measures comport substantially with the statutory and regulatory policies that define the constitutional thorough and efficient education.

Disputes inevitably will occur and judicial intervention undoubtedly will be sought in the administration of the public education that will evolve under these remedial standards. Nevertheless, because of the Commissioner's strong proposals for educational reform and the Legislature's clear recognition of the need for comprehensive substantive educational programs and standards, we anticipate that these reforms will be undertaken and pursued vigorously and in good faith. Given those commitments, this decision should be the last major judicial involvement in the long and tortuous history of the State's extraordinary effort to bring a thorough and efficient education to the children in its poorest school districts. . . .

On January 22, 1998, Judge King issued his report and recommendation. After reviewing the different proposals put forth by the parties, he recommended that the following programs be implemented: whole-school reform, full-day kindergarten for five-year-olds, full-day pre-kindergarten for four- and three-year olds, summer school, school-based health and social services, an accountability system, and added security. The Court now addresses those recommended reforms and other proposed remedial measures.

II

The Commissioner proposed that elementary schools in the Abbott districts undergo "whole-school reform," a comprehensive approach to education that fundamentally alters the way in which decisions about education are made. A school implements whole-school reform by integrating reform throughout the school as a total institution rather than by simply adding reforms piecemeal. If carried out successfully, whole-school reform affects the culture of the entire school, including instruction, curriculum, and assessment. The reform covers education from the earliest levels, including pre-school, and can be particularly effective in enabling the disadvantaged children in poor urban communities to reach higher educational standards. . . .

Because the evidence in support of the success of whole-school reform . . . is impressive, we adopt Judge King's recommendation "that the State require the Abbott districts to adopt some version of a proven, effective whole school design. . . ." We direct that implementation proceed according to the schedule proposed by the Commissioner and . . . contain the essential elements identified by the Commissioner. Finally, we direct the Commissioner to implement as soon as feasible a comprehensive formal evaluation program . . . to verify that [whole-school reform] is being implemented successfully and is resulting in the anticipated levels of improvement in the Abbott elementary schools.

B.

This Court has consistently recognized and emphasized that early childhood education is essential for children in the [districts]. *See, e.g., Abbott* IV, *supra,* 149 N.J. at 183. Accordingly, both parties submitted major proposals in respect of early childhood education. The parties clearly recognized that early childhood programs are critically important and address the fact that, if at-risk children are to have any chance of achieving educational success, they must be education-ready. As recommended by the Commissioner and contemplated by the State's experts and the Special Master, early childhood education is consistent with whole-school reform's focus on early educational initiatives and grade-by-grade continuity and improvement. Early childhood education in the special needs districts is an integral component of whole-school reform.

1.

Both parties recommended full-day kindergarten for all Abbott five-year olds. According to the Commissioner's report, "[s]tudies have shown that well-planned, developmentally appropriate full-day kindergarten programs for five-year-olds clearly provide one of the most cost-effective strategies for lowering the dropout rate and helping children at-risk become more effective learners in elementary school, particularly in first grade." The Commissioner's report also indicated that studies showed that students in full-day programs benefit more academically than students in half-day programs. Judge King "strongly endorse[d] the State's commitment to full-day kindergarten." We concur.

Full-day kindergarten comports with the requirements of [whole-school reform]. Dr. Slavin testified that schools implementing [whole-school reform] should increase their half-day kindergarten programs to full-day ones. Further, full-day kindergarten comports with statutory policy. . . .

Finally, research clearly supports the notion that full-day kindergarten is an essential part of a thorough and efficient education for the Abbott children. Not only will the children benefit in the long-run, as the empirical evidence demonstrates, but they will also be better prepared to enter first grade and take advantage of the opportunities presented by . . . whole-school reform.

Full-day kindergarten is not yet available in all Abbott districts. The demonstrated need for this program is acute. Because [whole-school reform] will be implemented in the Abbott schools without further delay, and because the Commissioner himself has indicated a willingness to ensure the availability of adequate temporary facilities, we affirm Judge King's recommendation that full-day kindergarten be "implemented *immediately*." In those schools unable promptly to locate or obtain adequate classroom space or instructional staff, full-day kindergarten shall be provided by the commencement of the September 1999 school year. The Commissioner's endorsement of full-day kindergarten signals and underscores the State's commitment to provide or secure the funds and resources essential for the effectuation of this early childhood initiative.

2.

There is no fundamental disagreement over the importance of pre-school education. The Commissioner proposed half-day pre-school for four-year olds, and the plaintiffs and Dr. Odden recommended full-day pre-school for both three- and four-year olds. As the Commissioner's research itself demonstrates: "Well-planned, high quality half-day preschool programs . . . help close the gap between the home and school environments and the educational expectations that lead to academic success."

Empirical evidence strongly supports the essentiality of pre-school education for children in impoverished urban school districts. That evidence demonstrates that the earlier education begins, the greater the likelihood that students will develop language skills and the discipline necessary to succeed in school. A review of two major studies on pre-school cited by the parties, the High/Scope Perry Preschool study and the Abecedarian study, also reveals that there is a strong correlation between the intensity and duration of pre-school and later educational progress and achievement. The Commissioner's expert on childhood education, Dr. Slavin, noted that "the programs that have shown the greatest success are ones that provide more intensive services" and "start with three-year-olds rather than four-year-olds." Common experience confirms this empirical evidence that pre-school attendance is linked to success in school.

A 1996 report by the Carnegie Task Force on Learning in the Primary Grades lends further support to that conclusion. Carnegie Corp. of New York, *Years of Promise: A Comprehensive Learning Strategy for America's Children* (1996). The Report recommends that high-quality learning opportunities for children ages three to five be made universally available:

> During the preschool years, children make the developmental leaps that form the basis of later achievement. To get all children ready for school and for an education that meets high standards of achievement, the task force

> recommends that the nation make a commitment to expanded high-quality public and private early care and education programs *for children ages three to five,* supported by national, state, and local mechanisms that are coordinated to assure adequate financing. [*Id.* at xi (emphasis added)]

Part of the basis of that recommendation is that one-third of children entering elementary school lack basic school-readiness skills. *Id.* at 17. One reason for this deficit is that poor areas suffer from a scarcity of quality, publicly-funded early care and early education for three- to five-year olds. *Id.* at 57.

The evidence also shows that one of the most important functions of early childhood education is language development. At the hearing, evidence was produced showing that children in low income families suffer greatly in language development. Key elements of language development begin when a child is three and four; therefore, opportunities for those children to learn are lost if early childhood education does not begin at those ages.

The Legislature itself has recognized the necessity of early childhood education for three- and four-year olds in the poorest school districts. N.J.S.A. 18A:7F-16 provides that for districts in which the concentration of low income pupils is greater than 20% but less than 40%, early childhood aid "shall be distributed" for "the purpose of providing full day kindergarten and preschool classes and other early childhood programs and services." The statute does not specify whether the pre-school aid should be used for three-year olds or four-year olds or both. For districts in which the concentration of low income pupils is equal to or greater than 40%, the statute directs that additional funds be used "for the purpose of expanding instructional services previously specified [*i.e.*, pre-school classes and other early childhood services] to 3 year olds." *Ibid.* For districts, then, with a 40% concentration of poor students, it is mandatory that . . . funds be expended for the pre-school education of three-year olds. The statute next provides that should extra funds remain, they may be used, "in addition to the instructional services previously specified" [*i.e.*, the just mentioned pre-school for three-year olds and the aforementioned "early childhood programs"], for "the purpose of" providing "transition and social services to primary grade students." *Ibid.* The statute thus contemplates three tiers of funding: (1) undifferentiated funds to be expended on pre-school in Abbott districts with 20% poor; (2) additional monies that must be spent on pre-school education for three-year olds in districts with 40% poor; and (3) extra funds to be used for services for elementary school students in districts with funds remaining after the mandates of (1) and (2) have been met.

This construction of the statute is borne out by administrative regulation. *See* N.J.A.C. 6:19-3.2d (providing that beginning in the 2001-2002 school year, [funds] may be used only for "preschool, full-day kindergarten and other early childhood programs and services"). Finally, we note that GoodStarts, a full-day pre-school program for three- and four-year olds developed under the Kean administration under the name "Urban Early Childhood Initiative," evidences the early recognition of the value of such programs and is reflective of the same educational policy concerns underlying [New Jersey's Comprehensive Educational Improvement and Financing Act "CEIFA"].

In the vast majority of Abbott districts, more than 40% of the population is low income. For these Abbott districts, then, pre-school for three-year olds is legislatively mandated. As for the remaining handful of Abbott districts where between 20% and 39% of their respective citizens are poor, we note the following. The record is undisputed and, indeed, uncontrovertible that the conditions that work to deprive children of their constitutional entitlement to a thorough and efficient education are pervasive [in *all* the Abbott districts.] . . . Given the documented and undisputed similarity of conditions that deleteriously impact the ability of children throughout the Abbott districts to receive a sound education, it would be inconsistent with the legislative mandate underlying CEIFA for the Commissioner not to use his power under N.J.S.A. 18A:7F-6b to direct [all] Abbott districts to restructure their curricula in order to provide pre-school education for three-year olds and to reallocate and apply . . . funds to the cost of providing pre-school education for three-year olds. . . .

This Court is convinced that pre-school for three- and four-year olds will have a significant and substantial positive impact on academic achievement in both early and later school years. As the experts described, the long-term benefits amply justify this investment. Also, the evidence strongly supports the conclusion that, in the poor urban school districts, the earlier children start pre-school, the better prepared they are to face the challenges of kindergarten and first grade. It is this year-to-year improvement that is a critical condition for the attainment of a thorough and efficient education once a child enters regular public school.

Stated conversely, because the absence of such early educational intervention deleteriously undermines educational performance once the child enters public school, the provision of pre-school education also has strong constitutional underpinning. In light of our construction of N.J.S.A. 18A:7F-16, however, and the powers of the Commissioner delineated in N.J.S.A. 18A:7F-6b, we need not reach the constitutional issue. The provision in CEIFA for education of three-year-olds is a clear indication that the Legislature understood and endorsed the strong empirical link between early education and later educational achievement.

We note that N.J.S.A. 18A:7F-16 does not unequivocally require districts receiving . . . funds to provide a full day of pre-school for either three- or four-year olds. Because whole-school reform must be implemented gradually and pre-school education must itself be integrated as part of that comprehensive reform, we concur in the Commissioner's determination that, as an initial reform, a half-day of pre-school should enable Abbott children to be education-ready when they enter primary school and thus allow them to take advantage of the opportunity to receive the thorough and efficient education that whole-school reform will provide. The Court directs the Commissioner to exercise his power under N.J.S.A. 18A:7F-6b and -16 to require all Abbott districts to provide half-day pre-school for three- and four-year olds. The Court authorizes the Commissioner to require the Abbott schools to implement these programs as expeditiously as possible. In directing the implementation of pre-school programs in the Abbott schools, the Commissioner must ensure that such programs are adequately funded and assist the schools in meeting the need for transportation and other services, support, and resources related to such programs. The Commissioner may authorize cooperation with or the use of existing early childhood and day-care programs in the community. If any Abbott schools are able to obtain the space, supplies, teaching faculty, staff, and means of transportation that are necessary to implement these programs for the 1998-1999 school year, they should be supplied with the necessary funding to enable them to do so. The Commissioner shall ensure that all other Abbott schools shall have the resources and additional funds that are necessary to implement pre-school education by the commencement of the 1999-2000 school year. . . .

In summary, and consistent with this opinion, we determine and direct that the Commissioner implement whole-school reform; implement full-day kindergarten and a half-day pre-school program for three- and four-year olds as expeditiously as possible; implement the technology, alternative school, accountability, and school-to-work and college-transition programs; prescribe procedures and standards to enable individual schools to adopt additional or extended supplemental programs and to seek and obtain the funds necessary to implement those programs for which they have demonstrated a particularized need; implement the facilities plan and timetable he proposed; secure funds to cover the complete cost of remediating identified life-cycle and infrastructure deficiencies in Abbott school buildings as well as the cost of providing the space necessary to house Abbott students adequately; and promptly initiate effective managerial responsibility over school construction, including necessary funding measures and fiscal reforms, such as may be achieved through amendment of the Educational Facilities Act.

In directing remedial relief in the areas of whole school reform, supplemental programs, and facilities improvements, the Court remains cognizant of the interests of the parties, particularly those of plaintiffs who speak for and represent the at-risk children of the special needs districts. The lessons of the history of the struggle to bring these children a thorough and efficient education render it essential that their interests remain prominent, paramount, and fully protected.

Whether the measures for education reform that are to be implemented will result in a thorough and efficient education for the children in the Abbott districts depends, in the final analysis, on the extent to which there is a top-to-bottom commitment to ensuring that the reforms are conscientiously undertaken and vigorously carried forward. That commitment on the part of the Executive Branch has been demonstrated by the Commissioner's strong proposals and positive avowals to see these reforms through. The Legislature's commitment is evidenced by the sound and comprehensive public education that is contemplated by the statute within which these reforms will be effected. It is not enough, however, that the three branches of government, sometimes working together and sometimes at apparent odds, have each responded to the challenge to carry out the Constitution's command of a thorough and efficient education. We must reach the point where it is possible to say with confidence that the most disadvantaged school children in the State will not be left out or left behind in the fulfillment of that constitutional promise. Success for all will come only when the roots of the educational system—the local schools and districts, the teachers, the administrators, the parents, and the children themselves—embrace the educational opportunity encompassed by these reforms.

VIII

The Court directs that remedial relief consistent with this opinion be promptly undertaken.

NOTES AND QUESTIONS

1. The New Jersey Constitution guarantees a thorough and efficient education to children ages 5 to 18. What reasoning did the *Abbott* court use to extend the state's constitutional obligation to children of pre-kindergarten age?
2. Prior to the *Abbott V* decision, the New Jersey legislature had adopted curriculum standards for its public schools. In *Abbott v. Burke,* 149 N.J. 145 (1997) (*Abbott IV*), the New Jersey Supreme Court declared that those curriculum standards establish the benchmark for determining whether students are receiving a constitutionally mandated "thorough and efficient" education. How are those curriculum standards also relevant to the state's constitutional obligation to provide high-quality preschool programs?
3. The New Jersey Supreme Court in *Abbott V* relied on empirical research regarding the benefits of high-quality pre-kindergarten education programs. According to the court, what is that evidence, and how does it inform the court's constitutional analysis? More generally, what is the relevance of such empirical research to the judicial interpretation of a constitutional provision?
4. The *Abbott V* preschool decision was the culmination of decades of litigation challenging the state's method of financing public education. In *Robinson v. Cahill,* 62 N.J. 473 (1973), the New Jersey Supreme Court first addressed challenges by the state's low-income school districts to the state's use of property taxes to fund public education, which resulted in inadequate and inequitable resources in those districts. In 1990, the New Jersey Supreme Court in *Abbott v. Burke,* 119 N.J. 287 (1990) (*Abbott II*), held unconstitutional the state's maintenance of inadequate educational opportunities for children in those low-income districts. The court specifically found that "[m]any poor children start school with an approximately two-year disadvantage compared to many suburban youngsters." *Abbott v. Burke,* 149 N.J. at 179. The court further declared that "an intensive preschool and all day kindergarten enrichment program [would help] to reverse the educational disadvantage these children start out with." 119 N.J. at 373. In *Burke v. Abbott,* 136 N.J. 444 (1994) (*Abbott III*), the New Jersey Supreme Court again declared the state's educational funding regime unconstitutional and indicated that the state should employ preschool as a supplemental program to remedy its constitutional violations. In response to that court decision, the New Jersey legislature then enacted the Comprehensive

Education Improvement and Financing Act (CEIFA), N.J.S.A. §18A: 7F-16. The CEIFA created a foundation level for funding a basic education and also provided additional funds for preschool and full-day kindergarten programs for low-income three- and four-year-olds. In *Abbott IV*, 149 N.J. 145 (1997), however, the New Jersey Supreme Court found that the legislation had not allocated sufficient funds to meet the actual needs of low-income children. In the absence of sufficient legislative action, the Court remanded the remedial matter to a supreme court judge to hold an evidentiary hearing determining the funding and programmatic steps required to satisfy the educational needs of those children. At the hearing, Dr. W. Steven Barrett of the National Institute for Early Education Research (NIEER) offered comprehensive expert testimony regarding the benefits of high-quality preschool programs. Based on the evidence at the hearing, the Supreme Court judge recommended that the state provide funding for a full-day preschool program for all three- and four-year-olds in low-income districts. Finally, in *Abbott V,* the New Jersey Supreme Court ordered the state to provide "high quality" half-day pre-K programs for all of those three- and four-year-olds.

5. By any measure, the court-mandated *Abbott* preschool programs have been a great success. By the 2005-2006 school year, 40,500 three- and four-year-olds were enrolled in the program through public schools, private providers and Head Start centers. In 2007, NIEER published the *Abbott Preschool Program Longitudinal Effects Study*. The study measures the effects of the learning gains attributable to the preschool programs for children as they enter kindergarten. According to the study, there is

> clear evidence of the following: (1) classroom quality in the Abbott Preschool Program continues, on the whole, to improve; (2) that children who attend the program, whether in public schools, private settings or Head Start, are improving in language, literacy, and math at least through the end of their kindergarten year; and (3) that children who attend preschool for two years at both age 3 and 4 significantly out-perform those who attend for only one year at 4 years of age or do not attend at all.

Study, at 3.

Hoke County Board of Education v. State of North Carolina and the State Board of Education

599 S.E.2d 365 (N.C. 2004)

ORR, Justice.

The State of North Carolina and the State Board of Education ("the State"), as defendants, appeal from a trial court order concluding that the State had failed in its constitutional duty to provide certain students with the opportunity to attain a sound basic education, as defined by this Court's holding in *Leandro v. State,* 346 N.C. 336, 488 S.E.2d 249 (1997). We affirm the trial court on this part of the State's appeal with modifications. . . .

[T]he State appeals those portions of the trial court's order that direct the State to remedy constitutional deficiencies relating to the public school education provided to students in Hoke County. In its memoranda of law, the trial court, in sum, ultimately ordered the State to: (1) assume the responsibility for, and correct, those educational methods and practices that contribute to the failure to provide students with a constitutionally-conforming education; and (2) expand pre-kindergarten educational programs so that they reach and serve all qualifying "at-risk" students. As for the trial court's first remedy, we affirm, with modifications. As for the trial court's second remedy, we reverse, concluding that the mandate requiring expanded pre-kindergarten programs amounts to a judicial interdiction that, under present circumstances, infringes on the constitutional duties and expectations of the legislative and executive branches of government.

On cross-appeal, plaintiff-intervenors argue that the trial court erred by including educational services provided by *federal* funds in making its determination of whether the State is meeting its constitutional obligation to provide North Carolina's children with a sound basic education. We disagree with plaintiff-intervenors' contention and, therefore, affirm the trial court.

I. Introduction

This case is a continuation of the landmark decision by this Court, unanimously interpreting the North Carolina Constitution to recognize that the legislative and executive branches have the duty to provide all the children of North Carolina the opportunity for a sound basic education. This litigation started primarily as a challenge to the educational funding mechanism imposed by the General Assembly that resulted in disparate funding outlays among low wealth counties and their more affluent counterparts. With the *Leandro* decision, however, the thrust of this litigation turned from a funding issue to one requiring the analysis of the qualitative educational services provided to the respective plaintiffs and plaintiff-intervenors. . . .

The *Leandro* decision and the ensuing trial have resulted in the thrust of the instant case breaking down into the following contingencies: (1) Does the evidence show that the State has failed to provide Hoke County school children with the opportunity to receive a sound basic education, as defined in *Leandro;* (2) if so, has the State demonstrated that its failure to provide such an opportunity is necessary to promote a compelling government interest; and (3) if the State has failed to provide Hoke County school children with the opportunity for a sound basic education *and* failed to demonstrate that its public educational shortcomings are necessary to promote a compelling government interest, does the relief granted by the trial court correct the failure with minimal encroachment on the other branches of government? . . .

We begin our examination under the umbrella of the State's first argument—namely, whether there was a clear showing of evidence supporting the trial court's conclusion that "the constitutional mandate of *Leandro* has been violated [in the Hoke County School System] and action must be taken by both the LEA [Local Educational Area] and the State to remedy the violation." After a comprehensive examination of the record and arguments of the parties, this Court concludes that the trial court was correct as to this issue and thus we affirm, albeit with modifications. . . .

In our view, the trial court conducted an appropriate and informative path of inquiry concerning the issue at hand. After determining that the evidence clearly showed that Hoke County students were failing, at an alarming rate, to obtain a sound basic education, the trial court in turn determined that the evidence presented also demonstrated that a combination of State action and inaction contributed significantly to the students' failings. Then, after concluding that the State's overall funding and resource provisions scheme was adequate on a statewide basis, the trial court determined that the evidence showed that the State's method of funding and providing for individual school districts such as Hoke County was such that it did not comply with *Leandro*'s mandate of ensuring that all children of the state be provided with the opportunity for a sound basic education. In particular, the trial court concluded the State's failing was essentially twofold in that the State: (1) failed to identify the inordinate number of "at-risk" students and provide a means for such students to avail themselves of the opportunity for a sound basic education; and (2) failed to oversee how educational funding and resources were being used and implemented in Hoke County schools.

At that point, the trial court also concluded that the State's failings, as demonstrated by the evidence, needed to be rectified. . . .

V. Proper School Age/Pre-Kindergarten

The next two issues of the instant appeal by the State are outgrowths of one another. As a consequence, we address them in tandem. Initially, the State contends that the trial court erred when it ruled that the proper age for school children was a justiciable issue. In the State's view, the proper age at which children should be permitted to attend public school is a nonjusticiable political question reserved for the General Assembly. To the extent that the State argues that establishing the proper age parameters for starting and completing school—i.e., kindergarten, the entering class for public school students, shall be composed of five-year-olds—we agree. Article IX, Section 3 of the North Carolina Constitution provides that "[t]he General Assembly shall provide that every child of appropriate age . . . shall attend the public schools." Pursuant to such authority, the General Assembly has determined that five-year-olds *may* attend school and that seven-year-olds *must* attend school. N.C.G.S. §§115C-364, -378 (2003). Our reading of the constitutional and statutory provisions leads us to conclude that the determination of the proper age for school children has indeed been squarely placed in the hands of the General Assembly. In addition, the United States Supreme Court has defined issues as nonjusticiable when either of the following circumstances is evident: (1) when the Constitution commits an issue, as here, to one branch of government; *or* (2) when satisfactory and manageable criteria or standards do not exist for judicial determination of the issue. *Baker v. Carr,* 369 U.S. 186, 210, 7 L. Ed. 2d 663, 682 (1962). In our view, not only are the applicable statutory and constitutional provisions persuasive in and of themselves, but the evidence in this case demonstrates that the trial court was without satisfactory or manageable judicial criteria that could justify mandating changes with regard to the proper age for school children. Thus, with regard to the issue of whether the trial court erred by interfering with the province of the

General Assembly—establishing the appropriate age for students entering the public school system—we conclude that the trial court did so err. First, our state's constitutional provisions and corresponding statutes serve to establish the issue as the exclusive province of the General Assembly and, second, there was no evidence at trial indicating the trial court had satisfactory or manageable criteria that would justify modifying legislative efforts. As a consequence, the Court holds that any trial court rulings that infringed on the legislative prerogative of establishing school-age eligibility were in error.

However, when considered in the context of the related issue of pre-kindergarten programs, the crux of this issue is less about whether school must be offered to four-year-olds than it is about whether the State must help prepare those students who enter the schools to avail themselves of an opportunity to obtain a sound basic education. While the General Assembly may be empowered to establish the actual age for beginning school, the question of whether the General Assembly must address the particular needs of children prior to entering the school system is a distinct and separate inquiry. For example, the General Assembly, in its discretion, could establish that mandatory school attendance begins at four years of age, five years of age, or six years of age. However, the State's power to establish such an age does not answer the question of whether or not it must address the particular needs of those children who are, or are approaching, the established age for school admission. Thus, the issue before us is less about at-risk four-year-olds than it is about at-risk children approaching and/or attaining school-age eligibility as established by the General Assembly.

In our view, the evidence presented at trial clearly supported these findings and conclusions by the trial court: (1) A large number of Hoke County students had failed to obtain a sound basic education; (2) a large number of Hoke County students were being denied their rightful opportunity to a sound basic education because the State had failed in its duty to provide the necessary means for such an opportunity; (3) there were an inordinate number of "at-risk" students attending Hoke County schools; (4) the special needs attendant to such "at-risk" students were not being met; and (5) it was ultimately the State's responsibility to meet the needs of "at-risk" students in order for such students to avail themselves of their right to the opportunity to obtain a sound basic education. In addition to ordering the State to reassess its resource allocations to Hoke County schools in an effort to improve them for students currently in attendance, the trial court heard evidence concerning the plight of those children who were about to enter the school system. Plaintiffs essentially argued that such evidence was relevant because it would show that the problem of "at-risk" students extended beyond those students already in school and would thereby support additional remedies that specifically targeted incoming students. Once the problems of "at-risk" students had been demonstrated at trial, it was not beyond the reach of the trial court to hear evidence concerning whether preemptive action on the part of the State might assist in resolving the problems of such "at-risk" students. Thus, we conclude that because the evidence presented showed that "at-risk" students in Hoke County were being denied their right to an opportunity to obtain a sound basic education, the trial court properly admitted additional evidence intended to show that preemptive action on the part of the State should target those children about to enroll, recognizing that preemptive action affecting such children prior to their entering the public schools might well be far more cost effective than waiting until they are actually in the educational system.

We now turn our attention to the trial court's findings and conclusions concerning "at-risk" children who are or were about to enter the Hoke County school system. In paragraph 74a of their complaint, plaintiffs alleged that "many ['at-risk'] children living in [Hoke County] begin public school kindergarten at a severe disadvantage. They do not have the basic skills and knowledge needed for kindergarten and as a foundation for the remainder of . . . school." Plaintiffs also alleged that "the lack of pre-kindergarten services and programs" offered in Hoke County deprived such students from receiving their opportunity for a sound basic education, and said that [Hoke County] schools "do not have sufficient resources to provide the pre-kindergarten and other programs and services needed for a sound basic education." As relief for the allegations raised in paragraph 74a, plaintiffs sought an order from the trial court that would, in essence, compel the State to provide remedial and preparatory pre-kindergarten services to "at-risk" four-year-olds in Hoke County.

In assessing the evidence presented at trial pertaining to the allegations of paragraph 74a, the trial court found: (1) that there was an inordinate number of "at-risk" children who were entering the Hoke County school district; (2) that such "at-risk" children were starting behind their non–"at-risk" counterparts; and (3) that such "at-risk" children were likely to stay behind, or fall further behind, their non–"at-risk" counterparts as they continued their education. In addition, the trial court found that the evidence showed that the State was providing inadequate resources for such "at-risk" prospective enrollees, and that the State's failings were contributing to the "at-risk" prospective enrollees' subsequent failure to avail themselves of the opportunity to obtain a sound basic education. In support of its findings, the trial court tracked and noted the number and percentage of prospective enrollees who ultimately entered Hoke County schools as "at-risk" students, and referred to other evidence demonstrating the students' lack of success as they continued through school. As for evidence concerning the State's failure to identify such "at-risk" prospective enrollees and its failure to provide remedial services so such "at-risk" students could avail themselves of a *Leandro*-conforming educational opportunity, the trial court found that the State's current remedial programs for "at-risk" prospective enrollees in Hoke County were limited to three pre-kindergarten classes serving eighteen students each. Other testimony at trial indicated that besides the fifty-four students who were attending such remedial classes, there were over 300 more who would benefit from such classes. The trial court additionally noted that the three class offerings were funded by a combination of state "Smart Start" and federal "Title One" monies.

As a consequence of its findings, the trial court concluded that State efforts towards providing remedial aid to "at-risk" prospective enrollees were inadequate. To that point in the proceedings, we agree with the trial court, and we hold that the evidence supports its findings of fact and that its findings support its conclusions of law. In our view, judging by its actions, it appears that even the State concedes that "at-risk" prospective enrollees in Hoke County are in need of assistance in order to avail themselves of their right to the opportunity for a sound basic education. Yet, there is a marked difference between the State's recognizing a need to assist "at-risk" students prior to enrollment in the public schools and a court order compelling the legislative and executive branches to address that need in a singular fashion. In our view, while the trial court's findings and conclusions concerning the problem of "at-risk" prospective enrollees are well supported by the evidence, a similar foundational support cannot be ascertained for the trial court's order requiring the State to provide pre-kindergarten classes for either all of the State's "at-risk" prospective enrollees or all of Hoke County's "at-risk" prospective enrollees. Certainly, when the State fails to live up to its constitutional duties, a court is empowered to order the deficiency remedied, and if the offending branch of government or its agents either fail to do so or have consistently shown an inability to do so, a court is empowered to provide relief by imposing a specific remedy and instructing the recalcitrant state actors to implement it. . . . However, such specific court-imposed remedies are rare, and strike this Court as inappropriate at this juncture of the instant case for two related reasons: (1) The subject matter of the instant case—public school education—is clearly designated in our state Constitution as the shared province of the legislative and executive branches; and (2) the evidence and findings of the trial court, while supporting a conclusion that "at-risk" children require additional assistance and that the State is obligated to provide such assistance, do not support the imposition of a narrow remedy that would effectively undermine the authority and autonomy of the government's other branches.

While this Court assuredly recognizes the gravity of the situation for "at-risk" prospective enrollees in Hoke County and elsewhere, and acknowledges the imperative need for a solution that will prevent existing circumstances from remaining static or spiraling further, we are equally convinced that the evidence indicates that the State shares our concerns and, more importantly, that the State has already begun to assume its responsibilities for implementing corrective measures. At the time of the trial, Smart Start, a public-private partnership that provides funds for early childhood welfare programs, was already in place. While Smart Start is not principally a pre-kindergarten education program, monies from the program often help LEAs establish and maintain pre-kindergarten classes. Hoke County and Charlotte-Mecklenburg schools were among a group of LEAs that operated such programs when this case was being heard. Although evidence at trial indicated that the State and Charlotte-Mecklenburg schools were at odds over the effectiveness of the latter's Bright Beginnings program, other testimony and evidence showed that State officials: (1) recognized the need for, and effectiveness of, early intervention programs like pre-kindergarten; and (2) had authorized the establishment of such programs by LEAs that desired them.

Meanwhile, plaintiffs, and even the trial court seem to suggest that the State's claims and evidence concerning the issue amounted to little more than lip service, and that the evidence at trial more accurately reflected a showing that the State, to the point of the trial, had done nothing to provide for a statewide pre-kindergarten program and had done nothing to expand pre-kindergarten services to the nearly 300 other Hoke County "at-risk" prospective enrollees who were eligible for such classes. In further support of that view, this Court notes that among all the reports submitted to the trial court by the State since the trial concluded, the State makes no mention of its efforts, continuing or otherwise, on behalf of "at-risk" prospective enrollees in Hoke County. But even if this Court were to concur fully with plaintiffs' view, we note that the question before us does not concern the extent of the State's compliance with the trial court's order regarding pre-kindergarten for "at-risk" prospective enrollees in Hoke County schools, but *whether the State must comply* with that portion of the order. In our view, there is inadequate foundational support for an order that compels the State to provide pre-kindergarten services for all "at-risk" prospective enrollees in Hoke County. At this juncture, the suggestion that pre-kindergarten is the sole vehicle or, for that matter, a proven effective vehicle by which the State can address the myriad problems associated with such "at-risk" prospective enrollees is, at best, premature.

The evidence shows that the State recognizes the extent of the problem—its deficiencies in affording "at-risk" prospective enrollees their guaranteed opportunity to obtain a sound basic education—and its obligation to address and correct it. However, a single or definitive means for achieving constitutional compliance for such students has yet to surface from the depths of the evidentiary sea. Certainly, both sides have conceded that pre-kindergarten is, and can be, an effective method for preparing "at-risk" prospective enrollees for the rigors of their forthcoming education. Nevertheless, neither side has demonstrated to the satisfaction of this Court that it is either the only qualifying means or even the only known qualifying means. The state's legislative and executive branches have been endowed by their creators, the people of North Carolina, with the authority to establish and maintain a public school system that ensures all the state's children will be given their chance to get a proper—that is, a *Leandro*-conforming—education. As a consequence of such empowerment, those two branches have developed a shared history and expertise in the field that dwarfs that of this and any other Court. While we remain the ultimate arbiters of our state's Constitution, and vigorously attend to our duty of protecting the citizenry from abridgments and infringements of its provisions, we simultaneously recognize our limitations in providing specific remedies for violations committed by other government branches in service to a subject matter, such as public school education, that is within their primary domain. Thus, we conclude that the trial court erred when it imposed at this juncture of the litigation and on this record the requirement that the State must provide pre-kindergarten classes for all "at-risk" prospective enrollees in Hoke County. In our view, based on the evidence presented at trial, such a remedy is premature, and its strict enforcement could undermine the State's ability to meet its educational obligations for "at-risk" prospective enrollees by alternative means. As a consequence, we reverse those portions of the trial court order that may be construed to the effect of requiring the State to provide pre-kindergarten services as the remedy for constitutional violations referenced in . . . this opinion. . . .

In closing, we recount in summary the Court's major conclusions and holdings concerning the issues of the case before us. Initially, this Court affirms the trial court's conclusion that plaintiffs have made a clear showing that an inordinate number of students in Hoke County are failing to obtain a sound basic education and that defendants have failed in their constitutional duty to provide such students with the opportunity to obtain a sound basic education. In addition, this Court affirms the trial court's ruling that the State must act to correct those deficiencies that were deemed by the trial court as contributing to the State's failure of providing a *Leandro*-comporting educational opportunity.

As for the State's contention that it is the sole arbiter of determining the proper age for attending schools, we agree. Concerning the trial court's remedy for the State's failure to provide Hoke County prospective enrollees with an opportunity to avail themselves of a sound basic education, we reverse. In our view, the trial court's mandate requiring the State to offer pre-kindergarten services to at-risk prospective enrollees would be, at this juncture, a premature judicial encroachment on a core function of our state's legislative and executive branches.

In addition, we affirm the trial court's ruling concerning the State's use of federal contributions in designing and implementing an education financing scheme. In our view, the question of whether federal funds are properly being utilized by the State is one best answered by consulting the federal statutory framework that provides for such funds. As the clear language of the applicable statutes expressly grants the Secretary the power to decide the question of whether state expenditures of federal education funds comports with federal law, we defer to the Secretary's judgment and note that there was no evidence at trial showing that the State's use of such funds had spurred retaliatory action by the Secretary. As a consequence, we can find no error in the trial court's ruling that the State's use of federal education funds did not violate either federal law or our state's Constitution.

As for the pending cases involving either other rural school districts or urban school districts, we order that they should proceed, as necessary, in a fashion that is consistent with the tenets outlined in this opinion.

Finally, the Court notes that the original Constitution of our state, adopted on 18 December 1776, included the specific provision "[t]hat a school or schools shall be established by the legislature, for the convenient instruction of youth." N.C. Const. of 1776, para. 41. Some months before, William Hooper, one of North Carolina's delegates to the Continental Congress in Philadelphia, had solicited information from John Adams as to his thoughts on what should be included in a soon-to-be drafted constitution for North Carolina. Modern historians note that at the time, Adams was considered a "renowned authority on constitutionalism," John V. Orth, *The North Carolina State Constitution: A Reference Guide* 2 (1993), and that as he contemplated the future of the country, Adams became convinced that its success rested on education, *see* David McCullough, *John Adams,* 364 (Simon & Schuster 2001).

Adams, in subsequent correspondence, wrote: "[A] memorable change must be made in the system of education[,] and knowledge must become so general as to raise the lower ranks of society nearer to the higher. The education of a nation[,] instead of being confined to a few schools and universities for the instruction of the few, must become the national care and expense for the formation of the many." *Id.*

This Court now remands to the lower court and ultimately into the hands of the legislative and executive branches, one more installment in the 200-plus year effort to provide an education to the children of North Carolina. Today's challenges are perhaps more difficult in many ways than when Adams articulated his vision for what was then a fledgling agrarian nation. The world economy and technological advances of the twenty-first century mandate the necessity that the State step forward, boldly and decisively, to see that all children, without regard to their socio-economic circumstances, have an educational opportunity and experience that not only meet the constitutional mandates set forth in *Leandro,* but fulfill the dreams and aspirations of the founders of our state and nation. Assuring that our children are afforded the chance to become contributing, constructive members of society is paramount. Whether the State meets this challenge remains to be determined.

AFFIRMED IN PART AS MODIFIED, AND REVERSED IN PART.

NOTES AND QUESTIONS

1. The North Carolina Supreme Court in *Hoke* reversed the trial court's remedial decision to require the state to provide preschool programs to at-risk children. The Court defined "at-risk" children as those who have "one or more of the following characteristics: (1) member of low-income family; (2) participate in free or reduced-cost lunch programs; (3) have parents with a low-level education; (4) show limited proficiency in English; (5) are a member of a racial or ethnic minority group; (6) live in a home headed by a single parent or guardian."
2. The *Hoke* Court found a judicially imposed remedy to be premature because the trial court record lacked an evidentiary foundation for such a remedy, and the legislature had not had an initial opportunity to develop a preschool program. What additional evidence would have provided the foundation for a judicially imposed remedy requiring the provision of preschool to at-risk children? Why did the *Hoke* court withdraw its remedial power and allow the legislature to design a preschool program, while the *Abbott* court imposed its own remedy?
3. After the trial court entered its order requiring the state to provide preschool to at-risk four-year-olds (but before that order was reversed), the North Carolina legislature in fact began a statewide preschool program for at-risk four-year-olds. The state's so-called More-at-Four program, which has been advanced by the legislature and the governor, serves 11,000 at-risk four-year-olds. The state's lawmakers and governor cite the

continuing threat of *Hoke* litigation as support for their efforts to expand the program.

4. In *High Quality Pre-Kindergarten as the First Step in Educational Adequacy: Using the Courts to Expand Access to State Pre-K Programs,* 27 Child. Legal Rts. J. 24 (Spring 2007), Ellen Boylan demonstrates how education finance litigation can be used to expand access to state-funded, high-quality pre-K programs, particularly for disadvantaged students. Through her work at the Education Law Center, Boylan has supported litigation challenging the inadequacy of state funding for preschool programs as a violation of the state's constitution. *See also* James E. Ryan, *A Constitutional Right to Preschool?,* 94 Cal. L. Rev. 49 (2006). The challenge begins by demonstrating the absence of minimally adequate, publicly funded pre-K programs for large segments of students. As the *Abbott* litigation suggests, in light of the overwhelming benefits of preschool, a state's failure to provide minimally adequate preschool programs for students violates the constitutional mandate in many states. Since *Abbott,* litigants have attacked inequitable and inadequate preschool funding and access head-on, and they have sought remedies specifically tailored to early childhood education. Boylan documents five state courts that already have issued decisions regarding pre-K funding inadequacies, and she is tracking pending school finance cases in at least ten other jurisdictions that include claims for increased preschool funding. *See* Boylan, 27 Child. Legal Rts. J. at 26; www.startingat3.org/news/Sa3news_080714_PreK_Litigation_Update.htm (Aug. 12, 2008).

B. THE POLITICAL LANDSCAPE OF PRESCHOOL

1. Evidence of the Benefits of High-Quality Pre-Kindergarten Educational Programs

The National Institute for Early Education Research (NIEER) has performed and compiled extensive research regarding the benefits and costs of early childhood education. That research is available at www.nieer.org. The evidence developed through myriad discrete and longitudinal studies demonstrates that the educational, social, emotional and long-term economic benefits of early childhood education are significant. Those benefits are particularly dramatic in children from poor socioeconomic conditions or minority groups. Yet the benefits are also significant for non-minority children from other socioeconomic conditions. The research further shows that the benefits of high-quality early-childhood education markedly outweigh the costs required to provide those benefits. An investment of resources in early childhood education produces an astonishing return on that investment.

As the result of his own pathbreaking research and his analysis of all of the available evidence, W. Steven Barnett of NIEER concludes:

> A solid body of evidence demonstrates that high quality preschool education can produce substantial gains in language, cognitive, social, and emotional

development. The largest amount of evidence pertains to children from lower-income families. For these children, it is clear that early gains can lead to long-term increases in educational success and, in turn, adult social and economic success. Several economic analyses show that these benefits substantially outweigh the costs. From a societal perspective, public investments in high quality preschool education are warranted on purely economic grounds. In addition, such investments have the potential to improve educational and economic equality.

It is clear from national data that children from lower-income families begin school far behind in their learning and development. This gap at the schoolhouse door makes it difficult for these children to succeed in school, and school failure makes it difficult for them to succeed socially and economically as adults. When the gap for children in poverty starting school is eighteen months, it is unreasonable to expect public education to close this gap after the fact. It makes more sense to prevent it from becoming so large in the first place.

Research suggests that it is possible to shrink the learning and development gap by the time children begin school with high quality preschool education. However, public policies are relatively weak in this regard. Not all children in poverty have access to programs and the programs they do have access to often are not high quality. Although evidence on the correlation between the effects of quality and quantity on child outcomes is mixed, the experimental evidence is less mixed. Intensive high quality programs can produce substantial gains. The Abecedarian study is about as direct a test of high quality versus current circumstances (many of the children attended what would be considered fairly good child care by current standards) as can be found, and the results are clear. Whether the concern is with economic efficiency or children's rights the conclusion is that our nation invests too little in providing children who can benefit the most with access to preschool education and assurance that those programs are of optimal quality.

Public action is needed to produce more optimal investments in the education of young children. Given their relatively low costs, Head Start and state pre-kindergarten programs might pass a simple cost-benefit test. However, they are still not optimal. They neglect the benefits from child care when they are offered only as part-day programs and they still fall short of desirable educational quality. Child care policy is in even worse shape because for all practical purposes, educational quality is ignored when the emphasis is on providing the maximum number of hours of care at the least cost. Even when child care programs are brought up to educational standards similar to those of state pre-kindergarten programs, high rates of turnover—which are partly due to rules requiring predetermination of eligibility based on income or employment status—can preclude educational continuity. The education and child care policies need to be brought together rationally to realize the potential gains from offering highly educational programs that meet parents' needs for child care.

Most public support for preschool education targets children in poverty or low-income families. This is supported by evidence that shows high returns for public investments in the education of these young children. Unfortunately, there are several problems with this approach in practice. First, programs are trying to target a status that changes fairly frequently with a service that must be provided consistently over a sustained time. The result is a

> failure to successfully serve much of the target population. Second, benefits to children's learning and development extend up the income ladder far beyond poverty. If the goal is to prevent the majority of school failure and dropout, this cannot be accomplished by ignoring the middle class. There is a very real sense that the dichotomy between the poor and everyone else is false when it comes to early childhood learning and development. There is no sharp dividing line, and exhausting resources to target certain children may not be an economically efficient strategy. Finally, there is ample evidence that programs for children in poverty are limited by weak public support. For example, after forty years, Head Start still does not reach all of the eligible population and its teachers are paid far less than those in universal public schools. Free high quality public preschool education for all children is one option that might actually prove a better economic investment than targeted programs for children in poverty.

W. Steven Barnett, *Benefits and Costs of Early Childhood Education,* 27 Child. Legal Rts. J. 7, 14-15 (2007).

2. The Movement toward Universal Preschool

In light of the overwhelming research demonstrating the benefits of high-quality early-education programs, the states have become increasingly receptive to the creation or expansion of such programs. According to NIEER, 49 states have instituted at least some pre-K initiatives, 38 states offer publicly funded pre-K programs, and 27 states offer pre-K programs that are targeted at low-income students. *The State of Preschool,* NIEER (2007). Enrollment in state-funded pre-K programs has steadily increased. Nonetheless, only 22 percent of four-year-olds and 3 percent of three-year-olds are being served. The chart on the following page summarizes NIEER's data regarding access to preschool programs throughout the country.

In its most comprehensive report, NIEER surveyed the landscape of early childhood education in America and concluded:

> Participation in preschool education has grown steadily over the past several decades in the United States. Most American children spend time in a pre-K classroom at age 4 and many attend at age 3 as well. This trend contributes to the development of the nation's children and has the potential to substantially reduce educational inequality in the United States. Yet, pre-K participation in the United States remains highly unequal, with many children starting out behind before they begin kindergarten. This inequality in preschool education participation seems likely to exacerbate rather than ameliorate educational inequality. The rising tide of preschool education participation has not lifted all boats equally and the factors that predicted inequality in 1991 still predicted inequality in 2005. In addition, strong regional differences in pre-K participation became apparent by the end of the decade.
>
> The children least likely to attend pre-K are those whose parents have the least education and least income, whose mothers do not work outside the home and who live in the western and midwestern regions of our country. Hispanic children appear to be particularly disadvantaged as they have a much lower rate of preschool education participation than other children but

ACCESS FOR 4-YEAR-OLDS RANK	STATE	PERCENT OF CHILDREN ENROLLED IN STATE PRE-KINDERGARTEN (2006-2007)			NUMBER OF CHILDREN ENROLLED IN STATE PRE-KINDERGARTEN (2006-2007)		
		4-year-olds	3-year-olds	Total (3s and 4s)	4-year-olds	3-year-olds	Total (3s and 4s)
1	Oklahoma	68.4%	0.0%	34.2%	34,375	0	34,375
2	Florida	56.7%	0.0%	28.3%	124,390	0	124,390
3	Georgia	53.3%	0.0%	26.6%	74,155	0	74,155
4	West Virginia	45.8%	5.1%	25.5%	9,586	1,073	10,659
5	Texas	45.2%	4.4%	24.7%	170,313	16,925	187,238
6	Vermont	44.9%	15.6%	30.1%	2,908	1,028	3,936
7	South Carolina	37.8%	0.6%	19.3%	21,367	349	21,716
8	Wisconsin	36.1%	0.8%	18.4%	24,878	550	25,428
9	New York	34.6%	0.5%	17.5%	83,505	1,155	84,660
10	Maryland	34.0%	1.2%	17.6%	24,825	849	25,674
11	Kentucky	29.3%	10.7%	19.9%	15,808	5,815	21,623
12	Illinois	26.7%	18.5%	22.6%	47,108	32,711	79,819
13	New Jersey	25.3%	15.1%	20.1%	28,240	17,259	45,499
14	Louisiana	24.4%	0.0%	12.3%	14,543	0	14,543
15	Arkansas	21.4%	10.8%	16.1%	8,148	4,068	12,216
16	Michigan	16.9%	0.0%	8.5%	21,801	0	21,801
17	Maine	16.3%	0.0%	8.1%	2,263	0	2,263
18	Connecticut	15.6%	4.5%	10.0%	6,625	1,907	8,532
19	Kansas	15.6%	0.0%	7.8%	5,971	0	5,971
20	Tennessee	15.6%	1.0%	8.3%	12,293	753	13,046
21	North Carolina	14.8%	0.0%	7.4%	17,961	0	17,961
22	Colorado	14.6%	3.1%	8.8%	9,784	2,084	11,868
23	Virginia	12.5%	0.0%	6.3%	12,501	0	12,501
24	California	10.8%	5.0%	7.9%	56,254	26,318	82,572
25	Massachusetts	10.3%	9.2%	9.8%	8,047	7,153	15,200
26	New Mexico	8.9%	0.9%	4.9%	2,497	242	2,739
27	Delaware	7.6%	0.0%	3.7%	843	0	843
28	Pennsylvania	7.2%	2.2%	4.7%	10,329	3,255	13,548
29	Washington	5.8%	1.4%	3.6%	4,671	1,163	5,834
30	Arizona	5.5%	0.0%	2.7%	5,076	0	5,076
31	Oregon	4.8%	2.6%	3.7%	2,235	1,203	3,438
32	Missouri	4.3%	2.2%	3.3%	3,262	1,710	4,972
33	Iowa	4.0%	1.4%	2.7%	1,515	518	2,033
34	Nebraska	4.0%	2.0%	3.0%	977	496	1,473
35	Ohio	3.4%	1.3%	2.3%	4,979	1,870	6,849
36	Nevada	2.2%	0.4%	1.3%	799	140	939
37	Minnesota	1.9%	1.3%	1.6%	1,245	864	2,109
38	Alabama	1.8%	0.0%	0.9%	1,062	0	1,062
No program	Alaska	0.0%	0.0%	0.0%	0	0	0
No program	Hawaii	0.0%	0.0%	0.0%	0	0	0
No program	Idaho	0.0%	0.0%	0.0%	0	0	0
No program	Indiana	0.0%	0.0%	0.0%	0	0	0
No program	Mississippi	0.0%	0.0%	0.0%	0	0	0
No program	Montana	0.0%	0.0%	0.0%	0	0	0
No program	New Hampshire	0.0%	0.0%	0.0%	0	0	0
No program	North Dakota	0.0%	0.0%	0.0%	0	0	0
No program	Rhode Island	0.0%	0.0%	0.0%	0	0	0
No program	South Dakota	0.0%	0.0%	0.0%	0	0	0
No program	Utah	0.0%	0.0%	0.0%	0	0	0
No program	Wyoming	0.0%	0.0%	0.0%	0	0	0
50 states' population		21.8%	3.2%	12.5%	877,139	131,458	1,008,597

apparently not because cultural values lead them to avoid such programs. African-American children have somewhat higher rates of participation than might be expected given their family resources and location.

In the most educated families, preschool education participation rates at age 4 are almost as high as kindergarten participation rates. Over the last decade, there has been progress in closing the attendance gap for 4-year-old children of the least educated parents. This likely reflects the growth of Head Start and state preschool education programs. However, these targeted programs have not fully accomplished their goals with respect to access. Targeted programs have enrolled far more children than the number who are in poverty or whose mothers are high school dropouts. However, targeted programs still do not reach many of those eligible.

Targeted programs fail to fully accomplish their goals. This is in part due to the dynamic nature of the population, which leads to difficulties in identification, changes in eligibility, and geographic mobility. Also, targeted programs do not adequately address issues of access for children whose families have modest incomes and have lower participation rates than even children in poverty.

In addition to the inequalities in overall access just noted, it is apparent that inequality in access to preschool education is greater at age 3 than at age 4. Improvements in access for the most disadvantaged children from 1991 to 2005 seem largely limited to 4-year-olds. Thus, more advantaged children are not just more likely to go to pre-K before they enter kindergarten; they are likely to have started at an earlier age. Although this could, at least in part, reflect differences in attitudes about the appropriate time for children to enter preschool education programs, public policy in the United States undoubtedly plays a role. Head Start serves considerably fewer children at age 3 than at age 4. Most state pre-K programs serve only or primarily 4-year-olds. The consequences are readily apparent.

How might public policy in the United States decrease inequities in preschool education participation at ages 3 and 4? One approach would be to expand targeted programs. This would mean increased funding for Head Start, state preschool education programs, and child care subsidies, including tax credits for families with moderate incomes. Western and midwestern states, in particular, could improve equality in access by investing much more in state-funded pre-K programs.

Greater attention could be focused on funds to expand the enrollment of children at age 3 in educationally effective programs. For most state preschool education programs, serving equal numbers at age 3 would essentially require doubling the size of the programs.

Obviously, the most effective approach would be to offer preschool education programs to all children. A preschool education program for all children would cost the public more, but the added benefits from serving more children could more than justify the added costs. In addition to reaching previously underserved disadvantaged children, newly served children from families that are not currently eligible also would benefit in ways that can contribute to the public good, such as increased school readiness and achievement. These families benefit from the enhanced educational opportunities their children receive even if they already had access to some preschool education or child care. For many middle-income families "preschool participation" does not mean high-quality education. They simply cannot afford high quality. Parents who need long hours of child care to stay afloat

> financially can face an especially difficult trade-off between quality and hours.
>
> Other studies have found that inequalities in access extend to quality as well as quantity. As highlighted in a recent NIEER report on state preschool education programs, quality and adequate funding continue to be major issues. The nation and its children will not benefit if quality is sacrificed to increase participation rates. Instead, the promised benefits will be lost and America will have only the illusion of progress in preschool education. Higher standards and added resources for quality are essential components of any effort to increase equality of access to effective preschool education.

See W. Steven Barnett and Donald J. Yarosz, *Who Goes to Preschool and Why Does It Matter?* at 13-14 (NIEER, 2007).

C. THE EDUCATIONAL LANDSCAPE OF PRESCHOOL: ALTERNATIVE APPROACHES TO THE DELIVERY OF EARLY-CHILDHOOD EDUCATION

Governmental recognition of the critical importance of early childhood education has raised the issue of the efficacy of various preschool educational approaches. Professor James Ryan, one of the nation's leading scholars in education law, characterizes the existing preschool delivery model as one of limited "school choice," in which parents select from a variety of options—including Head Start, public schools, private providers, religious institutions and private-public partnerships. Ryan, *The Political Economy of School Choice* (with Michael Heise), 111 Yale L.J. 2043 (2002). *See also* Brown, *School Choice, and the Suburban Veto,* 90 Va. L. Rev. 1635 (2004). Most preschools are privately operated, and parents decide to pay tuition to the school of their choosing. Ryan, 111 Yale L.J. at 2130. At the same time, legislation has provided publicly supported preschool programs at the federal level. Head Start provides funds, and sometimes staff and facilities, to local agencies to provide preschool for children below the poverty line. The Individuals with Disabilities in Education Act provides financial assistance to public and private preschool programs that educate children with disabilities. In addition, Congress has provided limited funding to high-poverty school districts for the provision of pre-kindergarten programs. Publicly funded preschool programs at the state level have grown as well. Professor Ryan cites the research supporting the short-term and long-term benefits from preschool, and he approves the trend toward increased government funding for preschool programs. He suggests that the expansion of government-funded preschool options for students across a wide spectrum of income levels will encourage the expansion of school choice at the elementary and secondary school levels as well. Ryan, 111 Yale L.J. at 2132-2135.

As preschool options expand, parents will seek information about the various preschool models and make an informed choice. Preschool programs offer a wide range of educational approaches.

1. Reggio Emilia

The Reggio Emilia approach to early childhood education has become the gold standard. According to Newsweek magazine, Reggio-inspired preschools are the best in the world. *See* Pia Hinckle, *The Best Schools in the World,* (Newsweek, Dec. 2, 1991). Developed in the 1940s in the Italian village of Reggio Emilia, this educational approach has spread throughout the world, and it is practiced in outstanding preschools in the United States. The approach begins with the creation of a learning environment that will facilitate a child's construction of his or her own cognitive, social and emotional powers by synthesizing all forms of communication and language. In particular, the Reggio approach involves (1) an emergent curriculum that springs from the interests of children as expressed throughout the school day, but also outside of school at community and family events; (2) projects that arise naturally from groups of children and that are as short or long as the children direct; (3) the representation and presentation of concepts in multiple forms of expression, including print, art, construction, music, puppetry, play and drama; (4) collaboration among children, among teachers and between children and teachers, including dialogue, negotiation, problem solving, listening and tolerance for different perspectives; (5) highly qualified teachers who learn along with students while listening, observing and documenting the growth of community in the classroom; (6) assessment through a display of a variety of experiences, which is then used as a tool for additional learning and advocacy for children; and (7) an environment that is itself a "teacher" because it links classrooms to a center "piazza," invites small and large group projects, celebrates the presentations of children and includes areas for dramatic play and artistic expression through an artist's studio, or "atelier."

In a Reggio-inspired preschool, not only are children respected, but they are given some control over their own learning. They are encouraged to use all of their senses to learn, through play, touching, dancing, moving, listening, seeing and creating. The Reggio school also welcomes parents as partners in the learning process. The school becomes the hub of the community fostering developmentally appropriate learning for children and adults.

Although Reggio-inspired schools have very high expectations for the growth of children, those expectations are not always verifiable by traditional forms of assessment for "academic" achievement. For example, students are not tested to determine whether they have acquired the "academic" skills sometimes thought necessary for kindergarten readiness. Nonetheless, the development experienced by children in a Reggio school is significantly more profound than that experienced by children in a preschool environment that stresses so-called academic achievement. Children emerge from a Reggio preschool better able to lead, to create, to problem solve, to collaborate, to express themselves, to negotiate, to build alliances, to focus, to listen, to absorb, to relate to adults and to find joy in learning. They also gain a deeply rooted sense of self-confidence and an authentic sense of self-respect and self-esteem. Accordingly, the Reggio approach is viewed around the world as the most effective preschool education for children.

2. Montessori

The Italian educator Maria Montessori founded the Montessori school movement in 1907. The Montessori view is that each child is an individual learner. The school environment is structured to enable children to direct their own learning by choosing an activity specifically designed to develop a discrete skill. The Montessori premise is that children learn best when learning alone. Children engage in an activity at their own pace, after the teacher has demonstrated the "right" way to perform that activity. The activity is repeated until the child is ready for the next structured activity. In this way the Montessori environment encourages independent and focused children who acquire select skills. The approach allows children to construct their own individual learning. Yet Montessori schools generally are not designed to enable children to find joy in their learning through collaboration or group work.

3. Waldorf

Based on the philosophy of Rudolf Steiner, Waldorf schools strive to create a predictable routine for children. Waldorf stresses creating learning through play, story, music, cooking and art. The "routine" is created by keeping students with the same teacher and peer group for a number of years. The school thereby allows the child to develop a relationship of trust with teachers and fellow students. The school is designed to replicate a child's home, contributing to the sense of a familiar environment for learning. The Waldorf method is also interdisciplinary. Children are encouraged to use their imagination and artistic expression as part of the learning process.

4. Head Start

In 1965 Congress created Head Start, a federally funded preschool program for low-income families. *See* Head Start Act, 42 U.S.C. §9801 *et seq.* (2007). Head Start currently supports more than 2,000 early-childhood education programs throughout the nation, serving nearly 1,000,000 children each year. The National Head Start Association has developed minimum guidelines for quality early-education programs, including:

- secure, supportive, nurturing environment
- small class size
- small adult:child ratio
- culturally sensitive curriculum and staff
- staff trained in child development and comprehensive services
- safe environment
- parent involvement in the child's education
- individualized approach, which builds on children's strengths and promotes positive self-image
- combination of individual, small group and large group activities
- child-initiated and child-directed activities
- class not segregated by language, handicap or behavior

- health, cognitive, emotional, social and physical development
- encouraging social relationships
- balance between children-initiated and teacher-initiated activities
- developmentally appropriate curriculum
- minimum teacher training standard

Head Start programs also aspire to take a comprehensive approach to early childhood education, including health services, nutrition, wellness, parent education and social services. *See, e.g.,* www.nhsa.org/research. Accordingly, many excellent Head Start programs are Reggio-inspired. In recent years, however, the federal Department of Health and Human Services has promulgated Head Start "performance standards" that emphasize academic achievement, particularly the development of literary skills. *See, e.g.,* 45 C.F.R. §1304.21 (2007). This shift toward academic achievement is unfortunate in light of the research demonstrating the overriding academic, social and emotional benefits of Head Start's prior comprehensive approach. *See, e.g.,* www.nhsa.org; www.acf.hhs.gov.

CHAPTER 6

THE ESTABLISHMENT CLAUSE AND THE LEMON TEST: PUBLIC RESOURCES FOR RELIGIOUS EDUCATION

The First Amendment to the U.S. Constitution provides in pertinent part: "Congress shall make no law respecting an establishment of religion, or prohibiting the free exercise thereof, . . ."

The origins of the First Amendment's language precluding the establishment of religion in public educational institutions and its underlying philosophy are often traced by scholars and judges to James Madison's 1785 *Memorial and Remonstrance Against Religious Assessments to the General Assembly of the Commonwealth of Virginia*. In his *Remonstrance*, Madison begins by declaring: "We, the subscribers, citizens of the said Commonwealth, having taken into serious consideration, a Bill printed by order of the last Session of General Assembly, entitled 'A Bill establishing a provision for teachers of the Christian Religion,' and conceiving that the same, if finally armed with the sanctions of a law, will be a dangerous abuse of power, are bound as faithful members of a free State, to remonstrate against it, and to declare the reasons by which we are determined." Madison proceeds to make six independent arguments against many forms of public involvement in religion and religious education.

First, there is natural right to be free to exercise or not exercise any particular religious practice. Each person has the right to exercise his conscience in matters of religion. This right is a "gift of nature" tantamount to the other inalienable rights asserted in the Declaration of Independence. All men are by their nature free and independent. When they enter into civil society, they are unable to give up their equal right to the free exercise of religion. This right is by its very nature inalienable because the conscience cannot yield to the dictates of others and the relationship between a person and his or her Creator creates a "duty" on the person to exercise free choice in the very decision whether to pay homage to the Creator. Moreover, the natural right to exercise freedom of religion also includes the right to choose *not* to follow any religion at all. As a natural right, the freedom to exercise religion (or not) predates civil society and cannot be abridged by civil society or its laws. *See Remonstrance* ¶¶ 1-4; 15.

Second, when civil society enacts laws that affect religion, religion is harmed. Legislation that favors or disadvantages religion is an offense against God because it denies the fundamental belief that the choice to believe should be arrived at freely. In addition, a civil judge is not a competent authority on religious doctrine or truth. The history of the world demonstrates that when the state meddles with religion, religion becomes depurified and debased. Nor does religion need the support of civil society to flourish. The principles and beliefs of religion predate civil society and thus will continue to exist regardless of any support from civil society. *See Remonstrance* ¶¶ 5-7; 12.

Third, when civil society enacts laws that affect religion, civil society is harmed. The legislative support for religion is dangerous to civil society. History demonstrates that such support leads to "spiritual tyranny." States that support religious institutions have not guarded liberty or equality. To the contrary, such societies have seen "torrents of blood" resulting from the effort to support religion. At a minimum, "intermeddling" law and religion destroys harmony and moderation among members of the society. *See Remonstrance,* ¶¶ 7-9; 11.

Fourth, enforcement of a law as dangerous as the establishment of religion undermines respect for the rule of law. Where law invades the private lives of citizens, those citizens lose respect for the rule of law and its province. That respect is all the more sacrificed when there are efforts to invade the private sphere of conscience, because those efforts at enforcement necessarily fail. *See Remonstrance* ¶¶ 4, 13.

Fifth, a law that favors one religion over others inhibits the diffusion of knowledge and creates an "obstacle to the victorious progress of truth." Here, Madison clearly alludes to the Enlightenment concept of human progress toward truth, a concept that Jefferson advances in his arguments for the general diffusion of knowledge. The framers also foreshadow John Stuart Mill's arguments that freedom of thought and speech must be protected from laws that would prohibit some thought and some speech in the name of orthodoxy. When the state establishes or even preferences one belief system, the state thereby inhibits the marketplace of ideas required for the evolution toward truth. *See Remonstrance* ¶ 12.

Finally, a law that favors one religion over others is a "signal of persecution." In this argument, Madison suggests that even the appearance of religious intolerance will act as a "signal" that deters people searching for freedom from coming to, or remaining in, America. *See Remonstrance* ¶¶ 9, 10.

The lesson from Madison's *Remonstrance* is that any governmental act that has the purpose or effect of supporting, disadvantaging or intermeddling with sectarian education would: (1) infringe the natural rights of all Americans to free and equal exercise of religion; (2) harm religion itself; (3) harm civil society; (4) undermine respect for the rule of law; (5) inhibit the diffusion of knowledge and the progressive search for truth; and (6) operate as a signal of

American persecution. To what extent are these arguments still persuasive? As you read the Supreme Court's evolving interpretations of the First Amendment's religion clauses in the context of education, consider carefully whether the Court has heeded Madison's warning.

This chapter begins with the Supreme Court's seminal cases regarding the allocation of public resources for sectarian educational purposes. Those cases hint at a developing constitutional test that invalidates governmental action in the educational context, where the action has the primary purpose or effect of advancing religion. Even in situations where the allocation of public resources toward religious educational purposes served secular purposes and had neutral effects, however, the courts began to articulate a different concern: the government's entanglement with religion. Part B of this chapter therefore displays the rise of that concern in the context of challenges to educational programs that allow for "release time" for religious education during the school day—both on site and off site. Ultimately, the Supreme Court's earlier prohibitions on nonsecular purposes and effects joined the Court's "entanglement" concern to form an often-criticized, three-part constitutional test in *Lemon v. Kurtzman*, 403 U.S. 602 (1971). In part C, the *Lemon* test and its application can be observed in a host of contests to governmental involvement in religious education.

Each case in this chapter addresses a specific attempt by the government to support sectarian education. In addition, however, the cases explored in this chapter should be approached from a broader perspective. Together, the cases in this chapter provide an exceptional example of how the law evolves from a case-specific issue to a broader concern to a theoretical pattern to a rigid test and finally to an overriding standard.

A. PUBLIC RESOURCES FOR SECTARIAN SCHOOLS: BOOKS AND BUSES; PURPOSES AND EFFECTS

When public resources are employed to assist parochial schools, is the benefit conferred on the parochial schools a private or public benefit? Is the benefit received by the private school or its students? Should the constitutionality of a legislative scheme depend on whether the beneficiaries are the students or the religious schools? Consider the Court's answer to these questions in *Cochran*, *Everson* and *Allen*.

In *Cochran v. Louisiana State Board of Education*, 281 U.S. 370 (1930), citizens and taxpayers of the State of Louisiana brought suit to restrain state officials from using tax dollars to purchase school books and supply them free of cost to the school children of the state. They contended that the legislation violated the Louisiana Constitution, as well as section 4 of Article IV and the Fourteenth Amendment of the federal Constitution. The plaintiffs argued that taxation for the purchase of school books constituted a taking of private property for the private purpose of furnishing textbooks to children attending non-public schools. In sustaining the law, however, the U.S. Supreme Court relied heavily upon the Louisiana State Supreme Court's finding that the purpose of the law was a "public" one because its "interest is education, broadly" of both public and private school children. The *Cochran* Court, like the Court in *Pierce v. Society of Sisters*, 268 U.S. 510 (1925), analyzes the challenged legislation to determine whether it involves a justifiable taking of private property for a public purpose. The First Amendment's establishment clause and free exercise clause are not directly at issue in either decision.

In *Everson*, by contrast, the Court begins its opinion with a familiar due process analysis, but proceeds to address head on the role of the religion clauses of the First Amendment. After declaring that the First Amendment's establishment and free exercise clauses are applicable to the states through the Fourteenth Amendment's protections of religious liberty from state encroachment, the *Everson* Court relies upon the "child benefit" concept enunciated in *Cochran* to uphold the use of public funds to provide transportation of students to parochial school. The *Everson* majority finds in the First Amendment the fundamental principle that the state should be *neutral* toward religion, neither favoring religious education nor disfavoring such education.

Everson v. Board of Education

330 U.S. 1 (1947)

Mr. Justice Black delivered the opinion of the Court.

A New Jersey statute authorizes its local school districts to make rules and contracts for the transportation of children to and from schools. The appellee, a township board of education, acting pursuant to this statute, authorized reimbursement to parents of money expended by them for the bus transportation of their children on regular busses operated by the public transportation system. Part of this money was for the payment of transportation of some children in the community to Catholic parochial schools. These church schools give their students, in addition to secular education, regular religious instruction conforming to the religious tenets and modes of worship of the Catholic Faith. The superintendent of these schools is a Catholic priest.

The only contention here is that the state statute and the resolution, insofar as they authorized reimbursement to parents of children attending parochial schools, violate the Federal Constitution [by forcing] . . . inhabitants to pay taxes to help support and maintain schools which are dedicated to, and which regularly teach, the Catholic Faith. This is alleged to be a use of state power to support church schools contrary to the prohibition of the First Amendment which the Fourteenth Amendment made applicable to the states. . . .

The First Amendment, as made applicable to the states by the Fourteenth, *Murdock v. Pennsylvania*, commands that a state "shall make no law respecting an establishment of religion, or prohibiting the free exercise thereof." . . . These words of the First Amendment reflected in the minds of early Americans a vivid mental picture of conditions and practices which they fervently wished to stamp out in order to preserve liberty for themselves and for their posterity. Doubtless their goal has not been entirely reached; but so far has the Nation moved toward it that the expression "law respecting an establishment of religion," probably does not so vividly remind present-day Americans of the evils, fears, and political problems that caused that expression to be written into our Bill of Rights. Whether this New Jersey law is one respecting an "establishment of religion" requires an understanding of the meaning of that language, particularly with respect to the imposition of taxes. Once again, therefore, it is not inappropriate briefly to review the background and environment of the period in which that constitutional language was fashioned and adopted.

A large proportion of the early settlers of this country came here from Europe to escape the bondage of laws which compelled them to support and attend government-favored churches. The centuries immediately before and contemporaneous with the colonization of America had been filled with turmoil, civil strife, and persecutions, generated in large part by established sects determined to maintain their absolute political and religious supremacy. With the power of government supporting them, at various times and places, Catholics had persecuted Protestants, Protestants had persecuted Catholics, Protestant sects had persecuted other Protestant sects, Catholics of one shade of belief had persecuted Catholics of another shade of belief, and all of these had from time to time persecuted Jews. In efforts to force loyalty to whatever religious group happened to be on top and in league with the government of a particular time and place, men and women had been fined, cast in jail, cruelly tortured, and killed. Among the offenses for which these punishments had been inflicted were such things as speaking disrespectfully of the views of ministers of government-established churches, non-attendance at those churches, expressions of non-belief in their doctrines, and failure to pay taxes and tithes to support them.

These practices of the old world were transplanted to and began to thrive in the soil of the new America. The very charters granted by the English Crown to the individuals and companies designated to make the laws which would control the destinies of the colonials authorized these individuals and companies to erect religious establishments which all, whether believers or non-believers, would be required to support and attend. An exercise of this authority was accompanied by a repetition of many of the old-world practices and persecutions. Catholics found themselves hounded and proscribed because of their faith; Quakers who followed their conscience went to jail; Baptists were peculiarly obnoxious to certain dominant Protestant sects; men and women of varied faiths who happened to be in a minority in a particular locality were persecuted because they steadfastly persisted in worshipping God only as their own consciences dictated. And all of these dissenters were compelled to pay tithes and taxes to support government-sponsored churches whose ministers preached inflammatory sermons designed to strengthen and consolidate the established faith by generating a burning hatred against dissenters.

These practices became so commonplace as to shock the freedom-loving colonials into a feeling of abhorrence. The imposition of taxes to pay ministers' salaries and to build and maintain churches and church property aroused their indignation. It was these feelings which found expression in the First Amendment. No one locality and no one group throughout the Colonies can rightly be given entire credit for having aroused the sentiment that culminated in adoption of the Bill of Rights' provisions embracing religious liberty. But Virginia, where the established church had achieved a dominant influence in political affairs and where many excesses attracted wide public attention, provided a great stimulus and able leadership for the movement. The people there, as elsewhere, reached the conviction that individual religious liberty could be achieved best under a government which was stripped of all power to tax, to support, or otherwise to assist any or all religions, or to interfere with the beliefs of any religious individual or group.

The movement toward this end reached its dramatic climax in Virginia in 1785-86 when the Virginia legislative body was about to renew Virginia's tax levy for the support of the established church. Thomas Jefferson and James Madison led the fight against this tax. Madison wrote his great Memorial and Remonstrance against the law. In it, he eloquently argued that a true religion did not need the support of law; that no person, either believer or nonbeliever, should be taxed to support a religious institution of any kind; that the best interest of a society required that the minds of men always be wholly free; and that cruel persecutions were the inevitable result of government established religions. Madison's Remonstrance received strong support throughout Virginia, and the Assembly postponed consideration of the proposed tax measure until its next session. When the proposal came up for consideration at that session, it not only died in committee, but the Assembly enacted the famous "Virginia Bill for Religious Liberty" originally written by Thomas Jefferson. The preamble to that Bill stated among other things that

> Almighty God hath created the mind free; that all attempts to influence it by temporal punishments or burthens, or by civil incapacitations, tend only to beget habits of hypocrisy and meanness, and are a departure from the plan of the Holy author of our religion, who being Lord both of body and mind, yet chose not to propagate it by coercions on either . . . ; that to compel a man to furnish contributions of money for the propagation of opinions which he disbelieves, is sinful and tyrannical; that even the forcing him to support this or that teacher of his own religious persuasion, is depriving him of the comfortable liberty of giving his contributions to the particular pastor, whose morals he would make his pattern. . . .

This Court has previously recognized that the provisions of the First Amendment, in the drafting and adoption of which Madison and Jefferson played such leading roles, had the same objective and were intended to provide the same protection against governmental intrusion on religious liberty as the Virginia statute. . . .

The "establishment of religion" clause of the First Amendment means at least this: Neither a state nor the Federal Government can set up a church. Neither can pass laws which aid one religion, aid all religions, or prefer one religion over another. Neither can force nor influence a person to go to or to remain away from church against his will or force him to profess a belief or disbelief in any religion. No person can be punished for entertaining or professing religious beliefs or disbeliefs, for church attendance or non-attendance. No tax in any amount, large or small, can be levied to support any religious activities or institutions, whatever they may be called, or whatever form they may adopt to teach or practice religion. Neither a state nor the Federal Government can, openly or secretly, participate in the affairs of any religious organizations or groups and *vice versa*. In the words of Jefferson, the clause against establishment of religion by law was intended to erect "a wall of separation between church and State."

We must consider the New Jersey statute in accordance with the foregoing limitations imposed by the First Amendment. But we must not strike that state statute down if it is within the State's constitutional power even though it approaches the verge of that power. . . . New Jersey cannot consistently with the "establishment of religion" clause of the First Amendment contribute tax-raised funds to the support of an institution which teaches the tenets and faith of any church. On the other hand, other language of the amendment commands that New Jersey cannot hamper its citizens in the free exercise of their own religion. Consequently, it cannot exclude individual Catholics, Lutherans, Mohammedans, Baptists, Jews, Methodists, Non-believers, Presbyterians, or the members of any other faith, *because of their faith, or lack of it*, from receiving the benefits of public welfare legislation. While we do not mean to intimate that a state could not provide transportation only to children attending public schools, we must be careful, in protecting the citizens of New Jersey against state-established churches, to be sure that we do not inadvertently prohibit New Jersey from extending its general state law benefits to all its citizens without regard to their religious belief.

Measured by these standards, we cannot say that the First Amendment prohibits New Jersey from spending tax-raised funds to pay the bus fares of parochial school pupils as a part of a general program under which it pays the fares of pupils attending public and other schools. It is undoubtedly true that children are helped to get to church schools. There is even a possibility that some of the children might not be sent to the church schools if the parents were compelled to pay their children's bus fares out of their own pockets when transportation to a public school would have been paid for by the State. . . . That Amendment requires the state to be a neutral in its relations with groups of religious believers and non-believers; it does not require the state to be their adversary. State power is no more to be used so as to handicap religions than it is to favor them.

This Court has said that parents may, in the discharge of their duty under state compulsory education laws, send their children to a religious rather than a public school if the school meets the secular educational requirements which the state has power to impose. See *Pierce v. Society of Sisters*. It appears that these parochial schools meet New Jersey's requirements. The State contributes no money to the schools. It does not support them. Its legislation, as applied, does no more than provide a general program to help parents get their children, regardless of their religion, safely and expeditiously to and from accredited schools.

The First Amendment has erected a wall between church and state. That wall must be kept high and impregnable. We could not approve the slightest breach. New Jersey has not breached it here.

Affirmed.

NOTES AND QUESTIONS

1. Where does the *Everson* Court's neutrality concept originate? Does the First Amendment's language and purpose preclude governmental education programs that are facially neutral toward religion, but have a nonneutral effect? If neutrality is the overriding test for First Amendment compliance, is the Court correct that New Jersey's law meets that test?
2. In his dissent in *Everson*, Justice Jackson traces the origins of American public schools to 1840 and Horace Mann's premise, "that secular education can be isolated from all religious teaching so that the school can inculcate all needed temporal knowledge and also maintain a strict and lofty neutrality as to religion. The assumption is that after the individual has been instructed in worldly wisdom he will be better fitted to choose his religion." How would Horace Mann have resolved the issue here? Justice Jackson also declares that the "basic fallacy in the Court's reasoning, which accounts for its failure to apply the principles it avows, is in ignoring the essentially religious test by which beneficiaries of this expenditure are selected." According to Justice Jackson, the First Amendment, "was set forth in absolute terms, and its strength is its rigidity. It was intended not only to keep the states' hands out of religion, but to keep religion's hands off the state, and, above all, to keep bitter religious controversy out of public life by denying to every denomination any advantage from getting control of public policy or the public purse. Those great ends I cannot but think are immeasurably compromised by today's decision." Is Justice Jackson's reasoning persuasive?
3. In his separate dissent, Justice Rutledge argues that the First Amendment's language, history and intent as evidenced by the founders' writings and historic condition, demonstrate the fallacy of the majority's reasoning. Consider first the plain language of the Amendment. Is Justice Rutledge correct that the word "respecting" an establishment of religion indicates that the Amendment's prohibitions are broader than the majority believes? According to Justice Rutledge, "the Amendment's purpose was not to strike merely at the official establishment of a single sect, creed or religion, outlawing only a formal relation such as had prevailed in England and some of the colonies. Necessarily it was to uproot all such relationships. But the object was broader than separating church and state in this narrow sense. It was to create a complete and permanent separation of the spheres of religious activity and civil authority by comprehensively forbidding every form of public aid or support for religion." How does the Amendment's language reveal that purpose?
4. Justice Rutledge also buttressed his dissent with evidence of the framers' intent, arguing that in documents like Madison's *Remonstrance*, "is to be found irrefutable confirmation of the Amendment's sweeping content." Reconsider Madison's arguments in the *Remonstrance*. Is Justice Rutledge correct that those sentiments would invalidate the use of public funds for parochial school transportation?
5. At one point in the drafting history of the First Amendment, the wording was proposed: "No religion shall be established by law, nor shall the equal rights of conscience be infringed." *See Everson* (Rutledge, J. dissenting),

citing 1 Annals of Congress 729. According to Justice Rutledge, Representative Huntington of Connecticut feared this might be construed to prevent judicial enforcement of private pledges. He stated "that he feared . . . that the words might be taken in such latitude as to be extremely hurtful to the cause of religion. To avoid any such possibility, Madison suggested inserting the word "national" before "religion," thereby not only again disclaiming intent to bring about the result Huntington feared but also showing unmistakably that "establishment" meant public "support" of religion in the financial sense. 1 Annals of Congress 731.

6. After exploring the language, intent and legislative history of the First Amendment, Justice Rutledge answers the question presented: "Does New Jersey's action furnish support for religion by use of the taxing power? Certainly it does, if the test remains undiluted as Jefferson and Madison made it, that money taken by taxation from one is not to be used or given to support another's religious training or belief, or indeed one's own." Do you agree with Justice Rutledge's interpretation? What is the role of language, intent and legislative history in interpreting the Constitution?
7. A key issue in the due process analysis is whether the education of children in a parochial school is a purely private objective, or instead serves a public purpose. The *Everson* Court, citing *Cochran*, finds a public purpose because the statute "facilitate[s] the opportunity of children to get a secular education." Where do "private" purposes end and "public" purposes begin? If private and public purposes, as the Court suggests, often "coincide," when will a statute ever be declared unconstitutional because it serves only a private purpose? To what extent should the education of children be a public matter? To what extent is the education of children, in reality, a private matter? Consider how the classical, modern, American and contemporary educational philosophers would answer that question.
8. Since *Everson*, the Supreme Court has debated intensely the history and intent behind the establishment and free exercise clauses of the First Amendment. The fact that the clause was adopted at a time when its adopters were "religious" people has been used to claim that the separation of state from church was not envisioned by the clause. Do you agree?
9. If the First Amendment's core principle is governmental neutrality toward religion, then how is that neutrality to be assessed? In the *Allen* case, which follows, the Supreme Court makes clear that the establishment clause precludes legislation that has either the purpose or the effect of advancing religious education.

BOARD OF EDUCATION V. ALLEN

392 U.S. 236 (1968)

Mr. Justice WHITE delivered the opinion of the Court.

A law of the State of New York requires local public school authorities to lend textbooks free of charge to all students in grades seven through 12; students attending private schools are included. This case presents the question whether this statute is a "law respecting an establishment of religion, or prohibiting the free exercise thereof," and so in conflict with the First and Fourteenth Amendments to the Constitution, because it authorizes the loan of textbooks to students attending parochial schools. We hold that the law is not in violation of the Constitution. . . .

Everson and later cases have shown that the line between state neutrality to religion and state support of religion is not easy to locate. . . .

> The test may be stated as follows: what are the purpose and the primary effect of the enactment? If either is the advancement or inhibition of religion then the enactment exceeds the scope of legislative power as circumscribed by the Constitution. That is to say that to withstand the strictures of the Establishment Clause there must be a secular legislative purpose and a primary effect that neither advances nor inhibits religion. *Everson v. Board of Education*. . . .

. . . The statute upheld in *Everson* would be considered a law having "a secular legislative purpose and a primary effect that neither advances nor inhibits religion." We reach the same result with respect to the New York law requiring school books to be loaned free of charge to all students in specified grades. The express purpose of [the law] was stated by the New York Legislature to be furtherance of the educational opportunities available to the young. Appellants have shown us nothing about the necessary effects of the statute that is contrary to its stated purpose. The law merely makes available to all children the benefits of a general program to lend school books free of charge. Books are furnished at the request of the pupil and ownership remains, at least technically, in the State. Thus no funds or books are furnished to parochial schools, and the financial benefit is to parents and children, not to schools.

Of course books are different from buses. Most bus rides have no inherent religious significance, while religious books are common. However, the language of [the law] does not authorize the loan of religious books, and the State claims no right to distribute religious literature. Although the books loaned are those required by the parochial school for use in specific courses, each book loaned must be approved by the public school authorities; only secular books may receive approval. The law was construed by the Court of Appeals of New York as "merely making available secular textbooks at the request of the individual student," and the record contains no suggestion that religious books have been loaned. Absent evidence, we cannot assume that school authorities, who constantly face the same problem in selecting textbooks for use in the public schools, are unable to distinguish between secular and religious books or that they will not honestly discharge their duties under the law. In judging the validity of the statute on this record we must proceed on the assumption that books loaned to students are books that are not unsuitable for use in the public schools because of religious content.

The major reason offered by appellants for distinguishing free textbooks from free bus fares is that books, but not buses, are critical to the teaching process, and in a sectarian school that process is employed to teach religion. However this Court has long recognized that religious schools pursue two goals, religious instruction and secular education. In the leading case of *Pierce v. Society of Sisters* . . . the Court held that although it would not question

Oregon's power to compel school attendance or require that the attendance be at an institution meeting State-imposed requirements as to quality and nature of curriculum, Oregon had not shown that its interest in secular education required that all children attend publicly operated schools. A premise of this holding was the view that the State's interest in education would be served sufficiently by reliance on the secular teaching that accompanied religious training in the schools maintained by the Society of Sisters. Since *Pierce,* a substantial body of case law has confirmed the power of the States to insist that attendance at private schools, if it is to satisfy state compulsory-attendance laws, be at institutions which provide minimum hours of instruction, employ teachers of specified training, and cover prescribed subjects of instruction. Indeed, the State's interest in assuring that these standards are being met has been considered a sufficient reason for refusing to accept instruction at home as compliance with compulsory education statutes. These cases were a sensible corollary of *Pierce v. Society of Sisters*: if the State must satisfy its interest in secular education through the instrument of private schools, it has a proper interest in the manner in which those schools perform their secular educational function. Another corollary was *Cochran* . . . where appellants said that a statute requiring school books to be furnished without charge to all students, whether they attended public or private schools, did not serve a "public purpose," and so offended the Fourteenth Amendment. Speaking through Chief Justice Hughes, the Court summarized as follows its conclusion that Louisiana's interest in the secular education being provided by private schools made provision of textbooks to students in those schools a properly public concern: "[The State's] interest is education, broadly; its method, comprehensive. Individual interests are aided only as the common interest is safeguarded."

Underlying these cases, and underlying also the legislative judgments that have preceded the court decisions, has been a recognition that private education has played and is playing a significant and valuable role in raising national levels of knowledge, competence, and experience. Americans care about the quality of the secular education available to their children. They have considered high quality education to be an indispensable ingredient for achieving the kind of nation, and the kind of citizenry, that they have desired to create. Considering this attitude, the continued willingness to rely on private school systems, including parochial systems, strongly suggests that a wide segment of informed opinion, legislative and otherwise, has found that those schools do an acceptable job of providing secular education to their students. This judgment is further evidence that parochial schools are performing, in addition to their sectarian function, the task of secular education.

Against this background of judgment and experience, unchallenged in the meager record before us in this case, we cannot agree with appellants either that all teaching in a sectarian school is religious or that the processes of secular and religious training are so intertwined that secular textbooks furnished to students by the public are in fact instrumental in the teaching of religion. . . . We are unable to hold, based solely on judicial notice, that this statute results in unconstitutional involvement of the State with religious instruction or . . . is a law respecting the establishment of religion within the meaning of the First Amendment.

The judgment is affirmed.

NOTES AND QUESTIONS

1. How would you answer the following question posed by Justice Douglas in his dissent:

   > . . . Whatever may be said of *Everson,* there is nothing ideological about a bus. There is nothing ideological about a school lunch, or a public nurse, or a scholarship. The constitutionality of such public aid to students in parochial schools turns on considerations not present in this textbook case. The textbook goes to the very heart of education in a parochial school. It is the chief, although not solitary, instrumentality for propagating a particular religious creed or faith. How can we possibly approve such state aid to a religion?

   Is there a fundamental distinction between books and buses? If so, does that distinction have constitutional significance?
2. Justice Douglas also argues that:

   > Even where the treatment given to a particular topic in a school textbook is not blatantly sectarian, it will necessarily have certain shadings that will lead a parochial school to prefer one text over another. The Crusades, for example, may be taught as a Christian undertaking to "save the Holy Land" from the Moslem Turks who "became a threat to Christianity and its holy places," which "they did not treat . . . with respect" . . . or as essentially a series of wars born out of political and materialistic motives. . . .

   Do you agree that school textbooks have different "shadings" that might lead a parochial school to choose one over the other? Can you develop a list of topics on which the parochial treatment of a subject might be very different from the secular?
3. In *Allen,* the majority teases from *Everson* and other prior cases a "test" for determining the constitutionality of state "involvement" with religion: "what are the purposes and the primary effect of the enactment? If either is the advancement or inhibition of religion then the enactment exceeds the scope of legislative power as circumscribed by the constitution." Does the language of the Constitution give rise to that "test"? Is the test consistent with the views expressed in founding principles such as those in Madison's *Remonstrance*? Apply the test articulated in *Allen* to the facts in *Cochran.* Would the analysis have been different?
4. The *Allen* Court stresses that parochial schools do an "acceptable job of providing secular education to their students," and observes that 22.2 percent of New York's students attend non-public schools. If the provision of secular education is an important public interest, then when will the provision of support for parochial schools ever have a nonsecular purpose and effect? The Court also states that the processes of religious and secular training are not so "intertwined" as to make the provision of support for parochial schools in this case unconstitutional. Can you envision

situations in which state and church would be so "intertwined" or entangled as to render the state assistance unconstitutional?

5. Consider the typical law school case book. Does that book have a "sectarian" perspective? Does law school have a "sectarian" perspective? How about law, or the rule of law?

B. RELEASE TIME FOR RELIGIOUS ACTIVITIES DURING THE PUBLIC SCHOOL DAY: TOWARD ENTANGLEMENT

School districts have attempted a variety of methods to utilize the public schools to support religious education. In the early 1900s, a number of districts began to set aside a portion of the school day for religious instruction. In its first form, "release-time" programs used public school facilities and public school administrators to give children religious classes. Those children who did not want to participate in the religious classes were ushered to a different part of the building during the "release-time." This practice became fairly common, and was not challenged in any significant way until the Supreme Court addressed the practice in *People ex rel. McCollum v. Board of Education*, 333 U.S. 203 (1948).

In *McCollum*, the Court declared unconstitutional the Illinois program of allowing religious teachers to come into the public school classroom for 30 minutes a week during the regular school day to provide religious teachings rather than secular education. The Court reasoned that:

> This is beyond all question a utilization of the tax-established and tax-supported public school system to aid religious groups to spread their faith. And it falls squarely under the ban of the First Amendment (made applicable to the States by the Fourteenth) as we interpreted it in *Everson v. Board of Education*. . . . The majority in the *Everson* case, and [even] the minority, agreed that the First Amendment's language, properly interpreted, had erected a wall of separation between Church and State. . . . For the First Amendment rests upon the premise that both religion and government can best work to achieve their lofty aims if each is left free from the other within its respective sphere. Or, as we said in the *Everson* case, the First Amendment has erected a wall between Church and State which must be kept high and impregnable. Here not only are the State's tax-supported public school buildings used for the dissemination of religious doctrines. The State also affords sectarian groups an invaluable aid in that it helps to provide pupils for their religious classes through use of the State's compulsory public school machinery. This is not separation of Church and State.

In the wake of the Supreme Court's ruling in *McCollum*, New York City created a different release-time program. The modified program was designed to cure the constitutional defects in the *McCollum* program. Accordingly, the revised New York regime afforded students the option of being released from the public schools during the school day to attend religious education classes off public school grounds. The constitutionality of this "release-time" program was addressed by the Supreme Court in *Zorach*.

Zorach v. Clauson

343 U.S. 306 (1952)

Mr. Justice Douglas delivered the opinion of the Court.

New York City has a program which permits its public schools to release students during the school day so that they may leave the school buildings and school grounds and go to religious centers for religious instruction or devotional exercises. A student is released on written request of his parents. Those not released stay in the classrooms. The churches make weekly reports to the schools, sending a list of children who have been released from public school but who have not reported for religious instruction.

This "released time" program involves neither religious instruction in public school classrooms nor the expenditure of public funds. All costs, including the application blanks, are paid by the religious organizations. The case is therefore unlike *McCollum v. Board of Education,* which involved a "released time" program from Illinois. In that case the classrooms were turned over to religious instructors. We accordingly held that the program violated the First Amendment which (by reason of the Fourteenth Amendment) prohibits the states from establishing religion or prohibiting its free exercise. . . .

There is a suggestion that the system involves the use of coercion to get public school students into religious classrooms. There is no evidence in the record before us that supports that conclusion. The present record indeed tells us that the school authorities are neutral in this regard and do no more than release students whose parents so request. If in fact coercion were used, if it were established that any one or more teachers were using their office to persuade or force students to take the religious instruction, a wholly different case would be presented. Hence we put aside that claim of coercion both as respects the "free exercise" of religion and "an establishment of religion" within the meaning of the First Amendment.

Moreover, apart from that claim of coercion, we do not see how New York by this type of "released time" program has made a law respecting an establishment of religion within the meaning of the First Amendment. There is much talk of the separation of Church and State in the history of the Bill of Rights and in the decisions clustering around the First Amendment. *See Everson v. Board of Education; McCollum v. Board of Education.* There cannot be the slightest doubt that the First Amendment reflects the philosophy that Church and State should be separated. And so far as interference with the "free exercise" of religion and an "establishment" of religion are concerned, the separation must be complete and unequivocal. The First Amendment within the scope of its coverage permits no exception; the prohibition is absolute. The First Amendment, however, does not say that in every and all respects there shall be a separation of Church and State. Rather, it studiously defines the manner, the specific ways, in which there shall be no concern or union or dependency one on the other. That is the common sense of the matter. Otherwise the state and religion would be aliens to each other—hostile, suspicious, and even unfriendly. Churches could not be required to pay even property taxes. Municipalities would not be permitted to render police or fire protection to religious groups. Policemen who helped parishioners into their places of worship would violate the Constitution. Prayers in our legislative halls; the appeals to the Almighty in the messages of the Chief Executive; the proclamations making Thanksgiving Day a holiday; "so help me God" in our courtroom oaths—these and all other references to the Almighty that run through our laws, our public rituals, our ceremonies would be flouting the First Amendment. A fastidious atheist or agnostic could even object to the supplication with which the Court opens each session: "God save the United States and this Honorable Court."

We would have to press the concept of separation of Church and State to these extremes to condemn the present law on constitutional grounds. The nullification of this law would have wide and profound effects. A Catholic student applies to his teacher for permission to leave the school during hours on a Holy Day of Obligation to attend a mass. A Jewish student asks his teacher for permission to be excused for Yom Kippur. A Protestant wants the afternoon off for a family baptismal ceremony. In each case the teacher requires parental consent in writing. In each case the teacher, in order to make sure the student is not a truant, goes further and requires a report from the priest, the rabbi, or the minister. The teacher in other words cooperates in a religious program to the extent of making it possible for her students to participate in it. Whether she does it occasionally for a few students, regularly for one, or pursuant to a systematized program designed to further the religious needs of all the students does not alter the character of the act.

We are a religious people whose institutions presuppose a Supreme Being. We guarantee the freedom to worship as one chooses. We make room for as wide a variety of beliefs and creeds as the spiritual needs of man deem necessary. We sponsor an attitude on the part of government that shows no partiality to any one group and that lets each flourish according to the zeal of its adherents and the appeal of its dogma. When the state encourages religious instruction or cooperates with religious authorities by adjusting the schedule of public events to sectarian needs, it follows the best of our traditions. For it then respects the religious nature of our people and accommodates the public service to their spiritual needs. To hold that it may not would be to find in the Constitution a requirement that the government show a callous indifference to religious groups. That would be preferring those who believe in no religion over those who do believe. Government may not finance religious groups nor undertake religious instruction nor blend secular and sectarian education nor use secular institutions to force one or some religion on any person. But we find no constitutional requirement which makes it necessary for government to be hostile to religion and to throw its weight against efforts to widen the effective scope of religious influence. The government must be neutral when it comes to competition between sects. It may not thrust any sect on any person. It may not make a religious observance compulsory. It may not coerce anyone to attend church, to observe a religious holiday, or to take religious instruction. But it can close its doors or suspend its operations as to those who want to repair to their religious sanctuary for worship or instruction. No more than that is undertaken here. . . .

In the *McCollum* case the classrooms were used for religious instruction and the force of the public school was used to promote that instruction. Here, as we have said, the public schools do no more than accommodate their schedules to a program of outside religious instruction. We follow the *McCollum* case. But we cannot expand it to cover the present released time program unless separation of Church and State means that public institutions can make no adjustments of their schedules to accommodate the religious needs of the people. We cannot read into the Bill of Rights such a philosophy of hostility to religion.

Affirmed.

NOTES AND QUESTIONS

1. Is the release time program upheld in *Zorach* fairly distinguishable from the one rejected in *McCollum*? In their dissents, Justices Black and Frankfurter declare that this case is indistinguishable from *McCollum*. In particular, consider Justice Black's argument:

   > I see no significant difference between the invalid Illinois system and that of New York here sustained. Except for the use of the school buildings in Illinois, there is no difference between the systems which I consider even worthy of mention. In the New York program, as in that of Illinois, the school authorities release some of the children on the condition that they attend the religious classes, get reports on whether they attend, and hold the other children in the school building until the religious hour is over. As we attempted to make categorically clear, the *McCollum* decision would have been the same if the religious classes had not been held in the school buildings. . . .

2. Is the distinction between *McCollum* and *Zorach* based upon the physical location of the religious education in the public schools? To what extent is the level of administrative involvement relevant to the constitutionality of a release-time program? Could a school district constitutionally operate a release-time program in which religious educators entered the public school to escort children to their off-site classrooms? What if the religious educators recruited students on school grounds? What if the classes were offered on public school property leased to the religious groups for their use? What if the public school facilities were leased to religious groups pursuant to a school district's policy which allowed the rental of its property? Could such a policy preclude the rental of public school facilities on the grounds that the lessee has a religious affiliation?
3. Consider Justice Jackson's dissenting opinion, stressing the "coercive" nature of the release time program:

   > This released time program is founded upon a use of the State's power of coercion, which, for me, determines its unconstitutionality. Stripped to its essentials, the plan has two stages: first, that the State compel each student to yield a large part of his time for public secular education; and, second, that some of it be "released" to him on condition that he devote it to sectarian religious purposes.

Where precisely is the "coercion" that Justice Jackson decries? How does the issue of "coercion" relate to the principles embodied in the First Amendment?

4. The majority opinion in *Zorach* concedes that the release-time program might be "unwise or improvident from an educational or community viewpoint." What are the educational advantages and disadvantages of such a program?
5. Justice Douglas affirms that Americans are a "religious people whose institutions presuppose a Supreme Being." First, what support is there for the idea that Americans are a "religious people"? Second, in what way do America's institutions presuppose a "Supreme Being"? Is it possible, given the American philosophic tradition leading to the First Amendment, that Americans are a religious people, but that their political institutions do *not* presuppose a deity?
6. In his dissent in *McCollum*, Justice Frankfurter offered the following history of American education:

> . . . The evolution of colonial education, largely in the service of religion, into the public school system of today is the story of changing conceptions regarding the American democratic society, of the functions of State-maintained education in such a society, and of the role therein of the free exercise of religion by the people. The modern public school derived from a philosophy of freedom reflected in the First Amendment. It is appropriate to recall that the Remonstrance of James Madison, an event basic in the history of religious liberty, was called forth by a proposal that involved support to religious education. . . .
>
> It is pertinent to remind that the establishment of this principle of separation in the field of education was not due to any decline in the religious beliefs of the people. Horace Mann was a devout Christian, and the deep religious feeling of James Madison is stamped upon the Remonstrance. The secular public school did not imply indifference to the basic role of religion in the life of the people, nor rejection of religious education as a means of fostering it. The claims of religion were not minimized by refusing to make the public schools agencies for their assertion. The non-sectarian or secular public school was the means of reconciling freedom in general with religious freedom. The sharp confinement of the public schools to secular education was a recognition of the need of a democratic society to educate its children, insofar as the State undertook to do so, in an atmosphere free from pressures in a realm in which pressures are most resisted and where conflicts are most easily and most bitterly engendered. Designed to serve as perhaps the most powerful agency for promoting cohesion among a heterogeneous democratic people, the public school must keep scrupulously free from entanglement in the strife of sects. The preservation of the community from divisive conflicts, of Government from irreconcilable pressures by religious groups, of religion from censorship and coercion however subtly exercised, requires strict confinement of the State to instruction other than religious, leaving to the individual's church and home, indoctrination in the faith of his choice.
>
> This development of the public school as a symbol of our secular unity was not a sudden achievement nor attained without violent conflict. While in small communities of comparatively homogeneous religious beliefs, the need for absolute separation presented no urgencies, elsewhere the growth

> of the secular school encountered the resistance of feeling strongly engaged against it. But the inevitability of such attempts is the very reason for Constitutional provisions primarily concerned with the protection of minority groups. And such sects are shifting groups, varying from time to time, and place to place, thus representing in their totality the common interest of the nation. . . .

7. Consider again the connection between the public school and the First Amendment. What is that link? How can a public school and the First Amendment together produce "unity" in a democracy? What does Justice Frankfurter mean by "our secular unity?" Finally, consider again the significance of the assumption that the drafters of the First Amendment were deeply religious. Should that have relevance in interpreting the Constitution itself?
8. Although the Supreme Court upheld the release-time program at issue in *Zorach,* its effort to distinguish the *Zorach* program from the *McCollum* program based in part on the degree of interdependence between religious and secular teachers may have set the stage for a new element in establishment clause jurisprudence. Should the constitutionality of a school program depend at all on the level of entanglement between public and parochial education?

C. PUBLIC ASSISTANCE FOR RELIGIOUS EDUCATION: THE *LEMON* TEST AND THE PROHIBITION ON ENTANGLEMENT

As the previous establishment clause cases reveal, the Supreme Court attempted to insure that legislation maintained neutrality toward religion by examining its purposes and effects. The "release-time" cases, however, raise an additional concern regarding increasing state interaction with religious instruction. In 1971, in *Lemon v. Kurtzman,* 403 U.S. 602 (1971), the Supreme Court articulated its concern by announcing a three-part test for determining whether legislation runs afoul of the establishment clause.

The Supreme Court in *Lemon* addresses state programs that provide financial assistance to church-related schools in the form of subsidizing the salaries of teachers at those schools. The so-called *Lemon* test has been applied in virtually every establishment clause challenge to educational programs since it was announced. Yet, as the cases that follow indicate, the test has undergone intense scrutiny and criticism. The Court has come close to abolishing the test, but instead has chosen to disregard it in recent days.

LEMON v. KURTZMAN

403 U.S. 602 (1971)

Mr. Chief Justice BURGER delivered the opinion of the Court.

These two appeals raise questions as to Pennsylvania and Rhode Island statutes providing state aid to church-related elementary and secondary schools. Both statutes are challenged as violative of the Establishment and Free Exercise Clauses of the First Amendment and the Due Process Clause of the Fourteenth Amendment. . . .

II

. . . The language of the Religion Clauses of the First Amendment is at best opaque, particularly when compared with other portions of the Amendment. Its authors did not simply prohibit the establishment of a state church or a state religion, an area history shows they regarded as very important and fraught with great dangers. Instead they commanded that there should be "no law *respecting* an establishment of religion." A law may be one "respecting" the forbidden objective while falling short of its total realization. A law "respecting" the proscribed result, that is, the establishment of religion, is not always easily identifiable as one violative of the Clause. A given law might not *establish* a state religion but nevertheless be one "respecting" that end in the sense of being a step that could lead to such establishment and hence offend the First Amendment.

In the absence of precisely stated constitutional prohibitions, we must draw lines with reference to the three main evils against which the Establishment Clause was intended to afford protection: "sponsorship, financial support, and active involvement of the sovereign in religious activity." *Walz v. Tax Commission*, 397 U.S. 664, 668 (1970).

Every analysis in this area must begin with consideration of the cumulative criteria developed by the Court over many years. Three such tests may be gleaned from our cases. First, the statute must have a secular legislative purpose; second, its principal or primary effect must be one that neither advances nor inhibits religion, *Board of Education v. Allen*. Finally, the statute must not foster "an excessive government entanglement with religion." *Walz*.

Inquiry into the legislative purposes of the Pennsylvania and Rhode Island statutes affords no basis for a conclusion that the legislative intent was to advance religion. On the contrary, the statutes themselves clearly state that they are intended to enhance the quality of the secular education in all schools covered by the compulsory attendance laws. There is no reason to believe the legislatures meant anything else. A State always has a legitimate concern for maintaining minimum standards in all schools it allows to operate. . . .

The legislatures of Rhode Island and Pennsylvania have concluded that secular and religious education are identifiable and separable. In the abstract we have no quarrel with this conclusion.

The two legislatures, however, have also recognized that church-related elementary and secondary schools have a significant religious mission and that a substantial portion of their activities is religiously oriented. They have therefore sought to create statutory restrictions designed to guarantee the separation between secular and religious educational functions and to ensure that State financial aid supports only the former. All these provisions are precautions taken in candid recognition that these programs approached, even if they did not intrude upon, the forbidden areas under the Religion Clauses. We need not decide whether these legislative precautions restrict the principal or primary effect of the programs to the point where they do not offend the Religion Clauses, for we conclude that the cumulative impact of the entire relationship arising under the statutes in each State involves excessive entanglement between government and religion.

III

In *Walz v. Tax Commission*, the Court upheld state tax exemptions for real property owned by religious organizations and used for religious worship. That holding, however, tended to confine rather than enlarge the area of permissible state involvement with religious institutions by calling for close scrutiny of the degree of entanglement involved in the relationship. The objective is to prevent, as far as possible, the intrusion of either into the precincts of the other.

Our prior holdings do not call for total separation between church and state; total separation is not possible in an absolute sense. Some relationship between government and religious organizations is inevitable. . . . Fire inspections, building and zoning regulations, and state requirements under compulsory school-attendance laws are examples of necessary and permissible contacts. . . . Judicial caveats against entanglement must recognize that the line of separation, far from being a "wall," is a blurred, indistinct, and variable barrier depending on all the circumstances of a particular relationship. . . .

In order to determine whether the government entanglement with religion is excessive, we must examine the character and purposes of the institutions that are benefited, the nature of the aid that the State provides, and the resulting relationship between the government and the religious authority. . . . Here we find that both statutes foster an impermissible degree of entanglement.

(a) Rhode Island program

The District Court made extensive findings on the grave potential for excessive entanglement that inheres in the religious character and purpose of the Roman Catholic elementary schools of Rhode Island, to date the sole beneficiaries of the Rhode Island Salary Supplement Act.

The church schools involved in the program are located close to parish churches. This understandably permits convenient access for religious exercises since instruction in faith and morals is part of the total educational process. The school buildings contain identifying religious symbols such as crosses on the exterior and crucifixes, and religious paintings and statues either in the classrooms or hallways. Although only approximately 30 minutes a day are devoted to direct religious instruction, there are religiously oriented extracurricular activities. Approximately two-thirds of the teachers in these schools are nuns of various religious orders. Their dedicated efforts provide an atmosphere in which religious instruction and religious vocations are natural and proper parts of life in such schools. Indeed, as the District Court found, the role of teaching nuns in enhancing the religious atmosphere has led the parochial school authorities to attempt to maintain a one-to-one ratio between nuns and lay teachers in all schools rather than to permit some to be staffed almost entirely by lay teachers.

On the basis of these findings the District Court concluded that the parochial schools constituted "an integral part of the religious mission of the Catholic Church." The various characteristics of the schools make them "a powerful vehicle for transmitting the Catholic faith to the next generation." This process of inculcating religious doctrine is, of course, enhanced by the impressionable age of the pupils, in primary schools particularly. In short, parochial schools involve substantial religious activity and purpose.

The substantial religious character of these church-related schools gives rise to entangling church-state relationships of the kind the Religion Clauses sought to avoid. Although the District Court found that concern for religious values did not inevitably or necessarily intrude into the content of secular subjects, the considerable religious activities of these schools led the legislature to provide for careful governmental controls and surveillance by state authorities in order to ensure that state aid supports only secular education.

The dangers and corresponding entanglements are enhanced by the particular form of aid that the Rhode Island Act provides. Our decisions from *Everson* to *Allen* have permitted the States to provide church-related schools with secular, neutral, or nonideological services, facilities, or materials. Bus transportation, school lunches, public health services, and secular textbooks supplied in common to all students were not thought to offend the Establishment Clause. . . .

In *Allen* the Court refused to make assumptions, on a meager record, about the religious content of the textbooks that the State would be asked to provide. We cannot, however, refuse here to recognize that teachers have a substantially different ideological character from books. In terms of potential for involving some aspect of faith or morals in secular subjects, a textbook's content is ascertainable, but a teacher's handling of a subject is not. We cannot ignore the danger that a teacher under religious control and discipline poses to the separation of the religious from the purely secular aspects of pre-college education. The conflict of functions inheres in the situation.

In our view the record shows these dangers are present to a substantial degree. The Rhode Island Roman Catholic elementary schools are under the general supervision of the Bishop of Providence and his appointed representative, the Diocesan Superintendent of Schools. In most cases, each individual parish, however, assumes the ultimate financial responsibility for the school, with the parish priest authorizing the allocation of parish funds. With only two exceptions, school principals are nuns appointed either by the Superintendent or the Mother Provincial of the order whose members staff the school. By 1969 lay teachers constituted more than a third of all teachers in the parochial elementary schools, and their number is growing. They are first interviewed by the superintendent's office and then by the school principal. The contracts are signed by the parish priest, and he retains some discretion in negotiating salary levels. Religious authority necessarily pervades the school system.

The schools are governed by the standards set forth in a "Handbook of School Regulations," which has the force of synodal law in the diocese.

It emphasizes the role and importance of the teacher in parochial schools: "The prime factor for the success or the failure of the school is the spirit and personality, as well as the professional competency, of the teacher." . . . The Handbook also states that: "Religious formation is not confined to formal courses; nor is it restricted to a single subject area." Finally, the Handbook advises teachers to stimulate interest in religious vocations and missionary work. Given the mission of the church school, these instructions are consistent and logical.

. . . The teacher is employed by a religious organization, subject to the direction and discipline of religious authorities, and works in a system dedicated to rearing children in a particular faith. These controls are not lessened by the fact that most of the lay teachers are of the Catholic faith. Inevitably some of a teacher's responsibilities hover on the border between secular and religious orientation.

We need not and do not assume that teachers in parochial schools will be guilty of bad faith or any conscious design to evade the limitations imposed by the statute and the First Amendment. We simply recognize that a dedicated religious person, teaching in a school affiliated with his or her faith and operated to inculcate its tenets, will inevitably experience great difficulty in remaining religiously neutral. Doctrines and faith are not inculcated or advanced by neutrals. With the best of intentions such a teacher would find it hard to make a total separation between secular teaching and religious doctrine. What would appear to some to be essential to good citizenship might well for others border on or constitute instruction in religion. Further difficulties are inherent in the combination of religious discipline and the possibility of disagreement between teacher and religious authorities over the meaning of the statutory restrictions.

We do not assume, however, that parochial school teachers will be unsuccessful in their attempts to segregate their religious beliefs from their secular educational responsibilities. But the potential for impermissible fostering of religion is present. The Rhode Island Legislature has not, and could not, provide state aid on the basis of a mere assumption that secular teachers under religious discipline can avoid conflicts. The State must be certain, given the Religion Clauses, that subsidized teachers do not inculcate religion—indeed the State here has undertaken to do so. To ensure that no trespass occurs, the State has therefore carefully conditioned its aid with pervasive restrictions. An eligible recipient must teach only those courses that are offered in the public schools and use only those texts and materials that are found in the public schools. In addition the teacher must not engage in teaching any course in religion.

A comprehensive, discriminating, and continuing state surveillance will inevitably be required to ensure that these restrictions are obeyed and the First Amendment otherwise respected. Unlike a book, a teacher cannot be inspected once so as to determine the extent and intent of his or her personal beliefs and subjective acceptance of the limitations imposed by the First Amendment. These prophylactic contacts will involve excessive and enduring entanglement between state and church.

There is another area of entanglement in the Rhode Island program that gives concern. The statute excludes teachers employed by non-public schools whose average per-pupil expenditures on secular education equal or exceed the comparable figures for public schools. In the event that the total expenditures of an otherwise eligible school exceed this norm, the program requires the government to examine the school's records in order to determine how much of the total expenditures is attributable to secular education and how much to religious activity. This kind of state inspection and evaluation of the religious content of a religious organization is fraught with the sort of entanglement that the Constitution forbids. It is a relationship pregnant with dangers of excessive government direction of church schools and hence of churches. . . .

(b) Pennsylvania program

The Pennsylvania statute also provides state aid to church-related schools for teachers' salaries. The complaint describes an educational system that is very similar to the one existing in Rhode Island. . . .

The Pennsylvania statute, moreover, has the further defect of providing state financial aid directly to the church-related school. This factor distinguishes both *Everson* and *Allen*, for in both those cases the Court was careful to point out that state aid was provided to the student and his parents—not to the church-related school. . . .

The history of government grants of a continuing cash subsidy indicates that such programs have almost always been accompanied by varying measures of control and surveillance. The government cash grants before us now provide no basis for predicting that comprehensive measures of surveillance and controls will not follow. In particular the government's post-audit power to inspect and evaluate a church-related school's financial records and to determine which expenditures are religious and which are secular creates an intimate and continuing relationship between church and state.

IV

A broader base of entanglement of yet a different character is presented by the divisive political potential of these state programs. In a community where such a large number of pupils are served by church-related schools, it can be assumed that state assistance will entail considerable political activity. Partisans of parochial schools, understandably concerned with rising costs and sincerely dedicated to both the religious and secular educational missions of their schools, will inevitably champion this cause and promote political action to achieve their goals. Those who oppose state aid, whether for constitutional, religious, or fiscal reasons, will inevitably respond and employ all of the usual political campaign techniques to prevail. Candidates will be forced to declare and voters to choose. It would be unrealistic to ignore the fact that many people confronted with issues of this kind will find their votes aligned with their faith.

Ordinarily political debate and division, however vigorous or even partisan, are normal and healthy manifestations of our democratic system of government, but political division along religious lines was one of the principal evils against which the First Amendment was intended to protect. Freund, Comment, Public Aid to Parochial Schools, 82 Harv. L. Rev. 1680, 1692 (1969). The potential divisiveness of such conflict is a threat to the normal political process. . . . To have States or communities divide on the issues presented by state aid to parochial schools would tend to confuse and obscure other issues of great urgency. We have an expanding array of vexing issues, local and national, domestic and international, to debate and divide on. It conflicts with our whole history and tradition to permit questions of the Religion Clauses to assume such importance in our legislatures and in our elections that they could divert attention from the myriad issues and problems that confront every level of government. The highways of church and state relationships are not likely to be one-way streets, and the Constitution's authors sought to protect religious worship from the pervasive power of government. The history of many countries attests to the hazards of religion's intruding into the political arena or of political power intruding into the legitimate and free exercise of religious belief.

Of course, as the Court noted in *Walz*, "adherents of particular faiths and individual churches frequently take strong positions on public issues." *Walz v. Tax Commission*. We could not expect otherwise, for religious values pervade the fabric of our national life. But in *Walz* we dealt with a status under state tax laws for the benefit of all religious groups. Here we are confronted with successive and very likely permanent annual appropriations that benefit relatively few religious groups. Political fragmentation and divisiveness on religious lines are thus likely to be intensified.

The potential for political divisiveness related to religious belief and practice is aggravated in these two statutory programs by the need for continuing annual appropriations and the likelihood of larger and larger demands as costs and populations grow. . . .

V

In *Walz* it was argued that a tax exemption for places of religious worship would prove to be the first step in an inevitable progression leading to the establishment of state churches and state religion. That claim could not stand up against more than 200 years of virtually universal practice imbedded in our colonial experience and continuing into the present.

The progression argument, however, is more persuasive here. We have no long history of state aid to church-related educational institutions comparable to 200 years of tax exemption for churches. Indeed, the state programs before us today represent something of an innovation. We have already noted that modern governmental programs have self-perpetuating and self-expanding propensities. These internal pressures are only enhanced when the schemes involve institutions whose legitimate needs are growing and whose interests have substantial political support. Nor can we fail to see that in constitutional adjudication some steps, which when taken were thought to approach "the verge," have become the platform for yet further steps. A certain momentum develops in constitutional theory and it can be a "downhill thrust" easily set in motion but difficult to retard or stop. Development by momentum is not invariably bad; indeed, it is the way the common law has grown, but it is a force to be recognized and reckoned with. The dangers are increased by the difficulty of perceiving in advance exactly where the "verge" of the precipice lies. As well as constituting an independent evil against which the Religion Clauses were intended to protect, involvement or entanglement between government and religion serves as a warning signal. . . .

NOTES AND QUESTIONS

1. In *Lemon,* the Supreme Court observes that the establishment clause was intended to protect against three main evils: sponsorship, financial support, and active involvement of the sovereign in religious activity. However, the Court also states that the language of the religion clauses of the First Amendment is "opaque." If the language is so unclear, then what is the origin of the Court's definition of the three "evils" the establishment clause was intended to guard against?
2. The "*Lemon* test" consists of a three-part analysis: the statute must have a secular legislative purpose, the principal or primary effect must not advance or inhibit religion, and the statute must not foster an excessive government entanglement with religion. Analyze the origin of the threepart test in *Lemon.* The test has been the subject of tremendous criticism. Indeed, its vitality is in serious doubt. How would you weigh the advantages and disadvantages of the test?
3. The Court declares that its prior holdings do not call for total separation between church and state, as complete separation is not possible in the absolute sense. Do you agree with this comment?
4. To determine whether a challenged statute excessively intertwines government and religion, the Court must examine the character and purposes of the benefiting institutions, the nature of the aid the state provides, and the resulting relationship between the government and religious authority. Do you agree with this analysis used to determine whether an "excessive" entanglement exists? Is there an alternative you would suggest for clarifying what is "excessive"?
5. The Court provides a laundry list of aid that states have been allowed in the past to provide to church-related schools without offending the religion clauses. The list of approved aid includes: secular, neutral, or nonideological services, facilities, or materials such as bus transportation, school lunches, public health services, and secular textbooks. What are additional examples of aid that you think would satisfy the First Amendment?
6. The Court had affirmed the constitutionality of tax exemptions for church property the previous year in *Walz v. Tax Commission,* 397 U.S. 664, 670 (1970). The Court explained that granting tax exemptions for church property did not constitute governmental support or sponsorship since the government did not transfer any of its revenues to churches. Rather, the tax exemption merely allowed the church to refrain from affirmatively supporting the state. Therefore, the Court held that federal or state tax exemption granted to churches was not a violation of

the religion clauses of the First Amendment. Do you agree with the Court's reasoning?

7. In *Tilton v. Richardson,* 403 U.S. 672 (1971), which was decided contemporaneously with *Lemon,* the Supreme Court applied its newly crafted three-part test to determine the constitutionality of Title I of the Higher Education Facilities Act of 1963. The Court first found a legitimate, secular purpose in the Act's creation of a program of construction grants for facilities at "institutions of higher education" which are not "primarily" used for religious purposes. The Court also found that the regime would not generally advance religion or create any excessive entanglement concerns. The Court, however, did declare unconstitutional a portion of the law which allowed a recipient of federal funds to use its facility for religious purposes 20 years after the completion of construction and therefore would have the unconstitutional effect of advancing religion.
8. In *Committee for Public Education v. Nyquist,* 413 U.S. 756 (1973), the Supreme Court applied its *Lemon* test to assess the constitutionality of New York's statutory scheme providing financial assistance to parochial schools in the form of grants for maintenance, repair and tuition, as well as income tax credits. After concluding that the statute's purpose of providing a healthy and safe environment for all school children was sufficiently secular, the Court found that "New York's maintenance and repair provisions violate the Establishment Clause because their effect, inevitably, is to subsidize and advance the religious mission of sectarian schools." In addition, the Court concluded that:

> New York's tuition reimbursement program also fails the "effect" test, for much the same reasons that govern its maintenance and repair grants. The state program is designed to allow direct, unrestricted grants of $50 to $100 per child (but no more than 50% of tuition actually paid) as reimbursement to parents in low-income brackets who send their children to nonpublic schools, the bulk of which is concededly sectarian in orientation. . . . By reimbursing parents for a portion of their tuition bill, the State seeks to relieve their financial burdens sufficiently to assure that they continue to have the option to send their children to religion-oriented schools. And while the other purposes for that aid—to perpetuate a pluralistic educational environment and to protect the fiscal integrity of overburdened public schools—are certainly unexceptionable, the effect of the aid is unmistakably to provide desired financial support for nonpublic, sectarian institutions.

The Court then turned to New York's system for providing income tax benefits to parents of children attending New York's non-public schools by allowing them to subtract from their adjusted gross income a specified amount if they do not receive a tuition reimbursement. Yet the Supreme Court invalidated these provisions as well:

> In practical terms there would appear to be little difference, for purposes of determining whether such aid has the effect of advancing religion, between the tax benefit allowed here and the tuition grant . . . [i]n both instances the money involved represents a charge made upon the state for

> the purpose of religious education. . . . A proper respect for both the Free Exercise and the Establishment Clauses compels the State to pursue a course of "neutrality" toward religion. . . . Special tax benefits, however, cannot be squared with the principle of neutrality by the decisions of this Court. To the contrary, insofar as such benefits render assistance to parents who send their children to sectarian schools, their purpose and inevitable effect are to aid and advance those religious institutions. . . . As the parties here must concede, tax reductions authorized by this law flow primarily to the parents of children attending sectarian, non-public schools. Without intimating whether this factor alone might have controlling significance in another context in some future case, it should be apparent that in terms of the potential divisiveness of any legislative measure the narrowness of the benefited class would be an important factor.

Finally, the *Nyquist* Court proceeded to analyze the entanglement prong of the *Lemon* test as well:

> The importance of the competing societal interests implicated here prompts us to make the further observation that, apart from any specific entanglement of the State in particular religious programs, assistance of the sort here involved carries grave potential for entanglement in the broader sense of continuing political strife over aid to religion.

9. The *Nyquist* and *Tilton* cases represent the heyday of the *Lemon* test. In both cases, the Court is able to use the concept of "entanglement" to conduct a case by case analysis of the effects of each provision of a challenged legislative scheme. Does "entanglement" allow for salutary precision in judicial analysis, or subjective assessments more suitable to legislators? Can you detect problems with the *Lemon* test even as the Court clings to its components?
10. *Meek v. Pittenger*, 421 U.S. 349 (1975), is another prime example of the application of *Lemon*. There, individuals and various organizations brought an action challenging, on First Amendment grounds, the constitutionality of Pennsylvania statutes providing for state loans for textbooks, instructional materials and equipment in connection with the education of students in non-public schools. The United States Supreme Court held that all but the textbook loan provisions of the statutes in question violated the establishment clause of the First Amendment.

    The Supreme Court first concluded that "the textbook loan provisions . . . are in every material respect identical to the loan program approved in *Allen*. Pennsylvania, like New York, 'merely makes available to all children the benefits of a general program to lend school books free of charge.' As such, those provisions . . . do not offend the constitutional prohibition against laws 'respecting an establishment of religion.'" The Court then proceeded to find, however, "that the direct loan of instructional material and equipment has the unconstitutional primary effect of advancing religion because of the predominantly religious character of the schools benefiting from the Act." The Court reasoned that "the primary beneficiaries" of the program are "nonpublic schools with a predominant sectarian character."

The Supreme Court further declared:

> We need not decide whether substantial state expenditures to enrich the curricula of church-related elementary and secondary schools, like the expenditure of state funds to support the basic educational program of those schools, necessarily result in the direct and substantial advancement of religious activity. For decisions of this Court make clear that the District Court erred in relying entirely on the good faith and professionalism of the secular teachers and counselors functioning in church-related schools to ensure that a strictly nonideological posture is maintained. . . . [T]he potential for impermissible fostering of religion is present. . . . The State must be certain, given the Religion Clauses, that subsidized teachers do not inculcate religion. . . . "A comprehensive, discriminating, and continuing state surveillance will inevitably be required to ensure that these restrictions are obeyed and the First Amendment otherwise respected. . . ."

The prophylactic contacts required to ensure that teachers play a strictly nonideological role, the Court held, give rise to an unconstitutional degree of entanglement between church and state. *See also Wolman v. Walter*, 433 U.S. 229 (1977) (upholding textbook lending and payments for student services not delivered on parochial school property, but nonetheless finding that state funding for teaching materials, equipment and field trips was unconstitutional because there was no way of insuring secular use without the type of ongoing monitoring prohibited as excessive entanglement).

11. In 1983, however, the Supreme Court began to loosen the *Lemon* test. In *Mueller v. Allen*, 463 U.S. 388 (1983), the Supreme Court found constitutional a Minnesota law that gave tax breaks for tuition, textbooks and transportation fees to parents with children in private schools. In distinguishing past decisions rejecting similar legislation, the Court found that because the deduction was available both to parents of children in private and public school, there was no violation. However, the Court did point out that it is likely that parents of private school children would benefit more than parents of public school children. In this decision, which seems to break with the *Lemon* test and its progeny, the Court noted that there is a benefit to having alternatives to public school and fostering "wholesome competition."

Mueller v. Allen

463 U.S. 388 (1983)

Justice Rehnquist delivered the opinion of the Court.

Minnesota allows taxpayers, in computing their state income tax, to deduct certain expenses incurred in providing for the education of their children.

. . . Minnesota, like every other State, provides its citizens with free elementary and secondary schooling. It seems to be agreed that about 820,000 students attended this school system in the most recent school year. During the same year, approximately 91,000 elementary and secondary students attended some 500 privately supported schools located in Minnesota, and about 95% of these students attended schools considering themselves to be sectarian.

Minnesota, by a law originally enacted in 1955 and revised in 1976 and again in 1978, permits state taxpayers to claim a deduction from gross income for certain expenses incurred in educating their children. The deduction is limited to actual expenses incurred for the "tuition, textbooks and transportation" of dependents attending elementary or secondary schools.

Today's case is no exception to our oft-repeated statement that the Establishment Clause presents especially difficult questions of interpretation and application. It is easy enough to quote the few words constituting that Clause—"Congress shall make no law respecting an establishment of religion." It is not at all easy, however, to apply this Court's various decisions construing the Clause to governmental programs of financial assistance to sectarian schools and the parents of children attending those schools. Indeed, in many of these decisions we have expressly or implicitly acknowledged that "we can only dimly perceive the lines of demarcation in this extraordinarily sensitive area of constitutional law." *Lemon.*

One fixed principle in this field is our consistent rejection of the argument that "any program which in some manner aids an institution with a religious affiliation" violates the Establishment Clause. . . . For example, it is now well established that a State may reimburse parents for expenses incurred in transporting their children to school, *Everson,* and that it may loan secular textbooks to all schoolchildren within the State, *Allen.*

Notwithstanding the repeated approval given programs such as those in *Allen* and *Everson,* our decisions also have struck down arrangements resembling, in many respects, these forms of assistance. *See, e.g., Lemon v. Kurtzman, supra; Meek v. Pittenger; Wolman v. Walter.* In this case we are asked to decide whether Minnesota's tax deduction bears greater resemblance to those types of assistance to parochial schools we have approved, or to those we have struck down. Petitioners place particular reliance on our decision in *Committee for Public Education v. Nyquist* where we held invalid a New York statute providing public funds for the maintenance and repair of the physical facilities of private schools and granting thinly disguised "tax benefits," actually amounting to tuition grants, to the parents of children attending private schools. As explained below, we conclude that [the Minnesota law], bears less resemblance to the arrangement struck down in *Nyquist* than it does to assistance programs upheld in our prior decisions and those discussed with approval in *Nyquist.*

The general nature of our inquiry in this area has been guided, since the decision in *Lemon v. Kurtzman, supra,* by the "threepart" test laid down in that case:

> First, the statute must have a secular legislative purpose; second, its principal or primary effect must be one that neither advances nor inhibits religion . . . ; finally, the statute must not foster "an excessive government entanglement with religion."

While this principle is well settled, our cases have also emphasized that it provides "no more than [a] helpful [signpost]" in dealing with Establishment Clause challenges. *Hunt v. McNair.* With this caveat in mind, we turn to the specific challenges raised . . . under the *Lemon* framework.

Little time need be spent on the question of whether the Minnesota tax deduction has a secular purpose. Under our prior decisions, governmental assistance programs have consistently survived this inquiry even when they have run afoul of other aspects of the *Lemon* framework. *See, e.g., Lemon v. Kurtzman; Wolman v. Walter.* This reflects, at least in part, our reluctance to attribute unconstitutional motives to the States, particularly when a plausible secular purpose for the State's program may be discerned from the face of the statute.

A State's decision to defray the cost of educational expenses incurred by parents—regardless of the type of schools their children attend—evidences a purpose that is both secular and understandable. An educated populace is essential to the political and economic health of any community, and a State's efforts to assist parents in meeting the rising cost of educational expenses plainly serves this secular purpose of ensuring that the State's citizenry is well educated. Similarly, Minnesota, like other States, could conclude that there is a strong public interest in assuring the continued financial health of private schools, both sectarian and nonsectarian. By educating a substantial number of students such schools relieve public schools of a correspondingly great burden—to the benefit of all taxpayers. In addition, private schools may serve as a benchmark for public schools, in a manner analogous to the "TVA yardstick" for private power companies. . . . All these justifications are readily available to support [the law], and each is sufficient to satisfy the secular purpose inquiry of *Lemon.*

We turn therefore to the more difficult but related question whether the Minnesota statute has "the primary effect of advancing the sectarian aims of the nonpublic schools." . . . In concluding that it does not, we find several features of the Minnesota tax deduction particularly significant. First, an essential feature of Minnesota's arrangement is the fact that [it], is only one among many deductions—such as those for medical expenses, and charitable contributions,—available under the Minnesota tax laws. Our decisions consistently have recognized that traditionally "[legislatures] have especially broad latitude in creating classifications and distinctions in tax statutes," . . . in part because the "familiarity with local conditions" enjoyed by legislators especially enables them to "achieve an equitable distribution of the tax burden." . . . Under our prior decisions, the Minnesota Legislature's judgment that a deduction for educational expenses fairly equalizes the tax burden of its citizens and encourages desirable expenditures for educational purposes is entitled to substantial deference.

. . . Most importantly, the deduction is available for educational expenses incurred by *all* parents, including those whose children attend public schools and those whose children attend nonsectarian private schools or sectarian private schools. . . .

In this respect, as well as others, this case is vitally different from the scheme struck down in *Nyquist.* There, public assistance amounting to tuition grants was provided only to parents of children in *non-public* schools. This fact had considerable bearing on our decision striking down the New York statute at issue; we explicitly distinguished both *Allen* and *Everson* on the grounds that "[in] both cases the class of beneficiaries included *all* schoolchildren, those in public as well as those in private schools." Moreover, we intimated that "public assistance (*e.g.*, scholarships) made available generally without regard to the sectarian-nonsectarian, or public-nonpublic nature of the institution benefited," might not offend the Establishment Clause. We think the tax deduction adopted by Minnesota is more similar to this latter type of program than it is to the arrangement struck down in *Nyquist*. Unlike the assistance at issue in *Nyquist*, [the Minnesota law], permits *all* parents—whether their children attend public school or private—to deduct their children's educational expenses. As *Widmar* and our other decisions indicate, a program, like [this one], that neutrally provides state assistance to a broad spectrum of citizens is not readily subject to challenge under the Establishment Clause.

We also agree with the Court of Appeals that, by channeling whatever assistance it may provide to parochial schools through individual parents, Minnesota has reduced the Establishment Clause objections to which its action is subject. It is true, of course, that financial assistance provided to parents ultimately has an economic effect comparable to that of aid given directly to the schools attended by their children. It is also true, however, that under Minnesota's arrangement public funds become available only as a result of numerous private choices of individual parents of school-age children. For these reasons, we recognized in *Nyquist* that the means by which state assistance flows to private schools is of some importance: we said that "the fact that aid is disbursed to parents rather than to . . . schools" is a material consideration in Establishment Clause analysis, albeit "only one among many factors to be considered." It is noteworthy that all but one of our recent cases invalidating state aid to parochial schools have involved the direct transmission of assistance from the State to the schools themselves. The exception, of course, was *Nyquist*, which, as discussed previously, is distinguishable from this case on other grounds. Where, as here, aid to parochial schools is available only as a result of decisions of individual parents no "imprimatur of state approval," *Widmar*, can be deemed to have been conferred on any particular religion, or on religion generally.

We find it useful, in the light of the foregoing characteristics of [Minnesota's law], to compare the attenuated financial benefits flowing to parochial schools from the section to the evils against which the Establishment Clause was designed to protect. These dangers are well described by our statement that "'[what] is at stake as a matter of policy [in Establishment Clause cases] is preventing that kind and degree of government involvement in religious life that, as history teaches us, is apt to lead to strife and frequently strain a political system to the breaking point.'" *Nyquist*, quoting *Walz v. Tax Comm'n* (opinion of Harlan, J.). It is important, however, to "keep these issues in perspective": "At this point in the 20th century we are quite far removed from the dangers that prompted the Framers to include the Establishment Clause in the Bill of Rights. See *Walz v. Tax Comm'n*. The risk of significant religious or denominational control over our democratic processes—or even of deep political division along religious lines—is remote, and when viewed against the positive contributions of sectarian schools, any such risk seems entirely tolerable in light of the continuing oversight of this Court." *Wolman*, (Powell, J., concurring in part, concurring in judgment in part, and dissenting in part).

The Establishment Clause of course extends beyond prohibition of a state church or payment of state funds to one or more churches. We do not think, however, that its prohibition extends to the type of tax deduction established by Minnesota. The historic purposes of the Clause simply do not encompass the sort of attenuated financial benefit, ultimately controlled by the private choices of individual parents, that eventually flows to parochial schools from the neutrally available tax benefit at issue in this case.

Petitioners argue that, notwithstanding the facial neutrality, the statute primarily benefits religious institutions. Petitioners rely, as they did below, on a statistical analysis of the type of persons claiming the tax deduction. They contend that most parents of public school children incur no tuition expenses, and that other expenses deductible under [the law], are negligible in value; moreover, they claim that 96% of the children in private schools in 1978-1979 attended religiously affiliated institutions. Because of all this, they reason, the bulk of deductions . . . , will be claimed by parents of children in sectarian schools. . . .

We need not consider these contentions in detail. We would be loath to adopt a rule grounding the constitutionality of a facially neutral law on annual reports reciting the extent to which various classes of private citizens claimed benefits under the law. Such an approach would scarcely provide the certainty that this field stands in need of, nor can we perceive principled standards by which such statistical evidence might be evaluated. . . .

Finally, private educational institutions, and parents paying for their children to attend these schools, make special contributions to the areas in which they operate. "Parochial schools, quite apart from their sectarian purpose, have provided an educational alternative for millions of young Americans; they often afford wholesome competition with our public schools; and in some States they relieve substantially the tax burden incident to the operation of public schools." *Wolman*, (Powell, J., concurring in part, concurring in judgment in part, and dissenting in part). If parents of children in private schools choose to take especial advantage of the relief provided by [the Minnesota law], it is no doubt due to the fact that they bear a particularly great financial burden in educating their children. More fundamentally, whatever unequal effect may be attributed to the statutory classification can fairly be regarded as a rough return for the benefits, discussed above, provided to the State and all taxpayers by parents sending their children to parochial schools. In the light of all this, we believe it wiser to decline to engage in the type of empirical inquiry into those persons benefited by state law which petitioners urge.

Thus, we hold that the Minnesota tax deduction for educational expenses satisfies the primary effect inquiry of our Establishment Clause cases.

Turning to the third part of the *Lemon* inquiry, we have no difficulty in concluding that the Minnesota statute does not "excessively entangle" the State in religion. The only plausible source of the "comprehensive, discriminating, and continuing state surveillance," necessary to run afoul of this standard would lie in the fact that state officials must determine whether particular textbooks qualify for a deduction. In making this decision, state officials must disallow deductions taken for "instructional books and materials used in the teaching of religious tenets, doctrines or worship, the purpose of which is to inculcate such tenets, doctrines or worship. . . ." Making decisions such as this does not differ substantially from making the types of decisions approved in earlier opinions of this Court. . . .

For the foregoing reasons, the judgment of the Court of Appeals is *Affirmed.*

NOTES AND QUESTIONS

1. Can the Court's decision upholding tax deductions for parochial school tuition be legitimately reconciled with its *Nyquist* decision invalidating grants and tax credits for parochial education?
2. In *Mueller*, the Minnesota statute allowed taxpayers to deduct expenses incurred for tuition, textbooks and transportation of their children attending elementary or secondary schools and the Supreme Court held this act did not offend the establishment clause of the First and Fourteenth Amendments. What are examples of public financial assistance to parochial schools that you think the Court would invalidate?
3. The Court commented that a state's efforts in assisting parents to meet the rising cost of educational expenses serves a secular purpose because educating the state's citizenry is essential to the survival of the community. Moreover, parochial schools sometimes have the effect of relieving the tax burden of operating public schools. Given this benefit of enhancing the entire education system, why would state assistance to a parochial school offend the establishment clause if the same type of aid was provided to parents who send their children to public schools? Keep in mind that the Court stated that one factor favoring the statute's constitutionality was that the deduction was available for educational expenses incurred by all parents.
4. The dissenting opinion in *Mueller* argued that the establishment clause prohibits a state from directly or indirectly subsidizing religious education and thus any tax benefit subsidizing tuition payments to sectarian schools or instructional materials used for sectarian purposes would be unconstitutional. Is there a meaningful constitutional difference between financial aid to parents whose children attend parochial schools in the form of a tax payment and more direct methods of aid? Do you think the dissent's point is valid?
5. Consider how the majority opinion employs each of the three components of the *Lemon* test. In light of the Court's dismissal of statistical evidence of the actual impact of the tax deductions, what is left of the "effects" component of the *Lemon* test? Is "facial neutrality" sufficient to satisfy the constitutional standard?
6. The Court's opinion in *Mueller* reiterates the following statement from the *Walz* case: "At this point in the 20th century we are quite far removed from

the dangers that prompted the Framers to include the Establishment Clause in the bill of rights." Do you agree that those "dangers" are "far removed"?

7. Consider the role of governmental monitoring in the Supreme Court's establishment clause cases. In *Meek*, the Supreme Court asserts that because the good faith of school administrators and teachers could not be assumed, the state would have to engage in excessive entangling and monitoring activities. In *Mueller*, however, the Court argues that entanglement will not be a concern because it is unwilling to assume that public and private school administrators will act in bad faith and require constant oversight. The issue of supervision is present in the next case as well. How does the *Aguilar* Court treat the relationship between the necessity of supervision and the issue of entanglement?

AGUILAR V. FELTON

473 U.S. 402 (1985)

Justice BRENNAN delivered the opinion of the Court.

The City of New York uses federal funds to pay the salaries of public employees who teach in parochial schools. In this companion case to *School District of Grand Rapids v. Ball*, [473 U.S. 373 (1985)] we determine whether this practice violates the Establishment Clause of the First Amendment.

I

A

The program at issue in this case, originally enacted as Title I of the Elementary and Secondary Education Act of 1965, authorizes the Secretary of Education to distribute financial assistance to local educational institutions to meet the needs of educationally deprived children from low-income families. . . .

II

In *School District of Grand Rapids v. Ball*, the Court has today held unconstitutional under the Establishment Clause two remedial and enhancement programs operated by the Grand Rapids Public School District, in which classes were provided to private school children at public expense in classrooms located in and leased from the local private schools. The New York City programs challenged in this case are very similar to the programs we examined in *Ball*. In both cases, publicly funded instructors teach classes composed exclusively of private school students in private school buildings. In both cases, an overwhelming number of the participating private schools are religiously affiliated. In both cases, the publicly funded programs provide not only professional personnel, but also all materials and supplies necessary for the operation of the programs. Finally, the instructors in both cases are told that they are public school employees under the sole control of the public school system.

Appellants attempt to distinguish this case on the ground that the City of New York, unlike the Grand Rapids Public School District, has adopted a system for monitoring the religious content of publicly funded Title I classes in the religious schools. At best, the supervision in this case would assist in preventing the Title I program from being used, intentionally or unwittingly, to inculcate the religious beliefs of the surrounding parochial school. But appellants' argument fails in any event, because the supervisory system established by the City of New York inevitably results in the excessive entanglement of church and state, an Establishment Clause concern distinct from that addressed by the effects doctrine. Even where state aid to parochial institutions does not have the primary effect of advancing religion, the provision of such aid may nonetheless violate the Establishment Clause owing to the nature of the interaction of church and state in the administration of that aid.

The principle that the state should not become too closely entangled with the church in the administration of assistance is rooted in two concerns. When the state becomes enmeshed with a given denomination in matters of religious significance, the freedom of religious belief of those who are not adherents of that denomination suffers, even when the governmental purpose underlying the involvement is largely secular. In addition, the freedom of even the adherents of the denomination is limited by the governmental intrusion into sacred matters. "[The] First Amendment rests upon the premise that both religion and government can best work to achieve their lofty aims if each is left free from the other within its respective sphere." *McCollum.*

In *Lemon v. Kurtzman*, the Court held that the supervision necessary to ensure that teachers in parochial schools were not conveying religious messages to their students would constitute the excessive entanglement of church and state. . . .

Similarly, in *Meek*, we invalidated a state program that offered, *inter alia*, guidance, testing, and remedial and therapeutic services performed by public employees on the premises of the parochial schools. As in *Lemon*, we observed that though a comprehensive system of supervision might conceivably prevent teachers from having the primary effect of advancing religion, such a system would inevitably lead to an unconstitutional administrative entanglement between church and state. . . .

The critical elements of the entanglement proscribed in *Lemon* and *Meek* are thus present in this case. First, as noted above, the aid is provided in a pervasively sectarian environment. Second, because assistance is provided in the form of teachers, ongoing inspection is required to ensure the absence of a religious message. . . . In short, the scope and duration of New York City's Title I program would require a permanent and pervasive state presence in the sectarian schools receiving aid.

This pervasive monitoring by public authorities in the sectarian schools infringes precisely those Establishment Clause values at the root of the prohibition of excessive entanglement. Agents of the city must visit and inspect the religious school regularly, alert for the subtle or overt presence of religious matter in Title I classes. . . . In addition, the religious school must obey these same agents when they make determinations as to what is and what is not a "religious symbol" and thus off limits in a Title I classroom. In short, the religious school, which has as a primary purpose the advancement and preservation of a particular religion must endure the ongoing presence of state personnel whose primary purpose is to monitor teachers and students in an attempt to guard against the infiltration of religious thought.

The administrative cooperation that is required to maintain the educational program at issue here entangles church and state in still another way that infringes interests at the heart of the Establishment Clause. Administrative personnel of the public and parochial school systems must work together in resolving matters related to schedules, classroom assignments, problems that arise in the implementation of the program, requests for additional services, and the dissemination of information regarding the program. Furthermore, the program necessitates "frequent contacts between the regular and the remedial teachers (or other professionals), in which each side reports on individual student needs, problems encountered, and results achieved."

We have long recognized that underlying the Establishment Clause is "the objective . . . to prevent, as far as possible, the intrusion of either [church or state] into the precincts of the other." *Lemon v. Kurtzman*. See also *McCollum v. Board of Education*. Although "[separation] in this context cannot mean absence of all contact," *Walz v. Tax Comm'n*, the detailed monitoring and close administrative contact required to maintain New York City's Title I program can only produce "a kind of continuing day-to-day relationship which the policy of neutrality seeks to minimize." The numerous judgments that must be made by agents of the city concern matters that may be subtle and controversial, yet may be of deep religious significance to the controlling denominations. As government agents must make these judgments, the dangers of political divisiveness along religious lines increase. At the same time, "[the] picture of state inspectors prowling the halls of parochial schools and auditing classroom instruction surely raises more than an imagined specter of governmental 'secularization of a creed.'" *Lemon v. Kurtzman*, (opinion of Brennan, J.).

III

Despite the well-intentioned efforts taken by the City of New York, the program remains constitutionally flawed owing to the nature of the aid, to the institution receiving the aid, and to the constitutional principles that they implicate—that neither the State nor Federal Government shall promote or hinder a particular faith or faith generally through the advancement of benefits or through the excessive entanglement of church and state in the administration of those benefits.

Affirmed.

NOTES AND QUESTIONS

1. This case allows the Court to flesh out the "entanglement" prong of the *Lemon* test. The Court identifies "critical elements" of the entanglement prohibited by *Lemon*: (1) aid provided in a "pervasively sectarian environment," and (2) "ongoing inspection" of teaching to insure the absence

of religious indoctrination. Is there a principled basis for these "critical elements"?

2. Justice Powell's concurrence in *Aguilar* stresses the "political divisiveness" aspect of the entanglement issue, arguing that direct aid to religious schools results in an impermissible risk of potential "strife" over the proper allocation of scarce resources. Do you agree? Where does Justice Powell's "political divisiveness" concern originate?
3. In this case, the majority felt the need to reaffirm the *Lemon* test, but did so by arguing that the test was particularly appropriate in cases involving the education of children. Why is that so? Do you agree? In the companion case of *School District of Grand Rapids v. Ball*, 473 U.S. 373 (1985), the Court assumes a valid secular purpose, allowing it to proceed to discuss the law's "effects" in detail. The Court in *Ball* announces three impermissible effects: (1) teachers become involved in inculcating religious beliefs; (2) a "symbolic link" between church and state which in the "eyes of impressionable youngsters" might give the impression of governmental support for religion, and (3) the provision of "subsidies" to the religious institutions affected. Is there any record or empirical support for these assumptions? Are these concerns unique to the education of young children?
4. Justice Brennan's opinion in *Ball* not only relies on distinctions between educational and noneducational institutions, it also relies on the distinction between "children in their formative years" and older students. Is the Court's distinction accurate? Even if it is accurate, should that distinction have constitutional relevance?
5. In their dissenting opinion in *Aguilar*, Justices O'Connor and Rehnquist argue that the "Court greatly exaggerates the degree of supervision necessary to prevent public school teachers from inculcating religion, and thereby demonstrates the flaws of a test that condemns benign cooperation between church and state." Further, the dissenters "disagree with the Court's analysis of entanglement, . . . and question the utility of entanglement as a separate Establishment Clause standard in most cases."
6. After *Aguilar*, the New York Board, like many such local educational agencies, began to offer Title I services to parochial school students at sites other than the parochial schools themselves, including public school sites. The cost of such means of avoiding *Aguilar*'s prohibitions was significant. As you will read shortly, the Supreme Court overturned the reasoning and result of *Aguilar* 12 years later in *Felton*. Can you discern the seeds of that reversal in the different opinions in *Aguilar*? Was the Court concerned with the cost of complying with the *Aguilar* rule? Or, is the reversal simply attributable to the changes in the Court's Justices?

CHAPTER 7

THE DECLINE OF LEMON *AND ENTANGLEMENT, AND THE RISE OF PRIVATE CHOICE AND VOUCHERS*

As discussed in Chapter 6, the *Lemon* test gave the courts a vehicle to police the interrelationship between governmental resources and religious education. Even as the *Lemon* test was embellished and applied, however, the seeds of its decline had been planted. As the Supreme Court refined the effects and entanglement elements of the *Lemon* test, it also began to focus on the level of pure governmental power involved in practices challenged under the First Amendment. If the decision to give resources for a religious educational purpose is made entirely by a private person, then arguably the government cannot be accused of violating the establishment clause. The Court used cases involving assistance to students with disabilities as the occasion for injecting a significant "private choice/governmental action" issue into establishment clause jurisprudence. After distinguishing impermissible, direct governmental support for religion from neutral governmental programs that allow private choices benefiting religion, the Court returned to its *Aguilar* decision and overturned it under a modified application of its *Lemon* test. Ultimately, the Court's emphasis on private choice and its deemphasis on the *Lemon* test lead it to approve vouchers in *Zelman*.

A. *LEMON* RECONSIDERED AND SHARED RESOURCES REVISITED

In *Witters v. Washington Dept. of Services for the Blind*, 474 U.S. 481 (1986), the Court held that the First Amendment does not preclude the state of Washington from extending assistance under a state vocational rehabilitation assistance program to a blind person studying at a Christian college and seeking to become a pastor, missionary, or youth director. After finding an "unmistakably secular purpose . . . to promote the well-being of the visually handicapped through the provision of vocational rehabilitation services," the Court concluded that the program did not have the effect of advancing religion: "[a]ny aid provided under Washington's program that ultimately flows to religious institutions does so only as a result of the genuinely independent and private choices of aid recipients. . . . In this case, the fact that aid goes to individuals means that the decision to support religious education is made by the individual, not by the State."

Justice O'Connor's concurring opinion in *Witters* emphasizes that when government aid supports a school's religious mission only because of independent decisions made by numerous individuals to guide their secular aid to that school, no reasonable observer is likely to draw an inference that the state itself is endorsing a religious practice or belief. In both Justice O'Connor's opinion and in the Court's opinion, there is the strong undercurrent distinguishing governmental action from independent decisions.

Similarly, in *Zobrest v. Catalina Foothills School District*, 509 U.S. 1 (1993), the Supreme Court upheld a public school district's provision of a sign-language interpreter to accompany a "special needs" student to classes at a Roman Catholic high school in Tucson, Arizona, pursuant to the Individuals with Disabilities Education Act (IDEA). Originally enacted in 1975, and amended in 1997, IDEA, 20 U.S.C. §§1400-1487, requires all children with learning disabilities to receive, "a free appropriate public education and related services designed to meet their unique needs." If necessary public facilities or services are not available in public school, then public funds must be channeled to private, even religious schools for the provision of those facilities or services.

Writing for the *Zobrest* Court, Justice Rehnquist reasoned:

> . . . We have never said that "religious institutions are disabled by the First Amendment from participating in publicly sponsored social welfare programs." For if the Establishment Clause did bar religious groups from receiving general government benefits, then "a church could not be protected by the police and fire departments, or have its public sidewalk kept in repair." Given that a contrary rule would lead to such absurd results, we have consistently held that government programs that neutrally provide benefits to a broad class of citizens defined without reference to religion are not readily subject to an Establishment Clause challenge just because sectarian institutions may also receive an attenuated financial benefit. Nowhere have we stated this principle more clearly than in *Mueller v. Allen*, . . . and *Witters v. Washington Dept. of Services for Blind*, . . . two cases dealing specifically with government programs offering general educational assistance. . . . That same reasoning applies with equal force here. The service at issue in this case is part of a general government program that distributes benefits neutrally to any child qualifying as "disabled" under the IDEA, without regard to the "sectarian-nonsectarian, or public-nonpublic nature" of the school the child attends. By according parents freedom to select a school of their choice, the statute ensures that a government-paid interpreter will be present in a sectarian school only as a result of the private decision of individual parents. In other words, because the IDEA creates no financial incentive for parents to choose a sectarian school, an interpreter's presence there cannot be attributed

> to state decision-making. . . . When the government offers a neutral service on the premises of a sectarian school as part of a general program that "is in no way skewed towards religion," it follows under our prior decisions that provision of that service does not offend the Establishment Clause. Indeed, this is an even easier case than *Mueller* and *Witters* in the sense that, under the IDEA, no funds traceable to the government ever find their way into sectarian schools' coffers. The only indirect economic benefit a sectarian school might receive by dint of the IDEA is the disabled child's tuition—and that is, of course, assuming that the school makes a profit on each student; that, without an IDEA interpreter, the child would have gone to school elsewhere; and that the school, then, would have been unable to fill that child's spot. . . . The IDEA creates a neutral government program dispensing aid not to schools but to individual handicapped children. If a handicapped child chooses to enroll in a sectarian school, we hold that the Establishment Clause does not prevent the school district from furnishing him with a sign-language interpreter there in order to facilitate his education. . . .

The Supreme Court in *Zobrest* reasons that the provision of governmental services to a religious school will survive a First Amendment challenge if: (1) the services are provided neutrally to any qualifying child without regard to religion, (2) the fact that services are provided in a sectarian school is solely the result of the parents' choice of educational institutions, and (3) no financial incentives exist for parents to choose a sectarian school. How does this analysis differ from the traditional *Lemon* test?

The Supreme Court distinguished *Zobrest* from earlier decisions because here the child, as opposed to the school, is the primary beneficiary. Justice Rehnquist emphasizes that the service at issue here is part of a general governmental program that distributes benefits "neutrally" to any child qualifying as "disabled" under IDEA. If every such child were to take their funds and use them to support a parochial education, would the service still be "neutral"? The Court again also stresses that the distribution of funds to parochial school is the product only of a private choice.

The *Zobrest* and *Witters* cases set the stage for a further, more explicit reconsideration of the *Lemon* test and its proper application. In *Agostini* and *Mitchell*, the Supreme Court reconsiders the issue of "resources-haring" between public and sectarian schools. In these decisions, several Justices become overtly critical of the *Lemon* test itself. The dramatic decline in the *Lemon* test eventually leads the Court to address the heated, contemporary issue of "vouchers" under a different construct. These cases wrestle with educational issues of immense political and practical significance. They also raise profound questions of constitutional jurisprudence and the Supreme Court's respect for its own precedent.

Agostini v. Felton

521 U.S. 203 (1997)

Justice O'Connor delivered the opinion of the Court.

In *Aguilar v. Felton*, this Court held that the Establishment Clause of the First Amendment barred the city of New York from sending public school teachers into parochial schools to provide remedial education to disadvantaged children pursuant to a congressionally mandated program. . . . Petitioners [now] maintain that *Aguilar* cannot be squared with our intervening Establishment Clause jurisprudence and ask that we explicitly recognize what our more recent cases already dictate: *Aguilar* is no longer good law. We agree with petitioners that *Aguilar* is not consistent with our subsequent Establishment Clause decisions and further conclude that, on the facts presented here, petitioners are entitled under Federal Rule of Civil Procedure 60(b)(5) to relief from the operation of the District Court's prospective injunction.

I

In 1965, Congress enacted Title I of the Elementary and Secondary Education Act of 1965, 79 Stat. 27, as modified, 20 U.S.C. §6301 *et seq.*, to "provide full educational opportunity to every child regardless of economic background." Toward that end, Title I channels federal funds, through the States, to "local educational agencies" (LEA's). The LEA's spend these funds to provide remedial education, guidance, and job counseling to eligible students. (LEA's must use funds to "help participating children meet . . . State student performance standards"), . . . (LEA's may use funds to provide "counseling, mentoring, and other pupil services") . . . Title I funds must be made available to *all* eligible children, regardless of whether they attend public schools, and the services provided to children attending private schools must be "equitable in comparison to services and other benefits for public school children."

A

. . . In order to evaluate whether *Aguilar* has been eroded by our subsequent Establishment Clause cases, it is necessary to understand the rationale upon which *Aguilar*, as well as its companion case, *Ball*, rested. . . .

Distilled to essentials, the Court's conclusion that the Shared Time program in *Ball* had the impermissible effect of advancing religion rested on three assumptions: (i) any public employee who works on the premises of a religious school is presumed to inculcate religion in her work; (ii) the presence of public employees on private school premises creates a symbolic union between church and state; and (iii) any and all public aid that directly aids the educational function of religious schools impermissibly finances religious indoctrination, even if the aid reaches such schools as a consequence of private decision making. Additionally, in *Aguilar* there was a fourth assumption: that New York City's Title I program necessitated an excessive government entanglement with religion because public employees who teach on the premises of religious schools must be closely monitored to ensure that they do not inculcate religion.

B

Our more recent cases have undermined the assumptions upon which *Ball* and *Aguilar* relied. To be sure, the general principles we use to evaluate whether government aid violates the Establishment Clause have not changed since *Aguilar* was decided. For example, we continue to ask whether the government acted with the purpose of advancing or inhibiting religion, and the nature of that inquiry has remained largely unchanged. . . . Likewise, we continue to explore whether the aid has the "effect" of advancing or inhibiting religion. What has changed since we decided *Ball* and *Aguilar* is our understanding of the criteria used to assess whether aid to religion has an impermissible effect.

1

As we have repeatedly recognized, government inculcation of religious beliefs has the impermissible effect of advancing religion. Our cases subsequent to *Aguilar* have, however, modified in two significant respects the approach we use to assess indoctrination. First, we have abandoned the presumption erected in *Meek* and *Ball* that the placement of public employees on parochial school grounds inevitably results in the impermissible effect of state-sponsored indoctrination or constitutes a symbolic union between government and religion. . . .

. . . Second, we have departed from the rule relied on in *Ball* that all government aid that directly aids the educational function of religious schools is invalid. . . .

[U]nder current law, the Shared Time program in *Ball* and New York City's Title I program in *Aguilar* will not, as a matter of law, be deemed to have the effect of advancing religion through indoctrination. Indeed, each of the premises upon which we relied in *Ball* to reach a contrary conclusion is no longer valid. First, there is no reason to presume that, simply because she enters a parochial school classroom, a full-time public employee such as a Title I teacher will depart from her assigned duties and instructions and embark on religious indoctrination. . . . Certainly, no evidence has ever shown that any New York City Title I instructor teaching on parochial school premises attempted to inculcate religion in students. . . .

Nor under current law can we conclude that a program placing full-time public employees on parochial campuses to provide Title I instruction would impermissibly finance religious indoctrination. . . . Accordingly, contrary to our conclusion in Aguilar, placing full-time employees on parochial school campuses does not as a matter of law have the impermissible effect of advancing religion through indoctrination.

2

Although we [have] examined . . . the criteria by which an aid program identifies its beneficiaries, we did so solely to assess whether any use of that aid to indoctrinate religion could be attributed to the State. A number of our Establishment Clause cases have found that the criteria used for identifying beneficiaries are relevant in a second respect, apart from enabling a court to evaluate whether the program subsidizes religion. Specifically, the criteria might themselves have the effect of advancing religion by creating a financial incentive to undertake religious indoctrination. . . .

In *Ball* and *Aguilar*, the Court gave this consideration no weight. Before and since those decisions, we have sustained programs that provided aid to *all* eligible children regardless of where they attended school. . . .

Applying this reasoning to New York City's Title I program, it is clear that Title I services are allocated on the basis of criteria that neither favor nor disfavor religion. The services are available to all children who meet the Act's eligibility requirements, no matter what their religious beliefs or where they go to school. The Board's program does not, therefore, give aid recipients any incentive to modify their religious beliefs or practices in order to obtain those services.

3

We turn now to *Aguilar*'s conclusion that New York City's Title I program resulted in an excessive entanglement between church and state. Whether a government aid program results in such an entanglement has consistently been an aspect of our Establishment Clause analysis. We have considered entanglement both in the course of assessing whether an aid program has an impermissible effect of advancing religion, and as a factor separate and apart from "effect," *Lemon v. Kurtzman*. Regardless of how we have characterized the issue, however, the factors we use to assess whether an entanglement is "excessive" are similar to the factors we use to examine "effect." That is, to assess entanglement, we have looked to "the character and purposes of the institutions that are benefited, the nature of the aid that the State provides, and the resulting relationship between the government and religious authority." Similarly, we have assessed a law's "effect" by examining the character of the institutions benefited (*e.g.*, whether the religious institutions were "predominantly religious"). . . . Indeed, in *Lemon* itself, the entanglement that the Court found "independently" to necessitate the program's invalidation also was found to have the effect of inhibiting religion. . . . Thus, it is simplest to recognize why entanglement is significant and treat it—as we did in *Walz*—as an aspect of the inquiry into a statute's effect.

Not all entanglements, of course, have the effect of advancing or inhibiting religion. Interaction between church and state is inevitable, and we have always tolerated some level of involvement between the two. Entanglement must be "excessive" before it runs afoul of the Establishment Clause. . . .

The pre-*Aguilar* Title I program does not result in an "excessive" entanglement that advances or inhibits religion. As discussed previously, the Court's finding of "excessive" entanglement in *Aguilar* rested on three grounds: (i) the program would require "pervasive monitoring by public authorities" to ensure that Title I employees did not inculcate religion; (ii) the program required "administrative cooperation" between the Board and parochial schools; and (iii) the program might increase the dangers of "political divisiveness." Under our current understanding of the Establishment Clause, the last two considerations are insufficient by themselves to create an "excessive" entanglement. They are present no matter where Title I services are offered, and no court has held that Title I services cannot be offered off-campus. Further, the assumption underlying the first consideration has been undermined. In *Aguilar*, the Court presumed that full-time public employees on parochial school grounds would be tempted to inculcate religion, despite the ethical standards they were required to uphold. Because of this risk *pervasive* monitoring would be required. . . . Since we have abandoned the assumption that properly instructed public employees will fail to discharge their duties faithfully, we must also discard the assumption that *pervasive* monitoring of Title I teachers is required. There is no suggestion in the record before us that unannounced monthly visits of public supervisors are insufficient to prevent or to detect inculcation of religion by public employees. Moreover, we have not found excessive entanglement in cases in which States imposed far more onerous burdens on religious institutions than the monitoring system at issue here.

To summarize, New York City's Title I program does not run afoul of any of three primary criteria we currently use to evaluate whether government aid has the effect of advancing religion: it does not result in governmental indoctrination; define its recipients by reference to religion; or create an excessive entanglement. We therefore hold that a federally funded program providing supplemental, remedial instruction to disadvantaged children on a neutral basis is not invalid under the Establishment Clause when such instruction is given on the premises of sectarian schools by government employees pursuant to a program containing safeguards such as those present here. The same considerations that justify this holding require us to conclude that this carefully constrained program also cannot reasonably be viewed as an endorsement of religion. . . . Accordingly, we must acknowledge that *Aguilar*, as well as the portion of *Ball* addressing Grand Rapids' Shared Time program, are no longer good law.

C

The doctrine of *stare decisis* does not preclude us from recognizing the change in our law and overruling *Aguilar* and those portions of *Ball* inconsistent with our more recent decisions. As we have often noted, "*stare decisis* is not an inexorable command," but instead reflects a policy judgment that "in most matters it is more important that the applicable rule of law be settled than that it be settled right." That policy is at its weakest when we interpret the Constitution because our interpretation can be altered only by constitutional amendment or by overruling our prior decisions. Thus, we have held in several cases that *stare decisis* does not prevent us from overruling a previous decision where there has been a significant change in or subsequent development of our constitutional law. As discussed above, our Establishment Clause jurisprudence has changed significantly since we decided *Ball* and *Aguilar*, so our decision to overturn those cases rests on far more than "a present doctrinal disposition to come out differently from the Court of [1985]." We therefore overrule *Ball* and *Aguilar* to the extent those decisions are inconsistent with our current understanding of the Establishment Clause. We therefore conclude that our Establishment Clause law has "significantly changed" since we decided *Aguilar*. We are only left to decide whether this change in law entitles petitioners to relief under Rule 60(b)(5). We conclude that it does.

MITCHELL v. HELMS

530 U.S. 793 (2000)

THOMAS, J., announced the judgment of the Court and delivered an opinion, in which REHNQUIST, C.J., and SCALIA and KENNEDY, JJ., joined. O'CONNOR, J., filed an opinion concurring in the judgment, in which BREYER, J., joined. SOUTER, J., filed a dissenting opinion, in which STEVENS and GINSBURG, JJ., joined.

As part of a longstanding school aid program known as Chapter 2, the Federal Government distributes funds to state and local governmental agencies, which in turn lend educational materials and equipment to public and private schools, with the enrollment of each participating school determining the amount of aid that it receives. The question is whether Chapter 2, as applied in Jefferson Parish, Louisiana, is a law respecting an establishment of religion, because many of the private schools receiving Chapter 2 aid in that parish are religiously affiliated. We hold that Chapter 2 is not such a law.

I

A

Chapter 2 of the Education Consolidation and Improvement Act of 1981, as amended, 20 U.S.C. §§7301-7373, has its origins in the Elementary and Secondary Education Act of 1965 (ESEA), and is a close cousin of the provision of the ESEA that we recently considered in *Agostini v. Felton*. Like the provision at issue in *Agostini*, Chapter 2 channels federal funds to local educational agencies (LEA's), which are usually public school districts, via state educational agencies (SEA's), to implement programs to assist children in elementary and secondary schools.

LEA's and SEA's must offer assistance to both public and private schools (although any private school must be nonprofit). Participating private schools receive Chapter 2 aid based on the number of children enrolled in each school, and allocations of Chapter 2 funds for those schools must generally be "equal (consistent with the number of children to be served) to expenditures for programs . . . for children enrolled in the public schools of the [LEA]." LEA's must in all cases "assure equitable participation" of the children of private schools "in the purposes and benefits" of Chapter 2. Further, Chapter 2 funds may only "supplement and, to the extent practical, increase the level of funds that would . . . be made available from non-Federal sources." §7371(b). LEA's and SEA's may not operate their programs "so as to supplant funds from non-Federal sources."

Several restrictions apply to aid to private schools. Most significantly, the "services, materials, and equipment" provided to private schools must be "secular, neutral, and nonideological." In addition, private schools may not acquire control of Chapter 2 funds or title to Chapter 2 materials, equipment, or property. A private school receives the materials and equipment . . . by submitting to the LEA an application detailing which items the school seeks and how it will use them; the LEA, if it approves the application, purchases those items from the school's allocation of funds, and then lends them to that school.

In Jefferson Parish, as in Louisiana as a whole, private schools have primarily used their allocations for nonrecurring expenses, usually materials and equipment. . . .

It appears that, in an average year, about 30% of Chapter 2 funds spent in Jefferson Parish are allocated for private schools. [41 of the 46 private schools are religious.]

B

Respondents filed suit in December 1985, alleging, among other things, that Chapter 2, as applied in Jefferson Parish, violated the Establishment Clause of the First Amendment of the Federal Constitution. . . .

II

The Establishment Clause of the First Amendment dictates that "Congress shall make no law respecting an establishment of religion." In the over 50 years since *Everson*, we have consistently struggled to apply these simple words in the context of governmental aid to religious schools. As we admitted in *Tilton v. Richardson*, 403 U.S. 672 (1971), "candor compels the acknowledgment that we can only dimly perceive the boundaries of permissible government activity in this sensitive area."

In *Agostini*, however, we brought some clarity to our case law, by overruling two anomalous precedents (one in whole, the other in part) and by consolidating some of our previously disparate considerations under a revised test. Whereas in *Lemon* we had considered whether a statute (1) has a secular purpose, (2) has a primary effect of advancing or inhibiting religion, or (3) creates an excessive entanglement between government and religion, in *Agostini* we modified *Lemon* for purposes of evaluating aid to schools and examined only the first and second factors. We acknowledged that our cases discussing excessive entanglement had applied many of the same considerations as had our cases discussing primary effect, and we therefore recast *Lemon*'s entanglement inquiry as simply one criterion relevant to determining a statute's effect. We also acknowledged that our cases had pared somewhat the factors that could justify a finding of excessive entanglement. . . .

In this case, our inquiry under *Agostini*'s purpose and effect test is a narrow one. Because respondents do not challenge the District Court's holding that Chapter 2 has a secular purpose, and because the Fifth Circuit also did not question that holding, we will consider only Chapter 2's effect. Further, in determining that effect, we will consider only the first two *Agostini* criteria, since neither respondents nor the Fifth Circuit has questioned the District Court's holding, that Chapter 2 does not create an excessive entanglement. Considering Chapter 2 in light of our more recent case law, we conclude that it neither results in religious indoctrination by the government nor defines its recipients by reference to religion. We therefore hold that Chapter 2 is not a "law respecting an establishment of religion." . . .

A

As we indicated in *Agostini*, and have indicated elsewhere, the question whether governmental aid to religious schools results in governmental indoctrination is ultimately a question whether any religious indoctrination that occurs in those schools could reasonably be attributed to governmental action. . . .

In distinguishing between indoctrination that is attributable to the State and indoctrination that is not, we have consistently turned to the principle of neutrality, upholding aid that is offered to a broad range of groups or persons without regard to their religion. . . . If the government is offering assistance to recipients who provide, so to speak, a broad range of indoctrination, the government itself is not thought responsible for any particular indoctrination. To put the point differently, if the government, seeking to further some legitimate secular purpose, offers aid on the same terms, without regard to religion, to all who adequately further that purpose, see *Allen* (discussing dual secular and religious purposes of religious schools), then it is fair to say that any aid going to a religious recipient only has the effect of furthering that secular purpose. The government, in crafting such an aid program, has had to conclude that a given level of aid is necessary to further that purpose among secular recipients and has provided no more than that same level to religious recipients.

As a way of assuring neutrality, we have repeatedly considered whether any governmental aid that goes to a religious institution does so "only as a result of the genuinely independent and private choices of individuals." *Agostini*. We have viewed as significant whether the "private choices of individual parents," as opposed to the "unmediated" will of government, *Ball*, determine what schools ultimately benefit from the governmental aid, and how much. For if numerous private choices, rather than the single choice of a government, determine the distribution of aid pursuant to neutral eligibility criteria, then a government cannot, or at least cannot easily, grant special favors that might lead to a religious establishment. Private choice also helps guarantee neutrality by mitigating the preference for pre-existing recipients that is arguably inherent in any governmental aid program, . . . and that could lead to a program inadvertently favoring one religion or favoring religious private schools in general over nonreligious ones. . . .

The tax deduction for educational expenses that we upheld in *Mueller* was, in these respects, the same as the tuition grant in *Witters*. We upheld it chiefly because it "neutrally provides state assistance to a broad spectrum of citizens," and because "numerous, private choices of individual parents of school-age children," determined which schools would benefit from the deductions. We explained that "where, as here, aid to parochial schools is available only as a result of decisions of individual parents no 'imprimatur of state approval' can be deemed to have been conferred on any particular religion, or on religion generally."

Agostini's second primary criterion for determining the effect of governmental aid is closely related to the first. The second criterion requires a court to consider whether an aid program "defines its recipients by reference to religion." As we briefly explained in *Agostini*, this second criterion looks to the same set of facts as does our focus, under the first criterion, on neutrality, but the second criterion uses those facts to answer a somewhat different question—whether the criteria for allocating the aid "create a financial incentive to undertake religious indoctrination." In *Agostini* we set out the following rule for answering this question:

> This incentive is not present, however, where the aid is allocated on the basis of neutral, secular criteria that neither favor nor disfavor religion, and is made available to both religious and secular beneficiaries on a nondiscriminatory basis. Under such circumstances, the aid is less likely to have the effect of advancing religion.

The cases on which *Agostini* relied for this rule, and *Agostini* itself, make clear the close relationship between this rule, incentives, and private choice. For to say that a program does not create an incentive to choose religious schools is to say that the private choice is truly "independent." . . . See *Agostini,* (holding that Title I did not create any impermissible incentive, because its services were "available to all children who meet the Act's eligibility requirements, no matter what their religious beliefs or where they go to school"). When such an incentive does exist, there is a greater risk that one could attribute to the government any indoctrination by the religious schools. . . .

We hasten to add, what should be obvious from the rule itself, that simply because an aid program offers private schools, and thus religious schools, a benefit that they did not previously receive does not mean that the program, by reducing the cost of securing a religious education, creates, under *Agostini*'s second criterion, an "incentive" for parents to choose such an education for their children. For *any* aid will have some such effect.

B

Respondents inexplicably make no effort to address Chapter 2 under the *Agostini* test. Instead, dismissing *Agostini* as factually distinguishable, they offer two rules that they contend should govern our determination of whether Chapter 2 has the effect of advancing religion. They argue first, and chiefly, that "direct, nonincidental" aid to the primary educational mission of religious schools is always impermissible. Second, they argue that provision to religious schools of aid that is divertible to religious use is similarly impermissible. Respondents' arguments are inconsistent with our more recent case law . . . and we therefore reject them. . . .

III

Applying the two relevant *Agostini* criteria, we see no basis for concluding that Jefferson Parish's Chapter 2 program "has the effect of advancing religion." Chapter 2 does not result in governmental indoctrination, because it determines eligibility for aid neutrally, allocates that aid based on the private choices of the parents of schoolchildren, and does not provide aid that has an impermissible content. Nor does Chapter 2 define its recipients by reference to religion.

Taking the second criterion first, it is clear that Chapter 2 aid "is allocated on the basis of neutral, secular criteria that neither favor nor disfavor religion, and is made available to both religious and secular beneficiaries on a nondiscriminatory basis." *Agostini*. Aid is allocated based on enrollment: "Private schools receive Chapter 2 materials and equipment based on the per capita number of students at each school," and allocations to private schools must "be equal (consistent with the number of children to be served) to expenditures for programs under this subchapter for children enrolled in the public schools of the [LEA]". . . .

Chapter 2 also satisfies the first *Agostini* criterion. The program makes a broad array of schools eligible for aid without regard to their religious affiliations or lack thereof. We therefore have no difficulty concluding that Chapter 2 is neutral with regard to religion. Chapter 2 aid also, like the aid in *Agostini*, *Zobrest*, and *Witters*, reaches participating schools only "as a consequence of private decision-making." Private decision-making controls because of the per capita allocation scheme, and those decisions are independent because of the program's neutrality. It is the students and their parents—not the government—who, through their choice of school, determine who receives Chapter 2 funds. The aid follows the child.

Because Chapter 2 aid is provided pursuant to private choices, it is not problematic that one could fairly describe Chapter 2 as providing "direct" aid. The materials and equipment provided under Chapter 2 are presumably used from time to time by entire classes rather than by individual students (although individual students are likely the chief consumers of library books and, perhaps, of computers and computer software), and students themselves do not need to apply for Chapter 2 aid in order for their schools to receive it, but, as we explained in *Agostini*, these traits are not constitutionally significant or meaningful. Nor, for reasons we have already explained, is it of constitutional significance that the schools themselves, rather than the students, are the bailees of the Chapter 2 aid. The ultimate beneficiaries of Chapter 2 aid are the students who attend the schools that receive that aid, and this is so regardless of whether individual students lug computers to school each day or, as Jefferson Parish has more sensibly provided, the schools receive the computers. Like the Ninth Circuit, and unlike the dissent, we "see little difference in loaning science kits to students who then bring the kits to school as opposed to loaning science kits to the school directly."

Finally, Chapter 2 satisfies the first *Agostini* criterion because it does not provide to religious schools aid that has an impermissible content. The statute explicitly bars anything of the sort, providing that all Chapter 2 aid for the benefit of children in private schools shall be "secular, neutral, and non-ideological," and the record indicates that the Louisiana SEA and the Jefferson Parish LEA have faithfully enforced this requirement insofar as relevant to this case. The chief aid at issue is computers, computer software, and library books. The computers presumably have no pre-existing content, or at least none that would be impermissible for use in public schools. Respondents do not contend otherwise. Respondents also offer no evidence that religious schools have received software from the government that has an impermissible content. . . .

IV

In short, Chapter 2 satisfies both the first and second primary criteria of *Agostini*. It therefore does not have the effect of advancing religion. For the same reason, Chapter 2 also "cannot reasonably be viewed as an endorsement of religion." Accordingly, we hold that Chapter 2 is not a law respecting an establishment of religion. Jefferson Parish need not exclude religious schools from its Chapter 2 program.

The judgment of the Fifth Circuit is reversed.

Justice O'CONNOR, with whom Justice BREYER joins, concurring in the judgment.

Three Terms ago, we held in *Agostini v. Felton*, that Title I, as applied in New York City, did not violate the Establishment Clause. I believe that *Agostini* likewise controls the constitutional inquiry respecting Title II presented here, and requires the reversal of the Court of Appeals' judgment that the program is unconstitutional as applied in Jefferson Parish, Louisiana. . . .

I

I write separately because, in my view, the plurality announces a rule of unprecedented breadth for the evaluation of Establishment Clause challenges to government school-aid programs. Reduced to its essentials, the plurality's rule states that government aid to religious schools does not have the effect of advancing religion so long as the aid is offered on a neutral basis and the aid is secular in content. The plurality also rejects the distinction between direct and indirect aid, and holds that the actual diversion of secular aid by a religious school to the advancement of its religious mission is permissible. Although the expansive scope of the plurality's rule is troubling, two specific aspects of the opinion compel me to write separately. First, the plurality's treatment of neutrality comes close to assigning that factor singular importance in the future adjudication of Establishment Clause challenges to government school-aid programs. Second, the plurality's approval of actual diversion of government aid to religious indoctrination is in tension with our precedents and, in any event, unnecessary to decide the instant case. . . .

Given the important similarities between the Chapter 2 program here and the Title I program at issue in *Agostini*, respondents' Establishment Clause challenge must fail. As in *Agostini*, the Chapter 2 aid is allocated on the basis of neutral, secular criteria; the aid must be supplementary and cannot supplant non-Federal funds; no Chapter 2 funds ever reach the coffers of religious schools; the aid must be secular; any evidence of actual diversion is *de minimis*; and the program includes adequate safeguards. Regardless of whether these factors are constitutional requirements, they are surely sufficient to find that the program at issue here does not have the impermissible effect of advancing religion. For the same reasons, "this carefully constrained program also cannot reasonably be viewed as an endorsement of religion." *Agostini*. Accordingly, I concur in the judgment.

NOTES AND QUESTIONS

1. Justice Thomas argues that private choices that result from a neutral legislative scheme cannot be attributable to government action. Do you agree? What is the relationship between neutrality and the "effects" component of the *Lemon* test? Should the constitutionality of a legislative

scheme depend upon the nature of the assistance provided? For instance, suppose the legislative regime allowed public resources to be diverted to construct sectarian schools to assist students with educational disabilities?

2. Justice Thomas's plurality opinion represents the views of only four Justices. Justice O'Connor's separate concurrence, therefore, becomes critical to the majority's current view of the law. What is the precise result in the case? Is there a single rule of law that can be discerned from reading the plurality opinion together with the concurrence?
3. In the wake of *Mitchell* and *Agostini*, is it possible to construct a test or template for the analysis of the constitutionality of any education statute under the establishment clause? For example, the analysis pursued by Justice Thomas in *Mitchell* proceeds in the following manner:

   First, the statute's expressed primary purpose must not be to either advance or inhibit religion. If so, the statute is unconstitutional.

   Second, assuming the statute's purposes are not unconstitutional, the statute's effects must be assessed. If the statute's primary effect is to advance or inhibit religion, the statute is unconstitutional.

   In performing that "effects" analysis, the following questions must be asked: (1) Does the statute have the effect of religious indoctrination attributable to the government?; (2) Does the statute define recipients in accordance with religion?; and (3) Does the statute so entangle government in religious education so as to have the effect of advancing or inhibiting religion?

   In answering each of these questions, the Court must determine whether the statute's effects are the product of private choices or the statute itself. If the effect of the statute is to advance religion because of the private choices made by citizens, then that effect cannot be attributable to improper governmental action.

B. VOUCHERS — THE BORDERLAND BETWEEN CHURCH AND STATE

The Supreme Court's evolving establishment clause case law distinguishing private choice from governmental benefits raises the issue whether educational resources can be redirected by parents to private, religious educational programs of their choosing. Such private initiatives may take the form of general school choice plans, charter schools or vouchers.

Vouchers enable parents to take some or all of the money that would have been allocated to a public school to educate their children and use it for private school education.[1] Vouchers typically do not represent cash payments directly to parents. Rather, the state or the district in which the child

[1] The National School Boards Association has prepared excellent materials regarding the political economy of vouchers. That material provides the authority for much of the information in this section. *See, e.g.* National School Boards Association Advocacy Tools on Vouchers, *www.nsba.org*.

otherwise would have been enrolled transfers funding from public to private school. The amount of the voucher often represents either some portion of state or local funding, or the amount of state aid that would have been paid for the child to attend public school in his or her school district. The actual cost to the school district can vary. In some proposals, those costs could exceed the amount of the voucher.

Although vouchers are frequently compared to tuition tax credit and tax deduction plans, they are different in several respects. Tax credit and deduction plans do not transfer funds from the state to a private institution. In effect, parents receive a discount from their tax obligations for tuition paid in a prior year rather than a grant or subsidy from a public agency that is remitted to a private school. Private schools tend to prefer vouchers because the schools receive the funds directly. Further, since vouchers are not derived from parents' income, they allow private schools to raise tuition more easily than do tax deductions or tax credits. Politically, vouchers are also more attractive than tax plans because many low-income parents cannot afford the upfront tuition costs needed to participate in a rebate program. Moreover, unless tax credits include negative or refundable income payments from the state, they are of no benefit to low-income people who pay little or no taxes. Tax deductions work to the disproportionate advantage of people in higher tax brackets and to the disadvantage of those who cannot benefit from a full tax deduction. Finally, tax plans operate as open-ended reductions in a state's revenue, whereas vouchers are paid for as deductions from a set level of state aid or local funding for education.

Vouchers also are often confused with charter schools and choice programs. More than half the states have passed laws allowing parents and teachers to establish charter schools at public expense. Charter schools operate relatively independently of the public school system, receive public funds on a per-pupil basis and involve student choice. At first glance, vouchers appear to resemble charter schools and thereby may add to state pressures to adopt them. However, there are several key distinctions. Most charters are granted by a public agency, such as a local school board. Charter schools are subject to criteria, expectations, operating conditions, and monitoring that are not required of private schools. Further, most charters are staffed by public employees, cannot charge tuition, and are subject to the same admissions requirements as public schools. However, there are some areas where the distinctions between charters and vouchers do become blurred. Several states, including Arizona, Minnesota, and Wisconsin, allow private schools to become charter schools. Depending on how it is implemented, a private school charter can operate as a "back-door" voucher. Additionally, a distinction should be made between public charter schools that are created by local school boards and those created by other entities, such as the state or a public university. Although public in character, these charter schools, like private school vouchers, redirect local school district finances without any legal, fiscal, or performance accountability to the voters in the community.

Finally, vouchers should not be confused with public school choice programs. Choice programs can include public charter schools, magnet schools and other public schools within the district and in other school districts.

In these choice programs, students remain within the public school system, and public resources are not redirected outside of the public school system.

In 1996, Cleveland, Ohio instituted a voucher program that limited eligibility to low-income students. In its *Zelman* decision, the United States Supreme Court voted 5-4 to uphold the constitutionality of the Cleveland voucher program.

ZELMAN v. SIMMONS-HARRIS

536 U.S. 639 (2002)

REHNQUIST, C.J., delivered the opinion of the Court, in which O'CONNOR, SCALIA, KENNEDY, and THOMAS, JJ., joined. O'CONNOR, J., and THOMAS, J., filed concurring opinions. STEVENS, J., filed a dissenting opinion. SOUTER, J., filed a dissenting opinion, in which STEVENS, GINSBURG, and BREYER, JJ., joined. BREYER, J., filed a dissenting opinion, in which STEVENS and SOUTER, JJ., joined.

Chief Justice REHNQUIST delivered the opinion of the Court.

The State of Ohio has established a pilot program designed to provide educational choices to families with children who reside in the Cleveland City School District. The question presented is whether this program offends the Establishment Clause of the United States Constitution. We hold that it does not. There are more than 75,000 children enrolled in the Cleveland City School District. The majority of these children are from low-income and minority families. Few of these families enjoy the means to send their children to any school other than an inner-city public school. For more than a generation, however, Cleveland's public schools have been among the worst performing public schools in the Nation. . . .

It is against this backdrop that Ohio enacted, among other initiatives, its Pilot Project Scholarship Program. The program provides financial assistance to families in any Ohio school district that is or has been "under federal court order requiring supervision and operational management of the district by the state superintendent." Cleveland is the only Ohio school district to fall within that category.

The program provides two basic kinds of assistance to parents of children in a covered district. First, the program provides tuition aid for students in kindergarten through third grade, expanding each year through eighth grade, to attend a participating public or private school of their parent's choosing. Second, the program provides tutorial aid for students who choose to remain enrolled in public school.

The tuition aid portion of the program is designed to provide educational choices to parents who reside in a covered district. Any private school, whether religious or nonreligious, may participate in the program and accept program students so long as the school is located within the boundaries of a covered district and meets statewide educational standards. Participating private schools must agree not to discriminate on the basis of race, religion, or ethnic background, or to "advocate or foster unlawful behavior or teach hatred of any person or group on the basis of race, ethnicity, national origin, or religion." Any public school located in a school district adjacent to the covered district may also participate in the program. Adjacent public schools are eligible to receive a $2,250 tuition grant for each program student accepted in addition to the full amount of per-pupil state funding attributable to each additional student. All participating schools, whether public or private, are required to accept students in accordance with rules and procedures established by the state superintendent.

Tuition aid is distributed to parents according to financial need. Families with incomes below 200% of the poverty line are given priority and are eligible to receive 90% of private school tuition up to $2,250. For these lowest-income families, participating private schools may not charge a parental co-payment greater than $250. For all other families, the program pays 75% of tuition costs, up to $1,875, with no co-payment cap. These families receive tuition aid only if the number of available scholarships exceeds the number of low-income children who choose to participate. Where tuition aid is spent depends solely upon where parents who receive tuition aid choose to enroll their child. If parents choose a private school, checks are made payable to the parents who then endorse the checks over to the chosen school.

The tutorial aid portion of the program provides tutorial assistance through grants to any student in a covered district who chooses to remain in public school. Parents arrange for registered tutors to provide assistance to their children and then submit bills for those services to the State for payment. Students from low-income families receive 90% of the amount charged for such assistance up to $360. All other students receive 75% of that amount. The number of tutorial assistance grants offered to students in a covered district must equal the number of tuition aid scholarships provided to students enrolled at participating private or adjacent public schools.

The program has been in operation within the Cleveland City School District since the 1996-1997 school year. In the 1999-2000 school year, 56 private schools participated in the program, 46 (or 82%) of which had a religious affiliation. None of the public schools in districts adjacent to Cleveland have elected to participate. More than 3,700 students participated in the scholarship program, most of whom (96%) enrolled in religiously affiliated schools. Sixty percent of these students were from families at or below the poverty line.

The program is part of a broader undertaking by the State to enhance the educational options of Cleveland's schoolchildren in response to the 1995 takeover. That undertaking includes programs governing community and magnet schools. Community schools are funded under state law but are run by their own school boards, not by local school districts. These schools enjoy academic independence to hire their own teachers and to determine their own curriculum. They can have no religious affiliation and are required to accept students by lottery.

Magnet schools are public schools operated by a local school board that emphasize a particular subject area, teaching method, or service to students. As of 1999, parents in Cleveland were able to choose from among 23 magnet schools, which together enrolled more than 13,000 students in kindergarten through eighth grade. These schools provide specialized teaching methods, such as Montessori, or a particularized curriculum focus, such as foreign language, computers, or the arts.

. . . In July 1999, respondents filed this action in United States District Court, seeking to enjoin the reenacted program on the ground that it violated the Establishment Clause of the United States Constitution.

The Establishment Clause of the First Amendment, applied to the States through the Fourteenth Amendment, prevents a State from enacting laws that have the "purpose" or "effect" of advancing or inhibiting religion. *Agostini v. Felton*. . . . There is no dispute that the program challenged here was enacted for the valid secular purpose of providing educational assistance to poor children in a demonstrably failing public school system. Thus, the question presented is whether the Ohio program nonetheless has the forbidden "effect" of advancing or inhibiting religion.

To answer that question, our decisions have drawn a consistent distinction between government programs that provide aid directly to religious schools, . . . and programs of true private choice, in which government aid reaches religious schools only as a result of the genuine and independent choices of private individuals. . . . While our jurisprudence with respect to the constitutionality of direct aid programs has "changed significantly" over the past two decades, our jurisprudence with respect to true private choice programs has remained consistent and unbroken. Three times we have confronted Establishment Clause challenges to neutral government programs that provide aid directly to a broad class of individuals, who, in turn, direct the aid to religious schools or institutions of their own choosing. Three times we have rejected such challenges. . . .

. . . *Mueller, Witters*, and *Zobrest* thus make clear that where a government aid program is neutral with respect to religion, and provides assistance directly to a broad class of citizens who, in turn, direct government aid to religious schools wholly as a result of their own genuine and independent private choice, the program is not readily subject to challenge under the Establishment Clause. A program that shares these features permits government aid to reach religious institutions only by way of the deliberate choices of numerous individual recipients. The incidental advancement of a religious mission, or the perceived endorsement of a religious message, is reasonably attributable to the individual recipient, not to the government, whose role ends with the disbursement of benefits. As a plurality of this Court recently observed: "[I]f numerous private choices, rather than the single choice of a government, determine the distribution of aid, pursuant to neutral eligibility criteria, then a government cannot, or at least cannot easily, grant special favors that might lead to a religious establishment." *Mitchell*. . . . It is precisely for these reasons that we have never found a program of true private choice to offend the Establishment Clause.

We believe that the program challenged here is a program of true private choice, consistent with *Mueller, Witters*, and *Zobrest*, and thus constitutional. As was true in those cases, the Ohio program is neutral in all respects toward religion. It is part of a general and multifaceted undertaking by the State of Ohio to provide educational opportunities to the children of a failed school district. It confers educational assistance directly to a broad class of individuals defined without reference to religion, i.e., any parent of a school-age child who resides in the Cleveland City School District. The program permits the participation of all schools within the district, religious or nonreligious. Adjacent public schools also may participate and have a financial incentive to do so. Program benefits are available to participating families on neutral terms, with no reference to religion. The only preference stated anywhere in the program is a preference for low-income families, who receive greater assistance and are given priority for admission at participating schools.

There are no "financial incentive[s]" that "ske[w]" the program toward religious schools. *Witters*. Such incentives "[are] not present . . . where the aid is allocated on the basis of neutral, secular criteria that neither favor nor disfavor religion, and is made available to both religious and secular beneficiaries on a nondiscriminatory basis." *Agostini*. The program here in fact creates financial disincentives for religious schools, with private schools receiving only half the government assistance given to community schools and one-third the assistance given to magnet schools. Adjacent public schools, should any choose to accept program students, are also eligible to receive two to three times the state funding of a private religious school. Families too have a financial disincentive to choose a private religious school over other schools. Parents that choose to participate in the scholarship program and then to enroll their children in a private school (religious or nonreligious) must copay a portion of the school's tuition. Families that choose a community school, magnet school, or traditional public school pay nothing. Although such features of the program are not necessary to its constitutionality, they clearly dispel the claim that the program "creates . . . financial incentive[s] for parents to choose a sectarian school." *Zobrest*.

Respondents suggest that even without a financial incentive for parents to choose a religious school, the program creates a "public perception that the State is endorsing religious practices and beliefs." But we have repeatedly recognized that no reasonable observer would think a neutral program of private choice, where state aid reaches religious schools solely as a result of the numerous independent decisions of private individuals, carries with it the imprimatur of government endorsement. *Mueller*; *Witters*; *Zobrest*; *Mitchell*. The argument is particularly misplaced here since "the reasonable observer in the endorsement inquiry must be deemed aware" of the "history and context" underlying a challenged program. Any objective observer familiar with the full history and context of the Ohio program would reasonably view it as one aspect of a broader undertaking to assist poor children in failed schools, not as an endorsement of religious schooling in general.

There also is no evidence that the program fails to provide genuine opportunities for Cleveland parents to select secular educational options for their school-age children. Cleveland schoolchildren enjoy a range of educational choices: They may remain in public school as before, remain in public school with publicly funded tutoring aid, obtain a scholarship and choose a religious school, obtain a scholarship and choose a nonreligious private school, enroll in a community school, or enroll in a magnet school. That 46 of the 56 private schools now participating in the program are religious schools does not condemn it as a violation of the Establishment Clause. The Establishment Clause question is whether Ohio is coercing parents into sending their children to religious schools, and that question must be answered by evaluating all options Ohio provides Cleveland schoolchildren, only one of which is to obtain a program scholarship and then choose a religious school.

Justice Souter [in dissent] speculates that because more private religious schools currently participate in the program, the program itself must somehow discourage the participation of private nonreligious schools. But Cleveland's preponderance of religiously affiliated private schools certainly did not arise as a result of the program; it is a phenomenon common to many American cities. . . . Indeed, by all accounts the program has captured a remarkable crosssection of private schools, religious and nonreligious. It is true that 82% of Cleveland's participating private schools are religious schools, but it is also true that 81% of private schools in Ohio are religious schools. To attribute constitutional significance to this figure, moreover, would lead to the absurd result that a neutral school-choice program might be permissible in some parts of Ohio, such as Columbus, where a lower percentage of private schools are religious schools, but not in inner-city Cleveland, where Ohio has deemed such programs most sorely needed, but where the preponderance of religious schools happens to be greater. . . . Likewise, an identical private choice program might be constitutional in some States, such as Maine or Utah, where less than 45% of private schools are religious schools, but not in other States, such as Nebraska or Kansas, where over 90% of private schools are religious schools.

Respondents and Justice Souter claim that even if we do not focus on the number of participating schools that are religious schools, we should attach constitutional significance to the fact that 96% of scholarship recipients have enrolled in religious schools. They claim that this alone proves parents lack genuine choice, even if no parent has ever said so. We need not consider this argument in detail, since it was flatly rejected in *Mueller*, where we found it irrelevant that 96% of parents taking deductions for tuition expenses paid tuition at religious schools. Indeed, we have recently found it irrelevant even to the constitutionality of a direct aid program that a vast majority of program benefits went to religious schools. See *Agostini*. . . . The constitutionality of a neutral educational aid program simply does not turn on whether and why, in a particular area, at a particular time, most private schools are run by religious organizations, or most recipients choose to use the aid at a religious school. As we said in *Mueller*, "[s]uch an approach would scarcely provide the certainty that this field stands in need of, nor can we perceive principled standards by which such statistical evidence might be evaluated."

This point is aptly illustrated here. The 96% figure upon which respondents and Justice Souter rely discounts entirely (1) the more than 1,900 Cleveland children enrolled in alternative community schools, (2) the more than 13,000 children enrolled in alternative magnet schools, and (3) the more than 1,400 children enrolled in traditional public schools with tutorial assistance. Including some or all of these children in the denominator of children enrolled in nontraditional schools during the 1999-2000 school year drops the percentage enrolled in religious schools from 96% to under 20%. *See also* J. Greene, *The Racial, Economic, and Religious Context of Parental Choice in Cleveland* 11, Table 4 (Oct. 8, 1999) (reporting that only 16.5% of nontraditional schoolchildren in Cleveland choose religious schools). The 96% figure also represents but a snapshot of one particular school year.

. . . The fluctuations seen in the Cleveland program are hardly atypical. Experience in Milwaukee, which since 1991 has operated an educational choice program similar to the Ohio program, demonstrates that the mix of participating schools fluctuates significantly from year to year based on a number of factors, one of which is the uncertainty caused by persistent litigation. Since the Wisconsin Supreme Court declared the Milwaukee program constitutional in 1998, *Jackson v. Benson*, 218 Wis. 2d 835, 578 N.W.2d 602 (1998), several nonreligious private schools have entered the Milwaukee market, and now represent 32% of all participating schools. Similarly, the number of program students attending nonreligious private schools increased from 2,048 to 3,582; these students now represent 33% of all program students. There are currently 34 nonreligious private schools participating in the Milwaukee program, a nearly five-fold increase from the 7 nonreligious schools that participated when the program began in 1990. And the total number of students enrolled in nonreligious schools has grown from 337 when the program began to 3,582 in the most recent school year. These numbers further demonstrate the wisdom of our refusal in *Mueller v. Allen*, to make the constitutionality of such a program depend on "annual reports reciting the extent to which various classes of private citizens claimed benefits under the law."

Justice Souter and Justice Stevens claim that community schools and magnet schools are separate and distinct from program schools, simply because the program itself does not include community and magnet school options. But none of the dissenting opinions explain how there is any perceptible difference between scholarship schools, community schools, or magnet schools from the perspective of Cleveland parents looking to choose the best educational option for their school-age children. Parents who choose a program school in fact receive from the State precisely what parents who choose a community or magnet school receive—the opportunity to send their children largely at state expense to schools they prefer to their local public school.

Respondents finally claim that we should look to *Nyquist* to decide these cases. We disagree for two reasons. First, the program in *Nyquist* was quite different from the program challenged here. *Nyquist* involved a New York program that gave a package of benefits exclusively to private schools and the parents of private school enrollees. . . . The program thus provided direct money grants to religious schools. It provided tax benefits "unrelated to the amount of money actually expended by any parent on tuition," ensuring a windfall to parents of children in religious schools. It similarly provided tuition reimbursements designed explicitly to "offe[r] . . . an incentive to parents to send their children to sectarian schools." Indeed, the program flatly prohibited the participation of any public school, or parent of any public school enrollee. Ohio's program shares none of these features.

Second, were there any doubt that the program challenged in *Nyquist* is far removed from the program challenged here, we expressly reserved judgment with respect to "a case involving some form of public assistance (e.g., scholarships) made available generally without regard to the sectarian-nonsectarian, or public-nonpublic nature of the institution benefited." That, of course, is the very question now before us, and it has since been answered, . . .

To the extent the scope of *Nyquist* has remained an open question in light of these later decisions, we now hold that *Nyquist* does not govern neutral educational assistance programs that, like the program here, offer aid directly to a broad class of individual recipients defined without regard to religion.

In sum, the Ohio program is entirely neutral with respect to religion. It provides benefits directly to a wide spectrum of individuals, defined only by financial need and residence in a particular school district. It permits such individuals to exercise genuine choice among options public and private, secular and religious. The program is therefore a program of true private choice. In keeping with an unbroken line of decisions rejecting challenges to similar programs, we hold that the program does not offend the Establishment Clause.

The judgment of the Court of Appeals is reversed.

It is so ordered.

Justice O'CONNOR, concurring.

The Court holds that Ohio's Pilot Project Scholarship Program survives respondents' Establishment Clause challenge. While I join the Court's opinion, I write separately for two reasons. First, although the Court takes an important step, I do not believe that today's decision, when considered in light of other longstanding government programs that impact religious organizations and our prior Establishment Clause jurisprudence, marks a dramatic break from the past. Second, given the emphasis the Court places on verifying that parents of voucher students in religious schools have exercised "true private choice," I think it is worth elaborating on the Court's conclusion that this inquiry should consider all reasonable educational alternatives to religious schools that are available to parents. To do otherwise is to ignore how the educational system in Cleveland actually functions. . . .

Based on the reasoning in the Court's opinion, which is consistent with the realities of the Cleveland educational system, I am persuaded that the Cleveland voucher program affords parents of eligible children genuine nonreligious options and is consistent with the Establishment Clause.

Justice THOMAS, concurring.

Frederick Douglass once said that "[e]ducation . . . means emancipation. It means light and liberty. It means the uplifting of the soul of man into the glorious light of truth, the light by which men can only be made free." Today many of our inner-city public schools deny emancipation to urban minority students. Despite this Court's observation nearly 50 years ago in *Brown v. Board of Education,* that "it is doubtful that any child may reasonably be expected to succeed in life if he is denied the opportunity of an education," 347 U.S. 483 (1954), urban children have been forced into a system that continually fails them. These cases present an example of such failures. Besieged by escalating financial problems and declining academic achievement, the Cleveland City School District was in the midst of an academic emergency when Ohio enacted its scholarship program.

The dissents and respondents wish to invoke the Establishment Clause of the First Amendment, as incorporated through the Fourteenth, to constrain a

State's neutral efforts to provide greater educational opportunity for underprivileged minority students. Today's decision properly upholds the program as constitutional, and I join it in full. . . .

While the romanticized ideal of universal public education resonates with the cognoscenti who oppose vouchers, poor urban families just want the best education for their children, who will certainly need it to function in our high-tech and advanced society. As Thomas Sowell noted 30 years ago: "Most black people have faced too many grim, concrete problems to be romantics. They want and need certain tangible results, which can be achieved only by developing certain specific abilities." *Black Education: Myths and Tragedies* 228 (1972). The same is true today. An individual's life prospects increase dramatically with each successfully completed phase of education. For instance, a black high school dropout earns just over $13,500, but with a high school degree the average income is almost $21,000. Blacks with a bachelor's degree have an average annual income of about $37,500, and $75,500 with a professional degree. See U.S. Dept. of Commerce, Bureau of Census, Statistical Abstract of the United States 140 (2001) (Table 218). Staying in school and earning a degree generates real and tangible financial benefits, whereas failure to obtain even a high school degree essentially relegates students to a life of poverty and, all too often, of crime. The failure to provide education to poor urban children perpetuates a vicious cycle of poverty, dependence, criminality, and alienation that continues for the remainder of their lives. If society cannot end racial discrimination, at least it can arm minorities with the education to defend themselves from some of discrimination's effects. . . .

Ten States have enacted some form of publicly funded private school choice as one means of raising the quality of education provided to underprivileged urban children. These programs address the root of the problem with failing urban public schools that disproportionately affect minority students. Society's other solution to these educational failures is often to provide racial preferences in higher education. Such preferences, however, run afoul of the Fourteenth Amendment's prohibition against distinctions based on race. See *Plessy*, (Harlan, J., dissenting). By contrast, school choice programs that involve religious schools appear unconstitutional only to those who would twist the Fourteenth Amendment against itself by expansively incorporating the Establishment Clause. Converting the Fourteenth Amendment from a guarantee of opportunity to an obstacle against education reform distorts our constitutional values and disserves those in the greatest need.

As Frederick Douglass poignantly noted "no greater benefit can be bestowed upon a long benighted people, than giving to them, as we are here earnestly this day endeavoring to do, the means of an education."

NOTES AND QUESTIONS

1. The Supreme Court concluded that Cleveland's voucher program involved strictly individual, private choices, and therefore did not offend the establishment clause of the First Amendment. If the primary goal of the Cleveland voucher program was to provide educational choices to

parents where statistics clearly illustrated a struggling public school system, why do you think the lower court argued that a parent's private, individual choice violated the establishment clause?

2. In order for a government aid program to pass constitutional muster, the program must be neutral with respect to religion, but it must also provide assistance directly to a broad class of citizens who channel government aid to religious schools. However, the Supreme Court failed to define what constitutes a "broad class of citizens." Do "families in financial need" qualify under the Court's definition of "broad class of citizens"? Should all parents, regardless of financial status, be eligible for government benefits supporting their private school choice for their children? For example, should wealthy parents who prefer private schools, regardless of whether they are religiously affiliated, be equally eligible for a tuition tax credit? How far should any government funding directed at religious schools extend, if at all?
3. The Supreme Court relies on *Agostini v. Felton* when it declares that a decisive factor in deciding whether government aid violates the establishment clause is whether the government acted with the purpose or effect of advancing religion. How has that standard been applied in *Zelman*?
4. In *Zelman*, the Supreme Court also drew a parallel from *Mueller*. The Court reasoned that in *Mueller*, the amount of government aid channeled to religious institutions by individual aid recipients was declared irrelevant to the program's constitutionality, and therefore the number of recipients choosing to utilize government aid at a religious school should be deemed an irrelevant factor in this case as well. Both cases resulted in the unintentional "effect" of advancing education in religious schools. Nonetheless, the Supreme Court held that since the parents in both cases have the ability to choose the particular school for their child to attend, the programs satisfied the establishment clause. In what ways are *Zelman* and *Mueller* distinguishable?
5. The Supreme Court established in *Zelman* that the voucher program was neutral toward religion and identified disincentives the program provided to parents who choose a private institution. Could parents argue that the financial disincentives of the voucher program toward parochial schools effectively inhibit religion, thus violating the Constitution? To remain "religious neutral" and satisfy the establishment clause, must the program treat all schools in the district equally, whether the school is public, Montessori, private, or parochial, and not offer any incentives to choose a particular type of school?
6. The Supreme Court declares that it has yet to find a program of true private choice in violation of the Establishment Clause. Is there any situation involving an individual's true private choice of schools that would cause the Court to declare the program unconstitutional?
7. Both Justice O'Connor's concurring opinion and Justice Souter's dissent debated the Court's consistency with its previous case, *Everson v. Board of Education of Ewing*, 330 U.S. 1 (1947). Recall that in *Everson*, the Court upheld a state statute that reimbursed the parents of parochial school

children for bus transportation. However, Justice Souter argued that the *Everson* Court also stated that no tax in any amount could be levied to support any religious activities or institutions, thus inaugurating the modern era of the establishment clause. Moreover, Justice Souter pointed out that there was no dissent in the *Everson* case. How would you answer his question: "how could the Court consistently let the *Everson* holding remain while simultaneously approving the Ohio voucher program"?

8. In his dissent, Justice Stevens argues that the majority was improperly influenced by three irrelevant facts: (1) Cleveland's educational crisis; (2) the range of choices available within the public school system, and (3) the voluntary character of the use of public funds to pay for religious education. Do you agree that these facts were both important to the majority and also irrelevant?
9. In his dissent, Justice Souter argues that the majority embraces the following evils which the establishment clause was designed by Jefferson and Madison to avoid: (1) disrespect for freedom of conscience; (2) the political corruption of religion; and (3) social conflict and division. How are these evils present here?
10. Milwaukee has operated a voucher program since 1990, and over the years, the legislature has expanded the original program. The Supreme Court refers to Milwaukee's voucher program, suggesting that it has been successful. The program was amended in 1995 to open the program to any child residing in Milwaukee whose family's income is below 125 percent of the poverty level. The program initially was open to all eligible public school children in grades K-12, with the maximum number of vouchers set at 7 percent of public school enrollment or a maximum of 7,250 students. The program was then allowed to double to 15 percent (or about 15,000 students in 1996-1997). Students are selected by random lottery.

    Enrollment of voucher students in any one school initially was limited to 50 percent, then to 65 percent. Currently, there is no limit on the portion of the student body that can include voucher students. The amount of the voucher, which is nearly $4,700 per pupil (full-time equivalent), is equal to the amount of per-pupil state aid that would have been paid to the Milwaukee school system, but not greater than the cost of educating a child at the private school.

    Over the first four years, the program grew from 341 to 802 students, or about half the authorized level. During that time, the number of participating schools expanded from 6 to 12. Currently, 1,600 students are using vouchers. By comparison, Milwaukee's 130 private schools enrolled more than 24,000 students in 1995, or about 30 percent of the city's middle- and upper-income children and 7 percent of the children from the city's poorest neighborhoods.

    The Wisconsin Supreme Court, in *Jackson v. Benson*, 578 N.W.2d 602 (Wis. 1998), upheld the voucher program against claims that the program violated well-settled Establishment Clause jurisprudence. The Supreme Court in *Zelman* appears to sanction this result.

11. There are now more than two dozen privately funded voucher programs in the country. Two of the more established are in San Antonio and Indianapolis. San Antonio set up a public school choice program emphasizing immersion into Latino language, culture and history. In addition, the business community created a program to allow 2,000 poor children to attend private schools through a private scholarship program. Parents pay about one-half the tuition cost. In this program, 99 percent of the students are enrolled in sectarian schools, mainly Catholic, and 95 percent of the parents rate religious training as very important or important.

    In Indianapolis, a privately financed trust was established in 1991 that supports the enrollment of about 1,000 children from low-income families in 67 private schools. As in San Antonio, parents pay about one-half the tuition cost. The private schools are overwhelmingly sectarian and enroll 75 percent of the children involved in the program. Forty percent of non-Catholic parents participating in the voucher program send their children to Catholic schools.

    Since *Zelman*, publicly funded voucher programs have been developed throughout the country. The D.C. program involves a five-year, federally funded experiment that will provide vouchers of up to $7,500 for public school students to attend private schools in the area. As is typical of the existing voucher programs, most of the students in the D.C. program are expected to use their publicly funded vouchers to attend parochial school. In fact, the Catholic Archdiocese of Washington alone is expecting to draw more than 80 percent of the eligible students. *See* Spencer S. Itsu and Justin Blum, *D.C. School Vouchers Win Final Approval*, Washington Post, at A01 (Jan. 23, 2004).

12. The Supreme Court's decision upholding the constitutionality of Cleveland's voucher program has shifted the voucher debate from the legal to the political arena. The legal arguments in favor of and in opposition to vouchers have now become political arguments. Consider the following political and economic issues raised by vouchers: (1) whether vouchers will enhance parental choice; (2) whether vouchers will spur competition between public and private education, thereby improving public education; (3) whether vouchers will increase parental control over tax dollars; (4) whether vouchers will open opportunities for minority and low-income families; (5) whether vouchers will offer help for low-income parents whose children are currently in private school; (6) whether vouchers will save money for public education; (7) whether vouchers can save taxpayers' money; and (8) whether vouchers will undermine public education.

13. In a position paper prepared in the wake of the relative popularity of vouchers by Michael A. Resnick for the National School Boards Association, the author identifies four reasons why vouchers will not work in the real world: (1) vouchers weaken public education; (2) vouchers undermine opportunity for all; (3) vouchers waste taxpayer dollars, and (4) vouchers promote a divided America. Resnick, *Why Vouchers Won't Work* (Natl. School Bds. Assn. 1998).

According to the National School Boards Association (NSBA), vouchers will weaken, not improve, public education because they will siphon off much-needed financial resources as well as the best students and the most engaged parents. As such, vouchers will not improve public education but rather will undermine the public schools' capacity to compete and improve. Vouchers also will encourage policymakers and others to give up on public education. They weaken the commitment to universal educational opportunity.

Moreover, the NSBA contends that vouchers are not really about universal parent choice. Geography and family finances will limit most low-income students to a very narrow range of private schools. Even then, the private school, not the parent, will determine which child is admitted and retained. Therefore, vouchers will not broaden the choices available to children from low-income families or those who do not meet the profile of private schools. Rather, vouchers will provide more choices to private institutions to determine which children to accept or reject. In fact, according to the NSBA, vouchers will reduce equity in educational opportunity. Even with vouchers, low-income families will still be financially, socially and geographically shut out of all but the cheapest neighborhood private schools.

In fact, vouchers arguably waste taxpayers' dollars. They will force taxpayers to support two education systems. With 4.8 million children currently enrolled in private schools (1993-1994), a universal voucher of $3,000 per child would immediately reallocate over $14 billion from public to private schools. Such a reduction in public school funds will hardly improve the education of children enrolled in public schools. In fact, such a shortfall is likely to force state legislatures and school boards to raise taxes to make up for at least some of the lost revenue. In effect, the NSBA concludes, taxpayers will be asked to support two education systems instead of one. Given a finite amount of public money, the pressure to fund this growing entitlement most likely will come at the expense of general funds for public schools.

In addition, according to U.S. Department of Education statistics, four out of every five students in private schools come from families whose annual incomes exceed $50,000. In the public schools, only about one out of five students come from families at that income level. High-income families, therefore, will become the primary beneficiaries of vouchers.

Furthermore, according to the NSBA, vouchers will lead to the balkanization of American education and culture. By encouraging more students to enroll in a diffuse collection of private schools, the public interest in promoting an American culture and identity will be ignored or diminished. Indeed, vouchers will foster the creation of publicly subsidized "niche" schools defined by ethnicity, language, or religion.

Vouchers may even resegregate American education. In many communities, universal vouchers will become a publicly funded ticket to end desegregation to the detriment of many students and the nation as a whole. While some private schools may have open admissions policies, unless they are required to maintain racial balance, their tuition, location, school culture, and mission can easily attract students along racial lines as well as undo public school desegregation plans.

Voucher opponents, of course, also argue that they will help tear down the wall that separates church and state. In 1993-1994, about 85 percent of the nation's 4.8 million private school students were enrolled in church-affiliated schools. Hence, the relationship between vouchers and public sponsorship of religion is a real issue. Using funds derived from all taxpayers to promote specific and conflicting religious beliefs in a diverse society has been criticized as bad public policy. Specifically, channeling public tax dollars to religious schools is arguably divisive and threatens to erode support from taxpayers who might disagree with the religious tenets and practices their tax dollars might be redirected to support.

The National School Boards Association further contends that vouchers should be rejected because they will invite the regulation of private education; create more government dependence by parents and private schools; lead to accreditation of private schools, certification of all teachers, and defined standards relating to all enrollment practices and curriculum; break down the funding barriers between government and private schools; lead to adherence to more government rules and regulations and ultimately decrease private school autonomy while increasing costs for everyone.

14. These final sweeping arguments attack vouchers as an assault on public education itself. As the breadth of the voucher debate suggests, the issue of vouchers raises questions about the fundamental value of public education, and the political will to share in the education of the community's children. As such, the debate revisits fundamental philosophic premises about the role of the state in providing for the education of its citizens. How would classical educational philosophers like Plato and Aristotle react to the voucher movement? What might Locke or Rousseau think? Would Dewey support the use of public resources for private, religious education? The answer may turn on whether the education of children in a democracy should be primarily a private, familial responsibility or primarily a shared, public responsibility.

15. *Zelman* holds that the establishment clause does not prevent the government from operating a voucher program which allows voucher recipients to choose to use their vouchers to attend a parochial institution. The Court had no occasion to reach the very different question of whether such a publicly funded voucher program may *preclude* recipients from using their vouchers to attend parochial institutions, without violating the free exercise clause. According to *Zelman*, the government *may* decide to include religious institutions in its voucher program, but *must* it do so? In *Locke v. Davey*, 124 S. Ct. 1307 (2004), the Supreme Court addressed the issue of whether the Constitution's free exercise clause compels a state to devote public funds to religious instruction in situations where it devotes public funds to secular instruction. Joshua Davey applied for a state of Washington scholarship to help him complete pastoral ministry training at a private college in the state. Although Davey was otherwise qualified for the scholarship, the state determined that he was not eligible because the state's constitution expressly prohibits the use of public money to fund religious instruction. The Ninth Circuit held that the state lacked a sufficiently compelling interest in enforcing its constitutional ban on funding religious education to justify a program that burdens religious exercise by denying funding for religious education. *Davey v. Locke*, 299 F.2d 748 (9th Cir. 2002). The Supreme Court, however, reversed.

16. Charter schools are "publicly funded elementary or secondary schools that have been freed from some of the rules, regulations, and statutes that apply to other public schools, in exchange for some type of accountability for producing certain results, which are set forth in each school's charter." *See* National Educational Association, *www.nea.org/charter*. The National Educational Association ("NEA") has recognized that "charter schools and other nontraditional public school options have the potential to facilitate education reforms and develop new and creative teaching methods that can be replicated in traditional public schools for the benefit of all children. Whether charter schools will fulfill this potential depends on how charter schools are designed and implemented, including the oversight and assistance provided by charter authorizers." *www.nea.org/charter* According to the NEA however,

- A charter should be granted only if the proposed school intends to offer an educational experience that is qualitatively different from what is available in traditional public schools.
- Local school boards should have the authority to grant or deny charter applications; the process should be open to the public, and applicants should have the right to appeal to a state agency decisions to deny or revoke a charter.
- Charter school funding should not disproportionately divert resources from traditional public schools.
- Charter schools should be monitored on a continuing basis and should be subject to modification or closure if children or the public interest is at risk.
- Private schools should not be allowed to convert to public charter schools, and private for-profit entities should not be eligible to receive a charter.
- Charter schools should be subject to the same public sector labor relations statutes as traditional public schools, and charter school employees should have the same collective bargaining rights as their counterparts in traditional public schools. . . .

Beginning with two charter schools in Minnesota in 1991, there were almost 3,000 charter schools by 2004, operating in 37 states plus the District of Columbia and Puerto Rico, and enrolling approximately 750,000 students. However, more than one-third of those schools had been in operation for three years or less, while more than 400 other charter schools had gone out of business between 1991 and 2004. . . .

Because charter schools vary as widely as traditional public schools, their academic achievement also varies widely. It is difficult–not to mention scientifically invalid–to make blanket comparisons of charter schools to traditional public schools. However, because charter schools promise to improve student achievement as a condition of relief from some of the rules and regulations that apply to traditional public schools, it is appropriate to evaluate their effectiveness.

In 2004, the National Assessment Governing Board (NAGB) released an analysis of charter school performance on he 2003 National Assessment of Educational Progress (NAEP), also known as "The Nation's Report Card." The report found that charter school students, on average, score lower than students in traditional public schools. While there was no measurable difference between charter school students and students in traditional public schools in the same racial/ethnic subgroup, charter school students who were eligible for free or reduced-price lunch scored lower than their peers in traditional public schools, and charter school students in central cities scored lower than their peers in math in 4th grade.

NAGB looked at the impact of school characteristics and found that:

- Charter schools that were part of the local school district had significantly higher scores than charter schools that served as their own district.
- Students taught by certified teachers had roughly comparable scores whether they attended charter schools or traditional public schools, but the scores of students taught by uncertified teachers in charter schools were significantly lower than those of charter school students with certified teachers.
- Students taught by teachers with at least five years' experience outperformed students with less experienced teachers, regardless of the type of school attended, but charter school students with inexperienced teachers did significantly worse than students in traditional public schools with less experienced teachers. (The impact of this finding is compounded by the fact that charter schools are twice as likely as traditional public schools to employ inexperienced teachers.)

In a study that followed North Carolina students for several years, professors Robert Bifulco and Helen Ladd found that students in charter schools actually made considerably smaller achievement gains in charter schools than they would have in traditional public schools.

Similarly, data from the National Assessment of Educational Progress (NAEP) released in December 2004 found that fourth-grade charter school students do no better than their public school counterparts on math and reading assessments and in some cases score lower.

While the report is credible and the results are important in what should be the ongoing monitoring of charter school performance, they should be viewed in perspective.

As National Assessment Governing Board Chairman Darvin Winick pointed out, "one snapshot in time cannot determine the achievement of students."

It's a noteworthy observation because that's exactly what the federal so-called "No Child Left Behind" law does. Under its provisions, the results of one test–"one snapshot in time"–are used to determine if a school or a whole district is performing acceptably or is "failing."

The NAEP study found that fourth-grade charter school students as a whole did not perform as well as public school fourth-graders in math, and performed about the same in reading. Breaking down the data to compare students of similar characteristics gives slight results:

- Among students of similar racial/ethnic backgrounds, the study found no difference in math or reading performance between charter school students and students in traditional public schools.
- Among students eligible for free or reduced-price lunch, the charter school fourth-graders scored lower in reading and mathematics, on average, than the fourth-graders in regular public school.
- The scores of students taught by uncertified teachers in charter schools were significantly lower than those of charter school students with certified teachers, and students taught by teachers with at least five years' experience outperformed students with less experienced teachers, regardless of the type of public school attended.

www.nea.org/charter

LOCKE v. DAVEY

540 U.S. 712 (2004)

Chief Justice REHNQUIST delivered the opinion of the Court.

The State of Washington established the Promise Scholarship Program to assist academically gifted students with postsecondary education expenses. In accordance with the State Constitution, students may not use the scholarship at an institution where they are pursuing a degree in devotional theology. We hold that such an exclusion from an otherwise inclusive aid program does not violate the Free Exercise Clause of the First Amendment.

. . . In 1999, to assist these high-achieving students, the legislature created the Promise Scholarship Program, which provides a scholarship, renewable for one year, to eligible students for post-secondary education expenses. Students may spend their secondary education expenses. Students may spend their funds on any education-related expense, including room and board. . . . To be eligible for the scholarship, a student must meet academic, income, and enrollment requirements. A student must graduate from a Washington public or private high school and either graduate in the top 15% of his graduating class, or attain on the first attempt a cumulative score of 1,200 or better on the Scholastic Assessment Test I or a score of 27 or better on the American College Test. The student's family income must be less than 135% of the State's median. Finally, the student must enroll "at least half time in an eligible postsecondary institution in the state of Washington," and may not pursue a degree in theology at that institution while receiving the scholarship. Private institutions, including those religiously affiliated, qualify as "eligible post-secondary institution[s]" if they are accredited by a nationally recognized accrediting body. A "degree in theology" is not defined in the statute, but, as both parties concede, the statute simply codifies the State's constitutional prohibition on providing funds to students to pursue degrees that are "devotional in nature or designed to induce religious faith."

. . . Once the students enroll in an eligible institution, the institution must certify that student is enrolled at least half time and that the student is not pursuing a degree in devotional theology. The institution, rather than the State, determines whether the student's major is devotional. If the student meets the enrollment requirements, the scholarship funds are sent to the institution for distribution to the student to pay for tuition or other educational expenses.

Respondent, Joshua Davey, was awarded a Promise Scholarship, and chose to attend Northwest College. Northwest is a private, Christian college affiliated with the Assemblies of God denomination, and is an eligible institution under the Promise Scholarship Program. Davey had "planned for many years to attend a Bible college and to prepare [himself] through that college training for a life-time of ministry, specifically as a church pastor." To that end, when he enrolled in Northwest College, he decided to pursue a double major in pastoral ministries and business management/administration. There is no dispute that the pastoral ministries degree is devotional and therefore excluded under the Promise Scholarship Program.

At the beginning of the 1999-2000 academic year, Davey met with Northwest's director of financial aid. He learned for the first time at this meeting that he could not use his scholarship to pursue a devotional theology degree. He was informed that to receive the funds appropriated for his use, he must certify in writing that he was not pursuing such a degree at Northwest. He refused to sign the form and did not receive any scholarship funds.

Davey then brought an action under 42 U.S.C. §1983 against various state officials (hereinafter State) in the District Court for the Western District of Washington to enjoin the State from refusing to award the scholarship solely because a student is pursuing a devotional theology degree, and for damages. He argued the denial of his scholarship based on his decision to pursue a theology degree violated, *inter alia*, the Free Exercise, Establishment, and Free Speech Clauses of the First Amendment, as incorporated by the Fourteenth Amendment, and the Equal Protection Clause of the Fourteenth Amendment. . . .

The Religion Clauses of the First Amendment provide: "Congress shall make no law respecting an establishment of religion, or prohibiting the free exercise thereof." These two Clauses, the Establishment Clause and the Free Exercise Clause, are frequently in tension. See *Norwood v. Harrison*, 413 U.S. 455, 469 (1973) (citing *Tilton v. Richardson*, 403 U.S. 672, 677 (1971)). Yet we have long said that "there is room for play in the joints" between them. *Walz v. Tax Comm'n of City of New York*, 397 U.S. 664, 669 (1970). In other words, there are some state actions permitted by the Establishment Clause but not required by the Free Exercise Clause.

This case involves that "play in the joints" described above. Under our Establishment Clause precedent, the link between government funds and religious training is broken by the independent and private choice of recipients. See *Zelman v. Simmons-Harris*, 536 U.S. 639, 652 (2002); *Zobrest v. Catalina Foothills School Dist.*, 509 U.S. 1, 13-14 (1993); *Witters v. Washington Dept. of Servs. for Blind*, 474 U.S. 481, 487 (1986); *Mueller v. Allen*, 463 U.S. 388, 399-400 (1983). As such, there is no doubt that the State could, consistent with the Federal Constitution, permit Promise Scholars to pursue a degree in devotional theology, see *Witters* at 489, and the State does not contend otherwise. The question before us, however, is whether Washington, pursuant to its own constitution,[2] which has been authoritatively interpreted as prohibiting even indirectly funding religious instruction that will prepare students for the ministry, . . . can deny them such funding without violating the Free Exercise Clause.

Davey urges us to answer that question in the negative. He contends that under the rule we enunciated in *Church of Lukumi Babalu Aye, Inc. v. Hialeah*, [508 U.S. 520 (1993)], the program is presumptively unconstitutional because it is not facially neutral with respect to religion. We reject his claim of presumptive unconstitutionality, however; to do otherwise would extend the *Lukumi* line of cases well beyond not only their facts but their reasoning. In *Lukumi*, the city of Hialeah made it a crime to engage in certain kinds of animal slaughter. We found that the law sought to suppress ritualistic animal sacrifices of the Santeria religion. 508 U.S., at 535. In the present case, the State's disfavor of religion (if it can be called that) is of a far milder kind. It imposes neither criminal nor civil sanctions on any type of religious service or rite. It does not deny to ministers the right to participate in the political affairs of the community. See *McDaniel v. Paty*, 435 U.S. 618 (1978). And it does not require students to choose between their religious beliefs and receiving a government benefit. . . . The State has merely chosen not to fund a distinct category of instruction.

Justice Scalia argues, however, that generally available benefits are part of the "baseline against which burdens on religion are measured." (dissenting opinion). Because the Promise Scholarship Program funds training for all secular professions, Justice Scalia contends the State must also fund training for religious professions. But training for religious professions and training for secular professions are not fungible. Training someone to lead a congregation is an essentially religious endeavor. Indeed, majoring in devotional theology is akin to a religious calling as well as an academic pursuit. . . . And the subject of religion is one in which both the United States and state constitutions embody distinct views—in favor of free exercise, but opposed to

---

[2] The relevant provision of the Washington Constitution, Art. I, §11, states:

> Religious Freedom. Absolute freedom of conscience in all matters of religious sentiment, belief and worship, shall be guaranteed to every individual, and no one shall be molested or disturbed in person or property on account of religion; but the liberty of conscience hereby secured shall not be construed as to excuse acts of licentiousness or justify practices inconsistent with the peace and safety of the state. No public money or property shall be appropriated for or applied to any religious worship, exercise or instruction, or the support of any religious establishment.

establishment—that find no counterpart with respect to other callings or professions. That a State would deal differently with religious education for the ministry than with education for other callings is a product of these views, not evidence of hostility toward religion.

Even though the differently worded Washington Constitution draws a more stringent line than that drawn by the United States Constitution, the interest it seeks to further is scarcely novel. In fact, we can think of few areas in which a State's antiestablishment interests come more into play. Since the founding of our country, there have been popular uprisings against procuring taxpayer funds to support church leaders, which was one of the hallmarks of an "established" religion. . . . J. Madison, *Memorial and Remonstrance Against Religious Assessments* reprinted in *Everson v. Board of Ed. of Ewing,* 330 U.S. 1, 65, 68 (1947) (appendix to dissent of Rutledge, J.) (noting the dangers to civil liberties from supporting clergy with public funds).

Most States that sought to avoid an establishment of religion around the time of the founding placed in their constitutions formal prohibitions against using tax funds to support the ministry. . . . The plain text of these constitutional provisions prohibited *any* tax dollars from supporting the clergy. We have found nothing to indicate, as Justice Scalia contends, that these provisions would not have applied so long as the State equally supported other professions or if the amount at stake was *de minimis.* That early state constitutions saw no problem in explicitly excluding *only* the ministry from receiving state dollars reinforces our conclusion that religious instruction is of a different ilk.

Far from evincing the hostility toward religion which was manifest in *Lukumi,* we believe that the entirety of the Promise Scholarship Program goes a long way toward including religion in its benefits. The program permits students to attend pervasively religious schools, so long as they are accredited. . . . And under the Promise Scholarship Program's current guidelines, students are still eligible to take devotional theology courses. . . .

In short, we find neither in the history or text of Article I, §11 of the Washington Constitution, nor in the operation of the Promise Scholarship Program, anything that suggests animus towards religion. Given the historic and substantial state interest at issue, we therefore cannot conclude that the denial of funding for vocational religious instruction alone is inherently constitutionally suspect.

Without a presumption of unconstitutionality, Davey's claim must fail. The State's interest in not funding the pursuit of devotional degrees is substantial and the exclusion of such funding places a relatively minor burden on Promise Scholars. If any room exists between the two Religion Clauses, it must be here. We need not venture further into this difficult area in order to uphold the Promise Scholarship Program as currently operated by the State of Washington.

The judgment of the Court of Appeals is therefore *Reversed.*

Justice SCALIA, with whom Justice THOMAS joins, dissenting.

. . . When the State makes a public benefit generally available, that benefit becomes part of the baseline against which burdens on religion are measured;

and when the State withholds that benefit from some individuals solely on the basis of religion, it violates the Free Exercise Clause no less than if it had imposed a special tax.

That is precisely what the State of Washington has done here. It has created a generally available public benefit, whose receipt is conditioned only on academic performance, income, and attendance at an accredited school. It has then carved out a solitary course of study for exclusion: theology. . . . No field of study but religion is singled out for disfavor in this fashion. Davey is not asking for a special benefit to which others are not entitled. . . . He seeks only *equal* treatment—the right to direct his scholarship to his chosen course of study, a right every other Promise Scholar enjoys.

. . . Let there be no doubt: This case is about discrimination against a religious minority. Most citizens of this country identify themselves as professing some religious belief, but the State's policy poses no obstacle to practitioners of only a tepid, civic version of faith. Those the statutory exclusion actually affects—those whose belief in their religion is so strong that they dedicate their study and their lives to its ministry—are a far narrower set. One need not delve too far into modern popular culture to perceive a trendy disdain for deep religious conviction. In an era when the Court is so quick to come to the aid of other disfavored groups, *see, e.g., Romer v. Evans*, 517 U.S. 620, 635 (1996), its indifference in this case, which involves a form of discrimination to which the Constitution actually speaks, is exceptional.

Today's holding is limited to training the clergy, but its logic is readily extendible, and there are plenty of directions to go. What next? Will we deny priests and nuns their prescription-drug benefits on the ground that taxpayers' freedom of conscience forbids medicating the clergy at public expense? This may seem fanciful, but recall that France has proposed banning religious attire from schools, invoking interests in secularism no less benign than those the Court embraces today. . . . When the public's freedom of conscience is invoked to justify denial of equal treatment, benevolent motives shade into indifference and ultimately into repression. Having accepted the justification in this case, the Court is less well equipped to fend it off in the future. I respectfully dissent.

NOTES AND QUESTIONS

1. To what extent does *Locke* resolve the issue of whether a publicly funded voucher program *may* bar recipients of vouchers from using them to attend parochial school? The Court allows states some room to "play" in deciding whether to include or exclude religious instruction and institutions in its public welfare programs. Yet, the free exercise clause still prevents the government from unduly burdening religious exercise in the absence of a substantial or compelling interest. The *Locke* Court concludes that the state's interest in "not funding the pursuit of devotional degrees" is "substantial" and that any burden on Davey's religious exercise is "relatively minor." Could the same be said of a state's decision to bar elementary or secondary school students from using vouchers to attend religious institutions?

2. During oral argument, Justice Scalia asked whether a state could create a scholarship program available for some forms of religious instruction, but not other forms of religious instruction (i.e., funding rabbinical training programs, but not funding training for the Catholic priesthood). How would you have answered that question?
3. Justice Breyer declared during oral argument that, "the implications of this case are breathtaking . . . if [Davey] wins . . . every program, not just educational programs . . . cannot be purely secular . . . they must fund all religions who want to do the same thing." *See http://www.firstamendmentcenter.org/faclibrary/case.aspx?case=Locke_v_Davey*. Do you agree with Justice Breyer's understanding of the consequences of any holding in favor of Davey?
4. The *Zelman* and *Locke* cases represent a crystallization of the Supreme Court's evolving establishment clause and free exercise clause doctrine. Recall the test for analyzing establishment clause issues suggested by Justice Thomas in his plurality opinion in *Mitchell*. Reconsider that test in light of the Court's most recent free exercise clause analysis in *Locke*. Is it possible to create a template that integrates the proper analysis under both the establishment clause and the free exercise clause? Consider how such a template might apply to the legal issues raised by the following "voucher" scenario. As you do so, do not lose sight of the underlying philosophical, political and practical issues raised by vouchers as well.

C. "SHARED RESOURCES AND VOUCHER" PRACTICUM

Wendy Norville is a ninth grader in the small town of Farmington. By all measures, the Farmington public school district is unsatisfactory. Farmington High School has a graduation rate of 20 percent. Furthermore, although Farmington's school system has a "special needs" program, Wendy Norville was not doing well in the small town environment. Mr. and Mrs. Norville wanted Wendy to attend a private, all girls' Catholic school in Loraine County, 40 minutes from Farmington. St. Mary's Academy led the state in academics and had tutors specializing in Wendy Norville's particular learning disabilities. Since Wendy's first day of kindergarten, the Norvilles received government funding to provide a state certified aid, Sarah Taylor, to help Wendy Norville at school. Happily, Wendy Norville was accepted to St. Mary's for the fall and her family filed the correct paperwork with the state so Sarah Taylor could continue to provide Wendy with educational assistance.

Unfortunately, Mr. and Mrs. Norville received notice a month into Wendy's semester at St. Mary's Academy informing them that Wendy was no longer eligible to receive government support for the state certified aid because she was attending a parochial school. Consequently, Mr. and Mrs. Norville brought an action on Wendy's behalf against the state to provide continued financial assistance. Wendy qualifies for government financial assistance to provide a certified aid under the federal Individuals with Disabilities Education

Act, regardless of what school she attends. The state answered the complaint, however, by claiming that providing financial assistance to supply Wendy with a publicly certified employee to assist her in her education at a religious institution would violate the establishment clause of the First Amendment. What arguments could the state advance to support its position? If you represented Wendy and Wendy's parents, what arguments would you make to challenge the withdrawal of public funds? Suppose St. Mary's called you to advise them about their legal and political posture. What advice would you offer St. Mary's? Finally, who would prevail?

Suppose the state in which Farmington is located passes legislation that allows for tuition aid to be distributed to parents according to the special needs of the student. For parents of children with no educational disabilities, the state pays 10 percent of the tuition cost of sending the child to a school other than the public school the child would otherwise attend. For students like Wendy who have educational disabilities, the state pays 50 percent of the tuition. Like most of the parents in this program, Wendy Norville's parents want to use the tuition voucher to send Wendy to a parochial school. Will the state's tuition aid program survive constitutional challenge? If so, is the program politically prudent?

What if the state also adopted a scholarship program which offers "gifted" students a stipend to attend "enrichment" classes. Like many children with learning disabilities, Wendy also is "gifted" in certain areas of cognitive reasoning. Suppose Wendy applies and receives a scholarship to help her pay tuition in an enrichment program, but the scholarship is rescinded by the state when Wendy announces that she will use the funds to attend St. Mary's institute for "gifted and talented" students. What arguments would you make challenging and supporting the state's decision to rescind Wendy's scholarship?

CHAPTER 8

RELIGIOUS OBSERVANCE IN THE PUBLIC SCHOOL

As the prior chapter displays, the Supreme Court has interpreted the establishment clause to permit legislatures to create programs that allow public funds to be used for religious education. At the same time, however, as the cases in this chapter indicate, the Court has steadfastly limited the reach of religious content and observance within the public school environment itself. The Court has wrestled with the issue of the constitutional limits placed on religious observance within a school in the context of school prayer, Bible study, religious symbols, moments of silence and instructional content in the classroom. The presence of religion in each of these school settings can fairly be described as curricular because in each situation students are exposed to the content of religion. In this context, the Supreme Court has been extremely skeptical of the purported "secular" purpose of the challenged initiatives, often piercing the face of a statute to uncover the actual, unconstitutional religious purpose lurking underneath. As the law has evolved in this area, the courts also have tried to draw a distinction between coerced and noncoerced religious observance, finding coercion particularly strong in the elementary classroom.

Even beyond the walls of the classroom, however, the Supreme Court has been skeptical of the presence of religious observance. As the second part of this chapter indicates, the Court has limited religious practices at school sponsored events. Finally, as demonstrated in the third section of this chapter, the logic of the Court's opinions has led one of its Justices and one federal appellate court to question the constitutionality of the recital of the Pledge of Allegiance. In considering the evolution of these cases, analyze carefully the judicial assumptions regarding the sources of compulsion in the classroom and throughout the school environment.

A. PRAYER, BIBLE READING, RELIGIOUS SYMBOLS, MOMENTS OF SILENCE AND RELIGIOUS INSTRUCTIONAL PRACTICES IN THE CLASSROOM

1. Prayer

Prior to 1962, it was not uncommon for states to require the school day to begin with a prayer or a reading from the Bible. In New York, students were required to recite: "Almighty God, we acknowledge our dependence upon Thee, and beg Thy blessings upon us, our parents, our teachers and our Country." In *Engel v. Vitale*, 370 U.S. 421 (1962), the Supreme Court addressed the constitutionality of this practice, declaring:

> We think that by using its public school system to encourage recitation of the Regents' prayer, the State of New York has adopted a practice wholly inconsistent with the Establishment Clause. There can, of course, be no doubt that New York's program of daily classroom invocation of God's blessings as prescribed in the Regents' prayer is a religious activity. It is a solemn avowal of divine faith and supplication for the blessings of the Almighty. . . .
>
> The petitioners contend among other things that the state laws requiring or permitting use of the Regents' prayer must be struck down as a violation of the Establishment Clause because that prayer was composed by governmental officials as a part of a governmental program to further religious beliefs. For this reason, petitioners argue, the State's use of the Regents' prayer in its public school system breaches the constitutional wall of separation between Church and State. We agree with that contention since we think that the constitutional prohibition against laws respecting an establishment of religion must at least mean that in this country it is no part of the business of government to compose official prayers for any group of the American people to recite as a part of a religious program carried on by government.
>
> It is a matter of history that this very practice of establishing governmentally composed prayers for religious services was one of the reasons which caused many of our early colonists to leave England and seek religious freedom in America. . . .
>
> It is an unfortunate fact of history that when some of the very groups which had most strenuously opposed the established Church of England found themselves sufficiently in control of colonial governments in this country to write their own prayers into law, they passed laws making their own religion the official religion of their respective colonies. Indeed, as late as the time of the Revolutionary War, there were established churches in at least eight of the thirteen former colonies and established religions in at least four of the other five. But the successful Revolution against English political domination was shortly followed by intense opposition to the practice of establishing religion by law. This opposition crystallized rapidly into an effective political force in Virginia where the minority religious groups such as Presbyterians, Lutherans, Quakers and Baptists had gained such strength that the adherents to the established Episcopal Church were actually a minority themselves. In 1785-1786, those opposed to the established Church, led by James Madison and Thomas Jefferson, who, though themselves not members of any of these dissenting religious groups, opposed all religious establishments by law on grounds of principle, obtained the enactment of the famous

"Virginia Bill for Religious Liberty" by which all religious groups were placed on an equal footing so far as the State was concerned. Similar though less far-reaching legislation was being considered and passed in other States.

By the time of the adoption of the Constitution, our history shows that there was a widespread awareness among many Americans of the dangers of a union of Church and State. These people knew, some of them from bitter personal experience, that one of the greatest dangers to the freedom of the individual to worship in his own way lay in the Government's placing its official stamp of approval upon one particular kind of prayer or one particular form of religious services. They knew the anguish, hardship and bitter strife that could come when zealous religious groups struggled with one another to obtain the Government's stamp of approval from each King, Queen, or Protector that came to temporary power. The Constitution was intended to avert a part of this danger by leaving the government of this country in the hands of the people rather than in the hands of any monarch. But this safeguard was not enough. Our Founders were no more willing to let the content of their prayers and their privilege of praying whenever they pleased be influenced by the ballot box than they were to let these vital matters of personal conscience depend upon the succession of monarchs. The First Amendment was added to the Constitution to stand as a guarantee that neither the power nor the prestige of the Federal Government would be used to control, support or influence the kinds of prayer the American people can say—that the people's religions must not be subjected to the pressures of government for change each time a new political administration is elected to office. Under that Amendment's prohibition against governmental establishment of religion, as reinforced by the provisions of the Fourteenth Amendment, government in this country, be it state or federal, is without power to prescribe by law any particular form of prayer which is to be used as an official prayer in carrying on any program of governmentally sponsored religious activity.

There can be no doubt that New York's state prayer program officially establishes the religious beliefs embodied in the Regents' prayer. The respondents' argument to the contrary, which is largely based upon the contention that the Regents' prayer is "non-denominational" and the fact that the program, as modified and approved by state courts, does not require all pupils to recite the prayer but permits those who wish to do so to remain silent or be excused from the room, ignores the essential nature of the program's constitutional defects. Neither the fact that the prayer may be denominationally neutral nor the fact that its observance on the part of the students is voluntary can serve to free it from the limitations of the Establishment Clause, as it might from the Free Exercise Clause, of the First Amendment, both of which are operative against the States by virtue of the Fourteenth Amendment. Although these two clauses may in certain instances overlap, they forbid two quite different kinds of governmental encroachment upon religious freedom. The Establishment Clause, unlike the Free Exercise Clause, does not depend upon any showing of direct governmental compulsion and is violated by the enactment of laws which establish an official religion whether those laws operate directly to coerce nonobserving individuals or not. This is not to say, of course, that laws officially prescribing a particular form of religious worship do not involve coercion of such individuals. When the power, prestige and financial support of government is placed behind a particular religious belief, the indirect coercive pressure upon religious minorities to conform to the prevailing officially approved religion is plain. But the purposes underlying the Establishment Clause go much further than that. Its first and most immediate purpose rested on the belief that a union of government and religion tends to destroy government and to degrade religion. The history of governmentally established religion, both in England and in this country, showed that whenever government had allied itself with one particular form of religion, the inevitable result had been that it had incurred the hatred, disrespect and even contempt of those who held contrary beliefs. That same history showed that many people had lost their respect for any religion that had relied upon the support of government to spread its faith. The Establishment Clause thus stands as an expression of principle on the part of the Founders of our Constitution that religion is too personal, too sacred, too holy, to permit its "unhallowed perversion" by a civil magistrate. Another purpose of the Establishment Clause rested upon an awareness of the historical fact that governmentally established religions and religious persecutions go hand in hand. . . . It was in large part to get completely away from this sort of systematic religious persecution that the Founders brought into being our Nation, our Constitution, and our Bill of Rights with its prohibition against any governmental establishment of religion. The New York laws officially prescribing the Regents' prayer are inconsistent both with the purposes of the Establishment Clause and with the Establishment Clause itself.

It has been argued that to apply the Constitution in such a way as to prohibit state laws respecting an establishment of religious services in public schools is to indicate a hostility toward religion or toward prayer. Nothing, of course, could be more wrong. The history of man is inseparable from the history of religion. . . . It is neither sacrilegious nor anti-religious to say that each separate government in this country should stay out of the business of writing or sanctioning official prayers and leave that purely religious function to the people themselves and to those the people choose to look to for religious guidance.

It is true that New York's establishment of its Regents' prayer as an officially approved religious doctrine of that State does not amount to a total establishment of one particular religious sect to the exclusion of all others—that, indeed, the governmental endorsement of that prayer seems relatively insignificant when compared to the governmental encroachments upon religion which were commonplace 200 years ago. To those who may subscribe to the view that because the Regents' official prayer is so brief and general there can be no danger to religious freedom in its governmental establishment, however, it may be appropriate to say in the words of James Madison, the author of the First Amendment:

> It is proper to take alarm at the first experiment on our liberties. . . . Who does not see that the same authority which can establish Christianity, in exclusion of all other Religions, may establish with the same ease any particular sect of Christians, in exclusion of all other Sects? That the same authority which can force a citizen to contribute three pence only of his property for the support of any one establishment, may force him to conform to any other establishment in all cases whatsoever?

The judgment of the Court of Appeals of New York is reversed and the cause remanded for further proceedings not inconsistent with this opinion.

NOTES AND QUESTIONS

1. In his opinion for the Court, Justice Black writes that the "Establishment Clause . . . does not depend upon any showing of direct governmental compulsion. . . ." Consider whether Justice Black's point has survived as the Court's cases develop a distinction between governmental and student initiated religious observation.
2. The Supreme Court places tremendous reliance on Madison's *Remonstrance* and its underlying principles. Is that reliance fairly placed? Does Madison's *Remonstrance* lend itself to a predictable test of the constitutionality of religious practices inside the school environment?
3. In footnote 21, the Court distinguishes the "religious exercise" in this case from "patriotic and ceremonial occasions" at which students are "officially encouraged" to "express love for our country" by reciting documents or anthems that "contain references to the Deity." Is this distinction meaningful? Is there a distinction between the school prayer invalidated here and the Pledge of Allegiance? In his dissent, Justice Stewart specifically mentions the fact that the Declaration of Independence refers to the "divine," that since 1954 the Pledge of Allegiance has contained the phrase "under God" and that since 1865 coins have contained the phrase "in God we trust." Can these phrases in these contexts be distinguished from the prayer invalidated in this case?

2. Bible Reading

In *Engel*, the state acknowledges that its compulsory school prayer was a "religious" exercise presumably without any "secular purpose." In light of the Supreme Court's holding and reasoning in *Engel*, does the constitutionality of state action requiring schools to begin each day with Bible reading become a particularly easy case?

SCHOOL DISTRICT OF ABINGTON TOWNSHIP, PENNSYLVANIA V. SCHEMPP

374 U.S. 203 (1963)

Once again we are called upon to consider the scope of the provision of the First Amendment to the United States Constitution which declares that "Congress shall make no law respecting an establishment of religion, or prohibiting the free exercise thereof." . . . These companion cases present the issues in the context of state action requiring that schools begin each day with readings from the Bible. . . . In light of the history of the First Amendment and of our cases interpreting and applying its requirements, we hold that the practices at issue and the laws requiring them are unconstitutional under the Establishment Clause, as applied to the States through the Fourteenth Amendment.

II.

It is true that religion has been closely identified with our history and government. As we said in *Engel*, "The history of man is inseparable from the history of religion. And . . . since the beginning of that history many people have devoutly believed that 'More things are wrought by prayer than this world dreams of.'" In *Zorach v. Clauson,* we gave specific recognition to the proposition that "[w]e are a religious people whose institutions presuppose a Supreme Being." The fact that the Founding Fathers believed devotedly that there was a God and that the unalienable rights of man were rooted in Him is clearly evidenced in their writings, from the Mayflower Compact to the Constitution itself. This background is evidenced today in our public life through the continuance in our oaths of office from the Presidency to the Alderman of the final supplication, "So help me God." Likewise each House of the Congress provides through its Chaplain an opening prayer, and the sessions of this Court are declared open by the crier in a short ceremony, the final phrase of which invokes the grace of God. Again, there are such manifestations in our military forces, where those of our citizens who are under the restrictions of military service wish to engage in voluntary worship. Indeed, only last year an official survey of the country indicated that 64% of our people have church membership, Bureau of the Census, U.S. Department of Commerce, *Statistical Abstract of the United States* (83d ed. 1962), 48, while less than 3% profess no religion whatever. *Id.,* at p. 46. It can be truly said, therefore, that today, as in the beginning, our national life reflects a religious people who, in the words of Madison, are "earnestly praying, as . . . in duty bound, that the Supreme Lawgiver of the Universe . . . guide them into every measure which may be worthy of his [blessing. . . .]"

This is not to say, however, that religion has been so identified with our history and government that religious freedom is not likewise as strongly imbedded in our public and private life. Nothing but the most telling of personal experiences in religious persecution suffered by our forebears, see *Everson v. Board of Education,* could have planted our belief in liberty of religious opinion any more deeply in our heritage. It is true that this liberty frequently was not realized by the colonists, but this is readily accountable by their close ties to the Mother Country. However, the views of Madison and Jefferson, preceded by Roger Williams, came to be incorporated not only in the Federal Constitution but likewise in those of most of our States. This freedom to worship was indispensable in a country whose people came from the four quarters of the earth and brought with them a diversity of religious opinion. Today authorities list 83 separate religious bodies, each with membership exceeding 50,000, existing among our people, as well as innumerable smaller groups.

. . . Before examining this "neutral" position in which the Establishment and Free Exercise Clauses of the First Amendment place our Government it is well that we discuss the reach of the Amendment under the cases of this Court. . . .

This Court has rejected unequivocally the contention that the Establishment Clause forbids only governmental preference of one religion over another. Almost 20 years ago . . . , the Court said that "neither a state nor the Federal Government can set up a church. Neither can pass laws which aid one religion, aid all religions, or prefer one religion over another." And Mr. Justice Jackson, dissenting, agreed:

> There is no answer to the proposition . . . that the effect of the religious freedom Amendment to our Constitution was to take every form of propagation of religion out of the realm of things which could directly or indirectly be made public business and thereby be supported in whole or in part at taxpayers' expense. . . . This freedom was first in the Bill of Rights because it was first in the fore-fathers' minds; it was set forth in absolute terms, and its strength is its rigidity.

Further, Mr. Justice Rutledge, joined by Justices Frankfurter, Jackson and Burton, declared:

> The [First] Amendment's purpose was not to strike merely at the official establishment of a single sect, creed or religion, outlawing only a formal relation such as had prevailed in England and some of the colonies. Necessarily it was to uproot all such relationships. But the object was broader than separating church and state in this narrow sense. It was to create a complete and permanent separation of the spheres of religious activity and civil authority by comprehensively forbidding every form of public aid or support for religion.

The same conclusion has been firmly maintained ever since that time, and we reaffirm it now.

While none of the parties to either of these cases has questioned these basic conclusions of the Court, both of which have been long established, recognized and consistently reaffirmed, others continue to question their history, logic and efficacy. Such contentions, in the light of the consistent interpretation in cases of this Court, seem entirely untenable and of value only as academic exercises.

IV.

The interrelationship of the Establishment and the Free Exercise Clauses was first touched upon by Mr. Justice Roberts for the Court in *Cantwell v. Connecticut,* where it was said that their "inhibition of legislation" had

> a double aspect. On the one hand, it forestalls compulsion by law of the acceptance of any creed or the practice of any form of worship. Freedom of conscience and freedom to adhere to such religious organization or form of worship as the individual may choose cannot be restricted by law. On the other hand, it safeguards the free exercise of the chosen form of religion. Thus the Amendment embraces two concepts, — freedom to believe and freedom to act. The first is absolute but, in the nature of things, the second cannot be. . . .

V.

The wholesome "neutrality" of which this Court's cases speak thus stems from a recognition of the teachings of history that powerful sects or groups might bring about a fusion of governmental and religious functions or a concert or dependency of one upon the other to the end that official support of the State or Federal Government would be placed behind the tenets of one or of all orthodoxies. This the Establishment Clause prohibits. And a further reason for neutrality is found in the Free Exercise Clause, which recognizes the value of religious training, teaching and observance and, more particularly, the right of every person to freely choose his own course with reference thereto, free of any compulsion from the state. This the Free Exercise Clause guarantees. Thus, as we have seen, the two clauses may overlap. As we have indicated, the Establishment Clause has been directly considered by this Court eight times in the past score of years and, with only one Justice dissenting on the point, it has consistently held that the clause withdrew all legislative power respecting religious belief or the expression thereof. The test may be stated as follows: what are the purpose and the primary effect of the enactment? If either is the advancement or inhibition of religion then the enactment exceeds the scope of legislative power as circumscribed by the Constitution. That is to say that to withstand the strictures of the Establishment Clause there must be a secular legislative purpose and a primary effect that neither advances nor inhibits religion. . . . The Free Exercise Clause, likewise considered many times here, withdraws from legislative power, state and federal, the exertion of any restraint on the free exercise of religion. Its purpose is to secure religious liberty in the individual by prohibiting any invasions thereof by civil authority. Hence it is necessary in a free exercise case for one to show the coercive effect of the enactment as it operates against him in the practice of his religion. The distinction between the two clauses is apparent—a violation of the Free Exercise Clause is predicated on coercion while the Establishment Clause violation need not be so attended.

Applying the Establishment Clause principles to the cases at bar we find that the States are requiring the selection and reading at the opening of the school day of verses from the Holy Bible and the recitation of the Lord's Prayer by the students in unison. These exercises are prescribed as part of the curricular activities of students who are required by law to attend school. They are held in the school buildings under the supervision and with the participation of teachers employed in those schools. . . . We agree with the trial court's finding as to the religious character of the exercises. Given that finding, the exercises and the law requiring them are in violation of the Establishment Clause. . . .

But even if its purpose is not strictly religious, it is sought to be accomplished through readings, without comment, from the Bible. Surely the place of the Bible as an instrument of religion cannot be gainsaid, and the State's recognition of the pervading religious character of the ceremony is evident from the rule's specific permission of the alternative use of the Catholic Douay version as well as the recent amendment permitting nonattendance at the exercises. None of these factors is consistent with the contention that the Bible is here used either as an instrument for nonreligious moral inspiration or as a reference for the teaching of secular subjects.

. . . Nor are these required exercises mitigated by the fact that individual students may absent themselves upon parental request, for that fact furnishes no defense to a claim of unconstitutionality under the Establishment Clause. See *Engel v. Vitale.* Further, it is no defense to urge that the religious practices here may be relatively minor encroachments on the First Amendment. The breach of neutrality that is today a trickling stream may all too soon become a raging torrent and, in the words of Madison, "it is proper to take alarm at the first experiment on our liberties." *Memorial and Remonstrance Against Religious Assessments,* quoted in *Everson.*

It is insisted that unless these religious exercises are permitted a "religion of secularism" is established in the schools. We agree of course that the State may not establish a "religion of secularism" in the sense of affirmatively opposing or showing hostility to religion, thus "preferring those who believe in no religion over those who do believe." *Zorach v. Clauson.* We do not agree, however, that this decision in any sense has that effect. In addition, it might well be said that one's education is not complete without a study of comparative religion or the history of religion and its relationship to the advancement of civilization. It certainly may be said that the Bible is worthy of study for its literary and historic qualities. Nothing we have said here indicates that such study of the Bible or of religion, when presented objectively as part of a secular program of education, may not be effected consistently with the First Amendment. But the exercises here do not fall into those categories. They are religious exercises, required by the States in violation of the command of the First Amendment that the Government maintain strict neutrality, neither aiding nor opposing religion.

Finally, we cannot accept that the concept of neutrality, which does not permit a State to require a religious exercise even with the consent of the majority of those affected, collides with the majority's right to free exercise of religion. While the Free Exercise Clause clearly prohibits the use of state action to deny the rights of free exercise to *anyone,* it has never meant that a majority could use the machinery of the State to practice its beliefs. Such a contention was effectively answered by Mr. Justice Jackson for the Court in *West Virginia Board of Education v. Barnette,* 319 U.S. 624, 638 (1943):

> The very purpose of a Bill of Rights was to withdraw certain subjects from the vicissitudes of political controversy, to place them beyond the reach of majorities and officials and to establish them as legal principles to be applied by the courts. One's right to . . . freedom of worship . . . and other fundamental rights may not be submitted to vote; they depend on the outcome of no elections.

The place of religion in our society is an exalted one, achieved through a long tradition of reliance on the home, the church and the inviolable citadel of the individual heart and mind. We have come to recognize through bitter experience that it is not within the power of government to invade that citadel, whether its purpose or effect be to aid or oppose, to advance or retard. In the relationship between man and religion, the State is firmly committed to a position of neutrality. Though the application of that rule requires interpretation of a delicate sort, the rule itself is clearly and concisely stated in the words of the First Amendment. . . . It is so ordered.

NOTES AND QUESTIONS

1. These school prayer and Bible-reading cases, like many challenging religious observance in the public schools, raise the issue of the balance between the First Amendment's establishment clause and the free exercise clause. Here, the Supreme Court attempts to reconcile the clauses by reading them together as a requirement that the government remain

neutral regarding religious observances in the schools. The Court also argues that the clauses together relegate religion to the private sector, forbidding any form of public involvement. Nonetheless, the Court distinguishes the two clauses by observing that a violation of the free exercise clause requires a showing of "coercion," while a violation of the establishment clause does not. In other words, the Court presumes coercion whenever the government establishes religion, but not when it inhibits the free exercise of religion. Reconsider the Supreme Court's establishment clause cases in light of this distinction. Did the Court presume coercion, for example, in *Mitchell* and *Zelman?*

2. In *Schempp,* the Court also makes abundantly clear that the First Amendment prohibits governmental support for religion generally, even if that support treats all religious affiliations equally. Where does the prohibition on equal governmental support for all religions, regardless of sect, originate? Is it consistent with the First Amendment's history?
3. The Court in *Schempp* rejects the argument that students can simply exit the classroom as an excuse for the religious observance. How does the Court's judgment here reflect its understanding of coercion in a classroom environment?

3. The Ten Commandments and Religious Symbols

In *Stone v. Graham,* 449 U.S. 39 (1980), the Supreme Court declared unconstitutional a Kentucky statute requiring the posting of a copy of the Ten Commandments, purchased with private contributions, on the wall of each public school classroom in the state. The Court applied its three-part *Lemon* test, concluding that the practice failed to meet the first requirement: "Kentucky's statute requiring the posting of the Ten Commandments in public school rooms has no secular legislative purpose, and is therefore unconstitutional."

The Court rejected Kentucky's claimed secular purpose:

> The preeminent purpose for posting the Ten Commandments on schoolroom walls is plainly religious in nature. The Ten Commandments are undeniably a sacred text in the Jewish and Christian faiths, and no legislative recitation of a supposed secular purpose can blind us to that fact. The Commandments do not confine themselves to arguably secular matters, such as honoring one's parents, killing or murder, adultery, stealing, false witness, and covetousness. . . . Rather, the first part of the Commandments concerns the religious duties of believers: worshipping the Lord God alone, avoiding idolatry, not using the Lord's name in vain, and observing the Sabbath Day. . . . This is not a case in which the Ten Commandments are integrated into the school curriculum, where the Bible may constitutionally be used in an appropriate study of history, civilization, ethics, comparative religion, or the like. *Abington School District v. Schempp.* Posting of religious texts on the wall serves no such educational function. If the posted copies of the Ten Commandments are to have any effect at all, it will be to induce the schoolchildren to read, meditate upon, perhaps to venerate and obey, the Commandments. However desirable this might be as a matter of private devotion, it is not a permissible state objective under the Establishment Clause.

Finally, the Court was not persuaded by the fact that the Ten Commandments were merely posted rather than read aloud, concluding that "relatively minor encroachments on the First Amendment" were still unconstitutional.

In his dissent in *Stone,* Justice Rehnquist criticized the majority's cavalier rejection of the state's legitimate secular purpose in exposing its students to a document that has had a significant impact on the development of "secular codes of the Western world." More generally, Justice Rehnquist challenged the Court's approach to religious observance in the public schools:

> I think it remains to be demonstrated whether it is possible, even if desirable, to comply with such demands as plaintiff's completely to isolate and cast out of secular education all that some people may reasonably regard as religious instruction. Perhaps subjects such as mathematics, physics or chemistry are, or can be, completely secularized. But it would not seem practical to teach either practice or appreciation of the arts if we are to forbid exposure of youth to any religious influences. Music without sacred music, architecture minus the cathedral, or painting without the scriptural themes would be eccentric and incomplete, even from a secular point of view. . . . I should suppose it is a proper, if not an indispensable, part of preparation for a worldly life to know the roles that religion and religions have played in the tragic story of mankind. The fact is that, for good or for ill, nearly everything in our culture worth transmitting, everything which gives meaning to life, is saturated with religious influences, derived from paganism, Judaism, Christianity—both Catholic and Protestant—and other faiths accepted by a large part of the world's peoples. One can hardly respect the system of education that would leave the student wholly ignorant of the currents of religious thought that move the world society for a part in which he is being prepared.

To what extent has Justice Rehnquist's dissent become the prevailing view of the Supreme Court? As you read the cases since *Stone,* consider the ways in which Justice Rehnquist has led the Court in the direction foreshadowed by his dissent.

In the following case, the Supreme Court reaffirmed *Stone* in the context of an establishment clause challenge to the posting of the Ten Commandments on courthouse walls.

McCreary County v. Aclu

545 U.S. 844 (2005)

Justice Souter delivered the opinion of the Court.

Executives of two counties posted a version of the Ten Commandments on the walls of their courthouses. After suits were filed charging violations of the Establishment Clause, the legislative body of each county adopted a resolution calling for a more extensive exhibit meant to show that the Commandments are Kentucky's "precedent legal code." The result in each instance was a modified display of the Commandments surrounded by texts containing religious references as their sole common element. After changing counsel, the counties revised the exhibits again by eliminating some documents, expanding the text set out in another, and adding some new ones. . . .

Twenty-five years ago in a case prompted by posting the Ten Commandments in Kentucky's public schools, this Court recognized that the Commandments "are undeniably a sacred text in the Jewish and Christian faiths" and held that their display in public classrooms violated the First Amendment's bar against establishment of religion. *Stone,* 449 U.S., at 41. *Stone* found a predominantly religious purpose in the government's posting of the Commandments, given their prominence as " 'an instrument of religion,' " *id.,* at 41, n.3 (quoting *School Dist. of Abington Township v. Schempp,* 374 U.S. 203, 224 (1963)). The Counties ask for a different approach here by arguing that official purpose is unknowable and the search for it inherently vain. In the alternative, the Counties would avoid the District Court's conclusion by having us limit the scope of the purpose enquiry so severely that any trivial rationalization would suffice, under a standard oblivious to the history of religious government action like the progression of exhibits in this case.

A

Ever since *Lemon v. Kurtzman* summarized the three familiar considerations for evaluating Establishment Clause claims, looking to whether government action has "a secular legislative purpose" has been a common, albeit seldom dispositive, element of our cases. Though we have found government action motivated by an illegitimate purpose only four times since *Lemon,* and "the secular purpose requirement alone may rarely be determinative . . . , it nevertheless serves an important function." *Wallace v. Jaffree,* 472 U.S. 38, 75 (1985) (O'Connor, J., concurring in judgment).

The touchstone for our analysis is the principle that the "First Amendment mandates governmental neutrality between religion and religion, and between religion and nonreligion." When the government acts with the ostensible and predominant purpose of advancing religion, it violates that central Establishment Clause value of official religious neutrality, there being no neutrality when the government's ostensible object is to take sides. Manifesting a purpose to favor one faith over another, or adherence to religion generally, clashes with the "understanding, reached . . . after decades of religious war, that liberty and social stability demand a religious tolerance that respects the religious views of all citizens. . . ." *Zelman v. Simmons-Harris,* 536 U.S. 639, 718 (2002) (Breyer, J., dissenting). By showing a purpose to favor religion, the government "sends the . . . message to . . . nonadherents 'that they are outsiders, not full members of the political community, and an accompanying message to adherents that they are insiders, favored members. . . .' " *Santa Fe Independent School Dist. v. Doe,* 530 U.S. 290, 309-310 (2000) (quoting *Lynch v. Donnelly,* 465 U.S. 668, 688 (1984) (O'Connor, J., concurring)).

Indeed, the purpose apparent from government action can have an impact more significant than the result expressly decreed: when the government maintains Sunday closing laws, it advances religion only minimally because many working people would take the day as one of rest regardless, but if the government justified its decision with a stated desire for all Americans to honor Christ, the divisive thrust of the official action would be inescapable. This is the teaching of *McGowan v. Maryland,* 366 U.S. 420 (1961), which upheld Sunday closing statutes on practical, secular grounds after finding that the government had forsaken the religious purposes behind centuries-old predecessor laws. *Id.,* at 449-451.

B

Despite the intuitive importance of official purpose to the realization of Establishment Clause values, the Counties ask us to abandon *Lemon*'s purpose test, or at least to truncate any enquiry into purpose here. Their first argument is that the very consideration of purpose is deceptive: according to them, true "purpose" is unknowable, and its search merely an excuse for courts to act selectively and unpredictably in picking out evidence of subjective intent. The assertions are as seismic as they are unconvincing.

Examination of purpose is a staple of statutory interpretation that makes up the daily fare of every appellate court in the country, and governmental purpose is a key element of a good deal of constitutional doctrine. With enquiries into purpose this common, if they were nothing but hunts for mares' nests deflecting attention from bare judicial will, the whole notion of purpose in law would have dropped into disrepute long ago.

But scrutinizing purpose does make practical sense, as in Establishment Clause analysis, where an understanding of official objective emerges from readily discoverable fact, without any judicial psychoanalysis of a drafter's heart of hearts. The eyes that look to purpose belong to an " 'objective observer,' " one who takes account of the traditional external signs that show up in the " 'text, legislative history, and implementation of the statute,' " or comparable official act. There is, then, nothing hinting at an unpredictable or disingenuous exercise when a court enquires into purpose after a claim is raised under the Establishment Clause.

The cases with findings of a predominantly religious purpose point to the straightforward nature of the test. In *Wallace,* for example, we inferred purpose from a change of wording from an earlier statute to a later one, each dealing with prayer in schools. And in *Edwards,* we relied on a statute's text and the detailed public comments of its sponsor, when we sought the purpose of a state law requiring creationism to be taught alongside evolution. In other cases, the government action itself bespoke the purpose, as in *Abington,* where the object of required Bible study in public schools was patently religious; in *Stone,* the Court held that the "[p]osting of religious texts on the wall serve[d] no . . . educational function," and found that if "the posted copies of the Ten Commandments [were] to have any effect at all, it [would] be to induce the schoolchildren to read, meditate upon, perhaps to venerate and obey, the Commandments." In each case, the government's action was held unconstitutional only because openly available data supported a commonsense conclusion that a religious objective permeated the government's action.

Nor is there any indication that the enquiry is rigged in practice to finding a religious purpose dominant every time a case is filed. In the past, the test has not been fatal very often, presumably because government does not generally act unconstitutionally, with the predominant purpose of advancing religion. That said, one consequence of the corollary that Establishment Clause analysis does not look to the veiled psyche of government officers could be that in some of the cases in which establishment complaints failed, savvy officials had disguised their religious intent so cleverly that the objective observer just missed it. But that is no reason for great constitutional concern. If someone in the government hides religious motive so well that the "'objective observer, acquainted with the text, legislative history, and implementation of the statute,'" cannot see it, then without something more the government does not make a divisive announcement that in itself amounts to taking religious sides. A secret motive stirs up no strife and does nothing to make outsiders of nonadherents, and it suffices to wait and see whether such government action turns out to have (as it may even be likely to have) the illegitimate effect of advancing religion.

C

After declining the invitation to abandon concern with purpose wholesale, we also have to avoid the Counties' alternative tack of trivializing the enquiry into it. The Counties would read the cases as if the purpose enquiry were so naive that any transparent claim to secularity would satisfy it, and they would cut context out of the enquiry, to the point of ignoring history, no matter what bearing it actually had on the significance of current circumstances. There is no precedent for the Counties' arguments, or reason supporting them.

1

Lemon said that government action must have "a secular . . . purpose," 403 U.S., at 612, and after a host of cases it is fair to add that although a legislature's stated reasons will generally get deference, the secular purpose required has to be genuine, not a sham, and not merely secondary to a religious objective. . . . As we said, the Court often does accept governmental statements of purpose, in keeping with the respect owed in the first instance to such official claims. But in those unusual cases where the claim was an apparent sham, or the secular purpose secondary, the unsurprising results have been findings of no adequate secular object, as against a predominantly religious one.

2

The Counties' second proffered limitation can be dispatched quickly. They argue that purpose in a case like this one should be inferred, if at all, only from the latest news about the last in a series of governmental actions, however close they may all be in time and subject. But the world is not made brand new every morning, and the Counties are simply asking us to ignore perfectly probative evidence; they want an absentminded objective observer, not one presumed to be familiar with the history of the government's actions and competent to learn what history has to show. . . .

We take *Stone* as the initial legal benchmark, our only case dealing with the constitutionality of displaying the Commandments. *Stone* recognized that the Commandments are an "instrument of religion" and that, at least on the facts before it, the display of their text could presumptively be understood as meant to advance religion: although state law specifically required their posting in public school classrooms, their isolated exhibition did not leave room even for an argument that secular education explained their being there. But *Stone* did not purport to decide the constitutionality of every possible way the Commandments might be set out by the government, and under the Establishment Clause detail is key. *County of Allegheny v. American Civil Liberties Union, Greater Pittsburgh Chapter,* 492 U.S. 573, 595 (1989) (opinion of Blackmun, J.) ("[T]he question is what viewers may fairly understand to be the purpose of the display. That inquiry, of necessity, turns upon the context in which the contested object appears") (internal quotation marks and citation omitted). Hence, we look to the record of evidence showing the progression leading up to the third display of the Commandments.

A

The display rejected in *Stone* had two obvious similarities to the first one in the sequence here: both set out a text of the Commandments as distinct from any traditionally symbolic representation, and each stood alone, not part of an arguably secular display. *Stone* stressed the significance of integrating the Commandments into a secular scheme to forestall the broadcast of an otherwise clearly religious message, and for good reason, the Commandments being a central point of reference in the religious and moral history of Jews and Christians. They proclaim the existence of a monotheistic god (no other gods). They regulate details of religious obligation (no graven images, no sabbath breaking, no vain oath swearing). And they unmistakably rest even the universally accepted prohibitions (as against murder, theft, and the like) on the sanction of the divinity proclaimed at the beginning of the text. Displaying that text is thus different from a symbolic depiction, like tablets with 10 roman numerals, which could be seen as alluding to a general notion of law, not a sectarian conception of faith. Where the text is set out, the insistence of the religious message is hard to avoid in the absence of a context plausibly suggesting a message going beyond an excuse to promote the religious point of view. The display in *Stone* had no context that might have indicated an object beyond the religious character of the text, and the Counties' solo exhibit here did nothing more to counter the sectarian implication than the postings at issue in *Stone*. See also *County of Allegheny,* ("Here, unlike in *Lynch* [*v. Donnelly*], nothing in the context of the display detracts from the creche's religious message"). Actually, the posting by the Counties lacked even the *Stone* display's implausible disclaimer that the Commandments were set out to show their effect on the civil law. What is more, at the ceremony for posting the framed Commandments in Pulaski County, the county executive was accompanied by his pastor, who testified to the certainty of the existence of God. The reasonable observer could only think that the Counties meant to emphasize and celebrate the Commandments' religious message.

This is not to deny that the Commandments have had influence on civil or secular law; a major text of a majority religion is bound to be felt. The point is simply that the original text viewed in its entirety is an unmistakably religious statement dealing with religious obligations and with morality subject to religious sanction. When the government initiates an effort to place this statement alone in public view, a religious object is unmistakable.

B

Once the Counties were sued, they modified the exhibits and invited additional insight into their purpose in a display that hung for about six months. This new one was the product of forthright and nearly identical Pulaski and McCreary County resolutions listing a series of American historical documents with theistic and Christian references, which were to be posted in order to furnish a setting for displaying the Ten Commandments and any "other Kentucky and American historical documen[t]" without raising concern about "any Christian or religious references" in them. As mentioned, the resolutions expressed support for an Alabama judge who posted the Commandments in his courtroom, and cited the fact the Kentucky Legislature once adjourned a session in honor of "Jesus Christ, Prince of Ethics."

In this second display, unlike the first, the Commandments were not hung in isolation, merely leaving the Counties' purpose to emerge from the pervasively religious text of the Commandments themselves. Instead, the second version was required to include the statement of the government's purpose expressly set out in the county resolutions, and underscored it by juxtaposing the Commandments to other documents with highlighted references to God as their sole common element. The display's unstinting focus was on religious passages, showing that the Counties were posting the Commandments precisely because of their sectarian content. That demonstration of the government's objective was enhanced by serial religious references and the accompanying resolution's claim about the embodiment of ethics in Christ. Together, the display and resolution presented an indisputable, and undisputed, showing of an impermissible purpose.

Today, the Counties make no attempt to defend their undeniable objective, but instead hopefully describe version two as "dead and buried." Their refusal to defend the second display is understandable, but the reasonable observer could not forget it.

C

1

After the Counties changed lawyers, they mounted a third display, without a new resolution or repeal of the old one. The result was the "Foundations of American Law and Government" exhibit, which placed the Commandments in the company of other documents the Counties thought especially significant in the historical foundation of American government. In trying to persuade the District Court to lift the preliminary injunction, the Counties cited several new purposes for the third version, including a desire "to educate the citizens of the county regarding some of the documents that played a significant role in the foundation of our system of law and government." The Counties' claims did not, however, persuade the court, intimately familiar with the details of this litigation, or the Court of Appeals, neither of which found a legitimizing secular purpose in this third version of the display. "'When both courts [that have already passed on the case] are unable to discern an arguably valid secular purpose, this Court normally should hesitate to find one.'"

These new statements of purpose were presented only as a litigating position, there being no further authorizing action by the Counties' governing boards. And although repeal of the earlier county authorizations would not have erased them from the record of evidence bearing on current purpose, the extraordinary resolutions for the second display passed just months earlier were not repealed or otherwise repudiated. Indeed, the sectarian spirit of the common resolution found enhanced expression in the third display, which quoted more of the purely religious language of the Commandments than the first two displays had done; for additions, ("I the LORD thy God am a jealous God") (text of Second Commandment in third display); ("the LORD will not hold him guiltless that taketh his name in vain") (from text of Third Commandment); and ("that thy days may be long upon the land which the LORD thy God giveth thee") (text of Fifth Commandment). No reasonable observer could swallow the claim that the Counties had cast off the objective so unmistakable in the earlier displays.

Nor did the selection of posted material suggest a clear theme that might prevail over evidence of the continuing religious object. In a collection of documents said to be "foundational" to American government, it is at least odd to include a patriotic anthem, but to omit the Fourteenth Amendment, the most significant structural provision adopted since the original Framing. And it is no less baffling to leave out the original Constitution of 1787 while quoting the 1215 Magna Carta even to the point of its declaration that "fish-weirs shall be removed from the Thames." If an observer found these choices and omissions perplexing in isolation, he would be puzzled for a different reason when he read the Declaration of Independence seeking confirmation for the Counties' posted explanation that the "Ten Commandments' . . . influence is clearly seen in the Declaration," *id.,* at 180a; in fact the observer would find that the Commandments are sanctioned as divine imperatives, while the Declaration of Independence holds that the authority of government to enforce the law derives "from the consent of the governed." If the observer had not thrown up his hands, he would probably suspect that the Counties were simply reaching for any way to keep a religious document on the walls of courthouses constitutionally required to embody religious neutrality.

2

In holding the preliminary injunction adequately supported by evidence that the Counties' purpose had not changed at the third stage, we do not decide that the Counties' past actions forever taint any effort on their part to deal with the subject matter. We hold only that purpose needs to be taken seriously under the Establishment Clause and needs to be understood in light of context; an implausible claim that governmental purpose has changed should not carry the day in a court of law any more than in a head with common sense. It is enough to say here that district courts are fully capable of adjusting preliminary relief to take account of genuine changes in constitutionally significant conditions.

Nor do we have occasion here to hold that a sacred text can never be integrated constitutionally into a governmental display on the subject of law, or American history. We do not forget, and in this litigation have frequently been reminded, that our own courtroom frieze was deliberately designed in the exercise of governmental authority so as to include the figure of Moses holding tablets exhibiting a portion of the Hebrew text of the later, secularly phrased Commandments; in the company of 17 other lawgivers, most of them secular figures, there is no risk that Moses would strike an observer as evidence that the National Government was violating neutrality in religion.

IV

The importance of neutrality as an interpretive guide is no less true now than it was when the Court broached the principle in *Everson v. Board of Ed. of Ewing,* 330 U.S. 1 (1947), and a word needs to be said about the different view taken in today's dissent. We all agree, of course, on the need for some interpretative help. The First Amendment contains no textual definition of "establishment," and the term is certainly not self-defining. No one contends that the prohibition of establishment stops at a designation of a national (or with Fourteenth Amendment incorporation, *Cantwell v. Connecticut,* 310 U.S. 296, 303 (1940), a state) church, but nothing in the text says just how much more it covers. There is no simple answer, for more than one reason.

The prohibition on establishment covers a variety of issues from prayer in widely varying government settings, to financial aid for religious individuals and institutions, to comment on religious questions. In these varied settings, issues [about] interpreting inexact Establishment Clause language, like difficult interpretative issues generally, arise from the tension of competing values, each constitutionally respectable, but none open to realization to the logical limit.

The First Amendment has not one but two clauses tied to "religion," the second forbidding any prohibition on the "the free exercise thereof," and sometimes, the two clauses compete: spending government money on the clergy looks like establishing religion, but if the government cannot pay for military chaplains a good many soldiers and sailors would be kept from the opportunity to exercise their chosen religions. See *Cutter v. Wilkinson,* 544 U.S. 709 (2005). At other times, limits on governmental action that might make sense as a way to avoid establishment could arguably limit freedom of speech when the speaking is done under government auspices. *Rosenberger v. Rector and Visitors of Univ. of Va.,* 515 U.S. 819 (1995). The dissent, then, is wrong to read cases like *Walz v. Tax Comm'n of City of New York,* 397 U.S. 664 (1970), as a rejection of neutrality on its own terms, *post,* at 7-8, for trade-offs are inevitable, and an elegant interpretative rule to draw the line in all the multifarious situations is not [to] be had.

Given the variety of interpretative problems, the principle of neutrality has provided a good sense of direction: the government may not favor one religion over another, or religion over irreligion, religious choice being the prerogative of individuals under the Free Exercise Clause. The principle has been helpful simply because it responds to one of the major concerns that prompted adoption of the Religion Clauses. The Framers and the citizens of their time intended not only to protect the integrity of individual conscience in religious matters, *Wallace v. Jaffree,* 472 U.S., at 52-54, and n.38, but to guard against the civic divisiveness that follows when the Government weighs in on one side of religious debate; nothing does a better job of roiling society, a point that needed no explanation to the descendants of English Puritans and Cavaliers (or Massachusetts Puritans and Baptists). *E.g., Everson, supra,* at 8 ("A large proportion of the early settlers of this country came here from Europe to escape [religious persecution]"). A sense of the past thus points to governmental neutrality as an objective of the Establishment Clause, and a sensible standard for applying it. To be sure, given its generality as a principle, an appeal to neutrality alone cannot possibly lay every issue to rest, or tell us what issues on the margins are substantial enough for constitutional significance, a point that has been clear from the Founding era to modern times. *E.g.,* Letter from J. Madison to R. Adams (1832), in 5 The Founders' Constitution at 107 (P. Kurland & R. Lerner eds. 1987) ("[In calling for separation] I must admit moreover that it may not be easy, in every possible case, to trace the line of separation between the rights of religion and the Civil authority with such distinctness as to avoid collisions & doubts on unessential points"); *Sherbert v. Verner,* 374 U.S. 398, 422 (1963) (Harlan, J., dissenting) ("The constitutional obligation of 'neutrality' . . . is not so narrow a channel that the slightest deviation from an absolutely straight course leads to condemnation"). But invoking neutrality is a prudent way of keeping sight of something the Framers of the First Amendment thought important.

The dissent, however, puts forward a limitation on the application of the neutrality principle, with citations to historical evidence said to show that the Framers understood the ban on establishment of religion as sufficiently narrow to allow the government to espouse submission to the divine will. The dissent identifies God as the God of monotheism, all of whose three principal strains (Jewish, Christian, and Muslim) acknowledge the religious importance of the Ten Commandments. On the dissent's view, it apparently follows that even rigorous espousal of a common element of this common monotheism, is consistent with the establishment ban.

But the dissent's argument for the original understanding is flawed from the outset by its failure to consider the full range of evidence showing what the Framers believed. The dissent is certainly correct in putting forward evidence that some of the Framers thought some endorsement of religion was compatible with the establishment ban; the dissent quotes the first President as stating that "national morality [cannot] prevail in exclusion of religious principle," for example, and it cites his first Thanksgiving proclamation giving thanks to God, (internal quotation marks omitted). Surely if expressions like these from Washington and his contemporaries were all we had to go on, there would be a good case that the neutrality principle has the effect of broadening the ban on establishment beyond the Framers' understanding of it (although there would, of course, still be the question of whether the historical case could overcome some 60 years of precedent taking neutrality as its guiding principle).

But the fact is that we do have more to go on, for there is also evidence supporting the proposition that the Framers intended the Establishment Clause to require governmental neutrality in matters of religion, including neutrality in statements acknowledging religion. The very language of the Establishment Clause represented a significant departure from early drafts that merely prohibited a single national religion, and, the final language instead "extended [the] prohibition to state support for 'religion' in general." See *Lee v. Weisman,* 505 U.S. 577, 614-615 (1992) (Souter, J., concurring) (tracing development of language).

The historical record, moreover, is complicated beyond the dissent's account by the writings and practices of figures no less influential than Thomas Jefferson and James Madison. Jefferson, for example, refused to issue Thanksgiving Proclamations because he believed that they violated the Constitution. See Letter to S. Miller (Jan. 23, 1808), in 5 The Founders' Constitution at 98. And Madison, whom the dissent claims as supporting its thesis, *post,* at 4, criticized Virginia's general assessment tax not just because it required people to donate "three pence" to religion, but because "it is itself a signal of persecution. It degrades from the equal rank of Citizens all those whose opinions in Religion do not bend to those of the Legislative authority." 505 U.S., at 622 (internal quotation marks omitted); see also Letter from J. Madison to E. Livingston (July 10, 1822), in 5 The Founders' Constitution, at 106 ("[R]eligion & Govt. will both exist in greater purity, the less they are mixed together"); Letter from J. Madison to J. Adams (Sept. 1833) in Religion and Politics in the Early Republic 120 (D. Dresibach ed. 1996) (stating that with respect to religion and government the "tendency to a usurpation on one side, or the other, or to a corrupting coalition or alliance between them, will be best guarded against by an entire abstinence of the Government from interference"); *Van Orden v. Perry,* 545 U.S. 677 (2005) (Stevens, J., dissenting).

The fair inference is that there was no common understanding about the limits of the establishment prohibition, and the dissent's conclusion that its narrower view was the original understanding stretches the evidence beyond tensile capacity. What the evidence does show is a group of statesmen, like others before and after them, who proposed a guarantee with contours not wholly worked out, leaving the Establishment Clause with edges still to be determined. And none the worse for that. Indeterminate edges are the kind to have in a constitution meant to endure, and to meet "exigencies which, if foreseen at all, must have been seen dimly, and which can be best provided for as they occur." *McCulloch v. Maryland,* 4 Wheat. 316, 415 (1819).

While the dissent fails to show a consistent original understanding from which to argue that the neutrality principle should be rejected, it does manage to deliver a surprise. As mentioned, the dissent says that the deity the Framers had in mind was the God of monotheism, with the consequence that government may espouse a tenet of traditional monotheism. This is truly a remarkable view. Other members of the Court have dissented on the ground that the Establishment Clause bars nothing more than governmental preference for one religion over another, *e.g., Wallace v. Jaffree,* 472 U.S., at 98-99 (Rehnquist, J., dissenting), but at least religion has previously been treated inclusively. Today's dissent, however, apparently means that government should be free to approve the core beliefs of a favored religion over the tenets of others, a view that should trouble anyone who prizes religious liberty. Certainly history cannot justify it; on the contrary, history shows that the religion of concern to the Framers was not that of the monotheistic faiths generally, but Christianity in particular, a fact that no member of this Court takes as a premise for construing the Religion Clauses. Justice Story probably reflected the thinking of the framing generation when he wrote in his Commentaries that the purpose of the Clause was "not to countenance, much less to advance, Mahometanism, or Judaism, or infidelity, by prostrating Christianity; but to exclude all rivalry among Christian sects." R. Cord, Separation of Church and State: Historical Fact and Current Fiction 13 (1988) (emphasis omitted). The Framers would, therefore, almost certainly object to the dissent's unstated reasoning that because Christianity was a monotheistic "religion," monotheism with Mosaic antecedents should be a touchstone of establishment interpretation. Even on originalist critiques of existing precedent, there is, it seems, no escape from interpretative consequences that would surprise the Framers. Thus, it appears to be common ground in the interpretation of a Constitution "intended to endure for ages to come," *McCulloch v. Maryland,* that applications unanticipated by the Framers are inevitable.

Historical evidence thus supports no solid argument for changing course (whatever force the argument might have when directed at the existing precedent), whereas public discourse at the present time certainly raises no doubt about the value of the interpretative approach invoked for 60 years now. We are centuries away from the St. Bartholomew's Day massacre and the treatment of heretics in early Massachusetts, but the divisiveness of religion in current public life is inescapable. This is no time to deny the prudence of understanding the Establishment Clause to require the Government to stay neutral on religious belief, which is reserved for the conscience of the individual.

4. Moments of Silence and "Voluntary Prayer"

Is there a difference in the level of coercion when a class recites the Pledge, reads the Bible together or posts the Ten Commandments on the classroom wall? If there is a difference, how should that difference be measured? Should the difference in the coercive power of religious observance be significant for both establishment clause and free exercise clause analysis? What about the coercive power of a moment of silence, or of "voluntary" prayer?

WALLACE V. JAFFREE

472 U.S. 38 (1985)

Justice STEVENS delivered the opinion of the Court.

. . . [T]he narrow question for decision is whether [that aspect of Alabama law], which authorizes a period of silence for "meditation or voluntary prayer," is a law respecting the establishment of religion within the meaning of the First Amendment. . . .

Before analyzing the precise issue that is presented to us, it is . . . appropriate to recall how firmly embedded in our constitutional jurisprudence is the proposition that the several States have no greater power to restrain the individual freedoms protected by the First Amendment than does the Congress of the United States. [The Court proceeded to reaffirm its view that the First Amendment's religion clauses apply fully to the states through the Fourteenth Amendment's protections of personal liberty.]

III

When the Court has been called upon to construe the breadth of the Establishment Clause, it has examined the criteria developed over a period of many years. Thus, in *Lemon v. Kurtzman,* we wrote:

> Every analysis in this area must begin with consideration of the cumulative criteria developed by the Court over many years. Three such tests may be gleaned from our cases. First, the statute must have a secular legislative purpose; second, its principal or primary effect must be one that neither advances nor inhibits religion; finally, the statute must not foster "an excessive government entanglement with religion."

It is the first of these three criteria that is most plainly implicated by this case. As the District Court correctly recognized, no consideration of the second or third criteria is necessary if a statute does not have a clearly secular purpose. For even though a statute that is motivated in part by a religious purpose may satisfy the first criterion, *see, e.g., Abington School District v. Schempp,* the First Amendment requires that a statute must be invalidated if it is entirely motivated by a purpose to advance religion.

In applying the purpose test, it is appropriate to ask "whether government's actual purpose is to endorse or disapprove of religion." In this case, the answer to that question is dispositive. For the record not only provides us with an unambiguous affirmative answer, but it also reveals that the enactment of [Alabama law] was not motivated by any clearly secular purpose—indeed, the statute had *no* secular purpose. . . . The sponsor of the bill . . . Senator Donald Holmes, inserted into the legislative record—apparently without dissent—a statement indicating that the legislation was an "effort to return voluntary prayer" to the public schools. . . . The addition of "or voluntary prayer" indicates that the State intended to characterize prayer as a favored practice. Such an endorsement is not consistent with the established principle that the government must pursue a course of complete neutrality toward religion.

The importance of that principle does not permit us to treat this as an inconsequential case involving nothing more than a few words of symbolic speech on behalf of the political majority. For whenever the State itself speaks on a religious subject, one of the questions that we must ask is "whether the government intends to convey a message of endorsement or disapproval of religion." The well-supported concurrent findings of the District Court and the Court of Appeals—that [the moment of silence for voluntary prayer] was intended to convey a message of state approval of prayer activities in the public schools—make it unnecessary, and indeed inappropriate, to evaluate the practical significance of the addition of the words "or voluntary prayer" to the statute. Keeping in mind, as we must, "both the fundamental place held by the Establishment Clause in our constitutional scheme and the myriad, subtle ways in which Establishment Clause values can be eroded," we conclude that [the law] violates the First Amendment.

NOTES AND QUESTIONS

1. The *Wallace* case again raises the issue of the meaning and vitality of the three-part *Lemon* test in the context of religious observance in the classroom. Justice Powell concurred in *Wallace* to defend the *Lemon* test, while Justice O'Connor recharacterizes that test:

   > Nothing in the United States Constitution as interpreted by this Court or in the laws of the State of Alabama prohibits public school students from voluntarily praying at any time before, during, or after the schoolday. . . . Perhaps because I am new to the struggle, I am not ready to abandon all aspects of the *Lemon* test. I do believe, however, that the standards announced in *Lemon* should be reexamined and refined in order to make them more useful in achieving the underlying purpose of the First Amendment . . . Choper, *Religion in the Public Schools: A Proposed Constitutional Standard,* 47 Minn. L. Rev. 329, 332-333 (1963) (footnotes omitted). Last Term, I proposed a refinement of the *Lemon* test with this goal in mind. . . . The religious liberty protected by the Establishment Clause is infringed when the government makes adherence to religion relevant to a person's standing in the political community. Direct government action endorsing religion or a particular religious practice is invalid under this approach because it "sends a message to nonadherents that they are outsiders, not full members of the political community, and an accompanying message to adherents that they are insiders, favored members of the political community." Under this view, *Lemon*'s inquiry as to the purpose and effect of a statute requires courts to examine whether government's purpose is to endorse religion and whether the statute actually conveys a message of endorsement. . . .

   Is Justice O'Connor's "endorsement" test compelling? Would it provide a clearer "signpost" than the *Lemon* test? Would it radically alter the outcome of the cases involving religious observance in the school?
2. Justice O'Connor proceeded to try to distinguish a "moment of silence" from school prayer or Bible reading:

   > The *Engel* and *Abington* decisions are not dispositive on the constitutionality of moment of silence laws. In those cases, public school teachers and students led their classes in devotional exercises. . . . The Court reviewed the purpose and effect of the statutes, concluded that they required religious exercises, and therefore found them to violate the Establishment Clause. Under all of these statutes, a student who did not share the religious beliefs expressed in the course of the exercise was left with the choice of participating, thereby compromising the nonadherent's beliefs, or withdrawing, thereby calling attention to his or her nonconformity. The decisions acknowledged the coercion implicit under the statutory schemes, but they expressly turned only on the fact that the government was sponsoring a manifestly religious exercise.
   >
   > A state-sponsored moment of silence in the public schools is different from state-sponsored vocal prayer or Bible reading. First, a moment of silence is not inherently religious. Silence, unlike prayer or Bible reading,

> need not be associated with a religious exercise. Second, a pupil who participates in a moment of silence need not compromise his or her beliefs. During a moment of silence, a student who objects to prayer is left to his or her own thoughts, and is not compelled to listen to the prayers or thoughts of others. For these simple reasons, a moment of silence statute does not stand or fall under the Establishment Clause according to how the Court regards vocal prayer or Bible reading. . . . By mandating a moment of silence, a State does not necessarily endorse any activity that might occur during the period. . . . The relevant issue is whether an objective observer, acquainted with the text, legislative history, and implementation of the statute, would perceive it as a state endorsement of prayer in public schools. . . . A moment of silence law that is clearly drafted and implemented so as to permit prayer, meditation, and reflection within the prescribed period, without endorsing one alternative over the others, should pass this test. . . . The analysis above suggests that moment of silence laws in many States should pass Establishment Clause scrutiny because they do not favor the child who chooses to pray during a moment of silence over the child who chooses to meditate or reflect. Alabama Code §16-1-20.1 (Supp. 1984) does not stand on the same footing. However deferentially one examines its text and legislative history, however objectively one views the message attempted to be conveyed to the public, the conclusion is unavoidable that the purpose of the statute is to endorse prayer in public schools. . . .

3. Justice O'Connor then joins Justice Rehnquist's broader reconsideration of establishment and free exercise clause jurisprudence:

> The primary issue raised by Justice Rehnquist's dissent is whether the historical fact that our Presidents have long called for public prayers of Thanks should be dispositive on the constitutionality of prayer in public schools. I think not. At the very least, Presidential Proclamations are distinguishable from school prayer in that they are received in a noncoercive setting and are primarily directed at adults, who presumably are not readily susceptible to unwilling religious indoctrination. This Court's decisions have recognized a distinction when government-sponsored religious exercises are directed at impressionable children who are required to attend school, for then government endorsement is much more likely to result in coerced religious beliefs. Although history provides a touchstone for constitutional problems, the Establishment Clause concern for religious liberty is dispositive here. . . .
>
> . . . The Court does not hold that the Establishment Clause is so hostile to religion that it precludes the States from affording schoolchildren an opportunity for voluntary silent prayer. To the contrary, the moment of silence statutes of many States should satisfy the Establishment Clause standard we have here applied. The Court holds only that Alabama has intentionally crossed the line between creating a quiet moment during which those so inclined may pray, and affirmatively endorsing the particular religious practice of prayer. This line may be a fine one, but our precedents and the principles of religious liberty require that we draw it. In my view, the judgment of the Court of Appeals must be affirmed.

Consider carefully the views expressed by Justice O'Connor. By what standard of constitutional law would a state be permitted to afford schoolchildren an opportunity for voluntary student prayer?

4. Finally, consider Justice Rehnquist's dissent, which sets the stage for the subsequent erosion of *Lemon* and a revised constitutional perspective:

> Thirty-eight years ago this Court, in *Everson v. Board of Education,* summarized its exegesis of Establishment Clause doctrine thus: "In the words of Jefferson, the clause against establishment of religion by law was intended to erect 'a wall of separation between church and State.' *Reynolds v. United States,* [98 U.S. 145, 164 (1879)]." This language from *Reynolds,* a case involving the Free Exercise Clause of the First Amendment rather than the Establishment Clause, quoted from Thomas Jefferson's letter to the Danbury Baptist Association the phrase "I contemplate with sovereign reverence that act of the whole American people which declared that their legislature should "make no law respecting an establishment of religion, or prohibiting the free exercise thereof," thus building a wall of separation between church and State." 8 *Writings of Thomas Jefferson* 113 (H. Washington ed. 1861). It is impossible to build sound constitutional doctrine upon a mistaken understanding of constitutional history, but unfortunately the Establishment Clause has been expressly freighted with Jefferson's misleading metaphor for nearly 40 years. . . . The language Madison proposed for what ultimately became the Religion Clauses of the First Amendment was this: "The civil rights of none shall be abridged on account of religious belief or worship, nor shall any national religion be established, nor shall the full and equal rights of conscience be in any manner, or on any pretext, infringed." On the same day that Madison proposed them, the amendments which formed the basis for the Bill of Rights were referred by the House to a Committee of the Whole, and after several weeks' delay were then referred to a Select Committee consisting of Madison and 10 others. The Committee revised Madison's proposal regarding the establishment of religion to read: "[No] religion shall be established by law, nor shall the equal rights of conscience be infringed." . . . The following week, without any apparent debate, the House voted to alter the language of the Religion Clauses to read "Congress shall make no law establishing religion, or to prevent the free exercise thereof, or to infringe the rights of conscience." . . . It seems indisputable from these glimpses of Madison's thinking, as reflected by actions on the floor of the House in 1789, that he saw the Amendment as designed to prohibit the establishment of a national religion, and perhaps to prevent discrimination among sects. He did not see it as requiring neutrality on the part of government between religion and irreligion. . . . "The real object of the [First] [Amendment] was not to countenance, much less to advance, Mahometanism, or Judaism, or infidelity, by prostrating Christianity; but to exclude all rivalry among Christian sects, and to prevent any national ecclesiastical establishment which should give to a hierarchy the exclusive patronage of the national government. It thus cut off the means of religious persecution (the vice and pest of former ages), and of the subversion of the rights of conscience in matters of religion, which had been trampled upon almost from the days of the Apostles to the present age." . . . The Establishment Clause did not require government neutrality between religion and irreligion nor did it prohibit the Federal Government from providing nondiscriminatory aid to religion. There is simply no historical foundation for the proposition that the Framers intended to build the "wall of separation" that was constitutionalized in *Everson*. . . . Whether due to its lack of

historical support or its practical unworkability, the *Everson* "wall" has proved all but useless as a guide to sound constitutional adjudication. It illustrates only too well the wisdom of Benjamin Cardozo's observation that "[metaphors] in law are to be narrowly watched, for starting as devices to liberate thought, they end often by enslaving it." *Berkey v. Third Avenue R. Co.,* 244 N.Y. 84, 94, 155 N.E. 58, 61 (1926).

But the greatest injury of the "wall" notion is its mischievous diversion of judges from the actual intentions of the drafters of the Bill of Rights. The "crucible of litigation," is well adapted to adjudicating factual disputes on the basis of testimony presented in court, but no amount of repetition of historical errors in judicial opinions can make the errors true. The "wall of separation between church and State" is a metaphor based on bad history, a metaphor which has proved useless as a guide to judging. It should be frankly and explicitly abandoned.

The Court has more recently attempted to add some mortar to *Everson*'s wall through the three-part test of *Lemon v. Kurtzman,* which served at first to offer a more useful test for purposes of the Establishment Clause than did the "wall" metaphor. Generally stated, the *Lemon* test proscribes state action that has a sectarian purpose or effect, or causes an impermissible governmental entanglement with religion. . . . The three-part test represents a determined effort to craft a workable rule from a historically faulty doctrine; but the rule can only be as sound as the doctrine it attempts to service. The three-part test has simply not provided adequate standards for deciding Establishment Clause cases, as this Court has slowly come to realize. Even worse, the *Lemon* test has caused this Court to fracture into unworkable plurality opinions, depending upon how each of the three factors applies to a certain state action. The results from our school services cases show the difficulty we have encountered in making the *Lemon* test yield principled results. . . . The true meaning of the Establishment Clause can only be seen in its history. As drafters of our Bill of Rights, the Framers inscribed the principles that control today. Any deviation from their intentions frustrates the permanence of that Charter and will only lead to the type of unprincipled decision-making that has plagued our Establishment Clause cases since *Everson.*

The Framers intended the Establishment Clause to prohibit the designation of any church as a "national" one. The Clause was also designed to stop the Federal Government from asserting a preference for one religious denomination or sect over others. Given the "incorporation" of the Establishment Clause as against the States via the Fourteenth Amendment in *Everson,* States are prohibited as well from establishing a religion or discriminating between sects. As its history abundantly shows, however, nothing in the Establishment Clause requires government to be strictly neutral between religion and irreligion, nor does that Clause prohibit Congress or the States from pursuing legitimate secular ends through nondiscriminatory sectarian means. . . . The State surely has a secular interest in regulating the manner in which public schools are conducted. Nothing in the Establishment Clause of the First Amendment, properly understood, prohibits any such generalized endorsement of prayer . . .

Justice Rehnquist not only attacks the *Lemon* test, he assails the entirety of the Supreme Court's jurisprudence in this area. First, consider whether such an attack is persuasive. Second, consider whether, even if such an attack is meritorious, it is appropriate in light of the years of established precedent it threatens to undermine. Third, what standard would replace the *Lemon* test? Does Justice Rehnquist suggest that any legislation will survive establishment clause scrutiny so long as it does not establish a governmental religion, or a governmental preference for one sect over another?

5. Religion in a School's Instructional Practices

The fundamental limits on the inclusion of religious matters in the public school classroom were further developed in the context of the endless battles between evolution and creationism. In 1925, John T. Scopes was prosecuted for violating a Tennessee law that prohibited the teaching of "any theory that denies the story of the Divine Creation of men as taught in the Bible." Although the great Scopes trial is often cited as the event that demonstrated the absurdity of such laws and the absurdity of the rejection of evolution as a scientific theory, the sentiments expressed in the Tennessee law still linger. In fact, the resilience of those who would inject religious doctrine into the public school classroom is remarkable. As the cases and materials that follow indicate, the courts have rejected such efforts at virtually every turn.

In *Epperson,* the Supreme Court articulates two competing themes that inform its treatment of the limits of religious instruction in the classroom. First, public education and decisions about curriculum are committed to the control of state and local authorities. Second, because the success of the American school depends on a free and vigorous exchange of ideas, a school's curriculum cannot cast a pall of orthodoxy or religious dogma over the school community.

EPPERSON V. ARKANSAS

393 U.S. 97 (1968)

I.

This appeal challenges the constitutionality of the "anti-evolution" statute which the State of Arkansas adopted in 1928 to prohibit the teaching in its public schools and universities of the theory that man evolved from other species of life. The statute was a product of the upsurge of "fundamentalist" religious fervor of the twenties. The Arkansas statute was an adaptation of the famous Tennessee "monkey law" which that State adopted in 1925. The constitutionality of the Tennessee law was upheld by the Tennessee Supreme Court in the celebrated *Scopes* case in 1927.

The Arkansas law makes it unlawful for a teacher in any state-supported school or university "to teach the theory or doctrine that mankind ascended or descended from a lower order of animals," or "to adopt or use in any such institution a textbook that teaches" this theory. Violation is a misdemeanor and subjects the violator to dismissal from his position.

The present case concerns the teaching of biology in a high school in Little Rock. According to the testimony, until the events here in litigation, the official textbook furnished for the high school biology course did not have a section on the Darwinian Theory. Then, for the academic year 1965-1966, the school administration, on recommendation of the teachers of biology in the school system, adopted and prescribed a textbook which contained a chapter setting forth "the theory about the origin . . . of man from a lower form of animal."

Susan Epperson, a young woman who graduated from Arkansas' school system and then obtained her master's degree in zoology at the University of Illinois, was employed by the Little Rock school system in the fall of 1964 to teach 10th grade biology at Central High School. At the start of the next academic year, 1965, she was confronted by the new textbook (which one surmises from the record was not unwelcome to her). She faced at least a literal dilemma because she was supposed to use the new textbook for classroom instruction and presumably to teach the statutorily condemned chapter; but to do so would be a criminal offense and subject her to dismissal.

She instituted the present action in the Chancery Court of the State, seeking a declaration that the Arkansas statute is void and enjoining the State and the defendant officials of the Little Rock school system from dismissing her for violation of the statute's provisions. H. H. Blanchard, a parent of children attending the public schools, intervened in support of the action. . . .

III.

The antecedents of today's decision are many and unmistakable. They are rooted in the foundation soil of our Nation. They are fundamental to freedom.

Government in our democracy, state and national, must be neutral in matters of religious theory, doctrine, and practice. It may not be hostile to any religion or to the advocacy of no-religion; and it may not aid, foster, or promote one religion or religious theory against another or even against the militant opposite. The First Amendment mandates governmental neutrality between religion and religion, and between religion and nonreligion.

As early as 1872, this Court said: "The law knows no heresy, and is committed to the support of no dogma, the establishment of no sect." *Watson v. Jones,* 13 Wall. 679, 728. This has been the interpretation of the great First Amendment which this Court has applied in the many and subtle problems which the ferment of our national life has presented for decision within the Amendment's broad command.

Judicial interposition in the operation of the public school system of the Nation raises problems requiring care and restraint. Our courts, however, have not failed to apply the First Amendment's mandate in our educational system where essential to safeguard the fundamental values of freedom of speech and inquiry and of belief. By and large, public education in our Nation is committed to the control of state and local authorities. Courts do not and cannot intervene in the resolution of conflicts which arise in the daily operation of school systems and which do not directly and sharply implicate basic constitutional values. On the other hand, "the vigilant protection of constitutional freedoms is nowhere more vital than in the community of American schools." . . . As this Court said in *Keyishian v. Board of Regents,* the

First Amendment "does not tolerate laws that cast a pall of orthodoxy over the classroom." 385 U.S. 589, 603 (1967). . . .

There is and can be no doubt that the First Amendment does not permit the State to require that teaching and learning must be tailored to the principles or prohibitions of any religious sect or dogma. In *Everson v. Board of Education,* this Court, in upholding a state law to provide free bus service to school children, including those attending parochial schools, said: "Neither [a State nor the Federal Government] can pass laws which aid one religion, aid all religions, or prefer one religion over another."

. . . While study of religions and of the Bible from a literary and historic viewpoint, presented objectively as part of a secular program of education, need not collide with the First Amendment's prohibition, the State may not adopt programs or practices in its public schools or colleges which "aid or oppose" any religion. This prohibition is absolute. It forbids alike the preference of a religious doctrine or the prohibition of theory which is deemed antagonistic to a particular dogma. As Mr. Justice Clark stated in *Joseph Burstyn, Inc. v. Wilson,* "the state has no legitimate interest in protecting any or all religions from views distasteful to them." . . . 343 U.S. 495, 505 (1952). The test was stated as follows in *Abington School District v. Schempp,* "What are the purpose and the primary effect of the enactment? If either is the advancement or inhibition of religion then the enactment exceeds the scope of legislative power as circumscribed by the Constitution."

These precedents inevitably determine the result in the present case. The State's undoubted right to prescribe the curriculum for its public schools does not carry with it the right to prohibit, on pain of criminal penalty, the teaching of a scientific theory or doctrine where that prohibition is based upon reasons that violate the First Amendment. It is much too late to argue that the State may impose upon the teachers in its schools any conditions that it chooses, however restrictive they may be of constitutional guarantees. *Keyishian v. Board of Regents.*

In the present case, there can be no doubt that Arkansas has sought to prevent its teachers from discussing the theory of evolution because it is contrary to the belief of some that the Book of Genesis must be the exclusive source of doctrine as to the origin of man. No suggestion has been made that Arkansas' law may be justified by considerations of state policy other than the religious views of some of its citizens. It is clear that fundamentalist sectarian conviction was and is the law's reason for existence. Its antecedent, Tennessee's "monkey law," candidly stated its purpose: to make it unlawful "to teach any theory that denies the story of the Divine Creation of man as taught in the Bible, and to teach instead that man has descended from a lower order of animals." Perhaps the sensational publicity attendant upon the *Scopes* trial induced Arkansas to adopt less explicit language. It eliminated Tennessee's reference to "the story of the Divine Creation of man" as taught in the Bible, but there is no doubt that the motivation for the law was the same: to suppress the teaching of a theory which, it was thought, "denied" the divine creation of man.

Arkansas' law cannot be defended as an act of religious neutrality. Arkansas did not seek to excise from the curricula of its schools and universities all discussion of the origin of man. The law's effort was confined to an attempt to blot out a particular theory because of its supposed conflict with the Biblical account, literally read. Plainly, the law is contrary to the mandate of the First, and in violation of the Fourteenth, Amendment to the Constitution.

NOTES AND QUESTIONS

1. The Supreme Court here balances the power of state and local governments to prescribe a curriculum against the value of a marketplace of ideas in the classroom. Does the establishment clause and its interpretation in this case help to define that balance?
2. The Court assumes that the Darwinian view of evolution is a purely secular one, and therefore a school district policy that requires the teaching of evolution would neither advance nor inhibit religion. Do you agree that evolution is religious-neutral?
3. In *Mozert v. Hawkins County Board of Education,* 827 F.2d 1058 (6th Cir. 1987), sixth grade students challenged the school's requirement that they read a story involving "mental telepathy" on the grounds that the reading violated their Christian beliefs. In particular, the students claimed that the messages of religious tolerance fostered by the school's curriculum were inconsistent with their own beliefs. The Sixth Circuit, however, found that mere exposure to a range of religious beliefs did not constitute the type of state "compulsion" violative of the First Amendment. *See also Smith v. Board of School Commissioners of Mobile County,* 827 F.2d 684 (11th Cir. 1987) (rejecting parent challenges to public school texts on the grounds that they advance the religion of "secular humanism" and finding the value of "tolerance of diverse views" to be religious-neutral).
4. If "neutrality" is the cornerstone of compliance with the First Amendment's establishment clause, then would a school district policy mandating the balanced treatment of *all* views of human evolution (including the religious view) survive constitutional challenge? Consider the Supreme Court's answer in *Aguillard.*

EDWARDS V. AGUILLARD

482 U.S. 578 (1987)

Justice BRENNAN delivered the opinion of the Court.

The question for decision is whether Louisiana's "Balanced Treatment for Creation-Science and Evolution-Science in Public School Instruction" Act (Creationism Act), is facially invalid as violative of the Establishment Clause of the First Amendment.

I

The Creationism Act forbids the teaching of the theory of evolution in public schools unless accompanied by instruction in "creation science." No school is required to teach evolution or creation science. If either is taught, however, the other must also be taught. The theories of evolution and creation science are statutorily defined as "the scientific evidences for [creation or evolution] and inferences from those scientific evidences."

Appellees, who include parents of children attending Louisiana public schools, Louisiana teachers, and religious leaders, challenged the constitutionality of the Act in District Court, seeking an injunction and declaratory relief. Appellants, Louisiana officials charged with implementing the Act, defended on the ground that the purpose of the Act is to protect a legitimate secular interest, namely, academic freedom. Appellees attacked the Act as facially invalid because it violated the Establishment Clause. . . .

II

The Establishment Clause forbids the enactment of any law "respecting an establishment of religion." The Court has applied a three-pronged test to determine whether legislation comports with the Establishment Clause. First, the legislature must have adopted the law with a secular purpose. Second, the statute's principal or primary effect must be one that neither advances nor inhibits religion. Third, the statute must not result in an excessive entanglement of government with religion. *Lemon v. Kurtzman,* State action violates the Establishment Clause if it fails to satisfy any of these prongs.

In this case, the Court must determine whether the Establishment Clause was violated in the special context of the public elementary and secondary school system. States and local school boards are generally afforded considerable discretion in operating public schools. . . . "At the same time . . . we have necessarily recognized that the discretion of the States and local school boards in matters of education must be exercised in a manner that comports with the transcendent imperatives of the First Amendment." *Board of Education, Island Trees Union Free School Dist. No. 26 v. Pico,* 457 U.S. 853, 864 (1982).

The Court has been particularly vigilant in monitoring compliance with the Establishment Clause in elementary and secondary schools. Families entrust public schools with the education of their children, but condition their trust on the understanding that the classroom will not purposely be used to advance religious views that may conflict with the private beliefs of the student and his or her family. Students in such institutions are impressionable and their attendance is involuntary. . . . The State exerts great authority and coercive power through mandatory attendance requirements, and because of the students' emulation of teachers as role models and the children's susceptibility to peer pressure. . . . Furthermore, "the public school is at once the symbol of our democracy and the most pervasive means for promoting our common destiny. In no activity of the State is it more vital to keep out divisive forces than in its schools." . . .

Consequently, the Court has been required often to invalidate statutes which advance religion in public elementary and secondary schools. . . .

Therefore, in employing the three-pronged *Lemon* test, we must do so mindful of the particular concerns that arise in the context of public elementary and secondary schools. We now turn to the evaluation of the Act under the *Lemon* test.

III

Lemon's first prong focuses on the purpose that animated adoption of the Act. "The purpose prong of the *Lemon* test asks whether government's actual purpose is to endorse or disapprove of religion." . . . A governmental intention to promote religion is clear when the State enacts a law to serve a religious purpose. This intention may be evidenced by promotion of religion in general, . . . or by advancement of a particular religious belief, . . . If the law was enacted for the purpose of endorsing religion, "no consideration of the second or third criteria [of *Lemon*] is necessary." . . . In this case, appellants have identified no clear secular purpose for the Louisiana Act.

True, the Act's stated purpose is to protect academic freedom. . . . This phrase might, in common parlance, be understood as referring to enhancing the freedom of teachers to teach what they will. The Court of Appeals, however, correctly concluded that the Act was not designed to further that goal. We find no merit in the State's argument that the "legislature may not [have] used the terms 'academic freedom' in the correct legal sense. They might have [had] in mind, instead, a basic concept of fairness; teaching all of the evidence." Even if "academic freedom" is read to mean "teaching all of the evidence" with respect to the origin of human beings, the Act does not further this purpose. The goal of providing a more comprehensive science curriculum is not furthered either by outlawing the teaching of evolution or by requiring the teaching of creation science.

While the Court is normally deferential to a State's articulation of a secular purpose, it is required that the statement of such purpose be sincere and not a sham. As Justice O'Connor stated in *Wallace:*

> It is not a trivial matter, however, to require that the legislature manifest a secular purpose and omit all sectarian endorsements from its laws. That requirement is precisely tailored to the Establishment Clause's purpose of assuring that Government not intentionally endorse religion or a religious practice. (concurring in judgment).

It is clear from the legislative history that the purpose of the legislative sponsor, Senator Bill Keith, was to narrow the science curriculum. During the legislative hearings, Senator Keith stated: "My preference would be that neither [creationism nor evolution] be taught." Such a ban on teaching does not promote—indeed, it undermines—the provision of a comprehensive scientific education.

It is equally clear that requiring schools to teach creation science with evolution does not advance academic freedom. The Act does not grant teachers a flexibility that they did not already possess to supplant the present science curriculum with the presentation of theories, besides evolution, about the origin of life. Indeed, the Court of Appeals found that no law prohibited Louisiana public school teachers from teaching any scientific theory. As the president of the Louisiana Science Teachers Association testified, "any scientific concept that's based on established fact can be included in our curriculum already, and no legislation allowing this is necessary." The Act provides Louisiana schoolteachers with no new authority. Thus the stated purpose is not furthered by it.

The Alabama statute held unconstitutional in *Wallace v. Jaffree* is analogous. In *Wallace,* the State characterized its new law as one designed to provide a 1-minute period for meditation. We rejected that stated purpose as insufficient, because a previously adopted Alabama law already provided for such a 1-minute period. Thus, in this case, as in *Wallace,* "appellants have not identified any secular purpose that was not fully served by [existing state law] before the enactment of [the statute in question]."

Furthermore, the goal of basic "fairness" is hardly furthered by the Act's discriminatory preference for the teaching of creation science and against the teaching of evolution. While requiring that curriculum guides be developed for creation science, the Act says nothing of comparable guides for evolution. Similarly, resource services are supplied for creation science but not for evolution. Only "creation scientists" can serve on the panel that supplies the resource services. The Act forbids school boards to discriminate against anyone who "chooses to be a creation-scientist" or to teach "creationism," but fails to protect those who choose to teach evolution or any other noncreation science theory, or who refuse to teach creation science.

If the Louisiana Legislature's purpose was solely to maximize the comprehensiveness and effectiveness of science instruction, it would have encouraged the teaching of all scientific theories about the origins of humankind. But under the Act's requirements, teachers who were once free to teach any and all facets of this subject are now unable to do so. Moreover, the Act fails even to ensure that creation science will be taught, but instead requires the teaching of this theory only when the theory of evolution is taught. Thus we agree with the Court of Appeals' conclusion that the Act does not serve to protect academic freedom, but has the distinctly different purpose of discrediting "evolution by counterbalancing its teaching at every turn with the teaching of creationism." . . .

As in *Stone* and *Abington,* we need not be blind in this case to the legislature's preeminent religious purpose in enacting this statute. There is a historic and contemporaneous link between the teachings of certain religious denominations and the teaching of evolution. It was this link that concerned the Court in *Epperson v. Arkansas,* which also involved a facial challenge to a statute regulating the teaching of evolution. In that case, the Court reviewed an Arkansas statute that made it unlawful for an instructor to teach evolution or to use a textbook that referred to this scientific theory. Although the Arkansas antievolution law did not explicitly state its predominate religious purpose, the Court could not ignore that "the statute was a product of the upsurge of 'fundamentalist' religious fervor" that has long viewed this particular scientific theory as contradicting the literal interpretation of the Bible. After reviewing the history of antievolution statutes, the Court determined that "there can be no doubt that the motivation for the [Arkansas] law was the same [as other antievolution statutes]: to suppress the teaching of a theory which, it was thought, 'denied' the divine creation of man." The Court found that there can be no legitimate state interest in protecting particular religions from scientific views "distasteful to them," and concluded "that the First Amendment does not permit the State to require that teaching and learning must be tailored to the principles or prohibitions of any religious sect or dogma."

These same historic and contemporaneous antagonisms between the teachings of certain religious denominations and the teaching of evolution are present in this case. The preeminent purpose of the Louisiana Legislature was clearly to advance the religious viewpoint that a supernatural being created humankind. The term "creation science" was defined as embracing this particular religious doctrine by those responsible for the passage of the Creationism Act. . . . The legislative history therefore reveals that the term "creation science," as contemplated by the legislature that adopted this Act, embodies the religious belief that a supernatural creator was responsible for the creation of humankind.

Furthermore, it is not happenstance that the legislature required the teaching of a theory that coincided with this religious view. The legislative history documents that the Act's primary purpose was to change the science curriculum of public schools in order to provide persuasive advantage to a particular religious doctrine that rejects the factual basis of evolution in its entirety. . . .

In this case, the purpose of the Creationism Act was to restructure the science curriculum to conform with a particular religious viewpoint. Out of many possible science subjects taught in the public schools, the legislature chose to affect the teaching of the one scientific theory that historically has been opposed by certain religious sects. As in *Epperson,* the legislature passed the Act to give preference to those religious groups which have as one of their tenets the creation of humankind by a divine creator. The "overriding fact" that confronted the Court in *Epperson* was "that Arkansas' law selects from the body of knowledge a particular segment which it proscribes for the sole reason that it is deemed to conflict with . . . a particular interpretation of the Book of Genesis by a particular religious group." Similarly, the Creationism Act is designed *either* to promote the theory of creation science which embodies a particular religious tenet by requiring that creation science be taught whenever evolution is taught *or* to prohibit the teaching of a scientific theory disfavored by certain religious sects by forbidding the teaching of evolution when creation science is not also taught. The Establishment Clause, however, "forbids *alike* the preference of a religious doctrine *or* the prohibition of theory which is deemed antagonistic to a particular dogma." Because the primary purpose of the Creationism Act is to advance a particular religious belief, the Act endorses religion in violation of the First Amendment.

We do not imply that a legislature could never require that scientific critiques of prevailing scientific theories be taught. Indeed, the Court acknowledged in *Stone* that its decision forbidding the posting of the Ten Commandments did not mean that no use could ever be made of the Ten Commandments, or that the Ten Commandments played an exclusively religious role in the history of Western Civilization. In a similar way, teaching a variety of scientific theories about the origins of humankind to schoolchildren might be validly done with the clear secular intent of enhancing the effectiveness of science instruction. But because the primary purpose of the Creationism Act is to endorse a particular religious doctrine, the Act furthers religion in violation of the Establishment Clause. . . .

The Louisiana Creationism Act advances a religious doctrine by requiring either the banishment of the theory of evolution from public school classrooms or the presentation of a religious viewpoint that rejects evolution in its entirety. The Act violates the Establishment Clause of the First Amendment because it seeks to employ the symbolic and financial support of government to achieve a religious purpose. . . .

NOTES AND QUESTIONS

1. Although the Court clearly invalidated the Louisiana law requiring teachers to give "equal time" to creation science when teaching evolution, the proponents of creation science were not deterred. What principle or language in the Court's opinion might give those proponents some hope for a renewed or recast effort to get creationism into the schools?
2. What does Justice Brennan mean when he says: "[t]eaching a variety of scientific theories about the origins of humankind to schoolchildren might be validly done with the clear secular intent of enhancing the effectiveness of science instruction"?
3. In their concurrence, Justices Powell and O'Connor write:

> As a matter of history, schoolchildren can and should properly be informed of all aspects of this Nation's religious heritage. I would see no constitutional problem if schoolchildren were taught the nature of the Founding Father's religious beliefs and how these beliefs affected the attitudes of the times and the structure of our government. Courses in comparative religion of course are customary and constitutionally appropriate. In fact, since religion permeates our history, a familiarity with the nature of religious beliefs is necessary to understand many historical as well as contemporary events. In addition, it is worth noting that the Establishment Clause does not prohibit *per se* the educational use of religious documents in public school education. Although this Court has recognized that the Bible is "an instrument of religion," *Abington School District v. Schempp,* it also has made clear that the Bible "may constitutionally be used in an appropriate study of history, civilization, ethics, comparative religion, or the like." *Stone v. Graham* (citing *Abington School District v. Schempp*). The book is, in fact, "the world's all-time best seller" with undoubted literary and historic value apart from its religious content. The Establishment Clause is properly understood to prohibit the use of the Bible and other religious documents in public school education only when the purpose of the use is to advance a particular religious belief.

4. Justices Powell and O'Connor also observe that

> there is an enormous variety of religions in the United States. The Encyclopedia of American Religions (2d ed. 1987) describes 1,347 religious organizations. The United States Census Bureau groups the major American religions into: Buddhist Churches of America; Eastern Churches; Jews; Old Catholic, Polish National Catholic, and Armenian Churches; The Roman Catholic Church; Protestants; and Miscellaneous. Statistical Abstract of the United States 50 (106th ed. 1986). Our country has become strikingly multireligious as well as multiracial and multiethnic. This fact, perhaps more than anything one could write, demonstrates the wisdom of including the Establishment Clause in the First Amendment.

5. In his vigorous dissent, Justice Scalia calls for abandoning the *Lemon* test altogether, and declares:

> Notwithstanding the majority's implication to the contrary, we do not presume that the sole purpose of a law is to advance religion merely because it was supported strongly by organized religions or by adherents of particular faiths. . . . Similarly, we will not presume that a law's purpose is to advance religion merely because it "happens to coincide or harmonize with the tenets of some or all religions," or because it benefits religion, even substantially. . . . Thus, the fact that creation science coincides with the beliefs of certain religions, a fact upon which the majority relies heavily, does not itself justify invalidation of the Act.

Is Justice Scalia correct that the majority unfairly "presumes" that the law has a religious purpose?

6. Justice Scalia also states that Louisiana citizens are "quite entitled, as a secular matter, to have whatever scientific evidence there may be against evolution presented in their schools. . . ." The consequence of this declaration was predictable. The proponents of creationism reformulated their beliefs into a "theory of intelligent design" and called this theory "evidence against evolution" to be studied by school children together with evolution. They also urged school districts to inform students through various "disclaimers" that the teaching of evolution does not mean an endorsement of that "theory" over other theories like "creation-science."
7. In *Freiler v. Tangipahoa Parish Board of Education,* 975 F. Supp. 819 (E.D. La. 1997), the district court declared unconstitutional a school board resolution requiring teachers to read to their students a disclaimer of any endorsement of the scientific theory of evolution before teaching the subject. The Court found no legitimate secular purpose for the policy:

> The School Board, in disclaiming evolution as an official orthodoxy, is expressing its view that, if the students believe or have been taught that the theory of evolution is essentially a religious teaching, the School Board officially denies approving of such spiritual doctrine. There is no secular purpose to this official denial. While many of diverse religious beliefs may disagree with such a characterization of evolution, the manner and the contemporaneous proposal and adoption of the disclaimer, the discussions and comments at the School Board meeting during which it was passed, the testimony submitted at trial, and the historical context in which the subject arises, demonstrate by a preponderance of the evidence that religious concerns motivated the disclaimer. In mandating this disclaimer, the School Board is endorsing religion by disclaiming the teaching of evolution in such a manner as to convey the message that evolution is a religious viewpoint that runs counter to the religious belief of the Biblical theory of Creation, or other religious views. An endorsement of religion is a violation of the Establishment Clause and thus must be invalidated.

How would the United States Supreme Court have treated the constitutionality of the disclaimer?

8. Consider Justice Scalia's specific attack on the "purpose" prong of the *Lemon* test and the Court's application of that prong in *Aguillard* and most recently in *McCreary*. Should a court *presume* a religious purpose and

require the state to provide evidence of a secular purpose, or should the court presume a secular purpose and require proof of a purpose to advance or inhibit religion? What significance should a court place on the political history of a school district's efforts to "avoid" or "evade" prior rulings of the Supreme Court?

9. Finally, consider the case law set forth throughout this section. Is it possible to glean from the cases a clear "test" or "template" for analyzing the constitutionality of practices that involve religion in the classroom? Would that test include all aspects of the *Lemon* test, or only some of them? Would the test distinguish speaking from listening? Would the test further distinguish recitals from curriculum? Would the test include some measure of coercion? Finally, would the test distinguish religious observance within the classroom from religious observance outside the classroom at school-sponsored events?

B. RELIGIOUS OBSERVANCE AT PUBLIC SCHOOL EVENTS

As displayed in the prior section, the Supreme Court has declared unconstitutional virtually all initiatives which expose students to religious observances in the classroom. Those initiatives are invalid because they are motivated by a non-secular purpose and have a coercive effect on vulnerable, school-age non-believers in the classroom. Do these same concerns exist, however, when prayers or benedictions are offered not by teachers in the classroom, but by students or outside speakers at school sponsored events?

LEE V. WEISMAN

505 U.S. 577 (1992)

KENNEDY, J., delivered the opinion of the Court, in which BLACKMUN, STEVENS, O'CONNOR, and SOUTER, JJ., joined. BLACKMUN, J., and SOUTER, J., filed concurring opinions, in which STEVENS and O'CONNOR, JJ., joined. SCALIA, J., filed a dissenting opinion, in which REHNQUIST, C.J., and WHITE and THOMAS, JJ., joined.

School principals in the public school system of the city of Providence, Rhode Island, are permitted to invite members of the clergy to offer invocation and benediction prayers as part of the formal graduation ceremonies for middle schools and for high schools. The question before us is whether including clerical members who offer prayers as part of the official school graduation ceremony is consistent with the Religion Clauses of the First Amendment, provisions the Fourteenth Amendment makes applicable with full force to the States and their school districts.

A

Deborah Weisman graduated from Nathan Bishop Middle School, a public school in Providence, at a formal ceremony in June 1989. She was about 14 years old. . . . Acting for himself and his daughter, Deborah's father, Daniel Weisman, objected to any prayers at Deborah's middle school graduation, but to no avail. The school principal, petitioner Robert E. Lee, invited a rabbi to deliver prayers at the graduation exercises for Deborah's class. Rabbi Leslie Gutterman, of the Temple Beth El in Providence, accepted.

It has been the custom of Providence school officials to provide invited clergy with a pamphlet entitled "Guidelines for Civic Occasions," prepared by the National Conference of Christians and Jews. The Guidelines recommend that public prayers at nonsectarian civic ceremonies be composed with "inclusiveness and sensitivity," though they acknowledge that "prayer of any kind may be inappropriate on some civic occasions." The principal gave Rabbi Gutterman the pamphlet before the graduation and advised him the invocation and benediction should be nonsectarian. . . .

These dominant facts mark and control the confines of our decision: State officials direct the performance of a formal religious exercise at promotional and graduation ceremonies for secondary schools. Even for those students who object to the religious exercise, their attendance and participation in the state-sponsored religious activity are in a fair and real sense obligatory, though the school district does not require attendance as a condition for receipt of the diploma.

This case does not require us to revisit the difficult questions dividing us in recent cases, questions of the definition and full scope of the principles governing the extent of permitted accommodation by the State for the religious beliefs and practices of many of its citizens. . . . For without reference to those principles in other contexts, the controlling precedents as they relate to prayer and religious exercise in primary and secondary public schools compel the holding here that the policy of the city of Providence is an unconstitutional one. We can decide the case without reconsidering the general constitutional framework by which public schools' efforts to accommodate religion are measured. Thus we do not accept the invitation of petitioners and *amicus* the United States to reconsider our decision in *Lemon v. Kurtzman*. The government involvement with religious activity in this case is pervasive, to the point of creating a state-sponsored and state-directed religious exercise in a public school. Conducting this formal religious observance conflicts with settled rules pertaining to prayer exercises for students, and that suffices to determine the question before us.

The principle that government may accommodate the free exercise of religion does not supersede the fundamental limitations imposed by the Establishment Clause. It is beyond dispute that, at a minimum, the Constitution guarantees that government may not coerce anyone to support or participate in religion or its exercise, or otherwise act in a way which "establishes a [state] religion or religious faith, or tends to do so." The State's involvement in the school prayers challenged today violates these central principles.

That involvement is as troubling as it is undenied. A school official, the principal, decided that an invocation and a benediction should be given; this is a choice attributable to the State, and from a constitutional perspective it is as if a state statute decreed that the prayers must occur. The principal chose the religious participant, here a rabbi, and that choice is also attributable to the State. The reason for the choice of a rabbi is not disclosed by the record, but the potential for divisiveness over the choice of a particular member of the clergy to conduct the ceremony is apparent.

Divisiveness, of course, can attend any state decision respecting religions, and neither its existence nor its potential necessarily invalidates the State's attempts to accommodate religion in all cases. The potential for divisiveness is of particular relevance here though, because it centers around an overt religious exercise in a secondary school environment where, as we discuss below, subtle coercive pressures exist and where the student had no real alternative which would have allowed her to avoid the fact or appearance of participation.

The State's role did not end with the decision to include a prayer and with the choice of a clergyman. Principal Lee provided Rabbi Gutterman with a copy of the "Guidelines for Civic Occasions," and advised him that his prayers should be nonsectarian. Through these means the principal directed and controlled the content of the prayers. . . . It is a cornerstone principle of our Establishment Clause jurisprudence that "it is no part of the business of government to compose official prayers for any group of the American people to recite as a part of a religious program carried on by government," and that is what the school officials attempted to do.

Petitioners argue, and we find nothing in the case to refute it, that the directions for the content of the prayers were a good-faith attempt by the school to ensure that the sectarianism which is so often the flashpoint for religious animosity be removed from the graduation ceremony. The concern is understandable, as a prayer which uses ideas or images identified with a particular religion may foster a different sort of sectarian rivalry than an invocation or benediction in terms more neutral. The school's explanation, however, does not resolve the dilemma caused by its participation. The question is not the good faith of the school in attempting to make the prayer acceptable to most persons, but the legitimacy of its undertaking that enterprise at all when the object is to produce a prayer to be used in a formal religious exercise which students, for all practical purposes, are obliged to attend.

We are asked to recognize the existence of a practice of nonsectarian prayer, prayer within the embrace of what is known as the Judeo-Christian tradition, prayer which is more acceptable than one which, for example, makes explicit references to the God of Israel, or to Jesus Christ, or to a patron saint. There may be some support, as an empirical observation, to the statement of the Court of Appeals for the Sixth Circuit, picked up by Judge Campbell's dissent in the Court of Appeals in this case, that there has emerged in this country a civic religion, one which is tolerated when sectarian exercises are not. . . . If common ground can be defined which permits once conflicting faiths to express the shared conviction that there is an ethic and a morality which transcend human invention, the sense of community and purpose sought by all decent societies might be advanced. But though the First Amendment does not allow the government to stifle prayers which aspire to these ends, neither does it permit the government to undertake that task for itself.

The First Amendment's Religion Clauses mean that religious beliefs and religious expression are too precious to be either proscribed or prescribed by the State. The design of the Constitution is that preservation and transmission of religious beliefs and worship is a responsibility and a choice committed to the private sphere, which itself is promised freedom to pursue that mission. It must not be forgotten then, that while concern must be given to define the protection granted to an objector or a dissenting nonbeliever, these same Clauses exist to protect religion from government interference. James Madison, the principal author of the Bill of Rights, did not rest his opposition to a religious establishment on the sole ground of its effect on the minority. A principal ground for his view was: "Experience witnesseth that ecclesiastical establishments, instead of maintaining the purity and efficacy of Religion, have had a contrary operation." *Memorial and Remonstrance Against Religious Assessments* (1785).

These concerns have particular application in the case of school officials, whose effort to monitor prayer will be perceived by the students as inducing a participation they might otherwise reject. Though the efforts of the school officials in this case to find common ground appear to have been a good-faith attempt to recognize the common aspects of religions and not the divisive ones, our precedents do not permit school officials to assist in composing prayers as an incident to a formal exercise for their students. And these same precedents caution us to measure the idea of a civic religion against the central meaning of the Religion Clauses of the First Amendment, which is that all creeds must be tolerated and none favored. The suggestion that government may establish an official or civic religion as a means of avoiding the establishment of a religion with more specific creeds strikes us as a contradiction that cannot be accepted.

The degree of school involvement here made it clear that the graduation prayers bore the imprint of the State and thus put school-age children who objected in an untenable position. We turn our attention now to consider the position of the students, both those who desired the prayer and she who did not.

To endure the speech of false ideas or offensive content and then to counter it is part of learning how to live in a pluralistic society, a society which insists upon open discourse towards the end of a tolerant citizenry. And tolerance presupposes some mutuality of obligation. It is argued that our constitutional vision of a free society requires confidence in our own ability to accept or reject ideas of which we do not approve, and that prayer at a high school graduation does nothing more than offer a choice. By the time they are seniors, high school students no doubt have been required to attend classes and assemblies and to complete assignments exposing them to ideas they find distasteful or immoral or absurd or all of these. Against this background, students may consider it an odd measure of justice to be subjected during the course of their educations to ideas deemed offensive and irreligious, but to be denied a brief, formal prayer ceremony that the school offers in return. This argument cannot prevail, however. It overlooks a fundamental dynamic of the Constitution.

The First Amendment protects speech and religion by quite different mechanisms. Speech is protected by ensuring its full expression even when the government participates, for the very object of some of our most important speech is to persuade the government to adopt an idea as its own. The method for protecting freedom of worship and freedom of conscience in religious matters is quite the reverse. In religious debate or expression the government is not a prime participant, for the Framers deemed religious establishment antithetical to the freedom of all. The Free Exercise Clause embraces a freedom of conscience and worship that has close parallels in the speech provisions of the First Amendment, but the Establishment Clause is a specific prohibition on forms of state intervention in religious affairs with no precise counterpart in the speech provisions. The explanation lies in the lesson of history that was and is the inspiration for the Establishment Clause, the lesson that in the hands of government what might begin as a tolerant expression of religious views may end in a policy to indoctrinate and coerce. A state-created orthodoxy puts at grave risk that freedom of belief and conscience which are the sole assurance that religious faith is real, not imposed.

The lessons of the First Amendment are as urgent in the modern world as in the 18th century when it was written. One timeless lesson is that if citizens are subjected to state-sponsored religious exercises, the State disavows its own duty to guard and respect that sphere of inviolable conscience and belief which is the mark of a free people. To compromise that principle today would be to deny our own tradition and forfeit our standing to urge others to secure the protections of that tradition for themselves.

As we have observed before, there are heightened concerns with protecting freedom of conscience from subtle coercive pressure in the elementary and secondary public schools. Our decisions . . . recognize, among other things, that prayer exercises in public schools carry a particular risk of indirect coercion. The concern may not be limited to the context of schools, but it is most pronounced there. . . . What to most believers may seem nothing more than a reasonable request that the nonbeliever respect their religious practices, in a school context may appear to the nonbeliever or dissenter to be an attempt to employ the machinery of the State to enforce a religious orthodoxy.

We need not look beyond the circumstances of this case to see the phenomenon at work. The undeniable fact is that the school district's supervision and control of a high school graduation ceremony places public pressure, as well as peer pressure, on attending students to stand as a group or, at least, maintain respectful silence during the invocation and benediction. This pressure, though subtle and indirect, can be as real as any overt compulsion. Of course, in our culture standing or remaining silent can signify adherence to a view or simple respect for the views of others. And no doubt some persons who have no desire to join a prayer have little objection to standing as a sign of respect for those who do. But for the dissenter of high school age, who has a reasonable perception that she is being forced by the State to pray in a manner her conscience will not allow, the injury is no less real. There can be no doubt that for many, if not most, of the students at the graduation, the act of standing or remaining silent was an expression of participation in the rabbi's prayer. That was the very point of the religious exercise. It is of little comfort to a dissenter, then, to be told that for her the act of standing or remaining in silence signifies mere respect, rather than participation. What matters is that, given our social conventions, a reasonable dissenter in this milieu could believe that the group exercise signified her own participation or approval of it.

Finding no violation under these circumstances would place objectors in the dilemma of participating, with all that implies, or protesting. We do not address whether that choice is acceptable if the affected citizens are mature adults, but we think the State may not, consistent with the Establishment Clause, place primary and secondary school children in this position. Research in psychology supports the common assumption that adolescents are often susceptible to pressure from their peers towards conformity, and that the influence is strongest in matters of social convention. . . . To recognize that the choice imposed by the State constitutes an unacceptable constraint only acknowledges that the government may no more use social pressure to enforce orthodoxy than it may use more direct means.

The injury caused by the government's action, and the reason why Daniel and Deborah Weisman object to it, is that the State, in a school setting, in effect required participation in a religious exercise. It is, we concede, a brief exercise during which the individual can concentrate on joining its message, meditate on her own religion, or let her mind wander. But the embarrassment and the intrusion of the religious exercise cannot be refuted by arguing that these prayers, and similar ones to be said in the future, are of a *de minimis* character. Assuming, as we must, that the prayers were offensive to the student and the parent who now object, the intrusion was both real and, in the context of a secondary school, a violation of the objectors' rights. That the intrusion was in the course of promulgating religion that sought to be civic or nonsectarian rather than pertaining to one sect does not lessen the offense or isolation to the objectors. At best it narrows their number, at worst increases their sense of isolation and affront.

There was a stipulation in the District Court that attendance at graduation and promotional ceremonies is voluntary. Petitioners and the United States, as *amicus,* made this a center point of the case, arguing that the option of not attending the graduation excuses any inducement or coercion in the ceremony itself. The argument lacks all persuasion. Law reaches past formalism. And to say a teenage student has a real choice not to attend her high school graduation is formalistic in the extreme. True, Deborah could elect not to attend commencement without renouncing her diploma; but we shall not allow the case to turn on this point. Everyone knows that in our society and in our culture high school graduation is one of life's most significant occasions. A school rule which excuses attendance is beside the point. Attendance may not be required by official decree, yet it is apparent that a student is not free to absent herself from the graduation exercise in any real sense of the term "voluntary," for absence would require forfeiture of those intangible benefits which have motivated the student through youth and all her high school years. Graduation is a time for family and those closest to the student to celebrate success and express mutual wishes of gratitude and respect, all to the end of impressing upon the young person the role that it is his or her right and duty to assume in the community and all of its diverse parts.

The importance of the event is the point the school district and the United States rely upon to argue that a formal prayer ought to be permitted, but it becomes one of the principal reasons why their argument must fail. Their contention, one of considerable force were it not for the constitutional constraints applied to state action, is that the prayers are an essential part of these ceremonies because for many persons an occasion of this significance lacks meaning if there is no recognition, however brief, that human achievements cannot be understood apart from their spiritual essence. We think the Government's position that this interest suffices to force students to choose between compliance or forfeiture demonstrates fundamental inconsistency in its argumentation. It fails to acknowledge that what for many of Deborah's classmates and their parents was a spiritual imperative was for Daniel and Deborah Weisman religious conformance compelled by the State. While in some societies the wishes of the majority might prevail, the Establishment Clause of the First Amendment is addressed to this contingency and rejects the balance urged upon us. The Constitution forbids the State to exact religious conformity from a student as the price of attending her own high school graduation. This is the calculus the Constitution commands.

The Government's argument gives insufficient recognition to the real conflict of conscience faced by the young student. The essence of the Government's position is that with regard to a civic, social occasion of this importance it is the objector, not the majority, who must take unilateral and private action to avoid compromising religious scruples, hereby electing to miss the graduation exercise. This turns conventional First Amendment analysis on its head. It is a tenet of the First Amendment that the State cannot require one of its citizens to forfeit his or her rights and benefits as the price of resisting conformance to state-sponsored religious practice. To say that a student must remain apart from the ceremony at the opening invocation and closing benediction is to risk compelling conformity in an environment analogous to the classroom setting, where we have said the risk of compulsion is especially high. Just as in *Engel v. Vitale,* and *School Dist. of Abington v. Schempp,* where we found that provisions within the challenged legislation permitting a student to be voluntarily excused from attendance or participation in the daily prayers did not shield those practices from invalidation, the fact that attendance at the graduation ceremonies is voluntary in a legal sense does not save the religious exercise.

. . . The atmosphere at the opening of a session of a state legislature where adults are free to enter and leave with little comment and for any number of reasons cannot compare with the constraining potential of the one school event most important for the student to attend. The influence and force of a formal exercise in a school graduation are far greater than the prayer exercise we condoned in *Marsh.* The *Marsh* majority in fact gave specific recognition to this distinction and placed particular reliance on it in upholding the prayers at issue there. Today's case is different. At a high school graduation, teachers and principals must and do retain a high degree of control over the precise contents of the program, the speeches, the timing, the movements, the dress, and the decorum of the students. . . . In this atmosphere the state-imposed character of an invocation and benediction by clergy selected by the school combine to make the prayer a state-sanctioned religious exercise in which the student was left with no alternative but to submit. This is different from *Marsh* and suffices to make the religious exercise a First Amendment violation. Our Establishment Clause jurisprudence remains a delicate and fact-sensitive one, and we cannot accept the parallel relied upon by petitioners and the United States between the facts of *Marsh* and the case now before us. Our decisions in *Engel v. Vitale,* and *School Dist. of Abington v. Schempp,* require us to distinguish the public school context.

We do not hold that every state action implicating religion is invalid if one or a few citizens find it offensive. People may take offense at all manner of religious as well as nonreligious messages, but offense alone does not in every case show a violation. We know too that sometimes to endure social isolation or even anger may be the price of conscience or nonconformity. But, by any reading of our cases, the conformity required of the student in this case was too high an exaction to withstand the test of the Establishment Clause. The prayer exercises in this case are especially improper because the State has in every practical sense compelled attendance and participation in an explicit religious exercise at an event of singular importance to every student, one the objecting student had no real alternative to avoid.

Our jurisprudence in this area is of necessity one of line-drawing, of determining at what point a dissenter's rights of religious freedom are infringed by the State. . . .

Our society would be less than true to its heritage if it lacked abiding concern for the values of its young people, and we acknowledge the profound belief of adherents to many faiths that there must be a place in the student's life for precepts of a morality higher even than the law we today enforce. We express no hostility to those aspirations, nor would our oath permit us to do so. A relentless and all-pervasive attempt to exclude religion from every aspect of public life could itself become inconsistent with the Constitution. We recognize that, at graduation time and throughout the course of the educational process, there will be instances when religious values, religious practices, and religious persons will have some interaction with the public schools and their students. . . . But these matters, often questions of accommodation of religion, are not before us. The sole question presented is whether a religious exercise may be conducted at a graduation ceremony in circumstances where, as we have found, young graduates who object are induced to conform. No holding by this Court suggests that a school can persuade or compel a student to participate in a religious exercise. That is being done here, and it is forbidden by the Establishment Clause of the First Amendment.

For the reasons we have stated, the judgment of the Court of Appeals is
Affirmed.

Justice Scalia, with whom The Chief Justice, Justice White, and Justice Thomas join, dissenting.

Three Terms ago, I joined an opinion recognizing that the Establishment Clause must be construed in light of the "government policies of accommodation, acknowledgment, and support for religion [that] are an accepted part of our political and cultural heritage." That opinion affirmed that "the meaning of the Clause is to be determined by reference to historical practices and understandings." It said that "[a] test for implementing the protections of the Establishment Clause that, if applied with consistency, would invalidate longstanding traditions cannot be a proper reading of the Clause."

These views of course prevent me from joining today's opinion, which is conspicuously bereft of any reference to history. In holding that the Establishment Clause prohibits invocations and benedictions at public school graduation ceremonies, the Court—with nary a mention that it is doing so—lays waste a tradition that is as old as public school graduation ceremonies themselves, and that is a component of an even more longstanding American tradition of nonsectarian prayer to God at public celebrations generally. As its instrument of destruction, the bulldozer of its social engineering, the Court invents a boundless, and boundlessly manipulable, test of psychological coercion, which promises to do for the Establishment Clause what the *Durham* rule did for the insanity defense. Today's opinion shows more forcefully than volumes of argumentation why our Nation's protection, that fortress which is our Constitution, cannot possibly rest upon the changeable philosophical predilections of the Justices of this Court, but must have deep foundations in the historic practices of our people.

I

. . . The history and tradition of our Nation are replete with public ceremonies featuring prayers of thanksgiving and petition. . . . From our Nation's origin, prayer has been a prominent part of governmental ceremonies and proclamations. The Declaration of Independence, the document marking our birth as a separate people, "appealed to the Supreme Judge of the world for the rectitude of our intentions" and avowed "a firm reliance on the protection of divine Providence."

In addition to this general tradition of prayer at public ceremonies, there exists a more specific tradition of invocations and benedictions at public school graduation exercises.

II

The Court presumably would separate graduation invocations and benedictions from other instances of public "preservation and transmission of religious beliefs" on the ground that they involve "psychological coercion." I find it a sufficient embarrassment that our Establishment Clause jurisprudence regarding holiday displays, has come to "require scrutiny more commonly associated with interior decorators than with the judiciary." But interior decorating is a rock-hard science compared to psychology practiced by amateurs. A few citations of "research in psychology" that have no particular bearing upon the precise issue here, cannot disguise the fact that the Court has gone beyond the realm where judges know what they are doing. . . .

. . . The opinion manifests that the Court itself has not given careful consideration to its test of psychological coercion. For if it had, how could it observe, with no hint of concern or disapproval, that students stood for the Pledge of Allegiance, which immediately preceded Rabbi Gutterman's invocation? The government can, of course, no more coerce political orthodoxy than religious orthodoxy. Moreover, since the Pledge of Allegiance has been revised since *Barnette* to include the phrase "under God," recital of the Pledge would appear to raise the same Establishment Clause issue as the invocation and benediction. If students were psychologically coerced to remain standing during the invocation, they must also have been psychologically coerced, moments before, to stand for (and thereby, in the Court's view, take part in or appear to take part in) the Pledge. Must the Pledge therefore be barred from the public schools (both from graduation ceremonies and from the classroom)? In *Barnette* we held that a public school student could not be compelled to *recite* the Pledge; we did not even hint that she could not be compelled to observe respectful silence—indeed, even to *stand* in respectful silence—when those who wished to recite it did so. Logically, that ought to be the next project for the Court's bulldozer. . . .

. . . The Court relies on our "school prayer" cases. . . . But whatever the merit of those cases, they do not support, much less compel, the Court's psycho-journey. In the first place, *Engel* and *Schempp* do not constitute an exception to the rule, distilled from historical practice, that public ceremonies may include prayer; rather, they simply do not fall within the scope of the rule (for the obvious reason that school instruction is not a public ceremony). Second, we have made clear our understanding that school prayer occurs within a framework in which legal coercion to attend school (*i.e.,* coercion under threat of penalty) provides the ultimate backdrop. . . . And finally, our school prayer cases turn in part on the fact that the classroom is inherently an instructional setting, and daily prayer there—where parents are not present to counter "the students' emulation of teachers as role models and the children's susceptibility to peer pressure,"—might be thought to raise special concerns regarding state interference with the liberty of parents to direct the religious upbringing of their children: "Families entrust public schools with the education of their children, but condition their trust on the understanding that the classroom will not purposely be used to advance religious views that may conflict with the private beliefs of the student and his or her family." Voluntary prayer at graduation—a one-time ceremony at which parents, friends, and relatives are present—can hardly be thought to raise the same concerns.

IV

Our Religion Clause jurisprudence has become bedeviled (so to speak) by reliance on formulaic abstractions that are not derived from, but positively conflict with, our long-accepted constitutional traditions. Foremost among these has been the so-called *Lemon* test, which has received well-earned criticism from many Members of this Court. . . . The Court today demonstrates the irrelevance of *Lemon* by essentially ignoring it, and the interment of that case may be the one happy byproduct of the Court's otherwise lamentable decision. Unfortunately, however, the Court has replaced *Lemon* with its psycho-coercion test, which suffers the double disability of having no roots whatever in our people's historic practice, and being as infinitely expandable as the reasons for psychotherapy itself. . . .

. . . I must add one final observation: The Founders of our Republic knew the fearsome potential of sectarian religious belief to generate civil dissension and civil strife. And they also knew that nothing, absolutely nothing, is so inclined to foster among religious believers of various faiths a toleration — no, an affection — for one another than voluntarily joining in prayer together, to the God whom they all worship and seek. Needless to say, no one should be compelled to do that, but it is a shame to deprive our public culture of the opportunity, and indeed the encouragement, for people to do it voluntarily.

For the foregoing reasons, I dissent.

NOTES AND QUESTIONS

1. Justice Kennedy indicates that the act of standing at graduation while a prayer is read is an act of participation rather than merely an act of respect. How would you define an act of "participation" in this context? May the state or federal government mandate "respect" for another's beliefs or nonbeliefs?
2. The majority relies on "special pressure" among adolescents to support its view of compulsion. How would the Court's reasoning change if such pressure were overstated? How does the Court's reasoning apply to non-adolescent aged children?
3. The majority writes that, "[l]aw reaches past formalism." To what extent is that true in the particular context of the First Amendment case-law governing public education?
4. What is the basis for the majority's distinction between a prayer at a graduation and a prayer at a legislative session? Compare *Marsh v. Chambers,* 463 U.S. 783 (1983) (upholding invocations and benedictions that open a legislative session). Significantly, Justice Kennedy's opinion for the Court does not analyze the issue by applying the three-part *Lemon* test, prompting a separate concurrence that declares the vitality of that test and applies it to the case at hand.
5. In his concurrence, Justice Souter responds directly to the arguments made by Justice Rehnquist regarding the textual history of the establishment clause. Justice Souter argues that that history confirms that the framers intended to prohibit any preferential aid to religion. Justice Rehnquist, by contrast, argues that the framer's intent was merely to prohibit a "national church" and to prohibit governmental assistance to one religious sect over another religious sect. *See Wallace* (Rehnquist, J. dissenting). Which argument do you find more persuasive? Should the Court's result depend on the textual history of the establishment clause? Do you agree with Justice Scalia that the meaning of the establishment clause and presumably any constitutional clause "is to be determined by reference to historical practices and understandings"? Does Justice Scalia rely on historical practices or understandings?
6. The majority carefully distinguishes the principles underlying the First Amendment's protection of religion from the principles underlying

the First Amendment's protection of speech. Unlike the protection of "speech," which assumes governmental involvement as a locutor, the protection of "religion" assumes the opposite: the establishment clause prohibits governmental involvement. Justice Kennedy infers from the design of the First Amendment that the constitutional protection of "freedom of belief and conscience" demands a prohibition on governmental involvement in religion. Is Justice Kennedy's distinction between the constitutional protection for speech and religion compelling?

7. The prayer at issue in the case was nondenominational. In their separate concurrence, therefore, Justices Souter, Stevens and O'Connor emphasize that the establishment clause not only forbids state practices that assist one religion over another, but also forbids state practices that assist all religions or that preference religion over nonreligion. If the establishment clause prohibits states from preferencing religion over nonreligion, does it also prohibit states from preferring nonreligion over religion?
8. In support of his view that the establishment clause prohibits even governmental preference of religion over non-religion, Justice Souter traces the history of the drafting of the establishment clause:

> When James Madison arrived at the First Congress with a series of proposals to amend the National Constitution, one of the provisions read that "the civil rights of none shall be abridged on account of religious belief or worship, nor shall any national religion be established, nor shall the full and equal rights of conscience be in any manner, or on any pretext, infringed." 1 Annals of Cong. 434 (1789). Madison's language did not last long. It was sent to a Select Committee of the House, which, without explanation, changed it to read that "no religion shall be established by law, nor shall the equal rights of conscience be infringed." Thence the proposal went to the Committee of the Whole, which was in turn dissatisfied with the Select Committee's language and adopted an alternative proposed by Samuel Livermore of New Hampshire: "Congress shall make no laws touching religion, or infringing the rights of conscience." Livermore's proposal would have forbidden laws having anything to do with religion and was thus not only far broader than Madison's version, but broader even than the scope of the Establishment Clause as we now understand it. . . .
>
> The House rewrote the amendment once more before sending it to the Senate, this time adopting, without recorded debate, language derived from a proposal by Fisher Ames of Massachusetts: "Congress shall make no law establishing Religion, or prohibiting the free exercise thereof, nor shall the rights of conscience be infringed." 1 *Documentary History of the First Federal Congress of the United States of America* 136 (Senate Journal) (L. de Pauw ed. 1972); *see* 1 Annals of Cong. 765 (1789). Perhaps, on further reflection, the Representatives had thought Livermore's proposal too expansive, or perhaps, as one historian has suggested, they had simply worried that his language would not "satisfy the demands of those who wanted something said specifically against establishments of religion." L. Levy, *The Establishment Clause* 81 (1986) (hereinafter Levy). We do not know; what we do know is that the House rejected the Select Committee's version, which arguably ensured only that "no religion" enjoyed an official preference over

others, and deliberately chose instead a prohibition extending to laws establishing "religion" in general. The sequence of the Senate's treatment of this House proposal, and the House's response to the Senate, confirm that the Framers meant the Establishment Clause's prohibition to encompass nonpreferential aid to religion. . . .

9. Justice Scalia suggests that the logic of the Court's opinion (its "bulldozer") would compel it to declare unconstitutional the reciting of the Pledge of Allegiance. As discussed in Section C of this chapter, the constitutionality of the Pledge in public schools is in doubt. How does the reasoning in *Lee* relate to the Pledge?
10. Can the school district, as Justice Scalia suggests, avoid the constitutional infirmity of a graduation prayer merely by announcing that no one is compelled to join in the prayer and that the failure to object to the prayer will not necessarily be deemed to be a participation in the prayer?

SANTA FE INDEPENDENT SCHOOL DISTRICT V. JANE DOE

530 U.S. 290 (2000)

Justice STEVENS delivered the opinion of the Court.

We granted the District's petition for certiorari, limited to the following question: "Whether petitioner's policy permitting student-led, student-initiated prayer at football games violates the Establishment Clause." We conclude, as did the Court of Appeals, that it does. . . .

II

The first Clause in the First Amendment to the Federal Constitution provides that "Congress shall make no law respecting an establishment of religion, or prohibiting the free exercise thereof." . . . In *Lee v. Weisman,* we held that a prayer delivered by a rabbi at a middle school graduation ceremony violated that Clause. Although this case involves student prayer at a different type of school function, our analysis is properly guided by the principles that we endorsed in *Lee*. . . .

These invocations are authorized by a government policy and take place on government property at government-sponsored school-related events. Of course, not every message delivered under such circumstances is the government's own. We have held, for example, that an individual's contribution to a government-created forum was not government speech.

In *Lee,* the school district made the related argument that its policy of endorsing only "civic or nonsectarian" prayer was acceptable because it minimized the intrusion on the audience as a whole. We rejected that claim by explaining that such a majoritarian policy "does not lessen the offense or isolation to the objectors. At best it narrows their number, at worst increases their sense of isolation and affront." Similarly, while Santa Fe's majoritarian election might ensure that *most* of the students are represented, it does nothing to protect the minority; indeed, it likely serves to intensify their offense.

Moreover, the District has failed to divorce itself from the religious content in the invocations. It has not succeeded in doing so, either by claiming that its policy is "'one of neutrality rather than endorsement'" or by characterizing the individual student as the "circuit-breaker" in the process. Contrary to the District's repeated assertions that it has adopted a "hands-off" approach to the pregame invocation, the realities of the situation plainly reveal that its policy involves both perceived and actual endorsement of religion. In this case, as we found in *Lee,* the "degree of school involvement" makes it clear that the pregame prayers bear "the imprint of the State and thus put school-age children who objected in an untenable position."

The District has attempted to disentangle itself from the religious messages by developing the two-step student election process. The text of the October policy, however, exposes the extent of the school's entanglement. The elections take place at all only because the school "board *has chosen to permit* students to deliver a brief invocation and/or message." The elections thus "shall" be conducted "by the high school student council" and "upon advice and direction of the high school principal." The decision whether to deliver a message is first made by majority vote of the entire student body, followed by a choice of the speaker in a separate, similar majority election. Even though the particular words used by the speaker are not determined by those votes, the policy mandates that the "statement or invocation" be "consistent with the goals and purposes of this policy," which are "to solemnize the event, to promote good sportsmanship and student safety, and to establish the appropriate environment for the competition."

In addition to involving the school in the selection of the speaker, the policy, by its terms, invites and encourages religious messages. The policy itself states that the purpose of the message is "to solemnize the event." A religious message is the most obvious method of solemnizing an event. Moreover, the requirements that the message "promote good citizenship" and "establish the appropriate environment for competition" further narrow the types of message deemed appropriate, suggesting that a solemn, yet nonreligious, message, such as commentary on United States foreign policy, would be prohibited. Indeed, the only type of message that is expressly endorsed in the text is an "invocation"—a term that primarily describes an appeal for divine assistance. In fact, as used in the past at Santa Fe High School, an "invocation" has always entailed a focused religious message. Thus, the expressed purposes of the policy encourage the selection of a religious message, and that is precisely how the students understand the policy. The results of the elections described in the parties' stipulation make it clear that the students understood that the central question before them was whether prayer should be a part of the pregame ceremony. We recognize the important role that public worship plays in many communities, as well as the sincere desire to include public prayer as a part of various occasions so as to mark those occasions' significance. But such religious activity in public schools, as elsewhere, must comport with the First Amendment.

The actual or perceived endorsement of the message, moreover, is established by factors beyond just the text of the policy. Once the student speaker is selected and the message composed, the invocation is then delivered to a large audience assembled as part of a regularly scheduled, school-sponsored function conducted on school property. The message is broadcast over the school's public address system, which remains subject to the control of school officials. It is fair to assume that the pregame ceremony is clothed in the traditional indicia of school sporting events, which generally include not just the team, but also cheerleaders and band members dressed in uniforms sporting the school name and mascot. The school's name is likely written in large print across the field and on banners and flags. The crowd will certainly include many who display the school colors and insignia on their school T-shirts, jackets, or hats and who may also be waving signs displaying the school name. It is in a setting such as this that "the board has chosen to permit" the elected student to rise and give the "statement or invocation."

In this context the members of the listening audience must perceive the pregame message as a public expression of the views of the majority of the student body delivered with the approval of the school administration. In cases involving state participation in a religious activity, one of the relevant questions is "whether an objective observer, acquainted with the text, legislative history, and implementation of the statute, would perceive it as a state endorsement of prayer in public schools." . . . Regardless of the listener's support for, or objection to, the message, an objective Santa Fe High School student will unquestionably perceive the inevitable pregame prayer as stamped with her school's seal of approval.

The text and history of this policy, moreover, reinforce our objective student's perception that the prayer is, in actuality, encouraged by the school. When a governmental entity professes a secular purpose for an arguably religious policy, the government's characterization is, of course, entitled to some deference. But it is nonetheless the duty of the courts to "distinguish a sham secular purpose from a sincere one." . . .

According to the District, the secular purposes of the policy are to "foster free expression of private persons . . . as well [as to] solemnize sporting events, promote good sportsmanship and student safety, and establish an appropriate environment for competition." We note, however, that the District's approval of only one specific kind of message, an "invocation," is not necessary to further any of these purposes. Additionally, the fact that only one student is permitted to give a content-limited message suggests that this policy does little to "foster free expression." Furthermore, regardless of whether one considers a sporting event an appropriate occasion for solemnity, the use of an invocation to foster such solemnity is impermissible when, in actuality, it constitutes prayer sponsored by the school. And it is unclear what type of message would be both appropriately "solemnizing" under the District's policy and yet nonreligious.

Most striking to us is the evolution of the current policy from the long-sanctioned office of "Student Chaplain" to the candidly titled "Prayer at Football Games" regulation. This history indicates that the District intended to preserve the practice of prayer before football games. The conclusion that the District viewed the October policy simply as a continuation of the previous policies is dramatically illustrated by the fact that the school did not conduct a new election, pursuant to the current policy, to replace the results of the previous election, which occurred under the former policy. Given these observations, and in light of the school's history of regular delivery of a student-led prayer at athletic events, it is reasonable to infer that the specific purpose of the policy was to preserve a popular "state-sponsored religious practice."

School sponsorship of a religious message is impermissible because it sends the ancillary message to members of the audience who are nonadherents "that they are outsiders, not full members of the political community, and an accompanying message to adherents that they are insiders, favored members of the political community." . . . The delivery of such a message—over the school's public address system, by a speaker representing the student body, under the supervision of school faculty, and pursuant to a school policy that explicitly and implicitly encourages public prayer—is not properly characterized as "private" speech.

III

The District next argues that its football policy is distinguishable from the graduation prayer in *Lee* because it does not coerce students to participate in religious observances. Its argument has two parts: first, that there is no impermissible government coercion because the pregame messages are the product of student choices; and second, that there is really no coercion at all because attendance at an extracurricular event, unlike a graduation ceremony, is voluntary.

The reasons just discussed explaining why the alleged "circuit-breaker" mechanism of the dual elections and student speaker do not turn public speech into private speech also demonstrate why these mechanisms do not insulate the school from the coercive element of the final message. In fact, this aspect of the District's argument exposes anew the concerns that are created by the majoritarian election system. The parties' stipulation clearly states that the issue resolved in the first election was "whether a student would deliver prayer at varsity football games," and the controversy in this case demonstrates that the views of the students are not unanimous on that issue.

One of the purposes served by the Establishment Clause is to remove debate over this kind of issue from governmental supervision or control. We explained in *Lee* that the "preservation and transmission of religious beliefs and worship is a responsibility and a choice committed to the private sphere." The two student elections authorized by the policy, coupled with the debates that presumably must precede each, impermissibly invade that private sphere. The election mechanism, when considered in light of the history in which the policy in question evolved, reflects a device the District put in place that determines whether religious messages will be delivered at home football games. The mechanism encourages divisiveness along religious lines in a public school setting, a result at odds with the Establishment Clause. Although it is true that the ultimate choice of student speaker is "attributable to the students," Brief for Petitioner 40, the District's decision to hold the constitutionally problematic election is clearly "a choice attributable to the State."

The District further argues that attendance at the commencement ceremonies at issue in *Lee* "differs dramatically" from attendance at high school football games, which it contends "are of no more than passing interest to many students" and are "decidedly extracurricular," thus dissipating any coercion. Attendance at a high school football game, unlike showing up for class, is certainly not required in order to receive a diploma. Moreover, we may assume that the District is correct in arguing that the informal pressure to attend an athletic event is not as strong as a senior's desire to attend her own graduation ceremony.

There are some students, however, such as cheerleaders, members of the band, and, of course, the team members themselves, for whom seasonal commitments mandate their attendance, sometimes for class credit. The District also minimizes the importance to many students of attending and participating in extracurricular activities as part of a complete educational experience. As we noted in *Lee,* "law reaches past formalism." To assert that high school students do not feel immense social pressure, or have a truly genuine desire, to be involved in the extracurricular event that is American high school football is "formalistic in the extreme." *Id.* We stressed in *Lee* the obvious observation that "adolescents are often susceptible to pressure from their peers towards conformity, and that the influence is strongest in matters of social convention." High school home football games are traditional gatherings of a school community; they bring together students and faculty as well as friends and family from years present and past to root for a common cause. Undoubtedly, the games are not important to some students, and they voluntarily choose not to attend. For many others, however, the choice between whether to attend these games or to risk facing a personally offensive religious ritual is in no practical sense an easy one. The Constitution, moreover, demands that the school may not force this difficult choice upon these students for "it is a tenet of the First Amendment that the State cannot require one of its citizens to forfeit his or her rights and benefits as the price of resisting conformance to state-sponsored religious practice."

Even if we regard every high school student's decision to attend a home football game as purely voluntary, we are nevertheless persuaded that the delivery of a pregame prayer has the improper effect of coercing those present to participate in an act of religious worship. For "the government may no more use social pressure to enforce orthodoxy than it may use more direct means." As in *Lee,* "what to most believers may seem nothing more than a reasonable request that the nonbeliever respect their religious practices, in a school context may appear to the nonbeliever or dissenter to be an attempt to employ the machinery of the State to enforce a religious orthodoxy." The constitutional command will not permit the District "to exact religious conformity from a student as the price" of joining her classmates at a varsity football game.

The Religion Clauses of the First Amendment prevent the government from making any law respecting the establishment of religion or prohibiting the free exercise thereof. By no means do these commands impose a prohibition on all religious activity in our public schools. Indeed, the common purpose of the Religion Clauses "is to secure religious liberty." Thus, nothing in the Constitution as interpreted by this Court prohibits any public school student from voluntarily praying at any time before, during, or after the school day. But the religious liberty protected by the Constitution is abridged when the State affirmatively sponsors the particular religious practice of prayer.

IV

Finally, the District argues repeatedly that the Does have made a premature facial challenge to the October policy that necessarily must fail. The District emphasizes, quite correctly, that until a student actually delivers a solemnizing message under the latest version of the policy, there can be no certainty that any of the statements or invocations will be religious. Thus, it concludes, the October policy necessarily survives a facial challenge.

This argument, however, assumes that we are concerned only with the serious constitutional injury that occurs when a student is forced to participate in an act of religious worship because she chooses to attend a school event. But the Constitution also requires that we keep in mind "the myriad, subtle ways in which Establishment Clause values can be eroded," and that we guard against other different, yet equally important, constitutional injuries. One is the mere passage by the District of a policy that has the purpose and perception of government establishment of religion. Another is the implementation of a governmental electoral process that subjects the issue of prayer to a majoritarian vote.

The District argues that the facial challenge must fail because "Santa Fe's Football Policy cannot be invalidated on the basis of some 'possibility or even likelihood' of an unconstitutional application." Our Establishment Clause cases involving facial challenges, however, have not focused solely on the possible applications of the statute, but rather have considered whether the statute has an unconstitutional purpose. . . . Under the *Lemon* standard, a court must invalidate a statute if it lacks "a secular legislative purpose." . . . It is therefore proper, as part of this facial challenge, for us to examine the purpose of the October policy.

As discussed, the text of the October policy alone reveals that it has an unconstitutional purpose. The plain language of the policy clearly spells out the extent of school involvement in both the election of the speaker and the content of the message. Additionally, the text of the October policy specifies only one, clearly preferred message—that of Santa Fe's traditional religious "invocation." Finally, the extremely selective access of the policy and other content restrictions confirm that it is not a content-neutral regulation that creates a limited public forum for the expression of student speech. Our examination, however, need not stop at an analysis of the text of the policy. . . .

The District, nevertheless, asks us to pretend that we do not recognize what every Santa Fe High School student understands clearly—that this policy is about prayer. The District further asks us to accept what is obviously untrue: that these messages are necessary to "solemnize" a football game and that this single-student, year-long position is essential to the protection of student speech. We refuse to turn a blind eye to the context in which this policy arose, and that context quells any doubt that this policy was implemented with the purpose of endorsing school prayer.

Therefore, the simple enactment of this policy, with the purpose and perception of school endorsement of student prayer, was a constitutional violation. We need not wait for the inevitable to confirm and magnify the constitutional injury. In *Wallace,* for example, we invalidated Alabama's as yet unimplemented and voluntary "moment of silence" statute based on our conclusion that it was enacted "for the sole purpose of expressing the State's endorsement of prayer activities for one minute at the beginning of each school day." . . . Therefore, even if no Santa Fe High School student were ever to offer a religious message, the October policy fails a facial challenge because the attempt by the District to encourage prayer is also at issue. Government efforts to endorse religion cannot evade constitutional reproach based solely on the remote possibility that those attempts may fail.

This policy likewise does not survive a facial challenge because it impermissibly imposes upon the student body a majoritarian election on the issue of prayer. Through its election scheme, the District has established a governmental electoral mechanism that turns the school into a forum for religious debate. It further empowers the student body majority with the authority to subject students of minority views to constitutionally improper messages. The award of that power alone, regardless of the students' ultimate use of it, is not acceptable. . . . [T]he election mechanism established by the District undermines the essential protection of minority viewpoints. Such a system encourages divisiveness along religious lines and threatens the imposition of coercion upon those students not desiring to participate in a religious exercise. Simply by establishing this school-related procedure, which entrusts the inherently nongovernmental subject of religion to a majoritarian vote, a constitutional violation has occurred. No further injury is required for the policy to fail a facial challenge.

To properly examine this policy on its face, we "must be deemed aware of the history and context of the community and forum." . . . Our examination of those circumstances above leads to the conclusion that this policy does not provide the District with the constitutional safe harbor it sought. The policy is invalid on its face because it establishes an improper majoritarian election on religion, and unquestionably has the purpose and creates the perception of encouraging the delivery of prayer at a series of important school events.

The judgment of the Court of Appeals is, accordingly, affirmed.

Chief Justice REHNQUIST, with whom Justice SCALIA and Justice THOMAS join, dissenting.

The Court distorts existing precedent to conclude that the school district's student-message program is invalid on its face under the Establishment Clause. But even more disturbing than its holding is the tone of the Court's opinion; it bristles with hostility to all things religious in public life. Neither the holding nor the tone of the opinion is faithful to the meaning of the Establishment Clause, when it is recalled that George Washington himself, at the request of the very Congress which passed the Bill of Rights, proclaimed a day of "public thanksgiving and prayer, to be observed by acknowledging with grateful hearts the many and signal favors of Almighty God."

Presidential Proclamation, 1 *Messages and Papers of the Presidents, 1789-1897,* p. 64 (J. Richardson ed. 1897).

NOTES AND QUESTIONS

1. The Court begins its analysis by defining the issue as whether the speech here is "government" speech forbidden by the establishment clause or "private" speech protected by the free exercise clause. The Court concludes that the "invocation" is governmental speech in part because it is (1) authorized by governmental policy; (2) takes place on government property, at a (3) government-sponsored school-related event. Do you agree that the invocation was governmental speech? In light of the Court's guidelines for distinguishing governmental speech from private speech, what kind of speech at a school or school event would be considered "private"? The Court calls the distinction between private and governmental speech "crucial." How would the Court's analysis have been different if the Court found the invocation to be "private"?
2. The Court's determination that the invocation is governmental speech leads it to consider whether the school has created a limited open forum. The Court concludes that the podium for the delivery of an invocation is not an open forum in this case. Do you agree? If the school had created a limited open forum, would it be barred from presenting the invocation?
3. The Court rejects the argument that the invocation represents student-initiated private speech, despite the fact that the speaker is elected by the student body. Under what circumstances can student-initiated speech constitute governmental endorsement of religion?
4. To what extent is the Court correct that student attendance at a school's home football game is involuntary?
5. In his dissent, Justice Rehnquist observes that *Lemon* has had a "checkered career," and then relies on Justice Souter's opinion in *Lee* for the proposition that if a school chooses its graduation speaker by wholly secular criteria and that speaker chooses to deliver a religious message, "it would be harder to attribute an endorsement of religion to the state." Do you agree? Even if it would be "harder" to find endorsement in a student's choice to deliver a religious message, could endorsement nonetheless be found?
6. In *Santa Fe* and elsewhere the Court refers to the metaphor of a "circuit-breaker." What is that metaphor and how is it being used in those cases?

C. THE PLEDGE OF ALLEGIANCE

The current debate regarding the constitutionality of the Pledge of Allegiance in American schools—both at school events and in the classroom—represents the culmination of the case law in this chapter. If the precedents established by the Supreme Court are taken seriously, it is very difficult to justify the continuation of the common practice of reciting the Pledge in public school. Nonetheless, the Pledge also raises political issues that threaten to transcend the legal ones.

In *Minersville v. Gobitis,* 310 U.S. 586 (1940), the United States Supreme Court reaffirmed the constitutionality of a compulsory flag salute and pledge. Three years later, however, in *Barnette,* the court changed direction and held that a state's requirement that all public school teachers and students salute the flag and recite the Pledge of Allegiance violates the First Amendment. The "Pledge" at issue in *Barnette* did not contain any reference to "God."

Since *Barnette,* Congress has altered the pledge language to include the now-familiar phrase "one nation under God. . . ." Although the Supreme Court has not precisely addressed the language of the revised Pledge, recall Justice Scalia's warning in *Lee v. Weisman* that the Court's recent reasoning would lead it to declare unconstitutional even nonmandatory recitation of a Pledge that refers to a deity.

Indeed, in *Newdow,* the Ninth Circuit scrupulously applied the establishment clause standards articulated by the Supreme Court and found the Pledge to be unconstitutional. The Supreme Court granted *certiorari* in the *Newdow* case, but a majority of the Court declined to reach the merits of Newdow's challenge, concluding that, as a noncustodial parent of the student, he lacked standing to bring claims on her behalf. *Elk Grove Unified School District v. Newdow,* 124 S. Ct. 2301 (2004). The *Newdow* litigation thus provides an excellent example of the uncertain application of the Supreme Court's current "tests" for determining the constitutional boundaries of religious observance in the public school environment.

1. Pledging Political Allegiance

West Virginia State Board of Education v. Barnette

319 U.S. 624 (1943)

Justice Jackson delivered the Opinion of the Court.

Following the decision by this Court on June 3, 1940, in *Minersville School District v. Gobitis,* the West Virginia legislature amended its statutes to require all schools therein to conduct courses of instruction in history, civics, and in the Constitutions of the United States and of the State "for the purpose of teaching, fostering and perpetuating the ideals, principles and spirit of Americanism, and increasing the knowledge of the organization and machinery of the government."

. . . The Board of Education on January 9, 1942, adopted a resolution containing recitals taken largely from the Court's *Gobitis* opinion and ordering that the salute to the flag become "a regular part of the program of activities in the public schools," that all teachers and pupils "shall be required to participate in the salute honoring the Nation represented by the Flag; provided, however, that refusal to salute the Flag be regarded as an act of insubordination, and shall be dealt with accordingly." . . .

Appellees, citizens of the United States and of West Virginia, brought suit in the United States District Court for themselves and others similarly situated asking its injunction to restrain enforcement of these laws and regulations against Jehovah's Witnesses. The Witnesses are an unincorporated body teaching that the obligation imposed by law of God is superior to that of laws enacted by temporal government. Their religious beliefs include a literal version of Exodus, Chapter 20, verses 4 and 5, which says: "Thou shalt not make unto thee any graven image, or any likeness of anything that is in heaven above, or that is in the earth beneath, or that is in the water under the earth; thou shalt not bow down thyself to them nor serve them." They consider that the flag is an "image" within this command. For this reason they refuse to salute it.

Children of this faith have been expelled from school and are threatened with exclusion for no other cause. Officials threaten to send them to reformatories maintained for criminally inclined juveniles. Parents of such children have been prosecuted and are threatened with prosecutions for causing delinquency.

This case calls upon us to reconsider a precedent decision, as the Court throughout its history often has been required to do. Before turning to the *Gobitis* case, however, it is desirable to notice certain characteristics by which this controversy is distinguished.

The freedom asserted by these appellees does not bring them into collision with rights asserted by any other individual. It is such conflicts which most frequently require intervention of the State to determine where the rights of one end and those of another begin. But the refusal of these persons to participate in the ceremony does not interfere with or deny rights of others to do so. Nor is there any question in this case that their behavior is peaceable and orderly. The sole conflict is between authority and rights of the individual. The State asserts power to condition access to public education on making a prescribed sign and profession and at the same time to coerce attendance by punishing both parent and child. The latter stand on a right of self-determination in matters that touch individual opinion and personal attitude.

As the present Chief Justice said in dissent in the *Gobitis* case, the State may "require teaching by instruction and study of all in our history and in the structure and organization of our government, including the guaranties of civil liberty, which tend to inspire patriotism and love of country." Here, however, we are dealing with a compulsion of students to declare a belief. They are not merely made acquainted with the flag salute so that they may be informed as to what it is or even what it means. The issue here is whether this slow and easily neglected route to aroused loyalties constitutionally may be short-cut by substituting a compulsory salute and slogan. This issue is not prejudiced by the Court's previous holding that where a State, without compelling attendance, extends college facilities to pupils who voluntarily enroll, it may prescribe military training as part of the course without offense to the Constitution. It was held that those who take advantage of its opportunities may not on ground of conscience refuse compliance with such conditions. . . . In the present case attendance is not optional. That case is also to be distinguished from the present one because, independently of college privileges or requirements, the State has power to raise militia and impose the duties of service therein upon its citizens.

There is no doubt that, in connection with the pledges, the flag salute is a form of utterance. Symbolism is a primitive but effective way of communicating ideas. The use of an emblem or flag to symbolize some system, idea, institution, or personality, is a short cut from mind to mind. Causes and nations, political parties, lodges and ecclesiastical groups seek to knit the loyalty of their followings to a flag or banner, a color or design. The State announces rank, function, and authority through crowns and maces, uniforms and black robes; the church speaks through the Cross, the Crucifix, the altar and shrine, and clerical raiment. Symbols of State often convey political ideas just as religious symbols come to convey theological ones. Associated with many of these symbols are appropriate gestures of acceptance or respect: a salute, a bowed or bared head, a bended knee. A person gets from a symbol the meaning he puts into it, and what is one man's comfort and inspiration is another's jest and scorn.

. . . Here it is the State that employs a flag as a symbol of adherence to government as presently organized. It requires the individual to communicate by word and sign his acceptance of the political ideas it thus bespeaks. Objection to this form of communication when coerced is an old one, well known to the framers of the Bill of Rights.

It is also to be noted that the compulsory flag salute and pledge requires affirmation of a belief and an attitude of mind. It is not clear whether the regulation contemplates that pupils forego any contrary convictions of their own and become unwilling converts to the prescribed ceremony or whether it will be acceptable if they simulate assent by words without belief and by a gesture barren of meaning. It is now a commonplace that censorship or suppression of expression of opinion is tolerated by our Constitution only when the expression presents a clear and present danger of action of a kind the State is empowered to prevent and punish. It would seem that involuntary affirmation could be commanded only on even more immediate and urgent grounds than silence. But here the power of compulsion is invoked without any allegation that remaining passive during a flag salute ritual creates a clear and present danger that would justify an effort even to muffle expression. To sustain the compulsory flag salute we are required to say that a Bill of Rights which guards the individual's right to speak his own mind, left it open to public authorities to compel him to utter what is not in his mind.

Whether the First Amendment to the Constitution will permit officials to order observance of ritual of this nature does not depend upon whether as a voluntary exercise we would think it to be good, bad or merely innocuous. Any credo of nationalism is likely to include what some disapprove or to omit what others think essential, and to give off different overtones as it takes on different accents or interpretations. If official power exists to coerce acceptance of any patriotic creed, what it shall contain cannot be decided by courts, but must be largely discretionary with the ordaining authority, whose power to prescribe would no doubt include power to amend. Hence validity of the asserted power to force an American citizen publicly to profess any statement of belief or to engage in any ceremony of assent to one, presents questions of power that must be considered independently of any idea we may have as to the utility of the ceremony in question.

Nor does the issue as we see it turn on one's possession of particular religious views or the sincerity with which they are held. While religion supplies appellees' motive for enduring the discomforts of making the issue in this case, many citizens who do not share these religious views hold such a compulsory rite to infringe constitutional liberty of the individual. It is not necessary to inquire whether non-conformist beliefs will exempt from the duty to salute unless we first find power to make the salute a legal duty.

The *Gobitis* decision, however, *assumed,* as did the argument in that case and in this, that power exists in the State to impose the flag salute discipline upon school children in general. The Court only examined and rejected a claim based on religious beliefs of immunity from an unquestioned general rule. The question which underlies the flag salute controversy is whether such a ceremony so touching matters of opinion and political attitude may be imposed upon the individual by official authority under powers committed to any political organization under our Constitution. We examine rather than assume existence of this power and, against this broader definition of issues in this case, reexamine specific grounds assigned for the *Gobitis* decision.

It was said that the flag-salute controversy confronted the Court with "the problem which Lincoln cast in memorable dilemma: 'Must a government of necessity be too *strong* for the liberties of its people, or too *weak* to maintain its own existence?' " and that the answer must be in favor of strength. *Minersville School District v. Gobitis.*

We think these issues may be examined free of pressure or restraint growing out of such considerations.

It may be doubted whether Mr. Lincoln would have thought that the strength of government to maintain itself would be impressively vindicated by our confirming power of the State to expel a handful of children from school. Such oversimplification, so handy in political debate, often lacks the precision necessary to postulates of judicial reasoning. If validly applied to this problem, the utterance cited would resolve every issue of power in favor of those in authority and would require us to override every liberty thought to weaken or delay execution of their policies.

Government of limited power need not be anemic government. Assurance that rights are secure tends to diminish fear and jealousy of strong government, and by making us feel safe to live under it makes for its better support. Without promise of a limiting Bill of Rights it is doubtful if our Constitution could have mustered enough strength to enable its ratification. To enforce those rights today is not to choose weak government over strong government. It is only to adhere as a means of strength to individual freedom of mind in preference to officially disciplined uniformity for which history indicates a disappointing and disastrous end.

The subject now before us exemplifies this principle. Free public education, if faithful to the ideal of secular instruction and political neutrality, will not be partisan or enemy of any class, creed, party, or faction. If it is to impose any ideological discipline, however, each party or denomination must seek to control, or failing that, to weaken the influence of the educational system. Observance of the limitations of the Constitution will not weaken government in the field appropriate for its exercise.

It was also considered in the *Gobitis* case that functions of educational officers in States, counties and school districts were such that to interfere with their authority "would in effect make us the school board for the country."

The Fourteenth Amendment, as now applied to the States, protects the citizen against the State itself and all of its creatures—Boards of Education not excepted. These have, of course, important, delicate, and highly discretionary functions, but none that they may not perform within the limits of the Bill of Rights. That they are educating the young for citizenship is reason for scrupulous protection of Constitutional freedoms of the individual, if we are not to strangle the free mind at its source and teach youth to discount important principles of our government as mere platitudes.

Such Boards are numerous and their territorial jurisdiction often small. But small and local authority may feel less sense of responsibility to the Constitution, and agencies of publicity may be less vigilant in calling it to account. The action of Congress in making flag observance voluntary and respecting the conscience of the objector in a matter so vital as raising the Army contrasts sharply with these local regulations in matters relatively trivial to the welfare of the nation. There are village tyrants as well as village Hampdens, but none who acts under color of law is beyond reach of the Constitution.

The *Gobitis* opinion reasoned that this is a field "where courts possess no marked and certainly no controlling competence," that it is committed to the legislatures as well as the courts to guard cherished liberties and that it is constitutionally appropriate to "fight out the wise use of legislative authority in the forum of public opinion and before legislative assemblies rather than to transfer such a contest to the judicial arena," since all the "effective means of inducing political changes are left free." *Id.* at 597-598, 600.

The very purpose of a Bill of Rights was to withdraw certain subjects from the vicissitudes of political controversy, to place them beyond the reach of majorities and officials and to establish them as legal principles to be applied by the courts. One's right to life, liberty, and property, to free speech, a free press, freedom of worship and assembly, and other fundamental rights may not be submitted to vote; they depend on the outcome of no elections.

In weighing arguments of the parties it is important to distinguish between the due process clause of the Fourteenth Amendment as an instrument for transmitting the principles of the First Amendment and those cases in which it is applied for its own sake. The test of legislation which collides with the Fourteenth Amendment, because it also collides with the principles of the First, is much more definite than the test when only the Fourteenth is involved. Much of the vagueness of the due process clause disappears when the specific prohibitions of the First become its standard. The right of a State to regulate, for example, a public utility may well include, so far as the due process test is concerned, power to impose all of the restrictions which a legislature may have a "rational basis" for adopting. But freedoms of speech and of press, of assembly, and of worship may not be infringed on such slender grounds. They are susceptible of restriction only to prevent grave and immediate danger to interests which the State may lawfully protect. It is important to note that while it is the Fourteenth Amendment which bears directly upon the State it is the more specific limiting principles of the First Amendment that finally govern this case.

Nor does our duty to apply the Bill of Rights to assertions of official authority depend upon our possession of marked competence in the field where the invasion of rights occurs. True, the task of translating the majestic generalities of the Bill of Rights, conceived as part of the pattern of liberal government in the eighteenth century, into concrete restraints on officials dealing with the problems of the twentieth century, is one to disturb self-confidence. These principles grew in soil which also produced a philosophy that the individual was the center of society, that his liberty was attainable through mere absence of governmental restraints, and that government should be entrusted with few controls and only the mildest supervision over men's affairs. We must transplant these rights to a soil in which the *laissez-faire* concept or principle of non-interference has withered at least as to economic affairs, and social advancements are increasingly sought through closer integration of society and through expanded and strengthened governmental controls. These changed conditions often deprive precedents of reliability and cast us more than we would choose upon our own judgment. But we act in these matters not by authority of our competence but by force of our commissions. We cannot, because of modest estimates of our competence in such specialties as public education, withhold the judgment that history authenticates as the function of this Court when liberty is infringed.

Lastly, and this is the very heart of the *Gobitis* opinion, it reasons that "National unity is the basis of national security," that the authorities have "the right to select appropriate means for its attainment," and hence reaches the conclusion that such compulsory measures toward "national unity" are constitutional. Upon the verity of this assumption depends our answer in this case.

National unity as an end which officials may foster by persuasion and example is not in question. The problem is whether under our Constitution compulsion as here employed is a permissible means for its achievement.

Struggles to coerce uniformity of sentiment in support of some end thought essential to their time and country have been waged by many good as well as by evil men. Nationalism is a relatively recent phenomenon but at other times and places the ends have been racial or territorial security, support of a dynasty or regime, and particular plans for saving souls. As first and moderate methods to attain unity have failed, those bent on its accomplishment must resort to an ever-increasing severity. As governmental pressure toward unity becomes greater, so strife becomes more bitter as to whose unity it shall be. Probably no deeper division of our people could proceed from any provocation than from finding it necessary to choose what doctrine and whose program public educational officials shall compel youth to unite in embracing. Ultimate futility of such attempts to compel coherence is the lesson of every such effort from the Roman drive to stamp out Christianity as a disturber of its pagan unity, the Inquisition, as a means to religious and dynastic unity, the Siberian exiles as a means to Russian unity, down to the fast failing efforts of our present totalitarian enemies. Those who begin coercive elimination of dissent soon find themselves exterminating dissenters.

Compulsory unification of opinion achieves only the unanimity of the graveyard.

It seems trite but necessary to say that the First Amendment to our Constitution was designed to avoid these ends by avoiding these beginnings. There is no mysticism in the American concept of the State or of the nature or origin of its authority. We set up government by consent of the governed, and the Bill of Rights denies those in power any legal opportunity to coerce that consent. Authority here is to be controlled by public opinion, not public opinion by authority.

The case is made difficult not because the principles of its decision are obscure but because the flag involved is our own. Nevertheless, we apply the limitations of the Constitution with no fear that freedom to be intellectually and spiritually diverse or even contrary will disintegrate the social organization. To believe that patriotism will not flourish if patriotic ceremonies are voluntary and spontaneous instead of a compulsory routine is to make an unflattering estimate of the appeal of our institutions to free minds. We can have intellectual individualism and the rich cultural diversities that we owe to exceptional minds only at the price of occasional eccentricity and abnormal attitudes. When they are so harmless to others or to the State as those we deal with here, the price is not too great. But freedom to differ is not limited to things that do not matter much. That would be a mere shadow of freedom. The test of its substance is the right to differ as to things that touch the heart of the existing order.

If there is any fixed star in our constitutional constellation, it is that no official, high or petty, can prescribe what shall be orthodox in politics, nationalism, religion, or other matters of opinion or force citizens to confess by word or act their faith therein. If there are any circumstances which permit an exception, they do not now occur to us.

We think the action of the local authorities in compelling the flag salute and pledge transcends constitutional limitations on their power and invades the sphere of intellect and spirit which it is the purpose of the First Amendment to our Constitution to reserve from all official control.

Affirmed.

Mr. Justice Frankfurter, dissenting:

One who belongs to the most vilified and persecuted minority in history is not likely to be insensible to the freedoms guaranteed by our Constitution. Were my purely personal attitude relevant I should wholeheartedly associate myself with the general libertarian views in the Court's opinion, representing as they do the thought and action of a lifetime. But as judges we are neither Jew nor Gentile, neither Catholic nor agnostic. We owe equal attachment to the Constitution and are equally bound by our judicial obligations whether we derive our citizenship from the earliest or the latest immigrants to these shores. As a member of this Court I am not justified in writing my private notions of policy into the Constitution, no matter how deeply I may cherish them or how mischievous I may deem their disregard. The duty of a judge who must decide which of two claims before the Court shall prevail, that of a State to enact and enforce laws within its general competence or that of an individual to refuse obedience because of the demands of his conscience, is not that of the ordinary person. It can never be emphasized too much that one's own opinion about the wisdom or evil of a law should be excluded altogether when one is doing one's duty on the bench. The only opinion of our own even looking in that direction that is material is our opinion whether legislators could in reason have enacted such a law. In the light of all the circumstances, including the history of this question in this Court, it would require more daring than I possess to deny that reasonable legislators could have taken the action which is before us for review. Most unwillingly, therefore, I must differ from my brethren with regard to legislation like this. I cannot bring my mind to believe that the "liberty" secured by the Due Process Clause gives this Court authority to deny to the State of West Virginia the attainment of that which we all recognize as a legitimate legislative end, namely, the promotion of good citizenship, by employment of the means here chosen.

. . . Under our constitutional system the legislature is charged solely with civil concerns of society. If the avowed or intrinsic legislative purpose is either to promote or to discourage some religious community or creed, it is clearly within the constitutional restrictions imposed on legislatures and cannot stand. But it by no means follows that legislative power is wanting whenever a general non-discriminatory civil regulation in fact touches conscientious scruples or religious beliefs of an individual or a group. Regard for such scruples or beliefs undoubtedly presents one of the most reasonable claims for the exertion of legislative accommodation.

What one can say with assurance is that the history out of which grew constitutional provisions for religious equality and the writings of the great exponents of religious freedom—Jefferson, Madison, John Adams, Benjamin Franklin—are totally wanting in justification for a claim by dissidents of exceptional immunity from civic measures of general applicability, measures not in fact disguised assaults upon such dissident views. The great leaders of the American Revolution were determined to remove political support from every religious establishment. They put on an equality the different religious sects—Episcopalians, Presbyterians, Catholics, Baptists, Methodists, Quakers, Huguenots—which, as dissenters, had been under the heel of the various orthodoxies that prevailed in different colonies. So far as the state was concerned, there was to be neither orthodoxy nor heterodoxy. And so Jefferson and those who followed him wrote guaranties of religious freedom into our constitutions. Religious minorities as well as religious majorities were to be equal in the eyes of the political state. But Jefferson and the others also knew that minorities may disrupt society. It never would have occurred to them to write into the Constitution the subordination of the general civil authority of the state to sectarian scruples.

The constitutional protection of religious freedom terminated disabilities, it did not create new privileges. It gave religious equality, not civil immunity. Its essence is freedom from conformity to religious dogma, not freedom from conformity to law because of religious dogma. Religious loyalties may be exercised without hindrance from the state, not the state may not exercise that which except by leave of religious loyalties is within the domain of temporal power. Otherwise each individual could set up his own censor against obedience to laws conscientiously deemed for the public good by those whose business it is to make laws.

The prohibition against any religious establishment by the government placed denominations on an equal footing—it assured freedom from support by the government to any mode of worship and the freedom of individuals to support any mode of worship. Any person may therefore believe or disbelieve what he pleases. He may practice what he will in his own house of worship or publicly within the limits of public order. But the lawmaking authority is not circumscribed by the variety of religious beliefs, otherwise the constitutional guaranty would be not a protection of the free exercise of religion but a denial of the exercise of legislation.

The essence of the religious freedom guaranteed by our Constitution is therefore this: no religion shall either receive the state's support or incur its hostility. Religion is outside the sphere of political government. This does not mean that all matters on which religious organizations or beliefs may pronounce are outside the sphere of government. Were this so, instead of the separation of church and state, there would be the subordination of the state on any matter deemed within the sovereignty of the religious conscience. . . .

An act compelling profession of allegiance to a religion, no matter how subtly or tenuously promoted, is bad. But an act promoting good citizenship and national allegiance is within the domain of governmental authority and is therefore to be judged by the same considerations of power and of constitutionality as those involved in the many claims of immunity from civil obedience because of religious scruples.

That claims are pressed on behalf of sincere religious convictions does not of itself establish their constitutional validity. Nor does waving the banner of religious freedom relieve us from examining into the power we are asked to deny the states. Otherwise the doctrine of separation of church and state, so cardinal in the history of this nation and for the liberty of our people, would mean not the disestablishment of a state church but the establishment of all churches and of all religious groups.

The subjection of dissidents to the general requirement of saluting the flag, as a measure conducive to the training of children in good citizenship, is very far from being the first instance of exacting obedience to general laws that have offended deep religious scruples.

. . . Law is concerned with external behavior and not with the inner life of man. It rests in large measure upon compulsion. Socrates lives in history partly because he gave his life for the conviction that duty of obedience to secular law does not presuppose consent to its enactment or belief in its virtue. The consent upon which free government rests is the consent that comes from sharing in the process of making and unmaking laws. The state is not shut out from a domain because the individual conscience may deny the state's claim. The individual conscience may profess what faith it chooses. It may affirm and promote that faith—in the language of the Constitution, it may "exercise" it freely—but it cannot thereby restrict community action through political organs in matters of community concern, so long as the action is not asserted in a discriminatory way either openly or by stealth. One may have the right to practice one's religion and at the same time owe the duty of formal obedience to laws that run counter to one's beliefs. . . .

Parents have the privilege of choosing which schools they wish their children to attend. And the question here is whether the state may make certain requirements that seem to it desirable or important for the proper education of those future citizens who go to schools maintained by the states, or whether the pupils in those schools may be relieved from those requirements if they run counter to the consciences of their parents. Not only have parents the right to send children to schools of their own choosing but the state has no right to bring such schools "under a strict governmental control" or give "affirmative direction concerning the intimate and essential details of such schools, entrust their control to public officers, and deny both owners and patrons reasonable choice and discretion in respect of teachers, curriculum, and textbooks." Why should not the state likewise have constitutional power to make reasonable provisions for the proper instruction of children in schools maintained by it?

When dealing with religious scruples we are dealing with an almost numberless variety of doctrines and beliefs entertained with equal sincerity by the particular groups for which they satisfy man's needs in his relation to the mysteries of the universe. There are in the United States more than 250 distinctive established religious denominations. In the State of Pennsylvania there are 120 of these, and in West Virginia as many as 65. But if religious scruples afford immunity from civic obedience to laws, they may be invoked by the religious beliefs of any individual even though he holds no membership in any sect or organized denomination. Certainly this Court cannot be called upon to determine what claims of conscience should be recognized and what should be rejected as satisfying the "religion" which the Constitution protects. That would indeed resurrect the very discriminatory treatment of religion which the Constitution sought forever to forbid.

. . . We are told that a flag salute is a doubtful substitute for adequate understanding of our institutions. The states that require such a school exercise do not have to justify it as the only means for promoting good citizenship in children, but merely as one of diverse means for accomplishing a worthy end. We may deem it a foolish measure, but the point is that this Court is not the organ of government to resolve doubts as to whether it will fulfill its purpose. Only if there be no doubt that any reasonable mind could entertain can we deny to the states the right to resolve doubts their way and not ours.

That which to the majority may seem essential for the welfare of the state may offend the consciences of a minority. But, so long as no inroads are made upon the actual exercise of religion by the minority, to deny the political power of the majority to enact laws concerned with civil matters, simply because they may offend the consciences of a minority, really means that the consciences of a minority are more sacred and more enshrined in the Constitution than the consciences of a majority.

We are told that symbolism is a dramatic but primitive way of communicating ideas. Symbolism is inescapable. Even the most sophisticated live by symbols. But it is not for this Court to make psychological judgments as to the effectiveness of a particular symbol in inculcating concededly indispensable feelings, particularly if the state happens to see fit to utilize the symbol that represents our heritage and our hopes. And surely only flippancy could be responsible for the suggestion that constitutional validity of a requirement to salute our flag implies equal validity of a requirement to salute a dictator. The significance of a symbol lies in what it represents. To reject the swastika does not imply rejection of the Cross. And so it bears repetition to say that it mocks reason and denies our whole history to find in the allowance of a requirement to salute our flag on fitting occasions the seeds of sanction for obeisance to a leader. To deny the power to employ educational symbols is to say that the state's educational system may not stimulate the imagination because this may lead to unwise stimulation.

. . . Of course patriotism can not be enforced by the flag salute. But neither can the liberal spirit be enforced by judicial invalidation of illiberal legislation. Our constant preoccupation with the constitutionality of legislation rather than with its wisdom tends to preoccupation of the American mind with a false value. The tendency of focusing attention on constitutionality is to make constitutionality synonymous with wisdom, to regard a law as all right if it is constitutional. Such an attitude is a great enemy of liberalism. Particularly in legislation affecting freedom of thought and freedom of speech much which should offend a free-spirited society is constitutional. Reliance for the most precious interests of civilization, therefore, must be found outside of their vindication in courts of law. Only a persistent positive translation of the faith of a free society into the convictions and habits and actions of a community is the ultimate reliance against unabated temptations to fetter the human spirit.

2. Pledging Religious Allegiance

The legal issue of whether a public school may require its students to participate in a flag salute or pledge may have been resolved in *Barnette,* but the political issue remained. In 1954, Congress amended the Pledge of Allegiance to contain the phrase "one Nation, under God." Across America, public schools routinely begin the school day by asking their students to stand and join together in the recitation of the Pledge. It was generally assumed that such a practice was beyond constitutional challenge.

In June of 2002, however, the Ninth Circuit Court of Appeals surprised much of the country by holding in *Newdow v. United States Congress,* 292 F.3d 597 (9th Cir. 2002), that the recitation of the words "under God" in the Pledge of Allegiance rendered the Pledge unconstitutional under the establishment clause. The court further held that a California school district's policy and practice of teacher-led recitation similarly violated the establishment clause. The court originally based its decision on an analysis of the law involving school prayer, applying the *Lemon* test, the endorsement test, and the coercion tests.

Public outcry over the holding was immediate and vociferous. Politicians and commentators attacked the court's decision. The morning after the decision came out, members of the House of Representatives gathered on the steps of the Capitol building to recite the Pledge; they later voted to deny all congressionally established courts the jurisdiction to hear First Amendment challenges to the Pledge. In response, the Ninth Circuit stayed the decision until it could consider an en banc rehearing. The court ultimately decided not to rehear the case en banc, but it did amend the initial decision. The court narrowed its holding to the conclusion that requiring students to recite or listen to the Pledge violates the establishment clause because it "impermissibly coerces a religious act. . . ."

NEWDOW V. UNITED STATES CONGRESS

328 F.3d 466 (9th Cir. 2003), *rev'd on other grounds, Elk Grove Unified School District v. Newdow,* 542 U.S. 1 (2004)

Amended Opinion

GOODWIN, Circuit Judge.

Michael Newdow appeals pro se a judgment dismissing his challenge to the constitutionality of the words "under God" in the Pledge of Allegiance to the Flag. Newdow argues that the addition of these words by a 1954 federal statute to the previous version of the Pledge of Allegiance (which made no reference to God) and the daily recitation in the classroom of the Pledge of Allegiance, with the added words included, by his daughter's public school teacher are violations of the Establishment Clause of the First Amendment to the United States Constitution.

Factual and Procedural Background

Newdow is an atheist whose daughter attends public elementary school in the Elk Grove Unified School District ("EGUSD") in California. In accordance with state law and a school district rule, EGUSD teachers begin each school day by leading their students in a recitation of the Pledge of Allegiance ("the Pledge"). The California Education Code requires that public schools begin each school day with "appropriate patriotic exercises" and that "[t]he giving of the Pledge of Allegiance to the Flag of the United States of America shall satisfy" this requirement. To implement the California statute, the school district that Newdow's daughter attends has promulgated a policy that states, in pertinent part: "Each elementary school class [shall] recite the pledge of allegiance to the flag once each day."

The classmates of Newdow's daughter in the EGUSD are led by their teacher in reciting the Pledge codified in federal law. On June 22, 1942, Congress first codified the Pledge as "I pledge allegiance to the flag of the United States of America and to the Republic for which it stands, one Nation indivisible, with liberty and justice for all." The Pledge is currently codified as "I pledge allegiance to the Flag of the United States of America, and to the Republic for which it stands, one nation under God, indivisible, with liberty and justice for all."

Newdow does not allege that his daughter's teacher or school district requires his daughter to participate in reciting the Pledge. Rather, he claims that his daughter is injured when she is compelled to "watch and listen as her state-employed teacher in her state-run school leads her classmates in a ritual proclaiming that there is a God, and that our's [sic] is 'one nation under God.' "

Newdow's complaint in the district court challenged the constitutionality, under the First Amendment, of the 1954 Act, the California statute, and the school district's policy requiring teachers to lead willing students in recitation of the Pledge. He sought declaratory and injunctive relief, but did not seek damages. . . .

Discussion

[Parts A, B, and C, containing discussion of the President of the United States and the State of California as defendants and the plaintiff's standing as a non-custodial parent are omitted.]

D. Establishment Clause

The Establishment Clause of the First Amendment states that "Congress shall make no law respecting an establishment of religion," a provision that "the Fourteenth Amendment makes applicable with full force to the States and their school districts." Over the last three decades, the Supreme Court has used three interrelated tests to analyze alleged violations of the Establishment Clause in the realm of public education: the three-prong test set forth in *Lemon v. Kurtzman;* the "endorsement" test, first articulated by Justice O'Connor in her concurring opinion in *Lynch v. Donnelly* and later adopted by a majority of the Court in *County of Allegheny v. ACLU;* and the "coercion" test first used by the Court in *Lee.*

In 1971, in the context of unconstitutional state aid to nonpublic schools, the Supreme Court in *Lemon* set forth the following test for evaluating alleged Establishment Clause violations. To survive the "*Lemon* test," the government conduct in question (1) must have a secular purpose, (2) must have a principal or primary effect that neither advances nor inhibits religion, and (3) must not foster an excessive government entanglement with religion. The Supreme Court applied the *Lemon* test to every Establishment case it decided between 1971 and 1984, with the exception of *Marsh v. Chambers,* the case upholding legislative prayer. In the 1984 *Lynch* case, which upheld the inclusion of a nativity scene in a city's Christmas display, Justice O'Connor wrote a concurring opinion in order to suggest a "clarification" of Establishment Clause jurisprudence.

Justice O'Connor's "endorsement" test effectively collapsed the first two prongs of the *Lemon* test:

> The Establishment Clause prohibits government from making adherence to a religion relevant in any way to a person's standing in the political community. Government can run afoul of that prohibition in two principal ways. One is excessive entanglement with religious institutions. . . . The second and more direct infringement is government endorsement or disapproval of religion. Endorsement sends a message to nonadherents that they are outsiders, not full members of the political community, and an accompanying message to adherents that they are insiders, favored members of the political community.

The Court formulated the "coercion test" when it held unconstitutional the practice of including invocations and benedictions in the form of "nonsectarian" prayers at public school graduation ceremonies. Declining to reconsider the validity of the *Lemon* test, the Court in *Lee* found it unnecessary to apply the *Lemon* test to find the challenged practices unconstitutional. Rather, it relied on the principle that "at a minimum, the Constitution guarantees that government may not coerce anyone to support or participate in religion or its exercise, or otherwise to act in a way which establishes a state religion or religious faith, or tends to do so." The Court first examined the degree of school involvement in the prayer, and found that "the graduation prayers bore the imprint of the State and thus put school-age children who objected in an untenable position." The next issue the Court considered was "the position of the students, both those who desired the prayer and she who did not." Noting that "there are heightened concerns with protecting freedom of conscience from subtle coercive pressure in the elementary and secondary public schools," the Court held that the school district's supervision and control of the graduation ceremony put impermissible pressure on students to participate in, or at least show respect during, the prayer. The Court concluded that primary and secondary school children may not be placed in the dilemma of either participating in a religious ceremony or protesting.

Finally, in its most recent school prayer case, the Supreme Court applied the *Lemon* test, the endorsement test, and the coercion test to strike down a school district's policy of permitting student-led "invocations" before high school football games. Citing *Lee,* the Court held that "the delivery of a pregame prayer has the improper effect of coercing those present to participate in an act of religious worship." Applying the *Lemon* test, the Court found that the school district policy was facially unconstitutional because it did not have a secular purpose. The Court also used language associated with the endorsement test.

We are free to apply any or all of the three tests, and to invalidate any measure that fails any one of them. Because we conclude that the school district policy impermissibly coerces a religious act and accordingly hold the policy unconstitutional, we need not consider whether the policy fails the endorsement test or the *Lemon* test as well.

In the context of the Pledge, the statement that the United States is a nation "under God" is a profession of a religious belief, namely, a belief in monotheism. The recitation that ours is a nation "under God" is not a mere acknowledgment that many Americans believe in a deity. Nor is it merely descriptive of the undeniable historical significance of religion in the founding of the Republic. Rather, the phrase "one nation under God" in the context of the Pledge is normative. To recite the Pledge is not to describe the United States; instead, it is to swear allegiance to the values for which the flag stands: unity, indivisibility, liberty, justice, and—since 1954—monotheism. A profession that we are a nation "under God" is identical, for Establishment Clause purposes, to a profession that we are a nation "under Jesus," a nation "under Vishnu," a nation "under Zeus," or a nation "under no god," because none of these professions can be neutral with respect to religion. The school district's practice of teacher-led recitation of the Pledge aims to inculcate in students a respect for the ideals set forth in the Pledge, including the religious values it incorporates.

The Supreme Court recognized the normative and ideological nature of the Pledge in *Barnette.* There, the Court held unconstitutional a school district's wartime policy of punishing students who refused to recite the Pledge and salute the flag. The Court noted that the school district was compelling the students "to declare a belief," and "requir[ing] the individual to communicate by word and sign his acceptance of the political ideas [the flag] . . . bespeaks," "[T]he compulsory flag salute and pledge requires affirmation of a belief and an attitude of mind." The Court emphasized that the political concepts articulated in the Pledge were idealistic, not descriptive: " '[L]iberty and justice for all,' if it must be accepted as descriptive of the present order rather than an ideal, might to some seem an overstatement." The Court concluded that: "If there is any fixed star in our constitutional constellation, it is that no official, high or petty, can prescribe what shall be orthodox in politics, nationalism, religion, or other matters of opinion or force citizens to confess by word or act their faith therein."

The school district's policy here, like the school's action in *Lee,* places students in the untenable position of choosing between participating in an exercise with religious content or protesting. The defendants argue that the religious content of "one nation under God" is minimal. To an atheist or a believer in non-Judeo-Christian religions or philosophies, however, this phrase may reasonably appear to be an attempt to enforce a "religious orthodoxy" of monotheism, and is therefore impermissible. As the Court observed with respect to the graduation prayer in *Lee:* "What to most believers may seem nothing more than a reasonable request that the nonbeliever respect their religious practices, in a school context may appear to the nonbeliever or dissenter to be an attempt to employ the machinery of the State to enforce a religious orthodoxy."

The coercive effect of the policy here is particularly pronounced in the school setting given the age and impressionability of schoolchildren, and their understanding that they are required to adhere to the norms set by their school, their teacher and their fellow students. Furthermore, under *Lee,* noncompulsory participation is no basis for distinguishing *Barnette* from the case at bar because, even without a recitation requirement for each child, the mere presence in the classroom every day as peers recite the statement "one nation under God" has a coercive effect. The coercive effect of the Pledge is also made even more apparent when we consider the legislative history of the Act that introduced the phrase "under God." These words were designed to be recited daily in school classrooms. President Eisenhower, during the Act's signing ceremony, stated: "From this day forward, the millions of our school children will daily proclaim in every city and town, every village and rural schoolhouse, the dedication of our Nation and our people to the Almighty." All in all, there can be little doubt that under the controlling Supreme Court cases the school district's policy fails the coercion test.

The Supreme Court has addressed the Pledge in passing, and we owe due deference to its dicta. Our opinion, however, is not inconsistent with this dicta. In *Allegheny,* the Court noted that it had "considered in dicta the motto and the pledge, characterizing them as consistent with the proposition that government may not communicate an endorsement of religious belief." And in *Lynch,* the Court observed that students recited the pledge daily, but only to support its point that there is a long tradition of "official acknowledgment" of religion. Neither of these two references speaks to the issue here. We may assume *arguendo* that public officials do not unconstitutionally endorse religion when they recite the Pledge, yet it does not follow that schools may coerce impressionable young schoolchildren to recite it, or even to stand mute while it is being recited by their classmates.

Our decision is not inconsistent with *Engel,* which approved of encouraging students to "recit[e] historical documents such as the Declaration of Independence which contain references to the Deity or . . . sing[ ] officially espoused anthems which include the composer's professions of faith in a Supreme Being." The Pledge differs from the Declaration and the anthem in that its reference to God, in textual and historical context, is not merely a reflection of the author's profession of faith. It is, by design, an affirmation by the person reciting it. "I pledge" is a performative statement. To pledge allegiance to something is to alter one's moral relationship to it, and not merely to repeat the words of an historical document or anthem.

The only other United States Court of Appeals to consider the issue is the Seventh Circuit, which held in *Sherman v. Community Consolidated School District 21* that a policy similar to the one before us regarding the recitation of the Pledge of Allegiance containing the words "one nation under God" was constitutional. The *Sherman* court first stated that:

> If as *Barnette* holds no state may require anyone to recite the Pledge, and if as the prayer cases hold the recitation by a teacher or rabbi of unwelcome words is coercion, then the Pledge of Allegiance becomes unconstitutional under all circumstances, just as no school may read from a holy scripture at the start of class.

It then concludes, however, that this reasoning is flawed because the First Amendment "[does] not establish general rules about speech or schools; [it] call[s] for religion to be treated differently." We have some difficulty understanding this statement; we do not believe that the Constitution prohibits compulsory patriotism as in *Barnette,* but permits compulsory religion as in this case. If government-endorsed religion is to be treated differently from government-endorsed patriotism, the treatment must be less favorable, not more.

The Seventh Circuit makes an even more serious error, however. It not only refuses to apply the *Lemon* test because of the Supreme Court's criticism of that test in *Lee,* but it also fails to apply the coercion test from *Lee.* Circuit courts are not free to ignore Supreme Court precedent in this manner. Instead of applying any of the tests announced by the Supreme Court, the Seventh Circuit simply frames the question as follows: "Must ceremonial references in civic life to a deity be understood as prayer, or support for all monotheistic religions, to the exclusion of atheists and those who worship multiple gods?" For the reasons we have already explained, this question is simply not dispositive of whether the school district policy impermissibly coerces a religious act.

In light of Supreme Court precedent, we hold that the school district's policy and practice of teacher-led recitation of the Pledge, with the inclusion of the added words "under God," violates the Establishment Clause. . . .

NOTES AND QUESTIONS

1. In *Elk Grove Unified School District v. Newdow,* 542 U.S. 1 (2004), a majority of the Supreme Court avoided resolving the merits of Newdow's challenge to the constitutionality of the Pledge of Allegiance by dismissing his claims on the procedural ground that he lacked sufficient custody of his daughter to have "standing" to sue on her behalf. The Court, however, observed that prior to the addition of the phrase "under God," the Pledge "evolved as a common public acknowledgement of the ideals that our flag symbolizes." The Court also recognized that the Congressional legislation adding the phrase "under God" to the Pledge was accompanied by a Report of the House of Representatives, declaring: "[f]rom the time of our earliest history our peoples and our institutions have reflected the traditional concept that our Nation was founded on a fundamental belief in God," citing H.R. Rep. No. 1693, 83d Cong., 2d Sess., p. 2 (1954). Finally, the Court also noted that the Elk Grove school district, "[c]onsistent with our case law, . . . permits students who object on religious grounds to abstain from the recitation," citing *West Virginia Board of Education v. Barnette,* 319 U.S. 624 (1943). Nonetheless, the Supreme Court ultimately refused to reach the underlying merits of the Ninth Circuit's acceptance of Newdow's constitutional challenge to the Pledge.

   Chief Justice Rehnquist, Justice Thomas and Justice O'Connor each wrote a separate concurrence finding that Newdow had "standing" to sue on his daughter's behalf, but rejecting his constitutional challenge to the Pledge on its merits. Justice Scalia did not participate in the case.

   Justice Rehnquist found that the recital of the Pledge was a purely "patriotic ceremony" that included the language "under God" merely as "descriptive" of the "recognition" that the history of the country reflects the understanding that our nation was founded on a belief in God. He concluded that the "Constitution only requires that school children be entitled to abstain from the ceremony if they choose to do so."

   Justice Thomas concurred separately to argue that the Supreme Court's entire establishment clause jurisprudence is flawed, and should be reconstructed to make clear that the Pledge is not unconstitutional simply because "the State has not created or maintained any religious establishment, and neither has it granted government authority to an existing religion. The Pledge policy does not expose anyone to the legal coercion associated with an established religion."

   Justice O'Connor also wrote separately to reaffirm her view that the constitutionality of the recital of the Pledge depends on whether the practice constitutes a governmental "endorsement" of religion. Calling it a "close question," Justice O'Connor concluded that the Pledge represents a non-coercive form of "ceremonial deism" rather than an endorsement of religion. In support of her conclusion that no reasonable observer would feel overt governmental coercion to participate in the Pledge, Justice O'Connor relied upon the Pledge's history and ubiquity, the absence of worship or prayer in the exercise, the absence of any reference to a particular religion and the Pledge's minimal religious content.

2. In light of the fact that in *Newdow* five Supreme Court justices refused to reach the merits of the establishment clause issue and only three justices affirmatively found the Pledge to be constitutional, is it possible to detect what the result would have been if the entire Court had reached the merits of the case? Do you agree with Chief Justice Rehnquist that the recital of the Pledge represents only a "patriotic ceremony" which is merely descriptive of the recognition of the place of God in our nation's history?
3. In his concurrence, Justice Thomas concedes that the Ninth Circuit's opinion declaring the Pledge unconstitutional is based on "a persuasive reading of our precedent," but he then proceeds to criticize that precedent. Do you agree that the Ninth Circuit's opinion is "persuasive" in light of the evolution of the Court's establishment clause cases?
4. If a future litigant with "standing" challenges the recital of the Pledge in a public school situated within the Ninth Circuit, what role would the dismissed Ninth Circuit opinion play in that litigation? Would a lower court within the Ninth Circuit be bound by the Circuit's underlying reasoning in its *Newdow* opinion? Would that reasoning be persuasive?
5. How would you advise a school district within the Ninth Circuit or elsewhere regarding the recital of the Pledge? May the school district continue to recite the Pledge? Must the district allow school children to abstain? If the district does allow school children to abstain, how should the abstaining children be treated? For example, should the district permit the abstaining children to arrive at school shortly after the Pledge is recited?
6. Why did the Ninth Circuit in *Newdow II* decline to apply the *Lemon* and endorsement tests? In *Newdow I,* the court applied all three school prayer tests, stating:

   > We are free to apply any or all of the three tests, and to invalidate any measure that fails any one of them. The Supreme Court has not repudiated *Lemon;* in *Santa Fe,* it found that the application of each of the three tests provided an independent ground for invalidating the statute at issue in that case; and in *Lee,* the Court invalidated the policy solely on the basis of the coercion test. Although this court has typically applied the *Lemon* test to alleged Establishment Clause violations, we are not required to apply it if a practice fails one of the other tests. Nevertheless, for purposes of completeness, we will analyze the school district policy and the 1954 Act under all three tests.

   Was the subsequent decision to use only the coercion test justified? How would you have analyzed these facts under the *Lemon* and endorsement tests? Is the Pledge more coercive when recited in schools than when recited by government officials in other contexts? Does the time and place of the recitation of the pledge — during school, in the classroom, as opposed to graduation ceremonies or football games — make a difference?
7. The Ninth Circuit's opinion was met with uncommon hostility. In fact, its author was vilified in the press. In this context, consider the thoughtful

view of historian Arthur Schlesinger, Jr., that appeared in the midst of the controversy surrounding the Ninth Circuit's opinion:

> As for the Constitution, more than a half-century ago the Supreme Court, in *West Virginia State Board of Education v. Barnette,* declared unconstitutional a law requiring schoolchildren to salute the flag and recite the Pledge of Allegiance. "If there is any fixed star in our constitutional constellation," Justice Robert H. Jackson memorably said for the court, "it is that no official, high or petty, can prescribe what shall be orthodox in politics, nationalism, religion, or other matters of opinion."
>
> The court handed down its decision against compulsory pledges of allegiance and flag salutes on Flag Day in 1943, when young Americans were fighting and dying for that flag around the planet. The American people then, far from denouncing the court, applauded the decision as a pretty good statement of what we were fighting for. Are we backsliding today? Perhaps the next step for those who identify patriotism with religion will be to try to amend the Constitution itself by mentioning God.

8. In *Newdow,* as well as the other recent Supreme Court decisions in this section, the Court is fundamentally divided about the role of religion in American history and in the constitutional regime. Reconsider the philosophic basis for American public education. Is the exposure to a deity in public education necessary for the protection of freedom? Does liberty in a democracy require "unity" among citizens in the belief in a Supreme Being? What would the founders think of the recital of the Pledge in public school? How would classical and modern educational theorists like Plato and Locke react? Is the Pledge a proper exercise of "authority" in the public school, or does it unduly repress "progressive" forms of education which would offer children the freedom to come to love their country and/or a deity naturally? Does permitting the Pledge serve or disserve the proper "end" of education in the American democracy?

D. RELIGION IN PUBLIC SCHOOL PRACTICUM: IMPLEMENTING THE NO CHILD LEFT BEHIND ACT'S RELIGIOUS GUIDANCE

The No Child Left Behind Act (NCLB) requires school districts to certify annually that their policies do not prevent, or otherwise deny participation in, constitutionally protected prayer as set forth in the U.S. Department of Education's *Guidance on Constitutionality Protected Prayer in Public Elementary and Secondary Schools.* On February 7, 2003, the Department issued its *Guidance,* which purports to codify much of the law addressed in this chapter. The *Guidance* declares:

- **Prayer during noninstructional time.** Students may pray when not engaged in instruction, as long as they do not cause a "material disruption." Students may pray, alone or together, during noninstructional time, to the same extent that they may engage in nonreligious activities.

- **Organized prayer groups and activities.** Students may organize prayer groups, religious clubs, and gatherings, to the same extent they are allowed to organize other non-curricular groups. Districts must give religious groups the same access to school facilities as they give other non-curricular groups. If a district allows nonreligious groups to advertise or announce meetings using the school newspaper, the public address system, or leaflets, it must grant religious groups the same privileges. A district may disclaim sponsorship of non-curricular groups and events, if it does so in a manner that neither favors nor disfavors religious groups.
- **Teachers, administrators, and other school employees.** School employees "in their official capacity" may not encourage or discourage prayer or actively participate in it with students. Teachers may participate in religious activities where the "overall context makes clear" they are not participating "in their official capacity."
- **Moments of silence.** Districts are permitted to have neutral "moments of silence," during which students may pray silently or do something else. School employees may not encourage or discourage students from praying during moments of silence.
- **Accommodation of prayer during instructional time.** A district may dismiss students for off-site religious instruction, as long as it does not encourage or discourage participation. Districts may excuse students from class for religious exercises, as long as this does not "materially burden" other students. If a district excuses students from attending class for nonreligious reasons, it may not treat religious requests less favorably.
- **Religious expression and prayer in class assignments.** Students may express religious beliefs in oral and written class assignments. Such assignments should be judged by ordinary academic standards and legitimate pedagogical concerns.
- **Student assemblies and extracurricular events.** Student speakers at assemblies and extracurricular events may not be selected on a basis that favors or disfavors religious speech. If student speakers are selected with "genuinely neutral, evenhanded criteria" and "retain primary control" over their expression, their speech is not attributable to the school and cannot be restricted because of a religious or anti-religious message. However, if district employees "determine or substantially control the content" of the speech, the speech *is* attributable to the school and may not contain a religious or anti-religious message. To avoid being perceived as endorsing student speech, a district may make an "appropriate, neutral disclaimer" clarifying that it does not endorse the speech. But it then must also issue such disclaimers for *non*religious speech.
- **Prayer at graduation.** Districts may not mandate or organize prayer at graduation or select speakers in a way that favors religious speech. However, if speakers are selected on the basis of "genuinely neutral, evenhanded criteria" and "retain primary control" over their expression, the speech is not attributable to the school and may not be restricted because of religious or anti-religious content.

- **Baccalaureate ceremonies.** A district may not mandate or organize religious baccalaureate ceremonies. If a district makes its facilities and related services available to other private groups, it must make them available on the same terms for religious baccalaureate ceremonies.

To what extent does this *Guidance* accurately reflect the current state of the law? In particular, consider the possible case authority for the language in each part of the *Guidance* and the accuracy of the interpretation of the case law in the *Guidance* itself.

As a school district's lawyer, how would you advise your district to proceed if you perceive that the *Guidance* is inconsistent with governing case law? Consider the following alternatives:

1. Ignore the *Guidance* and rely on your own view of the law;
2. Draft new policy language that affirmatively certifies compliance with the *Guidance;*
3. Review the district's existing policies to insure compliance with the *Guidance;*
4. Draft policy language on each issue that attempts to reconcile the *Guidance* and the case law;
5. Make the school board aware of the risk of liability if it follows, or does not follow, the *Guidance;*
6. Contact the state educational agency to inquire about their attitude regarding enforcement of the *Guidance,* and/or
7. Advise the school board to begin an open community discussion about the *Guidance.*

Assume that after receiving general advice about the implementation of the *Guidance,* the school district seeks particular advice about an issue raised in conjunction with the annual high school musical. The teachers in the high school's drama department have selected *Les Miserables* as the student musical performance this year. The play's climactic moment occurs when the "hero" of the story, while facing death, passionately sings: "To love another person is to see the face of God." The high school's superintendent and the president of the school board are concerned that the religious message of the musical may be improper. Based on the case law and the *Guidance* controlling the separation of church and state in the public school, what advice would you offer the school district? Can the play go on? Should it?

Assuming that the district decides to stage the musical, are there any limitations on the manner in which the drama department teachers can teach the drama students about the play's religious messages? Suppose the head of the drama department at a public banquet announcing the decision to put on *Les Miserables* wants to inform the community that, "I have always loved this show because it renews my faith in God"? Suppose further that the head of the drama department wishes to distribute a short note attached to the programs distributed at the performance that reads: "This show was selected because it has the capacity to teach and to inspire students to an understanding of the place of faith in God in their lives"? How would you advise the district to proceed?

CHAPTER 9

THE USE OF SCHOOL FACILITIES

A school district's decision whether to allow its facilities to be used by nonschool groups involves reconciling legal, political and economic issues. As is true of much of the law governing education, the legal concerns here often involve accommodating religious groups and views. The cases set forth in this chapter suggest that a school district is not required to open its facilities to nondistrict uses, but once it decides to do so, it must insure that its policies are consistent with the First Amendment. *See Widmar v. Vincent,* 454 U.S. 263 (1981).

The precise requirements of that amendment in this context are manifest in the Supreme Court's recent decisions in *Board of Education of the Westside Community Schools v. Mergens,* 496 U.S. 226 (1990); *Lamb's Chapel v. Center Moriches Union Free School District,* 508 U.S. 384 (1993); *Rosenberger v. University of Virginia,* 515 U.S. 819 (1995); and *Good News Club v. Milford Central School,* 533 U.S. 98 (2001). Together, these cases require public educational institutions to allow equal access to their facilities regardless of the religious affiliation of the user or the content of the user's purposes. As the material in the remainder of this chapter indicates, the governing law presents a framework within which a school district or any public educational institution must make difficult political and economic choices.

A. THE LAW GOVERNING THE USE OF SCHOOL FACILITIES

WIDMAR V. VINCENT

454 U.S. 263(1981)

Justice POWELL delivered the opinion of the court.

This case presents the question whether a state university, which makes its facilities generally available for the activities of registered student groups, may close its facilities to a registered student group desiring to use the facilities for religious worship and religious discussion.

I

It is the stated policy of the University of Missouri at Kansas City to encourage the activities of student organizations. The University officially recognizes over 100 student groups. It routinely provides University facilities for the meetings of registered organizations.

From 1973 until 1977 a registered religious group named Cornerstone regularly sought and received permission to conduct its meetings in University facilities. In 1977, however, the University informed the group that it could no longer meet in University buildings. The exclusion was based on a regulation, adopted by the Board of Curators in 1972, that prohibits the use of University buildings or grounds "for purposes of religious worship or religious teaching."

II

Through its policy of accommodating their meetings, the University has created a forum generally open for use by student groups. Having done so, the University has assumed an obligation to justify its discriminations and exclusions under applicable constitutional norms. The Constitution forbids a State to enforce certain exclusions from a forum generally open to the public, even if it was not required to create the forum in the first place.

The University's institutional mission, which it describes as providing a "*secular* education" to its students, does not exempt its actions from constitutional scrutiny. With respect to persons entitled to be there, our cases leave no doubt that the First Amendment rights of speech and association extend to the campuses of state universities.

Here UMKC has discriminated against student groups and speakers based on their desire to use a generally open forum to engage in religious worship and discussion. These are forms of speech and association protected by the First Amendment. In order to justify discriminatory exclusion from a public forum based on the religious content of a group's intended speech, the University must therefore satisfy the standard of review appropriate to content-based exclusions. It must show that its regulation is necessary to serve a compelling state interest and that it is narrowly drawn to achieve that end.

III

In this case the University claims a compelling interest in maintaining strict separation of church and State. It derives this interest from the "Establishment Clauses" of both the Federal and Missouri Constitutions.

A

The University first argues that it cannot offer its facilities to religious groups and speakers on the terms available to other groups without violating the Establishment Clause of the Constitution of the United States. We agree that the interest of the University in complying with its constitutional obligations may be characterized as compelling. It does not follow, however, that an "equal access" policy would be incompatible with this Court's Establishment Clause cases. Those cases hold that a policy will not offend the Establishment Clause if it can pass a three-pronged test: "First, the [governmental policy] must have a secular legislative purpose; second, its principal or primary effect must be one that neither advances nor inhibits religion . . . ; finally, the [policy] must not foster 'an excessive government entanglement with religion.'" *Lemon v. Kurtzman,* 403 U.S. 602, 612-613 (1971).

In this case two prongs of the test are clearly met. Both the District Court and the Court of Appeals held that an open-forum policy, including non-discrimination against religious speech, would have a secular purpose and would avoid entanglement with religion. But the District Court concluded, and the University argues here, that allowing religious groups to share the limited public forum would have the "primary effect" of advancing religion.

The University's argument misconceives the nature of this case. The question is not whether the creation of a religious forum would violate the Establishment Clause. The University has opened its facilities for use by student groups, and the question is whether it can now exclude groups because of the content of their speech. See *Healy v. James,* 408 U.S. 169 (1972). In this context we are unpersuaded that the primary effect of the public forum, open to all forms of discourse, would be to advance religion.

We are not oblivious to the range of an open forum's likely effects. It is possible—perhaps even foreseeable—that religious groups will benefit from access to University facilities. But this Court has explained that a religious organization's enjoyment of merely "incidental" benefits does not violate the prohibition against the "primary advancement" of religion. *Committee for Public Education v. Nyquist,* 413 U.S. 756, 771 (1973).

We are satisfied that any religious benefits of an open forum at UMKC would be "incidental" within the meaning of our cases. Two factors are especially relevant.

First, an open forum in a public university does not confer any imprimatur of state approval on religious sects or practices. As the Court of Appeals quite aptly stated, such a policy "would no more commit the University . . . to religious goals" than it is "now committed to the goals of the Students for a Democratic Society, the Young Socialist Alliance," or any other group eligible to use its facilities.

Second, the forum is available to a broad class of nonreligious as well as religious speakers; there are over 100 recognized student groups at UMKC. The provision of benefits to so broad a spectrum of groups is an important index of secular effect. If the Establishment Clause barred the extension of general benefits to religious groups, "a church could not be protected by the police and fire departments, or have its public sidewalk kept in repair." At least in the absence of empirical evidence that religious groups will dominate UMKC's open forum, we agree with the Court of Appeals that the advancement of religion would not be the forum's "primary effect."

B

On one hand, respondents' First Amendment rights are entitled to special constitutional solicitude. Our cases have required the most exacting scrutiny in cases in which a State undertakes to regulate speech on the basis of its content. . . . On the other hand, the state interest asserted here—in achieving greater separation of church and State than is already ensured under the

Establishment Clause of the Federal Constitution—is limited by the Free Exercise Clause and in this case by the Free Speech Clause as well. In this constitutional context, we are unable to recognize the State's interest as sufficiently "compelling" to justify content-based discrimination against respondents' religious speech.

IV

Our holding in this case in no way undermines the capacity of the University to establish reasonable time, place, and manner regulations. Nor do we question the right of the University to make academic judgments as to how best to allocate scarce resources or "to determine for itself on academic grounds who may teach, what may be taught, how it shall be taught, and who may be admitted to study." Finally, we affirm the continuing validity of cases that recognize a university's right to exclude even First Amendment activities that violate reasonable campus rules or substantially interfere with the opportunity of other students to obtain an education.

The basis for our decision is narrow. Having created a forum generally open to student groups, the University seeks to enforce a content-based exclusion of religious speech. Its exclusionary policy violates the fundamental principle that a state regulation of speech should be content-neutral, and the University is unable to justify this violation under applicable constitutional standards.

For this reason, the decision of the Court of Appeals is *Affirmed.*

NOTES AND QUESTIONS

1. The Court states that Cornerstone's claim "implicates First Amendment rights of speech and association, and it is on the bases of speech and association rights that we decide the case." 454 U.S. 273, at n.13. What are those "rights" and how do they resolve this case? The Court acknowledges that Cornerstone's claim also rests on the free exercise clause of the First Amendment, yet specifically declines to decide the case under that clause. Why did the Court apparently go out of its way to avoid a decision based on the free exercise clause? To what extent did the Court want to avoid reconciling its free exercise jurisprudence with its establishment clause jurisprudence?
2. The Court recognizes that a university campus possesses many of the characteristics of a "public forum" and is "peculiarly the marketplace of ideas." 454 U.S. at 263, n.5. Nonetheless, the Court observes that there are "special characteristics" of a "school environment" that make it different from public forums such as streets or parks. What are they?
3. The Court suggests that because university students are "less impressionable than younger students," they are able to discern that the mere presence on campus of a religious group does not mean that the public university has placed its "imprimatur" on the group's message. 454 U.S. at 274, n.14. Do you agree? Suppose the group is allowed to use the same auditorium that houses critical university activities such as commencement?

4. Would the Court's result have been different if the school were a public elementary school with presumably more impressionable students? Suppose, for example, that Dewey Elementary School opens its music room to evening performances by local church choirs.
5. Does the number of organizations permitted access to facilities matter? Suppose Dewey Elementary School allows only two groups to use its multipurpose room: the chess club and the local church group.
6. In 1984, in the wake of *Widmar,* Congress enacted the Equal Access Act, which provides:

   > It shall be unlawful for any public secondary school which receives Federal financial assistance and which has a limited open forum to deny equal access or a fair opportunity to, or to discriminate against, any students who wish to conduct a meeting within that limited open forum on the basis of the religious, political, philosophical, or other content of the speech at such meetings. 20 U.S.C. §4071(a).

   The Act extends the holding of *Widmar* to all public "secondary" schools, not just universities. A "limited open forum" exists whenever a public secondary school "grants an offering to or opportunity for one or more non-curriculum related student groups to meet on school premises during noninstructional time." §4071(b). "Meeting" is defined to include "those activities of student groups which are permitted under a school's limited open forum and are not directly related to the school curriculum." §4072(3). "Noninstructional time" is defined to mean "time set aside by the school before actual classroom instruction begins or after actual classroom instruction ends." §4072(4). Thus, even if a public secondary school allows only one "noncurriculum related student group" to meet, the Act's obligations are triggered and the school may not deny other clubs, on the basis of the content of their speech, equal access to meet on school premises during noninstructional time.

   The Act further specifies that "schools shall be deemed to offer a fair opportunity to students who wish to conduct a meeting within its limited open forum" if the school uniformly provides that the meetings are voluntary and student-initiated; are not sponsored by the school, the government, or its agents or employees; do not materially and substantially interfere with the orderly conduct of education activities within the school; and are not directed, controlled, conducted, or regularly attended by "nonschool persons." §§4071(c)(1), (2), (4), and (5). "Sponsorship" is defined to mean "the act of promoting, leading, or participating in a meeting. The assignment of a teacher, administrator, or other school employee to a meeting for custodial purposes does not constitute sponsorship of the meeting." §4072(2). If the meetings are religious, employees or agents of the school or government may attend only in a "nonparticipatory capacity." §4071(c)(3). Moreover, a state may not influence the form of any religious activity, require any person to participate in such activity, or compel any school agent or employee to attend a meeting if the content of the speech at the meeting is contrary to that person's beliefs. §§4071(d)(1), (2), and (3).

Finally, the Act does not "authorize the United States to deny or withhold Federal financial assistance to any school," §4071(e), or "limit the authority of the school, its agents or employees, to maintain order and discipline on school premises, to protect the well-being of students and faculty, and to assure that attendance of students at the meetings is voluntary," §4071(f).

7. In *Mergens,* the Supreme Court interpreted the Equal Access Act, concluding that if a school creates a limited open form by allowing its facilities to be used by just one noncurricular group during noninstructional time, it must allow equal access to those facilities to other groups regardless of the "content" of their speech. A majority of the Court also agreed that an interpretation of the Equal Access Act that prohibits a school from denying religious groups access to a limited public forum would not violate the establishment clause.

Board of Education of the Westside Community Schools v. Mergens

496 U.S. 226 (1990)

Justice O'Connor, J., delivered the opinion of the Court with respect to Parts I, II-A, II-B, and II-C, in which Rehnquist, C.J., and White, Blackmun, Scalia, and Kennedy, JJ., joined, and an opinion with respect to Part III, in which Rehnquist, C.J., and White and Blackmun, JJ., joined.

This case requires us to decide whether the Equal Access Act, 20 U.S.C. §§4071-4074, prohibits Westside High School from denying a student religious group permission to meet on school premises during noninstructional time, and if so, whether the Act, so construed, violates the Establishment Clause of the First Amendment.

I

Respondents are current and former students at Westside High School, a public secondary school in Omaha, Nebraska.

Students at Westside High School are permitted to join various student groups and clubs, all of which meet after school hours on school premises. The students may choose from approximately 30 recognized groups on a voluntary basis.

School Board Policy 5610 concerning "Student Clubs and Organizations" recognizes these student clubs as a "vital part of the total education program as a means of developing citizenship, wholesome attitudes, good human relations, knowledge and skills." Board Policy 5610 also provides that each club shall have faculty sponsorship and that "clubs and organizations shall not be sponsored by any political or religious organization, or by any organization which denies membership on the basis of race, color, creed, sex or political belief." Board Policy 6180 on "Recognition of Religious Beliefs and Customs" requires that "students adhering to a specific set of religious beliefs or holding to little or no belief shall be alike respected." In addition, Board Policy 5450 recognizes its students' "Freedom of Expression," consistent with the authority of the Board.

. . . In January 1985, respondent Bridget Mergens met with Westside's principal, Dr. Findley, and requested permission to form a Christian club at the school. The proposed club would have the same privileges and meet on the same terms and conditions as other Westside student groups, except that the proposed club would not have a faculty sponsor. According to the students' testimony at trial, the club's purpose would have been, among other things, to permit the students to read and discuss the Bible, to have fellowship, and to pray together. Membership would have been voluntary and open to all students regardless of religious affiliation. [After the school district denied the request, Mergens challenged the district's policy as a violation of both the Equal Access Act and the First Amendment.]

II

A

In *Widmar v. Vincent,* we invalidated, on free speech grounds, a state university regulation that prohibited student use of school facilities "'for purposes of religious worship or religious teaching.'" In doing so, we held that an "equal access" policy would not violate the Establishment Clause under our decision in *Lemon v. Kurzman.* In particular, we held that such a policy would have a secular purpose, would not have the primary effect of advancing religion, and would not result in excessive entanglement between government and religion. We noted, however, that "university students are, of course, young adults. They are less impressionable than younger students and should be able to appreciate that the University's policy is one of neutrality toward religion."

In 1984, Congress extended the reasoning of *Widmar* to public secondary schools. Under the Equal Access Act, a public secondary school with a "limited open forum" is prohibited from discriminating against students who wish to conduct a meeting within that forum on the basis of the "religious, political, philosophical, or other content of the speech at such meetings."

B

The parties agree that Westside High School receives federal financial assistance and is a public secondary school within the meaning of the Act. The Act's obligation to grant equal access to student groups is therefore triggered if Westside maintains a "limited open forum"—i.e., if it permits one or more "noncurriculum related student groups" to meet on campus before or after classes.

Unfortunately, the Act does not define the crucial phrase "noncurriculum related student group." Our immediate task is therefore one of statutory interpretation. We begin, of course, with the language of the statute. The common meaning of the term "curriculum" is "the whole body of courses offered by an educational institution or one of its branches." . . . Any sensible interpretation of "noncurriculum related student group" must therefore be anchored in the notion that such student groups are those that are not related to the body of courses offered by the school. The difficult question is the degree of "unrelatedness to the curriculum" required for a group to be considered "noncurriculum related."

The Act's definition of the sort of "meetings" that must be accommodated under the statute, §40 71 (a), sheds some light on this question. "The term 'meeting' includes those activities of student groups which are . . . not directly related to the school curriculum." §4072(3) . . . Congress' use of the phrase "directly related" implies that student groups directly related to the subject matter of courses offered by the school do not fall within the "noncurriculum related" category and would therefore be considered "curriculum related."

The logic of the Act also supports this view, namely, that a curriculum related student group is one that has more than just a tangential or attenuated relationship to courses offered by the school. Because the purpose of granting equal access is to prohibit discrimination between religious or political clubs on the one hand and other noncurriculum-related student groups on the other, the Act is premised on the notion that a religious or political club is itself likely to be a noncurriculum-related student group. It follows, then, that a student group that is "curriculum related" must at least have a more direct relationship to the curriculum than a religious or political club would have.

Although the phrase "noncurriculum related student group" nevertheless remains sufficiently ambiguous that we might normally resort to legislative history, we find the legislative history on this issue less than helpful.

. . . We think it significant, however, that the Act, which was passed by wide, bipartisan majorities in both the House and the Senate, reflects at least some consensus on a broad legislative purpose. The committee reports indicate that the Act was intended to address perceived widespread discrimination against religious speech in public schools, and, as the language of the Act indicates, its sponsors contemplated that the Act would do more than merely validate the status quo. . . . A broad reading of the Act would be consistent with the views of those who sought to end discrimination by allowing students to meet and discuss religion before and after classes.

In light of this legislative purpose, we think that the term "noncurriculum related student group" is best interpreted broadly to mean any student group that does not directly relate to the body of courses offered by the school. In our view, a student group directly relates to a school's curriculum if the subject matter of the group is actually taught, or will soon be taught, in a regularly offered course; if the subject matter of the group concerns the body of courses as a whole; if participation in the group is required for a particular course; or if participation in the group results in academic credit. We think this limited definition of groups that directly relate to the curriculum is a commonsense interpretation of the Act that is consistent with Congress' intent to provide a low threshold for triggering the Act's requirements.

For example, a French club would directly relate to the curriculum if a school taught French in a regularly offered course or planned to teach the subject in the near future. A school's student government would generally relate directly to the curriculum to the extent that it addresses concerns, solicits opinions, and formulates proposals pertaining to the body of courses offered by the school. If participation in a school's band or orchestra were required for the band or orchestra classes, or resulted in academic credit, then those groups would also directly relate to the curriculum. The existence of such groups at a school would not trigger the Act's obligations.

On the other hand, unless a school could show that groups such as a chess club, a stamp collecting club, or a community service club fell within our description of groups that directly relate to the curriculum, such groups would be "noncurriculum related student groups" for purposes of the Act. The existence of such groups would create a "limited open forum" under the Act and would prohibit the school from denying equal access to any other student group on the basis of the content of that group's speech. Whether a specific student group is a "noncurriculum related student group" will therefore depend on a particular school's curriculum, but such determinations would be subject to factual findings well within the competence of trial courts to make.

Petitioners contend that our reading of the Act unduly hinders local control over schools and school activities, but we think that schools and school districts nevertheless retain a significant measure of authority over the type of officially recognized activities in which their students participate. First, schools and school districts maintain their traditional latitude to determine appropriate subjects of instruction. To the extent that a school chooses to structure its course offerings and existing student groups to avoid the Act's obligations, that result is not prohibited by the Act. On matters of statutory interpretation, "our task is to apply the text, not to improve on it." Second, the Act expressly does not limit a school's authority to prohibit meetings that would "materially and substantially interfere with the orderly conduct of educational activities within the school." The Act also preserves "the authority of the school, its agents or employees, to maintain order and discipline on school premises, to protect the well-being of students and faculty, and to assure that attendance of students at meetings is voluntary." Finally, because the Act applies only to public secondary schools that receive federal financial assistance, a school district seeking to escape the statute's obligations could simply forgo federal funding. Although we do not doubt that in some cases this may be an unrealistic option, Congress clearly sought to prohibit schools from discriminating on the basis of the content of a student group's speech, and that obligation is the price a federally funded school must pay if it opens its facilities to noncurriculum-related student groups. . . .

C

[W]e think it clear that Westside's existing student groups include one or more "noncurriculum related student groups." Although Westside's physical education classes apparently include swimming, counsel stated at oral argument that scuba diving is not taught in any regularly offered course at the school. Based on Westside's own description of the group, Subsurfers does not directly relate to the curriculum as a whole in the same way that a student government or similar group might. Moreover, participation in Subsurfers is not required by any course at the school and does not result in extra academic credit. Thus, Subsurfers is a "noncurriculum related student group" for purposes of the Act. Similarly, although math teachers at Westside have encouraged their students to play chess, chess is not taught in any regularly offered course at the school, and participation in the chess club is not required for any class and does not result in extra credit for any class. The chess club is therefore another "noncurriculum related student group" at Westside. Moreover, Westside's principal acknowledged at trial that the Peer Advocates program—a service group that works with special education classes—does not directly relate to any courses offered by the school and is not required by any courses offered by the school. Peer Advocates would therefore also fit within our description of a "noncurriculum related student group." The record therefore supports a finding that Westside has maintained a limited open forum under the Act.

Although our definition of "noncurriculum related student activities" looks to a school's actual practice rather than its stated policy, we note that our conclusion is also supported by the school's own description of its student activities. . . . These descriptions constitute persuasive evidence that these student clubs directly relate to the curriculum. By inference, however, the fact that the descriptions of student activities such as Subsurfers and chess do not include such references strongly suggests that those clubs do not, by the school's own admission, directly relate to the curriculum. We therefore conclude that Westside permits "one or more noncurriculum related student groups to meet on school premises during noninstructional time." Because Westside maintains a "limited open forum" under the Act, it is prohibited from discriminating, based on the content of the students' speech, against students who wish to meet on school premises during noninstructional time.

The remaining statutory question is whether petitioners' denial of respondents' request to form a religious group constitutes a denial of "equal access" to the school's limited open forum. Although the school apparently permits respondents to meet informally after school, respondents seek equal access in the form of official recognition by the school. Official recognition allows student clubs to be part of the student activities program and carries with it access to the school newspaper, bulletin boards, the public address system, and the annual Club Fair. Given that the Act explicitly prohibits denial of "equal access . . . to . . . any students who wish to conduct a meeting within [the school's] limited open forum" on the basis of the religious content of the speech at such meetings, we hold that Westside's denial of respondents' request to form a Christian club denies them "equal access" under the Act.

Because we rest our conclusion on statutory grounds, we need not decide—and therefore express no opinion on—whether the First Amendment requires the same result.

III

Petitioners contend that even if Westside has created a limited open forum within the meaning of the Act, its denial of official recognition to the proposed Christian club must nevertheless stand because the Act violates the Establishment Clause of the First Amendment, as applied to the States through the Fourteenth Amendment. Specifically, petitioners maintain that because the school's recognized student activities are an integral part of its educational mission, official recognition of respondents' proposed club would effectively incorporate religious activities into the school's official program, endorse participation in the religious club, and provide the club with an official platform to proselytize other students.

We disagree. In *Widmar,* we applied the three-part *Lemon* test to hold that an "equal access" policy, at the university level, does not violate the Establishment Clause. We concluded that "an open-forum policy including nondiscrimination against religious speech, would have a secular purpose," and would in fact avoid entanglement with religion. ("The University would risk greater 'entanglement' by attempting to enforce its exclusion of 'religious worship' and 'religious speech.' ") We also found that although incidental benefits accrued to religious groups who used university facilities, this result did not amount to an establishment of religion. First, we stated that a university's forum does not "confer any imprimatur of state approval on religious sects or practices." Indeed, the message is one of neutrality rather than endorsement; if a State refused to let religious groups use facilities open to others, then it would demonstrate not neutrality but hostility toward religion. "The Establishment Clause does not license government to treat religion and those who teach or practice it, simply by virtue of their status as such, as subversive of American ideals and therefore subject to unique disabilities." Second, we noted that "the [University's] provision of benefits to [a] broad . . . spectrum of groups"—both nonreligious and religious speakers—was "an important index of secular effect."

We think the logic of *Widmar* applies with equal force to the Equal Access Act. As an initial matter, the Act's prohibition of discrimination on the basis of "political, philosophical, or other" speech as well as religious speech is a sufficient basis for meeting the secular purpose prong of the *Lemon* test. *See Edwards v. Aguillard,* 482 U.S. 578, 586 (1987). Congress' avowed purpose—to prevent discrimination against religious and other types of speech—is undeniably secular. . . . Even if some legislators were motivated by a conviction that religious speech in particular was valuable and worthy of protection, that alone would not invalidate the Act, because what is relevant is the legislative purpose of the statute, not the possibly religious motives of the legislators who enacted the law. Because the Act on its face grants equal access to both secular and religious speech, we think it clear that the Act's purpose was not to " 'endorse or disapprove of religion."'

. . . Petitioners' principal contention is that the Act has the primary effect of advancing religion. Specifically, petitioners urge that, because the student religious meetings are held under school aegis, and because the state's compulsory attendance laws bring the students together (and thereby provide a ready-made audience for student evangelists), an objective observer in the position of a secondary school student will perceive official school support for such religious meetings.

We disagree. First, although we have invalidated the use of public funds to pay for teaching state-required subjects at parochial schools, in part because of the risk of creating "a crucial symbolic link between government and religion, thereby enlisting—at least in the eyes of impressionable youngsters—the powers of government to the support of the religious denomination operating the school," *Grand Rapids School Dist. v. Ball,* 473 U.S. 373, 385 (1985), there is a crucial difference between government speech endorsing religion, which the Establishment Clause forbids, and private speech endorsing religion, which the Free Speech and Free Exercise Clauses protect. We think that secondary school students are mature enough and are likely to understand that a school does not endorse or support student speech that it merely permits on a nondiscriminatory basis. *Cf. Tinker v. Des Moines Independent Community School Dist.,* 393 U.S. 503 (1969) (no danger that high school students' symbolic speech implied school endorsement); *West Virginia State Bd. of Ed. v. Barnette,* 319 U.S. 624 (1943) (same). *See generally Note,* 92 Yale. L.J. 499, 507-509 (1983) (summarizing research in adolescent psychology). The proposition that schools do not endorse everything they fail to censor is not complicated. "Particularly in this age of massive media information . . . the few years difference in age between high school and college students [does not] justify departing from *Widmar." Bender v. Williamsport Area School Dist.,* 475 U.S. 534, 556 (1986) (Powell, J. dissenting). Indeed, we note that Congress specifically rejected the argument that high school students are likely to confuse an equal access policy with state sponsorship of religion. Given the deference due "the duly enacted and carefully considered decision of a coequal and representative branch of our Government," we do not lightly second-guess such legislative judgments, particularly where the judgments are based in part on empirical determinations.

Second, we note the Act expressly limits participation by school officials at meetings of student religious groups, and that any such meetings must be held during "noninstructional time." The Act therefore avoids the problems of "the students' emulation of teachers as role models" and "mandatory attendance requirements. . . ." To be sure, the possibility of student peer pressure remains, but there is little if any risk of official state endorsement or coercion where no formal classroom activities are involved and no school officials actively participate. Moreover, petitioners' fear of a mistaken inference of endorsement is largely self-imposed, because the school itself has control over any impressions it gives its students. To the extent a school makes clear that its recognition of respondents' proposed club is not an endorsement of the views of the club's participants, see *Widmar* (noting that university student handbook states that the university's name will not be identified with the aims, policies, or opinions of any student organization or its members), students will reasonably understand that the school's official recognition of the club evinces neutrality toward, rather than endorsement of, religious speech.

Third, the broad spectrum of officially recognized student clubs at Westside, and the fact that Westside students are free to initiate and organize additional student clubs, counteract any possible message of official endorsement of or preference for religion or a particular religious belief. See *Widmar* ("The provision of benefits to so broad a spectrum of groups is an important index of secular effect"). Although a school may not itself lead or direct a religious club, a school that permits a student-initiated and student-led religious club to meet after school, just as it permits any other student group to do, does not convey a message of state approval or endorsement of the particular religion. Under the Act, a school with a limited open forum may not lawfully deny access to a Jewish students' club, a Young Democrats club, or a philosophy club devoted to the study of Neitzsche. To the extent that a religious club is merely one of many different student-initiated voluntary clubs, students should perceive no message of government endorsement of religion. Thus, we conclude that the Act does not, at least on its face and as applied to Westside, have the primary effect of advancing religion.

Petitioners' final argument is that by complying with the Act's requirement, the school risks excessive entanglement between government and religion. The proposed club, petitioners urge, would be required to have a faculty sponsor who would be charged with actively directing the activities of the group, guiding its leaders, and ensuring balance in the presentation of controversial ideas. Petitioners claim that this influence over the club's religious program would entangle the government in day-to-day surveillance of religion of the type forbidden by the Establishment Clause.

Under the Act, however, faculty monitors may not participate in any religious meetings, and nonschool persons may not direct, control, or regularly attend activities of student groups. Moreover, the Act prohibits school "sponsorship" of any religious meetings, which means that school officials may not promote, lead, or participate in any such meeting. Although the Act permits "the assignment of a teacher, administrator, or other school employee to the meeting for custodial purposes," such custodial oversight of the student-initiated religious group, merely to ensure order and good behavior, does not impermissibly entangle government in the day-to-day surveillance or administration of religious activities. See *Tony and Susan Alamo Foundation v. Secretary of Labor,* 471 U.S. 290, 305-306 (1985). Indeed, as the Court noted in *Widmar,* a denial of equal access to religious speech might well create greater entanglement problems in the form of invasive monitoring to prevent religious speech at meetings at which such speech might occur.

Accordingly, we hold that the Equal Access Act does not on its face contravene the Establishment Clause. Because we hold that petitioners have violated the Act, we do not decide respondents' claims under the Free Speech and Free Exercise Clauses. For the foregoing reasons, the judgment of the Court of Appeals is affirmed.

NOTES AND QUESTIONS

1. The Court's first narrow task is to interpret the Equal Access Act's language. In particular, the Court must define "curriculum related" and therefore must define "curriculum." Are you satisfied with the Court's definition? The Court argues that if "curriculum related" meant "anything remotely related to abstract educational goals," then the Act would become "hortatory." The Court, however, also declares that, "[t]o the extent that a school chooses to structure its course offerings and existing student groups to avoid the Act's obligations, that result is not prohibited by the Act." If a school district defines its curriculum ("the whole body of courses offered by the school") broadly enough, could it include every group *except* religious groups as a curriculum offering and maintain a closed forum?
2. Suppose Rousseau Middle School defines its curriculum as "all practices that satisfy the academic, social, emotional and physical needs of the whole child." Suppose, further, that its instructional practices are consistent with its defined "whole-child" curriculum. Could that school claim

that the chess club is curriculum related? What about after-school sports? Yoga? To the extent that these programs are related to the school's curriculum broadly defined, the school has not opened its facilities to any "non-curriculum related student group." Would it be justified in precluding religious groups from using its facilities? Would the school be *barred* by the establishment clause from allowing religious groups to use its facilities, which are otherwise used only by curriculum-related programs?

3. The *Mergens* Court explains that the Equal Access Act was "intended to address perceived widespread discrimination against religious speech in public schools." Is the perception of such discrimination in public schools based upon reality? Is there in fact such widespread discrimination? If so, on what level does it exist: district to faculty, faculty to student, and/or student to student?
4. As in *Widmar,* the *Mergens* Court confronts the issue of the impressionability of students, concluding that secondary students are "mature" enough to understand that a school does not "endorse" a religious viewpoint by allowing access to its facilities. Have the courts and Congress implicitly concluded that *elementary* school students are not mature enough to understand the lack of endorsement from access?
5. In their separate concurrence, Justices Marshall and Brennan challenged the plurality's estimation of the subtle forms of endorsement created by peer pressure:

   > The plurality concedes that there is a "possibility of student peer pressure," but maintains that this does not amount to "official state endorsement." This dismissal is too facile. We must remain sensitive, especially in the public schools, to "the numerous more subtle ways that government can show favoritism to particular beliefs or convey a message of disapproval to others." *County of Allegheny v. ACLU,* 492 U.S. 573, (1989) (O'Connor, J., concurring in part and in judgment). When the government, through mandatory attendance laws, brings students together in a highly controlled environment every day for the better part of their waking hours and regulates virtually every aspect of their existence during that time, we should not be so quick to dismiss the problem of peer pressure as if the school environment had nothing to do with creating and fostering it. The State has structured an environment in which students holding mainstream views may be able to coerce adherents of minority religions to attend club meetings or to adhere to club beliefs. Thus, the State cannot disclaim its responsibility for those resulting pressures.

   Do you agree with Justices Brennan and Marshall's understanding of the coercive nature of peer pressure?
6. In his dissent, Justice Stevens criticizes the Court for a construction of the Equal Access Act that:

   > alters considerably the balance between state and federal authority over education, a balance long respected by both Congress and this Court. *See, e.g., Board of Education, Island Trees Union Free School Dist. No. 26 v. Pico,* 457 U.S. 853, 863-864 (1982). The traditional allocation of responsibility makes sense for pedagogical, political, and ethical reasons. . . . We have, of course, sometimes found it necessary to limit local control over schools in order to

> protect the constitutional integrity of public education. "That [Boards of Education] are educating the young for citizenship is reason for scrupulous protection of Constitutional freedoms of the individual, if we are not to strangle the free mind at its source and teach youth to discount important principles of our government as mere platitudes." *West Virginia Bd. of Educ. v. Barnette,* 319 U.S., at 637; *see also Brown v. Topeka Bd. of Education,* 347 U.S. 483 (1954); *Missouri v. Jenkins,* 495 U.S. 33 (1990). Congress may make similar judgments, and has sometimes done so, finding it necessary to regulate public education in order to achieve important national goals.

What does Justice Stevens mean by the "constitutional integrity of public education"?

7. According to Justice Stevens, local control over education serves educational, political and even ethical purposes:

> As a matter of pedagogy, delicate decisions about immersing young students in ideological cross-currents ought to be made by educators familiar with the experience and needs of the particular children affected, and with the culture of the community in which they are likely to live as adults. . . . As a matter of politics, public schools are often dependent for financial support upon local communities. The schools may be better able to retain local favor if they are free to shape their policies in response to local preferences. *See San Antonio Independent School Dist. v. Rodriguez,* 411 U.S. 1, 49-53 (1973). As a matter of ethics, it is sensible to respect the desire of parents to guide the education of their children without surrendering control to distant politicians. *See Meyer v. Nebraska,* 262 U.S. 390, 399-403 (1923). . . .
>
> The Court's construction of this Act, however, leads to a sweeping intrusion by the federal government into the operation of our public schools, and does so despite the absence of any indication that Congress intended to divest local school districts of their power to shape the educational environment. If a high school administration continues to believe that it is sound policy to exclude controversial groups, such as political clubs, the Ku Klux Klan, and perhaps gay rights advocacy groups, from its facilities, it now must also close its doors to traditional extracurricular activities that are noncontroversial but not directly related to any course being offered at the school. Congress made frequent reference to the primacy of local control in public education, and the legislative history of the Act is thus inconsistent with the Court's rigid definition of "noncurriculum related groups." Indeed, the very fact that Congress omitted any definition in the statute itself is persuasive evidence of an intent to allow local officials broad discretion in deciding whether or not to create limited public fora. I see no reason—and no evidence of congressional intent—to constrain that discretion any more narrowly than our holding in *Widmar* requires.

Do you agree with Justice Steven's arguments supporting "local control" of school matters and their application in this case?

8. Since *Mergens,* the lower federal courts have interpreted the Equal Access Act to require religious clubs to receive the same financial and administrative treatment as nonreligious clubs. *See, e.g., Prince v. Jacoby,* 303 F.3d 1074 (9th Cir. 2002).
9. The concepts of public forum and viewpoint neutrality suggested in *Mergens* and *Widmar* are borrowed from the freedom of expression

jurisprudence. In free speech cases, the courts have prohibited public institutions from discriminating based on the "content" of the speech. Does the principle of content neutrality fit in the context of educational facilities?

Lamb's Chapel v. Center Moriches Union Free School District

508 U.S. 384 (1993)

Justice White, *J.,* delivered the opinion of the Court. New York Educ. Law §414 authorizes local school boards to adopt reasonable regulations for the use of school property for 10 specified purposes when the property is not in use for school purposes. Among the permitted uses is the holding of "social, civic and recreational meetings and entertainments, and other uses pertaining to the welfare of the community; but such meetings, entertainment and uses shall be nonexclusive and shall be open to the general public." §414(c). The list of permitted uses does not include meetings for religious purposes, . . . [T]he Board of Center Moriches Union Free School District (District) has issued rules and regulations with respect to the use of school property when not in use for school purposes. . . . Rule 7, however, consistent with the judicial interpretation of state law, provides that "the school premises shall not be used by any group for religious purposes."

The issue in this case is whether, against this background of state law, it violates the Free Speech Clause of the First Amendment, made applicable to the States by the Fourteenth Amendment, to deny a church access to school premises to exhibit for public viewing and for assertedly religious purposes, a film series dealing with family and child-rearing issues faced by parents today.

I

Petitioners (Church) are Lamb's Chapel, an evangelical church in the community of Center Moriches, and its pastor John Steigerwald. Twice the Church applied to the District for permission to use school facilities to show a six-part film series containing lectures by Doctor James Dobson. . . . The brochure stated that the film series would discuss Dr. Dobson's views on the undermining influences of the media that could only be counterbalanced by returning to traditional, Christian family values instilled at an early stage. . . . The District denied the . . . application, saying that "this film does appear to be church related and thereof your request must be refused.". . .

The Church brought suit in the District Court, challenging the denial as a violation of the Freedom of Speech and Assembly Clauses, the Free Exercise Clause, and the Establishment Clause of the First Amendment, as well as the Equal Protection Clause of the Fourteenth Amendment. As to each cause of action, the Church alleged that the actions were undertaken under color of state law, in violation of 42 U.S.C. §1983.

II

There is no question that the District, like the private owner of property, may legally preserve the property under its control for the use to which it is dedicated. . . . It is also common ground that the District need not have permitted after-hours use of its property for any of the uses permitted by N.Y. Educ. Law §414. The District, however, did open its property for 2 of the 10 uses permitted by §414. The Church argued below that because under Rule 10 of the rules issued by the District, school property could be used for "social, civic, and recreational" purposes, the District had opened its property for such a wide variety of communicative purposes that restrictions on communicative uses of the property were subject to the same constitutional limitations as restrictions in traditional public forums such as parks and sidewalks. Hence, its view was that subject matter or speaker exclusions on District property were required to be justified by a compelling state interest and to be narrowly drawn to achieve that end. Both the District Court and the Court of Appeals rejected this submission, which is also presented to this Court. The argument has considerable force, for the District's property is heavily used by a wide variety of private organizations, including some that presented a "close question," which the Court of Appeals resolved in the District's favor, as to whether the District had in fact already opened its property for religious uses. We need not rule on this issue, however, for even if the courts below were correct in this respect—and we shall assume for present purposes that they were—the judgment below must be reversed.

With respect to public property that is not a designated public forum open for indiscriminate public use for communicative purposes, we have said that "control over access to a nonpublic forum can be based on subject matter and speaker identity so long as the distinctions drawn are reasonable in light of the purpose served by the forum and are viewpoint neutral." . . . The Court of Appeals appeared to recognize that the total ban on using District property for religious purposes could survive First Amendment challenge only if excluding this category of speech was reasonable and viewpoint neutral. The court's conclusion in this case was that Rule 7 met this test. We cannot agree with this holding, for Rule 7 was unconstitutionally applied in this case.

The Court of Appeals thought that the application of Rule 7 in this case was viewpoint neutral because it had been, and would be, applied in the same way to all uses of school property for religious purposes. That all religions and all uses for religious purposes are treated alike under Rule 7, however, does not answer the critical question whether it discriminates on the basis of viewpoint to permit school property to be used for the presentation of all views about family issues and child rearing except those dealing with the subject matter from a religious standpoint. . . . The film series involved here no doubt dealt with a subject otherwise permissible under Rule 10, and its exhibition was denied solely because the series dealt with the subject from a religious standpoint. The principle that has emerged from our cases "is that the First Amendment forbids the government to regulate speech in ways that favor some viewpoints or ideas at the expense of others." . . . That principle applies in the circumstances of this case; . . .

The District, as a respondent, would save its judgment below on the ground that to permit its property to be used for religious purposes would be an establishment of religion forbidden by the First Amendment.

. . . We have no more trouble than did the *Widmar* Court in disposing of the claimed defense on the ground that the posited fears of an Establishment Clause violation are unfounded. The showing of this film series would not have been during school hours, would not have been sponsored by the school, and would have been open to the public, not just to church members. The District property had repeatedly been used by a wide variety of private organizations. Under these circumstances, as in *Widmar,* there would have been no realistic danger that the community would think that the District was endorsing religion or any particular creed, and any benefit to religion or to the Church would have been no more than incidental. As in *Widmar,* permitting District property to be used to exhibit the film series involved in this case would not have been an establishment of religion under the three-part test articulated in *Lemon v. Kurtzman.* The challenged governmental action has a secular purpose, does not have the principal or primary effect of advancing or inhibiting religion, and does not foster an excessive entanglement with religion.

The District also submits that it justifiably denied use of its property to a "radical" church for the purpose of proselytizing, since to do so would lead to threats of public unrest and even violence. There is nothing in the record to support such a justification, which in any event would be difficult to defend as a reason to deny the presentation of a religious point of view about a subject the District otherwise opens to discussion on District property. . . .

For the reasons stated in this opinion, the judgment of the Court of Appeals is *Reversed.*

NOTES AND QUESTIONS

1. Several Justices used this case as an occasion to debate the continuing vitality of the *Lemon* test. Justice Kennedy, for example, writes in his separate concurrence:

> Given the issues presented as well as the apparent unanimity of our conclusion that this overt, viewpoint-based discrimination contradicts the Free Speech Clause of the First Amendment and that there has been no substantial showing of a potential Establishment Clause violation, I agree with JUSTICE SCALIA that the Court's citation of *Lemon v. Kurtzman,* is unsettling and unnecessary.

2. Justice Scalia, with whom Justice Thomas joins, concurs in the judgment, and writes separately to attack the *Lemon* legacy:

> I join the Court's conclusion that the District's refusal to allow use of school facilities for petitioners' film viewing, while generally opening the schools for community activities, violates petitioners' First Amendment free-speech rights to the extent it compelled the District's denial. I also agree with the Court that allowing Lamb's Chapel to use school facilities poses "no realistic danger" of a violation of the Establishment Clause, but I cannot accept most of its reasoning in this regard. The Court explains that the showing of petitioners' film on school property after school hours would not cause the community to "think that the District was endorsing religion

> or any particular creed," and further notes that access to school property would not violate the three-part test articulated in *Lemon v. Kurtzman.*
>
> As to the Court's invocation of the *Lemon* test: Like some ghoul in a late-night horror movie that repeatedly sits up in its grave and shuffles abroad, after being repeatedly killed and buried, *Lemon* stalks our Establishment Clause jurisprudence once again, frightening the little children and school attorneys of Center Moriches Union Free School District. Its most recent burial, only last Term, was, to be sure, not fully six feet under: Our decision in *Lee v. Weisman,* 505 U.S. 577, 586-587 (1992), conspicuously avoided using the supposed "test" but also declined the invitation to repudiate it. Over the years, however, no fewer than five of the currently sitting Justices have, in their own opinions, personally driven pencils through the creature's heart (the author of today's opinion repeatedly), and a sixth has joined an opinion doing so. . . .
>
> The secret of the *Lemon* test's survival, I think, is that it is so easy to kill. It is there to scare us (and our audience) when we wish it to do so, but we can command it to return to the tomb at will. When we wish to strike down a practice it forbids, we invoke it . . . when we wish to uphold a practice it forbids, we ignore it entirely, . . . Sometimes, we take a middle course, calling its three prongs "no more than helpful signposts." Such a docile and useful monster is worth keeping around, at least in a somnolent state; one never knows when one might need him.
>
> For my part, I agree with the long list of constitutional scholars who have criticized *Lemon* and bemoaned the strange Establishment Clause geometry of crooked lines and wavering shapes its intermittent use has produced. See, *e.g.,* Choper, *The Establishment Clause and Aid to Parochial Schools—An Update,* 75 Calif. L. Rev. 5 (1987); Marshall, *"We Know It When We See It": The Supreme Court and Establishment,* 59 S. Cal. L. Rev. 495 (1986); McConnell, *Accommodation of Religion,* 1985 S. Ct. Rev. 1; Kurland, *The Religion Clauses and the Burger Court,* 34 Cath. U.L. Rev. 1 (1984); R. Cord, *Separation of Church and State* (1982); Choper, *The Religion Clauses of the First Amendment: Reconciling the Conflict,* 41 U. Pitt. L. Rev. 673 (1980). I will decline to apply *Lemon*—whether it validates or invalidates the government action in question—and therefore cannot join the opinion of the Court today.

3. The majority responded to Justice Scalia's "evening at the cinema" by reminding him that, "*Lemon,* however, frightening it may be to some, has not been overruled." 508 U.S. at 384, n.7. Do you think it should be overruled?
4. Justice Scalia's separate opinion invites multiple levels of analysis. On a rhetorical level, is his language and tone persuasive? On a historic level, is Justice Scalia's reliance on the pro-religious "view of those who adopted our Constitution" valid? He writes that "it suffices" to make his point, that while Congress debated the language of the First Amendment, it enacted the Northwest Territory Ordinance, which refers to "religion, morality and knowledge being necessary to good government" in the same sentence as "education." What principle of statutory or constitutional interpretation would permit one to argue that the meaning of the language of the First Amendment can be inferred from what the *adopter* (not the drafters) of that language enacted in a separate, distinct context?

5. How does the Constitution's language give "preferential treatment" to religion? Assuming that Justice Scalia infers preferential treatment for religion from the free exercise clause, how does that clause alone allow *endorsement* of religion? In particular, how can an endorsement of religion be inferred from reading the First Amendment as a whole, reconciling the free exercise clause with the strength of the establishment clause? Even if Justice Scalia's inferences from the history surrounding the First Amendment were legitimate, is his understanding of history complete?
6. In *Good News Club v. Milford Central School,* 533 U.S. 98 (2001), the Supreme Court again addressed the constitutional limits of a school district's power to deny religious groups access to its facilities. There, Milford School operated a limited public forum, opening its facilities to private and public groups for educational, social, civic, recreational and community purposes. The school, however, denied access to the Good News Club, a group of residents who wanted to get together to pray, read the Bible and sing religious songs. The Supreme Court held that the denial was unconstitutional under the First Amendment's free speech clause, because that denial was based on the content of the group's expression. Finding the school's policy to discriminate against the content of protected speech, the Court precluded the school from trying to justify its policy based on some legitimate, educational purpose. Furthermore, the Court held that the establishment clause was not violated by allowing the Good News Club to meet at school, because the meetings were held after school hours and were not sponsored by the school itself. Accordingly, the elementary-aged children at the school would not feel that the school had endorsed the clubs views in any way.
7. Consider the Supreme Court's reliance on the same "free speech" reasoning in the next case, which involves access not to physical facilities, but to a source of funding for student publications. Is there a distinction between access and resources that is relevant to free speech clause or establishment clause analysis?

ROSENBERGER v. RECTOR AND VISITORS OF THE UNIVERSITY OF VIRGINIA

515 U.S. 819 (1995)

Justice KENNEDY delivered the opinion of the Court.

The University of Virginia, an instrumentality of the Commonwealth for which it is named and thus bound by the First and Fourteenth Amendments, authorizes the payment of outside contractors for the printing costs of a variety of student publications. It withheld any authorization for payments on behalf of petitioners for the sole reason that their student paper ["Wide Awake"] "primarily promotes or manifests a particular belief in or about a deity or an ultimate reality." That the paper did promote or manifest views within the defined exclusion seems plain enough. The challenge is to the University's regulation and its denial of authorization, the case raising issues under the Speech and Establishment Clauses of the First Amendment. . . .

II

It is axiomatic that the government may not regulate speech based on its substantive content or the message it conveys. . . . Other principles follow from this precept. In the realm of private speech or expression, government regulation may not favor one speaker over another. . . . Discrimination against speech because of its message is presumed to be unconstitutional. . . . These rules informed our determination that the government offends the First Amendment when it imposes financial burdens on certain speakers based on the content of their expression. . . . When the government targets not subject matter, but particular views taken by speakers on a subject, the violation of the First Amendment is all the more blatant. . . . Viewpoint discrimination is thus an egregious form of content discrimination. The government must abstain from regulating speech when the specific motivating ideology or the opinion or perspective of the speaker is the rationale for the restriction. . . .

These principles provide the framework forbidding the State from exercising viewpoint discrimination, even when the limited public forum is one of its own creation. In a case involving a school district's provision of school facilities for private uses, we declared that "there is no question that the District, like the private owner of property, may legally preserve the property under its control for the use to which it is dedicated." *Lamb's Chapel.* The necessities of confining a forum to the limited and legitimate purposes for which it was created may justify the State in reserving it for certain groups or for the discussion of certain topics. Once it has opened a limited forum, however, the State must respect the lawful boundaries it has itself set. The State may not exclude speech where its distinction is not "reasonable in light of the purpose served by the forum," nor may it discriminate against speech on the basis of its viewpoint. Thus, in determining whether the State is acting to preserve the limits of the forum it has created so that the exclusion of a class of speech is legitimate, we have observed a distinction between, on the one hand, content discrimination, which may be permissible if it preserves the purposes of that limited forum, and, on the other hand, viewpoint discrimination, which is presumed impermissible when directed against speech otherwise within the forum's limitations.

The [Student Activities Fund, "SAF"] is a forum more in a metaphysical than in a spatial or geographic sense, but the same principles are applicable. The most recent and most apposite case is our decision in *Lamb's Chapel.* There, a school district had opened school facilities for use after school hours by community groups for a wide variety of social, civic, and recreational purposes. The district, however, had enacted a formal policy against opening facilities to groups for religious purposes. Invoking its policy, the district rejected a request from a group desiring to show a film series addressing various child-rearing questions from a "Christian perspective." There was no indication in the record in *Lamb's Chapel* that the request to use the school facilities was "denied, for any reason other than the fact that the presentation would have been from a religious perspective." Our conclusion was unanimous: "It discriminates on the basis of viewpoint to permit school property to be used for the presentation of all views about family issues and child rearing except those dealing with the subject matter from a religious standpoint."

The University does acknowledge (as it must in light of our precedents) that "ideologically driven attempts to suppress a particular point of view are presumptively unconstitutional in funding, as in other contexts," but insists that this case does not present that issue because the Guidelines draw lines based on content, not viewpoint. As we have noted, discrimination against one set of views or ideas is but a subset or particular instance of the more general phenomenon of content discrimination. And, it must be acknowledged, the distinction is not a precise one. It is, in a sense, something of an understatement to speak of religious thought and discussion as just a viewpoint, as distinct from a comprehensive body of thought. The nature of our origins and destiny and their dependence upon the existence of a divine being have been subjects of philosophic inquiry throughout human history. We conclude, nonetheless, that here, as in *Lamb's Chapel,* viewpoint discrimination is the proper way to interpret the University's objections to Wide Awake. By the very terms of the SAF prohibition, the University does not exclude religion as a subject matter but selects for disfavored treatment those student journalistic efforts with religious editorial viewpoints. Religion may be a vast area of inquiry, but it also provides, as it did here, a specific premise, a perspective, a standpoint from which a variety of subjects may be discussed and considered. The prohibited perspective, not the general subject matter, resulted in the refusal to make third-party payments, for the subjects discussed were otherwise within the approved category of publications.

The dissent's assertion that no viewpoint discrimination occurs because the Guidelines discriminate against an entire class of viewpoints reflects an insupportable assumption that all debate is bipolar and that antireligious speech is the only response to religious speech. Our understanding of the complex and multifaceted nature of public discourse has not embraced such a contrived description of the marketplace of ideas. If the topic of debate is, for example, racism, then exclusion of several views on that problem is just as offensive to the First Amendment as exclusion of only one. It is as objectionable to exclude both a theistic and an atheistic perspective on the debate as it is to exclude one, the other, or yet another political, economic, or social viewpoint. The dissent's declaration that debate is not skewed so long as multiple voices are silenced is simply wrong; the debate is skewed in multiple ways.

The University's denial of [the] request for third-party payments in the present case is based upon viewpoint discrimination not unlike the discrimination the school district relied upon in *Lamb's Chapel* and that we found invalid. The church group in *Lamb's Chapel* would have been qualified as a social or civic organization, save for its religious purposes. Furthermore, just as the school district in *Lamb's Chapel* pointed to nothing but the religious views of the group as the rationale for excluding its message, so in this case the University justifies its denial . . . on the ground that the contents of Wide Awake reveal an avowed religious perspective. . . .

The University tries to escape the consequences of our holding in *Lamb's Chapel* by urging that this case involves the provision of funds rather than access to facilities. The University begins with the unremarkable proposition that the State must have substantial discretion in determining how to allocate scarce resources to accomplish its educational mission. [T]he University argues that content-based funding decisions are both inevitable and lawful. Were the reasoning of *Lamb's Chapel* to apply to funding decisions as well as to those involving access to facilities, it is urged, its holding "would become a judicial juggernaut, constitutionalizing the ubiquitous content-based decisions that schools, colleges, and other government entities routinely make in the allocation of public funds."

To this end the University relies on our assurance in *Widmar v. Vincent.* There, in the course of striking down a public university's exclusion of religious groups from use of school facilities made available to all other student groups, we stated: "Nor do we question the right of the University to make academic judgments as to how best to allocate scarce resources." The quoted language in *Widmar* was but a proper recognition of the principle that when the State is the speaker, it may make content-based choices. When the University determines the content of the education it provides, it is the University speaking, and we have permitted the government to regulate the content of what is or is not expressed when it is the speaker or when it enlists private entities to convey its own message. In the same vein, in *Rust v. Sullivan,* we upheld the government's prohibition on abortion-related advice applicable to recipients of federal funds for family planning counseling. There, the government did not create a program to encourage private speech but instead used private speakers to transmit specific information pertaining to its own program. We recognized that when the government appropriates public funds to promote a particular policy of its own it is entitled to say what it wishes. When the government disburses public funds to private entities to convey a governmental message, it may take legitimate and appropriate steps to ensure that its message is neither garbled nor distorted by the grantee.

It does not follow, however, and we did not suggest in *Widmar,* that viewpoint-based restrictions are proper when the University does not itself speak or subsidize transmittal of a message it favors but instead expends funds to encourage a diversity of views from private speakers. A holding that the University may not discriminate based on the viewpoint of private persons whose speech it facilitates does not restrict the University's own speech, which is controlled by different principles. . . . The University's regulation now before us, however, has a speech-based restriction as its sole rationale and operative principle.

The distinction between the University's own favored message and the private speech of students is evident in the case before us. The University itself has taken steps to ensure the distinction in the agreement each CIO must sign. The University declares that the student groups eligible for SAF support are not the University's agents, are not subject to its control, and are not its responsibility. Having offered to pay the third-party contractors on behalf of private speakers who convey their own messages, the University may not silence the expression of selected viewpoints.

The University urges that, from a constitutional standpoint, funding of speech differs from provision of access to facilities because money is scarce and physical facilities are not. Beyond the fact that in any given case this proposition might not be true as an empirical matter, the underlying premise that the University could discriminate based on viewpoint if demand for space exceeded its availability is wrong as well. The government cannot justify viewpoint discrimination among private speakers on the economic fact of scarcity. Had the meeting rooms in *Lamb's Chapel* been scarce, had the demand been greater than the supply, our decision would have been no different. It would have been incumbent on the State, of course, to ration or allocate the scarce resources on some acceptable neutral principle; but nothing in our decision indicated that scarcity would give the State the right to exercise viewpoint discrimination that is otherwise impermissible.

Vital First Amendment speech principles are at stake here. The first danger to liberty lies in granting the State the power to examine publications to determine whether or not they are based on some ultimate idea and, if so, for the State to classify them. The second, and corollary, danger is to speech from the chilling of individual thought and expression. That danger is especially real in the University setting, where the State acts against a background and tradition of thought and experiment that is at the center of our intellectual and philosophic tradition. In ancient Athens, and, as Europe entered into a new period of intellectual awakening, in places like Bologna, Oxford, and Paris, universities began as voluntary and spontaneous assemblages or concourses for students to speak and to write and to learn. *See generally* R. Palmer & J. Colton, *A History of the Modern World* 39 (7th ed. 1992). The quality and creative power of student intellectual life to this day remains a vital measure of a school's influence and attainment. For the University, by regulation, to cast disapproval on particular viewpoints of its students risks the suppression of free speech and creative inquiry in one of the vital centers for the Nation's intellectual life, its college and university campuses.

The Guideline invoked by the University to deny third-party contractor payments on behalf of [Wide Awake] effects a sweeping restriction on student thought and student inquiry in the context of University sponsored publications. The prohibition on funding on behalf of publications that "primarily promote or manifest a particular belief in or about a deity or an ultimate reality," in its ordinary and common-sense meaning, has a vast potential reach. The term "promotes" as used here would comprehend any writing advocating a philosophic position that rests upon a belief in a deity or ultimate reality. See *Webster's Third New International Dictionary* 1815 (1961) (defining "promote" as "to contribute to the growth, enlargement, or prosperity of: further, encourage"). And the term "manifests" would bring within the scope of the prohibition any writing that is explicable as resting upon a premise that presupposes the existence of a deity or ultimate reality. 1375 (defining "manifest" as "to show plainly: make palpably evident or certain by showing or displaying"). Were the prohibition applied with much vigor at all, it would bar funding of essays by hypothetical student contributors named Plato, Spinoza, and Descartes. And if the regulation covers, as the University says it does, those student journalistic efforts that primarily manifest or promote a belief that there is no deity and no ultimate reality, then undergraduates named Karl Marx, Bertrand Russell, and Jean-Paul Sartre would likewise have some of their major essays excluded from student publications. If any manifestation of beliefs in first principles disqualifies the writing, as seems to be the case, it is indeed difficult to name renowned thinkers whose writings would be accepted, save perhaps for articles disclaiming all connection to their ultimate philosophy. Plato could contrive perhaps to submit an acceptable essay on making pasta or peanut butter cookies, provided he did not point out their (necessary) imperfections.

Based on the principles we have discussed, we hold that the regulation invoked to deny SAF support, both in its terms and in its application to these petitioners, is a denial of their right of free speech guaranteed by the First Amendment. It remains to be considered whether the violation following from the University's action is excused by the necessity of complying with the Constitution's prohibition against state establishment of religion. We turn to that question.

III

. . . If there is to be assurance that the Establishment Clause retains its force in guarding against those governmental actions it was intended to prohibit, we must in each case inquire first into the purpose and object of the governmental action in question and then into the practical details of the program's operation. Before turning to these matters, however, we can set forth certain general principles that must bear upon our determination.

A central lesson of our decisions is that a significant factor in upholding governmental programs in the face of Establishment Clause attack is their neutrality towards religion. . . . The governmental program here is neutral toward religion. There is no suggestion that the University created it to advance religion or adopted some ingenious device with the purpose of aiding a religious cause. The object of the SAF is to open a forum for speech and to support various student enterprises, including the publication of newspapers, in recognition of the diversity and creativity of student life. The University's SAF Guidelines have a separate classification for, and do not make third-party payments on behalf of, "religious organizations," which are those "whose purpose is to practice a devotion to an acknowledged ultimate reality or deity." The category of support here is for "student news, information, opinion, entertainment, or academic communications media groups," of which [Wide Awake] was 1 of 15 in the 1990 school year. Wide Awake did not seek a subsidy because of its Christian editorial viewpoint; it sought funding as a student journal, which it was.

The neutrality of the program distinguishes the student fees from a tax levied for the direct support of a church or group of churches. A tax of that sort, of course, would run contrary to Establishment Clause concerns dating from the earliest days of the Republic. The apprehensions of our predecessors involved the levying of taxes upon the public for the sole and exclusive purpose of establishing and supporting specific sects. The exaction here, by contrast, is a student activity fee designed to reflect the reality that student life in its many dimensions includes the necessity of wide-ranging speech and inquiry and that student expression is an integral part of the University's educational mission. The fee is mandatory, and we do not have before us the question whether an objecting student has the First Amendment right to demand a pro rata return to the extent the fee is expended for speech to which he or she does not subscribe. We must treat it, then, as an exaction upon the students. But the $14 paid each semester by the students is not a general tax designed to raise revenue for the University. The SAF cannot be used for unlimited purposes, much less the illegitimate purpose of supporting one religion. Much like the arrangement in *Widmar,* the money goes to a special fund from which . . .students . . . can draw for purposes consistent with the University's educational mission; and to the extent the student is interested in speech, withdrawal is permitted to cover the whole spectrum of speech, whether it manifests a religious view, an antireligious view, or neither. Our decision, then, cannot be read as addressing an expenditure from a general tax fund. Here, the disbursements from the fund go to private contractors for the cost of printing that which is protected under the Speech Clause of the First Amendment. This is a far cry from a general public assessment designed and effected to provide financial support for a church.

Government neutrality is apparent in the State's overall scheme in a further meaningful respect. The program respects the critical difference "between *government* speech endorsing religion, which the Establishment Clause forbids, and *private* speech endorsing religion, which the Free Speech and Free Exercise Clauses protect." *Mergens,* (opinion of O'Connor, J.). In this case, "the government has not fostered or encouraged" any mistaken impression that the student newspapers speak for the University. The University has taken pains to disassociate itself from the private speech involved in this case. The Court of Appeals' apparent concern that Wide Awake's religious orientation would be attributed to the University is not a plausible fear, and there is no real likelihood that the speech in question is being either endorsed or coerced by the State.

The Court of Appeals (and the dissent) are correct to extract from our decisions the principle that we have recognized special Establishment Clause dangers where the government makes direct money payments to sectarian institutions. The error is not in identifying the principle, but in believing that it controls this case. Even assuming that [Wide Awake] is no different from a church and that its speech is the same as the religious exercises conducted in *Widmar* (two points much in doubt), the Court of Appeals decided a case that was, in essence, not before it, and the dissent would have us do the same. We do not confront a case where, even under a neutral program that includes nonsectarian recipients, the government is making direct money payments to an institution or group that is engaged in religious activity. Neither the Court of Appeals nor the dissent, we believe, takes sufficient cognizance of the undisputed fact that no public funds flow directly to [Wide Awake's] coffers.

It does not violate the Establishment Clause for a public university to grant access to its facilities on a religion-neutral basis to a wide spectrum of student groups, including groups that use meeting rooms for sectarian activities, accompanied by some devotional exercises. See *Widmar; Mergens.* This is so even where the upkeep, maintenance, and repair of the facilities attributed to those uses is paid from a student activities fund to which students are required to contribute. *Widmar.* The government usually acts by spending money. Even the provision of a meeting room, as in *Mergens* and *Widmar,* involved governmental expenditure, if only in the form of electricity and heating or cooling costs. The error made by the Court of Appeals, as well as by the dissent, lies in focusing on the money that is undoubtedly expended by the government, rather than on the nature of the benefit received by the recipient. If the expenditure of governmental funds is prohibited whenever those funds pay for a service that is, pursuant to a religion-neutral program, used by a group for sectarian purposes, then *Widmar, Mergens,* and *Lamb's Chapel* would have to be overruled. Given our holdings in these cases, it follows that a public university may maintain its own computer facility and give student groups access to that facility, including the use of the printers, on a religion neutral, say first-come-first-served, basis. If a religious student organization obtained access on that religion-neutral basis and used a computer to compose or a printer or copy machine to print speech with a religious content or viewpoint, the State's action in providing the group with access would no more violate the Establishment Clause than would giving those groups access to an assembly hall. See *Lamb's Chapel; Widmar, supra; Mergens.* There is no difference in logic or principle, and no difference of constitutional significance, between a school using its funds to operate a facility to which students have access, and a school paying a third-party contractor to operate the facility on its behalf. The latter occurs here. The University provides printing services to a broad spectrum of student newspapers qualified as CIO's by reason of their officers and membership. Any benefit to religion is incidental to the government's provision of secular services for secular purposes on a religion-neutral basis. Printing is a routine, secular, and recurring attribute of student life.

By paying outside printers, the University in fact attains a further degree of separation from the student publication, for it avoids the duties of supervision, escapes the costs of upkeep, repair, and replacement attributable to student use, and has a clear record of costs. As a result, and as in *Widmar,* the University can charge the SAF, and not the taxpayers as a whole, for the discrete activity in question. It would be formalistic for us to say that the University must forfeit these advantages and provide the services itself in order to comply with the Establishment Clause. It is, of course, true that if the State pays a church's bills it is subsidizing it, and we must guard against this abuse. That is not a danger here, based on the considerations we have advanced and for the additional reason that the student publication is not a religious institution, at least in the usual sense of that term as used in our case law, and it is not a religious organization as used in the University's own regulations. It is instead a publication involved in a pure forum for the expression of ideas, ideas that would be both incomplete and chilled were the Constitution to be interpreted to require that state officials and courts scan the publication to ferret out views that principally manifest a belief in a divine being.

Were the dissent's view to become law, it would require the University, in order to avoid a constitutional violation, to scrutinize the content of student speech, lest the expression in question—speech otherwise protected by the Constitution—contain too great a religious content. The dissent, in fact, anticipates such censorship as "crucial" in distinguishing between "works characterized by the evangelism of Wide Awake and writing that merely happens to express views that a given religion might approve." That eventuality raises the specter of governmental censorship, to ensure that all student writings and publications meet some baseline standard of secular orthodoxy. To impose that standard on student speech at a university is to imperil the very sources of free speech and expression. As we recognized in *Widmar,* official censorship would be far more inconsistent with the Establishment Clause's dictates than would governmental provision of secular printing services on a religion-blind basis. . . .

To obey the Establishment Clause, it was not necessary for the University to deny eligibility to student publications because of their viewpoint. The neutrality commanded of the State by the separate Clauses of the First Amendment was compromised by the University's course of action. The viewpoint discrimination inherent in the University's regulation required public officials to scan and interpret student publications to discern their underlying philosophic assumptions respecting religious theory and belief. That course of action was a denial of the right of free speech and would risk fostering a pervasive bias or hostility to religion, which could undermine the very neutrality the Establishment Clause requires. There is no Establishment Clause violation in the University's honoring its duties under the Free Speech Clause.

B. POLITICAL AND PRACTICAL ISSUES REGARDING THE USE OF SCHOOL FACILITIES

In *Lamb's Chapel,* the Supreme Court reviews the following settled principles of law. First, a school district may preserve the property under its control for district purposes. Second, a school district need not open up its property to uses by any organizations other than the district. Third, a district may open up its facilities for nondistrict purposes. Fourth, if a district opens its property to a wide variety of nondistrict users, the property becomes tantamount to a public forum. As such, the district would be prohibited from denying access to its facilities based on the subject matter of the proposed use, unless the district could show that the denial was based upon a compelling state interest, narrowly drawn to achieve that end.

The Court assumes that in the *Lamb's Chapel* case itself, the school district did *not* open its facilities to indiscriminate nondistrict uses. Rather, the Court assumes that the district created a "limited" open forum. Accordingly, the district may control access to its facilities based on the subject matter of potential uses, so long as the distinctions it draws are "reasonable" in light of the purposes served by the forum and are viewpoint neutral. The narrow issue in the case as framed by Justice White is whether the district's decision to bar a church access to its facilities was viewpoint neutral. The court assumed that the church's purpose in using the facility to display a film on child-rearing was "church related." The Court then concluded that a ban based on a religious viewpoint was not viewpoint neutral.

In light of *Lamb's Chapel* and the governing case law, districts attempted to bar groups from their open forums on the ground that the group's policies or practices violated *other* district policies, particularly those prohibiting discrimination. A number of school districts took this approach in refusing to allow the Boy Scouts of America to utilize their otherwise open facilities on the ground that the Boy Scouts of America's refusal to allow gay members violated the district's policy prohibiting discrimination against sexual orientation or preference. In 2002, however, the No Child Left Behind (NCLB) Act was enacted which, among other things, prevents school districts receiving Title I funds from denying the Boy Scouts of America and its official affiliates equal access to, and a fair opportunity to meet in, a district's otherwise open or limited open facilities. 20 U.S.C. §7905.

The *Lamb's Chapel* decision, the NCLB Act and the law governing access to school district facilities present districts with significant policy decisions. The initial policy question is whether a district should open its facilities at all to nondistrict organizations and users. A district that decides to preclude nondistrict users of course maintains complete control over its physical assets. That control has the advantage of protecting the district's facilities from deteriorating, and thus from an increase in short-term and long-term maintenance costs. In addition, the district can maintain control over all of the explicit and implicit messages conveyed in its facilities. No speech takes place in the facilities other than speech directed by the district as part of its curricular or co-curricular activities.

Against these advantages of maintaining complete control over the district's facilities, however, the following disadvantages must be weighed. From an economic standpoint, a school district's facilities typically are its most valuable resource. The district's buildings and playfields can be attractive to a number of organizations willing to rent the facilities for a healthy fee. From a political standpoint, the school district may want to present itself as an important part of the whole community. As such, the district may consider its physical assets to be those of the community at large. The district may even position its schools as the "hub of the community." A skilled school district attorney will help guide the district toward policies and practices that maximize the political and legal advantages of allowing nondistrict use of school facilities, while minimizing the disadvantages. There are at least three ways an effective school lawyer can help in this area. First, the attorney may be called upon to help draft policy language governing the use of district facilities. Second, the school lawyer will be asked to draft intergovernmental agreements that allow other taxing bodies to use district facilities in return for monetary or nonmonetary consideration. Third, the district may ask its attorney to draft leases or license agreements between the district and third-party users of the facilities.

1. The School District's Community Use Policy

If the school district determines that its facilities should not be made available for any nondistrict user, the district should nonetheless have a policy evidencing that position. The policy language might simply declare in positive terms that the district's facilities shall be available for the exclusive use of district programs. That language would preclude any inference that the district has converted its facilities into an open forum or even a limited open forum.

Assuming, however, that the district decides to accept the economic and political advantages of opening its facilities to nondistrict users, the policy language may be more difficult to construct. The language must preserve the district's control over its facilities, while insuring that the district does not unlawfully discriminate among users. One common method of reconciling these interests involves a priority schedule. The district's policy may provide, for example, that its facilities will be available first to the district, and only if the district is not utilizing the facilities, second to other governmental bodies and third to other potential users.

a. Policy Language

Consider the following priority schedule policy language:

Community Use of School Facilities

In general, the buildings and grounds shall be made available to the public of the School District for activities which benefit the students and/or residents of the District and do not interfere with the regular school program, when the buildings and grounds are not being used for school programs or activities, or those of school-related organizations.

Buildings and grounds are available, in the following priority, for the following usages. No other outside usages may be approved under this policy.

1. Government-sponsored activities, through lease, intergovernmental agreement, or otherwise, by another governmental entity.
2. Not-for-profit recreational or social programs, including child care, which primarily serve students of the District.
3. Recreational or social programs, including child care, offered by for-profit organizations, which primarily serve students of the District.
4. Not-for-profit recreational or social programs, including child care, which primarily serve residents of the District.
5. Recreational or social programs, including child care, offered by for-profit organizations, which primarily serve residents of the District.

Persons who desire to use school facilities shall make application, in writing, to the individual school Principal and Director of Buildings and Director of Buildings and Grounds. Usage shall be subject to payment of a rental rate. Rates for such charges shall be determined by the Board and shall be on file at the Principal's office at each school. The facility rental rate for the requested facility will be in addition to the minimum two hour custodial charge. Rental charges may be waived when the user is a District Resident or governmental entity. Custodial charges may not be waived.

A custodial charge, set annually by the Superintendent, shall be paid as part of all rentals. A minimum of two hours will be charged per event. A minimum of 24 hours notice must be given for any and all cancellations. Any violations to this rule will result in the minimum two hour charge.

All initial requests for building usage shall be made through the Principal's office. Final approval and custodian assignments are made by the Director of

> Buildings and Grounds. The Principal and/or Director of Buildings and Grounds is authorized to reject any/all requests which do not meet the requirements set forth by the District for usage.
>
> In all cases of facility use, the user is responsible for maintaining the facility and will be charged for any damages resulting from negligence or abusive behavior. Charges will also be levied against the user if extra time must be spent cleaning up after the use of the facility. An indemnification clause shall be included in the application for facility use. Alcoholic beverages will not be permitted on the grounds of any school facility. The Superintendent is authorized to develop procedures and regulations to implement this policy.

How does this policy language balance control and flexibility? Could you draft language that provides more control without sacrificing flexibility? Generally, is it possible to create language that offers greater flexibility without sacrificing control? This language clearly preferences users pursuant to intergovernmental agreements. What policy rationale supports that priority? Do you agree that governmental bodies should have priority?

This policy clearly opens the district's facilities to nondistrict users, thereby creating at least a limited open forum. Could the district further limit the forum to "educational purposes"? What about limiting the forum to "curriculum-related purposes"? Would it be advisable to create an Exhibit to the policy that lists the types of organizations that fall within the policy language?

b. Policy Language Practicum

In light of this policy language, consider the following scenario in a district governed by that language:

> District 100 has three schools. Each school has a gymnasium, a multipurpose room and about 1.5 acres of playfields. The School District operates a summer school program at one of its schools, but there are no District programs in any of the other schools during the summer months. Pursuant to an intergovernmental agreement the District "rents" one of its schools to the local Park District for summer camp programs.
>
> The School District has been approached by a local Church. The Church has run out of space to conduct its popular summer school program. The Church now would like to rent the District's remaining unused school building for its summer school program. Because of the demand for the program among its members, the Church's summer school program will be available only to members of the Church, and not to nonmembers. The Church's daily summer school program consists of recreation, religious instruction and a prayer service. The Church is willing to pay the same "per square foot" rent as the Park District pays for its use of district facilities. The Church, however, claims that it cannot afford to pay more.
>
> Immediately after being contacted by the Church, the District received another request for the use of that same school during the summer months. The "Diligent Student" organization for gifted students would like to conduct its summer enrichment program in the school. This nonsectarian organization only admits students to its program who have scored in the top 5 percent on state or national achievement tests. The organization is willing to pay twice what the Park District pays on a "square foot" basis to rent the school.

How would you advise the district to proceed? Should it reject both offers? Can it preference the nonsectarian gifted program over the sectarian summer school program? Must it do so, or is it legally obligated to treat those groups without regard to their sectarian or nonsectarian status? Can the district distinguish between the two groups based on the price they are willing to pay for the facilities? Can the district eliminate the sectarian organization from its facilities on the grounds that its sectarian admission practices violate *other* school district policies barring discrimination in the use of its facilities? Would your analysis of the situation change if the enrichment program were operated by the Boy Scouts of America?

2. The School District's Intergovernmental Agreements

School districts often adopt policies or practices that involve allowing other governmental bodies priority over the use of their facilities when they are not being used for district purposes. For instance, the city's elected officials (i.e., the mayor and city council) may wish to use a school for their public meetings, or a secondary school district may wish to use a primary school district's facilities, or perhaps the park district may wish to use the school's facilities for its recreational programs. These governmental units generally have the power to tax the school district's constituents. These bodies also are elected by some, if not all, of these constituents. Accordingly, some school districts believe that the district's assets are the community's assets and should be used cooperatively by the governmental agencies that serve the community.

In addition, to the extent that such governmental bodies already tax the community, some districts feel that to charge other governmental bodies significant fees for the use of district facilities is tantamount to a double tax on the community. Suppose, for example, an elementary school district charges the community's secondary school district a rental fee for the use of an auditorium for a high school play. The taxpayers already are taxed by the high school district and taxed by the elementary school district. When the high school district is charged a fee by the elementary school district, that fee is arguably an additional tax on the high school district (and its constituents) by the elementary school district. Alternatively, the community may view such rental fees as an efficient "value = maximizing" exchange of assets between two taxing bodies, each of which is separately entrusted to maximize the value of its resources.

In light of these competing perspectives on intergovernmental contracts, it is perhaps not surprising that the contracts tend to be based on in-kind consideration or below market consideration. The typical intergovernmental agreement can be divided into the following basic sections: (a) the Recitals and Incorporation of Recitals; (b) the Term and Termination Clause; (c) The Exchange of Consideration, including maintenance and use provisions; (d) Risk Allocation in the Context of Indemnity and Insurance; (e) Incorporation and/or Preservation of Prior Agreements; (f) Nondiscrimination; and (g) Signature. How should each section be drafted to reflect an agreement that benefits the school district and all of its stakeholders?

a. The Recitals and Incorporation of Recitals

Consider the following recitals in a proposed intergovernmental agreement between a school district and a park district in which the school district is willing to allow the park district to use school facilities in exchange for maintenance services.

Recitals

WHEREAS, the School and the Park are units of local government authorized to enter into this Intergovernmental Agreement;

WHEREAS, the School does currently own, and may acquire in the future, certain real property within the limits of and/or within two miles of its district boundaries; and

WHEREAS, the School owns certain buildings on said real property within the boundaries of the District; and

WHEREAS, the School and the Park desire to enter into an Intergovernmental Agreement pursuant to which the Park will fulfill certain responsibilities with respect to maintenance of the School's property that is within the boundaries of the District; and

WHEREAS, the School and the Park further desire to enter into an Intergovernmental Agreement pursuant to which the Park will provide to the School certain maintenance services and pursuant to which the Park will have permission to utilize the School's buildings and grounds that are within the boundaries of the District for park programs and activities, subject to certain restrictions and limitations; and

NOW, THEREFORE, for consideration set out below in this Agreement and other valuable consideration the receipt and sufficiency of which is hereby acknowledged and in the spirit of good faith and intergovernmental cooperation, the School and the Park agree as follows. . . .

These recitals include positive language regarding intergovernmental cooperation and even the "spirit of good faith." Do you agree that such language is appropriate? What function do these recitals serve? Does it matter if the recitals are incorporated into the agreement?

b. The Term and Termination Clause

How long should this agreement operate? Typically, the term of such an agreement would be five years. What are the advantages and disadvantages of longer or shorter terms? The term clause often is related to the extension and termination provisions. What should happen if the parties do nothing after the five year term has expired? What are the circumstances in which the parties can terminate the agreement? Can you create language that serves the parties' mutual interests?

c. The Exchange of Consideration

This clause is the core of the deal. When all is said and done, the school simply wants to allow the park to use its facilities in return for the park's maintenance services. The maintenance services are usually defined in Exhibits incorporated by reference in the Agreement. More importantly, consider how the parties should define the school's obligations. The school is willing to give the park and its defined list of permittees the right to use its facilities for "supervised public recreational programs and activities," but only when the school's facilities are not being used for "educational purposes." The agreement's language should clearly indicate that: (1) the school gives the park the right to use its facilities whenever the school is not using those facilities for educational purposes; (2) the school gives the park priority over all other noneducational users of its facilities; and (3) the school preserves its prior right and obligation to use the facilities for its own programs and for any other educational program. Can you draft a clause that strikes a fair balance between the school and the park? Should this agreement be reciprocal? Can you draft language obligating the park district to allow the school district to use park district facilities when they are not being used for recreational programs?

d. Risk Allocation

As with most agreements that involve the use of property, an intergovernmental agreement typically contains provisions regarding indemnification and insurance for liability associated with the use of the property. How should these provisions allocate risk? In the absence of any contractual allocation of risk, how would the common law allocate the risk of liability for injuries on the school's premises?

e. Incorporation and/or Preservation of Prior Agreements

This common term typically makes clear that the Agreement supercedes all prior agreements between the parties. This provision also preserves all other contracts entered by the school with other parties. What purposes are served by such clauses? In this case, should this clause preserve *existing* contracts between the school and *other* users of its facilities, even though those contracts would bar the park from using those facilities?

f. Discrimination

This clause is also routine in intergovernmental agreements. It makes clear that any nondistrict user may not discriminate in violation of federal and state law. Such a clause is one way in which the school can try to insulate itself from any unlawful, discriminatory use of its facilities. What should the nondiscrimination clause in this agreement require? Might this clause incorporate the school's policy governing the use of its facilities? Can this clause be used by the school to dictate the content of the programs offered by the users of its facilities?

3. The School District's Lease or License Agreements

If a school district ultimately decides to allow a nondistrict organization (not governed by an intergovernmental agreement) to use its facilities, the district's attorney will be asked to draft the lease or licensing agreement. These contracts often have the following sections: (1) recitals; (2) incorporation of recitals; (3) relationship among the parties; (4) supervision of the facilities; (5) payment terms; (6) utilities fees; (7) custodial services; (8) penalties for alteration of the premises or damage to the premises; (9) validity of occupant's licenses and permits; (10) subletting; (11) insurance; (12) nondiscrimination; (13) indemnification; (14) termination; (15) removal rights; (16) use of school district's name; (17) governing law, and (18) acceptable uses of the facilities.

Accordingly, the license or lease agreement raises many of the same drafting issues raised by the intergovernmental agreement. Consider the substance and form of each of these terms for a proposed lease agreement between the school district and a religiously affiliated summer day camp. The day camp is willing to rent one of the school district's schools and play fields at an acceptable market rate to operate a six-week summer camp. Perhaps the most important term of this license/lease agreement (and the most difficult to draft) involves the acceptable uses to which the summer camp may put the premises. What language would you suggest? Consider the relative bargaining power of the school district and the licensee. Will that difference result in an exchange of consideration that is unlike the exchange negotiated among governmental bodies? Should the district enter into a single six-week agreement, or should it attempt to enter into a longer term arrangement with the summer camp?

Finally, consider the following scenario. Suppose the park district wishes to utilize the same school and playfields that is the subject of the license agreement with the day camp. Will the school district's intergovernmental agreement with the park district obligate the school district to allow the park district to use that school and playfields? If so, the intergovernmental agreement would preclude the school district from renting its facilities to the summer camp, and would cost the school district the revenue generated from the license. In light of the district's intergovernmental agreement with the park district, and the park district's stated desire to use the school and playfields, would you advise the school district to enter into any license agreement with the summer camp?

SECTION III

THE LEGAL AND PRACTICAL ASPECTS OF PUBLIC SCHOOL GOVERNANCE

The ultimate authority for the regulation of education emanates from the United States Constitution. The Constitution limits the power of Congress to federalize educational policy, and it limits the power of the both the federal and state governments to enact educational schemes that interfere with the independent constitutional rights of students and teachers. Where Congress has been authorized by the Constitution to govern educational matters, the resulting federal legislation trumps any state laws that are inconsistent with that legislation.

Assuming that the states do not violate federal statutory or constitutional mandates, however, they are free to govern the education of students within the state in light of their own policies. The states are empowered to create their own educational system, so long as the elements of that system do not run afoul of federal law. In exercising their broad power over education, the states uniformly have enacted legislation creating a system of statewide public schools and a statewide education authority to oversee those schools. The state legislatures also have subdivided the state into local school districts, usually governed by elected local school boards or trustees. Those local school boards, in turn, have been give then power to enact polices governing their school districts and to employ administrators to implement those policies. These administrators manage the district's affairs and are authorized to recommend to the school board decisions affecting the actual education of children.

In light of these layers of control over the educational process, the following hierarchy of authority can be charted: (1) the U.S. Constitution; (2) federal statutes and regulations enacted pursuant to constitutional authority; (3) state constitutions and statutes compatible with federal mandates; (4) policies adopted by statewide and local school districts pursuant to their state statutory authority; and (5) the actions taken by school district administrators, principals and teachers in implementing lawful district policies.

In this section, this hierarchy of authority is traced from the Constitution to the classroom. Chapter 10 begins with an exploration of the limits of federal control over education and concludes with an analysis of the sources of local school district governance. Chapter 11 looks closely at how a local school board actually governs a school district. As the practical exercises through this section suggest, each level in the hierarchy of authority must be understood by the school lawyer before providing any advice about a course of action.

CHAPTER 10

THE LEGAL STRUCTURE OF SCHOOL GOVERNANCE

The first question raised by action taken by a public university, college, school district or school is whether the governmental authority for that action is compatible with the federal constitution. As we have seen, the constitutional questions can be difficult where governmental action touches upon religious matters. We will see, as well, that constitutional issues of due process and student rights permeate education law. In this chapter, the constitutional question is more basic but no less controversial. Here, the threshold issue is whether the federal government through Congress has the power to regulate activity that takes place on or around school grounds.

A. THE CONSTITUTIONAL LIMITS OF FEDERAL REGULATION OF EDUCATION

The Constitution leaves to the states and their local governments "a residuary of inviolable sovereignty." *See New York v. United States,* 505 U.S. 144, 190 (1992) (citing *The Federalist Papers,* No. 39). That sovereignty is protected by the Tenth Amendment to the Constitution, which declares that the "powers not delegated to the United States by the Constitution, nor prohibited by it to the states, are reserved to the states respectively or to the people." In addition, the Eleventh Amendment, as interpreted by the current Supreme Court, has become a "fundamental aspect of the sovereignty which the states enjoy" because it protects the states from being sued in federal court for failing to comply with a range of federal statutory requirements. *See Alden v. Maine,* 527 U.S. 706 (1999).

These constitutional protections of state authority limit federal involvement in educational matters. The Constitution does not grant to the federal system any direct power to regulate education. That power inheres in the states under the Tenth Amendment. Moreover, absent clear language from Congress, states cannot be sued in federal court for their failure to comply with federal directives. The Supreme Court thus has made clear that the federal government may not directly compel a state to enact a federal educational program. *New York,* 505 U.S. at 190.

Nonetheless, the Constitution allows Congress to "influence" state educational matters. The Constitution's "supremacy clause" provides that if Congress enacts valid legislation, that legislation will preempt states laws that are contrary to the federal legislative objectives. (Article VI, clause 2 provides that federal law "shall be the Supreme Law of the Land.") The supremacy clause, however, is not an independent grant of legislative power to Congress. Rather, that clause insures that statutes passed by Congress pursuant to a direct grant of legislative power will supersede any irreconcilable state laws. In the education field, Congress has attempted to influence state educational policies and practices primarily through its "spending" power and its power to regulate interstate commerce. The Constitution's "spending clause" permits Congress to attach conditions to a state's receipt of federal funds. *See* art. I, §8, cl. 1. Congress also may influence state action by regulating the commerce that takes place between different states. Art. I, §8, cl. 3.

1. The Supremacy Clause

The supremacy clause precludes a state from passing any law that is incompatible with the terms or purposes of congressional legislation. *See, e.g., Alden v. Maine,* 527 U.S. 706 (1999). Federal statutes governing education therefore may preempt state laws that are inconsistent with the federal regime.

In *Shepheard v. Godwin,* 280 F. Supp. 869 (E.D. Va. 1968), for example, the state of Virginia attempted to reallocate money received by local school districts pursuant to a federal statute mandating the payment of "impact fees" to the local district in proportion to the number of children of federal employees who attended the district's schools. The federal statutory regime was designed to provide additional funding ("impact aid") to those school districts that lose tax revenue because federal employees are exempt from local property taxes. Such impact fees are particularly important to school districts that educate children of military families. Families who live on military bases do not pay property taxes, nor are their purchases on the base subject to local sales taxes. School districts which must educate children of military families therefore are not afforded sufficient local tax revenue from which to do so. The federal scheme at issue in *Shepheard* was designed to provide an additional source of revenue to local districts to help them educate children of federal employees within the district. The Court, however, determined that Virginia's effort to redirect these federal funds to statewide uses was inconsistent with the language and intent of the federal statute. Accordingly, the Court concluded that under the supremacy clause, the federal educational funding legislation must preempt the inconsistent state provisions.

Cases like *Shepheard* are the exception rather than the rule. Although the supremacy clause insures that state laws will not frustrate a congressional educational regime, the courts generally endeavor to reconcile federal and state law. *See, e.g., Wheeler v. Barrera,* 417 U.S. 402 (1974) (reading Title I of the

Elementary and Secondary Education Act, 20 U.S.C. §241a, flexibly to allow a variety of state legislated pedagogical methods for meeting its federal objectives). Unless the federal law expressly preempts state law in an area, or is entirely inconsistent with a contrary state provision, the state statute or practice generally will survive a supremacy clause challenge. *See, e.g., Geier v. American Honda Motor Co.,* 529 U.S. 861 (2000) (preemption required where state law frustrates congressional objectives or makes it impossible to comply with both federal and state laws); *CTS Corp. v. Dynamics Corp. of America,* 481 U.S. 69 (1987) (preemption occurs only if Congress expressly requires it, or if the state law would conflict with the fundamental objectives of the federal scheme).

If Congress exercises legitimate constitutional power to regulate state education, therefore, the resulting legislation would preempt state laws that are irreconcilable with the federal regime. In order for the supremacy clause to serve any function, however, Congress must first exercise legitimate legislative power. Congress has tried to influence local educational affairs primarily through its legislative power under the Constitution's commerce clause and spending clause.

2. The Commerce Clause Power

United States v. Lopez

514 U.S. 549 (1995)

Chief Justice Rehnquist delivered the opinion of the Court.

In the Gun-Free School Zones Act of 1990, Congress made it a federal offense "for any individual knowingly to possess a firearm at a place that the individual knows, or has reasonable cause to believe, is a school zone." The Act neither regulates a commercial activity nor contains a requirement that the possession be connected in any way to interstate commerce. We hold that the Act exceeds the authority of Congress "to regulate Commerce . . . among the several States. . . ." U.S. Const., Art. I, §8, cl. 3.

On March 10, 1992, respondent, who was then a 12th-grade student, arrived at Edison High School in San Antonio, Texas, carrying a concealed .38 caliber handgun and five bullets. Acting upon an anonymous tip, school authorities confronted respondent, who admitted that he was carrying the weapon. . . .

A federal grand jury indicted respondent on one count of knowing possession of a firearm at a school zone, in violation of §922(q) [of the Gun-Free School Zones Act of 1990]. Respondent moved to dismiss his federal indictment on the ground that §922(q) "is unconstitutional as it is beyond the power of Congress to legislate control over our public schools." . . .

We start with first principles. The Constitution creates a Federal Government of enumerated powers. *See* Art. I, §8. As James Madison wrote, "the powers delegated by the proposed Constitution to the federal government are few and defined. Those which are to remain in the State governments are numerous and indefinite." *The Federalist* No. 45, pp. 292-293 (C. Rossiter ed. 1961).

This constitutionally mandated division of authority "was adopted by the Framers to ensure protection of our fundamental liberties." . . . "Just as the separation and independence of the coordinate branches of the Federal Government serve to prevent the accumulation of excessive power in any one branch, a healthy balance of power between the States and the Federal Government will reduce the risk of tyranny and abuse from either front." The Constitution delegates to Congress the power "to regulate Commerce with foreign Nations, and among the several States, and with the Indian Tribes." Art. I, §8, cl. 3. . . .

[W]e have identified three broad categories of activity that Congress may regulate under its commerce power. First, Congress may regulate the use of the channels of interstate commerce. . . . Second, Congress is empowered to regulate and protect the instrumentalities of interstate commerce, or persons or things in interstate commerce, even though the threat may come only from intrastate activities. Finally, Congress' commerce authority includes the power to regulate those activities . . . that substantially affect interstate commerce.

Within this final category, admittedly, our case law has not been clear whether an activity must "affect" or "substantially affect" interstate commerce in order to be within Congress' power to regulate it under the Commerce Clause. We conclude, consistent with the great weight of our case law, that the proper test requires an analysis of whether the regulated activity "substantially affects" interstate commerce.

We now turn to consider the power of Congress, in the light of this framework, to enact §922(q). The first two categories of authority may be quickly disposed of: §922(q) is not a regulation of the use of the channels of interstate commerce, nor is it an attempt to prohibit the interstate transportation of a commodity through the channels of commerce; nor can §922(q) be justified as a regulation by which Congress has sought to protect an instrumentality of interstate commerce or a thing in interstate commerce. Thus, if §922(q) is to be sustained, it must be under the third category as a regulation of an activity that substantially affects interstate commerce.

First, we have upheld a wide variety of congressional Acts regulating intrastate economic activity where we have concluded that the activity substantially affected interstate commerce. Examples include the regulation of intrastate coal mining; intrastate extortionate credit transactions, restaurants utilizing substantial interstate supplies, inns and hotels catering to interstate guests, and production and consumption of homegrown wheat. These examples are by no means exhaustive, but the pattern is clear. Where economic activity substantially affects interstate commerce, legislation regulating that activity will be sustained. . . .

Section 922(q) is a criminal statute that by its terms has nothing to do with "commerce" or any sort of economic enterprise, however broadly one might define those terms. Section 922(q) is not an essential part of a larger regulation of economic activity, in which the regulatory scheme could be undercut unless the intrastate activity were regulated. It cannot, therefore, be sustained under our cases upholding regulations of activities that arise out of or are connected with a commercial transaction, which viewed in the aggregate, substantially affects interstate commerce.

Second, §922(q) contains no jurisdictional element which would ensure, through case-by-case inquiry, that the firearm possession in question affects interstate commerce. Although as part of our independent evaluation of constitutionality under the Commerce Clause we of course consider legislative findings, and indeed even congressional committee findings, regarding effect on interstate commerce, the Government concedes that "neither the statute nor its legislative history contain [s] express congressional findings regarding the effects upon interstate commerce of gun possession in a school zone." We agree with the Government that Congress normally is not required to make formal findings as to the substantial burdens that an activity has on interstate commerce. ("Congress need [not] make particularized findings in order to legislate.") But to the extent that congressional findings would enable us to evaluate the legislative judgment that the activity in question substantially affected interstate commerce, even though no such substantial effect was visible to the naked eye, they are lacking here. . . .

The Government's essential contention, *in fine,* is that we may determine here that §922(q) is valid because possession of a firearm in a local school zone does indeed substantially affect interstate commerce. The Government argues that possession of a firearm in a school zone may result in violent crime and that violent crime can be expected to affect the functioning of the national economy in two ways. First, the costs of violent crime are substantial, and, through the mechanism of insurance, those costs are spread throughout the population. Second, violent crime reduces the willingness of individuals to travel to areas within the country that are perceived to be unsafe. The Government also argues that the presence of guns in schools poses a substantial threat to the educational process by threatening the learning environment. A handicapped educational process, in turn, will result in a less productive citizenry. That, in turn, would have an adverse effect on the Nation's economic well-being. As a result, the Government argues that Congress could rationally have concluded that §922(q) substantially affects interstate commerce.

We pause to consider the implications of the Government's arguments. The Government admits, under its "costs of crime" reasoning, that Congress could regulate not only all violent crime, but all activities that might lead to violent crime, regardless of how tenuously they relate to interstate commerce. Similarly, under the Government's "national productivity" reasoning, Congress could regulate any activity that it found was related to the economic productivity of individual citizens: family law (including marriage, divorce, and child custody), for example. Under the theories that the Government presents in support of §922(q), it is difficult to perceive any limitation on federal power, even in areas such as criminal law enforcement or education where States historically have been sovereign. Thus, if we were to accept the Government's arguments, we are hard pressed to posit any activity by an individual that Congress is without power to regulate.

Although Justice Breyer argues that acceptance of the Government's rationales would not authorize a general federal police power, he is unable to identify any activity that the States may regulate but Congress may not. Justice Breyer posits that there might be some limitations on Congress' commerce power, such as family law or certain aspects of education. These suggested limitations, when viewed in light of the dissent's expansive analysis, are devoid of substance.

Justice Breyer focuses, for the most part, on the threat that firearm possession in and near schools poses to the educational process and the potential economic consequences flowing from that threat. Specifically, the dissent reasons that (1) gun-related violence is a serious problem; (2) that problem, in turn, has an adverse effect on classroom learning; and (3) that adverse effect on classroom learning, in turn, represents a substantial threat to trade and commerce. This analysis would be equally applicable, if not more so, to subjects such as family law and direct regulation of education.

For instance, if Congress can, pursuant to its Commerce Clause power, regulate activities that adversely affect the learning environment, then, *a fortiori,* it also can regulate the educational process directly. Congress could determine that a school's curriculum has a "significant" effect on the extent of classroom learning. As a result, Congress could mandate a federal curriculum for local elementary and secondary schools because what is taught in local schools has a significant "effect on classroom learning," and that, in turn, has a substantial effect on interstate commerce.

Justice Breyer rejects our reading of precedent and argues that "Congress . . . could rationally conclude that schools fall on the commercial side of the line." Again, Justice Breyer's rationale lacks any real limits because, depending on the level of generality, any activity can be looked upon as commercial. Under the dissent's rationale, Congress could just as easily look at child rearing as "falling on the commercial side of the line" because it provides a "valuable service— namely, to equip [children] with the skills they need to survive in life and, more specifically, in the workplace." We do not doubt that Congress has authority under the Commerce Clause to regulate numerous commercial activities that substantially affect interstate commerce and also affect the educational process. That authority, though broad, does not include the authority to regulate each and every aspect of local schools.

Admittedly, a determination whether an intrastate activity is commercial or noncommercial may in some cases result in legal uncertainty. But, so long as Congress' authority is limited to those powers enumerated in the Constitution, and so long as those enumerated powers are interpreted as having judicially enforceable outer limits, congressional legislation under the Commerce Clause always will engender "legal uncertainty." . . .

To uphold the Government's contentions here, we would have to pile inference upon inference in a manner that would bid fair to convert congressional authority under the Commerce Clause to a general police power of the sort retained by the States. Admittedly, some of our prior cases have taken long steps down that road, giving great deference to congressional action. The broad language in these opinions has suggested the possibility of additional expansion, but we decline here to proceed any further. To do so would require us to conclude that the Constitution's enumeration of powers does not presuppose something not enumerated, and that there never will be a distinction between what is truly national and what is truly local. . . . This we are unwilling to do. . . .

NOTES AND QUESTIONS

1. To what extent is education a national, as opposed to an intrastate, concern? In his dissenting opinion, Justice Stevens writes that the future character of America's commerce "is vitally dependent on the character of the education of our children." Do you agree?
2. Is education a "commercial" endeavor?
3. Would Congress, acting pursuant to its power to regulate interstate commerce, have the power to criminalize the use of cell phones or pagers on school grounds for drug-trafficking purposes?
4. The Court concludes that Congress cannot employ its commerce clause power to regulate an activity which "affects" interstate commerce, but may employ that power to regulate an activity which "substantially" affects interstate commerce. Why did the Court reject the lesser standard? How does the Court define "substantially"?
5. The Court rejects the government's attempt to establish that possession of a firearm in a local school zone substantially affects interstate commerce. Do you agree with the Court's rejection? Are there any additional arguments that the government could have made to establish the requisite substantial affect on interstate commerce?

3. The Congressional Spending Power, the Limits of Congressional Regulation of Curriculum and the No Child Left Behind Act

(a) The Congressional Spending Power

The Constitution grants to Congress the power to spend money to provide for the "general welfare of the United States". *See* art. 1, §8, cl. 1. In *Buckley v. Valeo,* 424 U.S. 1, 90-91 (1976), the Supreme Court declared that the congressional power to spend money to provide for the general welfare is "quite expansive," and "it is for Congress to decide which expenditures will promote the general welfare." *See also South Dakota v. Dole,* 483 U.S. 203 (1987) (spending power permits Congress to condition highway funds on a state's adoption of a minimum drinking age). Nonetheless, the Supreme Court also has imposed four doctrinal limits on Congress's spending clause power. First, the expenditures must be used by the states for the general welfare, as opposed to a purely local concern. *See New York v. United States,* 505 U.S. 144, 171 (1992). Second, the conditions imposed by Congress on funding must be "unambiguous," *see Pennhurst State School & Hospital v. Halderman,* 451 U.S. 1 (1981). Third, the conditions imposed must be reasonably related to the purpose of the expenditure. *New York,* 505 U.S. at 171. Fourth, the conditions may not violate any independent constitutional prohibition. *See Lawrence County v. Lead-Deadwood School Dist. No. 40-1,* 469 U.S. 256, 269-280 (1985). *See also* D. Engdahl, *Basis of the Spending Power,* 18 Seattle U.L. Rev. 215 (1995).

Congress has taken advantage of the generality of the language of the Constitution's spending clause and the powerful leverage of funding to influence a broad range of local educational matters. Many of the congressional statutes regulating education stem from Congress's power to spend money to provide for the educational welfare of students. In these statutes, Congress provides to the states, public universities and local school districts funds only on the condition that the states, universities and districts meet certain substantive statutory requirements. For example, the Individuals with Disabilities Education Act, 20 U.S.C. §1400-1487 (IDEA), allocates to the states funds only on the condition that the states comply with the mandates of that federal law protecting students with educational disabilities. In fact, one of the "strings" that Congress has attached to the receipt of federal money under IDEA is that the state forfeit its immunity from suit under the Eleventh Amendment and submit itself to federal court jurisdiction. *See Board of Education of Oak Park v. Kelly E.,* 207 F.3d 931, 935 (7th Cir. 2000) (citing 20 U.S.C. §604(c), which expressly removes a state's Eleventh Amendment immunity from suits).

Each of Congress's efforts to regulate education thus far have complied with the Supreme Court's requirements for a valid exercise of the spending power. In 2001, however, Congress enacted the No Child Left Behind Act, presumably pursuant to its spending clause power. As you analyze the Act's requirements, consider whether Congress has exceeded its broad spending power in enacting this statute.

(b) The No Child Left Behind Act and the Limits of Federal Regulation of Education

(1) The Act's Requirements

On January 8, 2002, the Elementary and Secondary Education Act Reauthorization, also known as the "No Child Left Behind Act of 2001," became law. The NCLB Act expands the federal government's involvement in the curriculum decisions of local school districts. The statute mandates that by the 2005-2006 school year, all students must be taught core subjects by "highly qualified" teachers and paraprofessionals. The Act also requires that starting in the 2005-2006 school year, all public school students in grades three through eight take annual tests in reading and math. Each state must administer these tests and then establish a minimum standard of performance. The school district is then given a period of twelve years to insure that all of its students reach that level of performance. In addition, a sample of students from each state will be required to take a National Assessment of Educational Progress to establish an acceptable range of performance on the state-administered tests. States must also report the results of their students' tests and their progress. The student test data must be disaggregated based on categories such as race, ethnicity, gender, socioeconomic status and language proficiency.

The consequences of a district's failure to achieve satisfactory student test results are significant. A school that fails to show "adequate yearly progress" for two years in a row is "identified for improvement," and is therefore required to develop a plan to strengthen student achievement. The school must notify the parents of the school's "identification" and must involve parents in the development of the improvement plan. Most significantly, the parents of children in "identified" schools must be given a range of options for the education of their children, including the choice to transfer to a school that has not been identified. The "identified" school district must pay for the transportation of children to a nonidentified school. If a school fails to remedy its failure to perform within a year of its identification, the district must also use its federal funding to finance private tutoring and summer school programs for their nonperforming students. The Act allows for these remedial programs to be administered by religious organizations.

If annual yearly progress is not shown by the end of the second year after identification, the school district must implement fairly dramatic corrective measures. The district may be required to replace the identified school's administration, faculty, staff or even curriculum. The district also will be required to offer and fund additional school attendance options for students. Finally, if the "identified" school cannot attain sufficient yearly progress by the end of the third year after its identification, the Act mandates restructuring. The district must alter the very nature of the school. The school's staff might be completely replaced. Alternatively, the school could be taken over by the state, operated as a charter school, or contracted out to a private organization. Each of these consequences of an individual school's failure to achieve yearly progress has a parallel in the Act if an entire district fails to show sufficient progress. The Act does, however, contain a safe harbor for both schools and districts. If the number of nonperforming students in each subgroup can be reduced by 10 percent or more from the prior year, the consequences of the Act are lessened.

(2) Legal Implications of the Act's Federal Curriculum

The Act's requirements of annual standardized testing in grades three through eight and its sanctions for failure to show "adequate yearly progress" raise important legal questions. Among the questions which are evident from the face of the statute alone are: (1) Does Congress's constitutional spending power extend to the Act's regulation of a school's performance?; (2) Does the Act's provisions for federal funding of remedial programs operated by religious groups violate the First Amendment's establishment clause?; (3) Do the Act's requirements that student achievement data be disaggregated by subgroups such as ethnicity and gender and that federally funded school choice options be available based in part on the performance of these subgroups raise equal protection concerns?; and (4) If, as a direct result of the Act's federally funded transfer options, the racial composition of schools significantly changes, will that result raise a new equal protection concern?

Finally, the NCLB Act's imposition of federal standards seems to divest school districts of local control over their district's curriculum and resources. Recall the value placed on "local control" in the *Rodriguez* case and throughout the law of education. In fact, local control was the state interest that justified marked disparities in the resources allocated to districts within a state. Does the Act leave the states with sovereignty over the education of their own citizens?

(3) Policy Questions Raised by the Act's Standards-Based Requirements

In addition to raising difficult legal questions, the Act also raises fundamental questions about educational policy and philosophy. The Act implements its stated purpose of insuring that all public school children receive an effective education by holding school districts accountable for the performance of their students on standardized tests. The Act thereby places into the law the "standards" movement in educational theory. It requires states, districts and schools to establish and test for standards, and it imposes consequences for the failure to meet standards. The Act's requirement that school districts demonstrate progress in the test scores of various subgroups of students is designed to provide incentives for school districts to improve these scores for all of its student population, regardless of race or gender. If a school or a district will be penalized when its children fail to meet standards, the curriculum in that school likely will become standards based. Nor can there be any doubt that some districts will evaluate their teachers in accordance with their students' test performance. The incentives and sanctions created by the Act thereby attempt to impose standards-based education in the schools throughout the states.

Some experts in the field of educational psychology argue that the so-called standards movement is actually counterproductive to authentic student learning. Equipped with a depth of empirical research and experience, Alfie Kohn has a written a host of books and articles challenging the political drive toward "standards" in education. In *The Schools Our Children Deserve: Moving Beyond Traditional Classrooms and "Tougher Standards,"* (1999) (hereinafter *The Schools),* Kohn begins by contending that the so-called standards movement carries with it disproven assumptions about the way children learn. The standards movement descends from a behavioralist psychology that holds that learning is the acquisition of observable skills and "bits of knowledge, a process that is linear, incremental, measurable." *The Schools* at 4. According to Kohn, that view was discredited, long ago by John Dewey, and more recently by Jean Piaget. A Swiss psychologist, Jean Piaget, showed that children learn in developmental stages, and that learning is always a two-way relationship between a person and the environment. *Id.* at 5. Students do not, as the standards movement presumes, digest knowledge; they construct their reality by allowing their perceptions to interact with their environment. *Id.* This fundamental understanding about the way children really learn informs the engaged learning, constructivist and differentiated instructional practices of sophisticated school districts and learning institutions. Genuine teaching and learning are antithetical to a standards approach to education. In other words, while the standards movement may be politically popular, it is educationally unsound.

Kohn finds several fatal "flaws" in the standards-based approach, each of which arguably appears in the structure of the NCLB Act: the standards-based curriculum's preoccupation with student achievement is detrimental to a focus on learning; its assumption that kids are inert receptacles of facts is not only outdated, it was never believed to be true; it relies on "tests," which themselves have proven to be erroneous measures of student learning; it coerces teachers and students to teach and learn to the test; and its premise that student learning and genuine success result from more information and harder tasks is simply false.

Each of these flaws, in turn, leads to practices that arguably harm students and their learning. For instance, the emphasis on student achievement as measured by test scores actually undermines student interest in learning, makes failure seem overwhelming, leads students to avoid challenging themselves, reduces the quality of learning, and invites students to value their intelligence, not their effort. *Id.* at 28. Similarly, the standards movement also is based on faulty assumptions about what genuine learning entails, including the erroneous view that learning can be segregated by subject or task or student.

Ultimately, Kohn argues that tests do not even accomplish their own questionable objectives. Kohn declares that it is "an open secret among educators that much of what the scores indicate is just the socio-economic status of the students who take them." *Id.* at 77. Indeed, the greatest predictors of high test results are family income and the educational level reached by the student's mother. *Id.* at 77, n.4. ("The richer the family, the higher the [SAT] score.") *See also* Gary Orfield & Mindy L. Kornhaber, eds., *Raising Standards or Raising Barriers?* (2001). Accordingly, from a political accountability perspective, a ranking of states, districts, or schools by test scores is not an accurate measure of the quality of education because those scores reflect too many external variables. *The Schools,* at 77. Moreover, because the tests at best are designed to reward only nonreflective, rapid-fire, shallow thinking, they do not even capture genuine learning or learning potential. *Id.* at 78-83.

The message that testing values shallow thinking is not lost on children. This is a particularly strong message because the testing environment has caused teachers to spend a tremendous amount of instructional time on test preparation, drill and kill, testing techniques, test-taking itself and test debriefing. Kohn presents evidence of what all educational professionals know to be true about standardized testing: teachers spend valuable instructional time simply teaching to the test. As Kohn concludes:

> *At best, high test scores for a given school or district are probably meaningless; at worst they're actually bad news because of the kind of teaching that was done to produce these scores* (emphasis in original). *Id.* at 91.

Kohn recognizes that the issue of whether standardized testing will continue to be abused is ultimately a "political" one. He does show that authentic assessment can be used as a tool to help children learn by giving to teachers useful insight into a student's learning style. Furthermore, Kohn answers the proponents of standardized testing by arguing that true "accountability" can be achieved in more effective ways. To that end, he insists that the quality of an educational environment can best be measured by visitors who know what to look for. In particular, Kohn demonstrates how the classroom climate can reveal a great deal about whether the school is effective in the most significant ways. A "good" school is one which meets the shared psychological needs of all students, meets the unique needs of each child, is likely to promote the *long-term* goals that parents and community members have for children, and reflects the fundamental purpose of democratic education, which is to prepare each student to participate equally as a contributing member of the community.

Do you find Kohn's attack on the standards movement to be persuasive? Consider your own educational experience with standards and testing. Are they consistent with Kohn's critique? If, in fact, the federalization of the standards movement is deleterious to students, what steps can be taken to mitigate its effects? Does this federalization of an arguably obsolete theory of education offer persuasive evidence favoring local control over education? Or, is it easier to rectify a failed experiment enacted at the federal level than it would be to reverse a state-by-state trend?

B. STATE AND LOCAL CONTROL OF EDUCATION

Because of the limits placed on congressional power to regulate internal state affairs, the states have authority over the education of persons within their borders. Under principles of federalism, in fact, the states are presumed to have the power to govern education within the state, and that presumption can be rebutted only if there is a clear limitation on that power from federal law.

The constitutions of every state provide for an educational system and give to the state legislatures a broad reservoir of power to control the school system. As a consequence, state legislatures have primary control over public education in America. The state legislatures have delegated to statewide educational agencies and to the local school districts broad powers otherwise reserved to the state itself. In fact, every state has created a statewide educational authority or board to govern education in the state, and has divided the state into local educational agencies or school districts. The statewide agency is managed by a state superintendent of schools, typically appointed by the governor. The local school districts are usually governed by school boards, the members of which are usually elected by the district.

1. The Strength of State and Local Control of Education

Local school districts are arms of the state. They are the vehicles by which the state realizes its educational objectives. Because school districts are established by the state and operate as the state's instrumentalities, their structure and very existence may be altered by the state itself. The legislature is free to change district boundaries so long as it violates no contrary directive from the state constitution, federal constitution, or federal statutes. For example, although the state may alter district boundaries for a myriad of rational purposes, it could not modify district boundaries to segregate school districts based on race, *see Akron Board of Education v. State Board of Education,* 490 F.2d 1285 (6th Cir. 1974). The U.S. Supreme Court has ruled, however, that a state's legislature has the power to establish and modify school districts without violating article I, section 10 of the U.S. Constitution, which precludes laws that impair the "obligation of contracts." *Attorney General of State of Michigan v. Lowrey,* 199 U.S. 233 (1905). In *Lowrey,* the Michigan legislature, acting pursuant to its authority under the state constitution to "establish and provide a system of public schools," attempted to redraw school district boundaries and reallocate assets to a newly defined district, taking those assets from the prior districts. The Supreme Court held that there was no constitutional limitation on the legislature's power to redraw school district boundaries:

> If the legislature of the State has the power to create and alter school districts and divide and apportion the property of such districts no contract can arise, no property of a district can be said to be taken, and the action of the legislature is compatible with a republican form of government even if it be admitted that Section 4, Article IV, of the Constitution applies to the creation of, or the powers or rights of property of, the subordinate municipalities of a State. We may omit, therefore, that Section and Article from further consideration. . . . [T]he legislature of a State has absolute power to make and change subordinate municipalities.

STATE EX REL. CLARK V. HAWORTH

122 Ind. 462, 23 N.E. 946 (Ind. 1890)

ELLIOTT, J.—The questions presented and argued in this case do not require us to do more than outline the pleadings, for the questions are general ones involving the validity and construction of a statute [requiring a designated series of books to be used throughout the state's schools and a uniform process for contracting to purchase those books]. It is sufficient to bring the questions clearly enough before the mind for investigation and consideration to say, that the realtor petitioned for a writ of mandate to compel the appellee, as school trustee of Monroe township, in the county of Howard, to certify to the county superintendent of schools the number of text-books required by the children of the township for use in the public schools, and to procure and furnish such books as the law requires; and that the return of the appellee to the alternative writ is so framed as to present the question of the constitutionality of the act of March 2d, 1889, and, also, the question as to the duties of the school trustee under that act.

The act assailed does not impinge in the slightest degree upon the right of local self-government. The right of local self-government is an inherent, and not a derivative one. Individualized, it is the right which a man possesses in virtue of his character as a freeman. It is not bestowed by legislatures, nor derived from statutes. But the courts which have carried to its utmost extent the doctrine of local self-government have never so much as intimated, that it exists as to a matter over which the Constitution has given the law-making power supreme control, nor have they gone beyond the line which separates matters of purely local concern from those of State control. Essentially and intrinsically the schools in which are educated and trained the children who are to become the rulers of the commonwealth are matters of State, and not of local jurisdiction. In such matters, the State is a unit, and the Legislature the source of power. The authority over schools and school affairs is not necessarily a distributive one to be exercised by local instrumentalities; but, on the contrary, it is a central power residing in the Legislature of the State. It is for the law-making power to determine whether the authority shall be exercised by a State board of education, or distributed to county, township, or city organizations throughout the State. With that determination the judiciary can no more rightfully interfere, than can the Legislature with a decree or judgment pronounced by a judicial tribunal. The decision is as conclusive and inviolable in the one case as in the other, and an interference with the legislative judgment would be a breach of the Constitution which no principle would justify, nor any precedent excuse. But we need not rest our conclusion that the control of schools and school affairs is vested in the law-making power of the State, upon the proposition that schools are intrinsically matters of State concern, and not of a local nature—although it may there be securely rested—for our Constitution, in language that can not be mistaken, declares that it is a matter of the State and not of the locality. The language of the Constitution is this: "Knowledge and learning, generally diffused throughout a community, being essential to the preservation of a free government, it shall be the duty of the General Assembly to encourage by all suitable means, moral, intellectual, scientific, and agricultural improvement, and to provide, by law, for a general and uniform system of common schools, wherein tuition shall be without charge, and equally open to all." Article VIII, Section 1. The Constitution enjoins a duty and confers a power. The duty and the power are coextensive, but the object they are designed to accomplish is unified, because the duty is to "provide, by law, for a general and a uniform system of common schools," and the power is granted to enable the General Assembly to effectively perform the duty. Both by the Constitution and by the intrinsic nature of the duty and the power, the authority is exclusively legislative, and the matter over which it is to be exercised solely of State concern. That this conclusion is sound, is so clear, that authorities are not required to fortify or support it, but authorities are not wanting, for the current of judicial decisions is unbroken.

Judge Cooley has examined the question with care, and discussed it with ability, and he declares that the Legislature has plenary power over the subject of the public schools. He says, in the course of his discussion, that: "To what degree the Legislature shall provide for the education of the people at the cost of the State or of its municipalities, is a question which, except as regulated by the Constitution, addresses itself to the legislative judgment exclusively." Again, he says: "The governing school boards derive all their authority from the statute, and can exercise no powers except those expressly granted and those which result by necessary implication from the grant." No case has been cited by counsel, and none has been discovered by us, although we have searched the reports with care, which denies the doctrine that the regulation of the public schools is a State matter exclusively within the domain of the Legislature.

If it be true that the power is a legislative one, then it is indisputably true, that the courts cannot control the legislative discretion. This principle is elementary in constitutional law, and it needs no support from precedents or decisions; but the principle has been so well expressed by Mr. Justice Bradley that we quote his language. Replying to an argument that the mode in which the power was exercised was improper, this great judge said: "The answer is, the legislative department, being the nation itself, speaking by its representatives, has a choice of methods, and is the master of its own discretion." We have adopted and applied this rule, and, indeed, we could not depart from it, without a disregard of principal, that no decision or precedent would excuse. As the power over schools is a legislative one, it is not exhausted by exercise. The Legislature having tried one plan is not precluded from trying another. It has a choice of methods, and may change its plans as often as it deems necessary or expedient; and for mistakes or abuses it is answerable to the people, but not to the courts. It is clear, therefore, that even if it were true, that the Legislature had uniformly entrusted the management of school affairs to local organizations, it would not authorize the conclusion, that it might not change the system. To deny the power to change, is to affirm that progress is impossible, and that we must move forever "in the dim footsteps of antiquity." But the legislative power moves in a constant stream, and is not exhausted by its exercise in any number of instances, however great. It is not true, however, that the authority over schools was originally regarded as a local one; on the contrary, the earlier cases asserted that the Legislature could not delegate the power to levy taxes for school purposes to local organizations, but must itself directly exercise the power; thus denying, in the strongest possible form, the theory of local control. This ruling was, for many years, regarded as the law of the State; but in the case of *Robinson v. Schenck,* it was held that the Legislature might either exercise the power itself, or delegate it to local governmental instrumentalities. It has, indeed, been the uniform course since the organization of the State, to regulate and control school affairs by legislation. All the public schools have been established under legislative enactments, and all rules and regulations have been made pursuant to statutory authority. Every school that has been established owes its existence to legislation; and every school officer owes his authority to the statute.

It is impossible to conceive of the existence of a uniform system of common schools without power lodged somewhere to make it uniform, and, even in the absence of express constitutional provisions, that power must necessarily reside in the Legislature. If it does reside there, then that body must have, as an incident of the principal power, the authority to prescribe the course of study and the system of instruction that shall be pursued and adopted, as well as the books which shall be used. This general doctrine is well entrenched by authority. Having this authority, the Legislature may not only prescribe regulations for using such books, but it may, also, declare how the books shall be obtained and distributed. If it may do this, then it may provide that they shall be obtained through the medium of a contract awarded to the best or lowest bidder, since, if it be true, as it unquestionably is, that the power is legislative, it must also be true that the Legislature has an unrestricted discretion and an unfettered choice of methods. It can not be possible that the courts can interfere with this legislative power, and adjudge that the Legislature shall not adopt this method or that method, for, if the question is at all legislative, it is so in its whole length and breadth. Under our form of government there is no such thing as a power partly judicial and partly legislative; the one power excludes the other, for each is distinct and independent. If the Legislature exercises its right to make a choice of methods, by enacting that the books for the schools shall be furnished by the person making the most acceptable bid, the courts can not interfere, because the power exercised is a purely legislative one, and within the legislative domain, courts are forbidden to enter. There is no escape from this conclusion, save by a denial of legislative independence, and an assertion of the right of judicial surveillance and control.

If the power over the school system is legislative and exclusive, then the Legislature has authority to impose upon all officers whose tenure is legislative, such duties respecting school affairs as it deems proper. All such officers take their offices *cum onere,* and must do what the Legislature commands or else resign. . . . We can find neither reason nor authority, that suggests a doubt as to the power of the Legislature to require a designated series of books to be used in the schools, and to require, that the books selected shall be obtained from the person to whom the contract for supplying them may be awarded. . . .

For the error in holding that the duty imposed upon school trustees is not imperative, the judgment must be reversed.

NOTES AND QUESTIONS

1. In his concurrence in *Haworth,* Justice Olds tracks the legal origins of the state's "common schools" as follows:

> The common schools of the State are in the main supported by the State, and the tuition is free. The Constitution expressly enjoins on the General Assembly the duty "to encourage by all suitable means, moral, intellectual, scientific and agricultural improvement, and to provide by law for a general and uniform system of common schools, wherein tuition shall be without charge and equally open to all." By the Constitution the common schools of the State are expressly placed under the control and supervision of the General Assembly. It is made the duty of that department of the State government to provide for a uniform system; this must relate to books, as it is manifestly essential that there must be a uniformity in books to secure proper efficiency in the schools, and such uniformity can only be brought about and maintained by legislation, providing for the adoption and use of certain books. Whether there should be a uniformity in the books of but a single school, or whether one system and the same class of books should extend to all schools in a township or county, or in the schools of the whole State, is a matter of policy to be considered by the General Assembly in the passage of laws to govern the common schools in this respect. This uniformity in books has always been controlled by legislation, and I think properly so, and it is committed to the General Assembly by the provisions of the Constitution. When once admitted that it is subject to legislative control at all, as it seems to me it must be, then it is exclusively within the province of the General

> Assembly to determine whether there shall be a uniformity of books in a single school or the schools of a township, county or State, and the manner by which the books to be used shall be adopted, and courts can in no way interfere.

2. In his dissenting opinion, Justice Berkshire argues that "local control" means local, not statewide control:

> This case clearly recognizes the right of local self-government in the control and management of the public schools, and agrees with what I have said already as to what is to be understood as a general school system under the Constitution, and is in line with the unbroken practical construction of the people of the State from the organization of the State government. But, I inquire, if the present law can be upheld, why may not the Legislature provide by law that all school-houses which the districts might be called upon to build for the following period of five years, or more, should be let through the State board of education to the lowest and best bidder, and in the same way all chalk for blackboard exercises furnished to the patrons of the schools; and the school trustees required to superintend the building of the school-houses and the distribution of the chalk among the patrons for the benefit of the contractors? This would have the effect to make the school system more general and uniform. But local control of the common schools by the people of the townships is in violation of no provision of the Constitution, but in harmony with the spirit and letter of that instrument.
>
> From the year 1824 to the passage of the act of 1889, the people of the districts and school townships have had unbroken control of their local school affairs, including the adoption and purchase of text-books without any claim by the Legislature that it had the power to deprive them of any of these privileges. In the individual opinion, to which we have referred, it is said: "Continued and uniform exposition, broken by this act for the first time in the whole history of our State, supports the views of the majority of the court upon the question of the right of the citizens of a *political corporation,* such as a county, township or city, to choose their own local officers. The essential and abiding principle of local self-government supports it. The rule that the people, whose property is liable for municipal debts, should choose those to whom they will entrust the management of their local affairs yields it support. The rule that the Constitution recognizes the principle that the people of a locality can govern themselves honestly and intelligently, without the direct guardianship of the persons representing the State at large, gives it support of no uncertain character."
>
> With what force the foregoing language comes to the law in question, whereby the Legislature has assumed to appoint a board of commissioners with power not only to say to the people the particular series of text-books which their children shall carry to school, but from whom they shall purchase them, the price to be paid, and the manner of payment.

3. The argument against national regulation of schools typically includes an argument in favor of the local control of schools. As the opinions in *Haworth* indicate, however, "local control" can mean different things, depending on the context. In light of the *Haworth* and *Lowrey* decisions, does "local control" mean "state" control or community-based, neighborhood control? Is the argument for local control based on federalism, or

is it instead based on each community's right to replicate its own, peculiar teachings to its students within that community, or is it both? Does the power of the state relative to local school districts depend on the theory supporting local control?

4. The arguments supporting local control of education have substantive political roots. Until the 1950s, education was undeniably the province of state and local governments. We have seen that historically the states have been intensely involved with the education of their children. In the mid-1950s, however, the federal government entered the educational arena in the form of judicial, legislative and executive initiatives. These initiatives were sparked by federal concern surrounding segregation, poverty and perceptions regarding a lack of student achievement relative to other countries. *See, e.g.,* S. Bailey & E. Mosher, *ESEA: The Office of Education Administers a Law* (1968). According to Bailey and Mosher, "[t]he historical Balkanization of the American school system into tens of thousands of districts—most of them of patently insufficient size—was unlikely to produce talents and economies of a scale relevant to the educational demands of the postwar years." *Id.* These sentiments led to the congressional enactment of the Elementary and Secondary Education Act of 1965, which nationalized the dialogue and response to the issues of educational funding, particularly for children with educational disabilities and economic disadvantages. The federal focus and philosophy was the provision of equality of opportunity for students.

   Yet, the nationalizing trend quickly waned during the 1980s, when local control reasserted itself under the guise of "federalism" and executive branch efforts to reduce the federal role in educational funding and decision making. *See* Birman & Ginsburg, *The Federal Role in Elementary and Secondary Education, New Directions and Continuing Concerns,* 14 Urban Lawyer 471 (Summer 1982).

   When decentralization of education failed to produce desirable results, however, the movement toward a sweeping, and hence national, reform resurfaced. This time, however, the federal focus shifted from equality of opportunity for children to standardized results and systemic accountability. *See* M. Heise, *Goals 2000: Educate America Act: The Federalization and Legalization of Educational Policy,* 63 Fordham L. Rev. 345 (1994). That shift ultimately produced the No Child Left Behind Act.

5. The NCLB Act appears to leave funding to the state and local governments, while nationalizing the achievement standards that each local district must satisfy. The Act influences local control by requiring each district to meet federally imposed standardized measures of achievement, upon penalty of forfeiting federal funds. The Act, however, leaves to the states and local school districts the responsibility for fully funding the educational opportunities which will help students to achieve these standards.

   In federalizing curriculum and achievement standards while preserving local control over funding, is the NCLB Act consistent with the underlying philosophy of local control? Consider the NCLB Act in light of the following commentary regarding federal efforts to impose nationwide standards:

> Traditionally, state and local governments, particularly local school boards, developed and implemented educational policies. After all, state and local governments bear the constitutional duty to educate their citizens, they provide most of the school funding, and presumably, state and local governments know more than Congress does about the specific needs of the students they serve . . . [Therefore] increased federal activity will not provide any long-term solutions to the pressing problems confronting America's schools. . . .

M. Heise, *Goals 2000: Educate America Act: The Federalization and Legalization of Educational Policy,* 63 Fordham L. Rev. 345, 368-372 (1994).

Heise's suggestion is that so long as funding is a local matter, educational reform at the national level will not be effective. Conversely, if the federal government wishes to impose its educational will on states and local school districts, it will likely have to fund its initiatives fully in order to be successful. Furthermore, recall the dramatic disparities of funding available in the local districts within most states. To impose national standards without removing the disparities in the local funding available to meet those standards is to guarantee that the underfunded districts will "fail" to meet the national standards. If the principle of "local control" were taken seriously, would the federal government inhibit the ability of each locality to both set and attain curricular goals? If that principle were taken seriously, what kind of federal reform initiatives would it engender?

2. The Constitution's Limits on State and Local Control of Education

(a) The Constitution's Limits on Local Control over Curriculum

In *Board of Education, Island Trees Union Free School District No. 26 v. Pico,* 457 U.S. 853 (1982), the Supreme Court addressed the constitutionality of a local school board's decision to remove books from its middle school and high school libraries. Although a majority of the Supreme Court could not agree on a single opinion, five Justices concurred that the school board's decision raised genuine issues of material fact as to whether its removal of the books was based on its disagreement with their political or social content, in violation of the students' first amendment rights to receive information.

Board of Education, Island Trees Union Free School District No. 26 v. Pico

457 U.S. 853 (1982)

Justice Brennan announced the judgment of the Court and delivered an opinion, in which Justice Marshall and Justice Stevens joined, and in which Justice Blackmun joined except for Part II-A-(1).

The principal question presented is whether the First Amendment imposes limitations upon the exercise by a local school board of its discretion to remove library books from high school and junior high school libraries. . . .

In September 1975, petitioners Ahrens, Martin, and Hughes attended a conference sponsored by Parents of New York United (PONYU), a politically conservative organization of parents concerned about education legislation in the State of New York. At the conference these petitioners obtained lists of books described by Ahrens as "objectionable," and by Martin as "improper fare for school students," It was later determined that the High School library contained nine of the listed books, and that another listed book was in the Junior High School library. In February 1976, at a meeting with the Superintendent of Schools and the Principals of the High School and Junior High School, the Board gave an "unofficial direction" that the listed books be removed from the library shelves and delivered to the Board's offices, so that Board members could read them. When this directive was carried out, it became publicized, and the Board issued a press release justifying its action. It characterized the removed books as "anti-American, anti-Christian, anti-[Semitic], and just plain filthy," and concluded that "[it] is our duty, our moral obligation, to protect the children in our schools from this moral danger as surely as from physical and medical dangers." . . .

Respondents reacted to the Board's decision by bringing the present action under 42 U.S.C. §1983 in the United States District Court for the Eastern District of New York. They alleged that petitioners had "ordered the removal of the books from school libraries and proscribed their use in the curriculum because particular passages in the books offended their social, political and moral tastes and not because the books, taken as a whole, were lacking in educational value."

Respondents [students at the school] claimed that the Board's actions denied them their rights under the First Amendment. . . .

II

We emphasize at the outset the limited nature of the substantive question presented by the case before us. Our precedents have long recognized certain constitutional limits upon the power of the State to control even the curriculum and classroom. For example, *Meyer v. Nebraska,* 262 U.S. 390 (1923), struck down a state law that forbade the teaching of modern foreign languages in public and private schools, and *Epperson v. Arkansas,* 393 U.S. 97 (1968), declared unconstitutional a state law that prohibited the teaching of the Darwinian theory of evolution in any state-supported school. But the current action does not require us to re-enter this difficult terrain, which *Meyer* and *Epperson* traversed without apparent misgiving. For as this case is presented to us, it does not involve textbooks, or indeed any books that Island Trees students would be required to read. Respondents do not seek in this Court to impose limitations upon their school Board's discretion to prescribe the curricula of the Island Trees schools. On the contrary, the only books at issue in this case are *library* books, books that by their nature are optional rather than required reading. Our adjudication of the present case thus does not intrude into the classroom, or into the compulsory courses taught there.

Furthermore, even as to library books, the action before us does not involve the *acquisition* of books. Respondents have not sought to compel their school Board to add to the school library shelves any books that students desire to read. Rather, the only action challenged in this case is the *removal* from school libraries of books originally placed there by the school authorities, or without objection from them. . . .

In sum, the issue before us in this case is a narrow one, both substantively and procedurally. It may best be restated as two distinct questions. First, does the First Amendment impose *any* limitations upon the discretion of petitioners to remove library books from the Island Trees High School and Junior High School? Second, if so, do the affidavits and other evidentiary materials before the District Court, construed most favorably to respondents, raise a genuine issue of fact whether petitioners might have exceeded those limitations? If we answer either of these questions in the negative, then we must reverse the judgment of the Court of Appeals and reinstate the District Court's summary judgment for petitioners. If we answer both questions in the affirmative, then we must affirm the judgment below. We examine these questions in turn.

A

(1)

The Court has long recognized that local school boards have broad discretion in the management of school affairs. *See, e.g., Meyer v. Nebraska, supra; Pierce v. Society of Sisters,* 268 U.S. 510, 534 (1925). *Epperson v. Arkansas,* reaffirmed that, by and large, "public education in our Nation is committed to the control of state and local authorities," and that federal courts should not ordinarily "intervene in the resolution of conflicts which arise in the daily operation of school systems." *Tinker v. Des Moines School Dist.,* 393 U.S. 503, 507 (1969), noted that we have "repeatedly emphasized . . . the comprehensive authority of the States and of school officials . . . to prescribe and control conduct in the schools." We have also acknowledged that public schools are vitally important "in the preparation of individuals for participation as citizens," and as vehicles for "inculcating fundamental values necessary to the maintenance of a democratic political system." *Ambach v. Norwick,* 441 U.S. 68, 76-77 (1979). We are therefore in full agreement with petitioners that local school boards must be permitted "to establish and apply their curriculum in such a way as to transmit community values," and that "there is a legitimate and substantial community interest in promoting respect for authority and traditional values be they social, moral, or political."

At the same time, however, we have necessarily recognized that the discretion of the States and local school boards in matters of education must be exercised in a manner that comports with the transcendent imperatives of the First Amendment. In *West Virginia Board of Education v. Barnette,* 319 U.S. 624 (1943), we held that under the First Amendment a student in a public school could not be compelled to salute the flag. We reasoned:

> Boards of Education . . . have, of course, important, delicate, and highly discretionary functions, but none that they may not perform within the limits of

> the Bill of Rights. That they are educating the young for citizenship is reason for scrupulous protection of Constitutional freedoms of the individual, if we are not to strangle the free mind at its source and teach youth to discount important principles of our government as mere platitudes.

Later cases have consistently followed this rationale. Thus *Epperson v. Arkansas* invalidated a State's anti-evolution statute as violative of the Establishment Clause, and reaffirmed the duty of federal courts "to apply the First Amendment's mandate in our educational system where essential to safeguard the fundamental values of freedom of speech and inquiry." And *Tinker v. Des Moines School Dist.,* held that a local school board had infringed the free speech rights of high school and junior high school students by suspending them from school for wearing black armbands in class as a protest against the Government's policy in Vietnam; we stated there that the "comprehensive authority . . . of school officials" must be exercised "consistent with fundamental constitutional safeguards." In sum, students do not "shed their constitutional rights to freedom of speech or expression at the schoolhouse gate," and therefore local school boards must discharge their "important, delicate, and highly discretionary functions" within the limits and constraints of the First Amendment.

The nature of students' First Amendment rights in the context of this case requires further examination. *West Virginia Board of Education v. Barnette, supra,* is instructive. There the Court held that students' liberty of conscience could not be infringed in the name of "national unity" or "patriotism." We explained that "the action of the local authorities in compelling the flag salute and pledge transcends constitutional limitations on their power and invades the sphere of intellect and spirit which it is the purpose of the First Amendment to our Constitution to reserve from all official control."

Similarly, *Tinker v. Des Moines School Dist.,* held that students' rights to freedom of expression of their political views could not be abridged by reliance upon an "undifferentiated fear or apprehension of disturbance" arising from such expression:

"Any departure from absolute regimentation may cause trouble. Any variation from the majority's opinion may inspire fear. Any word spoken, in class, in the lunchroom, or on the campus, that deviates from the views of another person may start an argument or cause a disturbance. But our Constitution says we must take this risk, *Terminiello v. Chicago,* 337 U.S. 1 (1949); and our history says that it is this sort of hazardous freedom—this kind of openness—that is the basis of our national strength and of the independence and vigor of Americans who grow up and live in this . . . often disputatious society."

In short, "First Amendment rights, applied in light of the special characteristics of the school environment, are available to . . . students."

Of course, courts should not "intervene in the resolution of conflicts which arise in the daily operation of school systems" unless "basic constitutional values" are "directly and sharply [implicated]" in those conflicts. *Epperson v. Arkansas,* 393 U.S., at 104. But we think that the First Amendment rights of students may be directly and sharply implicated by the removal of books from the shelves of a school library. Our precedents have focused "not only on the role of the First Amendment in fostering individual self-expression but also on its role in affording the public access to discussion, debate, and the dissemination of information and ideas." *First National Bank of Boston v. Bellotti,* 435 U.S. 765, 783 (1978). And we have recognized that "the State may not, consistently with the spirit of the First Amendment, contract the spectrum of available knowledge." *Griswold v. Connecticut,* 381 U.S. 479, 482 (1965). In keeping with this principle, we have held that in a variety of contexts "the Constitution protects the right to receive information and ideas." *Stanley v. Georgia,* 394 U.S. 557, 564 (1969); *see Kleindienst v. Mandel,* 408 U.S. 753, 762-763 (1972) (citing cases). This right is an inherent corollary of the rights of free speech and press that are explicitly guaranteed by the Constitution, in two senses. First, the right to receive ideas follows ineluctably from the *sender's* First Amendment right to send them: "The right of freedom of speech and press . . . embraces the right to distribute literature, and necessarily protects the right to receive it." *Martin v. Struthers,* 319 U.S. 141, 143 (1943) (citation omitted). "The dissemination of ideas can accomplish nothing if otherwise willing addressees are not free to receive and consider them. It would be a barren marketplace of ideas that had only sellers and no buyers." *Lamont v. Postmaster General,* 381 U.S. 301, 308 (1965) (Brennan, *J.,* concurring).

More importantly, the right to receive ideas is a necessary predicate to the *recipient's* meaningful exercise of his own rights of speech, press, and political freedom. Madison admonished us:

> A popular Government, without popular information, or the means of acquiring it, is but a Prologue to a Farce or a Tragedy; or, perhaps both. Knowledge will forever govern ignorance: And a people who mean to be their own Governors, must arm themselves with the power which knowledge gives. 9 *Writings of James Madison* 103 (G. Hunt ed. 1910).

As we recognized in *Tinker,* students too are beneficiaries of this principle:

> In our system, students may not be regarded as closed-circuit recipients of only that which the State chooses to communicate. . . . [School] officials cannot suppress "expressions of feeling with which they do not wish to contend." 393 U.S., at 511 (quoting *Burnside v. Byars,* 363 F.2d 744, 749 (CA5 1966)).

In sum, just as access to ideas makes it possible for citizens generally to exercise their rights of free speech and press in a meaningful manner, such access prepares students for active and effective participation in the pluralistic, often contentious society in which they will soon be adult members. Of course all First Amendment rights accorded to students must be construed "in light of the special characteristics of the school environment." *Tinker v. Des Moines School Dist.,* 393 U.S., at 506. But the special characteristics of the school *library* make that environment especially appropriate for the recognition of the First Amendment rights of students.

A school library, no less than any other public library, is "a place dedicated to quiet, to knowledge, and to beauty." *Brown v. Louisiana,* 383 U.S. 131, 142 (1966) (opinion of Fortas, J.). *Keyishian v. Board of Regents,* 385 U.S. 589

(1967), observed that "students must always remain free to inquire, to study and to evaluate, to gain new maturity and understanding." The school library is the principal locus of such freedom. As one District Court has well put it, in the school library "a student can literally explore the unknown, and discover areas of interest and thought not covered by the prescribed curriculum. . . . [The] student learns that a library is a place to test or expand upon ideas presented to him, in or out of the classroom." *Right to Read Defense Committee v. School Committee,* 454 F. Supp. 703, 715 (Mass. 1978).

Petitioners emphasize the inculcative function of secondary education, and argue that they must be allowed *unfettered* discretion to "transmit community values" through the Island Trees schools. But that sweeping claim overlooks the unique role of the school library. It appears from the record that use of the Island Trees school libraries is completely voluntary on the part of students. Their selection of books from these libraries is entirely a matter of free choice; the libraries afford them an opportunity at self-education and individual enrichment that is wholly optional. Petitioners might well defend their claim of absolute discretion in matters of *curriculum* by reliance upon their duty to inculcate community values. But we think that petitioners' reliance upon that duty is misplaced where, as here, they attempt to extend their claim of absolute discretion beyond the compulsory environment of the classroom, into the school library and the regime of voluntary inquiry that there holds sway.

(2)

In rejecting petitioners' claim of absolute discretion to remove books from their school libraries, we do not deny that local school boards have a substantial legitimate role to play in the determination of school library content. We thus must turn to the question of the extent to which the First Amendment places limitations upon the discretion of petitioners to remove books from their libraries. In this inquiry we enjoy the guidance of several precedents. *West Virginia Board of Education v. Barnette* stated:

> If there is any fixed star in our constitutional constellation, it is that no official, high or petty, can prescribe what shall be orthodox in politics, nationalism, religion, or other matters of opinion. . . . If there are any circumstances which permit an exception, they do not now occur to us. 319 U.S., at 642.

This doctrine has been reaffirmed in later cases involving education. For example, *Keyishian v. Board of Regents,* noted that "the First Amendment . . . does not tolerate laws that cast a pall of orthodoxy over the classroom"; *see also Epperson v. Arkansas,* 393 U.S., at 104-105. And *Mt. Healthy City Board of Ed. v. Doyle,* 429 U.S. 274 (1977), recognized First Amendment limitations upon the discretion of a local school board to refuse to rehire a nontenured teacher. The school board in *Mt. Healthy* had declined to renew respondent Doyle's employment contract, in part because he had exercised his First Amendment rights. Although Doyle did not have tenure, and thus "could have been discharged for no reason whatever," *Mt. Healthy* held that he could "nonetheless establish a claim to reinstatement if the decision not to rehire him was made by reason of his exercise of constitutionally protected First

Amendment freedoms." We held further that once Doyle had shown "that his conduct was constitutionally protected, and that this conduct was a "substantial factor" . . . in the Board's decision not to rehire him," the school board was obliged to show "by a preponderance of the evidence that it would have reached the same decision as to respondent's reemployment even in the absence of the protected conduct."

With respect to the present case, the message of these precedents is clear. Petitioners rightly possess significant discretion to determine the content of their school libraries. But that discretion may not be exercised in a narrowly partisan or political manner. If a Democratic school board, motivated by party affiliation, ordered the removal of all books written by or in favor of Republicans, few would doubt that the order violated the constitutional rights of the students denied access to those books. The same conclusion would surely apply if an all-white school board, motivated by racial animus, decided to remove all books authored by blacks or advocating racial equality and integration. Our Constitution does not permit the official suppression of *ideas*. Thus whether petitioners' removal of books from their school libraries denied respondents their First Amendment rights depends upon the motivation behind petitioners' actions. If petitioners *intended* by their removal decision to deny respondents access to ideas with which petitioners disagreed, and if this intent was the decisive factor in petitioners' decision, then petitioners have exercised their discretion in violation of the Constitution. To permit such intentions to control official actions would be to encourage the precise sort of officially prescribed orthodoxy unequivocally condemned in *Barnette*. On the other hand, respondents implicitly concede that an unconstitutional motivation would *not* be demonstrated if it were shown that petitioners had decided to remove the books at issue because those books were pervasively vulgar. And again, respondents concede that if it were demonstrated that the removal decision was based solely upon the "educational suitability" of the books in question, then their removal would be "perfectly permissible." In other words, in respondents' view such motivations, if decisive of petitioners' actions, would not carry the danger of an official suppression of ideas, and thus would not violate respondents' First Amendment rights.

As noted earlier, nothing in our decision today affects in any way the discretion of a local school board to choose books to *add* to the libraries of their schools. Because we are concerned in this case with the suppression of ideas, our holding today affects only the discretion to *remove* books. In brief, we hold that local school boards may not remove books from school library shelves simply because they dislike the ideas contained in those books and seek by their removal to "prescribe what shall be orthodox in politics, nationalism, religion, or other matters of opinion." *West Virginia Board of Education v. Barnette,* 319 U.S., at 642. Such purposes stand inescapably condemned by our precedents.

B

We now turn to the remaining question presented by this case: Do the evidentiary materials that were before the District Court, when construed most favorably to respondents, raise a genuine issue of material fact whether petitioners exceeded constitutional limitations in exercising their discretion to remove the books from the school libraries? We conclude that the materials do raise such a question, which forecloses summary judgment in favor of petitioners. . . .

This would be a very different case if the record demonstrated that petitioners had employed established, regular, and facially unbiased procedures for the review of controversial materials. But the actual record in the case before us suggests the exact opposite. Petitioners' removal procedures were vigorously challenged below by respondents, and the evidence on this issue sheds further light on the issue of petitioners' motivations. Respondents alleged that in making their removal decision petitioners ignored "the advice of literary experts," the views of "librarians and teachers within the Island Trees School system," the advice of the Superintendent of Schools, and the guidance of publications that rate books for junior and senior high school students. Respondents also claimed that petitioners' decision was based solely on the fact that the books were named on the PONYU list received by petitioners Ahrens, Martin, and Hughes, and that petitioners "did not undertake an independent review of other books in the [school] libraries." Evidence before the District Court lends support to these claims. The record shows that immediately after petitioners first ordered the books removed from the library shelves, the Superintendent of Schools reminded them that "we already have a policy . . . designed expressly to handle such problems," and recommended that the removal decision be approached through this established channel. But the Board disregarded the Superintendent's advice, and instead resorted to the extraordinary procedure of appointing a Book Review Committee—the advice of which was later rejected without explanation. In sum, respondents' allegations and some of the evidentiary materials presented below do not rule out the possibility that petitioners' removal procedures were highly irregular and ad hoc—the antithesis of those procedures that might tend to allay suspicions regarding petitioners' motivations.

Construing these claims, affidavit statements, and other evidentiary materials in a manner favorable to respondents, we cannot conclude that petitioners were "entitled to a judgment as a matter of law." The evidence plainly does not foreclose the possibility that petitioners' decision to remove the books rested decisively upon disagreement with constitutionally protected ideas in those books, or upon a desire on petitioners' part to impose upon the students of the Island Trees High School and Junior High School a political orthodoxy to which petitioners and their constituents adhered. Of course, some of the evidence before the District Court might lead a finder of fact to accept petitioners' claim that their removal decision was based upon constitutionally valid concerns. But that evidence at most creates a genuine issue of material fact on the critical question of the credibility of petitioners' justifications for their decision: On that issue, it simply cannot be said that there is no genuine issue as to any material fact.

The mandate shall issue forthwith.

Affirmed.

Justice BLACKMUN, concurring in part and concurring in the judgment.

While I agree with much in today's plurality opinion, and while I accept the standard laid down by the plurality to guide proceedings on remand, I write separately because I have a somewhat different perspective on the nature of the First Amendment right involved.

I

To my mind, this case presents a particularly complex problem because it involves two competing principles of constitutional stature. On the one hand, as the dissenting opinions demonstrate, and as we all can agree, the Court has acknowledged the importance of the public schools "in the preparation of individuals for participation as citizens, and in the preservation of the values on which our society rests." Because of the essential socializing function of schools, local education officials may attempt "to promote civic virtues," and to "[awaken] the child to cultural values." *Brown v. Board of Education,* 347 U.S. 483, 493 (1954). Indeed, the Constitution presupposes the existence of an informed citizenry prepared to participate in governmental affairs, and these democratic principles obviously are constitutionally incorporated into the structure of our government. It therefore seems entirely appropriate that the State use "public schools [to] . . . [inculcate] fundamental values necessary to the maintenance of a democratic political system."

On the other hand, as the plurality demonstrates, it is beyond dispute that schools and school boards must operate within the confines of the First Amendment. In a variety of academic settings the Court therefore has acknowledged the force of the principle that schools, like other enterprises operated by the State, may not be run in such a manner as to "prescribe what shall be orthodox in politics, nationalism, religion, or other matters of opinion." While none of these cases define the limits of a school board's authority to choose a curriculum and academic materials, they are based on the general proposition that "state-operated schools may not be enclaves of totalitarianism. . . . In our system, students may not be regarded as closed-circuit recipients of only that which the State chooses to communicate." . . .

In combination with more generally applicable First Amendment rules, most particularly the central proscription of content-based regulations of speech, *see Police Department of Chicago v. Mosley,* 408 U.S. 92 (1972), the cases outlined above yield a general principle: the State may not suppress exposure to ideas—for the sole *purpose* of suppressing exposure to those ideas—absent sufficiently compelling reasons. Because the school board must perform all its functions "within the limits of the Bill of Rights," this principle necessarily applies in at least a limited way to public education. Surely this is true in an extreme case: as the plurality notes, it is difficult to see how a school board, consistent with the First Amendment, could refuse for political reasons to buy books written by Democrats or by Negroes, or books that are "anti-American" in the broadest sense of that term. . . .

In my view, then, the principle involved here is both narrower and more basic than the "right to receive information" identified by the plurality. . . . Instead, I suggest that certain forms of state discrimination *between* ideas are improper. In particular, our precedents command the conclusion that the

State may not act to deny access to an idea simply because state officials disapprove of that idea for partisan or political reasons. . . .

Justice POWELL, dissenting.

The plurality opinion today rejects a basic concept of public school education in our country: that the States and locally elected school boards should have the responsibility for determining the educational policy of the public schools. After today's decision any junior high school student, by instituting a suit against a school board or teacher, may invite a judge to overrule an educational decision by the official body designated by the people to operate the schools.

I

School boards are uniquely local and democratic institutions. Unlike the governing bodies of cities and counties, school boards have only one responsibility: the education of the youth of our country during their most formative and impressionable years. Apart from health, no subject is closer to the hearts of parents than their children's education during those years. For these reasons, the governance of elementary and secondary education traditionally has been placed in the hands of a local board, responsible locally to the parents and citizens of school districts. Through parent-teacher associations (PTA's), and even less formal arrangements that vary with schools, parents are informed and often may influence decisions of the board. Frequently, parents know the teachers and visit classes. It is fair to say that no single agency of government at any level is closer to the people whom it serves than the typical school board.

I therefore view today's decision with genuine dismay. Whatever the final outcome of this suit and suits like it, the resolution of educational policy decisions through litigation, and the exposure of school board members to liability for such decisions, can be expected to corrode the school board's authority and effectiveness. As is evident from the generality of the plurality's "standard" for judicial review, the decision as to the educational worth of a book is a highly subjective one. Judges rarely are as competent as school authorities to make this decision; nor are judges responsive to the parents and people of the school district.

The new constitutional right, announced by the plurality, is described as a "right to receive ideas" in a school. As the dissenting opinions of the Chief Justice and Justice Rehnquist so powerfully demonstrate, however, this newfound right finds no support in the First Amendment precedents of this Court. And even apart from the inappropriateness of judicial oversight of educational policy, the new constitutional right is framed in terms that approach a meaningless generalization. It affords little guidance to courts, if they—as the plurality now authorizes them—are to oversee the inculcation of ideas. The plurality does announce the following standard: A school board's "discretion may not be exercised in a narrowly partisan or political manner." But this is a standardless standard that affords no more than subjective guidance to school boards, their counsel, and to courts that now will be required to decide whether a particular decision was made in a "narrowly partisan or political manner." Even the "chancellor's foot" standard in ancient equity jurisdiction was never this fuzzy.

As Justice Rehnquist tellingly observes, how does one limit—on a principled basis—today's new constitutional right? If a 14-year-old child may challenge a school board's decision to remove a book from the library, upon what theory is a court to prevent a like challenge to a school board's decision not to purchase that identical book? And at the even more "sensitive" level of "receiving ideas," does today's decision entitle student oversight of which courses may be added or removed from the curriculum, or even of what a particular teacher elects to teach or not teach in the classroom? Is not the "right to receive ideas" as much—or indeed even more—implicated in these educational questions?

II

The plurality's reasoning is marked by contradiction. It purports to acknowledge the traditional role of school boards and parents in deciding what should be taught in the schools. It states the truism that the schools are "vitally important in the preparation of individuals for participation as citizens," and as vehicles for "inculcating fundamental values necessary to the maintenance of a democratic political system." Yet when a school board, as in this case, takes its responsibilities seriously and seeks to decide what the fundamental values are that should be imparted, the plurality finds a constitutional violation.

Just this Term the Court held, in an opinion I joined, that the children of illegal aliens must be permitted to attend the public schools. See *Plyler v. Doe.* Quoting from earlier opinions, the Court noted that the "public [school is] a most vital civic institution for the preservation of democratic system of government" and that the public schools are "the primary vehicle for transmitting the values on which our society rests." By denying to illegal aliens the opportunity "to absorb the values and skills upon which our social order rests" the law under review placed a lifelong disability upon these illegal alien children.

Today the plurality drains much of the content from these apt phrases. A school board's attempt to instill in its students the ideas and values on which a democratic system depends is viewed as an impermissible suppression of other ideas and values on which other systems of government and other societies thrive. Books may not be removed because they are indecent; extol violence, intolerance, and racism; or degrade the dignity of the individual. Human history, not the least that of the 20th century, records the power and political life of these very ideas. But they are not our ideas or values. Although I would leave this educational decision to the duly constituted board, I certainly would not *require* a school board to promote ideas and values repugnant to a democratic society or to teach such values to *children.*

In different contexts and in different times, the destruction of written materials has been the symbol of despotism and intolerance. But the removal of nine vulgar or racist books from a high school library by a concerned local school board does not raise this specter. For me, today's decision symbolizes a debilitating encroachment upon the institutions of a free people.

NOTES AND QUESTIONS

1. Justice White joined the Court's affirmance, but only because he believed that the Court of Appeals correctly rejected the district court's summary judgment order in light of the lack of a fully developed factual record. Accordingly, Justice Brennan's opinion on the merits of the constitutional issues presented did not attract a majority of the Court. How would you characterize the Court's holding?
2. The plurality stresses the fact that the action involves a library's materials. Media centers have since become an increasingly vital center of the educational environment. Teachers employed in the media center must decide which books to place on a list of books to be purchased by the school or the school district. Are media centers and their directors entitled to different constitutional protection than classroom teachers?
3. In *Pico,* the books removed from the school libraries included: Kurt Vonnegut, *Slaughterhouse Five;* Desmond Morris, *The Naked Ape;* Pri Thomas, *Down These Mean Streets;* Langston Hughes, ed., *Best Short Stories of Negro Writers;* Anonymous, *Go Ask Alice;* Olive LaFarge, *Laughing Boy;* Richard Wright, *Black Boy;* Alice Childress, *A Hero Ain't Nothin' But a Sandwich;* Eldridge Cleaver, *Soul on Ice,* and Bernard Malamud, *The Fixer. See Pico,* 457 U.S. at 856, n.3.
4. In *Lies My Teacher Told Me* (1995), James W. Loewen dissects virtually every history textbook used across classrooms in America and finds in them an orthodox approach to historic events which is both mind numbing and utterly false. For example, Loewen shows that widely used texts are littered with remarkable distortions about Christopher Columbus, the first Thanksgiving, the "invisibility of racism" in America, the land of "opportunity," big brother, and even historical progress itself. Loewen concludes that these books are worse than propaganda. They deprive American students of the ability to learn from a "true history" and to judge for themselves what will secure or endanger their freedom. *Id.* at 318. What does Loewen's insight suggest about a standardized, national curriculum? What does it suggest about the value in allowing teachers the freedom to teach, apart from the settled orthodoxy of a state-imposed curriculum?

STEIRER V. BETHLEHEM AREA SCHOOL DISTRICT

987F.2d989 (3dCir. 1993)

SLOVITER, Chief Judge.

May a public high school constitutionally require its students to complete sixty hours of community service before graduation? On this issue of first impression for an appellate court, plaintiffs, two high school students and their parents, argue that the mandatory community service program compels expression in violation of the First and Fourteenth Amendments and constitutes involuntary servitude in violation of the Thirteenth Amendment. The district court rejected both challenges.

I. Facts and Procedural History

The facts are not in dispute. On April 30, 1990, the Bethlehem Area School District, by a majority vote of its Board of Directors, adopted a graduation requirement that every public high school student, except those in special education classes, complete a total of sixty hours of community service during the student's four years of high school. These hours may be completed after school hours, on weekends, or during the summer. Students must complete this requirement through participation in a course entitled the "Community Service Program" (the Program), which requires them to "perform sixty (60) hours of unpaid service to organizations or experiential situations approved by the Bethlehem Area School District."

The stated goal of the Program is to "help students acquire life skills and learn about the significance of rendering services to their communities . . . [and] gain a sense of worth and pride as they understand and appreciate the functions of community organizations." The four objectives of the Program are described in the Curriculum Course Guide as:

1. Students will understand their responsibilities as citizens in dealing with community issues.
2. Students will know that their concern about people and events in the community can have positive effects.
3. Students will develop pride in assisting others.
4. Students will provide services to the community without receiving pay.

The Program is jointly administered by the high school principal, the district coordinator, and the school counselor. In addition, parents are "fully informed" of the Program and are expected to encourage their children to successfully complete the sixty hours of service, to encourage them to continue performing community service after completing the course requirements, to assist in identifying appropriate organizations or experiential situations, and to provide transportation to the placement site. . . .

As an alternative to providing service to an approved community service organization, a student may choose to participate in an "experiential situation." This option allows a student to "develop [his or her] own individual community service experience." This alternative experience requires parental approval, the recommendation of the school counselor, and verification by a responsible adult. *Id.* It may involve the arts, community special events, aid to the elderly, the handicapped or the homeless, emergency services, the environment, library/historical research, recreation activities, or tutoring.

After completing the sixty hours of community service, the student must complete a written Experience Summary Form describing and evaluating his or her community service activity. Once the school counselor (i) certifies that the sixty hours of service were completed; and (ii) reviews and approves the student's Experience Summary Form, the student receives half a unit of course credit and a grade of Satisfactory (S). A student who does not satisfactorily complete the Program will not receive a high school diploma.

Barbara and Thomas Steirer and Thomas and Barbara Moralis, individually and as parents and guardians of Lynn Ann Steirer and David Stephen Moralis, respectively, and their two children brought suit in federal district court challenging the constitutionality of the Program and seeking a permanent injunction against its enforcement. . . .

II. Discussion

The Bethlehem Area's mandatory community service program is not unique,[4] but we are aware of no federal appellate court decision addressing the constitutionality of such programs in public schools.[5] We exercise plenary review over a district court's grant of summary judgment. *Wheeler v. Towanda Area School Dist.,* 950 F.2d 128, 129 (3d Cir. 1991). We turn to plaintiffs' challenges to the mandatory nature of the Program.

A. First Amendment

The district court granted summary judgment for defendants on plaintiffs' First Amendment claim on the ground that the community service required by the school district is non-expressive conduct. Plaintiffs contend on appeal that performing mandatory community service is expressive conduct because it forces them to declare a belief in the value of altruism. Proceeding on this premise, plaintiffs argue that heightened scrutiny should be applied and that the school board's reasons for making the program mandatory are not sufficiently compelling to outweigh the infringement of the students' First Amendment right to refrain from expressing such a belief.

The freedom of speech protected by the First Amendment, though not absolute, "includes both the right to speak freely and the right to refrain from speaking at all." *Wooleyv. Maynard,* 430 U.S. 705 (1977). As the Supreme Court has written:

> If there is any fixed star in our constitutional constellation, it is that no official, high or petty, can prescribe what shall be orthodox in politics, nationalism, religion, or other matters of opinion or force citizens to confess by word or act their faith therein.

---

[4] See, e.g., Marc Fisher, *Serving the Community; A Developing Curriculum Requirement,* Wash. Post, Apr. 10, 1988, at R6 (270-hour community service requirement over four years for Banneker High in Washington, D.C.); Roxana Kopetman, *Unusual Graduation Requirement; 100 Seniors Set for Community Service Project,* L.A. Times, Dec. 22, 1988, at 13 (Long Beach Unified School District high school students must dedicate three school days to community service); Lisa Leff, *Maryland Mandates Public Service by Students,* Wash. Post, July 30, 1992, at A1 (75-hour community service requirement for high school graduation adopted in Maryland); *Students on Compulsory Community Service,* Wash. Post, Sept. 5, 1991, at A20 (Georgetown Day High School students have 60-hour community service graduation requirement); Priscilla Van Tassel, *Students Do Community Work in School Hours,* N.Y. Times, Feb. 16, 1992, §12NJ, at 1 (state senator has sponsored bill to impose community service graduation requirement; currently students at Princeton High School can choose between community service and career exploration one day a week for one semester).

[5] Similar, although not identical, issues are raised by mandatory pro bono requirements at state law schools or for the bar. *See* John C. Scully, *Mandatory Pro Bono: An Attack on the Constitution,* 19 Hofstra L. Rev. 1229, 1245 (1991); Michael Millemann, *Mandatory Pro Bono in Civil Cases: A Partial Answer to the Right Question,* 49 Md. L. Rev. 18, 65, 70 (1990).

West Virginia State Bd. of Educ. v. Barnette, 319 U.S. 624 (1943); *see also Wooley,* 430 U.S. at 713 (unconstitutional to "require an individual to participate in the dissemination of an ideological message by displaying it on his private property [automobile license plate] in a manner and for the express purpose that it be observed and read by the public").

To support their position that the required community service is expressive of the school district's ideological viewpoint favoring altruism, plaintiffs point to statements made by individual members of the school board expressing a favorable view of altruism. Plaintiffs argue that the ideology of altruism is a matter of opinion not shared by all, and that "when a student goes out and works for others in his community, it is natural for an observer to assume that the student supports the idea that helping others and serving the community are desirable." Thus, plaintiffs conclude, a student who participates in the community service program is being forced to engage in expressive conduct.

We may assume arguendo that the members of the school board who approved the mandatory community service program believed that there was a value in community service, and that this belief may be equated with what plaintiffs choose to call the philosophy of altruism. It does not follow that requiring students to engage in a limited period of community service as an experiential program that is part of the school curriculum is constitutionally invalid. The gamut of courses in a school's curriculum necessarily reflects the value judgments of those responsible for its development, yet requiring students to study course materials, write papers on the subjects, and take the examinations is not prohibited by the First Amendment.

The Supreme Court has noted that "states and local school boards are generally afforded considerable discretion in operating public schools," *Edwards v. Aguillard,* 482 U.S. 578, 583 (1987), and it has discouraged judicial intervention in the day-to-day operation of public schools. As the Court stated:

> By and large, public education in our Nation is committed to the control of state and local authorities. Courts do not and cannot intervene in the resolution of conflicts which arise in the daily operation of school systems and which do not directly and sharply implicate constitutional values.

Epperson v. Arkansas, 393 U.S. 97, 104 (1968). . . . The mere fact that the course content itself reflects a particular ideology does not necessarily trench upon First Amendment proscriptions.

On the other hand, we do not accept the suggestion made by defendants at oral argument that once the educational purpose of the Program is established, the Program is ipso facto constitutional. Even "teaching values" must conform to constitutional standards. The constitutional line is crossed when, instead of merely teaching, the educators demand that students express agreement with the educators' values. The Supreme Court explained in *Tinker v. Des Moines Indep. Community School Dist.,* 393 U.S. 503 (1969), that in our system, state-operated schools may not be enclaves of totalitarianism. School officials do not possess absolute authority over their students. Students in school as well as out of school are "persons" under our Constitution. They are possessed of fundamental rights which the State must respect, just as they themselves must respect their obligation to the State. In our system, students may not be regarded as closed-circuit recipients of only that which the State chooses to communicate. They may not be confined to the expression of those sentiments that are officially approved.

The Court applied this principle in *Barnette,* where it held that requiring students in public school to salute the flag and recite the Pledge of Allegiance, with punishment of expulsion and possible delinquency proceedings for those who refused, was unconstitutional. The Court noted initially that the protection granted by the First Amendment is not limited to verbal utterances but extends as well to expressive conduct. Thus, because the Court viewed saluting the flag in connection with the recital of the Pledge of Allegiance as a "form of utterance," it held that the required salute as well as the recitation was a "compulsion . . . to declare a belief" that violated the students' freedom of speech. It explained:

> Symbolism is a primitive but effective way of communicating ideas. The use of an emblem or flag to symbolize some system, idea, institution, or personality, is a short cut from mind to mind.

In concluding that a compulsory flag salute and pledge "requires affirmation of a belief and an attitude of mind," the Court stated:

> We think the action of the local authorities in compelling the flag salute and pledge transcends constitutional limitations on their power and invades the sphere of intellect and spirit which it is the purpose of the First Amendment to our Constitution to reserve from all official control.

Thus, the question presented by this appeal is whether the performance of community service as a required school program carries with it the same "affirmation of a belief and an attitude of mind" that is a prerequisite for First Amendment protection. *Barnette,* 319 U.S. at 633. Unlike the act of community service, the activity involved in cases holding compelled conduct to be violative of the First Amendment included an obviously expressive element. . . . Similarly, a state-required contribution by public school teachers to a labor union's activities was deemed expressive conduct, but only to the extent those union activities involved the expression of political views, the support of political candidates or the advancement of other ideological causes. *See Abood v. Detroit Bd. of Educ.,* 431 U.S. 209, 234-36 (1977).

We find additional guidance for resolution of the question before us in the Court's opinion in *Spence v. Washington,* 418 U.S. 405 (1974). The issue in that case was whether displaying the American flag with two peace symbols attached to either side of the flag was expressive conduct. In holding that it was, the Court followed the precedent of *Barnette,* explaining that it had "for decades . . . recognized the communicative connotations of the use of flags." *Spence,* 418 U.S. at 410; *see also Texas v. Johnson,* 491 U.S. 397, 405-06 (1989) (burning American flag in political demonstration is expressive conduct).

The Court explained that conduct is protected by the First Amendment only if it is "sufficiently imbued with elements of communication." *Spence,* 418 U.S. at 409. Specifically, the actor must have "an intent to convey a particularized message . . . and in the surrounding circumstances the likelihood [must be] great that the message would be understood by those who viewed it." *Id.* at 410-11. Thus, in deciding whether conduct is expressive, we must look to the nature of the activity in conjunction with the factual context and environment in which it is undertaken. . . .

However, while acknowledging that the First Amendment protects more than "pure" speech, the Supreme Court has also consistently rejected the view that "an apparently limitless variety of conduct can be labeled 'speech' whenever the person engaging in the conduct intends thereby to express an idea." *See O'Brien,* 391 U.S. at 376. More recently in *City of Dallas v. Stanglin,* 490 U.S. 19 (1989), the Court held that dance-hall patrons coming together to engage in recreational dancing were not engaged in "expressive association" protected by the First Amendment. The Court stated, it is possible to find some kernel of expression in almost every activity a person undertakes—for example, walking down the street or meeting one's friends at a shopping mall—but such a kernel is not sufficient to bring the activity within the protection of the First Amendment. *Id.* at 25.

The boundaries of expressive conduct have been particularly cabined when the conduct is associated with school curricula. For example, we have held that although teachers have a First Amendment right to advocate the use of particular teaching methods outside of the classroom, this right does not "extend to choosing their own curriculum or classroom management techniques in contravention of school policy or dictates." *Bradley v. Pittsburgh Bd. Of Educ.,* 910 F.2d 1172, 1176 (3d Cir. 1990) (no First Amendment right to use "Learnball" in classroom); *see also Kirkland v. Northside Indep. School Dist.,* 890 F.2d 794, 795 (5th Cir. 1989) (teacher's use of a supplemental reading list did not "fall within the rubric of constitutionally protected speech"), cert. denied, 496 U.S. 926 (1990); *Fowler v. Board of Educ.,* 819 F.2d 657, 662-63 (6th Cir.) (opinion of Milburn, J.) (teacher's conduct in showing a film was not expressive or communicative where she had shown the film on a noninstructional day, left the room while the film was being shown, and made no attempt to explain to the students a message that could be derived from the film), cert. denied, 484 U.S. 986 (1987).

Moreover, courts have consistently found that hair and dress codes do not infringe students' First Amendment rights in the absence of any showing that a student's appearance was intended as the symbolic expression of an idea. *See, e.g., Bishop v. Colaw,* 450 F.2d 1069, 1074 (8th Cir. 1971); *see also Karr v. Schmidt,* 460 F.2d 609, 613 (5th Cir.) (expressing doubt "that the wearing of long hair has sufficient communicative content to entitle it to the protection of the First Amendment"), cert. denied, 409 U.S. 989 (1972); *New Rider v. Board of Educ.,* 480 F.2d 693, 698 (10th Cir.) ("wearing of long hair is not akin to pure speech"), cert. denied, 414 U.S. 1097 (1973); *East Hartford Educ. Ass'n v. Board of Educ.,* 562 F.2d 838, 842-44 (2d Cir. 1977) (public school teachers' dress code does not violate First Amendment).

Nonetheless, we do not discount entirely the possibility that a school-imposed requirement of community service could, in some contexts, implicate First Amendment considerations. Arguably, a student who was required to provide community service to an organization whose message conflicted with the student's contrary view could make that claim. Plaintiffs in this case do not make that argument, and the record is to the contrary. The Program does not limit students to providing service to a particular type of community service organization. Students have a multitude of service options which allows them to provide services to organizations with a wide range of political, religious, and moral views. Activities range from playing in a band to walking a dog for the SPCA. The list of approved organizations is extensive and open to additions. Furthermore, students are free to design their own experiential situations.

Thus, plaintiffs do not contend that the students are obliged to adopt an organization's objectionable philosophy. Instead they limit their First Amendment challenge to the argument that students must "affirm the philosophy that serving others and helping the community are what life is all about."

There is no basis in the record to support the argument that the students who participate in the program are obliged to express their belief, either orally or in writing, in the value of community service. Thus, they are not "confined to the expression of those sentiments that are officially approved." *Tinker,* 393 U.S. at 511. To the contrary, as plaintiff Thomas Moralis admitted in his deposition, there is no indication that a student who criticized the Program would not receive a passing grade. Nothing in the record contradicts Moralis' understanding that the students who participate in the Program need not express their agreement with its objectives in order to receiving a passing grade.

Finally, plaintiffs have produced no evidence that people in the community who see these students performing community service are likely to perceive their actions as an intended expression of a particularized message of their belief in the value of community service and altruism. We cannot accept plaintiffs' ipse dixit. It is just as likely that students performing community service under the auspices of a highly publicized required school program will be viewed merely as students completing their high school graduation requirements.

Because we conclude that the act of performing community service in the context of the Bethlehem Area School District high school graduation requirement is not an expressive act that "directly and sharply implicates constitutional values," *Epperson,* 393 U.S. at 104, we think that it is not our role to say that a school system cannot seek to expose its students to community service by requiring them to perform it. To the extent that there is an implicit value judgment underlying the program it is not materially different from that underlying programs that seek to discourage drug use and premature sexual activity, encourage knowledge of civics and abiding in the rule of law, and even encourage exercise and good eating habits. Schools have traditionally undertaken to point students toward values generally shared by the community. In fact, the Supreme Court has stated that public schools have a long history and tradition of teaching values to their students, including those associated with community responsibility. Public schools are important "in the preparation of individuals for participation as citizens, [] in the preservation of the values on which our society rests" and for "inculcating fundamental values necessary to the maintenance of a democratic political system." *Ambach v. Norwick,* 441 U.S. 68, 77 (1979) (upholding a citizenship requirement for public school teachers); *see also Brown v. Board of Educ.,* 347 U.S. 483, 493 (1954) (education is "the very foundation of good citizenship").

Having decided that the Program does not compel expression protected by the First Amendment, it is unnecessary to consider whether the state has a compelling interest in implementing a mandatory community service graduation requirement. Accordingly, we find that the district court properly granted summary judgment for defendants on plaintiffs' claim that the mandatory community service program violates the First and Fourteenth Amendments.

B. Thirteenth Amendment

Plaintiffs' second contention is that a mandatory community service program in a public high school constitutes "involuntary servitude" in violation of the Thirteenth Amendment. . . .

There is no basis in fact or logic which would support analogizing a mandatory community service program in a public high school to slavery. The record amply supports the defendants' claim that the community service program is primarily designed for the students' own benefit and education, notwithstanding some incidental benefit to the recipients of the services. An educational requirement does not become involuntary servitude merely because one of the stated objectives of the Program is that the students will work "without receiving pay."

Accordingly, we hold that the mandatory community service program instituted in the Bethlehem Area School District as a high school graduation requirement does not constitute involuntary servitude prohibited by the Thirteenth Amendment.

NOTES AND QUESTIONS

1. The *Steirer* case involves a student's challenge to the school's community service requirement. The Court relied in part on the cases that limit a *teacher's* rights to freedom of expression. Is there a difference between a *teacher's* freedom to not express a curriculum value, and a student's right not to do so? Suppose a teacher fundamentally abhors the philosophy of community service. Does that teacher have a protected right to abstain from the program?
2. Are there any other constitutional rights or concerns implicated by mandatory community service programs? Suppose a teacher or a student harbored a genuine objection to such programs on religious grounds?
3. Many school districts have implemented highly structured character education programs. One such popular program is called "Character Counts." The program is based on the school-wide and community-wide inculcation of six so-called pillars of character: trustworthiness, respect, responsibility, fairness, caring and citizenship. The program claims that these "pillars" are non-sectarian and, in fact, reflect all religious perspectives. Is there nonetheless a possible constitutional problem in asking a teacher or a student to

express these values? Is that concern based on the freedom of expression or the prohibition on the establishment of religion?

(b) The Constitution's Process Limits on Local Control

HORTONVILLE JOINT SCHOOL DISTRICT NO. 1 v. HORTONVILLE EDUCATION ASS'N

426 U.S. 482 (1976)

We granted certiorari in this case to determine whether School Board members, vested by state law with the power to employ and dismiss teachers, could, consistent with the Due Process Clause of the Fourteenth Amendment, dismiss teachers engaged in a strike prohibited by state law.

I

The petitioners are a Wisconsin school district, the seven members of its School Board, and three administrative employees of the district. Respondents are teachers suing on behalf of all teachers in the district and the Hortonville Education Association (HEA), the collective-bargaining agent for the district's teachers.

During the 1972-1973 school year Hortonville teachers worked under a master collective-bargaining agreement; negotiations were conducted for renewal of the contract, but no agreement was reached for the 1973-1974 school year. The teachers continued to work while negotiations proceeded during the year without reaching agreement. On March 18, 1974, the members of the teachers' union went on strike, in direct violation of Wisconsin law. On March 20, the district superintendent sent all teachers a letter inviting them to return to work; a few did so. On March 23, he sent another letter, asking the 86 teachers still on strike to return, and reminding them that strikes by public employees were illegal; none of these teachers returned to work. After conducting classes with substitute teachers on March 26 and 27, the Board decided to conduct disciplinary hearings for each of the teachers on strike. Individual notices were sent to each teacher setting hearings for April 1, 2, and 3.

On April 1, most of the striking teachers appeared before the Board with counsel. Their attorney indicated that the teachers did not want individual hearings, but preferred to be treated as a group. Although counsel agreed that the teachers were on strike, he raised several procedural objections to the hearings. He also argued that the Board was not sufficiently impartial to exercise discipline over the striking teachers and that the Due Process Clause of the Fourteenth Amendment required an independent, unbiased decision-maker. An offer of proof was tendered to demonstrate that the strike had been provoked by the Board's failure to meet teachers' demands, and respondents' counsel asked to cross-examine Board members individually. The Board rejected the request, but permitted counsel to make the offer of proof, aimed at showing that the Board's contract offers were unsatisfactory, that the Board used coercive and illegal bargaining tactics, and that teachers in the district had been locked out by the Board.

On April 2, the Board voted to terminate the employment of striking teachers, and advised them by letter to that effect. However, the same letter invited all teachers on strike to reapply for teaching positions. One teacher accepted the invitation and returned to work; the Board hired replacements to fill the remaining positions.

Respondents then filed suit against petitioners in state court, alleging, among other things, that the notice and hearing provided them by the Board were inadequate to comply with due process requirements. . . .

II

The Hortonville School District is a common school district under Wisconsin law, financed by local property taxes and state school aid and governed by an elected seven-member School Board. . . . The Board has broad power over "the possession, care, control and management of the property and affairs of the school district." . . . The Board negotiates terms of employment with teachers under the Wisconsin Municipal Employment Relations Act, and contracts with individual teachers on behalf of the district. The Board is the only body vested by statute with the power to employ and dismiss teachers.

The sole issue in this case is whether the Due Process Clause of the Fourteenth Amendment prohibits this School Board from making the decision to dismiss teachers admittedly engaged in a strike and persistently refusing to return to their duties. The Wisconsin Supreme Court held that state law prohibited the strike and that termination of the striking teachers' employment was within the Board's statutory authority. We are, of course, bound to accept the interpretation of Wisconsin law by the highest court of the State. The only decision remaining for the Board therefore involved the exercise of its discretion as to what should be done to carry out the duties the law placed on the Board.

Respondents argue, and the Wisconsin Supreme Court held, that the choice presented for the Board's decision is analogous to that involved in revocation of parole in *Morrissey v. Brewer* that the decision could be made only by an impartial decisionmaker, and that the Board was not impartial. In *Morrissey* the Court considered a challenge to state procedures employed in revoking the parole of state prisoners. There we noted that the parole revocation decision involved two steps: First, an inquiry whether the parolee had in fact violated the conditions of his parole; second, determining whether the violations found were serious enough to justify revocation of parole and the consequent deprivation of the parolee's conditional liberty. With respect to the second step, the Court observed:

> The second question involves the application of expertise by the parole authority in making a prediction as to the ability of the individual to live in society without committing antisocial acts. This part of the decision, too, depends on facts, and therefore it is important for the board to know not only that some violation was committed but also to know accurately how many and how serious the violations were. Yet this second step, deciding what to do about the violation once it is identified, is not purely factual but also predictive and discretionary.

Nothing in this case is analogous to the first step in *Morrissey,* since the teachers admitted to being on strike. But respondents argue that the School Board's decision in this case is, for constitutional purposes, the same as the second aspect of the decision to revoke parole. The Board cannot make a "reasonable" decision on this issue, the Wisconsin Supreme Court held and respondents argue, because its members are biased in some fashion that the due process guarantees of the Fourteenth Amendment prohibit.

Morrissey arose in a materially different context. We recognized there that a parole violation could occur at a place distant from where the parole revocation decision would finally be made; we also recognized the risk of factual error, such as misidentification. To minimize this risk, we held: "[D]ue process requires that after the arrest [for parole violation], the determination that reasonable ground exists for revocation of parole should be made by someone not directly involved in the case." But this holding must be read against our earlier discussion in *Morrissey* of the parole officer's role as counselor for and confidant of the parolee; it is this same officer who, on the basis of preliminary information, decides to arrest the parolee. A school board is not to be equated with the parole officer as an arresting officer; the school board is more like the parole board, for it has ultimate plenary authority to make its decisions derived from the state legislature. General language about due process in a holding concerning revocation of parole is not a reliable basis for dealing with the School Board's power as an employer to dismiss teachers for cause. We must focus more clearly on, first, the nature of the bias respondents attribute to the Board, and, second, the nature of the interests at stake in this case.

B

Respondents' argument rests in part on doctrines that have no application to this case. They seem to argue that the Board members had some personal or official stake in the decision whether the teachers should be dismissed, . . . and that Board has manifested some personal bitterness toward the teachers, aroused by teacher criticism of the Board during the strike. Even assuming that Respondents state the governing standards when the decisionmaker is a public employer dealing with employees, the teachers did not show, and the Wisconsin courts did not find, that the Board members had the kind of personal or financial stake in the decision that might create a conflict of interest, and there is nothing in the record to support charges of personal animosity. The Wisconsin Supreme Court was careful "not to suggest . . . that the board members were anything but dedicated public servants, trying to provide the district with quality education . . . within its limited budget." That court's analysis would seem to be confirmed by the Board's repeated invitations for striking teachers to return to work, the final invitation being contained in the letter that notified them of their discharge.

The only other factor suggested to support the claim of bias is that the School Board was involved in the negotiations that preceded and precipitated the striking teachers' discharge. Participation in those negotiations was a statutory duty of the Board. The Wisconsin Supreme Court held that this involvement, without more, disqualified the Board from deciding whether the teachers should be dismissed:

> The board was the collective bargaining agent for the school district and thus was engaged in the collective bargaining process with the teachers' representative, the HEA. It is not difficult to imagine the frustration on the part of the board members when negotiations broke down, agreement could not be reached and the employees resorted to concerted activity. . . . They were . . . not uninvolved in the events which precipitated decisions they were required to make.

Mere familiarity with the facts of a case gained by an agency in the performance of its statutory role does not, however, disqualify a decisionmaker. Nor is a decisionmaker disqualified simply because he has taken a position, even in public, on a policy issue related to the dispute, in the absence of a showing that he is not "capable of judging a particular controversy fairly on the basis of its own circumstances."

Respondents' claim and the Wisconsin Supreme Court's holding reduce to the argument that the Board was biased because it negotiated with the teachers on behalf of the school district without reaching agreement and learned about the reasons for the strike in the course of negotiating. From those premises the Wisconsin court concluded that the Board lost its statutory power to determine that the strike and persistent refusal to terminate it amounted to conduct serious enough to warrant discharge of the strikers. Wisconsin statutes vest in the Board the power to discharge its employees, a power of every employer, whether it has negotiated with the employees before discharge or not. The Fourteenth Amendment permits a court to strip the Board of the otherwise unremarkable power the Wisconsin Legislature has given it only if the Board's prior involvement in negotiating with the teachers means that it cannot act consistently with due process.

C

Due process, as this Court has repeatedly held, is a term that "negates any concept of inflexible procedures universally applicable to every imaginable situation." *Cafeteria Workers v. McElroy,* 367 U.S. 886, 895 (1961). Determining what process is due in a given setting requires the Court to take into account the individual's stake in the decision at issue as well as the State's interest in a particular procedure for making it. *See Mathews v. Eldridge,* 424 U.S. 319 (1976); *Arnettv. Kennedy,* 416 U.S. 134, 168 (1974) (Powell, J., concurring); *id.,* at 188 (White, J., concurring and dissenting); *Goldberg v. Kelly,* 397 U.S. 254, 263-266 (1970). Our assessment of the interests of the parties in this case leads to the conclusion that this is a very different case from *Morrissey v. Brewer,* and that the Board's prior role as negotiator does not disqualify it to decide that the public interest in maintaining uninterrupted classroom work required that teachers striking in violation of state law be discharged.

The teachers' interest in these proceedings is, of course, self-evident. They wished to avoid termination of their employment, obviously an important interest, but one that must be examined in light of several factors. Since the teachers admitted that they were engaged in a work stoppage, there was no possibility of an erroneous factual determination on this critical threshold issue. Moreover, what the teachers claim as a property right was the expectation that the jobs they had left to go and remain on strike in violation of law would remain open to them. The Wisconsin court accepted at least the essence of that claim in defining the property right under state law, and we do not quarrel with its conclusion. But even if the property interest claimed here is to be compared with the liberty interest at stake in *Morrissey,* we note that both "the risk of an erroneous deprivation" and "the degree of potential deprivation" differ in a qualitative sense and in degree from those in *Morrissey. Mathews v. Eldridge.*

The governmental interests at stake in this case also differ significantly from the interests at stake in *Morrissey.* The Board's decision whether to dismiss striking teachers involves broad considerations, and does not in the main turn on the Board's view of the "seriousness" of the teachers' conduct or the factors they urge mitigated their violation of state law. It was not an adjudicative decision, for the Board had an obligation to make a decision based on its own answer to an important question of policy: What choice among the alternative responses to the teachers' strike will best serve the interests of the school system, the interests of the parents and children who depend on the system, and the interests of the citizens whose taxes support it? The Board's decision was only incidentally a disciplinary decision; it had significant governmental and public policy dimensions as well. *See* Summers, *Public Employee Bargaining: A Political Perspective,* 83 Yale L.J. 1156 (1974).

State law vests the governmental, or policymaking, function exclusively in the School Board and the State has two interests in keeping it there. First, the Board is the body with overall responsibility for the governance of the school district; it must cope with the myriad day-to-day problems of a modern public school system including the severe consequences of a teachers' strike; by virtue of electing them the constituents have declared the Board members qualified to deal with these problems, and they are accountable to the voters for the manner in which they perform. Second, the state legislature has given to the Board the power to employ and dismiss teachers, as a part of the balance it has struck in the area of municipal labor relations; altering those statutory powers as a matter of federal due process clearly changes that balance. Permitting the Board to make the decision at issue here preserves its control over school district affairs, leaves the balance of power in labor relations where the state legislature struck it, and assures that the decision whether to dismiss the teachers will be made by the body responsible for that decision under state law.

III

Respondents have failed to demonstrate that the decision to terminate their employment was infected by the sort of bias that we have held to disqualify other decisionmakers as a matter of federal due process. A showing that the Board was "involved" in the events preceding this decision, in light of the important interest in leaving with the Board the power given by the state legislature, is not enough to overcome the presumption of honesty and integrity in policymakers with decisionmaking power. . . . Accordingly, we hold that the Due Process Clause of the Fourteenth Amendment did not guarantee respondents that the decision to terminate their employment would be made or reviewed by a body other than the School Board.

The judgment of the Wisconsin Supreme Court is reversed, and the case is remanded for further proceedings not inconsistent with this opinion.

Reversed and remanded.

NOTES AND QUESTIONS

1. In *Hortonville,* the Supreme Court initially appears to address the extent of adjudicative power of a local school district. Should the extent of a school district's power vary depending on whether it acts in an adjudicative, legislative, or executive manner?
2. In the *Hortonville* case, the Supreme Court assumes that state law has given to the school district the power to dismiss the striking teachers as part of the district's broad authority over the "possession, care, control and management of the property and affairs of the school district." The only issue is how the board goes about exercising its power. As such, the Court assumes that Wisconsin's legislature has delegated to the school board the power to adjudicate the dispute in this case. That power is analogized to the power of the parole board, rather than the power of the parole officer in *Morrissey*. By that same analogy, who in a school district would occupy the role analogous to the parole officer?
3. Ultimately, the Supreme Court declares that the board did not have to exercise its adjudicative power because there was no dispute about whether the teachers have in fact engaged in prohibited conduct. Would the board's prior role as a negotiator preclude it from impartially adjudicating that issue?
4. The *Hortonville* Court also recognizes the following "important interests" served by the legislature's decision to delegate to a local school board the "governmental, or policy making, function" in this case:

    1. it is administratively efficient to allow a local board to "cope" with the daily problems of school governance;
    2. as elected officials, board members have been deemed by their constituents to be "qualified" to handle the governance of a school district; and
    3. as elected officials, board members are "accountable" to the voters for their performance.

    Notice that the Court does not directly argue that the school board is qualified by its special expertise in the area to govern the school district. The reality is that school board members usually do not have any expertise in the education field. *See* S. Sarason, *Parental Involvement and the Political Principle* (1995). Should that affect the level of deference they are given by the judiciary?
5. The Court presumes that board members have "honesty and integrity" and therefore are capable of making policy decisions in an unbiased manner. The Court's analogy to the parole board also indicates that it believes that the school board's role is different from that of the school's professional administrators and managers. In other words, the Court suggests that school boards are not necessarily aligned with school administrators. Yet

the reality of school governance is that school boards are typically considered by teachers to be, and play the role of, "management." School board members receive virtually all of their information from the district's administrative team, and thus some may tend to act as the agents of the superintendent, rather than as servants of a broader constituency. *See* S. Sarason, *Parental Involvement and the Political Principle* (1995); S. Sarason, *Political Leadership and Educational Failure* (1998); Lutz, *The Politics of School/Community Relations* (1992). The role of school board as employer or manager is particularly evident in its labor relations. Is it likely that a board, which has in fact negotiated vigorously in its role as "management" in labor negotiations, could divorce itself from that role and become an independent policy maker or adjudicator? As attorney for a school district, what methods would you advise the school board to adopt that would help distinguish itself from management and help insure that it had enough detachment from management to be able to review management's recommendations from an independent perspective?

3. The Role of the State Board of Education Relative to Local School Boards

Each state has created a central educational agency or board charged by statute to implement the educational policies of the state. The state board of education typically has the power to administer the state's education system, to advance regulations consistent with the authorizing legislation, to execute the educational laws and regulations and, at times, to adjudicate disputes. *See, e.g., Tyska v. Board of Education,* 117 Ill. App. 3d 917, 73 Ill. Dec. 209, 453 N.E.2d 1344 (1983) (delegation to local educational agency of oversight of public schools is a legislative perogative).

Board of Education of School District No. 1 in the City and County of Denver v. Booth

984 P.2d 639 (Colo. 1999)

Chief Justice Mullarkey delivered the Opinion of the Court.

This case involves a challenge to the constitutionality of the second-appeal provision of the Charter Schools Act. *See* 22-30.5-108(3), 7 C.R.S. (1998). The question is whether the General Assembly constitutionally may authorize the State Board of Education to order a local school board to approve a charter school application that the local board has rejected when the State Board finds approval to be in the best interests of the pupils, school district, or community. We hold that the second-appeal provision is constitutional. . . .

On December 21, 1993, members of the Denver Public Schools (DPS) community submitted an application for the Thurgood Marshall Charter Middle School (Thurgood Marshall School). The charter applicants proposed implementing a core DPS curriculum in a nontraditional manner. The application describes a school that operates on a "limited resource model." Four or five teachers are assigned to "teams" of approximately seventy-two students. Students learn in integrated "blocks" according to their learning needs. In addition, small class sizes would permit students with a range of backgrounds and abilities to learn together. This structure anticipates addressing both special education and gifted and talented learning needs within the regular classroom rather than through separate programs.

The DPS improvement and accountability council, evaluating conceptual merit, ranked Thurgood Marshall School second among the charter applications submitted in 1993. Nevertheless, on February 17, 1994, the Denver Board denied Thurgood Marshall School's application. The Denver Board's concerns included the lack of an appropriate site for the school, inadequacies in the budget, "excessive per pupil funding requests," and inconsistencies in the proposed teacher grievance procedure.

The charter applicants appealed the Denver Board's decision to the State Board pursuant to Section 22-30.5-108(1). On April 6, 1994, the State Board reversed the Denver Board's decision and remanded for reconsideration. The remand included instructions for the parties to reevaluate and negotiate several issues related primarily to the proposed school's site and its financial relationship with the district.

After the first State Board appeal, the charter applicants worked primarily to address the issue of site. DPS informed them that, among other possibilities, Slavens Elementary School (Slavens) might become available. At the time, Slavens housed administrative offices.

In their application submitted for reconsideration, the charter applicants proposed using Slavens. On May 19, the Denver Board issued a resolution recognizing "the community support of and interest in the education philosophy" of the proposed school, but denying the application for the 1994-95 school year because the Denver Board's initial concerns had not been resolved. The Denver Board encouraged the charter applicants to reapply for the following school year.

The charter applicants filed a second appeal with the State Board. *See* 22-30.5-108(3)(c). On July 18, 1994, the State Board found the Denver Board's decision to be contrary to the best interests of the pupils, school district, or local community; ordered approval of the Thurgood Marshall School charter application; and directed the parties "to submit a status report outlining their progress with respect to budget, site, enrollment, and employment on or before December 1, 1994." . . .

III. Article IX: Education

The Denver Board's first constitutional challenge requires us to consider the interplay between the second-appeal provision . . . of the Charter Schools Act and two Sections of Article IX of the Colorado Constitution. Article IX, Section 1 vests "general supervision" of public schools in the State Board. The Education Article also requires the General Assembly to organize school districts "of convenient size," whose local boards "shall have control of instruction." Colo. Const. Art. IX, 15. The central issue is whether the second-appeal provision is a legitimate means of attaining the General Assembly's goals in light of Article IX, Sections 1 and 15.

The Denver Board asserts that any State Board decision ordering a local board to approve a specific charter application exceeds the state's general supervisory power and impermissibly encroaches on a local board's control of instruction, including its educational resources. The charter applicants contend that the State Board's authority . . . is consistent with its general supervisory powers. They assert that the General Assembly's plenary power to create, abolish, and define the territory of school districts implies the power to modify or withdraw the local district's powers "as it pleases."

Neither of these sweeping categorical arguments is persuasive because each fails to recognize or reconcile the potential for competing responsibilities created by the constitution. First, the Denver Board's argument, taken literally, would render the General Assembly powerless to regulate public education in a manner consistent with its constitutional obligations. The General Assembly is charged with "providing for the establishment and maintenance of a thorough and uniform system of free public schools throughout the state." Colo. Const. Art. IX, 2. Any meaningful regulation in furtherance of this responsibility, whether it involves curriculum, facilities, programs, management, services, or employment, will inevitably influence the allocation of resources. Yet the Denver Board suggests that any impact violates its control of instruction. We will not seriously entertain the notion that the General Assembly's constitutional responsibility for public education can be carried out only to the extent that its regulations have no discernible effect on local resources.

Similarly, with respect to the charter applicants, we cannot read Article IX, Section 1 as broadly and Article IX, Section 15 as narrowly as they suggest. It is beyond dispute that local governments assume a central role in administering public education. The United States Supreme Court has consistently emphasized principles of local control, separate and distinct from issues of federalism, in the context of public schools. *See San Antonio Indep. Sch. Dist. v. Rodriguez,* 411 U.S. 1, 42 (1973) (noting that local control permits tailoring of educational programs to local needs); *Wright v. Council of the City of Emporia,* 407 U.S. 451, 469 (1972) (recognizing that "direct control over decisions vitally affecting the education of one's children is a need that is strongly felt in our society"); *Wright,* 407 U.S. at 478 (Burger, C.J. dissenting) (arguing that "local control is not only vital to continued public support of the schools, but it is of overriding importance from an educational standpoint as well"); *see also Brown v. Board of Educ.,* 347 U.S. 483, 493 (1954) (recognizing public education as "perhaps the most important function" of local as well as state governments).

The framers' inclusion of Article IX, Section 15 makes Colorado one of only six states with an express constitutional provision for local governance, underscoring the importance of the concept to our state. As a result, this court has consistently emphasized principles of local control. *See, e.g., Lujan v. Colorado State Bd. of Educ.,* 649 P.2d 1005, 1021 (Colo. 1982) ("The historical development of public education in Colorado has been centered on the philosophy of local control.").

As long as a school district exists, the local board has undeniable constitutional authority. However, just as even core constitutional rights are not absolute, this constitutional authority is subject to limits. The contours of constitutional rights are typically determined by balancing competing interests. This is true particularly, as here, in the context of administrative agencies. In this case, the constitution requires balancing the local board's interest in exercising control over instruction with the State Board's interest in asserting its general supervisory authority. It is a balance that first must be struck by the legislature and, if challenged, reviewed by the courts.

A. Article IX, Section 1: General Supervision

The first clause of the Education Article of the Colorado Constitution reads: "The general supervision of the public schools of the state shall be vested in a board of education whose powers and duties shall be as now or hereafter prescribed by law." Colo. Const. Art. IX, 1(1). The meaning of the phrase "general supervision" is central to this dispute. Yet we have never been called previously to define it, either independently or in relation to a local board's control of instruction. We do so now, using the common meaning of the language as a foundation for implementing "the intent of the [constitution's] adopters." . . .

We conclude that, pursuant to Article IX, Section 1(1), the constitutional framers contemplated general supervision to include direction, inspection, and critical evaluation of Colorado's public education system from a statewide perspective, that they intended the State Board to serve as both a conduit of and a source for educational information and policy, and that they intended the General Assembly to have broad but not unlimited authority to delegate to the State Board "powers and duties" consistent with this intent. Colo. Const. Art. IX, 1(1).

In addition to relying on contemporaneous legislative definitions of "general supervision," we also gain insight from the powers assigned originally to the State Board. Of the new State Board's few designated responsibilities, one is particularly relevant here. In 1877, the legislature established a procedure by which "any person aggrieved by any decision or order" of a local school board could appeal that decision first to the county superintendent and then to the State Board. Colo. G.L. 2533, 81. The law provided that the State Board's decision "shall be final." Colo. G.L. 2533, 87.

This statutory assignment of authority to the State Board in 1877 is analogous to the role given the State Board in the second-appeal provision now before us. Our research has not revealed any cases interpreting the effect of the 1877 act's delegation of final decision-making authority to the State Board. Nevertheless, because this delegation was contemporaneous with the constitutional framers' creation of the State Board in 1876, it is suggestive of the framers' intent regarding the permissible scope of the State Board's powers and duties, and it provides legislative precedent for the Charter Schools Act's designation of the State Board as final arbiter of disputes involving local boards.

B. Article IX, Section 15: Control of Instruction

Having considered the contours of the State Board's constitutional authority, we now turn to the role of local boards. A local board of education has one primary source of constitutional authority: The general assembly shall, by law, provide for organization of school districts of convenient size, in each of which shall be established a board of education, to consist of three or more directors to be elected by the qualified electors of the district. Said directors shall have control of instruction in the public schools of their respective districts. Colo. Const. Art. IX, 15. As with "general supervision," we look initially to the common meaning of "control" and "instruction." "Control" means "power or authority to guide or manage." *Webster's* 496. "Instruction" is generally defined as "the action, practice, or profession of one that instructs," and "the quality or state of being instructed." *Id.* at 1172. Thus, control of instruction requires power or authority to guide and manage both the action and practice of instruction as well as the quality and state of instruction.

In contrast with the lack of prior case law interpreting the State Board's general supervision, we have made numerous decisions that required us to consider the extent of a local board's control in specific circumstances. In one early line of cases, we determined that the General Assembly cannot require money raised in one district to be expended for instruction in another district without the first district's consent. . . . Thus, control of instruction requires substantial discretion regarding the character of instruction that students will receive at the district's expense.

More recently, we have encountered control of instruction concerns in a line of cases involving administrative review of teacher employment decisions. *See, e.g., Blaine v. Moffat County Sch. Dist. Re No. 1,* 748 P.2d 1280, 1286 (Colo. 1988) (noting the local school board's "constitutional responsibility for the educational program in the public schools of the district"). The Denver Board relies on language in these cases emphasizing local control. The charter applicants, on the other hand, point to the relevant statutes in these decisions as illustrating analogous permissible checks on local board authority.

The points made by both sides are well taken. Our decisions interpreting the Teacher Employment, Compensation, and Dismissal Act, *see* 22-63-101 to -403, 7 C.R.S. (1998) (Teacher Tenure Act), have consistently upheld statutory schemes that limit local board authority, but they have also reflected an acute awareness that legislation must not usurp a local board's decision-making authority.

For example, we have clearly stated that ultimate findings of fact are within a local board's domain because it must retain "the power to determine what facts constitute the statutory grounds for dismissal." *Blair v. Lovett,* 196 Colo. 118, 125, 582 P.2d 668, 673 (1978). Similarly, we have emphasized that the General Assembly must reserve to local boards "the necessary latitude to determine whether . . . the teacher's conduct on the occasion in question was sufficiently serious or aggravated to warrant an ultimate finding of insubordination and the serious sanction of dismissal." *Ware v. Morgan County Sch. Dist. No. Re-3,* 748 P.2d 1295, 1300 (Colo. 1988) (citation omitted); *see also* Blaine, 748 P.2d at 1286 (finding that one purpose of the Teacher Tenure Act is to provide a school board with "the necessary means to carry out its constitutional responsibility for the education program in the public schools of the district").

In *Adams County School Dist. No. 50 v. Heimer,* 919 P.2d 786 (Colo. 1996), we construed the scope of the court of appeals' review narrowly in teacher tenure cases to avoid "usurping the role of the board, either by elevating the hearing officer's recommendation to an equal plane with the board decision or by requiring the court of appeals to decline to give deference to the board decision." . . .

From these decisions, we derive several guiding principles. First, a local board's resolution of individual cases such as teacher employment decisions inherently implicates its ability to control instruction. Second, as a corollary, generally applicable law triggers control of instruction concerns when applied to specific local board decisions likely to implicate important education policy. Third, local board discretion can be restricted or limited in such circumstances by statutory criteria and/or judicial review. Fourth, such general statutory or judicial constraints, if they exist, must not have the effect of usurping the local board's decision-making authority or its ability to implement, guide, or manage the educational programs for which it is ultimately responsible.

For circumstances in which the State Board and local boards have potentially conflicting authority, the reviewing court must strike a balance between local control of instruction and the State Board's general supervision. That balance will rarely be rigid. Indeed, it cannot be. Both local boards and the State Board exist to promote and serve the educational welfare of public school students in this state and, more broadly, to serve the state's democratic interest in a well-educated population. Inevitably, there will be instances in which the efforts of the two entities to fulfill their respective obligations will coincide or overlap. Occasionally, this overlap may generate conflict. As is evident from the fact that we have never previously been called to interpret "general supervision," these occasions are rare and their particular circumstances may be unforeseeable. Therefore, in the context of novel education reform legislation, we cannot attempt a definitive constitutional demarcation. Instead, taking the general principles identified above, we must review each case on its facts. Given this understanding, we turn to the statute whose language and operation are specifically before us.

IV. Second-Appeal Provision

The General Assembly has the constitutional authority and obligation to "provide for the establishment and maintenance of a thorough and uniform system of free public schools." Colo. Const. Art. IX, 2. Pursuant to the Charter Schools Act, the General Assembly's effort to improve the quality of public education includes a specific allocation of authority between the State Board and local boards. The issue is whether this allocation maintains a constitutionally permissible balance between the two entities.

To begin, we consider the Act's purpose. . . . The General Assembly intended the Charter Schools Act to create opportunities for innovation, autonomy, and reform in public schools. The declared legislative purposes include "encouraging diverse approaches to learning and education, and the use of different, proven, or innovative teaching methods," "the development of different and innovative forms of measuring pupil learning and achievement," and "providing parents and children with expanded choices in the types of education opportunities that are available within the public school system." The Act provides opportunities for individuals to organize public schools with independently designed curricula, program, and management structures that operate with substantial autonomy. . . .

None of the parties disputes the validity of the statutory purpose, and we likewise recognize that the goals are undoubtedly legitimate. . . . The Denver Board's contention is that the General Assembly has implemented the policy in a manner that infringes unconstitutionally on a local board's control of instruction.

In a case such as this, where the General Assembly has allocated authority between the State Board and local boards in order to further a legitimate educational purpose, we will give deference to the balance that it sought to maintain between the two entities. That is, we will presume the allocation is valid unless it clearly impedes the capacity of either the State Board or a local board to exercise its independent constitutional authority.

With this principle in mind, we consider the State Board's role on a second appeal: the scope of its review, the extent of its authority to issue orders, and the effect of an order instructing a local board to approve a charter application. The Denver Board has the burden of proving the statute unconstitutional beyond a reasonable doubt. *See Winslow Constr. Co. v. City & County of Denver*, 960 P.2d 685, 692 (Colo. 1998).

A. Scope of the "Best Interests" Review

The Denver Board argues that the "best interests" standard permits the State Board to make substantive determinations regarding a school's educational program that invade a local board's constitutional control of instruction. The charter applicants contend vigorously that the second-appeal provision is consistent with the State Board's supervisory authority, but they do so without addressing the scope of the State Board's review under Section 22-30.5-108(3)(d). . . .

We agree with the Denver Board that the second-appeal provision in Section 108(3)(d) plainly requires the State Board to substitute its judgment for that of the local board. . . . Although the General Assembly has not previously used the "best interests" standard in the education context, the fact that statutory language is new or has not been used in a particular context before does not make it ambiguous. . . . Rather, we must adhere to the presumption that "the words express the intent of the legislature."

The second-appeal provision authorizes the State Board to order a charter application's approval if it finds the local board's decision denying the application to be "contrary to the best interests of the pupils, school district, or community." The phrase "pupils, school district, [and] community" aptly identifies the groups to whom a local school board is directly accountable. It is precisely these constituents to whom a local board answers when making educational policy decisions. That is, the local board was elected to approve or deny charter applications according to the best interests of its pupils, school district, and community. Under Section 108(3)(d), the General Assembly has charged the State Board with deciding whether or not a local board made the correct decision.

Related statutes applying the same standard confirm our understanding of the plain meaning. In other contexts, the General Assembly has provided for decisions to be made in the "best interests" of children. . . . Decisions regarding the best interests of children are typically made in a court of law, are substantive, and require no deference to a prior decision maker. In addition, when the General Assembly has sought to constrain discretion, it has done so by providing specific criteria that must guide a particular decision. The General Assembly has required no such adherence to statutory criteria for the State Board's review of a local board's charter application decisions.

We conclude that the "best interests" language is not reasonably susceptible to different meanings. Therefore, for purposes of our constitutional analysis, we hold that the State Board is authorized to substitute its judgment for that of a local board.

B. Scope of State Board Instructions

Next we consider the State Board's statutory authority once it determines, on a second appeal, that the local board's decision was contrary to the best interests of the pupils, school district, or community. . . . We hold that when the State Board reverses a local board decision, the plain language of Section 108(3)(d) authorizes the State Board only to require approval of the charter application as submitted. As the court of appeals observed, the entire application process indicates legislative intent for efficiency and decisiveness. . . . The General Assembly clearly defined the State Board's role: If the State Board finds the local board's decision to be "contrary to the best interests . . . it shall remand such final decision . . . with instructions to approve the charter application." 22-30.5-108(3)(d). It does not authorize other action. . . .

C. Effect of Charter Approval

The Denver Board asserts that an approved charter entitles the applicants to implement every element of the application regardless of concerns expressed by a local board. It argues that this result conflicts with a local board's constitutional control of instruction as well as its statutory authority "to determine which schools of the district shall be operated and maintained."

If the Denver Board's interpretation of the statute is correct, the Thurgood Marshall School could open against the Denver Board's wishes and would be entitled to use the Slavens Elementary site. In addition to its broader legal challenges, the Denver Board has a specific concern that this site is unavailable because it is currently used for administrative purposes.

The charter applicants contend that the approved application serves as a blueprint for the school rather than as a binding contract. They suggest that the General Assembly intended the elements of a charter to be non-binding and negotiable between charter applicants and local boards even after approval. In effect, they assert that an approved charter provides the charter applicants with no guarantee that they will be able to open a charter school. . . .

The possibility that a complete application could leave site and funding issues unresolved indicates that the General Assembly did not intend an approved application to serve as a binding contract. Rather, an application's approval was intended to be an interim step toward creation of that contract.

In other words, we hold that the State Board's order instructing a local board to approve a charter application requires the charter applicants and the local board to resolve any issues necessary to permit the applicants to open a charter school. Therefore, when the State Board orders a local board to approve a charter application it is not requiring the local board to open a school. Rather, the State Board's action is consistent with its general supervisory authority requiring knowledge and dissemination of desirable improvements for the public education system. Expressing its judgment that a proposed school would serve the interests of an education community represents a valid means of disseminating its knowledge and stimulating desirable improvement. It is also consistent with the State Board's historic role as final arbiter of disputes involving local boards. . . .

This understanding of a State Board order to approve a charter application avoids constitutional infirmity. A local board has two opportunities to deny a charter and, in doing so, must state its reasons for the denial. Denial of an application implicates a local board's control of instruction because it applies general education policy to the guidance and management of instruction in an individual case: the decision whether to open a particular school. The local board's concerns, reflected in its reasons for denying the application, do not lose their validity simply because the State Board finds that approval of the application, taken as a whole, is in the best interests of the education community. Rather, a local board can comply with a State Board order to approve a charter application and still expect resolution of its initial grounds for denial in a satisfactory final agreement with the charter school applicants. At the same time, the holders of an approved application have a reasonable expectation that the problems identified by the local board in its statement of grounds for denial can be resolved, an agreement on a final contract can be reached, and a charter school will open.

D. The Thurgood Marshall School Application

When the Denver Board reviewed the formal application, both initially and on reconsideration, it expressed no reservations regarding the potential benefits of a limited resource model. It explicitly recognized "the community support of and interest in the education philosophy." The Denver Board denied the application primarily because of concerns about the applicants' ability to implement the program effectively.

Two of the Denver Board's concerns went to site and per pupil funding. We have recognized already that these issues are critical to a complete plan for a school. We also have noted that the Charter Schools Act does not require these issues to be resolved as part of a charter application. Nevertheless, the charter proponents included specific site and per pupil funding requests in their application. Their inclusion, and the fact that the Denver Board found both of them to generate substantial resource concerns, identifies them as problems remaining to be resolved.

In the course of this process the Denver Board has expressed other concerns that merit note here. For example, the Denver Board found that, apart from the per-pupil funding figure, the Thurgood Marshall School's proposed budget was inadequate because it relied on access to DPS equipment, such as computers, that was not available for the school's use. The charter proponents offered no evidence or arguments to contradict these conclusions.

In addition, the Denver Board expressed concern regarding the charter proponents' teacher grievance procedure. The proposed procedure included resolution of disputes by a principal, but the school's administrative structure does not include a principal. The charter proponents did not account for this discrepancy.

Compliance with the State Board's order instructing the Denver Board to approve the charter application does not invalidate these concerns. Instead, the order creates a good faith commitment on the part of the local board to work with the charter applicants toward resolving any remaining concerns and producing a satisfactory final contract that would permit the applicants to open the Thurgood Marshall School.

In conclusion, we hold that the State Board did not infringe unconstitutionally on the Denver Board's control of instruction when it ordered approval of the charter application. Furthermore, we disagree with the court of appeals' judgment that the State Board's decision on second appeal requires reconsideration. The primary effect of the State Board's order is consistent with our holding today. The order to approve the charter application implicitly recognized that approval would not constitute a final contract and that the parties would be required to work together in good faith to resolve the Denver Board's remaining concerns. The State Board's request for status reports exceeded its statutory authority, but this ultra vires act does not affect the substance of its decision. Therefore, on remand, the State Board need not reconsider its decision. Rather, it can modify its order to comply with the limits of its authority as defined in this opinion.

V. Textbook Prescription

The Denver Board's second constitutional challenge relates to textbook selection. The constitution specifically excludes textbook selection from the State Board's supervisory powers: "Neither the general assembly nor the state board of education shall have power to prescribe textbooks to be used in the public schools." Colo. Const. Art. IX, 16.

The Denver Board argues that a State Board order to approve a charter application has the effect of prescribing whatever textbooks the charter application proposes to use. The Denver Board asserts that such a prescription is a facial violation of Article IX, Section 16. The charter applicants respond that the Denver Board's challenge presents only hypothetical conflicts, does not amount to a facial challenge, and does not undermine the statute's application in this case. . . .

Under the Charter Schools Act, the State Board's statutory review of a local board decision is limited to those grounds for denial specified by the local board. *See* 22-30.5-108(2). In this case, the charter applicants' proposed choice of textbooks was not relevant either to the Denver Board's grounds for denial or to the State Board's reversal of that denial. In fact, the Denver Board could not have raised a plausible objection to the charter applicants' textbook selection because the charter applicants proposed to use the same textbooks used by other middle schools in the DPS system. Therefore, the State Board's review of the Denver Board's denial cannot be construed to implicate Article IX, Section 16 of the Colorado Constitution in this case. . . .

VI. Conclusion

We . . . conclude that the second-appeal provision strikes an appropriate balance between the respective constitutional powers of the State Board and local boards. In other words, it does not infringe unconstitutionally on a local board's control of instruction. We agree with the court of appeals' interpretation of the State Board's authority on a second appeal and its ruling that the State Board exceeded its authority in this case. However, on remand from the district court, the State Board is not required to reconsider its decision; it need only modify its order to comply with the limits of its authority as defined here.

NOTES AND QUESTIONS

1. How does Colorado allocate power and responsibility between state and local governments? What principles of local control guide the Colorado Supreme Court's decision? Colorado apparently leaves the issue of textbook selection to local school districts, but allows the state to control instructional practices. What justifies that distinction?
2. Consider the nature of the instructional practices in the proposed charter school. The practices include integrated, block sessions that envision small, inclusive classes of students with diverse learning styles. Do these practices have educational validity? Do you think the character of the proposed charter school influenced the court's decision? Will the instructional practices of the proposed school influence its choice of textbooks or other instructional materials?
3. The Colorado Supreme Court declines to reach the Denver Board's argument that the legislative scheme would improperly allow the State Board to grant a charter to a school, even after the local board denied that charter based on the proposed school's choice of textbooks. The court calls that argument "hypothetical." How would the court have resolved that issue if it had reached the question?
4. The New York Court of Appeals in *Older v. Board of Education of Union Free School District No. 1, Mamaroneck,* 27 N.Y.2d 333, 266 N.E.2d 812, 318 N.Y.S.2d 129 (1971), provides a classic judicial statement about the extraordinary reach of local school district power over "all" aspects of the management and control of the educational affairs of the district, including the creation of student attendance zones and the assignment and transfer of students within those zones.
5. School districts and their governing boards, however, are created by state statutes, and their authority therefore is limited to the powers expressly or impliedly delegated to them by statute. *See, e.g., McGilvra v. Seattle School District No. 1,* 113 Wash. 619, 194 P. 817 (Wash. 1921) (enjoining school district from utilizing its facilities for health care purposes); *Board of*

Education of Bath County v. Goodpaster, 260 Ky. 198, 84 S.W.2d 55 (1935) (legislation delegating power to school board necessarily delegates administrative rather than law-making power); *Tax Deferred Annuities Corp. v. Cleveland Board of Education,* 24 Ohio App. 3d 105, 493 N.E.2d 305 (1985) (boards of education are creatures of statute with power limited to that granted by statute).

6. ***School District Governance, Counseling, Policy Drafting and Litigation Practicum.*** In a highly publicized incident involving high school students who injured other students during a violent "hazing" exercise at Glenbrook North High School in Illinois, the school district initially took the position that it had no jurisdiction to punish the students because the conduct did not occur on school property or at a school-sponsored event. The district later changed its position, however, claiming authority to punish students under its policy prohibiting "secret societies." Assuming that the district's policy does in fact prohibit the students' conduct, is that policy subject to challenge for its broad reach into nonschool conduct? If you were asked to represent one of the students facing discipline, what arguments would you make about the limits of school district authority?

As you read the following typical school district policy establishing prohibited conduct and district power to sanction that conduct, consider the source of the power asserted by the district and its legitimacy.

Prohibited Student Conduct

Disciplinary action may be taken against any student guilty of gross disobedience or misconduct, including, but not limited to, the following:

1. Using, possessing, distributing, purchasing, or selling tobacco materials.
2. Using, possessing, distributing, purchasing, or selling alcoholic beverages. Students who are under the influence are not permitted to attend school or school functions and are treated as though they had alcohol in their possession.
3. Using, possessing, distributing, purchasing, or selling illegal drugs or controlled substances, look-alike drugs or drug paraphernalia. A "look-alike" drug is defined as a substance not containing an illegal drug or controlled substance, but one (a) that a student believes to be, or represents to be, an illegal drug or controlled substance or would lead a reasonable person to believe that the substance is a controlled substance, or (b) about which a student engaged in behavior that would lead a reasonable person to believe that the student expressly or impliedly represented to be an illegal drug or controlled substance. Students who are under the influence of any prohibited substance or drug or knowingly in possession of any drug paraphernalia are not permitted to attend school or school functions and are treated as though they had drugs or paraphernalia, as applicable, in their possession.
4. Using, possessing, controlling, or transferring a weapon in violation of the "weapons" section of this policy.
5. Using or possessing electronic signaling and cellular radio-telecommunication devices unless authorized and approved by the Building Principal. Electronic signaling devices include pocket—and

all similar — electronic paging devices. Exceptions may be granted by the Building Principal at his or her discretion, upon parental request in circumstances of emergency or demonstrated necessity.

6. Using or possessing a laser pointer unless under a staff member's supervision and in the context of instruction.
7. Disobeying directives from staff members or school officials and/or rules and regulations governing student conduct.
8. Using any form or type of aggressive behavior including, but not limited to, the use of violence, force, noise, coercion, threats, intimidation, fear, bullying, or other comparable conduct.
9. Causing or attempting to cause damage to, or stealing or attempting to steal, school property or another person's personal property.
10. Unexcused absenteeism.
11. Being a member of or joining or promising to join, or becoming pledged to become a member of, soliciting any other person to join, promise to join, or be pledged to become a member of any public school fraternity, sorority or secret society.
12. Involvement in gangs or gang-related activities, including the display of gang symbols or paraphernalia.
13. Engaging in any activity that constitutes an interference with school purposes or an educational function or any disruptive activity.

For purposes of this policy, the term "possession" includes having control, custody, or care, currently or in the past, of an object or substance, regardless of whether or not the item is (a) on the student's person, or (b) contained in another item belonging to, or under the control of the student, such as in the student's clothing, backpack, automobile, or (c) in a school's student locker, desk, or other school property, or (d) in any other location on school property or at a school-sponsored event.

These grounds for disciplinary action apply whenever the student's conduct is reasonably related to school or school activities, including, but not limited to:

1. On, or within sight of, school grounds before, during, or after school hours or at any other time when the school is being used by a school group;
2. Off school grounds at a school-sponsored activity, or event, or any activity or event which bears a reasonable relationship to school;
3. Traveling to or from school or a school activity, function or event; or
4. Anywhere, if the conduct may reasonably be considered to be a threat or an attempted intimidation of a staff member, or an interference with school purposes or an educational function.

Disciplinary Measures
Disciplinary measures include:

1. Disciplinary conference.
2. Withholding of privileges.
3. Seizure of illegal materials.
4. Suspension from school and all school activities for up to 10 days, provided that appropriate procedures are followed. A suspended student is prohibited from being on school grounds.

In light of this policy, could the district discipline a student who engages in bullying behavior during an intramural basketball game between the school's intramural team and a neighboring school's team that takes place on Saturday at the neighboring school's gym? What arguments would you make on behalf of the student facing the possibility of school discipline in this situation?

4. Local School District Control and the Limits of Education

Subject to the limits of federal and state law, local school districts and their governing boards have been granted broad power to regulate the educational affairs of the district. State statutes typically delegate to local boards of education the power to: (1) control and convey district property and other assets; (2) adopt districtwide and school-specific educational programs; (3) establish, organize and operate the district's schools; (4) establish attendance zones and enrollment plans for specific school sites; (5) eliminate or consolidate schools; (6) provide free and adequate school facilities; (7) set the hours of the school day and the length of the school year and holiday schedules; (8) designate and fill administrative, teaching, support staff and transportation positions; (9) provide for the transportation of all students; (10) select school sites; (11) construct or expand school sites; (12) rent school space; (13) finance education through investment, general borrowing and bond issuance; (14) adopt a school budget; (15) levy taxes to meet school district needs; (16) seek tax increases and voter funding through referenda; (17) contract for insurance of school property, personnel and board members; (18) enter into, and pay in accordance with, contracts with personnel and third-party vendors; (19) maintain a school food program; (20) cooperate and contract with other school districts and governmental entities; and (21) adopt rules and regulations implementing each of these powers. *See, e.g.,* Florida Stat. §1001.42 (enumerating a long list of local district powers).

Assuming that a state has delegated to a local school district and its school board sweeping authority to administer educational programs within the district, how are educational programs to be defined? The Washington Supreme Court, for instance, has held that school district power to regulate education does not include the power to run a healthcare facility in one of its school buildings. *McGilvra v. Seattle,* 113 Wash. 619, 194 P. 817 (Wash. 1921). Is "child care" an educational function within the power of local districts?

Clark v. Jefferson County Board of Education

410 So. 2d 23 (Ala. 1982)

Judge Maddox delivered the Opinion of the Court.

Does a county board of education have legal authority to operate a child-care center? That is the sole question presented by this appeal.

The Jefferson County Board of Education offers childcare services as an adjunct to its regular academic program. These services are rendered in response to requests from community members in twelve "Human Resource Zones" in the county. The child care services are offered under the auspices of the Community Education Department of the Board, and while the scope and nature of the child care programs offered by the Board vary somewhat from zone to zone, in accordance with the needs and desires of the local community, the basic child care services include supervision of recreational activities, including physical activity, feeding of a snack, assistance with homework, and, when requested, special tutorial programs coordinated with regular school work.

Participation in these programs is voluntary and on a fee basis. The community education program of the Board and the childcare program, in particular, are "self-sufficient" in that all expenses are met by fees generated from the programs. All programs are conducted within existing school facilities.

Appellant Clara Clark owns two day care centers in Jefferson County and one in Shelby County under the name of Happy House Day Care Center, Inc. The Jefferson County facilities owned and operated by Clark are in Irondale and Hoover. Clark identified several facilities which she contends are in competition with her Irondale facility, including at least one child care program operated by the Jefferson County Board of Education.

Clark filed suit against the Board of Education, and sought an injunction to prohibit the continued operation by the Board of Education of the childcare programs. Clark, in her suit, claimed that the Board was not empowered to operate the childcare centers. . . .

We first state, in summary form, Clark's argument that the Board has no authority to operate a childcare program. She says that county boards of education, creatures of statute, can exercise only those powers which are expressly conferred upon them, that the powers granted to county boards by Code 1975, §§16-8-8, and 16-8-9, to administer and supervise is limited to *public schools,* and that a day care program is not a part of a *public school* because "public schools" are those established and maintained for persons between the ages of 7 and 21. Basically, Clark argues that if the legislature had intended for county boards of education to have authority to offer educational or other opportunities to pre-scholars, it would have authorized such activities, by law, as it did with kindergartens, elementary, junior and senior high schools, grades 1 through 12, adult education, rehabilitation of handicapped children and adults, and special education. Clark's position is aptly stated by this quote from her brief: "No statute authorizes the education of children between one day and 5 years old."

The County Board contends that "the curricular and extracurricular offerings of the public school systems within this state, as in all states, are established by local boards of education in the exercise of their broad discretionary authority conferred by statute" and that in Alabama, this grant of authority is manifested throughout Chapter 8 of Title 16 of the Alabama Code.

The Board specifically claims that the following Code sections grant to it the necessary power to operate a day care center:

> The general administration and supervision of the public schools of the educational interest of each county, with the exception of cities having a city board of education, shall be vested in the county board of education.

Code 1975, §16-8-8.

> The county board of education shall exercise through its executive officer, the county superintendent of education [,] and his professional assistants, control and supervision of the public school system of the county. The board shall consult and advise through its executive officer and his professional assistants with school trustees, principals, teachers and interested citizens and shall seek in every way to promote the interest of the schools under its jurisdiction.

Code 1975, §16-8-9.

> The county board of education shall determine and establish a written educational policy for the county and shall prescribe rules and regulations for the conduct and management of the schools.

Code 1975, §16-8-10.

The Board argues that the establishment of a community education program, of which the child care specifically challenged by plaintiff is a part, constitutes a classic example of the exercise of administrative discretion, adopted in furtherance of what this lawfully constituted board of education deems to be in the best interest of the school system and its patrons.

The Board, therefore, says that where there is a broad grant of statutory authority, no specific grant of authority to operate a childcare program is required. The Board, in its brief, argues:

> Apparently, appellant contends that a public school system is without authority to devote its facilities or resources to any use other than those specifically prescribed somewhere in the education code. Clearly, the Legislature did not see fit to enumerate or to limit the multifarious programs and activities, both academic and nonacademic, which are enjoying record levels of public participation and support in this County and throughout the State. For example, review of Chapter 8 of Title 16 reveals no specific statute which authorizes county boards of education to support and maintain varsity athletic programs, band programs, or even lunchroom facilities. However, no one would seriously argue that the maintenance of such activities is not within the discretionary prerogative of county boards of education. The program attacked in the instant case is no less an exercise of the Board's proper discretionary authority. Like a band or varsity athletic program, it offers an opportunity for an enriching though not strictly academic experience which is made possible only through the availability of school facilities and the continuing support of the local board of education.

Although the Board takes the position that its childcare program is properly established and maintained under the Board's general discretionary authority, it cites other statutes which it says inferentially support its position. It says that the provisions of Code 1975, §16-8-41, which grants county boards authority to establish and maintain kindergartens and *playgrounds* is an example. It also cites Code 1975, §38-7-2(8), which defines a day care center, but which specifically excludes:

> a. Kindergartens or nursery schools or *other daytime programs operated by public elementary systems or secondary level school units* or institutions of higher learning. [Emphasis added.]

The Board contends that the foregoing statute constitutes express legislative acknowledgement and approval of the existence of "other daytime programs" operated by public schools which are similar to private day care centers. "Clearly," says the Board, "knowledge of the existence of such daytime programs as are being challenged in this case must be imputed to the legislature on the basis of this express exclusion from the coverage of the Child Care Act.

The Board also calls our attention to evidence introduced during the trial which shows that the State Board of Education has actively and officially supported the implementation and development of Community Education in local school systems. Illustrative of this evidence is a position statement adopted by the Alabama State Board of Education on March 23, 1977, which reads as follows:

> The State Board of Education in its efforts to provide the highest quality education for the citizens of Alabama recognizes the components of community education as a most positive influence on the lifelong learning process and the democratic way of life. The State Board of Education also sees the development of positive attitudes toward education, schools, schooling and community agencies as one of the strongest products of the community education philosophy. This philosophy includes increased use of public facilities, increased contacts between school personnel and the community, and citizen involvement in the decision making process that ultimately affects their lives. The community school therefore, represents the best interests of our public schools in Alabama.

Other exhibits included a publication which showed that the Alabama State Department of Education defines "community education" as follows:

> **What is Community Education?**
> Community education is a concept that stresses an expanded role for public education and provides a dynamic approach to individual and community improvement. Community education encourages the development of a comprehensive and coordinated delivery system for providing educational, recreational, social and cultural services for all people in a community. Although communities vary greatly with some being richer than others, all have tremendous human and physical resources that can be identified and mobilized to obtain workable solutions to problems. Inherent in the community education philosophy is the belief that each community education program should reflect the needs of its particular community. The philosophy advocates a process which produces essential modifications as times and problems change.

The publication includes a page which shows that "day care" is one of the activities under the umbrella of "people of all ages together using a community school and community resources."

The concept of community education is probably best expressed in a publication entitled "Community Education: A Position Statement," which was adopted by the Alabama State Board of Education in March, 1977, and which is included in the record. . . . The publication states that "the State Board of Education, recognizing the importance of and supporting the concepts involved in Community Education, adopted a resolution in March, 1975, urging all local school systems 'to actively pursue the community education concept. . . .' "

In the position statement, under a heading "Rationale" is the following:

> The 1972 President's Commission on School Finance suggested that Community Schools are a means of developing a closer linkage between school children, parents and other citizens in the education community. Involvement of community residents in programs in which they are highly interested and frequently have a voice in developing, naturally "bridges the gap" between school and community. In addition, it fosters positive feelings toward supporting education.
>
> Community Education is a process by which we can enhance cooperation with other community and social agencies and can provide maximum utilization of the tax dollar. The Community Education concept is based on the fundamental premise that the public schools belong to all the people, from pre-scholars through senior citizens. By means of Community Schools, local resources can be harnessed to provide a forum as a means to work with community problems, while bringing back a sense of community identity whereby adults, students and community members can work, play and learn together." . . .
>
> The neighborhood school facilities are owned by the community. They may be used for a whole range of community activities which support, strengthen and augment the basic program for which the educational system exists. The Community School expands the role of the school from a formal learning center for the young, operating six hours a day, five days a week, thirty-five weeks a year, to a total community opportunity center for the young and old, operating virtually around the clock throughout the calendar year. Summarily, it relates the operation of the school to those particular needs of that community.

The purpose of community education is summed up in the publication as follows:

> Encourage maximum use of school and other facilities for educational, cultural, recreational and social activity.
>
> Demonstrate that Community Education is an effective administrative structure for assessing, planning, developing and delivering community (education) services.
>
> Generate sufficient local interest in our public schools to the extent that they become the focal point for facilitating community involvement.
>
> Provide the leadership in bringing agencies and organizations together for joint planning and program operations that provide a choice to the public in the delivery of services.
>
> Implement a State Advisory Council for Community Education with the major objective advising the State Superintendent of Education on Community Education.

Based on the foregoing facts, and applying the law to those facts, we conclude that the judgment of the trial court is due to be affirmed.

The legislature has made broad grants of authority to the Alabama State Board of Education, the Alabama State Department of Education and to the individual county boards of education to administer and supervise the public schools. It is apparent that the Alabama State Board of Education, pursuant to authority granted it by law, has encouraged the development of "community education," of which "day care" is a part, and has determined that community education is in the best interest of the public schools in Alabama.

This Court has long recognized that the power to administer and supervise the school systems is vested in the various boards of education. . . . We have carefully considered Clark's argument that a public body, without statutory authority, is encroaching upon an area of private enterprise.

Upon consideration of the facts and the law, we hold that while there is no specific statutory grant of authority to local boards of education to operate day care centers, there is authority for such activity under the broad grants of power which we have evaluated and discussed in this opinion. We, therefore, affirm the judgment of the trial court.

Affirmed.

NOTES AND QUESTIONS

1. Reconsider the materials in Chapter 8 regarding the use of school facilities. Does a broad authorization to a school district of the power to operate educational facilities allow it to utilize its facilities for noneducational purposes?
2. The court in *Clark* stresses that the "community education" philosophy supports the school district's operation of a day care facility. Consider the merits of such a philosophy. Would it have been helpful for the district to have drafted policy language expressly adopting that philosophy?
3. How broad is the school district's discretionary power? Under the umbrella of a community education philosophy, could the district operate health club facilities for students and their parents? Could a district operate a health care clinic for its students under a general grant of authority to administer "educational" programs?
4. Apart from the legal issues raised by the "community education" approach, what are its political and practical advantages and disadvantages?
5. ***District Policy Drafting Practicum.*** Assuming that a school district client asks you as its attorney to provide draft policy language expressing its "community education" mission, what language should be used?

C. CONDEMNATION, ZONING AND THE LIMITS OF SCHOOL DISTRICT POWER

The school board is vested with authority to acquire any property that the school board deems necessary for "proper school purposes." The power given to local school districts by the state also includes the power to acquire such property by condemnation or eminent domain. *See, e.g., Dare County Board of Education v. Sakaria,* 118 N.C. App. 609, 456 S.E.2d 842 (1995). In taking private property for a public educational purpose, the school district must provide to the owner "just compensation." The power of a school board has been broadly interpreted to allow condemnation, and quick possession of condemned land for any purpose that is school related, including the development of administrative offices, stadiums, gymnasiums and parking. *See, e.g., In re Condemnation of School District of Pittsburgh,* 430 Pa. 566, 244 A.2d 42 (Pa. 1968) (acquisition of land for parking for school district administrative facilities constitutes a "proper school purpose" permitting condemnation); *Alexander v. Phillips,* 31 Ariz. 503, 254 P. 1056 (Ariz. 1927) (stadium); *Ranier v. Board of Education,* 273 S.W.2d 577 (Ky. 1954) (gymnasium); *Smith v. Board of Education,* 272 Ala. 227, 130 So. 2d 29 (Ala. 1961) (administrative offices). *See also Goldman v. Moore,* 35 Ill. 2d 450, 220 N.E.2d 466 (Ill. 1966). The power of condemnation is broad enough to permit a district to acquire property even outside of the district's borders. *See, e.g., In re Board of Public Instruction,* 160 Fla. 490, 35 So. 2d 579 (Fla. 1948).

A school district's power to take property for educational purposes often creates significant legal and political issues in a community. That power creates tensions between school districts and the municipalities in which they reside. Local school districts may have geographical borders that coincide with the municipalities that they serve, but often district and municipal boundaries are not the same. School districts which are commonly drawn around county lines may encompass more than one municipality.

Municipalities, like school districts, are creatures of the state. They only have those powers which have been delegated to them by the state. One of the powers invariably assigned to a municipality is the power to create zoning districts within the borders of the municipality. This legitimate city or village power, however, may be incompatible with the school districts' power to establish school sites and school structures within the municipality.

Many schools sit in residential areas. They take advantage of their residential location to create a neighborhood school community. The areas surrounding those neighborhood schools, however, are typically zoned "residential" by the municipality. The zoning ordinances passed by the city in such an area will require that structures built in that "zone" meet certain height, set-back, density, width and even aesthetic restrictions. School buildings will rarely meet those residential zoning requirements. Must public schools be built to satisfy local zoning ordinances, or are schools "exempt" from local zoning limitations?

In communities where elected school board members have a cooperative relationship with elected municipal officials, this potential conflict can be resolved through healthy dialogue and intergovernmental agreement. In most circumstances, shrewd city officials will recognize the supreme value that their constituents place on the education of the community's children and will not even attempt to impose zoning restrictions on a school building. Similarly, shrewd school officials will recognize the value of legitimate zoning guidelines and will attempt to plan school buildings so as to be sensitive to the place of the building in the community.

Suppose, however, that vacant land is scarce in a school district, and the district has no choice but to build a needed school in violation of the zoning restrictions on an available piece of property. Or suppose that the local municipal officials, in a power grab, attempt to impose zoning restrictions on the school site in order to scale back a desperately needed school addition to mollify complaining neighbors. Does the district have the authority to build its school addition despite the municipality's objection? As the following opinion demonstrates, school districts, which obtain their authority directly from the state and often encompass more than one municipality, cannot be subjected to any single municipality's zoning ordinances.

North Cook Intermediate Service Center v. Village of Skokie

Cir. Ct., Cook County, Ill.—Chancery Division, No. 99 CH 12107 (2000)

The parties are before the court on the motion for summary judgment filed by the plaintiff, North Cook Intermediate Service Center (hereinafter referred to as "NCISC"). The issues are whether the Village of Skokie may use its zoning powers to prevent the plaintiff from operating a public school on property within its village and, if so, whether the Village's decision to not allow the school to operate at its location [is] reasonable. . . . For the reasons stated herein, the court concludes that the plaintiff is an agent of state government and that the Village may not utilize its zoning power to prohibit the operation of the school on the subject premises. Additionally, the court also concludes that the purported exercise of that zoning power was arbitrary and unreasonable, and cannot be approved. Accordingly, the plaintiff's motion for summary judgment should be granted.

NCISC is established by the Illinois State Board of Education pursuant to Section 2-3.62 of the Illinois School Code. On September 2, 1998, NCISC entered into a lease for property located at 5270-72 Lincoln Ave., Skokie, Illinois, to be used as an alternative school. The school provides a smaller, more structured environment for students who have been identified as at-risk of failure or students who have been the subject of repeated disciplinary problems in traditional school settings.

The Village of Skokie through its Zoning Board has enacted certain zoning ordinances that regulate the use of property within the Village. NCISC was informed by the Village that it had to petition the Village for a text amendment to the zoning ordinance adding alternative educational schools as a special use in the zone where the property is located. NCISC also petitioned for a special use permit. After a lengthy public hearing, the Plan Commission voted 7-2 to approve the text change and approve the special use application. However, the Village Board subsequently voted unanimously to deny the NCISC request to add the text amendment to the ordinance allowing an alternative school as a special use. Through these actions the Village denied NCISC operation of the alternative school on the property. . . .

NCISC argues that school districts are not subject to the zoning laws of municipalities and that the Illinois Constitution does not permit a local government entity to exercise any control over or impose any burden upon a school district because of the State's interest in promoting and fostering Illinois schools. . . . The NCISC position is that the local entity, the Village, cannot impose a zoning violation on the alternative school because this action frustrates the purpose of the School Code which grants to the school districts the authority to operate schools. . . .

The Illinois Constitution has granted explicit authority to the Legislature to establish and maintain schools in Illinois. The Legislature in turn passed the School Code and established school districts to foster the operation of Illinois schools. Through the School Code, school districts are empowered to acquire sites for school purposes either with or without the owner's consent by condemnation or otherwise. The Supreme Court ruled in *City of Des Plaines v. Metropolitan Sanitary District,* 48 Ill. 2d 11 (1971) that the [Metropolitan Sanitary] District was exercising its power within its statutory grant, such exercise is not subject to zoning restrictions imposed by the host municipality. Here, NCISC is exercising its power authorized under the School Code as a branch of the state government and it should not be subject to zoning restrictions imposed by the Village of Skokie when it is clear that the Village is using its zoning authority to frustrate the power of NCISC to operate alternative schools.

Having decided the first issue in favor of the plaintiff resolves the entire case. Even so, the court finds, holds and rules further that the Village of Skokie's decision was unreasonable and arbitrary, and that NCISC is also entitled to summary judgment on Count II. The Village first asserts that it can find it inappropriate for the alternative school to be in the B2 commercial district because it is adjacent to residential areas. It then claims that the school poses a threat to the residents of the adjacent residential zoned area on account of the students being classified as "disruptive students." This apprehension ignores the fact that the alternative schools were designed and established for the sole purpose of addressing the greater educational and supervisory needs of such children. The disingenuous nature of this position is further demonstrated by the plaintiff having pointed out that since any school could have been located within a residential area, the alternative school could have been located directly within the residentially zoned community as a permitted use. The placement of the school in the adjacent B2 area can hardly be a violation of the zoning ordinance; particularly when commercial and trade schools, including music, dance, business, commercial, trade or technical subjects are permitted uses in the B2 commercial zones. Skokie's attempts to distinguish these schools from the alternative school which, as discussed, could have been located within the residential area, is unpersuasive.

For reasons stated above the plaintiff's motion for summary judgment is granted.

NOTES AND QUESTIONS

1. The *North Cook* court relies on the fact that the state, through its legislation, has given school districts the power to condemn property for school purposes. Does the existence of that power necessarily mean that a school district also has the power to avoid zoning restrictions on its property? In what ways, if any, are the legal and political issues associated with condemnation different from the issues associated with zoning?

2. Are there any limits to a school district's power to avoid zoning restrictions suggested by the *North Cook* opinion? Should there be?
3. Suppose a school district plans to build a 12-story middle school housing all 4,000 district students in a residential area. Do the neighbors have any redress?
4. The *North Cook* court's conclusion that local school districts may construct school buildings to suit educational purposes without interference from the cities or villages in which they sit is in keeping with a consistent line of case law. *See, e.g., School Dist. of Pittsburgh v. City of Pittsburgh,* 23 Pa. Commw. Ct. 405, 352 A.2d 223 (1976) (state authority delegated to schools superior to any authority given to municipalities with respect to construction permits); *Murnick v. Board of Education of City of Asbury Park,* 235 N.J. Super. 225, 561 A.2d 1193 (1989) (school boards are immune from municipal zoning regulations related to school sites); *City of Bloomfield v. Davis County Community School District,* 254 Iowa 900, 119 N.W.2d 909 (Iowa 1963) (as a state agency, a school district is not subject to a local municipal zoning ordinance).
5. How is "just compensation" measured when a school district acquires private property for educational purposes? The definition of "just" can be an intense subject of litigation. Should the landowner receive: (1) the appraised fair market value of the taken property (2) the replacement value of the property and its uses (3) the lost profits occasioned by the disruption, and/or (4) the cost of relocating? *See, e.g., United States v. Cors,* 337 U.S. 325 (1949) (rejecting the appraised market value approach as a talisman and indicating that the cost of providing "substitute" property may be considered in any award of compensation).

D. STRUCTURAL GOVERNANCE PRACTICUM: CHOOSING A NEW SCHOOL SITE, EXPANDING INTO PRE-K EDUCATION AND RESPONDING TO A CITY'S ZONING CHALLENGES

In light of a school district's apparently broad powers, consider the following scenarios:

1. A school district currently operates an elementary school that can barely accommodate its 400 students. A new housing development has been constructed in the area, bringing 120 new students to the school. The developer for the project has agreed with the municipality to pay some "impact aid" to the district to help the district accommodate the new students at the existing school. The school, however, cannot accommodate these additional students. Vacant land in the district is scarce.

   Research reveals two possible sites. The school could be rebuilt on the existing site by expanding that site to accommodate a larger facility. The existing site is surrounded by ten small houses, each valued at about $200,000. Those houses could be condemned and a larger school could be built at the current location. Alternatively, the school could be built on a large portion of a nearby golf course that is currently being used for maintenance and storage. The land itself is valued at only $500,000, but the school district is concerned that the owners of the golf course and its neighbors may be able to create additional political and financial costs.

As the school district's lawyer, how would you advise the district to proceed? First, what *process* would you create for the decision itself? Secondly, what are the various substantive options that are available? Should the district approach each "neighbor" and offer to buy the houses surrounding the existing site one at a time? Does the district have the power to condemn the surrounding houses and build an addition to the school? Should it do so? Should the district purchase homes from willing sellers and condemn the rest?

With respect to the golf course option, what arguments might the golf course owners and its neighbors make against condemnation, and how should the district respond? Finally, after the board decides which path to take, what advice would you offer the board about community relations as it proceeds down that path?

2. Assume that the board of a K-8 school district has decided that it would like to create partnerships with the preschool providers in the area. The preschool providers have no land of their own. They have been using space in the basements of churches, synagogues and the like. The district believes that early childhood education is vital to a child's future educational development, and that effective early childhood education will actually save the district money in the long run. Therefore, the district would like to create a facility to house all of the existing preschool programs in the community. Land in the community, however, is scarce. Can the district condemn a series of townhomes in order to construct a preschool building? Should it do so?
3. Finally, assume that the school district operates ten schools located in three different cities. One of the cities has threatened to pass an ordinance amending its existing zoning classifications. The amended ordinance would create a new zoning category known as a "Public Activity Zone." The zone would cover all of the buildings owned and operated by nonprivate entities in the city, including schools, houses of worship, park district facilities, libraries and governmental offices. The zone places rigid procedural and substantive restrictions on all existing and future "public" facilities. Most of the substantive restrictions are entirely incompatible with traditional school facilities.

The school board seeks legal and political advice. First, can the city impose its new zoning ordinance on the school district? Second, even assuming that the city has no power to force the schools to comply with its new classification, how would you advise the school board to approach the city's elected officials? Third, assuming that the school board works to resolve this potential conflict by means other than litigation between the school district and the city, what agreement could be created to settle this dispute? Draft a proposed intergovernmental agreement between the school district and the city that you believe satisfies the needs of *both* parties. The draft agreement should include at least the following terms: (1) recitals; (2) definitions; (3) length of term and termination provisions; (4) a statement regarding waiver or nonwaiver of legal rights; and most importantly (5) a *process* for school district and city cooperation that will take the place of the city's unilateral imposition of its new zoning ordinance on the district.

CHAPTER 11

THE LEGAL AND PRACTICAL MECHANICS OF SCHOOL BOARD GOVERNANCE

In the previous chapter, the role of the school board within the legal structure of school governance was identified. Subject only to a limited number of restrictions from federal and state law, local school boards have plenary power to regulate schools within their districts. In light of that power, the way in which school board members are selected and make decisions is an extremely important ingredient in the character of education in America. This chapter looks carefully at the composition of the school board and the methods of board governance.

A. BOARD MEMBER ELECTIONS, QUALIFICATIONS AND CONFLICTS

The law in virtually every state delegates to a state board of education and to local boards of education the governance of educational districts within the state. Eighty-five percent of the states have created local school boards. *See* Wirt & Kirst, *Schools in Conflict: The Politics of Education* (1982) (hereinafter, Wirt & Kirst). School boards consist of between five and seven members. In most states, school boards have seven members who are elected to four-year terms by voters within the district they serve. Elections are nonpartisan, and voter turnout is relatively low. *See* Wirt & Kirst. School board members invariably have occupations outside of the education area, and have little or no experience in educational matters. *See* S. Sarason, *Parental Involvement and the Political Principle: Why the Existing Governance Structure of Schools Should Be Abolished* (1995). The states are free to establish their own rules governing board elections, qualifications and disabling conflicts, within the confines of constitutional voting rights requirements.

1. Elections

In *Hadley v. Junior College District of Metropolitan Kansas City,* 397 U.S. 50, 56 (1970), the Supreme Court held that its one-person, one-vote principle applies fully to school board elections: "whenever a state or local government decides to select persons by popular election to perform governmental functions, the Equal Protection Clause of the Fourteenth Amendment requires that each qualified voter must be given an equal opportunity to participate in that election, and when members of an elected body are chosen from separate districts, each district must be established on a basis that will insure, as far as is practicable, that equal numbers of voters can vote for proportionately equal numbers of officials." The Court made clear, however, that a state could choose to select the members of its statewide or local school boards by appointment, rather than popular vote. *See Sailors v. Board of Education of Kent County,* 387 U.S. 105 (1967). Once the state decides to select board members by popular vote, it must conduct its elections in accordance with the equal protection clause's voting rights protections. As such, the state cannot limit the class of voters in school board elections to parents of public school children. *See Kramer v. Union Free School District No. 15,* 395 U.S. 621 (1969). Nor can a state limit school board voting to "property taxpayers." *See Cipriano v. City of Houma,* 395 U.S. 701 (1969).

Kramer v. Union Free School District No. 15

395 U.S. 621 (1969)

Mr. Chief Justice Warren delivered the opinion of the Court.

In this case we are called on to determine whether §2012 of the New York Education Law is constitutional. The legislation provides that in certain New York school districts residents who are otherwise eligible to vote in state and federal elections may vote in the school district election only if they (1) own (or lease) taxable real property within the district, or (2) are parents (or have custody of) children enrolled in the local public schools. Appellant, a bachelor who neither owns nor leases taxable real property, filed suit in federal court claiming that §2012 denied him equal protection of the laws in violation of the Fourteenth Amendment. With one judge dissenting, a three-judge District Court dismissed appellant's complaint. Finding that §2012 does violate the Equal Protection Clause of the Fourteenth Amendment, we reverse.

I.

New York law provides basically three methods of school board selection. In some large city districts, the school board is appointed by the mayor or city council. N.Y. Educ. Law §2553, subds. 2, 4 (1953), as amended (Supp. 1968). On the other hand, in some cities, primarily those with less than 125,000 residents, the school board is elected at general or municipal elections in which all qualified city voters may participate. N.Y. Educ. Law §§2502, subd. 2,

2553, subd. 3 (1953). Cf. N.Y. Educ. Law §2531 (1953). Finally, in other districts such as the one involved in this case, which are primarily rural and suburban, the school board is elected at an annual meeting of qualified school district voters.

The challenged statute is applicable only in the districts which hold annual meetings. To be eligible to vote at an annual district meeting, an otherwise qualified district resident must either (1) be the owner or lessee of taxable real property located in the district (2) be the spouse of one who owns or leases qualifying property, or (3) be the parent or guardian of a child enrolled for a specified time during the preceding year in a local district school.

Although the New York State Department of Education has substantial responsibility for education in the State, the local school districts maintain significant control over the administration of local school district affairs. Generally, the board of education has the basic responsibility for local school operation, including prescribing the courses of study, determining the textbooks to be used, and even altering and equipping a former schoolhouse for use as a public library. N.Y. Educ. Law §1709 (1953). Additionally, in districts selecting members of the board of education at annual meetings, the local voters also pass directly on other district matters. For example, they must approve the school budget submitted by the school board. N.Y. Educ. Law §§2021, 2022 (1953). Moreover, once the budget is approved, the governing body of the villages within the school district must raise the money which has been declared "necessary for teachers' salaries and the ordinary contingent expenses [of the schools]." N.Y. Educ. Law §1717 (1953). The voters also may "authorize such acts and vote such taxes as they shall deem expedient . . . for . . . equipping for library use any former schoolhouse . . . [and] for the purchase of land and buildings for agricultural, athletic, playground or social center purposes. . . ." N.Y. Educ. Law §416 (1953).

Appellant is a 31-year-old college-educated stockbroker who lives in his parents' home in the Union Free School District No. 15, a district to which §2012 applies. He is a citizen of the United States and has voted in federal and state elections since 1959. However, since he has no children and neither owns nor leases taxable real property, appellant's attempts to register for and vote in the local school district elections have been unsuccessful. After the school district rejected his 1965 application, appellant instituted the present class action challenging the constitutionality of the voter eligibility requirements. . . .

II.

Appellant agrees that the States have the power to impose reasonable citizenship, age, and residency requirements on the availability of the ballot. Cf. *Carrington v. Rash,* 380 U.S. 89, 91 (1965); *Pope v. Williams,* 193 U.S. 621 (1904). The sole issue in this case is whether the *additional* requirements of §2012—requirements which prohibit some district residents who are otherwise qualified by age and citizenship from participating in district meetings and school board elections—violate the Fourteenth Amendment's command that no State shall deny persons equal protection of the laws.

"In determining whether or not a state law violates the Equal Protection Clause, we must consider the facts and circumstances behind the law, the interests which the State claims to be protecting, and the interests of those who are disadvantaged by the classification." *Williams v. Rhodes,* 393 U.S. 23, 30 (1968). And, in this case, we must give the statute a close and exacting examination. "Since the right to exercise the franchise in a free and unimpaired manner is preservative of other basic civil and political rights, any alleged infringement of the right of citizens to vote must be carefully and meticulously scrutinized." *Reynolds v. Sims,* 377 U.S. 533, 562 (1964). See *Williams v. Rhodes, supra,* at 31; *Wesberry v. Sanders,* 376 U.S. 1, 17 (1964). This careful examination is necessary because statutes distributing the franchise constitute the foundation of our representative society. Any unjustified discrimination in determining who may participate in political affairs or in the selection of public officials undermines the legitimacy of representative government.

Thus, state apportionment statutes, which may *dilute* the effectiveness of some citizens' votes, receive close scrutiny from this Court. *Reynolds v. Sims, supra. See Avery v. Midland County,* 390 U.S. 474 (1968). No less rigid an examination is applicable to statutes *denying* the franchise to citizens who are otherwise qualified by residence and age. Statutes granting the franchise to residents on a selective basis always pose the danger of denying some citizens any effective voice in the governmental affairs which substantially affect their lives. Therefore, if a challenged state statute grants the right to vote to some bona fide residents of requisite age and citizenship and denies the franchise to others, the Court must determine whether the exclusions are necessary to promote a compelling state interest. *See Carrington v. Rash, supra,* at 96.

And, for these reasons, the deference usually given to the judgment of legislators does not extend to decisions concerning which resident citizens may participate in the election of legislators and other public officials. Those decisions must be carefully scrutinized by the Court to determine whether each resident citizen has, as far as is possible, an equal voice in the selections. Accordingly, when we are reviewing statutes which deny some residents the right to vote, the general presumption of constitutionality afforded state statutes and the traditional approval given state classifications if the Court can conceive of a "rational basis" for the distinctions made are not applicable. *See Harper v. Virginia Bd. of Elections,* 383 U.S. 663, 670 (1966). The presumption of constitutionality and the approval given "rational" classifications in other types of enactments are based on an assumption that the institutions of state government are structured so as to represent fairly all the people. However, when the challenge to the statute is in effect a challenge of this basic assumption, the assumption can no longer serve as the basis for presuming constitutionality. And, the assumption is no less under attack because the legislature which decides who may participate at the various levels of political choice is fairly elected. Legislation which delegates decision making to bodies elected by only a portion of those eligible to vote for the legislature can cause unfair representation. Such legislation can exclude a minority of voters from any voice in the decisions just as effectively as if the decisions were made by legislators the minority had no voice in selecting.

The need for exacting judicial scrutiny of statutes distributing the franchise is undiminished simply because, under a different statutory scheme, the offices subject to election might have been filled through appointment. States do have latitude in determining whether certain public officials shall be selected by election or chosen by appointment and whether various questions shall be submitted to the voters. In fact, we have held that where a county school board is an administrative, not legislative, body, its members need not be elected. *Sailors v. Kent Bd. of Education,* 387 U.S. 105, 108 (1967). However, "once the franchise is granted to the electorate, lines may not be drawn which are inconsistent with the Equal Protection Clause of the Fourteenth Amendment." *Harper v. Virginia Bd. of Elections, supra,* at 665.

Nor is the need for close judicial examination affected because the district meetings and the school board do not have "general" legislative powers. Our exacting examination is not necessitated by the subject of the election; rather, it is required because some resident citizens are permitted to participate and some are not. For example, a city charter might well provide that the elected city council appoint a mayor who would have broad administrative powers. Assuming the council were elected consistent with the commands of the Equal Protection Clause, the delegation of power to the mayor would not call for this Court's exacting review. On the other hand, if the city charter made the office of mayor subject to an election in which only some resident citizens were entitled to vote, there would be presented a situation calling for our close review.

III.

Besides appellant and others who similarly live in their parents' homes, the statute also disenfranchises the following persons (unless they are parents or guardians of children enrolled in the district public school): senior citizens and others living with children or relatives; clergy, military personnel, and others who live on tax-exempt property; boarders and lodgers; parents who neither own nor lease qualifying property and whose children are too young to attend school; parents who neither own nor lease qualifying property and whose children attend private schools.

Appellant asserts that excluding him from participation in the district elections denies him equal protection of the laws. He contends that he and others of his class are substantially interested in and significantly affected by the school meeting decisions. All members of the community have an interest in the quality and structure of public education, appellant says, and he urges that "the decisions taken by local boards . . . may have grave consequences to the entire population." Appellant also argues that the level of property taxation affects him, even though he does not own property, as property tax levels affect the price of goods and services in the community.

We turn therefore to question whether the exclusion is necessary to promote a compelling state interest. First, appellees argue that the State has a legitimate interest in limiting the franchise in school district elections to "members of the community of interest"—those "primarily interested in such elections." Second, appellees urge that the State may reasonably and permissibly conclude that "property taxpayers" (including lessees of taxable property who share the tax burden through rent payments) and parents of the children enrolled in the district's schools are those "primarily interested" in school affairs.

We do not understand appellees to argue that the State is attempting to limit the franchise to those "subjectively concerned" about school matters. Rather, they appear to argue that the State's legitimate interest is in restricting a voice in school matters to those "directly affected" by such decisions. The State apparently reasons that since the schools are financed in part by local property taxes, persons whose out-of-pocket expenses are "directly" affected by property tax changes should be allowed to vote. Similarly, parents of children in school are thought to have a "direct" stake in school affairs and are given a vote.

Appellees argue that it is necessary to limit the franchise to those "primarily interested" in school affairs because "the ever increasing complexity of the many interacting phases of the school system and structure make it extremely difficult for the electorate fully to understand the whys and wherefores of the detailed operations of the school system." Appellees say that many communications of school boards and school administrations are sent home to the parents through the district pupils and are "not broadcast to the general public"; thus, nonparents will be less informed than parents. Further, appellees argue, those who are assessed for local property taxes (either directly or indirectly through rent) will have enough of an interest "through the burden on their pocketbooks, to acquire such information as they may need."

We need express no opinion as to whether the State in some circumstances might limit the exercise of the franchise to those "primarily interested" or "primarily affected." Of course, we therefore do not reach the issue of whether these particular elections are of the type in which the franchise may be so limited. For, assuming, *arguendo,* that New York legitimately might limit the franchise in these school district elections to those "primarily interested in school affairs," close scrutiny of the §2012 classifications demonstrates that they do not accomplish this purpose with sufficient precision to justify denying appellant the franchise.

Whether classifications allegedly limiting the franchise to those resident citizens "primarily interested" deny those excluded equal protection of the laws depends, *inter alia,* on whether all those excluded are in fact substantially less interested or affected than those the statute includes. In other words, the classifications must be tailored so that the exclusion of appellant and members of his class is necessary to achieve the articulated state goal. Section 2012 does not meet the exacting standard of precision we require of statutes which selectively distribute the franchise. The classifications in §2012 permit inclusion of many persons who have, at best, a remote and indirect interest in school affairs and, on the other hand, exclude others who have a distinct and direct interest in the school meeting decisions.[15]

Nor do appellees offer any justification for the exclusion of seemingly interested and informed residents—other than to argue that the §2012 classifications include those "whom the State could understandably deem to be the most intimately interested in actions taken by the school board,"

[15] For example, appellant resides with his parents in the school district, pays state and federal taxes and is interested in and affected by school board decisions; however, he has no vote. On the other hand, an uninterested unemployed young man who pays no state or federal taxes, but who rents an apartment in the district, can participate in the election.

and urge that "the task of . . . balancing the interest of the community in the maintenance of orderly school district elections against the interest of any individual in voting in such elections should clearly remain with the Legislature."[16]

But the issue is not whether the legislative judgments are rational. A more exacting standard obtains. The issue is whether the §2012 requirements do in fact sufficiently further a compelling state interest to justify denying the franchise to appellant and members of his class. The requirements of §2012 are not sufficiently tailored to limiting the franchise to those "primarily interested" in school affairs to justify the denial of the franchise to appellant and members of his class.

The judgment of the United States District Court for the Eastern District of New York is therefore reversed. The case is remanded for further proceedings consistent with this opinion.

NOTES AND QUESTIONS

1. The Court indicates that a state could structure the governance of its schools so as to permit the appointment rather than the election of local school officials. What are the advantages and disadvantages of appointment of officials in the particular setting of school governance?
2. The Court suggests that a state could limit voting for school board membership to those who are primarily interested or affected by the actions of the school board. How could such a class of voters be defined? Could statutory language defining that class of primarily interested voters be drafted so as to be finely tailored to an articulated state interest in restricting voting to that class? How would the state interest be articulated?
3. Consider the following members of a community: students, parents of students, grandparents of students, teachers in district schools, teachers in non-district schools, taxpayers who used to have school-aged children, and taxpayers who never had school-aged children. Is each group "primarily" interested in educational issues? Are some more than others?

2. Qualifications

The qualifications for service on a school board are dictated by fairly uniform state laws. In most states, board members must be a citizen of the United States, at least 18 years of age, and a resident of the school district for at least six months (in some states a year) immediately preceding the election. *See, e.g.,* Florida Stat. §§1001.34-1001.38; *Vittoria v. West Orange Board of Education,* 122 N.J. 340, 300 A.2d 356 (1973). In Texas, for instance, a person is eligible for election to the board if the candidate: does not hold an office with the state or any of its political subdivisions; is a bona fide resident of the district in which he or she will serve with one year's continuous residence before election; is a qualified voter of the district in which he or she resides; is at least 26 years of

[16] We were informed at oral argument, however, that a very small proportion of the eligible voters attend the meetings.

age; and is not required to register as a lobbyist by virtue of his or her activities for compensation in or on behalf of a profession, business, or association related to the operation of the Board. (Tex. Educ. Code §7.103 (2003).) In Florida, each school board candidate: must be a resident of the area from which the candidate seeks election; must be a qualified elector of the district in which he or she serves; and must maintain that residency throughout the term of office. (Fla. Stat. §1001.34 (2002).) In New York, every school district officer must: be able to read and write; be a qualified voter of the district; and be a resident of the school district for at least one year prior to the election. (N.Y. Educ. Law §2012 (Consol. 2003).) Finally, the state law in California provides that, any person, regardless of sex, is eligible to be elected or appointed to a governing board of a school district, without further qualifications, if he or she is: 18 years or older; a citizen of the state; a resident of the school district; a registered voter; and not disqualified by the Constitution or laws of the state from holding a civil office. (Cal. Educ. Code §35107 (2003).)

Candidates for the board of education generally cannot be employed by the school district, and, in some states, cannot be related to employees of the district. Board members typically serve as volunteers without compensation.

State law also provides for circumstances that disqualify a sitting board member. A board position typically becomes vacant when the incumbent dies, submits a resignation in writing filed with the secretary or clerk of the board, becomes legally disabled, ceases to be an inhabitant of the school district, is convicted of a crime or is removed from office for misconduct.

Although the states may determine their own rules governing the qualifications and disqualifications of local school board members, those rules cannot establish unconstitutional requirements. A state, for example, certainly could not make a particular race or gender a qualification for board service. Nor can a state require board members to be owners of property in the district as a prerequisite to board candidacy. *Turner v. Fouche,* 396 U.S. 346 (1970).

3. Board Contracts and Board Member Conflicts

As a public body, an elected school board is charged with authorizing the school district to enter into contracts with administrators, teachers and third-party vendors. When the school district enters into these contracts, the district must expend public funds. As such, the public has a vital interest in the process used to arrive at these contracts and in the substantial fairness of the actual transactions. State laws invariably require that board action on such contracts be taken in public session and require that the terms of the contract be made available for public inspection. *See, e.g., Santa Monica School District v. Persh,* 5 Cal. App. 3d 945, 85 Cal. Rptr. 463 (1970) (authorization to enter contract, even to purchase property, must be given by legal vote of school board at public meeting); *Attorney General v. School Committee of Northhampton, Mass.,* 375 Mass. 127, 375 N.E.2d 1188 (Mass. 1970) (holding that the entire process for entering a contract with the district's superintendent, including the names of the finalists, should be open to the public).

State law also requires the school board to undergo an elaborate bidding process before entering into most third-party contracts. *See, e.g.,* Florida Stat.

§1001.42. The board must establish a procedure for advertising its willingness to accept bids from qualified contractors. The notice that the district is "going out for bid" must be accompanied by specifications and qualifications for the project that are not designed solely to eliminate a competitive bidding process. The board may specify, however, that the bidder must comply with all other district policies, including a district policy against employment discrimination. *See, e.g., Weiner v. Cuyahoga Community College,* 19 Ohio St. 2d 35, 249 N.E.2d 907 (1969). Once the bids are recorded, the district opens all of the bids at the same time, on a certain predetermined date in a public setting. The school board then selects which of the qualifying bids to accept at its public meeting. The board may strictly enforce its bidding deadlines and time periods. *See, e.g., Great Lakes Heating v. Troy School District,* 197 Mich. App. 312, 494 N.W.2d 863 (1992).

State law and political prudence both usually dictate that the school board accept the "lowest responsible bidder" for a contract or project. *See, e.g.,* Iowa School Code. §723; Oregon Attorney General's Model Public Contract Rules, Or. Admin. R. ch. 137, div. 30 (1998). The requirement that the board select the "lowest responsible bidder," by definition, means that the board need not always enter into a contract at the lowest price. The concept of a "responsible" bidder is broad enough to allow the school board some discretion in deciding which bidders will do the best job on a particular project, based on prior experience in the district or references from work outside the district. *See, e.g., Hibbs v. Arensberg,* 276 Pa. 24, 119 A. 727 (1923) (board may consider potential contractor's financing, standing, reputation, experience, resources, facilities, judgment and efficiency). Accordingly, the board may first select those bidders it deems to be "responsible" in a qualitative way, and then choose the lowest price from among only those responsible bidders. Most states also allow the board to exercise unfettered discretion in entering into contracts for professional services.

The board's failure to select the lowest responsible bidder may present a political problem for the board, but it is generally not a basis for voiding the contract itself. Nor does a rejected bidder generally have any cause of action for resulting losses. *Noonan Inc. v. School District of New York,* 400 Pa. 391, 162 A.2d 623 (1960).

The process of accepting bids for significant contracts guides virtually all decisions made by the school board to expend public funds. State law allows school boards broad power to enter into specific contracts on behalf of the district, including the power to contract for: (1) transportation of students "to and from school" and school-sponsored extracurricular activities, *see, e.g., State ex rel. North Carolina Utilities Commission v. McKinnon,* 254 N.C. 1, 118 S.E.2d 134 (1961); (2) food service and food programs primarily for students, *see, e.g., Krueger v. Board of Education,* 310 Mo. 239, 274 S.W. 811 (1925); (3) insurance covering district liability, property damage and teacher health and disability, *see, e.g., Nohl v. Board of Education,* 27 N.M. 232, 199 P. 373 (1921); (4) purchased services and equipment for particular school-related purposes or functions, *see, e.g., LaPorte v. Escanaba Area Public Schools,* 51 Mich. App. 305, 214 N.W.2d 840 (1974); (5) immediate medical care for students and employees, *see, e.g., Stineman v. Fontbonne College,* 664 F.2d 1082

(8th Cir. 1981); (6) legal services on behalf of the school district, *see, e.g., Errington v. Mansfield Township Board of Education,* 100 N.J. Super. 130, 241 A.2d 271 (1968); and (7) indemnification and insurance for board members for civil liability incurred in the scope of their board business; *see, e.g., Cobb v. City of Cape May,* 113 N.J. Super. 590, 274 A.2d 622 (1971).

In exercising its broad discretion to expend public funds by entering into contracts, the school board is entrusted to act in the district's best interests. The requirement that boards generally accept the "lowest responsible bidder" for an important contract helps to insure that the board will serve those interests. Nonetheless, two factors—the extent of the authority given to boards to enter into a variety of contracts and the fact that board members typically have ties to the business community surrounding their district—often lead to situations in which board members are tempted to place their own financial interests (or those of their friends and relations) above those of the district. In such situations, the board and its attorneys must confront difficult conflict of interest problems in the contracting process.

The most common conflict of interest occurs when board members provide materials, merchandise, property, services or labor to their school district in return for money or other consideration. State school codes generally make it illegal for board members to have any interest, either directly or indirectly, in any contract, work or business of the school district or in the purchase of any property which belongs to the district. *See, e.g.,* Florida Stat. §1001.42; Illinois Statutes, 105 ILCS 5/10-9. Further, no board member may represent, as agent or otherwise, any party with respect to the application or bid for any contract or work in regard to which the member may be called upon to vote. Merely abstaining from a vote may be insufficient to cure a board member's conflict of interest. Board members may also violate state conflict of interest provisions by purchasing property owned by the school district, selling books, apparatus or furniture to the district or accepting inducements in return for influence on the choice of instructional materials.

The law in most states, however, allows board members to have an interest in contracts with the district in certain exceptional circumstances. For instance, state law may permit board members to do business with the district (i.e., provide materials, merchandise, property, services or labor) if the amount of the contract does not exceed $ 1,000, or the aggregate amount per fiscal year does not exceed $5,000 if there are no other available suppliers in the district.

In any event, the interested board member typically must publicly disclose the nature and extent of the interest prior to, or during, board deliberations concerning the proposed award of the contract. The board member also must abstain from voting, and the award of the contract must be approved by a majority of the entire board. The sanctions for violations of the prohibition on board member contracts can be severe.

In light of the fact that school board members reside in the local school district, there is also a great potential for board members to cause their districts to enter into employment arrangements with neighbors or family members. How should those transactions be analyzed from a conflict of interest perspective? Most states have statutes that expressly prohibit school boards from taking action on employment issues affecting a board member's relative. These laws are designed to "engender confidence in public bodies and to eliminate situations in which preference or undue influence could come to bear in the operation of government." *Williams v. Augusta County School Board,* 248 Va. 124, 445 S.E.2d 118 (Va. 1994).

SMITH V. DORSEY

530 So. 2d 5 (Miss. 1988)

En Banc

GRIFFIN, Justice, for the Court:

In this appeal this Court is asked to construe Section 109 [of the Mississippi Constitution] as applied to contracts of teachers whose spouses are school board members. Stated differently, may a local school board contract with the spouses of its members?

In *Frazier v. State by and through Pittman,* 504 So. 2d 675 (Miss. 1987), we held that as between a legislator and spouse as a public school teacher, no such conflict of interest exists. We held that Section 109 was never intended to prohibit any individual from serving in the legislature and voting on general public school laws and appropriations therefor simply because his or her spouse is employed as a public school teacher in this state.

Here we have a different factual situation, requiring another answer, therefore, we affirm the order of the chancery court . . . finding that each of the defendants has been and is in violation of Section 109; declaring null and void all contracts between defendants' spouses and the Claiborne County School District; and enjoining the payment of any further salaries or payments of money to these spouses while the defendants are members of the Claiborne County Board of Education and for a period of one year after defendants shall leave said official capacities.

We reverse as to the chancellor's order requiring restitution from the defendants for compensation received in violation of Section 109.

Facts

Testimony at trial and stipulated exhibits include documents issued to defendants by the Secretary of State certifying them as Claiborne County School Board members; contracts for employment for their spouses . . . as teachers in the Claiborne County School District, at the time defendants served as board members; the teachers' payroll records from 1980-1986; and minutes of the Claiborne County School Board from 1980-1986.

On direct examination Dr. John Noble, the Claiborne County Superintendent of Education, stated that, following his recommendations of applicants for teaching positions within the district, the Claiborne County School Board had the authority to reach contracts of employment with these prospective teachers. The salaries for these teachers come from two separate sources, local funds and the State Minimum Program Fund. The contracts for employment contain within them the salary to be paid to the individual, as approved by the Board.

On October 10, 1986, the chancellor entered an order finding all defendants to be in violation of Section 109. He further adjudicated the defendants' spouses' contracts to be null and void, and that each defendant had an indirect interest in these contracts as he had been a Trustee of the Claiborne County Board of Education when said Board approved one or more contracts for the employment of the defendants' spouses.

Finally, the chancellor ordered that claims of restitution be made against the spouses of the defendants because of the Section 109 violations. The Court found that these violations as to all defendants and their spouses had existed for several years up to and including the present date. This appeal followed.

Law

Article 4, Section 109 of the Mississippi Constitution of 1890 provides:

> No public officer or member of the legislature shall be interested, directly or indirectly, in any contract with the state, or any district, county, city or town thereof, authorized by any law passed or order made by any board of which he may be or may have been a member, during the term for which he shall have been chosen, or within one year after the expiration of such term.

In *Frazier,* we said that this section prohibits any officer from:

(a) having any direct or indirect interest in any contract
(b) with the state or any political subdivision
(c) executed during his term of office or one year thereafter, and
(d) unauthorized by any law, or order of any board of which he was a member.

We noted that while there is no difficulty in ascertaining (b) and (c), and while (a) and (d) have not always been so clear-cut, the answer "usually [being] simple, . . . it is (a) and (d) where the gray areas are encountered." *Id.*

The chancellor found that each defendant had an indirect interest in his spouse's contract as prohibited by Section 109. We would agree.

In *Frazier,* we declined to go so far as to hold that the rational purpose and intent of the 1890 constitution prohibited James Nunnally, appellant therein, from running for the legislature and serving as a member of that governmental branch, which voted on several public school laws at the time when his wife, Betty Jo Nunnally, was employed as a public school teacher in this state.

Whatever might be said of the logic supporting the contention that Sec. 109 was violated because (1) Mr. Nunnally was in the Legislature (2) which passed a law authorizing his wife's public school employment contract (3) in which he manifestly had some interest, it simply defies practical wisdom to carry this section to such an extreme. As Justice Brandeis once observed, "the logic of words should yield to the logic of realities." *DiSanto v. Pennsylvania,* 273 U.S. 34, 43 (1927).

However, without hesitation we find that logic dictates some manifest interest by appellants herein in the public school employment contracts of their wives. Appellants are directly responsible for the hiring and firing of their spouses. Additionally, the record indicates that these school board members share fully in the process behind which the salaries are awarded to public school teachers in their district. This is not to say that we question the integrity or fairness of these board members in any way; we simply recognize that each has an indirect interest in his wife's contract which violates the constitutional provision.

In *Frazier,* this Court said the following:

> We hold that where a portion of the salaries derived by public school teachers under their teaching contracts comes from *discretionary* local tax levies, a teacher cannot make a valid contract with a school district while he is on the board of the governing authority which makes such tax levies, or within one year after his term on the governing board expires. Such a contract violates Sec. 109.
>
> It therefore follows that insofar as Miss. Code Ann. §25-4-105(3)(h) attempts to make an exception and authorize such a contract, it is at cross purposes with Sec. 109 and unconstitutional.
>
> As was aptly stated in *Commonwealth v. Withers,* 266 Ky. 29, 98 S.W.2d 24, 25 (1936):
>
>> It is a salutary doctrine that he who is entrusted with the business of others cannot be allowed to make such business as object of profit to himself. This is based upon principles of reason, of morality, and of public policy. These are principles of the common law and of equity which have been supplemented and made more emphatic by the foregoing and other statutory enactments. 504 So. 2d at 700.

And while this interpretation of Sec. 109 addresses the situation in which a school board member votes his own salary out of discretionary local tax levies, no distinction can be made by his voting that of his wife—the interest therein is one and the same.

Next, we address the question of restitution ordered by the lower court and brought up on appeal. In the trial below plaintiffs and appellees herein neither plead nor raised the question of any bad faith committed by appellants for their role in the employment of their spouses. Nor did the chancellor make any finding of such.

In our review of the record, we can see no allegation by these Claiborne County taxpayers that they did not receive value for services performed by the teachers, whose time of employment ranged from two (2) to thirty-three (33) years. Further, in at least one instance the record shows that a spouse of one board member had been teaching long before his election to that body. . . .

We, therefore, uphold the chancellor's order finding appellants herein have been and are in violation of Sec. 109; declaring the contracts of appellants' spouses to be null and void; and enjoining any further payment of salaries, etc. to said spouses while appellants remain as members of the Board of the Claiborne County School District and for a period of one year after the defendants shall leave their official capacities, . . . We reverse the chancellor's order of restitution. . . .

NOTES AND QUESTIONS

1. How deep into a familial relationship should the conflict rules extend? In *Williams v. Augusta County School Board,* 248 Va. 124, 445 S.E.2d 118 (Va. 1994), the Virginia Supreme Court construed the language of Virginia's law prohibiting school boards to employ relatives of board members, and concluded that the board had no power to hire the sister-in-law of a board member. How should a board policy be drafted to insure the public trust without depriving a school district of the flexibility it may need to hire otherwise qualified faculty? What about close personal friends of board members who apply to be teachers in the district? Should that create a debilitating conflict as well?
2. Of what significance is the timing of the hiring decision? In *Williams,* the court noted that the state's conflict rules create an exception allowing the employment of relatives of board members who have been "regularly employed at the time the employee becomes a member of the Board." If the board approves salary and promotion for teachers on an annual basis, what difference does it make that the teacher was hired before the board member was elected to the board?
3. The concept of incompatibility of offices is a doctrine created by the courts which precludes the holding of two public offices simultaneously if the two offices conflict. For example, the courts have held that the offices of county board member and deputy county coroner are incompatible, *see People ex rel. Teros v. Verbeck,* 106 Ill. Dec. 757, 506 N.E.2d 464 (1987), and that the offices of village trustee and police officer are incompatible. *Rogers v. Tinley Park,* 72 Ill. Dec. 1 451, N.E.2d 1324 (1983).

The attorney generals in some states have issued opinions addressing the compatibility of the office of school board member with other public offices. Consider whether the following offices are incompatible with the office of school board member: mayor, city council member, park board member, county board member, library district trustee and town trustee. What is the effect of such a conflict in each situation?

4. Board Conflicts and the Private Corporation Model Policy Practicum

As the examples of state law ethics provisions included in the prior section make clear, school board members are governed by the laws and regulations pertaining to elected, public officials. The "model" of legal constraints on board decision making, therefore, is the "elected official model." It is typically not the private sector, corporate board model. Nonetheless, as the push toward fiscal accountability and privatization in public education increases, so too has the tendency to conflate school board process with corporate board process. Should a school board be governed by state laws passed to regulate the boards of private corporations, or state laws passed to regulate public officials, or both?

The issue of the proper regulatory model has particular relevance to the treatment of school board conflicts of interest. Under the law governing the private business organization, a member of the board of directors may enter into a transaction with that director's own corporation, but must establish that the transaction was procedurally and substantively "fair" to the corporation. Under the Revised Model Business Corporations Act (the RMBCA), for example, a board member can avoid any liability for a conflicted transaction if the transaction has been fully disclosed and independently ratified. The RMBCA establishes alternative mechanisms for "independent" ratification, including the majority vote of independent board members, the recommendation of a committee of independent board members or the majority vote of shares held by independent shareholders. *See* RMBCA §8.31. Moreover, the RMBCA allows the board member to avoid liability even in the absence of showing independent ratification, if the board member can prove that the transaction was substantively "fair" to the corporation.

If the RMBCA were applied by analogy to the work of school board members, board members could insulate themselves from sanctions for a "conflicted" transaction by proving either that the decision was reached by an independent process or was substantively fair to the school district. Suppose, for example, a school board member was also the chair of the board, chief executive officer and majority shareholder of a corporation that has patented and now sells a new form of "dustless chalk" for use in the classroom. Under the RMBCA model, the district could approve a contract for the purchase of that chalk after being informed of the board member's conflict. Approval could be accomplished by a majority vote of independent board members, a committee of independent board members or (by analogy) a referendum of the district's taxpaying voters. Alternatively, the board members could attempt to establish the substantive "fairness" of the transaction, proving for example that the chalk was an invaluable product and only available from the board member's own company.

In most situations, this private corporate model for handling conflicts will allow for transactions barred by the far less flexible public official model. What are the advantages and disadvantages of applying the corporate law model to school board members?

Assuming that your school board client has asked you to draft policy language which establishes board governance procedures, particularly involving potential conflict of interest transactions, what language would you suggest?

B. SCHOOL BOARD ACTION AND PROCEDURES

In order to be legitimate, any action taken by the school board must occur at a validly constituted meeting. The meetings must be properly scheduled, noticed, conducted and recorded. As a public body, school boards generally must conduct their meetings in public view. School boards may set their own meeting procedures or may use more formal procedures, such as those contained in *Robert's Rules of Order*. If a school board adopts its own rules for meeting procedures, those rules should be filed for public inspection in the district's administrative office, along with other rules and policies adopted by the board.

1. Scheduling of Meetings

The state school codes typically require that the time and place of regular meetings be set by the new board at its first meeting. This organizational meeting must occur shortly (usually within seven days) after a school board election. At that meeting, the board must canvass the votes cast for new board members, declare victorious the winners and administer the oath of office. The newly organized board must then adopt a schedule of regular meetings for the year. *See, e.g.,* Florida Stat. §1001.372; Illinois Statutes, 105 ILCS 5/10-16.

The state's Open Meetings Act invariably also requires that a schedule of the dates, times and places of regular meetings be prepared and made available by the board at the beginning of every calendar or fiscal year. *See, e.g.,* Illinois Statutes, 5 ILCS 120/2.02, 2.03. In Texas, for example, every governmental body must provide written notice of the date, hour, place, and subject of each meeting held by that body. (Tex. Govt. §551.041.) In Florida, as well, all meetings must be open meetings at all times; the board must provide reasonable notice of all such meetings; minutes of a meeting must be promptly recorded and open to public inspection, and the board is prohibited from holding meetings at any facility or location which discriminates on the basis of sex, age, race, creed, color, origin or economic status or which operates in such a manner as to unreasonably restrict public access to such a facility. (Fla. Stat. §286.011 (2002).)

The board may also call "special" meetings on lesser notice. *See, e.g.,* Florida Stat. §1001.372. A special meeting may be called by the board president or by any three board members at any time by serving written notice upon board members either by mail 48 hours before the meeting or by personal service 24 hours before the meeting. This notice must state the time, place and purpose of the special meeting. *See, e.g.,* Illinois Statutes, 105 ILCS 5/10-16.

A board must mail copies of its board agenda, school budgets, and audits to any constituent annually requesting to be on an established school district mailing list. *See, e.g.,* Illinois Statutes, 105 ILCS 5/10-21.6. It must also mail copies of approved board minutes promptly after the board meeting at which the minutes were approved. The state's Open Meetings Act may require minutes of approved meetings to be available to the public shortly after their approval. A board may charge an annual subscription fee for those persons who request to be placed on the mailing list.

2. The Typical School Board Meeting Agenda

The following is a template for the typical school board meeting.

A. Call to Order by Presiding Officer
The board president is responsible for conducting the board meetings. The president is elected from among the board members for a one or

two-year term. *See, e.g.,* 105 ILCS 5/10-3. The vice president, also elected from among the board members, serves as president *pro tempore* if the president is absent or unable to act. *See, e.g.,* 105 ILCS 5/10-13.1.

B. Roll Call
The secretary takes the roll call of board members and keeps all official minutes and records of meetings. *See, e.g.,* 105 ILCS 5/10-7. The secretary is elected by the board, but need not be a member of the board, and serves for a two-year term, unless a one-year term is determined by resolution as board policy. The board secretary may be compensated for duties performed, but payment is typically limited if the secretary is a member of the board. *See, e.g.,* 105 ILCS 5/10-14 (no more than $500).

C. Quorum
At common law, a quorum equals a majority of the full membership of the board. Most states have codified this common law rule in their school codes. *See Matawan Regional Teachers Ass'n v. Matawan-Aberdeen Regional Board of Education,* 223 N.J. Super. 504, 538 A.2d 1331 (1988) (common law rule of majority is default rule, absent statute). If a quorum is not present, no official meeting or board action can occur.

D. Approval of Minutes
As required by the Open Meetings Act, minutes must be kept of both open and closed session meetings and of board-appointed committee meetings. Board minutes may be amended before being approved, but only to correct the recording of what actually occurred at the meeting, not to change votes or to amend an action of the board. Board minutes are not deemed to be official until they have been approved by the school board.

E. Visitors
At each regular and special meeting open to the public, members of the public and district employees must be given reasonable time to comment or ask questions of the board. Rules for public participation may be set by the board. *See, e.g.,* 105 ILCS 5/10-16.

F. Action Items

1. Procedures
A board may use procedures outlined in *Robert's Rules,* or may develop board policy regulating meeting procedures regarding the process for taking action.

2. Motions
Most actions are introduced by motions which are seconded, discussed, voted upon and recorded in the minutes. The process is as follows: (1) motion made (may be written ahead of time); (2) motion seconded; and (3) discussion held. Finally, at the end of the discussion, either a vote is taken or the matter may be tabled.

3. Consent Agenda
Some recurring items may be grouped for efficiency, such as personnel appointments, and approval of payment of monthly bills and salaries. However, the items grouped should be publicly mentioned or itemized in an agenda made available to the public before the meeting so that the board vote on the consent agenda items can be understood.

4. Resolutions
Some actions may require resolutions conforming to legal specifications. For example, the following matters may require a resolution rather than a simple motion: non-reemployment and dismissal of personnel; authorization of a teacher notice; bond issuance, and transfer of monies between funds.

5. Voting
   a. If a quorum is present, a majority of the votes of the members voting on an issue shall determine the outcome, unless a specific law provides otherwise. In other words, the votes cast in favor of a motion must exceed the votes cast in opposition to the motion. *See Collins v. Janey,* 147 Tenn. 477, 249 S.W. 801 (1922) (vote of three to two passes resolution on a seven-member board). All board members, including the president, may vote on any action. A roll call vote often is required on all questions involving the expenditure of money. In some states, four votes (a majority of the full board) may be required to dismiss a tenured teacher. *See, e.g.,* 105 ILCS 5/24-12. Leasing real property for school purposes or leasing real property to another governmental body, if the lease term exceeds ten years, or leasing equipment and machinery, often requires a two-thirds vote of the full board (five members). *See, e.g.,* 105 ILCS 5/10-22.11, 10-22.12, 10-23.4a. Similarly, the sale or exchange of school property requires a two-thirds vote of the full board (five members). *See, e.g.,* 105 ILCS 5/5-22 and 5/23. Invocation of the emergency exception to the public bidding procedures requires approval by three-fourths of the board (six members). 105 ILCS 5/10-20.21. An abstention vote does not count as a vote, but does count for determination of whether a quorum is present. If several members abstain, a board may not have the majority votes necessary to pass a measure that requires a majority vote of the *full* board. If several members abstain on a vote that requires a simple majority of a quorum, then the measure could pass with only one "aye" vote. *See, e.g.,* 105 ILCS 5/10-12. If a tie vote occurs, of course, the motion fails.

6. Rescinding Prior Board Action
"Undoing" of a board action may not occur by rewriting or amending the minutes originally approving the action. Rather, rescission or revocation of a prior official action requires a

board vote on a new motion to rescind or revoke the earlier action.

G. Discussion Items
Items not requiring action, or requiring action at a later date, may be discussed without a vote, such as the first reading of a board policy to be adopted at a later meeting.

H. Information Items
Boards typically require their administrators and staff to report periodically on matters such as school events, curriculum, new programs, and student assessment data. At each regular board meeting, the president or superintendent must report on any requests made of the district under the *Freedom of Information Act* and the status of the district's response. The board generally informs the public of any correspondence it has received.

I. Closed Session
There is a strong presumption that school board business must take place in open session. Nonetheless, portions of meetings closed to the public may be called and entered pursuant to the state's Open Meetings Act. Discussion must be kept confidential. No action may be taken in closed session; resulting action must be taken at a public meeting. *See, e.g., Dryden v. Marcellus Community Schools,* 401 Mich. 76, 257 N.W.2d 79 (Mich. 1977) (official action even on a closed session item must be taken in open session).

J. Old Business
Discussion of items previously before the board are often handled separately as "old business" matters on the meeting agenda.

K. New Business
Any member of a board may place items of new business on the agenda at any meeting in accordance with local district procedures.

L. Requests From Residents
Many states require the board to respond promptly to requests for action by community members. Typically, if the board president or superintendent receives from a resident of the district a written request to consider a specific matter before the board, an appointed board official must respond formally in writing to the request no later than 60 days from its receipt. The formal board response must state the board's position on the resident's request and shall either establish a meeting before the board or list the reasons for denying the request. *See, e.g.,* 105 ILCS 5/10-6.

M. Adjournment
The adjournment of a meeting may be announced by the president or may be done by motion of a board member. The board may move to adjourn and reconvene in closed session for matters that are appropriate for nonpublic discussion under the state's Open Meetings Act.

3. The Open Meetings Act

Most states require through an Open Meetings Act that school boards conduct business in public. The Open Meetings Act is based on the policy that public bodies exist to aid in the conduct of the people's business and that the people have a right to be informed as to the conduct of their business. The Act insures that the actions of public bodies are taken openly and that their deliberations are also conducted openly. In addition, citizens must be given advance notice of, and the right to attend, all meetings at which any business of a public body is discussed or acted upon in any way. As a result, the provisions of the Act usually are to be construed narrowly against closed meetings.

The Open Meetings Act in most states governs "meetings" of public bodies, defined as any gathering of a majority of a quorum of the members of a public body held for the purpose of discussing public business. For purposes of the Act, boards of education and their committees are considered public bodies. Consequently, when a majority of a quorum of the board or a committee appointed by the board meets to discuss public business, the provisions of the Act must be strictly followed, including adherence to notice, open session, and written minutes requirements.

(a) Time and Place for Meetings

Meetings must be held at specified times and places which are convenient and open to the public. The Americans With Disabilities Act, 42 U.S.C. §12101 *et seq.*, requires that meetings of public entities be held in locations accessible to individuals with disabilities. Meetings cannot be held on a legal holiday unless the regular meeting day falls on that holiday.

(b) Notice Requirements

Notice must be provided to the public of all meetings of a school board or its committees, including notice of the schedule of regular meetings and notices of any special, emergency, rescheduled or reconvened meetings. Such notice must be posted at the district's principal office or, if no such office exists, at the building where the meeting is to be held. The posted notice of meetings should include notice of the availability of accommodations (such as interpreters) to meet the district's disability notice and accommodation obligations under the Americans With Disabilities Act, 42 U.S.C. §12101 *et seq.* The public body also must supply notice of all meetings to any news medium that has filed an annual request for such notice. In addition, an agenda for each meeting must be posted at the principal office of the public body and at the location where the meeting is to be held, usually at least 48 hours in advance of holding the meeting. The requirement of a regular meeting agenda does not preclude the consideration of items not specifically set forth in the agenda.

The state's Open Meetings Act generally requires the following specific notices:

1. **Regular Meetings.** Public notice of the schedule of regular meetings is required at the beginning of each calendar or fiscal year, stating the

regular dates, times and places of such meetings. A list of the time and places of all regular meetings also must be prepared and made available at the beginning of each calendar or fiscal year. Changes in regular meeting dates require notice in advance of the meeting by publication in a newspaper of general circulation in the area in which the public body functions. Changes in regular meeting dates also must be posted at the district's principal office (or where the meeting is to be held if no such office exists) and supplied to any news medium which has filed an annual request.

2. **Special, Rescheduled Regular, and Reconvened Meetings.** Public notice of any special meeting, rescheduled regular meeting, or reconvened meeting is required in advance of the meeting. The notice must include the agenda of the meeting. The notice must be posted at the district's principal office or, if no such office exists, at the building where the meeting is to be held. In addition, the notice should be given to any news medium that has filed an annual request.
3. **Emergency Meetings.** Emergency meetings can be held only for bona fide reasons. Notice of an emergency meeting must be given as soon as practicable, but in any event prior to holding such an emergency meeting.

4. Minutes of Meetings

(a) Written Minutes Requirements

All public bodies and their committees are required to keep written minutes of all meetings, whether open or closed. *Harkenson v. Board of Education,* 10 Ill. App. 2d 79, 134 N.E.2d 356 (1956), *rev'd. on other grounds,* 10 Ill. 2d 560, 141 N.E.2d 5 (1957). At a minimum, the minutes must include the following: the date and time of the meeting; the members of the public body recorded as present or absent from the meeting; a summary of the discussion on all matters proposed, deliberated, or decided, and a record of any vote taken.

(b) Closed Session Minutes

Closed session minutes must also include the following when appropriate:

1. Minutes of a closed session called by a school board to respond to an actual danger to the safety of the students, staff or school premises must include a description of the actual danger, which was part of the motion to close the meeting.
2. Minutes of a closed session called to discuss litigation that is "probable and imminent" must include the basis for such a finding.

(c) Availability of Minutes

1. Minutes of open meetings must be made available for public inspection promptly after approval of those minutes.
2. Minutes of closed meetings must be made available for public inspection after the board determines in an open session that their

confidentiality is no longer required. Public bodies must meet at least semiannually to review minutes of closed sessions. At such meetings a determination must be made and reported in open session either that (1) the need for confidentiality still exists as to all or part of those minutes, or (2) the minutes or portions thereof no longer require confidential treatment and are available for public inspection. Either all or a portion of the minutes may be retained as confidential or released.

(d) Recordings of Meetings

Any person may record an open meeting by tape, film or other means pursuant to reasonable rules prescribed by the school board.

5. Exceptions to the Public Meeting Requirement: Closed Session

A limited number of exceptions to the Open Meetings Act exist. In light of the presumption favoring open meetings, however, a closed meeting may be held only where a specific reference to a statutory exception can be cited. *See, e.g., Hovet v. Hebron Public School District,* 419 N.W.2d 189 (N.D. 1988) (holding that a teacher's personnel file must be disclosed because no legislative directive specifically protects such files, despite the teacher's claims to privacy). The exceptions to the Open Meetings Act potentially applicable to school boards allow closed session consideration of the following:

- "The appointment, employment, compensation, discipline, performance, or dismissal of specific employees of the public body, including hearing testimony on a complaint lodged against an employee to determine its validity." *See, e.g.,* 5 ILCS 120/2(c)(1).
- "Collective negotiating matters between the public body and its employees or their representatives, or deliberations concerning salary schedules for one or more classes of employees." *See, e.g.,* 5 ILCS 120/2(c)(2).
- "The selection of a person to fill a public office . . . including a vacancy in a public office. . . ." *See, e.g.,* 5 ILCS 120/2(c)(3).
- "Evidence or testimony presented in open hearing, or in closed hearing where specifically authorized by law, to a quasi-adjudicative body, provided that the body prepares and makes available for public inspection a written decision setting forth its determinative reasoning." *See, e.g.,* 5 ILCS 120/2(c)(4).
- "The purchase or lease of real property for the use of the public body, including meetings held for the purpose of discussing whether a particular parcel should be acquired." *See, e.g.,* 5 ILCS 120/2(c)(5).
- "The setting of a price for sale or lease of property owned by the public body." 5 ILCS 120/2(c)(6).
- "The sale or purchase of securities, investments, or investment contracts." 5 ILCS 120/2(c)(7).
- "Security procedures and the use of personnel and equipment to respond to actual, a threatened, or a reasonably potential danger to the safety of employees, students, staff or public property." 5 ILCS 120/2(c)(8).

- "Student disciplinary cases." 5 ILCS 120/2(c)(9).
- "The placement of individual students in special education programs and other matters relating to individual students." 5 ILCS 120/2(c)(10).
- "Litigation, when an action against, affecting or on behalf of the particular public body has been filed and is pending before a court or administrative tribunal, or when the public body finds that an action is probable or imminent, in which case the basis for the finding shall be recorded and entered into the minutes of the closed meeting." 5 ILCS 120/(c)(11).
- "The establishment of reserves or settlement of claims as provided in the Local Governmental and Governmental Employees Tort Immunity Act, if otherwise the disposition of a claim or potential claim might be prejudiced, or the review or discussion of claims, loss or risk management information records, data, advice or communications from or with respect to any insurer of the public body or any intergovernmental risk management association or self insurance pool of which the public body is a member." 5 ILCS 120/2(c)(12).
- "Self evaluation, practices and procedures or professional ethics, when meeting with a representative of a statewide association of which the public body is a member." 5 ILCS 120/2(c)(16).
- "Discussion of minutes of meetings lawfully closed . . . whether for purposes of approval by the body of the minutes or semi-annual review of the minutes. . . ." 5 ILCS 120/2(c)(21).
- Negotiations meetings and grievance arbitration hearings may be conducted in closed session without specific public notice.

Consider each one of these exceptions to the requirement that school boards deliberate and act in public. What is its rationale? In *ACLU v. Bernasconi,* 557 A.2d 1232 (R.I. 1989), the Rhode Island Supreme Court upheld the school board's power to discuss and approve a plan to search student lockers for drugs in a closed session meeting. The court reasoned that the issue involved "security matters" that were exempt from the state's open meeting requirement. Do you agree?

What constitutes a "meeting" of board members that must comply with state process requirements? Suppose board members gather at a concert and begin deliberating board business? *Compare Harris v. Nordquist,* 96 Ore. App. 19, 771 P.2d 637 (1989) (no meeting at restaurant unless board members meet for the purpose of making "a decision") *with Paulton v. Volkmann,* 141 Wis. 2d 370, 415 N.W.2d 528 (1987) (attendance at another public body's meeting where board business discussed not improper).

In *Gosnell v. Hogan,* 179 Ill. App. 3d 161, 128 Ill. Dec. 252, 534 N.E.2d 434 (1989), the court declared that the interest in openness must give way to the greater interest in school board conduct that truly benefits the public. In interpreting ambiguous language in the Open Meetings Act, the court asks whether the *best decision* will be reached in public view or in executive session. Which forum do you believe is usually the most likely to produce such a decision?

Many states are beginning to adopt or to consider adopting legislation requiring school boards to tape or transcribe closed session meetings. What are the advantages and disadvantages to such legislation?

Finally, state law generally makes clear that e-mail communications between board members regarding board issues can constitute meetings within the ambit of the state's Open Meetings Act. *See* D. Stover, *School Boards in Hot Water,* School Board News (Natl. School Boards Assn. Mar. 18, 2003). The Open Meetings Act in most states does not yet take e-mail into account. How should e-mail communications be treated?

6. Freedom of Information Act Requirements

A state's Freedom of Information Act (FOIA) further requires public bodies, including school districts, to provide public records promptly for inspection or copying to any person who makes a written request. Like the Open Meetings Act, the FOIA recognizes that the people have a right to know the decisions, policies, procedures, rules, standards and other aspects of government activity that affect their lives. In Florida, every person who has custody of a public record must permit the record to be inspected and examined by any person desiring to do so at a reasonable time, under reasonable conditions, and under supervision by the custodian of the public record or the custodian's designee. (Fla. Stat. §119.07.) Similarly, in New York, the Freedom of Information Law provides:

i. The legislature hereby finds that a free society is maintained when government is responsive and responsible to the public, and when the public is aware of governmental actions. The more open a government is with its citizenry, the greater the understanding and participation of the public in government.

ii. The people's right to know the process of governmental decision-making and to review the documents and statistics leading to determination is basic to our society. Access to such information should not be thwarted by shrouding it with the cloak of secrecy or confidentiality.

iii. The legislature, therefore declares that government is the public's business and that the public, individually and collectively and represented by free press, should have access to the record of government in accordance with the provisions of this article. (N.Y. C.L.S. Pub. O. §86 *et seq.)*

(a) Documents Subject to Disclosure

The state's FOIA typically defines the term "public records" as records and documents in any form that have been prepared, have been used, are being used by, have been received, or are in the possession or control of the public body. This extremely broad definition includes more than just books or paper records. Public records include tape recordings, microfilm, and electronic data processing records. Examples of commonly requested public records include board meeting minutes and budget materials; procedural manuals for staff members; policies; administrative recommendations and decisions, and statements or interpretations of them; reports, documents and studies prepared by or for the district; and information regarding accounts or contracts that involve the expenditure of public funds (including the names, positions, dates of employment and salaries of all employees). School districts, however, generally are not required to create new documents in response to a FOIA request.

The FOIA contains a list of numerous exemptions to the general public disclosure requirement. Most of these exemptions, however, fall into four general categories:

1. Information which, if disclosed, would constitute an unwarranted invasion of privacy;
2. Certain preliminary and investigatory records;
3. Trade secrets and other confidential commercial or financial information; and
4. Information protected by law or privilege.

If a document that is exempt from disclosure contains material that is not exempt, the exempt material must be deleted and the remaining information disclosed. Many of the enumerated exceptions to the disclosure requirements pertain directly to school districts. For example, districts are not required to disclose records concerning faculty and staff evaluations, discipline matters (staff or student), or collective bargaining (except for final labor contracts). Also, districts may keep confidential certain discussions with their auditors and attorneys and notes and minutes from closed meetings held in accordance with the Open Meetings Act. Moreover, school districts are not required to allow inspection of tests or other examination data or materials. Finally, student and certain personnel records maintained by the district must be kept confidential except when the person about whom the record is maintained consents to disclosure or when disclosure is required by law. These exceptions are narrowly construed.

School districts are also required to prepare, display, and make available a brief description of the district. The description must include the district's purpose, the number of its employees, a diagram illustrating its organizational structure, its operating budget, and the names of board members. This notice should also contain a description of the methods by which the public may request records. Finally, districts are required to maintain a reasonably detailed and current list of all types and categories of records under its control.

(b) Procedure

The FOIA mandates that specific procedures be followed by a school district in responding to requests for public documents. The district is required to respond to a written request promptly, often within seven working days after receipt. If the request is unduly burdensome, the district is entitled to additional response time. If a district denies a request for information or requires an extension for providing the information, the district must notify the requesting person in writing of the decision and the specific reason for the delay or denial.

A school district may charge fees reasonably calculated to reimburse its actual costs for reproducing and certifying copies of any public records requested. The fee schedule must be made public. Reduction or waiver of the fee may be required if the person requesting the documents indicates that the request is in the public interest.

(c) Remedies

A person denied access to records may file suit for injunctive and declaratory relief. If successful, the applicant can receive attorney's fees if the sought-after records were clearly of significant interest to the general public and if the public body lacked a reasonable basis for withholding the records in question.

7. Board Procedures Practicum: Drafting Policies Governing Board Process

The state law requirements governing school board process restrict the board's discretion in the mechanics of its business. Nevertheless, state law does permit some discretion with respect to the conduct of board meetings and the board's communications with the community.

A school district attorney will be asked to distinguish those areas of board process that are mandatory from those that are discretionary. For example, the board has no choice but to meet in open session in taking action, but has great discretion in deciding how to allow public comments during board meetings. Similarly, the board must respond to FOIA requests, but has some latitude in drafting policy language governing the mechanics of its response.

Assume that the president of the board seeks legal and political advice regarding such an issue. A number of community members who are unable to attend board meetings in person have requested that the meetings be televised live and by periodic replay on the cable television's local access channel. The cable company is willing to do whatever it takes to accommodate the board's wishes. Must the board televise its meetings? If it has the choice whether to televise or not, how should it proceed? What are the pros and cons to televised board meetings?

C. BOARD-SUPERINTENDENT RELATIONS AND THE LIMITS OF ADMINISTRATION POWER

The school board has broad authority to govern the affairs of its school district. In reality, however, the board will delegate its own power to a chief executive officer or superintendent. That chief administrator will actually "manage" the district. The relationship between the popularly elected school board and its appointed educational professional often produces both legal and political issues that may be difficult to resolve.

FREMONT RE-1 SCHOOL DISTRICT v. JACOBS

737 P.2d 816 (Colo. 1987)

Justice ROVIRA delivered the Opinion of the Court.

Respondent Joyce Jacobs, a bus driver for the Fremont RE-1 School District, filed suit in May 1983 after she was fired by Norman Lemons, the school district's director of business services, in February 1983. She alleged that her firing was unlawful because the school board could not delegate to the director of business services the power to discharge her. The trial court disagreed and granted summary judgment for the school district and Lemons. In *Jacobs v. Fremont RE-1 School District,* the court of appeals reversed, concluding that the school board could lawfully delegate the authority to dismiss bus drivers because the function was administrative or ministerial in nature and not legislative or judicial. However, it found that the delegation would be valid only if it were accompanied by specific standards which left little or nothing to the discretion or judgment of the school administrators. Since the question of adequate standards had not been resolved by the trial court, the court of appeals found that summary judgment was inappropriate. We now conclude that the school board could lawfully delegate to its agents the task of firing bus drivers and that the standards set forth by the Fremont School Board in this case were adequate as a matter of law. Therefore, we affirm in part and reverse in part the judgment of the court of appeals.

I

Undisputed facts in the record show that prior to the firing of Jacobs the Fremont Board of Education had adopted a policy for the discharge of "classified personnel"—which included bus drivers like Jacobs and also secretaries, office clerks, bookkeepers, and maintenance employees. The policy, which was published in an employee handbook, provided that:

> The Board of Education delegates to the Superintendent of Schools the authority to dismiss classified personnel. Further, the Superintendent of Schools may delegate this authority to the Director of Business Services and/or the Director of Personnel. Classified employees shall be employed for such time as the District is in need of, or desirous of, the services of such employees. The duration of employment is unspecified and solely rests at the discretion of the District.

. . . Dismissal of classified employees shall be unaffected by the employee's religious beliefs, marital status, racial or ethnic background, sex, or participation in community affairs.

In February 1983, following a disagreement between Jacobs and her superiors stemming from a disciplinary action Jacobs had taken on her bus, she was discharged by Lemons. Later, after Jacobs filed suit, the school board ratified her discharge.

II

The sole question presented for review here is whether the board of education could lawfully delegate to the superintendent of schools and, through him, to Lemons the authority to dismiss Jacobs. An examination of the relevant statutes discloses that the legislature has imposed upon school boards certain "duties," and has granted them certain "powers." The Fremont school board points out that the legislature has granted school boards the "power" to discharge personnel under Section 22-32-110(h), but has not made employee discharge a "duty" of school boards under Section 22-32-109. It argues, therefore, that the school board was authorized to delegate the responsibility for discharging employees.

We disagree with this line of argument. As we read the statutes, Section 22-32-109 sets forth mandatory "duties" of school boards and Section 22-32-110 sets forth discretionary "powers." The listing of employee discharge as a "power" under Section 22-32-110 indicates only that a school board may, but need not, exercise its authority to fire employees. The statutes, as we read them, do not specify the scope of a school board's authority to delegate its duties and powers—they merely indicate which powers a school board *may* exercise and which duties it *must* perform.

We turn, therefore, to the rule of construction we adopted in *Big Sandy School District No. 100-J v. Carroll,* a case which presented us with a similar issue. In that case, members of a school board informally authorized the superintendent to hire a principal-teacher and provided him with a signed, blank contract. Thereafter, the superintendent apparently hired one Barney Carroll for the post, but discharged him ten days later. Carroll sued for breach of contract. The issue, as a result, was whether the superintendent had authority to hire a principal-teacher without the school board's explicit approval of the job applicant and his rate of pay. In examining the Colorado statute then in effect, we initially noted that it was the school board's "duty" to employ teachers. We then discussed and applied the established rule of construction applicable to quasi-municipal corporations like the school district:

> The general rule is that . . . a quasi-municipal corporation . . . may delegate to subordinate officers and boards powers and functions which are ministerial or administrative in nature, where there is a fixed and certain standard or rule which leaves little or nothing to the judgment or discretion of the subordinate. However, legislative or judicial powers, involving judgment and discretion on the part of the municipal body, which have been vested by statute in a municipal corporation may *not* be delegated unless such has been expressly authorized by the legislature.

Big Sandy, 164 Colo. at 178-79, 433 P.2d at 328. Analyzing the facts under this standard, we concluded that the power to employ teachers and fix their wages is a nondelegable statutory power which the legislature has conferred solely on the school board. It was thus not subject to delegation without explicit legislative authorization.

The principle announced in *Big Sandy* serves several salutary purposes. By placing limits on the delegation of power by school boards, it assures the public that school board members—who are subject to public election—must take responsibility for significant policy decisions associated with management of the school district. Further, the rule protects school districts from incurring significant liabilities based on actions taken by school administrators without the full considered approval of the school board. Lastly, by limiting delegation as a rule of statutory construction, questions concerning the constitutionality of delegation of legislative powers are avoided.

However, we are convinced that the *Big Sandy* rule should not be extended beyond the limited purposes it serves. As a practical matter, school districts require a significant degree of administrative flexibility in order to function smoothly on a day-to-day basis between meetings of their school boards. As school organizations have grown in size and their functions have become more diverse and complex, the need for administrative delegation has become all the more imperative. If the law were to insist on strict limitations on delegation of authority, school board members might tend to become mired in the details of routine operations, and the effectiveness and usefulness of school administrators might be hampered. As a result, the trend in this area of the law has been to allow greater flexibility and away from the insistence on detailed and definite standards. O. Reynolds, *Local Government Law* §57, at 166-68 (1982). In this vein, we have said:

> The modern tendency of the courts is toward greater liberality in permitting grants of discretion to administrative officials in order to facilitate the administration of the laws as the complexity of governmental and economic conditions increases.

Asphalt Paving Co. v. Board of County Commissioners. In a somewhat different context, we have held that:

> The [School] Board can select reasonable means to carry out its duties and responsibilities incidental to the sound development of employer-employee relations, as long as the means selected are not prohibited by law or against public policy.

Littleton Education Association v. Arapahoe County School District, 191 Colo. 411, 416, 553 P.2d 793, 797 (1976) (citing, *Louisiana Teachers' Association v. New Orleans Parish School Board,* 303 So. 2d 564 (La. App. 1974)).

Analyzing the question before us with these principles in mind, we conclude that the discharge of a bus driver is an administrative function subject to delegation by the school board. In our view, this action was not significantly related to the policy-making duties of the Fremont school board. In reaching this conclusion, we note that the character of this action—the discharge of a bus driver—is collateral to the school board's educational mission and the significance of this action is not so great that the law should demand the formal accountability of school board members before recognizing the validity of the action.

We recognize that in the past we have held that the power to hire teachers and fix their wages and the power to dismiss them are nondelegable powers. However, the hiring and firing of teachers directly affect the educational mission of the school district, and a central purpose for the election of school board members is to obtain their judgment on such matters. Actions that do not have a significant impact on institutional policy, on the other hand, are properly characterized as administrative in character and therefore are delegable. *Kreith v. University of Colorado,* 689 P.2d 718 (Colo. App. 1984) (holding that the authority to accept teacher resignation or retirement offers is delegable). We do not believe the discharge of a bus driver significantly affects the Fremont school board's institutional policy; therefore, we agree with the court of appeals that the power to discharge Jacobs was properly delegable.

However, we disagree with the holding of the court of appeals that further investigation of the adequacy of the standards limiting the discretion of the school administrators is required in this case. In our view, the standards set forth by the Fremont school board were adequate as a matter of law. Under the school board's employee handbook, "classified employees" served at the will of the district except that they could not be dismissed on account of their religious beliefs, marital status, racial or ethnic background, sex or participation in community affairs.

Ordinarily, a delegation of discretion this broad might run afoul of even the liberalized rules that have been applied to administrative delegation in recent cases. The requirement of standards to limit administrative discretion is designed to assure that administrative action will be rational and consistent and that subsequent judicial review will be available and effective. However, the law has traditionally accorded employers—including government agencies—broad discretion in the discharge of employees who are terminable at will. The general rule is that, absent a violation of constitutional rights, judicial review is not available to review the firing of an employee who is terminable at will. Such an employee may be dismissed without any justifying cause whatever.

Further, the traditional rule with respect to local government employees has been that:

> Local government employees hold their posts at the pleasure of the proper local government authorities and can be dismissed without cause, in the absence of restrictions or limitations provided by law.

Here, no additional restrictions or limitations relevant to this case have been provided by law. To the contrary, the Colorado legislature has explicitly provided tenure for specified teachers but has adopted no comparable protections for "classified employees" like Jacobs. Furthermore, the Fremont school board has explicitly categorized classified employees as terminable at will with a few limitations not pertinent here. As a result, we are not convinced the rule of construction applied in *Big Sandy* should operate to override the considered policy choices of the legislature and the school board.

The court of appeals' insistence on specific standards for dismissal, however, might indirectly convert Fremont's terminable at will employees to employees terminable only for cause—unless the school board were willing to decide itself every case involving the discharge of a "classified employee." Further, the adoption of more specific standards for dismissal could well create "property" rights for classified employees that would entitle them to a panoply of procedural due process protections. *E.g., Board of Regents v. Roth,* 408 U.S. 564, 33 L. Ed. 2d 548, 92 S. Ct. 2701 (1972); *Perry v. Sindermann,* 408 U.S. 593, 33 L. Ed. 2d 570, 92 S. Ct. 2694 (1972); *see also Bishop v. Wood,* 426 U.S. 341, 48 L. Ed. 2d 684, 96 S. Ct. 2074 (1976); *Arnett v. Kennedy,* 416 U.S. 134, 40 L. Ed. 2d 15, 94 S. Ct. 1633 (1974). Additionally, the adoption of specific dismissal standards might convert what is now an administrative function into a judicial function, which is not subject to delegation under the *Big Sandy* rule absent explicit legislative authorization. Consequently, it may be meaningless to hold that the discharge power may be delegated if more specific standards are adopted; if more specific standards are adopted, the power may no longer be delegable. We decline to overrule the policy decisions of the Colorado legislature and the

Fremont school board in such a roundabout fashion. In our view, the standards adopted by the school board are sufficient as a matter of law.

Accordingly, the judgment of the court of appeals is affirmed in part and reversed in part, and we remand to the court with instructions that it reinstate summary judgment on behalf of the petitioners.

NOTES AND QUESTIONS

1. The court appears to distinguish matters of "judgment and discretion," which are not delegable, from "administrative" functions, which are delegable. Is this distinction meaningful?
2. Most boards of education do not evaluate personnel. Instead, they delegate the evaluation of teachers, principals and administrative officers to the superintendent or like central administrator. Is the evaluation of personnel a purely "administrative" function, or does it involve matters of judgment? If the evaluation of personnel involves professional judgment, is the board safe in its delegation of that evaluation?
3. How would you counsel a board of education in its decision to delegate various responsibilities, such as: (1) instructional practices, (2) finance, (3) contract negotiations, (4) intergovernmental relations, and (5) media relations?

D. INTERNAL GOVERNANCE PRACTICUM: POLICY GOVERNANCE AND STRATEGIC PLANNING

1. Policy Governance

Attorneys who represent school districts spend a great deal of their time counseling school boards regarding process issues related to governance. In addition, "school lawyers" help school districts adopt board policies. Indeed the most significant method by which a school board governs a school district is through school board policies. Some such policies are required by federal statutes. For example, the Federal Drug Free Workplace Act requires a board policy establishing a drug-free workplace. Some policies are required by state law. For instance, the Open Meetings Act in virtually every state requires school boards to adopt a policy mandating that board meetings be reduced to minutes. As to those policies required by federal or state law, school lawyers must counsel their school board clients to adopt such policies and typically will draft the policies for adoption.

The great bulk of school board policies, however, are not required by law. Rather, they represent a political or educational judgment of the board. Nonetheless, effective school lawyers will strongly recommend to their clients the adoption of a host of "optional policies." In most cases, these policies will articulate legal requirements. While the law may not require the adoption of the policy, the law may require the practice reflected in the policy. Attorneys representing school districts, therefore, often draft such policies and strongly recommend that their clients adopt them. For instance, federal and state law defines residency requirements for determining a district's responsibility to educate a child. A clear policy articulating these residency requirements will:

1. communicate to the public that the district understands the legal requirements;
2. communicate to the superintendent and the educational organization the steps they must take to insure compliance with the law; and
3. communicate to parents and guardians information from which they can determine their child's residency for educational purposes.

Finally, there may be board policies that are neither required by law nor reflect legal requirements. These policies instead reflect the board's political or educational judgment. For example, a board of education may decide that each school within its district should conduct an annual "climate survey" to obtain an understanding of the organizational health of that school and to foster school improvement. Rather than informally communicating that desire to the superintendent or speaking about that desire at a board meeting, the board may decide to adopt a board policy that formally states its position. This type of governance, which is sometimes called "policy governance," has the following advantages:

1. The process of drafting a proposed policy itself forces the board to focus on its objectives;
2. The process of consideration of adopting the policy insures public discussion among board members and the public about the proposed policy;
3. Once the policy is adopted, the district's administrators have a clear, tangible direction from the board;
4. The district's administrators can literally point to the policy itself to help them in moving the entire system toward the objectives articulated in the policy;
5. The policy may give administrators some "cover" or protection in implementing measures that may not be popular with parents, faculty or staff; and
6. Policy governance helps to define the separate roles played by the board and administrators; once the board has performed its function of setting policy, it can withdraw and allow the administration to perform its function of implementing the policy.

2. Strategic Planning

Consistent with the principles of policy governance, well-functioning school boards do not micromanage the district's daily operations. Rather, they hold the superintendent accountable for the successes and failures of the district. The board, however, must develop standards by which to measure the superintendent's performance. A sophisticated board will insure that those standards are not unilaterally imposed by the board. The standards should come about as part of a cycle of goal setting. That cycle requires a commitment to a strategic planning process.

School districts have embraced private sector models of organizational growth and often devote a great deal of time to the strategic planning process. While school district attorneys typically do not actually participate in the planning meetings, they are often called on for advice about the process itself and its relationship to performance goals written into administrative and teacher contracts. Accordingly, school lawyers should be familiar with the strategic planning process. An effective school district strategic plan should be: widely publicized and understood; clear and unambiguous; attainable within the existing economic, political, and organizational contexts; attainable within the general time frame that has been articulated; manageable in scope; philosophically consistent with the vision of the district's leadership, and concentrated on planned instructional improvement and student growth.

Strategic planning is a management approach that uses a wide range of stakeholders to create plans based on assumptions about the future. Six processes are associated with the development of a strategic plan. An external analysis examines, among other things, social, economic, and demographic trends. An internal analysis explores management and operational processes, organizational resources and future needs. Together the internal and external analyses indicate the current status of the district and provide the basis for a strategic direction. The strategic direction is expressed in the development of goals and strategic plans. The strategic plans are implemented by committees chaired by the administrative team. At periodic intervals the plan is evaluated and the results are shared openly with a professional staff, a steering committee, the community and the school board. All steps in the plan must involve board members, administrators, teachers, parents, students and community members.

The strategic plan will encompass the district's mission statement, beliefs, three- to five-year goals and annual objectives. The following four strategic plans are representative of the different types of strategic plans employed throughout the country.

(a) Peters Township School District (15 miles south of Pittsburgh, Pennsylvania)

MISSION STATEMENT

In a cooperative partnership with a community that values excellence in education, the Peters Township School District will insure that all students acquire the knowledge base and skills necessary to become contributing members of society and life-long learners by providing the highest quality resources and staff within a comprehensive, result-oriented program implemented by caring people.

Educational Goals

Goal 1: Peters Township School District students will acquire knowledge at a high level.

Goal 2: Peters Township School District students will work independently and cooperatively.

Goal 3: Peters Township School District students will set and achieve personal goals.

Goal 4: Peters Township School District will obtain, train, and retain high quality personnel.

Goal 5: Peters Township School District will meet the educational needs of all students.

Goal 6: Peters Township High School students will meet new graduation requirements set by the State Board of Education.

Organizational Goals

Goal 1: Peters Township School District will provide facility and transportation services to support educational programs.

Goal 2: Peters Township School District will optimize the use of resources to meet district goals.

Goal 3: Peters Township School District will revise policies to reflect the needs and desires of the community.

Technology Goals

Goal 1: Peters Township School District will explore the use of technology in student learning.

Goal 2: Peters Township School District will use technology to optimize administrative and management functions.

Goal 3: Peters Township School District will use technology to enhance communication with parents and the community.

(b) Inter-Lakes School District (ILSD), New Hampshire

The mission of ILSD is to foster quality teaching and learning, promote social responsibility and encourage personal growth. We have our final list of FOCUS AREAS:

A. We will develop and implement a district-wide assessment plan.
B. We will research and promote a learning environment and academic program that best meets the needs of students in the middle grades.
C. We will build unity and cohesiveness within our communities and throughout our district.

Belief Statements

The following are some belief statements that we hope are universally true and accepted by all members of our communities.

1. All people are expected to act with reason, respect and responsibility.
2. Families share in the responsibility for the education of their children.

3. Better decisions are made from multiple sources of information including data, financial analysis, alignment with the mission statement, and input from shareholders.
4. District resources must be used as efficiently and effectively as possible.
5. We are committed to continuous school and self-improvement.
6. Instructional programs should be appropriate to the cognitive, social and emotional needs of students.
7. Curriculum development is an ongoing process.
8. Every student is expected to make continuous progress.

(c) Sulton School District, Sultan, Washington

"WORKING TOGETHER, ACHIEVING EXCELLENCE!"
STRATEGIC PLAN
SULTON SCHOOL DISTRICT

Beliefs

Students
We Believe all Students

- can achieve excellence.
- will be exposed to and explore a variety of post high school options.
- deserve to be respected and valued for their innate aptitudes.
- deserve to have ongoing learning challenges that motivate their pursuit to excellence.
- deserve a school system that is actively aligned with the State reform efforts.
- deserve to be treated with respect and civility, and are expected to respond in kind.
- will be prepared to compete at a high level in the career pathway of their choice, upon graduation.
- are individuals whose learning styles vary.
- share responsibility for maximizing their educational opportunities.
- will be contributing members of their community.

Schools
We Believe our Schools

- are academically and socially enriching environments.
- are the foundation for community pride and success.
- provide a safe environment.
- provide easy access to current policy, performance and information.
- recruit, develop, support, recognize, and reward quality staff and faculty.
- are accountable for implementing policies and curriculum, which will result in successful educational outcomes.
- are community learning and activity centers.
- reflect the values of the communities we serve.

Community
We Believe the Community

- provides an excellent quality of life.
- and parents are equal partners and key components of a successful school district.

Goals & Objectives
Improve Student Achievement in Skill Areas Necessary for a Successful Adult Life.

- Promote mastery and ongoing application of Washington Stated Learning Goals.
- Promote technological literacy.
- Provide vocational training opportunities.
- Promote fitness, health and individual well-being.
- Accommodate diverse student population.
- Increase graduation rate.
- Prepare all students to pass the Washington Assessment of Student Learning (WASL).
- Other advanced placement coursework. . . .

(d) Indiana Area School District

STRATEGIC PLAN
2002-2008

Indiana Area School District's Strategic Plan includes eight priority goal areas. Four goals are state-mandated: Assessment, Curriculum and Instruction, Graduation Requirements, and Professional Education Plan. The four remaining Strategic Plan goals are local priorities: Citizenship and Diversity, Continuous Improvement/ Restructuring, Parent and Community Involvement, and Technology.

Assessment
We will develop a comprehensive assessment plan that measures student achievement and provides for continuous improvement.

Curriculum and Instruction
We will implement curriculum and instruction that meets or exceeds the state academic standards for student achievement.

Graduation Requirements
We will establish a review process to validate our graduation requirements and to develop remediation plans for students who do not achieve at proficient levels on the state assessments.

Professional Education Plan
We will meet the staff development needs of professional and support staff, and connect staff development to our curriculum review cycle.

Citizenship and Diversity

We will create and promote an environment that encourages responsible citizenship, democratic ideals, community service, and respect for all.

Continuous Improvement/Restructuring

We will link a K-12 . . . accreditation process to student achievement, introduce a teaming initiative at the 7th and 8th grade level, and provide facilities that support delivery of our educational program.

Parent and Community Involvement

We will expand parent and community involvement in our schools, and increase parent-teacher communication.

Technology

We will implement a district technology plan that is designed to expand student learning opportunities and promote operational efficiency.

3. Strategic Plan Drafting Practicum

The mission statements in these different districts touch upon the same themes, sometimes employing similar language. How are they different? Do the differences create different beliefs and goals?

All of the strategic planning documents include a statement indicating that the strategic planning process was an inclusive one. Which stakeholders should be included in the process?

In order to insure that all stakeholders enroll or buy in to the goals set by the process, the process itself must be fair and respectful. How should such a process be structured? Should the board create an initial draft of the document and enlist feedback from the district's constituencies? Should the administrative team present the plan to the board for its approval? Should the entire document be the product of an inclusive planning retreat or off-site working meeting? Should the process be facilitated by someone outside the district? How should priorities among competing goals be established?

Law schools tend to lag behind elementary and secondary schools in recognizing the need for organizational growth and strategic planning. Nonetheless, law schools are beginning to embrace this process as well, particularly as it relates to funding for school initiatives. Assume that your own law school is about to embark on its first strategic planning exercise. Construct a process for that exercise. Who would be involved and how? Assume that you were asked to write a first draft of the law school's plan for review and acceptance by the faculty, administrators, alumni, community and fellow law students. First, draft a proposed mission statement for the law school. Second, draft a statement of ten beliefs that the entire law school community would share. Finally, propose a set of five key goals to be achieved by the law school over the next five-year period.

SECTION IV

THE RIGHTS AND RESPONSIBILITIES OF STUDENTS

CHAPTER 12

EQUAL EDUCATIONAL OPPORTUNITIES

The equal protection clause in the United States Constitution and in the constitutions of most states prohibits states and their public educational institutions from denying to students the "equal protection" of the laws. Nonetheless, as discussed in Chapter 4, the absence of a fundamental constitutional right to educational opportunities has permitted the states some degree of deference in their unequal allocation of educational resources to students. In this chapter, the issue of equal educational opportunity is reconsidered in the context of statutes and policies that classify students based upon constitutionally suspect categories such as race and gender.

A. RACIAL SEGREGATION, DESEGREGATION AND RESEGREGATION

1. Establishing the Constitutional Violation

BROWN v. BOARD OF EDUCATION OF TOPEKA

347 U.S. 483 (1954)

Mr. Chief Justice WARREN delivered the opinion of the Court.

These cases come to us from the States of Kansas, South Carolina, Virginia, and Delaware. They are premised on different facts and different local conditions, but a common legal question justifies their consideration together in this consolidated opinion.

In each of the cases, minors of the Negro race, through their legal representatives, seek the aid of the courts in obtaining admission to the public schools of their community on a non-segregated basis. In each instance, they had been denied admission to schools attended by white children under laws requiring or permitting segregation according to race. This segregation was alleged to deprive the plaintiffs of the equal protection of the laws under the

Fourteenth Amendment. In each of the cases other than the Delaware case, a three-judge federal district court denied relief to the plaintiffs on the so-called "separate but equal" doctrine announced by this Court in *Plessy v. Ferguson*, 163 U.S. 537. Under that doctrine, equality of treatment is accorded when the races are provided substantially equal facilities, even though these facilities be separate. In the Delaware case, the Supreme Court of Delaware adhered to that doctrine, but ordered that the plaintiffs be admitted to the white schools because of their superiority to the Negro schools.

The plaintiffs contend that segregated public schools are not "equal" and cannot be made "equal," and that hence they are deprived of the equal protection of the laws. . . .

Reargument was largely devoted to the circumstances surrounding the adoption of the Fourteenth Amendment in 1868. It covered exhaustively consideration of the Amendment in Congress, ratification by the states, then existing practices in racial segregation, and the views of proponents and opponents of the Amendment. This discussion and our own investigation convince us that, although these sources cast some light, it is not enough to resolve the problem with which we are faced. At best, they are inconclusive. . . .

An additional reason for the inconclusive nature of the Amendment's history, with respect to segregated schools, is the status of public education at that time.[4] In the South, the movement toward free common schools, supported by general taxation, had not yet taken hold. Education of white children was largely in the hands of private groups. Education of Negroes was almost nonexistent, and practically all of the race were illiterate. In fact, any education of Negroes was forbidden by law in some states. Today, in contrast, many Negroes have achieved outstanding success in the arts and sciences as well as in the business and professional world. It is true that public school education at the time of the Amendment had advanced further in the North, but the effect of the Amendment on Northern States was generally ignored in the congressional debates. Even in the North, the conditions of public education did not approximate those existing today. The curriculum was usually rudimentary; ungraded schools were common in rural areas; the school term was but three months a year in many states; and compulsory school attendance was virtually unknown. As a consequence, it is not surprising that there should be so little in the history of the Fourteenth Amendment relating to its intended effect on public education.

In the first cases in this Court construing the Fourteenth Amendment, decided shortly after its adoption, the Court interpreted it as proscribing all

---

[4] . . . Although the demand for free public schools followed substantially the same pattern in both the North and the South, the development in the South did not begin to gain momentum until about 1850, some twenty years after that in the North. The reasons for the somewhat slower development in the South [include] the rural character of the South and the different regional attitudes toward state assistance. . . . In the country as a whole, but particularly in the South, the War virtually stopped all progress in public education. The low status of Negro education in all sections of the country, both before and immediately after the War, is described in Beale, *A History of Freedom of Teaching in American Schools* (1941), 112-132, 175-195. Compulsory school attendance laws were not generally adopted until after the ratification of the Fourteenth Amendment, and it was not until 1918 that such laws were in force in all the states. . . .

state-imposed discriminations against the Negro race. The doctrine of "separate but equal" did not make its appearance in this Court until 1896 in the case of *Plessy v. Ferguson,* involving not education but transportation.[6] American courts have since labored with the doctrine for over half a century. . . .

In the instant cases, that question is directly presented. Here, . . . there are findings below that the Negro and white schools involved have been equalized, or are being equalized, with respect to buildings, curricula, qualifications and salaries of teachers, and other "tangible" factors. Our decision, therefore, cannot turn on merely a comparison of these tangible factors in the Negro and white schools involved in each of the cases. We must look instead to the effect of segregation itself on public education.

In approaching this problem, we cannot turn the clock back to 1868 when the Amendment was adopted, or even to 1896 when *Plessy v. Ferguson* was written. We must consider public education in the light of its full development and its present place in American life throughout the Nation. Only in this way can it be determined if segregation in public schools deprives these plaintiffs of the equal protection of the laws.

Today, education is perhaps the most important function of state and local governments. Compulsory school attendance laws and the great expenditures for education both demonstrate our recognition of the importance of education to our democratic society. It is required in the performance of our most basic public responsibilities, even service in the armed forces. It is the very foundation of good citizenship. Today it is a principal instrument in awakening the child to cultural values, in preparing him for later professional training, and in helping him to adjust normally to his environment. In these days, it is doubtful that any child may reasonably be expected to succeed in life if he is denied the opportunity of an education. Such an opportunity, where the state has undertaken to provide it, is a right which must be made available to all on equal terms.

We come then to the question presented: Does segregation of children in public schools solely on the basis of race, even though the physical facilities and other "tangible" factors may be equal, deprive the children of the minority group of equal educational opportunities? We believe that it does.

In *Sweatt v. Painter,* in finding that a segregated law school for Negroes could not provide them equal educational opportunities, this Court relied in large part on "those qualities which are incapable of objective measurement but which make for greatness in a law school." In *McLaurin v. Oklahoma State Regents,* the Court, in requiring that a Negro admitted to a white graduate school be treated like all other students, again resorted to intangible considerations: ". . . his ability to study, to engage in discussions and exchange views with other students, and, in general, to learn his profession." Such

[6] The doctrine apparently originated in *Roberts v. City of Boston,* 59 Mass. 198, 206 (1850), upholding school segregation against attack as being violative of a state constitutional guarantee of equality. Segregation in Boston public schools was eliminated in 1855. . . . But elsewhere in the North segregation in public education has persisted in some communities until recent years. It is apparent that such segregation has long been a nationwide problem, not merely one of sectional concern.

considerations apply with added force to children in grade and high schools. To separate them from others of similar age and qualifications solely because of their race generates a feeling of inferiority as to their status in the community that may affect their hearts and minds in a way unlikely ever to be undone. The effect of this separation on their educational opportunities was well stated by a finding in the Kansas case by a court which nevertheless felt compelled to rule against the Negro plaintiffs:

> Segregation of white and colored children in public schools has a detrimental effect upon the colored children. The impact is greater when it has the sanction of the law; for the policy of separating the races is usually interpreted as denoting the inferiority of the negro group. A sense of inferiority affects the motivation of a child to learn. Segregation with the sanction of law, therefore, has a tendency to [retard] the educational and mental development of negro children and to deprive them of some of the benefits they would receive in a racial[ly] integrated school system.[10]

We conclude that in the field of public education the doctrine of "separate but equal" has no place. Separate educational facilities are inherently unequal. Therefore, we hold that the plaintiffs and others similarly situated for whom the actions have been brought are, by reason of the segregation complained of, deprived of the equal protection of the laws guaranteed by the Fourteenth Amendment. This disposition makes unnecessary any discussion whether such segregation also violates the Due Process Clause of the Fourteenth Amendment.

NOTES AND QUESTIONS

1. In reaching its result in *Brown,* the Supreme Court could have articulated several different arguments for the unconstitutionality of racially segregated public schools, including: (1) students who are members of a racial minority learn better when they are integrated in classrooms with children who are not members of a racial minority; (2) separate educational facilities assigned to minority children are, or inevitably become, tangibly worse than facilities assigned to majority children; (3) precluding members of a racial minority and members of a racial majority from congregating in the same educational environment denies to all students their First Amendment rights to freedom of association; and/or (4) the perpetuation of separate educational facilities, regardless of their relative quality, harms children who are members of a racial minority by stigmatizing them. *See, e.g.,* Laurence H. Tribe, *American Constitutional Law* §16-15, at 1476-1480 (2d ed. 1988); Herbert Wechsler, *Toward Neutral Principles of Constitutional Law,* 73 Harv. L. Rev. 1, 34 (1959); Derrick Bell, *Serving Two Masters: Integration Ideals and Client Interests in School Desegregation Litigation,* 85 Yale L.J. 470 (1976); Nathaniel R. Jones, *Correspondence,* 86 Yale L.J. 378-384 (1976). What are the relative strengths and weaknesses of each of these arguments? Which argument did the *Brown* Court ultimately accept?

---

[10] Whatever may have been the extent of psychological knowledge at the time of *Plessy v. Ferguson,* this finding is amply supported by modern authority. Any language in *Plessy v. Ferguson* contrary to this finding is rejected.

2. The Court in *Brown* relies on both *Sweatt v. Painter,* 339 U.S. 629 (1950), and *McLaurin v. Oklahoma State Regents for Higher Education,* 339 U.S. 637 (1950). In *Sweatt,* the Supreme Court held that the equal protection clause prohibits the state of Texas from denying to African-American students admission to the University of Texas Law School because of their race. The Court's reasoning was based in large part on the fact that the separate law schools that the state made available to African-American students lacked "substantial equality in the educational opportunities offered. . . ." 339 U.S. at 633-634. The Court found that the tangible facilities and intangible qualities of the state's African-American law schools were, in fact, unequal to those available at the University of Texas Law School. The Court also observed that because the African-American law schools excluded "most" of the state's lawyers, judges and officials with whom future lawyers inevitably deal, those law schools were not "substantially equal" to law schools that include such a "substantial and significant segment of society." 339 U.S. at 634.

   In *McLaurin,* the Supreme Court concluded that the equal protection clause also prevents states from treating students differently within the educational environment because of their race. In that case, McLaurin enrolled as a graduate student at the University of Oklahoma, pursuing a doctorate in education. The state forced him to sit in a seat in the classroom assigned to African-American students, to sit at a library table assigned to African-American students and to eat at a "special" cafeteria table assigned to African-American students. 339 U.S. at 640. Although the Court assumed that these separations were "nominal" and resulted in no "disadvantage of location," it nonetheless declared: "[t]he result is that appellant is handicapped in his pursuit of an effective graduate instruction." 339 U.S. at 641. The state's practices violated the equal protection clause because, in setting McLaurin "apart from the other students," the state had imposed "restrictions" that "impair and inhibit his ability to study, to engage in discussions and exchange views with other students, and, in general, to learn his profession." *Id.* According to the Court, state-imposed restrictions "which prohibit the intellectual commingling of students" based on race produce "inequalities" that cannot be sustained. *Id.*

   Unlike in *Sweatt,* the Supreme Court in *Brown* assumed that "the physical facilities and other 'tangible' factors" in the segregated African-American schools were "equal" to those of the all-white schools. What is the significance of that assumption in the *Brown* case? Does the *Brown* Court suggest what the result might have been if the facilities and other tangible factors were demonstratively unequal among the races? To what extent does the reasoning in *Brown* rely upon or depart from the reasoning in *Sweatt* and *McLaurin?*

3. The petitioners in *Brown* made a strategic decision to attack the segregated aspects of public education rather than the tangible disparities in the quality of education between white and African-American students. Why do you think the petitioners chose that strategy? Consider the consequences of that strategy as you analyze the history of the remedial aspects of implementing the Court's desegregation rulings.

4. Two weeks before the Supreme Court issued its *Brown* decision, it decided *Hernandez v. Texas,* 347 U.S. 475 (1954). In that case, the Court held that the systematic exclusion of persons of Mexican descent from jury service constituted a denial of the equal protection of the laws guaranteed by the Fourteenth Amendment. According to the Court, the "groups" requiring the "aid of the courts in securing equal treatment under the laws" include those who are "singled out" or subjugated by the attitudes of community members. Significantly, the Court recognized that the equal protection clause does not just prohibit discriminatory laws. Rather, the clause also prohibits discriminatory community practices and attitudes that injure minority groups by segregating them and denying them access to important economic benefits. The Court understood the equal protection clause to protect minority groups from subordination caused by social norms and constraints.

   The *Brown* court has been criticized because its language does not make clear that the Constitution precludes practices of racial oppression, subordination and injury. *See, e.g.,* Derrick Bell, *Silent Covenants:* Brown v. Board of Education *and the Unfulfilled Hopes for Racial Reform* (2004); Sheryll Cashin, *The Failures of Integration: How Race and Class Are Undermining the American Dream* (2004). Instead, *Brown's* focus appears to be only (albeit importantly) on laws that formally separate the races. The critics of *Brown* often applaud the case as a monument to racial and educational equality, but lament the fact that its reasoning has allowed subsequent courts to frustrate the goal of genuine integration and educational equality. As you read the cases since *Brown,* consider whether these criticisms are fair.
5. What does "inherently unequal" mean? Are segregated schools unconstitutional because they are "inherently unequal," or because they in reality injure racial minorities by denying to them educational opportunities? According to the Court, what are the reasons that separate public educational facilities are not equal? The Court argues that even if tangible factors may be equal, segregation of children in public schools solely on the basis of race deprives the "children of the minority group of equal educational opportunities." List the ways in which it does so. The Court does not reach the issue of whether segregation adversely affects the children of the majority group. Do you believe that it does? Nor does the Court consider whether a diverse educational environment is valuable to all students. If the *Brown* decision is not rooted in the value of diversity, where does *that* value originate? What would diversity mean in this context? Could the benefits of a diverse student population for all students support a court order to achieve that diversity?
6. By focusing on the harm to African-American children caused by racial segregation, has the *Brown* Court and its progeny inadvertently divided the races on the *issue* of segregation itself? As the materials in Chapter 4 regarding the racial component to inequalities in educational funding demonstrate, the condition of racial segregation persists in the public schools throughout America. Does that condition allow white children and their parents to divorce themselves from the political and legal question of racial segregation? In other words, if racial segregation only harms

African-American children, what incentive is there for white children to become invested in the problem? If, by contrast, the Supreme Court had recognized that the lack of diversity in schools harms *all* children, might that recognition have led to deeper political and legal opposition to segregation?

7. In *Brown v. Bd. of Educ.*, 349 U.S. 294 (1955) *(Brown II)*, the Supreme Court addressed the issue of remedy:

> Full implementation of these constitutional principles may require solution of varied local school problems. School authorities have the primary responsibility for elucidating, assessing, and solving these problems; courts will have to consider whether the action of school authorities constitutes good faith implementation of the governing constitutional principles. . . .
>
> In fashioning and effectuating the decrees, the courts will be guided by equitable principles. Traditionally, equity has been characterized by a practical flexibility in shaping its remedies and by a facility for adjusting and reconciling public and private needs. These cases call for the exercise of these traditional attributes of equity power. At stake is the personal interest of the plaintiffs in admission to public schools as soon as practicable on a nondiscriminatory basis. To effectuate this interest may call for elimination of a variety of obstacles in making the transition to school systems operated in accordance with the constitutional principles set forth in our May 17, 1954, decision. Courts of equity may properly take into account the public interest in the elimination of such obstacles in a systematic and effective manner. But it should go without saying that the vitality of these constitutional principles cannot be allowed to yield simply because of disagreement with them.
>
> While giving weight to these public and private considerations, the courts will require that the defendants make a prompt and reasonable start toward full compliance with our May 17, 1954, ruling. Once such a start has been made, the courts may find that additional time is necessary to carry out the ruling in an effective manner. The burden rests upon the defendants to establish that such time is necessary in the public interest and is consistent with good faith compliance at the earliest practicable date. To that end, the courts may consider problems related to administration, arising from the physical condition of the school plant, the school transportation system, personnel, revision of school districts and attendance areas into compact units to achieve a system of determining admission to the public schools on a nonracial basis, and revision of local laws and regulations which may be necessary in solving the foregoing problems. They will also consider the adequacy of any plans the defendants may propose to meet these problems and to effectuate a transition to a racially nondiscriminatory school system. During this period of transition, the courts will retain jurisdiction of these cases. . . . [T]he cases are remanded to the District Courts to take such proceedings and enter such orders and decrees consistent with this opinion as are necessary and proper to admit to public schools on a racially nondiscriminatory basis with all deliberate speed the parties to these cases.

8. Can you detect even in this initial remedial language in *Brown II* the source of ongoing litigation about the scope of the remedy required by the Court's rulings? Interestingly, prior drafts of the opinion reveal that the Court

originally wrote that desegregation must occur with "all appropriate speed," but the word "appropriate" was changed to "deliberate" in the final version of *Brown II.* See *http://www.landmarkcases.org/brown/frankfurter_2.html.* Indeed, there was little speed and much resistance to the federal court orders implementing *Brown II.* In *Green v. County Sch. Bd. of New Kent County,* 391 U.S. 430 (1968), however, the Court rejected the school board's "freedom-of-choice" plan, which allowed students to choose their own public school. The board failed to show that its plan resulted in an effective transition to a unitary district and therefore the board failed to demonstrate its compliance with its responsibility "to achieve a system of determining admission to the public schools on a nonracial basis. . . ." The Supreme Court concluded that school districts must eliminate racial discrimination in public education "root and branch." In *Alexander v. Holmes County Bd. of Educ.,* 396 U.S. 1218 (1969), in the wake of concerted efforts by southern states to avoid integration, the Supreme Court denounced its "all deliberate speed" standard as a "soft euphemism for delay" that allowed too much deliberation and not enough speed. The Court ordered all southern school districts to become unitary on an immediate basis.

2. The Rise of Remedial Power

SWANN V. CHARLOTTE-MECKLENBURG BOARD OF EDUCATION

402 U.S. 1 (1971)

Mr. Chief Justice BURGER delivered the opinion of the Court.

We granted certiorari in this case to review important issues as to the duties of school authorities and the scope of powers of federal courts under this Court's mandates to eliminate racially separate public schools established and maintained by state action. *Brown v. Board of Education (Brown I).*

This case and those argued with it arose in States having a long history of maintaining two sets of schools in a single school system deliberately operated to carry out a governmental policy to separate pupils in schools solely on the basis of race. That was what *Brown v. Board of Education* was all about. These cases present us with the problem of defining in more precise terms than heretofore the scope of the duty of school authorities and district courts in implementing *Brown I* and the mandate to eliminate dual systems and establish unitary systems at once. . . .

II

Nearly 17 years ago this Court held, in explicit terms, that state-imposed segregation by race in public schools denies equal protection of the laws. At no time has the Court deviated in the slightest degree from that holding or its constitutional underpinnings. . . .

Over the 16 years since *Brown II,* many difficulties were encountered in implementation of the basic constitutional requirement that the State not discriminate between public school children on the basis of their race. Nothing in our national experience prior to 1955 prepared anyone for dealing with changes and adjustments of the magnitude and complexity encountered since then. Deliberate resistance of some to the Court's mandates has impeded the good-faith efforts of others to bring school systems into compliance. The detail and nature of these dilatory tactics have been noted frequently by this Court and other courts.

By the time the Court considered *Green v. County School Board.,* 391 U.S. 430, in 1968, very little progress had been made in many areas where dual school systems had historically been maintained by operation of state laws. In *Green,* the Court was confronted with a record of a freedom-of-choice program that the District Court had found to operate in fact to preserve a dual system more than a decade after *Brown II.* While acknowledging that a freedom-of-choice concept could be a valid remedial measure in some circumstances, its failure to be effective in *Green* required that:

> The burden on a school board today is to come forward with a plan that promises realistically to work . . . *now* . . . until it is clear that state-imposed segregation has been completely removed. . . .

III

The objective today remains to eliminate from the public schools all vestiges of state-imposed segregation. Segregation was the evil struck down by *Brown I* as contrary to the equal protection guarantees of the Constitution. That was the violation sought to be corrected by the remedial measures of *Brown II.* That was the basis for the holding in *Green* that school authorities are "clearly charged with the affirmative duty to take whatever steps might be necessary to convert to a unitary system in which racial discrimination would be eliminated root and branch."

If school authorities fail in their affirmative obligations under these holdings, judicial authority may be invoked. Once a right and a violation have been shown, the scope of a district court's equitable powers to remedy past wrongs is broad, for breadth and flexibility are inherent in equitable remedies.

. . . In seeking to define even in broad and general terms how far this remedial power extends it is important to remember that judicial powers may be exercised only on the basis of a constitutional violation. Remedial judicial authority does not put judges automatically in the shoes of school authorities whose powers are plenary. Judicial authority enters only when local authority defaults.

School authorities are traditionally charged with broad power to formulate and implement educational policy and might well conclude, for example, that in order to prepare students to live in a pluralistic society each school should have a prescribed ratio of Negro to white students reflecting the proportion for the district as a whole. To do this as an educational policy is within the broad discretionary powers of school authorities; absent a finding of a constitutional violation, however, that would not be within the authority of a federal court. As with any equity case, the nature of the violation determines the scope of the remedy. In default by the school authorities of their obligation to proffer acceptable remedies, a district court has broad power to fashion a remedy that will assure a unitary school system. . . .

IV

We turn now to the problem of defining with more particularity the responsibilities of school authorities in desegregating a state-enforced dual school system in light of the equal protection clause. Although the several related cases before us are primarily concerned with problems of student assignment, it may be helpful to begin with a brief discussion of other aspects of the process.

In *Green,* we pointed out that existing policy and practice with regard to faculty, staff, transportation, extracurricular activities, and facilities were among the most important indicia of a segregated system. Independent of student assignment, where it is possible to identify a "white school" or a "Negro school" simply by reference to the racial composition of teachers and staff, the quality of school buildings and equipment, or the organization of sports activities, a *prima facie* case of violation of substantive constitutional rights under the Equal Protection Clause is shown.

When a system has been dual in these respects, the first remedial responsibility of school authorities is to eliminate invidious racial distinctions. With respect to such matters as transportation, supporting personnel, and extracurricular activities, no more than this may be necessary. Similar corrective action must be taken with regard to the maintenance of buildings and the distribution of equipment. In these areas, normal administrative practice should produce schools of like quality, facilities, and staffs. Something more must be said, however, as to faculty assignment and new school construction.

In the companion case, the Mobile school board has argued that the Constitution requires that teachers be assigned on a "color blind" basis. It also argues that the Constitution prohibits district courts from using their equity power to order assignment of teachers to achieve a particular degree of faculty desegregation. We reject that contention. . . .

The construction of new schools and the closing of old ones are two of the most important functions of local school authorities and also two of the most complex. They must decide questions of location and capacity in light of population growth, finances, land values, site availability, through an almost endless list of factors to be considered. The result of this will be a decision which, when combined with one technique or another of student assignment, will determine the racial composition of the student body in each school in the system. Over the long run, the consequences of the choices will be far reaching. People gravitate toward school facilities, just as schools are located in response to the needs of people. The location of schools may thus influence the patterns of residential development of a metropolitan area and have important impact on composition of inner-city neighborhoods.

In the past, choices in this respect have been used as a potent weapon for creating or maintaining a state-segregated school system. In addition to the classic pattern of building schools specifically intended for Negro or white students, school authorities have sometimes, since *Brown,* closed schools which appeared likely to become racially mixed through changes in neighborhood residential patterns. This was sometimes accompanied by building new schools in the areas of white suburban expansion farthest from Negro population centers in order to maintain the separation of the races with a minimum departure from the formal principles of "neighborhood zoning." Such a policy does more than simply influence the short-run composition of the student body of a new school. It may well promote segregated residential patterns which, when combined with "neighborhood zoning," further lock the school system into the mold of separation of the races. Upon a proper showing a district court may consider this in fashioning a remedy.

In ascertaining the existence of legally imposed school segregation, the existence of a pattern of school construction and abandonment is thus a factor of great weight. In devising remedies where legally imposed segregation has been established, it is the responsibility of local authorities and district courts to see to it that future school construction and abandonment are not used and do not serve to perpetuate or re-establish the dual system. When necessary, district courts should retain jurisdiction to assure that these responsibilities are carried out. . . .

V

The central issue in this case is that of student assignment, and there are essentially four problem areas. . . .

(1) Racial Balances or Racial Quotas

The constant theme and thrust of every holding from *Brown I* to date is that state-enforced separation of races in public schools is discrimination that violates the Equal Protection Clause. The remedy commanded was to dismantle dual school systems.

We are concerned in these cases with the elimination of the discrimination inherent in the dual school systems, not with myriad factors of human existence which can cause discrimination in a multitude of ways on racial, religious, or ethnic grounds. The target of the cases from *Brown I* to the present was the dual school system. The elimination of racial discrimination in public schools is a large task and one that should not be retarded by efforts to achieve broader purposes lying beyond the jurisdiction of school authorities. One vehicle can carry only a limited amount of baggage. It would not serve the important objective of *Brown I* to seek to use school desegregation cases for purposes beyond their scope, although desegregation of schools ultimately will have impact on other forms of discrimination. . . .

Our objective in dealing with the issues presented by these cases is to see that school authorities exclude no pupil of a racial minority from any school, directly or indirectly, on account of race; it does not and cannot embrace all the problems of racial prejudice, even when those problems contribute to disproportionate racial concentrations in some schools. . . .

We see therefore that the use made of mathematical ratios was no more than a starting point in the process of shaping a remedy, rather than an inflexible requirement. From that starting point the District Court proceeded to frame a decree that was within its discretionary powers, as an equitable remedy for the particular circumstances. As we said in *Green,* a school authority's remedial plan or a district court's remedial decree is to be judged by its effectiveness. Awareness of the racial composition of the whole school system is likely to be a useful starting point in shaping a remedy to correct past constitutional violations. In sum, the very limited use made of mathematical ratios was within the equitable remedial discretion of the District Court.

(2) One-Race Schools

The record in this case reveals the familiar phenomenon that in metropolitan areas minority groups are often found concentrated in one part of the city. In some circumstances certain schools may remain all or largely of one race until new schools can be provided or neighborhood patterns change. Schools all or predominately of one race in a district of mixed population will require close scrutiny to determine that school assignments are not part of state-enforced segregation.

In light of the above, it should be clear that the existence of some small number of one-race, or virtually one-race, schools within a district is not in and of itself the mark of a system that still practices segregation by law. The district judge or school authorities should make every effort to achieve the greatest possible degree of actual desegregation and will thus necessarily be concerned with the elimination of one-race schools. *No per se* rule can adequately embrace all the difficulties of reconciling the competing interests involved; but in a system with a history of segregation the need for remedial criteria of sufficient specificity to assure a school authority's compliance with its constitutional duty warrants a presumption against schools that are substantially disproportionate in their racial composition. Where the school authority's proposed plan for conversion from a dual to a unitary system contemplates the continued existence of some schools that are all or predominately of one race, they have the burden of showing that such school assignments are genuinely nondiscriminatory. The court should scrutinize such schools, and the burden upon the school authorities will be to satisfy the court that their racial composition is not the result of present or past discriminatory action on their part.

An optional majority-to-minority transfer provision has long been recognized as a useful part of every desegregation plan. Provision for optional transfer of those in the majority racial group of a particular school to other schools where they will be in the minority is an indispensable remedy for those students willing to transfer to other schools in order to lessen the impact on them of the state-imposed stigma of segregation. In order to be effective, such a transfer arrangement must grant the transferring student free transportation and space must be made available in the school to which he desires to move.

(3) Remedial Altering of Attendance Zones

The maps submitted in these cases graphically demonstrate that one of the principal tools employed by school planners and by courts to break up the dual school system has been a frank—and sometimes drastic—gerrymandering of school districts and attendance zones. An additional step was pairing, "clustering," or "grouping" of schools with attendance assignments made deliberately to accomplish the transfer of Negro students out of formerly segregated Negro schools and transfer of white students to formerly all-Negro schools. More often than not, these zones are neither compact nor contiguous; indeed they may be on opposite ends of the city. As an interim corrective measure, this cannot be said to be beyond the broad remedial powers of a court.

Absent a constitutional violation there would be no basis for judicially ordering assignment of students on a racial basis. All things being equal, with no history of discrimination, it might well be desirable to assign pupils to schools nearest their homes. But all things are not equal in a system that has been deliberately constructed and maintained to enforce racial segregation. The remedy for such segregation may be administratively awkward, inconvenient, and even bizarre in some situations and may impose burdens on some; but all awkwardness and inconvenience cannot be avoided in the interim period when remedial adjustments are being made to eliminate the dual school systems.

No fixed or even substantially fixed guidelines can be established as to how far a court can go, but it must be recognized that there are limits. The objective is to dismantle the dual school system. "Racially neutral" assignment plans proposed by school authorities to a district court may be inadequate; such plans may fail to counteract the continuing effects of past school segregation resulting from discriminatory location of school sites or distortion of school size in order to achieve or maintain an artificial racial separation. When school authorities present a district court with a "loaded game board," affirmative action in the form of remedial altering of attendance zones is proper to achieve truly nondiscriminatory assignments. In short, an assignment plan is not acceptable simply because it appears to be neutral.

In this area, we must of necessity rely to a large extent, as this Court has for more than 16 years, on the informed judgment of the district courts in the first instance and on courts of appeals.

We hold that the pairing and grouping of noncontiguous school zones is a permissible tool and such action is to be considered in light of the objectives sought. . . .

(4) Transportation of Students

The scope of permissible transportation of students as an implement of a remedial decree has never been defined by this Court and by the very nature of the problem it cannot be defined with precision. No rigid guidelines as to student transportation can be given for application to the infinite variety of problems presented in thousands of situations. Bus transportation has been an integral part of the public education system for years, and was perhaps the single most important factor in the transition from the one-room schoolhouse to the consolidated school. Eighteen million of the Nation's public school children, approximately 39%, were transported to their schools by bus in 1969-1970 in all parts of the country.

The importance of bus transportation as a normal and accepted tool of educational policy is readily discernible in this and the companion case. . . . The District Court's conclusion that assignment of children to the school nearest their home serving their grade would not produce an effective dismantling of the dual system is supported by the record.

Thus the remedial techniques used in the District Court's order were within that court's power to provide equitable relief; implementation of the decree is well within the capacity of the school authority. . . .

VI

On the facts of this case, we are unable to conclude that the order of the District Court is not reasonable, feasible and workable. However, in seeking to define the scope of remedial power or the limits on remedial power of courts in an area as sensitive as we deal with here, words are poor instruments to convey the sense of basic fairness inherent in equity. Substance, not semantics, must govern, and we have sought to suggest the nature of limitations without frustrating the appropriate scope of equity.

At some point, these school authorities and others like them should have achieved full compliance with this Court's decision in *Brown I.* The systems would then be "unitary" in the sense required by our decisions. . . .

It does not follow that the communities served by such systems will remain demographically stable, for in a growing, mobile society, few will do so. Neither school authorities nor district courts are constitutionally required to make year-by-year adjustments of the racial composition of student bodies once the affirmative duty to desegregate has been accomplished and racial discrimination through official action is eliminated from the system. This does not mean that federal courts are without power to deal with future problems; but in the absence of a showing that either the school authorities or some other agency of the State has deliberately attempted to fix or alter demographic patterns to affect the racial composition of the schools, further intervention by a district court should not be necessary.

NOTES AND QUESTIONS

1. The Supreme Court in *Swann* finds the following four remedial devices to be within a district court's equitable power under the circumstances of this case: (1) racial quotas; (2) maintaining single-race schools; (3) altering attendance zones; and (4) cross-district transportation. Which of these devices is the most effective means of remedying racial segregation in the public schools? Which device is likely to result in the maintenance of integrated schools for the longest period of time?
2. Notice that in *Swann,* which was decided seven years before *Regents of the University of California v. Bakke,* 438 U.S. 265 (1978), the Supreme Court concludes that "affirmative action" is proper to achieve true nondiscrimination, particularly where the racial configuration of a district is a "loaded game board." How does the Court employ the concept of "affirmative action" in this context?
3. Apart from the court-ordered remedies approved by the Supreme Court in *Swann,* what other remedial measures could be implemented to achieve racial desegregation?

3. De Facto Segregation and Remedial Difficulties

KEYES V. SCHOOL DISTRICT NO. 1, DENVER, COLORADO

413 U.S. 189 (1973)

Mr. Justice BRENNAN delivered the opinion of the Court.

This school desegregation case concerns the Denver, Colorado, school system. That system has never been operated under a constitutional or statutory provision that mandated or permitted racial segregation in public education. Rather, the gravamen of this action, brought in June 1969 in the District Court for the District of Colorado by parents of Denver schoolchildren, is that respondent School Board alone, by use of various techniques such as the manipulation of student attendance zones, school site selection and a neighborhood school policy, created or maintained racially or ethnically (or both racially and ethnically) segregated schools throughout the school district, entitling petitioners to a decree directing desegregation of the entire school district. . . .

Before turning to the primary question we decide today, a word must be said about the District Court's method of defining a "segregated" school. Denver is a tri-ethnic, as distinguished from a bi-racial, community. The overall racial and ethnic composition of the Denver public schools is 66% Anglo, 14% Negro, and 20% Hispano. The District Court, in assessing the question of *de jure* segregation in the core city schools, preliminarily resolved that Negroes and Hispanos should not be placed in the same category to establish the segregated character of a school. . . .

We conclude, however, that the District Court erred in separating Negroes and Hispanos for purposes of defining a "segregated" school. We have held that Hispanos constitute an identifiable class for purposes of the Fourteenth Amendment. . . . Indeed, the District Court recognized this in classifying predominantly Hispano schools as "segregated" schools in their own right. But there is also much evidence that in the Southwest Hispanos and Negroes have a great many things in common. The United States Commission on Civil Rights has recently published two Reports on Hispano education in the Southwest. Focusing on students in the States of Arizona, California, Colorado, New Mexico, and Texas, the Commission concluded that Hispanos suffer from the same educational inequities as Negroes and American Indians. In fact, the District Court itself recognized that "one of the things which the Hispano has in common with the Negro is economic and cultural deprivation and discrimination." This is agreement that, though of different origins, Negroes and Hispanos in Denver suffer identical discrimination in treatment when compared with the treatment afforded Anglo students. In that circumstance, we think petitioners are entitled to have schools with a combined predominance of Negroes and Hispanos included in the category of "segregated" schools.

II

In our view, the only other question that requires our decision at this time is . . . whether the District Court and the Court of Appeals applied an incorrect legal standard in addressing petitioners' contention that respondent School Board engaged in an unconstitutional policy of deliberate segregation in the core city schools. Our conclusion is that those courts did not apply the correct standard in addressing that contention. . . .

This is not a case, however, where a statutory dual system has ever existed. Nevertheless, where plaintiffs prove that the school authorities have carried out a systematic program of segregation affecting a substantial portion of the students, schools, teachers, and facilities within the school system, it is only common sense to conclude that there exists a predicate for a finding of the existence of a dual school system. Several considerations support this conclusion. First, it is obvious that a practice of concentrating Negroes in certain schools by structuring attendance zones or designating "feeder" schools on the basis of race has the reciprocal effect of keeping other nearby schools predominantly white. Similarly, the practice of building a school—such as the Barrett Elementary School in this case—to a certain size and in a certain location, "with conscious knowledge that it would be a segregated school," has a substantial reciprocal effect on the racial composition of other nearby schools. So also, the use of mobile classrooms, the drafting of student transfer policies, the transportation of students, and the assignment of faculty and staff, on racially identifiable bases, have the clear effect of earmarking schools according to their racial composition, and this, in turn, together with the elements of student assignment and school construction, may have a profound reciprocal effect on the racial composition of residential neighborhoods within a metropolitan area, thereby causing further racial concentration within the schools. . . .

In short, common sense dictates the conclusion that racially inspired school board actions have an impact beyond the particular schools that are the subjects of those actions. This is not to say, of course, that there can never be a case in which the geographical structure of, or the natural boundaries within, a school district may have the effect of dividing the district into separate, identifiable and unrelated units. Such a determination is essentially a question of fact to be resolved by the trial court in the first instance, but such cases must be rare. In the absence of such a determination, proof of state-imposed segregation in a substantial portion of the district will suffice to support a finding by the trial court of the existence of a dual system. Of course, where that finding is made, as in cases involving statutory dual systems, the school authorities have an affirmative duty "to effectuate a transition to a racially nondiscriminatory school system." *Brown II.*

On remand, therefore, the District Court should decide in the first instance whether respondent School Board's deliberate racial segregation policy with respect to the Park Hill schools constitutes the entire Denver school system a dual school system. We observe that on the record now before us there is indication that Denver is not a school district which might be divided into separate, identifiable and unrelated units. This suggests that the official segregation in Park Hill affected the racial composition of schools throughout the district. . . .

On the question of segregative intent, petitioners presented evidence tending to show that the Board, through its actions over a period of years, intentionally created and maintained the segregated character of the core city schools. Respondents countered this evidence by arguing that the segregation in these schools is the result of a racially neutral "neighborhood school policy" and that the acts of which petitioners complain are explicable within the bounds of that policy. Accepting the School Board's explanation, the District Court and the Court of Appeals agreed that a finding of *de jure* segregation as to the core city schools was not permissible since petitioners had failed to prove "(1) a racially discriminatory purpose and (2) a causal relationship between the acts complained of and the racial imbalance admittedly existing in those schools." This assessment of petitioners' proof was clearly incorrect.

Although petitioners had already proved the existence of intentional school segregation in the Park Hill schools, this crucial finding was totally ignored when attention turned to the core city schools. Plainly, a finding of intentional segregation as to a portion of a school system is not devoid of probative value in assessing the school authorities' intent with respect to other parts of the same school system. On the contrary, where, as here, the case involves one school board, a finding of intentional segregation on its part in one portion of a school system is highly relevant to the issue of the board's intent with respect to other segregated schools in the system. . . .

Applying these principles in the special context of school desegregation cases, we hold that a finding of intentionally segregative school board actions in a meaningful portion of a school system, as in this case, creates a presumption that other segregated schooling within the system is not adventitious. It establishes, in other words, a prima facie case of unlawful segregative design on the part of school authorities, and shifts to those authorities the burden of proving that other segregated schools within the system are not also the result of intentionally segregative actions. This is true even if it is determined that different areas of the school district should be viewed independently of each other because, even in that situation, there is high probability that where school authorities have effectuated an intentionally segregative policy in a meaningful portion of the school system, similar impermissible considerations have motivated their actions in other areas of the system. We emphasize that the differentiating factor between *de jure* segregation and so-called *de facto* segregation to which we referred in *Swann* is *purpose* or *intent* to segregate. Where school authorities have been found to have practiced purposeful segregation in part of a school system, they may be expected to oppose system-wide desegregation, as did the respondents in this case, on the ground that their purposefully segregative actions were isolated and individual events, thus leaving plaintiffs with the burden of proving otherwise. But at that point where an intentionally segregative policy is practiced in a meaningful or significant segment of a school system, as in this case, the school authorities cannot be heard to argue that plaintiffs have proved only "isolated and individual" unlawfully segregative actions. In that circumstance, it is both fair and reasonable to require that the school authorities bear the burden of showing that their actions as to other segregated schools within the system were not also motivated by segregative intent. . . .

In discharging that burden, it is not enough, of course, that the school authorities rely upon some allegedly logical, racially neutral explanation for their actions. Their burden is to adduce proof sufficient to support a finding that segregative intent was not among the factors that motivated their actions. The courts below attributed much significance to the fact that many of the Board's actions in the core city area antedated our decision in *Brown.* We reject any suggestion that remoteness in time has any relevance to the issue of intent. If the actions of school authorities were to any degree motivated by segregative intent and the segregation resulting from those actions continues to exist, the fact of remoteness in time certainly does not make those actions any less "intentional."

This is not to say, however, that the prima facie case may not be met by evidence supporting a finding that a lesser degree of segregated schooling in the core city area would not have resulted even if the Board had not acted as it did. In *Swann,* we suggested that at some point in time the relationship between past segregative acts and present segregation may become so attenuated as to be incapable of supporting a finding of *de jure* segregation warranting judicial intervention. . . . We made it clear, however, that a connection between past segregative acts and present segregation may be present even when not apparent and that close examination is required before concluding that the connection does not exist. Intentional school segregation in the past may have been a factor in creating a natural environment for the growth of further segregation. Thus, if respondent School Board cannot disprove segregative intent, it can rebut the prima facie case only by showing that its past segregative acts did not create or contribute to the current segregated condition of the core city schools.

The respondent School Board invoked at trial its "neighborhood school policy" as explaining racial and ethnic concentrations within the core city schools, arguing that since the core city area population had long been Negro and Hispano, the concentrations were necessarily the result of residential patterns and not of purposefully segregative policies. We have no occasion to consider in this case whether a "neighborhood school policy" of itself will justify racial or ethnic concentrations in the absence of a finding that school authorities have committed acts constituting *de jure* segregation. It is enough that we hold that the mere assertion of such a policy is not dispositive where, as in this case, the school authorities have been found to have practiced *de jure* segregation in a meaningful portion of the school system by techniques that indicate that the "neighborhood school" concept has not been maintained free of manipulation. . . .

Thus, respondent School Board having been found to have practiced deliberate racial segregation in schools attended by over one-third of the Negro school population, that crucial finding establishes a prima facie case of intentional segregation in the core city schools. In such case, respondent's neighborhood school policy is not to be determinative "simply because it appears to be neutral."

IV

In summary, the District Court on remand, *first,* will afford respondent School Board the opportunity to prove its contention that the Park Hill area is a separate, identifiable and unrelated section of the school district that should be treated as isolated from the rest of the district. If respondent School Board fails to prove that contention, the District Court, *second,* will determine whether respondent School Board's conduct over almost a decade after 1960 in carrying out a policy of deliberate racial segregation in the Park Hill schools constitutes the entire school system a dual school system. If the District Court determines that the Denver school system is a dual school system, respondent School Board has the affirmative duty to desegregate the entire system "root and branch." . . . If the District Court determines, however, that the Denver school system is not a dual school system by reason of the Board's actions in Park Hill, the court, *third,* will afford respondent School Board the opportunity to rebut petitioners' prima facie case of intentional segregation in the core city schools raised by the finding of intentional segregation in the Park Hill schools. There, the Board's burden is to show that its policies and practices with respect to school site location, school size, school renovations and additions, student-attendance zones, student assignment and transfer options, mobile classroom units, transportation of students, assignment of faculty and staff, etc., considered together and premised on the Board's so-called "neighborhood school" concept, either were not taken in effectuation of a policy to create or maintain segregation in the core city schools, or, if unsuccessful in that effort, were not factors in causing the existing condition of segregation in these schools. Considerations of "fairness" and "policy" demand no less in light of the Board's intentionally segregative actions. If respondent Board fails to rebut petitioners' prima facie case, the District Court must, as in the case of Park Hill, decree all-out desegregation of the core city schools. . . .

NOTES AND QUESTIONS

1. The *Keyes* decision represents the Supreme Court's first major ruling regarding the issue of racially segregated schools in a northern state without a history of legally mandated segregation. Accordingly, the *Keyes* case is often characterized as a northern *de facto* discrimination case, as opposed to a southern de jure discrimination case.
2. Because racial segregation was not required as a matter of Colorado law, the initial question in *Keyes* is whether the school district harbored the intent to effectuate a dual school system. The Court concludes that a school board's intent to create racially segregated schools is tantamount to state- mandated segregation. In other words, the intentional creation of *de facto* segregation is the same as de jure segregation from a constitutional perspective, except that any challenge to a *de facto* segregated system must begin with proof of intentional school district behavior. Do you agree that *de facto* segregation should be the legal equivalent of de jure discrimination? Should the remedies required to alleviate the two types of constitutional wrongs be identical?
3. Consider the Court's summary in Section IV of its opinion. That summary specifically identifies the order and burden of proof in a school desegregation case. Envision what the actual trial of the case might look like given the Court's parameters.

4. In *Keyes,* the Supreme Court treats the Hispanic students like the African-American students because both groups have suffered similar "economic and cultural deprivation and discrimination." What other racial or ethnic groups would be included under that standard?
5. Is intent to *perpetuate* a dual system of segregation sufficient for a constitutional violation, or must there be an intent to *create* such a system? In *Columbus Bd. of Educ. v. Penick,* 443 U.S. 449 (1979) and *Dayton Board of Education v. Brinkman,* 443 U.S. 526 (1979), the Supreme Court found de jure segregation in the Ohio districts based upon the fact that Ohio public officials had knowledge of the existence of segregated schools and failed to take affirmative steps to dismantle that dual system. The Court suggested that the failure to remedy an existing dual school system was itself a constitutional violation. What is the difference between a constitutional violation and a constitutional remedy? It is clear that "affirmative," race-conscious devices may, and indeed must, be employed to remedy a constitutional violation caused by the maintenance of a dual school system. Can the failure to take those affirmative steps itself be a violation of the Constitution? If so, then race-conscious decision making by public officials in their efforts to *avoid* maintaining an unconstitutional, dual school system cannot be unconstitutional. When should a public body be permitted to take race into account in its decision making?
6. In *Milliken v. Bradley,* 418 U.S. 717 (1974), the Supreme Court made it clear that a federal court may *not*

   > impose a multi-district, area wide remedy to a single-district *de jure* segregation problem absent any finding that the other included school districts have failed to operate unitary school systems within their districts, absent any claim or finding that the boundary lines of any affected school district were established with the purpose of fostering racial segregation in public schools, absent any finding that the included districts committed acts which effected segregation within the other districts, and absent a meaningful opportunity for the included neighboring school districts to present evidence or be heard on the propriety of a multi-district remedy or on the question of constitutional violations by those neighboring districts.

7. The *Milliken* Court's reasoning was based in large part on the principle of local control:

   > no single tradition in public education is more deeply rooted than local control over the operation of schools; local autonomy has long been thought essential both to the maintenance of community concern and support for public schools and to quality of the educational process. Thus, in *San Antonio School District v. Rodriguez,* 411 U.S. 1, 50 (1973), we observed that local control over the educational process affords citizens an opportunity to participate in decision-making, permits the structuring of school programs to fit local needs, and encourages experimentation, innovation, and a healthy competition for educational excellence.

   What is the meaning of local control here? Does the concept of local control really carry weight, or is it simply employed by the Court to justify its result?

8. The *Milliken* Court also addressed the issue of remedy:

> The controlling principle consistently expounded in our holdings is that the scope of the remedy is determined by the nature and extent of the constitutional violation. Before the boundaries of separate and autonomous school districts may be set aside by consolidating the separate units for remedial purposes or by imposing a cross-district remedy, it must first be shown that there has been a constitutional violation within one district that produces a significant segregative effect in another district. Specifically, it must be shown that racially discriminatory acts of the state or local school districts, or of a single school district have been a substantial cause of interdistrict segregation. Thus an interdistrict remedy might be in order where the racially discriminatory acts of one or more school districts caused racial segregation in an adjacent district, or where district lines have been deliberately drawn on the basis of race. In such circumstances an interdistrict remedy would be appropriate to eliminate the interdistrict segregation directly caused by the constitutional violation. Conversely, without an interdistrict violation and interdistrict effect, there is no constitutional wrong calling for an interdistrict remedy.

4. Resegregation, Retrenchment and Evolving Remedial Limits

Freeman v. Pitts

503 U.S. 467 (1992)

Justice Kennedy delivered the opinion of the Court.

DeKalb County, Georgia, is a major suburban area of Atlanta. This case involves a court-ordered desegregation decree for the DeKalb County School System (DCSS). DCSS now serves some 73,000 students in kindergarten through high school and is the 32d largest elementary and secondary school system in the Nation. . . .

II

Two principal questions are presented. The first is whether a district court may relinquish its supervision and control over those aspects of a school system in which there has been compliance with a desegregation decree if other aspects of the system remain in noncompliance. As we answer this question in the affirmative, the second question is whether the Court of Appeals erred in reversing the District Court's order providing for incremental withdrawal of supervision in all the circumstances of this case.

A

The duty and responsibility of a school district once segregated by law is to take all steps necessary to eliminate the vestiges of the unconstitutional *de jure* system. This is required in order to ensure that the principal wrong of the *de jure* system, the injuries and stigma inflicted upon the race disfavored by the violation, is no longer present. This was the rationale and the objective of

Brown I and *Brown II.* In *Brown I* we said: "To separate [black students] from others of similar age and qualifications solely because of their race generates a feeling of inferiority as to their status in the community that may affect their hearts and minds in a way unlikely ever to be undone" . . .

The objective of *Brown I* was made more specific by our holding in *Green* that the duty of a former *de jure* district is to "take whatever steps might be necessary to convert to a unitary system in which racial discrimination would be eliminated root and branch." We also identified various parts of the school system which, in addition to student attendance patterns, must be free from racial discrimination before the mandate of *Brown* is met: faculty, staff, transportation, extracurricular activities, and facilities. The *Green* factors are a measure of the racial identifiability of schools in a system that is not in compliance with *Brown,* and we instructed the District Courts to fashion remedies that address all these components of elementary and secondary school systems.

The concept of unitariness has been a helpful one in defining the scope of the district courts' authority, for it conveys the central idea that a school district that was once a dual system must be examined in all of its facets, both when a remedy is ordered and in the later phases of desegregation when the question is whether the district courts' remedial control ought to be modified, lessened, or withdrawn. But, as we explained last Term in *Board of Ed. of Oklahoma City Public Schools v. Dowell,* 498 U.S. 237, 245-246 (1991), the term "unitary" is not a precise concept:

> It is a mistake to treat words such as "dual" and "unitary" as if they were actually found in the Constitution. . . . Courts have used the terms "dual" to denote a school system which has engaged in intentional segregation of students by race, and "unitary" to describe a school system which has been brought into compliance with the command of the Constitution. We are not sure how useful it is to define these terms more precisely, or to create subclasses within them.

It follows that we must be cautious not to attribute to the term a utility it does not have. The term "unitary" does not confine the discretion and authority of the District Court in a way that departs from traditional equitable principles.

That the term "unitary" does not have fixed meaning or content is not inconsistent with the principles that control the exercise of equitable power. The essence of a court's equity power lies in its inherent capacity to adjust remedies in a feasible and practical way to eliminate the conditions or redress the injuries caused by unlawful action. Equitable remedies must be flexible if these underlying principles are to be enforced with fairness and precision. In this respect, as we observed in *Swann,* "a school desegregation case does not differ fundamentally from other cases involving the framing of equitable remedies to repair the denial of a constitutional right. The task is to correct, by a balancing of the individual and collective interests, the condition that offends the Constitution." *Swann.* The requirement of a unitary school system must be implemented according to this prescription.

Our application of these guiding principles in *Pasadena Bd. of Education v. Spangler,* 427 U.S. 424 (1976), is instructive. There we held that a District

Court exceeded its remedial authority in requiring annual readjustment of school attendance zones in the Pasadena school district when changes in the racial makeup of the schools were caused by demographic shifts "not attributed to any segregative acts on the part of the [school district]." In so holding we said:

> It may well be that petitioners have not yet totally achieved the unitary system contemplated by . . . *Swann*. . . . In this case the District Court approved a plan designed to obtain racial neutrality in the attendance of students at Pasadena's public schools. No one disputes that the initial implementation of this plan accomplished *that* objective. That being the case, the District Court was not entitled to require the [Pasadena Unified School District] to rearrange its attendance zones each year so as to ensure that the racial mix desired by the court was maintained in perpetuity. For having once implemented a racially neutral attendance pattern in order to remedy the perceived constitutional violations on the part of the defendants, the District Court had fully performed its function of providing the appropriate remedy for previous racially discriminatory attendance patterns. . . .

Today, we make explicit the rationale that was central in *Spangler*. A federal court in a school desegregation case has the discretion to order an incremental or partial withdrawal of its supervision and control. This discretion derives both from the constitutional authority which justified its intervention in the first instance and its ultimate objectives in formulating the decree. The authority of the court is invoked at the outset to remedy particular constitutional violations. In construing the remedial authority of the district courts, we have been guided by the principles that "judicial powers may be exercised only on the basis of a constitutional violation," and that "the nature of the violation determines the scope of the remedy." *Swann*. A remedy is justifiable only insofar as it advances the ultimate objective of alleviating the initial constitutional violation.

We have said that the court's end purpose must be to remedy the violation and, in addition, to restore state and local authorities to the control of a school system that is operating in compliance with the Constitution. *Milliken v. Bradley*. . . . Partial relinquishment of judicial control, where justified by the facts of the case, can be an important and significant step in fulfilling the district court's duty to return the operations and control of schools to local authorities. In *Dowell,* we emphasized that federal judicial supervision of local school systems was intended as a "temporary measure." 498 U.S. at 247. Although this temporary measure has lasted decades, the ultimate objective has not changed—to return school districts to the control of local authorities. Just as a court has the obligation at the outset of a desegregation decree to structure a plan so that all available resources of the court are directed to comprehensive supervision of its decree, so too must a court provide an orderly means for withdrawing from control when it is shown that the school district has attained the requisite degree of compliance. A transition phase in which control is relinquished in a gradual way is an appropriate means to this end.

As we have long observed, "local autonomy of school districts is a vital national tradition." *Dayton Bd. of Education v. Brinkman,* 433 U.S. 406, 410 (1977) *(Dayton I)*. Returning schools to the control of local authorities at the earliest practicable date is essential to restore their true accountability in our governmental system. When the school district and all state entities participating with it in operating the schools make decisions in the absence of judicial supervision, they can be held accountable to the citizenry, to the political process, and to the courts in the ordinary course. As we discuss below, one of the prerequisites to relinquishment of control in whole or in part is that a school district has demonstrated its commitment to a course of action that gives full respect to the equal protection guarantees of the Constitution. Yet it must be acknowledged that the potential for discrimination and racial hostility is still present in our country, and its manifestations may emerge in new and subtle forms after the effects of *de jure* segregation have been eliminated. It is the duty of the State and its subdivisions to ensure that such forces do not shape or control the policies of its school systems. Where control lies, so too does responsibility.

We hold that, in the course of supervising desegregation plans, federal courts have the authority to relinquish supervision and control of school districts in incremental stages, before full compliance has been achieved in every area of school operations. While retaining jurisdiction over the case, the court may determine that it will not order further remedies in areas where the school district is in compliance with the decree. That is to say, upon a finding that a school system subject to a court-supervised desegregation plan is in compliance in some but not all areas, the court in appropriate cases may return control to the school system in those areas where compliance has been achieved, limiting further judicial supervision to operations that are not yet in full compliance with the court decree. In particular, the district court may determine that it will not order further remedies in the area of student assignments where racial imbalance is not traceable, in a proximate way, to constitutional violations.

A court's discretion to order the incremental withdrawal of its supervision in a school desegregation case must be exercised in a manner consistent with the purposes and objectives of its equitable power. Among the factors which must inform the sound discretion of the court in ordering partial withdrawal are the following: whether there has been full and satisfactory compliance with the decree in those aspects of the system where supervision is to be withdrawn; whether retention of judicial control is necessary or practicable to achieve compliance with the decree in other facets of the school system; and whether the school district has demonstrated, to the public and to the parents and students of the once disfavored race, its good-faith commitment to the whole of the court's decree and to those provisions of the law and the Constitution that were the predicate for judicial intervention in the first instance.

In considering these factors, a court should give particular attention to the school system's record of compliance. A school system is better positioned to demonstrate its good-faith commitment to a constitutional course of action when its policies form a consistent pattern of lawful conduct directed to eliminating earlier violations. And, with the passage of time, the degree to which racial imbalances continue to represent vestiges of a constitutional violation may diminish, and the practicability and efficacy of various remedies can be evaluated with more precision. . . .

That there was racial imbalance in student attendance zones was not tantamount to a showing that the school district was in noncompliance with the decree or with its duties under the law. Racial balance is not to be achieved for its own sake. It is to be pursued when racial imbalance has been caused by a constitutional violation. Once the racial imbalance due to the *de jure* violation has been remedied, the school district is under no duty to remedy imbalance that is caused by demographic factors. *Swann,* 402 U.S. at 31-32. If the unlawful *de jure* policy of a school system has been the cause of the racial imbalance in student attendance, that condition must be remedied. The school district bears the burden of showing that any current imbalance is not traceable, in a proximate way, to the prior violation. . . .

The effect of changing residential patterns on the racial composition of schools, though not always fortunate, is somewhat predictable. Studies show a high correlation between residential segregation and school segregation. Wilson & Taeuber, *Residential and School Segregation: Some Tests of Their Association,* in *Demography and Ethnic Groups* 57-58 (F. Bean & W. Frisbie eds. 1978). The District Court in this case heard evidence tending to show that racially stable neighborhoods are not likely to emerge because whites prefer a racial mix of 80% white and 20% black, while blacks prefer a 50-50 mix.

Where resegregation is a product not of state action but of private choices, it does not have constitutional implications. It is beyond the authority and beyond the practical ability of the federal courts to try to counteract these kinds of continuous and massive demographic shifts. To attempt such results would require ongoing and never-ending supervision by the courts of school districts simply because they were once *de jure* segregated. Residential housing choices, and their attendant effects on the racial composition of schools, present an ever-changing pattern, one difficult to address through judicial remedies.

In one sense of the term, vestiges of past segregation by state decree do remain in our society and in our schools. Past wrongs to the black race, wrongs committed by the State and in its name, are a stubborn fact of history. And stubborn facts of history linger and persist. But though we cannot escape our history, neither must we overstate its consequences in fixing legal responsibilities. The vestiges of segregation that are the concern of the law in a school case may be subtle and intangible but nonetheless they must be so real that they have a causal link to the *de jure* violation being remedied. It is simply not always the case that demographic forces causing population change bear any real and substantial relation to a *de jure* violation. And the law need not proceed on that premise.

As the *de jure* violation becomes more remote in time and these demographic changes intervene, it becomes less likely that a current racial imbalance in a school district is a vestige of the prior *de jure* system. The causal link between current conditions and the prior violation is even more attenuated if the school district has demonstrated its good faith. In light of its finding that the demographic changes in DeKalb County are unrelated to the prior violation, the District Court was correct to entertain the suggestion that DCSS had no duty to achieve system wide racial balance in the student population. . . .

We next consider whether retention of judicial control over student attendance is necessary or practicable to achieve compliance in other facets of the school system. Racial balancing in elementary and secondary school student assignments may be a legitimate remedial device to correct other fundamental inequities that were themselves caused by the constitutional violation. . . .

There was no showing that racial balancing was an appropriate mechanism to cure other deficiencies in this case. It is true that the school district was not in compliance with respect to faculty assignments, but the record does not show that student reassignments would be a feasible or practicable way to remedy this defect. To the contrary, the District Court suggests that DCSS could solve the faculty assignment problem by reassigning a few teachers per school. The District Court, not having our analysis before it, did not have the opportunity to make specific findings and conclusions on this aspect of the case, however. Further proceedings are appropriate for this purpose.

The requirement that the school district show its good-faith commitment to the entirety of a desegregation plan so that parents, students, and the public have assurance against further injuries or stigma also should be a subject for more specific findings. We stated in *Dowell* that the good-faith compliance of the district with the court order over a reasonable period of time is a factor to be considered in deciding whether or not jurisdiction could be relinquished. . . . A history of good-faith compliance is evidence that any current racial imbalance is not the product of a new *de jure* violation, and enables the district court to accept the school board's representation that it has accepted the principle of racial equality and will not suffer intentional discrimination in the future. . . .

When a school district has not demonstrated good faith under a comprehensive plan to remedy ongoing violations, we have without hesitation approved comprehensive and continued district court supervision. . . .

[T]he District Court in this case stated that throughout the period of judicial supervision it has been impressed by the successes DCSS has achieved and its dedication to providing a quality education for all students, and that DCSS "has traveled the often long road to unitary status almost to its end." With respect to those areas where compliance had not been achieved, the District Court did not find that DCSS had acted in bad faith or engaged in further acts of discrimination since the desegregation plan went into effect. This, though, may not be the equivalent of a finding that the school district has an affirmative commitment to comply in good faith with the entirety of a desegregation plan, and further proceedings are appropriate for this purpose as well. . . .

NOTES AND QUESTIONS

1. In *Freeman,* the Court signals its relaxation regarding the urgency of court-mandated dismantling of all vestiges of a dual educational system. The Court relies on *Board of Education of Oklahoma City Public Schools v. Dowell,* 498 U.S. 237 (1991), for its position that the creation of a racially "unitary" school district in all its dimensions is not a *constitutional* requirement.

In *Dowell,* the Supreme Court concluded that a school desegregation remedy is a "temporary" measure that should be dissolved after "local authorities have operated in compliance with it for a reasonable period of time. . . ." 498 U.S. at 247-248. In *Freeman,* the Court returns to the principles of equitable remedies to insure that a federal court's remedial plan is finely tailored to the actual constitutional violation. Where the constitutional violation has been redressed by a remedy, the district court may and should withdraw its jurisdiction over the monitoring and maintenance of that remedy. In other words, if resegregation has occurred by virtue of private choices, the court has no equitable power to devise additional remedies to redirect those private choices. Accordingly, a federal court's remedy for a constitutional violation can be entirely frustrated by "white flight." Moreover, because a state or school district apparently cannot take affirmative steps to desegregate its students *absent* a proven constitutional violation, a state or district may be unable to attempt to improve an obvious condition of *de facto* segregation.

2. Once again, the Court relies upon the principles of local school district control and autonomy to support its result. Are those principles persuasive in this context?
3. The *Freeman* Court indicates that a federal court's remedial power may weaken as the condition of resegregation becomes more and more removed in time from the original constitutional violation. Can you detect an evolving time limit on a federal court's exercise of remedial power in the Supreme Court's cases? Will the evolution of that concept lead the court to conclude that any race-conscious conduct by any governmental body (including the courts) must be temporary and must be specifically designed to remedy a constitutional violation?
4. What does the Court in *Freeman* mean when it declares that, "[r]acial balance is not to be achieved for its own sake"? Is the Court rejecting "racial balance" as a legitimate educational goal, or merely suggesting that a federal court's remedial power cannot be exercised merely to achieve such a goal (no matter how desirable), unless that goal is required to remedy a proven constitutional violation?
5. There is significant evidence showing that the academic achievement levels of African-American students, as measured by standardized tests, increased dramatically as the result of their ability to learn in an integrated educational environment. *See* G. Orfield & C. Lee, Brown *at 50: King's Dream* or Plessy's *Nightmare?,* Harv. Civil Rights Project, at 53 (Jan. 2004); R. Crain & R. Mahard, *Desegregation Plans That Raise Black Achievement: A Review of the Research* 35-45 (1982); Taylor, Brown, *Equal Protection and the Isolation of the Poor,* 95 Yale L.J. 1700, 1710-1711 (1986). As this research suggests, "racial balance" improves the academic performance of African-American students. Can a school district take voluntary, affirmative steps to achieve "racial balance" for that "sake"?
6. In the following *Jenkins* opinion, the Supreme Court traces ten years of litigation and court rulings in the case. How has the judicial approach to the issue of segregation changed over that time?

Missouri v. Jenkins

15 U.S. 70 (1995)

Chief Justice Rehnquist delivered the opinion of the Court.

As this school desegregation litigation enters its 18th year, we are called upon again to review the decisions of the lower courts. In this case, the State of Missouri has challenged the District Court's order of salary increases for virtually all instructional and noninstructional staff within the Kansas City, Missouri, School District (KCMSD) and the District Court's order requiring the State to continue to fund remedial "quality education" programs because student achievement levels were still "at or below national norms at many grade levels."

A general overview of this litigation is necessary for proper resolution of the issues upon which we granted certiorari. This case has been before the same United States District Judge since 1977. *Missouri v. Jenkins,* 491 U.S. 274, 276 (1989) *(Jenkins I).* In that year, the KCMSD, the school board, and the children of two school board members brought suit against the State and other defendants. Plaintiffs alleged that the State, the surrounding suburban school districts (SSD's), and various federal agencies had caused and perpetuated a system of racial segregation in the schools of the Kansas City metropolitan area. . . .

After a trial that lasted 7½ months, the District Court dismissed the case against the federal defendants and the SSD's, but determined that the State and the KCMSD were liable for an intradistrict violation, i.e., they had operated a segregated school system within the KCMSD. The District Court determined that prior to 1954 "Missouri mandated segregated schools for black and white children." Furthermore, the KCMSD and the State had failed in their affirmative obligations to eliminate the vestiges of the State's dual school system within the KCMSD.

In June 1985, the District Court issued its first remedial order and established as its goal the "elimination of all vestiges of state imposed segregation." The District Court determined that "segregation had caused a system wide *reduction* in student achievement in the schools of the KCMSD." . . .

The District Court . . . ordered a wide range of quality education programs for all students attending the KCMSD. First, the District Court ordered that the KCMSD be restored to an AAA classification, the highest classification awarded by the State Board of Education. Second, it ordered that the number of students per class be reduced so that the student-to-teacher ratio was below the level required for AAA standing. . . .

The District Court also ordered programs to expand educational opportunities for all KCMSD students: full-day kindergarten; expanded summer school; before- and after-school tutoring; and an early childhood development program. Finally, the District Court implemented a state-funded "effective schools" program that consisted of substantial yearly cash grants to each of the schools within the KCMSD. . . .

The KCMSD was awarded an AAA rating in the 1987-1988 school year, and there is no dispute that since that time it has "'maintained and greatly exceeded AAA requirements.'" The total cost for these quality education programs has exceeded $220 million.

The District Court also set out to desegregate the KCMSD but believed that "to accomplish desegregation within the boundary lines of a school district whose enrollment remains 68.3% black is a difficult task." Because it had found no interdistrict violation, the District Court could not order mandatory interdistrict redistribution of students between the KCMSD and the surrounding SSD's. The District Court refused to order additional mandatory student reassignments because they would "increase the instability of the KCMSD and reduce the potential for desegregation." Relying on favorable precedent from the Eighth Circuit, the District Court determined that "achievement of AAA status, improvement of the quality of education being offered at the KCMSD schools, magnet schools, as well as other components of this desegregation plan can serve to maintain and hopefully attract non-minority student enrollment."

In November 1986, the District Court approved a comprehensive magnet school and capital improvements plan and held the State and the KCMSD jointly and severally liable for its funding. Under the District Court's plan, every senior high school, every middle school, and one-half of the elementary schools were converted into magnet schools. The District Court adopted the magnet-school program to "provide a greater educational opportunity to *all* KCMSD students," and because it believed "that the proposed magnet plan [was] so attractive that it would draw non-minority students from the private schools who have abandoned or avoided the KCMSD, and draw in additional non-minority students from the suburbs." The District Court felt that "the long-term benefit of all KCMSD students of a greater educational opportunity in an integrated environment is worthy of such an investment." Since its inception, the magnet school program has operated at a cost, including magnet transportation, in excess of $448 million. . . .

In June 1985, the District Court ordered substantial capital improvements to combat the deterioration of the KCMSD's facilities. In formulating its capital-improvements plan, the District Court dismissed as "irrelevant" the "State's argument that the present condition of the facilities [was] not traceable to unlawful segregation." Instead, the District Court focused on its responsibility to "remedy the vestiges of segregation" and to "implement a desegregation plan which would maintain and attract non-minority enrollment."

As part of its desegregation plan, the District Court has ordered salary assistance to the KCMSD. In 1987, the District Court initially ordered salary assistance only for teachers within the KCMSD. Since that time, however, the District Court has ordered salary assistance to all but three of the approximately 5,000 KCMSD employees. The total cost of this component of the desegregation remedy since 1987 is over $200 million.

The District Court's desegregation plan has been described as the most ambitious and expensive remedial program in the history of school desegregation. The annual cost per pupil at the KCMSD far exceeds that of the neighboring SSD's or of any school district in Missouri. Nevertheless, the KCMSD, which has pursued a "friendly adversary" relationship with the plaintiffs, has continued to propose ever more expensive programs. As a result, the desegregation costs have escalated and now are approaching an annual cost of $200 million. These massive expenditures have financed "high schools in which every classroom will have air conditioning, an alarm system, and 15 microcomputers; a 2,000-square-foot planetarium; green houses and vivariums; a 25-acre farm with an air-conditioned meeting room for 104 people; a Model United Nations wired for language translation; broadcast capable radio and television studios with an editing and animation lab; a temperature controlled art gallery; movie editing and screening rooms; a 3,500-square-foot dust-free diesel mechanics room; 1,875-square-foot elementary school animal rooms for use in a zoo project; swimming pools; and numerous other facilities."

Not surprisingly, the cost of this remedial plan has "far exceeded KCMSD's budget, or for that matter, its authority to tax." The State, through the operation of joint-and-several liability, has borne the brunt of these costs. . . .

II

With this background, we turn to the present controversy. First, the State has challenged the District Court's requirement that it fund salary increases for KCMSD instructional and noninstructional staff. The State claimed that funding for salaries was beyond the scope of the District Court's remedial authority. Second, the State has challenged the District Court's order requiring it to continue to fund the remedial quality education programs for the 1992-1993 school year. The State contended that under *Freeman v. Pitts,* it had achieved partial unitary status with respect to the quality education programs already in place. As a result, the State argued that the District Court should have relieved it of responsibility for funding those programs. . . .

III

. . . Proper analysis of the District Court's orders challenged here . . . must rest upon their serving as proper means to the end of restoring the victims of discriminatory conduct to the position they would have occupied in the absence of that conduct and their eventual restoration of "state and local authorities to the control of a school system that is operating in compliance with the Constitution." We turn to that analysis.

The State argues that the order approving salary increases is beyond the District Court's authority because it was crafted to serve an "interdistrict goal," in spite of the fact that the constitutional violation in this case is "intradistrict" in nature. "The nature of the desegregation remedy is to be determined by the nature and scope of the constitutional violation." . . . The proper response to an intradistrict violation is an intradistrict remedy, that serves to eliminate the racial identity of the schools within the effected school district by eliminating, as far as practicable, the vestiges of *de jure* segregation in all facets of their operations.

Here, the District Court has found, and the Court of Appeals has affirmed, that this case involved no interdistrict constitutional violation that would support interdistrict relief. . . . Thus, the proper response by the District Court should have been to eliminate to the extent practicable the vestiges of prior *de jure* segregation within the KCMSD: a system wide reduction in student achievement and the existence of 25 racially identifiable schools with a population of over 90% black students.

The District Court and Court of Appeals, however, have felt that because the KCMSD's enrollment remained 68.3% black, a purely intradistrict remedy would be insufficient. But, as noted in *Milliken I,* we have rejected the suggestion "that schools which have a majority of Negro students are not 'desegregated' whatever the racial makeup of the school district's population and however neutrally the district lines have been drawn and administered."

Instead of seeking to remove the racial identity of the various schools within the KCMSD, the District Court has set out on a program to create a school district that was equal to or superior to the surrounding SSD's. Its remedy has focused on "desegregative attractiveness," coupled with "suburban comparability." Examination of the District Court's reliance on "desegregative attractiveness" and "suburban comparability" is instructive for our ultimate resolution of the salary-order issue.

The purpose of desegregative attractiveness has been not only to remedy the system wide reduction in student achievement, but also to attract nonminority students not presently enrolled in the KCMSD. This remedy has included an elaborate program of capital improvements, course enrichment, and extracurricular enhancement not simply in the formerly identifiable black schools, but in schools throughout the district. The District Court's remedial orders have converted every senior high school, every middle school, and one-half of the elementary schools in the KCMSD into "magnet" schools. The District Court's remedial order has all but made the KCMSD itself into a magnet district.

We previously have approved of intradistrict desegregation remedies involving magnet schools. *See, e.g., Milliken I.* Magnet schools have the advantage of encouraging voluntary movement of students within a school district in a pattern that aids desegregation on a voluntary basis, without requiring extensive busing and redrawing of district boundary lines. As a component in an intradistrict remedy, magnet schools also are attractive because they promote desegregation while limiting the withdrawal of white student enrollment that may result from mandatory student reassignment.

The District Court's remedial plan in this case, however, is not designed solely to redistribute the students within the KCMSD in order to eliminate racially identifiable schools within the KCMSD. Instead, its purpose is to attract non-minority students from outside the KCMSD schools. But this interdistrict goal is beyond the scope of the intradistrict violation identified by the District Court. In effect, the District Court has devised a remedy to accomplish indirectly what it admittedly lacks the remedial authority to mandate directly: the interdistrict transfer of students. . . .

In *Milliken I* we determined that a desegregation remedy that would require mandatory interdistrict reassignment of students throughout the Detroit metropolitan area was an impermissible interdistrict response to the intradistrict violation identified. . . .

What we meant in *Milliken I* by an interdistrict violation was a violation that caused segregation between adjoining districts. Nothing in *Milliken I* suggests that the District Court in that case could have circumvented the limits on its remedial authority by requiring the State of Michigan, a constitutional violator, to implement a magnet program designed to achieve the same interdistrict transfer of students that we held was beyond its remedial authority. Here, the District Court has done just that: created a magnet district of the KCMSD in order to serve the interdistrict goal of attracting nonminority students from the surrounding SSD's and redistributing them within the KCMSD. The District Court's pursuit of "desegregative attractiveness" is beyond the scope of its broad remedial authority.

Respondents argue that the District Court's reliance upon desegregative attractiveness is justified in light of the District Court's statement that segregation has "led to white flight from the KCMSD to suburban districts." The lower courts' "findings" as to "white flight" are both inconsistent internally, and inconsistent with the typical supposition, bolstered here by the record evidence, that "white flight" may result from desegregation, not *de jure* segregation. . . .

In *Freeman,* we stated that "the vestiges of segregation that are the concern of the law in a school case may be subtle and intangible but nonetheless they must be so real that they have a causal link to the *de jure* violation being remedied." The record here does not support the District Court's reliance on "white flight" as a justification for a permissible expansion of its intradistrict remedial authority through its pursuit of desegregative attractiveness. . . .

The District Court's pursuit of "desegregative attractiveness" cannot be reconciled with our cases placing limitations on a district court's remedial authority. It is certainly theoretically possible that the greater the expenditure per pupil within the KCMSD, the more likely it is that some unknowable number of non-minority students not presently attending schools in the KCMSD will choose to enroll in those schools. Under this reasoning, however, every increased expenditure, whether it be for teachers, noninstructional employees, books, or buildings, will make the KCMSD in some way more attractive, and thereby perhaps induce nonminority students to enroll in its schools. But this rationale is not susceptible to any objective limitation. . . .

Nor are there limits to the duration of the District Court's involvement. . . . Each additional program ordered by the District Court—and financed by the State—to increase the "desegregative attractiveness" of the school district makes the KCMSD more and more dependent on additional funding from the State; in turn, the greater the KCMSD's dependence on state funding, the greater its reliance on continued supervision by the District Court. But our cases recognize that local autonomy of school districts is a vital national tradition, and that a district court must strive to restore state and local authorities to the control of a school system operating in compliance with the Constitution.

The District Court's pursuit of the goal of "desegregative attractiveness" results in so many imponderables and is so far removed from the task of eliminating the racial identifiability of the schools within the KCMSD that we believe it is beyond the admittedly broad discretion of the District Court. In this posture, we conclude that the District Court's order of salary increases, which was "grounded in remedying the vestiges of segregation by improving the desegregative attractiveness of the KCMSD," is simply too far removed from an acceptable implementation of a permissible means to remedy previous legally mandated segregation.

Similar considerations lead us to conclude that the District Court's order requiring the State to continue to fund the quality education programs because student achievement levels were still "at or below national norms at many grade levels" cannot be sustained. The State does not seek from this Court a declaration of partial unitary status with respect to the quality education programs. It challenges the requirement of indefinite funding of a quality education program until national norms are met, based upon the assumption that while a mandate for significant educational improvement, both in teaching and in facilities, may have been justified originally, its indefinite extension is not. . . .

In reconsidering this order, the District Court should apply our three-part test from *Freeman v. Pitts*. The District Court should consider that the State's role with respect to the quality education programs has been limited to the funding, not the implementation, of those programs. As all the parties agree that improved achievement on test scores is not necessarily required for the State to achieve partial unitary status as to the quality education programs, the District Court should sharply limit, if not dispense with, its reliance on this factor. Just as demographic changes independent of *de jure* segregation will affect the racial composition of student assignments, *Freeman,* so too will numerous external factors beyond the control of the KCMSD and the State affect minority student achievement. So long as these external factors are not the result of segregation, they do not figure in the remedial calculus. . . . Insistence upon academic goals unrelated to the effects of legal segregation unwarrantably postpones the day when the KCMSD will be able to operate on its own.

The District Court also should consider that many goals of its quality education plan already have been attained: the KCMSD now is equipped with "facilities and opportunities not available anywhere else in the country." . . . It may be that in education, just as it may be in economics, a "rising tide lifts all boats," but the remedial quality education program should be tailored to remedy the injuries suffered by the victims of prior *de jure* segregation. . . .

On remand, the District Court must bear in mind that its end purpose is not only "to remedy the violation" to the extent practicable, but also "to restore state and local authorities to the control of a school system that is operating in compliance with the Constitution."

Justice GINSBURG, dissenting. . . .

The Court stresses that the present remedial programs have been in place for seven years. But compared to more than two centuries of firmly entrenched official discrimination, the experience with the desegregation remedies ordered by the District Court has been evanescent.

In 1724, Louis XV of France issued the Code Noir, the first slave code for the Colony of Louisiana, an area that included Missouri. . . . When Missouri entered the Union in 1821, it entered as a slave State.

Before the Civil War, Missouri law prohibited the creation or maintenance of schools for educating blacks: "No person shall keep or teach any school for the instruction of negroes or mulattoes, in reading or writing, in this State."

Beginning in 1865, Missouri passed a series of laws requiring separate public schools for blacks. The Missouri Constitution first permitted, then required, separate schools.

After this Court announced its decision in *Brown v. Board of Education,* Missouri's Attorney General declared these provisions mandating segregated schools unenforceable. The statutes were repealed in 1957 and the constitutional provision was rescinded in 1976. Nonetheless, 30 years after *Brown,* the District Court found that "the inferior education indigenous of the state-compelled dual school system has lingering effects in the Kansas City, Missouri School District." The District Court concluded that "the State . . . cannot defend its failure to affirmatively act to eliminate the structure and effects of its past dual system on the basis of restrictive state law." Just ten years ago, in June 1985, the District Court issued its first remedial order.

Today, the Court declares illegitimate the goal of attracting nonminority students to the Kansas City, Missouri, School District, and thus stops the District Court's efforts to integrate a school district that was, in the 1984/1985 school year, sorely in need and 68.3% black. Given the deep, inglorious history of segregation in Missouri, to curtail desegregation at this time and in this manner is an action at once too swift and too soon. . . .

NOTES AND QUESTIONS

1. In *Missouri v. Jenkins,* 495 U.S. 33 (1990) *(Jenkins II),* the Supreme Court rejected the district court's order requiring the Kansas City Metropolitan School District to increase its tax rate to raise the funds required to implement the court's ambitious plans. The Supreme Court, however, indicated that such a tax increase could be within the federal court's remedial power if "no permissible alternative would have accomplished the required task." Moreover, the Court made clear that a remedial order that does not impose its own tax increase but instead directs "a local government body to levy its own taxes is plainly a judicial act within the power of the federal court. . . ." What type of constitutional violation would justify such a remedy?
2. The district court creatively employed the concept of "magnet schools" to assist in its remedial plan. The Supreme Court defines a magnet school as "public schools of voluntary enrollment designed to promote integration by drawing students away from their neighborhoods and private schools through distinctive curricula and high quality." The Court declares that "[w]e have approved of intradistrict desegregation remedies involving magnet schools." Nonetheless, the Court rejects the district court's reliance on magnet schools here. Why?
3. After *Jenkins,* what is the law governing the responsibility of a state or school district to remedy a previous finding of intentional desegregation

by achieving a condition of integration? What are the limits to a court's remedial power?

4. Reflect on the path of the Supreme Court's rulings since *Brown.* The Court's recent rejection of challenges to segregation and resegregation has had a significant impact on the racial composition of American schools. American "schools are becoming more segregated in all regions for both African American and Latino students." G. Orfield and C. Lee, Brown *at 50: King's Dream or* Plessy's *Nightmare?,* Harv. Civil Rights Project, at 2 (Jan. 2004). In particular, the evidence shows that since the early 1990s, when the Supreme Court began to dilute court-ordered desegregation efforts, "there has been a major increase in segregation." *Id.* Throughout the nation, "Blacks and Latinos attend schools where two-thirds of the students are Black and Latino and most students are from their own group." *Id.,* at 17. Since 1988, the percentage of African-American students attending a majority white school declined from 43.5 percent to 30.2 percent. *Id.,* at 21.

   Moreover, there is a stunning link between racial segregation and poverty. While only 15 percent of the intensely segregated white students attend schools with concentrated poverty, 88 percent of the intensely segregated minority students attend schools with concentrated poverty. *Id.,* at 21. Furthermore, minority children in highly segregated minority schools with concentrated poverty "tend to be less healthy, to have weaker preschool experiences, to have only one parent, to move frequently and have unstable educational experiences, to attend classes taught by less experienced or unqualified teachers, to have friends and classmates with lower levels of achievement, to be in schools with fewer demanding pre-collegiate courses and more remedial courses, and to have higher teacher turnover. Many of these schools are also deteriorated and lack key resources." *Id.,* at 21-22. *See also* K. Carey, *The Funding Gap: Low-income and Minority Students Still Receive Fewer Dollars, in Many States,* The Education Trust, at 6-9 (Fall 2003). If *Brown* had challenged the inequality of tangible resources available to most minority students, would more progress have been made in the past 50 years? On the other hand, the evidence indicates that in an era when the Supreme Court took seriously *Brown's* commitment to integration, significant progress was made in both the racial balance of schools and in the academic achievement of minority students. Among the recommendations made by Orfield and Lee is a call for presidential leadership on the issue of school desegregation, including the appointment of "judges and civil rights enforcement officials who understand that the Supreme Court was right in *Brown* and that the job is far from over." Harvard Civil Rights Project, at 40. Do you agree with that recommendation? Finally, as you think about the link between poverty and segregation, reconsider the issues of inequitable and inadequate funding addressed in Chapter 4. To what extent would the recognition of a federal or state constitutional "right to education" create a climate of adequate and equitable funding that might help to bridge the racial divide?

B. AFFIRMATIVE ACTION FROM *BAKKE* TO *BOLLINGER*

In *Regents of the University of California v. Bakke,* 438 U.S. 265 (1978), the Court first addressed the constitutionality of race-conscious university admissions programs. In *Bakke,* a divided court delivered a plurality opinion with no clear mandate. Twenty-five years later, the Supreme Court endorsed Justice Powell's opinion in *Bakke* that "student body diversity is a compelling state interest that can justify the use of race in university admissions." *Grutter v. Bollinger,* 539 U.S. 306 (2003). While race-conscious admissions policies raise constitutional issues to be decided by the courts, they also have been the focus of political debate. When studying these cases, consider how the courts have handled both the legal and the political dimensions of these issues.

REGENTS OF THE UNIVERSITY OF CALIFORNIA V. BAKKE

438 U.S. 265 (1978)

Mr. Justice POWELL announced the judgment of the Court.

This case presents a challenge to the special admissions program of the petitioner, the Medical School of the University of California at Davis, which is designed to assure the admission of a specified number of students from certain minority groups. The Superior Court of California sustained respondent's challenge, holding that petitioner's program violated the California Constitution, Title VI of the Civil Rights Act of 1964, 42 U.S.C. §2000d et seq., and the Equal Protection Clause of the Fourteenth Amendment.

For the reasons stated in the following opinion, I believe that so much of the judgment of the California court as holds petitioner's special admissions program unlawful and directs that respondent be admitted to the Medical School must be affirmed. For the reasons expressed in a separate opinion, my Brothers The Chief Justice, Mr. Justice Stewart, Mr. Justice Rehnquist and Mr. Justice Stevens concur in this judgment.

I also conclude for the reasons stated in the following opinion that the portion of the court's judgment enjoining petitioner from according any consideration to race in its admissions process must be reversed. For reasons expressed in separate opinions, my Brothers Mr. Justice Brennan, Mr. Justice White, Mr. Justice Marshall, and Mr. Justice Blackmun concur in this judgment.

I

The Medical School of the University of California at Davis opened in 1968 with an entering class of 50 students. In 1971, the size of the entering class was increased to 100 students, a level at which it remains. No admissions program for disadvantaged or minority students existed when the school opened, and the first class contained three Asians but no blacks, no Mexican-Americans, and no American Indians. Over the next two years, the faculty devised a special admissions program to increase the representation of "disadvantaged" students in each Medical School class. The special program consisted of a separate admissions system operating in coordination with the regular admissions process. . . .

The special admissions program operated with a separate committee, a majority of whom were members of minority groups. On the 1973 application form, candidates were asked to indicate whether they wished to be considered as "economically and/or educationally disadvantaged" applicants; on the 1974 form the question was whether they wished to be considered as members of a "minority group," which the Medical School apparently viewed as "Blacks," "Chicanos," "Asians," and "American Indians." . . . No formal definition of "disadvantaged" was ever produced, but the chairman of the special committee screened each application to see whether it reflected economic or educational deprivation. Having passed this initial hurdle, the applications then were rated by the special committee in a fashion similar to that used by the general admissions committee, except that special candidates did not have to meet the 2.5 grade point average cutoff applied to regular applicants. . . . While the overall class size was still 50, the prescribed number was 8; in 1973 and 1974, when the class size had doubled to 100, the prescribed number of special admissions also doubled, to 16.

Although disadvantaged whites applied to the special program in large numbers, none received an offer of admission through that process. Indeed, in 1974, at least, the special committee explicitly considered only "disadvantaged" special applicants who were members of one of the designated minority groups.

II

En route to this crucial battle over the scope of judicial review, the parties fight a sharp preliminary action over the proper characterization of the special admissions program. Petitioner prefers to view it as establishing a "goal" of minority representation in the Medical School. Respondent, echoing the courts below, labels it a racial quota.

This semantic distinction is beside the point: The special admissions program is undeniably a classification based upon race and ethnic background. To the extent that there existed a pool of at least minimally qualified minority applicants to fill the 16 special admissions seats, white applicants could compete only for 84 seats in the entering class, rather than the 100 open to minority applicants. Whether this limitation is described as a quota or a goal, it is a line drawn on the basis of race and ethnic status.

The guarantees of the Fourteenth Amendment extend to all persons. Its language is explicit: "No State shall . . . deny to any person within its jurisdiction the equal protection of the laws." It is settled beyond question that the "rights created by the first section of the Fourteenth Amendment are, by its terms, guaranteed to the individual. The rights established are personal rights." . . . The guarantee of equal protection cannot mean one thing when applied to one individual and something else when applied to a person of another color. If both are not accorded the same protection, then it is not equal.

Nevertheless, petitioner argues that the court below erred in applying strict scrutiny to the special admissions program because white males, such as respondent, are not a "discrete and insular minority" requiring extraordinary protection from the majoritarian political process. *Carolene Products Co., supra,* 304 U.S., at 152-153 n.4,. . . . This rationale, however, has never been invoked in our decisions as a prerequisite to subjecting racial or ethnic distinctions to strict scrutiny. Nor has this Court held that discreteness and insularity constitute necessary preconditions to a holding that a particular classification is invidious.

B

It is far too late to argue that the guarantee of equal protection to all persons permits the recognition of special wards entitled to a degree of protection greater than that accorded others. "The Fourteenth Amendment is not directed solely against discrimination due to a 'two-class theory'—that is, based upon differences between 'white' and Negro." . . .

Once the artificial line of a "two-class theory" of the Fourteenth Amendment is put aside, the difficulties entailed in varying the level of judicial review according to a perceived "preferred" status of a particular racial or ethnic minority are intractable. The concepts of "majority" and "minority" necessarily reflect temporary arrangements and political judgments. [T]he white "majority" itself is composed of various minority groups, most of which can lay claim to a history of prior discrimination at the hands of the State and private individuals. Not all of these groups can receive preferential treatment and corresponding judicial tolerance of distinctions drawn in terms of race and nationality, for then the only "majority" left would be a new minority of white Anglo-Saxon Protestants. There is no principled basis for deciding which groups would merit "heightened judicial solicitude" and which would not. Courts would be asked to evaluate the extent of the prejudice and consequent harm suffered by various minority groups. Those whose societal injury is thought to exceed some arbitrary level of tolerability then would be entitled to preferential classifications at the expense of individuals belonging to other groups. Those classifications would be free from exacting judicial scrutiny. As these preferences began to have their desired effect, and the consequences of past discrimination were undone, new judicial rankings would be necessary. The kind of variable sociological and political analysis necessary to produce such rankings simply does not lie within the judicial competence—even if they otherwise were politically feasible and socially desirable.

III

We have held that in "order to justify the use of a suspect classification, a State must show that its purpose or interest is both constitutionally permissible and substantial, and that its use of the classification is 'necessary . . . to the accomplishment' of its purpose or the safeguarding of its interest." . . . The special admissions program purports to serve the purposes of: (i) "reducing the historic deficit of traditionally disfavored minorities in medical schools and in the medical profession," . . . ; (ii) countering the effects of societal discrimination; (iii) increasing the number of physicians who will practice in communities currently underserved; and (iv) obtaining the educational benefits that flow from an ethnically diverse student body. It is necessary to decide which, if any, of these purposes is substantial enough to support the use of a suspect classification.

A

If petitioner's purpose is to assure within its student body some specified percentage of a particular group merely because of its race or ethnic origin, such a preferential purpose must be rejected not as insubstantial but as facially invalid. Preferring members of any one group for no reason other than race or ethnic origin is discrimination for its own sake. This the Constitution forbids.

B

The State certainly has a legitimate and substantial interest in ameliorating, or eliminating where feasible, the disabling effects of identified discrimination. The line of school desegregation cases, commencing with *Brown,* attests to the importance of this state goal and the commitment of the judiciary to affirm all lawful means toward its attainment. In the school cases, the States were required by court order to redress the wrongs worked by specific instances of racial discrimination. That goal was far more focused than the remedying of the effects of "societal discrimination," an amorphous concept of injury that may be ageless in its reach into the past.

Hence, the purpose of helping certain groups whom the faculty of the Davis Medical School perceived as victims of "societal discrimination" does not justify a classification that imposes disadvantages upon persons like respondent, who bear no responsibility for whatever harm the beneficiaries of the special admissions program are thought to have suffered. To hold otherwise would be to convert a remedy heretofore reserved for violations of legal rights into a privilege that all institutions throughout the Nation could grant at their pleasure to whatever groups are perceived as victims of societal discrimination. That is a step we have never approved.

C

Petitioner identifies, as another purpose of its program, improving the delivery of health-care services to communities currently underserved. It may be assumed that in some situations a State's interest in facilitating the health care of its citizens is sufficiently compelling to support the use of a suspect classification. But there is virtually no evidence in the record indicating that petitioner's special admissions program is either needed or geared to promote that goal. The court below addressed this failure of proof:

> Petitioner simply has not carried its burden of demonstrating that it must prefer members of particular ethnic groups over all other individuals in order to promote better health-care delivery to deprived citizens. Indeed, petitioner has not shown that its preferential classification is likely to have any significant effect on the problem.

D

The fourth goal asserted by petitioner is the attainment of a diverse student body. This clearly is a constitutionally permissible goal for an institution of higher education. Academic freedom, though not a specifically enumerated constitutional right, long has been viewed as a special concern of the

First Amendment. The freedom of a university to make its own judgments as to education includes the selection of its student body. Mr. Justice Frankfurter summarized the "four essential freedoms" that constitute academic freedom:

> It is the business of a university to provide that atmosphere which is most conducive to speculation, experiment and creation. It is an atmosphere in which there prevail "the four essential freedoms" of a university—to determine for itself on academic grounds who may teach, what may be taught, how it shall be taught, and who may be admitted to study. . . .

Our national commitment to the safeguarding of these freedoms within university communities was emphasized in *Keyishian v. Board of Regents,* 385 U.S. 589, 603 (1967):

> Our Nation is deeply committed to safeguarding academic freedom which is of transcendent value to all of us and not merely to the teachers concerned. That freedom is therefore a special concern of the First Amendment. . . . The Nation's future depends upon leaders trained through wide exposure to that robust exchange of ideas which discovers truth "out of a multitude of tongues, [rather] than through any kind of authoritative selection." . . .

The president of Princeton University has described some of the benefits derived from a diverse student body:

> [A] great deal of learning occurs informally. It occurs through interactions among students of both sexes; of different races, religions, and backgrounds; who come from cities and rural areas, from various states and countries; who have a wide variety of interests, talents, and perspectives; and who are able, directly or indirectly, to learn from their differences and to stimulate one another to reexamine even their most deeply held assumptions about themselves and their world. As a wise graduate of ours observed in commenting on this aspect of the educational process, "People do not learn very much when they are surrounded only by the likes of themselves."

Thus, in arguing that its universities must be accorded the right to select those students who will contribute the most to the "robust exchange of ideas," petitioner invokes a countervailing constitutional interest, that of the First Amendment. In this light, petitioner must be viewed as seeking to achieve a goal that is of paramount importance in the fulfillment of its mission.

It may be argued that there is greater force to these views at the undergraduate level than in a medical school where the training is centered primarily on professional competency. But even at the graduate level, our tradition and experience lend support to the view that the contribution of diversity is substantial. In *Sweatt v. Painer,* the Court made a similar point with specific reference to legal education:

> The law school, the proving ground for legal learning and practice, cannot be effective in isolation from the individuals and institutions with which the law interacts. Few students and no one who has practiced law would choose to study in an academic vacuum, removed from the interplay of ideas and the exchange of views with which the law is concerned.

Ethnic diversity, however, is only one element in a range of factors a university properly may consider in attaining the goal of a heterogeneous student body. Although a university must have wide discretion in making the sensitive judgments as to who should be admitted, constitutional limitations protecting individual rights may not be disregarded. Respondent urges—and the courts below have held—that petitioner's dual admissions program is a racial classification that impermissibly infringes his rights under the Fourteenth Amendment. As the interest of diversity is compelling in the context of a university's admissions program, the question remains whether the program's racial classification is necessary to promote this interest.

IV

It may be assumed that the reservation of a specified number of seats in each class for individuals from the preferred ethnic groups would contribute to the attainment of considerable ethnic diversity in the student body. But petitioner's argument that this is the only effective means of serving the interest of diversity is seriously flawed. In a most fundamental sense the argument misconceives the nature of the state interest that would justify consideration of race or ethnic background. It is not an interest in simple ethnic diversity, in which a specified percentage of the student body is in effect guaranteed to be members of selected ethnic groups, with the remaining percentage an undifferentiated aggregation of students. The diversity that furthers a compelling state interest encompasses a far broader array of qualifications and characteristics of which racial or ethnic origin is but a single though important element. Petitioner's special admissions program, focused *solely* on ethnic diversity, would hinder rather than further attainment of genuine diversity.

Nor would the state interest in genuine diversity be served by expanding petitioner's two-track system into a multitrack program with a prescribed number of seats set aside for each identifiable category of applicants. Indeed, it is inconceivable that a university would thus pursue the logic of petitioner's two-track program to the illogical end of insulating each category of applicants with certain desired qualifications from competition with all other applicants.

The experience of other university admissions programs, which take race into account in achieving the educational diversity valued by the First Amendment, demonstrates that the assignment of a fixed number of places to a minority group is not a necessary means toward that end. An illuminating example is found in the Harvard College program.

In such an admissions program, race or ethnic background may be deemed a "plus" in a particular applicant's file, yet it does not insulate the individual from comparison with all other candidates for the available seats. The file of a particular black applicant may be examined for his potential contribution to diversity without the factor of race being decisive when compared, for example, with that of an applicant identified as an Italian-American if the latter is thought to exhibit qualities more likely to promote beneficial educational pluralism. Such qualities could include exceptional personal talents, unique work or service experience, leadership potential, maturity, demonstrated compassion, a history of overcoming disadvantage, ability to communicate with the poor, or other qualifications deemed important. In short, an admissions program operated in this way is flexible enough to consider all pertinent elements of diversity in light of the particular qualifications of each applicant, and to place them on the same footing for consideration, although not necessarily according them the same weight. Indeed, the weight attributed to a particular quality may vary from year to year depending upon the "mix" both of the student body and the applicants for the incoming class.

This kind of program treats each applicant as an individual in the admissions process. The applicant who loses out on the last available seat to another candidate receiving a "plus" on the basis of ethnic background will not have been foreclosed from all consideration for that seat simply because he was not the right color or had the wrong surname. It would mean only that his combined qualifications, which may have included similar non-objective factors, did not outweigh those of the other applicant. His qualifications would have been weighed fairly and competitively, and he would have no basis to complain of unequal treatment under the Fourteenth Amendment.

It has been suggested that an admissions program which considers race only as one factor is simply a subtle and more sophisticated—but no less effective—means of according racial preference than the Davis program. A facial intent to discriminate, however, is evident in petitioner's preference program and not denied in this case. No such facial infirmity exists in an admissions program where race or ethnic background is simply one element—to be weighed fairly against other elements—in the selection process. . . . And a court would not assume that a university, professing to employ a facially non-discriminatory admissions policy, would operate it as a cover for the functional equivalent of a quota system. In short, good faith would be presumed in the absence of a showing to the contrary in the manner permitted by our cases.

B

In summary, it is evident that the Davis special admissions program . . . tells applicants who are not Negro, Asian, or Chicano that they are totally excluded from a specific percentage of the seats in an entering class. No matter how strong their qualifications, quantitative and extracurricular, including their own potential for contribution to educational diversity, they are never afforded the chance to compete with applicants from the preferred groups for the special admissions seats. At the same time, the preferred applicants have the opportunity to compete for every seat in the class.

The fatal flaw in petitioner's preferential program is its disregard of individual rights as guaranteed by the Fourteenth Amendment. Such rights are not absolute. But when a State's distribution of benefits or imposition of burdens hinges on ancestry or the color of a person's skin, that individual is entitled to a demonstration that the challenged classification is necessary to promote a substantial state interest. Petitioner has failed to carry this burden. For this reason, that portion of the California court's judgment holding petitioner's special admissions program invalid under the Fourteenth Amendment must be affirmed.

Opinion of Mr. Justice BRENNAN, Mr. Justice WHITE, Mr. Justice MARSHALL, and Mr. Justice BLACKMUN, concurring in the judgment in part and dissenting in part.

The Court today, in reversing in part the judgment of the Supreme Court of California, affirms the constitutional power of Federal and State Governments to act affirmatively to achieve equal opportunity for all. The difficulty of the issue presented—whether government may use race-conscious programs to redress the continuing effects of past discrimination and the mature consideration which each of our Brethren has brought to it have resulted in many opinions, no single one speaking for the Court. But this should not and must not mask the central meaning of today's opinions: Government may take race into account when it acts not to demean or insult any racial group, but to remedy disadvantages cast on minorities by past racial prejudice, at least when appropriate findings have been made by judicial, legislative, or administrative bodies with competence to act in this area.

The Chief Justice and our Brothers Stewart, Rehnquist, and Stevens, have concluded that Title VI of the Civil Rights Act of 1964 . . . prohibits programs such as that at the Davis Medical School. On this statutory theory alone, they would hold that respondent Allan Bakke's rights have been violated and that he must, therefore, be admitted to the Medical School. Our Brother Powell, reaching the Constitution, concludes that, although race may be taken into account in university admissions, the particular special admissions program used by petitioner, which resulted in the exclusion of respondent Bakke, was not shown to be necessary to achieve petitioner's stated goals. Accordingly, these Members of the Court form a majority of five affirming the judgment of the Supreme Court of California insofar as it holds that respondent Bakke "is entitled to an order that he be admitted to the University."

We agree with Mr. Justice Powell that, as applied to the case before us, Title VI goes no further in prohibiting the use of race than the Equal Protection Clause of the Fourteenth Amendment itself. We also agree that the effect of the California Supreme Court's affirmance of the judgment of the Superior Court of California would be to prohibit the University from establishing in the future affirmative-action programs that take race into account. Since we conclude that the affirmative admissions program at the Davis Medical School is constitutional, we would reverse the judgment below in all respects. Mr. Justice Powell agrees that some uses of race in university admissions are permissible and, therefore, he joins with us to make five votes reversing the judgment below insofar as it prohibits the University from establishing race-conscious programs in the future.[1]

I

The Fourteenth Amendment, the embodiment in the Constitution of our abiding belief in human equality, has been the law of our land for only slightly more than half its 200 years. And for half of that half, the Equal

[1] We also agree with Mr. Justice Powell that a plan like the "Harvard" plan, . . . is constitutional under our approach, at least so long as the use of race to achieve an integrated student body is necessitated by the lingering effects of past discrimination.

Protection Clause of the Amendment was largely moribund so that, as late as 1927, Mr. Justice Holmes could sum up the importance of that Clause by remarking that it was the "last resort of constitutional arguments." *Buck v. Bell, 274* U.S. 200, 208 (1927). Worse than desuetude, the Clause was early turned against those whom it was intended to set free, condemning them to a "separate but equal" status before the law, a status always separate but seldom equal. Not until 1954—only 24 years ago—was this odious doctrine interred by our decision in *Brown v. Board of Education,* 347 U.S. 483 *(Brown I),* and its progeny, which proclaimed that separate schools and public facilities of all sorts were inherently unequal and forbidden under our Constitution.

Against this background, claims that law must be "color-blind" or that the datum of race is no longer relevant to public policy must be seen as aspiration rather than as description of reality. This is not to denigrate aspiration; for reality rebukes us that race has too often been used by those who would stigmatize and oppress minorities. Yet we cannot—and, as we shall demonstrate, need not under our Constitution or Title VI, which merely extends the constraints of the Fourteenth Amendment to private parties who receive federal funds—let color blindness become myopia which masks the reality that many "created equal" have been treated within our lifetimes as inferior both by the law and by their fellow citizens.

II

In our view, Title VI prohibits only those uses of racial criteria that would violate the Fourteenth Amendment if employed by a State or its agencies; it does not bar the preferential treatment of racial minorities as a means of remedying past societal discrimination to the extent that such action is consistent with the Fourteenth Amendment.

First, no decision of this Court has ever adopted the proposition that the Constitution must be colorblind.

Second, even if it could be argued in 1964 that the Constitution might conceivably require color blindness, Congress surely would not have chosen to codify such a view unless the Constitution clearly required it.

Third, the legislative history shows that Congress specifically eschewed any static definition of discrimination in favor of broad language that could be shaped by experience, administrative necessity, and evolving judicial doctrine.

A

The Court has also declined to adopt a "color-blind" interpretation of other statutes containing nondiscrimination provisions similar to that contained in Title VI. We have held under Title VII that where employment requirements have a disproportionate impact upon racial minorities they constitute a statutory violation, even in the absence of discriminatory intent, unless the employer is able to demonstrate that the requirements are sufficiently related to the needs of the job. More significantly, the Court has required that preferences be given by employers to members of racial minorities as a remedy for past violations of Title VII, even where there has been no finding that the employer has acted with a discriminatory intent. . . .

III

A

The assertion of human equality is closely associated with the proposition that differences in color or creed, birth or status, are neither significant nor relevant to the way in which persons should be treated. Nonetheless, the position that such factors must be "constitutionally an irrelevance," *Edwards v. California,* 314 U.S. 160, 185 (1941) (Jackson, J., concurring), summed up by the shorthand phrase "[o]ur Constitution is color-blind," *Plessy v. Ferguson,* 163 U.S. 537, 559 (1896) (Harlan, J., dissenting), has never been adopted by this Court as the proper meaning of the Equal Protection Clause. Indeed, we have expressly rejected this proposition on a number of occasions.

We conclude, therefore, that racial classifications are not per se invalid under the Fourteenth Amendment. Accordingly, we turn to the problem of articulating what our role should be in reviewing state action that expressly classifies by race.

B

Respondent argues that racial classifications are always suspect and, consequently, that this Court should weigh the importance of the objectives served by Davis' special admissions program to see if they are compelling. In addition, he asserts that this Court must inquire whether, in its judgment, there are alternatives to racial classifications which would suit Davis' purposes. Petitioner, on the other hand, states that our proper role is simply to accept petitioner's determination that the racial classifications used by its program are reasonably related to what it tells us are its benign purposes. We reject petitioner's view, but, because our prior cases are in many respects inapposite to that before us now, we find it necessary to define with precision the meaning of that inexact term, "strict scrutiny."

Unquestionably we have held that a government practice or statute which restricts "fundamental rights" or which contains "suspect classifications" is to be subjected to "strict scrutiny" and can be justified only if it furthers a compelling government purpose and, even then, only if no less restrictive alternative is available. But no fundamental right is involved here. Nor do whites as a class have any of the "traditional indicia of suspectness: the class is not saddled with such disabilities, or subjected to such a history of purposeful unequal treatment, or relegated to such a position of political powerlessness as to command extraordinary protection from the majoritarian political process." *Id.,* at 28.

IV

A

At least since [1968] it has been clear that a public body which has itself been adjudged to have engaged in racial discrimination cannot bring itself into compliance with the Equal Protection Clause simply by ending its unlawful acts and adopting a neutral stance. Three years later, [this court] reiterated that racially neutral remedies for past discrimination were inadequate where consequences of past discriminatory acts influence or control present decisions. And the Court further held both that courts could enter desegregation orders which assigned students and faculty by reference to race, and that local school boards could voluntarily adopt desegregation plans which made express reference to race if this was necessary to remedy the effects of past discrimination. Moreover, we stated that school boards, even in the absence of a judicial finding of past discrimination, could voluntarily adopt plans which assigned students with the end of creating racial pluralism by establishing fixed ratios of black and white students in each school. In each instance, the creation of unitary school systems, in which the effects of past discrimination had been "eliminated root and branch," was recognized as a compelling social goal justifying the overt use of race.

Finally, the conclusion that state educational institutions may constitutionally adopt admissions programs designed to avoid exclusion of historically disadvantaged minorities, even when such programs explicitly take race into account, finds direct support in our cases construing congressional legislation designed to overcome the present effects of past discrimination. Congress can and has outlawed actions which have a disproportionately adverse and unjustified impact upon members of racial minorities and has required or authorized race-conscious action to put individuals disadvantaged by such impact in the position they otherwise might have enjoyed. Such relief does not require as a predicate proof that recipients of preferential advancement have been individually discriminated against; it is enough that each recipient is within a general class of persons likely to have been the victims of discrimination. Nor is it an objection to such relief that preference for minorities will upset the settled expectations of nonminorities. See Franks, supra. In addition, we have held that Congress, to remove barriers to equal opportunity, can and has required employers to use test criteria that fairly reflect the qualifications of minority applicants vis-à-vis non-minority applicants, even if this means interpreting the qualifications of an applicant in light of his race.

B

Properly construed, therefore, our prior cases unequivocally show that a state government may adopt race-conscious programs if the purpose of such programs is to remove the disparate racial impact its actions might otherwise have and if there is reason to believe that the disparate impact is itself the product of past discrimination, whether its own or that of society at large. There is no question that Davis' program is valid under this test.

Certainly, on the basis of the undisputed factual submissions before this Court, Davis had a sound basis for believing that the problem of under representation of minorities was substantial and chronic and that the problem was attributable to handicaps imposed on minority applicants by past and present racial discrimination. Until at least 1973, the practice of medicine in this country was, in fact, if not in law, largely the prerogative of whites.

It cannot be questioned that, in the absence of the special admissions program, access of minority students to the Medical School would be severely limited and, accordingly, race-conscious admissions would be deemed an appropriate response under these federal regulations.

C

The second prong of our test—whether the Davis program stigmatizes any discrete group or individual and whether race is reasonably used in light of the program's objectives—is clearly satisfied by the Davis program.

It is not even claimed that Davis' program in any way operates to stigmatize or single out any discrete and insular, or even any identifiable, non-minority group. Nor will harm comparable to that imposed upon racial minorities by exclusion or separation on grounds of race be the likely result of the program. It does not, for example, establish an exclusive preserve for minority students apart from and exclusive of whites. Rather, its purpose is to overcome the effects of segregation by bringing the races together. True, whites are excluded from participation in the special admissions program, but this fact only operates to reduce the number of whites to be admitted in the regular admissions program in order to permit admission of a reasonable percentage—less than their proportion of the California population—of otherwise underrepresented qualified minority applicants.

Nor was Bakke in any sense stamped as inferior by the Medical School's rejection of him. Indeed, it is conceded by all that he satisfied those criteria regarded by the school as generally relevant to academic performance better than most of the minority members who were admitted. Moreover, there is absolutely no basis for concluding that Bakke's rejection as a result of Davis' use of racial preference will affect him throughout his life in the same way as the segregation of the Negro schoolchildren in *Brown I* would have affected them. Unlike discrimination against racial minorities, the use of racial preferences for remedial purposes does not inflict a pervasive injury upon individual whites in the sense that wherever they go or whatever they do there is a significant likelihood that they will be treated as second-class citizens because of their color. This distinction does not mean that the exclusion of a white resulting from the preferential use of race is not sufficiently serious to require justification; but it does mean that the injury inflicted by such a policy is not distinguishable from disadvantages caused by a wide range of government actions, none of which has ever been thought impermissible for that reason alone.

In addition, there is simply no evidence that the Davis program discriminates intentionally or unintentionally against any minority group which it purports to benefit. The program does not establish a quota in the invidious sense of a ceiling on the number of minority applicants to be admitted. Nor can the program reasonably be regarded as stigmatizing the program's beneficiaries or their race as inferior. The Davis program does not simply advance less qualified applicants; rather, it compensates applicants, who it is uncontested are fully qualified to study medicine, for educational disadvantages which it was reasonable to conclude were a product of state-fostered discrimination.

D

We disagree with the lower courts' conclusion that the Davis program's use of race was unreasonable in light of its objectives. First, as petitioner argues, there are no practical means by which it could achieve its ends in the foreseeable future without the use of race-conscious measures. . . . Moreover, while race is positively correlated with differences in GPA and MCAT scores, economic disadvantage is not. Thus, it appears that economically disadvantaged whites do not score less well than economically advantaged whites, while economically advantaged blacks score less well than do disadvantaged whites. These statistics graphically illustrate that the University's purpose to integrate its classes by compensating for past discrimination could not be achieved by a general preference for the economically disadvantaged or the children of parents of limited education unless such groups were to make up the entire class.

Second, the Davis admissions program does not simply equate minority status with disadvantage. Rather, Davis considers on an individual basis each applicant's personal history to determine whether he or she has likely been disadvantaged by racial discrimination. The record makes clear that only minority applicants likely to have been isolated from the mainstream of American life are considered in the special program; other minority applicants are eligible only through the regular admissions program.

E

Finally, Davis' special admissions program cannot be said to violate the Constitution simply because it has set aside a predetermined number of places for qualified minority applicants rather than using minority status as a positive factor to be considered in evaluating the applications of disadvantaged minority applicants. For purposes of constitutional adjudication, there is no difference between the two approaches. In any admissions program which accords special consideration to disadvantaged racial minorities, a determination of the degree of preference to be given is unavoidable, and any given preference that results in the exclusion of a white candidate is no more or less constitutionally acceptable than a program such as that at Davis. Furthermore, the extent of the preference inevitably depends on how many minority applicants the particular school is seeking to admit in any particular year so long as the number of qualified minority applicants exceeds that number. There is no sensible, and certainly no constitutional, distinction between, for example, adding a set number of points to the admissions rating of disadvantaged minority applicants as an expression of the preference with the expectation that this will result in the admission of an approximately determined number of qualified minority applicants and setting a fixed number of places for such applicants as was done here.

The "Harvard" program, see ante, as those employing it readily concede, openly and successfully employs a racial criterion for the purpose of ensuring that some of the scarce places in institutions of higher education are allocated to disadvantaged minority students. That the Harvard approach does not also make public the extent of the preference and the precise workings of the system while the Davis program employs a specific, openly stated number, does not condemn the latter plan for purposes of Fourteenth Amendment adjudication. It may be that the Harvard plan is more acceptable to the public than is the Davis "quota." If it is, any State, including California, is free to adopt it in preference to a less acceptable alternative, just as it is generally free, as far as the Constitution is concerned, to abjure granting any racial preferences in its admissions program. But there is no basis for preferring a particular preference program simply because in achieving the same goals that the Davis Medical School is pursuing, it proceeds in a manner that is not immediately apparent to the public.

Mr. Justice BLACKMUN.

I yield to no one in my earnest hope that the time will come when an "affirmative action" program is unnecessary and is, in truth, only a relic of the past. I would hope that we could reach this stage within a decade at the most. But the story of *Brown v. Board of Education,* 347 U.S. 483 (1954), decided almost a quarter of a century ago, suggests that that hope is a slim one. At some time, however, beyond any period of what some would claim is only transitional inequality, the United States must and will reach a stage of maturity where action along this line is no longer necessary. Then persons will be regarded as persons, and discrimination of the type we address today will be an ugly feature of history that is instructive but that is behind us.

The number of qualified, indeed highly qualified, applicants for admission to existing medical schools in the United States far exceeds the number of places available. Wholly apart from racial and ethnic considerations, therefore, the selection process inevitably results in the denial of admission to many qualified persons, indeed, to far more than the number of those who are granted admission. Obviously, it is a denial to the deserving. This inescapable fact is brought into sharp focus here because Allan Bakke is not himself charged with discrimination and yet is the one who is disadvantaged, and because the Medical School of the University of California at Davis itself is not charged with historical discrimination.

One theoretical solution to the need for more minority members in higher education would be to enlarge our graduate schools. Then all who desired and were qualified could enter, and talk of discrimination would vanish. Unfortunately, this is neither feasible nor realistic. The vast resources that apparently would be required simply are not available. And the need for more professional graduates, in the strict numerical sense, perhaps has not been demonstrated at all.

I am not convinced, as Mr. Justice Powell seems to be, that the difference between the Davis program and the one employed by Harvard is very profound or constitutionally significant. The line between the two is a thin and indistinct one. In each, subjective application is at work. Because of my conviction that admission programs are primarily for the educators, I am willing to accept the representation that the Harvard program is one where good faith in its administration is practiced as well as professed. I agree that such a program, where race or ethnic background is only one of many factors, is a program better formulated than Davis' two-track system. The cynical, of course, may say that under a program such as Harvard's one may accomplish covertly what Davis concedes it does openly. I need not go that far, for despite its two-track aspect, the Davis program, for me, is within constitutional bounds, though perhaps barely so. It is surely free of stigma, and, as in United Jewish Organizations, I am not willing to infer a constitutional violation.

I suspect that it would be impossible to arrange an affirmative-action program in a racially neutral way and have it successful. To ask that this be so is to demand the impossible. In order to get beyond racism, we must first take account of race. There is no other way. And in order to treat some persons equally, we must treat them differently. We cannot—we dare not—let the Equal Protection Clause perpetuate racial supremacy.

Mr. Justice STEVENS, with whom The Chief Justice, Mr. Justice STEWART, and Mr. Justice REHNQUIST join, concurring in the judgment in part and dissenting in part.

V

The University, through its special admissions policy, excluded Bakke from participation in its program of medical education because of his race. The University also acknowledges that it was, and still is, receiving federal financial assistance. The plain language of the statute therefore requires affirmance of the judgment below. A different result cannot be justified unless that language misstates the actual intent of the Congress that enacted the statute or the statute is not enforceable in a private action. Neither conclusion is warranted.

Title VI is an integral part of the far-reaching Civil Rights Act of 1964. No doubt, when this legislation was being debated, Congress was not directly concerned with the legality of "reverse discrimination" or "affirmative action" programs. Its attention was focused on the problem at hand, the "glaring . . . discrimination against Negroes which exists throughout our Nation," and, with respect to Title VI, the federal funding of segregated facilities. The genesis of the legislation, however, did not limit the breadth of the solution adopted. Just as Congress responded to the problem of employment discrimination by enacting a provision that protects all races, . . . so, too, its answer to the problem of federal funding of segregated facilities stands as a broad prohibition against the exclusion of any individual from a federally funded program "on the ground of race."

Petitioner contends, however, that exclusion of applicants on the basis of race does not violate Title VI if the exclusion carries with it no racial stigma. No such qualification or limitation of §601's categorical prohibition of "exclusion" is justified by the statute or its history. The language of the entire section is perfectly clear; the words that follow "excluded from" do not modify or qualify the explicit outlawing of any exclusion on the stated grounds.

In giving answers such as these, it seems clear that the proponents of Title VI assumed that the Constitution itself required a colorblind standard on the part of government, but that does not mean that the legislation only codifies an existing constitutional prohibition. The statutory prohibition against discrimination in federally funded projects contained in §601 is more than a simple paraphrasing of what the Fifth or Fourteenth Amendment would require. The Act's proponents plainly considered Title VI consistent with their view of the Constitution and they sought to provide an effective weapon to implement that view.

As with other provisions of the Civil Rights Act, Congress' expression of its policy to end racial discrimination may independently proscribe conduct that the Constitution does not. However, we need not decide the congruence—or lack of congruence—of the controlling statute and the Constitution since the meaning of the Title VI ban on exclusion is crystal clear: Race cannot be the basis of excluding anyone from participation in a federally funded program.

NOTES AND QUESTIONS

1. In addition to Fourteenth Amendment questions, the *Bakke* court also addresses Title VI of the Civil Rights Act. Justice Powell stated that Title VI prohibited government actions that violated the equal protection clause. Justice Stevens stated in his opinion that this case could be decided on statutory grounds and that the constitutional question should therefore be avoided because Title VI prohibits the medical school's admissions program. Accordingly, Title VI has been interpreted to prohibit all conduct that would violate the equal protection clause, but only such conduct.
2. In *Alexander v. Sandoval,* 532 U.S. 275 (2001), the Supreme Court held that private individuals may not sue to enforce disparate-impact regulations promulgated under Title VI of the Civil Rights Act of 1964, and described the legal structure of Title VI:

> Section 601 of that Title provides that no person shall, "on the ground of race, color, or national origin, be excluded from participation in, be denied the benefits of, or be subjected to discrimination under any program or activity" covered by Title VI. 42 U.S.C. §2000d. Section 602 authorizes federal agencies "to effectuate the provisions of [§601] . . . by issuing rules, regulations, or orders of general applicability," 42 U.S.C. §2000d-1. . . .
>
> Although Title VI has often come to this Court, it is fair to say (indeed, perhaps an understatement) that our opinions have not eliminated all uncertainty regarding its commands. For purposes of the present case, however, it is clear from our decisions, from Congress's amendments of Title VI, and from the parties' concessions that three aspects of Title VI must be taken as given. First, private individuals may sue to enforce §601 of Title VI and obtain both injunctive relief and damages. In *Cannon v. University of Chicago,* 441 U.S. 677 (1979), the Court held that a private right of action existed to enforce Title IX of the Education Amendments of 1972, 86 Stat. 373, as amended, 20 U.S.C. §1681 *et seq.* The reasoning of that decision embraced the existence of a private right to enforce Title VI as well. "Title IX," the Court noted, "was patterned after Title VI of the Civil Rights Act of 1964." 441 U.S. at 694. And, "in 1972 when Title IX was enacted, the [parallel] language in Title VI had already been construed as creating a private remedy." *Id.,* at 696. That meant, the Court reasoned, that Congress had intended Title IX, like Title VI, to provide a private cause of action. *Id.,* at 699, 703, 710-711. Congress has since ratified *Cannon's* holding. Section 1003 of the Rehabilitation Act Amendments of 1986, 100 Stat. 1845, 42 U.S.C. §2000d-7, expressly abrogated States' sovereign immunity against suits brought in federal court to enforce Title VI and provided that in a suit against a State "remedies (including remedies both at law and in equity) are available . . . to the same extent as such remedies are available . . . in the suit against any public or private entity other than a State," §2000d-7(a)(2). We recognized in *Franklin v. Gwinnett County Public Schools,* that §2000d-7 "cannot be read

except as a validation of *Cannon's* holding." It is thus beyond dispute that private individuals may sue to enforce §601.

Second, it is similarly beyond dispute—and no party disagrees—that §601 prohibits only intentional discrimination. In *Regents of Univ. of Cal. v. Bakke,* 438 U.S. 265, 57 L. Ed. 2d 750, 98 S. Ct. 2733 (1978), the Court reviewed a decision of the California Supreme Court that had enjoined the University of California Medical School from "according any consideration to race in its admissions process." Essential to the Court's holding reversing that aspect of the California court's decision was the determination that §601 "proscribes only those racial classifications that would violate the Equal Protection Clause or the Fifth Amendment." *Id.,* at 287 (opinion of Powell, J.); see also *id.,* at 325, 328, 352 (opinion of Brennan, White, Marshall, and Blackmun, JJ.). In *Guardians Assn. v. Civil Serv. Comm'n of New York City,* 463 U.S. 582, 77 L. Ed. 2d 866, 103 S. Ct. 3221 (1983), the Court made clear that under *Bakke* only intentional discrimination was forbidden by §601. What we said in *Alexander v. Choate,* 469 U.S. 287, 293, 83 L. Ed. 2d 661, 105 S. Ct. 712 (1985), is true today: "Title VI itself directly reaches only instances of intentional discrimination."

Third, we must assume for purposes of deciding this case that regulations promulgated under §602 of Title VI may validly proscribe activities that have a disparate impact on racial groups, even though such activities are permissible under §601. Though no opinion of this Court has held that, five Justices in *Guardians* voiced that view of the law at least as alternative grounds for their decisions, and dictum in *Alexander v. Choate* is to the same effect. These statements are in considerable tension with the rule of *Bakke* and *Guardians* that §601 forbids only intentional discrimination, *see, e.g., Guardians Assn. v. Civil Serv. Comm'n of New York City, supra,* at 612-613 (O'Connor, J., concurring in judgment), but petitioners have not challenged the regulations here. We therefore assume for the purposes of deciding this case that the DOJ and DOT regulations proscribing activities that have a disparate impact on the basis of race are valid. . . .

Nor does it follow straightaway from the three points we have taken as given that Congress must have intended a private right of action to enforce disparate-impact regulations. We do not doubt that regulations applying §601's ban on intentional discrimination are covered by the cause of action to enforce that section. Such regulations, if valid and reasonable, authoritatively construe the statute itself, and it is therefore meaningless to talk about a separate cause of action to enforce the regulations apart from the statute. A Congress that intends the statute to be enforced through a private cause of action intends the authoritative interpretation of the statute to be so enforced as well. . . . Our decision in *Lau v. Nichols,* 414 U.S. 563 (1974), falls within the same category. The Title VI regulations at issue in *Lau,* similar to the ones at issue here, forbade funding recipients to take actions which had the effect of discriminating on the basis of race, color, or national origin. Unlike our later cases, however, the Court in *Lau* interpreted §601 itself to proscribe disparate-impact discrimination, saying that it "relied solely on §601 . . . to reverse the Court of Appeals," and that the disparate-impact regulations simply "[made] sure that recipients of federal aid . . . conducted any federally financed projects consistently with §601."

We must face now the question avoided by *Lau,* because we have since rejected Lau's interpretation of §601 as reaching beyond intentional discrimination. It is clear now that the disparate-impact regulations do not

> simply apply §601—since they indeed forbid conduct that §601 permits—and therefore clear that the private right of action to enforce §601 does not include a private right to enforce these regulations. That right must come, if at all, from the independent force of §602. As stated earlier, we assume for purposes of this decision that §602 confers the authority to promulgate disparate-impact regulations; the question remains whether it confers a private right of action to enforce them. If not, we must conclude that a failure to comply with regulations promulgated under §602 that is not also a failure to comply with §601 is not actionable. . . .
>
> Neither as originally enacted nor as later amended does Title VI display an intent to create a freestanding private right of action to enforce regulations promulgated under §602. We therefore hold that no such right of action exists. . . .

3. In *Bakke,* Justice Powell and Justice Brennan disagree on what is an acceptable justification for race-based admissions. According to Justice Powell "the attainment of a diverse student body . . . clearly is a constitutionally permissible goal for an institution of higher education. Academic freedom, though not a specifically enumerated constitutional right, long has been viewed as a special concern of the First Amendment." However, Justice Brennan writes that, "prior cases unequivocally show that a state government may adopt race-conscious programs if the purpose of such programs is to remove the disparate racial impact [the state's] actions might otherwise have and if there is reason to believe that the disparate impact is itself the product of past discrimination, whether its own or that of society at large." Are the differences between the two justifications or purposes purely academic constitutional arguments if the end result is the same, namely that race-conscious admissions are allowed? Consider a school's dilemma when trying to adopt a race conscious admissions policy after *Bakke.* When deciding which racial groups to target for preferential treatment, do the different purposes impact which racial groups a school can include?
4. In *Bakke,* Justice Blackmun, concurring with Brennan, wrote "I yield to no one in my earnest hope that the time will come when an 'affirmative action' program is unnecessary and is, in truth, only a relic of the past. I would hope that we could reach this stage within a decade at the most. But the story of *Brown v. Board of Education,* decided almost a quarter of a century ago, suggests that that hope is a slim one. At some time, however, beyond any period of what some would claim is only transitional inequality, the United States must and will reach a stage of maturity where action along this line is no longer necessary. Then persons will be regarded as per sons, and discrimination of the type we address today will be an ugly feature of history that is instructive but that is behind us." Does the difference between Justice Brennan and Justice Powell's justifications for race-based admissions change the limited duration described by Justice Blackmun? If a school can consider race to create a diverse student body, as Justice Powell suggests, then is there any limit to when that policy is no longer allowable?
5. Since *Bakke,* the court has addressed preferential racial classifications in the area of employment or awarding government contracts. In *Adarand Constructors, Inc. v. Peña,* 515 U.S. 200 (1995), the plaintiff was denied a

construction contract to install highway guardrails in Colorado under a federal policy that gave preference to minority contracts. The Court held "that all racial classifications, imposed by whatever federal, state, or local governmental actor, must be analyzed by a reviewing court under strict scrutiny. In other words, such classifications are constitutional only if they are narrowly tailored measures that further compelling governmental interests." *See also City of Richmond v. J.A. Croson Co.,* 488 U.S. 469 (1989).

6. Justice Brennan provides for a lower level of scrutiny for benign discrimination in favor of a disadvantaged minority. One argument against Brennan's position is the difficulty in determining when a group is a minority. After the *Brown* decision in 1954 and the Civil Rights Act of 1964, historically black colleges and universities have lost students to traditionally white schools. Now, white students are actively recruited at traditionally black schools. At Tennessee State, white students are considered minorities and are given preferential treatment for awarding scholarships. Dahleen Glanton, *Black Colleges Fight to Survive,* Chicago Tribune, Oct. 21, 1996, sec. 1, at 1. Would the Tennessee State plan be constitutional according to Justice Brennan or Justice Powell?
7. Justice Powell emphasized that the goal of "the attainment of a diverse student body . . . is clearly is a constitutionally permissible goal for an institution of higher education. Academic freedom . . . long has been viewed as a special concern of the First Amendment. The freedom of a university to make its own judgments as to education includes the selection of its student body." Compare Justice Powell's reasoning to *United States v. Virginia,* 518 U.S. 515 (1996). In that case, Virginia defended the male-only admissions policy of the Virginia Military Institute, a public military college with the mission of producing "citizen-soldiers." The school argued that its methods would be changed, physical requirements would be altered, changes in personal privacy would be necessary, and the adversative environment would not survive if women were admitted. In its decision, the Supreme Court ordered the admission of female applicants and rejected the schools plan to open a separate, female military college. Is *United States v. Virginia* reconcilable with Justice Powell's reasoning on race-conscious admissions?
8. Justice Powell invalidates the Davis admissions program because some positions were set aside and only minorities could compete for those positions. Is the difference between a quota and a target or "critical mass" enough to determine the constitutionality of an admissions program? For Justice Powell, there is no "facial intent to discriminate . . . in an admissions program where race or ethnic background is simply [a "plus"] — to be weighed fairly against other elements — in the selection process." However, the amount of the "plus" factor is directly proportional to the amount of minorities admitted because of the race-conscious program. In other words, the larger the target or critical mass, then the larger the plus factor. If the plus factor is only a tie breaker between equally qualified candidates, then the only tie would be for the last position to be filled; in any other tie, both applicants would be either accepted or rejected. For the Harvard plan to have any significant impact, the plus factor must be large enough to

insure that more minority students are admitted. Under that circumstance, does the Harvard plan become a *de facto* quota system?

9. Between *Bakke* in 1978 and its landmark Michigan cases in 2003, the Supreme Court issued a series of rulings that were difficult to reconcile. In 1980, the Court upheld a federal statutory program that required the Commerce Department to set aside 10 percent of its grants to minority-owned or minority-controlled businesses. *See Fullilove v. Klutznick,* 448 U.S. 448 (1980). In *Johnson v. Transportation Agency Santa Clara County,* 480 U.S. 616 (1987), the Court affirmed the constitutionality of affirmative action programs for women. That same year, the Court also upheld a governmental policy requiring the promotion of an equal number of white and African-American state police troopers. *See United States v. Paradise,* 480 U.S. 149 (1987). In *City of Richmond v. J. A. Croson Co.,* 488 U.S. 469 (1989), however, the Court declared unconstitutional a city program that set aside 30 percent of building contract funds for minority contractors, and in *Adarand Constructors Inc. v. Peña,* 515 U.S. 200 (1995), the Court seemed to indicate clearly that the only racial affirmative action program that could survive "strict scrutiny" was one tailored to redress specific acts of proven past racial discrimination. Given this apparently ambiguous case law regarding affirmative action generally and the lack of any controlling authority after *Bakke* regarding affirmative action in education, it is not surprising that the lower federal courts clung dearly to language in *Bakke* and ultimately reached conflicting results. In 1996, the Fifth Circuit struck down the University of Texas Law School's race-based admissions policy, *see Hopwood v. Texas,* 78 F.3d 932 (5th Cir. 1996). In 2002, however, the Sixth Circuit upheld the University of Michigan Law School's "affirmative action" regime. *See Bollinger v. Grutter,* 288 F.3d 732 (6th Cir. 2002).

GRUTTER V. BOLLINGER

539 U.S. 306 (2003)

Justice O'CONNOR delivered the opinion of the Court.

This case requires us to decide whether the use of race as a factor in student admissions by the University of Michigan Law School (Law School) is unlawful.

I

A

The Law School ranks among the Nation's top law schools. It receives more than 3,500 applications each year for a class of around 350 students. Seeking to "admit a group of students who individually and collectively are among the most capable," the Law School looks for individuals with "substantial promise for success in law school" and "a strong likelihood of succeeding in the practice of law and contributing in diverse ways to the well-being of others." More broadly, the Law School seeks "a mix of students with varying backgrounds and experiences who will respect and learn from each other." In 1992, the dean of the Law School charged a faculty committee with crafting a written admissions policy to implement these goals. In particular, the Law School sought to ensure that its efforts to achieve student body diversity complied with this Court's most recent ruling on the use of race in university admissions. *See Regents of Univ. of Cal. v. Bakke,* 438 U.S. 265 (1978). Upon the unanimous adoption of the committee's report by the Law School faculty, it became the Law School's official admissions policy.

The hallmark of that policy is its focus on academic ability coupled with a flexible assessment of applicants' talents, experiences, and potential "to contribute to the learning of those around them." The policy requires admissions officials to evaluate each applicant based upon all the information available in the file, including a personal statement, letters of recommendation, and an essay describing the ways in which the applicant will contribute to the life and diversity of the Law School. In reviewing an applicant's file, admissions officials must consider the applicant's undergraduate grade point average (GPA) and Law School Admissions Test (LSAT) score because they are important (if imperfect) predictors of academic success in law school. The policy stresses that "no applicant should be admitted unless we expect that applicant to do well enough to graduate with no serious academic problems."

The policy makes clear, however, that even the highest possible score does not guarantee admission to the Law School. Nor does a low score automatically disqualify an applicant. Rather, the policy requires admissions officials to look beyond grades and test scores to other criteria that are important to the Law School's educational objectives. So-called " 'soft' variables" such as "the enthusiasm of recommenders, the quality of the undergraduate institution, the quality of the applicant's essay, and the areas and difficulty of undergraduate course selection" are all brought to bear in assessing an "applicant's likely contributions to the intellectual and social life of the institution."

The policy aspires to "achieve that diversity which has the potential to enrich everyone's education and thus make a law school class stronger than the sum of its parts." The policy does not restrict the types of diversity contributions eligible for "substantial weight" in the admissions process, but instead recognizes "many possible bases for diversity admissions." The policy does, however, reaffirm the Law School's longstanding commitment to "one particular type of diversity," that is, "racial and ethnic diversity with special reference to the inclusion of students from groups which have been historically discriminated against, like African-Americans, Hispanics and Native Americans, who without this commitment might not be represented in our student body in meaningful numbers." By enrolling a " 'critical mass' of [underrepresented] minority students," the Law School seeks to "ensur[e] their ability to make unique contributions to the character of the Law School."

The policy does not define diversity "solely in terms of racial and ethnic status." Nor is the policy "insensitive to the competition among all students for admission to the [L]aw [S]chool." Rather, the policy seeks to guide admissions officers in "producing classes both diverse and academically outstanding, classes made up of students who promise to continue the tradition of outstanding contribution by Michigan Graduates to the legal profession."

B

Petitioner Barbara Grutter is a white Michigan resident who applied to the Law School in 1996 with a 3.8 grade point average and 161 LSAT score. The Law School initially placed petitioner on a waiting list, but subsequently rejected her application. In December 1997, petitioner filed suit in the United States District Court for the Eastern District of Michigan against the Law School, the Regents of the University of Michigan, Lee Bollinger (Dean of the Law School from 1987 to 1994, and President of the University of Michigan from 1996 to 2002), Jeffrey Lehman (Dean of the Law School), and Dennis Shields (Director of Admissions at the Law School from 1991 until 1998). Petitioner alleged that respondents discriminated against her on the basis of race in violation of the Fourteenth Amendment; Title VI of the Civil Rights Act of 1964, 78 Stat. 252, 42 U.S.C. §2000d; and Rev. Stat. §1977, as amended, 42 U.S.C. §1981. . . .

During the 15-day bench trial, the parties introduced extensive evidence concerning the Law School's use of race in the admissions process. Dennis Shields, Director of Admissions when petitioner applied to the Law School, testified that he did not direct his staff to admit a particular percentage or number of minority students, but rather to consider an applicant's race along with all other factors. . . *Id.,* at 206a. Shields testified that at the height of the admissions season, he would frequently consult the so-called "daily reports" that kept track of the racial and ethnic composition of the class (along with other information such as residency status and gender). *Id.,* at 207a. This was done, Shields testified, to ensure that a critical mass of underrepresented minority students would be reached so as to realize the educational benefits of a diverse student body. *Ibid.* Shields stressed, however, that he did not seek to admit any particular number or percentage of underrepresented minority students. *Ibid.* Erica Munzel, who succeeded Shields as Director of Admissions, testified that " 'critical mass' " means " 'meaningful numbers' " or " 'meaningful representation,' " which she understood to mean a number that encourages underrepresented minority students to participate in the classroom and not feel isolated. . . .

The current Dean of the Law School, Jeffrey Lehman, also testified. Like the other Law School witnesses, Lehman did not quantify critical mass in terms of numbers or percentages. He indicated that critical mass means numbers such that underrepresented minority students do not feel isolated or like spokespersons for their race. When asked about the extent to which race is considered in admissions, Lehman testified that it varies from one applicant to another. In some cases, according to Lehman's testimony, an applicant's race may play no role, while in others it may be a " 'determinative' " factor.

The District Court heard extensive testimony from Professor Richard Lempert, who chaired the faculty committee that drafted the 1992 policy. Lempert emphasized that the Law School seeks students with diverse interests and backgrounds to enhance classroom discussion and the educational experience both inside and outside the classroom. When asked about the policy's " 'commitment to racial and ethnic diversity with special reference to the inclusion of students from groups which have been historically discriminated against,'" Lempert explained that this language did not purport to remedy past discrimination, but rather to include students who may bring to the Law School a perspective different from that of members of groups which have not been the victims of such discrimination. Lempert acknowledged that other groups, such as Asians and Jews, have experienced discrimination, but explained they were not mentioned in the policy because individuals who are members of those groups were already being admitted to the Law School in significant numbers.

Kent Syverud [a professor at the Law School when the admissions policy was adopted] was the final witness to testify about the Law School's use of race in admissions decisions. . . . Syverud's testimony indicated that when a critical mass of underrepresented minority students is present, racial stereotypes lose their force because non-minority students learn there is no "'minority viewpoint'" but rather a variety of viewpoints among minority students.

In an attempt to quantify the extent to which the Law School actually considers race in making admissions decisions, the parties introduced voluminous evidence at trial. Relying on data obtained from the Law School, petitioner's expert, Dr. Kinley Larntz, . . . concluded that membership in certain minority groups "'is an extremely strong factor in the decision for acceptance,'" and that applicants from these minority groups "'are given an extremely large allowance for admission'" as compared to applicants who are members of nonfavored groups. Dr. Larntz conceded, however, that race is not the predominant factor in the Law School's admissions calculus.

Dr. Stephen Raudenbush, the Law School's expert, focused on the predicted effect of eliminating race as a factor in the Law School's admission process. In Dr. Raudenbush's view, a race-blind admissions system would have a "'very dramatic,'" negative effect on underrepresented minority admissions. He testified that in 2000, 35 percent of underrepresented minority applicants were admitted. Dr. Raudenbush predicted that if race were not considered, only 10 percent of those applicants would have been admitted. Under this scenario, underrepresented minority students would have comprised 4 percent of the entering class in 2000 instead of the actual figure of 14.5 percent.

In the end, the District Court concluded that the Law School's use of race as a factor in admissions decisions was unlawful. . . .

Sitting en banc, the Court of Appeals reversed the District Court's judgment and vacated the injunction. The Court of Appeals first held that Justice Powell's opinion in *Bakke* was binding precedent establishing diversity as a compelling state interest. . . . The Court of Appeals also held that the Law School's use of race was narrowly tailored because race was merely a "potential 'plus' factor" and because the Law School's program was "virtually identical" to the Harvard admissions program described approvingly by Justice Powell and appended to his *Bakke* opinion. . . .

We granted certiorari, . . . to resolve the disagreement among the Courts of Appeals on a question of national importance: Whether diversity is a compelling interest that can justify the narrowly tailored use of race in selecting applicants for admission to public universities. *Compare Hopwood v. Texas,* 78 F.3d 932 (CA5 1996) *(Hopwood I)* (holding that diversity is not a compelling state interest), *with Smith v. University of Wash. Law School,* 233 F.3d 1188 (CA9 2000) (holding that it is).

II

A

We last addressed the use of race in public higher education over 25 years ago. In the landmark *Bakke* case, we reviewed a racial set-aside program that reserved 16 out of 100 seats in a medical school class for members of certain minority groups. The decision produced six separate opinions, none of which commanded a majority of the Court. Four Justices would have upheld the program against all attack on the ground that the government can use race to "remedy disadvantages cast on minorities by past racial prejudice" (joint opinion of Brennan, White, Marshall, and Blackmun, JJ., concurring in judgment in part and dissenting in part). Four other Justices avoided the constitutional question altogether and struck down the program on statutory grounds (opinion of Stevens, J., joined by Burger, C.J., and Stewart and Rehnquist, JJ., concurring in judgment in part and dissenting in part). Justice Powell provided a fifth vote not only for invalidating the set-aside program, but also for reversing the state court's injunction against any use of race whatsoever. The only holding for the Court in *Bakke* was that a "State has a substantial interest that legitimately may be served by a properly devised admissions program involving the competitive consideration of race and ethnic origin." Thus, we reversed that part of the lower court's judgment that enjoined the university "from any consideration of the race of any applicant."

Since this Court's splintered decision in *Bakke,* Justice Powell's opinion announcing the judgment of the Court has served as the touchstone for constitutional analysis of race-conscious admissions policies. Public and private universities across the Nation have modeled their own admissions programs on Justice Powell's views on permissible race-conscious policies. . . . We therefore discuss Justice Powell's opinion in some detail.

Justice Powell began by stating that "[t]he guarantee of equal protection cannot mean one thing when applied to one individual and something else when applied to a person of another color. If both are not accorded the same protection, then it is not equal." InJustice Powell's view, when governmental decisions "touch upon an individual's race or ethnic background, he is entitled to a judicial determination that the burden he is asked to bear on that basis is precisely tailored to serve a compelling governmental interest." Under this exacting standard, only one of the interests asserted by the university survived Justice Powell's scrutiny.

First, Justice Powell rejected an interest in " 'reducing the historic deficit of traditionally disfavored minorities in medical schools and in the medical profession' " as an unlawful interest in racial balancing. Second, Justice Powell rejected an interest in remedying societal discrimination because such measures would risk placing unnecessary burdens on innocent third parties "who bear no responsibility for whatever harm the beneficiaries of the special admissions program are thought to have suffered." Third, Justice Powell rejected an interest in "increasing the number of physicians who will practice in communities currently underserved," concluding that even if such an interest could be compelling in some circumstances the program under review was not "geared to promote that goal."

Justice Powell approved the university's use of race to further only one interest: "the attainment of a diverse student body." With the important proviso that "constitutional limitations protecting individual rights may not be disregarded," Justice Powell grounded his analysis in the academic freedom that "long has been viewed as a special concern of the First Amendment." Justice Powell emphasized that nothing less than the "'nation's future depends upon leaders trained through wide exposure' to the ideas and mores of students as diverse as this Nation of many peoples." In seeking the "right to select those students who will contribute the most to the 'robust exchange of ideas,'" a university seeks "to achieve a goal that is of paramount importance in the fulfillment of its mission." Both "tradition and experience lend support to the view that the contribution of diversity is substantial."

Justice Powell was, however, careful to emphasize that in his view race "is only one element in a range of factors a university properly may consider in attaining the goal of a heterogeneous student body." For Justice Powell, "[i]t is not an interest in simple ethnic diversity, in which a specified percentage of the student body is in effect guaranteed to be members of selected ethnic groups," that can justify the use of race. Rather, "[t]he diversity that furthers a compelling state interest encompasses a far broader array of qualifications and characteristics of which racial or ethnic origin is but a single though important element."

. . . [F]or the reasons set out below, today we endorse Justice Powell's view that student body diversity is a compelling state interest that can justify the use of race in university admissions.

B

The Equal Protection Clause provides that no State shall "deny to any person within its jurisdiction the equal protection of the laws." U.S. Const., Amdt. 14, §2. Because the Fourteenth Amendment "protect[s] persons, not groups," all "governmental action based upon race—a group classification long recognized as in most circumstances irrelevant and therefore prohibited—should be subjected to detailed judicial inquiry to ensure that the personal right to equal protection of the laws has not been infringed." *Adarand Constructors, Inc. v. Peña,* 515 U.S. 200, 227 (1995). We are a "free people whose institutions are founded upon the doctrine of equality." *Loving v. Virginia,* 388 U.S. 1, 11 (1967). It follows from that principle that "government may treat people differently because of their race only for the most compelling reasons." *Adarand Constructors, Inc.*

We have held that all racial classifications imposed by government "must be analyzed by a reviewing court under strict scrutiny." This means that such classifications are constitutional only if they are narrowly tailored to further compelling governmental interests. "Absent searching judicial inquiry into the justification for such race-based measures," we have no way to determine what "classifications are 'benign' or 'remedial' and what classifications are in fact motivated by illegitimate notions of racial inferiority or simple racial politics." *Richmond v. J. A. Croson Co.,* 488 U.S. 469, 493 (1989) (plurality opinion). We apply strict scrutiny to all racial classifications to " 'smoke out' illegitimate uses of race by assuring that [government] is pursuing a goal important enough to warrant use of a highly suspect tool."

Strict scrutiny is not "strict in theory, but fatal in fact." *Adarand Constructors, Inc. v. Peña.* Although all governmental uses of race are subject to strict scrutiny, not all are invalidated by it. As we have explained, "whenever the government treats any person unequally because of his or her race, that person has suffered an injury that falls squarely within the language and spirit of the Constitution's guarantee of equal protection." But that observation "says nothing about the ultimate validity of any particular law; that determination is the job of the court applying strict scrutiny." When race-based action is necessary to further a compelling governmental interest, such action does not violate the constitutional guarantee of equal protection so long as the narrow-tailoring requirement is also satisfied.

Context matters when reviewing race-based governmental action under the Equal Protection Clause. . . . In *Adarand Constructors, Inc. v. Peña,* we made clear that strict scrutiny must take " 'relevant differences' into account." Indeed, as we explained, that is its "fundamental purpose." Not every decision influenced by race is equally objectionable and strict scrutiny is designed to provide a framework for carefully examining the importance and the sincerity of the reasons advanced by the governmental decision maker for the use of race in that particular context.

III

A

With these principles in mind, we turn to the question whether the Law School's use of race is justified by a compelling state interest. Before this Court, as they have throughout this litigation, respondents assert only one justification for their use of race in the admissions process: obtaining "the educational benefits that flow from a diverse student body." In other words, the Law School asks us to recognize, in the context of higher education, a compelling state interest in student body diversity.

We first wish to dispel the notion that the Law School's argument has been foreclosed, either expressly or implicitly, by our affirmative-action cases decided since *Bakke.* It is true that some language in those opinions might be read to suggest that remedying past discrimination is the only permissible justification for race-based governmental action. *See, e.g., Richmond v. J. A. Croson Co.* (plurality opinion) (stating that unless classifications based upon race are "strictly reserved for remedial settings, they may in fact promote notions of racial inferiority and lead to a politics of racial hostility"). But we have never held that the only governmental use of race that can survive strict scrutiny is remedying past discrimination. Nor, since *Bakke,* have we directly addressed the use of race in the context of public higher education. Today, we hold that the Law School has a compelling interest in attaining a diverse student body.

The Law School's educational judgment that such diversity is essential to its educational mission is one to which we defer. The Law School's assessment that diversity will, in fact, yield educational benefits is substantiated by respondents and their amici. Our scrutiny of the interest asserted by the Law School is no less strict for taking into account complex educational judgments in an area that lies primarily within the expertise of the university. Our holding today is in keeping with our tradition of giving a degree of deference to a university's academic decisions, within constitutionally prescribed limits. . . .

We have long recognized that, given the important purpose of public education and the expansive freedoms of speech and thought associated with the university environment, universities occupy a special niche in our constitutional tradition. . . . In announcing the principle of student body diversity as a compelling state interest, Justice Powell invoked our cases recognizing a constitutional dimension, grounded in the First Amendment, of educational autonomy: "The freedom of a university to make its own judgments as to education includes the selection of its student body." *Bakke.* From this premise, Justice Powell reasoned that by claiming "the right to select those students who will contribute the most to the 'robust exchange of ideas,'" a university "seek[s] to achieve a goal that is of paramount importance in the fulfillment of its mission." 438 U.S., at 313 (quoting *Keyishian v. Board of Regents of Univ. of State of N.Y.).* Our conclusion that the Law School has a compelling interest in a diverse student body is informed by our view that attaining a diverse student body is at the heart of the Law School's proper institutional mission, and that "good faith" on the part of a university is "presumed" absent "a showing to the contrary."

As part of its goal of "assembling a class that is both exceptionally academically qualified and broadly diverse," the Law School seeks to "enroll a 'critical mass' of minority students." The Law School's interest is not simply "to assure within its student body some specified percentage of a particular group merely because of its race or ethnic origin." *Bakke,* 438 U.S., at 307 (opinion of Powell, J.). That would amount to outright racial balancing, which is patently unconstitutional. *Ibid.; Freeman v. Pitts,* 503 U.S. 467, 494 (1992) ("Racial balance is not to be achieved for its own sake"); *Richmond v. J. A. Croson Co.,* 488 U.S., at 507. Rather, the Law School's concept of critical mass is defined by reference to the educational benefits that diversity is designed to produce.

These benefits are substantial. As the District Court emphasized, the Law School's admissions policy promotes "cross-racial understanding," helps to break down racial stereotypes, and "enables [students] to better understand persons of different races." These benefits are "important and laudable," because "classroom discussion is livelier, more spirited, and simply more enlightening and interesting" when the students have "the greatest possible variety of backgrounds."

The Law School's claim of a compelling interest is further bolstered by its amici, who point to the educational benefits that flow from student body diversity. In addition to the expert studies and reports entered into evidence at trial, numerous studies show that student body diversity promotes learning outcomes, and "better prepares students for an increasingly diverse workforce and society, and better prepares them as professionals."

See, e.g., W. Bowen & D. Bok, *The Shape of the River* (1998); *Diversity Challenged: Evidence on the Impact of Affirmative Action* (G. Orfield & M. Kurlaender eds. 2001); *Compelling Interest: Examining the Evidence on Racial Dynamics in Colleges and Universities* (M. Chang, D. Witt, J.Jones, & K. Hakuta eds. 2003). . . .

These benefits are not theoretical but real, as major American businesses have made clear that the skills needed in today's increasingly global marketplace can only be developed through exposure to widely diverse people, cultures, ideas, and viewpoints. What is more, high-ranking retired officers and civilian leaders of the United States military assert that, "[b]ased on [their] decades of experience," a "highly qualified, racially diverse officer corps . . . is essential to the military's ability to fulfill its principle mission to provide national security." The primary sources for the Nation's officer corps are the service academies and the Reserve Officers Training Corps (ROTC), the latter comprising students already admitted to participating colleges and universities. At present, "the military cannot achieve an officer corps that is both highly qualified and racially diverse unless the service academies and the ROTC used limited race-conscious recruiting and admissions policies." To fulfill its mission, the military "must be selective in admissions for training and education for the officer corps, and it must train and educate a highly qualified, racially diverse officer corps in a racially diverse setting." We agree that "[i]t requires only a small step from this analysis to conclude that our country's other most selective institutions must remain both diverse and selective."

We have repeatedly acknowledged the overriding importance of preparing students for work and citizenship, describing education as pivotal to "sustaining our political and cultural heritage" with a fundamental role in maintaining the fabric of society. *Plyler v. Doe,* 457 U.S. 202, 221 (1982). This Court has long recognized that "education . . . is the very foundation of good citizenship." *Brown v. Board of Education,* 347 U.S. 483, 493 (1954). For this reason, the diffusion of knowledge and opportunity through public institutions of higher education must be accessible to all individuals regardless of race or ethnicity. The United States, as amicus curiae, affirms that "[e]nsuring that public institutions are open and available to all segments of American society, including people of all races and ethnicities, represents a paramount government objective." And, "[n]owhere is the importance of such openness more acute than in the context of higher education." Effective participation by members of all racial and ethnic groups in the civic life of our Nation is essential if the dream of one Nation, indivisible, is to be realized.

Moreover, universities, and in particular, law schools, represent the training ground for a large number of our Nation's leaders. *Sweatt v. Painter,* 339 U.S. 629, 634 (1950) (describing law school as a "proving ground for legal learning and practice"). Individuals with law degrees occupy roughly half the state governorships, more than half the seats in the United States Senate, and more than a third of the seats in the United States House of Representatives. The pattern is even more striking when it comes to highly selective law schools. A handful of these schools accounts for 25 of the 100 United States Senators, 74 United States Courts of Appeals judges, and nearly 200 of the more than 600 United States District Court judges.

In order to cultivate a set of leaders with legitimacy in the eyes of the citizenry, it is necessary that the path to leadership be visibly open to talented and qualified individuals of every race and ethnicity. All members of our heterogeneous society must have confidence in the openness and integrity of the educational institutions that provide this training. As we have recognized, law schools "cannot be effective in isolation from the individuals and institutions with which the law interacts." *See Sweatt v. Painter.* Access to legal education (and thus the legal profession) must be inclusive of talented and qualified individuals of every race and ethnicity, so that all members of our heterogeneous society may participate in the educational institutions that provide the training and education necessary to succeed in America.

The Law School does not premise its need for critical mass on "any belief that minority students always (or even consistently) express some characteristic minority viewpoint on any issue." To the contrary, diminishing the force of such stereotypes is both a crucial part of the Law School's mission, and one that it cannot accomplish with only token numbers of minority students. Just as growing up in a particular region or having particular professional experiences is likely to affect an individual's views, so too is one's own, unique experience of being a racial minority in a society, like our own, in which race unfortunately still matters. The Law School has determined, based upon its experience and expertise, that a "critical mass" of underrepresented minorities is necessary to further its compelling interest in securing the educational benefits of a diverse student body.

B

Even in the limited circumstance when drawing racial distinctions is permissible to further a compelling state interest, government is still "constrained in how it may pursue that end: [T]he means chosen to accomplish the [government's] asserted purpose must be specifically and narrowly framed to accomplish that purpose." *Shaw v. Hunt,* 517 U.S. 899, 908 (1996). The purpose of the narrow tailoring requirement is to ensure that "the means chosen 'fit' . . . th[e] compelling goal so closely that there is little or no possibility that the motive for the classification was illegitimate racial prejudice or stereotype." *Richmond v. J. A. Croson Co.*

Since *Bakke,* we have had no occasion to define the contours of the narrow-tailoring inquiry with respect to race-conscious university admissions programs. That inquiry must be calibrated to fit the distinct issues raised by the use of race to achieve student body diversity in public higher education. Contrary to Justice Kennedy's assertions, we do not "abandon strict scrutiny" (dissenting opinion). Rather, as we have already explained, we adhere to *Adarand's* teaching that the very purpose of strict scrutiny is to take such "relevant differences into account."

To be narrowly tailored, a race-conscious admissions program cannot use a quota system—it cannot "insulat[e] each category of applicants with certain desired qualifications from competition with all other applicants." *Bakke* (opinion of Powell, J.). Instead, a university may consider race or ethnicity only as a "'plus' in a particular applicant's file," without "insulat[ing] the individual from comparison with all other candidates for the available seats."

In other words, an admissions program must be "flexible enough to consider all pertinent elements of diversity in light of the particular qualifications of each applicant, and to place them on the same footing for consideration, although not necessarily according them the same weight."

We find that the Law School's admissions program bears the hallmarks of a narrowly tailored plan. As Justice Powell made clear in *Bakke,* truly individualized consideration demands that race be used in a flexible, nonmechanical way. It follows from this mandate that universities cannot establish quotas for members of certain racial groups or put members of those groups on separate admissions tracks. Nor can universities insulate applicants who belong to certain racial or ethnic groups from the competition for admission. Universities can, however, consider race or ethnicity more flexibly as a "plus" factor in the context of individualized consideration of each and every applicant.

We are satisfied that the Law School's admissions program, like the Harvard plan described by Justice Powell, does not operate as a quota. Properly understood, a "quota" is a program in which a certain fixed number or proportion of opportunities are "reserved exclusively for certain minority groups." *Richmond v. J. A. Croson Co.* (plurality opinion). Quotas " 'impose a fixed number or percentage which must be attained, or which cannot be exceeded,' " *Sheet Metal Workers v. EEOC,* 478 U.S. 421, 495 (1986) (O'Connor, J., concurring in part and dissenting in part), and "insulate the individual from comparison with all other candidates for the available seats." *Bakke* (opinion of Powell, J.). In contrast, "a permissible goal . . . require[s] only a good-faith effort . . . to come within a range demarcated by the goal itself," *Sheet Metal Workers v. EEOC,* and permits consideration of race as a "plus" factor in any given case while still ensuring that each candidate "compete[s] with all other qualified applicants," *Johnson v. Transportation Agency, Santa Clara Cty.,* 480 U.S. 616, 638 (1987).

Justice Powell's distinction between the medical school's rigid 16-seat quota and Harvard's flexible use of race as a "plus" factor is instructive. Harvard certainly had minimum goals for minority enrollment, even if it had no specific number firmly in mind. *See Bakke* (opinion of Powell, J.) ("10 or 20 black students could not begin to bring to their classmates and to each other the variety of points of view, backgrounds and experiences of blacks in the United States"). What is more, Justice Powell flatly rejected the argument that Harvard's program was "the functional equivalent of a quota" merely because it had some " 'plus' " for race, or gave greater "weight" to race than to some other factors, in order to achieve student body diversity.

The Law School's goal of attaining a critical mass of underrepresented minority students does not transform its program into a quota. As the Harvard plan described by Justice Powell recognized, there is of course "some relationship between numbers and achieving the benefits to be derived from a diverse student body, and between numbers and providing a reasonable environment for those students admitted." "[S]ome attention to numbers," without more, does not transform a flexible admissions system into a rigid quota. Nor, as Justice Kennedy posits, does the Law School's consultation of the "daily reports," which keep track of the racial and ethnic composition of the class (as well as of residency and gender), "suggest [ ] there was no further attempt at individual review save for race itself" during the final stages of the admissions process. To the contrary, the Law School's admissions officers testified without contradiction that they never gave race any more or less weight based upon the information contained in these reports. Moreover, as Justice Kennedy concedes, between 1993 and 2000, the number of African-American, Latino, and Native-American students in each class at the Law School varied from 13.5 to 20.1 percent, a range inconsistent with a quota.

The Chief Justice believes that the Law School's policy conceals an attempt to achieve racial balancing, and cites admissions data to contend that the Law School discriminates among different groups within the critical mass. But, as The Chief Justice concedes, the number of underrepresented minority students who ultimately enroll in the Law School differs substantially from their representation in the applicant pool and varies considerably for each group from year to year.

That a race-conscious admissions program does not operate as a quota does not, by itself, satisfy the requirement of individualized consideration. When using race as a "plus" factor in university admissions, a university's admissions program must remain flexible enough to ensure that each applicant is evaluated as an individual and not in a way that makes an applicant's race or ethnicity the defining feature of his or her application. The importance of this individualized consideration in the context of a race-conscious admissions program is paramount. *See Bakke* (opinion of Powell, J.) (identifying the "denial . . . of th[e] right to individualized consideration" as the "principal evil" of the medical school's admissions program).

Here, the Law School engages in a highly individualized, holistic review of each applicant's file, giving serious consideration to all the ways an applicant might contribute to a diverse educational environment. The Law School affords this individualized consideration to applicants of all races. There is no policy, either de jure or *de facto,* of automatic acceptance or rejection based upon any single "soft" variable. Unlike the program at issue in *Gratz v. Bollinger,* the Law School awards no mechanical, predetermined diversity "bonuses" based upon race or ethnicity. *See* [Powell's *Bakke* opinion] (distinguishing a race-conscious admissions program that automatically awards 20 points based upon race from the Harvard plan, which considered race but "did not contemplate that any single characteristic automatically ensured a specific and identifiable contribution to a university's diversity"). Like the Harvard plan, the Law School's admissions policy "is flexible enough to consider all pertinent elements of diversity in light of the particular qualifications of each applicant, and to place them on the same footing for consideration, although not necessarily according them the same weight." *Bakke* (opinion of Powell, J.).

We also find that, like the Harvard plan Justice Powell referenced in *Bakke,* the Law School's race-conscious admissions program adequately ensures that all factors that may contribute to student body diversity are meaningfully considered alongside race in admissions decisions. With respect to the use of race itself, all underrepresented minority students admitted by the Law School have been deemed qualified. By virtue of our Nation's struggle with racial inequality, such students are both likely to have experiences of particular importance to the Law School's mission, and less likely to be admitted in meaningful numbers on criteria that ignore those experiences.

The Law School does not, however, limit in any way the broad range of qualities and experiences that may be considered valuable contributions to student body diversity. To the contrary, the 1992 policy makes clear "[t]here are many possible bases for diversity admissions," and provides examples of admittees who have lived or traveled widely abroad, are fluent in several languages, have overcome personal adversity and family hardship, have exceptional records of extensive community service, and have had successful careers in other fields. The Law School seriously considers each "applicant's promise of making a notable contribution to the class by way of a particular strength, attainment, or characteristic—e.g., an unusual intellectual achievement, employment experience, nonacademic performance, or personal background." All applicants have the opportunity to highlight their own potential diversity contributions through the submission of a personal statement, letters of recommendation, and an essay describing the ways in which the applicant will contribute to the life and diversity of the Law School.

What is more, the Law School actually gives substantial weight to diversity factors besides race. The Law School frequently accepts non-minority applicants with grades and test scores lower than underrepresented minority applicants (and other non-minority applicants) who are rejected. This shows that the Law School seriously weighs many other diversity factors besides race that can make a real and dispositive difference for non-minority applicants as well. By this flexible approach, the Law School sufficiently takes into account, in practice as well as in theory, a wide variety of characteristics besides race and ethnicity that contribute to a diverse student body. Justice Kennedy speculates that "race is likely outcome determinative for many members of minority groups" who do not fall within the upper range of LSAT scores and grades. But the same could be said of the Harvard plan discussed approvingly by Justice Powell in *Bakke,* and indeed of any plan that uses race as one of many factors. ("'When the Committee on Admissions reviews the large middle group of applicants who are "admissible" and deemed capable of doing good work in their courses, the race of an applicant may tip the balance in his favor'").

Petitioner and the United States argue that the Law School's plan is not narrowly tailored because race-neutral means exist to obtain the educational benefits of student body diversity that the Law School seeks. We disagree. Narrow tailoring does not require exhaustion of every conceivable race-neutral alternative. Nor does it require a university to choose between maintaining a reputation for excellence or fulfilling a commitment to provide educational opportunities to members of all racial groups. *See Wygant v. Jackson Bd. of Ed.,* 476 U.S. 267, 280, n.6 (1986) (alternatives must serve the interest "'about as well'"); *Richmond v. J. A. Croson Co.,* 488 U.S., at 509-510 (plurality opinion) (city had a "whole array of race-neutral" alternatives because changing requirements "would have [had] little detrimental effect on the city's interests"). Narrow tailoring does, however, require serious, good faith consideration of workable race-neutral alternatives that will achieve the diversity the university seeks. *See id.,* at 507 (set-aside plan not narrowly tailored where "there does not appear to have been any consideration of the use of race-neutral means"); *Wygant v. Jackson Bd. of Ed.,* n.6 (narrow tailoring "require[s] consideration" of "lawful alternative and less restrictive means").

We agree with the Court of Appeals that the Law School sufficiently considered workable race-neutral alternatives. The District Court took the Law School to task for failing to consider race-neutral alternatives such as "using a lottery system" or "decreasing the emphasis for all applicants on undergraduate GPA and LSAT scores." But these alternatives would require a dramatic sacrifice of diversity, the academic quality of all admitted students, or both.

The Law School's current admissions program considers race as one factor among many, in an effort to assemble a student body that is diverse in ways broader than race. Because a lottery would make that kind of nuanced judgment impossible, it would effectively sacrifice all other educational values, not to mention every other kind of diversity. So too with the suggestion that the Law School simply lower admissions standards for all students, a drastic remedy that would require the Law School to become a much different institution and sacrifice a vital component of its educational mission. The United States advocates "percentage plans," recently adopted by public undergraduate institutions in Texas, Florida, and California to guarantee admission to all students above a certain class-rank threshold in every high school in the State. The United States does not, however, explain how such plans could work for graduate and professional schools. Moreover, even assuming such plans are race-neutral, they may preclude the university from conducting the individualized assessments necessary to assemble a student body that is not just racially diverse, but diverse along all the qualities valued by the university. We are satisfied that the Law School adequately considered race-neutral alternatives currently capable of producing a critical mass without forcing the Law School to abandon the academic selectivity that is the cornerstone of its educational mission.

We acknowledge that "there are serious problems of justice connected with the idea of preference itself." *Bakke,* 438 U.S., at 298 (opinion of Powell, J.). Narrow tailoring, therefore, requires that a race-conscious admissions program not unduly harm members of any racial group. Even remedial race-based governmental action generally "remains subject to continuing oversight to assure that it will work the least harm possible to other innocent persons competing for the benefit." *Id.* To be narrowly tailored, a race-conscious admissions program must not "unduly burden individuals who are not members of the favored racial and ethnic groups." *Metro Broadcasting, Inc. v. FCC,* 497 U.S. 547, 630 (1990) (O'Connor, J., dissenting).

We are satisfied that the Law School's admissions program does not. Because the Law School considers "all pertinent elements of diversity," it can (and does) select non-minority applicants who have greater potential to enhance student body diversity over underrepresented minority applicants. *See Bakke, supra,* at 317 (opinion of Powell, J.). As Justice Powell recognized in *Bakke,* so long as a race-conscious admissions program uses race as a "plus" factor in the context of individualized consideration, a rejected applicant "will not have been foreclosed from all consideration for that seat simply because he was not the right color or had the wrong surname. . . . His qualifications would have been weighed fairly and competitively, and he would have no basis to complain of unequal treatment under the Fourteenth Amendment."

We agree that, in the context of its individualized inquiry into the possible diversity contributions of all applicants, the Law School's race-conscious admissions program does not unduly harm non-minority applicants.

We are mindful, however, that "[a] core purpose of the Fourteenth Amendment was to do away with all governmentally imposed discrimination based upon race." *Palmore v. Sidoti,* 466 U.S. 429, 432 (1984). Accordingly, race-conscious admissions policies must be limited in time. This requirement reflects that racial classifications, however compelling their goals, are potentially so dangerous that they may be employed no more broadly than the interest demands. Enshrining a permanent justification for racial preferences would offend this fundamental equal protection principle. We see no reason to exempt race-conscious admissions programs from the requirement that all governmental use of race must have a logical end point. The Law School, too, concedes that all "race-conscious programs must have reasonable durational limits."

In the context of higher education, the durational requirement can be met by sunset provisions in race-conscious admissions policies and periodic reviews to determine whether racial preferences are still necessary to achieve student body diversity. Universities in California, Florida, and Washington State, where racial preferences in admissions are prohibited by state law, are currently engaged in experimenting with a wide variety of alternative approaches. Universities in other States can and should draw on the most promising aspects of these race-neutral alternatives as they develop. *Cf. United States v. Lopez,* 514 U.S. 549, 581 (1995) (Kennedy, J., concurring) ("[T]he States may perform their role as laboratories for experimentation to devise various solutions where the best solution is far from clear").

The requirement that all race-conscious admissions programs have a termination point "assure [s] all citizens that the deviation from the norm of equal treatment of all racial and ethnic groups is a temporary matter, a measure taken in the service of the goal of equality itself." *Richmond v. J. A. Croson Co*

We take the Law School at its word that it would "like nothing better than to find a race-neutral admissions formula" and will terminate its race-conscious admissions program as soon as practicable. . . . It has been 25 years since Justice Powell first approved the use of race to further an interest in student body diversity in the context of public higher education. Since that time, the number of minority applicants with high grades and test scores has indeed increased. We expect that 25 years from now, the use of racial preferences will no longer be necessary to further the interest approved today.

IV

In summary, the Equal Protection Clause does not prohibit the Law School's narrowly tailored use of race in admissions decisions to further a compelling interest in obtaining the educational benefits that flow from a diverse student body. Consequently, petitioner's statutory claims based upon Title VI and 42 U.S.C. §1981 also fail. *See Bakke, supra,* at 287 (opinion of Powell, J.) ("Title VI . . . proscribe[s] only those racial classifications that would violate the Equal Protection Clause or the Fifth Amendment"); *General*

Building Contractors Assn., Inc. v. Pennsylvania, 458 U.S. 375, 389-391 (1982) (the prohibition against discrimination in §1981 is co-extensive with the Equal Protection Clause). The judgment of the Court of Appeals for the Sixth Circuit, accordingly, is affirmed.

It is so ordered.

Justice GINSBURG, with whom Justice BREYER joins, concurring.

The Court further observes that "[i]t has been 25 years since Justice Powell [in *Regents of Univ. of Cal. v. Bakke,* 438 U.S. 265 (1978)] first approved the use of race to further an interest in student body diversity in the context of public higher education." For at least part of that time, however, the law could not fairly be described as "settled," and in some regions of the Nation, overtly race-conscious admissions policies have been proscribed. . . . Moreover, it was only 25 years before *Bakke* that this Court declared public school segregation unconstitutional, a declaration that, after prolonged resistance, yielded an end to a law-enforced racial caste system, itself the legacy of centuries of slavery. . . .

It is well documented that conscious and unconscious race bias, even rank discrimination based upon race, remain alive in our land, impeding realization of our highest values and ideals. . . . As to public education, data for the years 2000-2001 show that 71.6% of African-American children and 76.3% of Hispanic children attended a school in which minorities made up a majority of the student body. *See* E. Frankenberg, C. Lee, & G. Orfield, *A Multiracial Society with Segregated Schools: Are We Losing the Dream?* p. 4 (Jan. 2003). And schools in predominantly minority communities lag far behind others measured by the educational resources available to them. *See Brief for National Urban League et al. as Amici Curiae* (citing General Accounting Office, *Per-Pupil Spending Differences Between Selected Inner City and Suburban Schools Varied by Metropolitan Area,* 17 (2002)).

However strong the public's desire for improved education systems may be, *see* P. Hart & R. Teeter, *A National Priority: Americans Speak on Teacher Quality* 2, 11 (2002) (public opinion research conducted for Educational Testing Service); *The No Child Left Behind Act of 2001,* Pub. L. 107-110, 115 Stat. 1425, 20 U.S.C.A. §7231 (2003 Supp. Pamphlet), it remains the current reality that many minority students encounter markedly inadequate and unequal educational opportunities. Despite these inequalities, some minority students are able to meet the high threshold requirements set for admission to the country's finest undergraduate and graduate educational institutions. As lower school education in minority communities improves, an increase in the number of such students may be anticipated. From today's vantage point, one may hope, but not firmly forecast, that over the next generation's span, progress toward nondiscrimination and genuinely equal opportunity will make it safe to sunset affirmative action.

Chief Justice REHNQUIST, with whom Justice SCALIA, Justice KENNEDY, and Justice THOMAS join, dissenting.

I agree with the Court that, "in the limited circumstance when drawing racial distinctions is permissible," the government must ensure that its means are narrowly tailored to achieve a compelling state interest. . . . I do not believe, however, that the University of Michigan Law School's (Law School) means are narrowly tailored to the interest it asserts. The Law School claims it must take the steps it does to achieve a " 'critical mass' " of underrepresented minority students. But its actual program bears no relation to this asserted goal. Stripped of its "critical mass" veil, the Law School's program is revealed as a naked effort to achieve racial balancing. . . .

Before the Court's decision today, we consistently applied the same strict scrutiny analysis regardless of the government's purported reason for using race and regardless of the setting in which race was being used. We rejected calls to use more lenient review in the face of claims that race was being used in "good faith" because " '[m]ore than good motives should be required when government seeks to allocate its resources by way of an explicit racial classification system.' " . . . We likewise rejected calls to apply more lenient review based upon the particular setting in which race is being used. Indeed, even in the specific context of higher education, we emphasized that "constitutional limitations protecting individual rights may not be disregarded." *Bakke.*

Although the Court recites the language of our strict scrutiny analysis, its application of that review is unprecedented in its deference. . . .

In practice, the Law School's program bears little or no relation to its asserted goal of achieving "critical mass." Respondents explain that the Law School seeks to accumulate a "critical mass" of each underrepresented minority group. . . . But the record demonstrates that the Law School's admissions practices with respect to these groups differ dramatically and cannot be defended under any consistent use of the term "critical mass". . . .

Only when the "critical mass" label is discarded does a likely explanation for these numbers emerge. The Court states that the Law School's goal of attaining a "critical mass" of underrepresented minority students is not an interest in merely " 'assur[ing] within its student body some specified percentage of a particular group merely because of its race or ethnic origin.' " The Court recognizes that such an interest "would amount to outright racial balancing, which is patently unconstitutional." The Court concludes, however, that the Law School's use of race in admissions, consistent with Justice Powell's opinion in *Bakke,* only pays " '[s]ome attention to numbers.' "

But the correlation between the percentage of the Law School's pool of applicants who are members of the three minority groups and the percentage of the admitted applicants who are members of these same groups is far too precise to be dismissed as merely the result of the school paying "some attention to [the] numbers." As the [data shows], from 1995 through 2000 the percentage of admitted applicants who were members of these minority groups closely tracked the percentage of individuals in the school's applicant pool who were from the same groups. . . .

For example, in 1995, when 9.7% of the applicant pool was African-American, 9.4% of the admitted class was African-American. By 2000, only 7.5% of the applicant pool was African-American, and 7.3% of the admitted class was African-American. This correlation is striking. Respondents themselves emphasize that the number of underrepresented minority students admitted to the Law School would be significantly smaller if the race of each applicant were not considered. But, as the examples above illustrate, the measure of the decrease would differ dramatically among the groups. The tight correlation between the percentage of applicants and admittees of a given race, therefore, must result from careful race based planning by the Law School. It suggests a formula for admission based upon the aspirational assumption that all applicants are equally qualified academically, and therefore that the proportion of each group admitted should be the same as the proportion of that group in the applicant pool. . . .

But the divergence between the percentages of underrepresented minorities in the applicant pool and in the enrolled classes is not the only relevant comparison. In fact, it may not be the most relevant comparison. The Law School cannot precisely control which of its admitted applicants decide to attend the university. But it can and, as the numbers demonstrate, clearly does employ racial preferences in extending offers of admission. Indeed, the ostensibly flexible nature of the Law School's admissions program that the Court finds appealing, appears to be, in practice, a carefully managed program designed to ensure proportionate representation of applicants from selected minority groups.

I do not believe that the Constitution gives the Law School such free rein in the use of race. The Law School has offered no explanation for its actual admissions practices and, unexplained, we are bound to conclude that the Law School has managed its admissions program, not to achieve a "critical mass," but to extend offers of admission to members of selected minority groups in proportion to their statistical representation in the applicant pool.

But this is precisely the type of racial balancing that the Court itself calls "patently unconstitutional."

Finally, I believe that the Law School's program fails strict scrutiny because it is devoid of any reasonably precise time limit on the Law School's use of race in admissions. . . . Our previous cases have required some limit on the duration of programs such as this because discrimination on the basis of race is invidious.

The Court suggests a possible 25-year limitation on the Law School's current program. Respondents, on the other hand, remain more ambiguous, explaining that "the Law School of course recognizes that race-conscious programs must have reasonable durational limits, and the Sixth Circuit properly found such a limit in the Law School's resolve to cease considering race when genuine race-neutral alternatives become available." These discussions of a time limit are the vaguest of assurances. In truth, they permit the Law School's use of racial preferences on a seemingly permanent basis. Thus, an important component of strict scrutiny—that a program be limited in time—is casually subverted.

The Court, in an unprecedented display of deference under our strict scrutiny analysis, upholds the Law School's program despite its obvious flaws. We have said that when it comes to the use of race, the connection between the ends and the means used to attain them must be precise. But here the flaw is deeper than that; it is not merely a question of "fit" between ends and means. Here the means actually used are forbidden by the Equal Protection Clause of the Constitution.

Justice SCALIA, with whom Justice THOMAS joins, concurring in part and dissenting in part.

I join the opinion of The Chief Justice. As he demonstrates, the University of Michigan Law School's mystical "critical mass" justification for its discrimination by race challenges even the most gullible mind. The admissions statistics show it to be a sham to cover a scheme of racially proportionate admissions.

I also join Parts I through VII of Justice Thomas's opinion. I find particularly unanswerable his central point: that the allegedly "compelling state interest" at issue here is not the incremental "educational benefit" that emanates from the fabled "critical mass" of minority students, but rather Michigan's interest in maintaining a "prestige" law school whose normal admissions standards disproportionately exclude blacks and other minorities. If that is a compelling state interest, everything is.

I add the following: The "educational benefit" that the University of Michigan seeks to achieve by racial discrimination consists, according to the Court, of "'cross-racial understanding,'" and "'better prepar[ation of] students for an increasingly diverse workforce and society,'" all of which is necessary not only for work, but also for good "citizenship." This is not, of course, an "educational benefit" on which students will be graded on their Law School transcript (Works and Plays Well with Others: B+) or tested by the bar examiners (Q: Describe in 500 words or less your cross-racial understanding). For it is a lesson of life rather than law—essentially the same lesson taught to (or rather learned by, for it cannot be "taught" in the usual sense) people three feet shorter and twenty years younger than the full-grown adults at the University of Michigan Law School, in institutions ranging from Boy Scout troops to public-school kindergartens. If properly considered an "educational benefit" at all, it is surely not one that is either uniquely relevant to law school or uniquely "teachable" in a formal educational setting. And therefore: If it is appropriate for the University of Michigan Law School to use racial discrimination for the purpose of putting together a "critical mass" that will convey generic lessons in socialization and good citizenship, surely it is no less appropriate—indeed, particularly appropriate—for the civil service system of the State of Michigan to do so. There, also, those exposed to "critical masses" of certain races will presumably become better Americans, better Michiganders, better civil servants. And surely private employers cannot be criticized—indeed, should be praised—if they also "teach" good citizenship to their adult employees through a patriotic, all-American system of racial discrimination in hiring. The non-minority individuals who are deprived of a legal education, a civil service job, or any job at all by reason of their skin color will surely understand.

Unlike a clear constitutional holding that racial preferences in state educational institutions are impermissible, or even a clear anticonstitutional holding that racial preferences in state educational institutions are OK, today's Grutter-Gratz split double header seems perversely designed to prolong the controversy and the litigation. Some future lawsuits will presumably focus on whether the discriminatory scheme in question contains enough evaluation of the applicant "as an individual," and sufficiently avoids "separate admissions tracks" to fall under Grutter rather than Gratz. Some will focus on whether a university has gone beyond the bounds of a "'good faith effort'" and has so zealously pursued its "critical mass" as to make it an unconstitutional *de facto* quota system, rather than merely "'a permissible goal.'" Other lawsuits may focus on whether, in the particular setting at issue, any educational benefits flow from racial diversity. . . . Still other suits may challenge the bona fides of the institution's expressed commitment to the educational benefits of diversity that immunize the discriminatory scheme in Grutter. (Tempting targets, one would suppose, will be those universities that talk the talk of multiculturalism and racial diversity in the courts but walk the walk of tribalism and racial segregation on their campuses—through minority-only student organizations, separate minority housing opportunities, separate minority student centers, even separate minority-only graduation ceremonies.) And still other suits may claim that the institution's racial preferences have gone below or above the mystical Grutter-approved "critical mass." Finally, litigation can be expected on behalf of minority groups intentionally short changed in the institution's composition of its generic minority "critical mass." I do not look forward to any of these cases. The Constitution proscribes government discrimination on the basis of race, and state-provided education is no exception.

Justice THOMAS, with whom Justice SCALIA joins as to Parts I-VII, concurring in part and dissenting in part.

Frederick Douglass, speaking to a group of abolitionists almost 140 years ago, delivered a message lost on today's majority:

> [I]n regard to the colored people, there is always more that is benevolent, I perceive, than just, manifested towards us. What I ask for the negro is not benevolence, not pity, not sympathy, but simply justice. The American people have always been anxious to know what they shall do with us. . . . I have had but one answer from the beginning. Do nothing with us! Your doing with us has already played the mischief with us. Do nothing with us! If the apples will not remain on the tree of their own strength, if they are worm-eaten at the core, if they are early ripe and disposed to fall, let them fall! . . . And if the negro cannot stand on his own legs, let him fall also. All I ask is, give him a chance to stand on his own legs! Let him alone! . . . [Y]our interference is doing him positive injury. *What the Black Man Wants: An Address Delivered in Boston, Massachusetts,* on 26 January 1865, reprinted in 4 *The Frederick Douglass Papers* 59, 68 (J. Blassingame & J. McKivigan eds. 1991).

Like Douglass, I believe blacks can achieve in every avenue of American life without the meddling of university administrators. Because I wish to see all students succeed whatever their color, I share, in some respect, the sympathies of those who sponsor the type of discrimination advanced by the University of Michigan Law School (Law School). The Constitution does not, however, tolerate institutional devotion to the status quo in admissions policies when such devotion ripens into racial discrimination. Nor does the Constitution countenance the unprecedented deference the Court gives to the Law School, an approach inconsistent with the very concept of "strict scrutiny."

No one would argue that a university could set up a lower general admission standard and then impose heightened requirements only on black applicants. Similarly, a university may not maintain a high admission standard and grant exemptions to favored races. The Law School, of its own choosing, and for its own purposes, maintains an exclusionary admissions system that it knows produces racially disproportionate results. Racial discrimination is not a permissible solution to the self-inflicted wounds of this elitist admissions policy.

The majority upholds the Law School's racial discrimination not by interpreting the people's Constitution, but by responding to a faddish slogan of the cognoscenti. Nevertheless, I concur in part in the Court's opinion. First, I agree with the Court insofar as its decision, which approves of only one racial classification, confirms that further use of race in admissions remains unlawful. Second, I agree with the Court's holding that racial discrimination in higher education admissions will be illegal in 25 years (stating that racial discrimination will no longer be narrowly tailored, or "necessary to further" a compelling state interest, in 25 years). I respectfully dissent from the remainder of the Court's opinion and the judgment, however, because I believe that the Law School's current use of race violates the Equal Protection Clause and that the Constitution means the same thing today as it will in 300 months. . . .

GRATZ V. BOLLINGER

539 U.S. 244 (2003)

Chief Justice REHNQUIST delivered the opinion of the Court.

We granted certiorari in this case to decide whether "the University of Michigan's use of racial preferences in undergraduate admissions violate[s] the Equal Protection Clause of the Fourteenth Amendment, Title VI of the Civil Rights Act of 1964 (42 U.S.C. §2000d), or 42 U.S.C. §1981." Because we find that the manner in which the University considers the race of applicants in its undergraduate admissions guidelines violates these constitutional and statutory provisions, we reverse that portion of the District Court's decision upholding the guidelines.

I

A

Petitioners Jennifer Gratz and Patrick Hamacher both applied for admission to the University of Michigan's (University) College of Literature, Science, and the Arts (LSA) as residents of the State of Michigan. Both petitioners are Caucasian. . . . Gratz was notified in April that the LSA was unable to offer her admission. . . . Hamacher's application was subsequently denied in April 1997, and he enrolled at Michigan State University. . . .

B

Petitioners argue, first and foremost, that the University's use of race in undergraduate admissions violates the Fourteenth Amendment. Specifically, they contend that this Court has only sanctioned the use of racial classifications to remedy identified discrimination, a justification on which respondents have never relied. Petitioners further argue that "diversity as a basis for employing racial preferences is simply too open-ended, ill-defined, and indefinite to constitute a compelling interest capable of supporting narrowly-tailored means." But for the reasons set forth today in *Grutter v. Bollinger,* the Court has rejected these arguments of petitioners.

Petitioners alternatively argue that even if the University's interest in diversity can constitute a compelling state interest, the District Court erroneously concluded that the University's use of race in its current freshman admissions policy is narrowly tailored to achieve such an interest. Petitioners argue that the guidelines the University began using in 1999 do not "remotely resemble the kind of consideration of race and ethnicity that Justice Powell endorsed in *Bakke.*" Respondents reply that the University's current admissions program *is* narrowly tailored and avoids the problems of the Medical School of the University of California at Davis program (U. C. Davis) rejected by Justice Powell. They claim that their program "hews closely" to both the admissions program described by Justice Powell as well as the Harvard College admissions program that he endorsed. Specifically, respondents contend that the LSA's policy provides the individualized consideration that "Justice Powell considered a hallmark of a constitutionally appropriate admissions program." For the reasons set out below, we do not agree. . . .

We find that the University's policy, which automatically distributes 20 points, or one-fifth of the points needed to guarantee admission, to every single "underrepresented minority" applicant solely because of race, is not narrowly tailored to achieve the interest in educational diversity that respondents claim justifies their program.

In *Bakke,* Justice Powell reiterated that "[p] referring members of any one group for no reason other than race or ethnic origin is discrimination for its own sake." 438 U.S., at 307. He then explained, however, that in his view it would be permissible for a university to employ an admissions program in which "race or ethnic background may be deemed a 'plus' in a particular applicant's file." *Id.,* at 317. He explained that such a program might allow for "[t]he file of a particular black applicant [to] be examined for his potential contribution to diversity without the factor of race being decisive when compared, for example, with that of an applicant identified as an Italian-American if the latter is thought to exhibit qualities more likely to promote beneficial educational pluralism." *Ibid.* Such a system, inJustice Powell's view, would be "flexible enough to consider all pertinent elements of diversity in light of the particular qualifications of each applicant." *Ibid.*

Justice Powell's opinion in *Bakke* emphasized the importance of considering each particular applicant as an individual, assessing all of the qualities that individual possesses, and in turn, evaluating that individual's ability to contribute to the unique setting of higher education. The admissions program Justice Powell described, however, did not contemplate that any single characteristic automatically ensured a specific and identifiable contribution to a university's diversity. . . . Instead, under the approach Justice Powell described, each characteristic of a particular applicant was to be considered in assessing the applicant's entire application.

The current LSA policy does not provide such individualized consideration. The LSA's policy automatically distributes 20 points to every single applicant from an "underrepresented minority" group, as defined by the University. The only consideration that accompanies this distribution of points is a factual review of an application to determine whether an individual is a member of one of these minority groups. Moreover, unlike Justice Powell's example, where the race of a "particular black applicant" could be considered without being decisive, see *Bakke,* the LSA's automatic distribution of 20 points has the effect of making "the factor of race . . . decisive" for virtually every minimally qualified underrepresented minority applicant.

Also instructive in our consideration of the LSA's system is the example provided in the description of the Harvard College Admissions Program, which Justice Powell both discussed in, and attached to, his opinion in *Bakke.* The example was included to "illustrate the kind of significance attached to race" under the Harvard College program. It provided as follows:

> The Admissions Committee, with only a few places left to fill, might find itself forced to choose between A, the child of a successful black physician in an academic community with promise of superior academic performance, and B, a black who grew up in an inner-city ghetto of semi-literate parents whose academic achievement was lower but who had demonstrated energy and leadership as well as an apparently abiding interest in black power. If a good number of black students much like A but few like B had already been admitted, the Committee might prefer B; and vice versa. If C, a white student with extraordinary artistic talent, were also seeking one of the remaining places, his unique quality might give him an edge over both A and B. Thus, the critical criteria are often individual qualities or experience *not dependent upon race but sometimes associated with it. Ibid.* (emphasis added).

This example further demonstrates the problematic nature of the LSA's admissions system. Even if student C's "extraordinary artistic talent" rivaled that of Monet or Picasso, the applicant would receive, at most, five points under the LSA's system. At the same time, every single underrepresented minority applicant, including students A and B, would automatically receive 20 points for submitting an application. Clearly, the LSA's system does not offer applicants the individualized selection process described in Harvard's example. Instead of considering how the differing backgrounds, experiences, and characteristics of students A, B, and C might benefit the University, admissions counselors reviewing LSA applications would simply award both A and B 20 points because their applications indicate that they are African-American, and student C would receive up to 5 points for his "extraordinary talent."

Respondents emphasize the fact that the LSA has created the possibility of an applicant's file being flagged for individualized consideration by the ARC. We think that the flagging program only emphasizes the flaws of the University's system as a whole when compared to that described by Justice Powell. Again, students A, B, and C illustrate the point. First, student A would never be flagged. This is because, as the University has conceded, the effect of automatically awarding 20 points is that virtually every qualified underrepresented minority applicant is admitted. Student A, an applicant "with promise of superior academic performance," would certainly fit this description. Thus, the result of the automatic distribution of 20 points is that the University would never consider student A's individual background, experiences, and characteristics to assess his individual "potential contribution to diversity," *Bakke*. Instead, every applicant like student A would simply be admitted.

It is possible that students B and C would be flagged and considered as individuals. This assumes that student B was not already admitted because of the automatic 20-point distribution, and that student C could muster at least 70 additional points. But the fact that the "review committee can look at the applications individually and ignore the points," once an application is flagged, is of little comfort under our strict scrutiny analysis. . . . Additionally, this individualized review is only provided *after* admissions counselors automatically distribute the University's version of a "plus" that makes race a decisive factor for virtually every minimally qualified underrepresented minority applicant.

Respondents contend that "[t]he volume of applications and the presentation of applicant information make it impractical for [LSA] to use the . . . admissions system" upheld by the Court today in *Grutter*. But the fact that the implementation of a program capable of providing individualized consideration might present administrative challenges does not render constitutional an otherwise problematic system. . . . Nothing in Justice Powell's opinion in *Bakke* signaled that a university may employ whatever means it desires to achieve the stated goal of diversity without regard to the limits imposed by our strict scrutiny analysis.

We conclude, therefore, that because the University's use of race in its current freshman admissions policy is not narrowly tailored to achieve respondents' asserted compelling interest in diversity, the admissions policy violates the Equal Protection Clause of the Fourteenth Amendment. We further find that the admissions policy also violates Title VI and 42 U.S.C. §1981. Accordingly, we reverse that portion of the District Court's decision granting respondents summary judgment with respect to liability and remand the case for proceedings consistent with this opinion.

Justice O'Connor, concurring.

I

Unlike the law school admissions policy the Court upholds today in *Grutter v. Bollinger*, the procedures employed by the University of Michigan's (University) Office of Undergraduate Admissions do not provide for a meaningful individualized review of applicants. *Cf. Regents of Univ. of Cal. v. Bakke*, 438 U.S. 265 (1978) (principal opinion of Powell, J.). The law school considers the various diversity qualifications of each applicant, including race, on a case-by-case basis. *See Grutter v. Bollinger*. By contrast, the Office of Undergraduate Admissions relies on the selection index to assign *every* underrepresented minority applicant the same, *automatic* 20-point bonus without consideration of the particular background, experiences, or qualities of each individual applicant. And this mechanized selection index score, by and large, automatically determines the admissions decision for each applicant.

The selection index thus precludes admissions counselors from conducting the type of individualized consideration the Court's opinion in *Grutter,* requires: consideration of each applicant's individualized qualifications, including the contribution each individual's race or ethnic identity will make to the diversity of the student body, taking into account diversity within and among all racial and ethnic groups. . . .

Justice GINSBURG, with whom Justice SOUTER joins, dissenting.

I

Educational institutions, the Court acknowledges, are not barred from any and all consideration of race when making admissions decisions. But the Court once again maintains that the same standard of review controls judicial inspection of all official race classifications. This insistence on "consistency," *Adarand,* 515 U.S., at 224, would be fitting were our Nation free of the vestiges of rank discrimination long reinforced by law. But we are not far distant from an overtly discriminatory past, and the effects of centuries of law-sanctioned inequality remain painfully evident in our communities and schools.

In the wake "of a system of racial caste only recently ended," large disparities endure. Unemployment, poverty, and access to health care vary disproportionately by race. Neighborhoods and schools remain racially divided. African-American and Hispanic children are all too often educated in poverty-stricken and underperforming institutions. Adult African-Americans and Hispanics generally earn less than whites with equivalent levels of education. Equally credentialed job applicants receive different receptions depending on their race. Irrational prejudice is still encountered in real estate markets and consumer transactions. "Bias both conscious and unconscious, reflecting traditional and unexamined habits of thought, keeps up barriers that must come down if equal opportunity and nondiscrimination are ever genuinely to become this country's law and practice." *[See]* generally Krieger, *Civil Rights Perestroika: Intergroup Relations After Affirmative Action,* 86 Calif. L. Rev. 1251, 1276-1291 (1998).

The Constitution instructs all who act for the government that they may not "deny to any person . . . the equal protection of the laws." Amdt. 14, §1. In implementing this equality instruction, as I see it, government decision makers may properly distinguish between policies of exclusion and inclusion. Actions designed to burden groups long denied full citizenship stature are not sensibly ranked with measures taken to hasten the day when entrenched discrimination and its after effects have been extirpated. *See* Carter, *When Victims Happen to Be Black, 97* Yale L. J. 420, 433-434 (1988) ("[T]o say that two centuries of struggle for the most basic of civil rights have been mostly about freedom from racial categorization rather than freedom from racial oppressio[n] is to trivialize the lives and deaths of those who have suffered under racism. To pretend . . . that the issue presented in *[Regents of Univ. of Cal. v. Bakke,* 438 U.S. 265 (1978)] was the same as the issue in *[Brown v. Board of Education,* 347 U.S. 483 (1954)] is to pretend that history never happened and that the present doesn't exist.").

Our jurisprudence ranks race a "suspect" category, "not because [race] is inevitably an impermissible classification, but because it is one which usually, to our national shame, has been drawn for the purpose of maintaining racial inequality." *Norwalk Core v. Norwalk Redevelopment Agency,* 395 F.2d 920, 931-932 (CA2 1968) (footnote omitted). But where race is considered "for the purpose of achieving equality," no automatic proscription is in order. For, as insightfully explained, "[t]he Constitution is both color blind and color conscious. To avoid conflict with the equal protection clause, a classification that denies a benefit, causes harm, or imposes a burden must not be based upon race. In that sense, the Constitution is colorblind. But the Constitution is color conscious to prevent discrimination being perpetuated and to undo the effects of past discrimination." *United States v. Jefferson County Bd. of Ed.,* 372 F.2d 836, 876 (CA5 1966) (Wisdom, J.); *see* Wechsler, *The Nationalization of Civil Liberties and Civil Rights,* Supp. to 12 Tex. Q. 10, 23 (1968) *(Brown* may be seen as disallowing racial classifications that "impl[y] an invidious assessment" while allowing such classifications when "not invidious in implication" but advanced to "correct inequalities"). Contemporary human rights documents draw just this line; they distinguish between policies of oppression and measures designed to accelerate *de facto* equality.

The mere assertion of a laudable governmental purpose, of course, should not immunize a race-conscious measure from careful judicial inspection. Close review is needed "to ferret out classifications in reality malign, but masquerading as benign," *Adarand,* 515 U.S., at 275 (Ginsburg, J., dissenting), and to "ensure that preferences are not so large as to trammel unduly upon the opportunities of others or interfere too harshly with legitimate expectations of persons in once-preferred groups."

II

Examining in this light the admissions policy employed by the University of Michigan's College of Literature, Science, and the Arts (College), and for the reasons well stated by Justice Souter, I see no constitutional infirmity. Like other top-ranking institutions, the College has many more applicants for admission than it can accommodate in an entering class. Every applicant admitted under the current plan, petitioners do not here dispute, is qualified to attend the College. The racial and ethnic groups to which the College accords special consideration (African-Americans, Hispanics, and Native-Americans) historically have been relegated to inferior status by law and social practice; their members continue to experience class-based discrimination to this day. There is no suggestion that the College adopted its current policy in order to limit or decrease enrollment by any particular racial or ethnic group, and no seats are reserved on the basis of race. Nor has there been any demonstration that the College's program unduly constricts admissions opportunities for students who do not receive special consideration based upon race. *Cf.* Liu, *The Causation Fallacy:* Bakke *and the Basic Arithmetic of Selective Admissions,* 100 Mich. L. Rev. 1045, 1049 (2002) ("In any admissions process where applicants greatly outnumber admittees, and where white applicants greatly outnumber minority applicants, substantial preferences for minority applicants will not significantly diminish the odds of admission facing white applicants.").

The stain of generations of racial oppression is still visible in our society, *see* Krieger, 86 Calif. L. Rev., at 1253, and the determination to hasten its removal remains vital. One can reasonably anticipate, therefore, that colleges and universities will seek to maintain their minority enrollment—and the networks and opportunities thereby opened to minority graduates—whether or not they can do so in full candor through adoption of affirmative action plans of the kind here at issue. . . .

NOTES AND QUESTIONS

1. In *Grutter,* Justice O'Connor begins her analysis by discussing in "detail" Justice Powell's opinion in *Bakke,* declaring that the opinion has provided the model of race-conscious admissions policies followed by public and private educational institutions. Recall that Justice Powell's opinion was not the Court's opinion in *Bakke.* Nonetheless, the lower courts, including the Sixth Circuit, had concluded that they were bound by that opinion because it represented the "narrowest grounds" on which five members of the *Bakke* Court agreed. In *Marks v. United States,* 430 U.S. 188 (1977), the Supreme Court ruled that when a "fragmented Court decides a case and no single rationale explaining the result enjoys the assent of five Justices, the holding of the Court may be viewed as that position taken by those members who concurred in the judgments on the narrowest grounds." 430 U.S. at 193. Do you agree that Justice Powell's opinion regarding the interest in diversity represents the "narrowest grounds" of concurrence in *Bakke?* In *Grutter,* the Supreme Court accepts the notion that the lower federal courts are bound under *Marks* by Justice Powell's opinion. As such, the Court could have affirmed the Sixth Circuit's opinion in *Grutter* based simply on the fact that the Sixth Circuit did not err in following the Powell opinion. Yet, the Court goes much further. It expressly converts Powell's view into the Court's view: "today we endorse Justice Powell's view that student body diversity is a compelling state interest that can justify the use of race in university admissions."
2. Many Supreme Court observers speculated before *Grutter* was decided that Justice O'Connor would provide the "swing" vote for the Court. They further conjectured that Justice O'Connor might well vote to uphold the University of Michigan Law School's admissions program because she had been a judicial clerk for Justice Powell, and because she may have felt herself benefited by affirmative action programs that encouraged her own entry into law school and the legal profession. Do you believe that this form of "legal realism" is appropriate in analyzing the Court's opinion?
3. Of what relevance is the fact that public and private institutions, according to the Court, have modeled their admissions programs in accordance with Justice Powell's opinion? Does the existence of race-conscious admissions policies create settled expectations that are difficult for the Court to undo in one stroke? In this context, does the Court's 25-year "sunset" declaration perhaps serve as a warning to educational institutions that any expectation that they may have of continuing their race-conscious admissions programs indefinitely would not be a legitimate one?
4. The majority rejects the concept implicit in *Croson* and *Adarand* that, "the only governmental use of race that can survive strict scrutiny is

remedying past discrimination." The Court proceeds to declare that there is a "compelling state interest in student body diversity." The Court is careful to qualify that interest as the "Law School's" interest and as an interest in the "context of higher education." Are these qualifications significant? Is there a compelling interest in student body diversity in preschool, elementary school, middle school or high school?

5. What are the benefits of a diverse student body that render that interest so compelling? The Court alludes to the following "substantial" benefits of a diverse student body: (1) educational benefits; (2) an increase in the "robust" exchange of ideas; (3) cross-racial understanding; (4) breaking down racial stereotypes; (5) livelier, more spirited, enlightening and interesting classroom discussions; (6) the promotion of learning "outcomes"; (7) better preparation of students to work and interact in an "increasingly diverse" society and workforce; (8) better preparation as professionals in an "increasingly global marketplace"; (9) helping the military to fulfill its very mission of "national security"; (10) facilitating the "diffusion of knowledge and opportunity through public institutions of higher education" to be accessible to all individuals and thereby sustaining our "political and cultural heritage"; (11) fostering the effective participation by members of all racial and ethnic groups which is vital to becoming *one* nation; (12) supporting the training in law school for diverse national leaders and thereby cultivating leaders with legitimacy; and (13) developing attorneys of diverse races and ethnicities who will be able, in turn, to help all members of a "heterogeneous society" succeed. Consider each one of these proffered benefits of a diverse student body. First, what is the support for the benefit advanced? Second, do you agree that the benefit offered is really a benefit? Third, which of the benefits are limited to the law school environment? Fourth, which of the benefits are limited to education generally?
6. In a portion of its opinion specifically ridiculed by the dissenters, the majority in *Grutter* defers to the educational expertise of the state of Michigan regarding the "educational" benefits flowing from a diverse student body. The majority relies on its tradition of deferring to local control and to the expertise of educational professionals. Is such deference appropriate here? Suppose, as Justice Thomas suggests, the state of Michigan reaches the educational judgment that single-race schools lead to better learning outcomes than diverse schools. Could that educational judgment compel an admissions policy that excludes white students from a particular state school?
7. What does a "diverse" student body mean? The Court makes clear that diversity is not just about race, but includes the variety of backgrounds and experiences which students bring to the educational environment. Could the benefits of a "diverse" student body still be achieved in a single-race school? Does the fact that an applicant is a member of an underrepresented racial minority mean that the admission of that student into law school would *automatically* advance the interest in diversity? Can race be used by an admissions committee as part of its judgment about the distance which the applicant most likely has traveled to get to higher

education? If, as some have suggested, race is a proxy for the "distance traveled" by an applicant, then the fact that the applicant is a member of an underrepresented minority could mean that the applicant has developed (out of struggle) a strength of character which makes that applicant *more* qualified for law school than applicants who have not had to develop such strength of character. The majority opinion, however, speaks little of how underrepresented minority applicants, by virtue of their history of underrepresentation, may have qualities that by definition enhance their law school qualifications. Instead, the Court speaks primarily of the state's interest in a diverse student body. Could the law school decide that membership in an underrepresented minority gives to an applicant a strength of character that is a more effective predictor of success in law school and the profession than any LSAT score? Would the Supreme Court defer to *that* educational judgment, and uphold an admissions policy that credits the strength of an individual's character resulting from membership in an underrepresented minority?

8. As the *Grutter* Court declares, the state must also demonstrate that its compelling governmental interest in student body diversity is pursued by means that are "specifically and narrowly framed to accomplish that purpose." The Court finds that the law school's use of race as a factor, even a "plus" factor, as part of its "truly individualized consideration" of each applicant "bears the hallmarks of a narrowly tailored plan." As long as the law school makes a "highly individualized, holistic review of each applicant's file," giving serious consideration to all the ways an applicant might contribute to a diverse educational environment, a race-conscious admissions policy will apparently satisfy the rigors of strict scrutiny. In *Gratz,* of course, the Supreme Court ruled that the state's undergraduate admissions policy which automatically distributes 20 points (or one-fifth of the points needed to guarantee admission) to every single underrepresented minority solely based upon race, was not narrowly tailored to achieve educational diversity. The absence of an "individualized assessment" of every applicant appears to be the fatal flaw in the undergraduate policy. But is it that simple? Do you agree with Justice Scalia's opinion in *Grutter,* that the line between valid Grutter-like admissions policies and invalid Gratz-like policies will be difficult to draw and will inevitably lead to litigation in the future?
9. The Supreme Court in *Grutter* ultimately rejects the notion that the law school must exhaust alternative, race-neutral means of attaining diversity before embarking on its admissions policy. In so doing, the Court specifically rejects the position advanced by the Bush administration in the case. The Bush administration, citing the Texas system of reserving a fixed percentage of spots in its undergraduate institutions for all high school students above a certain class rank, claimed that the law school should have pursued such so-called race-neutral means of obtaining diversity. Not only did the Court reject the Bush administration's legal argument, however, it also rejected the administration's premise. The Court indicates that such a "percentage plan" is itself highly suspect because it completely precludes the kind of "individualized assessments necessary to

assemble a student body that is not just racially diverse, but diverse along all the qualities valued by the university."

10. Compare Justice Thomas's approach to race and his use of the Frederick Douglass quote with Justice Ginsburg's approach distinguishing between invidious use of race and the salutary use of race in political decision making. Which Justice has the better argument? Consider, too, the view expressed by Professor Peter Westen in *The Empty Idea of Equality,* 95 Harv. L. Rev. 537 (1982). Westen argues that the principle of equality is meaningless without reference to substantive goals that are anterior to equality itself. He shows that *all* laws discriminate by treating some people differently than others. Indeed, laws are *designed* to treat people unequally. The equal protection inquiry therefore is whether the substantive value advanced by unequal treatment justifies that unequal treatment. By this logic, the affirmative action issue cannot hinge on whether or not a law (or an admissions policy) treats people unequally based upon their race. Rather, the question must be *why* the law or policy does so. If the unequal treatment serves a strong enough substantive value, then it should be sustained. Accordingly, a law that treats people of different races differently in order to achieve a salutary substantive value like educational opportunity should be sustained. By contrast, if the law treats people of different races differently so as to perpetuate *barriers* to educational opportunity (for instance) that law should be struck down. Westen's argument challenges students of the Supreme Court's affirmative action decisions to attempt to discover in each Justice's approach to the issue a *substantive value* that is really unrelated to the issue of equality itself. What substantive value judgments inform the decisions in *Grutter* and *Gratz?* Is Westen correct that the principle of equality is meaningless, or is equality a substantive value to be independently protected?
11. In his separate *Grutter* opinion, Justice Thomas relies heavily on a quotation from Frederick Douglass, arguing that Douglass insisted that African-Americans would be better off if they were just left alone. Thomas quotes Douglass to say: "Let him alone! . . . [Y]our interference is doing him positive injury." Justice Thomas, however, selectively deleted important language from that Douglass quotation. What Douglass said in the portion deleted by Thomas was: "Let him alone! If you see him on his way to school, let him alone, don't disturb him! If you see him going to a dinner table at a hotel, let him go! If you see him going to a ballot box, let him alone, don't disturb him! If you see him going into a workshop, just let him alone—your interference is doing him a positive injury." Do the words which Thomas excised from his quotation change the meaning of that quotation?
12. Recall Justice Blackmun's opinion in *Bakke* in 1978, where he declared his "hope" that affirmative action programs would be unnecessary within "a decade at most." In *Grutter,* the majority indicates that Justice Blackmun's hope has not been realized, and declares its own hope that such programs will not be needed 25 years from 2003. Is the *Grutter* majority merely announcing its hope, or is it serious that its opinion will have a "sunset" 25 years from its issuance? On balance, is the Supreme Court in 2003

more, or less, optimistic than the *Bakke* Court was about the prospects of racial progress in America?

13. How will educational institutions know that the necessity for affirmative action programs no longer exists? Is the objective to equalize secondary school graduation rates between majority and underrepresented minority students? Are underrepresented minority students currently just African-Americans and Hispanics? Will those groups change over the next 25 years? Will the necessity for affirmative action be removed only when the striking disparities in per-pupil funding among majority and minority students are eradicated? Those disparities have a significant racial component. School districts attended by African-American and Hispanic children devote $902 less per student than predominantly white districts. *See* Holmes & Winter, *Fixing the Race Gap in 25 Years or Less,* N.Y. Times, June 29, 2003, at 4:1 (hereinafter Holmes & Winter).
14. In a surprisingly candid interview in the immediate aftermath of her *Grutter* opinion, Justice O'Connor expressed her hope that we will not need "artificial" help in making graduate school classrooms diverse if "we do our job of educating young people. . . ." *See* Holmes & Winter. Justice O'Connor seems to redirect the national dialogue about affirmative action to the primary grades. If only the elementary schools, middle schools and secondary schools were themselves diverse, and did their job of fostering achievement in a diverse student body, she suggests, there would be no need for affirmative action at the graduate and professional school levels. What are the impediments to creating a diverse student body in precollegiate classrooms?
15. In light of Justice O'Connor's focus on elementary education, consider the composition of public school classrooms in America. In 2000, the U.S. Department of Education reported that white students constitute 61.2 percent of the public school population, while 17.2 percent are African-American, 16.3 percent are Hispanic, 4.1 percent are Asian or Pacific Islander, and 1.2 percent are American Indian or Alaskan Native. *See* U.S.A. Today, Lifeline at 1-2 (July 2, 2003). At the same time, the composition of educational professionals is significantly less diverse: 84.3 percent of public school teachers are white. What's more, 90 percent of all elementary school teachers are women. While gender and racial diversity among teachers is improving, it still lags behind diversity among students. What accounts for that difference?
16. Under the Supreme Court's rulings in *Grutter* and *Gratz,* is a state *compelled* to use race-conscious means to obtain diversity? If not, has the Court gone far enough to insure that the states maintain policies and practices that do not frustrate diversity in education? In other words, diversity is an interest that may justify race-conscious federal admissions policies, but diversity apparently is not a goal strong enough to compel them?
17. Recall that in *Hopwood v. Texas,* 78 F.3d 932 (5th Cir. 1996), the Fifth Circuit had declared unconstitutional the University of Texas School of Law's race-conscious admissions program, reasoning:

> With the best of intentions, in order to increase the enrollment of certain favored classes of minority students, the University of Texas School of Law

> ("the law school") discriminates in favor of those applicants by giving substantial racial preferences in its admissions program. The beneficiaries of this system are blacks and Mexican-Americans, to the detriment of whites and non-preferred minorities. The question we decide today is whether the Fourteenth Amendment permits the school to discriminate in this way.
>
> We hold that it does not. The law school has presented no compelling justification, under the Fourteenth Amendment or Supreme Court precedent, that allows it to continue to elevate some races over others, even for the wholesome purpose of correcting perceived racial imbalance in the student body. . . .

In light of the Supreme Court's rulings in *Grutter* and *Gratz,* consider the constitutionality of the following system, as described by the Fifth Circuit in *Hopwood:*

> Numbers are therefore paramount for admission. In the early 1990's, the law school largely based its initial admissions decisions upon an applicant's so-called Texas Index ("TI") number, a composite of undergraduate grade point average ("GPA") and Law School Aptitude Test ("LSAT") score. The law school used this number as a matter of administrative convenience in order to rank candidates and to predict, roughly, one's probability of success in law school. Moreover, the law school relied heavily upon such numbers to estimate the number of offers of admission it needed to make in order to fill its first-year class.
>
> Blacks and Mexican-Americans were treated differently from other candidates, however. First, compared to whites and non-preferred minorities, the TI ranges that were used to place them into the three admissions categories were lowered to allow the law school to consider and admit more of them. In March 1992, for example, the presumptive TI admission score for resident whites and non-preferred minorities was 199. Mexican Americans and blacks needed a TI of only 189 to be presumptively admitted. The difference in the presumptive-deny ranges is even more striking. The presumptive denial score for "nonminorities" was 192; the same score for blacks and Mexican Americans was 179.
>
> These disparate standards greatly affected a candidate's chance of admission. For example, by March 1992, because the presumptive denial score for whites was a TI of 192 or lower, and the presumptive admit TI for minorities was 189 or higher, a minority candidate with a TI of 189 or above almost certainly would be admitted, even though his score was considerably below the level at which a white candidate almost certainly would be rejected. Out of the pool of resident applicants who fell within this range (189-192 inclusive), 100% of blacks and 90% of Mexican-Americans, but only 6% of whites, were offered admission.
>
> The stated purpose of this lowering of standards was to meet an "aspiration" of admitting a class consisting of 10% Mexican Americans and 5% blacks, proportions roughly comparable to the percentages of those races graduating from Texas colleges. The law school found meeting these "goals" difficult, however, because of uncertain acceptance rates and the variable quality of the applicant pool. In 1992, for example, the entering class contained 41 blacks and 55 Mexican-Americans, respectively 8% and 10.7% of the class.

> In addition to maintaining separate presumptive TI levels for minorities and whites, the law school ran a segregated application evaluation process. Upon receiving an application form, the school color-coded it according to race. If a candidate failed to designate his race, he was presumed to be in a nonpreferential category. Thus, race was always an overt part of the review of any applicant's file.
>
> The law school reviewed minority candidates within the applicable discretionary range differently from whites. Instead of being evaluated and compared by one of the various discretionary zone subcommittees, black and Mexican American applicants' files were reviewed by a minority subcommittee of three, which would meet and discuss every minority candidate.

18. In light of *Grutter* and *Gratz,* how would you advise educational institutions to conduct their admissions practices? As you develop a strategy that complies with the *Grutter-Gratz* precedent, assume that the institution strives for a student body which is both talented and diverse. Further, recall the concern advanced in *Gratz* that an admissions policy which requires an "individualized assessment" of every applicant in the context of an institution with many applicants may require resources which are simply unavailable. Is it possible to devise a cost-effective admissions policy that stays on the correct side of the *Grutter-Gratz* line?

19. *Anti-Affirmative Action Ballot Initiatives.* In 1996, the state of California passed Proposition 209, a ballot initiative that amends the California constitution to provide the state "shall not discriminate against, or grant preferential treatment to, any individual or group on the basis of race, sex, color, ethnicity, or national origin in the operation of . . . public education. . . ." The prohibition includes all California school districts and universities. In 1998, the state of Washington passed a virtually identical ballot initiative. On November 7, 2006, the State of Michigan then passed Proposal 2, a similar ballot initiative containing the same prohibitions. Thus far, the courts have upheld these anti-affirmative action ballot initiatives against constitutional challenges. *See, e.g., Coalition for Economic Equality v. Wilson,* 122 F.3d 692, 702 (9th Cir. 1997) ("Rather than classifying individuals by race or gender, Proposition 209 *prohibits* the State from classifying individuals by race or gender."); *Coalition to Defend Affirmative Action v. Granholm,* 473 F.3d 237, 249 (6th Cir. 2006) ("the color-blind goal of the Equal Protection Clause is to do away with all governmentally imposed discrimination based on race.").

The language of these ballot initiatives appears to prohibit public educational institutions from granting any preferential treatment to any student or applicant "on the basis of" race or gender. By contrast, the Equal Protection Clause permits public educational institutions to give preferential treatment on the basis of race if narrowly tailored to achieve a compelling interest, and permits public educational institutions to give preferential treatment on the basis of gender if supported by an exceedingly persuasive justification. Accordingly, a public educational institution governed by these ballot initiatives may not be able to defend its racial or gender preferences by asserting compelling or persuasive interests such as the educational benefits of student body diversity. On the other hand, the language of these initiatives only prohibits "preferences" on "the basis of" race or gender. That language does not prohibit preferences based on other characteristics, which may be proxies for race and gender. For example, a decision to admit an African-American applicant to the University of Michigan Law School for a host of reasons of which race is merely one part can be defended because that decision was not made on the basis of race. Race was not the causal factor, or even a substantial factor, in the decision. As such, the use of race (or gender) as one of many factors in reaching an admissions decision (or a student assignment decision) need not run afoul of these ballot initiatives. For an outstanding collection of articles and presentations regarding these ballot initiatives, *see* "From Proposition 209 to Proposal 2: Examining the Effects of Anti-Affirmative Action Voter Initiatives," 13 U. Mich. J. Race & Law 461 (Spring 2008).

C. VOLUNTARY INTEGRATION AND THE CONSTITUTIONALITY OF RACE-CONSCIOUS EDUCATIONAL DECISIONS

Parents Involved in Community Schools v. Seattle School District No. 1 et al.,

Crystal D. Meredith, custodial parent and next friend of Joshua Ryan McDonald v. Jefferson County Board of Education et al.,

127 S.Ct. 2738 (2007)

Roberts, C.J. announced the judgment of the Court and delivered the opinion of the Court with respect to Parts I, II, III-A, and III-C, in which Scalia, Kennedy, Thomas, and Alito, JJ., joined and an opinion with respect to Parts III-B and IV, in which Scalia, Thomas, and Alito, JJ., joined. Thomas, J., filed a concurring opinion. Kennedy, J., filed an opinion concurring in part and concurring in the judgment. Stevens, J., filed a dissenting opinion. Breyer, J., filed a dissenting opinion, in which Stevens, Souter, and Ginsburg, JJ., joined.

The school districts in these cases voluntarily adopted student assignment plans that rely upon race to determine which public schools certain children may attend. The Seattle school district classifies children as white or nonwhite; the Jefferson County school district as black or "other." In Seattle, this racial classification is used to allocate slots in oversubscribed high schools. In Jefferson County, it is used to make certain elementary school assignments and to rule on transfer requests. In each case, the school district relies upon an individual student's race in assigning that student to a particular school, so that the racial balance at the school falls within a predetermined range based on the racial composition of the school district as a whole. Parents of students denied assignment to particular schools under these plans solely because of their race brought suit, contending that allocating children to different public schools on the basis of race violated the Fourteenth Amendment guarantee of equal protection. The Courts of Appeals below upheld the plans. We granted certiorari, and now reverse.

I

Both cases present the same underlying legal question — whether a public school that had not operated legally segregated schools or has been found to be unitary may choose to classify students by race and rely upon that classification in making school assignments. Although we examine the plans under the same legal framework, the specifics of the two plans, and the circumstances surrounding their adoption, are in some respects quite different.

A

Seattle School District No. 1 operates 10 regular public high schools. In 1998, it adopted the plan at issue in this case for assigning students to these schools. The plan allows incoming ninth graders to choose from among any of the district's high schools, ranking however many schools they wish in order of preference.

Some schools are more popular than others. If too many students list the same school as their first choice, the district employs a series of "tiebreakers" to determine who will fill the open slots at the oversubscribed school. The first tiebreaker selects for admission students who have a sibling currently enrolled in the chosen school. The next tiebreaker depends upon the racial composition of the particular school and the race of the individual student. In the district's public schools approximately 41 percent of enrolled students are white; the remaining 59 percent, comprising all other racial groups, are classified by Seattle for assignment purposes as nonwhite. If an oversubscribed school is not within 10 percentage points of the district's overall white/nonwhite racial balance, it is what the district calls "integration positive," and the district employs a tiebreaker that selects for assignment students whose race "will serve to bring the school into balance." If it is still necessary to select students for the school after using the racial tiebreaker, the next tiebreaker is the geographic proximity of the school to the student's residence.

Seattle has never operated segregated schools — legally separate schools for students of different races — nor has it ever been subject to court-ordered desegregation. It nonetheless employs the racial tiebreaker in an attempt to address the effects of racially identifiable housing patterns on school assignments. Most white students live in the northern part of Seattle, most students of other racial backgrounds in the southern part. Four of Seattle's high schools are located in the north — Ballard, Nathan Hale, Ingraham, and Roosevelt — and five in the south — Rainier Beach, Cleveland, West Seattle, Chief Sealth, and Franklin. One school — Garfield — is more or less in the center of Seattle.

For the 2000-2001 school year, five of these schools were oversubscribed — Ballard, Nathan Hale, Roosevelt, Garfield, and Franklin — so much so that 82 percent of incoming ninth graders ranked one of these schools as their first choice. Three of the oversubscribed schools were "integration positive" because the school's white enrollment the previous school year was greater than 51 percent—Ballard, Nathan Hale, and Roosevelt. Thus, more nonwhite students (107, 27, and 82, respectively) who selected one of these three schools as a top choice received placement at the school than would have been the case had race not been considered, and proximity been the next tiebreaker. Franklin was "integration positive" because its nonwhite enrollment the previous school year was greater than 69 percent; 89 more white students were assigned to Franklin by operation of the racial tiebreaker in the 2000–2001 school year than otherwise would have been. Garfield was the only oversubscribed school whose composition during the 1999-2000 school year was within the racial guidelines, although in previous years Garfield's enrollment had been predominantly nonwhite, and the racial tiebreaker had been used to give preference to white students.

Petitioner Parents Involved in Community Schools (Parents Involved) is a nonprofit corporation comprising the parents of children who have been or may be denied assignment to their chosen high school in the district because of their race. The concerns of Parents Involved are illustrated by Jill Kurfirst, who sought to enroll her ninth-grade son, Andy Meeks, in Ballard High School's special Biotechnology Career Academy. Andy suffered from attention deficit hyperactivity disorder and dyslexia, but had made good progress with hands-on instruction, and his mother and middle school teachers thought that the smaller biotechnology program held the most promise for his continued success. Andy was accepted into this selective program but, because of the racial tiebreaker, was denied assignment to Ballard High School. Parents Involved commenced this suit in the Western District of Washington, alleging that Seattle's use of race in assignments violated the Equal Protection Clause of the Fourteenth Amendment, Title VI of the Civil Rights Act of 1964, and the Washington Civil Rights Act.

The District Court granted summary judgment to the school district, finding that state law did not bar the district's use of the racial tiebreaker and that the plan survived strict scrutiny on the federal constitutional claim because it was narrowly tailored to serve a compelling government interest. . . .

A panel of the Ninth Circuit then . . . reversed the District Court. . . . The panel determined that while achieving racial diversity and avoiding racial isolation are compelling government interests, Seattle's use of the racial tiebreaker was not narrowly tailored to achieve these interests. The Ninth Circuit granted rehearing en banc, and overruled the panel decision, affirming the District Court's determination that Seattle's plan was narrowly tailored to serve a compelling government interest. We granted certiorari.

B

Jefferson County Public Schools operates the public school system in metropolitan Louisville, Kentucky. In 1973 a federal court found that Jefferson County had maintained a segregated school system, and in 1975, reinstated with modifications, the District Court entered a desegregation decree. Jefferson County operated under this decree until 2000, when the District Court dissolved the decree after finding that the district had achieved unitary status by eliminating "[t]o the greatest extent practicable" the vestiges of its prior policy of segregation.

In 2001, after the decree had been dissolved, Jefferson County adopted the voluntary student assignment plan at issue in this case. Approximately 34 percent of the district's 97,000 students are black; most of the remaining 66 percent are white. The plan requires all nonmagnet schools to maintain a minimum black enrollment of 15 percent, and a maximum black enrollment of 50 percent.

At the elementary school level, based on his or her address, each student is designated a "resides" school to which students within a specific geographic area are assigned; elementary resides schools are "grouped into clusters in order to facilitate integration." The district assigns students to nonmagnet schools in one of two ways: Parents of kindergartners, first-graders, and students new to the district may submit an application indicating a first and second choice among the schools within their cluster; students who do not submit such an application are assigned within the cluster by the district. "Decisions to assign students to schools within each cluster are based on available space within the schools and the racial guidelines in the District's current student assignment plan." If a school has reached the "extremes of the racial guidelines," a student whose race would contribute to the school's racial imbalance will not be assigned there. After assignment, students at all grade levels are permitted to apply to transfer between nonmagnet schools in the district. Transfers may be requested for any number of reasons, and may be denied because of lack of available space or on the basis of the racial guidelines.

When petitioner Crystal Meredith moved into the school district in August 2002, she sought to enroll her son, Joshua McDonald, in kindergarten for the 2002–2003 school year. His resides school was only a mile from his new home, but it had no available space—assignments had been made in May, and the class was full. Jefferson County assigned Joshua to another elementary school in his cluster, Young Elementary. This school was 10 miles from home, and Meredith sought to transfer Joshua to a school in a different cluster, Bloom Elementary, which—like his resides school—was only a mile from home. Space was available at Bloom, and intercluster transfers are allowed, but Joshua's transfer was nonetheless denied because, in the words of Jefferson County, "[t]he transfer would have an adverse effect on desegregation compliance" of Young.

Meredith brought suit in the Western District of Kentucky, alleging violations of the Equal Protection Clause of the Fourteenth Amendment. The District Court found that Jefferson County had asserted a compelling interest in maintaining racially diverse schools, and that the assignment plan was (in all relevant respects) narrowly tailored to serve that compelling interest. The Sixth Circuit affirmed in a *per curiam* opinion relying upon the reasoning of the District Court, concluding that a written opinion "would serve no useful purpose." We granted certiorari.

II

As a threshold matter, we must assure ourselves of our jurisdiction. Seattle argues that Parents Involved lacks standing because none of its current members can claim an imminent injury. Even if the district maintains the current plan and reinstitutes the racial tiebreaker, Seattle argues, Parents Involved members will only be affected if their children seek to enroll in a Seattle public high school and choose an oversubscribed school that is integration positive — too speculative a harm to maintain standing.

This argument is unavailing. The group's members have children in the district's elementary, middle, and high schools, and the complaint sought declaratory and injunctive relief on behalf of Parents Involved members whose elementary and middle school children may be "denied admission to the high schools of their choice when they apply for those schools in the future," The fact that it is possible that children of group members will not be denied admission to a school based on their race — because they choose an undersubscribed school or an oversubscribed school in which their race is an advantage — does not eliminate the injury claimed. Moreover, Parents Involved also asserted an interest in not being "forced to compete for seats at certain high schools in a system that uses race as a deciding factor in many of its admissions decisions." As we have held, one form of injury under the Equal Protection Clause is being forced to compete in a race-based system that may prejudice the plaintiff, *Adarand Constructors, Inc.* v. *Pena,* 515 U.S. 200, 211 (1995); *Northeastern Fla. Chapter, Associated Gen. Contractors of America* v. *Jacksonville,* 508 U.S. 656, 666 (1993), an injury that the members of Parents Involved can validly claim on behalf of their children.

In challenging standing, Seattle also notes that it has ceased using the racial tiebreaker pending the outcome of this litigation. But the district vigorously defends the constitutionality of its race-based program, and nowhere suggests that if this litigation is resolved in its favor it will not resume using race to assign students. Voluntary cessation does not moot a case or controversy unless "subsequent events ma[ke] it absolutely clear that the allegedly wrongful behavior could not reasonably be expected to recur," a heavy burden that Seattle has clearly not met.

Jefferson County does not challenge our jurisdiction, but we are nonetheless obliged to ensure that it exists. Although apparently Joshua has now been granted a transfer to Bloom, the school to which transfer was denied under the racial guidelines, the racial guidelines apply at all grade levels. Upon Joshua's enrollment in middle school, he may again be subject to assignment based on his race. In addition, Meredith sought damages in her complaint, which is sufficient to preserve our ability to consider the question.

III

A

It is well established that when the government distributes burdens or benefits on the basis of individual racial classifications, that action is reviewed under strict scrutiny. *Johnson* v. *California,* 543 U.S. 499, 505–506 (2005); *Grutter* v. *Bollinger,* 539 U.S. 306, 326 (2003); *Adarand, supra,* at 224. As the Court recently reaffirmed, "'racial classifications are simply too pernicious to permit any but the most exact connection between justification and classification.'" *Gratz* v. *Bollinger,* 539 U.S. 244, 270 (2003) (quoting *Fullilove* v. *Klutznick,* 448 U.S. 448, 537 (1980) (Stevens, J., dissenting); brackets omitted).

In order to satisfy this searching standard of review, the school districts must demonstrate that the use of individual racial classifications in the assignment plans here under review is "narrowly tailored" to achieve a "compelling" government interest. *Adarand, supra,* at 227.

Without attempting in these cases to set forth all the interests a school district might assert, it suffices to note that our prior cases, in evaluating the use of racial classifications in the school context, have recognized two interests that qualify as compelling. The first is the compelling interest of remedying the effects of past intentional discrimination. See *Freeman* v. *Pitts,* 503 U.S. 467, 494 (1992). Yet the Seattle public schools have not shown that they were ever segregated by law, and were not subject to court-ordered desegregation decrees. The Jefferson County public schools were previously segregated by law and were subject to a desegregation decree entered in 1975. In 2000, the District Court that entered that decree dissolved it, finding that Jefferson County had "eliminated the vestiges associated with the former policy of segregation and its pernicious effects," and thus had achieved "unitary" status. Jefferson County accordingly does not rely upon an interest in remedying the effects of past intentional discrimination in defending its present use of race in assigning students.

Nor could it. We have emphasized that the harm being remedied by mandatory desegregation plans is the harm that is traceable to segregation, and that "the Constitution is not violated by racial imbalance in the schools, without more." *Milliken* v. *Bradley,* 433 U.S. 267, n.14 (1977). See also *Freeman, supra,* at 495–496; *Dowell,* 498 U.S., at 248; *Milliken* v. *Bradley,* 418 U.S. 717, 746 (1974). Once Jefferson County achieved unitary status, it had remedied the constitutional wrong that allowed race-based assignments. Any continued use of race must be justified on some other basis.

The second government interest we have recognized as compelling for purposes of strict scrutiny is the interest in diversity in higher education upheld in *Grutter,* 539 U.S., at 328. The specific interest found compelling in *Grutter* was student body diversity "in the context of higher education." *Ibid.* The diversity interest was not focused on race alone but encompassed "all factors that may contribute to student body diversity." *Id.,* at 337. We described the various types of diversity that the law school sought:

"[The law school's] policy makes clear there are many possible bases for diversity admissions, and provides examples of admittees who have lived or traveled widely abroad, are fluent in several languages, have overcome personal adversity and family hardship, have exceptional records of extensive community service, and have had successful careers in other fields." *Id.,* at 338 (brackets and internal quotation marks omitted).

The Court quoted the articulation of diversity from Justice Powell's opinion in *Regents of the University of California* v. *Bakke,* 438 U.S. 265 (1978), noting that "it is not an interest in simple ethnic diversity, in which a specified percentage of the student body is in effect guaranteed to be members of selected ethnic groups, that can justify the use of race." *Grutter, supra,* at 324–325 (citing and quoting *Bakke, supra,* at 314–315 (opinion of Powell, J.); brackets and internal quotation marks omitted). Instead, what was upheld in *Grutter* was consideration of "a far broader array of qualifications and characteristics of which racial or ethnic origin is but a single though important element." 539 U.S., at 325 (quoting *Bakke, supra,*at 315 (opinion of Powell, J.); internal quotation marks omitted).

The entire gist of the analysis in *Grutter* was that the admissions program at issue there focused on each applicant as an individual, and not simply as a member of a particular racial group. The classification of applicants by race upheld in *Grutter* was only as part of a "highly individualized, holistic review," 539 U.S., at 337. As the Court explained, "[t]he importance of this individualized consideration in the context of a race-conscious admissions program is paramount." *Ibid.* The point of the narrow tailoring analysis in which the *Grutter* Court engaged was to ensure that the use of racial classifications was indeed part of a broader assessment of diversity, and not simply an effort to achieve racial balance, which the Court explained would be "patently unconstitutional." *Id.,* at 330.

In the present cases, by contrast, race is not considered as part of a broader effort to achieve "exposure to widely diverse people, cultures, ideas, and viewpoints," *ibid.*; race, for some students, is determinative standing alone. The districts argue that other factors, such as student preferences, affect assignment decisions under their plans, but under each plan when race comes into play, it is decisive by itself. It is not simply one factor weighed with others in reaching a decision, as in *Grutter*; it is *the* factor. Like the University of Michigan undergraduate plan struck down in *Gratz,* 539 U.S., at 275, the plans here "do not provide for a meaningful individualized review of applicants" but instead rely on racial classifications in a "nonindividualized, mechanical" way. *Id.,* at 276, 280 (O'Connor, J., concurring).

Even when it comes to race, the plans here employ only a limited notion of diversity, viewing race exclusively in white/nonwhite terms in Seattle and black/"other" terms in Jefferson County. But see *Metro Broadcasting, Inc.* v. *FCC,* 497 U.S. 547, 610 (1990) ("We are a Nation not of black and white alone, but one teeming with divergent communities knitted together with various traditions and carried forth, above all, by individuals") (O'Connor, J., dissenting). The Seattle "Board Statement Reaffirming Diversity Rationale" speaks of the "inherent educational value" in "[p]roviding students the opportunity to attend schools with diverse student enrollment." But under the Seattle plan, a school with 50 percent Asian-American students and 50 percent white students but no African-American, Native-American, or Latino students would qualify as balanced, while a school with 30 percent Asian-American, 25 percent African-American, 25 percent Latino, and 20 percent white students would not. It is hard to understand how a plan that could allow these results can be viewed as being concerned with achieving enrollment that is " 'broadly diverse,' " *Grutter, supra,* at 329. . . .

In upholding the admissions plan in *Grutter,* . . . this Court relied upon considerations unique to institutions of higher education, noting that in light of "the expansive freedoms of speech and thought associated with the university environment, universities occupy a special niche in our constitutional tradition." 539 U.S., at 329. See also *Bakke, supra,* at 312, 313 (opinion of Powell, J.). The Court explained that "[c]ontext matters" in applying strict scrutiny, and repeatedly noted that it was addressing the use of race "in the context of higher education." *Grutter, supra,* at 327, 328, 334. The Court in *Grutter* expressly articulated key limitations on its holding — defining a specific type of broad-based diversity and noting the unique context of higher education — but these limitations were largely disregarded by the lower courts in extending *Grutter* to uphold race-based assignments in elementary and secondary schools. The present cases are not governed by *Grutter.*

B

Perhaps recognizing that reliance on *Grutter* cannot sustain their plans, both school districts assert additional interests, distinct from the interest upheld in *Grutter,* to justify their race-based assignments. In briefing and argument before this Court, Seattle contends that its use of race helps to reduce racial concentration in schools and to ensure that racially concentrated housing patterns do not prevent nonwhite students from having access to the most desirable schools. Jefferson County has articulated a similar goal, phrasing its interest in terms of educating its students "in a racially integrated environment." Each school district argues that educational and broader socialization benefits flow from a racially diverse learning environment, and each contends that because the diversity they seek is racial diversity — not the broader diversity at issue in *Grutter* — it makes sense to promote that interest directly by relying on race alone.

The parties and their *amici* dispute whether racial diversity in schools in fact has a marked impact on test scores and other objective yardsticks or achieves intangible socialization benefits. The debate is not one we need to resolve, however, because it is clear that the racial classifications employed by the districts are not narrowly tailored to the goal of achieving the educational and social benefits asserted to flow from racial diversity. In design and operation, the plans are directed only to racial balance, pure and simple, an objective this Court has repeatedly condemned as illegitimate.

The plans are tied to each district's specific racial demographics, rather than to any pedagogic concept of the level of diversity needed to obtain the asserted educational benefits. In Seattle, the district seeks white enrollment of between 31 and 51 percent (within 10 percent of "the district white average" of 41 percent), and nonwhite enrollment of between 49 and 69 percent (within 10 percent of "the district minority average" of 59 percent). In Jefferson County, by contrast, the district seeks black enrollment of no less than 15 or more than 50 percent, a range designed to be "equally above and below Black student enrollment systemwide," based on the objective of achieving at "all schools . . . an African-American enrollment equivalent to the average district-wide African-American enrollment" of 34 percent. In Seattle, then, the benefits of racial diversity require enrollment of at least 31 percent white students; in Jefferson County, at least 50 percent. There must be at least 15 percent nonwhite students under Jefferson County's plan; in Seattle, more than three times that figure. This comparison makes clear that the racial demographics in each district — whatever they happen to be — drive the required "diversity" numbers. The plans here are not tailored to achieving a degree of diversity necessary to realize the asserted educational benefits; instead the plans are tailored, in the words of Seattle's Manager of Enrollment

Planning, Technical Support, and Demographics, to "the goal established by the school board of attain-ing a level of diversity within the schools that approximates the district's overall demographics."

The districts offer no evidence that the level of racial diversity necessary to achieve the asserted educational benefits happens to coincide with the racial demographics of the respective school districts—or rather the white/non-white or black/"other" balance of the districts, since that is the only diversity addressed by the plans. Indeed, in its brief Seattle simply assumes that the educational benefits track the racial breakdown of the district. ("For Seattle, 'racial balance' is clearly not an end in itself but rather a measure of the extent to which the educational goals the plan was designed to foster are likely to be achieved"). When asked for "a range of percentage that would be diverse," however, Seattle's expert said it was important to have "sufficient numbers so as to avoid students feeling any kind of specter of exceptionality." The district did not attempt to defend the proposition that anything outside its range posed the "specter of exceptionality." Nor did it demonstrate in any way how the educational and social benefits of racial diversity or avoidance of racial isolation are more likely to be achieved at a school that is 50 percent white and 50 percent Asian-American, which would qualify as diverse under Seattle's plan, than at a school that is 30 percent Asian-American, 25 percent African-American, 25 percent Latino, and 20 percent white, which under Seattle's definition would be racially concentrated.

Similarly, Jefferson County's expert referred to the importance of having "at least 20 percent" minority group representation for the group "to be visible enough to make a difference," and noted that "small isolated minority groups in a school are not likely to have a strong effect on the overall school." The Jefferson County plan, however, is based on a goal of replicating at each school "an African-American enrollment equivalent to the average district-wide African-American enrollment." Joshua McDonald's requested transfer was denied because his race was listed as "other" rather than black, and allowing the transfer would have had an adverse effect on the racial guideline compliance of Young Elementary, the school he sought to leave. At the time, however, Young Elementary was 46.8 percent black. The transfer might have had an adverse effect on the effort to approach district-wide racial proportionality at Young, but it had nothing to do with preventing either the black or "other" group from becoming "small" or "isolated" at Young.

In fact, in each case the extreme measure of relying on race in assignments is unnecessary to achieve the stated goals, even as defined by the districts. For example, at Franklin High School in Seattle, the racial tiebreaker was applied because nonwhite enrollment exceeded 69 percent, and resulted in an incoming ninth-grade class in 2000–2001 that was 30.3 percent Asian-American, 21.9 percent African-American, 6.8 percent Latino, 0.5 percent Native-American, and 40.5 percent Caucasian. Without the racial tiebreaker, the class would have been 39.6 percent Asian-American, 30.2 percent African-American, 8.3 percent Latino, 1.1 percent Native-American, and 20.8 percent Caucasian. When the actual racial breakdown is considered, enrolling students without regard to their race yields a substantially diverse student body under any definition of diversity.

In *Grutter*, the number of minority students the school sought to admit was an undefined "meaningful number" necessary to achieve a genuinely diverse student body. 539 U.S., at 316, 335–336. Although the matter was the subject of disagreement on the Court, see *id.,* at 346–347 (Scalia, J., concurring in part and dissenting in part); *id.,* at 382–383 (Rehnquist, C.J., dissenting); *id.,* at 388–392 (Kennedy, J., dissenting), the majority concluded that the law school did not count back from its applicant pool to arrive at the "meaningful number" it regarded as necessary to diversify its student body. *Id.,* at 335–336. Here the racial balance the districts seek is a defined range set solely by reference to the demographics of the respective school districts.

This working backward to achieve a particular type of racial balance, rather than working forward from some demonstration of the level of diversity that provides the purported benefits, is a fatal flaw under our existing precedent. We have many times over reaffirmed that "[r]acial balance is not to be achieved for its own sake." *Freeman*, 503 U.S., at 494. See also *Richmond* v. *J. A. Croson Co.*, 488 U.S. 469, 507 (1989); *Bakke*, 438 U.S., at 307 (opinion of Powell, J.) ("If petitioner's purpose is to assure within its student body some specified percentage of a particular group merely because of its race or ethnic origin, such a preferential purpose must be rejected . . . as facially invalid"). *Grutter* itself reiterated that "outright racial balancing" is "patently unconstitutional." 539 U.S., at 330.

Accepting racial balancing as a compelling state interest would justify the imposition of racial proportionality throughout American society, contrary to our repeated recognition that "[a]t the heart of the Constitution's guarantee of equal protection lies the simple command that the Government must treat citizens as individuals, not as simply components of a racial, religious, sexual or national class." *Miller* v. *Johnson*, 515 U.S. 900, 911 (1995) (quoting *Metro Broadcasting*, 497 U.S., at 602 (O'Connor, J., dissenting); internal quotation marks omitted).[14] Allowing racial balancing as a compelling end in itself would "effectively assur[e] that race will always be relevant in American life, and that the 'ultimate goal' of 'eliminating entirely from governmental decisionmaking such irrelevant factors as a human being's race' will never be achieved." *Croson, supra*, at 495 (plurality opinion of O'Connor, J.) (quoting *Wygant* v. *Jackson Bd. of Ed.*, 476 U.S. 267, 320 (1986) (Stevens, J., dissenting), in turn quoting *Fullilove,* 448 U.S., at 547 (Stevens, J., dissenting); brackets and citation omitted). An interest "linked to nothing other than proportional representation of various races . . . would support indefinite use of racial classifications, employed first to obtain the appropriate mixture of racial views and then to ensure that the [program] continues to reflect that mixture." *Metro Broadcasting, supra*, at 614 (O'Connor, J., dissenting).

The validity of our concern that racial balancing has "no logical stopping point," *Croson, supra*, at 498 (quoting *Wygant, supra*, at 275 (plurality opinion); internal quotation marks omitted); see also *Grutter, supra*, at 343, is demonstrated here by the degree to which the districts tie their racial guidelines to their demographics. As the districts' demographics shift, so too will their definition of racial diversity. (describing application of racial tiebreaker based on "*current* white percentage" of 41 percent and "*current* minority percentage" of 59 percent (emphasis added)).

The Ninth Circuit below stated that it "share[d] in the hope" expressed in *Grutter* that in 25 years racial preferences would no longer be necessary to further the interest identified in that case. But in Seattle the plans are defended as necessary to address the consequences of racially identifiable housing patterns. The sweep of the mandate claimed by the district is contrary to our rulings that remedying past societal discrimination does not justify race-conscious government action. See, *e.g., Shaw* v. *Hunt,* 517 U.S. 899, 909–910 (1996) ("[A]n effort to alleviate the effects of societal discrimination is not a compelling interest"); *Croson, supra,* at 498–499; *Wygant,* 476 U.S., at 276 (plurality opinion) ("Societal discrimination, without more, is too amorphous a basis for imposing a racially classified remedy"); *id.,* at 288 (O'Connor, J., concurring in part and concurring in judgment) ("[A] governmental agency's interest in remedying 'societal' discrimination, that is, discrimination not traceable to its own actions, cannot be deemed sufficiently compelling to pass constitutional muster").

The principle that racial balancing is not permitted is one of substance, not semantics. Racial balancing is not transformed from "patently unconstitutional" to a compelling state interest simply by relabeling it "racial diversity." While the school districts use various verbal formulations to describe the interest they seek to promote—racial diversity, avoidance of racial isolation, racial integration—they offer no definition of the interest that suggests it differs from racial balance. ("Q. What's your understanding of when a school suffers from racial isolation? A. I don't have a definition for that"); *id.,* at 228a–229a ("I don't think we've ever sat down and said, 'Define racially concentrated school exactly on point in quantitative terms.' I don't think we've ever had that conversation"); ("Q. How does the Jefferson County School Board define diversity . . . ?" "A. Well, we want to have the schools that make up the percentage of students of the population").

Jefferson County phrases its interest as "racial integration," but integration certainly does not require the sort of racial proportionality reflected in its plan. Even in the context of mandatory desegregation, we have stressed that racial proportionality is not required, see *Milliken,* 433 U.S., at 280, n.14 ("[A desegregation] order contemplating the substantive constitutional right [to a] particular degree of racial balance or mixing is . . . infirm as a matter of law" (internal quotation marks omitted)); *Swann* v. *Charlotte-Mecklenburg Bd. of Ed.,* 402 U.S. 1, 24 (1971) ("The constitutional command to desegregate schools does not mean that every school in every community must always reflect the racial composition of the school system as a whole"), and here Jefferson County has already been found to have eliminated the vestiges of its prior segregated school system.

The en banc Ninth Circuit declared that "when a racially diverse school system is the goal (or racial concentration or isolation is the problem), there is no more effective means than a consideration of race to achieve the solution." For the foregoing reasons, this conclusory argument cannot sustain the plans. However closely related race-based assignments may be to achieving racial balance, that itself cannot be the goal, whether labeled "racial diversity" or anything else. To the extent the objective is sufficient diversity so that students see fellow students as individuals rather than solely as members of a racial group, using means that treat students solely as members of a racial group is fundamentally at cross-purposes with that end.

C

The districts assert, as they must, that the way in which they have employed individual racial classifications is necessary to achieve their stated ends. The minimal effect these classifications have on student assignments, however, suggests that other means would be effective. Seattle's racial tiebreaker results, in the end, only in shifting a small number of students between schools. Approximately 307 student assignments were affected by the racial tiebreaker in 2000-2001; the district was able to track the enrollment status of 293 of these students. Of these, 209 were assigned to a school that was one of their choices, 87 of whom were assigned to the same school to which they would have been assigned without the racial tiebreaker. Eighty-four students were assigned to schools that they did not list as a choice, but 29 of those students would have been assigned to their respective school without the racial tiebreaker, and 3 were able to attend one of the oversubscribed schools due to waitlist and capacity adjustments. In over one-third of the assignments affected by the racial tiebreaker, then, the use of race in the end made no difference, and the district could identify only 52 students who were ultimately affected adversely by the racial tiebreaker in that it resulted in assignment to a school they had not listed as a preference and to which they would not otherwise have been assigned.

As the panel majority in *Parents Involved VI* concluded:

"[T]he tiebreaker's annual effect is thus merely to shuffle a few handfuls of different minority students between a few schools—about a dozen additional Latinos into Ballard, a dozen black students into Nathan Hale, perhaps two dozen Asians into Roosevelt, and so on. The District has not met its burden of proving these marginal changes . . . outweigh the cost of subjecting hundreds of students to disparate treatment based solely upon the color of their skin."

Similarly, Jefferson County's use of racial classifications has only a minimal effect on the assignment of students. Elementary school students are assigned to their first- or second-choice school 95 percent of the time, and transfers, which account for roughly 5 percent of assignments, are only denied 35 percent of the time—and presumably an even smaller percentage are denied on the basis of the racial guidelines, given that other factors may lead to a denial. *McFarland I*, 330 F.Supp. 2d, at 844–845, nn. 16, 18. Jefferson County estimates that the racial guidelines account for only 3 percent of assignments. As Jefferson County explains, "the racial guidelines have minimal impact in this process, because they 'mostly influence student assignment in subtle and indirect ways.' "

While we do not suggest that *greater* use of race would be preferable, the minimal impact of the districts' racial classifications on school enrollment casts doubt on the necessity of using racial classifications. In *Grutter*, the consideration of race was viewed as indispensable in more than tripling minority representation at the law school—from 4 to 14.5 percent. See 539 U.S., at 320. Here the most Jefferson County itself claims is that "because the guidelines provide a firm definition of the Board's goal of racially integrated schools, they 'provide administrators with the authority to facilitate, negotiate and collaborate with principals and staff to maintain schools within the 15–50% range.'" Classifying and assigning schoolchildren according to a binary conception of race is an extreme approach in light of our precedents and our Nation's history of using race in public schools, and requires more than such an amorphous end to justify it.

The districts have also failed to show that they considered methods other than explicit racial classifications to achieve their stated goals. Narrow tailoring requires "serious, good faith consideration of workable race-neutral alternatives," *Grutter, supra,* at 339, and yet in Seattle several alternative assignment plans—many of which would not have used express racial classifications—were rejected with little or no consideration. Jefferson County has failed to present any evidence that it considered alternatives, even though the district already claims that its goals are achieved primarily through means other than the racial classifications. Compare *Croson,* 488 U.S., at 519 (Kennedy, J., concurring in part and concurring in judgment) (racial classifications permitted only "as a last resort").

IV

Justice Breyer's dissent takes a different approach to these cases, one that fails to ground the result it would reach in law. Instead, it selectively relies on inapplicable precedent and even dicta while dismissing contrary holdings, alters and misapplies our well-established legal framework for assessing equal protection challenges to express racial classifications, and greatly exaggerates the consequences of today's decision.

To begin with, Justice Breyer seeks to justify the plans at issue under our precedents recognizing the compelling interest in remedying past intentional discrimination. Not even the school districts go this far, and for good reason. The distinction between segregation by state action and racial imbalance caused by other factors has been central to our jurisprudence in this area for generations. See, *e.g., Milliken,* 433 U.S., at 280, n.14; *Freeman,* 503 U.S., at 495–496 ("Where resegregation is a product not of state action but of private choices, it does not have constitutional implications"). The dissent elides this distinction between *de jure* and *de facto* segregation, casually intimates that Seattle's school attendance patterns reflect illegal segregation, and fails to credit the judicial determination—under the most rigorous standard—that Jefferson County had eliminated the vestiges of prior segregation. The dissent thus alters in fundamental ways not only the facts presented here but the established law. . . .

Justice Breyer's dissent also asserts that these cases are controlled by *Grutter,* claiming that the existence of a compelling interest in these cases "follows *a fortiori*" from *Grutter,* at 41, 64–66, and accusing us of tacitly overruling that case. The dissent overreads *Grutter,* however, in suggesting that it renders pure racial balancing a constitutionally compelling interest; *Grutter* itself recognized that using race simply to achieve racial balance would be "patently unconstitutional," 539 U.S., at 330. The Court was exceedingly careful in describing the interest furthered in *Grutter* as "not an interest in simple ethnic diversity" but rather a "far broader array of qualifications and characteristics" in which race was but a single element. 539 U.S., at 324–325 (internal quotation marks omitted). We take the *Grutter* Court at its word. We simply do not understand how Justice Breyer can maintain that classifying every schoolchild as black or white, and using that classification as a determinative factor in assigning children to achieve pure racial balance, can be regarded as "less burdensome, and hence more narrowly tailored" than the consideration of race in *Grutter*, when the Court in *Grutter* stated that "[t]he importance of . . . individualized consideration" in the program was "paramount," and consideration of race was one factor in a "highly individualized, holistic review." 539 U.S., at 337. Certainly if the constitutionality of the stark use of race in these cases were as established as the dissent would have it, there would have been no need for the extensive analysis undertaken in *Grutter*. In light of the foregoing, Justice Breyer's appeal to *stare decisis* rings particularly hollow.

At the same time it relies on inapplicable desegregation cases, misstatements of admitted dicta, and other noncontrolling pronouncements, Justice Breyer's dissent candidly dismisses the significance of this Court's repeated *holdings* that all racial classifications must be reviewed under strict scrutiny, arguing that a different standard of review should be applied because the districts use race for beneficent rather than malicious purposes.

This Court has recently reiterated, however, that " '*all* racial classifications [imposed by government] . . . must be analyzed by a reviewing court under strict scrutiny.' " *Johnson*, 543 U.S., at 505 (quoting *Adarand*, 515 U.S., at 227; emphasis added by *Johnson* Court). See also *Grutter, supra*, at 326 ("[G]overnmental action based on race—a group classification long recognized as in most circumstances irrelevant and therefore prohibited—should be subjected to detailed judicial inquiry" Justice Breyer nonetheless relies on the good intentions and motives of the school districts, stating that he has found "no case that . . . repudiated this constitutional asymmetry between that which seeks to *exclude* and that which seeks to *include* members of minority races." (emphasis in original). We have found many. Our cases clearly reject the argument that motives affect the strict scrutiny analysis. See *Johnson, supra*, at 505 ("We have insisted on strict scrutiny in every context, even for so-called 'benign' racial classifications"); *Adarand*, 515 U.S., at 227 (rejecting idea that " 'benign' " racial classifications may be held to "different standard"); *Croson*, 488 U.S., at 500 ("Racial classifications are suspect, and that means that simple legislative assurances of good intention cannot suffice").

This argument that different rules should govern racial classifications designed to include rather than exclude is not new; it has been repeatedly pressed in the past, see, *e.g.*, *Gratz*, 539 U.S., at 282 (Breyer, J., concurring in judgment); *id.*, at 301 (Ginsburg, J., dissenting); *Adarand, supra*, at 243 (Stevens, J., dissenting); *Wygant*, 476 U.S., at 316–317 (Stevens, J., dissenting), and has been repeatedly rejected. See also *Bakke*, 438 U.S., at 289–291 (opinion of Powell, J.) (rejecting argument that strict scrutiny should be applied only to classifications that disadvantage minorities, stating "[r]acial and ethnic distinctions of any sort are inherently suspect and thus call for the most exacting judicial examination").

The reasons for rejecting a motives test for racial classifications are clear enough. "The Court's emphasis on 'benign racial classifications' suggests confidence in its ability to distinguish good from harmful governmental uses of racial criteria. History should teach greater humility. . . . '[B]enign' carries with it no independent meaning, but reflects only acceptance of the current generation's conclusion that a politically acceptable burden, imposed on particular citizens on the basis of race, is reasonable." *Metro Broadcasting,* 497 U.S., at 609–610 (O'Connor, J., dissenting). See also *Adarand, supra,* at 226 ("'[I]t may not always be clear that a so-called preference is in fact benign'" (quoting *Bakke, supra,* at 298 (opinion of Powell, J.))). Accepting Justice Breyer's approach would "do no more than move us from 'separate but equal' to 'unequal but benign.'" *Metro Broadcasting, supra,* at 638 (Kennedy, J., dissenting).

Justice Breyer speaks of bringing "the races" together (putting aside the purely black-and-white nature of the plans), as the justification for excluding individuals on the basis of their race. Again, this approach to racial classifications is fundamentally at odds with our precedent, which makes clear that the Equal Protection Clause "protect[s] *persons,* not *groups,*" *Adarand,* 515 U.S., at 227 (emphasis in original).

Justice Breyer also suggests that other means for achieving greater racial diversity in schools are necessarily unconstitutional if the racial classifications at issue in these cases cannot survive strict scrutiny. These other means—*e.g.,* where to construct new schools, how to allocate resources among schools, and which academic offerings to provide to attract students to certain schools—implicate different considerations than the explicit racial classifications at issue in these cases, and we express no opinion on their validity—not even in dicta. Rather, we employ the familiar and well-established analytic approach of strict scrutiny to evaluate the plans at issue today, an approach that in no way warrants the dissent's cataclysmic concerns. Under that approach, the school districts have not carried their burden of showing that the ends they seek justify the particular extreme means they have chosen—classifying individual students on the basis of their race and discriminating among them on that basis. . . .

If the need for the racial classifications embraced by the school districts is unclear, even on the districts' own terms, the costs are undeniable. "[D]istinctions between citizens solely because of their ancestry are by their very nature odious to a free people whose institutions are founded upon the doctrine of equality." *Adarand,* 515 U.S., at 214 (internal quotation marks omitted). Government action dividing us by race is inherently suspect because such classifications promote "notions of racial inferiority and lead to a politics of racial hostility," *Croson, supra,* at 493, "reinforce the belief, held by too many for too much of our history, that individuals should be judged by the color of their skin," *Shaw* v. *Reno,* 509 U.S. 630, 657 (1993), and "endorse race-based reasoning and the conception of a Nation divided into racial blocs, thus contributing to an escalation of racial hostility and conflict." *Metro Broadcasting,* 497 U.S., at 603 (O'Connor, J., dissenting). As the Court explained in *Rice* v. *Cayetano,* 528 U.S. 495, 517 (2000), "[o]ne of the principal reasons race is treated as a forbidden classification is that it demeans the dignity and worth of a person to be judged by ancestry instead of by his or her own merit and essential qualities."

All this is true enough in the contexts in which these statements were made—government contracting, voting districts, allocation of broadcast licenses, and electing state officers—but when it comes to using race to assign children to schools, history will be heard. In *Brown* v. *Board of Education*, 347 U.S. 483 (1954) (*Brown I*), we held that segregation deprived black children of equal educational opportunities regardless of whether school facilities and other tangible factors were equal, because government classification and separation on grounds of race themselves denoted inferiority. *Id.*, at 493–494. It was not the inequality of the facilities but the fact of legally separating children on the basis of race on which the Court relied to find a constitutional violation in 1954. See *id.*, at 494 ("'The impact [of segregation] is greater when it has the sanction of the law'"). The next Term, we accordingly stated that "full compliance" with *Brown I* required school districts "to achieve a system of determining admission to the public schools *on a nonracial basis*." *Brown II*, 349 U.S., at 300-301 (emphasis added).

The parties and their *amici* debate which side is more faithful to the heritage of *Brown*, but the position of the plaintiffs in *Brown* was spelled out in their brief and could not have been clearer: "[T]he Fourteenth Amendment prevents states from according differential treatment to American children on the basis of their color or race." What do the racial classifications at issue here do, if not accord differential treatment on the basis of race? As counsel who appeared before this Court for the plaintiffs in *Brown* put it: "We have one fundamental contention which we will seek to develop in the course of this argument, and that contention is that no State has any authority under the equal-protection clause of the Fourteenth Amendment to use race as a factor in affording educational opportunities among its citizens." There is no ambiguity in that statement. And it was that position that prevailed in this Court, which emphasized in its remedial opinion that what was "[a]t stake is the personal interest of the plaintiffs in admission to public schools as soon as practicable *on a non-discriminatory basis*," and what was required was "determining admission to the public schools *on a nonracial basis*." *Brown II*, *supra*, at 300-301 (emphasis added). What do the racial classifications do in these cases, if not determine admission to a public school on a racial basis? Before *Brown*, schoolchildren were told where they could and could not go to school based on the color of their skin. The school districts in these cases have not carried the heavy burden of demonstrating that we should allow this once again—even for very different reasons. For schools that never segregated on the basis of race, such as Seattle, or that have removed the vestiges of past segregation, such as Jefferson County, the way "to achieve a system of determining admission to the public schools on a nonracial basis," *Brown II*, 349 U.S., at 300-301, is to stop assigning students on a racial basis. The way to stop discrimination on the basis of race is to stop discriminating on the basis of race.

The judgments of the Courts of Appeals for the Sixth and Ninth Circuits are reversed, and the cases are remanded for further proceedings.

It is so ordered.

JUSTICE KENNEDY, concurring in part and concurring in the judgment.

The Nation's schools strive to teach that our strength comes from people of different races, creeds, and cultures uniting in commitment to the freedom of all. In these cases two school districts in different parts of the country seek to teach that principle by having classrooms that reflect the racial makeup of the surrounding community. That the school districts consider these plans to be necessary should remind us our highest aspirations are yet unfulfilled. But the solutions mandated by these school districts must themselves be lawful. To make race matter now so that it might not matter later may entrench the very prejudices we seek to overcome. In my view the state-mandated racial classifications at issue, official labels proclaiming the race of all persons in a broad class of citizens—elementary school students in one case, high school students in another—are unconstitutional as the cases now come to us.

I agree with The Chief Justice that we have jurisdiction to decide the cases before us and join Parts I and II of the Court's opinion. I also join Parts III-A and III-C for reasons provided below. My views do not allow me to join the balance of the opinion by The Chief Justice, which seems to me to be inconsistent in both its approach and its implications with the history, meaning, and reach of the Equal Protection Clause. Justice Breyer's dissenting opinion, on the other hand, rests on what in my respectful submission is a misuse and mistaken interpretation of our precedents. This leads it to advance propositions that, in my view, are both erroneous and in fundamental conflict with basic equal protection principles. As a consequence, this separate opinion is necessary to set forth my conclusions in the two cases before the Court.

I

The opinion of the Court and Justice Breyer's dissenting opinion (hereinafter dissent) describe in detail the history of integration efforts in Louisville and Seattle. These plans classify individuals by race and allocate benefits and burdens on that basis; and as a result, they are to be subjected to strict scrutiny. See *Johnson* v. *California*, 543 U.S. 499, 505-506 (2005); *ante*, at 11. The dissent finds that the school districts have identified a compelling interest in increasing diversity, including for the purpose of avoiding racial isolation. See *post*, at 37-45. The plurality, by contrast, does not acknowledge that the school districts have identified a compelling interest here. See *ante*, at 17–25. For this reason, among others, I do not join Parts III-B and IV. Diversity, depending on its meaning and definition, is a compelling educational goal a school district may pursue.

It is well established that when a governmental policy is subjected to strict scrutiny, "the government has the burden of proving that racial classifications 'are narrowly tailored measures that further compelling governmental interests.'" *Johnson, supra*, at 505 (quoting *Adarand Constructors, Inc.* v. *Pena*, 515 U.S. 200, 227 (1995)). "Absent searching judicial inquiry into the justification for such race-based measures, there is simply no way of determining what classifications are 'benign' or 'remedial' and what classifications are in fact motivated by illegitimate notions of racial inferiority or simple racial politics." *Richmond* v. *J. A. Croson Co.*, 488 U.S. 469, 493 (1989) (plurality opinion). And the inquiry into less restrictive alternatives demanded by the narrow tailoring analysis requires in many cases a thorough understanding of how a plan works. The government bears the burden of justifying its use of individual racial classifications. As part of that burden it must establish, in detail, how decisions based on an individual student's race are made in a challenged governmental program. The Jefferson County Board of Education fails to meet this threshold mandate.

Petitioner Crystal Meredith challenges the district's decision to deny her son Joshua McDonald a requested transfer for his kindergarten enrollment. The district concedes it denied his request "under the guidelines," which is to say, on the basis of Joshua's race. Yet the district also maintains that the guidelines do not apply to "kindergartens," and it fails to explain the discrepancy. Resort to the record, including the parties' Stipulation of Facts, further confuses the matter.

The discrepancy identified is not some simple and straightforward error that touches only upon the peripheries of the district's use of individual racial classifications. To the contrary, Jefferson County in its briefing has explained how and when it employs these classifications only in terms so broad and imprecise that they cannot withstand strict scrutiny. While it acknowledges that racial classifications are used to make certain assignment decisions, it fails to make clear, for example, who makes the decisions; what if any oversight is employed; the precise circumstances in which an assignment decision will or will not be made on the basis of race; or how it is determined which of two similarly situated children will be subjected to a given race-based decision.

When litigation, as here, involves a "complex, comprehensive plan that contains multiple strategies for achieving racially integrated schools," Brief for Respondents in No. 05–915, at 4, these ambiguities become all the more problematic in light of the contradictions and confusions that result.

One can attempt to identify a construction of Jefferson County's student assignment plan that, at least as a logical matter, complies with these competing propositions; but this does not remedy the underlying problem. Jefferson County fails to make clear to this Court—even in the limited respects implicated by Joshua's initial assignment and transfer denial—whether in fact it relies on racial classifications in a manner narrowly tailored to the interest in question, rather than in the far-reaching, inconsistent, and *ad hoc* manner that a less forgiving reading of the record would suggest. When a court subjects governmental action to strict scrutiny, it cannot construe ambiguities in favor of the State.

As for the Seattle case, the school district has gone further in describing the methods and criteria used to determine assignment decisions on the basis of individual racial classifications. The district, nevertheless, has failed to make an adequate showing in at least one respect. It has failed to explain why, in a district composed of a diversity of races, with fewer than half of the students classified as "white," it has employed the crude racial categories of "white" and "non-white" as the basis for its assignment decisions.

The district has identified its purposes as follows: "(1) to promote the educational benefits of diverse school enrollments; (2) to reduce the potentially harmful effects of racial isolation by allowing students the opportunity to opt out of racially isolated schools; and (3) to make sure that racially segregated housing patterns did not prevent non-white students from having equitable access to the most popular over-subscribed schools." Yet the school district does not explain how, in the context of its diverse student population, a blunt distinction between "white" and "non-white" furthers these goals. As the Court explains, "a school with 50 percent Asian-American students and 50 percent white students but no African-American, Native-American, or Latino students would qualify as balanced, while a school with 30 percent Asian-American, 25 percent African-American, 25 percent Latino, and 20 percent white students would not." Far from being narrowly tailored to its purposes, this system threatens to defeat its own ends, and the school district has provided no convincing explanation for its design. Other problems are evident in Seattle's system, but there is no need to address them now. As the district fails to account for the classification system it has chosen, despite what appears to be its ill fit, Seattle has not shown its plan to be narrowly tailored to achieve its own ends; and thus it fails to pass strict scrutiny.

II

Our Nation from the inception has sought to preserve and expand the promise of liberty and equality on which it was founded. Today we enjoy a society that is remarkable in its openness and opportunity. Yet our tradition is to go beyond present achievements, however significant, and to recognize and confront the flaws and injustices that remain. This is especially true when we seek assurance that opportunity is not denied on account of race. The enduring hope is that race should not matter; the reality is that too often it does.

This is by way of preface to my respectful submission that parts of the opinion by The Chief Justice imply an all-too-unyielding insistence that race cannot be a factor in instances when, in my view, it may be taken into account. The plurality opinion is too dismissive of the legitimate interest government has in ensuring all people have equal opportunity regardless of their race. The plurality's postulate that "[t]he way to stop discrimination on the basis of race is to stop discriminating on the basis of race," is not sufficient to decide these cases. Fifty years of experience since *Brown* v. *Board of Education,* 347 U.S. 483 (1954), should teach us that the problem before us defies so easy a solution. School districts can seek to reach *Brown*'s objective of equal educational opportunity. The plurality opinion is at least open to the interpretation that the Constitution requires school districts to ignore the problem of *de facto* resegregation in schooling. I cannot endorse that conclusion. To the extent the plurality opinion suggests the Constitution mandates that state and local school authorities must accept the status quo of racial isolation in schools, it is, in my view, profoundly mistaken.

The statement by Justice Harlan that "[o]ur Constitution is color-blind" was most certainly justified in the context of his dissent in *Plessy* v. *Ferguson,* 163 U.S. 537, 559 (1896). The Court's decision in that case was a grievous error it took far too long to overrule. *Plessy,* of course, concerned official classification by race applicable to all persons who sought to use railway carriages. And, as an aspiration, Justice Harlan's axiom must command our assent. In the real world, it is regrettable to say, it cannot be a universal constitutional principle.

In the administration of public schools by the state and local authorities it is permissible to consider the racial makeup of schools and to adopt general policies to encourage a diverse student body, one aspect of which is its racial composition. Cf. *Grutter* v. *Bollinger,* 539 U.S. 306 (2003); *id.,* at 387–388 (Kennedy, J., dissenting). If school authorities are concerned that the student-body compositions of certain schools interfere with the objective of offering an equal educational opportunity to all of their students, they are free to devise race-conscious measures to address the problem in a general way and without treating each student in different fashion solely on the basis of a systematic, individual typing by race.

School boards may pursue the goal of bringing together students of diverse backgrounds and races through other means, including strategic site selection of new schools; drawing attendance zones with general recognition of the demographics of neighborhoods; allocating resources for special programs; recruiting students and faculty in a targeted fashion; and tracking enrollments, performance, and other statistics by race. These mechanisms are race conscious but do not lead to different treatment based on a classification that tells each student he or she is to be defined by race, so it is unlikely any of them would demand strict scrutiny to be found permissible. See *Bush* v. *Vera,* 517 U.S. 952, 958 (1996) (plurality opinion) ("Strict scrutiny does not apply merely because redistricting is performed with consciousness of race. . . . Electoral district lines are 'facially race neutral' so a more searching inquiry is necessary before strict scrutiny can be found applicable in redistricting cases than in cases of 'classifications based explicitly on race' " (quoting *Adarand,* 515 U.S., at 213)). Executive and legislative branches, which for generations now have considered these types of policies and procedures, should be permitted to employ them with candor and with confidence that a constitutional violation does not occur whenever a decisionmaker considers the impact a given approach might have on students of different races. Assigning to each student a personal designation according to a crude system of individual racial classifications is quite a different matter; and the legal analysis changes accordingly.

Each respondent has asserted that its assignment of individual students by race is permissible because there is no other way to avoid racial isolation in the school districts. Yet, as explained, each has failed to provide the support necessary for that proposition. Cf. *Croson,* 488 U.S., at 501 ("The history of racial classifications in this country suggests that blind judicial deference to legislative or executive pronouncements of necessity has no place in equal protection analysis"). And individual racial classifications employed in this manner may be considered legitimate only if they are a last resort to achieve a compelling interest. See *id.,* at 519 (Kennedy, J., concurring in part and concurring in judgment).

In the cases before us it is noteworthy that the number of students whose assignment depends on express racial classifications is limited. I join Part III-C of the Court's opinion because I agree that in the context of these plans, the small number of assignments affected suggests that the schools could have achieved their stated ends through different means. These include the facially race-neutral means set forth above or, if necessary, a more nuanced, individual evaluation of school needs and student characteristics that might include race as a component. The latter approach would be informed by *Grutter,* though of course the criteria relevant to student placement would differ based on the age of the students, the needs of the parents, and the role of the schools.

III

The dissent rests on the assumptions that these sweeping race-based classifications of persons are permitted by existing precedents; that its confident endorsement of race categories for each child in a large segment of the community presents no danger to individual freedom in other, prospective realms of governmental regulation; and that the racial classifications used here cause no hurt or anger of the type the Constitution prevents. Each of these premises is, in my respectful view, incorrect.

A

The dissent's reliance on this Court's precedents to justify the explicit, sweeping, classwide racial classifications at issue here is a misreading of our authorities that, it appears to me, tends to undermine well-accepted principles needed to guard our freedom. And in his critique of that analysis, I am in many respects in agreement with The Chief Justice. The conclusions he has set forth in Part III-A of the Court's opinion are correct, in my view, because the compelling interests implicated in the cases before us are distinct from the interests the Court has recognized in remedying the effects of past intentional discrimination and in increasing diversity in higher education. As the Court notes, we recognized the compelling nature of the interest in remedying past intentional discrimination in *Freeman* v. *Pitts*, 503 U.S. 467, 494 (1992), and of the interest in diversity in higher education in *Grutter*. At the same time, these compelling interests, in my view, do help inform the present inquiry. And to the extent the plurality opinion can be interpreted to foreclose consideration of these interests, I disagree with that reasoning.

As to the dissent, the general conclusions upon which it relies have no principled limit and would result in the broad acceptance of governmental racial classifications in areas far afield from schooling. The dissent's permissive strict scrutiny (which bears more than a passing resemblance to rational-basis review) could invite widespread governmental deployment of racial classifications. There is every reason to think that, if the dissent's rationale were accepted, Congress, assuming an otherwise proper exercise of its spending authority or commerce power, could mandate either the Seattle or the Jefferson County plans nationwide. There seems to be no principled rule, moreover, to limit the dissent's rationale to the context of public schools. The dissent emphasizes local control, see *post*, at 48-49, the unique history of school desegregation, see *post*, at 2, and the fact that these plans make less use of race than prior plans, see *post*, at 57, but these factors seem more rhetorical than integral to the analytical structure of the opinion.

This brings us to the dissent's reliance on the Court's opinions in *Gratz* v. *Bollinger*, 539 U.S. 244 (2003), and *Grutter*, 539 U.S. 306. If today's dissent said it was adhering to the views expressed in the separate opinions in *Gratz* and *Grutter*, see *Gratz*, 539 U.S., at 281 (Breyer, J., concurring in judgment); *id.*, at 282 (Stevens, J., dissenting); *id.*, at 291 (Souter, J., dissenting); *id.*, at 298

(Ginsburg, J., dissenting); *Grutter, supra*, at 344 (Ginsburg, J., concurring),that would be understandable, and likely within the tradition—to be invoked, in my view, in rare instances—that permits us to maintain our own positions in the face of *stare decisis* when fundamental points of doctrine are at stake. See, *e.g., Federal Maritime Comm'n* v. *South Carolina Ports Authority*, 535 U.S. 743, 770 (2002) (Stevens, J., dissenting). To say, however, that we must ratify the racial classifications here at issue based on the majority opinions in *Gratz* and *Grutter* is, with all respect, simply baffling.

Gratz involved a system where race was not the entire classification. The procedures in *Gratz* placed much less reliance on race than do the plans at issue here. The issue in *Gratz* arose, moreover, in the context of college admissions where students had other choices and precedent supported the proposition that First Amendment interests give universities particular latitude in defining diversity. See *Regents of Univ. of Cal.* v. *Bakke*, 438 U.S. 265, 312-314 (1978) (opinion of Powell, J.). Even so the race factor was found to be invalid. *Gratz, supra*, at 251. If *Gratz* is to be the measure, the racial classification systems here are *a fortiori* invalid. If the dissent were to say that college cases are simply not applicable to public school systems in kindergarten through high school, this would seem to me wrong, but at least an arguable distinction. Under no fair reading, though, can the majority opinion in *Gratz* be cited as authority to sustain the racial classifications under consideration here.

The same must be said for the controlling opinion in *Grutter*. There the Court sustained a system that, it found, was flexible enough to take into account "all pertinent elements of diversity," 539 U.S., at 341 (internal quotation marks omitted), and considered race as only one factor among many, *id.*, at 340. Seattle's plan, by contrast, relies upon a mechanical formula that has denied hundreds of students their preferred schools on the basis of three rigid criteria: placement of siblings, distance from schools, and race. If those students were considered for a whole range of their talents and school needs with race as just one consideration, *Grutter* would have some application. That, though, is not the case. The only support today's dissent can draw from *Grutter* must be found in its various separate opinions, not in the opinion filed for the Court.

B

To uphold these programs the Court is asked to brush aside two concepts of central importance for determining the validity of laws and decrees designed to alleviate the hurt and adverse consequences resulting from race discrimination. The first is the difference between *de jure* and *de facto* segregation; the second, the presumptive invalidity of a State's use of racial classifications to differentiate its treatment of individuals.

In the immediate aftermath of *Brown* the Court addressed other instances where laws and practices enforced *de jure* segregation. See, *e.g., Loving* v. *Virginia*, 388 U.S. 1 (1967) (marriage); *New Orleans City Park Improvement Assn.* v. *Detiege*, 358 U.S. 54 (1958) *(per curiam)* (public parks); *Gayle* v. *Browder*, 352 U.S. 903 (1956) *(per curiam)* (buses); *Holmes* v. *Atlanta*, 350 U.S. 879 (1955) *(per curiam)* (golf courses); *Mayor of Baltimore* v. *Dawson*, 350 U.S. 877 (1955) *(per curiam)* (beaches). But with reference to schools, the effect of the legal wrong proved most difficult to correct. To remedy the wrong, school districts that had been segregated by law had no choice, whether under court supervision or pursuant to voluntary desegregation efforts, but to resort to extraordinary measures including individual student and teacher assignment to schools based on race. See, *e.g., Swann* v. *Charlotte-Mecklenburg Bd. of Ed.*, 402 U.S. 1, 8-10 (1971); see also *Croson*, 488 U.S., at 519 (KENNEDY, J., concurring in part and concurring in judgment) (noting that racial classifications "may be the only adequate remedy after a judicial determination that a State or its instrumentality has violated the Equal Protection Clause"). So it was, as the dissent observes, that Louisville classified children by race in its school assignment and busing plan in the 1970's.

Our cases recognized a fundamental difference between those school districts that had engaged in *de jure* segregation and those whose segregation was the result of other factors. School districts that had engaged in *de jure* segregation had an affirmative constitutional duty to desegregate; those that were *de facto* segregated did not. Compare *Green* v. *School Bd. of New Kent Cty.*, 391 U.S. 430, 437-438 (1968), with *Milliken* v. *Bradley*, 418 U.S. 717, 745 (1974). The distinctions between *de jure* and *de facto* segregation extended to the remedies available to governmental units in addition to the courts. For example, in *Wygant* v. *Jackson Bd. of Ed.*, 476 U.S. 267, 274 (1986), the plurality noted: "This Court never has held that societal discrimination alone is sufficient to justify a racial classification. Rather, the Court has insisted upon some showing of prior discrimination by the governmental unit involved before allowing limited use of racial classifications in order to remedy such discrimination." The Court's decision in *Croson, supra,* reinforced the difference between the remedies available to redress *de facto* and *de jure* discrimination:

"To accept [a] claim that past societal discrimination alone can serve as the basis for rigid racial preferences would be to open the door to competing claims for 'remedial relief' for every disadvantaged group. The dream of a Nation of equal citizens in a society where race is irrelevant to personal opportunity and achievement would be lost in a mosaic of shifting preferences based on inherently unmeasurable claims of past wrongs." *Id.*, at 505-506.

From the standpoint of the victim, it is true, an injury stemming from racial prejudice can hurt as much when the demeaning treatment based on race identity stems from bias masked deep within the social order as when it is imposed by law. The distinction between government and private action, furthermore, can be amorphous both as a historical matter and as a matter of present-day finding of fact. Laws arise from a culture and vice versa. Neither can assign to the other all responsibility for persisting injustices.

Yet, like so many other legal categories that can overlap in some instances, the constitutional distinction between *de jure* and *de facto* segregation has been thought to be an important one. It must be conceded its primary function in school cases was to delimit the powers of the Judiciary in the fashioning of remedies. See, *e.g., Milliken, supra,* at 746. The distinction ought not to be altogether disregarded, however, when we come to that most sensitive of all racial issues, an attempt by the government to treat whole classes of persons differently based on the government's systematic classification of each individual by race. There, too, the distinction serves as a limit on the exercise of a power that reaches to the very verge of constitutional authority. Reduction of an individual to an assigned racial identity for differential treatment is among the most pernicious actions our government can undertake. The allocation of governmental burdens and benefits, contentious under any circumstances, is even more divisive when allocations are made on the basis of individual racial classifications. See, *e.g., Regents of Univ. of Cal.* v. *Bakke*, 438 U.S. 265 (1978); *Adarand*, 515 U.S. 200.

Notwithstanding these concerns, allocation of benefits and burdens through individual racial classifications was found sometimes permissible in the context of remedies for *de jure* wrong. Where there has been *de jure* segregation, there is a cognizable legal wrong, and the courts and legislatures have broad power to remedy it. The remedy, though, was limited in time and limited to the wrong. The Court has allowed school districts to remedy their prior *de jure* segregation by classifying individual students based on their race. See *North Carolina Bd. of Ed.* v. *Swann*, 402 U.S. 43, 45-46 (1971). The limitation of this power to instances where there has been *de jure* segregation serves to confine the nature, extent, and duration of governmental reliance on individual racial classifications.

The cases here were argued upon the assumption, and come to us on the premise, that the discrimination in question did not result from *de jure* actions. And when *de facto* discrimination is at issue our tradition has been that the remedial rules are different. The State must seek alternatives to the classification and differential treatment of individuals by race, at least absent some extraordinary showing not present here.

C

The dissent refers to an opinion filed by Judge Kozinski in one of the cases now before us, and that opinion relied upon an opinion filed by Chief Judge Boudin in a case presenting an issue similar to the one here. Though this may oversimplify the matter a bit, one of the main concerns underlying those opinions was this: If it is legitimate for school authorities to work to avoid racial isolation in their schools, must they do so only by indirection and general policies? Does the Constitution mandate this inefficient result? Why may the authorities not recognize the problem in candid fashion and solve it altogether through resort to direct assignments based on student racial classifications? So, the argument proceeds, if race is the problem, then perhaps race is the solution.

The argument ignores the dangers presented by individual classifications, dangers that are not as pressing when the same ends are achieved by more indirect means. When the government classifies an individual by race, it must first define what it means to be of a race. Who exactly is white and who is nonwhite? To be forced to live under a state-mandated racial label is inconsistent with the dignity of individuals in our society. And it is a label that an individual is powerless to change. Governmental classifications that command people to march in different directions based on racial typologies can cause a new divisiveness. The practice can lead to corrosive discourse, where race serves not as an element of our diverse heritage but instead as a bargaining chip in the political process. On the other hand race-conscious measures that do not rely on differential treatment based on individual classifications present these problems to a lesser degree.

The idea that if race is the problem, race is the instrument with which to solve it cannot be accepted as an analytical leap forward. And if this is a frustrating duality of the Equal Protection Clause it simply reflects the duality of our history and our attempts to promote freedom in a world that sometimes seems set against it. Under our Constitution the individual, child or adult, can find his own identity, can define her own persona, without state intervention that classifies on the basis of his race or the color of her skin. . . .

This Nation has a moral and ethical obligation to fulfill its historic commitment to creating an integrated society that ensures equal opportunity for all of its children. A compelling interest exists in avoiding racial isolation, an interest that a school district, in its discretion and expertise, may choose to pursue. Likewise, a district may consider it a compelling interest to achieve a diverse student population. Race may be one component of that diversity, but other demographic factors, plus special talents and needs, should also be considered. What the government is not permitted to do, absent a showing of necessity not made here, is to classify every student on the basis of race and to assign each of them to schools based on that classification. Crude measures of this sort threaten to reduce children to racial chits valued and traded according to one school's supply and another's demand.

That statement, to be sure, invites this response: A sense of stigma may already become the fate of those separated out by circumstances beyond their immediate control. But to this the replication must be: Even so, measures other than differential treatment based on racial typing of individuals first must be exhausted.

The decision today should not prevent school districts from continuing the important work of bringing together students of different racial, ethnic, and economic backgrounds. Due to a variety of factors—some influenced by government, some not—neighborhoods in our communities do not reflect the diversity of our Nation as a whole. Those entrusted with directing our public schools can bring to bear the creativity of experts, parents, administrators, and other concerned citizens to find a way to achieve the compelling interests they face without resorting to widespread governmental allocation of benefits and burdens on the basis of racial classifications.

With this explanation I concur in the judgment of the Court.

JUSTICE BREYER, with whom JUSTICE STEVENS, JUSTICE SOUTER, and JUSTICE GINSBURG join, dissenting.

These cases consider the longstanding efforts of two local school boards to integrate their public schools. The school board plans before us resemble many others adopted in the last 50 years by primary and secondary schools throughout the Nation. All of those plans represent local efforts to bring about the kind of racially integrated education that *Brown* v. *Board of Education*, 347 U.S. 483 (1954), long ago promised—efforts that this Court has repeatedly required, permitted, and encouraged local authorities to undertake. This Court has recognized that the public interests at stake in such cases are "compelling." We have approved of "narrowly tailored" plans that are no less race-conscious than the plans before us. And we have understood that the Constitution *permits* local communities to adopt desegregation plans even where it does not *require* them to do so.

The plurality pays inadequate attention to this law, to past opinions' rationales, their language, and the contexts in which they arise. As a result, it reverses course and reaches the wrong conclusion. In doing so, it distorts precedent, it misapplies the relevant constitutional principles, it announces legal rules that will obstruct efforts by state and local governments to deal effectively with the growing resegregation of public schools, it threatens to substitute for present calm a disruptive round of race-related litigation, and it undermines *Brown*'s promise of integrated primary and secondary education that local communities have sought to make a reality. This cannot be justified in the name of the Equal Protection Clause. . . .

Conclusions

To show that the school assignment plans here meet the requirements of the Constitution, I have written at exceptional length. But that length is necessary. I cannot refer to the history of the plans in these cases to justify the use of race-conscious criteria without describing that history in full. I cannot rely upon *Swann*'s statement that the use of race-conscious limits is permissible without showing, rather than simply asserting, that the statement represents a constitutional principle firmly rooted in federal and state law. Nor can I explain my disagreement with the Court's holding and the plurality's opinion, without offering a detailed account of the arguments they propound and the consequences they risk.

Thus, the opinion's reasoning is long. But its conclusion is short: The plans before us satisfy the requirements of the Equal Protection Clause. And it is the plurality's opinion, not this dissent that "fails to ground the result it would reach in law."

Four basic considerations have led me to this view. *First*, the histories of Louisville and Seattle reveal complex circumstances and a long tradition of conscientious efforts by local school boards to resist racial segregation in public schools. Segregation at the time of *Brown* gave way to expansive remedies that included busing, which in turn gave rise to fears of white flight and resegregation. For decades now, these school boards have considered and adopted and revised assignment plans that sought to rely less upon race, to emphasize greater student choice, and to improve the conditions of all schools for all students, no matter the color of their skin, no matter where they happen to reside. The plans under review—which are less burdensome, more egalitarian, and more effective than prior plans—continue in that tradition. And their history reveals school district goals whose remedial, educational, and democratic elements are inextricably intertwined each with the others.

Second, since this Court's decision in *Brown*, the law has consistently and unequivocally approved of both voluntary and compulsory race-conscious measures to combat segregated schools. The Equal Protection Clause, ratified following the Civil War, has always distinguished in practice between state action that excludes and thereby subordinates racial minorities and state action that seeks to bring together people of all races. From *Swann* to *Grutter*, this Court's decisions have emphasized this distinction, recognizing that the fate of race relations in this country depends upon unity among our children, "for unless our children begin to learn together, there is little hope that our people will ever learn to live together." *Milliken*, 418 U.S., at 783 (Marshall, J., dissenting). See also C. Sumner, Equality Before the Law: Unconstitutionality of Separate Colored Schools in Massachusetts, in 2 The Works of Charles Sumner 327, 371 (1849) ("The law contemplates not only that all be taught, but that all shall be taught together").

Third, the plans before us, subjected to rigorous judicial review, are supported by compelling state interests and are narrowly tailored to accomplish those goals. Just as diversity in higher education was deemed compelling in *Grutter*, diversity in public primary and secondary schools—where there is even more to gain—must be, *a fortiori*, a compelling state interest. Even apart from *Grutter*, five Members of this Court agree that "avoiding racial isolation" and "achiev[ing] a diverse student population" remain today compelling interests. *Ante*, at 17-18 (opinion of Kennedy, J.). These interests combine remedial, educational, and democratic objectives. For the reasons discussed above, however, I disagree with Justice Kennedy that Seattle and Louisville have not done enough to demonstrate that their present plans are necessary to continue upon the path set by *Brown*. These plans are *more* "narrowly tailored" than the race-conscious law school admissions criteria at issue in *Grutter*. Hence, their lawfulness follows *a fortiori* from this Court's prior decisions.

Fourth, the plurality's approach risks serious harm to the law and for the Nation. Its view of the law rests either upon a denial of the distinction between exclusionary and inclusive use of race-conscious criteria in the context of the Equal Protection Clause, or upon such a rigid application of its "test" that the distinction loses practical significance. Consequently, the Court's decision today slows down and sets back the work of local school boards to bring about racially diverse schools.

Indeed, the consequences of the approach the Court takes today are serious. Yesterday, the plans under review were lawful. Today, they are not. Yesterday, the citizens of this Nation could look for guidance to this Court's unanimous pronouncements concerning desegregation. Today, they cannot. Yesterday, school boards had available to them a full range of means to combat segregated schools. Today, they do not.

The Court's decision undermines other basic institutional principles as well. What has happened to *stare decisis?* The history of the plans before us, their educational importance, their highly limited use of race—all these and more—make clear that the compelling interest here is stronger than in *Grutter*. The plans here are more narrowly tailored than the law school admissions program there at issue. Hence, applying *Grutter*'s strict test, their lawfulness follows *a fortiori*. To hold to the contrary is to transform that test from "strict" to "fatal in fact"—the very opposite of what *Grutter* said. And what has happened to *Swann?* To *McDaniel?* To *Crawford?* To *Harris?* To *School Committee of Boston?* To *Seattle School Dist. No. 1?* After decades of vibrant life, they would all, under the plurality's logic, be written out of the law.

And what of respect for democratic local decisionmaking by States and school boards? For several decades this Court has rested its public school decisions upon *Swann's*basic view that the Constitution grants local school districts a significant degree of leeway where the inclusive use of race-conscious criteria is at issue. Now localities will have to cope with the difficult problems they face (including resegregation) deprived of one means they may find necessary.

And what of law's concern to diminish and peacefully settle conflict among the Nation's people? Instead of accommodating different good-faith visions of our country and our Constitution, today's holding upsets settled expectations, creates legal uncertainty, and threatens to produce considerable further litigation, aggravating race-related conflict.

And what of the long history and moral vision that the Fourteenth Amendment itself embodies? The plurality cites in support those who argued in *Brown* against segregation, and Justice Thomas likens the approach that I have taken to that of segregation's defenders. See (plurality opinion) (comparing Jim Crow segregation to Seattle and Louisville's integration polices); (Thomas, J., concurring). But segregation policies did not simply tell schoolchildren "where they could and could not go to school based on the color of their skin," (plurality opinion); they perpetuated a caste system rooted in the institutions of slavery and 80 years of legalized subordination. The lesson of history, (plurality opinion), is not that efforts to continue racial segregation are constitutionally indistinguishable from efforts to achieve racial integration. Indeed, it is a cruel distortion of history to compare Topeka, Kansas, in the 1950's to Louisville and Seattle in the modern day—to equate the plight of Linda Brown (who was ordered to attend a Jim Crow school) to the circumstances of Joshua McDonald (whose request to transfer to a school closer to home was initially declined). This is not to deny that there is a cost in applying "a state-mandated racial label." (KENNEDY, J., concurring in part and concurring in judgment). But that cost does not approach, in degree or in kind, the terrible harms of slavery, the resulting caste system, and 80 years of legal racial segregation. . . .

Finally, what of the hope and promise of *Brown?* For much of this Nation's history, the races remained divided. It was not long ago that people of different races drank from separate fountains, rode on separate buses, and studied in separate schools. In this Court's finest hour, *Brown* v. *Board of Education* challenged this history and helped to change it. For *Brown* held out a promise. It was a promise embodied in three Amendments designed to make citizens of slaves. It was the promise of true racial equality—not as a matter of fine words on paper, but as a matter of everyday life in the Nation's cities and schools. It was about the nature of a democracy that must work for all Americans. It sought one law, one Nation, one people, not simply as a matter of legal principle but in terms of how we actually live.

Not everyone welcomed this Court's decision in *Brown*. Three years after that decision was handed down, the Governor of Arkansas ordered state militia to block the doors of a white schoolhouse so that black children could not enter. The President of the United States dispatched the 101st Airborne Division to Little Rock, Arkansas, and federal troops were needed to enforce a desegregation decree. See *Cooper* v. *Aaron,* 358 U.S. 1 (1958). Today, almost 50 years later, attitudes toward race in this Nation have changed dramatically. Many parents, white and black alike, want their children to attend schools with children of different races. Indeed, the very school districts that once spurned integration now strive for it. The long history of their efforts reveals the complexities and difficulties they have faced. And in light of those challenges, they have asked us not to take from their hands the instruments they have used to rid their schools of racial segregation, instruments that they believe are needed to overcome the problems of cities divided by race and poverty. The plurality would decline their modest request.

The plurality is wrong to do so. The last half-century has witnessed great strides toward racial equality, but we have not yet realized the promise of *Brown.* To invalidate the plans under review is to threaten the promise of *Brown.* The plurality's position, I fear, would break that promise. This is a decision that the Court and the Nation will come to regret.

I must dissent.

NOTES AND QUESTIONS

1. What is the precise holding in this case? Justice Roberts writes the opinion for the Court. Five members of the Court, including Justice Kennedy, seem to join that opinion. Yet, Justice Kennedy also writes separately and clearly does not agree with significant portions of Justice Roberts's opinion.
2. The first merits-based issue the Court confronts is the level of judicial scrutiny appropriate to the constitutional challenge in the case. Justice Roberts declares that all racial classifications demand strict scrutiny, requiring the proponents of the classification to show that the classification is "narrowly tailored" to achieve a "compelling" governmental interest. What arguments does Justice Roberts advance for his view that *all* racial classifications demand the same level of strict scrutiny? How many members of the Court agree?
3. Justice Roberts finds two interests that have been held to be compelling enough to justify race-conscious governmental decisions: (1) remedying the effects of past intentional discrimination; and (2) student body diversity. Why does Justice Roberts believe that neither interest is at issue here?
4. Justice Roberts recognizes that the school districts assert other interests that might prove compelling, including reducing racial isolation, giving non-white students access to the most desirable schools, educating students in a racially integrated environment, and the educational and broader socialization benefits that flow from a racially diverse learning environment. Significantly, Justice Roberts—and therefore the Court—never decides whether these interests might be compelling enough to justify narrowly tailored race-conscious student assignments. Why not? How many members of the Supreme Court did in fact conclude that these additional interests asserted by the school districts are "compelling"?
5. Justice Roberts ultimately concludes that the "racial classifications employed by the districts are not narrowly tailored to the goal of

achieving the educational and social benefits asserted to flow from racial diversity." How many members of the Court agreed with that conclusion? Do you find Justice Roberts's narrow tailoring arguments persuasive?

6. In his dissent, for four members of the Court, Justice Breyer suggests that strict scrutiny need not be applied in this context, but concludes in any event that the interests asserted by the districts are compelling. In particular, which interests are compelling enough to justify race-conscious decisions? The dissent also finds the methods employed by the school districts to be sufficiently tailored to achieve the stated objectives. Do you agree?
7. In what precise ways does Justice Kennedy agree with the four dissenters?
8. If in fact five justices agreed only that the school district's plans were not "narrowly tailored" to achieve their interests, how could those plans have been changed to satisfy the Court?
9. Justice Kennedy's separate opinion appears to provide a fifth vote for portions of Justice Roberts's opinion, and a fifth vote for portions of Justice Breyer's opinion. Justice Kennedy agrees with Justice Roberts's ultimate conclusion that the means chosen by the school districts to achieve their objectives were not "narrowly tailored." Significantly, however, Justice Kennedy agrees with the four dissenters that the following "interests" are compelling: (1) encouraging a diverse student body, one aspect of which is its "racial composition"; (2) removing obstacles to "equal educational opportunity" to all students; (3) bringing together students of diverse races and backgrounds; and (4) avoiding racial isolation in schooling. Those interests justify race-conscious educational decisions. If a school district attempts to achieve these goals through classifications of individual students by their race, that racial classification will be upheld only if it survives strict scrutiny and is narrowly tailored to achieve the goals. According to Justice Kennedy, however, some *race-conscious* programs designed to achieve these compelling interests will not even require strict scrutiny. In a critical passage, he declares:

    > School boards may pursue the goal of bringing together students of diverse backgrounds and races through other means including strategic site selection of new schools; drawing attendance zones with general recognition of the demographics of neighborhoods; allocating resources for special programs; recruiting students and faculty in a targeted fashion; and tracking enrollments, performance, and other statistics by race. These mechanisms are race-conscious but do not lead to a different treatment based on a classification that tells each student he or she is to be defined by race, so it is unlikely any of them would demand strict scrutiny to be found permissive.

    If these policies and practices are *race conscious*, why does Justice Kennedy indicate that they should escape strict scrutiny?
10. In light of the various opinions in *PICS*, what advice would you give to a school district that would like to create racially diverse learning environments because the district genuinely believes—as the research indicates—that such environments are in the educational best interests of students?

Is the district entirely precluded from employing racial classifications of individual students in order to produce the educational benefits of student body diversity?

11. Suppose a school district determines that one of its primary educational objectives is to teach students "racial literacy." The district also has reached the data-driven judgment that students only achieve authentic racial literacy through daily contact with meaningful numbers of students of different races in a racially diverse environment. In the wake of *PICS*, can such a district establish that its assignment of individual students to educational environments based on their race is narrowly tailored to achieve the precise educational outcome of racial literacy? *See, e.g.*, Kaufman, *PICS in Focus: A Majority of the Supreme Court Reaffirms the Constitutionality of Race-Conscious School Integration Strategies*, 35 Hast. Const. L.Q. 1 (2007); Kaufman, *(Still) Constitutional Desegregation Strategies: Teaching Racial Literacy to Secondary School Students and Preferencing Racially-literate Applicants to Higher Education*, 13 U.Mich. J. Race & L. 147 (2007).

12. In its *PICS* Opinion, the Supreme Court declared unconstitutional the school assignment plan employed by the Jefferson County, Kentucky, school district. That district had been under a federal court order *requiring* it to utilize effective race-conscious decisions to integrate its schools, including individual classifications of students based on race. The court order was dissolved in 2001 because of the district's success in achieving racial integration. The district, however, continued its student assignment plans after the court order was lifted. The district determined that its sustained effort to desegregate its schools had produced significant educational benefits for all students, and decided to continue its strategies. The Supreme Court, however, concluded that the district's voluntary continuation of its race conscious student assignment strategies was unconstitutional. Accordingly, the constitution *required* those strategies until they were successful, and then *prohibited* their continuation. After *PICS*, the Jefferson County school district, which encompasses Louisville, found itself in an unenviable position. After pursuing educationally beneficial policies for decades as required by the courts, the district was told that it may no longer continue those policies. Nonetheless, the district has responded to *PICS* by declaring its intention to remain committed to finding a constitutionally permissible method of achieving the racial integration of its schools, including student assignment strategies based on income levels rather than race. *See* Emily Bazelon, "The Next Kind of Integration," *New York Times* (July 20, 2008), www.nytimes.com/2008/07/20/magazine/20integration. As this article demonstrates, school districts generally believe that racial diversity in educational environments is in the educational best interests of all students and are working with their lawyers to pursue strategies designed to achieve that diversity within the constraints of *PICS*. *See also* James E. Ryan, *The Supreme Court and Voluntary Integration*, 121 Harv. L. Rev. 131 (2007). What advice would you offer such a district?

13. Beyond the practical implications of *PICS,* the opinion raises profound questions about the proper interpretation of both the equal protection clause and *Brown v. Board of Education.* Justice Roberts argues that the equal protection clause requires that all governmental decisions and programs be "color blind." He finds in *Brown* the principle that no state may assign children to its schools based on their race. Accordingly, he concludes his opinion with the statement that, "[t]he way to stop discrimination on the basis of race is to stop discriminating on the basis of race." The dissenters, of course, find in the equal protection clause a precise prohibition on government action that excludes or subordinates children because of their race. Calling Justice Roberts's opinion a "cruel distortion of history," the dissenters show that the equal protection clause distinguishes between prohibited efforts to continue racial segregation and lawful efforts to achieve racial integration. As such, the dissent argues that *Brown* declared unconstitutional the legalized separation and subordination of African-American school children, a constitutional violation remedied by strong, effective and race-conscious measures designed to achieve racial integration. If racial integration is the remedy to the constitutional violation found in *Brown,* how could *Brown* then be read to declare unconstitutional efforts to achieve that integration? The dissent concludes that the Court's ruling threatens the "promise of *Brown.*" Which of the opinions in *PICS* regarding the equal protection clause and *Brown* do you find most persuasive?

D. GENDER EQUALITY IN EDUCATIONAL INSTITUTIONS

1. The Constitutional Protections and Their Limits

In *Craig v. Boren,* 429 U.S. 190, 197 (1976), the Supreme Court concluded that: "[c]lassifications by gender must serve important governmental objectives and must be substantially related to achievement of those objectives." Although the Court refused to apply the rigorous strict scrutiny standard it has used to analyze racial classifications, it nonetheless determined that gender discrimination is offensive enough to warrant a more searching analysis than that given to laws that do not distinguish based upon race or gender.

In *Mississippi University for Women v. Hogan,* 458 U.S. 718, 724 (1982), the Court later reaffirmed that a statute that classifies people based upon gender can survive an equal protection challenge only if there is an "exceedingly persuasive justification" for the classification. In *Hogan,* the Court struck down a Mississippi statute that excluded males from enrolling in a state-supported professional nursing school. The state's primary justification for its exclusion of men from its nursing program was that it "compensates for discrimination against women and, therefore, constitutes educational affirmative action." *Id.* at 727. The Court declared that in "limited circumstances, a gender-based classification favoring one sex can be justified if it intentionally and directly assists members of the sex that is disproportionately burdened." *Id.* at 728. The class benefited by the state's regime, however, must be shown to "actually suffer a disadvantage related to the classification." *Id.* In *Hogan,* the state failed to persuade the Court that its actual purpose was to "compensate for discriminatory barriers faced by women" because women typically are overrepre-sented in the nursing profession. *Id.* at 728-731. Nor could the state establish that its gender-based classification was sufficiently related to its purported compensatory objective. *Id.*

In *United States v. Virginia,* 518 U.S. 515 (1996), the Supreme Court, in an opinion authored by Justice Ginsburg, held that the equal protection clause also precludes Virginia from excluding women from the Virginia Military Institute (VMI). The Court found no "exceedingly persuasive justification" for Virginia's exclusion of women from its "incomparable" military academy. The Court presumed that single-sex education affords "pedagogical benefits to at least some students," and declared that "diversity among public educational institutions can serve the public good." Nonetheless, the Court found that Virginia's exclusion of women from VMI served neither legitimate purpose.

United States v. Virginia

518 U.S. 515 (1996)

Justice Ginsburg delivered the opinion of the Court.

Virginia's public institutions of higher learning include an incomparable military college, Virginia Military Institute (VMI). The United States maintains that the Constitution's equal protection guarantee precludes Virginia from reserving exclusively to men the unique educational opportunities VMI affords. We agree.

I

Founded in 1839, VMI is today the sole single-sex school among Virginia's 15 public institutions of higher learning. VMI's distinctive mission is to produce "citizen-soldiers," men prepared for leadership in civilian life and in military service. VMI pursues this mission through pervasive training of a kind not available anywhere else in Virginia. Assigning prime place to character development, VMI uses an "adversative method" modeled on English public schools and once characteristic of military instruction. VMI constantly endeavors to instill physical and mental discipline in its cadets and impart to them a strong moral code. The school's graduates leave VMI with heightened comprehension of their capacity to deal with duress and stress, and a large sense of accomplishment for completing the hazardous course.

VMI has notably succeeded in its mission to produce leaders; among its alumni are military generals, Members of Congress, and business executives. The school's alumni overwhelmingly perceive that their VMI training helped them to realize their personal goals. VMI's endowment reflects the loyalty of its graduates; VMI has the largest per-student endowment of all public undergraduate institutions in the Nation.

Neither the goal of producing citizen-soldiers nor VMI's implementing methodology is inherently unsuitable to women. And the school's impressive record in producing leaders has made admission desirable to some women. Nevertheless, Virginia has elected to preserve exclusively for men the advantages and opportunities a VMI education affords.

II

A

From its establishment in 1839 as one of the Nation's first state military colleges, . . . VMI has remained financially supported by Virginia and "subject to the control of the [Virginia] General Assembly." First southern college to teach engineering and industrial chemistry, . . . VMI once provided teachers for the Commonwealth's schools,. . . . [1] Civil War strife threatened the school's vitality, but a resourceful superintendent regained legislative support by highlighting "VMI's great potential[,] through its technical know-how," to advance Virginia's postwar recovery.

VMI today enrolls about 1,300 men as cadets. Its academic offerings in the liberal arts, sciences, and engineering are also available at other public colleges and universities in Virginia. But VMI's mission is special. It is the mission of the school

> to produce educated and honorable men, prepared for the varied work of civil life, imbued with love of learning, confident in the functions and attitudes of leadership, possessing a high sense of public service, advocates of the American democracy and free enterprise system, and ready as citizen-soldiers to defend their country in time of national peril.

In contrast to the federal service academies, institutions maintained "to prepare cadets for career service in the armed forces," VMI's program "is directed at preparation for both military and civilian life"; "only about 15% of VMI cadets enter career military service."

VMI produces its "citizen-soldiers" through "an adversative, or doubting, model of education" which features "physical rigor, mental stress, absolute equality of treatment, absence of privacy, minute regulation of behavior, and indoctrination in desirable values." As one Commandant of Cadets described it, the adversative method "dissects the young student," and makes him aware of his "limits and capabilities," so that he knows "how far he can go with his anger, . . . how much he can take under stress, . . . exactly what he can do when he is physically exhausted."

VMI cadets live in spartan barracks where surveillance is constant and privacy nonexistent; they wear uniforms, eat together in the mess hall, and regularly participate in drills. Entering students are incessantly exposed to the rat line, "an extreme form of the adversative model," comparable in intensity to Marine Corps boot camp. Tormenting and punishing, the rat line bonds

---

[1] During the Civil War, school teaching became a field dominated by women. *See* A. Scott, *The Southern Lady: From Pedestal to Politics,* 1830-1930, p. 82 (1970).

new cadets to their fellow sufferers and, when they have completed the 7-month experience, to their former tormentors. . . .

VMI attracts some applicants because of its reputation as an extraordinarily challenging military school, and "because its alumni are exceptionally close to the school." . . . "Women have no opportunity anywhere to gain the benefits of [the system of education at VMI]."

B

In 1990, prompted by a complaint filed with the Attorney General by a female high-school student seeking admission to VMI, the United States sued the Commonwealth of Virginia and VMI, alleging that VMI's exclusively male admission policy violated the Equal Protection Clause of the Fourteenth Amendment.

III

The cross-petitions in this case present two ultimate issues. First, does Virginia's exclusion of women from the educational opportunities provided by VMI's extraordinary opportunities for military training and civilian leadership development—deny to women "capable of all of the individual activities required of VMI cadets," the equal protection of the laws guaranteed by the Fourteenth Amendment? Second, if VMI's "unique" situation—as Virginia's sole single-sex public institution of higher education—offends the Constitution's equal protection principle, what is the remedial requirement?

IV

We note, once again, the core instruction of this Court's path marking decisions in *J. E. B. v. Alabama ex rel. T. B.,* 511 U.S. 127, 136-137, and n.6 (1994), and *Mississippi Univ. for Women,* 458 U.S. at 724: Parties who seek to defend gender-based government action must demonstrate an "exceedingly persuasive justification" for that action.

Today's skeptical scrutiny of official action denying rights or opportunities based upon sex responds to volumes of history. As a plurality of this Court acknowledged a generation ago, "our Nation has had a long and unfortunate history of sex discrimination." *Frontiero v. Richardson,* 411 U.S. 677, 684 (1973). Through a century plus three decades and more of that history, women did not count among voters composing "We the People"; not until 1920 did women gain a constitutional right to the franchise. And for a half century thereafter, it remained the prevailing doctrine that government, both federal and state, could withhold from women opportunities accorded men so long as any "basis in reason" could be conceived for the discrimination. . . .

In 1971, for the first time in our Nation's history, this Court ruled in favor of a woman who complained that her State had denied her the equal protection of its laws. *Reed v. Reed,* 404 U.S. 71 (1971). . . . Since *Reed,* the Court has repeatedly recognized that neither federal nor state government acts compatibly with the equal protection principle when a law or official policy denies to women, simply because they are women, full citizenship stature—equal opportunity to aspire, achieve, participate in and contribute to society based upon their individual talents and capacities. . . .

Without equating gender classifications, for all purposes, to classifications based upon race or national origin,[6] the Court, in post-Reed decisions, has carefully inspected official action that closes a door or denies opportunity to women (or to men). . . . To summarize the Court's current directions for cases of official classification based upon gender: Focusing on the differential treatment or denial of opportunity for which relief is sought, the reviewing court must determine whether the proffered justification is "exceedingly persuasive." The burden of justification is demanding and it rests entirely on the State. The State must show "at least that the [challenged] classification serves 'important governmental objectives and that the discriminatory means employed' are 'substantially related to the achievement of those objectives.' " The justification must be genuine, not hypothesized or invented *post hoc* in response to litigation. And it must not rely on overbroad generalizations about the different talents, capacities, or preferences of males and females.

The heightened review standard our precedent establishes does not make sex a proscribed classification. Supposed "inherent differences" are no longer accepted as a ground for race or national origin classifications. Physical differences between men and women, however, are enduring: "The two sexes are not fungible; a community made up exclusively of one [sex] is different from a community composed of both."

"Inherent differences" between men and women, we have come to appreciate, remain cause for celebration, but not for denigration of the members of either sex or for artificial constraints on an individual's opportunity. Sex classifications may be used to compensate women "for particular economic disabilities [they have] suffered," to "promote equal employment opportunity," to advance full development of the talent and capacities of our Nation's people. But such classifications may not be used, as they once were, to create or perpetuate the legal, social, and economic inferiority of women.

Measuring the record in this case against the review standard just described, we conclude that Virginia has shown no "exceedingly persuasive justification" for excluding all women from the citizen-soldier training afforded by VMI. We therefore affirm the Fourth Circuit's initial judgment, which held that Virginia had violated the Fourteenth Amendment's Equal Protection Clause. Because the remedy proffered by Virginia—the Mary Baldwin VWIL program—does not cure the constitutional violation, *i.e.,* it does not provide equal opportunity, we reverse the Fourth Circuit's final judgment in this case.

V

The Fourth Circuit initially held that Virginia had advanced no state policy by which it could justify, under equal protection principles, its determination "to afford VMI's unique type of program to men and not to women." Virginia challenges that "liability" ruling and asserts two justifications in defense of VMI's exclusion of women. First, the Commonwealth contends, "single-sex education provides important educational benefits," and the option of single-sex education contributes to "diversity in educational approaches." Second, the

---

[6] The Court has thus far reserved most stringent judicial scrutiny for classifications based upon race or national origin, but last Term observed that strict scrutiny of such classifications is not inevitably "fatal in fact." *Adarand Constructors, Inc. v. Peña,* 515 U.S. 200, 237 (1995).

Commonwealth argues, "the unique VMI method of character development and leadership training," the school's adversative approach, would have to be modified were VMI to admit women. We consider these two justifications in turn.

A

Single-sex education affords pedagogical benefits to at least some students, Virginia emphasizes, and that reality is uncontested in this litigation.[8] Similarly, it is not disputed that diversity among public educational institutions can serve the public good. But Virginia has not shown that VMI was established, or has been maintained, with a view to diversifying, by its categorical exclusion of women, educational opportunities within the Commonwealth. In cases of this genre, our precedent instructs that "benign" justifications proffered in defense of categorical exclusions will not be accepted automatically; a tenable justification must describe actual state purposes, not rationalizations for actions in fact differently grounded.

Mississippi Univ. for Women is immediately in point. There the State asserted, in justification of its exclusion of men from a nursing school, that it was engaging in "educational affirmative action" by "compensating for discrimination against women." Undertaking a "searching analysis," the Court found no close resemblance between "the alleged objective" and "the actual purpose underlying the discriminatory classification." Pursuing a similar inquiry here, we reach the same conclusion.

Neither recent nor distant history bears out Virginia's alleged pursuit of diversity through single-sex educational options. In 1839, when the Commonwealth established VMI, a range of educational opportunities for men and women was scarcely contemplated. Higher education at the time was considered dangerous for women;[9] reflecting widely held views about

---

[8] On this point, the dissent sees fire where there is no flame. "Both men and women can benefit from a single-sex education," the District Court recognized, although "the beneficial effects" of such education, the court added, apparently "are stronger among women than among men." The United States does not challenge that recognition. Cf. C. Jencks & D. Riesman, *The Academic Revolution* 297-298 (1968):

> The pluralistic argument for preserving all-male colleges is uncomfortably similar to the pluralistic argument for preserving all-white colleges. . . . The all-male college would be relatively easy to defend if it emerged from a world in which women were established as fully equal to men. But it does not. It is therefore likely to be a witting or unwitting device for preserving tacit assumptions of male superiority—assumptions for which women must eventually pay.

[9] Dr. Edward H. Clarke of Harvard Medical School, whose influential book, *Sex in Education* [(1873)], went through 17 editions, was perhaps the most well-known speaker from the medical community opposing higher education for women. He maintained that the physiological effects of hard study and academic competition with boys would interfere with the development of girls' reproductive organs. *See* E. Clarke, *Sex in Education* 38-39, 62-63 (1873); *id.*, at 127 ("identical edu cation of the two sexes is a crime before God and humanity, that physiology protests against, and that experience weeps over"); *see also* H. Maudsley, *Sex in Mind and in Education* 17 (1874) ("It is not that girls have not ambition, nor that they fail generally to run the intellectual race [in coeducational settings], but it is asserted that they do it at a cost to their strength and health which entails life-long suffering, and even incapacitates them for the adequate performance of the natural functions of their sex."); C. Meigs, *Females and Their Diseases* 350 (1848) (after five or six weeks of "mental and educational discipline," a healthy woman would "lose . . . the habit of menstruation" and suffer numerous ills as a result of depriving her body for the sake of her mind).

women's proper place, the Nation's first universities and colleges—for example, Harvard in Massachusetts, William and Mary in Virginia—admitted only men. VMI was not at all novel in this respect: In admitting no women, VMI followed the lead of the Commonwealth's flagship school, the University of Virginia, founded in 1819. . . .

Virginia eventually provided for several women's seminaries and colleges. Farmville Female Seminary became a public institution in 1884. Two women's schools, Mary Washington College and James Madison University, were founded in 1908; another, Radford University, was founded in 1910. By the mid-1970's, all four schools had become coeducational.

Debate concerning women's admission as undergraduates at the main university continued well past the century's midpoint. Familiar arguments were rehearsed. If women were admitted, it was feared, they "would encroach on the rights of men; there would be new problems of government, perhaps scandals; the old honor system would have to be changed; standards would be lowered to those of other coeducational schools; and the glorious reputation of the university, as a school for men, would be trailed in the dust."

Ultimately, in 1970, "the most prestigious institution of higher education in Virginia," the University of Virginia, introduced coeducation and, in 1972, began to admit women on an equal basis with men. . . .

Virginia describes the current absence of public single-sex higher education for women as "an historical anomaly." But the historical record indicates action more deliberate than anomalous: First, protection of women against higher education; next, schools for women far from equal in resources and stature to schools for men; finally, conversion of the separate schools to coeducation. . . .

In sum, we find no persuasive evidence in this record that VMI's male-only admission policy "is in furtherance of a state policy of 'diversity.'" No such policy, the Fourth Circuit observed, can be discerned from the movement of all other public colleges and universities in Virginia away from single-sex education. That court also questioned "how one institution with autonomy, but with no authority over any other state institution, can give effect to a state policy of diversity among institutions." A purpose genuinely to advance an array of educational options, as the Court of Appeals recognized, is not served by VMI's historic and constant plan—a plan to "afford a unique educational benefit only to males." However "liberally" this plan serves the Commonwealth's sons, it makes no provision whatever for her daughters. That is not *equal* protection.

B

Virginia next argues that VMI's adversative method of training provides educational benefits that cannot be made available, unmodified, to women. Alterations to accommodate women would necessarily be "radical," so "drastic," Virginia asserts, as to transform, indeed "destroy," VMI's program. Neither sex would be favored by the transformation, Virginia maintains: Men would be deprived of the unique opportunity currently available to them; women would not gain that opportunity because their participation would "eliminate the very aspects of [the] program that distinguish [VMI] from . . . other institutions of higher education in Virginia."

The District Court forecast from expert witness testimony, and the Court of Appeals accepted, that coeducation would materially affect "at least these three aspects of VMI's program—physical training, the absence of privacy, and the adversative approach." And it is uncontested that women's admission would require accommodations, primarily in arranging housing assignments and physical training programs for female cadets. It is also undisputed, however, that "the VMI methodology could be used to educate women." The District Court even allowed that some women may prefer it to the methodology a women's college might pursue. . . . The parties, furthermore, agree that "*some* women can meet the physical standards [VMI] now impose[s] on men." In sum, as the Court of Appeals stated, "neither the goal of producing citizen soldiers," VMI's *raison d'etre,* "nor VMI's implementing methodology is inherently unsuitable to women."

In support of its initial judgment for Virginia, a judgment rejecting all equal protection objections presented by the United States, the District Court made "findings" on "gender-based developmental differences." These "findings" restate the opinions of Virginia's expert witnesses, opinions about typically male or typically female "tendencies." For example, "males tend to need an atmosphere of adversativeness," while "females tend to thrive in a cooperative atmosphere." *Ibid.* "I'm not saying that some women don't do well under [the] adversative model," VMI's expert on educational institutions testified, "undoubtedly there are some [women] who do"; but educational experiences must be designed "around the rule," this expert maintained, and not "around the exception."

The United States does not challenge any expert witness estimation on average capacities or preferences of men and women. Instead, the United States emphasizes that time and again since this Court's turning point decision in *Reed v. Reed,* we have cautioned reviewing courts to take a "hard look" at generalizations or "tendencies" of the kind pressed by Virginia, and relied upon by the District Court. *See* O'Connor, *Portia's Progress,* 66 N.Y.U. L. Rev. 1546, 1551 (1991). State actors controlling gates to opportunity, we have instructed, may not exclude qualified individuals based upon "fixed notions concerning the roles and abilities of males and females." *Mississippi Univ. for Women.*

It may be assumed, for purposes of this decision, that most women would not choose VMI's adversative method. As Fourth Circuit Judge Motz observed, however, in her dissent from the Court of Appeals' denial of rehearing en banc, it is also probable that "many men would not want to be educated in such an environment." Education, to be sure, is not a "one size fits all" business. The issue, however, is not whether "women—or men—should be forced to attend VMI"; rather, the question is whether the Commonwealth can constitutionally deny to women who have the will and capacity, the training and attendant opportunities that VMI uniquely affords.

The notion that admission of women would downgrade VMI's stature, destroy the adversative system and, with it, even the school, is a judgment hardly proved, a prediction hardly different from other "self-fulfilling prophec[ies]," *see Mississippi Univ. for Women,* once routinely used to deny rights or opportunities. When women first sought admission to the bar and access to legal education, concerns of the same order were expressed.

For example, in 1876, the Court of Common Pleas of Hennepin County, Minnesota, explained why women were thought ineligible for the practice of law. Women train and educate the young, the court said, which

> forbids that they shall bestow that time (early and late) and labor, so essential in attaining to the eminence to which the true lawyer should ever aspire. It cannot therefore be said that the opposition of courts to the admission of females to practice . . . is to any extent the outgrowth of . . . "old fogyism[.]" . . . It arises rather from a comprehension of the magnitude of the responsibilities connected with the successful practice of law, and a desire to *grade up* the profession.

A like fear, according to a 1925 report, accounted for Columbia Law School's resistance to women's admission, although

> the faculty . . . never maintained that women could not master legal learning. . . . No, its argument has been . . . more practical. If women were admitted to the Columbia Law School, [the faculty] said, then the choicer, more manly and red-blooded graduates of our great universities would go to the Harvard Law School!

Medical faculties similarly resisted men and women as partners in the study of medicine. . . . More recently, women seeking careers in policing encountered resistance based upon fears that their presence would "undermine male solidarity," deprive male partners of adequate assistance and lead to sexual misconduct. Field studies did not confirm these fears.

Women's successful entry into the federal military academies, and their participation in the Nation's military forces, indicate that Virginia's fears for the future of VMI may not be solidly grounded. The Commonwealth's justification for excluding all women from "citizen-soldier" training for which some are qualified, in any event, cannot rank as "exceedingly persuasive," as we have explained and applied that standard.

Virginia and VMI trained their argument on "means" rather than "end," and thus misperceived our precedent. Single-sex education at VMI serves an "important governmental objective," they maintained, and exclusion of women is not only "substantially related," it is essential to that objective. By this notably circular argument, the "straightforward" test *Mississippi Univ. for Women* described was bent and bowed.

The Commonwealth's misunderstanding and, in turn, the District Court's, is apparent from VMI's mission: to produce "citizen-soldiers," individuals

> imbued with love of learning, confident in the functions and attitudes of leadership, possessing a high sense of public service, advocates of the American democracy and free enterprise system, and ready . . . to defend their country in time of national peril.

Surely that goal is great enough to accommodate women, who today count as citizens in our American democracy equal in stature to men. Just as surely, the Commonwealth's great goal is not substantially advanced by women's categorical exclusion, in total disregard of their individual merit, from the Commonwealth's premier "citizen-soldier" corps. Virginia, in sum, "has fallen far short of establishing the 'exceedingly persuasive justification,'" *Mississippi Univ. for Women,* that must be the solid base for any gender-defined classification.

VI

In the second phase of the litigation, Virginia presented its remedial plan—maintain VMI as a male-only college and create VWIL as a separate program for women. The plan met District Court approval. The Fourth Circuit, in turn, deferentially reviewed the Commonwealth's proposal and decided that the two single-sex programs directly served Virginia's reasserted purposes: single-gender education, and "achieving the results of an adversative method in a military environment." Inspecting the VMI and VWIL educational programs to determine whether they "afforded to both genders benefits comparable in substance, [if] not in form and detail," the Court of Appeals concluded that Virginia had arranged for men and women opportunities "sufficiently comparable" to survive equal protection evaluation. The United States challenges this "remedial" ruling as pervasively misguided.

A

A remedial decree, this Court has said, must closely fit the constitutional violation; it must be shaped to place persons unconstitutionally denied an opportunity or advantage in "the position they would have occupied in the absence of [discrimination]." *See Milliken v. Bradley,* 433 U.S. 267 (1977). The constitutional violation in this case is the categorical exclusion of women from an extraordinary educational opportunity afforded men. A proper remedy for an unconstitutional exclusion, we have explained, aims to "eliminate [so far as possible] the discriminatory effects of the past" and to "bar like discrimination in the future." *Louisiana v. United States,* 380 U.S. 145, 154 (1965).

Virginia chose not to eliminate, but to leave untouched, VMI's exclusionary policy. For women only, however, Virginia proposed a separate program, different in kind from VMI and unequal in tangible and intangible facilities. Having violated the Constitution's equal protection requirement, Virginia was obliged to show that its remedial proposal "directly addressed and related to" the violation, *see Milliken,* the equal protection denied to women ready, willing, and able to benefit from educational opportunities of the kind VMI offers. Virginia described VWIL as a "parallel program," and asserted that VWIL shares VMI's mission of producing "citizen-soldiers" and VMI's goals of providing "education, military training, mental and physical discipline, character . . . and leadership development." . . . If the VWIL program could not "eliminate the discriminatory effects of the past," could it at least "bar like discrimination in the future"? . . . A comparison of the programs said to be "parallel" informs our answer. In exposing the character of, and differences in, the VMI and VWIL programs, we recapitulate facts earlier presented.

VWIL affords women no opportunity to experience the rigorous military training for which *VMI is famed.* Instead, the VWIL program "deemphasize[s]" military education and uses a "cooperative method" of education "which reinforces self-esteem." . . .

B

In myriad respects other than military training, VWIL does not qualify as VMI's equal. VWIL's student body, faculty, course offerings, and facilities hardly match VMI's. Nor can the VWIL graduate anticipate the benefits associated with VMI's 157-year history, the school's prestige, and its influential alumni network. . . .

Virginia, in sum, while maintaining VMI for men only, has failed to provide any "comparable single-gender women's institution." Instead, the Commonwealth has created a VWIL program fairly appraised as a "pale shadow" of VMI in terms of the range of curricular choices and faculty stature, funding, prestige, alumni support and influence.

Virginia's VWIL solution is reminiscent of the remedy Texas proposed 50 years ago, in response to a state trial court's 1946 ruling that, given the equal protection guarantee, African Americans could not be denied a legal education at a state facility. *See Sweatt v. Painter,* 339 U.S. 629 (1950). Reluctant to admit African Americans to its flagship University of Texas Law School, the State set up a separate school for Heman Sweatt and other black law students. As originally opened, the new school had no independent faculty or library, and it lacked accreditation. Nevertheless, the state trial and appellate courts were satisfied that the new school offered Sweatt opportunities for the study of law "substantially equivalent to those offered by the State to white students at the University of Texas." . . .

Facing the marked differences reported in the *Sweatt* opinion, the Court unanimously ruled that Texas had not shown "substantial equality in the [separate] educational opportunities" the State offered. Accordingly, the Court held, the Equal Protection Clause required Texas to admit African Americans to the University of Texas Law School. In line with *Sweatt,* we rule here that Virginia has not shown substantial equality in the separate educational opportunities the Commonwealth supports at VWIL and VMI.

C

When Virginia tendered its VWIL plan, the Fourth Circuit did not inquire whether the proposed remedy, approved by the District Court, placed women denied the VMI advantage in "the position they would have occupied in the absence of [discrimination]." *Milliken.* Instead, the Court of Appeals considered whether the Commonwealth could provide, with fidelity to the equal protection principle, separate and unequal educational programs for men and women. . . .

The Fourth Circuit plainly erred in exposing Virginia's VWIL plan to a deferential analysis, for "all gender-based classifications today" warrant "heightened scrutiny." Valuable as VWIL may prove for students who seek the program offered, Virginia's remedy affords no cure at all for the opportunities and advantages withheld from women who want a VMI education and can make the grade. In sum, Virginia's remedy does not match the constitutional violation; the Commonwealth has shown no "exceedingly persuasive justification" for withholding from women qualified for the experience premier training of the kind VMI affords. . . .

VII

. . . Women seeking and fit for a VMI-quality education cannot be offered anything less, under the Commonwealth's obligation to afford them genuinely equal protection.

A prime part of the history of our Constitution, historian Richard Morris recounted, is the story of the extension of constitutional rights and protections to people once ignored or excluded.[21] VMI's story continued as our comprehension of "We the People" expanded. There is no reason to believe that the admission of women capable of all the activities required of VMI cadets would destroy the Institute rather than enhance its capacity to serve the "more perfect Union."

. . . *It is so ordered.*

Justice THOMAS took no part in the consideration or decision of this case.

Chief Justice REHNQUIST, concurring in the judgment.

The Court holds first that Virginia violates the Equal Protection Clause by maintaining the Virginia Military Institute's (VMI's) all-male admissions policy, and second that establishing the Virginia Women's Institute for Leadership (VWIL) program does not remedy that violation. While I agree with these conclusions, I disagree with the Court's analysis and so I write separately. . . .

Before this Court, Virginia has sought to justify VMI's single-sex admissions policy primarily on the basis that diversity in education is desirable, and that while most of the public institutions of higher learning in the Commonwealth are coeducational, there should also be room for single-sex institutions. I agree with the Court that there is scant evidence in the record that this was the real reason that Virginia decided to maintain VMI as men only. But, unlike the majority, I would consider only evidence that postdates our decision in *Hogan,* and would draw no negative inferences from the Commonwealth's actions before that time. I think that after *Hogan,* the Commonwealth was entitled to reconsider its policy with respect to VMI, and not to have earlier justifications, or lack thereof, held against it.

Even if diversity in educational opportunity were the Commonwealth's actual objective, the Commonwealth's position would still be problematic. The difficulty with its position is that the diversity benefited only one sex; there was single-sex public education available for men at VMI, but no corresponding single-sex public education available for women. When *Hogan* placed Virginia on notice that VMI's admissions policy possibly was unconstitutional, VMI could have dealt with the problem by admitting women; but its governing body felt strongly that the admission of women would have seriously harmed the institution's educational approach. Was there something else the Commonwealth could have done to avoid an equal protection

---

[21] R. Morris, The Forging of the Union, 1781-1789, p. 193 (1987); see *id.,* at 191, setting out letter to a friend from Massachusetts patriot (later second President) John Adams, on the subject of qualifications for voting in his home State:

> It is dangerous to open so fruitful a source of controversy and altercation as would be opened by attempting to alter the qualifications of voters; there will be no end of it. New claims will arise; women will demand a vote; lads from twelve to twenty-one will think their rights not enough attended to; and every man who has not a farthing, will demand an equal voice with any other, in all acts of state. It tends to confound and destroy all distinctions, and prostrate all ranks to one common level. Letter from John Adams to James Sullivan (May 26, 1776), in 9 *Works of John Adams* 378 (C. Adams ed. 1854).

violation? Since the Commonwealth did nothing, we do not have to definitively answer that question.

I do not think, however, that the Commonwealth's options were as limited as the majority may imply. . . . Had Virginia made a genuine effort to devote comparable public resources to a facility for women, and followed through on such a plan, it might well have avoided an equal protection violation. I do not believe the Commonwealth was faced with the stark choice of either admitting women to VMI, on the one hand, or abandoning VMI and starting from scratch for both men and women, on the other. . . .

Virginia offers a second justification for the single-sex admissions policy: maintenance of the adversative method. I agree with the Court that this justification does not serve an important governmental objective. A State does not have substantial interest in the adversative methodology unless it is pedagogically beneficial. While considerable evidence shows that a single-sex education is pedagogically beneficial for some students, and hence a State may have a valid interest in promoting that methodology, there is no similar evidence in the record that an adversative method is pedagogically beneficial or is any more likely to produce character traits than other methodologies.

II

The Court defines the constitutional violation in these cases as "the categorical exclusion of women from an extraordinary educational opportunity afforded to men." By defining the violation in this way, and by emphasizing that a remedy for a constitutional violation must place the victims of discrimination in "'the position they would have occupied in the absence of [discrimination],'" the Court necessarily implies that the only adequate remedy would be the admission of women to the all-male institution. As the foregoing discussion suggests, I would not define the violation in this way; it is not the "exclusion of women" that violates the Equal Protection Clause, but the maintenance of an all-men school without providing any—much less a comparable—institution for women.

Accordingly, the remedy should not necessarily require either the admission of women to VMI or the creation of a VMI clone for women. An adequate remedy in my opinion might be a demonstration by Virginia that its interest in educating men in a single-sex environment is matched by its interest in educating women in a single-sex institution. . . . It would be a sufficient remedy, I think, if the two institutions offered the same quality of education and were of the same overall caliber.

If a State decides to create single-sex programs, the State would, I expect, consider the public's interest and demand in designing curricula. And rightfully so. But the State should avoid assuming demand based upon stereotypes; it must not assume *a priori,* without evidence, that there would be no interest in a women's school of civil engineering, or in a men's school of nursing.

In the end, the women's institution Virginia proposes, VWIL, fails as a remedy, because it is distinctly inferior to the existing men's institution and will continue to be for the foreseeable future. . . . I therefore ultimately agree with the Court that Virginia has not provided an adequate remedy.

Justice SCALIA, dissenting.

Today the Court shuts down an institution that has served the people of the Commonwealth of Virginia with pride and distinction for over a century and a half. To achieve that desired result, it rejects (contrary to our established practice) the factual findings of two courts below, sweeps aside the precedents of this Court, and ignores the history of our people. As to facts: It explicitly rejects the finding that there exist "gender-based developmental differences" supporting Virginia's restriction of the "adversative" method to only a men's institution, and the finding that the all-male composition of the Virginia Military Institute (VMI) is essential to that institution's character. As to precedent: It drastically revises our established standards for reviewing sex-based classifications. And as to history: It counts for nothing the long tradition, enduring down to the present, of men's military colleges supported by both States and the Federal Government.

Much of the Court's opinion is devoted to deprecating the closed-mind-ed-ness of our forebears with regard to women's education, and even with regard to the treatment of women in areas that have nothing to do with education. . . . Today it enshrines the notion that no substantial educational value is to be served by an all-men's military academy—so that the decision by the people of Virginia to maintain such an institution denies equal protection to women who cannot attend that institution but can attend others. Since it is entirely clear that the Constitution of the United States—the old one—takes no sides in this educational debate, I dissent. . . .

[I]n my view the function of this Court is to *preserve* our society's values regarding (among other things) equal protection, not to *revise* them; to prevent backsliding from the degree of restriction the Constitution imposed upon democratic government, not to prescribe, on our own authority, progressively higher degrees. For that reason it is my view that, whatever abstract tests we may choose to devise, they cannot supersede—and indeed ought to be crafted so *as to reflect*—those constant and unbroken national traditions that embody the people's understanding of ambiguous constitutional texts. More specifically, it is my view that "when a practice not expressly prohibited by the text of the Bill of Rights bears the endorsement of a long tradition of open, widespread, and unchallenged use that dates back to the beginning of the Republic, we have no proper basis for striking it down." . . .

The all-male constitution of VMI comes squarely within such a governing tradition. Founded by the Commonwealth of Virginia in 1839 and continuously maintained by it since, VMI has always admitted only men. And in that regard it has not been unusual. For almost all of VMI's more than a century and a half of existence, its single-sex status reflected the uniform practice for government-supported military colleges.

. . . And the same applies, more broadly, to single-sex education in general, which, as I shall discuss, is threatened by today's decision with the cutoff of all state and federal support. Government-run nonmilitary educational institutions for the two sexes have until very recently also been part of our national tradition. "[It is] [c]oeducation, historically, [that] is a novel educational theory. From grade school through high school, college, and graduate and professional training, much of the Nation's population during much of our history has been educated in sexually segregated classrooms." These traditions may of course be changed by the democratic decisions of the people, as they largely have been.

Today, however, change is forced upon Virginia, and reversion to single-sex education is prohibited nationwide, not by democratic processes but by order of this Court. Even while bemoaning the sorry, bygone days of "fixed notions" concerning women's education, the Court favors current notions so fixedly that it is willing to write them into the Constitution of the United States by application of custom-built "tests." This is not the interpretation of a Constitution, but the creation of one.

II

To reject the Court's disposition today, however, it is not necessary to accept my view that the Court's made-up tests cannot displace longstanding national traditions as the primary determinant of what the Constitution means. It is only necessary to apply honestly the test the Court has been applying to sex-based classifications for the past two decades. . . .

III

A

It is beyond question that Virginia has an important state interest in providing effective college education for its citizens. That single-sex instruction is an approach substantially related to that interest should be evident enough from the long and continuing history in this country of men's and women's colleges. But beyond that, as the Court of Appeals here stated: "That single-gender education at the college level is beneficial to both sexes is a *fact established in this case.*"

But besides its single-sex constitution, VMI is different from other colleges in another way. It employs a "distinctive educational method," sometimes referred to as the "adversative, or doubting, model of education." . . .

There can be no serious dispute that, as the District Court found, single-sex education and a distinctive educational method "represent legitimate contributions to diversity in the Virginia higher education system." As a theoretical matter, Virginia's educational interest would have been *best* served (insofar as the two factors we have mentioned are concerned) by six different types of public colleges—an all-men's, an all-women's, and a coeducational college run in the "adversative method," and an all-men's, an all-women's, and a coeducational college run in the "traditional method." But as a practical matter, of course, Virginia's financial resources, like any State's, are not limitless, and the Commonwealth must select among the available options. Virginia thus has decided to fund, in addition to some 14 coeducational 4-year colleges, one college that is run as an all-male school on the adversative model: the Virginia Military Institute.

Virginia did not make this determination regarding the make-up of its public college system on the unrealistic assumption that no other colleges exist. Substantial evidence in the District Court demonstrated that the Commonwealth has long proceeded on the principle that " 'higher education resources should be viewed as a whole—public and private' "—because such an approach enhances diversity and because "'it is academic and economic waste to permit unwarranted duplication.'" It is thus significant that, whereas there are "four all-female private [colleges] in Virginia," there is only "one private all-male college," which "indicates that the private sector is providing for the [former] form of education to a much greater extent that it provides for all-male education." In these circumstances, Virginia's election to fund one public all-male institution and one on the adversative model—and to concentrate its resources in a single entity that serves both these interests in diversity—is substantially related to the Commonwealth's important educational interests. . . .

IV

As is frequently true, the Court's decision today will have consequences that extend far beyond the parties to the litigation. What I take to be the Court's unease with these consequences, and its resulting unwillingness to acknowledge them, cannot alter the reality.

A

Under the constitutional principles announced and applied today, single-sex public education is unconstitutional. By going through the motions of applying a balancing test—asking whether the State has adduced an "exceedingly persuasive justification" for its sex-based classification—the Court creates the illusion that government officials in some future case will have a clear shot at justifying some sort of single-sex public education. Indeed, the Court seeks to create even a greater illusion than that: It purports to have said nothing of relevance to *other* public schools at all. "We address specifically and only an educational opportunity recognized . . . as 'unique.'"

The Supreme Court of the United States does not sit to announce "unique" dispositions. Its principal function is to establish *precedent*—that is, to set forth principles of law that every court in America must follow. . . .

And the rationale of today's decision is sweeping: for sex-based classifications, a redefinition of intermediate scrutiny that makes it indistinguishable from strict scrutiny. . . .

In any event, regardless of whether the Court's rationale leaves some small amount of room for lawyers to argue, it ensures that single-sex public education is functionally dead. . . . This is especially regrettable because, as the District Court here determined, educational experts in recent years have increasingly come to "support [the] view that substantial educational benefits flow from a single-gender environment, be it male or female, *that cannot be replicated in a coeducational setting.*" Until quite recently, some public officials have attempted to institute new single-sex programs, at least as experiments. In 1991, for example, the Detroit Board of Education announced a program to establish three boys-only schools for inner-city youth; it was met with a lawsuit, a preliminary injunction was swiftly entered by a District Court that purported to rely on *Hogan, see Garrett v. Board of Ed. of School Dist. of Detroit, 775* F. Supp. 1004, 1006 (ED Mich. 1991), and the Detroit Board of Education voted to abandon the litigation and thus abandon the plan. . . . Today's opinion assures that no such experiment will be tried again. . . .

Justice Brandeis said it is "one of the happy incidents of the federal system that a single courageous State may, if its citizens choose, serve as a laboratory; and try novel social and economic experiments without risk to the rest of the country." *New State Ice Co. v. Liebmann,* 285 U.S. 262, 311 (1932) (dissenting opinion). But it is one of the unhappy incidents of the federal system that a self-righteous Supreme Court, acting on its Members' personal view of what would make a " 'more perfect Union,' " can impose its own favored social and economic dispositions nationwide. . . .

NOTES AND QUESTIONS

1. Although the Court struck down Virginia's single-sex institution, it left open the possibility that such an institution could survive constitutional challenge if it were supported by an "exceedingly persuasive justification." Apparently one persuasive justification would be the sincere effort to take affirmative action to compensate for the proven past discriminatory barriers or disproportionate burdens that have been suffered by women. Reading *Virginia* with *Hogan,* the Supreme Court seems to approve of affirmative action programs that are gender-conscious. Presumably, a school that excludes men would survive an equal protection challenge to the extent that the school's policy was finely tailored to achieve the purpose of compensating for a proven history of barriers to women. By that reasoning, could a state legitimately operate a female-only law school on the ground that it was attempting to compensate women for the history of barriers to their entry into the legal profession?
2. The "intermediate" scrutiny applied to gender classifications may lead to anomalous results, particularly when juxtaposed with the "strict" scrutiny applied to racial classifications. In *Freeman* and *Jenkins,* the Supreme Court indicates that a federal court has no power to require school districts to take affirmative steps to maintain a desegregated condition, even where that condition was the source of an original, proven constitutional violation. In *Hogan* and *Virginia,* the Court seems to permit state remedial plans that employ affirmative action both to remedy past discrimination and perhaps to achieve the "public good" of diversity. In fact, the language of these opinions suggests that so long as the state can establish that it has a sincere belief that women have been disadvantaged in a particular context, the state can take affirmative, gender-based compensatory steps even absent any proven constitutional violation. As such, the lesser scrutiny applied to gender discrimination seems to allow for greater use of gender-conscious remedies. Does the strict scrutiny applied to racial classifications actually limit the use of race-conscious remedies? Is this state of the law backwards, or does it make sense in light of the evolution of the cases?
3. Do male and female students learn differently? There is evidence demon strating significant differences in the way in which men and women (and boys and girls) process information. *See, e.g.,* Carol Gilligan, *In a Different Voice: Psychological Theory and Women's Development* (1982); Michael Gurian, *Boys and Girls Learn Differently!* (2001) (hereinafter Gurian). In typical elementary school classrooms, girls outperform boys in nearly

every subject. By middle school, however, girls' standardized test scores drop relative to boys, especially in math and science. Linda L. Peter, *What Remains of Public Choice and Parental Rights: Does the* VMI *Decision Preclude Exclusive Schools or Classes Based upon Gender?,* 33 Cal. Western L. Rev. 249, 263 (1997) (hereinafter Peter). This disparity grows throughout the education process. In 2000, the National Center for Educational Statistics confirmed that after elementary school, boys acquire a significant advantage over girls in math and science. *Trends in Educational Equity of Girls and Women* 60-69 (Mar. 3, 2000). Some commentators attribute such testing disparities to inherent biological differences in learning styles between the sexes. Peter, at 263. Others suggest that this disparity results from the preferential treatment boys receive from their teachers, either because they raise their hands more often in class, speak out of turn, or are otherwise less disciplined than girls. Peter, at 264. *See also* Myra Sadker & David Sadker, *Failing at Fairness: How America's Schools Cheat Girls* 138 (1994) (hereinafter Sadker).

Michael Gurian attributes the differences to evolved biological gender dissimilarities in the brain that influence learning. *See* Gurian, at 57-59. ("brain systems explain why girls on average don't like math as much as boys and boys generally don't like reading and writing as much"). In particular, Gurian argues that boys and girls learn in fundamentally different ways and at different rates. For example, in elementary grades, girls are superior to boys in seeing in low light and in hearing. Boys are superior at certain visual tasks in bright light. The development of the female brain allows girls to read better and sooner than boys. Girls are better at tests that require listening to questions. Boys perform better on tests requiring circling of answers, and on standardized, multiple choice assessments. Gurian, at 36-37, 59. Girls comprise 5 percent of all hyperactive children, while boys comprise 95 percent of all hyperactive children. Girls are better at learning a foreign language. Boys are better at reading maps and deciphering directions. Girls focus on relationships and communication. Boys focus on action, exploration, and things. Girls solve math problems with language help. Boys solve math problems without talking. Gurian, at 36-37. In middle school, the estrogen level in girls generates greater activity in the brain (particularly during the first phase of menstruation), leading to increased concentration. At the same time, a significant increase in the testosterone level in boys tends to induce aggressive behavior. In high school, elevated estrogen levels in girls can generate disadvantages in brain activity. *See* Gurian, at 36-38. Gurian concludes that because of their different brain compositions and different learning styles, "*both* boys and girls are victims of gender disadvantage in our schools." Gurian, at 63. According to Gurian, therefore, the ultimate educational environment would confront the disadvantages in the brain chemistry of both males and females and adjust instructional practices to meet the specific educational needs of each type of student. Gurian, at 66, 294.

If, as the research suggests, girls and boys really do learn differently, should they be treated differently by educational professionals? Is Gurian right that instructional practices should be adjusted to address gender differences? What objective is served by teaching boys and girls the same way in the classroom, if they are not the same in their learning styles? Does the principle of "equality" require that boys and girls be treated the same way even if they are fundamentally different?

4. Is single-sex education designed to achieve a legitimate governmental objective? The dissent in *Virginia* and several amici argued that diversity in educational opportunities is an altogether appropriate governmental pursuit and that single-sex schools can contribute to such diversity. Indeed, it is the mission of some single-sex schools "to dissipate, rather than perpetuate, traditional gender classifications." In footnote 7, the *Virginia* Court observed as follows:

> We do not question the Commonwealth's prerogative evenhandedly to support diverse educational opportunities. We address specifically and only an educational opportunity recognized by the District Court and the Court of Appeals as "unique," an opportunity available only at Virginia's premier military institute, the Commonwealth's sole single-sex public university or college. Cf. *Mississippi Univ. for Women v. Hogan,* 458 U.S. 718, 720, n.1, 73 L. Ed. 2d 1090, 102 S. Ct. 3331 (1982) ("Mississippi maintains no other single-sex public university or college. Thus, we are not faced with the question of whether States can provide 'separate but equal' undergraduate institutions for males and females.").

The No Child Left Behind Act, enacted on January 8, 2002, makes it clear that single-sex public education in the United States is legal, provided that comparable courses, services, and facilities are made available to both sexes. In fact, the Act did more than merely legalize single-sex education in public schools; it also makes single-sex programs eligible to compete for up to $450 million dollars per year in specially targeted federal funding. *See, e.g.,* National Association for Single-Sex Public Education, *www.singlesexschools.org.*

Some research suggests that girls and boys alike benefit from segregated classrooms. A nationwide survey reported that girls' school graduates felt more confident, assertive and had a stronger sense of identity than girls who graduated from coeducational schools. *Peter,* at 264, citing *Sadker,* at 233. In a 2000 survey of 4,200 girls' school graduates, more than 80 percent reported they were better prepared to succeed in the coed world precisely because they went to a single sex school. Moulton & Ransome, *With few distractions, students will do better,* Aug. 26, 2003, available at *www.ncgs.org/ type2.php?pid=news* (hereinafter Moulton & Ransome). Without boys in the classroom, girls speak up more, take more science and math courses, obtain more advanced degrees and hold more high ranking positions in large companies. *Id. See also* Kay Bailey Hutchinson, *The Lesson of Single-Sex Public Education: Both Successful and Constitutional,* 50 Am. U.L. Rev. 1075, 1077 (Oct. 11, 2001) citing Susan Estrich, *Ideologues Decry Single-Sex Education, But Girls Benefit,* Denver Post, May 22, 1998, at B11. According to statistics published by The National Coalition of Girls' Schools, girls attending single-sex schools typically score 30 percent higher on SAT tests than the girls' national average. In addition, almost 100 percent of girls' school graduates go on to college and are twice as likely to earn doctorates. *Julia Morgan School for Girls, Why a Girls' School?,* available at *http://www.juliamorganschool. org/girls.html.* Some commentators suggest that boys also benefit from single-sex education because they are more likely to focus on their studies, express themselves more freely, and pursue nontraditional arts and literature degrees. *See Peter at* 264, nn.107, 108.

Adolescent women offer a variety of perspectives regarding single-sex education. Some adolescent girls are worried about the environment of a single-sex school. According to 14-year-old Diana Keiser, "[g]irls, all they talk about is what's new, who's doing what with who . . . I don't think I could stand every single day with all girls." Stefanie Weiss, The University of Maryland's Academy of Leadership, *Sex and Scholarship,* July 21, 2002, Wash. Post, at W-18, available at *http://www.washingtonpost.com/ac2/wp-dyn/A15181-2002Jull6?language=printer.* "Notions of 'fitting in' or 'being cool' fade into the background, while academic achievement, intellectual inquiry and a child's natural desire to learn regain the prominence they deserve." Moulton & Ransome. In Senator Hutchinson's article, a 14-year-old girl was quoted, stating that "[w]hen you are in high school with boys, it's a distraction. Girls try to look good instead of trying to do well in school." Kay Bailey Hutchinson, *The Lesson of Single-Sex Public Education: Both Successful and Constitutional,* 50 Am. U.L. Rev. 1075, 1077 (Oct. 11, 2001). Christopher Wadsworth, executive director of the International Boy's School Coalition, quoted in the Washington Post, stated that "[t]he girls dumb themselves down, the boys posture. It's all mating behavior, and it's all very appropriate. [But] the object of education is to instruct." Stefanie Weiss, the University of Maryland's Academy of Leadership, *Sex and Scholarship,* Wash. Post, at W-18, July 21, 2002, available at *http://www.washingtonpost.com/ac2/wp-dyn/A1518l-2002Jull6?language=printer.* Based upon your own educational experience, do you agree that "girls dumb themselves down" in a coeducational setting?

These studies provide some evidence that single-sex education may indeed benefit both boys and girls. Does this evidence provide the type of "exceedingly persuasive justification" required by *Virginia* for the creation of gender-segregated schools?

5. On the other hand, the American Civil Liberties Union (ACLU), provides a contrary analysis. The ACLU concludes that "[s]ingle-sex education is at best a 'sound-good method' because it is based upon misconceptions about the abilities and preferences of girls and boys rather than empirical evidence." Laura W. Murphy, *Single-Sex Notice of Intent, Comments to the Department of Education,* available at *http://www.aclu.org/WomensRights/Womensrights.cfm?ID=10481&c=174,* July 8, 2002. The ACLU observes that if similar characteristics found in single-sex schools, such as smaller class rooms, extensive resources, well-trained teachers, and advanced educational methods, were available in public (co-ed) schools, measurable differences between single-sex education and co-educational programs would disappear. *Id.* The ACLU also argues that single-sex schools undermine Title IX, violate the Equal Protection Clause of the U.S. Constitution and foster sex

discrimination. *Id.* Are single-sex schools and coeducational schools operating on unequal playing fields? Would the national education system be better off if the resources utilized for single-sex schools were instead used in public coeducational programs?

2. Title IX Statutory Protections and Their Limits

(a) Title IX's Scope

In the Education Amendments of 1972, 20 U.S.C. §§1681-1683, Congress included Title IX's directive preventing gender-based discrimination in federally funded schools. 20 U.S.C. §1681(a) (2002). *See also* Maryann Ahranjani, Mary Daly v. Boston College: *The Impermissibility of Single-Sex Classrooms Within a Private University,* 9 Am. U.S. Gender Soc. Poly. & L., 179, 188 (2001) (hereinafter Ahranjani). Title IX provides that students attending "educational institutions" that "receiv[e] Federal financial assistance" shall not be "excluded from participation in, be denied the benefits of, or be subjected to discrimination under any education program or activity" because of their sex. 20 U.S.C. §1681(a). Section (c) of the statute defines an "educational institution" to include both public and private schools, from preschools to graduate schools. 20 U.S.C. §1681(c). While the language of the statute may seem clear, the actual scope of Title IX has been the subject of much debate among scholars and the courts. *See* Ahranjani, at 188; Julie M. Amstein, United States v. Virginia: *The Case of Coeducation at Virginia Military Institute,* 3 Am. U.S. Gender Soc. Poly. & L. 69 (1999).

First, what does it mean to "receiv[e]" federal funding? In *Grove City College v. Bell,* 465 U.S. 555 (1984), the Supreme Court examined the statute's language, congressional intent and previous judicial constructions to conclude that any money originally disbursed by the federal government and subsequently collected by an educational institution could constitute "recei [pt of] Federal financial assistance" for purposes of Title IX. *Id.* at 568, n.18, quoting Sex Discrimination Regulations: Hearings Before the Subcomm. on Postsecondary Education of the House Comm. on Education and Labor, 94th Cong., 1st Sess. 482 (1975) (1975 Hearings) ("assistance that the Government furnishes, that goes directly or indirectly to an institution, is Government aid within the meaning of Title IX"). The *Grove City* Court cautioned that, as a consequence of Title IX's broadly construed financial assistance clause, federal aid awarded to one student could subject an entire college to the Title IX requirements simply because the federal financial assistance would eventually reach the school's general operating budget. *Grove City,* 465 U.S. at 571-573. Hence, the entire college would be the "educational program or activity" subject to regulation. That interpretation would effectively require students to attend a private college without the benefit of federal financial aid, or subject the college, which might otherwise be exempt from Title IX oversight, to disciplinary action by the Office of Civil Rights (OCR), the regulatory arm of the Department of Education. The Supreme Court held that such a construction was contrary to the "program-specific" language of the Act. *Grove City,* 465 U.S. at 570. The Court therefore limited the application of Title IX to the particular department that receives the federal monies; in Grove City's case, the specific financial aid program. *Grove City,* 465 U.S. at 573-574.

Nonetheless, in direct response to the *Grove City* ruling, Congress passed the Civil Rights Restoration Act of 1987, which "restore [d] the prior consistent and long-standing executive branch interpretation of broad, institution-wide application" of Title IX requirements. Pub. L. No. 100-259, 1988 S. 557. ("Certain aspects of recent decisions and opinions of the Supreme Court have unduly narrowed or cast doubt upon the broad application of title IX of the Education Amendments of 1972 . . ."). Specifically, because the educational institution is the intended recipient of the federal money, it is subject to Title IX requirements. Congress thereby expanded Title IX's reach to include nearly every educational institution in the country (both public and private) because, on average, federal funds comprise 43 percent of the revenue received by private universities. *See, e.g.,* U.S. Department of Education, NCES, Current-fund revenue of private degree-granting institutions, by source: 1980-81 to 1995-96, Table 331, available at *http://nces.ed.gov/pubs2003/digest02/tables/dt331.asp.*

If compliance with Title IX proves too onerous, the institutions are free to "terminate [their] participation in the federal grant program and thus avoid the requirements of Title IX." 20 U.S.C. §1681(a)(5). While Title IX may be described as a "contractual relationship with Congress," *see* Allison Herren Lee, *Title IX, Equal Protection, and the Richter Scale: Will* VMI's *Vibration Topple Single-Sex Education,* 7 Tex. J. Women & the Law 37, 69 (1997) (hereinafter Lee), the statute's funding mechanism allows Congress to implement substantive educational policies.

In order to receive government funds, institutions are required by Title IX to submit a Certificate of Assurance, indicating that their programs and activities treat all students equally with respect to gender. 28 C.F.R. §54.115. Each particular funding agency issues the terms of an educational institution's endowment according to Title IX's official interpretation, and cautions that failing to comply with the policy will cause funds to be revoked. Lee, at 69. Generally, institutions must not discriminate between male and female admissions, athletic programs, access to financial aid, counseling or campus housing. *Id. See also Mercer v. Duke University,* 190 F.3d 643 (4th Cir. 1999). Title IX's regulations, however, allow an educational institution to maintain separate athletic teams for men and women where selection is based upon competitive skill or where the teams participate in a contact sport. 34 C.F.R. §106.41(b). *See Horner v. Kentucky High School Athletic Ass'n,* 206 F.3d 685 (6th Cir. 2000) (athletic association's refusal to sanction separate girls' fast-pitch softball team did not violate Title IX where girls were given opportunities to compete for spots on the boys' team).

The Supreme Court has made clear that individuals may bring a private right of action for damages against an educational institution for violating Title IX. *Cannon v. University of Chicago,* 441 U.S. 677, 717 (1979). In *Cannon,* the Court inferred from the language, intent and structure of Title IX a private remedy under federal law for Title IX violations. *Id.* at 708. Because Title IX binds both public and private institutions, a private right of action extends to both types of institutions as well. The *Cannon* Court found support for a private remedy in the plain language of the statute: it specifically confers a remedy to that class of people wronged by an act of gender discrimination. *Id.* at 694. Additionally, Congress intended to treat Title IX the same as Title VI of the Civil Rights Act of 1964, which itself implied a private right of action. *Id.* at 694-696 (see, *e.g.,* pp. 695-696, noting that the only difference between Title IX and Title VI was that the word "sex" replaced the words "race, color, or national origin"). Furthermore, Title IX was originally drafted as an amendment to Title VI until it had been sufficiently modified to require treatment as an independent provision. *Id.* at 694, 703. In fact, Title VI's legislative history so convincingly implied a private remedy that the Supreme Court could "no[t] hesitat[e] [to] conclud[e]" that such a right be allowed. *Id.* at 703, n.34. Furthermore, the Court found that a private remedy was consistent with Title IX's goals of eliminating the appearance of federal support for illegal discrimination and providing victims with recourse against discriminatory schools. *Id.* at 704. Finally, the Court concluded that a private remedy under federal law does not interfere with the states' rights to pursue alternative remedies for two reasons: (1) the federal government historically protects citizens from discrimination, *id.* at 708, and (2) the federal action arises under a statute that regulates recipients of federal money. *Id.*

In *Franklin v. Gwinnett County Public Schools,* 503 U.S. 60 (1992), the Court reaffirmed the existence of an implied private right of action under Title IX and made clear that the traditional remedy of monetary damages is available to victims of Title IX violations. In *Franklin,* the plaintiff, a tenth-grader, sought monetary damages against the school district, alleging that she was the victim of "continual sexual harassment" by the district's sports coach. Reasoning that Congress enacted Title IX against a backdrop of traditional damages remedies and declined to amend Title IX to reject a private remedy after the Court implied such a remedy in *Cannon,* the Supreme Court held that the plaintiff was entitled to pursue a claim for damages against the district.

In its most recent Title IX decisions, the Supreme Court has assumed the existence of a private remedy, and has defined the contours of that remedy. In *Gebser v. Lago Vista Independent School District,* 524 U.S. 274 (1998), the Court established the elements of a Title IX claim involving sexual harassment of a student by a teacher. In *Davis v. Monroe County Board of Education,* 526 U.S. 629 (1999), the Court defined the essential elements of a private action under Title IX involving sexual harassment of a student by another student.

Gebser v. Lago Vista Independent School District

524 U.S. 274(1998)

Justice O'Connor delivered the opinion of the Court.

The question in this case is when a school district may be held liable in damages in an implied right of action under Title IX for the sexual harassment of a student by one of the district's teachers. We conclude that damages may not be recovered in those circumstances unless an official of the school district who at a minimum has authority to institute corrective measures on the district's behalf has actual notice of, and is deliberately indifferent to, the teacher's misconduct.

I

In the spring of 1991, when petitioner Alida Star Gebser was an eighth-grade student at a middle school in respondent Lago Vista Independent School District (Lago Vista), she joined a high school book discussion group led by Frank Waldrop, a teacher at Lago Vista's high school. Lago Vista received federal funds at all pertinent times. During the book discussion sessions, Waldrop often made sexually suggestive comments to the students. Gebser entered high school in the fall and was assigned to classes taught by Waldrop in both semesters. Waldrop continued to make inappropriate remarks to the students, and he began to direct more of his suggestive comments toward Gebser, including during the substantial amount of time that the two were alone in his classroom. He initiated sexual contact with Gebser in the spring, when, while visiting her home ostensibly to give her a book, he kissed and fondled her. The two had sexual intercourse on a number of occasions during the remainder of the school year. Their relationship continued through the summer and into the following school year, and they often had intercourse during class time, although never on school property.

Gebser did not report the relationship to school officials, testifying that while she realized Waldrop's conduct was improper, she was uncertain how to react and she wanted to continue having him as a teacher. In October 1992, the parents of two other students complained to the high school principal about Waldrop's comments in class. The principal arranged a meeting, at which, according to the principal, Waldrop indicated that he did not believe he had made offensive remarks but apologized to the parents and said it would not happen again. The principal also advised Waldrop to be careful about his classroom comments and told the school guidance counselor about the meeting, but he did not report the parents' complaint to Lago Vista's superintendent, who was the district's Title IX coordinator. A couple of months later, in January 1993, a police officer discovered Waldrop and Gebser engaging in sexual intercourse and arrested Waldrop. Lago Vista terminated his employment, and subsequently, the Texas Education Agency revoked his teaching license. During this time, the district had not promulgated or distributed an official grievance procedure for lodging sexual harassment complaints; nor had it issued a formal anti-harassment policy.

Gebser and her mother filed suit against Lago Vista and Waldrop in state court in November 1993, raising claims against the school district under Title IX. . . .

II

Title IX provides in pertinent part that, "no person . . . shall, on the basis of sex, be excluded from participation in, be denied the benefits of, or be subjected to discrimination under any education program or activity receiving Federal financial assistance." The express statutory means of enforcement is administrative: The statute directs federal agencies who distribute education funding to establish requirements to effectuate the nondiscrimination mandate, and permits the agencies to enforce those requirements through "any . . . means authorized by law," including ultimately the termination of federal funding. The Court held in *Cannon v. University of Chicago,* 441 U.S. 677 (1979), that Title IX is also enforceable through an implied private right of action, a conclusion we do not revisit here. We subsequently established in *Franklin v. Gwinnett County Public Schools,* 503 U.S. 60 (1992), that monetary damages are available in the implied private action.

Franklin . . . establishes that a school district can be held liable in damages in cases involving a teacher's sexual harassment of a student; the decision, however, does not purport to define the contours of that liability. We face that issue squarely in this case. . . .

III

Because the private right of action under Title IX is judicially implied, we have a measure of latitude to shape a sensible remedial scheme that best comports with the statute. . . . That endeavor inherently entails a degree of speculation, since it addresses an issue on which Congress has not specifically spoken. . . . To guide the analysis, we generally examine the relevant statute to ensure that we do not fashion the parameters of an implied right in a manner at odds with the statutory structure and purpose. . . .

Those considerations, we think, are pertinent not only to the scope of the implied right, but also to the scope of the available remedies. . . . We suggested as much in *Franklin,* where we recognized "the general rule that all appropriate relief is available in an action brought to vindicate a federal right," but indicated that the rule must be reconciled with congressional purpose. The "general rule," that is, "yields where necessary to carry out the intent of Congress or to avoid frustrating the purposes of the statute involved." . . .

Applying those principles here, we conclude that it would "frustrate the purposes" of Title IX to permit a damages recovery against a school district for a teacher's sexual harassment of a student based upon principles of *respondeat superior* or constructive notice, *i.e.,* without actual notice to a school district official. Because Congress did not expressly create a private right of action under Title IX, the statutory text does not shed light on Congress' intent with respect to the scope of available remedies. Instead, "we attempt to infer how the [1972] Congress would have addressed the issue had the . . . action been included as an express provision in the" statute. . . .

As a general matter, it does not appear that Congress contemplated unlimited recovery in damages against a funding recipient where the recipient is unaware of discrimination in its programs. When Title IX was enacted in 1972, the principal civil rights statutes containing an express right of action did not provide for recovery of monetary damages at all, instead allowing only injunctive and equitable relief. *See* 42 U.S.C. §2000a-3(a) (1970 ed.); §2000e-5(e), (g) (1970 ed., Supp. II). It was not until 1991 that Congress made damages available under Title VII, and even then, Congress carefully limited the amount recoverable in any individual case, calibrating the maximum recovery to the size of the employer. *See* 42 U.S.C. §1981a(b)(3). Adopting petitioners' position would amount, then, to allowing unlimited recovery of damages under Title IX where Congress has not spoken on the subject of either the right or the remedy, and in the face of evidence that when Congress expressly considered both in Title VII it restricted the amount of damages available.

Congress enacted Title IX in 1972 with two principal objectives in mind: "to avoid the use of federal resources to support discriminatory practices" and "to provide individual citizens effective protection against those practices." *Cannon.* The statute was modeled after *Title VI of the Civil Rights Act of 1964,* which is parallel to Title IX except that it prohibits race discrimination, not sex discrimination, and applies in all programs receiving federal funds, not only in education programs. *See* 42 U.S.C. §2000d *et seq.* The two statutes operate in the same manner, conditioning an offer of federal funding on a promise by the recipient not to discriminate, in what amounts essentially to a contract between the Government and the recipient of funds. . . .

That contractual framework distinguishes Title IX from Title VII, which is framed in terms not of a condition but of an outright prohibition. Title VII applies to all employers without regard to federal funding and aims broadly to "eradicate discrimination throughout the economy." *Landgrafv. USI Film Products,* 511 U.S. 244, 254, (1994). Title VII, moreover, seeks to "make persons whole for injuries suffered through past discrimination." Thus, whereas Title VII aims centrally to compensate victims of discrimination, Title IX focuses more on "protecting" individuals from discriminatory practices carried out by recipients of federal funds. That might explain why, when the Court first recognized the implied right under Title IX in *Cannon,* the opinion referred to injunctive or equitable relief in a private action, but not to a damages remedy.

Title IX's contractual nature has implications for our construction of the scope of available remedies. When Congress attaches conditions to the award of federal funds under its spending power, U.S. Const., Art. I, §8, cl. 1, as it has in Title IX and Title VI, we examine closely the propriety of private actions holding the recipient liable in monetary damages for noncompliance with the condition. Our central concern in that regard is with ensuring "that the receiving entity of federal funds [has] notice that it will be liable for a monetary award." . . . If a school district's liability for a teacher's sexual harassment rests on principles of constructive notice or *respondeat superior,* it will likewise be the case that the recipient of funds was unaware of the discrimination. It is sensible to assume that Congress did not envision a recipient's liability in damages in that situation. . . .

Most significantly, Title IX contains important clues that Congress did not intend to allow recovery in damages where liability rests solely on principles of vicarious liability or constructive notice. Title IX's express means of enforcement—by administrative agencies—operates on an assumption of actual notice to officials of the funding recipient. The statute entitles agencies who disburse education funding to enforce their rules implementing the nondiscrimination mandate through proceedings to suspend or terminate funding or through "other means authorized by law." 20 U.S.C. §1682. Significantly, however, an agency may not initiate enforcement proceedings until it "has advised the appropriate person or persons of the failure to comply with the requirement and has determined that compliance cannot be secured by voluntary means." The administrative regulations implement that obligation, requiring resolution of compliance issues "by informal means whenever possible," 34 CFR §100.7(d) (1997), and prohibiting commencement of enforcement proceedings until the agency has determined that voluntary compliance is unobtainable and "the recipient . . . has been notified of its failure to comply and of the action to be taken to effect compliance," §100.8(d); *see* §100.8(c).

In the event of a violation, a funding recipient may be required to take "such remedial action as [is] deemed necessary to overcome the effects of [the] discrimination." §106.3. While agencies have conditioned continued funding on providing equitable relief to the victim, the regulations do not appear to contemplate a condition ordering payment of monetary damages, and there is no indication that payment of damages has been demanded as a condition of finding a recipient to be in compliance with the statute. . . .

Presumably, a central purpose of requiring notice of the violation "to the appropriate person" and an opportunity for voluntary compliance before administrative enforcement proceedings can commence is to avoid diverting education funding from beneficial uses where a recipient was unaware of discrimination in its programs and is willing to institute prompt corrective measures. The scope of private damages relief proposed by petitioners is at odds with that basic objective. When a teacher's sexual harassment is imputed to a school district or when a school district is deemed to have "constructively" known of the teacher's harassment, by assumption the district had no actual knowledge of the teacher's conduct. Nor, of course, did the district have an opportunity to take action to end the harassment or to limit further harassment. It would be unsound, we think, for a statute's *express* system of enforcement to require notice to the recipient and an opportunity to come into voluntary compliance while a judicially *implied* system of enforcement permits substantial liability without regard to the recipient's knowledge or its corrective actions upon receiving notice. . . . Moreover, an award of damages in a particular case might well exceed a recipient's level of federal funding. Where a statute's express enforcement scheme hinges its most severe sanction on notice and unsuccessful efforts to obtain compliance, we cannot attribute to Congress the intention to have implied an enforcement scheme that allows imposition of greater liability without comparable conditions.

IV

Because the express remedial scheme under Title IX is predicated upon notice to an "appropriate person" and an opportunity to rectify any violation, 20 U.S.C. §1682, we conclude, in the absence of further direction from Congress, that the implied damages remedy should be fashioned along the same lines. An "appropriate person" under §1682 is, at a minimum, an official of the recipient entity with authority to take corrective action to end the discrimination. Consequently, in cases like this one that do not involve official policy of the recipient entity, we hold that a damages remedy will not lie under Title IX unless an official who at a minimum has authority to address the alleged discrimination and to institute corrective measures on the recipient's behalf has actual knowledge of discrimination in the recipient's programs and fails adequately to respond.

We think, moreover, that the response must amount to deliberate indifference to discrimination. The administrative enforcement scheme presupposes that an official who is advised of a Title IX violation refuses to take action to bring the recipient into compliance. The premise, in other words, is an official decision by the recipient not to remedy the violation. That framework finds a rough parallel in the standard of deliberate indifference. Under a lower standard, there would be a risk that the recipient would be liable in damages not for its own official decision but instead for its employees' independent actions. Comparable considerations led to our adoption of a deliberate indifference standard for claims under §1983 alleging that a municipality's actions in failing to prevent a deprivation of federal rights was the cause of the violation.

Applying the framework to this case is fairly straightforward, as petitioners do not contend they can prevail under an actual notice standard. The only official alleged to have had information about Waldrop's misconduct is the high school principal. That information, however, consisted of a complaint from parents of other students charging only that Waldrop had made inappropriate comments during class, which was plainly insufficient to alert the principal to the possibility that Waldrop was involved in a sexual relationship with a student. Lago Vista, moreover, terminated Waldrop's employment upon learning of his relationship with Gebser. Justice Stevens points out in his dissenting opinion that Waldrop of course had knowledge of his own actions. Where a school district's liability rests on actual notice principles, however, the knowledge of the wrongdoer himself is not pertinent to the analysis. *See* Restatement [Second of Agency] §280.

Petitioners focus primarily on Lago Vista's asserted failure to promulgate and publicize an effective policy and grievance procedure for sexual harassment claims. They point to Department of Education regulations requiring each funding recipient to "adopt and publish grievance procedures providing for prompt and equitable resolution" of discrimination complaints, 34 CFR §106.8(b) (1997), and to notify students and others "that it does not discriminate on the basis of sex in the educational programs or activities which it operates," §106.9(a). Lago Vista's alleged failure to comply with the regulations, however, does not establish the requisite actual notice and deliberate indifference. And in any event, the failure to promulgate a grievance procedure does not itself constitute "discrimination" under Title IX. Of course, the Department of Education could enforce the requirement administratively: Agencies generally have authority to promulgate and enforce requirements that effectuate the statute's non-discrimination mandate, 20 U.S.C. §1682, even if those requirements do not purport to represent a definition of discrimination under the statute. . . . We have never held, however, that the implied private right of action under Title IX allows recovery in damages for violation of those sorts of administrative requirements.

V

The number of reported cases involving sexual harassment of students in schools confirms that harassment unfortunately is an all too common aspect of the educational experience. No one questions that a student suffers extraordinary harm when subjected to sexual harassment and abuse by a teacher, and that the teacher's conduct is reprehensible and undermines the basic purposes of the educational system. The issue in this case, however, is whether the independent misconduct of a teacher is attributable to the school district that employs him under a specific federal statute designed primarily to prevent recipients of federal financial assistance from using the funds in a discriminatory manner. Our decision does not affect any right of recovery that an individual may have against a school district as a matter of state law or against the teacher in his individual capacity under state law or under 42 U.S.C. §1983. Until Congress speaks directly on the subject, however, we will not hold a school district liable in damages under Title IX for a teacher's sexual harassment of a student absent actual notice and deliberate indifference. We therefore affirm the judgment of the Court of Appeals.

It is so ordered.

NOTES AND QUESTIONS

1. The *Gebser* decision provides school districts with a blueprint for avoiding liability under Title IX for acts of discrimination against students based upon gender. Based upon the language in the decision, what policies and administrative procedures should every school district enact to conform to the Court's ruling?
2. The *Gebser* Court reasons that traditional agency principles of vicarious liability and respondeat superior, which would render a school district strictly liable for the acts of its teachers in the scope of their employment, are not appropriate in this case. Why not? Would the conduct of a teacher who engages in sexual harassment of a student be within the scope of that teacher's employment?
3. The Court also makes clear that its decision does not "affect any right of recovery that an individual may have against a school district as a matter of state law or against the teacher in his individual capacity under state law or under 42 U.S.C. §1983." The materials in Chapters 14 and 15 address the state law and §1983 claims that might be pursued by students who are victims of sexual harassment.
4. The regulations promulgated pursuant to Title IX provide that a school "may take affirmative action to overcome the effects of conditions which resulted in limited participation therein by persons of a particular sex." 34 C.F.R. §106.3 (2000). Is this compatible with the Supreme Court's view of affirmative action in the context of equal protection analysis?

Davis v. Monroe County Board of Education

526 U.S. 629 (1999)

Justice O'Connor delivered the opinion of the Court.

Petitioner brought suit against the Monroe County Board of Education and other defendants, alleging that her fifth-grade daughter had been the victim of sexual harassment by another student in her class. Among petitioner's claims was a claim for monetary and injunctive relief under Title IX. The District Court dismissed petitioner's Title IX claim on the ground that "student-on-student," or peer, harassment provides no ground for a private cause of action under the statute. The Court of Appeals for the Eleventh Circuit, sitting en banc, affirmed. We consider here whether a private damages action may lie against the school board in cases of student-on-student harassment. We conclude that it may, but only where the funding recipient acts with deliberate indifference to known acts of harassment in its programs or activities. Moreover, we conclude that such an action will lie only for harassment that is so severe, pervasive, and objectively offensive that it effectively bars the victim's access to an educational opportunity or benefit. . . .

Petitioner's minor daughter, LaShonda, was allegedly the victim of a prolonged pattern of sexual harassment by one of her fifth-grade classmates at Hubbard Elementary School, a public school in Monroe County, Georgia. According to petitioner's complaint, the harassment began in December 1992, when the classmate, G. F., attempted to touch LaShonda's breasts and genital area and made vulgar statements such as " 'I want to get in bed with you' " and " 'I want to feel your boobs.' " Similar conduct allegedly occurred on or about January 4 and January 20, 1993. LaShonda reported each of these incidents to her mother and to her classroom teacher, Diane Fort. Petitioner, in turn, also contacted Fort, who allegedly assured petitioner that the school principal, Bill Querry, had been informed of the incidents. Petitioner contends that, notwithstanding these reports, no disciplinary action was taken against G. F.

G. F.'s conduct allegedly continued for many months. In early February, G. F. purportedly placed a door stop in his pants and proceeded to act in a sexually suggestive manner toward LaShonda during physical education class. LaShonda reported G. F.'s behavior to her physical education teacher, Whit Maples. Approximately one week later, G. F. again allegedly engaged in harassing behavior, this time while under the supervision of another classroom teacher, Joyce Pippin. Again, LaShonda allegedly reported the incident to the teacher, and again petitioner contacted the teacher to follow up.

Petitioner alleges that G. F. once more directed sexually harassing conduct toward LaShonda in physical education class in early March, and that LaShonda reported the incident to both Maples and Pippen. In mid-April 1993, G. F. allegedly rubbed his body against LaShonda in the school hallway in what LaShonda considered a sexually suggestive manner, and LaShonda again reported the matter to Fort.

The string of incidents finally ended in mid-May, when G. F. was charged with, and pleaded guilty to, sexual battery for his misconduct. The complaint alleges that LaShonda had suffered during the months of harassment, however; specifically, her previously high grades allegedly dropped as she became unable to concentrate on her studies, and, in April 1993, her father discovered that she had written a suicide note. The complaint further alleges that, at one point, LaShonda told petitioner that she " 'didn't know how much longer she could keep [G. F.] off her.' "

Nor was LaShonda G. F.'s only victim; it is alleged that other girls in the class fell prey to G. F.'s conduct. At one point, in fact, a group composed of

LaShonda and other female students tried to speak with Principal Querry about G. F.'s behavior. According to the complaint, however, a teacher denied the students' request with the statement, "'If [Querry] wants you, he'll call you.'"

Petitioner alleges that no disciplinary action was taken in response to G. F.'s behavior toward LaShonda. In addition to her conversations with Fort and Pippen, petitioner alleges that she spoke with Principal Querry in mid-May 1993. When petitioner inquired as to what action the school intended to take against G. F., Querry simply stated, "'I guess I'll have to threaten him a little bit harder.'" Yet, petitioner alleges, at no point during the many months of his reported misconduct was G. F. disciplined for harassment. Indeed, Querry allegedly asked petitioner why LaShonda "'was the only one complaining.'"

Nor, according to the complaint, was any effort made to separate G. F. and LaShonda. On the contrary, notwithstanding LaShonda's frequent complaints, only after more than three months of reported harassment was she even permitted to change her classroom seat so that she was no longer seated next to G. F. Moreover, petitioner alleges that, at the time of the events in question, the Monroe County Board of Education (Board) had not instructed its personnel on how to respond to peer sexual harassment and had not established a policy on the issue.

B

On May 4, 1994, petitioner filed suit in the United States District Court for the Middle District of Georgia against the Board, Charles Dumas, the school district's superintendent, and Principal Querry. The complaint alleged that the Board is a recipient of federal funding for purposes of Title IX, that "the persistent sexual advances and harassment by the student G. F. upon [LaShonda] interfered with her ability to attend school and perform her studies and activities," and that "the deliberate indifference by Defendants to the unwelcome sexual advances of a student upon LaShonda created an intimidating, hostile, offensive and abusive school environment in violation of Title IX." The complaint sought compensatory and punitive damages, attorney's fees, and injunctive relief. . . .

We granted certiorari, in order to resolve a conflict in the Circuits over whether, and under what circumstances, a recipient of federal educational funds can be liable in a private damages action arising from student-on-student sexual harassment. . . .

II

Title IX provides, with certain exceptions not at issue here, that

> no person in the United States shall, on the basis of sex, be excluded from participation in, be denied the benefits of, or be subjected to discrimination under any education program or activity receiving Federal financial assistance. 20 U.S.C. §1681(a).

Congress authorized an administrative enforcement scheme for Title IX. Federal departments or agencies with the authority to provide financial assistance are entrusted to promulgate rules, regulations, and orders to enforce the objectives of §1681, *see* §1682, and these departments or agencies may rely on "any . . . means authorized by law," including the termination of funding, *ibid.* to give effect to the statute's restrictions.

There is no dispute here that the Board is a recipient of federal education funding for Title IX purposes. Nor do respondents support an argument that student-on-student harassment cannot rise to the level of "discrimination" for purposes of Title IX. Rather, at issue here is the question whether a recipient of federal education funding may be liable for damages under Title IX under any circumstances for discrimination in the form of student-on-student sexual harassment.

A

Petitioner urges that Title IX's plain language compels the conclusion that the statute is intended to bar recipients of federal funding from permitting this form of discrimination in their programs or activities. She emphasizes that the statute prohibits a student from being "*subjected to discrimination* under any education program or activity receiving Federal financial assistance." 20 U.S.C. §1681 (emphasis supplied). It is Title IX's "unmistakable focus on the benefited class," *Cannon v. University of Chicago,* 441 U.S. 677, 691 (1979), rather than the perpetrator, that, in petitioner's view, compels the conclusion that the statute works to protect students from the discriminatory misconduct of their peers.

Here, however, we are asked to do more than define the scope of the behavior that Title IX proscribes. We must determine whether a district's failure to respond to student-on-student harassment in its schools can support a private suit for money damages. . . . This Court has indeed recognized an implied private right of action under Title IX, *see Cannon v. University of Chicago,* and we have held that money damages are available in such suits, *Franklin v. Gwinnett County Public Schools.* Because we have repeatedly treated Title IX as legislation enacted pursuant to Congress' authority under the Spending Clause, however, private damages actions are available only where recipients of federal funding had adequate notice that they could be liable for the conduct at issue. When Congress acts pursuant to its spending power, it generates legislation "much in the nature of a contract: in return for federal funds, the States agree to comply with federally imposed conditions." *Pennhurst State School and Hospital v. Halderman,* 451 U.S. 1, 17 (1981). In interpreting language in spending legislation, we thus "insist that Congress speak with a clear voice," recognizing that "there can, of course, be no knowing acceptance [of the terms of the putative contract] if a State is unaware of the conditions [imposed by the legislation] or is unable to ascertain what is expected of it."

Invoking *Pennhurst,* respondents urge that Title IX provides no notice that recipients of federal educational funds could be liable in damages for harm arising from student-on-student harassment. Respondents contend, specifically, that the statute only proscribes misconduct by grant recipients, not third parties. Respondents argue, moreover, that it would be contrary to the very purpose of Spending Clause legislation to impose liability on a funding recipient for the misconduct of third parties, over whom recipients exercise little control.

We agree with respondents that a recipient of federal funds may be liable in damages under Title IX only for its own misconduct. The recipient itself must "exclude [persons] from participation in, . . . deny [persons] the benefits of, or . . . subject [persons] to discrimination under" its "programs or activities" in order to be liable under Title IX. The Government's enforcement power may only be exercised against the funding recipient, and we have not extended damages liability under Title IX to parties outside the scope of this power. . . .

We disagree with respondents' assertion, however, that petitioner seeks to hold the Board liable for G. F.'s actions instead of its own. Here, petitioner attempts to hold the Board liable for its *own* decision to remain idle in the face of known student-on-student harassment in its schools. In *Gebser,* we concluded that a recipient of federal education funds may be liable in damages under Title IX where it is deliberately indifferent to known acts of sexual harassment by a teacher. In that case, a teacher had entered into a sexual relationship with an eighth grade student, and the student sought damages under Title IX for the teacher's misconduct. We recognized that the scope of liability in private damages actions under Title IX is circumscribed by *Pennhurst's* requirement that funding recipients have notice of their potential liability. 524 U.S. at 287-288. Invoking *Pennhurst, Guardians Assn.,* and *Franklin,* in *Gebser* we once again required "that 'the receiving entity of federal funds [have] notice that it will be liable for a monetary award'" before subjecting it to damages liability. We also recognized, however, that this limitation on private damages actions is not a bar to liability where a funding recipient intentionally violates the statute. In particular, we concluded that *Pennhurst* does not bar a private damages action under Title IX where the funding recipient engages in intentional conduct that violates the clear terms of the statute.

Accordingly, we rejected the use of agency principles to impute liability to the district for the misconduct of its teachers. Likewise, we declined the invitation to impose liability under what amounted to a negligence standard—holding the district liable for its failure to react to teacher-student harassment of which it knew or *should have* known. Rather, we concluded that the district could be liable for damages only where the district itself intentionally acted in clear violation of Title IX by remaining deliberately indifferent to acts of teacher-student harassment of which it had actual knowledge. Contrary to the dissent's suggestion, the misconduct of the teacher in *Gebser* was not "treated as the grant recipient's actions." Liability arose, rather, from "an official decision by the recipient not to remedy the violation." By employing the "deliberate indifference" theory already used to establish municipal liability under Rev. Stat. §1979, 42 U.S.C. §1983, we concluded in *Gebser* that recipients could be liable in damages only where their own deliberate indifference effectively "caused" the discrimination. The high standard imposed in *Gebser* sought to eliminate any "risk that the recipient would be liable in damages not for its own official decision but instead for its employees' independent actions."

Gebser thus established that a recipient intentionally violates Title IX, and is subject to a private damages action, where the recipient is deliberately indifferent to known acts of teacher-student discrimination. Indeed, whether viewed as "discrimination" or "subjecting" students to discrimination,

Title IX "unquestionably . . . placed on [the Board] the duty not" to permit teacher-student harassment in its schools, *Franklin v. Gwinnett County Public Schools,* and recipients violate Title IX's plain terms when they remain deliberately indifferent to this form of misconduct.

We consider here whether the misconduct identified in *Gebser*—deliberate indifference to known acts of harassment—amounts to an intentional violation of Title IX, capable of supporting a private damages action, when the harasser is a student rather than a teacher. We conclude that, in certain limited circumstances, it does. As an initial matter, in *Gebser we* expressly rejected the use of agency principles in the Title IX context, noting the textual differences between Title IX and Title VII. 524 U.S. at 283; cf. *Faragher v. Boca Raton,* 524 U.S. 775-792 (1998) (invoking agency principles on ground that definition of "employer" in Title VII includes agents of employer); *Meritor Savings Bank, FSB v. Vinson, 477* U.S. 57, 72 (1986) (same). Additionally, the regulatory scheme surrounding Title IX has long provided funding recipients with notice that they may be liable for their failure to respond to the discriminatory acts of certain non-agents. The Department of Education requires recipients to monitor third parties for discrimination in specified circumstances and to refrain from particular forms of interaction with outside entities that are known to discriminate. *See, e.g.,* 34 CFR §§106.31(b)(6), 106.31(d), 106.37(a)(2), 106.38(a), 106.51(a)(3) (1998).

The common law, too, has put schools on notice that they may be held responsible under state law for their failure to protect students from the tortious acts of third parties. *See* Restatement (Second) of Torts §320, and Comment *a* (1965). In fact, state courts routinely uphold claims alleging that schools have been negligent in failing to protect their students from the torts of their peers. *See, e.g., Rupp v. Bryant,* 417 So. 2d 658, 666-667 (Fla. 1982); *Brahatcek v. Millard School Dist.,* 202 Neb. 86, 99-100, 273 N.W.2d 680, 688 (1979); *McLeod v. Grant County School Dist. No. 128,* 42 Wn.2d 316, 320, 255 P.2d 360, 362-363 (1953).

This is not to say that the identity of the harasser is irrelevant. On the contrary, both the "deliberate indifference" standard and the language of Title IX narrowly circumscribe the set of parties whose known acts of sexual harassment can trigger some duty to respond on the part of funding recipients. Deliberate indifference makes sense as a theory of direct liability under Title IX only where the funding recipient has some control over the alleged harassment. A recipient cannot be directly liable for its indifference where it lacks the authority to take remedial action.

The language of Title IX itself—particularly when viewed in conjunction with the requirement that the recipient have notice of Title IX's prohibitions to be liable for damages—also cabins the range of misconduct that the statute proscribes. The statute's plain language confines the scope of prohibited conduct based upon the recipient's degree of control over the harasser and the environment in which the harassment occurs. If a funding recipient does not engage in harassment directly, it may not be liable for damages unless its deliberate indifference "subjects" its students to harassment. That is, the deliberate indifference must, at a minimum, "cause [students] to undergo" harassment or "make them liable or vulnerable" to it. *Random House Dictionary of the English Language* 1415 (1966) (defining "subject" as "to cause to undergo the action of something specified; expose" or "to make liable or vulnerable; lay open; expose"); *Webster's Third New International Dictionary of the English Language 2275* (1961) (defining "subject" as "to cause to undergo or submit to: make submit to a particular action or effect: EXPOSE"). Moreover, because the harassment must occur "under" "the operations of" a funding recipient, *see* 20 U.S.C. §1681(a); §1687 (defining "program or activity"), the harassment must take place in a context subject to the school district's control, *Webster's Third New International Dictionary of the English Language, supra,* at 2487 (defining "under" as "in or into a condition of subjection, regulation, or subordination"; "subject to the guidance and instruction of"); *Random House Dictionary of the English Language, supra,* at 1543 (defining "under" as "subject to the authority, direction, or supervision of").

These factors combine to limit a recipient's damages liability to circumstances wherein the recipient exercises substantial control over both the harasser and the context in which the known harassment occurs. Only then can the recipient be said to "expose" its students to harassment or "cause" them to undergo it "under" the recipient's programs. We agree with the dissent that these conditions are satisfied most easily and most obviously when the offender is an agent of the recipient. We rejected the use of agency analysis in *Gebser,* however, and we disagree that the term "under" somehow imports an agency requirement into Title IX. As noted above, the theory in *Gebser* was that the recipient was *directly* liable for its deliberate indifference to discrimination. Liability in that case did not arise because the "teacher's actions [were] treated" as those of the funding recipient, the district was directly liable for its *own* failure to act. The terms "subject" and "under" impose limits, but nothing about these terms requires the use of agency principles.

Where, as here, the misconduct occurs during school hours and on school grounds—the bulk of G. F.'s misconduct, in fact, took place in the classroom—the misconduct is taking place "under" an "operation" of the funding recipient.

In these circumstances, the recipient retains substantial control over the context in which the harassment occurs. More importantly, however, in this setting the Board exercises significant control over the harasser. We have observed, for example, "that the nature of [the State's] power [over public schoolchildren] is custodial and tutelary, permitting a degree of supervision and control that could not be exercised over free adults." *Vernonia School Dist. 47J v. Acton,* 515 U.S. 646, 655 (1995). On more than one occasion, this Court has recognized the importance of school officials' "comprehensive authority . . . , consistent with fundamental constitutional safeguards, to prescribe and control conduct in the schools." *Tinker v. Des Moines Independent Community School Dist.,* 393 U.S. 503, 507 (1969); *see also New Jersey v. T.L.O.,* 469 U.S. 325, 342, n.9 (1985). The common law, too, recognizes the school's disciplinary authority. See Restatement (Second) of Torts §152 (1965). We thus conclude that recipients of federal funding may be liable for "subjecting" their students to discrimination where the recipient is deliberately indifferent to known acts of student-on-student sexual harassment and the harasser is under the school's disciplinary authority. . . .

We stress that our conclusion here—that recipients may be liable for their deliberate indifference to known acts of peer sexual harassment—does not mean that recipients can avoid liability only by purging their schools of actionable peer harassment or that administrators must engage in particular disciplinary action. We thus disagree with respondents' contention that, if Title IX provides a cause of action for student-on-student harassment, "nothing short of expulsion of every student accused of misconduct involving sexual overtones would protect school systems from liability or damages." Likewise, the dissent erroneously imagines that victims of peer harassment now have a Title IX right to make particular remedial demands. In fact, as we have previously noted, courts should refrain from second guessing the disciplinary decisions made by school administrators.

School administrators will continue to enjoy the flexibility they require so long as funding recipients are deemed "deliberately indifferent" to acts of student-on-student harassment only where the recipient's response to the harassment or lack thereof is clearly unreasonable in light of the known circumstances. The dissent consistently mischaracterizes this standard to require funding recipients to "remedy" peer harassment, and to "ensure that . . . students conform their conduct to" certain rules. Title IX imposes no such requirements. On the contrary, the recipient must merely respond to known peer harassment in a manner that is not clearly unreasonable. This is not a mere "reasonableness" standard, as the dissent assumes. In an appropriate case, there is no reason why courts, on a motion to dismiss, for smmary judgment, or for a directed verdict, could not identify a response as not "clearly unreasonable" as a matter of law.

Like the dissent, we acknowledge that school administrators shoulder substantial burdens as a result of legal constraints on their disciplinary authority. To the extent that these restrictions arise from federal statutes, Congress can review these burdens with attention to the difficult position in which such legislation may place our Nation's schools. We believe, however, that the standard set out here is sufficiently flexible to account both for the level of disciplinary authority available to the school and for the potential liability arising from certain forms of disciplinary action. A university might not, for example, be expected to exercise the same degree of control over its students that a grade school would enjoy, and it would be entirely reasonable for a school to refrain from a form of disciplinary action that would expose it to constitutional or statutory claims.

While it remains to be seen whether petitioner can show that the Board's response to reports of G. F.'s misconduct was clearly unreasonable in light of the known circumstances, petitioner may be able to show that the Board "subjected" LaShonda to discrimination by failing to respond in any way over a period of five months to complaints of G. F.'s in-school misconduct from LaShonda and other female students. . . .

B

Having previously determined that "sexual harassment" is "discrimination" in the school context under Title IX, we are constrained to conclude that student-on-student sexual harassment, if sufficiently severe, can likewise rise to the level of discrimination actionable under the statute. The statute's other prohibitions, moreover, help give content to the term "discrimination" in this context. Students are not only protected from discrimination, but also specifically shielded from being "excluded from participation in" or "denied the benefits of" any "education program or activity receiving Federal financial assistance." §1681(a). The statute makes clear that, whatever else it prohibits, students must not be denied access to educational benefits and opportunities on the basis of gender. We thus conclude that funding recipients are properly held liable in damages only where they are deliberately indifferent to sexual harassment, of which they have actual knowledge, that is so severe, pervasive, and objectively offensive that it can be said to deprive the victims of access to the educational opportunities or benefits provided by the school.

The most obvious example of student-on-student sexual harassment capable of triggering a damages claim would thus involve the overt, physical deprivation of access to school resources. Consider, for example, a case in which male students physically threaten their female peers every day, successfully preventing the female students from using a particular school resource—an athletic field or a computer lab, for instance. District administrators are well aware of the daily ritual, yet they deliberately ignore requests for aid from the female students wishing to use the resource. The district's knowing refusal to take any action in response to such behavior would fly in the face of Title IX's core principles, and such deliberate indifference may appropriately be subject to claims for monetary damages. It is not necessary, however, to show physical exclusion to demonstrate that students have been deprived by the actions of another student or students of an educational opportunity on the basis of sex. Rather, a plaintiff must establish sexual harassment of students that is so severe, pervasive, and objectively offensive, and that so undermines and detracts from the victims' educational experience, that the victim-students are effectively denied equal access to an institution's resources and opportunities.

Whether gender-oriented conduct rises to the level of actionable "harassment" thus "depends on a constellation of surrounding circumstances, expectations, and relationships," *Oncale v. Sundowner Offshore Services, Inc.*, 523 U.S. 75, 82 (1998), including, but not limited to, the ages of the harasser and the victim and the number of individuals involved, *see* OCR Title IX Guidelines 12041-12042. Courts, moreover, must bear in mind that schools are unlike the adult workplace and that children may regularly interact in a manner that would be unacceptable among adults. *See, e.g.*, Brief for National School Boards Association et al. as *Amici Curiae* 11 (describing "dizzying array of immature . . . behaviors by students"). Indeed, at least early on, students are still learning how to interact appropriately with their peers. It is thus understandable that, in the school setting, students often engage in insults, banter, teasing, shoving, pushing, and gender-specific conduct that is upsetting to the students subjected to it. Damages are not available for simple acts of teasing and name-calling among school children, however, even where these comments target differences in gender. Rather, in the context of student-on-student harassment, damages are available only where the behavior is so severe, pervasive, and objectively offensive that it denies its victims the equal access to education that Title IX is designed to protect.

The dissent fails to appreciate these very real limitations on a funding recipient's liability under Title IX. It is not enough to show, as the dissent would read this opinion to provide, that a student has been "teased," or "called . . . offensive names." Comparisons to an "overweight child who skips gym class because the other children tease her about her size," the student "who refuses to wear glasses to avoid the taunts of 'four-eyes,'" and "the child who refuses to go to school because the school bully calls him a 'scardy-cat' at recess," are inapposite and misleading. Nor do we contemplate, much less hold, that a mere "decline in grades is enough to survive" a motion to dismiss. The drop-off in LaShonda's grades provides necessary evidence of a potential link between her education and G. F.'s misconduct, but petitioner's ability to state a cognizable claim here depends equally on the alleged persistence and severity of G. F.'s actions, not to mention the Board's alleged knowledge and deliberate indifference. We trust that the dissent's characterization of our opinion will not mislead courts to impose more sweeping liability than we read Title IX to require.

Moreover, the provision that the discrimination occur "under any education program or activity" suggests that the behavior be serious enough to have the systemic effect of denying the victim equal access to an educational program or activity. Although, in theory, a single instance of sufficiently severe one-on-one peer harassment could be said to have such an effect, we think it unlikely that Congress would have thought such behavior sufficient to rise to this level in light of the inevitability of student misconduct and the amount of litigation that would be invited by entertaining claims of official indifference to a single instance of one-on-one peer harassment. By limiting private damages actions to cases having a systemic effect on educational programs or activities, we reconcile the general principle that Title IX prohibits official indifference to known peer sexual harassment with the practical realities of responding to student behavior, realities that Congress could not have meant to be ignored. Even the dissent suggests that Title IX liability may arise when a funding recipient remains indifferent to severe, gender-based mistreatment played out on a "widespread level" among students.

The fact that it was a teacher who engaged in harassment in *Franklin* and *Gebser* is relevant. The relationship between the harasser and the victim necessarily affects the extent to which the misconduct can be said to breach Title IX's guarantee of equal access to educational benefits and to have a systemic effect on a program or activity. Peer harassment, in particular, is less likely to satisfy these requirements than is teacher-student harassment.

C

Applying this standard to the facts at issue here, we conclude that the Eleventh Circuit erred in dismissing petitioner's complaint. Petitioner alleges that her daughter was the victim of repeated acts of sexual harassment by G. F. over a 5-month period, and there are allegations in support of the conclusion that G. F.'s misconduct was severe, pervasive, and objectively offensive. The harassment was not only verbal; it included numerous acts of objectively offensive touching, and, indeed, G. F. ultimately pleaded guilty to criminal sexual misconduct. Moreover, the complaint alleges that there were multiple victims who were sufficiently disturbed by G. F.'s misconduct to seek an audience with the school principal. Further, petitioner contends that the harassment had a concrete, negative effect on her daughter's ability to receive an education. The complaint also suggests that petitioner may be able to show both actual knowledge and deliberate indifference on the part of the Board, which made no effort whatsoever either to investigate or to put an end to the harassment. . . .

Accordingly, the judgment of the United States Court of Appeals for the Eleventh Circuit is reversed, and the case is remanded for further proceedings consistent with this opinion.

It is so ordered.

NOTES AND QUESTIONS

1. Reconsider the language of Title IX in light of the Court's reasoning in *Davis*. The statute prohibits three independent forms of conduct based upon "sex": (1) exclusion from participation in; (2) denial of the benefits of, *and* (3) subjection to discrimination under any education program or activity. In concluding that the level of harassment must be "so severe, pervasive and objectively offensive" that it denies the victim access to educational benefits provided by the school, the Court argues that Title IX prohibits conduct that denies students educational benefits based upon gender. Yet, while Title IX clearly prohibits such conduct, it also independently prohibits schools from subjecting students to discrimination based upon gender. In fact, the Court acknowledges that the Department of Education's Office for Civil Rights Guidelines provide that student-on-student harassment falls within the scope of Title IX's proscriptions. *See* Department of Education, Office of Civil Rights, *Sexual Harassment Guidance: Harassment of Students by School Employees, Other Students, or Third Parties,* 62 Fed. Reg. 12034, 12039-40 (1997) (OCR Title IX Guidelines); *see also* Department of Education, *Racial Incidents and Harassment Against Students at Educational Institutions,* 59 Fed. Reg. 11448, 11449 (1994). If, as the Court argues, sexual harassment is a form of gender discrimination, then why is proof of sexual harassment alone not sufficient to make out a Title IX claim? Why must the sexual harassment *also* deny the victim access to educational benefits?
2. How are private women's colleges affected by Title IX and the equal protection clause? Title IX prohibits discrimination in admitting students to *public* colleges; unless the private colleges receive federal funds, they are generally exempt from oversight. Moreover, courts decline to apply the equal protection clause to private colleges because constitutional challenges impose limitations only on governmental actors.

   Professor Christopher Pyle, however, argues that it is anomalous to subject public colleges to constitutional oversight, but to immunize the ostensibly private colleges that receive nearly as much state funding as public colleges. Christopher H. Pyle, *Women's Colleges: Is Segregation by Sex*

Still Justifiable after United States v. Virginia?, 77 B.U.L. Rev. 209, 226-227 (1997). He contends that women's colleges should justify their exclusionary policies just as the male academies did in *Virginia.* Pyle suggests that *Virginia* may actually lead women's colleges to believe that they are beyond the reach of its holding because the Court implies that the academy discriminated for some "invidious" purpose, preserving an all-male tradition at women's expense, while women's colleges exclude men for a "benign" purpose. *Id.* at 217. Nevertheless, he emphasizes that women's colleges should be aware that the real issue in *Virginia* was whether the institutions improperly relied on outdated stereotypes in "exclud[ing] all members of one sex in order to achieve a legitimate educational end," suggesting that women's colleges are now still permitted to rely on illegitimate generalizations. *Id. at 217.*

To that end, Pyle ultimately concludes that, in theory, *Virginia* created a "skeptical scrutiny" standard, which is somewhere between intermediate scrutiny and strict scrutiny, and does not appear to treat women's colleges and male academies equally. *Id.* at 230-233. The Court demands an "exceedingly persuasive justification" for denying admission to members of one gender; however, it appears that women's colleges may indeed rely on generalizations about men's and women's education styles and preferences to support their justification, while male academies cannot. *Id.* at 231-232. Pyle speculates that as this standard is applied in the future, the Court will not, in fact, allow women's colleges to rely on such evidence to make their arguments for segregation. *Id.* at 271. He suggests that women's colleges affirmatively address their discrimination issues *now* in order to avoid future litigation. *Id.* As an attorney for a private women's college how would you advise your client to proceed?

3. The American Association of University Women (the AAUW) reported in 1993 that 85 percent of girls surveyed in 79 public school grades eight through eleven acknowledged that they had experienced unwelcome peer sexual advances in school. *Hostile Hallways: The AAUW Survey on Sexual Harassment in America's Schools* (1993). According to 31 percent of the girls surveyed, such unwelcome sexual encounters happened "often." *Id.* Although most of the experiences involved expressions or gestures, 13 percent of the girls reported being forced into engaging in sexual activity other than kissing. *Id. See also How Schools Shortchange Girls,* AAUW Educational Foundation and National Education Association, 106-112, 114-126 (1995) (hereinafter AAUW Report). When does the level of such unwelcome sexual behavior become harassment? The majority opinion in *Davis* responds to the dissent's warnings about the expanded scope of Title IX remedies by making clear that peer sexual harassment must be more "severe, pervasive, and objectively offensive" than gender-based teasing or offensive name calling. Is it possible that gender-based peer harassment contributes to the decline in academic achievement among adolescent girls in coeducational environments? If so, how "severe," must such "teasing" become to deny to adolescent girls the "equal access to education that Title IX is designed to protect"?

4. The AAUW Report presents the available research regarding curriculum and instructional materials in American classrooms and finds evidence of pervasive gender bias. Textbooks still generally exclude women, stereotype members of both sexes, depict the subordination of women, isolate materials regarding women, slight contemporary policy issues related to women and falsely portray the history of women. *See* AAUW Report at 106-112, 114-127. In the classroom as well, evidence indicates that teacher-student interactions are characterized by double standards for men and women, condescension toward women, tokenism, denial of achieved status or authority to women, backlashes against successful women, and strategies that attempt to separate successful women from others in their gender group. *Id.* The AAUW Report also concludes: "research spanning the past twenty years consistently reveals that males receive more teacher attention than do females" from preschool through college. *Id.* Are these findings consistent with your own educational experience? Are they consistent with your own law school or graduate school experience? Is an educational institution's "deliberate indifference" to such forms of gender bias in the curriculum and the classroom actionable under Title IX?
5. Under the "deliberate indifference" standard created by *Davis,* how should a school district react to parental complaints about gender-based teasing in the classroom? Is a policy prohibiting such behavior sufficient to establish an educational institution's lack of "deliberate indifference"? How should the "deliberate indifference" standard of liability be applied to a school which is so inept that it never gains knowledge or actual notice of pervasive sexual harassment? *See, e.g., Massey v. Akron City Board of Education,* 82 F. Supp. 2d 735 (N.D. Ohio 2000) (no deliberate indifference when school district was unaware of inappropriate sexual contact between teacher and student); *Doe v. Dallas Independent School District,* 153 F.3d 211, 219 (5th Cir. 1998) (merely "inept" actions by school do not constitute deliberate indifference). In *Wills v. Brown University,* 184 F.3d 20 (1st Cir. 1999), however, the First Circuit found deliberate indifference in the university's failure to take "timely and reasonable measures to end the harassment."
6. Does a school's disciplinary action against a student for "severe" expressions of gender-based harassment raise First Amendment concerns? In Chapter 12, the issue of a student's right to freedom of expression is addressed in the context of school anti harassment policies, some of which have been invalidated because they violate the speech rights of students. How can a school proactively prevent sexual harassment in the classroom without unnecessarily curtailing student speech? *See* N. Stein, *Secrets in Public: Sexual Harassment in Public (and Private) Schools* (1997) (rejecting criticisms of school district efforts to police students' acts of sexual harassment in the schools as misplaced given the pervasive nature of the problem).
7. Does Title IX protect gay men from sexual harassment? The statute clearly protects men from harassment based upon gender. Moreover, in *Nabozny v. Podlesny,* 92 F.3d 446 (7th Cir. 1996), the Seventh Circuit held that a school district and its administrator could be liable for their deliberate indifference to the peer harassment of a gay middle school student. The

Court reasoned that the school's failure to enforce its sexual harassment policy equally for incidents of male-female and male-male harassment constituted unjustifiable gender discrimination. *See also* Lovell, *Other Students Always Used to Say, "Look at the Dykes": Protecting Students from Peer Sexual Orientation Harassment,* 86 Cal. L. Rev. 617 (1998).

E. RACE AND GENDER DISCRIMINATION PRACTICUMS: THE REALITY OF DISCRIMINATION IN THE CLASSROOM

1. School District Policies and Interventions

In light of the legal requirements placed on school districts, consider the following school district policy and determine whether it is sufficient:

> No student shall, on the basis of his or her sex, sexual orientation, race, color, national origin, ancestry, ethnicity, language barrier, religious beliefs or religious affiliation, physical and mental handicap or disability, status as homeless, economic and social conditions, or actual or potential marital or parental status be denied equal access to programs, activities, services or benefits, or be limited in the exercise of any right, privilege, advantage or opportunity. *See* Title IX, 20 U.S.C. §1681 *et seq.;* 34 C.F.R. Part 106. Sexual harassment of students is prohibited. Any person, including a District employee or agent, or student, engages in sexual harassment whenever he or she makes sexual advances, requests sexual favors, and engages in other verbal or physical conduct of a sexual or sex-based nature, imposed on the basis of sex, that:
>
> 1. denies or limits the provision of educational aid, benefits, services, or treatment; or that makes such conduct a condition of a student's academic status; or
> 2. has the purpose or effect of:
>   a. substantially interfering with a student's educational environment;
>   b. creating an intimidating, hostile, or offensive educational environment;
>   c. depriving a student of educational aid, benefits, services, or treatment; or
>   d. making submission to or rejection of such conduct the basis for academic decisions affecting a student.
>
> The terms "intimidating," "hostile," and "offensive" include conduct that has the effect of humiliation, embarrassment, or discomfort. Examples of sexual harassment include touching, crude jokes or pictures, discussions of sexual experiences, teasing related to sexual characteristics, and spreading rumors related to a person's alleged sexual activities. *See* Title IX of the Educational Amendments, 20 U.S.C. §1681 *et seq.;* 34 C.F.R. Part 106.

What process must be established to provide internal remedies to victims of violations of these policies? Assuming that these policies are adequate to satisfy the district's legal obligations, can those policies alone protect students from acts of discrimination or harassment in the classroom? What steps would you advise a school district to take to insure that male and female students are not subjected to conscious gender bias and subconscious gender disadvantage within the classroom? Would those steps be similar to the steps taken to insure the absence of any racial bias and stereotyping in the classroom?

2. A School District's Voluntary Integration Strategy

Round Tree School District is a large district that houses three elementary schools and two middle schools. Round Tree is predominantly white, but has a large Hispanic population concentrated at the northern end of the district. Currently, virtually all of the district's Hispanic children attend North Elementary School and Northside Middle School, as those schools are closest to where they live. The district has never been found to have violated any legal requirements regarding its racial composition. The district, however, would like to achieve diversity throughout its schools. It is considering ways in which to attract white students to the north side schools and Hispanic students to the other schools, hoping to spread the Hispanic population throughout the district. The school board through its president seeks legal advice before considering alternative strategies for doing so. Based upon the law governing racial segregation and desegregation, may the school district act with a purpose to achieve racial diversity throughout its district?

Assume that the district decides to make its north side schools into "magnet schools" by creating a "dual language" (English/Spanish) immersion program for both native-English and native-Spanish speaking students. It hopes that the dual language program will attract white students to the north schools. Further, it plans to create similar dual language opportunities at the other schools, and would offer Hispanic children the option of being transported to the other schools to achieve a significant native-Spanish speaking population at the other schools. May the district proceed with its "dual language" magnet program for the purpose of achieving diversity in each of its schools?

3. International and Comparative Law Perspective on Gender Equity in Education

Gender disparities in education remain "pervasive" worldwide. *See* Education for All Global Monitoring Report, UNESCO (2008). Most of the 73 million children who do not go to any primary school are girls. *Id.* Only about one-third of the countries report gender parity in educational opportunities. *Id.* In sub-Saharan Africa, only 20% of the girls receive a primary school education. *Id. See also* Jonathan Alter, "It's Not Just About the Boys. Get Girls into School," at 50-51 (*Newsweek* Sept. 29, 2008) (citing UNICEF data, 2001-2005). According to Alter, "[t]he biggest barrier to primary and secondary education in the developing world remains the fees that too many countries continue to charge parents for each child in school." Alter, at 51-52. These "fees" are not always direct; education often requires payment for uniforms, books and transportation. In rural areas, where schools are spread out, transportation is a significant impediment. According to Alter, the "effect is that poor families (disproportionately in rural areas, where school attendance is lightest) send their oldest, healthiest boys to school with the hope that they will support their parents in old age. This often deprives girls—the ones actually much more likely to help their families—of the chance to go to school." *Id.* Gender equity in the developing world requires the abolition of direct and indirect costs, followed by the creation of a safe, clean and well-staffed primary school infrastructure that can accommodate the influx of additional students.

The UNESCO Report also finds that gender equality is difficult to achieve because many girls are affected by an unsafe and hostile school environment, including sexual violence and harassment that leads them to withdraw from school. *See* Report, Summary, Goal 5. As a general rule, girls are more likely to attend school in countries with higher percentages of female teachers. *Id.* Throughout the world, 94% of pre-school teachers are women, 62% of primary school teachers are women, 53% of secondary teachers are women and 41% of higher education teachers are women. *Id.* The Report observes:

> Boys generally enjoy more challenging interactions with teachers, dominate classroom activities and receive more attention than girls through criticism, praise and constructive feedback. Studies of rural pupils in Kenya, Malawi and Rwanda found that teachers have low expectations of female students. Both teachers and students contributed to a pattern tha[t] gives girls fewer opportunities to participate actively in class.

Id. Moreover, UNESCO also reports that throughout the world:

> Contents analysis of textbooks points to gender bias against girls and women regardless of the level of education, subject matter, country or region. Girls and women are systematically under-represented in textbooks and still shown in highly stereotyped roles, even in countries that have achieved gender parity in primary education.

Id.

CHAPTER 13

THE RIGHTS OF STUDENTS

In this chapter, the school's legitimate interest in maintaining discipline must be reconciled with the fundamental constitutional or statutory rights of students to freedom of expression, freedom from unreasonable searches and seizures, due process and privacy. Where does the legitimate authority of school districts to govern the education environment end and the rights of students begin?

A student's right to attend school and claim the benefits afforded by the public school system is subject to the school's legitimate policies and administrative regulations. *Leonard v. School Committee of Attleboro,* 212 N.E.2d 468 (Mass. 1965); *Coggins v. Board of Education of City of Durham,* 28 S.E.2d 527 (N.C. 1944). Because of the state's custodial authority over students, public school students are subject to a greater degree of control and supervision than is permitted over nonstudents. *State v. J.A.,* 679 So. 2d 316 (Fla. App. 1996); *Hoff v. Vacaville Unified School District,* 968 P.2d 522 (Cal. 1998); *Plesnicar v. Kovach,* 430 N.E.2d 648 (Ill. App. 1981). The school district may exercise such powers of control, restraint and discipline over pupils as is reasonably necessary to enable the educators to perform their duties and to accomplish the purposes of education. A reasonable school regulation is one that is essential to maintaining order and discipline on school property and which contributes to the maintenance of order and decorum within the educational environment. *Blackwell v. Issaquena County Board of Education,* 363 F.2d 749 (5th Cir. 1966). The courts will not interfere in such matters unless there is a clear abuse of discretion, *Wilson v. Abilene Independent School District,* 190 S.W.2d 406 (Tex. App. 1945), or unless the district interferes with a student's constitutional rights. *See, e.g., Phoenix Elementary School District No. 1 v. Green,* 943 P.2d 836 (Ariz. 1997).

A. FREEDOM OF EXPRESSION

In the public school system, students enjoy some, but not all, of the protections of the First Amendment. In the seminal *Tinker* case, the Supreme Court ruled that students were entitled to wear black armbands in school as a silent, nondisruptive protest. *Tinker v. Des Moines Independent County School District,* 393 U.S. 503 (1969). First Amendment rights also include newspapers, clubs and handouts. However, these rights are not without limits. Students are guaranteed the right to express their opinions unless it "materially and substantially" disrupts classes or other school activities. In *Bethel,* the Supreme Court concluded that a school district may censor a student's speech during an assembly if the contents are "vulgar" or "indecent" and thus "substantially" interfere with school activities. *Bethel School District No. 403 v. Fraser,* 478 U.S. 675 (1986). In *Hazelwood,* the Court further expanded the power of schools to regulate student expression. *Hazelwood School District v. Kuhlmeier,* 488 U.S. 260 (1988). If a publication or activity, such as a school play, newspaper, student government speech delivered in a schoolwide forum or yearbook, is considered an "official" school function, the administration may censor controversial items if they merely view the contents as "inappropriate" or "harmful." School dress codes also are commonly challenged under the First Amendment. Dress codes regulate symbolic speech because a student's style of dress is an articulation of the student's opinions and sense of self. Nevertheless, many schools have dress codes that restrict specific clothing, hair length, skirt length and even clothing color. Courts are unlikely to invalidate a school's dress code unless it is extremely unreasonable or discriminatory.

1. Political Expression That Does Not Substantially Interfere with School

TINKER V. DES MOINES INDEPENDENT COMMUNITY SCHOOL DISTRICT

---

393 U.S. 503 (1969)

Mr. Justice FORTAS delivered the opinion of the Court.

Petitioner John F. Tinker, 15 years old, and petitioner Christopher Eckhardt, 16 years old, attended high schools in Des Moines, Iowa. Petitioner Mary Beth Tinker, John's sister, was a 13-year-old student in junior high school.

In December 1965, a group of adults and students . . . [were] determined to publicize their objections to the hostilities in Vietnam and their support for a truce by wearing black armbands during the holiday season. . . .

The principals of the Des Moines schools became aware of the plan to wear armbands. On December 14, 1965, they met and adopted a policy that any student wearing an armband to school would be asked to remove it, and if he refused he would be suspended until he returned without the armband. . . .

On December 16, Mary Beth and Christopher wore black armbands to their schools. John Tinker wore his armband the next day. They were all sent home and suspended from school until they would come back without their armbands. . . .

This complaint was filed in the United States District Court by petitioners, through their fathers, under §1983 of Title 42 of the United States Code.

It prayed for an injunction restraining the respondent school officials and the respondent members of the board of directors of the school district from disciplining the petitioners, and it sought nominal damages. After an evidentiary hearing the District Court dismissed the complaint. It upheld the constitutionality of the school authorities' action on the ground that it was reasonable in order to prevent disturbance of school discipline. The court referred to but expressly declined to follow the Fifth Circuit's holding in a similar case that the wearing of symbols like the armbands cannot be prohibited unless it "materially and substantially interfere(s) with the requirements of appropriate discipline in the operation of the school." *Burnside v. Byars,* 363 F.2d 744, 479 (1966).

On appeal, the Court of Appeals for the Eighth Circuit considered the case en banc. The court was equally divided, and the District Court's decision was accordingly affirmed, without opinion. We granted certiorari.

I

The District Court recognized that the wearing of an armband for the purpose of expressing certain views is the type of symbolic act that is within the Free Speech Clause of the First Amendment. . . . As we shall discuss, the wearing of armbands in the circumstances of this case was entirely divorced from actually or potentially disruptive conduct by those participating in it. It was closely akin to "pure speech" which, we have repeatedly held, is entitled to comprehensive protection under the First Amendment. . . .

First Amendment rights, applied in light of the special characteristics of the school environment, are available to teachers and students. It can hardly be argued that either students or teachers shed their constitutional rights to freedom of speech or expression at the schoolhouse gate. This has been the unmistakable holding of this Court for almost 50 years. In *Meyer v. Nebraska,* 262 U.S. 390, 43 S. Ct. 625, 67 L. Ed. 1042 (1923), and *Bartels v. Iowa,* 262 U.S. 404, 43 S. Ct. 628, 67 L. Ed. 1047 (1923), this Court, in opinions by Mr. Justice McReynolds, held that the Due Process Clause of the Fourteenth Amendment prevents States from forbidding the teaching of a foreign language to young students. Statutes to this effect, the Court held, unconstitutionally interfere with the liberty of teacher, student, and parent. . . .

In *West Virginia State Board of Education v. Barnette,* this Court held that under the First Amendment, the student in public school may not be compelled to salute the flag. Speaking through Mr. Justice Jackson, the Court said:

> The Fourteenth Amendment, as now applied to the States, protects the citizen against the State itself and all of its creatures—Boards of Education not excepted. These have, of course, important, delicate, and highly discretionary functions, but none that they may not perform within the limits of the Bill of Rights. That they are educating the young for citizenship is reason for scrupulous protection of Constitutional freedoms of the individual, if we are not to strangle the free mind at its source and teach youth to discount important principles of our government as mere platitudes. . . .

On the other hand, the Court has repeatedly emphasized the need for affirming the comprehensive authority of the States and of school officials, consistent with fundamental constitutional safeguards, to prescribe and control conduct in the schools. . . . Our problem lies in the area where students in the exercise of First Amendment rights collide with the rules of the school authorities.

II

The problem posed by the present case does not relate to regulation of the length of skirts or the type of clothing, to hair style, or deportment. . . . It does not concern aggressive, disruptive action or even group demonstrations. Our problem involves direct, primary First Amendment rights akin to "pure speech."

The school officials banned and sought to punish petitioners for a silent, passive expression of opinion, unaccompanied by any disorder or disturbance on the part of petitioners. There is here no evidence whatever of petitioners' interference, actual or nascent, with the schools' work or of collision with the rights of other students to be secure and to be let alone. Accordingly, this case does not concern speech or action that intrudes upon the work of the schools or the rights of other students.

Only a few of the 18,000 students in the school system wore the black armbands. Only five students were suspended for wearing them. There is no indication that the work of the schools or any class was disrupted. Outside the classrooms, a few students made hostile remarks to the children wearing armbands, but there were no threats or acts of violence on school premises.

The District Court concluded that the action of the school authorities was reasonable because it was based upon their fear of a disturbance from the wearing of the armbands. But, in our system, undifferentiated fear or apprehension of disturbance is not enough to overcome the right to freedom of expression. Any departure from absolute regimentation may cause trouble. Any variation from the majority's opinion may inspire fear. Any word spoken, in class, in the lunchroom, or on the campus, that deviates from the views of another person may start an argument or cause a disturbance. But our Constitution says we must take this risk, . . . and our history says that it is this sort of hazardous freedom—this kind of openness—that is the basis of our national strength and of the independence and vigor of Americans who grow up and live in this relatively permissive, often disputatious, society.

In order for the State in the person of school officials to justify prohibition of a particular expression of opinion, it must be able to show that its action was caused by something more than a mere desire to avoid the discomfort and unpleasantness that always accompany an unpopular viewpoint. Certainly where there is no finding and no showing that engaging in the forbidden conduct would "materially and substantially interfere with the requirements of appropriate discipline in the operation of the school," the prohibition cannot be sustained. . . .

In the present case, the District Court made no such finding, and our independent examination of the record fails to yield evidence that the school authorities had reason to anticipate that the wearing of the armbands would substantially interfere with the work of the school or impinge upon the rights of other students. Even an official memorandum prepared after the suspension that listed the reasons for the ban on wearing the armbands made no reference to the anticipation of such disruption.

On the contrary, the action of the school authorities appears to have been based upon an urgent wish to avoid the controversy which might result from the expression, even by the silent symbol of armbands, of opposition to this Nation's part in the conflagration in Vietnam. It is revealing, in this respect, that the meeting at which the school principals decided to issue the contested regulation was called in response to a student's statement to the journalism teacher in one of the schools that he wanted to write an article on Vietnam and have it published in the school paper. (The student was dissuaded.)

It is also relevant that the school authorities did not purport to prohibit the wearing of all symbols of political or controversial significance. The record shows that students in some of the schools wore buttons relating to national political campaigns, and some even wore the Iron Cross, traditionally a symbol of Nazism. The order prohibiting the wearing of armbands did not extend to these. Instead, a particular symbol—black armbands worn to exhibit opposition to this Nation's involvement in Vietnam—was singled out for prohibition. Clearly, the prohibition of expression of one particular opinion, at least without evidence that it is necessary to avoid material and substantial interference with schoolwork or discipline, is not constitutionally permissible.

In our system, state-operated schools may not be enclaves of totalitarianism. School officials do not possess absolute authority over their students. Students in school as well as out of school are "persons" under our Constitution. They are possessed of fundamental rights which the State must respect, just as they themselves must respect their obligations to the State. In our system, students may not be regarded as closed-circuit recipients of only that which the State chooses to communicate. They may not be confined to the expression of those sentiments that are officially approved. In the absence of a specific showing of constitutionally valid reasons to regulate their speech, students are entitled to freedom of expression of their views. . . . [S]chool officials cannot suppress "expressions of feelings with which they do not wish to contend."

In *Meyer v. Nebraska,* Mr. Justice McReynolds expressed this Nation's repudiation of the principle that a State might so conduct its schools as to "foster a homogeneous people." He said:

> In order to submerge the individual and develop ideal citizens, Sparta assembled the males at seven into barracks and in trusted their subsequent education and training to official guardians. Although such measures have been deliberately approved by men of great genius, their ideas touching the relation between individual and State were wholly different from those upon which our institutions rest; and it hardly will be affirmed that any Legislature could impose such restrictions upon the people of a state without doing violence to both letter and spirit of the Constitution.

This principle has been repeated by this Court on numerous occasions during the intervening years. In *Keyishian v. Board of Regents,* Mr. Justice Brennan, speaking for the Court, said:

> The vigilant protection of constitutional freedoms is nowhere more vital than in the community of American schools. . . . The classroom is peculiarly the

> "marketplace of ideas." The Nation's future depends upon leaders trained through wide exposure to that robust exchange of ideas which discovers truth "out of a multitude of tongues, [rather] than through any kind of authoritative selection."

The principle of these cases is not confined to the supervised and ordained discussion which takes place in the classroom. The principal use to which the schools are dedicated is to accommodate students during prescribed hours for the purpose of certain types of activities. Among those activities is personal intercommunication among the students. This is not only an inevitable part of the process of attending school; it is also an important part of the educational process. A student's rights, therefore, do not embrace merely the classroom hours. When he is in the cafeteria, or on the playing field, or on the campus during the authorized hours, he may express his opinions, even on controversial subjects like the conflict in Vietnam, if he does so without "materially and substantially interfer(ing) with the requirements of appropriate discipline in the operation of the school" and without colliding with the rights of others. . . . But conduct by the student, in class or out of it, which for any reason—whether it stems from time, place, or type of behavior—materially disrupts classwork or involves substantial disorder or invasion of the rights of others is, of course, not immunized by the constitutional guarantee of freedom of speech. . . .

Under our Constitution, free speech is not a right that is given only to be so circumscribed that it exists in principle but not in fact. Freedom of expression would not truly exist if the right could be exercised only in an area that a benevolent government has provided as a safe haven for crackpots. The Constitution says that Congress (and the States) may not abridge the right to free speech. This provision means what it says. We properly read it to permit reasonable regulation of speech-connected activities in carefully restricted circumstances. But we do not confine the permissible exercise of First Amendment rights to a telephone booth or the four corners of a pamphlet, or to supervised and ordained discussion in a school classroom.

If a regulation were adopted by school officials forbidding discussion of the Vietnam conflict, or the expression by any student of opposition to it anywhere on school property except as part of a prescribed classroom exercise, it would be obvious that the regulation would violate the constitutional rights of students, at least if it could not be justified by a showing that the students' activities would materially and substantially disrupt the work and discipline of the school. . . . In the circumstances of the present case, the prohibition of the silent, passive "witness of the armbands," as one of the children called it, is no less offensive to the constitution's guarantees.

As we have discussed, the record does not demonstrate any facts which might reasonably have led school authorities to forecast substantial disruption of or material interference with school activities, and no disturbances or disorders on the school premises in fact occurred. These petitioners merely went about their ordained rounds in school. Their deviation consisted only in wearing on their sleeve a band of black cloth, not more than two inches wide. They wore it to exhibit their disapproval of the Vietnam hostilities and their advocacy of a truce, to make their views known, and, by their example, to influence others to adopt them. They neither interrupted school activities nor sought to intrude in the school affairs or the lives of others. They caused discussion outside of the classrooms, but no interference with work and no disorder. In the circumstances, our Constitution does not permit officials of the State to deny their form of expression. . . . We reverse and remand for further proceedings consistent with this opinion.

NOTES AND QUESTIONS

1. In *Tinker,* the Supreme Court noted that the wearing of armbands was considered "symbolic speech" which is closely akin to "pure speech," which it repeatedly held, is entitled to comprehensive protection under the First Amendment. Can you think of any other instances where an act should be considered "symbolic speech" and therefore protected by the First Amendment?
2. The Supreme Court reasoned that students do not shed their constitutional rights to freedom of speech or expression at the schoolhouse gate. Nonetheless, it must be recognized that the First Amendment rights of students in public schools are not automatically co-extensive with the rights of adults. *Bethel School District No. 403 v. Fraser,* 478 U.S. 675, 682 (1986). Do you believe that students are entitled to their full First Amendment rights? Or should schools be permitted to regulate the extent of their First Amendment rights?
3. One of the main holdings of *Tinker* that has stood the test of time is the holding that a "student may express his opinions, even on controversial subjects like the conflict in Vietnam, if he does so without 'materially and substantially interfering with the requirements of appropriate discipline in the operation of the school' and without colliding with the rights of others." What if the students in *Tinker* had tried to recruit others to wear the armbands; would this still have passed constitutional muster? Can you think of other forms of expression that may materially and substantially interfere with the operation of a school?
4. According to the Supreme Court, the *Tinker* school officials incorrectly "fore casted" substantial disruption and material interference when they enacted the school policy against armbands. If you were a school official faced with the armband issue, would you have made a similar forecast or recognized the students only wanted to silently voice their disapproval of the war?
5. Justice Stewart, in his concurring opinion, notes that students are a captive audience and as a result of their situation are not possessed of that full capacity for individual choice that is the presupposition of First Amendment guarantees. What justifies the diminished power of a student's First Amendment rights?
6. Justice Black, in his dissenting opinion, states that the majority opinion will subject all the public schools in the country to the whims and caprices of their loudest-mouthed, but maybe not their brightest, students. Do you

agree with Justice Black? Do you think that the majority holding subjects students to the opinions and impulses of more aggressive students? Or should the students be exposed to all beliefs, not just those of their parents and teachers?

7. In *Hernandez v. Hanson,* 430 F. Supp. 1154 (D. Neb. 1977), the federal district court analyzed the constitutionality of a school policy that required students to obtain prior approval before distributing literature at school on behalf of nonschool sponsored organizations. Building on the holding in *Tinker,* the court held that the policy was overbroad for two reasons. First, the policy established a blanket restraint on distributions without attempting to "forecast" if the circulation would interfere in a "material and substantial" way with the administration of school activity and discipline. Second, the policy prohibited *any* distribution of literature concerning non-school events or organizations. Since students are a "captive audience," do you think the court's decision is appropriate? Or should the school be permitted to screen and ban nonschool advertising in order to stop potential abuse or damaging exploitation of the students?

2. Offensively Lewd and Indecent Speech

Bethel School District No. 403 v. Fraser

478 U.S. 675 (1986)

Chief Justice Burger delivered the opinion of the Court.

We granted certiorari to decide whether the First Amendment prevents a school district from disciplining a high school student for giving a lewd speech at a school assembly.

I

A

On April 26, 1983, respondent Matthew N. Fraser, a student at Bethel High School in Pierce County, Washington, delivered a speech nominating a fellow student for student elective office. Approximately 600 high school students, many of whom were 14-year-olds, attended the assembly. Students were required to attend the assembly or to report to the study hall. The assembly was part of a school-sponsored educational program in self-government. . . . During the entire speech, Fraser referred to his candidate in terms of an elaborate, graphic, and explicit sexual metaphor. . . .

During Fraser's delivery of the speech, a school counselor observed the reaction of students to the speech. Some students hooted and yelled; some by gestures graphically simulated the sexual activities pointedly alluded to in respondent's speech. Other students appeared to be bewildered and embarrassed by the speech. One teacher reported that on the day following the speech, she found it necessary to forgo a portion of the scheduled class lesson in order to discuss the speech with the class.

A Bethel High School disciplinary rule prohibiting the use of obscene language in the school provides:

> Conduct which materially and substantially interferes with the educational process is prohibited, including the use of obscene, profane language or gestures.

The morning after the assembly, the Assistant Principal called Fraser into her office and notified him that the school considered his speech to have been a violation of this rule. Fraser was then informed that he would be suspended for three days, and that his name would be removed from the list of candidates for graduation speaker at the school's commencement exercises. . . .

II

This Court acknowledged in *Tinker v. Des Moines,* that students do not "shed their constitutional rights to freedom of speech or expression at the schoolhouse gate." . . . The Court of Appeals read that case as precluding any discipline of Fraser for indecent speech and lewd conduct in the school assembly. That court appears to have proceeded on the theory that the use of lewd and obscene speech in order to make what the speaker considered to be a point in a nominating speech for a fellow student was essentially the same as the wearing of an armband in *Tinker* as a form of protest or the expression of a political position.

The marked distinction between the political "message" of the armbands in *Tinker* and the sexual content of respondent's speech in this case seems to have been given little weight by the Court of Appeals. In upholding the students' right to engage in a nondisruptive, passive expression of a political viewpoint in *Tinker,* this Court was careful to note that the case did "not concern speech or action that intrudes upon the work of the schools or the rights of other students." . . .

It is against this background that we turn to consider the level of First Amendment protection accorded to Fraser's utterances and actions before an official high school assembly attended by 600 students.

III

The role and purpose of the American public school system were well described by two historians, who stated: "[P]ublic education must prepare pupils for citizenship in the Republic. . . . It must inculcate the habits and manners of civility as values in themselves conducive to happiness and as indispensable to the practice of self-government in the community and the nation." C. Beard & M. Beard, *New Basic History of the United States* 228 (1968). In *Ambach v. Norwick,* 441 U.S. 68 (1979), we echoed the essence of this statement of the objectives of public education as the "inculcat[ion of] fundamental values necessary to the maintenance of a democratic political system."

These fundamental values of "habits and manners of civility" essential to a democratic society must, of course, include tolerance of divergent political and religious views, even when the views expressed may be unpopular. But these "fundamental values" must also take into account consideration of the sensibilities of others, and, in the case of a school, the sensibilities of fellow students. The undoubted freedom to advocate unpopular and controversial views in schools and classrooms must be balanced against the society's countervailing interest in teaching students the boundaries of socially appropriate behavior. Even the most heated political discourse in a democratic society requires consideration for the personal sensibilities of the other participants and audiences.

In our Nation's legislative halls, where some of the most vigorous political debates in our society are carried on, there are rules prohibiting the use of expressions offensive to other participants in the debate. . . . Can it be that what is proscribed in the halls of Congress is beyond the reach of school officials to regulate?

The First Amendment guarantees wide freedom in matters of adult public discourse. A sharply divided Court upheld the right to express an antidraft viewpoint in a public place, albeit in terms highly offensive to most citizens. *See Cohen v. California,* 403 U.S. 15 (1971). It does not follow, however, that simply because the use of an offensive form of expression may not be prohibited to adults making what the speaker considers a political point, the same latitude must be permitted to children in a public school. In *New Jersey v. T.L.O.,* 469 U.S. 325, 340-342 (1985), we reaffirmed that the constitutional rights of students in public school are not automatically coextensive with the rights of adults in other settings. As cogently expressed by Judge Newman, "the First Amendment gives a high school student the classroom right to wear Tinker's armband, but not Cohen's jacket." *Thomas v. Board of Education, Granville Central School Dist.,* 607 F.2d 1043, 1057 (CA2 1979).

Surely it is a highly appropriate function of public school education to prohibit the use of vulgar and offensive terms in public discourse. Indeed, the "fundamental values necessary to the maintenance of a democratic political system" disfavor the use of terms of debate highly offensive or highly threatening to others. Nothing in the Constitution prohibits the states from insisting that certain modes of expression are inappropriate and subject to sanctions. The inculcation of these values is truly the "work of the schools." *Tinker,* 393 U.S., at 508. The determination of what manner of speech in the classroom or in school assembly is inappropriate properly rests with the school board.

The process of educating our youth for citizenship in public schools is not confined to books, the curriculum, and the civics class; schools must teach by example the shared values of a civilized social order. Consciously or otherwise, teachers — and indeed the older students — demonstrate the appropriate form of civil discourse and political expression by their conduct and deportment in and out of class. Inescapably, like parents, they are role models. The schools, as instruments of the state, may determine that the essential lessons of civil, mature conduct cannot be conveyed in a school that tolerates lewd, indecent, or offensive speech and conduct such as that indulged in by this confused boy.

The pervasive sexual innuendo in Fraser's speech was plainly offensive to both teachers and students — indeed to any mature person. By glorifying male sexuality, and in its verbal content, the speech was acutely insulting to teenage girl students. The speech could well be seriously damaging to its less mature audience, many of whom were only 14 years old and on the threshold of awareness of human sexuality. Some students were reported as bewildered by the speech and the reaction of mimicry it provoked.

This Court's First Amendment jurisprudence has acknowledged limitations on the otherwise absolute interest of the speaker in reaching an unlimited audience where the speech is sexually explicit and the audience may include children. . . . These cases recognize the obvious concern on the part of parents, and school authorities acting *in loco parentis,* to protect children — especially in a captive audience — from exposure to sexually explicit, indecent, or lewd speech. . . .

We hold that petitioner School District acted entirely within its permissible authority in imposing sanctions upon Fraser in response to his offensively lewd and indecent speech. Unlike the sanctions imposed on the students wearing armbands in *Tinker,* the penalties imposed in this case were unrelated to any political viewpoint. The First Amendment does not prevent the school officials from determining that to permit a vulgar and lewd speech such as respondent's would undermine the school's basic educational mission. A high school assembly or classroom is no place for a sexually explicit monologue directed towards an unsuspecting audience of teenage students. Accordingly, it was perfectly appropriate for the school to disassociate itself to make the point to the pupils that vulgar speech and lewd conduct is wholly inconsistent with the "fundamental values" of public school education. Justice Black, dissenting in *Tinker,* made a point that is especially relevant in this case:

> I wish therefore, . . . to disclaim any purpose to hold that the Federal Constitution compels the teachers, parents, and elected school officials to surrender control of the American public school system to public school students. 393 U.S. at 526.

IV

Respondent contends that the circumstances of his suspension violated due process because he had no way of knowing that the delivery of the speech in question would subject him to disciplinary sanctions. This argument is wholly without merit. We have recognized that "maintaining security and order in the schools requires a certain degree of flexibility in school disciplinary procedures, and we have respected the value of preserving the informality of the student-teacher relationship." *New Jersey v. T.L.O.* . . . Given the school's need to be able to impose disciplinary sanctions for a wide range of unanticipated conduct disruptive of the educational process, the school disciplinary rules need not be as detailed as a criminal code which imposes criminal sanctions. . . . Two days' suspension from school does not rise to the level of a penal sanction calling for the full panoply of procedural due process protections applicable to a criminal prosecution. . . . The school disciplinary rule proscribing "obscene" language and the prespeech admonitions of teachers gave adequate warning to Fraser that his lewd speech could subject him to sanctions.

The judgment of the Court of Appeals for the Ninth Circuit is *Reversed.*

NOTES AND QUESTIONS

1. In *Bethel,* the quintessential freedom of speech case, Fraser was reprimanded and suspended following his delivery of a questionable nomination speech for a classmate. School officials classified the speech as a violation of a disciplinary rule prohibiting "conduct which materially and substantially interferes with the educational process, including the use of obscene, profane language or gestures." Fraser admitted to using sexual innuendos in the speech. Does this qualify as "obscene, profane language or gestures?" Should the bewilderment and embarrassment of a handful of students warrant the revocation of one student's freedom of speech?
2. Justice Brennan, in a concurring opinion, included Fraser's speech to allow individuals to make their own judgment concerning the nature of the case:

   > "I know a man who is firm—he's firm in his pants, he's firm in his shirt, his character is firm—but most . . . of all, his belief in you, the students of Bethel, is firm. Jeff Kuhlman is a man who takes his point and pounds it in. If necessary, he'll take an issue and nail it to the wall. He doesn't attack things in spurts—he drives hard, pushing and pushing until finally—he succeeds. Jeff is a man who will go to the very end—even the climax, for each and every one of you. So vote for Jeff for A.S.B. vice-president—he'll never come between you and the best our high school can be."

   Do you find the speech "vulgar," "lewd," "obscene?" Do you agree with Justice Brennan and find it hard to equate the speech described by the Court as the same one you just read? Regardless of your opinion of the speech, do you think it was necessary for the administration to punish Fraser?
3. If Fraser tried to deliver this speech in the hall after school, or in a classroom during math, would the result have been the same?
4. If anyone else besides a student delivered this speech in a park or town hall, what would the outcome be? Does the speech appear tame and appropriate considering the music on the radio and the programs on television?
5. The Internet has created a bevy of new issues that the framers never could have fathomed. In *Coy v. Board of Education of the North Canton City Schools,* 205 F. Supp. 2d 791 (N.D. Ohio 2002), Coy claimed the defendants violated his First Amendment rights when they disciplined him for accessing his personal website from a school computer. The website, created on his own computer, contained information about Coy and his friends, as well as a section titled "losers" that contained pictures and insults concerning three classmates. Students alerted the administration to the website's existence and after reviewing its contents, the school suspended Coy. The court ruled that summary judgment was not appropriate because defendants had offered two different explanations for their conduct. One plausible explanation for the suspension is that Coy violated the school's Internet policy and displayed vulgar speech at school. The other possible rationalization for the suspension is that the school disapproved of the website's content. If the school disciplined Coy purely because it did not like what was contained in his personal website, Coy will prevail. Do you agree with the court's reasoning?

6. Courts considering school officials' ability to discipline students for offensive communications created on home computers have generally held that this type of misbehavior cannot be punished unless it has a demonstrable nexus to school. School officials must be able to show that the student's speech disrupted, or at least, could reasonably be expected to disrupt, school activities. In *Killion v. Franklin Regional School District,* 136 F. Supp. 2d 446 (W.D. Pa. 2001), for example, the court overturned the suspension of a student who composed a list of vulgar but nonthreatening insults directed at his high school's athletic director and e-mailed the list to friends from his home computer. Disciplined after an acquaintance distributed the list on school grounds, the student sued under 42 U.S.C. §1983, asserting that the district's actions infringed his freedom of expression under the First Amendment. The court agreed. According to *Killion,* the student's off-campus speech was protected by the First Amendment because defendants failed to prove that the "speech" disrupted school or that there was a substantial reason to anticipate a disruption. *See also Emmett v. Kent School District No. 415,* 92 F. Supp. 2d 1088 (W.D. Wash. 2000) (enjoining suspension of student for creating Web page on Internet from his home; although high school population was target audience, nonviolent mock obituaries posted on site were not intended to nor did they actually threaten anyone); *Beussink v. Woodland R-IV School District,* 30 F. Supp. 2d 1175 (E.D. Mo. 1998) (enjoining suspension when student's criticisms of school administrators posted on home computer did not materially interfere with or give rise to reasonable fear of interference with school discipline).
7. A student may not be expelled from school for having possession of a publication that contains certain four-letter words, when the same four-letter words appear both in a book that is assigned as required reading to tenth grade students and in a magazine found in the school library. *Vought v. Van Buren Public Schools,* 306 F. Supp. 1388 (E.D. Mich. 1969). However, student language in public schools that is vulgar and lewd is not protectable speech under the First Amendment, regardless of the context in which it is uttered. *Heller v. Hodgin,* 928 F. Supp. 789 (S.D. Ind. 1996). Thus, a high school student's First Amendment rights are not violated by a suspension for uttering an obscenity, particularly when the words are clearly disruptive as they were heard by students in the cafeteria and, in the opinion of an assistant principal, were "fighting words." *Id.*
8. A student may properly be suspended for violating the school's racial harassment and intimidation policy. *West v. Derby Unified School Dist. No. 260,* 23 F. Supp. 2d 1223 (D. Kan. 1998) (wearing a jacket with the Confederate battle flag on it, when racial incidents have recently occurred in the school and the jacket could cause a disruption); *Phillips v. Anderson County School District Five,* 987 F. Supp. 488 (D.S.C. 1997) (wearing sagging pants in violation of school dress code). *Bivens by and Through Green v. Albuquerque Public Schools,* 899 F. Supp. 556 (D.N.M. 1995). Students, however, may not be suspended solely because they silently refuse to rise and stand for the playing or singing of the national anthem, when the conduct of the students is not disorderly and does not materially disrupt the conduct and discipline of the school, and when there is no evidence that it would do so in the future. *Sheldon v. Fannin,* 221 F. Supp. 766 (D. Ariz. 1963).

3. School-Sponsored Expressive Activities

Hazelwood School District v. Kuhlmeier

484 U.S. 260 (1988)

Justice White delivered the opinion of the Court.

This case concerns the extent to which educators may exercise editorial control over the contents of a high school newspaper produced as part of the school's journalism curriculum.

I

Petitioners are the Hazelwood School District in St. Louis County, Missouri; various school officials; . . . , the principal of Hazelwood East High School; and . . . , a teacher in the school district. Respondents are three former Hazelwood East students who were staff members of Spectrum, the school newspaper. They contend that school officials violated their First Amendment rights by deleting two pages of articles from the May 13, 1983, issue of Spectrum. [The school's principal, Reynolds, barred the publication of the articles because they described three Hazelwood students' experiences with pregnancy and the impact of divorce on some of the students.] . . .

II

Students in the public schools do not "shed their constitutional rights to freedom of speech or expression at the schoolhouse gate." *Tinker.* They cannot be punished merely for expressing their personal views on the school premises—whether "in the cafeteria, or on the playing field, or on the campus during the authorized hours,"—unless school authorities have reason to believe that such expression will "substantially interfere with the work of the school or impinge upon the rights of other students."

We have nonetheless recognized that the First Amendment rights of students in the public schools "are not automatically coextensive with the rights of adults in other settings," *Bethel,* and must be "applied in light of the special characteristics of the school environment." *Tinker; New Jersey v. T.L.O.* A school need not tolerate student speech that is inconsistent with its "basic educational mission," *Fraser,* even though the government could not censor similar speech outside the school. Accordingly, we held in Fraser that a student could be disciplined for having delivered a speech that was "sexually explicit" but not legally obscene at an official school assembly, because the school was entitled to "disassociate itself" from the speech in a manner that would demonstrate to others that such vulgarity is "wholly inconsistent with the 'fundamental values' of public school education." We thus recognized that "[t]he determination of what manner of speech in the classroom or in school assembly is inappropriate properly rests with the school board," rather than with the federal courts. It is in this context that respondents' First Amendment claims must be considered.

A

We deal first with the question whether Spectrum may appropriately be characterized as a forum for public expression. The public schools do not possess all of the attributes of streets, parks, and other traditional public forums that "time out of mind, have been used for purposes of assembly, communicating thoughts between citizens, and discussing public questions." . . . Hence, school facilities may be deemed to be public forums only if school authorities have "by policy or by practice" opened those facilities "for indiscriminate use by the general public" . . . or by some segment of the public, such as student organizations. If the facilities have instead been reserved for other intended purposes, "communicative or otherwise," then no public forum has been created, and school officials may impose reasonable restrictions on the speech of students, teachers, and other members of the school community. "The government does not create a public forum by inaction or by permitting limited discourse, but only by intentionally opening a nontraditional forum for public discourse." . . .

In sum, the evidence relied upon by the Court of Appeals fails to demonstrate the "clear intent to create a public forum," that existed in cases in which we found public forums to have been created. . . . School officials did not evince either "by policy or by practice," . . . any intent to open the pages of Spectrum to "indiscriminate use," by its student reporters and editors, or by the student body generally. Instead, they "reserve[d] the forum for its intended purpos[e]," as a supervised learning experience for journalism students. Accordingly, school officials were entitled to regulate the contents of Spectrum in any reasonable manner. It is this standard, rather than our decision in *Tinker,* that governs this case.

B

The question whether the First Amendment requires a school to tolerate particular student speech—the question that we addressed in *Tinker*—is different from the question whether the First Amendment requires a school affirmatively to promote particular student speech. The former question addresses educators' ability to silence a student's personal expression that happens to occur on the school premises. The latter question concerns educators' authority over school-sponsored publications, theatrical productions, and other expressive activities that students, parents, and members of the public might reasonably perceive to bear the imprimatur of the school. These activities may fairly be characterized as part of the school curriculum, whether or not they occur in a traditional classroom setting, so long as they are supervised by faculty members and designed to impart particular knowledge or skills to student participants and audiences.

Educators are entitled to exercise greater control over this second form of student expression to assure that participants learn whatever lessons the activity is designed to teach, that readers or listeners are not exposed to material that may be inappropriate for their level of maturity, and that the views of the individual speaker are not erroneously attributed to the school. Hence, a school may in its capacity as publisher of a school newspaper or producer of a school play "disassociate itself," *Fraser,* not only from speech that would "substantially interfere with [its] work . . . or impinge upon the rights of other students," *Tinker,* but also from speech that is, for example, ungrammatical, poorly written, inadequately researched, biased or prejudiced, vulgar or profane, or unsuitable for immature audiences. A school must be able to set high standards for the student speech that is disseminated under its auspices—standards that may be higher than those demanded by some newspaper publishers or theatrical producers in the "real" world—and may refuse to disseminate student speech that does not meet those standards. In addition, a school must be able to take into account the emotional maturity of the intended audience in determining whether to disseminate student speech on potentially sensitive topics, which might range from the existence of Santa Claus in an elementary school setting to the particulars of teenage sexual activity in a high school setting. A school must also retain the authority to refuse to sponsor student speech that might reasonably be perceived to advocate drug or alcohol use, irresponsible sex, or conduct otherwise inconsistent with "the shared values of a civilized social order," *Fraser,* or to associate the school with any position other than neutrality on matters of political controversy. Otherwise, the schools would be unduly constrained from fulfilling their role as "a principal instrument in awakening the child to cultural values, in preparing him for later professional training, and in helping him to adjust normally to his environment." *Brown v. Board of Education.*

Accordingly, we conclude that the standard articulated in *Tinker* for determining when a school may punish student expression need not also be the standard for determining when a school may refuse to lend its name and resources to the dissemination of student expression. Instead, we hold that educators do not offend the First Amendment by exercising editorial control over the style and content of student speech in school-sponsored expressive activities so long as their actions are reasonably related to legitimate pedagogical concerns.

This standard is consistent with our oft-expressed view that the education of the Nation's youth is primarily the responsibility of parents, teachers, and state and local school officials, and not of federal judges. . . . It is only when the decision to censor a school-sponsored publication, theatrical production, or other vehicle of student expression has no valid educational purpose that the First Amendment is so "directly and sharply implicate[d]," as to require judicial intervention to protect students' constitutional rights. . . .

III

In sum, we cannot reject as unreasonable Principal Reynolds' conclusion that neither the pregnancy article nor the divorce article was suitable for publication in Spectrum. Reynolds could reasonably have concluded that the students who had written and edited these articles had not sufficiently mastered those portions of the Journalism II curriculum that pertained to the treatment of controversial issues and personal attacks, the need to protect the privacy of individuals whose most intimate concerns are to be revealed in the newspaper, and "the legal, moral, and ethical restrictions imposed upon journalists within [a] school community" that includes adolescent subjects and readers. Finally, we conclude that the principal's decision to delete two pages of Spectrum, rather than to delete only the offending articles or to require that they be modified, was reasonable under the circumstances as he understood them. Accordingly, no violation of First Amendment rights occurred.

NOTES AND QUESTIONS

1. In *Hazelwood,* the Supreme Court distinguished *Tinker* and held that educators do not offend the First Amendment by exercising editorial control over the style and content of student speech in school-sponsored expressive activities so long as their actions are reasonably related to legitimate pedagogical concerns. If the school is judging the reasonableness of the educational concerns, will it always find a way to censor the students? Should the Supreme Court have taken the opportunity to outline acceptable and unacceptable instances of censorship?
2. The Court agreed that a school should be able to censor the publication of a newspaper article that is "ungrammatical, poorly written, inadequately researched, biased or prejudiced." Do you agree with this holding? If the school sponsors the newspaper and has its name on the paper, should it be allowed to regulate the quality of the newspaper? Or is the regulation of the quality of the articles a step in the direction of content censorship?
3. The dissent observes that the newspaper was not touted as a class exercise in honing writing skills, but as a forum established to give students an opportunity to express their views while gaining an appreciation for the First Amendment. Does the school's censorship of the newspaper fulfill the goals of the newspaper?
4. The students working on the newspaper were also registered for Journalism II. The school board guaranteed the Journalism II students an atmosphere conducive to exercising the full panoply of rights associated with a free student press. Did the censorship of the newspaper break the school board's promise? If the purpose of Journalism II is to help the students gain real world experience, what is the school's censorship teaching the students?
5. *Desilets v. Clearview Regional Board of Education,* 266 N.J. Super. 531, 630 A.2d 333 (1993), is similar to *Hazelwood.* In *Desilets,* the plaintiff alleged a violation of his First Amendment rights after the school board censored his movie reviews of R-rated movies for the school paper. The board defended its censorship, claiming the school paper was part of the regular educational curriculum and related to a legitimate pedagogical concern. The court disagreed with the school board since the censoring of movie reviews had no valid educational purpose. The significant distinction between *Hazelwood* and *Desilets* is that the material in *Hazelwood* was censored because of its content and journalistic style. Alternatively, in *Desilets,* the censorship had nothing to do with the style or the content (what is written) of the review, only its subject matter (what is written about). As a result, the court followed the *Hazelwood* holding where the pedagogical interests of the school do not extend beyond style and content of the article. Thus, the school board's censorship violated the student's First Amendment rights. Do you agree with the court's holding? Do you think that reviews of R-rated movies should be allowed in junior high school newspapers even though the students cannot watch the movies without adult supervision?

4. Speech Encouraging Illegal Drug Use

Morse v. Frederick

127 S.Ct. 2618 (2007)

Chief Justice Roberts delivered the opinion of the Court.

At a school-sanctioned and school-supervised event, a high school principal saw some of her students unfurl a large banner conveying a message she reasonably regarded as promoting illegal drug use. Consistent with established school policy prohibiting such messages at school events, the principal directed the students to take down the banner. One student—among those who had brought the banner to the event—refused to do so. The principal confiscated the banner and later suspended the student. The Ninth Circuit held that the principal's actions violated the First Amendment, and that the student could sue the principal for damages.

Our cases make clear that students do not "shed their constitutional rights to freedom of speech or expression at the schoolhouse gate." *Tinker v. Des Moines Independent Community School Dist.*, 393. At the same time, we have held that "the constitutional rights of students in public school are not automatically coextensive with the rights of adults in other settings," *Bethel School Dist. No. 403 v. Fraser,* and that the rights of students "must be 'applied in light of the special characteristics of the school environment.' " *Hazelwood School Dist. v. Kuhlmeier*. Consistent with these principles, we hold that schools may take steps to safeguard those entrusted to their care from speech that can reasonably be regarded as encouraging illegal drug use. We conclude that the school officials in this case did not violate the First Amendment by confiscating the pro-drug banner and suspending the student responsible for it.

I

On January 24, 2002, the Olympic Torch Relay passed through Juneau, Alaska, on its way to the winter games in Salt Lake City, Utah. The torchbearers were to proceed along a street in front of Juneau-Douglas High School (JDHS) while school was in session. Petitioner Deborah Morse, the school principal, decided to permit staff and students to participate in the Torch Relay as an approved social event or class trip. Students were allowed to leave class to observe the relay from either side of the street. Teachers and administrative officials monitored the students' actions.

Respondent Joseph Frederick, a JDHS senior, was late to school that day. When he arrived, he joined his friends (all but one of whom were JDHS students) across the street from the school to watch the event. Not all the students waited patiently. Some became rambunctious, throwing plastic cola bottles and snowballs and scuffling with their classmates. As the torchbearers and camera crews passed by, Frederick and his friends unfurled a 14-foot banner bearing the phrase: "BONG HiTS 4 JESUS." The large banner was easily readable by the students on the other side of the street.

Principal Morse immediately crossed the street and demanded that the banner be taken down. Everyone but Frederick complied. Morse confiscated the banner and told Frederick to report to her office, where she suspended him for 10 days. Morse later explained that she told Frederick to take the banner down because she thought it encouraged illegal drug use, in violation of established school policy. Juneau School Board Policy No. 5520 states: "The Board specifically prohibits any assembly or public expression that . . . advocates the use of substances that are illegal to minors. . . ." In addition, Juneau School Board Policy No. 5850 subjects "[p]upils who participate in approved social events and class trips" to the same student conduct rules that apply during the regular school program.

Frederick administratively appealed his suspension, but the Juneau School District Superintendent upheld it, limiting it to time served (8 days). In a memorandum setting forth his reasons, the superintendent determined that Frederick had displayed his banner "in the midst of his fellow students, during school hours, at a school-sanctioned activity." He further explained that Frederick "was not disciplined because the principal of the school 'disagreed' with his message, but because his speech appeared to advocate the use of illegal drugs."

The superintendent continued:

"The common-sense understanding of the phrase 'bong hits' is that it is a reference to a means of smoking marijuana. Given [Frederick's] inability or unwillingness to express any other credible meaning for the phrase, I can only agree with the principal and countless others who saw the banner as advocating the use of illegal drugs. [Frederick's] speech was not political. He was not advocating the legalization of marijuana or promoting a religious belief. He was displaying a fairly silly message promoting illegal drug usage in the midst of a school activity, for the benefit of television cameras covering the Torch Relay. [Frederick's] speech was potentially disruptive to the event and clearly disruptive of and inconsistent with the school's educational mission to educate students about the dangers of illegal drugs and to discourage their use."

Relying on our decision in *Fraser, supra,* the superintendent concluded that the principal's actions were permissible because Frederick's banner was "speech or action that intrudes upon the work of the schools." The Juneau School District Board of Education upheld the suspension.

Frederick then filed suit under 42 U.S.C. § 1983, alleging that the school board and Morse had violated his First Amendment rights. He sought declaratory and injunctive relief, unspecified compensatory damages, punitive damages, and attorney's fees. The District Court granted summary judgment for the school board and Morse, ruling that they were entitled to qualified immunity and that they had not infringed Frederick's First Amendment rights. The court found that Morse reasonably interpreted the banner as promoting illegal drug use — a message that "directly contravened the Board's policies relating to drug abuse prevention." Under the circumstances, the court held that "Morse had the authority, if not the obligation, to stop such messages at a school-sanctioned activity."

The Ninth Circuit reversed. Deciding that Frederick acted during a "school-authorized activit[y]," and "proceed[ing] on the basis that the banner expressed a positive sentiment about marijuana use," the court nonetheless found a violation of Frederick's First Amendment rights because the school punished Frederick without demonstrating that his speech gave rise to a "risk of substantial disruption." The court further concluded that Frederick's right to display his banner was so "clearly established" that a reasonable principal in Morse's position would have understood that her actions were unconstitutional, and that Morse was therefore not entitled to qualified immunity.

We granted certiorari on two questions: whether Frederick had a First Amendment right to wield his banner, and, if so, whether that right was so clearly established that the principal may be held liable for damages. . . . We resolve the first question against Frederick, and therefore have no occasion to reach the second.[1]

II

At the outset, we reject Frederick's argument that this is not a school speech case — as has every other authority to address the question. The event occurred during normal school hours. It was sanctioned by Principal Morse "as an approved social event or class trip," and the school district's rules expressly provide that pupils in "approved social events and class trips are subject to district rules for student conduct." Teachers and administrators were interspersed among the students and charged with supervising them. The high school band and cheerleaders performed. Frederick, standing among other JDHS students across the street from the school, directed his banner toward the school, making it plainly visible to most students. Under these circumstances, we agree with the superintendent that Frederick cannot "stand in the midst of his fellow students, during school hours, at a school-sanctioned activity and claim he is not at school." There is some uncertainty at the outer boundaries as to when courts should apply school-speech precedents, see *Porter* v. *Ascension Parish School Bd.*, 393 F.3d 608, 615, n.22 (CA5 2004), but not on these facts.

III

The message on Frederick's banner is cryptic. It is no doubt offensive to some, perhaps amusing to others. To still others, it probably means nothing at all. Frederick himself claimed "that the words were just nonsense meant to attract television cameras." But Principal Morse thought the banner would be interpreted by those viewing it as promoting illegal drug use, and that interpretation is plainly a reasonable one.

---

[1] Justice Breyer would rest decision on qualified immunity without reaching the underlying First Amendment question. The problem with this approach is the rather significant one that it is inadequate to decide the case before us. Qualified immunity shields public officials from money damages only. See *Wood v. Strickland*, 420 U.S. 308, n.6 (1975). In this case, Frederick asked not just for damages, but also for declaratory and injunctive relief. Justice Breyer's proposed decision on qualified immunity grounds would dispose of the damages claims, but Frederick's other claims would remain unaddressed. To get around that problem, Justice Breyer hypothesizes that Frederick's suspension — the target of his request for injunctive relief — "may well be justified on non-speech-related grounds." That hypothesis was never considered by the courts below, never raised by any of the parties, and is belied by the record, which nowhere suggests that the suspension would have been justified solely on non-speech-related grounds.

As Morse later explained in a declaration, when she saw the sign, she thought that "the reference to a 'bong hit' would be widely understood by high school students and others as referring to smoking marijuana." She further believed that "display of the banner would be construed by students, District personnel, parents and others witnessing the display of the banner, as advocating or promoting illegal drug use"—in violation of school policy. ("I told Frederick and the other members of his group to put the banner down because I felt that it violated the [school] policy against displaying . . . material that advertises or promotes use of illegal drugs").

We agree with Morse. At least two interpretations of the words on the banner demonstrate that the sign advocated the use of illegal drugs. First, the phrase could be interpreted as an imperative: "[Take] bong hits . . ."—a message equivalent, as Morse explained in her declaration, to "smoke marijuana" or "use an illegal drug." Alternatively, the phrase could be viewed as celebrating drug use—"bong hits [are a good thing]," or "[we take] bong hits"—and we discern no meaningful distinction between celebrating illegal drug use in the midst of fellow students and outright advocacy or promotion.

The pro-drug interpretation of the banner gains further plausibility given the paucity of alternative meanings the banner might bear. The best Frederick can come up with is that the banner is "meaningless and funny." The dissent similarly refers to the sign's message as "curious," "ambiguous," "nonsense," "ridiculous," "obscure," "silly," "quixotic," and "stupid." Gibberish is surely a possible interpretation of the words on the banner, but it is not the only one, and dismissing the banner as meaningless ignores its undeniable reference to illegal drugs.

The dissent mentions Frederick's "credible and uncontradicted explanation for the message—he just wanted to get on television." But that is a description of Frederick's *motive* for displaying the banner; it is not an interpretation of what the banner says. The *way* Frederick was going to fulfill his ambition of appearing on television was by unfurling a pro-drug banner at a school event, in the presence of teachers and fellow students.

Elsewhere in its opinion, the dissent emphasizes the importance of political speech and the need to foster "national debate about a serious issue," as if to suggest that the banner is political speech. But not even Frederick argues that the banner conveys any sort of political or religious message. Contrary to the dissent's suggestion, this is plainly not a case about political debate over the criminalization of drug use or possession.

IV

The question thus becomes whether a principal may, consistent with the First Amendment, restrict student speech at a school event, when that speech is reasonably viewed as promoting illegal drug use. We hold that she may.

In *Tinker,* this Court made clear that "First Amendment rights, applied in light of the special characteristics of the school environment, are available to teachers and students." *Tinker* involved a group of high school students who decided to wear black armbands to protest the Vietnam War. School officials learned of the plan and then adopted a policy prohibiting students from wearing armbands. When several students nonetheless wore armbands to school, they were suspended. The students sued, claiming that their First Amendment rights had been violated, and this Court agreed.

Tinker held that student expression may not be suppressed unless school officials reasonably conclude that it will "materially and substantially disrupt the work and discipline of the school." The essential facts of *Tinker* are quite stark, implicating concerns at the heart of the First Amendment. The students sought to engage in political speech, using the armbands to express their "disapproval of the Vietnam hostilities and their advocacy of a truce, to make their views known, and, by their example, to influence others to adopt them." Political speech, of course, is "at the core of what the First Amendment is designed to protect." *Virginia v. Black*, 538 U.S. 343, 365 (2003). The only interest the Court discerned underlying the school's actions was the "mere desire to avoid the discomfort and unpleasantness that always accompany an unpopular viewpoint," or "an urgent wish to avoid the controversy which might result from the expression." *Tinker*, 393 U.S., at 509, 510. That interest was not enough to justify banning "a silent, passive expression of opinion, unaccompanied by any disorder or disturbance." *Id.,* at 508.

This Court's next student speech case was *Fraser*. Matthew Fraser was suspended for delivering a speech before a high school assembly in which he employed what this Court called "an elaborate, graphic, and explicit sexual metaphor." Analyzing the case under *Tinker*, the District Court and Court of Appeals found no disruption, and therefore no basis for disciplining Fraser. This Court reversed, holding that the "School District acted entirely within its permissible authority in imposing sanctions upon Fraser in response to his offensively lewd and indecent speech."

The mode of analysis employed in *Fraser* is not entirely clear. The Court was plainly attuned to the content of Fraser's speech, citing the "marked distinction between the political 'message' of the armbands in *Tinker* and the sexual content of [Fraser's] speech." But the Court also reasoned that school boards have the authority to determine "what manner of speech in the classroom or in school assembly is inappropriate." (Brennan, J., concurring in judgment) ("In the present case, school officials sought only to ensure that a high school assembly proceed in an orderly manner. There is no suggestion that school officials attempted to regulate [Fraser's] speech because they disagreed with the views he sought to express").

We need not resolve this debate to decide this case. For present purposes, it is enough to distill from *Fraser* two basic principles. First, *Fraser*'s holding demonstrates that "the constitutional rights of students in public school are not automatically coextensive with the rights of adults in other settings." Had Fraser delivered the same speech in a public forum outside the school context, it would have been protected. In school, however, Fraser's First Amendment rights were circumscribed "in light of the special characteristics of the school environment." Second, *Fraser* established that the mode of analysis set forth in *Tinker* is not absolute. Whatever approach *Fraser* employed, it certainly did not conduct the "substantial disruption" analysis prescribed by *Tinker*.

Our most recent student speech case, *Kuhlmeier,* concerned "expressive activities that students, parents, and members of the public might reasonably perceive to bear the imprimatur of the school." Staff members of a high school newspaper sued their school when it chose not to publish two of their articles. The Court of Appeals analyzed the case under *Tinker*, ruling in favor of the students because it found no evidence of material disruption to classwork or school discipline. This Court reversed, holding that "educators do not offend the First Amendment by exercising editorial control over the style and content of student speech in school-sponsored expressive activities so long as their actions are reasonably related to legitimate pedagogical concerns."

Kuhlmeier does not control this case because no one would reasonably believe that Frederick's banner bore the school's imprimatur. The case is nevertheless instructive because it confirms both principles cited above. *Kuhlmeier* acknowledged that schools may regulate some speech "even though the government could not censor similar speech outside the school." And, like *Fraser*, it confirms that the rule of *Tinker* is not the only basis for restricting student speech.

Drawing on the principles applied in our student speech cases, we have held in the Fourth Amendment context that "while children assuredly do not 'shed their constitutional rights . . . at the schoolhouse gate,' . . . the nature of those rights is what is appropriate for children in school." *Vernonia School Dist. 47J v. Acton*, 515 U.S. 646, 655-656 (1995) (quoting *Tinker, supra,* at 506). In particular, "the school setting requires some easing of the restrictions to which searches by public authorities are ordinarily subject." *New Jersey v. T.L.O.*, 469 U.S. 325, 340 (1985). See *Vernonia, supra,* at 656 ("Fourth Amendment rights, no less than First and Fourteenth Amendment rights, are different in public schools than elsewhere . . ."); *Board of Ed. of Independent School Dist. No. 92 of Pottawatomie Cty. v. Earls*, 536 U.S. 822, 829-830 (2002) ("special needs' inhere in the public school context"; "[w]hile schoolchildren do not shed their constitutional rights when they enter the schoolhouse, Fourth Amendment rights . . . are different in public schools than elsewhere; the 'reasonableness' inquiry cannot disregard the schools' custodial and tutelary responsibility for children" (quoting *Vernonia*, 515 U.S., at 656; citation and some internal quotation marks omitted).

Even more to the point, these cases also recognize that deterring drug use by schoolchildren is an "important—indeed, perhaps compelling" interest. Drug abuse can cause severe and permanent damage to the health and well-being of young people:

"School years are the time when the physical, psychological, and addictive effects of drugs are most severe. Maturing nervous systems are more critically impaired by intoxicants than mature ones are; childhood losses in learning are lifelong and profound; children grow chemically dependent more quickly than adults, and their record of recovery is depressingly poor. And of course the effects of a drug-infested school are visited not just upon the users, but upon the entire student body and faculty, as the educational process is disrupted."

Just five years ago, we wrote: "The drug abuse problem among our Nation's youth has hardly abated since *Vernonia* was decided in 1995. In fact, evidence suggests that it has only grown worse." *Earls, supra,* at 834, and n.5.

The problem remains serious today. See generally 1 National Institute on Drug Abuse, National Institutes of Health, Monitoring the Future: National

Survey Results on Drug Use, 1975–2005, Secondary School Students (2006). About half of American 12th graders have used an illicit drug, as have more than a third of 10th graders and about one-fifth of 8th graders. *Id.,* at 99. Nearly one in four 12th graders has used an illicit drug in the past month. *Id.,* at 101. Some 25% of high schoolers say that they have been offered, sold, or given an illegal drug on school property within the past year. Dept. of Health and Human Services, Centers for Disease Control and Prevention, Youth Risk Behavior Surveillance—United States, 2005, 55 Morbidity and Mortality Weekly Report, Surveillance Summaries, No. SS-5, p. 19 (June 9, 2006).

Congress has declared that part of a school's job is educating students about the dangers of illegal drug use. It has provided billions of dollars to support state and local drug-prevention programs, Brief for United States as *Amicus Curiae* 1, and required that schools receiving federal funds under the Safe and Drug-Free Schools and Communities Act of 1994 certify that their drug prevention programs "convey a clear and consistent message that . . . the illegal use of drugs [is] wrong and harmful." 20 U.S.C. § 7114(d)(6) (2000 ed., Supp. IV).

Thousands of school boards throughout the country—including JDHS—have adopted policies aimed at effectuating this message. Those school boards know that peer pressure is perhaps "the single most important factor leading schoolchildren to take drugs," and that students are more likely to use drugs when the norms in school appear to tolerate such behavior. Student speech celebrating illegal drug use at a school event, in the presence of school administrators and teachers, thus poses a particular challenge for school officials working to protect those entrusted to their care from the dangers of drug abuse.

The "special characteristics of the school environment," *Tinker,* 393 U.S., at 506, and the governmental interest in stopping student drug abuse—reflected in the policies of Congress and myriad school boards, including JDHS—allow schools to restrict student expression that they reasonably regard as promoting illegal drug use. *Tinker* warned that schools may not prohibit student speech because of "undifferentiated fear or apprehension of disturbance" or "a mere desire to avoid the discomfort and unpleasantness that always accompany an unpopular viewpoint." *Id.,* at 508, 509. The danger here is far more serious and palpable. The particular concern to prevent student drug abuse at issue here, embodied in established school policy, extends well beyond an abstract desire to avoid controversy.

Petitioners urge us to adopt the broader rule that Frederick's speech is proscribable because it is plainly "offensive" as that term is used in *Fraser.* We think this stretches *Fraser* too far; that case should not be read to encompass any speech that could fit under some definition of "offensive." After all, much political and religious speech might be perceived as offensive to some. The concern here is not that Frederick's speech was offensive, but that it was reasonably viewed as promoting illegal drug use.

Although accusing this decision of doing "serious violence to the First Amendment" by authorizing "viewpoint discrimination," the dissent concludes that "it might well be appropriate to tolerate some targeted viewpoint discrimination in this unique setting." Nor do we understand the dissent to take the position that schools are required to tolerate student advocacy of illegal drug use at school events, even if that advocacy falls short of inviting "imminent" lawless action. ("[I]t is possible that our rigid imminence requirement ought to be relaxed at schools"). And even the dissent recognizes that the issues here are close enough that the principal should not be held liable in damages, but should instead enjoy qualified immunity for her actions. Stripped of rhetorical flourishes, then, the debate between the dissent and this opinion is less about constitutional first principles than about whether Frederick's banner constitutes promotion of illegal drug use. We have explained our view that it does. The dissent's contrary view on that relatively narrow question hardly justifies sounding the First Amendment bugle. . . .

School principals have a difficult job, and a vitally important one. When Frederick suddenly and unexpectedly unfurled his banner, Morse had to decide to act—or not act—on the spot. It was reasonable for her to conclude that the banner promoted illegal drug use—in violation of established school policy—and that failing to act would send a powerful message to the students in her charge, including Frederick, about how serious the school was about the dangers of illegal drug use. The First Amendment does not require schools to tolerate at school events student expression that contributes to those dangers.

The judgment of the United States Court of Appeals for the Ninth Circuit is reversed, and the case is remanded for further proceedings consistent with this opinion.

It is so ordered.

Justice THOMAS, concurring.

The Court today decides that a public school may prohibit speech advocating illegal drug use. I agree and therefore join its opinion in full. I write separately to state my view that the standard set forth in *Tinker v. Des Moines Independent Community School Dist.,* 393 U.S. 503 (1969), is without basis in the Constitution.

I

The First Amendment states that "Congress shall make no law . . . abridging the freedom of speech." As this Court has previously observed, the First Amendment was not originally understood to permit all sorts of speech; instead, "[t]here are certain well-defined and narrowly limited classes of speech, the prevention and punishment of which have never been thought to raise any Constitutional problem." *Chaplinsky v. New Hampshire,* 315 U.S. 568, 571-572 (1942); *see also Cox v. Louisiana,* 379 U.S. 536, 554 (1965). In my view, the history of public education suggests that the First Amendment, as originally understood, does not protect student speech in public schools. Although colonial schools were exclusively private, public education proliferated in the early 1800's. By the time the States ratified the Fourteenth Amendment, public schools had become relatively common. W. Reese, America's Public Schools: From the Common School to "No Child Left Behind" 11-12 (2005) (hereinafter Reese). If students in public schools were originally understood as having free-speech rights, one would have expected

19th-century public schools to have respected those rights and courts to have enforced them. They did not.

A

During the colonial era, private schools and tutors offered the only educational opportunities for children, and teachers managed classrooms with an iron hand. R. Butts & L. Cremin, *A History of Education in American Culture* 121, 123 (1953) (hereinafter Butts). Public schooling arose, in part, as a way to educate those too poor to afford private schools. See Kaestle & Vinovskis, *From Apron Strings to ABCs: Parents, Children, and Schooling in Nineteenth-Century Massachusetts,* 84 Am. J. Sociology S39, S49 (Supp. 1978). Because public schools were initially created as substitutes for private schools, when States developed public education systems in the early 1800's, no one doubted the government's ability to educate and discipline children as private schools did. Like their private counterparts, early public schools were not places for freewheeling debates or exploration of competing ideas. Rather, teachers instilled "a core of common values" in students and taught them self-control. Reese 23; A. Potter & G. Emerson, *The School and the Schoolmaster: A Manual* 125 (1843) ("By its discipline it contributes, insensibly, to generate a spirit of subordination to lawful authority, a power of self-control, and a habit of postponing present indulgence to a greater future good . . ."); D. Parkerson & J. Parkerson, *The Emergence of the Common School in the U.S. Countryside* 6 (1998) (hereinafter Parkerson) (noting that early education activists, such as Benjamin Rush, believed public schools "help[ed] control the innate selfishness of the individual").

Teachers instilled these values not only by presenting ideas but also through strict discipline. Butts 274-275. Schools punished students for behavior the school considered disrespectful or wrong. Parkerson 65 (noting that children were punished for idleness, talking, profanity, and slovenliness). Rules of etiquette were enforced, and courteous behavior was demanded. Reese 40. To meet their educational objectives, schools required absolute obedience. C. Northend, *The Teacher's Assistant or Hints and Methods in School Discipline and Instruction* 44, 52 (1865) ("I consider a school judiciously governed, where order prevails; where the strictest sense of propriety is manifested by the pupils towards the teacher, and towards each other . . ." (internal quotation marks omitted)).

In short, in the earliest public schools, teachers taught, and students listened. Teachers commanded, and students obeyed. Teachers did not rely solely on the power of ideas to persuade; they relied on discipline to maintain order.

B

Through the legal doctrine of *in loco parentis,* courts upheld the right of schools to discipline students, to enforce rules, and to maintain order. Rooted in the English common law, in loco parentis originally governed the legal rights and obligations of tutors and private schools. 1 W. Blackstone, *Commentaries on the Laws of England* 441 (1765) ("[A parent] may also delegate part of his parental authority, during his life, to the tutor or schoolmaster of his child; who is then in loco parentis, and has such a portion of the power of the parent committed to his charge, viz. that of restraint and correction, as may be necessary to answer the purposes for which he is employed"). Chancellor James Kent noted the acceptance of the doctrine as part of American law in the early 19th century. 2 J. Kent, Commentaries on American Law *205, *206-*207 ("So the power allowed by law to the parent over the person of the child may be delegated to a tutor or instructor, the better to accomplish the purpose of education").

As early as 1837, state courts applied the in loco parentis principle to public schools:

"One of the most sacred duties of parents, is to train up and qualify their children, for becoming useful and virtuous members of society; this duty cannot be effectually performed without the ability to command obedience, to control stubbornness, to quicken diligence, and to reform bad habits. . . . The teacher is the substitute of the parent; . . . and in the exercise of these delegated duties, is invested with his power." *State v. Pendergrass,* 19 N.C. 365, 365-366, (1837).

Applying in loco parentis, the judiciary was reluctant to interfere in the routine business of school administration, allowing schools and teachers to set and enforce rules and to maintain order. Sheehan v. Sturges, 53 Conn. 481, 483-484, 2A. 841, 842 (1885). Thus, in the early years of public schooling, schools and teachers had considerable discretion in disciplinary matters:

"To accomplish th[e] desirable ends [of teaching self-restraint, obedience, and other civic virtues], the master of a school is necessarily invested with much discretionary power. . . . He must govern these pupils, quicken the slothful, spur the indolent, restrain the impetuous, and control the stubborn. He must make rules, give commands, and punish disobedience. What rules, what commands, and what punishments shall be imposed, are necessarily largely within the discretion of the master, where none are defined by the school board." *Patterson v. Nutter,* 78 Me. 509, 511, 7A. 273, 274 (1886).

A review of the case law shows that in loco parentis allowed schools to regulate student speech as well. Courts routinely preserved the rights of teachers to punish speech that the school or teacher thought was contrary to the interests of the school and its educational goals. For example, the Vermont Supreme Court upheld the corporal punishment of a student who called his teacher "Old Jack Seaver" in front of other students. *Lander v. Seaver,* 32Vt. 114, 115 (1859). The court explained its decision as follows: . . .

II

Tinker effected a sea change in students' speech rights, extending them well beyond traditional bounds. . . .

Of course, *Tinker*'s reasoning conflicted with the traditional understanding of the judiciary's role in relation to public schooling, a role limited by in loco parentis. Perhaps for that reason, the Court has since scaled back *Tinker*'s standard, or rather set the standard aside on an ad hoc basis.

. . . Today, the Court creates another exception. In doing so, we continue to distance ourselves from *Tinker*, but we neither overrule it nor offer an explanation of when it operates and when it does not. I am afraid that our jurisprudence now says that students have a right to speak in schools except when they don't—a standard continuously developed through litigation against local schools and their administrators. In my view, petitioners could prevail for a much simpler reason: As originally understood, the Constitution does not afford students a right to free speech in public schools.

III

In light of the history of American public education, it cannot seriously be suggested that the First Amendment "freedom of speech" encompasses a student's right to speak in public schools. Early public schools gave total control to teachers, who expected obedience and respect from students. And courts routinely deferred to schools' authority to make rules and to discipline students for violating those rules. Several points are clear: (1) under in loco parentis, speech rules and other school rules were treated identically; (2) the in loco parentis doctrine imposed almost no limits on the types of rules that a school could set while students were in school; and (3) schools and teachers had tremendous discretion in imposing punishments for violations of those rules.

It might be suggested that the early school speech cases dealt only with slurs and profanity. But that criticism does not withstand scrutiny. First, state courts repeatedly reasoned that schools had discretion to impose discipline to maintain order. The substance of the student's speech or conduct played no part in the analysis. Second, some cases involved punishment for speech on weightier matters, for instance a speech criticizing school administrators for creating a fire hazard. Yet courts refused to find an exception to in loco parentis even for this advocacy of public safety.

To be sure, our educational system faces administrative and pedagogical challenges different from those faced by 19th-century schools. And the idea of treating children as though it were still the 19th century would find little support today. But I see no constitutional imperative requiring public schools to allow all student speech. Parents decide whether to send their children to public schools. If parents do not like the rules imposed by those schools, they can seek redress in school boards or legislatures; they can send their children to private schools or home school them; or they can simply move. Whatever rules apply to student speech in public schools, those rules can be challenged by parents in the political process.

In place of that democratic regime, *Tinker* substituted judicial oversight of the day-to-day affairs of public schools. The *Tinker* Court made little attempt to ground its holding in the history of education or in the original understanding of the First Amendment. Instead, it imposed a new and malleable standard: Schools could not inhibit student speech unless it "substantially interfere[d] with the requirements of appropriate discipline in the operation of the school." 393 U.S., at 509 (internal quotation marks omitted). Inherent in the application of that standard are judgment calls about what constitutes interference and what constitutes appropriate discipline. See id., at 517-518 (Black, J., dissenting) (arguing that the armbands in fact caused a disruption). Historically, courts reasoned that only local school districts were entitled to make those calls. The *Tinker* Court usurped that traditional authority for the judiciary.

And because *Tinker* utterly ignored the history of public education, courts (including this one) routinely find it necessary to create ad hoc exceptions to its central premise. This doctrine of exceptions creates confusion without fixing the underlying problem by returning to first principles. Just as I cannot accept *Tinker*'s standard, I cannot subscribe to *Kuhlmeier*'s alternative. Local school boards, not the courts, should determine what pedagogical interests are "legitimate" and what rules "reasonably relat[e]" to those interests. . . .

In the name of the First Amendment, *Tinker* has undermined the traditional authority of teachers to maintain order in public schools. "Once a society that generally respected the authority of teachers, deferred to their judgment, and trusted them to act in the best interest of school children, we now accept defiance, disrespect, and disorder as daily occurrences in many of our public schools." Dupre, *Should Students Have Constitutional Rights? Keeping Order in the Public Schools*, 65 Geo. Wash. L. Rev. 49, 50 (1996). We need look no further than this case for an example: *Frederick* asserts a constitutional right to utter at a school event what is either "[g]ibberish," or an open call to use illegal drugs. To elevate such impertinence to the status of constitutional protection would be farcical and would indeed be to "surrender control of the American public school system to public school students." . . .

I join the Court's opinion because it erodes *Tinker*'s hold in the realm of student speech, even though it does so by adding to the patchwork of exceptions to the *Tinker* standard. I think the better approach is to dispense with *Tinker* altogether, and given the opportunity, I would do so.

NOTES AND QUESTIONS

1. In reaching its conclusion, the Court traces its controlling precedent regarding student speech, including *Tinker, Fraser,* and *Kuhlmeier*. Is the Court's result a logical extension of those cases?
2. After *Morse,* what are the circumstances under which a public educational institution can regulate student speech?
3. In his separate concurrence, Justice Thomas argues that the Court's precedent establishing the limits of governmental regulation of student speech should be discarded because "the history of public education suggests that the First Amendment as originally understood, does not protect student speech in public schools." According to Justice Thomas, therefore, the First Amendment's protection of speech simply does not apply to public schools.
4. In his dissent, Justice Stevens contends that the Court ignores its previous cases and takes a "ham-handed categorical approach" that is "deaf to the constitutional imperative to permit unfettered debate, even among high school students, about the wisdom of the war on drugs, or of legalizing marijuana for medicinal use." Was Joseph Frederick's banner part of a "debate" about the wisdom of government drug policy? Justice Stevens also suggests that the Court's reasoning would enable a school district to prohibit student speech promoting other harmful practices, including consumption of alcohol or even fatty foods. Do you agree?

5. Speech Codes and Appearance Codes

(a) Speech Codes and Antiharassment Policies

Based upon the Supreme Court's reasoning in *Fraser, Hazelwood* and *Tinker,* many school districts and universities began to develop codes governing student-speech. These codes typically are called "antiharassment policies" to indicate that their objective is to prohibit abusive behavior among students and thereby to create a safer learning environment. *See, e.g.,* Henry Louis Gates, Jr., *Speaking of Race, Speaking of Sex: Hate Speech, Civil Rights and Civil Liberties* (1994); Catherine A. MacKinnin, *Only Words* (1993).

The campus speech codes have taken two different forms. Some early policies tracked the language of the Equal Opportunity Employment Commission's (EEOC) guidelines regarding sexual harassment in the workplace. The initial University of Michigan's code was typical of this approach. The policy prohibited "[a]ny behavior . . . verbal or physical, that, (1) stigmatizes or victimizes an individual" on the basis of race, ethnicity, religion, gender or sexual orientation; (2) "involves an express or implied threat"; and (3) "[h]as the purpose or reasonably foreseeable effect of interfering with an individual's academic efforts, employment, participation in University sponsored extracurricular affairs or personal safety." In *Doe v. University of Michigan,* 721 F. Supp. 852 (E.D. Mich. 1989), however, the federal court declared the policy unconstitutional on the ground that it restricted speech protected by the First Amendment and was unconstitutionally vague in its use of language like "stigmatize," "victimize," "interference," and "threat to . . . academic efforts." The federal courts have consistently followed *Doe's* rejection of similar EEOC language in campus speech codes. *See, e.g.,* The *UWMPost, Inc. v. Board of Regents of the University of Wisconsin, 774* F. Supp. 1163 (E.D. Wis. 1991); *Iota Xi Chapter of Sigma Chi Fraternity v. George Mason University,* 773 F. Supp. 792 (E.D. Va. 1991), *aff'd.,* 993 F.2d 386 (4th Cir. 1993).

In the wake of the rejection of the University of Michigan's campus speech code, Stanford University Law Professor Thomas Grey attempted to draft a constitutionally sound speech code based upon the Supreme Court's "fighting words" doctrine from *Chaplinsky v. New Hampshire,* 315 U.S. 568 (1942). In *Chaplinsky,* the Supreme Court held that words that "by their very utterance inflict injury or tend to incite an immediate breach of the peace" are not necessarily entitled to First Amendment protection. This "fighting words" doctrine, however, was virtually discarded by the Supreme Court in *R.A.V. v. City of St. Paul, Minn.,* 505 U.S. 377 (1992), invalidating a local ordinance that prohibited the use of certain "fighting words" that "arouse anger, alarm, or resentment in others on the basis of race, color, creed, religion, or gender. . . ." The Stanford Code prohibited harassment by personal "vilification," and defined such harassment as any speech or expression that: (1) is "intended to insult or stigmatize an individual . . . on the basis of their sex, race, etc."; (2) is "addressed directly to the individual . . . when it insults or stigmatizes"; and (3) makes use of "insulting" or "fighting" words or nonverbal symbols. Nonetheless, the policy was enjoined under a California law that mandated the application of full First Amendment speech rights even to private universities like Stanford. *See Corry v. The Leland Stanford Junior University,* Case No. 740309 Order on Preliminary Injunction (Cal. Super. Ct., County of Santa Clara, Feb. 27, 1995). The court reasoned that under the Supreme Court's *R.A.V.* decision, the Stanford Code impermissibly reached speech that, although harmful, did not necessarily incite an immediate breach of the peace. The court also found terms like "insult" and "stigmatize" to be unconstitutionally vague. *See also Dambrot v. Central Michigan University,* 55 F.3d 1177 (6th Cir. 1995).

In 1999, the State College Areas Public School District in Pennsylvania adopted an antiharassment policy that was expressly intended to provide high school students "with a safe, secure, and nurturing school environment." The policy itself declared that "disrespect among members of the school community is unacceptable behavior which threatens to disrupt the school environment and well being of the individual." The policy defined harassment as "verbal or physical conduct based upon one's actual or perceived race, religion, color, national origin, gender, sexual orientation, disability or other personal characteristics, and which has the purpose or effect of substantially interfering with a student's educational performance or creating an intimidating, hostile or offensive environment." The policy also gave several examples: "harassment can include any unwelcome verbal, written or physical conduct that offends, denigrates or belittles an individual because of any of the characteristics described above. Such conduct includes, but is not limited to, unsolicited derogatory remarks, jokes, demeaning comments or behaviors, slurs, mimicking, name calling, graffiti, innuendo, gestures, physical contact, stalking, threatening, bullying, extorting or the display or circulation of written materials or pictures." Another section of the policy prohibited harassment on the basis of characteristics such as "clothing, physical appearance, social skills, peer group, intellect, educational program, hobbies or values."

David Saxe, a member of the Pennsylvania State Board of Education, challenged the policy in federal court, arguing that the policy violated the First Amendment on its face. The district court dismissed the complaint, concluding that the policy was facially constitutional. *Saxe v. State College Area School District,* 77 F. Supp. 2d 621 (M.D. Pa. 1999). The district court reasoned that the policy's definition of harassment was similar to the standard for harassment under federal civil rights laws, Title VII and Title IX, and the Pennsylvania Human Relations Act. The district court observed that "harassment has never been considered to be protected activity under the First Amendment."

The Third Circuit, however, reversed. *Saxe v. State College Area School District,* 240 F.3d 200 (3d Cir. 2001). The court rejected the district court's ruling that harassment is never protected under the First Amendment: "The District Court's categorical pronouncement exaggerates the current state of the law in this area. . . . Such a categorical rule is without precedent in the decisions of the Supreme Court or this Court, and it belies the very real tension between anti-harassment laws and the Constitution's guarantee of freedom of speech."

The Third Circuit reasoned that the district's antiharassment policy prohibited harassment based upon "personal characteristics" not protected under federal civil rights law, including "appearance, clothing, and social skills." The court declared: "[b]y prohibiting disparaging speech directed at a person's 'values,' the Policy strikes at the heart of moral and political discourse—the lifeblood of constitutional self-government (and democratic education) and the core concern of the First Amendment." The Third Circuit thus found that the policy targeted more speech than school officials could prohibit under the Supreme Court's freedom of speech case law. The Court warned that a school must be prepared to justify any such antiharassment policy under *Tinker v. Des Moines Independent Community School District,* 393 U.S. 503 (1969). In *Tinker,* the Court ruled that school officials could censor student expression if that student expression would cause a substantial disruption of school activities. The school district's policy encompassed speech that did not necessarily meet *Tinker's* substantial disruption standard. The Third Circuit found that the policy could be read to prohibit "core political and religious speech" that does not create a substantial disruption, but merely offends another student.

In the wake of *Saxe,* is it possible to draft an antiharassment policy that would survive judicial scrutiny? *See, e.g.,* Jon B. Gould, *The Precedent That Wasn't: College Hate Speech Codes and the Two Faces of Legal Compliance,* 35 Law & Soc. Rev. 345 (2001). Assuming that a university or school district genuinely desires to create an educational environment free from harassing speech, what policy language would you suggest that the institution adopt? Consider whether the following policy language would survive constitutional challenge:

> The District will not tolerate harassing or intimidating conduct, whether verbal, physical, or visual, that affects tangible benefits of education, that unreasonably interferes with a student's educational performance, or that creates an intimidating, hostile, or offensive educational environment. No person, including a District employee or agent, or student, shall harass or intimidate another student based upon a student's gender, color, race, religion, creed, ancestry, national origin, physical or mental disability, sexual orientation, or other protected group status. Examples of prohibited conduct include name-calling, using derogatory slurs, or wearing or possessing items depicting or implying hatred or prejudice of one of the characteristics stated above.

(b) Appearance Codes and Dress Codes

Vines v. Board of Education of Zion School District No. 6

2002 U.S. Dist. LEXIS 228 (N.D. Ill. 2002)

Plaintiffs, Barbara and Robert Vines (Vines), filed suit, *pro se,* against defendant, the Board of Education of Zion School District No. 6 (Board), on behalf of themselves and their daughter, Kathryn Vines (Kathryn), alleging that the Board's dress code violates the United States Constitution. . . .

Central Junior High School instituted a dress code effective the 2001-2002 school year. The dress code states that it was instituted "to create a school environment that fosters the academic and social growth of its students."

The students are required to dress in solid black, solid white, or a combination of black and white clothing. Logos, patches, pins, imprinted slogans, words and designs on the clothing are not permitted. Allowable tops include T-shirts, blouses and shirts. Black and/or white jeans, shorts, and appropriate skirts are allowed. Students who violate the dress code may be asked to return home and change, may be required to wear their gym uniform, and may be "subject to additional consequences."

Students new to the school are permitted a "grace period" to comply with the dress code. Students who are unable to comply with the dress code due to financial hardship are accommodated or otherwise provided "appropriate resources." Students whose parents or legal guardians object to the dress code on religious grounds are not required to comply with the dress code provided that the parent or legal guardian present a signed statement of objection detailing the grounds for the objection to the Board.

Plaintiffs allege that the Board's dress code violates Kathryn's First Amendment right of free speech and freedom of religion and infringes upon the Vines' "right to self-regulation." . . .

B. First Amendment Claim

. . . In the instant case, plaintiffs do not allege, nor can it be inferred, that Central Junior High School has been opened for "indiscriminate use" by the general public. Accordingly, Central Junior High School is a nonpublic forum, and the appropriate test is whether the dress code is "reasonably related to legitimate pedagogical concerns." *Hazelwood.*

"Pedagogical concerns" include the structured transmission of a body of knowledge in an orderly environment and the inculcation of civility and traditional moral, social, and political norms. . . . Here, the Board's policy states that a student's dress must meet health and safety standards and may not be disruptive to the educational program. School uniforms may be instituted if uniforms "would contribute to attaining and maintaining a positive and productive school learning environment." The Board states that the students' dress code improves the safety of schools and the academic and social growth of students by discouraging gang affiliations, reducing peer pressure and socioeconomic competition; by improving students' self-concepts, classroom behavior, and academic performance; and by reducing vulgar, profane, or obscene disruptions to the educational process. These constitute legitimate pedagogical concerns, and the dress code's restrictions of Kathryn's expression are reasonably related to these legitimate pedagogical concerns. Accordingly, the Board's dress code constitutionally regulates Kathryn's First Amendment free speech rights in the nonpublic forum of her school. . . .

C. Fourteenth Amendment Claim

The Vines also allege that the dress code "constitutes an unreasonable infringement upon our family's right to self-regulation." In their response to the Board's motion, the Vines argue that the school must share the responsibility of dressing and grooming with a student's parents.

The Fourteenth Amendment's Due Process Clause includes the fundamental liberty "interest of parents in the care, custody, and control of their children." *Troxel v. Granville,* 530 U.S. 57, 65-66 (2000). However, parental rights are not absolute in the public school context and can be subject to reasonable regulation. *See, e.g., Runyon v. McCary,* 427 U.S. 160, 177 (1976) (recognizing no parental right to educate children in private segregated academies); *Fleischfresser v. Directors of Sch. Dist. 20,* 15 F.3d 680, 690 (7th Cir. 1994). A rational-basis review is the appropriate standard in analyzing parental rights in the context of public education and school dress codes. *See Littlefield [v. Forney Independent School District,* 268 F.3d 275, 291 (5th Cir. 2001)]; *Herndon v. Chapel Hill-Carrboro City Bd. of Educ.,* 89 F.3d 174, 177-79 (4th Cir. 1996); *Immediato v. Rye Neck Sch. Dist.,* 73 F.3d 454, 461 (2nd Cir. 1996).

As found above, the Board's dress code is rationally related to the Board's interest in fostering the education of its students and furthering the legitimate goals of improving student safety.

For the foregoing reasons, the Board's Motion for Judgment on the Pleadings is granted. . . .

NOTES AND QUESTIONS

1. In *Littlefield v. Forney Independent School District,* 268 F.3d 275 (5th Cir. 2001), the Fifth Circuit held that a school's mandatory uniform policy did not violate students' First Amendment rights to freedom of expression. The Court reasoned that even if student dress were an act of expression, a school is entitled to regulate dress for legitimate pedagogical reasons. The plaintiffs unsuccessfully argued that the district's policy was a form of "coerced speech" and a "prior restraint." The "coerced speech" argument implies that the uniforms convey a particular message that the school district wishes to express. As to the "prior restraint" argument, the students claimed that the uniform policy precludes the use of clothing to express any message — no matter how specific or particularized — and that because school children do wear clothing that sends political, cultural and social messages, this restriction is a content-based prior restraint on speech. Would you categorize your style of dress as symbolic speech? Does wearing a uniform convey a particular message that the school district wishes to express? What would that message be? Are uniforms more practical for students since they enable everyone to dress the same, regardless of their parents' income? Do uniforms reduce stereotyping and eliminate social, economic and fashion pressures? Do a pair of name brand sneakers and a t-shirt from a rock concert send an important message to society? If so, is it political, cultural, or social?
2. The *Vines* court concentrates on the pedagogical interests arguably served by appearance and dress codes. Those interests include reducing peer pressure, reducing vulgar and profane disruptions in the educational process, discouraging gang affiliations and eliminating socio-economic competition. Can you think of any other pedagogical concerns that the court could have identified? If students are dressed similarly and thus are not concerned about who wears the latest fashions, do you think it may add to a student's self-confidence? Do the advantages of dress and appearance codes outweigh the disadvantages?

3. In *East High Gay/Straight Alliance v. Board of Education of Salt Lake City School District,* 81 F. Supp. 2d 1166 (D. Utah 1999), the court explores First Amendment issues in the context of student clubs. In *East High,* a club with a "gay-positive" perspective challenged the school's policy that denied access to school facilities to "non-curricular" groups. The club members argued that the school made past exceptions for other "non-curricular" groups, but refused to make an exception due to the club's viewpoint. As a result, the club claimed that the blanket exclusion of the expression of "gay-positive views" as well as the Rainbow Club from the existing forum for curricular-related student groups constituted impermissible viewpoint discrimination in violation of the First Amendment. The court reasoned that the school's policy designating a forum for "curriculum-related" student groups does not violate the First Amendment in light of its reasonableness. However, the court noted that it needed to further explore whether the student group was wrongfully excluded under the terms of the First Amendment and the Equal Access Act, which prohibits public schools with a "limited open forum" from discriminating against students wishing to meet in that forum based upon the "religious, political, philosophical, or other content of the speech at such meetings" 20 U.S.C. §§4071-4074. Summary judgment was denied for the school district because the court followed *Tinker's* rationale that the prohibition of expression of one particular opinion, without evidence that it is necessary to avoid material and substantial interference with schoolwork or the rights of others, is unconstitutional. *East High,* 81 F. Supp. 2d at 1195. *See also Colin v. Orange Unified School District,* 83 F. Supp. 2d 1135 (C.D. Cal. 2000) (failure to give Gay/Straight Alliance access to limited open form in school violates the Equal Access Act). Would you have denied summary judgment as well? Do clubs fall under the umbrella of "school-sponsored speech" or school newspapers? If yes, should that have affected the court's decision? Does a school "lend its name and resources" to clubs?

6. Freedom of Expression Practicum

Marie Clare is a staff member of the Tuckerville High School newspaper. Marie's love of food has compelled her to do an investigative story on the Tuckerville High School cafeteria. Marie thoroughly investigated the inner workings of the cafeteria. She interviewed cafeteria cooks, servers and suppliers. Marie even went so far as to visit the supplier's plant to examine the ingredients of the food and observe the freezing and packaging processes. Once her research was completed, Marie wrote an exposé on the negative quality and fat content of the food the cafeteria serves. The staff was astounded by Marie's discoveries and moved up the article date to make an earlier edition. Once the newspaper had gone to print, but before the distribution of the newspaper, the principal conducted his customary perusal of the articles. The principal was horrified at Marie's article and demanded the students delete Marie's article from the edition. When asked for a reason, the principal responded, "I found four typos in her article, and I demand perfection." The students do not believe that typos were the principal's sole reason for deleting Marie's article. Marie files a lawsuit claiming a violation of her First Amendment rights. Who will prevail?

B. FREEDOM FROM UNREASONABLE SEARCHES AND SEIZURES

The Fourth Amendment to the United States Constitution insures individuals will be free from unreasonable searches and seizures. This right, however, does not fully extend to students in the American public school system. Students are not afforded the same protections guaranteed by the Fourth Amendment inside the schoolhouse gate as they are outside that gate. Students may be subjected to drug testing as a condition to participating in extracurricular activities and may be subjected to random locker searches. The Supreme Court and many lower courts have upheld such policies, because the policies qualify under the "special needs" exception to the Fourth Amendment recognized in *New Jersey v. T.L.O.,* 469 U.S. 325 (1985). Thus, in order to maintain stability and discipline in schools, teachers and administrators no longer must demonstrate probable cause for searches and seizures, but only that "the measures adopted are reasonably related to the objectives of the search and not excessively intrusive."

The departure from Fourth Amendment protections has persisted as the courts continue to take a more aggressive approach in the balance between government interests and students' rights. The encroachment on student rights began with a simple purse search and evolved into athlete drug testing. The erosion of constitutional protections then expanded beyond athletes to students involved in all extracurricular activities. The "special needs" doctrine also has been used to justify random drug testing of students. According to the courts, students have a lower expectation of privacy than other Americans. Moreover, student athletes and students involved in certain extracurricular activities are said to have even lower expectations of privacy. The courts attribute these lower expectations to "communal undress" frequent in locker rooms, minimum grade point average requirements and preseason physical exams. These factors, coupled with the "special needs" vital to protecting our youth from ever-present drug concerns, have enabled the courts to justify their contraction of Fourth Amendment protections in the school setting.

1. The Fourth Amendment's Reasonableness Standard Governs the School Setting

NEW JERSEY v. T.L.O.

469 U.S. 325 (1985)

Justice WHITE delivered the opinion of the Court.

We granted certiorari in this case to examine the appropriateness of the exclusionary rule as a remedy for searches carried out in violation of the

Fourth Amendment by public school authorities. Our consideration of the proper application of the Fourth Amendment to the public schools, however, has led us to conclude that the search that gave rise to the case now before us did not violate the Fourth Amendment. Accordingly, we here address only the questions of the proper standard for assessing the legality of searches conducted by public school officials and the application of that standard to the facts of this case.

I

On March 7, 1980, a teacher at Piscataway High School in Middlesex County, N.J., discovered two girls smoking in a lavatory. One of the two girls was the respondent T.L.O., who at that time was a 14-year-old high school freshman. Because smoking in the lavatory was a violation of a school rule, the teacher took the two girls to the Principal's office, where they met with Assistant Vice Principal Theodore Choplick. In response to questioning by Mr. Choplick, T.L.O.'s companion admitted that she had violated the rule. T.L.O., however, denied that she had been smoking in the lavatory and claimed that she did not smoke at all.

Mr. Choplick asked T.L.O. to come into his private office and demanded to see her purse. Opening the purse, he found a pack of cigarettes, which he removed from the purse and held before T.L.O. as he accused her of having lied to him. As he reached into the purse for the cigarettes, Mr. Choplick also noticed a package of cigarette rolling papers. In his experience, possession of rolling papers by high school students was closely associated with the use of marihuana. Suspecting that a closer examination of the purse might yield further evidence of drug use, Mr. Choplick proceeded to search the purse thoroughly. The search revealed a small amount of marihuana, a pipe, a number of empty plastic bags, a substantial quantity of money in one-dollar bills, an index card that appeared to be a list of students who owed T.L.O. money, and two letters that implicated T.L.O. in marihuana dealing.

Mr. Choplick notified T.L.O.'s mother and the police, and turned the evidence of drug dealing over to the police. At the request of the police, T.L.O.'s mother took her daughter to police headquarters, where T.L.O. confessed that she had been selling marihuana at the high school. On the basis of the confession and the evidence seized by Mr. Choplick, the State brought delinquency charges against T.L.O. in the Juvenile and Domestic Relations Court of Middlesex County. Contending that Mr. Choplick's search of her purse violated the Fourth Amendment, T.L.O. moved to suppress the evidence found in her purse as well as her confession, which, she argued, was tainted by the allegedly unlawful search. The Juvenile Court denied the motion to suppress. . . .

II

In determining whether the search at issue in this case violated the Fourth Amendment, we are faced initially with the question whether that Amendment's prohibition on unreasonable searches and seizures applies to searches conducted by public school officials. We hold that it does.

It is now beyond dispute that "the Federal Constitution, by virtue of the Fourteenth Amendment, prohibits unreasonable searches and seizures by state officers." . . . Equally indisputable is the proposition that the Fourteenth Amendment protects the rights of students against encroachment by public school officials:

> The Fourteenth Amendment, as now applied to the States, protects the citizen against the State itself and all of its creatures—Boards of Education not excepted. These have, of course, important, delicate, and highly discretionary functions, but none that they may not perform within the limits of the Bill of Rights. That they are educating the young for citizenship is reason for scrupulous protection of Constitutional freedoms of the individual, if we are not to strangle the free mind at its source and teach youth to discount important principles of our government as mere platitudes. *West Virginia State Bd. of Ed. v. Barnette.*

These two propositions—that the Fourth Amendment applies to the States through the Fourteenth Amendment, and that the actions of public school officials are subject to the limits placed on state action by the Fourteenth Amendment—might appear sufficient to answer the suggestion that the Fourth Amendment does not proscribe unreasonable searches by school officials. On reargument, however, the State of New Jersey has argued that the history of the Fourth Amendment indicates that the Amendment was intended to regulate only searches and seizures carried out by law enforcement officers; accordingly, although public school officials are concededly state agents for purposes of the Fourteenth Amendment, the Fourth Amendment creates no rights enforceable against them.

It may well be true that the evil toward which the Fourth Amendment was primarily directed was the resurrection of the pre-Revolutionary practice of using general warrants or "writs of assistance" to authorize searches for contraband by officers of the Crown. . . .

Notwithstanding the general applicability of the Fourth Amendment to the activities of civil authorities, a few courts have concluded that school officials are exempt from the dictates of the Fourth Amendment by virtue of the special nature of their authority over schoolchildren. . . . Teachers and school administrators, it is said, act *in loco parentis* in their dealings with students: their authority is that of the parent, not the State, and is therefore not subject to the limits of the Fourth Amendment.

Such reasoning is in tension with contemporary reality and the teachings of this Court. We have held school officials subject to the commands of the First Amendment, *see Tinker,* and the Due Process Clause of the Fourteenth Amendment, *see Goss v. Lopez,* 419 U.S. 565 (1975). If school authorities are state actors for purposes of the constitutional guarantees of freedom of expression and due process, it is difficult to understand why they should be deemed to be exercising parental rather than public authority when conducting searches of their students. More generally, the Court has recognized that "the concept of parental delegation" as a source of school authority is not entirely "consonant with compulsory education laws." *Ingraham v. Wright,* 430 U.S. 651 (1977). Today's public school officials do not merely exercise authority voluntarily conferred on them by individual parents; rather, they act in furtherance of publicly mandated educational and disciplinary policies. . . . In carrying out searches and other disciplinary functions pursuant to such policies, school officials act as representatives of the State, not merely as surrogates for the parents, and they cannot claim the parents' immunity from the strictures of the Fourth Amendment.

III

To hold that the Fourth Amendment applies to searches conducted by school authorities is only to begin the inquiry into the standards governing such searches. Although the underlying command of the Fourth Amendment is always that searches and seizures be reasonable, what is reasonable depends on the context within which a search takes place. The determination of the standard of reasonableness governing any specific class of searches requires "balancing the need to search against the invasion which the search entails." . . . On one side of the balance are arrayed the individual's legitimate expectations of privacy and personal security; on the other, the government's need for effective methods to deal with breaches of public order.

We have recognized that even a limited search of the person is a substantial invasion of privacy. . . . We have also recognized that searches of closed items of personal luggage are intrusions on protected privacy interests, for "the Fourth Amendment provides protection to the owner of every container that conceals its contents from plain view." . . . A search of a child's person or of a closed purse or other bag carried on her person,[5] no less than a similar search carried out on an adult, is undoubtedly a severe violation of subjective expectations of privacy.

Of course, the Fourth Amendment does not protect subjective expectations of privacy that are unreasonable or otherwise "illegitimate." . . . To receive the protection of the Fourth Amendment, an expectation of privacy must be one that society is "prepared to recognize as legitimate." The State of New Jersey has argued that because of the pervasive supervision to which children in the schools are necessarily subject, a child has virtually no legitimate expectation of privacy in articles of personal property "unnecessarily" carried into a school. This argument has two factual premises: (1) the fundamental incompatibility of expectations of privacy with the maintenance of a sound educational environment; and (2) the minimal interest of the child in

---

[5] We do not address the question, not presented by this case, whether a schoolchild has a legitimate expectation of privacy in lockers, desks, or other school property provided for the storage of school supplies. Nor do we express any opinion on the standards (if any) governing searches of such areas by school officials or by other public authorities acting at the request of school officials. *Compare Zamora v. Pomeroy*, 639 F.2d 662, 670 (CA10 1981) ("Inasmuch as the school had assumed joint control of the locker it cannot be successfully maintained that the school did not have a right to inspect it"), *and People v. Overton*, 24 N.Y.2d 522, 249 N.E.2d 366, 301 N.Y.S.2d 479 (1969) (school administrators have power to consent to search of a student's locker), *with State v. Engerud*, 94 N.J. 331, 348, 463 A.2d 934, 943 (1983) ("We are satisfied that in the context of this case the student had an expectation of privacy in the contents of his locker. . . . For the four years of high school, the school locker is a home away from home. In it the student stores the kind of personal 'effects' protected by the Fourth Amendment").

bringing any items of personal property into the school. Both premises are severely flawed.

Although this Court may take notice of the difficulty of maintaining discipline in the public schools today, the situation is not so dire that students in the schools may claim no legitimate expectations of privacy. We have recently recognized that the need to maintain order in a prison is such that prisoners retain no legitimate expectations of privacy in their cells, but it goes almost without saying that "[t]he prisoner and the schoolchild stand in wholly different circumstances, separated by the harsh facts of criminal conviction and incarceration." . . . We are not yet ready to hold that the schools and the prisons need be equated for purposes of the Fourth Amendment.

Nor does the State's suggestion that children have no legitimate need to bring personal property into the schools seem well anchored in reality. Students at a minimum must bring to school not only the supplies needed for their studies, but also keys, money, and the necessaries of personal hygiene and grooming. In addition, students may carry on their persons or in purses or wallets such nondisruptive yet highly personal items as photographs, letters, and diaries. Finally, students may have perfectly legitimate reasons to carry with them articles of property needed in connection with extracurricular or recreational activities. In short, schoolchildren may find it necessary to carry with them a variety of legitimate, noncontraband items, and there is no reason to conclude that they have necessarily waived all rights to privacy in such items merely by bringing them onto school grounds.

Against the child's interest in privacy must be set the substantial interest of teachers and administrators in maintaining discipline in the classroom and on school grounds. Maintaining order in the classroom has never been easy, but in recent years, school disorder has often taken particularly ugly forms: drug use and violent crime in the schools have become major social problems. . . . Even in schools that have been spared the most severe disciplinary problems, the preservation of order and a proper educational environment requires close supervision of schoolchildren, as well as the enforcement of rules against conduct that would be perfectly permissible if undertaken by an adult. "Events calling for discipline are frequent occurrences and sometimes require immediate, effective action." Accordingly, we have recognized that maintaining security and order in the schools requires a certain degree of flexibility in school disciplinary procedures, and we have respected the value of preserving the informality of the student-teacher relationship.

How, then, should we strike the balance between the schoolchild's legitimate expectations of privacy and the school's equally legitimate need to maintain an environment in which learning can take place? It is evident that the school setting requires some easing of the restrictions to which searches by public authorities are ordinarily subject. The warrant requirement, in particular, is unsuited to the school environment: requiring a teacher to obtain a warrant before searching a child suspected of an infraction of school rules (or of the criminal law) would unduly interfere with the maintenance of the swift and informal disciplinary procedures needed in the schools. Just as we have in other cases dispensed with the warrant requirement when "the burden of obtaining a warrant is likely to frustrate the governmental purpose behind the search," we hold today that school officials need not obtain a warrant before searching a student who is under their authority.

The school setting also requires some modification of the level of suspicion of illicit activity needed to justify a search. Ordinarily, a search—even one that may permissibly be carried out without a warrant—must be based upon "probable cause" to believe that a violation of the law has occurred. However, "probable cause" is not an irreducible requirement of a valid search. The fundamental command of the Fourth Amendment is that searches and seizures be reasonable, and although "both the concept of probable cause and the requirement of a warrant bear on the reasonableness of a search, . . . in certain limited circumstances neither is required." Thus, we have in a number of cases recognized the legality of searches and seizures based upon suspicions that, although "reasonable," do not rise to the level of probable cause. Where a careful balancing of governmental and private interests suggests that the public interest is best served by a Fourth Amendment standard of reasonableness that stops short of probable cause, we have not hesitated to adopt such a standard.

We join the majority of courts that have examined this issue in concluding that the accommodation of the privacy interests of schoolchildren with the substantial need of teachers and administrators for freedom to maintain order in the schools does not require strict adherence to the requirement that searches be based upon probable cause to believe that the subject of the search has violated or is violating the law. Rather, the legality of a search of a student should depend simply on the reasonableness, under all the circumstances, of the search. Determining the reasonableness of any search involves a twofold inquiry: first, one must consider "whether the . . . action was justified at its inception," second, one must determine whether the search as actually conducted "was reasonably related in scope to the circumstances which justified the interference in the first place." Under ordinary circumstances, a search of a student by a teacher or other school official will be justified at its inception" when there are reasonable grounds for suspecting that the search will turn up evidence that the student has violated or is violating either the law or the rules of the school.[8] Such a search will be permissible in its scope when the measures adopted are reasonably related to the objectives of the search and not excessively intrusive in light of the age and sex of the student and the nature of the infraction.

This standard will, we trust, neither unduly burden the efforts of school authorities to maintain order in their schools nor authorize unrestrained intrusions upon the privacy of schoolchildren. By focusing attention on the question of reasonableness, the standard will spare teachers and school administrators the necessity of schooling themselves in the niceties of probable

---

[8] We do not decide whether individualized suspicion is an essential element of the reasonableness standard we adopt for searches by school authorities.

cause and permit them to regulate their conduct according to the dictates of reason and common sense. At the same time, the reasonableness standard should ensure that the interests of students will be invaded no more than is necessary to achieve the legitimate end of preserving order in the schools.

IV

There remains the question of the legality of the search in this case. We recognize that the "reasonable grounds" standard applied by the New Jersey Supreme Court in its consideration of this question is not substantially different from the standard that we have adopted today. Nonetheless, we believe that the New Jersey court's application of that standard to strike down the search of T.L.O.'s purse reflects a somewhat crabbed notion of reasonableness. Our review of the facts surrounding the search leads us to conclude that the search was in no sense unreasonable for Fourth Amendment purposes. . . .

NOTES AND QUESTIONS

1. The Supreme Court in *T.L.O.* specifically stated that it would not address the question of whether a schoolchild has a right to privacy in lockers, desks or other school property provided for the storage of school supplies. How would you expect the Court to have analyzed a student's privacy right in those "effects"?
2. The Supreme Court reasoned that schools must maintain a balance between schoolchildren's legitimate expectations of privacy and the school's equally legitimate need to establish a safe and disciplined environment. However, the school must acknowledge the fine line that exists between a healthy learning environment and a prison. The Supreme Court stated "it was not yet ready to hold that the schools and the prisons need be equated for the purposes of the Fourth Amendment."
3. The Supreme Court ruled that prior to searching a student's possessions, school officials need not obtain a warrant or demonstrate probable cause. A teacher or administrator need only have "reasonable grounds" in order to conduct the search. Do you feel that this exception to the Fourth Amendment best serves the public interest or leaves too much room for interpretation?
4. Considering that the same children who lack many of the Fourth Amendment protections in school enjoy those protections outside of the schoolhouse gate, would you characterize this duality as a strength or a weakness with the legal system?
5. Justices Brennan and Marshall dissent in part in *T.L.O.* because the "reasonableness" standard differs from the "probable cause" standard found in the Fourth Amendment. The Justices brand the majority decision as an "unclear, unprecedented, and unnecessary departure from generally applicable Fourth Amendment standards." Do you agree?
6. In footnote 8, the *T.L.O.* Court leaves for another day the issue whether "individualized suspicion" is necessary to justify a warrantless search at school. Can you predict how the Court will resolve that issue in the future?

2. Drug Testing of Students

VERNONIA SCHOOL DISTRICT 47J v. ACTON

515 U.S. 646 (1995)

Justice SCALIA delivered the opinion of the Court.

The Student Athlete Drug Policy adopted by School District 47J in the town of Vernonia, Oregon, authorizes random urinalysis drug testing of students who participate in the District's school athletics programs. We granted certiorari to decide whether this violates the Fourth and Fourteenth Amendments to the United States Constitution.

I

A

Petitioner Vernonia School District 47J (District) operates one high school and three grade schools in the logging community of Vernonia, Oregon. As elsewhere in small-town America, school sports play a prominent role in the town's life, and student athletes are admired in their schools and in the community.

Drugs had not been a major problem in Vernonia schools. In the mid-to-late 1980's, however, teachers and administrators observed a sharp increase in drug use. Students began to speak out about their attraction to the drug culture, and to boast that there was nothing the school could do about it. Along with more drugs came more disciplinary problems. . . .

Not only were student athletes included among the drug users but, as the District Court found, athletes were the leaders of the drug culture. This caused the District's administrators particular concern, since drug use increases the risk of sports-related injury. . . .

Initially, the District responded to the drug problem by offering special classes, speakers, and presentations designed to deter drug use. It even brought in a specially trained dog to detect drugs, but the drug problem persisted. . . .

At that point, District officials began considering a drug-testing program. . . . The school board approved the Policy for implementation in the fall of 1989. Its expressed purpose is to prevent student athletes from using drugs, to protect their health and safety, and to provide drug users with assistance programs.

B

The Policy applies to all students participating in interscholastic athletics. Students wishing to play sports must sign a form consenting to the testing and must obtain the written consent of their parents. Athletes are tested at the beginning of the season for their sport. In addition, once each week of the season the names of the athletes are placed in a "pool" from which a student, with the supervision of two adults, blindly draws the names of 10% of the athletes for random testing. Those selected are notified and tested that same day, if possible.

The student to be tested completes a specimen control form which bears an assigned number. Prescription medications that the student is taking must be identified by providing a copy of the prescription or a doctor's authorization. The student then enters an empty locker room accompanied by an adult monitor of the same sex. Each boy selected produces a sample at a urinal, remaining fully clothed with his back to the monitor, who stands approximately 12 to 15 feet behind the student. Monitors may (though do not always) watch the student while he produces the sample, and they listen for normal sounds of urination. Girls produce samples in an enclosed bathroom stall, so that they can be heard but not observed. After the sample is produced, it is given to the monitor, who checks it for temperature and tampering and then transfers it to a vial.

The samples are sent to an independent laboratory, which routinely tests them for amphetamines, cocaine, and marijuana. Other drugs, such as LSD, may be screened at the request of the District, but the identity of a particular student does not determine which drugs will be tested. The laboratory's procedures are 99.94% accurate. The District follows strict procedures regarding the chain of custody and access to test results. The laboratory does not know the identity of the students whose samples it tests. It is authorized to mail written test reports only to the superintendent and to provide test results to District personnel by telephone only after the requesting official recites a code confirming his authority. Only the superintendent, principals, vice-principals, and athletic directors have access to test results, and the results are not kept for more than one year.

If a sample tests positive, a second test is administered as soon as possible to confirm the result. If the second test is negative, no further action is taken. If the second test is positive, the athlete's parents are notified, and the school principal convenes a meeting with the student and his parents, at which the student is given the option of (1) participating for six weeks in an assistance program that includes weekly urinalysis, or (2) suffering suspension from athletics for the remainder of the current season and the next athletic season. The student is then retested prior to the start of the next athletic season for which he or she is eligible. The Policy states that a second offense results in automatic imposition of option (2); a third offense in suspension for the remainder of the current season and the next two athletic seasons.

C

In the fall of 1991, respondent James Acton, then a seventh grader, signed up to play football at one of the District's grade schools. He was denied participation, however, because he and his parents refused to sign the testing consent forms. The Actons filed suit, seeking declaratory and injunctive relief from enforcement of the Policy on the grounds that it violated the Fourth and Fourteenth Amendments to the United States Constitution and Article I, §9, of the Oregon Constitution. After a bench trial, the District Court entered an order denying the claims on the merits and dismissing the action. The United States Court of Appeals for the Ninth Circuit reversed, holding that the Policy violated both the Fourth and Fourteenth Amendments and Article I, §9, of the Oregon Constitution.

II

The Fourth Amendment to the United States Constitution provides that the Federal Government shall not violate "[t]he right of the people to be secure in their persons, houses, papers, and effects, against unreasonable searches and seizures. . . ." We have held that the Fourteenth Amendment extends this constitutional guarantee to searches and seizures by state officers, including public school officials. . . .

As the text of the Fourth Amendment indicates, the ultimate measure of the constitutionality of a governmental search is "reasonableness." At least in a case such as this, where there was no clear practice, either approving or disapproving the type of search at issue, at the time the constitutional provision was enacted, whether a particular search meets the reasonableness standard, " 'is judged by balancing its intrusion on the individual's Fourth Amendment interests against its promotion of legitimate governmental interests.' ". . . Where a search is undertaken by law enforcement officials to discover evidence of criminal wrongdoing, this Court has said that reasonableness generally requires the obtaining of a judicial warrant, . . . A search unsupported by probable cause can be constitutional, we have said, "when special needs, beyond the normal need for law enforcement, make the warrant and probable-cause requirement impracticable."

We have found such "special needs" to exist in the public school context. There, the warrant requirement "would unduly interfere with the maintenance of the swift and informal disciplinary procedures [that are] needed," and "strict adherence to the requirement that searches be based upon probable cause" would undercut "the substantial need of teachers and administrators for freedom to maintain order in the schools." *T.L.O.* The school search we approved in *T.L.O.*, while not based upon probable cause, *was* based upon individualized *suspicion* of wrongdoing. As we explicitly acknowledged, however, " 'the Fourth Amendment imposes no irreducible requirement of such suspicion,' " . . . We have upheld suspicionless searches and seizures to conduct drug testing of railroad personnel involved in train accidents, to conduct random drug testing of federal customs officers who carry arms or are involved in drug interdiction, and to maintain automobile checkpoints looking for illegal immigrants and contraband, and drunk drivers.

III

The first factor to be considered is the nature of the privacy interest upon which the search here at issue intrudes. The Fourth Amendment does not protect all subjective expectations of privacy, but only those that society recognizes as "legitimate." *T.L.O.* What expectations are legitimate varies, of course, with context, depending, for example, upon whether the individual asserting the privacy interest is at home, at work, in a car, or in a public park. In addition, the legitimacy of certain privacy expectations vis-à-vis the State may depend upon the individual's legal relationship with the State. . . . Central, in our view, to the present case is the fact that the subjects of the Policy are (1) children, who (2) have been committed to the temporary custody of the State as schoolmaster.

Traditionally at common law, and still today, unemancipated minors lack some of the most fundamental rights of self-determination—including even the right of liberty in its narrow sense, *i.e.,* the right to come and go at will. They are subject, even as to their physical freedom, to the control of their parents or guardians. . . . When parents place minor children in private schools for their education, the teachers and administrators of those schools stand *in loco parentis* over the children entrusted to them. In fact, the tutor or schoolmaster is the very prototype of that status. As Blackstone describes it, a parent "may . . . delegate part of his parental authority, during his life, to the tutor or schoolmaster of his child; who is then *in loco parentis,* and has such a portion of the power of the parent committed to his charge, viz. that of restraint and correction, as may be necessary to answer the purposes for which he is employed." 1 W. Blackstone, *Commentaries on the Laws of England* 441 (1769).

In *T.L.O.* we rejected the notion that public schools, like private schools, exercise only parental power over their students, which of course is not subject to constitutional constraints. Such a view of things, we said, "is not entirely 'consonant with compulsory education laws,'" and is inconsistent with our prior decisions treating school officials as state actors for purposes of the Due Process and Free Speech Clauses. But while denying that the State's power over schoolchildren is formally no more than the delegated power of their parents, *T.L.O.* did not deny, but indeed emphasized, that the nature of that power is custodial and tutelary, permitting a degree of supervision and control that could not be exercised over free adults. "[A] proper educational environment requires close supervision of schoolchildren, as well as the enforcement of rules against conduct that would be perfectly permissible if undertaken by an adult." While we do not, of course, suggest that public schools as a general matter have such a degree of control over children as to give rise to a constitutional "duty to protect," we have acknowledged that for many purposes "school authorities ac[t] *in loco parentis,*" *Bethel,* with the power and indeed the duty to "inculcate the habits and manners of civility." Thus, while children assuredly do not "shed their constitutional rights . . . at the schoolhouse gate," *Tinker,* the nature of those rights is what is appropriate for children in school. *See, e.g., Goss v. Lopez* (due process for a student challenging disciplinary suspension requires only that the teacher "informally discuss the alleged misconduct with the student minutes after it has occurred"); *Fraser* ("[I]t is a highly appropriate function of public school education to prohibit the use of vulgar and offensive terms in public discourse"); *Hazelwood* (public school authorities may censor school-sponsored publications, so long as the censorship is "reasonably related to legitimate pedagogical concerns"); *Ingraham* ("Imposing additional administrative safeguards [upon corporal punishment] . . . would . . . entail a significant intrusion into an area of primary educational responsibility").

Fourth Amendment rights, no less than First and Fourteenth Amendment rights, are different in public schools than elsewhere; the "reasonableness" inquiry cannot disregard the schools' custodial and tutelary responsibility for children. For their own good and that of their classmates, public school children are routinely required to submit to various physical examinations, and to be vaccinated against various diseases. According to the American Academy of Pediatrics, most public schools "provide vision and hearing screening and dental and dermatological checks. . . . Others also mandate scoliosis screening at appropriate grade levels." Committee on School Health, American Academy of Pediatrics, *School Health: A Guide for Health Professionals 2* (1987). In the 1991-1992 school year, all 50 States required public school students to be vaccinated against diphtheria, measles, rubella, and polio. U.S. Dept. of Health & Human Services, Public Health Service, Centers for Disease Control, State Immunization Requirements 1991-1992, p. 1. Particularly with regard to medical examinations and procedures, therefore, "students within the school environment have a lesser expectation of privacy than members of the population generally." *T.L.O.* (Powell, J., concurring).

Legitimate privacy expectations are even less with regard to student athletes. School sports are not for the bashful. They require "suiting up" before each practice or event, and showering and changing afterwards. Public school locker rooms, the usual sites for these activities, are not notable for the privacy they afford. The locker rooms in Vernonia are typical: No individual dressing rooms are provided; shower heads are lined up along a wall, unseparated by any sort of partition or curtain; not even all the toilet stalls have doors. As the United States Court of Appeals for the Seventh Circuit has noted, there is "an element of 'communal undress' inherent in athletic participation," *Schaill by Kross v. Tippecanoe County School Corp.,* 864 F.2d 1309, 1318 (1988).

There is an additional respect in which school athletes have a reduced expectation of privacy. By choosing to "go out for the team," they voluntarily subject themselves to a degree of regulation even higher than that imposed on students generally. In Vernonia's public schools, they must submit to a preseason physical exam, they must acquire adequate insurance coverage or sign an insurance waiver, maintain a minimum grade point average, and comply with any "rules of conduct, dress, training hours and related matters as may be established for each sport by the head coach and athletic director with the principal's approval." Somewhat like adults who choose to participate in a "closely regulated industry," students who voluntarily participate in school athletics have reason to expect intrusions upon normal rights and privileges, including privacy.

IV

Having considered the scope of the legitimate expectation of privacy at issue here, we turn next to the character of the intrusion that is complained of. We recognized in *Skinner* that collecting the samples for urinalysis intrudes upon "an excretory function traditionally shielded by great privacy." We noted, however, that the degree of intrusion depends upon the manner in which production of the urine sample is monitored. *Ibid.* Under the District's Policy, male students produce samples at a urinal along a wall. They remain fully clothed and are only observed from behind, if at all. Female students produce samples in an enclosed stall, with a female monitor standing outside listening only for sounds of tampering. These conditions are nearly identical to those typically encountered in public restrooms, which men, women, and especially schoolchildren use daily. Under such conditions, the privacy interests compromised by the process of obtaining the urine sample are in our view negligible.

The other privacy-invasive aspect of urinalysis is, of course, the information it discloses concerning the state of the subject's body, and the materials he has ingested. In this regard it is significant that the tests at issue here look only for drugs, and not for whether the student is, for example, epileptic, pregnant, or diabetic. Moreover, the drugs for which the samples are screened are standard, and do not vary according to the identity of the student. And finally, the results of the tests are disclosed only to a limited class of school personnel who have a need to know; and they are not turned over to law enforcement authorities or used for any internal disciplinary function.

Respondents argue, however, that the District's Policy is in fact more intrusive than this suggests, because it requires the students, if they are to avoid sanctions for a falsely positive test, to identify *in advance* prescription medications they are taking. We agree that this raises some cause for concern. In *Von Raab,* we flagged as one of the salutary features of the Customs Service drug-testing program the fact that employees were not required to disclose medical information unless they tested positive, and, even then, the information was supplied to a licensed physician rather than to the Government employer. On the other hand, we have never indicated that requiring advance disclosure of medications is *per se* unreasonable. Indeed, in *Skinner* we held that it was not "a significant invasion of privacy." It can be argued that, in *Skinner,* the disclosure went only to the medical personnel taking the sample, and the Government personnel analyzing it, and that disclosure to teachers and coaches—to persons who personally *know* the student—is a greater invasion of privacy. Assuming for the sake of argument that both those propositions are true, we do not believe they establish a difference that respondents are entitled to rely on here.

The General Authorization Form that respondents refused to sign, which refusal was the basis for James's exclusion from the sports program, said only (in relevant part): "I . . . authorize the Vernonia School District to conduct a test on a urine specimen which I provide to test for drugs and/or alcohol use. I also authorize the release of information concerning the results of such a test to the Vernonia School District and to the parents and/or guardians of the student." While the practice of the District seems to have been to have a school official take medication information from the student at the time of the test, see *id.,* at 29, 42, that practice is not set forth in, or required by, the Policy, which says simply: "Student athletes who . . . are or have been taking prescription medication must provide verification (either by a copy of the prescription or by doctor's authorization) prior to being tested." It may well be that, if and when James was selected for random testing at a time that he was taking medication, the School District would have permitted him to provide the requested information in a confidential manner—for example, in a sealed envelope delivered to the testing lab. Nothing in the Policy contradicts that, and when respondents choose, in effect, to challenge the Policy on its face, we will not assume the worst. Accordingly, we reach the same conclusion as in *Skinner* that the invasion of privacy was not significant.

V

Finally, we turn to consider the nature and immediacy of the governmental concern at issue here, and the efficacy of this means for meeting it. . . . Whether that relatively high degree of government concern is necessary in this case or not, we think it is met.

That the nature of the concern is important—indeed, perhaps compelling—can hardly be doubted. Deterring drug use by our Nation's schoolchildren is at least as important as enhancing efficient enforcement of the Nation's laws against the importation of drugs, which was the governmental concern in *Von Raab,* or deterring drug use by engineers and trainmen, which was the governmental concern in *Skinner.* School years are the time when the physical, psychological, and addictive effects of drugs are most severe. "Maturing nervous systems are more critically impaired by intoxicants than mature ones are; childhood losses in learning are lifelong and profound"; "children grow chemically dependent more quickly than adults, and their record of recovery is depressingly poor." . . . And of course the effects of a drug-infested school are visited not just upon the users, but upon the entire student body and faculty, as the educational process is disrupted. In the present case, moreover, the necessity for the State to act is magnified by the fact that this evil is being visited not just upon individuals at large, but upon children for whom it has undertaken a special responsibility of care and direction. Finally, it must not be lost sight of that this program is directed more narrowly to drug use by school athletes, where the risk of immediate physical harm to the drug user or those with whom he is playing his sport is particularly high. Apart from psychological effects, which include impairment of judgment, slow reaction time, and a lessening of the perception of pain, the particular drugs screened by the District's Policy have been demonstrated to pose substantial physical risks to athletes. . . .

As for the immediacy of the District's concerns: We are not inclined to question—indeed, we could not possibly find clearly erroneous—the District Court's conclusion that "a large segment of the student body, particularly those involved in interscholastic athletics, was in a state of rebellion," that "[d]isciplinary actions had reached 'epidemic proportions,'" and that "the rebellion was being fueled by alcohol and drug abuse as well as by the student's misperceptions about the drug culture." That is an immediate crisis of greater proportions than existed in *Skinner,* where we upheld the Government's drug-testing program based upon findings of drug use by railroad employees nationwide, without proof that a problem existed on the particular railroads whose employees were subject to the test. And of much greater proportions than existed in *Von Raab,* where there was no documented history of drug use by any customs officials.

As to the efficacy of this means for addressing the problem: It seems to us self-evident that a drug problem largely fueled by the "role model" effect of athletes' drug use, and of particular danger to athletes, is effectively addressed by making sure that athletes do not use drugs. Respondents argue that a "less intrusive means to the same end" was available, namely, "drug testing on suspicion of drug use." We have repeatedly refused to declare that only the "least intrusive" search practicable can be reasonable under the Fourth Amendment. . . . Respondents' alternative entails substantial difficulties—if it is indeed practicable at all. It may be impracticable, for one thing, simply because the parents who are willing to accept random drug testing for athletes are not willing to accept accusatory drug testing for all students, which transforms the process into a badge of shame. Respondents' proposal brings the risk that teachers will impose testing arbitrarily upon troublesome but not drug-likely students. It generates the expense of defending lawsuits that charge such arbitrary imposition, or that simply demand greater process before accusatory drug testing is imposed. And not least of all, it adds to the ever-expanding diversionary duties of schoolteachers the new function of spotting and bringing to account drug abuse, a task for which they are ill prepared, and which is not readily compatible with their vocation. . . . In many respects, we think, testing based upon "suspicion" of drug use would not be better, but worse.

VI

Taking into account all the factors we have considered above—the decreased expectation of privacy, the relative unobtrusiveness of the search, and the severity of the need met by the search—we conclude Vernonia's Policy is reasonable and hence constitutional. We caution against the assumption that suspicionless drug testing will readily pass constitutional muster in other contexts. The most significant element in this case is the first we discussed: that the Policy was undertaken in furtherance of the government's responsibilities, under a public school system, as guardian and tutor of children entrusted to its care. Just as when the government conducts a search in its capacity as employer (a warrantless search of an absent employee's desk to obtain an urgently needed file, for example), the relevant question is whether that intrusion upon privacy is one that a reasonable employer might engage in; so also when the government acts as guardian and tutor the relevant question is whether the search is one that a reasonable guardian and tutor might undertake. Given the findings of need made by the District Court, we conclude that in the present case it is.

We may note that the primary guardians of Vernonia's schoolchildren appear to agree. The record shows no objection to this district wide program by any parents other than the couple before us here—even though, as we have described, a public meeting was held to obtain parents' views. We find insufficient basis to contradict the judgment of Vernonia's parents, its school board, and the District Court, as to what was reasonably in the interest of these children under the circumstances.

NOTES AND QUESTIONS

1. The Supreme Court in *Vernonia* built on its decision in *T.L.O.* finding that suspicionless drug testing of student athletes passed constitutional muster. The Supreme Court reasoned that because of student athletes' decreased expectation of privacy, the relative unobtrusiveness of the search, the importance of testing, and the "special need" that existed because of the

drug crisis, the school district's urinalysis policy for student athletes was permissible under Fourth Amendment.

2. The Supreme Court found that student athletes have an even lower privacy expectation than other students. The Court looked to the element of communal undress, how sports are not for the bashful, preseason physical exams which require urine samples, and a laundry list of other factors germane to a student athlete. Do you believe these reasons justify a lesser degree of privacy? Or should student athletes be given more respect and freedom because they balance schoolwork with the rigors of athletics?
3. The dissent explored an alternative to *Vernonia's* suspicionless drug testing. Justice O'Connor wrote that suspicion-based drug testing would have been a viable alternative since the school collected evidence of drug use in specific students and student groups. *Id.* at 679. For example, Justice O'Connor noted that teachers observed students passing joints, coaches smelled marijuana smoke in hotel rooms and students were observed acting inebriated and high on the school premises. As a result of this evidence, Justice O'Connor found a substantial basis for suspicion-based drug testing. Do you agree with the dissent's less intrusive solution?
4. In a factually similar case, the Seventh Circuit held that the suspicionless drug testing program of students involved in extracurricular activities did not violate the Fourth Amendment. *Todd v. Rush County Schools,* 133 F.3d 984, 986 (7th Cir. 1998). However, the extracurricular activities were not limited to athletics. The program covered all students who were members of a school club or who drove to school. Moreover, the drug use in the Rush County schools was far less rampant than the compelling, out of control, drug epidemic existent in the Vernonia school system. The court relied heavily on *Vernonia* despite the fact that *Vernonia* "cautioned against the assumption that suspicionless drug testing will readily pass constitutional muster in other contexts." Do the discrepancies in the cases force you to reexamine the Seventh Circuit's decision, or are the "special needs" in both cases similar? What level of drug problem should exist in the school district before allowing suspicionless drug testing? Is any level of drug use in schools sufficient to mandate suspicionless drug testing due to "special needs"?
5. Consider the factors that the *Vernonia* Court focused upon: the nature of the privacy interest upon which the search at issue intrudes; the character of the intrusion; the nature and immediacy of the government concern, and the efficacy of the means utilized to address that concern. Do you agree with the Court's use of each of these factors?

Board of Education of Independent School District No. 92 of Pottawatomie County v. Earls

536 U.S. 822 (2002)

Justice Thomas delivered the opinion of the Court.

The Student Activities Drug Testing Policy implemented by the Board of Education of Independent School District No. 92 of Pottawatomie County

(School District) requires all students who participate in competitive extracurricular activities to submit to drug testing. Because this Policy reasonably serves the School District's important interest in detecting and preventing drug use among its students, we hold that it is constitutional.

I

The city of Tecumseh, Oklahoma, is a rural community located approximately 40 miles southeast of Oklahoma City. The School District administers all Tecumseh public schools. In the fall of 1998, the School District adopted the Student Activities Drug Testing Policy (Policy), which requires all middle and high school students to consent to drug testing in order to participate in any extracurricular activity. In practice, the Policy has been applied only to competitive extracurricular activities sanctioned by the Oklahoma Secondary Schools Activities Association, such as the Academic Team, Future Farmers of America, Future Homemakers of America, band, choir, pom pom, cheerleading, and athletics. Under the Policy, students are required to take a drug test before participating in an extracurricular activity, must submit to random drug testing while participating in that activity, and must agree to be tested at any time upon reasonable suspicion. The urinalysis tests are designed to detect only the use of illegal drugs, including amphetamines, marijuana, cocaine, opiates, and barbiturates, not medical conditions or the presence of authorized prescription medications.

At the time of their suit, both respondents attended Tecumseh High School. Respondent Lindsay Earls was a member of the show choir, the marching band, the Academic Team, and the National Honor Society. Respondent Daniel James sought to participate in the Academic Team. Together with their parents, Earls and James brought a 42 U.S.C. §1983 action against the School District, challenging the Policy both on its face and as applied to their participation in extracurricular activities. They alleged that the Policy violates the Fourth Amendment as incorporated by the Fourteenth Amendment and requested injunctive and declarative relief. They also argued that the School District failed to identify a special need for testing students who participate in extracurricular activities, and that the "Drug Testing Policy neither addresses a proven problem nor promises to bring any benefit to students or the school."

Applying the principles articulated in *Vernonia,* in which we upheld the suspicionless drug testing of school athletes, the United States District Court for the Western District of Oklahoma rejected respondents' claim that the Policy was unconstitutional and granted summary judgment to the School District. The court noted that "special needs" exist in the public school context and that, although the School District did "not show a drug problem of epidemic proportions," there was a history of drug abuse starting in 1970 that presented "legitimate cause for concern." The District Court also held that the Policy was effective because "[i]t can scarcely be disputed that the drug problem among the student body is effectively addressed by making sure that the large number of students participating in competitive, extracurricular activities do not use drugs."

The United States Court of Appeals for the Tenth Circuit reversed, holding that the Policy violated the Fourth Amendment. The Court of Appeals agreed with the District Court that the Policy must be evaluated in the "unique environment of the school setting," but reached a different conclusion as to the Policy's constitutionality. Before imposing a suspicionless drug testing program, the Court of Appeals concluded that a school "must demonstrate that there is some identifiable drug abuse problem among a sufficient number of those subject to the testing, such that testing that group of students will actually redress its drug problem." The Court of Appeals then held that because the School District failed to demonstrate such a problem existed among Tecumseh students participating in competitive extracurricular activities, the Policy was unconstitutional. We granted certiorari, and now reverse.

II

The Fourth Amendment to the United States Constitution protects "[t]he right of the people to be secure in their persons, houses, papers, and effects, against unreasonable searches and seizures." Searches by public school officials, such as the collection of urine samples, implicate Fourth Amendment interests. *See Vernonia, T.L.O.* We must therefore review the School District's Policy for "reasonableness," which is the touchstone of the constitutionality of a governmental search.

In the criminal context, reasonableness usually requires a showing of probable cause. . . . The probable-cause standard, however, "is peculiarly related to criminal investigations" and may be unsuited to determining the reasonableness of administrative searches where the "Government seeks to *prevent* the development of hazardous conditions." . . .

The Court has also held that a warrant and finding of probable cause are unnecessary in the public school context because such requirements " 'would unduly interfere with the maintenance of the swift and informal disciplinary procedures [that are] needed.' " *Vernonia,* quoting *T.L.O.*

Given that the School District's Policy is not in any way related to the conduct of criminal investigations, respondents do not contend that the School District requires probable cause before testing students for drug use. Respondents instead argue that drug testing must be based at least on some level of individualized suspicion. It is true that we generally determine the reasonableness of a search by balancing the nature of the intrusion on the individual's privacy against the promotion of legitimate governmental interests. But we have long held that "the Fourth Amendment imposes no irreducible requirement of [individualized] suspicion." "[I]n certain limited circumstances, the Government's need to discover such latent or hidden conditions, or to prevent their development, is sufficiently compelling to justify the intrusion on privacy entailed by conducting such searches without any measure of individualized suspicion." Therefore, in the context of safety and administrative regulations, a search unsupported by probable cause may be reasonable "when 'special needs, beyond the normal need for law enforcement, make the warrant and probable-cause requirement impracticable.' " . . .

Significantly, this Court has previously held that "special needs" inhere in the public school context. *See Vernonia, T.L.O.* While schoolchildren do not shed their constitutional rights when they enter the schoolhouse, *see Tinker v. Des Moines Independent Community School Dist.,* "Fourth Amendment rights . . . are different in public schools than elsewhere; the 'reasonableness' inquiry cannot disregard the schools' custodial and tutelary responsibility for children." *Vernonia.* In particular, a finding of individualized suspicion may not be necessary when a school conducts drug testing.

In *Vernonia,* this Court held that the suspicionless drug testing of athletes was constitutional. The Court, however, did not simply authorize all school drug testing, but rather conducted a fact-specific balancing of the intrusion on the children's Fourth Amendment rights against the promotion of legitimate governmental interests. Applying the principles of *Vernonia* to the somewhat different facts of this case, we conclude that Tecumseh's Policy is also constitutional.

We first consider the nature of the privacy interest allegedly compromised by the drug testing. As in *Vernonia* the context of the public school environment serves as the backdrop for the analysis of the privacy interest at stake and the reasonableness of the drug testing policy in general. ("Central . . . is the fact that the subjects of the Policy are (1) children, who (2) have been committed to the temporary custody of the State as schoolmaster"); ("The most significant element in this case is the first we discussed: that the Policy was undertaken in furtherance of the government's responsibilities, under a public school system, as guardian and tutor of children entrusted to its care"); ("[W]hen the government acts as guardian and tutor the relevant question is whether the search is one that a reasonable guardian and tutor might undertake").

A student's privacy interest is limited in a public school environment where the State is responsible for maintaining discipline, health, and safety. Schoolchildren are routinely required to submit to physical examinations and vaccinations against disease. Securing order in the school environment sometimes requires that students be subjected to greater controls than those appropriate for adults. *See T.L.O.* (Powell, J., concurring) ("Without first establishing discipline and maintaining order, teachers cannot begin to educate their students. And apart from education, the school has the obligation to protect pupils from mistreatment by other children, and also to protect teachers themselves from violence by the few students whose conduct in recent years has prompted national concern").

Respondents argue that because children participating in nonathletic extracurricular activities are not subject to regular physicals and communal undress, they have a stronger expectation of privacy than the athletes tested in *Vernonia.* This distinction, however, was not essential to our decision in *Vernonia,* which depended primarily upon the school's custodial responsibility and authority.

In any event, students who participate in competitive extracurricular activities voluntarily subject themselves to many of the same intrusions on their privacy as do athletes. Some of these clubs and activities require occasional off-campus travel and communal undress. All of them have their own rules and requirements for participating students that do not apply to the student body as a whole. For example, each of the competitive extracurricular activities governed by the Policy must abide by the rules of the Oklahoma Secondary Schools Activities Association, and a faculty sponsor monitors the students for compliance with the various rules dictated by the clubs and activities. This regulation of extracurricular activities further diminishes the expectation of privacy among schoolchildren. Cf. *Vernonia* ("Somewhat like adults who choose to participate in a closely regulated industry, students who voluntarily participate in school athletics have reason to expect intrusions upon normal rights and privileges, including privacy" (internal quotation marks omitted)). We therefore conclude that the students affected by this Policy have a limited expectation of privacy.

B

Next, we consider the character of the intrusion imposed by the Policy. See *Vernonia*. Urination is "an excretory function traditionally shielded by great privacy." *Skinner*. But the "degree of intrusion" on one's privacy caused by collecting a urine sample "depends upon the manner in which production of the urine sample is monitored." *Vernonia*.

Under the Policy, a faculty monitor waits outside the closed restroom stall for the student to produce a sample and must "listen for the normal sounds of urination in order to guard against tampered specimens and to insure an accurate chain of custody." The monitor then pours the sample into two bottles that are sealed and placed into a mailing pouch along with a consent form signed by the student. This procedure is virtually identical to that reviewed in *Vernonia,* except that it additionally protects privacy by allowing male students to produce their samples behind a closed stall. Given that we considered the method of collection in *Vernonia* a "negligible" intrusion, the method here is even less problematic.

In addition, the Policy clearly requires that the test results be kept in confidential files separate from a student's other educational records and released to school personnel only on a "need to know" basis. Respondents nonetheless contend that the intrusion on students' privacy is significant because the Policy fails to protect effectively against the disclosure of confidential information and, specifically, that the school "has been careless in protecting that information: for example, the Choir teacher looked at students' prescription drug lists and left them where other students could see them." But the choir teacher is someone with a "need to know," because during off-campus trips she needs to know what medications are taken by her students. Even before the Policy was enacted the choir teacher had access to this information. In any event, there is no allegation that any other student did see such information. This one example of alleged carelessness hardly increases the character of the intrusion.

Moreover, the test results are not turned over to any law enforcement authority. Nor do the test results here lead to the imposition of discipline or have any academic consequences. Rather, the only consequence of a failed drug test is to limit the student's privilege of participating in extracurricular activities. Indeed, a student may test positive for drugs twice and still be allowed to participate in extracurricular activities. After the first positive test, the school contacts the student's parent or guardian for a meeting. The student may continue to participate in the activity if within five days of the meeting the student shows proof of receiving drug counseling and submits to a second drug test in two weeks. For the second positive test, the student is suspended from participation in all extracurricular activities for 14 days, must complete four hours of substance abuse counseling, and must submit to monthly drug tests. Only after a third positive test will the student be suspended from participating in any extracurricular activity for the remainder of the school year, or 88 school days, whichever is longer.

Given the minimally intrusive nature of the sample collection and the limited uses to which the test results are put, we conclude that the invasion of students' privacy is not significant.

C

Finally, this Court must consider the nature and immediacy of the government's concerns and the efficacy of the Policy in meeting them. *See Vernonia.* This Court has already articulated in detail the importance of the governmental concern in preventing drug use by schoolchildren. The drug abuse problem among our Nation's youth has hardly abated since *Vernonia* was decided in 1995. In fact, evidence suggests that it has only grown worse.[5] As in *Vernonia,* "the necessity for the State to act is magnified by the fact that this evil is being visited not just upon individuals at large, but upon children for whom it has undertaken a special responsibility of care and direction." The health and safety risks identified in *Vernonia* apply with equal force to Tecumseh's children. Indeed, the nationwide drug epidemic makes the war against drugs a pressing concern in every school.

Additionally, the School District in this case has presented specific evidence of drug use at Tecumseh schools. Teachers testified that they had seen students who appeared to be under the influence of drugs and that they had heard students speaking openly about using drugs. A drug dog found marijuana cigarettes near the school parking lot. Police officers once found drugs or drug paraphernalia in a car driven by a Future Farmers of America member. And the school board president reported that people in the community were calling the board to discuss the "drug situation." We decline to second-guess the finding of the District Court that "[v]iewing the evidence as a whole, it cannot be reasonably disputed that the [School District] was faced with a 'drug problem' when it adopted the Policy."

Respondents consider the proffered evidence insufficient and argue that there is no "real and immediate interest" to justify a policy of drug testing nonathletes. We have recognized, however, that "[a] demonstrated problem of drug abuse . . . [is] not in all cases necessary to the validity of a testing

---

[5] For instance, the number of 12th graders using any illicit drug increased from 48.4 percent in 1995 to 53.9 percent in 2001. The number of 12th graders reporting they had used marijuana jumped from 41.7 percent to 49.0 percent during that same period. See Department of Health and Human Services, *Monitoring the Future: National Results on Adolescent Drug Use,* Overview of Key Findings (2001) (Table 1).

regime," but that some showing does "shore up an assertion of special need for a suspicionless general search program." *Chandler v. Miller,* 520 U.S. 305, 319 (1997). The School District has provided sufficient evidence to shore up the need for its drug testing program.

Furthermore, this Court has not required a particularized or pervasive drug problem before allowing the government to conduct suspicionless drug testing. . . . Likewise, the need to prevent and deter the substantial harm of childhood drug use provides the necessary immediacy for a school testing policy. Indeed, it would make little sense to require a school district to wait for a substantial portion of its students to begin using drugs before it was allowed to institute a drug testing program designed to deter drug use.

Given the nationwide epidemic of drug use, and the evidence of increased drug use in Tecumseh schools, it was entirely reasonable for the School District to enact this particular drug testing policy. We reject the Court of Appeals' novel test that "any district seeking to impose a random suspicionless drug testing policy as a condition to participation in a school activity must demonstrate that there is some identifiable drug abuse problem among a sufficient number of those subject to the testing, such that testing that group of students will actually redress its drug problem." Among other problems, it would be difficult to administer such a test. As we cannot articulate a threshold level of drug use that would suffice to justify a drug testing program for schoolchildren, we refuse to fashion what would in effect be a constitutional quantum of drug use necessary to show a "drug problem."

Respondents also argue that the testing of nonathletes does not implicate any safety concerns, and that safety is a "crucial factor" in applying the special needs framework. They contend that there must be "surpassing safety interests," or "extraordinary safety and national security hazards," in order to override the usual protections of the Fourth Amendment. Respondents are correct that safety factors into the special needs analysis, but the safety interest furthered by drug testing is undoubtedly substantial for all children, athletes and nonathletes alike. We know all too well that drug use carries a variety of health risks for children, including death from overdose.

We also reject respondents' argument that drug testing must presumptively be based upon an individualized reasonable suspicion of wrongdoing because such a testing regime would be less intrusive. In this context, the Fourth Amendment does not require a finding of individualized suspicion, and we decline to impose such a requirement on schools attempting to prevent and detect drug use by students. Moreover, we question whether testing based upon individualized suspicion in fact would be less intrusive. Such a regime would place an additional burden on public school teachers who are already tasked with the difficult job of maintaining order and discipline. A program of individualized suspicion might unfairly target members of unpopular groups. The fear of lawsuits resulting from such targeted searches may chill enforcement of the program, rendering it ineffective in combating drug use. . . . In any case, this Court has repeatedly stated that reasonableness under the Fourth Amendment does not require employing the least intrusive means, because "[t]he logic of such elaborate less-restrictive-alternative arguments could raise insuperable barriers to the exercise of virtually all search-and-seizure powers." . . .

Finally, we find that testing students who participate in extracurricular activities is a reasonably effective means of addressing the School District's legitimate concerns in preventing, deterring, and detecting drug use. While in *Vernonia* there might have been a closer fit between the testing of athletes and the trial court's finding that the drug problem was "fueled by the 'role model' effect of athletes' drug use," such a finding was not essential to the holding. *Vernonia* did not require the school to test the group of students most likely to use drugs, but rather considered the constitutionality of the program in the context of the public school's custodial responsibilities. Evaluating the Policy in this context, we conclude that the drug testing of Tecumseh students who participate in extracurricular activities effectively serves the School District's interest in protecting the safety and health of its students.

III

Within the limits of the Fourth Amendment, local school boards must assess the desirability of drug testing schoolchildren. In upholding the constitutionality of the Policy, we express no opinion as to its wisdom. Rather, we hold only that Tecumseh's Policy is a reasonable means of furthering the School District's important interest in preventing and deterring drug use among its schoolchildren. Accordingly, we reverse the judgment of the Court of Appeals.

Justice O'CONNOR, with whom Justice SOUTER joins, dissenting.

I dissented in *Vernonia,* and continue to believe that case was wrongly decided. Because *Vernonia* is now this Court's precedent, and because I agree that petitioners' program fails even under the balancing approach adopted in that case, I join Justice GINSBURG's dissent.

Justice GINSBURG, with whom Justice STEVENS, Justice O'CONNOR, and Justice SOUTER join, dissenting.

Seven years ago, in *Vernonia,* this Court determined that a school district's policy of randomly testing the urine of its student athletes for illicit drugs did not violate the Fourth Amendment. In so ruling, the Court emphasized that drug use "increase[d] the risk of sports-related injury" and that Vernonia's athletes were the "leaders" of an aggressive local "drug culture" that had reached " 'epidemic proportions.' " Today, the Court relies upon *Vernonia* to permit a school district with a drug problem its superintendent repeatedly described as "not . . . major," *see* App. 180, 186, 191, to test the urine of an academic team member solely by reason of her participation in a nonathletic, competitive extracurricular activity—participation associated with neither special dangers from, nor particular predilections for, drug use.

"[T]he legality of a search of a student," this Court has instructed, "should depend simply on the reasonableness, under all the circumstances, of the search." *New Jersey v. T.L.O.* . . . Although " 'special needs' inhere in the public school context," those needs are not so expansive or malleable as to render reasonable any program of student drug testing a school district elects to install.

The particular testing program upheld today is not reasonable, it is capricious, even perverse: Petitioners' policy targets for testing a student population least likely to be at risk from illicit drugs and their damaging effects. I therefore dissent.

NOTES AND QUESTIONS

1. The *Pottawatomie* ruling expands on the *Vernonia* ruling since the court reasoned that those students who participate in competitive extracurricular activities voluntarily subject themselves to many of the same intrusions on their privacy as student athletes. Do you believe that the travel and "communal undress" involved in certain extracurricular activities validates the Court's equating them with athletics?
2. The dissent stated that enrollment in public school, and election to participate in school activities beyond the bare minimum that the curriculum requires, are indeed factors relevant to reasonableness, but they do not on their own justify intrusive, suspicionless searches. Can you offer any additional factors that the dissenters might consider as reasons justifying suspicionless searches?
3. What type of situations would have arisen if the *Vernonia* court had ruled that the only prerequisite necessary to permit a school to conduct drug tests is a child's attendance at a public school? Would the parents have been outraged or relieved?
4. The Supreme Court has recognized that a demonstrated problem of drug abuse is not always necessary to validate a drug testing program, but that some showing does shore up an assertion of special need for a suspicionless general search program. *Chandler v. Miller,* 520 U.S. 305, 319 (1997). Do you think the Supreme Court should have taken this opportunity to outline what situations may be acceptable as special needs and what situations cannot be considered special needs?
5. In *Gruenke v. Seip,* 225 F.3d 290 (3d Cir. 2000), a member of the high school swim team, who was asked by her swim team coach to take a pregnancy test after he suspected she was pregnant, brought suit along with her mother against the coach, in which they asserted §1983 and state law claims. The district court granted summary judgment for the coach on the §1983 claims based upon qualified immunity, and dismissed the state law claims without prejudice. Plaintiffs appealed. The Court of Appeals held that: (1) the coach's actions violated the team member's clearly established Fourth Amendment right to be free from unreasonable searches; (2) the coach was not entitled to qualified immunity with respect to claims based upon a violation of the team member's clearly established due process rights to be free from disclosure of personal matters and medical information; (3) the allegations stated a claim for violation of the mother's due process right to manage the upbringing of her child; but (4) the mother's due process right was not clearly established, so that the coach was entitled to qualified immunity; and (5) the coach did not violate the team member's First Amendment associational rights.

6. Fourth Amendment issues are not limited to drug tests and bag searches; they also encompass locker searches and "sniffer" dogs. In *Zamora v. Pomeroy,* 639 F.2d 662 (10th Cir. 1981), the Tenth Circuit upheld as reasonable a dog search of a student's locker. The Court in *Zamora* reasoned that the student handbook contained regulations concerning locker usage, and the school retained control and access to all lockers, including maintaining a file of all lockers and their combinations. If the students paid a yearly fee for the lockers, similar to rent, would the outcome have been the same? What if the students supplied their own locks for the lockers and the school did not maintain a file with the combinations? Is searching a locker a minimally intrusive exercise or are locker contents usually personal?
7. In a case with facts similar to those in *Zamora,* a school district instituted locker searches in an attempt to combat a growing drug problem and to maintain a safe and secure environment for the students. *Commonwealth of Pennsylvania v. Cass,* 551 Pa. 25, 29, 709 A.2d 350, 352 (Pa. 1998). The court ruled that the locker searches were constitutional since the decision to search was reasonable under the circumstances. One of the glaring differences between *Cass* and *Zamora* is who conducted the actual locker search. In *Zamora,* although "sniffer" dogs were used to locate the offending lockers, the principal actually opened the locker. Alternatively, in *Cass,* a police officer along with school officials opened the lockers indicated by the dog. Does the officer's active involvement in opening the lockers change the situation?
8. The above cases each discuss the constitutionality of locker searches. In each case, the lockers were selected because of "sniffer" dogs. However, in *B.C. v. Plumas Unified School District,* 192 F.3d 1260 (9th Cir. 1999), the school district used "sniffer" dogs to search students' belongings rather than their lockers. After the students were called out of their classrooms, the dogs entered the classroom and proceeded to sniff their backpacks, jackets and other personal items. *Id.* On the claim that the dog sniff search violated the students' Fourth Amendment rights, the court held that there was an abuse of the students' rights, but granted qualified immunity for the defendants. The court analyzed the *Vernonia* factors and determined that the dog sniff was highly intrusive because the body and its odors are highly personal and dogs often engender irrational fear. Also, because the search was completely involuntary, the students' privacy interests were not minimal. Additionally, the court noted that the district had no drug problem or drug crisis that might otherwise justify the dog sniff. However, because it was not clearly established that the use of dogs to sniff students in a school setting constituted a search, the defendants were entitled to qualified immunity. Moreover, since the plaintiff did not leave his belongings in the classroom there was no actual seizure of his property. Furthermore, the students were directed to a covered snack bar for the duration of the search, where they received suitable supervision. Accordingly, there was no actionable seizure of "person." Do you agree with the court's decision?
9. In *Anders v. Fort Wayne Community Schools,* 124 F. Supp. 2d 618 (N.D. Ind. 2000), the Court upheld the school's search of a student's car. The search

was justified by the school's reasonable belief that the student was smoking in the car, and by the student's implied consent to the search by obtaining a school parking permit.

3. Search and Seizure Practicum

In 2002, the federal government's Office of Drug Control Policy published a guide for schools as they consider whether and how to conduct drug tests of their students. The publication, entitled *What You Need to Know About Drug Testing in Schools, www.whitehousedrugpolicy.gov/publications/drug%5Ftesting/index.html* (hereinafter *Drug Testing),* reports that more than 50 percent of all high school students have used illegal substances, and recommends the following:

> Schools should proceed with caution before testing students for drugs. Screenings are not 100 percent accurate, so every positive screen should be followed by a laboratory-based confirming test. Before going ahead with tests, schools should also have a good idea of precisely what drugs their students are using. Testing for just one set of illegal drugs when others pose an equal or greater threat would do little to address a school's drug problem.
>
> Confidentiality is a major concern with students and their parents. Schools have a responsibility to respect students' privacy, so it is vital that only the people who need to know the test results see them—parents and school administrators, for example. The results should not be shared with anyone else, not even teachers.
>
> The decision of whether to implement a drug-testing program should not be left to one individual, or even to a school board. It should involve the entire community. In fact, by making the effort to include everyone, a school can greatly increase its chances of adopting a successful testing program.
>
> It is not enough to have a general sense that student drug testing sounds like a good idea. Schools must first determine whether there is a real need for testing. Such a need can be determined from student drug-use surveys, reports by teachers and other school staff about student drug use, reports about drug use from parents and others in the community, and from discoveries of drug paraphernalia or drug residue at school.
>
> If student drug use is found to be a significant problem, schools will want to consult early in their deliberations with an attorney familiar with laws regarding student drug testing. They should seek the advice of drug prevention and treatment professionals, and also contact officials at schools that already have drug-testing programs to learn what works and what doesn't.
>
> Schools considering testing will want plenty of public input. They should bring together members of the board of education, school administrators and staff, parents, community leaders, local healthcare agencies, local businesses, students and anyone else who has an interest in reducing student drug use—even those who are against the idea. Listening to opponents and including their views can strengthen the testing programs and improve its chances of success. *See Drug Testing.*

In light of this guidance, how would you advise East York High School, a large school with a significant history of drug use among its students, to proceed? Suggest policy language and administrative procedures for the district.

Now, assume that Mary Sunshine is a member of the East York High School marching band. Mary is in the eleventh grade and has played the tuba in the marching band since she was in ninth grade. As a result of her love for the marching band, Mary enrolled in two for-credit band classes, one of which is contingent on her participation in the marching band and the other is conducted solely during school hours with band and nonband members. At the beginning of the school semester, the East York School District mandated a suspicionless urinalysis drug testing policy for all students, in grades six through twelve, participating in extracurricular activities, including the marching band. Mary refused to consent to the mandatory drug testing. Consequently, Mary received a suspension from band classes and the marching band. Accordingly, Mary, by and through her parents, filed a complaint alleging that the policy violated her right to be free from unreasonable searches and seizures, guaranteed by the Fourth Amendment. Do you think Mary will win her case against the school district?

Suppose further that the school district adopted its drug testing policy following a three-year study which reported that 40 percent of all students in grades six through twelve had used an illegal drug during the year. Moreover, the students in the school district far exceeded the national average for drug usage. Additionally, band members never undergo "communal undress" since they always wear t-shirts and shorts underneath the uniform and Mary's high school does not require students to shower following physical education. The marching band director also stated on the record that he had never seen or heard of a member of his marching band using drugs. Finally, the district's policy also affected students who were enrolled in the for-credit instrumental music class who did not participate in the marching band or any other extracurricular activity.

C. DUE PROCESS RIGHTS OF STUDENTS

The right to attend public school is not a fundamental constitutional right. *C.B. by and through Breeding v. Driscoll,* 82 F.3d 383 (11th Cir. 1996). Nonetheless, state constitutions and statutes have given to students a protectable liberty and property interest in attending public school. As such, the suspension and expulsion of a student from a public school deprives him or her of a constitutionally protected liberty and property interest. *L.Q.A. by and through Arrington v. Eberhart,* 920 F. Supp. 1208 (M.D. Ala. 1996); *Packer v. Board of Education of Town of Thomaston,* 717 A.2d 117 (Conn. 1998). Therefore, although local educational agencies have been granted broad authority to discipline, suspend or expel students for a host of legitimate reasons, the *process* by which those agencies determine that such disciplinary steps are required is dictated by the "due process" clause of the constitution.

In *Goss,* the Supreme Court established minimal due process protections for students subjected to the disciplinary authority of a public, educational institution.

Goss v. Lopez

419 U.S. 565 (1975)

Mr. Justice White delivered the opinion of the Court.

This appeal by various administrators of the Columbus, Ohio, Public School System (CPSS) challenges the judgment of a three-judge federal court, declaring that appellees—various high school students in the CPSS—were denied due process of law contrary to the command of the Fourteenth Amendment in that they were temporarily suspended from their high schools without a hearing either prior to suspension or within a reasonable time thereafter, and enjoining the administrators to remove all references to such suspensions from the students' records.

I

Ohio law, Rev. Code Ann. §3313.64 (1972), provides for free education to all children between the ages of six and 21. Section 3313.66 of the Code empowers the principal of an Ohio public school to suspend a pupil for misconduct for up to 10 days or to expel him. In either case, he must notify the student's parents within 24 hours and state the reasons for his action. A pupil who is expelled, or his parents, may appeal the decision to the Board of Education and in connection therewith shall be permitted to be heard at the board meeting. The Board may reinstate the pupil following the hearing. No similar procedure is provided in §3313.66 or any other provision of state law for a suspended student. Aside from a regulation tracking the statute, at the time of the imposition of the suspensions in this case the CPSS itself had not issued any written procedure applicable to suspensions. Nor, so far as the record reflects, had any of the individual high schools involved in this case. Each, however, had formally or informally described the conduct for which suspension could be imposed.

The nine named appellees, each of whom alleged that he or she had been suspended from public high school in Columbus for up to 10 days without a hearing pursuant to §3313.66, filed an action under 42 U.S.C. §1983 against the Columbus Board of Education and various administrators of the CPSS. The complaint sought a declaration that §3313.66 was unconstitutional in that it permitted public school administrators to deprive plaintiffs of their rights to an education without a hearing of any kind, in violation of the procedural due process component of the Fourteenth Amendment. It also sought to enjoin the public school officials from issuing future suspensions pursuant to §3313.66 and to require them to remove references to the past suspensions from the records of the students in question.

The proof below established that the suspensions arose out of a period of widespread student unrest in the CPSS during February and March 1971. Six of the named plaintiffs . . . , were students at the Marion-Franklin High School and were each suspended for 10 days on account of disruptive or disobedient conduct committed in the presence of the school administrator who ordered the suspension. . . .

II

At the outset, appellants contend that because there is no constitutional right to an education at public expense, the Due Process Clause does not protect against expulsions from the public school system. This position misconceives the nature of the issue and is refuted by prior decisions. The Fourteenth Amendment forbids the State to deprive any person of life, liberty, or property without due process of law. Protected interests in property are normally "not created by the Constitution. Rather, they are created and their dimensions are defined" by an independent source such as state statutes or rules entitling the citizen to certain benefits. *Board of Regents v. Roth,* 408 U.S. 564, 577 (1972). . . .

Here, on the basis of state law, appellees plainly had legitimate claims of entitlement to a public education. Ohio Rev. Code Ann. §§3313.48 and 3313.64 (1972 and Supp. 1973) direct local authorities to provide a free education to all residents between five and 21 years of age, and a compulsory-attendance law requires attendance for a school year of not less than 32 weeks. Ohio Rev. Code Ann. §3321.04 (1972). It is true that §3313.66 of the Code permits school principals to suspend students for up to 10 days; but suspensions may not be imposed without any grounds whatsoever. All of the schools had their own rules specifying the grounds for expulsion or suspension. Having chosen to extend the right to an education to people of appellees' class generally, Ohio may not withdraw that right on grounds of misconduct, absent fundamentally fair procedures to determine whether the misconduct has occurred. . . .

Although Ohio may not be constitutionally obligated to establish and maintain a public school system, it has nevertheless done so and has required its children to attend. Those young people do not "shed their constitutional rights" at the schoolhouse door. *Tinker v. Des Moines School Dist.,* 393 U.S. 503, 506 (1969). "The Fourteenth Amendment, as now applied to the States, protects the citizen against the State itself and all of its creatures—Boards of Education not excepted." *West Virginia Board of Education v. Barnette,* 319 U.S. 624, 637 (1943). The authority possessed by the State to prescribe and enforce standards of conduct in its schools although concededly very broad, must be exercised consistently with constitutional safeguards. Among other things, the State is constrained to recognize a student's legitimate entitlement to a public education as a property interest which is protected by the Due Process Clause and which may not be taken away for misconduct without adherence to the minimum procedures required by that Clause.

The Due Process Clause also forbids arbitrary deprivations of liberty. "Where a person's good name, reputation, honor, or integrity is at stake because of what the government is doing to him," the minimal requirements of the Clause must be satisfied. *Wisconsin v. Constantineau,* 400 U.S. 433, 437 (1971); *Board of Regents v. Roth.* School authorities here suspended appellees from school for periods of up to 10 days based upon charges of misconduct. If sustained and recorded, those charges could seriously damage the students' standing with their fellow pupils and their teachers as well as interfere with later opportunities for higher education and employment. It is apparent that the claimed right of the State to determine unilaterally and without process whether that misconduct has occurred immediately collides with the requirements of the Constitution.

Appellants proceed to argue that even if there is a right to a public education protected by the Due Process Clause generally, the Clause comes into play only when the State subjects a student to a "severe detriment or grievous loss." The loss of 10 days, it is said, is neither severe nor grievous and the Due Process Clause is therefore of no relevance. Appellants' argument is again refuted by our prior decisions; for in determining "whether due process requirements apply in the first place, we must look not to the 'weight' but to the *nature* of the interest at stake." *Board of Regents v. Roth.* Appellees were excluded from school only temporarily, it is true, but the length and consequent severity of a deprivation, while another factor to weigh in determining the appropriate form of hearing, "is not decisive of the basic right" to a hearing of some kind. *Fuentes v. Shevin,* 407 U.S. 67, 86 (1972). The Court's view has been that as long as a property deprivation is not *de minimis,* its gravity is irrelevant to the question whether account must be taken of the Due Process Clause. . . . A 10-day suspension from school is not *de minimis* in our view and may not be imposed in complete disregard of the Due Process Clause.

A short suspension is, of course, a far milder deprivation than expulsion. But, "education is perhaps the most important function of state and local governments," *Brown v. Board of Education,* 347 U.S. 483, 493 (1954), and the total exclusion from the educational process for more than a trivial period, and certainly if the suspension is for 10 days, is a serious event in the life of the suspended child. Neither the property interest in educational benefits temporarily denied nor the liberty interest in reputation, which is also implicated, is so insubstantial that suspensions may constitutionally be imposed by any procedure the school chooses, no matter how arbitrary.

III

"Once it is determined that due process applies, the question remains what process is due." . . . We turn to that question, fully realizing as our cases regularly do that the interpretation and application of the Due Process Clause are intensely practical matters and that "[the] very nature of due process negates any concept of inflexible procedures universally applicable to every imaginable situation." . . . We are also mindful of our own admonition:

> Judicial interposition in the operation of the public school system of the Nation raises problems requiring care and restraint. . . . By and large, public education in our Nation is committed to the control of state and local authorities. *Epperson v. Arkansas,* 393 U.S. 97, 104 (1968).

There are certain bench marks to guide us, however. *Mullane v. Central Hanover Trust Co.,* 339 U.S. 306 (1950), a case often invoked by later opinions, said that "[many] controversies have raged about the cryptic and abstract words of the Due Process Clause but there can be no doubt that at a minimum they require that deprivation of life, liberty or property by adjudication be preceded by notice and opportunity for hearing appropriate to the nature of the case." "The fundamental requisite of due process of law is the opportunity to be heard," *Grannis v. Ordean,* 234 U.S. 385, 394 (1914), a right that "has little reality or worth unless one is informed that the matter is pending and can choose for himself whether to . . . contest." At the very minimum, therefore, students facing suspension and the consequent interference with a protected property interest must be given *some* kind of notice and afforded *some* kind of hearing. "Parties whose rights are to be affected are entitled to be heard; and in order that they may enjoy that right they must first be notified." *Baldwin v. Hale,* 1 Wall. 223, 233 (1864).

It also appears from our cases that the timing and content of the notice and the nature of the hearing will depend on appropriate accommodation of the competing interests involved. The student's interest is to avoid unfair or mistaken exclusion from the educational process, with all of its unfortunate consequences. The Due Process Clause will not shield him from suspensions properly imposed, but it disserves both his interest and the interest of the State if his suspension is in fact unwarranted. The concern would be mostly academic if the disciplinary process were a totally accurate, unerring process, never mistaken and never unfair. Unfortunately, that is not the case, and no one suggests that it is. Disciplinarians, although proceeding in utmost good faith, frequently act on the reports and advice of others; and the controlling facts and the nature of the conduct under challenge are often disputed. The risk of error is not at all trivial, and it should be guarded against if that may be done without prohibitive cost or interference with the educational process.

The difficulty is that our schools are vast and complex. Some modicum of discipline and order is essential if the educational function is to be performed. Events calling for discipline are frequent occurrences and sometimes require immediate, effective action. Suspension is considered not only to be a necessary tool to maintain order but a valuable educational device. The prospect of imposing elaborate hearing requirements in every suspension case is viewed with great concern, and many school authorities may well prefer the untrammeled power to act unilaterally, unhampered by rules about notice and hearing. But it would be a strange disciplinary system in an educational institution if no communication was sought by the disciplinarian with the student in an effort to inform him of his dereliction and to let him tell his side of the story in order to make sure that an injustice is not done. "[Fairness] can rarely be obtained by secret, one-sided determination of facts decisive of rights. . . ." "Secrecy is not congenial to truth-seeking and self-righteousness gives too slender an assurance of rightness. No better instrument has been devised for arriving at truth than to give a person in jeopardy of serious loss notice of the case against him and opportunity to meet it." *McGrath, supra,* at 170, 171-172 (Frankfurter, J., concurring).

We do not believe that school authorities must be totally free from notice and hearing requirements if their schools are to operate with acceptable efficiency. Students facing temporary suspension have interests qualifying for protection of the Due Process Clause, and due process requires, in connection with a suspension of 10 days or less, that the student be given oral or written notice of the charges against him and, if he denies them, an explanation of the evidence the authorities have and an opportunity to present his side of the story. The Clause requires at least these rudimentary precautions against unfair or mistaken findings of misconduct and arbitrary exclusion from school.

There need be no delay between the time "notice" is given and the time of the hearing. In the great majority of cases the disciplinarian may informally discuss the alleged misconduct with the student minutes after it has occurred. We hold only that, in being given an opportunity to explain his version of the facts at this discussion, the student first be told what he is accused of doing and what the basis of the accusation is. Lower courts which have addressed the question of the *nature* of the procedures required in short suspension cases have reached the same conclusion. Since the hearing may occur almost immediately following the misconduct, it follows that as a general rule notice and hearing should precede removal of the student from school. We agree with the District Court, however, that there are recurring situations in which prior notice and hearing cannot be insisted upon. Students whose presence poses a continuing danger to persons or property or an ongoing threat of disrupting the academic process may be immediately removed from school. In such cases, the necessary notice and rudimentary hearing should follow as soon as practicable, as the District Court indicated.

In holding as we do, we do not believe that we have imposed procedures on school disciplinarians which are inappropriate in a classroom setting. Instead we have imposed requirements which are, if anything, less than a fair-minded school principal would impose upon himself in order to avoid unfair suspensions. Indeed, according to the testimony of the principal of Marion-Franklin High School, that school had an informal procedure, remarkably similar to that which we now require, applicable to suspensions generally but which was not followed in this case. Similarly, according to the most recent memorandum applicable to the entire CPSS, school principals in the CPSS are now required by local rule to provide at least as much as the constitutional minimum which we have described.

We stop short of construing the Due Process Clause to require, country-wide, that hearings in connection with short suspensions must afford the student the opportunity to secure counsel, to confront and cross-examine witnesses supporting the charge, or to call his own witnesses to verify his version of the incident. Brief disciplinary suspensions are almost countless. To impose in each such case even truncated trial-type procedures might well overwhelm administrative facilities in many places and, by diverting resources, cost more than it would save in educational effectiveness. Moreover, further formalizing the suspension process and escalating its formality and adversary nature may not only make it too costly as a regular disciplinary tool but also destroy its effectiveness as part of the teaching process.

On the other hand, requiring effective notice and informal hearing permitting the student to give his version of the events will provide a meaningful hedge against erroneous action. At least the disciplinarian will be alerted to the existence of disputes about facts and arguments about cause and effect. He may then determine himself to summon the accuser, permit cross-examination, and allow the student to present his own witnesses. In more difficult cases, he may permit counsel. In any event, his discretion will be more informed and we think the risk of error substantially reduced.

Requiring that there be at least an informal give-and-take between student and disciplinarian, preferably prior to the suspension, will add little to the fact finding function where the disciplinarian himself has witnessed the conduct forming the basis for the charge. But things are not always as they seem to be, and the student will at least have the opportunity to characterize his conduct and put it in what he deems the proper context.

We should also make it clear that we have addressed ourselves solely to the short suspension, not exceeding 10 days. Longer suspensions or expulsions for the remainder of the school term, or permanently, may require more formal procedures. Nor do we put aside the possibility that in unusual situations, although involving only a short suspension, something more than the rudimentary procedures will be required.

IV

The District Court found each of the suspensions involved here to have occurred without a hearing, either before or after the suspension, and that each suspension was therefore invalid and the statute unconstitutional insofar as it permits such suspensions without notice or hearing. Accordingly, the judgment is *Affirmed.*

NOTES AND QUESTIONS

1. In *Goss,* the Supreme Court finds from state laws mandating a free public education a protectable "property" interest in the form of an "entitlement to a public education. . . ." In light of the fact that all states have similar laws mandating free public education, can it be said that there is a constitutionally-protected property right to an education in this country? If so, how can the existence of such a constitutionally protected right be reconciled with the Supreme Court's conclusion in *San Antonio Independent School District v. Rodriguez,* 411 U.S. 1 (1973) that there is no fundamental constitutional right to an education?
2. The Court in *Goss* also finds a constitutionally protected "liberty" interest in a student's "good name, reputation, honor, or integrity" as it affects the "student's standing" and "later opportunities." Where does that interest originate? Is there a liberty interest in "reputation" that is distinct from "opportunities"?
3. The Court ultimately concludes that students confronted with a suspension from school of any length must receive at least "*some* kind of notice and afforded *some* kind of hearing." The notice can be oral or written. Moreover, the Court suggests that the student must receive "an explanation of the evidence the authorities have and an opportunity to present his side of the story." Such notice and hearing generally should "precede" removal of the student from school. What policy language would you draft for a school district based upon this Supreme Court ruling?
4. The Court immediately crafts an exception for its result: "Students whose presence poses a continuing danger to persons or property or an ongoing

threat of disrupting the academic process may be immediately removed from school. In such cases, the necessary notice and rudimentary hearing should follow as soon as practicable, . . ." Can you draft policy language defining such exceptional circumstances?

5. Is it significant that the school district in *Goss* suspended the students for disciplinary rather than academic reasons? In *Board of Curators of Missouri v. Horowitz,* 435 U.S. 78 (1978), the Court held that a medical student could be deprived of continuing enrollment because of substandard academic performance without any predeprivation process protections. The Court found that the decision to dismiss Horowitz, unlike the decisions in *Goss,* "rested on the academic judgment of school officials . . . [and] require[d] an expert evaluation . . . not readily adopted to the procedural tests of judicial or administrative decision making." *See also Regents of University of Michigan v. Ewing,* 474 U.S. 214 (1985) *(substantive* due process analysis does not govern judgments regarding academic performance). Do you agree? The distinction between procedural due process and substantive due process challenges to a school district's conduct is addressed in the next case.

DUNN & MCCULLOUGH v. FAIRFIELD COMMUNITY HIGH SCHOOL DISTRICT NO. 225

158 F.3d 962 (7th Cir. 1998)

Before POSNER, Chief Judge, and CUMMINGS and DIANE P. WOOD, Circuit Judges.

Diane P. Wood, Circuit Judge. Shaun Dunn and Bill McCullough were both budding musicians who participated as guitar players in the high school band program at Fairfield Community High School. . . . Fairfield prohibited its band members from departing from the planned musical program during band performances, and it specifically forbade guitar solos during the performances. In direct defiance of those rules and their teacher's explicit orders, Dunn and McCullough (along with two other students) played two unauthorized guitar pieces (instrumentals, with no words) at a February 10, 1995, band program. In due course, the discipline they received for this infraction caused them both to receive an "F" for the band course, and that "F" prevented McCullough from graduating with honors. This lawsuit under 42 U.S.C. §§1983 and 1988 followed. . . . While as a practical matter the school may have overreacted to the spectacle of two young musicians playing the "wrong" pieces, we conclude that its actions violated no right cognizable under the federal civil rights statutes, and we therefore affirm the district court. . . .

II

The students' complaint alleged that Fairfield had violated their constitutional rights in two ways: first, that it violated their "right to substantive due process . . . by imposing disciplinary measures unrelated to academic conduct and . . . outside the parameters and intent of the Illinois School Code and [Fairfield's] disciplinary policy," . . . In essence, they claimed that Fairfield had transgressed the Constitution when it imposed the drastic measure of expulsion from class, knowing that it would inevitably lead to a failing grade in the course, for one single disciplinary incident. . . . The disciplinary action in question, the [district] court concluded, bore a rational relation to the school's interest in maintaining order and providing an education. The court also commented in a footnote that if the plaintiffs were to prevail, "almost every disciplinary action could become a federal case." . . .

III

. . . The fundamental flaw in their theory of the case arises from their failure to appreciate the difference between the procedural protections afforded by the Fourteenth Amendment against state deprivations and the far more limited substantive standards that Amendment imposes on state actors. If this had been a case (as it is not) in which Dunn and McCullough had complained that Fairfield threw them out of Band class and effectively condemned them to an "F" in the course without giving them some kind of notice and a hearing, we would delve into the nature of the property interest Illinois law creates in a public education. Assuming a protectible interest exists (as it undoubtedly does, *see* . . . *Goss v. Lopez,* 419 U.S. 565, 574-75), we would then assess Fairfield's procedures. . . .

But that is not the students' claim. Instead, they assert that the federal Constitution places substantive restrictions on the type of disciplinary measures public school districts may use for conceded violations of rules of student conduct. At some extreme, that is certainly true; the question here is where the outer boundaries lie. The students seem to think that federal constitutional protection is co-extensive with the right recognized under Illinois law to a free public education through the end of high school. The Supreme Court's recent decision in *County of Sacramento v. Lewis,* 523 U.S. 833 (1998), definitively shows that they are wrong. *Lewis* involved a far more serious deprivation than anything Dunn or McCullough suffered: 16-year-old Philip Lewis was killed by a police officer during the course of the officer's high-speed pursuit of the motorcycle Lewis was riding as a passenger. Lewis's parents sued under §1983, claiming that Lewis had been deprived of his life in violation of substantive due process. In other words, they alleged that no matter how much procedure the state used, it was simply not entitled under the federal Constitution to allow its agents to engage in such risky, reckless behavior. . . .

The Supreme Court rejected the Lewises' claim in an opinion that emphasized once again how limited the scope of the substantive due process doctrine is. . . . In so doing, it relied on two independent grounds: first, that substantive due process does not apply when a particular part of the Constitution "provides an explicit textual source of constitutional protection against a particular sort of government behavior," and second, that "in any event the allegations are insufficient to state a substantive due process violation through executive abuse of power." We turn to the latter part of the Court's opinion, because no one claims that Fairfield's actions should be judged under a more specific part of the federal Constitution.

The touchstone of due process, the Court explained, is "protection of the individual against arbitrary action of government," whether the problem is the denial of fundamental procedural fairness or the exercise of governmental power without any reasonable justification. The criteria that govern what is fatally arbitrary in the latter cases depend upon whether legislation or a specific act of a governmental officer is at issue. In *Lewis,* the focus was on the specific act of a governmental officer, and in those cases, the Court said that "only the most egregious official conduct" is arbitrary in the constitutional sense. At least since *Rochin v. California,* 342 U.S. 165 (1952) the Court has looked for an abuse of power that "shocks the conscience"; it reaffirmed that benchmark in *Lewis.* Looked at from the opposite point of view, the Court reiterated that "the due process guarantee does not entail a body of constitutional law imposing liability whenever someone cloaked with state authority causes harm." Negligent conduct can virtually never meet the constitutional threshold. Instead, the Court said, "conduct intended to injure in some way unjustifiable by any governmental interest" would be most likely to rise to the conscience-shocking level. In the (literally) fast-moving and fluid situation faced by a police officer on the street, the Court found that "even precipitate recklessness fails to inch close enough to harmful purpose" for purposes of substantive due process analysis. It therefore found that the Lewises' complaint on behalf of their deceased son did not state a constitutional claim.

One is tempted to say that if a police officer's "precipitate recklessness," which caused the deprivation of someone's life, was not sufficiently shocking to satisfy substantive due process standards, then it would be nearly absurd to say that a school principal's decision effectively to give two students an "F" in Band class did. It may be worth acknowledging that this in no way necessarily implies approval of the state official's action; we are certain that no member of the Supreme Court thought in hindsight that the police officer in *Lewis* had responded prudently to the young motorcycle speeders, and we may have similar doubts about the wisdom of the severity of Fairfield's sanctions against the rebel musicians here.

Although the briefs are not entirely clear on this point, we understand from oral argument that Dunn and McCullough are also asserting a legislative violation of substantive due process rights, insofar as they are attacking Fairfield's written disciplinary classifications and penalty structure. In *[Walsh v. Glucksberg,* 521 U.S. 702 (1997)], the Court reaffirmed that "the Due Process Clause guarantees more than fair process, and the 'liberty' it protects includes more than the absence of physical restraint". . . . The substantive component of the clause, the Court explained, "provides heightened protection against governmental interference with certain fundamental rights and liberty interests," including things like the right to marry, to have children, to direct the education and upbringing of one's children, to marital privacy, to use contraception, to bodily integrity, and to choose an abortion. Once again, measured by that standard the school policy that the students attack comes nowhere close to a constitutional violation. Although students may have some substantive due process rights while they are in school, *see Wood v. Strickland,* 420 U.S. 308, 326 (1975), education itself is not a fundamental right, see *San Antonio Indep. Schl. Dist. v. Rodriguez,* 411 U.S. 1 (1973). That means that Fairfield's decision to stack the deck so that these students would fail Band must be sustained unless it is wholly arbitrary. Here, however, Dunn and McCullough freely conceded that they had violated a school rule, that the rule was designed to preserve discipline in the classroom and to punish student insubordination, and that these were legitimate interests on the part of the school district. That alone is enough to show that their claim cannot possibly succeed. The Constitution does not guarantee these or any other students the right not to receive an "F" in a course from which they were excluded because of misbehavior. . . .

On a practical level, we share the district court's concern about transforming the federal courts into an appellate arm of the schools throughout the country, but this is not a "floodgates" inspired decision. . . .

NOTES AND QUESTIONS

1. "A clear majority of the courts" has held that students do not have a substantive constitutional entitlement to participate in interscholastic athletics. *Brands v. Sheldon Community School,* 671 F. Supp. 627 (N.D. Iowa 1987); *Colorado Seminary v. NCAA,* 570 F.2d 320 (10th Cir. 1978); *Hamilton v. Tennessee Secondary School Athletic Assn.,* 552 F.2d 681 (6th Cir. 1976); *Mitchell v. Louisiana High School Athletic Assn.,* 430 F.2d 1155 (5th Cir. 1970). The Eighth Circuit has observed that "a student's interest in participating in a single year of interscholastic athletics amounts to a mere expectation rather than a constitutionally protected claim of entitlement." *In re United States ex rel. Missouri State High School Activities Assn.,* 682 F.2d 147 (8th Cir. 1982), quoting *Walsh v. Louisiana High School Athletic Assn.,* 616 F.2d 152, 159-160 (5th Cir. 1980).
2. The *Fairfield* Court alludes to the possibility that a school district's exercise of power could be challenged under a "specific part of the federal constitution." What are examples of "explicit textual" sources of constitutional protections for students?
3. The Court indicates that "wholly arbitrary" exercises of school district power could be challenged as violations of substantive due process. What are examples of school district conduct that would be "wholly arbitrary"?
4. The power of school authorities to suspend or expel pupils is not limited to acts done by pupils in school, but may be exercised, in proper cases, as to offenses committed outside of school hours and not in the presence of a teacher. *Pollnow v. Glennon,* 594 F. Supp. 220 (S.D.N.Y. 1984). Under a statute authorizing the suspension of a student for behavior detrimental to the education, welfare, safety or morals of other students, a high school student may properly be suspended and placed on probation for using his or her automobile to harass a school bus on a public highway. *Clements v. Board of Trustees of Sheridan County School District No. 2,* 585 P.2d 197 (Wyo. 1978). A school board's regulation prohibiting students from attending parties at which alcohol is served is valid, since such a regulation is rationally related to the school board's interest in deterring student alcohol consumption. *Bush by and through Bush v. Dassel-Cokato Board of Education,* 745 F. Supp. 562 (D. Minn. 1990). However, the expulsion of a student for possession of marijuana in a car parked adjacent to the school campus is

void and unenforceable when the expulsion is not made pursuant to any rule or regulation promulgated by the school board, and when the students were not fairly apprised that they could be expelled for the possession of marijuana off the school campus. *Galveston Independent School District v. Boothe,* 590 S.W.2d 553 (Tex. App. 1979). A student may properly be suspended or expelled for fighting; *Donaldson v. Board of Education for Danville School District No. 118,* 424 N.E.2d 737 (Ill. App. 1981), or for possessing a dangerous weapon at a school-sponsored event so long as the student's constitutional and statutory process rights are not abridged. *Wood by and through Wood v. Henry County Public Schools,* 495 S.E.2d 255 (Va. 1998). Thus, students have been found properly expelled or suspended for using a stun gun during an altercation with another student during school hours, even though the altercation took place at a school other than that which the expelled student attended, *Fremont Union High School District v. Santa Clara County Board of Education,* 235 Cal. App. 3d 1182 (Ca. App. 1991); for knowingly possessing a knife on school property; *Kolesnick by and through Shaw v. Omaha Public School District,* 558 N.W.2d 807 (Neb. 1997); and for carrying a pocket knife on a school field trip. *Wood by and through Wood v. Henry County Public Schools,* 495 S.E.2d 255 (Va. 1998). Moreover, a statute that provides for the expulsion from school for up to 12 months of students who bring weapons to school is facially constitutional under a state constitutional guarantee of a "thorough and efficient school system," since the state has a compelling interest in providing a safe and secure environment to school children under that constitutional guarantee, and such an expulsion is a reasonably necessary and narrowly tailored method to further that interest. *Cathe A. v. Doddridge County Board of Education,* 490 S.E.2d 340 (W. Va. 1997). Similarly, the expulsion of a student from a public school for the knowing possession of a knife on school property is rationally related to the school board's interest in protecting the other students and the staff from violence, and therefore does not violate the student's state or federal constitutional rights. *Kolesnick by and through Shaw v. Omaha Public School District,* 558 N.W.2d 807 (Neb. 1997).

5. Zero-tolerance discipline policies and practices, which assign uniform punishment for specific acts of misconduct regardless of mitigating factors, have been challenged on due process grounds with mixed results. *Compare Doe v. Board of Education of Oak Park & River Forest High School District 200,* 115 F.3d 1273, 1282 (7th Cir. 1997) (affirming one-semester expulsion for student who brought pipe and marijuana to school dance); *Kolesnick by and through Shaw v. Omaha Public School District,* 558 N.W.2d 807 (Neb. 1997) (upholding two-semester expulsion of eighth grader who brought knife to school; that board opted for consistency of punishment rather than tailoring punishment of the child did not implicate the due process clause of U.S. Constitution); *E.M. through S.M. v. Briggs,* 922 P.2d 754 (Utah 1996) (affirming expulsion to end of year pursuant to board's zero-tolerance drug and alcohol policy); *Colvin by and through Colvin v. Lowndes County, Mississippi School District,* 114 F. Supp. 2d 504 (N.D. Miss. 2000) (one-year expulsion per zero-tolerance policy of academically struggling student for possession of Swiss Army knife violated due process when board did not

consider mitigating circumstances); *Lyons v. Penn Hills School District,* 723 A.2d 1073 (Pa. Commw. 1999) (setting aside one-year expulsion of seventh grader for Swiss Army knife possession and invalidating district's zero-tolerance policy, which afforded superintendent no discretion to tailor punishment). *See also Seal v. Morgan,* 229 F.3d 567 (6th Cir. 2000) (reversing summary judgment for school officials in a discipline case involving expulsion of a student on a zero-tolerance-for-weapons rationale after a friend's knife was found in his car in the campus parking lot). The *Seal* Court rebuked the board of education for asserting that the student's claimed unawareness of the weapon was a legally irrelevant "technicality" and that the zero-tolerance policy required expulsion regardless of whether the student knew the knife was in his car. "Suspending or expelling a student for weapons possession, even if the student did not knowingly possess any weapon, would not be rationally related to any legitimate state interest. . . . We would have thought this principle so obvious that it would go without saying." 229 F.3d at 575-576.

D. STUDENT PRIVACY RIGHTS AND FERPA

The Federal Family Educational Rights and Privacy Act of 1974 (FERPA), 20 U.S. C. §1232g, authorizes federal funds to be withheld from public and private educational institutions that permit students' "education records (or personally identifiable information contained therein)" to be released without a parent's written consent. 20 U.S.C. §1232g(b)(2)(A). FERPA thus encourages school officials and educators to protect student records from public view. In the following two recent cases, the U.S. Supreme Court addresses the extent of FERPA's protections and remedies.

Owasso Public Schools v. Falvo

534 U.S. 426 (2002)

Justice Kennedy delivered the opinion of the Court.

Teachers sometimes ask students to score each other's tests, papers, and assignments as the teacher explains the correct answers to the entire class. Respondent contends this practice, which the parties refer to as peer grading, violates the Family Educational Rights and Privacy Act of 1974 (FERPA or Act), 88 Stat. 571, 20 U.S.C. §1232g. We took this case to resolve the issue.

I

Under FERPA, schools and educational agencies receiving federal financial assistance must comply with certain conditions. §1232g(a)(3). One condition specified in the Act is that sensitive information about students may not be released without parental consent. The Act states that federal funds are to be withheld from school districts that have "a policy or practice of permitting the release of education records (or personally identifiable information contained therein . . .) of students without the written consent of their parents."

§1232g(b)(1). The phrase "education records" is defined, under the Act, as "records, files, documents, and other materials" containing information directly related to a student, which "are maintained by an educational agency or institution or by a person acting for such agency or institution." §1232g(a)(4)(A). The definition of education records contains an exception for "records of instructional, supervisory, and administrative personnel . . . which are in the sole possession of the maker thereof and which are not accessible or revealed to any other person except a substitute." §1232g(a)(4)(B)(i). The precise question for us is whether peer-graded classroom work and assignments are education records.

Three of respondent Kristja J. Falvo's children are enrolled in Owasso Independent School District No. I-011, in a suburb of Tulsa, Oklahoma. The children's teachers, like many teachers in this country, use peer grading. In a typical case, the students exchange papers with each other and score them according to the teacher's instructions, then return the work to the student who prepared it. The teacher may ask the students to report their own scores. In this case it appears the student could either call out the score or walk to the teacher's desk and reveal it in confidence, though by that stage, of course, the score was known at least to the one other student who did the grading. Both the grading and the system of calling out the scores are in contention here.

Respondent claimed the peer grading embarrassed her children. She asked the school district to adopt a uniform policy banning peer grading and requiring teachers either to grade assignments themselves or at least to forbid students from grading papers other than their own. The school district declined to do so, and respondent brought a class action pursuant to Rev. Stat. §1979, 42 U.S.C. §1983 (1994 ed., Supp. V), against the school district, Superintendent Dale Johnson, Assistant Superintendent Lynn Johnson, and Principal Rick Thomas (petitioners). Respondent alleged the school district's grading policy violated FERPA and other laws not relevant here. . . .

We granted certiorari to decide whether peer grading violates FERPA. . . . Finding no violation of the Act, we reverse. . . .

II

The parties appear to agree that if an assignment becomes an education record the moment a peer grades it, then the grading, or at least the practice of asking students to call out their grades in class, would be an impermissible release of the records under §1232g(b)(1). . . . Without deciding the point, we assume for the purposes of our analysis that they are correct. The parties disagree, however, whether peer-graded assignments constitute education records at all. The papers do contain information directly related to a student, but they are records under the Act only when and if they "are maintained by an educational agency or institution or by a person acting for such agency or institution." §1232g(a)(4)(A).

Petitioners, supported by the United States as *amicus curiae,* contend the definition covers only institutional records—namely, those materials retained in a permanent file as a matter of course. They argue that records "maintained by an educational agency or institution" generally would include final course grades, student grade point averages, standardized test scores, attendance records, counseling records, and records of disciplinary actions—but not student homework or classroom work. . . .

Respondent, adopting the reasoning of the Court of Appeals, contends student-graded assignments fall within the definition of education records. That definition contains an exception for "records of instructional, supervisory, and administrative personnel . . . which are in the sole possession of the maker thereof and which are not accessible or revealed to any other person except a substitute." §1232g(a)(4)(B)(i). The Court of Appeals reasoned that if grade books are not education records, then it would have been unnecessary for Congress to enact the exception. Grade books and the grades within, the court concluded, are "maintained" by a teacher and so are covered by FERPA. . . . The court recognized that teachers do not maintain the grades on individual student assignments until they have recorded the result in the grade books. It reasoned, however, that if Congress forbids teachers to disclose students' grades once written in a grade book, it makes no sense to permit the disclosure immediately beforehand. . . . The court thus held that student graders maintain the grades until they are reported to the teacher. . . .

The Court of Appeals' logic does not withstand scrutiny. Its interpretation, furthermore, would effect a drastic alteration of the existing allocation of responsibilities between States and the National Government in the operation of the Nation's schools. We would hesitate before interpreting the statute to effect such a substantial change in the balance of federalism unless that is the manifest purpose of the legislation. This principle guides our decision.

Two statutory indicators tell us that the Court of Appeals erred in concluding that an assignment satisfies the definition of education records as soon as it is graded by another student. First, the student papers are not, at that stage, "maintained" within the meaning of §1232g(a)(4)(A). The ordinary meaning of the word "maintain" is "to keep in existence or continuance; preserve; retain." *Random House Dictionary of the English Language* 1160 (2d ed. 1987). Even assuming the teacher's grade book is an education record—a point the parties contest and one we do not decide here—the score on a student-graded assignment is not "contained therein," §1232g(b)(1), until the teacher records it. The teacher does not maintain the grade while students correct their peers' assignments or call out their own marks. Nor do the student graders maintain the grades within the meaning of §1232g(a)(4)(A). The word "maintain" suggests FERPA records will be kept in a filing cabinet in a records room at the school or on a permanent secure database, perhaps even after the student is no longer enrolled. The student graders only handle assignments for a few moments as the teacher calls out the answers. It is fanciful to say they maintain the papers in the same way the registrar maintains a student's folder in a permanent file.

The Court of Appeals was further mistaken in concluding that each student grader is "a person acting for" an educational institution for purposes of §1232g(a)(4)(A). . . . The phrase "acting for" connotes agents of the school, such as teachers, administrators, and other school employees. Just as it does not accord with our usual understanding to say students are "acting for" an educational institution when they follow their teacher's direction to take a quiz, it is equally awkward to say students are "acting for" an educational institution when they follow their teacher's direction to score it. Correcting a classmate's work can be as much a part of the assignment as taking the test itself. It is a way to teach material again in a new context, and it helps show students how to assist and respect fellow pupils. By explaining the answers to the class as the students correct the papers, the teacher not only reinforces the lesson but also discovers whether the students have understood the material and are ready to move on. We do not think FERPA prohibits these educational techniques. We also must not lose sight of the fact that the phrase "by a person acting for [an educational] institution" modifies "maintain." Even if one were to agree students are acting for the teacher when they correct the assignment, that is different from saying they are acting for the educational institution in maintaining it.

Other sections of the statute support our interpretation. *See Davis v. Michigan Dept. of Treasury,* 489 U.S. 803, 809 (1989) ("It is a fundamental canon of statutory construction that the words of a statute must be read in their context and with a view to their place in the overall statutory scheme"). FERPA, for example, requires educational institutions to "maintain a record, kept with the education records of each student." §1232g(b)(4)(A). This record must list those who have requested access to a student's education records and their reasons for doing so. *Ibid.* The record of access "shall be available only to parents, [and] to the school official and his assistants who are responsible for the custody of such records." *Ibid.*

Under the Court of Appeals' broad interpretation of education records, every teacher would have an obligation to keep a separate record of access for each student's assignments. Indeed, by that court's logic, even students who grade their own papers would bear the burden of maintaining records of access until they turned in the assignments. We doubt Congress would have imposed such a weighty administrative burden on every teacher, and certainly it would not have extended the mandate to students.

Also FERPA requires "a record" of access for each pupil. This single record must be kept "with the education records." This suggests Congress contemplated that education records would be kept in one place with a single record of access. By describing a "school official" and "his assistants" as the personnel responsible for the custody of the records, FERPA implies that education records are institutional records kept by a single central custodian, such as a registrar, not individual assignments handled by many student graders in their separate classrooms.

FERPA also requires recipients of federal funds to provide parents with a hearing at which they may contest the accuracy of their child's education records. §1232g(a)(2). The hearings must be conducted "in accordance with regulations of the Secretary," *ibid.,* which in turn require adjudication by a disinterested official and the opportunity for parents to be represented by an attorney. 34 CFR §99.22 (2001). It is doubtful Congress would have provided parents with this elaborate procedural machinery to challenge the accuracy of the grade on every spelling test and art project the child completes.

Respondent's construction of the term "education records" to cover student homework or classroom work would impose substantial burdens on teachers across the country. It would force all instructors to take time, which otherwise could be spent teaching and in preparation, to correct an assortment of daily student assignments. Respondent's view would make it much more difficult for teachers to give students immediate guidance. The interpretation respondent urges would force teachers to abandon other customary practices, such as group grading of team assignments. Indeed, the logical consequences of respondent's view are all but unbounded. At argument, counsel for respondent seemed to agree that if a teacher in any of the thousands of covered classrooms in the Nation puts a happy face, a gold star, or a disapproving remark on a classroom assignment, federal law does not allow other students to see it. . . .

We doubt Congress meant to intervene in this drastic fashion with traditional state functions. Under the Court of Appeals' interpretation of FERPA, the federal power would exercise minute control over specific teaching methods and instructional dynamics in classrooms throughout the country. The Congress is not likely to have mandated this result, and we do not interpret the statute to require it.

For these reasons, even assuming a teacher's grade book is an education record, the Court of Appeals erred, for in all events the grades on students' papers would not be covered under FERPA at least until the teacher has collected them and recorded them in his or her grade book. We limit our holding to this narrow point, and do not decide the broader question whether the grades on individual student assignments, once they are turned in to teachers, are protected by the Act.

The judgment of the Court of Appeals is reversed, and the case is remanded for further proceedings consistent with this opinion.

NOTES AND QUESTIONS

1. The Family Educational Rights and Privacy Act of 1974 (FERPA) also known as the Buckley Amendment, regulates student records kept by most United States schools, both public and private, at the elementary, secondary or higher education (including law school) levels. It is called the Buckley Amendment after Senator James Buckley, the man who introduced this law as a Senate floor amendment to legislation extending the Elementary and Secondary Education Act Amendments of 1965.
2. *Owasso* focused on the language used in §1232g of FERPA. Specifically, §1232g(a)(4)(A) states "the term 'educational records' means, except as may be provided otherwise in subparagraph (B), those records, files, documents, and other materials which—(i) contain information directly related to a student; and (ii) are maintained by an educational agency or institution or by a person acting for such agency or institution." 20 U.S.C. §1232g(a)(4)(A) (1974). The Supreme Court also examined the language of §1232g(b)(4)(A), which states "each educational agency or institution shall maintain a record, kept with the education records of each student . . . available only to parents, to the school official and his assistants who are responsible for the custody of such records. . . ." 20 U.S.C. §1232g(b)(4)(A) (1974).

3. Although peer grading may be embarrassing to students, the Supreme Court reasoned that this practice did not violate FERPA since the students are not "acting for" a school employee and the graded papers are not "maintained" within the meaning of §1232g(a)(4)(A). Additionally, the Supreme Court concluded if the term "educational records" included classroom work and homework, the result would be a substantial burden on educators. Do you think that daily class work should be included in "educational records"?
4. The Supreme Court briefly touched upon a real world scenario where tests, homework and classroom work were considered educational records. Under FERPA, participating schools must provide parents with a hearing to contest their child's educational records. In that case, parents would be entitled to a forum to challenge their child's grades. This scenario may also enable parents to question the educator's method of teaching and testing. What are the practical consequences of allowing this degree of intervention?
5. FERPA also provides protection "against the releasing or providing access to, any personally identifiable information in education records other than directory information . . . without parental consent. . . ." 20 U.S.C. §1232g(b)(2) (1974). As a result, cases such as *Rios v. Read,* 73 F.R.D. 589 (E.D.N.Y. 1977), have held that the release of pupils' names or other distinguishing information is unlawful unless there is a legitimate need for the information and proper notice has been received. *Rios,* 73 F.R.D. at 597-598. The *Rios* Court referenced the remarks of Senator Buckley in which he emphasized the need for balancing the protection of students' rights with the legitimate federal need for the information. *Id.* at 599; *see also* Sen. Rep. No. 93-1026, 93d Cong., 2d sess. 187, *reprinted* in 1974 U.S. Code Cong. & Admin. News 4251. Accordingly, the *Rios* plaintiffs established a need for the information because it was integral to gauging the progress of students receiving bilingual training. *Id.* at 599. The court ruled that notice must be given to the students and their parents, and they must be given an opportunity to object to the disclosure. *Id.* at 597. The court also held that the type of notice will depend on the circumstances of each case; however, the notice must constitute a reasonable effort to notify the parent in advance of any disclosure. *Id.* Do you think that FERPA sufficiently protects the students' privacy rights? What would you change in order to protect students from illegitimate disclosures?

GONZAGA UNIVERSITY V. JOHN DOE

536 U.S. 273 (2002)

Chief Justice REHNQUIST delivered the opinion of the Court.

The question presented is whether a student may sue a private university for damages under 42 U.S.C. §1983 to enforce provisions of the Family Educational Rights and Privacy Act of 1974 (FERPA or Act), 20 U.S.C. §1232g, which prohibit the federal funding of educational institutions that have a policy or practice of releasing education records to unauthorized persons.

We hold such an action foreclosed because the relevant provisions of FERPA create no personal rights to enforce under 42 U.S.C. §1983.

Respondent John Doe is a former undergraduate in the School of Education at Gonzaga University, a private university in Spokane, Washington. He planned to graduate and teach at a Washington public elementary school. Washington at the time required all of its new teachers to obtain an affidavit of good moral character from a dean of their graduating college or university. In October 1993, Roberta League, Gonzaga's "teacher certification specialist," overheard one student tell another that respondent engaged in acts of sexual misconduct against Jane Doe, a female undergraduate. League launched an investigation and contacted the state agency responsible for teacher certification, identifying respondent by name and discussing the allegations against him. Respondent did not learn of the investigation, or that information about him had been disclosed, until March 1994, when he was told by League and others that he would not receive the affidavit required for certification as a Washington schoolteacher.

Respondent then sued Gonzaga and League (petitioners) in state court. He alleged violations of Washington tort and contract law, as well as a pendent violation of §1983 for the release of personal information to an "unauthorized person" in violation of FERPA. A jury found for respondent on all counts, awarding him $1,155,000, including $150,000 in compensatory damages and $300,000 in punitive damages on the FERPA claim. . . .

Congress enacted FERPA under its spending power to condition the receipt of federal funds on certain requirements relating to the access and disclosure of student educational records. The Act directs the Secretary of Education to withhold federal funds from any public or private "educational agency or institution" that fails to comply with these conditions. As relevant here, the Act provides:

> No funds shall be made available under any applicable program to any educational agency or institution which has a policy or practice of permitting the release of education records (or personally identifiable information contained therein . . .) of students without the written consent of their parents to any individual, agency, or organization. 20 U.S.C. §1232g(b)(1).

The Act directs the Secretary of Education to enforce this and other of the Act's spending conditions. §1232g(f). The Secretary is required to establish an office and review board within the Department of Education for "investigating, processing, reviewing, and adjudicating violations of [the Act]." §1232g(g). Funds may be terminated only if the Secretary determines that a recipient institution "is failing to comply substantially with any requirement of [the Act]" and that such compliance "cannot be secured by voluntary means." §§1234c(a), 1232g(f).

Respondent contends that this statutory regime confers upon any student enrolled at a covered school or institution a federal right, enforceable in suits for damages under §1983, not to have "education records" disclosed to unauthorized persons without the student's express written consent. But we have never before held, and decline to do so here, that spending legislation drafted in terms resembling those of FERPA can confer enforceable rights. . . .

We made clear that unless Congress "speaks with a clear voice," and manifests an "unambiguous" intent to confer individual rights, federal funding provisions provide no basis for private enforcement by §1983. . . .

Accordingly, where the text and structure of a statute provide no indication that Congress intends to create new individual rights, there is no basis for a private suit, whether under §1983 or under an implied right of action. . . .

With this principle in mind, there is no question that FERPA's nondisclosure provisions fail to confer enforceable rights. To begin with, the provisions entirely lack the sort of "rights-creating" language critical to showing the requisite congressional intent to create new rights. . . . Unlike the individually focused terminology of Titles VI and IX ("no person shall be subjected to discrimination"), FERPA's provisions speak only to the Secretary of Education, directing that "no funds shall be made available" to any "educational agency or institution" which has a prohibited "policy or practice." 20 U.S.C. §1232g(b)(1). This focus is two steps removed from the interests of individual students and parents and clearly does not confer the sort of "*individual* entitlement" that is enforceable under §1983. . . .

FERPA's nondisclosure provisions further speak only in terms of institutional policy and practice, not individual instances of disclosure. *See* 1232g(b)(1)-(2) (prohibiting the funding of "any educational agency or institution which has a *policy or practice* of permitting the release of education records" (emphasis added)). Therefore, . . . they have an "aggregate" focus, . . . they are not concerned with "whether the needs of any particular person have been satisfied," and they cannot "give rise to individual rights," . . . Recipient institutions can further avoid termination of funding so long as they "comply substantially" with the Act's requirements. §1234c(a). . . . Respondent directs our attention to subsection (b)(2), but the text and structure of subsections (b)(1) and (b)(2) are essentially the same. In each provision the reference to individual consent is in the context of describing the type of "policy or practice" that triggers a funding prohibition. For reasons expressed repeatedly in our prior cases, however, such provisions cannot make out the requisite congressional intent to confer individual rights enforceable by §1983. . . .

Our conclusion that FERPA's nondisclosure provisions fail to confer enforceable rights is buttressed by the mechanism that Congress chose to provide for enforcing those provisions. Congress expressly authorized the Secretary of Education to "*deal with violations*" of the Act, §1232g(f) (emphasis added), and required the Secretary to "establish or designate [a] review board" for investigating and adjudicating such violations, §1232g(g). Pursuant to these provisions, the Secretary created the Family Policy Compliance Office (FPCO) "to act as the Review Board required under the Act and to enforce the Act with respect to all applicable programs." 34 CFR 99.60(a) and (b) (2001). The FPCO permits students and parents who suspect a violation of the Act to file individual written complaints. §99.63. If a complaint is timely and contains required information, the FPCO will initiate an investigation, §§99.64(a)-(b), notify the educational institution of the charge, §99.65(a), and request a written response, §99.65. If a violation is found, the FPCO distributes a notice of factual findings and a "statement of the specific steps that the agency or institution must take to comply" with FERPA. §§99.66(b) and (c)(1). These administrative procedures . . . further counsel against our finding a congressional intent to create individually enforceable private rights.

Congress finally provided that "except for the conduct of hearings, none of the functions of the Secretary under this section shall be carried out in any of the regional offices" of the Department of Education. 20 U.S.C. §1232g(g). This centralized review provision was added just four months after FERPA's enactment due to "concern that regionalizing the enforcement of [FERPA] may lead to multiple interpretations of it, and possibly work a hardship on parents, students, and institutions." 120 Cong. Rec. 39863 (1974) (joint statement). . . . It is implausible to presume that the same Congress nonetheless intended private suits to be brought before thousands of federal- and state-court judges, which could only result in the sort of "multiple interpretations" the Act explicitly sought to avoid.

In sum, if Congress wishes to create new rights enforceable under §1983, it must do so in clear and unambiguous terms—no less and no more than what is required for Congress to create new rights enforceable under an implied private right of action. FERPA's nondisclosure provisions contain no rights-creating language, they have an aggregate, not individual, focus, and they serve primarily to direct the Secretary of Education's distribution of public funds to educational institutions. They therefore create no rights enforceable under §1983. Accordingly, the judgment of the Supreme Court of Washington is reversed, and the case is remanded for further proceedings not inconsistent with this opinion.

E. STUDENT PRIVACY PRACTICUM

In light of *Gonzaga* and the other cases in this section, analyze the following realistic scenario. On September 14, 2001, Darryl Toms and Kate Deeds petitioned the members of the Oak Village School Board for the names, addresses, ages and grade point averages of all the students enrolled at Village schools. Darryl, an employee of the state's tourism office, approached the board because he wanted to use the students' records to send the top students invitations and tickets for the new, state-funded theme park "Genius Mountain." Kate, on the other hand, contacted the board because she needed the students' records to acquire statistics for the state. Kate, a member of the governor's staff, explained that state officials asked her to compile data on the students' opinions on the curriculum. Additionally, her questionnaire would poll the students on their favorite subjects and the topics they would like to learn about. Kate would then compare how the students perform in school with their answers to the questionnaire. The surveys will provide statistics, either for or against, the governor's initiative for revamping the statewide curriculum. The board decided to give both Darryl and Kate the information in late December. However, the board currently has no intention of notifying the parents of its decision to release the information. The students' parents have taken the school board to court to stop the release of the students' personal information. If you were a judge in Oak Village, how would you rule based upon your knowledge of education law and the details provided in the problem?

CHAPTER 14

STUDENTS WITH EDUCATIONAL DISABILITIES

A. THE HISTORY OF EDUCATING CHILDREN WITH EDUCATIONAL DISABILITIES

In the early 1970s, there were roughly eight million disabled children in the United States. Of these children, at least one million were completely excluded from the public school system, and more than half were not receiving an appropriate education. Some states had passed laws to improve the education available to disabled students, but most had not. In 1971 and 1972, however, two highly influential cases were decided.

In the first case, *Pennsylvania Association for Retarded Children (PARC) v. Commonwealth,* 334 F. Supp. 1257 (E.D. Pa. 1971) and 343 F. Supp. 279 (E.D. Pa. 1972), a disabilities group filed suit challenging the constitutionality of a Pennsylvania statute that excluded "retarded" children from public education and training. A federal district court enjoined the state from denying mentally retarded children access to free public education. The federal court declared that these children must, whenever practicable, be integrated into the regular classroom rather then segregated from that classroom. The Court created a presumption that placement of children with educational disabilities "in a regular public school class is preferable to placement in a special public school class. . . . "

In the second case, *Mills v. Board of Education of District of Columbia,* 348 F. Supp. 866 (D.C. 1972), which was also filed on behalf of disabled children, the district court held that no disabled child should be excluded from public education unless the school (1) provided that child adequate alternative educational services suited to the child's needs and (2) held a prior hearing and periodic review of the child's status, progress and the adequacy of any educational alternative. In *Mills,* the district court extended the reasoning of *PARC* to children with educational disabilities who were "not being furnished with programs of specialized education." The *Mills* court ordered the school district to provide to those students a free and appropriate education, individualized educational plans and due process protections. According to the court, the district's conduct in denying "exceptional" children "all publicly supported education while providing such education to other children, is violative of the Due Process Clause." That clause also requires that students receive "a hearing prior to exclusion, termination [or] classification into a special program. . . . " The court specifically ordered the District of Columbia to "provide to each child of school age a free and suitable publicly supported education regardless of the degree of the child's mental, physical or emotional disability or impairment. Furthermore, defendants shall not exclude any child resident in the District of Columbia from such publicly supported education on the basis of a claim of insufficient resources."

These two lawsuits, and a national political campaign for better educational services, spurred Congress to pass three major federal statutes: the Rehabilitation Act of 1973 (RHA), the Individuals with Disabilities Education Act (IDEA) (originally passed in 1975 under the name Education for all Handicapped Children Act) and the Americans with Disabilities Act of 1990 (ADA). These laws provide the legal framework for the education of students with educational disabilities.

The RHA provides, in Section 504, that "[n]o otherwise qualified individual . . . shall solely by reason of his or her handicap, be excluded from the participation in, be denied the benefits of, or be subjected to discrimination under any program or activity receiving Federal financial assistance. . . . " 29 U.S.C. §794. The Act protects any person who has a qualifying mental or physical impairment, a record of such impairment, or is regarded as having such impairment. 29 U.S.C. §705. It applies to all public and private schools receiving federal funding, and covers teachers and school employees as well as students. Generally, a school's compliance with IDEA will satisfy the RHA requirements.

IDEA is a spending program through which the federal government funds state efforts to support the education of disabled children. States and local educational agencies (LEAs) must construct specific statutory policies and procedures in order to receive federal funding. All states now participate. IDEA requires that all disabled students, ages three through 21, receive a "free appropriate public education." 20 U.S.C. §§1401, 1414. Students with disabilities include those with mental impairments, physical impairments or learning disabilities, "who, by reason thereof, need special education and related services." 20 U.S.C. §1401. This mandate covers disabled children who attend public or private schools, home schools and those students who are expelled or suspended from school.

The statute also requires states and LEAs to identify and evaluate disabled students and create an Individualized Educational Program (IEP) for each disabled child. An IEP is a written report that includes, among other things, the school's annual goals and short-term instructional objectives for a student, the special education and related services to be provided, and any assistive technology needed. The special education program specified must constitute a "free appropriate public education." 20 U.S.C. §1401. The IDEA also erects mandatory process protections for students with educational disabilities. 20 U.S.C §1415. Parents have a right to participate in their child's educational plan and to receive an impartial hearing to resolve any disputes. *Id.* The IDEA requires that students be allowed to remain, or to "stay put," in their current placement, during the pendency of any proceeding under IDEA to review that placement. 20 U.S.C. §1415(j). Parents also have the right to bring a civil action challenging their child's placement. 20 U.S.C. §1415(i)(2). The federal court's jurisdiction over such civil actions extends to claims against the state and its agencies because IDEA expressly abrogates any Eleventh Amendment immunity afforded the state for violations of the statute. 20 U.S.C. §1403. The federal court also may award attorney fees to parents, if they prevail. 20 U.S.C.

While the RHA and the IDEA apply only to schools, the ADA covers all public entities and "places of public accommodation." Such "places" include private businesses and organizations providing goods and services to the public, as well as almost all public and private schools except religious schools. The ADA provides that "no qualified individual with a disability shall, by reason of such disability, be excluded from participation in or be denied the benefits of the services, programs or activities of a public entity or be subjected to discrimination by any such entity." 42 U.S.C. §§12131-34.

B. THE FEDERAL STATUTORY STRUCTURE AND GOVERNING CASE LAW

The primary goal of these statutes is to improve the education of, and opportunities for, disabled Americans. With respect to the education of students with educational disabilities, Congress has created statutory duties to provide: (1) reasonable accommodation in educational programs and facilities; (2) a free, appropriate education; (3) special education and related services; (4) the least restrictive educational environment; (5) alternative appropriate placements; and (6) procedural protections which, among other things, permit such students to "stay put" in their placements pending any review of those placements.

As the cases in this section indicate, however, the courts have wrestled with questions regarding the proper nature and scope of these congressional mandates. The challenge for the courts has been to balance the interest of school districts in managing their scarce resources with the goal of serving the needs of students with educational disabilities.

Achieving that balance requires an examination of the principle of equality itself. The congressional statutes recognize that students with educational disabilities may have exceptional needs, and that meeting those needs may require school districts to offer these students more resources than those provided to students without educational disabilities. In other words, the statutory mandates are built on the philosophy that the needs of students with educational disabilities are unlike those of students without such disabilities, and that those unequal needs justify the provision of unequal services. What are the arguments supporting and refuting that philosophy?

Assuming that different educational needs justify different levels of educational services, what is the ultimate objective of those services? Do the statutory mandates require the provision of services that are necessary to allow students with educational disabilities to reach the "same" level of educational performance as students without disabilities? Is the goal to enable students with educational disabilities to receive at least some benefit from their education or is it to insure that they are able to maximize their own potential? Should the goal of education be the same for *all* students regardless of need?

1. The Statutory Duty to Accommodate Students with Educational Disabilities

The ADA and the RHA both require educational institutions to make reasonable accommodation for students with educational disabilities. As the *Davis* case indicates, however, that duty to provide reasonable accommodation apparently does not extend to the provision of resources that would constitute a substantial modification of an existing program. Nor are school districts apparently required to offer accommodations that would create an undue financial or administrative burden.

Southeastern Community College v. Davis

442 U.S. 397(1979)

Mr. Justice Powell delivered the opinion of the Court.

This case presents a matter of first impression for this Court: Whether §504 of the Rehabilitation Act of 1973, which prohibits discrimination against an "otherwise qualified handicapped individual" in federally funded programs "solely by reason of his handicap," forbids professional schools from imposing physical qualifications for admission to their clinical training programs.

I

Respondent, who suffers from a serious hearing disability, seeks to be trained as a registered nurse. During the 1973-1974 academic year she was enrolled in the College Parallel program of Southeastern Community College, a state institution that receives federal funds. Respondent hoped to progress to Southeastern's Associate Degree Nursing program, completion of which would make her eligible for state certification as a registered nurse. In the course of her application to the nursing program, she was interviewed by a member of the nursing faculty. It became apparent that respondent had difficulty understanding questions asked, and on inquiry she acknowledged a history of hearing problems and dependence on a hearing aid. She was advised to consult an audiologist.

On the basis of an examination at Duke University Medical Center, respondent was diagnosed as having a "bilateral, sensori-neural hearing loss." A change in her hearing aid was recommended, as a result of which it was expected that she would be able to detect sounds "almost as well as a person would who has normal hearing." But this improvement would not mean that she could discriminate among sounds sufficiently to understand normal spoken speech. Her lip-reading skills would remain necessary for effective communication: "While wearing the hearing aid, she is well aware of gross sounds occurring in the listening environment. However, she can only be responsible for speech spoken to her, when the talker gets her attention and allows her to look directly at the talker."

Southeastern next consulted Mary McRee, Executive Director of the North Carolina Board of Nursing. On the basis of the audiologist's report, McRee recommended that respondent not be admitted to the nursing program. In McRee's view, respondent's hearing disability made it unsafe for her to practice as a nurse. In addition, it would be impossible for respondent to participate safely in the normal clinical training program, and those modifications that would be necessary to enable safe participation would prevent her from realizing the benefits of the program: "To adjust patient learning experiences in keeping with [respondent's] hearing limitations could, in fact, be the same as denying her full learning to meet the objectives of your nursing programs."

. . . Respondent then filed suit in the United States District Court for the Eastern District of North Carolina, alleging both a violation of §504 of the Rehabilitation Act of 1973, 87 Stat. 394, as amended, 29 U.S.C. §794 (1976 ed., Supp. II), and a denial of equal protection and due process. After a bench trial, the District Court entered judgment in favor of Southeastern. . . .

II

As previously noted, this is the first case in which this Court has been called upon to interpret §504. It is elementary that "[t]he starting point in every case involving construction of a statute is the language itself." Section 504 by its terms does not compel educational institutions to disregard the disabilities of handicapped individuals or to make substantial modifications in their programs to allow disabled persons to participate. Instead, it requires only that an "otherwise qualified handicapped individual" not be excluded from participation in a federally funded program "solely by reason of his handicap," indicating only that mere possession of a handicap is not a permissible ground for assuming an inability to function in a particular context.

The court below, however, believed that the "otherwise qualified" persons protected by §504 include those who would be able to meet the requirements of a particular program in every respect except as to limitations imposed by their handicap. Taken literally, this holding would prevent an institution from taking into account any limitation resulting from the handicap, however disabling. It assumes, in effect, that a person need not meet legitimate physical requirements in order to be "otherwise qualified." We think the understanding of the District Court is closer to the plain meaning of the statutory language. An otherwise qualified person is one who is able to meet all of a program's requirements in spite of his handicap.

The regulations promulgated by the Department of HEW to interpret §504 reinforce, rather than contradict, this conclusion. According to these regulations, a "[q]ualified handicapped person" is, "[w]ith respect to postsecondary and vocational education services, a handicapped person who meets the academic and technical standards requisite to admission or participation in the [school's] education program or activity. . . . " 45 CFR §84.3(k)(3) (1978). An explanatory note states: "The term 'technical standards' refers to all non-academic admissions criteria that are essential to participation in the program in question."

A further note emphasizes that legitimate physical qualifications may be essential to participation in particular programs.[2] We think it clear, therefore, that HEW interprets the "other" qualifications which a handicapped person may be required to meet as including necessary physical qualifications.

III

The remaining question is whether the physical qualifications Southeastern demanded of respondent might not be necessary for participation in its nursing program. It is not open to dispute that, as Southeastern's Associate Degree Nursing program currently is constituted, the ability to understand speech without reliance on lip-reading is necessary for patient safety during the clinical phase of the program. As the District Court found, this ability also is indispensable for many of the functions that a registered nurse performs.

Respondent contends nevertheless that §504, properly interpreted, compels Southeastern to undertake affirmative action that would dispense with the need for effective oral communication. First, it is suggested that respondent can be given individual supervision by faculty members whenever she attends patients directly. Moreover, certain required courses might be dispensed with altogether for respondent. It is not necessary, she argues, that Southeastern train her to undertake all the tasks a registered nurse is licensed to perform. Rather, it is sufficient to make §504 applicable if respondent might be able to perform satisfactorily some of the duties of a registered nurse or to hold some of the positions available to a registered nurse.

Respondent finds support for this argument in portions of the HEW regulations discussed above. In particular, a provision applicable to postsecondary educational programs requires covered institutions to make "modifications" in their programs to accommodate handicapped persons, and to provide "auxiliary aids" such as sign-language interpreters. Respondent argues that this regulation imposes an obligation to ensure full participation in covered programs by handicapped individuals and, in particular, requires

---

[2] The note states:

> Paragraph (k) of §84.3 defines the term "qualified handicapped person." Throughout the regulation, this term is used instead of the statutory term "otherwise qualified handicapped person." The Department believes that the omission of the word "otherwise" is necessary in order to comport with the intent of the statute because, read literally, "otherwise" qualified handicapped persons include persons who are qualified except for their handicap, rather than in spite of their handicap. Under such a literal reading, a blind person possessing all the qualifications for driving a bus except sight could be said to be "otherwise qualified" for the job of driving. Clearly, such a result was not intended by Congress. In all other respects, the terms "qualified" and "otherwise qualified" are intended to be interchangeable.

Southeastern to make the kind of adjustments that would be necessary to permit her safe participation in the nursing program.

We note first that on the present record it appears unlikely respondent could benefit from any affirmative action that the regulation reasonably could be interpreted as requiring. Section 84.44(d)(2), for example, explicitly excludes "devices or services of a personal nature" from the kinds of auxiliary aids a school must provide a handicapped individual. Yet the only evidence in the record indicates that nothing less than close, individual attention by a nursing instructor would be sufficient to ensure patient safety if respondent took part in the clinical phase of the nursing program. Furthermore, it also is reasonably clear that §84.44(a) does not encompass the kind of curricular changes that would be necessary to accommodate respondent in the nursing program. In light of respondent's inability to function in clinical courses without close supervision, Southeastern, with prudence, could allow her to take only academic classes. Whatever benefits respondent might realize from such a course of study, she would not receive even a rough equivalent of the training a nursing program normally gives. Such a fundamental alteration in the nature of a program is far more than the "modification" the regulation requires.

Moreover, an interpretation of the regulations that required the extensive modifications necessary to include respondent in the nursing program would raise grave doubts about their validity. If these regulations were to require substantial adjustments in existing programs beyond those necessary to eliminate discrimination against otherwise qualified individuals, they would do more than clarify the meaning of §504. Instead, they would constitute an unauthorized extension of the obligations imposed by that statute.

The language and structure of the Rehabilitation Act of 1973 reflect a recognition by Congress of the distinction between the evenhanded treatment of qualified handicapped persons and affirmative efforts to overcome the disabilities caused by handicaps. Section 501(b), governing the employment of handicapped individuals by the Federal Government, requires each federal agency to submit "an affirmative action program plan for the hiring, placement, and advancement of handicapped individuals. . . . " These plans "shall include a description of the extent to which and methods whereby the special needs of handicapped employees are being met." Similarly, §503(a), governing hiring by federal contractors, requires employers to "take affirmative action to employ and advance in employment qualified handicapped individuals. . . . " The President is required to promulgate regulations to enforce this section.

Under §501(c) of the Act, by contrast, state agencies such as Southeastern are only "encourage[d] . . . to adopt and implement such policies and procedures." Section 504 does not refer at all to affirmative action, and except as it applies to federal employers it does not provide for implementation by administrative action. A comparison of these provisions demonstrates that Congress understood accommodation of the needs of handicapped individuals may require affirmative action and knew how to provide for it in those instances where it wished to do so.

Although an agency's interpretation of the statute under which it operates is entitled to some deference, "this deference is constrained by our obligation to honor the clear meaning of a statute, as revealed by its language, purpose, and history." Here, neither the language, purpose, nor history of §504 reveals an intent to impose an affirmative-action obligation on all recipients of federal funds. Accordingly, we hold that even if HEW has attempted to create such an obligation itself, it lacks the authority to do so.

IV

We do not suggest that the line between a lawful refusal to extend affirmative action and illegal discrimination against handicapped persons always will be clear. It is possible to envision situations where an insistence on continuing past requirements and practices might arbitrarily deprive genuinely qualified handicapped persons of the opportunity to participate in a covered program. Technological advances can be expected to enhance opportunities to rehabilitate the handicapped or otherwise to qualify them for some useful employment. Such advances also may enable attainment of these goals without imposing undue financial and administrative burdens upon a State. Thus, situations may arise where a refusal to modify an existing program might become unreasonable and discriminatory. Identification of those instances where a refusal to accommodate the needs of a disabled person amounts to discrimination against the handicapped continues to be an important responsibility of HEW.

In this case, however, it is clear that Southeastern's unwillingness to make major adjustments in its nursing program does not constitute such discrimination. The uncontroverted testimony of several members of Southeastern's staff and faculty established that the purpose of its program was to train persons who could serve the nursing profession in all customary ways. This type of purpose, far from reflecting any animus against handicapped individuals is shared by many if not most of the institutions that train persons to render professional service. It is undisputed that respondent could not participate in Southeastern's nursing program unless the standards were substantially lowered. Section 504 imposes no requirement upon an educational institution to lower or to effect substantial modifications of standards to accommodate a handicapped person.

One may admire respondent's desire and determination to overcome her handicap, and there well may be various other types of service for which she can qualify. In this case, however, we hold that there was no violation of §504 when Southeastern concluded that respondent did not qualify for admission to its program. Nothing in the language or history of §504 reflects an intention to limit the freedom of an educational institution to require reasonable physical qualifications for admission to a clinical training program. Nor has there been any showing in this case that any action short of a substantial change in Southeastern's program would render unreasonable the qualifications it imposed. . . .

NOTES AND QUESTIONS

1. The first issue in analyzing any claim under the ADA or RHA is whether the student is disabled. The statutory definition requires a showing that a

specific learning disability substantially limits at least one of the student's major life activities. If the student, through hard work and coping mechanisms, has managed to meet basic academic requirements despite the disability, is that student disabled? In *Price v. National Board of Medical Examiners,* 966 F. Supp. 419 (S.D. W. Va. 1997), the court determined that students diagnosed with attention deficit hyperactivity disorder (ADHD) were not disabled because their impairments did not significantly restrict regular life activities, as measured by the fact that their academic performance was not significantly worse than students without that disorder. Do you agree?

2. According to the Supreme Court in *Davis,* §504 does not compel educational institutions to "make substantial modifications" to their programs to allow disabled students to participate. What constitutes a "substantial" modification and how should courts make this determination? *See, e.g., Maczaczyj v. New York,* 956 F. Supp. 403 (W.D.N.Y. 1997) (college not required to provide student who suffered from a social phobia with a "satellite uplink" so that student could avoid attending regular class because such a modification would be "substantial").
3. The *Davis* Court defines an "otherwise qualified" student as one who can meet all of a program's requirements despite a handicap. What if only additional help or services would allow a disabled student to be "otherwise qualified"? Is that student actually "otherwise qualified"?
4. While *Davis* established a definition of "otherwise qualified," questions still remained. In *Brookhart v. Illinois State Board of Education,* 697 F.2d 179 (7th Cir. 1983), the Seventh Circuit further defined the concepts of "otherwise qualified" and "reasonable accommodation." The court found that a school board could require disabled students to pass a minimum competency test (M.C.T.) to graduate from high school. The court stated:

> Plaintiffs in this case have no grounds on which to argue that the contents of the M.C.T. are discriminatory solely because handicapped students who are incapable of attaining a level of minimal competency will fail the test. Altering the content of the M.C.T. to accommodate an individual's inability to learn the tested material because of his handicap would be a "substantial modification" . . . as well as a "perversion" of the diploma requirement. . . . A student who is unable to learn because of his handicap is surely not an individual who is qualified in spite of his handicap. Thus denial of a diploma because of the inability to pass the M.C.T. is not discrimination under the RHA. . . .
>
> However, an otherwise qualified student who is unable to disclose the degree of learning he actually possesses because of the test format or environment would be the object of discrimination solely on the basis of his handicap. . . . [F]ederal law requires administrative modification to minimize the effects of plaintiffs' handicaps on any future examinations.

According to the Seventh Circuit, therefore, schools do not have to change their expectations regarding their students' knowledge base, only the methods they use to measure that knowledge base. Reasonable accommodation may require schools to design special testing or other services to give disabled students the chance to demonstrate their abilities.

See also Darian v. University of Massachusetts, 980 F. Supp. 77 (D. Mass. 1997) (educational institution's duty to make reasonable accommodation for student who became pregnant during coursework required modifications in instructional practices and examinations, but did not include elimination of degree requirements).

5. Schools may also require disabled students to satisfy general standards in other areas. In *Bercovitch v. Baldwin School, Inc.,* 133 F.3d 141 (1st Cir. 1998), the First Circuit held that to be "otherwise qualified," disabled students must not only meet a school's knowledge expectations, but also its conduct requirements. The case involved an 11-year-old boy with Attention Deficit Hyperactivity Disorder (ADHD) who was suspended indefinitely after a series of disciplinary violations. The school attempted to accommodate his behavior for years, providing for unique punishments and encouraging medical treatment, but eventually concluded that he could not return. The First Circuit held that the school was not required to alter its code of conduct to allow the boy to continue his education there, stating that "if more than reasonable modifications are required of an institution in order to accommodate an individual, then that individual is not qualified for the program. . . . The law does not require an academic program to compromise its integral criteria to accommodate a disabled individual." Who does this decision benefit? Disabled students? Nondisabled students? Schools? How should schools or courts measure the reasonableness of any modifications?
6. ***Accommodation Practicum.*** Suppose a school's blind music teacher asks the school to accommodate the teacher's disability by allowing her to bring a guide dog to class each day. The school agrees, but quickly receives complaints from parents of a student who suffers a severe allergic reaction to the dog. What legal and practical advice would you give the school district, the teacher and the student's parents? In *Clark County School District v. Buchanan,* 924 P.2d 716 (Nev. 1996), the Nevada Supreme Court found that such a teacher would be entitled to an injunction requiring the school district to allow her to bring a guide dog to class, but indicated that the school could place reasonable restrictions on the teacher to prevent any legitimate health problems experienced by students or other faculty. What reasonable restrictions could be negotiated?
7. In *School Board of Nassau County v. Arline,* 480 U.S. 273 (1987), the Supreme Court held that an elementary school teacher with tuberculosis was a "handicapped individual" within the meaning of the RHA, because her contagious disease constituted an actual impairment and a "record of impairment" that substantially limited her ability to perform "major life activities," such as breathing. The Court found insufficient evidence in the record, however, as to whether Arline was "otherwise qualified" for her job. In its footnotes, the court indicated how that issue should be resolved on remand. First, the Court observed that, in the employment context, "otherwise qualified" means the ability to perform the "essential functions" of the job in question, in spite of an impairment. The Court then declared that when a handicapped person is unable to perform those essential functions, the employer must nevertheless provide "reasonable accommodation" to the employee that would allow the employee to

perform those functions: "Employers have an affirmative obligation to make a reasonable accommodation for a handicapped employee." 480 U.S. at 287-289, and notes 17 and 19. Reasonable accommodations, however, do not include an alteration of facilities or the provision of services that would impose "undue financial and administrative burdens" or require "a fundamental alteration in the nature of the program." Finally, the court made clear that a "person who poses a significant risk of communicating an infectious disease to others in the work-place will not be otherwise qualified for his or her job if reasonable accommodation will not eliminate that risk. The Act would not require a school board to place a teacher with active, contagious tuberculosis in a classroom with elementary school children." 480 U.S. at 287, n.16.

8. Although the *Arline* case involved issues of employment discrimination, its reasoning clearly applies by analogy to a school district's obligation to offer reasonable accommodation to handicapped students. What is a school district's "affirmative obligation" to accommodate a student with an active, contagious disease in the classroom?
9. In *Arline,* the Supreme Court expressly declined to reach the question of whether a "carrier of contagious disease such as AIDS" would be considered to have a "physical impairment" or would be considered "handicapped" solely based upon the "contagiousness" of the disease. Since *Arline,* however, the courts have uniformly concluded that even an asymptomatic carrier of the AIDS virus would be "handicapped" due to impairment of major life activities, including reproduction. *See, e.g., Martinez v. School Board of Hillsborough County, Florida,* 861 F.2d 1502 (11th Cir. 1988); *Doe v. Dolton Elementary School Dist. No. 148,* 694 F. Supp. 440 (N.D. Ill. 1988); *Thomas v. Atascadero Unified School District,* 662 F. Supp. 376 (C.D. Cal. 1986). In *Martinez,* the Eleventh Circuit further declared that a child in the "late stages of AIDS" was "otherwise qualified" to be educated in the regular classroom in spite of her handicap, because the possibility of transmission of the virus through "tears, saliva and urine" was not "significant."

2. The Statutory Duty to Provide a Free, Appropriate Education for Students with Educational Disabilities

In the ADA, RHA and IDEA, Congress clearly requires school districts to offer to students with disabilities services that are not offered to students without such disabilities. Unlike the ADA and RHA, however, IDEA specifically defines a disabled student as one "who by reason of" a mental impairment, physical impairment, emotional disturbance or specific learning disability "need[s] special education and related services." 20 U.S.C. §1401(3). The statute's definition of eligible students thus is specifically tailored to cover those students who will benefit from special education and related services. If the student suffers from any disability that affects education or related services, the state and local district must provide "special education and related services."

Must the district provide services designed to allow students with educational disabilities to achieve their maximum potential, or merely enough services to allow these students to receive some benefit from the educational program?

Board of Education of Hendrick Hudson Central School District v. Rowley

458 U.S. 176 (1982)

Justice Rehnquist delivered the opinion of the Court.

This case presents a question of statutory interpretation. Petitioners contend that the Court of Appeals and the District Court misconstrued the requirements imposed by Congress upon States which receive federal funds under the Education of the Handicapped Act. We agree and reverse the judgment of the Court of Appeals.

I

The Education of the Handicapped Act (Act), 84 Stat. 175, as amended, 20 U.S.C. §1401 *et seq.* (1976 ed. and Supp. IV), provides federal money to assist state and local agencies in educating handicapped children, and conditions such funding upon a State's compliance with extensive goals and procedures. The Act represents an ambitious federal effort to promote the education of handicapped children, and was passed in response to Congress' perception that a majority of handicapped children in the United States "were either totally excluded from schools or [were] sitting idly in regular classrooms awaiting the time when they were old enough to 'drop out.'" The Act's evolution and major provisions shed light on the question of statutory interpretation which is at the heart of this case.

Congress first addressed the problem of educating the handicapped in 1966 when it amended the Elementary and Secondary Education Act of 1965 to establish a grant program "for the purpose of assisting the States in the initiation, expansion, and improvement of programs and projects . . . for the education of handicapped children." That program was repealed in 1970 by the Education of the Handicapped Act, Part B of which established a grant program similar in purpose to the repealed legislation. Neither the 1966 nor the 1970 legislation contained specific guidelines for state use of the grant money; both were aimed primarily at stimulating the States to develop educational resources and to train personnel for educating the handicapped.

Dissatisfied with the progress being made under these earlier enactments, and spurred by two District Court decisions holding that handicapped children should be given access to a public education, Congress in 1974 greatly increased federal funding for education of the handicapped and for the first time required recipient States to adopt "a goal of providing full educational opportunities to all handicapped children." The 1974 statute was recognized as an interim measure only, adopted "in order to give the Congress an additional year in which to study what if any additional Federal assistance [was] required to enable the States to meet the needs of handicapped children." The ensuing year of study produced the Education for All Handicapped Children Act of 1975.

In order to qualify for federal financial assistance under the Act, a State must demonstrate that it "has in effect a policy that assures all handicapped children the right to a free appropriate public education." 20 U.S.C. §1412(1). That policy must be reflected in a state plan submitted to and approved by the Secretary of Education, §1413, which describes in detail the goals, programs, and timetables under which the State intends to educate handicapped children within its borders. States receiving money under the Act must provide education to the handicapped by priority, first "to handicapped children who are not receiving an education" and second "to handicapped children . . . with the most severe handicaps who are receiving an inadequate education," and "to the maximum extent appropriate" must educate handicapped children "with children who are not handicapped." The Act broadly defines "handicapped children" to include "mentally retarded, hard of hearing, deaf, speech impaired, visually handicapped, seriously emotionally disturbed, orthopedically impaired, [and] other health impaired children, [and] children with specific learning disabilities."

The "free appropriate public education" required by the Act is tailored to the unique needs of the handicapped child by means of an "individualized educational program" (IEP). §1401(18). The IEP, which is prepared at a meeting between a qualified representative of the local educational agency, the child's teacher, the child's parents or guardian, and, where appropriate, the child, consists of a written document containing:

> (A) a statement of the present levels of educational performance of such child, (B) a statement of annual goals, including short-term instructional objectives, (C) a statement of the specific educational services to be provided to such child, and the extent to which such child will be able to participate in regular educational programs, (D) the projected date for initiation and anticipated duration of such services, and (E) appropriate objective criteria and evaluation procedures and schedules for determining, on at least an annual basis, whether instructional objectives are being achieved. §1401(19).

Local or regional educational agencies must review, and where appropriate revise, each child's IEP at least annually.

In addition to the state plan and the IEP already described, the Act imposes extensive procedural requirements upon States receiving federal funds under its provisions. Parents or guardians of handicapped children must be notified of any proposed change in "the identification, evaluation, or educational placement of the child or the provision of a free appropriate public education to such child," and must be permitted to bring a complaint about "any matter relating to" such evaluation and education. §§1415(b)(1)(D) and (E). Complaints brought by parents or guardians must be resolved at "an impartial due process hearing," and appeal to the state educational agency must be provided if the initial hearing is held at the local or regional level. §§1415(b)(2) and (c). Thereafter, "[a]ny party aggrieved by the findings and decision" of the state administrative hearing has "the right to bring a civil action with respect to the complaint . . . in any State court of competent jurisdiction or in a district court of the United States without regard to the amount in controversy." §1415(e)(2).

Thus, although the Act leaves to the States the primary responsibility for developing and executing educational programs for handicapped children, it imposes significant requirements to be followed in the discharge of that responsibility. Compliance is assured by provisions permitting the withholding of federal funds upon determination that a participating state or local agency has failed to satisfy the requirements of the Act, §§1414(b)(2)(A), 1416, and by the provision for judicial review. At present, all States except New Mexico receive federal funds under the portions of the Act at issue today.

II

This case arose in connection with the education of Amy Rowley, a deaf student at the Furnace Woods School in the Hendrick Hudson Central School District, Peekskill, N.Y. Amy has minimal residual hearing and is an excellent lip-reader. During the year before she began attending Furnace Woods, a meeting between her parents and school administrators resulted in a decision to place her in a regular kindergarten class in order to determine what supplemental services would be necessary to her education. Several members of the school administration prepared for Amy's arrival by attending a course in sign-language interpretation, and a Teletype machine was installed in the principal's office to facilitate communication with her parents who are also deaf. At the end of the trial period it was determined that Amy should remain in the kindergarten class, but that she should be provided with an FM hearing aid which would amplify words spoken into a wireless receiver by the teacher or fellow students during certain classroom activities. Amy successfully completed her kindergarten year.

As required by the Act, an IEP was prepared for Amy during the fall of her first-grade year. The IEP provided that Amy should be educated in a regular classroom at Furnace Woods, should continue to use the FM hearing aid, and should receive instruction from a tutor for the deaf for one hour each day and from a speech therapist for three hours each week. The Rowleys agreed with parts of the IEP, but insisted that Amy also be provided a qualified sign-language interpreter in all her academic classes in lieu of the assistance proposed in other parts of the IEP. Such an interpreter had been placed in Amy's kindergarten class for a 2-week experimental period, but the interpreter had reported that Amy did not need his services at that time. The school administrators likewise concluded that Amy did not need such an interpreter in her first-grade classroom. They reached this conclusion after consulting the school district's Committee on the Handicapped, which had received expert evidence from Amy's parents on the importance of a sign-language interpreter, received testimony from Amy's teacher and other persons familiar with her academic and social progress, and visited a class for the deaf.

When their request for an interpreter was denied, the Rowleys demanded and received a hearing before an independent examiner. After receiving evidence from both sides, the examiner agreed with the administrators' determination that an interpreter was not necessary because "Amy was achieving educationally, academically, and socially" without such assistance. The examiner's decision was affirmed on appeal by the New York Commissioner of Education on the basis of substantial evidence in the record. Pursuant to the Act's provision for judicial review, the Rowleys then brought an action in the United States District Court for the Southern District of New York, claiming that the administrators' denial of the sign-language interpreter constituted a denial of the "free appropriate public education" guaranteed by the Act. . . .

We granted certiorari to review the lower courts' interpretation of the Act. Such review requires us to consider two questions: What is meant by the Act's requirement of a "free appropriate public education"? And what is the role of state and federal courts in exercising the review granted by 20 U.S.C. §1415? . . .

III

A

This is the first case in which this Court has been called upon to interpret any provision of the Act. As noted previously, the District Court and the Court of Appeals concluded that "[t]he Act itself does not define 'appropriate education,'" but leaves "to the courts and the hearing officers" the responsibility of "giv[ing] content to the requirement of an 'appropriate education.'" Petitioners contend that the definition of the phrase "free appropriate public education" used by the courts below overlooks the definition of that phrase actually found in the Act. Respondents agree that the Act defines "free appropriate public education," but contend that the statutory definition is not "functional" and thus "offers judges no guidance in their consideration of controversies involving 'the identification, evaluation, or educational placement of the child or the provision of a free appropriate public education.'" The United States, appearing as *amicus curiae* on behalf of respondents, states that "[a]lthough the Act includes definitions of a 'free appropriate public education' and other related terms, the statutory definitions do not adequately explain what is meant by 'appropriate.'"

We are loath to conclude that Congress failed to offer any assistance in defining the meaning of the principal substantive phrase used in the Act. It is beyond dispute that, contrary to the conclusions of the courts below, the Act does expressly define "free appropriate public education":

> The term "free appropriate public education" means *special education* and *related services* which (A) have been provided at public expense, under public supervision and direction, and without charge, (B) meet the standards of the State educational agency, (C) include an appropriate preschool, elementary, or secondary school education in the State involved, and (D) are provided in conformity with the individualized education program required under section 1414(a)(5) of this title. §1401(18) (emphasis added).

"Special education," as referred to in this definition, means "specially designed instruction, at no cost to parents or guardians, to meet the unique needs of a handicapped child, including classroom instruction, instruction in physical education, home instruction, and instruction in hospitals and institutions.""Related services" are defined as "transportation, and such developmental, corrective, and other supportive services . . . as may be required to assist a handicapped child to benefit from special education."

Like many statutory definitions, this one tends toward the cryptic rather than the comprehensive, but that is scarcely a reason for abandoning the quest for legislative intent. Whether or not the definition is a "functional" one, as respondents contend it is not, it is the principal tool which Congress has given us for parsing the critical phrase of the Act. We think more must be made of it than either respondents or the United States seems willing to admit.

According to the definitions contained in the Act, a "free appropriate public education" consists of educational instruction specially designed to meet the unique needs of the handicapped child, supported by such services as are necessary to permit the child "to benefit" from the instruction. Almost as a checklist for adequacy under the Act, the definition also requires that such instruction and services be provided at public expense and under public supervision, meet the State's educational standards, approximate the grade levels used in the State's regular education, and comport with the child's IEP. Thus, if personalized instruction is being provided with sufficient supportive services to permit the child to benefit from the instruction, and the other items on the definitional checklist are satisfied, the child is receiving a "free appropriate public education" as defined by the Act.

Other portions of the statute also shed light upon congressional intent. Congress found that of the roughly eight million handicapped children in the United States at the time of enactment, one million were "excluded entirely from the public school system" and more than half were receiving an inappropriate education. In addition, as mentioned in Part I, the Act requires States to extend educational services first to those children who are receiving no education and second to those children who are receiving an "inadequate education." When these express statutory findings and priorities are read together with the Act's extensive procedural requirements and its definition of "free appropriate public education," the face of the statute evinces a congressional intent to bring previously excluded handicapped children into the public education systems of the States and to require the States to adopt *procedures* which would result in individualized consideration of and instruction for each child.

Noticeably absent from the language of the statute is any substantive standard prescribing the level of education to be accorded handicapped children. Certainly the language of the statute contains no requirement like the one imposed by the lower courts—that States maximize the potential of handicapped children "commensurate with the opportunity provided to other children." That standard was expounded by the District Court without reference to the statutory definitions or even to the legislative history of the Act. Although we find the statutory definition of "free appropriate public education" to be helpful in our interpretation of the Act, there remains the question of whether the legislative history indicates a congressional intent that such education meet some additional substantive standard. For an answer, we turn to that history.

B

(i)

As suggested in Part I, federal support for education of the handicapped is a fairly recent development. Before passage of the Act some States had passed laws to improve the educational services afforded handicapped children, but many of these children were excluded completely from any form of public education or were left to fend for themselves in classrooms designed for education of their nonhandicapped peers. As previously noted, the House Report begins by emphasizing this exclusion and misplacement, noting that millions of handicapped children "were either totally excluded from schools or [were] sitting idly in regular classrooms awaiting the time when they were old enough to 'drop out.'" One of the Act's two principal sponsors in the Senate urged its passage in similar terms:

> While much progress has been made in the last few years, we can take no solace in that progress until all handicapped children are, in fact, receiving an education. The most recent statistics provided by the Bureau of Education for the Handicapped estimate that . . . 1.75 million handicapped children do not receive any educational services, and 2.5 million handicapped children are not receiving an appropriate education (remarks of Sen. Williams).

This concern, stressed repeatedly throughout the legislative history, confirms the impression conveyed by the language of the statute: By passing the Act, Congress sought primarily to make public education available to handicapped children. But in seeking to provide such access to public education, Congress did not impose upon the States any greater substantive educational standard than would be necessary to make such access meaningful. Indeed, Congress expressly "recognize[d] that in many instances the process of providing special education and related services to handicapped children is not guaranteed to produce any particular outcome." Thus, the intent of the Act was more to open the door of public education to handicapped children on appropriate terms than to guarantee any particular level of education once inside. . . .

That the Act imposes no clear obligation upon recipient States beyond the requirement that handicapped children receive some form of specialized education is perhaps best demonstrated by the fact that Congress, in explaining the need for the Act, equated an "appropriate education" to the receipt of some specialized educational services. The Senate Report states: "[T]he most recent statistics provided by the Bureau of Education for the Handicapped estimate that of the more than 8 million children. . . . with handicapping conditions requiring special education and related services, only 3.9 million such children are receiving an appropriate education." This statement, which reveals Congress' view that 3.9 million handicapped children were "receiving an appropriate education" in 1975, is followed immediately in the Senate Report by a table showing that 3.9 million handicapped children were "served" in 1975 and a slightly larger number were "unserved." A similar statement and table appear in the House Report.

By characterizing the 3.9 million handicapped children who were "served" as children who were "receiving an appropriate education," the

Senate and House Reports unmistakably disclose Congress' perception of the type of education required by the Act: an "appropriate education" is provided when personalized educational services are provided.

(ii)

Respondents contend that "the goal of the Act is to provide each handicapped child with an equal educational opportunity." We think, however, that the requirement that a State provide specialized educational services to handicapped children generates no additional requirement that the services so provided be sufficient to maximize each child's potential "commensurate with the opportunity provided other children." Respondents and the United States correctly note that Congress sought "to provide assistance to the States in carrying out their responsibilities under . . . the Constitution of the United States to provide equal protection of the laws." But we do not think that such statements imply a congressional intent to achieve strict equality of opportunity or services.

The educational opportunities provided by our public school systems undoubtedly differ from student to student, depending upon a myriad of factors that might affect a particular student's ability to assimilate information presented in the classroom. The requirement that States provide "equal" educational opportunities would thus seem to present an entirely unworkable standard requiring impossible measurements and comparisons. Similarly, furnishing handicapped children with only such services as are available to non-handicapped children would in all probability fall short of the statutory requirement of "free appropriate public education"; to require, on the other hand, the furnishing of every special service necessary to maximize each handicapped child's potential is, we think, further than Congress intended to go. Thus to speak in terms of "equal" services in one instance gives less than what is required by the Act and in another instance more. The theme of the Act is "free appropriate public education," a phrase which is too complex to be captured by the word "equal" whether one is speaking of opportunities or services.

The legislative conception of the requirements of equal protection was undoubtedly informed by *[Mills* and *PARC]*. But cases such as *Mills* and *PARC* held simply that handicapped children may not be excluded entirely from public education. In *Mills,* the District Court said:

> If sufficient funds are not available to finance all of the services and programs that are needed and desirable in the system then the available funds must be expended equitably in such a manner that no child is entirely excluded from a publicly supported education consistent with his needs and ability to benefit therefrom.

The *PARC* court used similar language, saying "[i]t is the commonwealth's obligation to place each mentally retarded child in a free, public program of education and training appropriate to the child's capacity. . . . " The right of access to free public education enunciated by these cases is significantly different from any notion of absolute equality of opportunity regardless of capacity. To the extent that Congress might have looked further than these cases which are mentioned in the legislative history, at the time of enactment of the Act this Court had held at least twice that the Equal Protection Clause of the Fourteenth Amendment does not require States to expend equal financial resources on the education of each child.

In explaining the need for federal legislation, the House Report noted that "no congressional legislation has required a precise guarantee for handicapped children, i.e. a basic floor of opportunity that would bring into compliance all school districts with the constitutional right of equal protection with respect to handicapped children." Assuming that the Act was designed to fill the need identified in the House Report—that is, to provide a "basic floor of opportunity" consistent with equal protection—neither the Act nor its history persuasively demonstrates that Congress thought that equal protection required anything more than equal access. Therefore, Congress' desire to provide specialized educational services, even in furtherance of "equality," cannot be read as imposing any particular substantive educational standard upon the States.

The District Court and the Court of Appeals thus erred when they held that the Act requires New York to maximize the potential of each handicapped child commensurate with the opportunity provided nonhandicapped children. Desirable though that goal might be, it is not the standard that Congress imposed upon States which receive funding under the Act. Rather, Congress sought primarily to identify and evaluate handicapped children, and to provide them with access to a free public education.

(iii)

Implicit in the congressional purpose of providing access to a "free appropriate public education" is the requirement that the education to which access is provided be sufficient to confer some educational benefit upon the handicapped child. It would do little good for Congress to spend millions of dollars in providing access to a public education only to have the handicapped child receive no benefit from that education. The statutory definition of "free appropriate public education," in addition to requiring that States provide each child with "specially designed instruction," expressly requires the provision of "such . . . supportive services . . . as may be required to assist a handicapped child *to benefit* from special education." §1401(17) (emphasis added). We therefore conclude that the "basic floor of opportunity" provided by the Act consists of access to specialized instruction and related services which are individually designed to provide educational benefit to the handicapped child.

The determination of when handicapped children are receiving sufficient educational benefits to satisfy the requirements of the Act presents a more difficult problem. The Act requires participating States to educate a wide spectrum of handicapped children, from the marginally hearing-impaired to the profoundly retarded and palsied. It is clear that the benefits obtainable by children at one end of the spectrum will differ dramatically from those obtainable by children at the other end, with infinite variations in between. One child may have little difficulty competing successfully in an academic setting with nonhandicapped children while another child may encounter great difficulty in acquiring even the most basic of self-maintenance skills. We do not attempt today to establish any one test for determining the adequacy of educational benefits conferred upon all children covered by the Act. Because in this case we are presented with a handicapped child who is receiving substantial specialized instruction and related services, and who is performing above average in the regular classrooms of a public school system, we confine our analysis to that situation.

The Act requires participating States to educate handicapped children with nonhandicapped children whenever possible. When that "mainstreaming" preference of the Act has been met and a child is being educated in the regular classrooms of a public school system, the system itself monitors the educational progress of the child. Regular examinations are administered, grades are awarded, and yearly advancement to higher grade levels is permitted for those children who attain an adequate knowledge of the course material. The grading and advancement system thus constitutes an important factor in determining educational benefit. Children who graduate from our public school systems are considered by our society to have been "educated" at least to the grade level they have completed, and access to an "education" for handicapped children is precisely what Congress sought to provide in the Act.

C

When the language of the Act and its legislative history are considered together, the requirements imposed by Congress become tolerably clear. Insofar as a State is required to provide a handicapped child with a "free appropriate public education," we hold that it satisfies this requirement by providing personalized instruction with sufficient support services to permit the child to benefit educationally from that instruction. Such instruction and services must be provided at public expense, must meet the State's educational standards, must approximate the grade levels used in the State's regular education, and must comport with the child's IEP. In addition, the IEP, and therefore the personalized instruction, should be formulated in accordance with the requirements of the Act and, if the child is being educated in the regular classrooms of the public education system, should be reasonably calculated to enable the child to achieve passing marks and advance from grade to grade. . . .

VI

Applying these principles to the facts of this case, we conclude that the Court of Appeals erred in affirming the decision of the District Court. Neither the District Court nor the Court of Appeals found that petitioners had failed to comply with the procedures of the Act, and the findings of neither court would support a conclusion that Amy's educational program failed to comply with the substantive requirements of the Act. On the contrary, the District Court found that the "evidence firmly establishes that Amy is receiving an 'adequate' education, since she performs better than the average child in her class and is advancing easily from grade to grade." . . . In light of this finding, and of the fact that Amy was receiving personalized instruction and related services calculated by the Furnace Woods school administrators to meet her educational needs, the lower courts should not have concluded that the Act requires the provision of a sign-language interpreter. Accordingly, the decision of the Court of Appeals is reversed, and the case is remanded for further proceedings consistent with this opinion.

Justice WHITE, with whom Justice BRENNAN and Justice MARSHALL join, dissenting.

In order to reach its result in this case, the majority opinion contradicts itself, the language of the statute, and the legislative history. Both the majority's standard for a "free appropriate education" and its standard for judicial review disregard congressional intent.

I

The majority first turns its attention to the meaning of a "free appropriate public education." . . . I agree that the language of the Act does not contain a substantive standard beyond requiring that the education offered must be "appropriate." However, if there are limits not evident from the face of the statute on what may be considered an "appropriate education," they must be found in the purpose of the statute or its legislative history. The Act itself announces it will provide a "*full* educational opportunity to all handicapped children." This goal is repeated throughout the legislative history, in statements too frequent to be "'passing references and isolated phrases.'" These statements elucidate the meaning of "appropriate." According to the Senate Report, for example, the Act does "guarantee that handicapped children are provided *equal* educational opportunity." This promise appears throughout the legislative history. Indeed, at times the purpose of the Act was described as tailoring each handicapped child's educational plan to enable the child "to achieve his or her maximum potential." . . . The legislative history thus directly supports the conclusion that the Act intends to give handicapped children an educational opportunity commensurate with that given other children.

The majority opinion announces a different substantive standard, that "Congress did not impose upon the States any greater substantive educational standard than would be necessary to make such access meaningful." While "meaningful" is no more enlightening than "appropriate," the Court purports to clarify itself. Because Amy was provided with *some* specialized instruction from which she obtained *some* benefit and because she passed from grade to grade, she was receiving a meaningful and therefore appropriate education. . . .

This falls far short of what the Act intended. The Act details as specifically as possible the kind of specialized education each handicapped child must receive. It would apparently satisfy the Court's standard of "access to specialized instruction and related services which are individually designed to provide educational benefit to the handicapped child," for a deaf child such as Amy to be given a teacher with a loud voice, for she would benefit from that service. The Act requires more. It defines "special education" to mean "specifically designed instruction, at no cost to parents or guardians, to *meet the unique needs* of a handicapped child. . . . " Providing a teacher with a loud voice would not meet Amy's needs and would not satisfy the Act. The basic floor of opportunity is instead, as the courts below recognized, intended to eliminate the effects of the handicap, at least to the extent that the child will be given an equal opportunity to learn if that is reasonably possible. Amy Rowley, without a sign-language interpreter, comprehends less than half of what is said in the classroom—less than half of what normal children comprehend. This is hardly an equal opportunity to learn, even if Amy makes passing grades. . . .

NOTES AND QUESTIONS

1. Would you agree with the petitioners here that the Act does not provide judges guidance in deciding questions of "appropriate" public education? The Court states that Congress recognized that some educational settings are simply not suitable for disabled children. How would you support or refute that congressional premise? Why does the Court hold that specialized education services need not be sufficient to maximize each child's potential? How much educational benefit is sufficient? Does this case present a "floor of opportunity" for disabled children or a ceiling? Is "some" specialized instruction meaningful? The dissenting justices in the case argued that "some" specialized instruction in this case would require only a teacher with a loud voice. Is this really what the majority envisioned?
2. In *Rowley,* the Supreme Court left unanswered the question of whether there are disabled children for whom no "appropriate education" is possible. The First Circuit addressed this issue in *Timothy W. v. Rochester, New Hampshire, School District,* 875 F.2d 954 (1st Cir. 1989), finding that no student may be denied an education. The court held:

   > The language the Act could not be more unequivocal. The statute is permeated with the words "*all* handicapped children" whenever it refers to the target population. It never speaks of any exceptions for severely handicapped children. Indeed . . . the Act gives priority to the most severely handicapped. Nor is there any language whatsoever which requires as a prerequisite to being covered by the Act, that a handicapped child must demonstrate that he or she will "benefit" from the educational program. Rather, the Act speaks of the state's responsibility to design a special education and related services program that will meet the unique "needs" of all handicapped children. The language of the Act in its entirety makes clear that a "zero-reject" policy is at the core of the Act, and that no child, regardless of the severity of his or her handicap, is to ever again be subjected to the deplorable state of affairs which existed at the time of the Act's passage, in which millions of handicapped children received inadequate education or none at all.

3. In *Ridgewood Board of Education v. N.E.,* 172 F.3d 238 (3d Cir. 1999), the Third Circuit held that the IDEA requires individualized educational services designed to provide *meaningful* educational benefits. There, a student was diagnosed with a learning disability when a discrepancy appeared between his extremely high intelligence and his relatively low test scores, particularly in reading. The district, after it first resisted identifying the

child as eligible for special educational services, offered the child trivial benefits in the form of placement in a resource center during his regular classes. The student made little progress, and the parents, through a due process hearing, persuaded an Administrative Law Judge that the district's services were inappropriate and inadequate. Ultimately, the Third Circuit agreed that IDEA requires an individualized educational plan that provides significant and meaningful educational benefits, including a district-funded private placement.

4. Although the Supreme Court concluded that IDEA does not itself require school districts to provide services that are designed to maximize a student's potential, the Supreme Court and the lower federal courts since *Rowley* have made clear that states and even local school districts could require higher standards than that required by the federal scheme. *See, e.g., Soraruf v. Pinckney Community Schools,* 208 F.3d 215 (6th Cir. 2000) (Michigan law, but not IDEA, requires services allowing students to reach their "maximum potential"); *Pink by Crider v. Mt. Diablo School District,* 738 F. Supp 345 (N.D. Cal. 1990) (California law requires services designed to allow students to achieve their "full potential").

3. The Statutory Duty to Provide "Special Education and Related Services" for Students with Educational Disabilities

In *Rowley,* the Supreme Court established a definition for appropriate education under the IDEA, but did not address the "related services" requirement included within an appropriate education. In *Tatro,* the Court turned to that question and the corresponding requirements in the Rehabilitation Act.

Irving Independent School District v. Tatro

468 U.S. 883 (1984)

Chief Justice Burger delivered the opinion of the Court.

We granted certiorari to determine whether the Education of the Handicapped Act or the Rehabilitation Act of 1973 requires a school district to provide a handicapped child with clean intermittent catheterization during school hours.

I

Amber Tatro is an 8-year-old girl born with a defect known as spina bifida. As a result, she suffers from orthopedic and speech impairments and a neurogenic bladder, which prevents her from emptying her bladder voluntarily. Consequently, she must be catheterized every three or four hours to avoid injury to her kidneys. In accordance with accepted medical practice, clean intermittent catheterization (CIC), a procedure involving the insertion of a catheter into the urethra to drain the bladder, has been prescribed. The procedure is a simple one that may be performed in a few minutes by a layperson with less than an hour's training. . . .

In 1979 petitioner Irving Independent School District agreed to provide special education for Amber, who was then three and one-half years old. In consultation with her parents, who are respondents here, petitioner developed an individualized education program for Amber under the requirements of the Education of the Handicapped Act, 84 Stat. 175, as amended significantly by the Education for All Handicapped Children Act of 1975, 20 U.S.C. §§1401(19), 1414(a)(5). The individualized education program provided that Amber would attend early childhood development classes and receive special services such as physical and occupational therapy. That program, however, made no provision for school personnel to administer CIC.

Respondents unsuccessfully pursued administrative remedies to secure CIC services for Amber during school hours. In October 1979 respondents brought the present action in District Court against petitioner, the State Board of Education, and others. They sought an injunction ordering petitioner to provide Amber with CIC and sought damages and attorney's fees. First, respondents invoked the Education of the Handicapped Act. Because Texas received funding under that statute, petitioner was required to provide Amber with a "free appropriate public education," which is defined to include "related services." Respondents argued that CIC is one such "related service." Second, respondents invoked §504 of the Rehabilitation Act of 1973, as amended, 29 U.S.C. §794, which forbids an individual, by reason of a handicap, to be "excluded from the participation in, be denied the benefits of, or be subjected to discrimination under" any program receiving federal aid. . . .

II

This case poses two separate issues. The first is whether the Education of the Handicapped Act requires petitioner to provide CIC services to Amber. The second is whether §504 of the Rehabilitation Act creates such an obligation. We first turn to the claim presented under the Education of the Handicapped Act.

States receiving funds under the Act are obliged to satisfy certain conditions. A primary condition is that the state implement a policy "that assures all handicapped children the right to a free appropriate public education." Each educational agency applying to a state for funding must provide assurances in turn that its program aims to provide "a free appropriate public education to all handicapped children."

A "free appropriate public education" is explicitly defined as "special education and related services." The term "special education" means

> specially designed instruction, at no cost to parents or guardians, to meet the unique needs of a handicapped child, including classroom instruction, instruction in physical education, home instruction, and instruction in hospitals and institutions.

"Related services" are defined as

> transportation, and such developmental, corrective, and other supportive services (including speech pathology and audiology, psychological services, physical and occupational therapy, recreation, and medical and counseling services, except that such medical services shall be for diagnostic and

> evaluation purposes only) as may be required to assist a handicapped child to benefit from special education, and includes the early identification and assessment of handicapping conditions in children.

The issue in this case is whether CIC is a "related service" that petitioner is obliged to provide to Amber. We must answer two questions: first, whether CIC is a "supportive servic[e] . . . required to assist a handicapped child to benefit from special education"; and second, whether CIC is excluded from this definition as a "medical servic[e]" serving purposes other than diagnosis or evaluation.

A

The Court of Appeals was clearly correct in holding that CIC is a "supportive servic[e] . . . required to assist a handicapped child to benefit from special education." It is clear on this record that, without having CIC services available during the school day, Amber cannot attend school and thereby "benefit from special education." CIC services therefore fall squarely within the definition of a "supportive service."

As we have stated before, "Congress sought primarily to make public education available to handicapped children" and "to make such access meaningful." *Board of Education of Hendrick Hudson Central School District v. Rowley.* A service that enables a handicapped child to remain at school during the day is an important means of providing the child with the meaningful access to education that Congress envisioned. The Act makes specific provision for services, like transportation, for example, that do no more than enable a child to be physically present in class; and the Act specifically authorizes grants for schools to alter buildings and equipment to make them accessible to the handicapped. Services like CIC that permit a child to remain at school during the day are no less related to the effort to educate than are services that enable the child to reach, enter, or exit the school.

We hold that CIC services in this case qualify as a "supportive servic[e] . . . required to assist a handicapped child to benefit from special education."

B

We also agree with the Court of Appeals that provision of CIC is not a "medical servic[e]," which a school is required to provide only for purposes of diagnosis or evaluation. We begin with the regulations of the Department of Education, which are entitled to deference. The regulations define "related services" for handicapped children to include "school health services," which are defined in turn as "services provided by a qualified school nurse or other qualified person.""Medical services" are defined as "services provided by a licensed physician." Thus, the Secretary has determined that the services of a school nurse otherwise qualifying as a "related service" are not subject to exclusion as a "medical service," but that the services of a physician are excludable as such.

This definition of "medical services" is a reasonable interpretation of congressional intent. Although Congress devoted little discussion to the "medical services" exclusion, the Secretary could reasonably have concluded that it was designed to spare schools from an obligation to provide a service that might well prove unduly expensive and beyond the range of their competence. From this understanding of congressional purpose, the Secretary could reasonably have concluded that Congress intended to impose the obligation to provide school nursing services.

Congress plainly required schools to hire various specially trained personnel to help handicapped children, such as "trained occupational therapists, speech therapists, psychologists, social workers and other appropriately trained personnel." School nurses have long been a part of the educational system, and the Secretary could therefore reasonably conclude that school nursing services are not the sort of burden that Congress intended to exclude as a "medical service." By limiting the "medical services" exclusion to the services of a physician or hospital, both far more expensive, the Secretary has given a permissible construction to the provision.

Petitioner's contrary interpretation of the "medical services" exclusion is unconvincing. In petitioner's view, CIC is a "medical service," even though it may be provided by a nurse or trained layperson; that conclusion rests on its reading of Texas law that confines CIC to uses in accordance with a physician's prescription and under a physician's ultimate supervision. Aside from conflicting with the Secretary's reasonable interpretation of congressional intent, however, such a rule would be anomalous. Nurses in petitioner School District are authorized to dispense oral medications and administer emergency injections in accordance with a physician's prescription. This kind of service for nonhandicapped children is difficult to distinguish from the provision of CIC to the handicapped. It would be strange indeed if Congress, in attempting to extend special services to handicapped children, were unwilling to guarantee them services of a kind that are routinely provided to the nonhandicapped.

To keep in perspective the obligation to provide services that relate to both the health and educational needs of handicapped students, we note several limitations that should minimize the burden petitioner fears. First, to be entitled to related services, a child must be handicapped so as to require special education. In the absence of a handicap that requires special education, the need for what otherwise might qualify as a related service does not create an obligation under the Act.

Second, only those services necessary to aid a handicapped child to benefit from special education must be provided, regardless how easily a school nurse or layperson could furnish them. For example, if a particular medication or treatment may appropriately be administered to a handicapped child other than during the school day, a school is not required to provide nursing services to administer it.

Third, the regulations state that school nursing services must be provided only if they can be performed by a nurse or other qualified person, not if they must be performed by a physician. It bears mentioning that here not even the services of a nurse are required; as is conceded, a layperson with minimal training is qualified to provide CIC.

Finally, we note that respondents are not asking petitioner to provide equipment that Amber needs for CIC. They seek only the services of a qualified person at the school.

We conclude that provision of CIC to Amber is not subject to exclusion as a "medical service," and we affirm the Court of Appeals' holding that CIC is a "related service" under the Education of the Handicapped Act.

NOTES AND QUESTIONS

1. Why do you think Congress distinguished supportive services from medical services? Does the limitation of medical services to diagnosis and evaluation make sense? What does the Court add to this definition?
2. The Supreme Court states here that related services allow the child to obtain a meaningful education. How does this fit with the definition of "meaningful" in *Rowley*?
3. Here, petitioners did not ask the school to provide any equipment for Amber's related services. What if they had? Would that fact have changed the outcome?
4. The Supreme Court further defined "related services" under IDEA in the following *Garret F.* case. Consider the Court's treatment of *Tatro* in *Garret F.*

CEDAR RAPIDS COMMUNITY SCHOOL DISTRICT v. GARRET F.

526 U.S. 66 (1999)

Justice STEVENS delivered the opinion of the Court.

The Individuals with Disabilities Education Act (IDEA), 84 Stat. 175, as amended, was enacted, in part, "to assure that all children with disabilities have available to them . . . a free appropriate public education which emphasizes special education and related services designed to meet their unique needs." Consistent with this purpose, the IDEA authorizes federal financial assistance to States that agree to provide disabled children with special education and "related services." The question presented in this case is whether the definition of "related services" in §1401(a)(17) requires a public school district in a participating State to provide a ventilator-dependent student with certain nursing services during school hours.

I

Respondent Garret F. is a friendly, creative, and intelligent young man. When Garret was four years old, his spinal column was severed in a motorcycle accident. Though paralyzed from the neck down, his mental capacities were unaffected. He is able to speak, to control his motorized wheelchair through use of a puff and suck straw, and to operate a computer with a device that responds to head movements. Garret is currently a student in the Cedar Rapids Community School District (District), he attends regular classes in a typical school program, and his academic performance has been a success. Garret is, however, ventilator dependent, and therefore requires a responsible individual nearby to attend to certain physical needs while he is in school.

During Garret's early years at school his family provided for his physical care during the school day. When he was in kindergarten, his 18-year-old aunt attended him; in the next four years, his family used settlement proceeds they received after the accident, their insurance, and other resources to employ a licensed practical nurse. In 1993, Garret's mother requested the District to accept financial responsibility for the health care services that Garret requires during the school day. The District denied the request, believing that it was not legally obligated to provide continuous one-on-one nursing services.

Relying on both the IDEA and Iowa law, Garret's mother requested a hearing before the Iowa Department of Education. An Administrative Law Judge (ALJ) received extensive evidence concerning Garret's special needs, the District's treatment of other disabled students, and the assistance provided to other ventilator-dependent children in other parts of the country. In his 47-page report, the ALJ found that the District has about 17,500 students, of whom approximately 2,200 need some form of special education or special services. Although Garret is the only ventilator-dependent student in the District, most of the health care services that he needs are already provided for some other students. "The primary difference between Garret's situation and that of other students is his dependency on his ventilator for life support." The ALJ noted that the parties disagreed over the training or licensure required for the care and supervision of such students, and that those providing such care in other parts of the country ranged from nonlicensed personnel to registered nurses. However, the District did not contend that only a licensed physician could provide the services in question.

The ALJ explained that federal law requires that children with a variety of health impairments be provided with "special education and related services" when their disabilities adversely affect their academic performance, and that such children should be educated to the maximum extent appropriate with children who are not disabled. In addition, the ALJ explained that applicable federal regulations distinguish between "school health services," which are provided by a "qualified school nurse or other qualified person," and "medical services," which are provided by a licensed physician. The District must provide the former, but need not provide the latter (except, of course, those "medical services" that are for diagnostic or evaluation purposes). According to the ALJ, the distinction in the regulations does not just depend on "the title of the person providing the service"; instead, the "medical services" exclusion is limited to services that are "in the special training, knowledge, and judgment of a physician to carry out." The ALJ thus concluded that the IDEA required the District to bear financial responsibility for all of the services in dispute, including continuous nursing services.

The District challenged the ALJ's decision in Federal District Court, but that court approved the ALJ's IDEA ruling and granted summary judgment against the District. The Court of Appeals affirmed. It noted that, as a recipient of federal funds under the IDEA, Iowa has a statutory duty to provide all disabled children a "free appropriate public education," which includes "related services." The Court of Appeals read our opinion in *Irving Independent School District v. Tatro,* 468 U.S. 883 (1984), to provide a two-step analysis of the "related services" definition in §1401(a)(17)—asking first, whether the requested services are included within the phrase "supportive services"; and second, whether the services are excluded as "medical services." The Court of

Appeals succinctly answered both questions in Garret's favor. The Court found the first step plainly satisfied, since Garret cannot attend school unless the requested services are available during the school day. As to the second step, the court reasoned that *Tatro* "established a bright-line test: the services of a physician (other than for diagnostic and evaluation purposes) are subject to the medical services exclusion, but services that can be provided in the school setting by a nurse or qualified layperson are not."

In its petition for certiorari, the District challenged only the second step of the Court of Appeals' analysis. The District pointed out that some federal courts have not asked whether the requested health services must be delivered by a physician, but instead have applied a multifactor test that considers, generally speaking, the nature and extent of the services at issue. We granted the District's petition to resolve this conflict.

II

The District contends that §1401(a)(17) does not require it to provide Garret with "continuous one-on-one nursing services" during the school day, even though Garret cannot remain in school without such care. However, the IDEA's definition of "related services," our decision in *Irving Independent School District v. Tatro,* and the overall statutory scheme all support the decision of the Court of Appeals.

The text of the "related services" definition, broadly encompasses those supportive services that "may be required to assist a child with a disability to benefit from special education." As we have already noted, the District does not challenge the Court of Appeals' conclusion that the in-school services at issue are within the covered category of "supportive services." As a general matter, services that enable a disabled child to remain in school during the day provide the student with "the meaningful access to education that Congress envisioned." *Tatro,* 468 U.S., at 891 ("'Congress sought primarily to make public education available to handicapped children' and 'to make such access meaningful'" (quoting *Board of Ed. of Hendrick Hudson Central School Dist., Westchester Cty. v. Rowley,* 458 U.S. 176, 192, 102 S. Ct. 3034, 73 L. Ed. 2d 690 (1982))).

This general definition of "related services" is illuminated by a parenthetical phrase listing examples of particular services that are included within the statute's coverage. §1401(a)(17). "[M]edical services" are enumerated in this list, but such services are limited to those that are "for diagnostic and evaluation purposes." The statute does not contain a more specific definition of the "medical services" that are excepted from the coverage of §1401(a)(17).

The scope of the "medical services" exclusion is not a matter of first impression in this Court. In *Tatro* we concluded that the Secretary of Education had reasonably determined that the term "medical services" referred only to services that must be performed by a physician, and not to school health services. Accordingly, we held that a specific form of health care (clean intermittent catheterization) that is often, though not always, performed by a nurse is not an excluded medical service. We referenced the likely cost of the services and the competence of school staff as justifications for drawing a line between physician and other services, but our endorsement of that line was unmistakable. It is thus settled that the phrase "medical services" in §1401(a)(17) does not embrace all forms of care that might loosely be described as "medical" in other contexts, such as a claim for an income tax deduction.

The District does not ask us to define the term so broadly. Indeed, the District does not argue that any of the items of care that Garret needs, considered individually, could be excluded from the scope of 20 U.S.C. §1401(a)(17). It could not make such an argument, considering that one of the services Garret needs (catheterization) was at issue in *Tatro,* and the others may be provided competently by a school nurse or other trained personnel. As the ALJ concluded, most of the requested services are already provided by the District to other students, and the in-school care necessitated by Garret's ventilator dependency does not demand the training, knowledge, and judgment of a licensed physician. While more extensive, the in-school services Garret needs are no more "medical" than was the care sought in *Tatro.*

Instead, the District points to the combined and continuous character of the required care, and proposes a test under which the outcome in any particular case would depend upon a series of factors, such as [1] whether the care is continuous or intermittent, [2] whether existing school health personnel can provide the service, [3] the cost of the service, and [4] the potential consequences if the service is not properly "performed."

The District's multifactor test is not supported by any recognized source of legal authority. The proposed factors can be found in neither the text of the statute nor the regulations that we upheld in *Tatro.* Moreover, the District offers no explanation why these characteristics make one service any more "medical" than another. The continuous character of certain services associated with Garret's ventilator dependency has no apparent relationship to "medical" services, much less a relationship of equivalence. Continuous services may be more costly and may require additional school personnel, but they are not thereby more "medical." Whatever its imperfections, a rule that limits the medical services exemption to physician services is unquestionably a reasonable and generally workable interpretation of the statute. Absent an elaboration of the statutory terms plainly more convincing than that which we reviewed in *Tatro,* there is no good reason to depart from settled law.

Finally, the District raises broader concerns about the financial burden that it must bear to provide the services that Garret needs to stay in school. The problem for the District in providing these services is not that its staff cannot be trained to deliver them; the problem, the District contends, is that the existing school health staff cannot meet all of their responsibilities and provide for Garret at the same time. Through its multifactor test, the District seeks to establish a kind of undue-burden exemption primarily based upon the cost of the requested services. The first two factors can be seen as examples of cost-based distinctions: Intermittent care is often less expensive than continuous care, and the use of existing personnel is cheaper than hiring additional employees. The third factor — the cost of the service — would then encompass the first two. The relevance of the fourth factor is likewise related to cost because extra care may be necessary if potential consequences are especially serious.

The District may have legitimate financial concerns, but our role in this dispute is to interpret existing law. Defining "related services" in a manner that *accommodates* the cost concerns Congress may have had, cf. *Tatro,* is altogether different from using cost *itself as* the definition. Given that §1401(a)(17) does not employ cost in its definition of "related services" or excluded "medical services," accepting the District's cost-based standard as the sole test for determining the scope of the provision would require us to engage in judicial law-making without any guidance from Congress. It would also create some tension with the purposes of the IDEA. The statute may not require public schools to maximize the potential of disabled students commensurate with the opportunities provided to other children, *see Rowley,* and the potential financial burdens imposed on participating States may be relevant to arriving at a sensible construction of the IDEA, *see Tatro.* But Congress intended "to open the door of public education" to all qualified children and "require[d] participating States to educate handicapped children with nonhandicapped children whenever possible."

This case is about whether meaningful access to the public schools will be assured, not the level of education that a school must finance once access is attained. It is undisputed that the services at issue must be provided if Garret is to remain in school. Under the statute, our precedent, and the purposes of the IDEA, the District must fund such "related services" in order to help guarantee that students like Garret are integrated into the public schools.

The judgment of the Court of Appeals is accordingly *Affirmed.*

NOTES AND QUESTIONS

1. As the Supreme Court suggests, Congress, in the Education for All Handicapped Children Act and IDEA, has mandated that "*all* handicapped children" must receive "special education and related services" at "public expense." 20 U.S.C. §1401(a)(18); 34 C.F.R. §300.4. In *Timothy W. v. Rochester, New Hampshire School District,* 875 F.2d 954 (1st Cir. 1989), the federal district court initially held that a "severely retarded and multiply handicapped" child is not eligible for special education and related services because there was no showing that the child could "benefit from that education." As we have seen, however, the Court of Appeals flatly rejected that interpretation of the Education for All Handicapped Children Act. The First Circuit declared: "a school district has a duty to provide an educational program for every handicapped child in the district, regardless of the severity of the handicap. . . . The district court erred in requiring a benefit/eligibility test. . . . "
2. Should the financial burdens on a school be influential in determining whether a disabled child will receive a particular benefit or service? In *Garret F.,* the Cedar Rapids school district proposed a multifactoral test that would have permitted the courts to weigh the financial burdens of providing "related services" in defining what is meant by "related services." The Supreme Court recognizes the district's "legitimate financial concerns" but finds no legal support for its legal position. Nonetheless, the Court

does indicate that defining related services "in a manner that *accommodates* the cost concerns" Congress may have had would be appropriate (emphasis in original). *See also Clevenger v. Oak Ridge School Board,* 744 F.2d 514 (6th Cir. 1984) ("cost can be a legitimate consideration . . . only . . . when choosing between several options, all of which offer an appropriate education."). What "cost concerns" might Congress have had that would be relevant to the definition of related services?

3. The courts have placed the burden squarely on school districts and their educational professionals to construct and implement an appropriate education for all students with educational disabilities. *See, e.g., M.C. on behalf of J.C. v. Central Regional School District,* 81 F.3d 389 (3d Cir. 1996) (burden of determining and instituting appropriate individualized educational plan on district, not parents); *Oberti v. Clementon School District Board of Education,* 995 F.2d 1204 (3d Cir. 1993) (school district bears burden of compliance with statutory requirements).

4. The Statutory Duty of Placement in the "Least Restrictive Environment" for Students with Educational Disabilities

Under IDEA, students with educational disabilities must be placed in an appropriate program of special education and related services. The IDEA, 20 U.S.C. §1412(a)(5)(A), expressly declares the congressional objective and philosophy that, whenever possible, students with educational disabilities should be "placed" in the same educational environment as children without educational disabilities: "To the maximum extent appropriate, children with disabilities . . . [must be] educated with children who are not disabled. . . ." *Id. See also* 34 C.F.R. §300.551.

Congress further provides that "removal of children with disabilities from the regular educational environment" may occur only when the "nature or severity of the disability of a child is such that education in regular classes with the use of supplementary aids and services cannot be achieved satisfactorily." 20 U.S.C. §1412(a)(5)(A). The federal regulations implementing this statute make clear that school districts must strive to place a child in the "least restrictive environment" on a "continuum of alternative placements." 34 C.F.R. §300.551.

The federal courts consistently have interpreted IDEA and its regulations to establish a strong congressional directive that school districts integrate children with educational disabilities into the so-called regular classroom. *See, e.g., Daniel R.R. v. State Board of Education,* 874 F.2d 1036 (5th Cir. 1989); *Roncker v. Walter,* 700 F.2d 1058 (6th Cir. 1983), *cert. denied,* 464 U.S. 864 (1983). The integration of disabled students into the regular classroom is often described by courts and educators as either "mainstreaming" or "inclusion." *See, e.g., Oberti v. Clementon School District Board of Education,* 995 F.2d 1204 (3d Cir. 1993) (recognizing that "inclusion" may be a more precise term than "mainstreaming" for keeping students with educational disabilities in the regular classroom, but nonetheless adopting the more frequently used term "mainstreaming").

The courts have developed alternative evidentiary tests to determine whether a school district has met its statutory burden of "mainstreaming" or "inclusion." In *Roncker v. Walter,* the Sixth Circuit established an influential test that requires the school district to justify any decision not to mainstream a student by affirmatively demonstrating that the benefits of mainstreaming for the child are "marginal" and are "far outweighed by the benefit gained from services which could not be feasibly provided in the nonsegregated setting." The Fourth and Eighth Circuits have adopted this *Roncker* approach. *See DeVries v. Fairfax County School Board,* 882 F.2d 876 (4th Cir. 1989); *A.W. v. Northwest R-1 School District,* 813 F.2d 158 (8th Cir. 1987).

In *Daniel R.R. v. State Board of Education,* 874 F.2d 1036 (5th Cir. 1989), however, the Fifth Circuit created an equally influential test that analyzes first whether education can be achieved in the regular classroom with the help of supplemental services. If so, the school must provide that educational environment and those services. Even if a child cannot fully be integrated into the regular classroom, the district still must include the child in that classroom "to the maximum extent appropriate." In *Oberti,* the Third Circuit considered the alternative tests developed by the federal courts and adopted the *Daniel R.R.* approach. In that case, the court concluded that the school district had violated the mainstreaming requirement of IDEA by failing to prove by a preponderance of the evidence that an eight-year-old child with Down's Syndrome "could not be educated satisfactorily in a regular classroom with supplementary aids and services."

In *Sacramento City School District v. Rachel H,* 14 F.3d 1398 (9th Cir. 1994), the Ninth Circuit appears to combine elements of the tests supplied by both the *Daniel R.R.* and *Roncker* cases. *See also Clyde K. v. Puyallup,* 35 F.3d 1396 (9th Cir. 1997).

Sacramento City Unified School District, Board of Education v. Rachel H.

14 F.3d 1398 (9th Cir. 1994)

Sneed, Circuit Judge:

The Sacramento Unified School District ("the District") timely appeals the district court's judgment in favor of Rachel Holland ("Rachel") and the California State Department of Education. The court found that the appropriate placement for Rachel under the Individuals with Disabilities Act ("IDEA") was full-time in a regular second grade classroom with some supplemental services. The District contends that the appropriate placement for Rachel is half-time in special education classes and half-time in a regular class. We affirm the judgment of the district court.

I. Facts and Prior Proceedings

Rachel Holland is now 11 years old and is moderately mentally retarded. She was tested with an I.Q. of 44. She attended a variety of special education programs in the District from 1985-89. Her parents sought to increase the time Rachel spent in a regular classroom, and in the fall of 1989, they requested that Rachel be placed full-time in a regular classroom for the 1989-90 school year. The District rejected their request and proposed a placement that would have divided Rachel's time between a special education class for academic subjects and a regular class for non-academic activities such as art, music, lunch, and recess. The district court found that this plan would have required moving Rachel at least 6 times each day between the two classrooms. The Hollands instead enrolled Rachel in a regular kindergarten class at the Shalom School, a private school. Rachel remained at the Shalom School in regular classes and at the time the district court rendered its opinion, was in the second grade.

The Hollands and the District were able to agree on an Individualized Education Program ("IEP") for Rachel. Although the IEP is required to be reviewed annually, *see* 20 U.S.C. §1401(20)(B), because of the dispute between the parties, Rachel's IEP has not been reviewed since January 1990.[3]

The Hollands appealed the District's placement decision to a state hearing officer pursuant to 20 U.S.C. §1415(b)(2). They maintained that Rachel best learned social and academic skills in a regular classroom and would not benefit from being in a special education class. The District contended Rachel was too severely disabled to benefit from full-time placement in a regular class. The hearing officer concluded that the District had failed to make an adequate effort to educate Rachel in a regular class pursuant to the IDEA. The officer found that (1) Rachel had benefitted from her regular kindergarten class—that she was motivated to learn and learned by imitation and modeling; (2) Rachel was not disruptive in a regular classroom; and (3) the District had overstated the cost of putting Rachel in regular education—that the cost would not be so great that it weighed against placing her in a regular classroom. The hearing officer ordered the District to place Rachel in a regular classroom with support services, including a special education consultant and a part-time aide.

The District appealed this determination to the district court. Pursuant to 20 U.S.C. §1415(e)(2), the parties presented additional evidence at an evidentiary hearing. The court affirmed the decision of the hearing officer that Rachel should be placed full-time in a regular classroom.

In considering whether the District proposed an appropriate placement for Rachel, the district court examined the following factors: (1) the educational benefits available to Rachel in a regular classroom, supplemented with appropriate aids and services, as compared with the educational benefits of a special education classroom; (2) the non-academic benefits of interaction with children who were not disabled; (3) the effect of Rachel's presence on the teacher and other children in the classroom; and (4) the cost of mainstreaming Rachel in a regular classroom.

---

[3] The 1990 IEP objectives include: speaking in 4 or 5 word sentences; repeating instructions of complex tasks; initiating and terminating conversations; stating her name, address and phone number; participating in a safety program with classmates; developing a 24 word sight vocabulary; counting to 25; printing her first and last names and the alphabet; playing co-operatively; participating in lunch without supervision; and identifying upper and lower case letters and the sounds associated with them.

1. Educational Benefits

The district court found the first factor, educational benefits to Rachel, weighed in favor of placing her in a regular classroom. Each side presented expert testimony which is summarized in the margin.[4] The court noted that the District's evidence focused on Rachel's limitations, but did not establish that the educational opportunities available through special education were better or equal to those available in a regular classroom. Moreover, the court found that the testimony of the Hollands' experts was more credible because they had more background in evaluating children with disabilities placed in regular classrooms, and they had a greater opportunity to observe Rachel over an extended period of time in normal circumstances. The district court also gave great weight to the testimony of Rachel's current teacher, Nina Crone, who the court found to be an experienced, skillful teacher. Ms. Crone stated that Rachel was a full member of the class and participated in all activities. Ms. Crone testified that Rachel was making progress on her IEP goals—that Rachel was learning one-to-one correspondence in counting, could recite the English and Hebrew alphabets, and that her communication abilities and sentence lengths were also improving.

The district court found that Rachel received substantial benefits in regular education and that all of her IEP goals could be implemented in a regular classroom with some modification to the curriculum and with the assistance of a part-time aide.

2. Non-academic Benefits

The district court next found that the second factor, non-academic benefits to Rachel, also weighed in favor of placing her in a regular classroom. The court noted that the Hollands' evidence indicated that Rachel had developed her social and communications skills as well as her self-confidence from placement in a regular class, while the District's evidence tended to show that Rachel was not learning from exposure to other children and that she was isolated from her classmates. The court concluded that the differing evaluations in large part reflected the predisposition of the evaluators. The court found the testimony of Rachel's mother and her current teacher to be the most credible. These witnesses testified regarding Rachel's excitement about school, learning, and her new friendships, and Rachel's improved self-confidence.

3. Effect on the Teacher and Children in the Regular Class

The district court next addressed the issue of whether Rachel had a detrimental effect on others in her regular classroom. The court looked at two aspects, (1) whether there was detriment because the child was disruptive, distracting or unruly, and (2) whether the child would take up so much of the teacher's time that the other students would suffer from lack of attention. The witnesses of both parties agreed that Rachel followed directions, was

---

[4] The Hollands' experts testified Rachel had made significant strides at the Shalom School, and suggested that her motivation stemmed from her regular classroom placement. They stated Rachel was learning language and other skills from modeling the behavior of the other students. The District's experts, from the state Diagnostic Center, testified that Rachel had made little progress toward her IEP goals, derived little benefit from regular class placement and suggested supplementary aids would be ineffective.

well-behaved and not a distraction in class. The court found the most germane evidence on the second aspect came from Rachel's second grade teacher, Nina Crone, who testified that Rachel did not interfere with her ability to teach the other children and in the future would require only a part-time aide. Accordingly, the district court determined that the third factor weighed in favor of placing Rachel in a regular classroom.

4. Cost

Finally, the district court found that the District had not offered any persuasive or credible evidence to support its claim that educating Rachel in a regular classroom with appropriate services would be significantly more expensive than educating her in the District's proposed setting.

The District contended that it would cost $109,000 to educate Rachel full-time in a regular classroom. This figure was based upon a full-time aide for Rachel and an estimate that it would cost over $80,000 to provide school-wide sensitivity training. The court found that the District did not establish that such training was necessary, and if it was, the court noted that there was evidence from the California Department of Education that the training could be had at no cost. Moreover, the court found it would be inappropriate to assign the total cost of the training to Rachel when other children with disabilities would benefit. In addition, the court concluded that the evidence did not suggest that Rachel required a full-time aide.

In addition, the court found that the comparison should have been between, on the one hand, the cost of placing Rachel in a special class with a full-time special education teacher and two full-time aides with approximately 11 other children, and, on the other hand, the cost of placing her in a regular class with a part-time aide. It noted, however, that the District had provided no evidence of this cost comparison.

The court also was not persuaded by the District's argument that it would lose significant funding if Rachel did not spend at least 51% of her time in a special education class. The court noted that a witness from the California Department of Education testified that waivers were available if a school district sought to adopt a program that did not fit neatly within the funding guidelines. The District had not applied for a waiver, however.

Thus, by inflating the cost estimates and failing to address the true comparison, the District did not meet its burden of proving that regular placement would burden the District's funds or adversely affect services available to other children. Therefore, the court found that the cost factor did not weigh against mainstreaming Rachel.

The district court concluded that the appropriate placement for Rachel was full-time in a regular second grade classroom with some supplemental services and affirmed the decision of the hearing officer. . . .

B. Mainstreaming Requirements of the IDEA

1. The Statute

The IDEA provides that each state must establish:

> Procedures to assure that, to the maximum extent appropriate, children with disabilities . . . are educated with children who are not disabled, and that

> special classes, separate schooling, or other removal of children with disabilities from the regular educational environment occurs only when the nature or severity of the disability is such that education in regular classes with the use of supplementary aids and services cannot be achieved satisfactorily. . . .

20 U.S.C. §1412(5)(B).

This provision sets forth Congress's preference for educating children with disabilities in regular classrooms with their peers. . . .

2. Burden of Proof

There is a conflict regarding which party bears the burden of proof. The Third Circuit has held that a school district has the initial burden of justifying its educational placement at the administrative level *and* the burden in the district court if the student is challenging the agency decision. Other circuits have held that the burden of proof in the district court rests with the party challenging the agency decision. *See Roland M. v. Concord Sch. Comm.,* 910 F.2d 983, 991 (1st Cir. 1990), *cert. denied,* 499 U.S. 912 (1991); *Kerkam v. McKenzie,* 862 F.2d 884, 887 (D.C. Cir. 1988). Under either approach, in this case the District, which was challenging the agency decision, had the burden of demonstrating in the district court that its proposed placement provided mainstreaming to "the maximum extent appropriate."

3. Test for Determining Compliance with the IDEA's Mainstreaming Requirement

We have not adopted or devised a standard for determining the presence of compliance with 20 U.S.C. §1412(5)(B). The Third, Fifth and Eleventh Circuits use what is known as the *Daniel R.R.* test. The Fourth, Sixth and Eighth Circuits apply the *Roncker* test. . . .

Although the district court relied principally on *Daniel R.R.* and *Greer,* it did not specifically adopt the *Daniel R.R.* test over the *Roncker* test. Rather, it employed factors found in both lines of cases in its analysis. The result was a four factor balancing test in which the court considered (1) the educational benefits of placement full-time in a regular class; (2) the non-academic benefits of such placement; (3) the effect Rachel had on the teacher and children in the regular class, and (4) the costs of mainstreaming Rachel. This analysis directly addresses the issue of the appropriate placement for a child with disabilities under the requirements of 20 U.S.C. §1412(5)(b). Accordingly, we approve and adopt the test employed by the district court.

4. The District's Contentions on Appeal

The District strenuously disagrees with the district court's findings that Rachel was receiving academic and non-academic benefits in a regular class and did not have a detrimental effect on the teacher or other students. It argues that the court's findings were contrary to the evidence of the state Diagnostic Center, and that the court should not have been persuaded by the testimony of Rachel's teacher, particularly her testimony that Rachel would need only a part-time aide in the future. The district court, however, conducted a full evidentiary hearing and made a thorough analysis. The court found the Hollands' evidence to be more persuasive. Moreover, the court asked Rachel's teacher extensive questions regarding Rachel's need for a part-time aide. We will not disturb the findings of the district court.

The District is also not persuasive on the issue of cost. The District now claims that it will lose up to $190,764 in state special education funding if Rachel is not enrolled in a special education class at least 51% of the day. However, the District has not sought a waiver pursuant to California Education Code §56101. This section provides that (1) any school district may request a waiver of any provision of the Education Code if the waiver is necessary or beneficial to the student's IEP, and (2) the Board may grant the waiver when failure to do so would hinder compliance with federal mandates for a free appropriate education for children with disabilities. Cal. Ed. Code §56101(a) & (b). (Deering 1992).

Finally, the District, citing *Wilson v. Marana Unified Sch. Dist.*, 735 F.2d 1178 (9th Cir. 1984), argues that Rachel must receive her academic and functional curriculum in special education from a specially credentialed teacher. *Wilson* does not stand for this proposition. Rather, the court in *Wilson* stated:

> The school district argues that under state law a child who qualifies for special education *must be* taught by a teacher who is certificated in that child's particular area of disability. We do not agree and do not reach a decision on that broad assertion. We hold only, under our standard of review, that the school district's decision was a reasonable one under the circumstances of this case.

735 F.2d at 1180 (emphasis in original). More importantly, the District's proposition that Rachel must be taught by a special education teacher runs directly counter to the congressional preference that children with disabilities be educated in regular classes with children who are not disabled. *See* 20 U.S.C. §1412(5)(B).

We affirm the judgment of the district court. While we cannot determine what the appropriate placement is for Rachel at the present time, we hold that the determination of the present and future appropriate placement for Rachel should be based upon the principles set forth in this opinion and the opinion of the district court.

Affirmed.

5. The Statutory Duty to Provide an Alternative, Appropriate Placement

Where a public school district or LEA is unable to provide a student with educational disabilities with an "appropriate" education in its own facilities, the district is nevertheless required to locate and pay for an appropriate alternative placement, including a private school placement. 20 U.S.C. §1412(a)(10)(B). Where the public school district or LEA decides to refer or place a student in a private school as a means of providing the required appropriate education and related services for that student, the district must reimburse the parents for the costs. 20 U.S.C. §1412(a)(10)(B).

In *School Committee of Burlington v. Massachusetts Department of Education*, 471 U.S. 359 (1985), the Supreme Court held that the federal courts have the power to enforce the IDEA by requiring school districts to fund private placements where the public school's individualized educational plans have been found to be inappropriate. In *Florence County School District v. Carter,* 510 U.S. 7 (1993), the Court extended its reasoning in *Burlington* to require public school districts to reimburse parents for the cost of a private placement for children with educational disabilities, even where the parents "unilaterally withdraw their child from a public school that provides an inappropriate education under IDEA and put the child in a private school that provides an education that is otherwise proper under IDEA." 510 U.S. at 9. Moreover, in *Board of Ed. of the City School Dist. of New York v. Tom F.,* 128 S.Ct. 1 (2007), the Supreme Court split 4-4, thereby affirming the lower court's opinion that a public school district must reimburse parents for the costs of an alternative, appropriate private placement, even if the child has not first attempted a public school placement.

These cases therefore require an analysis of two issues: (1) whether the public school district has developed an appropriate individualized educational placement under IDEA, and (2) whether the alternative placement provides such an appropriate program under IDEA. If the public school placement is inappropriate, the parents have the unilateral right to remove their child and require the school district to fund an alternative, appropriate placement in a private school. *See also Muller v. Committee on Special Education,* 145 F.3d 95 (2d Cir. 1998).

In response to these court decisions, Congress enacted Amendments to IDEA, which routinize the process of securing an alternative placement. 20 U.S.C. §1412(a)(10)(C). The statute now reaffirms that a public school district is not required to fund a private school placement unilaterally selected by the parents so long as the public school itself is able to offer the student with educational disabilities an "appropriate" education under IDEA. 20 U.S.C. §1412(a)(10)(C). If, however, a hearing officer or court determines that the public school has failed to provide such an appropriate education, the public school may be ordered to reimburse the parents for the costs of their unilaterally chosen private school placement. *Id.* Reimbursement may now be reduced or denied, however, if the parents fail to give the district sufficient written notice of their intent to remove the child from the public school placement or if the parents have otherwise acted in an "unreasonable" manner. 20 U.S.C. §1412(a)(10)(C)(iii).

Moreover, these Amendments to IDEA do not necessarily require a public school to administer or fund the full services given the student on the site of the private school in which the student voluntarily enrolls. *See, e.g., Russman v. Board of Education,* 150 F.3d 219, 222 (2d Cir. 1998); *Cefalu v. East Baton Rouge Parish School Board,* 117 F.3d 231, 233 (5th Cir. 1997). Rather, the public school is required to "purchase" those services with a "proportionate amount" of the federal funds allocated to the district under IDEA. *Foley v. Special School District of St. Louis County,* 153 F.3d 863, 865 (8th Cir. 1998); *Fowler v. Unified School District No. 259,* 128 F.3d 1431, 1437 (10th Cir. 1997).

As we have seen, the issues of placement and funding for special education students become more complicated when the private school placement has a religious affiliation. The Amendments to IDEA make clear that any special education services required by IDEA "may be provided to children . . . on the premises of private, including parochial schools, to the extent consistent with law." 20 U.S.C. §1412(a)(10)(A)(i)(II). The "law" governing the constitutionality of a public school's provision of special education services at a parochial school is reflected in *Zobrest v. Catalina Foothills School District,* 509 U.S. 1 (1993). Recall that in that case, the Supreme Court held that the establishment clause of the First Amendment does not prevent a public school district from furnishing a student with a sign-language interpreter on the site of a parochial school pursuant to the mandates of IDEA. The Supreme Court characterized IDEA as a general government program that distributes benefits on a religiously neutral basis to any child qualifying for services under the statute. Consistent with *Zobrest,* the IDEA Amendments allow, but do not require, special education services to be provided at a parochial school. 20 U.S.C. §1412(a)(10)(A)(i)(II). *See also KDM v. Reedsport School District,* 196 F.3d 1046 (9th Cir. 1999).

Accordingly, under IDEA, the placement and funding responsibilities with respect to parochial schools are identical to those regarding any private school. First, where the public school district chooses to refer or place a student with educational disabilities into a private school with a religious affiliation, the district will be required to reimburse parents for the cost of that placement. 20 U.S.C. §1412(a)(10)(B). Second, if the parents voluntarily choose to place their child in a parochial school, the public school district will be required to expend only a proportionate amount of its federal funding under IDEA on services for the child, and only if the public school district itself has been unable to provide an appropriate education for the child.

6. The Statutory Duty to Provide Procedural Protections for Students with Educational Disabilities, Including the Duty to Allow Them to "Stay Put" in Their Placements

The federal statutes governing educational disabilities have both a substantive and procedural dimension. These statutes require school districts and LEAs to meet important substantive obligations, including the provision of a free, appropriate education and related services in the least restrictive educational environment. In addition, however, the statutes include a network of procedural protections designed to insure that parents of children with educational disabilities are fully involved in placement decisions affecting their children, and have the ability to challenge those decisions in a due process hearing before a neutral arbiter, and ultimately in court.

These process protections raise difficult legal and practical issues and have given rise to significant litigation. The IDEA procedural safeguards are particularly problematic in situations in which a school district unilaterally determines that a student with an educational disability should be immediately removed from a given placement for disciplinary reasons. Must the school district allow the student to "stay put" in his or her existing placement until the completion of the fair process and review procedures otherwise required by IDEA, or may a school district immediately remove a disruptive child before those procedures have run their course?

Honig, California Superintendent of Public Instruction v. Doe

484 U.S. 305 (1988)

Justice Brennan delivered the opinion of the Court.

As a condition of federal financial assistance, the Education of the Handicapped Act requires States to ensure a "free appropriate public education" for all disabled children within their jurisdictions. In aid of this goal, the Act establishes a comprehensive system of procedural safeguards designed to ensure parental participation in decisions concerning the education of their disabled children and to provide administrative and judicial review of any decisions with which those parents disagree. Among these safeguards is the so-called "stay-put" provision, which directs that a disabled child "shall remain in [his or her] then current educational placement" pending completion of any review proceedings, unless the parents and state or local educational agencies otherwise agree. 20 U.S.C. §1415(e)(3). Today we must decide whether, in the face of this statutory proscription, state or local school authorities may nevertheless unilaterally exclude disabled children from the classroom for dangerous or disruptive conduct growing out of their disabilities. In addition, we are called upon to decide whether a district court may, in the exercise of its equitable powers, order a State to provide educational services directly to a disabled child when the local agency fails to do so.

In the Education of the Handicapped Act (EHA or the Act), 20 U.S.C. §1400 *et seq.,* Congress sought "to assure that all handicapped children have available to them . . . a free appropriate public education which emphasizes special education and related services designed to meet their unique needs, [and] to assure that the rights of handicapped children and their parents or guardians are protected." §1400(c). When the law was passed in 1975, Congress had before it ample evidence that such legislative assurances were sorely needed: 21 years after this Court declared education to be "perhaps the most important function of state and local governments," *Brown v. Board of Education,* 347 U.S. 483, 493 (1954), congressional studies revealed that better than half of the Nation's 8 million disabled children were not receiving appropriate educational services. §1400(b)(3). Indeed, one out of every eight of these children was excluded from the public school system altogether, §1400(b)(4); many others were simply "warehoused" in special classes or were neglectfully shepherded through the system until they were old enough to drop out. See H.R. Rep. No. 94-332, p. 2 (1975). Among the most poorly served of disabled students were emotionally disturbed children: Congressional statistics revealed that for the school year immediately preceding passage of the Act, the educational needs of 82 percent of all children with emotional disabilities went unmet. *See* S. Rep. No. 94-168, p. 8 (1975) (hereinafter S. Rep.).

Although these educational failings resulted in part from funding constraints, Congress recognized that the problem reflected more than a lack of financial resources at the state and local levels. Two federal-court decisions, which the Senate Report characterized as "landmark," demonstrated that many disabled children were excluded pursuant to state statutes or local rules and policies, typically without any consultation with, or even notice to, their parents. *See Mills v. Board of Education of District of Columbia, Pennsylvania Ass'n for Retarded Children v. Pennsylvania*. Indeed, by the time of the EHA's enactment, parents had brought legal challenges to similar exclusionary practices in 27 other States.

In responding to these problems, Congress did not content itself with passage of a simple funding statute. Rather, the EHA confers upon disabled students an enforceable substantive right to public education in participating States, *see Board of Education of Hendrick Hudson Central School Dist. v. Rowley*, 458 U.S. 176 (1982), and conditions federal financial assistance upon a State's compliance with the substantive and procedural goals of the Act. Accordingly, States seeking to qualify for federal funds must develop policies assuring all disabled children the "right to a free appropriate public education," and must file with the Secretary of Education formal plans mapping out in detail the programs, procedures, and timetables under which they will effectuate these policies. 20 U.S.C. §§1412(1), 1413(a). Such plans must assure that, "to the maximum extent appropriate," States will "mainstream" disabled children, *i.e.*, that they will educate them with children who are not disabled, and that they will segregate or otherwise remove such children from the regular classroom setting "only when the nature or severity of the handicap is such that education in regular classes . . . cannot be achieved satisfactorily." §1412(5).

Envisioning the IEP as the centerpiece of the statute's education delivery system for disabled children, and aware that schools had all too often denied such children appropriate educations without in any way consulting their parents, Congress repeatedly emphasized throughout the Act the importance and indeed the necessity of parental participation in both the development of the IEP and any subsequent assessments of its effectiveness. *See* §§1400(c), 1401(19), 1412(7), 1415(b)(1)(A), (C), (D), (E), and 1415(b)(2). Accordingly, the Act establishes various procedural safeguards that guarantee parents both an opportunity for meaningful input into all decisions affecting their child's education and the right to seek review of any decisions they think inappropriate. These safeguards include the right to examine all relevant records pertaining to the identification, evaluation, and educational placement of their child; prior written notice whenever the responsible educational agency proposes (or refuses) to change the child's placement or program; an opportunity to present complaints concerning any aspect of the local agency's provision of a free appropriate public education; and an opportunity for "an impartial due process hearing" with respect to any such complaints. §§1415(b)(1), (2).

At the conclusion of any such hearing, both the parents and the local educational agency may seek further administrative review and, where that proves unsatisfactory, may file a civil action in any state or federal court. §§1415(c), (e)(2). In addition to reviewing the administrative record, courts are empowered to take additional evidence at the request of either party and to "grant such relief as [they] determine[ ] is appropriate." §1415(e)(2). The "stay-put" provision at issue in this case governs the placement of a child while these often lengthy review procedures run their course. It directs that: "During the pendency of any proceedings conducted pursuant to [§1415], unless the State or local educational agency and the parents or guardian otherwise agree, the child shall remain in the then current educational placement of such child. . . . " §1415(e)(3).

The present dispute grows out of the efforts of certain officials of the San Francisco Unified School District (SFUSD) to expel two emotionally disturbed children from school indefinitely for violent and disruptive conduct related to their disabilities. In November 1980, respondent John Doe assaulted another student at the Louise Lombard School, a developmental center for disabled children. Doe's April 1980 IEP identified him as a socially and physically awkward 17-year-old who experienced considerable difficulty controlling his impulses and anger. Among the goals set out in his IEP was "[i]mprovement in [his] ability to relate to [his] peers [and to] cope with frustrating situations without resorting to aggressive acts." Frustrating situations, however, were an unfortunately prominent feature of Doe's school career: physical abnormalities, speech difficulties, and poor grooming habits had made him the target of teasing and ridicule as early as the first grade; his 1980 IEP reflected his continuing difficulties with peers, noting that his social skills had deteriorated and that he could tolerate only minor frustration before exploding.

On November 6, 1980, Doe responded to the taunts of a fellow student in precisely the explosive manner anticipated by his IEP: he choked the student with sufficient force to leave abrasions on the child's neck, and kicked out a school window while being escorted to the principal's office afterwards. Doe admitted his misconduct and the school subsequently suspended him for five days. Thereafter, his principal referred the matter to the SFUSD Student Placement Committee (SPC or Committee) with the recommendation that Doe be expelled. On the day the suspension was to end, the SPC notified Doe's mother that it was proposing to exclude her child permanently from SFUSD and was therefore extending his suspension until such time as the expulsion proceedings were completed. The Committee further advised her that she was entitled to attend the November 25 hearing at which it planned to discuss the proposed expulsion.

After unsuccessfully protesting these actions by letter, Doe brought this suit against a host of local school officials and the State Superintendent of Public Instruction. Alleging that the suspension and proposed expulsion violated the EHA, he sought a temporary restraining order canceling the SPC hearing and requiring school officials to convene an IEP meeting. The District Judge granted the requested injunctive relief and further ordered defendants to provide home tutoring for Doe on an interim basis; shortly thereafter, she issued a preliminary injunction directing defendants to return Doe to his then current educational placement at Louise Lombard School pending completion of the IEP review process. Doe reentered school on December 15, 5½ weeks, and 24 schooldays, after his initial suspension.

Respondent Jack Smith was identified as an emotionally disturbed child by the time he entered the second grade in 1976. School records prepared that year indicated that he was unable "to control verbal or physical outburst[s]" and exhibited a "[s]evere disturbance in relationships with peers and adults." Further evaluations subsequently revealed that he had been physically and emotionally abused as an infant and young child and that, despite above average intelligence, he experienced academic and social difficulties as a result of extreme hyperactivity and low self-esteem. Of particular concern was Smith's propensity for verbal hostility; one evaluator noted that the child reacted to stress by "attempt[ing] to cover his feelings of low self worth through aggressive behavior[,] . . . primarily verbal provocations."

Based upon these evaluations, SFUSD placed Smith in a learning center for emotionally disturbed children. His grandparents, however, believed that his needs would be better served in the public school setting and, in September 1979, the school district acceded to their requests and enrolled him at A. P. Giannini Middle School. His February 1980 IEP recommended placement in a Learning Disability Group, stressing the need for close supervision and a highly structured environment. Like earlier evaluations, the February 1980 IEP noted that Smith was easily distracted, impulsive, and anxious; it therefore proposed a half-day schedule and suggested that the placement be undertaken on a trial basis.

At the beginning of the next school year, Smith was assigned to a full-day program; almost immediately thereafter he began misbehaving. School officials met twice with his grandparents in October 1980 to discuss returning him to a half-day program; although the grandparents agreed to the reduction, they apparently were never apprised of their right to challenge the decision through EHA procedures. The school officials also warned them that if the child continued his disruptive behavior—which included stealing, extorting money from fellow students, and making sexual comments to female classmates—they would seek to expel him. On November 14, they made good on this threat, suspending Smith for five days after he made further lewd comments. His principal referred the matter to the SPC, which recommended exclusion from SFUSD. . . .

After learning of Doe's action, Smith sought and obtained leave to intervene in the suit. The District Court subsequently entered summary judgment in favor of respondents on their EHA claims and issued a permanent injunction. In a series of decisions, the District Judge found that the proposed expulsions and indefinite suspensions of respondents for conduct attributable to their disabilities deprived them of their congressionally mandated right to a free appropriate public education, as well as their right to have that education provided in accordance with the procedures set out in the EHA. The District Judge therefore permanently enjoined the school district from taking any disciplinary action other than a 2- or 5-day suspension against any disabled child for disability-related misconduct, or from effecting any other change in the educational placement of any such child without parental consent pending completion of any EHA proceedings. In addition, the judge barred the State from authorizing unilateral placement changes and directed it to establish an EHA compliance-monitoring system or, alternatively, to enact guidelines governing local school responses to disability-related misconduct. Finally, the judge ordered the State to provide services directly to disabled children when, in any individual case, the State determined that the local educational agency was unable or unwilling to do so.

The Court first concluded that the action was "moot" as to Doe because Doe was 24 years old when the case reached the Supreme Court, and the EHA limits eligibility to children between 3 and 21 years old. The Court, however, found that Smith, who was 20 years old when the case reached the Supreme Court, still presented a live controversy because he, "has demonstrated both "a sufficient likelihood that he will again be wronged in a similar way, . . . " and that any resulting claim he may have for relief will surely evade our review. . . . "

III

The language of §1415(e)(3) is unequivocal. It states plainly that during the pendency of any proceedings initiated under the Act, unless the state or local educational agency and the parents or guardian of a disabled child otherwise agree, "the child *shall* remain in the then current educational placement." §1415(e)(3) (emphasis added). Faced with this clear directive, petitioner asks us to read a "dangerousness" exception into the stay-put provision on the basis of either of two essentially inconsistent assumptions: first, that Congress thought the residual authority of school officials to exclude dangerous students from the classroom too obvious for comment; or second, that Congress inadvertently failed to provide such authority and this Court must therefore remedy the oversight. Because we cannot accept either premise, we decline petitioner's invitation to rewrite the statute.

Petitioner's arguments proceed, he suggests, from a simple, commonsense proposition: Congress could not have intended the stay-put provision to be read literally, for such a construction leads to the clearly unintended, and untenable, result that school districts must return violent or dangerous students to school while the often lengthy EHA proceedings run their course. We think it clear, however, that Congress very much meant to strip schools of the *unilateral* authority they had traditionally employed to exclude disabled students, particularly emotionally disturbed students, from school. In so doing, Congress did not leave school administrators powerless to deal with dangerous students; it did, however, deny school officials their former right to "self-help," and directed that in the future the removal of disabled students could be accomplished only with the permission of the parents or, as a last resort, the courts.

As noted above, Congress passed the EHA after finding that school systems across the country had excluded one out of every eight disabled children from classes. In drafting the law, Congress was largely guided by the recent decisions in *Mills v. Board of Education of District of Columbia,* and *PARC,* both of which involved the exclusion of hard-to-handle disabled students. *Mills* in particular demonstrated the extent to which schools used disciplinary measures to bar children from the classroom. There, school officials had labeled four of the seven minor plaintiffs "behavioral problems," and had excluded them from classes without providing any alternative education to them or any notice to their parents. After finding that this practice was not limited to the named plaintiffs but affected in one way or another an estimated class of 12,000 to 18,000 disabled students, the District Court enjoined future exclusions, suspensions, or expulsions "on grounds of discipline."

Congress attacked such exclusionary practices in a variety of ways. It required participating States to educate *all* disabled children, regardless of the severity of their disabilities, 20 U.S.C. §1412(2)(C), and included within the definition of "handicapped" those children with serious emotional disturbances. §1401(1). It further provided for meaningful parental participation in all aspects of a child's educational placement, and barred schools, through the stay-put provision, from changing that placement over the parent's objection until all review proceedings were completed. Recognizing that those proceedings might prove long and tedious, the Act's drafters did not intend §1415(e)(3) to operate inflexibly, *see* 121 Cong. Rec. 37412 (1975) (remarks of Sen. Stafford), and they therefore allowed for interim placements where parents and school officials are able to agree on one. Conspicuously absent from §1415(e)(3), however, is any emergency exception for dangerous students. This absence is all the more telling in light of the injunctive decree issued in *PARC,* which permitted school officials unilaterally to remove students in "'extraordinary circumstances.'" Given the lack of any similar exception in *Mills,* and the close attention Congress devoted to these "landmark" decisions, *see* S. Rep., at 6, we can only conclude that the omission was intentional; we are therefore not at liberty to engraft onto the statute an exception Congress chose not to create.

Our conclusion that §1415(e)(3) means what it says does not leave educators hamstrung. The Department of Education has observed that, "[w]hile the [child's] placement may not be changed [during any complaint proceeding], this does not preclude the agency from using its normal procedures for dealing with children who are endangering themselves or others." Comment following 34 CFR §300.513 (1987). Such procedures may include the use of study carrels, timeouts, detention, or the restriction of privileges. More drastically, where a student poses an immediate threat to the safety of others, officials may temporarily suspend him or her for up to 10 schooldays. This authority, which respondent in no way disputes, not only ensures that school administrators can protect the safety of others by promptly removing the most dangerous of students, it also provides a "cooling down" period during which officials can initiate IEP review and seek to persuade the child's parents to agree to an interim placement. And in those cases in which the parents of a truly dangerous child adamantly refuse to permit any change in placement, the 10-day respite gives school officials an opportunity to invoke the aid of the courts under §1415(e)(2), which empowers courts to grant any appropriate relief. . . .

As the EHA's legislative history makes clear, one of the evils Congress sought to remedy was the unilateral exclusion of disabled children by *schools,* not courts, and one of the purposes of §1415(e)(3), therefore, was "to prevent *school* officials from removing a child from the regular public school classroom over the parents' objection pending completion of the review proceedings." *Burlington School Committee v. Massachusetts Dept. of Education,* 471

U.S., at 373 (emphasis added). The stay-put provision in no way purports to limit or pre-empt the authority conferred on courts by §1415(e)(2), *see Doe v. Brookline School Committee,* 722 F.2d 910, 917 (CA1 1983); indeed, it says nothing whatever about judicial power.

In short, then, we believe that school officials are entitled to seek injunctive relief under §1415(e)(2) in appropriate cases. In any such action, §1415(e)(3) effectively creates a presumption in favor of the child's current educational placement which school officials can overcome only by showing that maintaining the child in his or her current placement is substantially likely to result in injury either to himself or herself, or to others. In the present case, we are satisfied that the District Court, in enjoining the state and local defendants from indefinitely suspending respondent or otherwise unilaterally altering his then current placement, properly balanced respondent's interest in receiving a free appropriate public education in accordance with the procedures and requirements of the EHA against the interests of the state and local school officials in maintaining a safe learning environment for all their students.

IV

We believe the courts below properly construed and applied §1415(e)(3), except insofar as the Court of Appeals held that a suspension in excess of 10 schooldays does not constitute a "change in placement." We therefore affirm the Court of Appeals' judgment on this issue as modified herein. . . .

NOTES AND QUESTIONS

1. The *Honig* Court argues that Congress has created a clear presumption in favor of a disabled child's current educational placement that can be overcome only if a school district affirmatively proves to a court in an injunction proceeding that the maintenance of the current placement is "substantially likely to result in injury" to the child or others. Recall that in *Goss v. Lopez,* 419 U.S. 565 (1975), the Supreme Court interpreted the procedural protections afforded all students under the Constitution's due process clause, and declared that "[s]tudents whose presence poses a continuing danger to persons or property or an ongoing threat of disrupting the academic process may be immediately removed" without prior notice or hearing. Do the procedural protections given to students with educational disabilities by the IDEA exceed those given to all other students by the due process clause? Should students with educational disabilities be entitled to more process protections than students without such disabilities?
2. After *Honig,* Congress amended IDEA to allow school districts more discretion in their treatment of students with educational disabilities during the pendency of any review of their placements. The statute now allows districts unilaterally to suspend a disabled student for up to ten days without providing notice and a hearing. 20 U.S.C. §1415(k)(1)(A)(i). In addition, the school may change a student's placement to an "interim" alternative placement for up to 45 days by demonstrating to a hearing officer that there is "substantial evidence that maintaining the current

placement . . . is substantially likely to result in injury to the child or to others." 20 U.S.C. §1415(k)(2). The school may unilaterally change the student's placement to an "interim" alternative placement for up to 45 days *without* a hearing, only if the student carries a weapon, or knowingly possesses, uses or sells illegal drugs at school. 20 U.S.C. §1415(k)(1)(A)(ii). The interim alterative placement must offer the student the same "general curriculum" and services directed by the student's IEP. 20 U.S.C. §415(K)(3)(B).

The child's parents may challenge the interim placement in a proceeding conducted by an impartial hearing officer, but the child will remain in the placement during the period of unilateral suspension. 20 U.S.C §1415(k)(7)(A). If that period of suspension expires before the hearing officer resolves the issue of any subsequent placement, however, the student must be returned to the original placement. 20 U.S.C. §1415(k)(7)(B). Accordingly, the statute also allows the school district to seek and receive an expedited hearing upon a showing that it is "dangerous" for the child to be returned to the original placement during the pendency of due process proceedings. 20 U.S.C. §1415(7)(c).

3. Do these process protections give students who do not have genuine educational disabilities an incentive to claim such a disability in order to take advantage of these protections in situations in which they face suspension or expulsion? *See, e.g.,* McKinney, *Disciplining Children With(out) Disabilities: Schools Behind the Eight Ball,* 130 Ed. L. Rep. 365 (1999); Rachelson, *Expelling Students Who Claim to Be Disabled: Escaping the Individuals with Disabilities Act's "Stay-Put" Provision,* 2 Mich. L. & Poly. Rev. 127(1997).
4. In *The Allure of Legalization Reconsidered: The Case of Special Education,* Neal and Kirp seriously challenge the benefits of the "legalization" of special education. *See* D. Neal et al., *School Days, Rule Days: The Legalization and Regulation of Education* (1980). They argue that due process hearings impose high economic and psychological costs, that separating disabled students for distinct legal treatment distorts the allocation of resources for the education of all students, that legalization demonstrates a mistrust of the exercise of professional judgment by experienced educators, and that the benefits of legalization for students are difficult to document. Do you find these arguments compelling? What are the benefits to "legalization" that might outweigh these disadvantages?
5. ***International and Comparative Law Perspective.*** The United Nations Convention on the Rights of the Child requires signing countries to recognize the "right of the disabled child to special care" and to ensure assistance "free of charge, whenever possible," including "education . . . in a manner conducive to the child's achieving the fullest possible social integration and individual development . . . " Article 23. For a fascinating description of the evolution of special education in China, *see* Yanhui Pang and Dean Richey, *The Development of Special Education in China,* 21 Int. Journal of Special Education 77 (2006) (finding progress toward inclusive education in the current special education programs, but also finding a lack of special education services for the 80% of China's population that live in rural areas, and a lack of qualified teachers.)

C. THE PRACTICE OF EDUCATING STUDENTS WITH EDUCATIONAL DISABILITIES: IMPLEMENTING THE LEGAL STRUCTURE

1. Individualized Education Plans

An "Individualized Education Plan" or IEP is a "written statement for a child with a disability that is developed, reviewed, and revised in a meeting. . . . " (34 C.F.R. §300.340.) An Individual Education Plan is a student's "curriculum" for the year, matching up the child's needs with a individualized, appropriate program. (34 C.F.R. §300 Appendix C.) An IEP informs the parents of the "good faith effort" the school district will take to assist the child in meeting the child's annual goals. (34 C.F.R. §300.350(a)(2).) In *Rowley,* the Supreme Court held that IEPs must be "reasonably calculated to enable the student with disabilities to receive educational benefits." The IEP is thus a legal obligation by the school to the child for whom the IEP is written.

(a) Who Is involved in the IEP?

The following stakeholders typically meet at the school district's office or at the student's school to develop an IEP: (1) The student's parents and/or legal guardians (if they choose not to attend then the school district must record attempts to have the parent(s) participate); (2) if parents cannot be located, surrogate parents must be appointed; (3) the student's special education teacher; (4) the student's regular education teacher (if the child is or may be participating in regular education); (5) the student (when appropriate); (6) a representative of the Local Education Agency or school district (i.e., case manager, principal or assistant principal); (7) an individual who can interpret the instructional implications of evaluation results; and (8) at the discretion of the parent or school district, other individuals who have special knowledge or expertise regarding the child (i.e., related service personnel), including an independent school psychologist and a lawyer. 34 C.F.R. §300.345.

(b) Who Gets an IEP?

For children with disabilities aged three through five, an Individualized Family Service Plan may serve as the IEP. Children aged five through 21 with disabilities who are determined eligible to receive an IEP must receive one.

(c) What Must an IEP Include?

The IEP must include the following: a statement of the child's present level of functioning and educational performance; a statement of the how the child's disability affects the child's involvement in the general education curriculum and participation in appropriate activities (34 C.F.R. §300.347(a)(1)); a statement of the measurable annual goals, including benchmarks (short-term objectives) (34 C.F.R. §300.347(a)(2)); a statement of the special education, related services, supplementary aids, program modifications and supports to be provided to the child (34 C.F.R. §300.347(a)(3)), including the projected starting date, along with the frequency, location and duration of the services; an explanation of the extent the child with disabilities will not be participating with nondisabled children in the regular education classroom (34 C.F.R. §300.347(a)(4)); a statement of the modifications required for the child to participate in state or district achievement assessments, if appropriate; a statement of how the child's progress toward the annual goals will be measured, and a statement of how the child's parent will be regularly informed (34 C.F.R. §300.347(a)(7)); and beginning at age 14, and updated annually thereafter, a statement of needed transition services (34 C.F.R. §300.347(b)(1)).

The IEP also contains a declaration of special factors to be considered in meeting the educational needs of the child, including:

1. positive behavioral interventions, strategies, and supports to address a child whose behavior impedes his or her learning (34 C.F.R. §300.346(a)(2)(i));
2. the language needs of the child, particularly limited English proficiency students (34 C.F.R. §300.346(a)(2)(ii));
3. appropriate instruction and use of Braille for blind or visually impaired children (34 C.F.R. §300.346(a)(2)(iii));
4. communication needs (i.e., direct communication), particularly of children who are deaf or hard of hearing (34 C.F.R. §300.346(a)(2)(iv)); and
5. assistive technology devices and services for children when deemed necessary and appropriate by the IEP team (34 C.F.R. §300.346(a)(2)(v)).

Finally, beginning at least one year before the child reaches the age of majority (18), a statement must be included that the child was informed of his or her rights under special education law, which rights will transfer to the child when the child reaches the age of majority. (34 C.F.R. §300.347(c).)

(d) What "Related Services" Must the District Provide?

The district must also provide related services such as transportation, speech and language services, audiology services, counseling services, social work services, physical or occupational therapy, related medical services for diagnosis, evaluation, and consultation, interpreters, special reader services, braillists and typists, transition services, vocational services and vocational programs.

(e) How Is an IEP Effectively Monitored?

At least annually, the child's IEP and placement must be monitored. The child's benchmarks and short-term objectives should be monitored quarterly. Parents should be kept aware of the child's progress. Reports of pupil progress must be given at a rate that is at least equivalent to that given to children without educational disabilities (i.e., quarterly, with progress reports and report cards) (34 C.F.R. §300.347(a)(7)(ii)).

(f) How Can the IEP Process Be Managed to Reduce Conflict?

The IEP process is often characterized by tension and conflict between the parents of a child with special educational needs and the school district. From the perspective of the parent or guardian, the process is emotionally difficult because it involves a disability in a child. That emotional strain often manifests itself in aggression toward the district and its professionals. In particular, parents may become assertive in their demand for individual services. This tension may be exacerbated if the parents have brought with them to the IEP meeting a legal or educational expert.

From the district's point of view, the provision of effective special education services can be extremely expensive. The administrators charged with monitoring the IEP process are often viewed by the school district as "gatekeepers." That label suggests that the school district's representatives in the process may bring with them a strong desire to contain costs. The district's motive to reduce costs is often incompatible with a parent's desire to obtain effective services for a child.

There are two ways to reduce this inherently tense situation. First, the district must provide the parents with sincere communication regarding the process. The communication must be clear, nonpatronizing, nonthreatening and honest. The tone of the administrators and educational professionals is vital. It must be conciliatory and it must manifest a genuine interest in serving the educational needs of the child.

As part of this communication, the district must also allow parents time to reflect on the IEP documents and on the dialogue at the IEP meetings. All too often, districts try to get parents to sign-off on an IEP plan for their children on the spot, right in the middle of a first meeting. This is simply unfair and will breed disharmony down the road.

Second, the district must make sure that at least one of its educational professionals involved in the IEP process really knows the child. Because special education tends to be separated administratively from "regular education," it is not unusual for a district's IEP representative to have had absolutely no contact with the child involved. Not only do parents justifiably resent the presence of district administrators who do not understand the needs of their children, these administrators have no ability to contribute to a legitimate educational plan for the child. As such, administrators who do not understand the child tend to fight for the district's cost-saving goal rather than for the educational needs of the child. That approach, in turn, creates tremendous hostility among parents at the IEP meetings and throughout the process.

2. Discipline

A student with disabilities may not be expelled or suspended for behavior or a condition that results from his or her disability. If the behavior is not a result of the student's disability, however, the child can be disciplined in accordance with the district's discipline policy (34 C.F.R. §300.524).

A school district may remove a student with disabilities from school for up to ten days, under circumstances that would allow the school to remove a nondisabled child. The removal, however, may not constitute a change in placement for the child with educational disabilities (34 C.F.R. §300.121(d)). If the disabled child has been removed from school for more than ten cumulative days in a school term, services must be provided to the extent necessary to assist the student in progressing in the general curriculum and achieving the IEP goals (34 C.F.R. §300.121 (d)) (34 C.F.R. §300.520).

"Changes in placement" require a determination that the change is necessary, as well as the development of a behavioral assessment plan or review of a student's current behavior assessment plan, within ten business days (34 C.F.R. §300.520); notification to the parent(s) (34 C.F.R. §300.523); and an alternative free appropriate public education (FAPE) (34 C.F.R. §300.121). A "change in placement" is *appropriate* if a child carries a weapon to school or a school function, or knowingly possesses or uses illegal drugs or sells or solicits controlled substances at school or a school function. A change of placement to an appropriate alternative education setting is necessary and acceptable, for the same amount of time as would be endured by a nondisabled student, but no more than 45 days (34 C.F.R. §300.520).

Alternatively, a district may effect a change in placement pursuant to the ruling of a hearing examiner. In an expedited due process hearing, a hearing officer may order an appropriate interim alternative education setting (IAES) if the hearing officer finds that injury to the student or others may result from the current placement (34 C.F.R. §300.521). With regard to appropriate interim alternative placements, (34 C.F.R. §300.522), the IEP determines the propriety of the alternative placement. Moreover, the alternative interim placement must enable the student to continue in the general curriculum, enable the student to continue to receive required services and modifications, including those in the student's IEP, and provide services and modifications addressing the student's behavior and focusing on prevention of the behavior's reoccurrence.

In determining whether and how to discipline a particular child with special needs, the school district and its personnel should consider the student's physical freedom and social interaction. The district should administer behavior interventions that respect human dignity and personal privacy and insure the student's right to the least restrictive environment. In order to establish institutional guarantees of appropriate disciplinary procedures, the school district through its school board should establish and maintain a committee to develop policies and procedures regarding the proper use of behavioral interventions. The school board's policies and procedures regarding the use of behavioral interventions must comply with the state board of education's rules. The school board's policies and procedures also should be developed with advice from parents of regular and special education students, teachers, administrators, advocates and experts in the field of behavior intervention. The practices should emphasize positive intervention, incorporate generally accepted behavior interventions in the field, include determination criteria, and include effective, but nonintrusive, monitoring procedures.

3. Process Rights

(a) Notice

The local district is required to provide the parent of a student with a disability with prior written notice: (1) when the district proposes to initiate or change the identification, evaluation, or educational placement of a student or the provision of a free, appropriate public education to a student; (2) when the district refuses to initiate or change the identification, evaluation, or educational placement of a student or the provision of a free, appropriate public education to a student; and (3) one year prior to the student reaching the age of majority at 18 years of age.

The written notice must be provided at least ten days prior to the proposed or refused action and must include: (1) a description of the action proposed or refused by the district, an explanation of why the district proposes or refuses to take the action, and a description of any other options the district considered and the reasons why those options were rejected; (2) a description of each evaluation procedure, test, record or report the district used as a basis for the proposed or refused action; (3) a description of any other factors that are relevant to the district's proposal or refusal; (4) a statement that the parent of a student with a disability has due process rights and, if the notice is not an initial referral for evaluation, the means by which a copy of the description of procedural safeguards can be obtained; and (5) sources for the parent to contact to obtain assistance in understanding his or her due process rights.

The notice must be written in language understandable to the general public and provided in the native language or other mode of communication used by the parent, unless it is clearly not feasible to do so. If the native language or other mode of communication of the parent is not a written language, the local district must take steps to insure that the notice is translated orally or by other means to the parent in his or her native language or other mode of communication, that the parent understands the content of the notice, and that there is written evidence that these requirements have been met.

(b) Parental Consent

The local district must obtain parental consent before conducting any evaluation and prior to the initial placement of a student with a disability in special education. Additionally, a local school district may not require parent or guardian consent as a condition of any benefit to the parent or guardian or the child except for the services or activity for which consent is required.

If a parent refuses consent for evaluation or initial placement in special education, the district may continue to pursue an evaluation or placement using mediation and due process hearing procedures. If the hearing officer supports the district, the district may evaluate or initially provide special education and related services to the student without parent consent, subject to the parent's right to appeal the decision and to have the student remain in his or her present educational placement pending the outcome of any administrative or judicial proceeding.

(c) Evaluations

The parent of a student with a disability has the right to obtain an independent educational evaluation of the student. A parent has the right to an independent educational evaluation at public expense if the parent disagrees with an evaluation obtained by the local district. However, the district may initiate a due process hearing to demonstrate that its evaluation is appropriate. If the final decision is that the evaluation is appropriate, the parent still has the right to an independent educational evaluation, but not at public expense. If the parent obtains an independent educational evaluation at private expense, the results of the evaluation must be considered by the district in any decision made with respect to the provision of a free, appropriate public education to the student and may be presented as evidence at a due process hearing regarding the student.

If a hearing officer requests an independent educational evaluation as part of a hearing, the cost of the evaluation must be at public expense. A district must provide to a parent, upon request, information about where an independent educational evaluation may be obtained. Whenever an independent evaluation is at public expense, the criteria under which the evaluation is obtained, including the location of the evaluation and the qualifications of the examiner, must be the same as the criteria which the district uses when it initiates an evaluation.

(d) Placement by Parent of Student in a Nonpublic School or Facility

A local district is not required to pay for the cost of education, including special education and related services, of a student with a disability at a nonpublic school or facility if the district made a free, appropriate public education available to the student and the parents instead elected to place the student in the nonpublic school or facility. If the parent of a student with a disability who previously received special education and related services enrolls the student in a nonpublic elementary or secondary school without consent or referral by the local district, a court or hearing officer may require the district to reimburse the parent for the cost of that enrollment, however, if it is found that the district did not make a free, appropriate public education available to the student in a timely manner prior to that enrollment.

(e) Protections for Students Not Yet Eligible for Special Education and Related Services

If, prior to a student engaging in behavior that violated any local district rule or code of conduct and resulted in disciplinary action, the local district had knowledge that the student was a student with a disability who has not been determined eligible to receive special education and related services, the student may claim protections afforded students who have been determined eligible.

A local district has knowledge that a student is a student with a disability if: (1) the student's parent has expressed concern in writing prior to the incident (unless the parent is illiterate or otherwise unable to comply) to appropriate school personnel that the student is in need of special education and related services; (2) the student's behavior or performance demonstrates the need for such services; (3) the student's parent has requested a case study evaluation of the student; or (4) the student's teacher or other school personnel has expressed concern about the student's behavior or performance to a designated director of special education or other local district personnel.

If, prior to taking disciplinary action against a student, the local district had no knowledge that the student was a student with a disability, the student may be subjected to the same disciplinary procedures as those applied to students without disabilities who engaged in comparable behaviors.

(f) Referral to and Action by Law Enforcement and Judicial Authorities

Local districts or other agencies are not prohibited from reporting a crime committed by a student with a disability to appropriate authorities. In addition, state law enforcement and judicial authorities are not prevented from exercising their responsibilities regarding the application of federal and state law to crimes committed by a student with a disability. Local districts or other agencies reporting a crime committed by a student with a disability must insure that copies of the special education and disciplinary records of the student are transmitted to the appropriate law enforcement authorities for their consideration.

(g) Complaint Resolution and Mediation

Complaints with respect to any matter relating to the identification, evaluation or educational placement of a student or the provision of a free, appropriate public education to a student should be referred to the local district. Many states and local school districts have established a mediation regime for resolving disputes in the IEP process. In mediation, neither party is asked to abandon basic beliefs about the student's ability. The parties are asked to consider alternatives that could be included in the student's program, to listen to the concerns and problems expressed by the other party, and to be realistic about the student's capabilities and the local district's obligations and resources. The mediator is an impartial third party and has no authority to force any action by either party. Mediation participants should include persons who have the authority to act on behalf of the student and of the local district. Efforts to mediate the disagreement are generally not admissible as evidence at any subsequent administrative or civil proceeding except for the purpose of noting the mediation that did occur and the terms of any written agreement(s) reached as a result of mediation. The mediator may not be called as a witness at any subsequent administrative or civil proceeding.

(h) Impartial Due Process Hearing

A parent or local district may initiate a due process hearing regarding the district's proposal or refusal to initiate or change the identification, evaluation or educational placement of a student or the provision of a free, appropriate public education. A request for a due process hearing cannot be denied for any reason. No person who is an employee of the local district involved in the education or care of a student whose services are the subject of a dispute may conduct the hearing. Prior to appointing the due process hearing officer, the state board of education typically must review the background of the prospective appointee in order to establish that: (1) the individual has never been employed by or administratively connected with the local district or special education joint agreement involved in the case; (2) is not a resident of the district involved; and (3) has no personal or professional interest that would conflict with his or her objectivity in the hearing.

Any party to a hearing has the right to:

1. a fair, impartial, and orderly hearing;
2. the opportunity to present evidence, testimony, and arguments necessary to support and clarify the issue in dispute;
3. close the hearing to the public;
4. have the student who is the subject of the hearing present at the hearing if requested by the parent;
5. confront and cross-examine witnesses;
6. be accompanied and advised by counsel and by individuals with special knowledge with respect to students with disabilities;
7. inspect and review all school records pertaining to the student and obtain copies of any such records;
8. have access to the district's list of independent evaluators and obtain an independent evaluation of the student at their own expense;
9. be advised at least five days prior to the hearing of any evidence to be introduced;
10. compel the attendance of any local school district employee at the hearing, or any other person who may have information relevant to the needs, abilities, proposed program or the status of the student;
11. request that an interpreter be available during the hearing;
12. maintain the placement and eligibility status of the student until the completion of all administrative and judicial proceedings; and
13. request an expedited hearing to change the placement of a dangerous student. A parent may also request an expedited hearing if the parent disagrees with the district's manifestation determination or the district's removal of the student to an interim alternative educational setting.

The Supreme Court has held that the burden of proof at the due process hearing rests with the party seeking relief. *Shaffer v. Weast,* 546 U.S. 49 (2005). Where a school district initiates a due process hearing, therefore, the district bears the burden of proving that its selected placement is appropriate. In most cases, however, parents or representatives of the student will seek a due process hearing to challenge a district's recommended plan. As such, the Court has shifted to the parents and student representatives the burden of proof in most due process hearings.

The state board of education must insure that a final hearing decision is reached and mailed to the parties promptly after receipt of a request for a hearing, unless the hearing officer grants a specific time extension at the request of either party. Within a short time (often ten days) after the conclusion of the hearing, the hearing officer must issue a written decision that sets forth the issues in dispute, findings of fact based upon the evidence and testimony presented and the hearing officer's conclusions of law and orders. The hearing officer must determine whether the evidence establishes that the student has needs that require special education services and, if so, whether the services and placement proposed or provided by the district are appropriate given the student's identified needs.

Any party to the impartial due process hearing aggrieved by the final written decision has the right to initiate a civil action with respect to the issues presented in the hearing. The civil action can be brought in any court of competent jurisdiction, within a short, statutorily prescribed time period after a copy of the decision is mailed to the parties. During a pending due process hearing or any judicial proceeding, the student generally must remain in his or her present educational placement. The student's present eligibility status and special education and related services must be continued. However, if school personnel maintain that it is dangerous for the student to be in the current placement during pending due process proceedings, the local district may request an expedited hearing.

(i) Attorneys' Fees

In any action or proceeding brought under the Individuals with Disabilities Education Act, the court may award reasonable attorneys' fees to the parent or guardian of a student with a disability if he or she is the prevailing party. Fees awarded must be based upon rates prevailing in the community in which the action or proceeding arose for the kind and quality of services furnished. No bonus or multiplier may be used in calculating the fees awarded.

Attorneys' fees may not be awarded and related costs may not be reimbursed in any action or proceeding for services performed subsequent to the time of a written offer of settlement to a parent if: (1) the offer is made within the time prescribed by Rule 68 of the Federal Rules of Civil Procedure or, in the case of an administrative proceeding, at any time more than ten days before the proceeding begins; (2) the offer is not accepted within ten days; and (3) the court or administrative hearing officer finds that the relief finally obtained by the parents is not more favorable to the parents than the offer of settlement.

Notwithstanding these restrictions, however, an award of attorneys' fees and related costs may be made to a parent who is the prevailing party and who was substantially justified in rejecting the settlement offer. The court may reduce, accordingly, the amount of the attorneys' fees awarded whenever the court finds that: (1) the parent, during the course of the action or proceeding, unreasonably protracted the final resolution of the controversy; (2) the amount of the attorneys' fees authorized to be awarded unreasonably exceeds the hourly rate prevailing in the community for similar services by attorneys of reasonably comparable skill, reputation, and experience; (3) the time spent and legal services furnished were excessive considering the nature of the action or proceeding; or (4) the attorney representing the parent did not provide the school district the appropriate information in the due process complaint.

(j) Surrogate Parents

A local school district must make reasonable attempts to contact the parent of a student who has been referred for, or is in need of, special education and related services. If the parent cannot be identified or located or the student is a ward of the state residing in a residential facility, an educational surrogate parent must be appointed to insure that the educational rights of the student are protected. A student residing in a foster home or relative caretaker setting no longer requires the appointment of an educational surrogate parent. The foster parent or relative caretaker may represent the educational needs of each child placed in his or her home.

The person selected as an educational surrogate parent cannot be an employee of a public agency involved in the education or care of the student, can have no interest that conflicts with the interest of the student he or she represents, and must have knowledge and skills to insure adequate representation of the student. An employee of a residential facility may be selected as an educational surrogate parent for a student residing in that facility if that facility only provides noneducational care for the student. The educational surrogate parent may represent the student in all matters relating to the identification, evaluation and educational placement of the student and the provision of a free, appropriate public education.

(k) Access to Records

A local district must permit a parent to inspect and review any educational records relating to his or her student which are collected, maintained or used by the district. The district must comply with a request to review the educational records without unnecessary delay and before any meeting relating to the identification, evaluation, or placement of the student. The right to inspect and review educational records includes: (1) the right to a response from the participating district to reasonable requests for explanations and interpretations of the records; (2) the right to have a representative of the parent inspect and review the records; and (3) the right to request that the school district provide copies of education records if failure to provide those copies would effectively prevent the parent from exercising his or her right to inspect and review the records at a location where they are normally maintained. A local school district may presume that the parent has authority to inspect and review records relating to his or her student unless the school district has been advised that the parent does not have the authority under applicable state law governing such matters as guardianship, separation and divorce.

(l) Amendment of Records at Parent's Request

A parent who believes that information in the education records collected, maintained or used is inaccurate or misleading or violates the privacy or other rights of the student may request the participating district to amend the record. The local school district must decide promptly whether to amend the information in accordance with the request, usually within 15 school days from the date of receipt of the request. If the district decides to refuse to amend the information in accordance with the request, it must inform the parent of the refusal and advise the parent of the right to a records hearing. The school district must, upon request, provide an opportunity for a records hearing to challenge information in education records to insure that it is not inaccurate, misleading, or otherwise in violation of the privacy or other rights of a student.

If, as the result of a records hearing, the school district decides that the information is inaccurate, misleading or otherwise in violation of the privacy or other rights of the student, it must amend the information and inform the parent in writing that it has done so. If, as a result of the records hearing, the school district decides that the information is not inaccurate, misleading or otherwise in violation of the privacy or other rights of the student, it must inform the parent of his or her right to place in the education records maintained on the student a statement commenting on the information or setting forth any reasons for disagreeing with the decision of the school district. Any explanation placed in the records of the student must be maintained by the school district as part of the student's records for as long as the record or contested portion is maintained by the school district. If the records of the student or contested portions are disclosed by the district to any party, the explanation must also be disclosed.

D. THE COST OF SPECIAL EDUCATION AND STRATEGIES FOR MEETING UNFUNDED MANDATES

1. Why Is Special Education so Expensive?

School districts often decry the costs of special education both in absolute dollar terms and also as a disproportionate percentage of their education fund budget. There is no doubting that the federal special education mandates can be expensive. First, school districts must provide and pay for a free *appropriate* public education (FAPE), not just a free public education. There is no clear definition of "appropriate," which may require costly nonpublic schools, nonpublic agencies, residential schools and one-to-one aides. Second, school districts must provide FAPE for students aged 3-21, not just those aged 5-18. Preschool intervention can be intense and expensive. Forty-hour per week programs for autistic students are not uncommon. Students requiring services at ages 18-21 are usually severally disabled and thus these services are extremely costly. Third, the district program must be consented to by the parent. If the parent does not agree, a due process hearing ensues, involving attorneys on both sides. If the parent prevails at due process, the district must pay the parent's attorneys' fees. Fourth, procedures for assessing students and developing IEPs, an annual requirement for each special education student, are complicated and require substantial staff time. (IEPs are often 20 pages.) A failure to comply with the required procedures can result in a negative due process hearing decision. Finally, parents often encourage districts to find that their students are eligible for special education to insure that the student receives the individual attention and parent participation that come with IEPs.

These federally mandated expenditures are not fully funded by the federal government. For most districts, virtually all of the revenues for special education derive from local sources, likely local property taxes.

2. The Allocation of Scarce Resources

In *Special Education—At What Cost to General Education?* (Center for Special Education Finance, Winter 1999-2000), Thomas B. Parish writes:

> Questions about the impact of rising costs of special education on general education programming are among the most contentious issues faced by the public education community today. In *Irreconcilable Differences? Defining the Rising Conflict Between Regular and Special Education,* (1995), Meredith and Underwood . . . conclude that "the cost of educating disabled students . . . is threatening our ability to educate nondisabled students in many districts and, therefore, is placing the entire public education edifice potentially at risk."

After surveying special education expenditures trends in the states, Parish concludes:

> nationally, special education as a percentage of total K-12 enrollments has continued to rise virtually every year since national data were first collected in 1976-77. Over the decade 1987-88 to 1996-97, the proportion of school-age children in special education has increased by about 19 percent.

Nonetheless, Parish offers the following caution:

> It is tempting to make special education the "whipping boy" in response to concern over rising costs. However, as much of the growing expenditures on special education seem attributable to continuously rising identification rates, it is insufficient to look to special education alone for the solution. For the most part, only those students not making appropriate progress in general education are referred to special education for supplemental services. To understand why special education is growing, we need a better understanding of why growing numbers of children are not finding success within general education. . . .
>
> To the extent that state and local officials continue to raise the bar for student achievement and heighten the sanctions for school failure, the more tempting it becomes for general educators to refer students for individualized treatment through special education. . . .
>
> The reaction of some states to rising special education expenditures is simply to cap state aid for special education. At the same time, they may be adopting statewide accountability measures that single out low-performing students, inadvertently driving them into special education. . . .

In addition, there is no doubt that special education expenditures per eligible student are also increasing in some districts, and perhaps nationally. It may be that more children are arriving in the public schools with a need for more complex interventions. In response to this relatively small number of high-cost children, Meredith and Underwood (1995) express concern over an increasing failure to amortize these special education costs. State and federal funding mechanisms need to provide differential funding for these extraordinarily high-cost cases. Otherwise, "the risk of random, devastating expenditures striking a particular school budget increases."

Accordingly, Parish concludes:

As general educators, we cannot increasingly refer students with diverse learning needs to special education and then look with alarm as this segment of the school budget rises. As state policymakers, we need to support programs that attempt to assist students prior to their referral to more costly special education interventions, especially in light of ever-increasing student standards and high-stakes accountability. We also need to target, supplementary special education aid to districts serving students with extraordinarily high-cost needs. At the same time, it is essential to begin bridging the gap between general and special education programs and providers to more fully address the educational needs of all children.

3. Educational Strategies for Efficiently Meeting the Needs of Children with Educational Disabilities

(a) Early Intervention

In 1981, Missouri became the first state to pilot a project (Parents as Teachers) designed to provide parent education and support services to families beginning at the child's birth. The project enrolled 350 families who represented a cross section of socio-economic status and family configurations. The benefits of the program were confirmed by an independent evaluation conducted in 1985. At age three, children in the pilot project were significantly more advanced than comparison group children in language, social development, problem solving and other cognitive abilities—competencies that are essential to later school success. Parents and children benefited regardless of socio-economic status and traditional risk factors. School districts were viewed more positively by project parents than by those in comparison groups. Presently, Missouri mandates all school districts to provide the Parents as Teachers Program and it has been replicated in more than 50 sites across the nation. M. Winter & J. Rouse, *Fostering Intergenerational Literacy: The Missouri Parents as Teachers Program,* The Reading Teacher (Feb. 1990).

The evidence is clear that a well administered preschool program with clearly stated goals will result in lasting benefits to at-risk children. Topics in Early Childhood Special Education: Demographic and Definitional Issues (vol. 8, no. 3, Fall 1988); I. Lazar, *Measuring the Effects of Early Childhood Programs;* Phi Delta Kappa: The Hot Topic Series Preschool Education (Center on Evaluation, Development, Research, Oct. 1989); J. Pfannenstiel & D. Seltzer, *New Parents as Teachers: Evaluation of an Early Parent Education Program.*

Early Childhood Res. Q. (vol. 4, no. 1, Mar. 1989); L. Schorr, *Early Interventions Aimed at Reducing Intergenerational Disadvantage: The New Social Policy,* Teachers College Record: The Care and Education of Young Children: Expanding Contexts, Sharpening Focus (vol. 90, no. 3, Spring, 1989); D. Schumacher, *Pay Now or Pay Later to Reach at Risk Kids, Demographer Warns.* Educ. Daily (Sept. 18, 1990); M. Winter & J. Rouse, *Fostering Inter-generational Literacy: The Missouri Parents as Teachers Program,* The Reading Teacher (Feb. 1990).

Children enrolled in early childhood programs were significantly more successful than their controls. The preschool program children were significantly less likely to be enrolled in special or remedial classes and significantly more likely to graduate from high school and to enroll in post secondary education. The differences were so large as to be cost-effective; the savings in special and remedial education alone were greater than the cost of the early childhood experience. There were also differences in labor-force participation after the completion of school, and even differences in the rate at which the young adults were exposed to child welfare and police agencies. Of significance is the fact that the differences between school accomplishments of the preschool program children and the controls became greater with the passage of time. On many measures the effects did not become statistically significant until after fourth grade.

In 1980, the state of Colorado conducted an extensive study of disabled children who had completed preschool. The state asked one question: How many educationally disabled children are served in regular education programs at the completion of preschool? The results of this study showed that 31.4 percent of the children were enrolled in regular education programs without any special education services, 37.1 percent were enrolled in resource settings where they received some special education services, while spending most of their time in regular settings, and 31 percent were placed in full-time self-contained special education programs. All control group children unserved in preschool required special education services. In summary, the data reflects the cost-effectiveness of early intervention and the long-term savings for society. *See, e.g.,* E. Edgar, M. Heggelund, & M. Fisher, *A Longitudinal Study of Graduates of Special Education Preschool: Educational Placement after Preschool,* Topics in Early Childhood Special Education, 61-64 (1988).

In light of the generally accepted premise that early childhood education is extremely cost-effective because it allows early intervention and prevents educational disabilities from developing, what efforts could be made by school districts to create early childhood education programs? How might school districts be able to partner with early childhood service providers in a community?

(b) Differentiation in the Classroom

Another method of reducing the costs of special education is to insure that differentiated instructional practices take place for *all* children throughout the school. Differentiation is a teacher's response to a learner's needs, guided by principles such as tailored tasks, flexible grouping and ongoing assessment and adjustment. Teachers can differentiate by altering the content of instruction, the process of delivery of materials and the expected outcomes. The key is to alter content, process and expected outcomes to meet each student's unique readiness, interests and learning style. Strategies employed to meet a student's learning needs include: recognition of multiple intelligences, varying materials, tiered or scaffolded lessons, small and flexible grouping, individual instruction and varying homework assignments.

Because differentiation properly practiced requires a classroom teacher to adapt teaching to meet the needs of each student, this approach to education can work extremely well with students who have learning disabilities. Differentiation *assumes* what educational professionals know to be true: every student learns differently. If every student learns differently, then differentiation will succeed in reaching students who are gifted, learning disabled or both.

Differentiation, of course, may be inconsistent with a standards-based, grade-level directed approach to education. Although the political trends as evidenced by the No Child Left Behind Act are "standards-based," true educational professionals understand that teaching to a grade level norm or a grade level test disserves all students, particularly those with learning disabilities. As such, standardized testing regimes tend to isolate special education students for special treatment apart from the "regular" classroom. Differentiation allows teachers to meet the needs of *all* students, including those with educational disabilities, in the regular classroom. As such, it serves the educational interests of all students, and coincidently saves the cost caused by unnecessarily isolating for special treatment a child with learning disabilities.

(c) Flex

The Flexible Service Delivery Model (Flex), which has been implemented on a trial basis in several path-breaking school districts, is a way of providing services and interventions to students who demonstrate a need for academic or behavioral support without going through a formal evaluation process. Flex is based upon a collaborative problem-solving approach where a team (which includes pupil services personnel, classroom teachers and administrators) meets to discuss student needs, develop strategies and goals and evaluate their effectiveness with established timelines. Interventions may be delivered in a variety of settings by a variety of people.

Flexible Service Delivery was adopted in an effort to offer a more flexible and responsive delivery system for students than the traditional model of service delivery. The traditional model generally follows a refer-test-place process in which a referred child is given standardized tests to determine eligibility for special education services. The Flex model was developed to overcome some of the weaknesses in the traditional model, including: (1) the necessity to place a label on a child; (2) rigid criteria for establishing eligibility for special education (if students are not found eligible, they may be sent back to the regular education teacher with little support); (3) the criteria for a given diagnosis is often unreliable and often varies across districts and states, and (4) the testing process results in time delays before service is initiated. Flexible Service Delivery allows districts to provide services to students without giving them a label or having to find them "eligible." Under Flexible Service

Delivery, the goal is to insure that every student who needs support receives support.

The current special education system also includes a number of problems that create unintended barriers to effective services for some students, including a referral and evaluation system driven by deficit labels that are not logically related to the development of effective interventions and rigid procedural requirements that make it difficult to offer preventive interventions or that result in unacceptable time delays before service is initiated.

Flexible Service Delivery involves implementation of alternative assessment practices that: place assistance to the child first and use intervention results as part of the evaluation process (as opposed to categorical labeling); use alternative assessments to accurately monitor student progress on a regular basis; and use data derived from students' responses to interventions to determine the need for further services. The Flex system integrates assessment and intervention activities to improve the effectiveness of services for students. Special education and any other compensatory services are employed more flexibly as intervention. Flex also allows flexibility regarding the provider of intervention services, the amount of intervention provided and the location of the services.

E. THE IEP PROCESS PRACTICUM

The Valley School District has a policy regarding special education that commits the district to the provision of services to the extent required by law. The district has interpreted its own policy to require no more than the provision of a "floor" of opportunity for children with educational disabilities. Alice is in the fourth grade and has been a model student throughout her school years, both behaviorally and academically. She scores extremely well in classroom assessments. In addition, Alice has always "met" expectations in the state's standardized tests. Finally, Alice scores in the 85th percentile on the Comprehensive Test of Basic Skills (CTBS/Terra-Nova), which the school administers every year.

Alice's fourth grade teacher, however, has observed that although Alice is extremely intelligent, she has difficulty absorbing written material, and appears to struggle with processing written cues. As an advocate for Alice, the teacher insists that Alice be tested for the possibility of a learning disability. Indeed, the teacher believes that Alice may be both "gifted" in some cognitive areas, and also learning disabled in other cognitive areas. The district's administrator charged with overseeing the district's special education practices and budget, however, takes a contrary view. The administrator believes that as long as Alice continues to "test" in the above-average range, the district has no responsibility to provide any special education services for Alice. Alice's parents complain to the president of the district's school board that the district has denied services to Alice, despite the contrary wishes of Alice's teacher. The school board president seeks your legal advice. What are the district's legal responsibilities to Alice? What practical advice would you offer in addition to your legal opinion?

SECTION V

THE EDUCATIONAL ENVIRONMENT

Educators are entrusted to provide a safe learning environment for children, and they generally succeed. Despite all of the media attention given to acts of violence in schools, the reality is that schools are a relatively safe place. Nonetheless, schools can be the site of physical and emotional harm to children. When a teacher, supervisor or parent volunteer commits an act or omission injuring a student on school grounds, or at a school-sponsored event, the law of torts generally provides a student with a remedy to seek compensation in the form of damages. The common law of torts allows a student to sue a teacher or other educational professional who breaches a duty that causes harm in the educational environment.

The evolution of common law tort duties in schools has been informed by two competing policy concerns. The teacher's "custody" over young students during the school day has led some courts to observe that teachers stand *in loco parentis* relative to their students and to impose upon teachers a duty of care that is greater than the general duty of care community members owe to each other. *See, e.g., Eastman v. Williams,* 124 Vt. 445, 207 A.2d 146 (Vt. 1965). ("The teacher stands in the parents' place in his relationship to the pupil.") On the other hand, the reality that the judgments entered in tort cases will likely be paid by the school district or its publicly elected officials from public funds has led some courts to cabin tort liability in the educational environment. *See, e.g., Donohue v. Copiague Union Free School District,* 47 N.Y.2d 440, 418 N.Y.S.2d 375, 391 N.E.2d 1352 (1979) (extension of tort liability to educational malpractice would "constitute blatant interference with the responsibility for the administration of the public school system").

These competing policy objectives shape the nature of the duties owed by educational professionals and the defenses to liability available to school districts and their officials. Chapter 14 in this section addresses traditional common law tort duties in the educational environment. As you explore these classic tort cases, analyze whether the school setting should alter the development and application of traditional tort concepts. Chapter 15 then raises the related, but distinct question of whether the school setting has produced, or should produce, unique, nontraditional duties. Certainly, section 1983 of the U.S. Code imposes unique duties on public schools. That federal law expressly allows students to sue school districts for injuries resulting from the district's violation of their constitutional rights, 42 U.S.C. §1983. In addition, the perception that the physical and emotional safety of school children has become more threatened has led to strong arguments for the recognition of enhanced duties to protect children from harm in the educational environment.

As you evaluate the cases and scholarship regarding recent trends in the evolution of legal duties in the school setting, reconsider the fundamental goals of education and the role of a safe and secure environment in achieving those goals. Consider, as well, the place of disparate resources in the evolution of duties in the educational environment. For instance, should a teacher's duty to supervise students depend on the number of students in the classroom? Should the duty to maintain a safe educational environment recognize distinctions in the resources available to operate and maintain a safe school?

CHAPTER 15

TRADITIONAL COMMON LAW TORTS IN THE EDUCATIONAL ENVIRONMENT

A. THE FRAMEWORK OF TORT CLAIMS AND DEFENSES IN THE EDUCATIONAL ENVIRONMENT

1. Tort Claims

There are four essential elements to every common law tort claim: (1) the defendant must owe a duty to the plaintiff; (2) the duty owed must be breached; (3) the breach of duty must be the proximate cause of the harm, and (4) the plaintiff tort victim must have suffered some cognizable injury. *See generally* Keeton et al., *Prosser and Keeton on Torts* (5th ed. 1984); Restatement (Second) of Torts (1977).

The liabilities created by the common law of torts are often divided into three different mental states. First, in rare situations, the courts may impose "strict liability." Strict liability means that a school district or its agents may be liable to students for injuries without any "fault," and regardless of whether the district or its agents had an intent to harm the student or breached any standard of care. Second, and far more significant in the school setting, teachers and school administrators will be held liable for their negligence—their failure to satisfy a standard of care which their profession or their community deems reasonable under the circumstances. In particular, teachers and other educational professionals have a common law duty to exercise reasonable care in the supervision of children. *See, e.g., Sheehan v. St. Peter's Catholic School,* 188 N.W.2d 868 (Minn. 1971) (teacher and school liable for failure to supervise children at recess where student was injured when a pebble thrown by another student went into her eye); *Gibbons v. Orleans Parish,* 391 So. 2d 976 (La. Ct. App. 1980) (school district liable for negligent placement of equipment, and failure to create adequate playground supervision). Finally, teachers and school administrators also may be liable for "intentional torts," where the student is injured as the result of an intentional (not merely careless) act.

2. Tort Defenses

The law of torts also recognizes defenses to each of these tort claims, which are generally applicable in the education setting.

(a) Defenses Based on the Victim's Own Conduct

Some of these defenses attack the conduct of the tort victim. The tortfeasor, for instance, may try to overcome liability by arguing that the victim's own negligence contributed to the injury, or that the victim's comparative negligence should be taken into consideration in the damages awarded, or that the victim's assumption of the risk should bar recovery.

Contributory negligence is conduct on the part of the plaintiff that falls below the standard of care the plaintiff should have exercised and which was a contributing cause of the harm. *See* Restatement (Second) of Torts §463 (1977). The standard of care for children, however, is not the same as that for adults. Accordingly, the courts are hesitant to find contributory negligence unless a student's lack of care constitutes a gross disregard for safety. *See, e.g., Cormier v. Sinegal,* 180 So. 2d 567 (La. Ct. App. 1965). Only where a student engages in dangerous conduct such as purposefully igniting or mixing dangerous chemicals in a science experiment or recklessly climbing on a sharp fence, therefore, will the courts be willing to permit a finding of contributory negligence. *See, e.g., Rixmann v. Somerset Public Schools,* 83 Wis. 2d 571, 266 N.W.2d 326 (Wis. 1978) (intentionally disrupting science experiment); *Wilhelm v. Board of Education of City of New York,* 16 A.D.2d 791, 227 N.Y.S.2d 791 (1962) (disrupting science lab); *Basmajian v. Board of Education,* 211 A.D. 347, 207 N.Y.S. 298 (1925) (reckless climbing). In those cases where "contributory negligence" is found, the consequences are harsh. The plaintiff is completely precluded from recovering any damages at all.

The doctrine of comparative negligence, by contrast, allows the fact-finder to reduce the *amount* of damages it awards to a tort victim by the degree to which the victim's own negligence causes the injury. Many states have passed comparative negligence statutes to avoid the draconian consequences of "contributory negligence." In these states, the fact-finder is required to apportion fault among the tortfeasor and the victim and award damages in an amount that corresponds to the percentage of fault attributed to the defendant.

Finally, the defense of "assumption of risk" permits a tortfeasor to escape liability by establishing that the victim knowingly and voluntarily assumed the risk of the injury that occurred. Unlike comparative and contributory negligence, this defense is not concerned with the plaintiff's relative carelessness. Rather, the "assumption of risk" theory concentrates on the plaintiff's knowledge of the risk and voluntary actions in taking on that risk. As such, courts have held that students playing intramural sports knowingly assume the risk of the normal hazards of athletics, but do not assume the risk that athletic equipment would fail or break. *Compare Maltz v. Board of Education of New York City,* 32 Misc. 2d 492, 114 N.Y.S.2d 856 (1952) (student assumes risk of sports injury while playing basketball); *Benedetto v. Travelers Insurance Co.,* 172 So. 2d 354 (La. Ct. App. 1965) (teammates assume risk of getting hit by balls and bats at baseball games) *with Stevens v. Central School District No. 1,* 25 A.D. 2d 871, 270 N.Y.S.2d 23 (1966) (no assumption of risk that glass door near basketball court would shatter).

(b) Immunity Defenses

In the education arena, there are also unique immunity defenses that may limit the practical reach of civil tort actions by students for damages. School districts and their governing boards are often sued for the tortious acts of their educators in the scope of employment. A school district's liability for such torts raises questions about the degree of immunity that should be afforded a governmental body charged with making and implementing discretionary policy judgments.

As arms of the state, school districts historically have enjoyed sovereign immunity from tort claims. This traditional, common law immunity is rooted in the notion that the "king can do no wrong." More recently, the doctrine has been rationalized on the ground that a school district's funds should be used only for educational purposes, and should not be used to pay tort damages. In addition, it has been argued that because a state agency could not authorize tortious conduct, a public school district should not be made liable vicariously for such conduct. *See Molitor v. Kaneland Community Unit School District No. 302,* 18 Ill. 2d 11, 163 N.E.2d 89 (Ill. 1959) (articulating the historic and contemporary justifications for the sovereign immunity of school districts).

As the judicial doctrine of governmental immunity evolved in the education setting, however, the courts began to create exceptions to that doctrine. Because the doctrine was designed to protect sovereign acts from liability, some courts recognized a distinction between protected governmental conduct by school districts and unprotected nongovernmental, "proprietary" conduct. In *Morris v. School District of Township of Mt. Lebanon,* 393 Pa. 633, 144 A.2d 737 (Pa. 1958), for example, the Pennsylvania Supreme Court held the school district liable for injuries to a child in the district's summer camp program, reasoning that the program was "proprietary" rather than governmental. *See also Sawaya v. Tucson High School District,* 78 Ariz. 389, 281 P.2d 105 (Az. 1955) (district liable for injuries at stadium it owned, but had rented to another party). *But see Kellam v. School Board of Norfolk,* 202 Va. 252, 117 S.E.2d 96 (Va. 1960) (district's act in renting its auditorium is governmental, and hence no liability ensues).

Some courts have decided to abolish the immunity doctrine altogether. *See Ayala v. Philadelphia Board of Public Education,* 453 Pa. 584, 305 A.2d 877 (Pa. 1973) (ultimately abolishing the common law immunity of school districts); *Molitor v. Kaneland Community Unit School District No. 302,* 18 Ill. 2d 11, 163 N.E.2d 89 (Ill. 1959) (abandoning the doctrine of sovereign immunity for school districts and holding the district liable for student injuries on a school bus). In *Molitor,* the court rejected the historic roots of sovereign immunity as an anachronistic throwback to the long-rejected doctrine of the divine right of kings. Moreover, the court argued that, "[we] do not believe that in this present day and age, when public education constitutes one of the biggest businesses in the country, that school immunity can be justified on the protection-of-public-funds theory." Finally, the *Molitor* court rejected the argument that sovereign immunity could be abolished only by the legislature, reasoning that the doctrine was judicially created and therefore could be judicially destroyed. Some courts, however, have declared that the task of abrogating sovereign immunity must be left to the legislature. *See Morash and Sons, Inc. v. Commonwealth,* 363 Mass. 612, 296 N.E.2d 461 (Mass. 1973).

The vast majority of states (30 or more) have now by common law or statute completely abolished sovereign immunity. *See* Keeton et al., *Prosser and Keeton on Torts* 1044-1045 (5th ed. 1984) ("The great majority [of states] have now consented to at least some liability for torts, in all cases retaining the immunity at least to some extent for basic policy or discretionary decisions."). Of those states that have not fully removed sovereign immunity, most offer immunity to school districts so long as the district or the state has secured insurance against harm to students. *See, e.g., Crowell v. School District No. 7,* 805 P.2d 522 (Mont. 1991) (Montana legislature has allowed school districts to waive immunity to the extent of insurance coverage); *Dugger v. Sprouse,* 257 Ga. 778, 364 S.E.2d 275 (Ga. 1988) (governmental entity waives sovereign immunity to extent of insurance coverage). Accordingly, in virtually every state, the traditional defense of sovereign immunity will no longer completely insulate school districts from their tortious conduct and from the tortious conduct of their educators in the scope of their employment.

Although sovereign immunity may no longer protect school districts, those districts and their officials generally are still protected from personal liability for their discretionary policy judgments. The courts have hesitated to impose tort liability on public and private school districts and administrators where the harm results from decisions within their educational judgment or discretion. *See, e.g., Nalepa v. Plymouth-Canton Community School District,* 525 N.E.2d 897 (Mich. Ct. App. 1994) (superintendent immune from liability under Michigan statute protecting educators from liability for conduct within the scope of their authority). School board members exercising judgment and discretion thus typically are not liable for the consequences of their conduct. *See, e.g., Mosley v. Portland School District, No. 1,* 315 Or. 85, 843 P.2d 415 (Or. 1992) (location of security personnel is a discretionary matter). Rather, they can be sued only for malicious conduct in the performance of their discretionary functions or tortious conduct outside of their discretionary authority.

Accordingly, one of the most significant issues regarding school district and school board liability is whether the conduct challenged was part of a school district's or a school board's discretionary authority. Discretionary authority is often defined by what it is not. Ministerial acts are not discretionary, and therefore can result in tort liability. *See, e.g., Adams v. Schneider,* 71 Ind. App. 249, 124 N.E. 718 (1919) (board members liable for negligence in building bleachers for field day event). Where statutory directives are mandatory and not discretionary, a board member's failure to comply with the directive can give rise to personal liability. *Compare Bronaugh v. Murray,* 294 Ky. 715, 172 S.W.2d 591 (1943) (failure to obtain insurance for bus accidents as required by statute results in liability) *with Nichols v. Zera,* 33 Mich. App. 274, 189 N.W.2d 751 (1971) (no statutory duty to prevent harm to students from fight with nonstudents).

In *Hopkins v. Spring Independent School District,* 736 S.W.2d 617 (Tex. 1987), for instance, the Texas Supreme Court addressed the issue of a school district's immunity from liability for conduct involving judgment and discretion. In that case, an elementary school student who suffers from cerebral palsy was pushed into a stack of chairs and sustained a head injury. She had mild convulsions, developed cold sweats and became dazed and incoherent. The teacher did not call for help or send her to the school nurse. At the end of the school day, the student suffered severe convulsions while on the bus. The bus driver contacted a supervisor, requesting a school nurse be provided at the next stop, but none was provided. The student's parent sued the school district, the bus supervisor, the school principal, the school nurse and the teacher, claiming the school personnel's negligence and gross negligence in failing to provide adequate care dramatically decreased the student's life expectancy.

The court ruled, however, that the school personnel could not be liable even for negligent acts that result in serious bodily injury to students under the following language from the Texas Education Code:

> No professional employee of any school district within this state shall be personally liable for any act incident to or within the scope of the duties of his position of employment, and which act involves the exercise of judgment or discretion on the part of the employee, except in circumstances where professional employees use excessive force in the discipline of students or negligence resulting in bodily injury to students.

Reconsider the policies supporting sovereign immunity and the countervailing policies supporting the imposition of traditional tort liability in the nation's schools. The *Hopkins* court does not address those policies head on. How would you have weighed those policies here?

In the absence of any sovereign immunity or discretionary authority defense, school districts retain liability for the tortious conduct of educators. As you analyze the following tort claims involving strict liability, negligence and intentional conduct in the educational environment, revisit the question of the nature of that environment itself. Is the school an extension of the home with educators acting as guardians, or is it a purely public forum?

B. STRICT LIABILITY TORTS AND THE DUTY TO PROTECT STUDENTS FROM DANGEROUS SITUATIONS

The tort law concept of "strict liability" applies where the defendant has manufactured or distributed a defective product, or where the defendant engages in an inherently dangerous or ultrahazardous activity. *See* Keeton et al., *Prosser and Keeton on Torts* 315 (5th ed. 1984). The defendant's creation of the dangerous circumstance which results in foreseeable harm alone renders that defendant liable without any fault. *See* Restatement (Second) of Torts 519-521 (1977). As the *Fallon* case indicates, however, the courts have been reluctant to impose strict liability on educational professionals.

FALLON V. INDIAN TRAIL SCHOOL

148 Ill. App. 3d 931, 500 N.E.2d 101, 102 Ill. Dec. 479 (1986)

Justice STROUSE delivered the opinion of the court:

The plaintiff, Mary Jane Fallon, appeals from the order of the circuit court which dismissed counts I, II, and III of her four-count amended complaint against the defendants, Indian Trail School (school), Addison Township School District No. 4 (school district), Maureen Roach and Louise Roynan-Leo (teachers). For the reasons set forth below, we affirm the decision of the circuit court.

The plaintiff's amended complaint sought to recover damages for spinal injuries suffered as a result of a trampoline accident which occurred on February 23, 1975. At that time the plaintiff was a sixth-grade student at the school and the defendants, Roach and Roynan-Leo, were physical education teachers. The incident occurred when the plaintiff attempted a "front drop" maneuver on the trampoline during her physical education class. In her attempt to perform the maneuver, the plaintiff sustained spinal injuries.

On appeal, the plaintiff contends that the trial court erroneously granted the motion to dismiss counts I and II, thereby preventing her from introducing evidence which would demonstrate that trampoline usage is an "abnormally dangerous" activity.

The plaintiff also contends that the trial court erroneously granted the motion to dismiss count III, as it properly included the elements of a negligent hiring and supervision claim.

. . . In count I, the plaintiff alleged that the trampoline was an abnormally dangerous instrumentality, and the school district should, therefore, be held accountable under strict tort liability for any injuries due to its use. In count II, the plaintiff charged the school and school district with negligence as a result of a violation of section 10.20.8 of the School Code . . . because the trampoline was an abnormally dangerous instrumentality. We must, therefore, decide whether the plaintiff has alleged sufficient facts to support the contention that the trampoline is an abnormally dangerous instrumentality and trampoline usage is an abnormally dangerous activity.

Illinois recognizes strict liability under two theories: unreasonably dangerous defective products and the theory which plaintiff alleges is applicable to this case, ultrahazardous activities. Sections 519 and 520 of the Restatement (Second) of Torts (1981) (Restatement) have formulated a definition of ultrahazardous activities. Under section 519(1) of the Restatement, "[o]ne who carries on an abnormally dangerous activity is subject to liability for harm to the person, land or chattels of another resulting from the activity, although he has exercised the utmost care to prevent the harm." (Restatement

(Second) of Torts sec. 519(1) (1981).) Section 520 of the Restatement considers: "[E]xistence of a high degree of risk of some harm . . . ; likelihood that the harm that results from it will be great; inability to eliminate the risk by the exercise of reasonable care; extent to which the activity is not a matter of common usage. . . ." Restatement (Second) of Torts sec. 520 (1981).

Illinois has long recognized strict liability for damages caused by engaging in an ultrahazardous activity, although it has never explicitly relied upon the Restatement factors in determining whether a given activity is abnormally dangerous. . . .

The plaintiff concedes that there is no Illinois authority discussing either whether (1) trampoline usage of this sort is an ultrahazardous activity, or (2) the trampoline is an abnormally dangerous instrumentality. Indeed, the trial court, in its written disposition dismissing counts I and II, noted that most of the discussion which related to this subject had to do with such obviously dangerous instrumentalities and activities as blasting, transport of explosives, maintenance of high electrical current, large animals, and maintenance of water reservoirs. In support of her argument, the plaintiff attached Exhibit A, "Trampoline-Related Quadriplegia: Review of the Literature and Reflections on the American Academy of Pediatrics' Position Statement," a review documenting cervical spine injuries resulting from trampoline-related accidents.

After reviewing Exhibit A, the trial court's disposition, as well as the plaintiff's amended complaint, we believe the trial court was correct in finding that trampoline usage, as alleged in the present case, does not fall within the parameter of an abnormally dangerous activity. We also agree that the trampoline, as a matter of law, is not an abnormally dangerous instrumentality. Trampolines are widely used in the school systems as well as other centers of gymnastic activity. The injuries that may be caused result not from the trampoline itself but rather from the manner of its use. The terms "ultra-hazardous," "abnormally dangerous," or "intrinsically dangerous," as traditionally used, refer to that type of danger which is inherent in the instrumentality itself at all times and do not mean danger which arises from mere casual or collateral negligence of others with respect to it under the particular circumstances. More concisely, it means dangerous in its normal or nondefective state. We conclude that although its negligent use can be the basis for liability, neither the trampoline itself nor its ordinary use is abnormally dangerous or ultrahazardous. Therefore, counts I and II were properly dismissed.

NOTES AND QUESTIONS

1. What are examples of activities in a school setting that would create a "danger which is inherent in the instrumentality itself"? A child has a severe allergy to a particular food. The student's medical records contain information as to this fact. The school cafeteria serves that food to the child; should there be liability for the creation of a dangerous circumstance, which results in a foreseeable harm?
2. In *Nottingham v. Akron Board of Education,* 81 Ohio App. 3d 319, 610 N.E.2d 1096 (1992), the court refused to impose liability on the school district for

its failure to protect a student from a dangerous dog on school grounds. In *Brown v. Tesack,* 566 So. 2d 955 (La. 1990), however, the Louisiana Supreme Court held the school district and its school board liable for injuries resulting when a child ignited duplicating fluid that the school's employees had placed into a dumpster. The court reasoned that the school district could foresee that children might misuse such an "inherently dangerous object" and cause harm. Accordingly, the court held the district liable for its disposal of a "dangerous substance" in the school's dumpster. Although the court mentions that the school district breached a "duty," its opinion makes clear that liability is being imposed for the foreseeable injuries created by ultra-hazardous items, conditions or activities.

C. NEGLIGENCE AND THE DUTY TO PROTECT STUDENTS FROM PHYSICAL HARM

Negligence in the school setting involves a breach of the duty of care that educational professionals and administrators owe to students. The common law has developed a standard of care unique to educational professionals that is characterized as a duty to supervise children. That duty of supervision appears to be the strongest when the teacher is in the classroom, supervising students engaged in a dangerous activity. The duty seems to weaken, but not disappear, outside the walls of the classroom.

1. The Duty to Supervise in the Classroom

JOHNSON V. SCHOOL DISTRICT OF MILLARD

253 Neb. 634, 573 N.W.2d 116 (Neb. 1998)

WRIGHT, Justice.

The plaintiff commenced this negligence action pursuant to the Nebraska Political Subdivisions Tort Claims Act, alleging that the defendant, through its employee, was negligent in that the employee failed to properly supervise students who were under her care. The defendant appeals from an award to the plaintiff in the amount of $21,226.10. . . .

Facts

On September 15, 1993, Robbie L. Johnson, a first grader at Willa Cather Elementary School, was injured while attending his music class. On this day, the teacher of the music class, Nancy Patton, taught her class the song and accompanying game of "London Bridge." London Bridge is a game in which two children, while singing a song, form a "bridge" by linking their arms. The children's linked arms are then lowered around a third child who is rocked back and forth. The children were taught how to sing the song, and then the teacher used two children to demonstrate how the accompanying game was played. The teacher picked two children at random and instructed them to link their arms together, explaining that they were to rock a third child within their linked arms. The teacher warned the children not to act silly and told them not to yell, scream, or swing their arms too much. After giving these instructions, the teacher allowed the children to play the game on their own. It was undisputed that this was the first time the students had played the game and that Johnson was the first child who was caught and rocked between the children's linked arms.

Johnson testified that he was swung "fast and hard" while caught in his classmates' arms. While swinging Johnson, the two children accidentally released their hands and threw Johnson into a bookcase at the end of the room, cutting his head above his right eyebrow. Johnson testified that he told the children swinging him to stop at least three times and asked for help twice before the accident occurred. He testified that he was trying to yell over the music, but everyone was talking, and some of the children were laughing and singing.

It is undisputed that the teacher was not watching Johnson when he was injured. Johnson testified that the teacher was writing on the blackboard, and he and another student testified that she had her back to the children when the accident occurred. The teacher testified that she saw Johnson caught within the children's arms but did not witness him being swung because she was aiding another child.

Johnson required 50 stitches to close the cut above his right eye. The cut extended to the bone and divided the muscle throughout its length. Johnson suffered blurred vision for a short period of time and continues to suffer headaches as a result of his injury.

The trial court held that the teacher's mere instruction to first grade children on how to play the game without direct supervision during at least the early portions of the game was negligent supervision. The court found that as a result of the accident Johnson sustained an injury and damages, and awarded him $1,226.10 for medical expenses, $15,000 for permanent disfigurement, and $5,000 for pain and suffering. The School District of Millard appeals from the judgment.

Assignments of Error

Summarized and restated, the school district asserts that the trial court erred (1) in holding the school district to a standard of care that required direct supervision of a nondangerous activity, rather than the standard of care of an ordinary prudent person; (2) in finding the school district negligent without requiring the use of expert testimony or other evidence to show that the school district was negligent; and (3) in finding that the school district's negligence proximately caused Johnson's injury.

Analysis

The school district argues that we should reverse the judgment of the trial court because the court failed to give proper weight to the testimony of the teacher, the only adult that testified, and therefore made findings of fact which are clearly wrong. In a bench trial of a law action, the court, as the trier of fact, is the sole judge of the credibility of the witnesses and the weight to be given their testimony. This court will not reweigh the testimony or reevaluate the credibility of the witnesses, but it will review the evidence to determine whether the trial court made findings which are clearly wrong.

The school district asserts that the trial court was clearly wrong in relying upon Johnson's testimony, since some of the estimates given by him appear to be in error. Johnson testified that his classmates swung him violently for 3 minutes before the accident occurred and that he was off the ground for 10 seconds before hitting the bookcase. In contrast, another student and the teacher testified that the incident occurred in 5 seconds or less, and the teacher testified that the London Bridge song takes only 7 to 12 seconds to sing.

Although Johnson's estimate regarding the length of time he was off the ground is not possible, we cannot say that the trial court was clearly wrong in relying upon other aspects of his testimony. The court's determination of liability was not based upon Johnson's estimate of how long he was off the ground before striking the bookcase and was not based upon his estimate of how long he was swung by his classmates before the accident. Liability was predicated on the court's finding that the teacher was in the blackboard area with her back to Johnson at the time of the accident, that Johnson was swung "fast and hard" by his classmates, and that this was the first time the children had played London Bridge in class. The court found that under these circumstances, the teacher was negligent in failing to directly supervise the students during at least the early portions of the game and in failing to stop the aggressive swinging of Johnson. The court found that under all of the attendant circumstances, the accident and injury were foreseeable, and that the negligence of the teacher was the proximate cause of Johnson's injury. Thus, the school district's claim that the court improperly weighed the evidence and made findings of fact which are clearly wrong is without merit.

Likewise, the school district's claim that the trial court gave too much weight to Johnson's testimony is without merit. In a bench trial, the court, as the trier of fact, is the sole judge of the weight to be given the testimony. Thus, we will not review the amount of weight which the trier of fact gave to either the teacher's or Johnson's testimony.

The proper standard of care regarding negligent supervision is whether the defendant acted as a reasonably prudent person would in a similar circumstance. The trial court found that the teacher was negligent in not directly supervising the children during at least the early portions of the game. The question is whether the teacher had a duty to directly supervise her students at this time.

The school district argues that the trial court incorrectly required the teacher to provide direct supervision, which imposed a higher standard of care than that of a reasonably prudent person. The cases cited by the school district imply that constant supervision of students at all times is not required by a teacher acting as a reasonably prudent person and that direct supervision is needed only when children are engaged in dangerous activities. By analogy, the school district argues that since London Bridge is not a dangerous activity, the court should not have required the teacher to provide constant and direct supervision.

We conclude that the trial court did not require the teacher to provide constant and direct supervision because the court's order states that the teacher needed to provide direct supervision to the children during only the "early portions of the game." The court did not hold the teacher to a higher standard of care than that of a reasonably prudent person. Instead, the court found that a reasonably prudent person would have given direct supervision to first graders during at least the early portions of a game which they were playing for the first time. We cannot say that the trial court was clearly wrong.

The school district claims that the teacher would not have had enough time to assist Johnson even if she had supervised him more closely and that, therefore, she is not responsible for Johnson's injury. We disagree. The trial court found that the teacher was in the blackboard area with her back to Johnson just prior to the injury and that Johnson did not trip and fall into the bookcase, but, rather, was propelled by the "fast and hard" swinging of the two children composing the bridge. The court found that Johnson told his classmates to stop and cried for help before the accident. The court found that the teacher was negligent in failing to stop the aggressive swinging by the two students making up the bridge and that this negligence was the proximate cause of Johnson's injury. As each of these findings is supported by the evidence, we cannot say that the trial court was clearly wrong.

We next address whether the school district's negligence was the proximate cause of Johnson's injury or whether the act of the other children constitutes an intervening cause which defeats causation. There are three basic requirements that must be met to establish causation: (1) that "but for" the defendant's negligence, the injury would not have occurred; (2) that the injury is the natural and probable result of the negligence; and (3) that there is no efficient intervening cause. The school district argues that the act of Johnson's classmates, who released their hands and propelled Johnson into the bookcase, is an intervening cause which defeats causation.

In order for the children's accidentally releasing their hands to be an intervening cause, this court must find that the children's act was unforeseeable. We conclude that it is reasonably foreseeable that children playing London Bridge might swing another child in such a manner that the sudden release of their hands could cause an accident. Therefore, the fact that the children released their hands and caused Johnson to hit his head is not an intervening cause.

Finally, the school district argues that the trial court erred in determining liability without the use of expert testimony regarding the teacher's standard of care. Neb. Evid. R. 702, states: "If scientific, technical, or other specialized knowledge will assist the trier of fact to understand the evidence or to determine a fact in issue, a witness qualified as an expert . . . may testify thereto in the form of an opinion or otherwise."

Scientific evidence is not needed to understand whether the teacher was negligent when she failed to watch a group of first graders play a game for the first time. There is nothing technical or scientific about a common children's game such as London Bridge. Accordingly, an expert witness would have been of little use to the trier of fact. The trial court was not clearly wrong when, without the use of expert testimony, it found that the teacher was negligent and that her negligence was a proximate cause of Johnson's injury.

NOTES AND QUESTIONS

1. The court distinguishes between the duty of constant supervision and the duty of reasonable supervision. What are the contours of that distinction? In the case itself, at what point did the teacher's duty change?
2. The court also distinguishes its facts from those involving dangerous situations. The duty of "constant supervision" apparently exists in circumstances involving unusual danger, while the duty of reasonable supervision exists in the routine classroom situation. Here, the court suggests that a reasonably prudent teacher would have been more vigilant, and that the failure to turn from the chalkboard was a breach of the standard of reasonable supervision. How much more care would have been required under a duty of "constant supervision"?
3. Consider whether the duty to supervise has been breached in the following common situations: (1) A student is misbehaving in class while the teacher is lecturing. The teacher sends the student out in the hallway for a timeout. While in the hallway and unsupervised, the student sustains an injury. Was there a failure to supervise the student? (2) Upon entering the school, the students are screened by a metal detector. The situation is often chaotic and rushed. Children slip through the metal detectors despite setting the alarm off. Does the school face liability because they completed a weapon search and had reason to believe that a weapon may have been taken into the school?

2. The Heightened Duty to Supervise in Dangerous School Situations

Norman v. Ogallala Public School District

259 Neb. 184, 609 N.W.2d 338 (Neb. 2002)

Hendry, C.J.

Introduction

David and Susan Norman, individually and on behalf of their son, Christopher Norman (Christopher), brought a negligence action against the Ogallala Public School District, Keith County District No. 1, and teacher Willis Hastings. Christopher suffered severe injuries when the shirt he was wearing during a welding class caught fire. The district court for Keith County found the school district and Hastings negligent and awarded damages in the amount of $342,290.80. The school district and Hastings then filed this appeal.

Factual Background

In November 1994, Christopher, a 15-year-old freshman, was enrolled in a welding class at the Ogallala High School. The class was taught by Hastings and included instruction in both arc and acetylene welding. Students in the class were beginning welders who had not yet become proficient at welding.

The school provided certain protective gear for students to wear during the welding class consisting of goggles, helmets, leather gloves, and leather leggings. Students were encouraged, but not required, to utilize this protective gear. The school did not provide leather aprons for students' use during the welding class.

Classroom instruction was provided as part of the welding class. Students were given a textbook and handouts, which discussed welding procedures and certain safety measures in setting up and using welding equipment. Students also took a variety of tests which included performance of certain welding operations. None of these tests defined what type of protective clothing should be worn while welding, and most of the tests made no reference to protective clothing.

Hastings told students that they needed to wear "protective clothing" while welding and provided them with handouts regarding protective clothing. These handouts made reference only to leather clothing or clothing made from "heavy fire resistant cloth." The handouts depicted a welder wearing a helmet, leather jacket, coveralls, and gloves. However, Hastings simply told students to bring an "old shirt" from home to wear during class. Hastings allowed students to decide what to wear during welding class and did not inspect their clothing. Students were not prevented from welding regardless of what they were wearing. Information about protective clothing was not provided to students' parents. Hastings' deposition was offered and admitted into evidence, without objection to the following testimony:

Q: You would agree it was your responsibility to ensure that the clothing worn by the student would minimize the risk of igniting themselves?
A: No.
Q: You would not agree with that?
A: No. . . .
Q: My question is, is it your duty to ensure that they are wearing proper protective clothing to minimize the risk of them igniting themselves?
A: No. No.
Q: That's not your job?
A: No.

On November 16, 1994, Christopher was acetylene welding while wearing a black T-shirt. Over this, he wore his "protective clothing," a long-sleeved cotton-flannel shirt which was buttoned to the neck, with the sleeves also buttoned. While Christopher was welding, his flannel shirt ignited on the left side. Hastings and another shop teacher realized that Christopher's shirt was on fire and, after a struggle, managed to remove the shirt. The cotton-flannel shirt and black T-shirt were both burned over the entire left side.

Christopher suffered second- and third-degree burns to his chest, left side, and left arm, constituting 10 percent of his body. Christopher was treated at the Greeley Burn Center in Greeley, Colorado, where he underwent a debridement process during which dead skin was scraped from the burn every day for 2 weeks, causing extreme pain. He underwent painful therapy for several months and eventually had to have a skin graft taken from his thigh to allow the burn to heal. Christopher also had to wear a pressure garment for

1½ years in order to reduce scarring and had to perform exercises to prevent tightening of the scarred area. The significant scarring from the burns is permanent, but Christopher's range of motion and activities have not been limited as a result of the scarring and it is unlikely that he will have to have any further medical treatment.

The Normans brought a negligence action under the Political Subdivisions Tort Claims Act, against the school and Hastings (hereinafter collectively the school), individually and on Christopher's behalf. The school denied any negligence and asserted that it was immune from any negligence claim pursuant to the discretionary function exemption of the Political Subdivisions Tort Claims Act. The case was tried to the court.

At trial, three expert witnesses testified regarding welding safety standards. The American Welding Society (AWS) has promulgated certain safety standards which have been adopted by the American National Standards Institute (ANSI) and published in an ANSI safety standard. We will refer to the advisory safety standard then in effect as "ANSI Z49.1-94." ANSI is an organization which acts as a depository of industry and trade standards. ANSI adopts standards submitted to it by industrial organizations and distributes these standards to the public. The three experts who testified at trial agreed that ANSI Z49.1-94 is applicable to anyone carrying out the welding process, including those in a school setting. ANSI Z49.1-94 was offered and admitted into evidence without objection.

C. Phillip Colver, one of the Normans' two expert witnesses, is a chemical engineering consultant who has studied the welding process during his professional career. . . . In Colver's opinion, the students were not properly trained or supervised regarding proper protective clothing and the school did not follow the ANSI safety standards regarding protective clothing. Colver also testified that in a school setting, when dealing with students who have less appreciation of welding hazards than a professional welder, the safest possible setting should be provided. It was also his opinion that the fact that Christopher was not wearing proper protective clothing was the proximate cause of Christopher's injuries.

James Rhone, director of environmental health and safety at the University of Nebraska-Lincoln, testified on behalf of the Normans about proper safety procedures. . . . Rhone testified that in his opinion there were no safety practices taught in Hastings' welding class, even though safety would be especially important when teaching young students to weld. It was Rhone's opinion that simply giving students handouts to read was not an adequate safety procedure. Rhone also testified that the term "should" as used in ANSI Z49.1-94, expresses a recommendation that cotton clothing be chemically treated to reduce combustibility. Rhone testified that the school's failure to provide proper protective clothing and use proper safety procedures was the proximate cause of Christopher's injuries. Both Rhone and Colver testified that had the school followed proper procedures with respect to protective clothing, Christopher would not have been burned.

Donald Lynn, a professional welding engineer, testified on behalf of the school. Lynn testified that the school was in compliance with ANSI Z49.1-94, on the day of Christopher's accident because it is not mandatory under ANSI

Z49.1-94, that leather or flame-retardant clothing be worn while welding. In Lynn's opinion, Christopher was properly dressed for welding, the school properly informed students and parents about protective clothing, and students were properly supervised during class. Lynn testified that there was no breach of duty by the school which caused this accident.

Testimony was also adduced on the issue of the pain Christopher endured due to his injuries. Christopher and his parents testified about the pain Christopher endured while undergoing the debridement process. Donald Hunter, an occupational therapist trained in burn care and therapy who treated Christopher, testified to the pain Christopher underwent during the debridement process and the skin-grafting. . . .

In its order issued on July 22, 1998, the court determined that the discretionary function exception to the Political Subdivisions Tort Claims Act did not apply in this case. The court further found that the school was negligent in allowing Christopher to wear an untreated cotton-flannel shirt while welding, in failing to ensure that students wore proper protective clothing, in failing to provide students and parents with sufficient information about protective clothing, and in failing to provide students with leather aprons to wear during the welding class. The court found that the school's negligence was a proximate cause of Christopher's injuries and awarded damages in the amount of $342,290.80.

The school made a motion for judgment notwithstanding the verdict or for a new trial, which was overruled. This appeal followed.

Assignments of Error

The school claims, restated and summarized, that the trial court erred in (1) determining that the discretionary function exception did not apply; (2) allowing the opinions of Colver and Rhone into evidence; (3) interpreting ANSI Z49.1-94; (4) finding the school negligent in allowing Christopher to wear an untreated cotton-flannel shirt while welding; (5) finding the school negligent in failing to ensure students wore proper clothing; (6) determining the school failed to provide students and parents with sufficient information about protective clothing; (7) determining that the school was negligent in failing to provide leather aprons to students; (8) determining that the school's negligence was a proximate cause of Christopher's injuries; and (9) awarding excessive damages.

Analysis

Discretionary Function Exemption

The school claims that it is immune from any alleged negligence in this case pursuant to the discretionary function exemption of the Political Subdivisions Tort Claims Act. Section 13-910(2) provides:

> The Political Subdivisions Tort Claims Act . . . shall not apply to: . . . any claim based upon the exercise or performance of or the failure to exercise or perform a discretionary function or duty on the part of the political subdivision or an employee of the political subdivision, whether or not the discretion is abused.

The purpose of the discretionary function exemption is to prevent judicial "second-guessing" of legislative and administrative decisions grounded in social, economic, and political policy through the medium of an action in tort. *Jasa, supra.* The discretionary function exemption extends only to basic policy decisions made in governmental activity, and not to ministerial activities implementing such policy decisions. Examples of discretionary functions include the initiation of programs and activities, establishment of plans and schedules, and judgmental decisions within a broad regulatory framework lacking specific standards. The discretionary function exemption in tort claims acts extends only to basic policy decisions and not to the exercise of discretionary acts at an operational level. The political subdivision remains liable for negligence of its employees at the operational level, where there is no room for policy judgment. The school claims that Hastings' decisions regarding supervision, materials, and clothing to be worn during the welding class involve an element of judgment or choice and are thus "policy decisions," to which the discretionary function exemption applies. However, Hastings' decisions involving the welding class are not basic policy decisions, but are discretionary acts at an operational level. Such decisions are not planning-level decisions involving social, economic, or political policy judgment and do not come within the discretionary function exemption. We conclude as a matter of law that the discretionary function exemption has no application in this case. . . .

ANSI Standard

The parties do not dispute that ANSI Z49.1-94 was relevant to the facts of this case. However, the school argues that the trial court erred in its interpretation of that standard. . . .

The standard of care in this case is that of ordinary negligence, or what a reasonable person would or would not do under similar circumstances. Advisory safety standards, such as the ANSI standard, may represent a consensus of what a reasonable person in a particular industry would do, and therefore may be helpful to the trier of fact in deciding whether the standard of care has been met. ANSI Z49.1-94, clearly expresses a recommendation that cotton clothing be chemically treated if it is used for protection. The school did not follow that recommendation, which may be considered as evidence of negligence. We determine that under the circumstances of this case, considering the sufficiency of the evidence in the light most favorable to the successful parties, the trial court's utilization of ANSI Z49.1-94, was not clearly wrong.

Findings of Negligence

The school claims the trial court erred in finding the school negligent in several respects. First, the school claims the trial court erred in finding that the school was negligent in allowing Christopher to wear an untreated cotton-flannel shirt while welding. The school claims that under ANSI Z49.1-94, it is not mandatory that cotton clothing be chemically treated and that thus, the school did not breach its duty by allowing Christopher to wear the untreated shirt. However, negligence must be measured against the particular set of facts and circumstances which are present in each case.

Students in the welding class were not professional welders and had not perfected their welding techniques. Colver testified that in a school setting, when dealing with students who have less appreciation of welding hazards than a professional welder, the safest possible setting should be provided. Chemical treatment reduces the risk of cotton clothing becoming ignited. The court recognized the importance of the particular circumstances of this case in finding that the school breached its duty of care by allowing inexperienced welders to wear untreated cotton shirts. Although ANSI Z49.1-94 may not make wearing chemically treated cotton "mandatory," we cannot say that the trial court's finding of negligence was clearly wrong based on the evidence.

The school next asserts that the trial court erred in finding that the school was negligent in failing to ensure students wore proper clothing. However, there is competent evidence in the record that students were not properly informed about the type of protective clothing to wear, that they were not prevented from welding regardless of what they were wearing, and that Hastings never inspected what types of clothing students wore. The trial court found that under the circumstances, the school was negligent in failing to ensure that students wore proper clothing. Based on the evidence, the trial court's finding in this respect was not clearly wrong.

The school further claims the trial court erred in finding the school negligent in failing to provide students and parents with sufficient information about protective clothing. The trial court found that even though Hastings was aware that ANSI Z49.1-94 recommended that cotton clothing be chemically treated if used for protection, he never provided this information to students or parents, which would have allowed them to make an informed choice as to the type of clothing to select. The record shows that Hastings provided no information to parents regarding protective clothing. Based on the evidence, the trial court's finding of negligence was not clearly wrong.

Finally, the school asserts that the trial court erred in finding that the school was negligent by failing to provide leather aprons for students to wear while welding. The school claims leather aprons were not required by ANSI Z49.1-94. However, ANSI Z49.1-94 provides, "Durable flame-resistant aprons made of leather or other suitable materials shall be used to protect the front of the body when additional protection against sparks and radiant energy is needed." The court noted in its order that the handouts students were given depicted a welder wearing leather clothing, recommended that leather aprons or jackets be worn, and provided no alternatives if leather clothing was not provided. Based on a review of these handouts, the court determined that a leather apron would have covered the area where Christopher's shirt caught fire, and had Christopher been wearing an apron, he would not have been burned. The trial court's finding that the school was negligent in failing to provide leather aprons, considered in the light most favorable to the successful parties, was not clearly wrong.

Proximate Cause

The school claims the trial court erred in finding that the school's negligence was the proximate cause of Christopher's injuries. A proximate cause is a cause that (1) produces a result in a natural and continuous sequence and

(2) without which the result would not have occurred. The determination of causation is ordinarily a question for the trier of fact.

The evidence presented by the Normans established that had the school followed proper safety procedures with regard to protective clothing, Christopher would not have been wearing the shirt in question, would not have been allowed to weld while wearing the shirt, or would have been wearing a leather apron which would have covered the area of the shirt which caught fire. Two expert witnesses testified that had Christopher not been wearing the cotton-flannel shirt on the day in question, he would not have been injured and that the school's negligence was the cause of Christopher's injuries. Based on the evidence presented, the trial court's finding that the school's negligence was the proximate cause of Christopher's injuries was not clearly wrong.

Damages

The school claims the trial courts' award of $342,290.80 in damages is excessive. On appeal, the fact finder's determination of damages is given great deference. . . .

The school claims the damages are excessive because Christopher has completely recovered from his injuries, has no limitations on his range of motion or his activities, and it is unlikely that he will incur future medical expenses. However, the record contains extensive evidence, including both testimony and photographs, demonstrating the pain that Christopher endured and the permanent scarring resulting from the burns. In addition to the pain Christopher endured, Christopher's parents incurred medical bills in the amount of $44,614.54 as a direct result of Christopher's injuries. The award of damages was not so excessive as to be the result of passion, prejudice, mistake, or some other means not apparent in the record. The trial court's determination of damages is supported by evidence and bears a reasonable relationship to the elements of damages proved and, thus, will not be disturbed on appeal. . . .

NOTES AND QUESTIONS

1. In this case, the Supreme Court of Nebraska held that a public school was negligent in failing to make sure that the inexperienced welding student wore proper clothing. Furthermore, the court concluded that the school failed to foresee the dangerous situation that arose and that the school's failure to require the protective clothing was the proximate cause of the student's injury. Do you think the court adequately supported its conclusion that each of the four elements of a valid cause of action for negligence had been established?
2. The *Norman* court reasoned that negligence must be measured against the particular set of circumstances present in each case. What circumstances, if any, would have to be changed in order for the court to find that the school has satisfied its duty of care?

3. The *Norman* case also contains a typical discussion of the limits of school district immunity for so-called discretionary conduct. The school claimed immunity from the negligence action, arguing that the teacher's decision regarding supervision, materials and clothing to be worn during the welding class was discretionary. However, the Supreme Court of Nebraska interpreted "discretionary" narrowly, and concluded that the discretionary function exemption was not applicable in this case. What are examples of decisions and choices teachers make daily in their classrooms that the court would deem discretionary, thus providing immunity for the school district?
4. As the reasoning in this case suggests, although the courts are unwilling to impose strict liability, they have created a higher duty of care on educational professionals to supervise their children in situations where potentially hazardous conditions are present. *See, e.g., Johnson v. City of Boston,* 22 Mass. App. 24, 490 N.E.2d 1204 (1986) (nonshatterproof glass); *Brooks v. Board of Education of N.Y.,* 12 N.Y.2d 971, 238 N.Y.S.2d 963, 189 N.E.2d 497 (1963) (contact sports in physical education programs require heightened care); *Mastrangelo v. West Side Union High School District, 2* Cal. 2d 540, 42 P.2d 634 (Cal. 1935) (chemistry experiments require strict supervision); *Dixon v. Chicago Board of Education,* 304 Ill. App. 3d 744, 710 N.E.2d 112, 237 Ill. Dec. 689 (1st Dist. 1999) (strict supervision of students during swimming team tryouts required, but sufficiently provided where swimming coach was present at all times while teenage girl drowned).
5. Recall that in *Johnson v. School District of Millard,* 253 Neb. 634, 573 N.W.2d 116 (Neb. 1998), as well, the court reasoned that the duty of reasonable supervision becomes a duty of direct and constant supervision when dangerous conditions are present. While trampolines and welding may present ready examples of dangerous situations, is it possible that virtually any activity engaged in by elementary school children is potentially dangerous?

3. The Duty to Supervise Outside the Classroom

The duty to supervise children clearly exists within the walls of the classroom and school buildings. The shape of that duty becomes more fluid, however, when children are escorted outside the school building. As a practical matter, the school day routinely extends beyond the limits of the classroom and the school building. Recess and playground activities are an integral part of the curriculum at most schools. Supervision of children on the playground therefore has become an important part of a teacher's responsibilities. Most districts, in fact, pay lunchroom or playground supervisors a separate stipend to insure adequate supervision. Similarly, districts attempt to insure adequate supervisors on field trips, often enlisting the help of parent volunteers. Should the increased possibility of harm to students at recess or on field trips, and the difficulty of preventing such harm, lead to a broadening or a contracting of tort liability?

Simonetti v. School District of Philadelphia

308 Pa. Super. 555, 454 A.2d 1038 (Pa. 1983)

Wieand, Judge.

Richard Simonetti, a fifth grade student, returned to the classroom from recess and was struck in the left eye by a pencil which had been propelled from the hand of a classmate when he tripped. The teacher, an employee of the School District of Philadelphia, was outside the classroom, standing at the door, when Simonetti was injured. There she was engaged in monitoring the return of her students from recess and talking with another teacher. The student who dropped or threw the pencil and two other students had been required to remain in the classroom during recess as punishment for misbehavior at breakfast. They had been talking with the teacher during the recess period and were instructed to take their seats when the teacher stepped outside the classroom to supervise the return of the students from recess.

In an action against the School District, it was contended by Simonetti that the teacher had been negligent in failing to provide adequate classroom supervision. The case was tried without a jury, and damages of $15,000 were awarded to the minor plaintiff and his mother. After the School District's exceptions had been dismissed and judgment entered on the verdict, this appeal followed.

In *Bottorf v. Waltz* . . . a case in which a student had been burned when melted wax was spilled on his back, this Court defined the standard of care required of a teacher . . . as follows:

> What constitutes proper supervision depends largely upon the circumstances attending the event. Thus, the fact that supervisory personnel present when an accident occurs could conceivably have prevented its occurrence does not necessarily render the school agency liable if the supervisory personnel was competent and acted reasonably under all the circumstances. . . .
>
> There is no liability predicated on lack or insufficiency of supervision where the event in connection with which the injury occurred was not reasonably foreseeable. . . . The courts frequently state that a teacher is not required to anticipate the myriad of unexpected acts which occur daily in and about school, to guard against all dangers inherent in the rashness of children, or to watch all movements of children.
>
> Where injury results from an unforeseen, sudden, impulsive, or spontaneous act of another pupil, such act has been held the intervening proximate cause of the injury notwithstanding lack, or possible inadequacy, of supervision. Thus, it has been said that failure of supervision is not that proximate cause of an accident where injury results from an unanticipated act of a fellow pupil, since the teacher cannot be expected to watch all movement of pupils in the absence of anything to place the teacher on notice to guard against the occurrence.

Although there is a paucity of Pennsylvania decisions, cases from other jurisdictions illustrate the application of these principles. In *Ohman v. Board of Education of City of New York,* the facts were remarkably similar to those of the instant case. There, a thirteen-year-old student sustained injury when struck in the eye by a pencil. The pencil had been thrown by one student to another, and when the boy for whom it was intended ducked, the pencil hit the minor plaintiff. The accident occurred while the teacher in charge of the classroom was temporarily absent for the purpose of sorting and storing supplies in a corridor closet. The court held that the teacher's absence from the room was insufficient to impose liability upon the Board of Education, saying:

> [A] teacher may be charged only with reasonable care such as a parent of ordinary prudence would exercise under comparable circumstances. Proper supervision depends largely on the circumstances attending the event but so far as the cases indicate there has been no departure from the usual rules of negligence.

In *Swaitkowski v. Board of Education of the City of Buffalo,* 36 A.D.2d 685, the Court held that the Board of Education was not liable for injuries sustained by a student who, upon returning to his seat, sat on the point of a pencil placed on the seat by another student while the teacher was absent from the classroom for a short period to assist another teacher locate books in a bookroom 10-½ feet away with the doors open. The Court said: Nor can respondents prevail on their claim of inadequate supervision by the teacher in leaving the classroom unattended for the short space of time she was required to be absent. As in *Ohman v. Board of Educ. of City of N.Y.,* the injury resulted from "the act of an intervening third party which under the circumstances could hardly have been anticipated in the reasonable exercise of the teacher's legal duty toward the plaintiff" and which act was "one of those events which could occur equally as well in the presence of the teacher as during her absence." We are, of course, mindful of the proposition that a school board is not the insurer of the safety of students and that a school or teacher may be charged only with reasonable care such as a parent of ordinary prudence would exercise under comparable circumstances.

In *Morris v. Ortiz,* a student in an auto mechanics class was injured when another student jumped on a car top which the former student was holding. The trial court directed a verdict in favor of the teacher and school district. In affirming, the Arizona Supreme Court said:

> To hold that [the teacher] had to anticipate [the student's] act and somehow circumvent it is to say that it is the responsibility of a school teacher to anticipate the myriad of unexpected acts which occur daily in and about schools and school premises, the penalty for failure of which would be financial responsibility in negligence. We do not think that either the teacher or the district should be subject to such harassment nor is there an invocable legal doctrine or principle which can lead to such an absurd result.

In *Butler v. District of Columbia,* 417 F.2d 1150 (D.C. Cir. 1969), a seventh grade student was struck in the left eye by a sharp piece of metal when he entered a printing classroom. The teacher was then absent because he had been assigned as a hall or cafeteria supervisor. The plaintiff's case was based on alleged negligent supervision of the classroom after the teacher and principal had prior knowledge that "horseplay" and throwing had occurred in the classroom. In holding that there could be no recovery, the Court took note of the district's dilemma of balancing "the need for a teacher to supervise several hundred students milling about the corridors and the cafeteria against the need to supervise fourteen students in a certain classroom for a period of time." Id., at 1153.

From these decisions it can safely be concluded that momentary absence from a classroom is not negligence. This is particularly true where, as in the instant case, the absence was for the authorized and compelling reason of monitoring the return of about thirty students from recess. The teacher, it may confidently be observed, could not have been at two places at the same time. With equal confidence, it can be said that it was not negligence for the teacher to give priority to an entire class of approximately thirty students returning from recess rather than to remain in the classroom to supervise three students who had been required to stay in the classroom during the recess period.

It is common knowledge that children may indulge in horseplay. They may throw a pencil, shoot a paper clip or snap a rubber band when a teacher is absent or turns his or her back. In the instant case, the teacher attempted to guard against any horseplay by instructing the three students who were in the classroom to return to their seats and remain there. While these students were capable of free spirits and were even being punished for unrelated misconduct at breakfast, there is no evidence that they were hellions who required constant custody.

To require the teacher to anticipate the events which occurred while she was outside the classroom door would be to hold that a teacher is required to anticipate the myriad of unexpected acts which occur daily in classrooms in every school in the land. This is not the law, and we perceive no good reason for imposing such an absolute standard on teachers and school districts.

The judgment is reversed and is now entered for the appellant.

NOTES AND QUESTIONS

1. The court seems to absolve the school district from liability on the theory that "children inevitably get hurt." Should that inevitability increase or decrease the standard of care?
2. The "educational environment" is hardly limited to the classroom. Even elementary school students travel throughout the school building to the library, media center, gym, auditorium and lunchroom. The school district is liable for failing to supervise children throughout the building and at school events. *See, e.g., Viveiros v. State,* 54 Haw. 611, 513 P.2d 487 (1973) (district liable for injuries to student at student performance in lecture hall). Suppose there is a student selling illegal drugs on a corner near the school. Other students purchase drugs from this individual. The drug dealing is visible and known to school personnel, though it occurs after school hours. Should the school be responsible? What if students are gossiping during the school day about a fight that is brewing between two rival groups after school. School personnel overhear facts regarding this fight, but do nothing to stop it because the fight has not occurred and the problem is not in school. A student who is part of the fight is seriously injured. Was there a breach of duty to supervise and protect the student?

A student who is not part of the fight is seriously injured when caught in the middle of the chaos. Was there a breach of duty to supervise and protect that student?

3. When does the duty to supervise students begin and end? Students often travel to school and congregate on school grounds well before the bell rings. Similarly, they linger on school grounds well after the school day ends. Should the school be responsible for injuries to students before and after school? *Compare Titus v. Lindberg,* 49 N.J. 66, 228 A.2d 65 (N.J. 1967) (school liable for injuries to students who commonly arrive at school before the day begins); *Kerwin v. County of San Mateo,* 176 Cal. App. 2d 304, 1 Cal. Rptr. 437 (1959) (school district has no duty to supervise students on their way home from school, unless it has undertaken to provide transportation); *Dailey v. Los Angeles Unified School District,* 2 Cal. 3d 741, 87 Cal. Rptr. 376, 470 P.2d 360 (Cal. 1970) (school district may be liable for foreseeable injuries to truant students off school grounds); *Nicholson v. Board of Education,* 36 N.Y.2d 798, 369 N.Y.S.2d 703, 330 N.E.2d 651 (1975) (school district liable for injuries caused by firecracker on school playground, after school hours) *with Lawes v. Board of Education,* 16 N.Y.2d 302, 266 N.Y.S.2d 364, 213 N.E.2d 667 (1965) (no liability for injuries to student who was hit by a snowball while walking to school); *Richard v. St. Landry Parish School Board,* 344 So. 2d 1116 (La. Ct. App. 1977) (no liability for student's use of knife taken from teacher's desk after school).
4. In *Lawes,* the New York Court of Appeals reasoned that the winter climate makes it inevitable that school children will throw snowballs on the way to and from school. The prevention of injuries therefore would require "intensive policing, almost child by child." The court was unwilling to "demand or expect such perfection from ordinary teachers or ordinary school management. . . ." Ultimately, the court declared that teachers owe their students the same level of care that a "parent of ordinary prudence would observe in comparable circumstances." The court proceeded to conclude that a parent would not ordinarily prevent a child from throwing snowballs, and in fact might encourage the activity. Do you agree? Even if the school could not prevent all injuries from childish activities, should it discipline children who are found to have engaged in those activities? Would a prudent parent discipline a child for throwing a snowball at another child? Might such discipline prevent future harm?

Glankler v. Rapides Parish School Board

610 So. 2d 1020 (La. Ct. App. 1992)

Knoll, Judge.

This appeal concerns questions of liability against the Rapides Parish School Board (School Board) and the State of Louisiana, Department of Health and Human Resources (DHHR), as a result of severe injuries a kindergarten student sustained while on a school field trip, and the excessiveness of the awards made for general and special damages, as well as for loss of consortium to the student's mother.

Nancy Glankler, the mother of Jennifer Mangel, individually and on behalf of her daughter, sued the School Board, its insurer, Audubon Insurance Company, and DHHR. Glankler alleged that her daughter, six years of age, a kindergarten student at Nachman Elementary School, broke her leg at the left hip joint on a class outing when she was struck by a 60 pound, metal two-person swing at DHHR's facility at the Parents' Park located on the campus of Pinecrest State School. As a result of this injury, her growth plate in the hip joint was permanently destroyed.

Since the School Board and DHHR were political subdivisions, Glankler's tort claims against them were tried without a jury. The trial court found the School Board and DHHR equally liable, and awarded the following: (1) $500,000 for Jennifer's physical pain and suffering, past and future; (2) $1,000,000 for Jennifer's emotional suffering, mental trauma, and loss of enjoyment of life; (3) $500,000 for Jennifer's disfigurement and permanent disability; (4) $131,536.25 for medical, hospital, and related health care expenses, past and future; and, (5) $250,000 for Glankler's loss of consortium. The trial court limited the School Board's liability for Jennifer's damages to $500,000, but found Glankler's loss of consortium award exempt from the damage limitation. DHHR's liability for damages was not limited by the trial court because it did not find that DHHR pleaded limitation of liability as an affirmative defense. . . .

We reverse the trial court's finding that DHHR was liable, and amend the judgment to bring Glankler's loss of consortium award under the $500,000 statutory limitation of liability, finding the loss of consortium award extinguished by the statutory cap. We also affirm the future medical award.

Facts

On May 25, 1988, the Nachman Elementary School kindergarten class took an end-of-year field trip to the Parents' Park at Pinecrest State School, a facility owned by DHHR. The Parents' Park is an acre and one-half fenced playground built primarily for the residents of Pinecrest and their families for use on visitation days. In addition, DHHR traditionally made the park available on designated days to schools and other organizations. The park, among other things, was equipped with slides, merry-go-rounds, a wading pool, and 47 metal glider-type swings.

On the day of the field trip, three kindergarten teachers, Janice Riggs, Janet Bakeler, and Earline Pearson, and approximately 11 parents supervised the outing of 78 kindergarten students, with an average age of 5 years. It is undisputed that for several days prior to the trip, the teachers instructed the children about the types of playground equipment that would be available and the different rules they needed to follow. In particular, the teachers instructed the children that they were not to push the swings. Before leaving the school, the teachers reviewed the safety rules with the children and several of the parents in attendance. Upon arrival at the park, a walking tour was conducted, showing the playground to the children and parents. The teachers told the children where to put their change of clothes, and pointed out the areas of the playground that the children were not to use. Again, the teachers instructed the children not to push the swings.

At approximately 10:30 a.m., Jennifer pushed a friend on the glider-type swing. As Jennifer pushed her friend, the swing knocked Jennifer down and struck her again twice on its return swing, severely injuring her.

Summarizing Jennifer's medical treatment, her recovery, and medical projections of future treatment, the trial court stated in its written reasons for judgment: "After being hit by the swing, some mothers ran and picked Jennifer up, put her under the pavilion and called her mother. Jennifer was unable to walk after the accident and was taken to Cabrini Hospital where it was determined the blow had caused a fracture of the base of the femoral neck. Internal fixation surgery [by Dr. Vanda Davidson, an orthopedist] was scheduled the next day in order to pin the broken bones together in the proper alignment. The injury sustained by the child will have a severe crippling effect on her for the rest of her life. . . ."

Expert Testimony

The School Board and DHHR, urging different reasons germane to an analysis of their respective liability, contend that the trial court erred in qualifying Paul Hogan as an expert. The School Board argues that Hogan was not qualified to testify in the area of child supervision; DHHR contests Hogan's expertise in the field of swing design. Because of our ultimate resolution of DHHR's liability favorable to DHHR, we pretermit discussion of DHHR's argument about Hogan's expertise.

LSA-C.E. Art. 702 allows experts to testify when scientific, technical, or other specialized knowledge will assist the trial court to understand the evidence or to determine a fact in issue if the witness is qualified as an expert "by knowledge, skill, experience, training, or education." Trial courts have great latitude in determining whether or not a person possesses the requisite background and experience to be considered as an expert. The United States Fifth Circuit Court of Appeal has recently interpreted F.R.E. 403, after which the Louisiana rules on expert testimony are patterned. The court delineated the following four inquiries for determining the admissibility of expert testimony: (1) whether the witness is qualified to express an expert opinion, (2) whether the facts upon which the expert relies are the same type as are relied upon by other experts in the field, (3) whether in reaching his conclusion the expert used well-founded methodology, and (4) assuming the expert's testimony passes these tests, whether the testimony's potential for unfair prejudice substantially outweighs its probative value under the relevant rules. *Id.*

For 30 years Hogan has authored books on the subject of play and playground construction, and has designed and built approximately 450 playgrounds. His books and audio-visual materials are used worldwide by persons, parental groups, and architects who are involved in early childhood education.

Hogan testified that the supervision of children is a topic which is inseparable from the design and construction of playgrounds. Furthermore, Hogan stated that he has testified as an expert in the field of supervision of children 20 to 30 times in both playground design and safety cases. He also stated that he has lectured on the proper supervision of children in the playground setting.

Viewing the record evidence in light of the delineated inquiry espoused in [our cases], we cannot say that the trial court was clearly erroneous in its acceptance of Paul Hogan as an expert in the field of child supervision on the playground.

[The Court of Appeals next concludes that the trial court erred in finding DHHR liable for Jennifer's damages, because there was no evidence that DHHR had actual or constructive notice of the unreasonably hazardous condition of the swing.]

School Board's Liability

The School Board contends that the trial court erred in finding it liable for Jennifer's damages. It argues that it afforded reasonable supervision of this kindergarten class activity and that is all that is required.

Although charged with the highest degree of care toward children placed in their custody, supervisors at schools are not absolute insurers of the children's safety and cannot be expected or required to prevent them from falling or striking each other during normal childhood play. . . . It is well established in school-related accident cases that supervising teachers must follow a reasonable standard of care commensurate with the age of the children under the attendant circumstances, and liability is imposed only where there is a causal connection between the lack of supervision and the accident that could have been avoided by the exercise of the required degree of supervision. . . . Likewise, the fulfillment of the obligation owed does not exact individual supervision of each child at all times and places.

Louisiana jurisprudence has time and again had an opportunity to discuss the ratio of teachers to students in child supervision cases. Synopsizing the holdings of the myriad of cases on this issue, we stated in *Rollins v. Concordia Parish School Bd.,* 465 So. 2d 213, 218 (La. App. 3rd Cir. 1985):

> Defendant argues that the children in this class were adequately supervised as a matter of law as the Louisiana courts have held that a school board provided adequate supervision where only one teacher had the responsibility of supervising anywhere from 50 to 120 children. A review of these and similar cases indicates that the courts actually based their findings of adequate supervision on an examination of whether the supervision was reasonable in light of the age of the children involved and the circumstances surrounding the accident.

. . . In the present case, the trial court concluded that the School Board did not provide adequate supervision of the students. The trial court did not include the 11 parents as supervisors finding that the parents were not sufficiently instructed to qualify as supervisors of children. Therefore, the trial court viewed the supervision of 78 kindergarten students by only three teachers. The trial court reasoned as follows:

> "The warnings to the parents that were present that morning were not specific enough to be sufficient. . . .
>
> The School Board argues there was proper supervision with the three (3) teachers along with eleven (11) parent supervisors. As stated before, the actual number of parent supervisors is highly questionable. Furthermore, the parents were neither trained nor skilled in the type of supervision required on the

> day in question. While their presence was sought by the school, it did not add to the professional supervision needed, and I am not really sure if any were aware of the absolute need to keep the children away from the type of swings that caused little Jennifer's injuries. The three (3) teachers on the field trip all have impressive credentials with excellent records in education. The parents of all the children in the Nachman kindergarten class sent their children with the belief and assurance that a sufficient number of trained qualified teachers would be there to look after their children. There were but three (3)! This responsibility is the School Board's alone and may not be delegated under any circumstances. The School Board, through its hiring practices and minimum requirement standard, knows the abilities and training of its employees and can exercise control over them. The School Board was negligent for relying upon the parent supervisors to look after the health and safety of seventy-eight (78) kindergarten children. The School Board had no knowledge of the training and background of these volunteer parents nor the authority to direct them. The School Board's negligence becomes even more apparent when at trial it is established some of these parents had no inkling as to their role or duty as designated parent supervisor. Therefore for the purposes of determining proper supervision, these parent supervisors will not be considered. Accordingly, it is the opinion of this Court that under the circumstances, three (3) teachers could not adequately supervise seventy-eight (78) kindergarten children scattered over one and a half (1½) acres. . . .
>
> The Court has personally visited Parent's Park to see the layout and feel the weight and blunt hardness of the swing. With one hundred (100) pieces of playground equipment spread over almost one and a half (1½) acres, it is a virtual children's wonderland. Within this one-and-a-half (1½)-acre area and one hundred (100) pieces of equipment are forty-seven (47) adult swings of the type that crippled Jennifer Mangel. After walking over the playground, I believe, that due to area and numerous obstacles blocking the line of sight of any overseer, it is imperative that many trained adults should be stationed throughout the playground. Each should have had a designated area to watch, so that there would be adequate supervision for safety. The School Board's negligence was therefore the cause of the injuries suffered by Jennifer Mangel.

We have carefully reviewed the record and find that although the School Board was negligent for reasons that we will discuss infra, we find that it was not for lack of supervision. We disagree with the learned trial court on this finding of fact. The record shows that the parents that were there were in fact supervising the children, and therefore, should have been included in determining whether the students were properly supervised. The trial court discounted the parents primarily because the parents did not receive warnings "specific enough to be sufficient." The record shows instances of parent supervision from parents who were not present when the teachers were giving supervisory instructions, and the parents intervened to prevent potential accidents which developed while the kindergarten students played at Parents' Park. Although the record preponderates that all of the parents were not given the safety instructions, we do not find that it was unreasonable for the School Board to complement the supervision with these adults. The parenting skills each adult brought, together with the guidance of the teachers as they walked around Parents' Park, augmented the degree of supervision offered and was reasonable. Therefore, the parents should have been included as supervisors.

It is unrefuted that the three kindergarten teachers began instructing the kindergarten children two to three weeks prior to the outing on safety considerations. With particularity, the teachers emphasized that the children were not allowed to run in front of the swings or to push them. These instructions were repeated on the day of the trip prior to the class' departure for the outing, and were reiterated after the class arrived at Parents' Park.

Three professional kindergarten teachers, having 23, 17 and 15 years' experience, at least one aide, and approximately 11 parents supervised the play activities of the 78 kindergartners at Parents' Park.

Glanker contends that the teachers were congregated at the time of the accident some distance from the swing where Jennifer was. Although the evidence shows that the teachers were together at the time of Jennifer's accident, the record does not preponderate that the three teachers were not supervising the play activity of the kindergartners, or that they abandoned their plan of supervision.

Glanker further contends that Paul Hogan analyzed the teachers' supervisory plan, and determined that it was flawed. Although Hogan may have been able to devise a better plan of supervision, we cannot say that the plan implemented by the teachers, the aide, and parents in the case subjudice did not meet a reasonable standard of care commensurate with the age of the children and the attendant circumstances. We find the plan of supervision used by the School Board to be reasonable and that is all that is required. It is always easier to come up with a better plan after the accident. To say that a better plan of supervision would have prevented the accident is too speculative because an accident can happen within a matter of a few seconds when, for example, a supervisor is correcting another child. Rather than try to arrive at a magic number of supervisors per number of children, the jurisprudence wisely requires a reasonable standard of care commensurate with the age of the children and the attendant circumstances. There is no requirement that the supervisor of children have each child under constant scrutiny. While we find the School Board provided reasonable supervision of the children, we find the School Board was negligent in allowing the kindergarten students to swing on swings that posed an unreasonable risk of harm to small children. This was the cause in fact that set this whole accident in motion.

In considering a defendant's duty to a particular person, consideration should be given to the person's age, maturity, experience, familiarity with the premises and its dangers, and other factors which might increase or decrease the risk of harm to that person.

It is undisputed that the swing Jennifer was pushing weighed approximately sixty pounds, was made of metal, and hung from steel straps suspended from posts which were anchored in a concrete slab beneath it. It was likewise unrefuted that the kindergartners' feet could not touch the ground when they sat in these adult swings. Even at the time of trial, approximately two years post-accident, Jennifer's feet still could not touch the ground when she sat in the swing. . . .

Hogan ultimately recognized that because the children's feet could not touch the ground, the repeated instructions given to the kindergarten students not only prior to the trip, but also on the day of the visit, were insufficient since it is the nature of children to attempt, in some way, to get the swings to move with them in it. Therefore, Hogan opined that by allowing the children to sit in the swings, the pushing of the swings, the forbidden activity, was inevitable. We agree. . . .

The inevitable question then is how were the children supposed to swing? The School Board offered no plan, but allowed the children to use the swings. This failure by the School Board to minimize the danger by taking necessary and reasonable precautions, e.g., to exclude the heavy metal swings for use or to require adults to swing with the children, constitutes negligence. Therefore, for these reasons we find no error in the trial court's conclusion that the School Board was liable for the damages Jennifer suffered.

NOTES AND QUESTIONS

1. The Court of Appeals of Louisiana stated that although supervisors are charged with the highest degree of care toward children placed in their custody, they are not absolute insurers of their safety and cannot be expected to protect them from falling or striking each other during normal childhood play. The court leaves to interpretation what is "normal childhood play" and fails to define "highest degree of care" or even when supervisors must be expected to observe this highest degree of care. How would you interpret or define these parameters when determining a supervisor's duty of care owed to students?
2. The trial court reasoned that the 11 parent volunteers would not be considered qualified supervisors of the children and therefore the school board was negligent in allowing only three teachers to accompany 78 students on the field trip. What are the arguments supporting and undermining the court's treatment of parent volunteers? Why would any school enlist the help of parent volunteers if they do not constitute qualified supervisors?
3. The appellate court noted that a teacher's standard of care is dependent on the child's age. Should the standard of care vary by age or grade level?
4. The court also found that the teachers' warnings indicated an awareness of the hazardous condition of the swings and that the school board failed to minimize the danger by taking necessary precautions. The court relied on two similar cases, *Comeaux v. Commercial Union Insurance Co.,* 269 So. 2d 500 (La. Ct. App. 1972), and *Drueding v. St. Paul Fire & Marine Insurance Co.,* 482 So. 2d 83 (La. Ct. App. 1986), to support its imposition of tort liability on the school board for negligently exposing students to such known dangers. *See also King v. Kartanson,* 720 S.W.2d 65 (Tenn. Ct. App. 1986) (school district not liable for injuries to 13-year-old student hit by car while crossing the street on a field trip; teachers properly cautioned students and had no duty to escort them across relatively safe street).
5. The potential for tort liability has led some districts to attempt to secure from their students "waivers" or "releases" from any claims resulting from injuries in the school setting. These efforts have almost universally failed. The courts have held that such releases are void as against public policy. *Wagenblast v. Odessa School District No. 105-157-166J,* 110 Wash. 2d 845, 758 P.2d 968 (Wash. 1988) (school district's control over students and duty

to protect them precludes requiring waiver as a condition to participation in extracurricular and athletic activities). *See also Adams v. Roark,* 686 S.W.2d 73 (Tenn. 1985); *Whittington v. Sowela Technical Institute,* 438 So. 2d 236 (La. Ct. App. 1983).

6. ***Negligent Entrustment.*** Should the school district be liable for selecting insufficient or unqualified educators under a theory of "negligent entrustment"? In count III of the plaintiff's complaint in the *Fallon* case, the plaintiff pursued a theory of negligent entrustment against the school and the school district. The court, however, rejected that theory of liability, reasoning:

> Remaining are the allegations that the school district carelessly and negligently: (1) failed to investigate the teachers' credentials and teaching abilities, and (2) allowed and permitted the teachers to teach when they were not qualified.
>
> We hold that these allegations are legally insufficient to support a cause of action for negligent hiring, and thus the trial court's dismissal was proper.
>
> There are many kinds of unfitness for employment that do not give rise to tort liability for negligent hiring. The right of an employer to make decisions about the qualifications of his employees does not establish, per se, a right for negligent hiring. For example, employers may hire the mentally and physically handicapped, who have some degree of unfitness. Such employers, however, do not assume liability because of their employees' unfitness. Liability for negligent hiring arises only when a particular unfitness of an applicant creates a danger of harm to a third person which the employer knew, or should have known, when he hired and placed this applicant in employment where he could injure others. *(See, e.g., Gregor v. Kleiser* (1982), 111 Ill. App. 3d 333, 67 Ill. Dec. 38, 443 N.E.2d 1162 (plaintiff attacked by bouncer who defendant hired knowing his reputation and vicious propensity for physical violence on others); *Easley v. Apollo Detective Agency, Inc.* (1979), 69 Ill. App. 3d 920, 26 Ill. Dec. 313, 387 N.E.2d 1241 (security guard used passkey to enter apartment and assaulted plaintiff).) Therefore, allegations that the school district failed to investigate or that the teachers were unqualified, are insufficient to state a cause of action for negligent hiring under the allegations here.

In *O'Brien v. Township High School District 214,* 83 Ill. 2d 462, 47 Ill. Dec. 702, 415 N.E.2d 1015 (Ill. 1980), however, the court held the school district liable for its negligence in entrusting an untrained employee with the treatment of a student's injured knee. Would a school district be liable for negligently entrusting untrained parent volunteers with the care of students on field trips?

7. ***Field Trip Supervision Policy Practicum.*** In light of the liability issues associated with field trips, what policy would you advise a school district to implement? Consider the language of the following policy. What changes, if any, would you suggest?

> The Board of Education encourages field trips when the experiences are an integral part of the school curriculum and contribute to the District's desired educational goals.

Student activities involving travel shall be authorized by the Superintendent. Each trip authorization shall be based on the written rationale of the travel's educational value as well as the safety and welfare of the students involved.

Guidelines for field trips are:

1. All field trips shall be adequately supervised by staff members and other adults.
2. Whenever entrance fees, food, lodging or other costs are involved, these costs shall be assumed by the student unless otherwise stipulated by the Superintendent, provided that no student shall be excluded from any trip because of a lack of funds. On all field trips, a bus fee to be set by the Superintendent may be charged to help defray the cost of transportation.
3. Parent/Guardian permission must be obtained in writing prior to the student's participation.

The teacher shall arrange for the supervision and appropriate alternative learning experiences for non-participating students.

8. ***Food Allergies in School Practicum.*** Does the duty to maintain a safe school environment and to protect children from foreseeable harm extend to eliminating the risk of dangerous allergic reactions to food in school? Food allergies affect 8% of school age children. Michael C. Young, *The Peanut Allergy Answer Book* (Fair Winds Press 2006). Nearly 80% of children outgrow milk and egg allergies by age 5. Yet, the opposite is true of peanut and tree nut allergies: 80% of children with nut allergies retain them through school age. *Id.* The level of peanut and tree nut allergies has doubled since 2005. *Id.* On average, children with nut allergies have serious reactions every three years. *Id.* Most children experience their first allergic reaction to nuts without any warning. *Id.* In fact, 25% of the administrations of epinephrine are for children who have never before experienced any allergic reaction. *Id.* Nut allergies are so dangerous that they make up 90% of the 150 food allergy fatalities each year. *Id.* Most of the fatal anaphylaxis occurs outside the home, including at school. *Id.*

   In light of the growing danger that a child will suffer a life-threatening allergic reaction to food products at school, what steps should a school district take to mitigate that risk? The school, of course, must be prepared to treat any allergic reaction at school, on school grounds or at school events. Preparation includes identifying children with known allergies, creating an emergency plan for treating anaphylactic reactions, having a full-time nurse in the school, training all staff in treatment, educating the entire school community about allergies, and ensuring that every student with a life-threatening allergy has an epinephrine autoinjector. Each of these preparation steps must be taken to reduce the consequences of an allergic reaction. *Id.*

   In addition, however, many schools are considering more aggressive prevention policies. The key issue is whether schools should ban peanuts and tree nuts entirely from the school environment. Schools that attempt to ban peanuts and tree nuts argue that the risk of exposure is so great that they should take every precaution practical to mitigate that risk. On the other hand, it may be impossible to create a truly peanut-free environment. Parents may inadvertently send their children to school with peanut butter or with products that have hidden peanut ingredients, despite any policy prohibiting peanuts. A peanut ban arguably may create a false sense of security among children and school staff. Some schools worry that a peanut ban may subject allergic students to bullying. How should a school district reconcile these competing interests? Assume that a school district is aware that three of the 400 children in one of its schools are severely allergic to peanuts. Beyond ensuring that the school is prepared to treat any reactions suffered by these children, should the district adopt a policy banning peanut products at that school, or perhaps even throughout all of the district's schools? Would the absence of such a policy expose the district to liability if a life-threatening reaction occurs? Would the existence of such a policy expose the school to liability if—despite the policy—a reaction occurs?

CHAPTER 16

EVOLVING DUTIES IN THE EDUCATIONAL ENVIRONMENT

A. THE EVOLVING DUTY TO PROTECT STUDENTS FROM EMOTIONAL AND PHYSICAL HARM

1. The Intentional Infliction of Emotional Harm

In situations where teachers and administrators have been extremely derelict in their care of children, parents and guardians have pursued intentional tort claims to redress emotional harm to students. In *Cardinale v. La Petite Academy, Inc.*, 207 F. Supp. 2d 1158 (D. Nev. 2002), the school's abuse and neglect of its students raised intentional infliction of emotional distress claims. In that case, Santino and Gianni Cardinale, and their parents asserted intentional infliction of emotional distress claims against the La Petite preschool. The Cardinale plaintiffs alleged that La Petite allowed Santino and Gianni Cardinale to "run around the pre-school facilities partially undressed, wet with water, and barefoot." Further, the Cardinale plaintiffs alleged that La Petite failed to apply diaper rash medication to Gianni Cardinale. The Cardinale plaintiffs also asserted that La Petite failed to administer doctor-prescribed medication to Santino and Gianni Cardinale, and that one of La Petite's pre-school teachers "regularly abuse[d], neglect[ed] and use[d] excessive force upon . . . Santino" Cardinale. The preschool moved to dismiss the parents' tort claims, arguing that "by-standers" could not bring such claims, and that the conduct alleged was not sufficiently "outrageous."

In ruling on the motion to dismiss, the federal district court declared that the conduct could give rise to intentional infliction of emotional distress claims, but that parents who had not been eyewitnesses to the conduct could not pursue such claims:

> In Nevada, [and in most jurisdictions] a claimant asserting an IIED claim must show: "(1) extreme and outrageous conduct with either the intention of, or reckless disregard for, causing emotional distress, (2) the plaintiff's having

suffered severe or extreme emotional distress and (3) actual or proximate causation. . . ." Nevada also provides that bystanders may recover on an IIED claim. . . . In addition to the requirements for a standard IIED claim, for bystander IIED, a party must show that the bystander him or her -self was a witness to the "outrageous act," and that the bystander is a "close relative" of "the person against whom the outrage was directed. . . ."

In the present case, all Plaintiffs have asserted claims for IIED. La Petite has only brought a Motion to Dismiss with respect to the IIED claim brought by the parent Plaintiffs—Tess and Leonard Cardinale, and Michelle and David Shoup. La Petite argues that Tess and Leonard Cardinal . . . do not allege that they were on the receiving end of the outrageous behavior. The Plaintiffs do not contest this assertion. Instead, Plaintiffs allege that they can prevail on an IIED claim because of the alleged harm to their children. Thus, the requirements with respect to bystanders of IIED apply.

To recover as a bystander on an IIED claim, a plaintiff must have a sufficiently "close relationship" with the person against whom the outrage is directed, and the plaintiff must be a witness to the outrage. . . . While the relationship between the parents and the children is undisputably one "close" enough for the purpose of this rule, Plaintiffs do not allege in their Complaint that they witnessed any of the allegedly outrageous acts. Indeed, the Complaint centers on alleged behavior by La Petite that necessarily occurred in the parents' absence; all of the alleged actions of La Petite occurred when the children were at the La Petite daycare facility. Because witnessing the alleged outrageous act is a necessary element of a bystander IIED claim, Plaintiffs cannot prevail, even presuming the allegations of material fact and drawing all reasonable inferences in favor of Plaintiffs. . . . La Petite's Motion to Dismiss the IIED claims by Tess and Leonard Cardinale . . . should be granted. . . .

La Petite argues that Plaintiffs' prayer for punitive damages is improper because to sustain a claim for punitive damages, a plaintiff must prove by "clear and convincing evidence" that a defendant used "oppression, fraud or malice, express or implied." Nev. Rev. Stat. 42.005. La Petite argues that the allegations in Plaintiffs' Complaint do not support the conclusion that La Petite's actions evidenced oppression, fraud, or malice. In response, Plaintiffs argue that because of the rules of notice pleading, specification of the precise facts that support a claim for punitive damages is unnecessary in the Complaint itself. Plaintiffs also argue that Affidavits attached to their Opposition provide evidence of conduct that a trier of fact could conclude constitutes conscious disregard, oppression, malice, and fraud, within the meaning of Nevada Revised Statute 42.005. . . .

By arguing that Plaintiffs' prayer for punitive damages should be struck, La Petite is asking this Court to weigh the sufficiency of the evidence—evidence which has not yet even been offered. Further, at this point in the proceedings, evaluation of the sufficiency of evidence is inappropriate. La Petite's Motion to Strike Plaintiffs' request for punitive damages should be denied. . . .

In *Cardinale,* the court therefore recognizes that the preschool's neglect and abuse of its children could give rise to intentional infliction of emotional distress claims, and even punitive damages. In the next case, the parties stipulated that the conduct of a physical education teacher was tortious, leaving only the question of appropriate relief.

Spears v. Jefferson Parish School Board

646 So. 2d 1104 (La. Ct. App. 1994)

Judge Gothard delivered the opinion of the court.

This appeal arises out of an action filed by the Plaintiffs, Joyce and Samuel Spears individually and on behalf of their minor son, Justin, for injuries sustained while Justin was a kindergarten student at Woodland West Elementary School, a part of the Jefferson Parish School System. Liability of the defendant was established by a joint stipulation of the parties and the matter went to trial on the issue of quantum. In due course the trial court rendered judgment, accompanied by written reasons, in favor of the Plaintiffs. . . .

On February 28, 1989, Justin Spears was a kindergarten student at Woodland West Elementary School. Because it was a rainy day, the students were seated on the floor of the Cafeteria watching a movie during their regularly scheduled Physical Education class under the supervision of Coach John Brooks and Coach Johnny Peyton. Justin and two friends of his began to be slightly disruptive. At that time Coach Brooks called the boys over to sit near him. The boys began to play with his hair and his ears. Coach Brooks told the boys that if they did not stop annoying him he would "kill them." Because the coach was experiencing management problems with the three boys, he took two of them into an adjacent office with him while he did some paperwork, leaving the rest of the class to watch the movie. Justin stayed behind talking to Coach Peyton. The boys began asking Coach Brooks how he would kill them. Coach Brooks told them he would probably tie the jump rope around their neck and push them off a chair in the office. Because Justin was talking to Coach Peyton during this discussion, Coach Brooks asked the boys if they wanted to play a trick on Justin and they agreed.

The testimony differs as to the events that followed, but it is clear that Coach Brooks led Justin to believe that his friends were dead. He told Justin he had hanged them by their neck with the jump rope, and at least one of the boys was lying on the floor pretending to be dead. When Justin saw the boy lying there he became upset and began to cry. Coach Brooks told Justin it was just a joke and that the boys were not really dead.

Plaintiffs introduced live testimony from Justin and both of his parents. They also introduced depositions from two psychologists who treated Justin. According to the evidence, Justin was a normal, well-adjusted five-year-old before the incident. However, in the weeks following the incident he began to exhibit infantile behavior. He refused to go to the bathroom alone and refused to wipe himself. He was afraid that Coach Brooks would come out of the mirror in the bathroom and harm him. He became overly dependent on his mother and was not comfortable when she was out of sight.

Justin was treated by Dr. Lynne Shwery, a psychologist at Children's Hospital. Dr. Shwery testified at her deposition that she treated Justin from the time of the incident until he moved with his family to Virginia in June, 1991. She opined that Justin had "experienced an event that was outside the range of usual human experience and that would be markedly distressing to almost anyone." She diagnosed Justin as having Post-Traumatic Stress

Disorder and explained that Justin was fearful and anxious. He had come to the realization that the world was not a safe place and that all adults could not be trusted.

From the time of the family's relocation to Virginia in 1991, Justin was treated by Dr. Tonya Fridy; that treatment was still on going at the time of trial. Dr. Fridy's professional diagnosis concurred with that of Dr. Shwery's. Additionally, Dr. Fridy stated that Justin had separation anxiety and social phobia disorder and would probably need three to five more years of therapy. The defendant offered testimony from their own expert, Dr. Vincent Carbone. He conducted an evaluation of Justin and concluded that Justin was "a very anxious child who was very fearful of things in his environment," but Dr. Carbone did not agree that Justin was suffering from Post-Traumatic Stress Disorder.

After considering all of the evidence, the trial court rendered judgment in favor of Plaintiff, accompanied by written reasons which included the finding that "this child has been effectively robbed of a normal, carefree childhood due to the careless actions of the coach."

In brief to this court the defendant assigns nine errors which can be placed into three arguments. First, it is argued that the trial court erred in its findings of fact concerning the magnitude of Justin's injuries and thus the award of damages is excessive. Second, it is argued that the award of loss of consortium to the parents is incorrect. The final argument concerns an evidentiary ruling on the defendant's assertion that Justin's parents failed to mitigate the damages. . . .

Given the circumstances of this case and the standard of review mandated by the Supreme Court, we do not find the trial court's award of general damages in the amount of $100,000 to Justin was an abuse of discretion. For the same reasons we cannot find that the award of $2,160 for future therapy was an abuse of discretion. Therefore, we will not overturn those portions of the judgment.

The defendant also complains of the award of $5,000 each to Justin's parents for loss of consortium. . . . Loss of consortium in the context of the parent/child relationship means loss of the aid, assistance and companionship of the child, or loss of affection, society and service. . . . It is clear from the record that the incident adversely affected the relationship between Justin and his parents. The child, who was developing normally before the incident, became a behavior problem as a direct result of defendant's actions. Injuries incurred by the child rendered the family life difficult afterward since Justin no longer wished to go on family outings. Consequently, we do not find error in the award on loss of consortium damages to the parents.

For the foregoing reasons the judgment of the trial court is affirmed.

NOTES AND QUESTIONS

1. In *Cardinale,* the failure to care for children resulted in the possibility of intentional tort claims. When does the failure to act become intentional conduct? The *Cardinale* court suggests that reckless disregard for the interests of children could be found to be intentional conduct, justifying

even punitive damages. What is the difference between reckless supervision and negligent supervision?

2. In *Spears,* the court had no need to address the merits of the plaintiff's tort claims because the parties stipulated to liability. What tort claims could the plaintiff have established in the case?
3. The coach's conduct in *Spears* displayed a serious lack of judgment. What disciplinary action should the school take? What training should the school provide for its educators to insure that similar conduct does not occur?
4. When does a teacher's joke or prank constitute an act of intentional infliction of emotional distress? Suppose a physical education teacher "punishes" a child who was disruptive in class by removing all of the available towels from the child after the child finishes a shower?
5. In his article, *Disability Harassment in the Public Schools,* 43 Wm. & Mary L. Rev. 1079 (2002), Mark C. Weber argues for a legal doctrine that acknowledges the harm caused when vulnerable students, particularly those with educational disabilities, are subjected to harassment:

> . . . It is a common mistake to view disability discrimination as mere thoughtlessness or failure to take extra steps to accommodate the unique needs of people with disabilities. In reality, much disability discrimination is the overt expression of hostility and the conscious effort to subordinate members of a group with less power and social standing than the majority. A key example of intentional discrimination against individuals with disabilities is harassment on the basis of differences in physical or mental characteristics. Courts, however, wedded to the idea that disability discrimination is the mere failure to accommodate, frequently fail to take seriously the damage that harassment inflicts and refuse to provide an adequate legal response. . . . The reality of disability harassment can be discerned from the reported cases on the subject and from everyday observations of what happens in the public schools. . . . The cases dealing with allegations of disability harassment in the schools fall into several categories: first, outright physical mistreatment and verbal abuse of highly vulnerable children by school personnel; second, conduct by teachers that treats children with disabilities unfairly and actively encourages fellow students to join in the ridicule; and third, failure to provide protection against known risks of physical or psychological harm by other students, often including the risk of physical assault. The fact that all of the cases described lost on at least one level and that many more cases also fail indicates . . . that many courts simply do not view disability harassment as a form of disability discrimination for which damages are the logical remedy.

   Should the logic of common law torts such as intentional infliction of emotional distress be extended to allow victims of harassment to recover damages against school officials for their failure to protect students from such abusive behavior at or near school?

6. Many educational institutions place students whose special needs cannot be met in the regular classroom into a "self-contained" special education classroom. These students are commonly subjected to harassment from their peers. Should the school be responsible for this harassment, which may be a foreseeable consequence of separating students? Suppose a teacher, in an

effort to aid a student with an attention deficient disorder, puts a study corral around the student to eliminate distractions. The student is extremely uncomfortable. Is this a form of intentional infliction of distress by the teacher? What if the teacher has all of the students write letters to a special education child regarding his behavior and how it upsets them? Has the teacher actively encouraged students to harass the special needs student?

2. The Duty to Maintain an Emotionally Safe Educational Environment

(a) The Duty to Prevent the Emotional Harm That May Lead to Violence

In 1999, in the wake of unthinkable violence at Columbine High School and other schools in America, the U.S. Department of Education began to study the climate of American schools toward providing a guide to maintaining "safe schools." The department published the results of its "Safe School Initiative" in *Threat Assessment in Schools: A Guide to Managing Threatening Situations and to Creating Safe School Climates* (2002) (hereinafter *Guide).* The *Guide* begins with "ten key findings" regarding violence in schools:

- Incidents of targeted violence at school are rarely sudden, impulsive acts.
- Prior to most incidents, other people knew about the attacker's idea and/or plan to attack.
- Most attackers did not threaten their targets directly prior to advancing the attack.
- There is no accurate or useful "profile" of students who engage in targeted school violence.
- Most attackers engaged in some behavior, prior to the incident, that caused concern or indicated a need for help.
- Most attackers were known to have difficulty coping with significant losses or personal failures. Many had considered or attempted suicide.
- Many attackers felt bullied, persecuted or injured by others prior to the attack.
- Most attackers had access to and had used weapons prior to the attack.
- In many cases, other students were involved in some capacity.
- Despite prompt law enforcement responses, most shooting incidents were stopped by means other than law enforcement intervention.

From these key findings, the *Guide* articulates the following principles:

- Targeted violence is the end result of an understandable, and oftentimes discernible, process of thinking and behavior.
- Targeted violence stems from an interaction among the individual, the situation, the setting and the target.
- An investigative, skeptical, inquisitive mindset is critical to successful threat assessment.
- Effective threat assessment is based upon facts, rather than on characteristics or "traits."

- An "integrated systems approach" should guide threat assessment inquiries and investigations.
- The central question in a threat assessment inquiry or investigation is whether a student *poses* a threat, not whether the student has *made* a threat.

Finally, the *Guide* advances the following "major components and tasks for creating a safe school climate":

- Assessment of the school's emotional climate;
- Emphasis on the importance of listening in schools;
- Adoption of a strong, but caring stance against the code of silence;
- Prevention of, and intervention in, bullying;
- Involvement of all members of the school community in planning, creating and sustaining a school culture of safety and respect;
- Development of trusting relationships between each student and at least one adult at school; and
- Creation of mechanisms for developing and sustaining safe school climates.

In addition to recommending that schools attempt to break the code of silence that inhibits students from disclosing serious concerns, the *Guide* stresses the importance of creating a culture of respect and meaningful connections between students and adult educational professionals:

> In educational settings that support climates of safety, adults and students respect each other. A safe school environment offers positive personal role models in its faculty. It provides a place for open discussion where diversity and difference are respected; communication between adults and students is encouraged and supported; and conflict is managed and mediated constructively. Cultures and climates of safety support environments in which teachers and administrators pay attention to students' social and emotional needs as well as their academic needs. Such environments emphasize "emotional intelligence," as well as educational or intellectual pursuits.[1] Students experience a sense of emotional "fit" and of respect within the school body, and may be less likely to engage in or be victimized by harmful behavior.[2]
>
> A culture of safety creates "shame free zones" in which daily teasing and bullying is not accepted as a normal part of the adolescent culture.[3] School environments characterized by bullying and meanness can lead to student isolation and fear. At best, school environments that turn a blind eye to bullying and teasing inhibit the work of school learning and growth. At the worst, such environments allow behavior that fosters fear and fury that stunts the healthy development of the victims of that behavior, and may lead to psychological and physical violence.

---

[1] D. Goleman, *Emotional Intelligence* (1995).

[2] See, for example, M.D. Resnick, P.S. Bearman, R.W. Blum, et. al., Protecting Adolescents from Harm, 278 JAMA 823-832 (1997). *See also http://www.allaboutkids.umn.edu.*

[3] See W. Pollack, *Real Boys: Rescuing Our Sons from the Myths of Boyhood;* W. Pollack & T. Shuster, Real Boys' Voices (2000); W. Pollack & K. Cushman, *Real Boys Workbook* (2001).

Creating Connections Between Adults and Students

Connection through human relationships is a central component of a culture of safety and respect. This connection is the critical emotional glue among students, and between students and adults charged with meeting students' educational, social, emotional, and safety needs.[4]

In a climate of safety, students have a positive connection to at least one adult in authority. Each student feels that there is an adult to whom he or she can turn for support and advice if things get tough, and with whom that student can share his or her concerns openly and without fear of shame or reprisal. Schools in which students feel able to talk to teachers, deans, secretaries, coaches, custodians, counselors, nurses, school safety officers, bus drivers, and other staff support communication between students and adults about concerns and problems.

Schools that emphasize personal contact and connection between school officials and students will take steps to identify and work with students who have few perceptible connections to the school.

International and Comparative Law Perspective

School violence is not a problem unique to American schools. In *Tackling School Violence Worldwide: A Comparative Perspective of Basic Issues and Challenges*, Toshio Ohsako concludes:

> Overall, the studies clearly reveal that violence is occurring at a high rate in developing countries and its impact on schooling, learning and living is certainly serious, which refutes the commonly-held view that violence is primarily an issue for industrialized countries. Furthermore, the findings show that the problem of violence seems to multiply the existing problems of national development in these countries. Although the economic loss caused by violence in the school is equally great in the industrialized and the developing countries, it is assumed that the impact on society, including on education, is more intensively and painfully felt in the latter, due to the problems that already exist with the development of economic, educational and human resources.
>
> Despite the importance attached to the issue of violence, placing a high priority on violence management in the developing countries is a difficult educational policy option—due mainly to the fact that other education priorities, such as literacy and basic education, occupy much of their efforts. Nonetheless, it is also clear from the results of the present studies that the issue of violence is also their major enemy, affecting the qualitative improvement of their schools, and it is a task that has to be tackled. The lessons of international development work generally caution us that social and educational development without peace in the minds of individuals is a fragile entity, which cannot be sustained. How the developing countries can control and manage violence without creating heavy burdens on their national human developmental work, and budget, is a fundamental issue for debate.

See Violence at School: Global Issues and Interventions, Studies in Comparative Education, (ed. Toshio Ohsako) at 8 (1997).

---

[4] W. Pollack, *Real Boys* (1998).

(b) The Duty to Prevent Bullying

Should a teacher, administrator or school district be liable for injuries caused by their toleration of an environment in which students are bullied or harassed by other students?

"Bullying" conduct is nothing new, but the attention paid to it among school districts and their attorneys is new. The evidence suggests that 85 percent of America's school children have reported witnessing a bullying incident at school. *See* Garrity & Baris, *Bullying Behaviors* (1992). Bullying techniques include acts of intimidation, verbal aggression, social alienation and physical aggression. Each of these weapons targets a child or group of children for repetitive negative actions where the victims feel powerless to defend themselves. Contrary to popular belief, bullies are not usually physically stronger than their victims. In fact, bullies often have learning or behavioral disabilities. Accordingly, bullies do not usually stop bullying on their own without skillful adult intervention.

The most common type of victim is a passive recipient of the targeted attacks. These victims tend to lack social skills, cry easily, lack the ability to use humor to diffuse conflict, may be lonely and depressed, are anxious, insecure and unable to defend themselves. As Professor Weber suggests, many bullying victims also have learning disabilities or behavioral problems. Accordingly, the typical victim of bullying is the student who is least able to employ defensive mechanisms. These mechanisms require a level of confidence and skill which, in a vicious cycle, is deflated by the constant bullying. The data further shows that bullying and teasing causes in children stress, anxiety, depression, low self-esteem, physical illness, school phobia, difficulties with peer relationships and perhaps rage and violence.

Professor Weber suggests that educators have a legal duty to prevent these serious injuries caused to students by such behavior. There is no doubt that educators usually are aware of bullying situations in their classrooms or on their playgrounds. Educators also know that the cycle of bullying behavior will not stop in the absence of adult intervention. Is it a breach of duty not to intervene to prevent the recurrence of bullying?

The prevention of bullying behavior can take two different forms. First, professional educators should intervene to stop an actual incident of bullying behavior and discipline the perpetrator. Second, and more importantly, the educator should create an educational environment in which bullying is not acceptable at any level, and in which students are given effective strategies for coping with situations in which they are the victims of teasing. Among the suggestions in the literature for creating a school environment which is emotionally safe for children are the following:

1. Conduct a teasing survey or questionnaire;
2. Use the classroom or small group setting to discuss the teasing. Consistent dialogue is the key for success;
3. Teach and consistently review and practice easing the teasing strategies;
4. Use literature as a springboard for discussion and reinforcement;
5. Discuss the nature and frequency of put-downs and ridicule on television and in the movies;

6. Encourage tolerance and the appreciation of difference;
7. If possible, provide the opportunity for playground and lunch supervisors to consult with the social worker, counselor, or principal regarding how to deal with teasing behavior;
8. Discuss the importance of children looking out for each other and offering their support if they witness a classmate being teased. Role-play and practice this situation;
9. Provide a box in a secure place where students can anonymously submit concerns about specific students who are teased;
10. Promote the awareness of kind behaviors by establishing a classroom or schoolwide program of "Random Acts of Kindness" or "Kindness is Contagious";
11. Engage older students and/or the safety patrol to monitor teasing in the hallways, in the locker areas, and on the school grounds. Discuss with them their appropriate responses when teasing is observed;
12. Elicit the help of older students to read relevant literature to the primary grades;
13. Discuss with school staff and parents the policy regarding teasing, bullying, or harassing behaviors;
14. Provide an opportunity for a meeting where parents can learn how they can help their kids cope with teasing situations and share concerns;
15. Provide consistent consequences for the teasers;
16. Teasers need to know that their behavior will not be tolerated;
17. Teasees need to know that they can turn to adults for help and support when necessary.

The research and literature regarding bullying in schools is consistent and widespread. For the seminal data on the subject and schoolwide prevention strategies, *see* Michelle Borba, *Esteem Builders* (1989); Larry Chase, *The Other Side of the Report Card* (1975); Naomi Drew, *Learning the Skills of Peacemaking* (1987); William Glasser, *Schools Without Failure* (1969); Daniel Goleman, *Emotional Intelligence* (1995); Bob Stanish, *The Giving Book: Creative Classroom Approaches to Caring, Valuing and Cooperating* (1988).

Bullying Practicum

Consider the language of the following district policy designed to prevent bullying:

> "Bullying diminishes a student's ability to learn and a school's ability to educate. Preventing students from engaging in this disruptive behavior is an important District goal. The District will not tolerate bullying whether verbal, physical or visual as bullying interferes with a student's educational performance by creating a hostile or offensive educational environment. Bullying is defined as a single or repeated act that intimidates or mistreats another for the purpose of making him or her feel or appear weak. Bullying creates a substantial interference with the operation of the school and affects the educational opportunities for an individual or group of students which results in:
>
> - Physical or psychological harm to a student, and/or

- Knowingly puts a student in reasonable anticipation of physical or psychological harm, and/or
- Creates a reasonable anticipation of harm to a student's property.

Bullying also includes directing threatening, vulgar, obscene, demeaning language in oral, written and/or electronic form, towards one or more students, whether or not the student(s) is physically present when the language is spoken or displayed. Bullying is prohibited on school grounds, on school transportation, at school-sponsored events, in school-sponsored publications and all other forums that may reasonably be perceived as sponsored by the school."

What changes, if any, would you make to this policy? How should this policy be implemented and enforced? What rules and regulations would you promulgate to assist the district's superintendent in effectuating this policy?

In light of the attention devoted to harassment and bullying in the school environment, educators know or should know that their failure to intervene will likely cause harm to a student. Should that failure give rise to civil liability? Consider the issue of civil liability in the context of bullying as you read the next section, which covers educational malpractice.

B. EDUCATIONAL MALPRACTICE

Do the classic tort elements of duty, breach, cause and injury apply when an educational professional fails to meet the standard of care typically employed by those in the profession, thereby causing injury to a student? The tort of malpractice has a rich history as applied to professionals like doctors, lawyers and accountants. Should that tort apply equally to educators? As you consider the rejection of the tort of educational malpractice in the next case, analyze whether that tort is truly distinct from other fully recognized torts involving professional malpractice.

Hunter v. Board of Education of Montgomery County

292 Md. 481, 439 A.2d 582 (Md. App. 1982)

This case primarily presents the troubling but nevertheless important question, which has not been previously addressed by this Court, of whether an action can be successfully asserted against a school board and various individual employees for improperly evaluating, placing or teaching a student. The Circuit Court for Montgomery County (Shearin, J.) and the Court of Special Appeals concluded that an educational negligence action could not be maintained. We agree with this determination and will affirm that portion of the judgment, but will reverse with respect to petitioners' allegations concerning the commission of an intentional tort by certain individual employees of the board.

. . . The Hunters filed this six count declaration on behalf of their child, Ross, naming as defendants the Montgomery County School Board as a corporate body, the principal of Hungerford Elementary School where young Hunter received his primary education, a board employee who engaged in diagnostic testing of the student in second grade, and the boy's sixth grade teacher at Hungerford. The action was instituted in October, 1977, shortly after Ross' sixteenth birthday. As best we can gather from the declaration, the parents (petitioners here) complain that the school system negligently evaluated the child's learning abilities and caused him to repeat first grade materials while being physically placed in the second grade. It is alleged that this misplacement, which continued at least through grade school, generally caused the student to feel "embarrassment," to develop "learning deficiencies," and to experience "depletion of ego strength." The petitioners further claim that the individual educators, acting intentionally and maliciously, furnished false information to them concerning the student's learning disability, altered school records to cover up their actions, and demeaned the child.

It is clear, however, that the gravamen of petitioners' claim in this case sounds in negligence, asserting damages for the alleged failure of the school system to properly educate young Hunter, and we first focus our attention on this aspect of it. In so doing, we note that these so-called "educational malpractice" claims have been unanimously rejected by those few jurisdictions considering the topic. See *D.S.W. v. Fairbanks No. Star Bor. Sch. Dist.,* 628 P.2d 554 (Alaska 1981); *Smith v. Alameda Cty. Soc. Serv. Agency,* 90 Cal. App. 3d 929, 153 Cal. Rptr. 712 (1979); *Peter W. v. San Francisco Unified School District,* 60 Cal. App. 3d 814, 131 Cal. Rptr. 854 (1976); *Hoffman v. Board of Ed. of City of N.Y.,* 49 N.Y.2d 121, 424 N.Y.S.2d 376, 400 N.E.2d 317 (1979); *Donohue v. Copiague Union Free School Dist.,* 47 N.Y.2d 440, 418 N.Y.S.2d 375, 391 N.E.2d 1352 (1979). These decisions generally hold that a cause of action seeking damages for acts of negligence in the educational process is precluded by considerations of public policy, among them being the absence of a workable rule of care against which the defendant's conduct may be measured, the inherent uncertainty in determining the cause and nature of any damages, and the extreme burden which would be imposed on the already strained resources of the public school system to say nothing of those of the judiciary. Thus, in *Peter W., supra,* where a high school graduate sought recovery in tort for a claimed inadequate education, the California court, viewing the problem as whether an actionable duty of care existed, noted that the "wrongful conduct and injuries allegedly involved in educational malfeasance" were neither comprehensible nor assessable within the judicial framework and explained as follows:

> Unlike the activity of the highway or the marketplace, classroom methodology affords no readily acceptable standards of care, or cause, or injury. The science of pedagogy itself is fraught with different and conflicting theories of how or what a child should be taught, and any layman might—and commonly does—have his own emphatic views on the subject. The "injury" claimed here is plaintiff's inability to read and write. Substantial professional authority attests that the achievement of literacy in the schools, or its failure, is influenced by a host of factors which affect the pupil subjectively, from outside the formal teaching process, and beyond the control of its ministers. They may be physical, neurological, emotional, cultural, environmental; they may be present but not perceived, recognized but not identified.
>
> We find in this situation no conceivable "workability of a rule of care" against which defendants' alleged conduct may be measured . . . no reasonable

> "degree of certainty that . . . plaintiff suffered injury" within the meaning of the law of negligence . . . ; and no such perceptible "connection between the defendant's conduct and the injury suffered," as alleged, which would establish a causal link between them within the same meaning. . . .

Although the just-articulated policy considerations alone sufficed to negate a legal duty of care in *Peter W.,* the court aptly identified additional, practical consequences of imposing such a duty upon the persons and agencies who administer our public educational system:

> Few of our institutions, if any, have aroused the controversies, or incurred the public dissatisfaction, which have attended the operation of the public schools during the last few decades. Rightly or wrongly, but widely, they are charged with outright failure in the achievement of their educational objectives; according to some critics, they bear responsibility for many of the social and moral problems of our society at large. Their public plight in these respects is attested in the daily media, in bitter governing board elections, in wholesale rejections of school bond proposals, and in survey upon survey. To hold them to an actionable "duty of care," in the discharge of their academic functions, would expose them to the tort claims—real or imagined—of disaffected students and parents in countless numbers. They are already beset by social and financial problems which have gone to major litigations, but for which no permanent solution has yet appeared. . . . The ultimate consequences, in terms of public time and money, would burden them—and society—beyond calculation. . . .

In *Donohue v. Copiague Union Free School Dist.,* the New York Court of Appeals addressed the identical proposition as that presented in *Peter W.,* but viewed the issue as presenting solely a question of public policy:

> The fact that a complaint alleging "educational malpractice" might on the pleadings state a cause of action within traditional notions of tort law does not, however, require that it be sustained. The heart of the matter is whether, assuming that such a cause of action may be stated, the courts should, as a matter of public policy, entertain such claims. We believe they should not. . . .

The New York court concluded that the action should not be permitted because to do so would "constitute blatant interference with the responsibility for the administration of the public school system lodged by [State] Constitution and statute in school administrative agencies." . . . Two subsequent cases, presenting somewhat more appealing circumstances, provided the respective New York and California courts the opportunity to revisit and strengthen the *Donohue* and *Peter W.* decisions. In *Hoffman v. Board of Ed. of City of N.Y.,* 49 N.Y.2d 121, 424 N.Y.S.2d 376, 400 N.E.2d 317 (1979), the plaintiff, who was of normal intelligence, was negligently placed in special classes for the mentally retarded where he remained for over ten years. The New York Court of Appeals reversed the Appellate Division, which had allowed recovery, and declared that "[t]he policy considerations which prompted our decision in *Donohue* apply with equal force to 'educational malpractice' actions based upon allegations of educational misfeasance and nonfeasance." Likewise, in *Smith v. Alameda Cty. Soc. Serv. Agency,* 90 Cal. App. 3d 929, 153 Cal. Reptr. 712 (1979), the plaintiff alleged that the school district negligently placed him in classes for the mentally handicapped under circumstances where the district either knew or should have known that he was not retarded. Declaring that the duty sought to be imposed in *Smith* was basically "indistinguishable from the one argued for in *Peter W.*," the court held that no cause of action was stated against the school district. 153 Cal. Reptr. at 719. *See also D.S.W. v. Fairbanks No. Star Bor. Sch. Dist.,* 628 P.2d 554 (Alaska 1981) (following the California and New York decisions, the court held that there exists no cause of action for negligent failure to diagnose dyslexia and termination of remedial classes).

We find ourselves in substantial agreement with the reasoning employed by the courts in *Peter W.* and *Donohue,* for an award of money damages, in our view, represents a singularly inappropriate remedy for asserted errors in the educational process. The misgivings expressed in these cases concerning the establishment of legal cause and the inherent immeasurability of damages that is involved in such educational negligence actions against the school systems are indeed well founded. Moreover, to allow petitioners' asserted negligence claims to proceed would in effect position the courts of this State as overseers of both the day-to-day operation of our educational process as well as the formulation of its governing policies. This responsibility we are loath to impose on our courts. Such matters have been properly entrusted by the General Assembly to the State Department of Education and the local school boards who are invested with authority over them. [The Maryland School Code] broadly delineates the supervisory responsibility of the State Department of Education, the local school boards, and their respective superintendents. In this regard, we have stated in another context, that "the totality of the various statutory provisions concerning the State Board [of Education] 'quite plainly . . . invests the . . . Board with the last word on any matter concerning educational policy or the administration of the system of public education.' "

Our conclusion on this point, however, does not imply that parents who feel aggrieved by an action of public educators affecting their child are without recourse. For example: (1) the General Assembly has provided a comprehensive scheme for reviewing a placement decision of a handicapped child including an appeal to the circuit court, (2) both parent and child have the right to review educational records and, if appropriate, insist that the documents be amended, (3) . . . the Education Article commands that each county superintendent, "without charge to the parties concerned . . . shall decide all controversies that involve: (i) [t]he rules and regulations of the county board; and (ii) [t]he proper administration of the county public school system," with the decision being appealable to the county board and then to the state board of education and further, if appropriate, to the courts through the administrative procedure act, and (4) county boards of education are required to establish "at least one" citizen committee "to advise the board and to facilitate its activities and programs in the public schools," and similar committees may be established for an individual school. Thus, it is preferable, in the legislature's view, to settle disputes concerning classification and placement of students and the like by resorting to these and similar informal measures than through the *post hoc* remedy of a civil action. With this we have no quarrel, for, as aptly noted by the Alaska Supreme Court in this regard, "[p]rompt administrative and judicial review may correct erroneous action in time so that any educational shortcomings suffered by a student may be corrected. Money damages, on the other hand, are a poor, and only tenuously related, substitute for a proper education." Consequently, we will affirm the judgment of the Court of Special Appeals concerning the dismissal of counts I, III, IV, V and VI of petitioners' amended declaration. This leaves the claim set forth in count II to which we now address our attention.

Count II represents the parents' somewhat amorphous claim that the respondents intentionally and maliciously acted to injure their child. Research reveals that none of the prior cases discussing educational malpractice have squarely confronted the question of whether public educators may be held responsible for their intentional torts arising in the educational context. In declining to entertain the educational negligence and breach of contract actions, we in no way intend to shield individual educators from liability for their intentional torts. It is our view that where an individual engaged in the educational process is shown to have willfully and maliciously injured a child entrusted to his educational care, such outrageous conduct greatly outweighs any public policy considerations which would otherwise preclude liability so as to authorize recovery. It may well be true that a claimant will usually face a formidable burden in attempting to produce adequate evidence to establish the intent requirement of the tort, but that factor alone cannot prevent a plaintiff from instituting the action. Thus, the petitioners are entitled to make such an attempt here.

Where, as here, it is alleged that the individual educators have willfully and maliciously acted to injure a student enrolled in a public school, such actions can never be considered to have been done in furtherance of the beneficent purposes of the educational system. Since such alleged intentional torts constitute an abandonment of employment, the Board is absolved of liability for these purported acts of its individual employees. Consequently, we are not called upon here to consider whether or to what extent the board has another defense available to it under the doctrine of governmental immunity.

NOTES AND QUESTIONS

1. In his separate opinion, Judge Davidson in the *Hunter* case tracked the development of malpractice claims against other professionals and argued for a similar claim against educators:

> In my view, public educators are professionals. They have special training and state certification is a prerequisite to their employment. They hold themselves out as possessing certain skills and knowledge not shared by noneducators. As a result, people who utilize their services have a right to expect them to use that skill and knowledge with some minimum degree of competence. In addition, like other professionals, they must often make educated judgments in applying their knowledge to specific individual needs. As professionals, they owe a professional duty of care to children who receive their services and a standard of care based upon customary conduct

is appropriate. There can be no question that negligent conduct on the part of a public educator may damage a child by inflicting psychological damage and emotional distress. Moreover, from the fact that public educators purport to teach it follows that some causal relationship may exist between the conduct of a teacher and the failure of a child to learn. Thus, it should be possible to maintain a viable tort action against such professionals for educational malpractice.

. . . Unlike my colleagues, I believe that public policy does not prohibit such claims from being entertained. It is common knowledge, and indeed the majority recognizes, that the failure of schools to achieve educational objectives has reached massive proportions. It is widely recognized that, as a result, not only are many persons deprived of the learning that both materially and spiritually enhances life, but also that society as a whole is beset by social and moral problems. These changed circumstances mandate a change in the common law. New and effective remedies must be devised if the law is to remain vital and viable.

Moreover, I do not agree with my colleagues that adequate internal administrative procedures designed for the achievement of educational goals are available within the educational system. In my view none of the available procedures adequately deal with incompetent teaching or provide adequate relief to an injured student. A cause of action for educational malpractice meets these social and individual needs.

In addition, I do not agree with the majority that recognition of such a cause of action will result in a flood of litigation imposing an impossible burden on the public educational system and the courts. Similar arguments appearing in cases that recognized the constitutional rights of students have not been validated by subsequent empirical evidence. *See Goss v. Lopez,* 419 U.S. 565, 600 n.22 (1975) (Powell, J., dissenting).

Finally, I do not agree with the majority that the recognition of such a cause of action "would in effect position the courts of this State as overseers of both the day-to-day operation of our educational process as well as the formulation of its governing policies," roles that have been "properly entrusted by the General Assembly to the State Department of Education and the local school boards." That the Legislature has delegated authority to administer a particular area to certain administrative agencies should not preclude judicial responsiveness to individuals injured by unqualified administrative functioning. In recognizing a cause of action for educational malpractice, this Court would do nothing more than what courts have traditionally done from time immemorial—namely provide a remedy to a person harmed by the negligent act of another. Our children deserve nothing less.

2. Judge Davidson responds to virtually every argument advanced by the courts to support their general rejection of educational malpractice claims. Do you find his reasoning persuasive?
3. How could the "injury" element of the tort of malpractice be established? Could an expert testify as to the loss of income potential caused by the breach of duty? What about a loss of confidence and self-esteem?
4. Does the fact that education is underfunded provide an excuse for malpractice?
5. If teachers could be held liable for failing to educate kids, how would the classroom environment change?

6. As the *Hunter* case indicates, the courts generally have been unwilling to recognize the common law tort of educational malpractice. *See also Torres v. Little Flower Children's Services,* 64 N.Y.2d 119, 485 N.Y.S.2d 15, 474 N.E.2d 223 (1984) (public policy forecloses educational malpractice claim against child care center). Nonetheless, the courts have entertained an educational malpractice claim where educational professionals or administrators have failed to meet statutory mandates regarding the placement, diagnoses or services required for special education students. *See, e.g., Agostine v. School Dist. of Philadelphia,* 106 Pa. Comm. 492, 527 A.2d 193 (1987) (failure to place child properly under special education statute creates basis for common law educational malpractice claim); *Savino v. Bd. of Ed.,* 123 A.D.2d 314, 506 N.Y.S.2d (1986) (same); *D.S.W. v. Fairbanks North Star Bor. School Dist.,* 628 P.2d 554 (Alaska 1981) (same).

C. THE DUTY TO REPORT CHILD ABUSE

1. The Legal Obligations

The National Child Abuse and Treatment Act of 1974 defines child abuse and neglect as "[p]hysical or mental injury, sexual abuse or exploitation, negligent treatment, or maltreatment of a child under the age of eighteen or the age specified by the child protection law of the state in question, by a person who is responsible for the child's welfare, under circumstances which indicate that the child's health or welfare is harmed or threatened thereby." This federal law, and more recent amendments of the law, allocate money to states which have enacted laws requiring that cases of child abuse and neglect be reported to appropriate local authorities. *See* 18 U.S.C. §2251; 42 U.S.C. §5101.

The states generally have responded by developing reporting standards and responsibilities. All states now require "educators" in public and private schools to report suspected incidents of child abuse and neglect. The reporting obligation is broad enough to include any person who works with children in a school setting and has "reasonable cause to believe" that abuse or neglect is taking place. *See* Fischer et. al., *Teachers and the Law* 99 (6th ed. 2003) (hereinafter Fischer).

The consequences of failing to report a case of child abuse or neglect are harsh. In most states, the willful or knowing failure to report such a case is a crime, punishable by fine or imprisonment. *See* Fischer, at 101. The failure to report can also result in proper disciplinary action against even a tenured teacher. *Pesce v. J. Sterling Morton High School,* 830 F.2d 789 (7th Cir. 1987). Moreover, the willful or, in some cases, the negligent failure to report cases of child abuse or neglect may give rise to civil liability when damages result. *See* Aaron, *Civil Liability for Teachers' Negligent Failure to Report Suspected Child Abuse,* 28 Wayne L. Rev. 183, 210-213 (1981); Fischer, at 101.

On the other hand, because allegations of child abuse can be defamatory, the states, as a condition to their receipt of federal funds, have uniformly granted to reporters of abuse immunity from liability for false reporting, unless there is proof that the report was made in bad faith. In fact, states affirmatively require educational professionals, including school counselors and social workers, to report cases of child abuse and neglect, even where doing so would breach any privilege that would otherwise attach to confidential communications. Fischer, at 100. Federal and state lawmakers have determined that the public policy of prevention of child abuse and neglect is more important than both the public policy supporting civil liability for false reporting and the public policy supporting preexisting professional obligations of protecting client-confidentiality.

Because educators are required to report suspected cases of child abuse, most school districts have created policies which reflect the reporting requirements. Districts also have promulgated administrative regulations which establish an effective reporting process and have developed training programs which help educators identify physical and behavioral signs of abuse. *See* Fischer, at 97-98, citing D.D. Broadhurst, *The Educator's Role in the Prevention and Treatment of Child Abuse and Neglect* (Wash. D.C. Natl. Center on Child Abuse and Neglect, U.S. Dep. of Health, Educ. & Welf. Pub. L. No. 79-30172, 1979) (providing an excellent catalogue of the physical and behavioral indicators of physical abuse, physical neglect, sexual abuse and emotional maltreatment).

While each state's reporting mechanism is different, most states require the educator to make an immediate (often within 24 hours) oral report of suspected cases of child abuse and neglect to the state's department of children and family services and to follow up the oral report with a detailed written record. Fischer, at 102.

2. Reporting Child Abuse and Neglect: Policy and Liability Practicum

Assume that in an effort to comply with the child abuse and neglect reporting requirement of its state, School District No. 10 has enacted the following policy:

> A District employee who has reasonable cause to suspect that a student may be an abused or neglected child shall report such a case to the State Department of Children and Family Services. The employee shall notify the Superintendent or Building Principal that a report has been made. Any employee hired shall sign a statement prior to the commencement of employment, to the effect that the employee has knowledge and understanding of the reporting requirements of the State's laws and of this Policy.

What rules and regulations should District No. 10 also adopt to implement its policy? Consider the following common forms of such rules and regulations:

Rules and Regulations — Abused and Neglected Children

I. General

All school personnel, including, but not limited to, teachers, counselors, social workers, nurses, psychologists, and administrators, are obligated by law to initiate a verbal and written report with the state Department of Children and Family Services (hereafter DCFS) when they have reasonable cause to believe that a child is an abused child or a neglected child.

II. Definitions

A. "Child" is defined as any person under the age of 18 years, unless legally emancipated.

B. "Abused child" means a child whose parent or immediate family member, or any person responsible for the child's welfare, or any individual residing in the same home as the child, or a paramour of the child's parent:

1. inflicts, causes to be inflicted, or allows to be inflicted upon such child physical injury, by other than accidental means, which causes death, disfigurement, impairment of physical or emotional health, or loss or impairment of any bodily function;
2. creates a substantial risk of physical injury to such child by other than accidental means which would be likely to cause death, disfigurement, impairment of physical or emotional health, or loss or impairment of any bodily function;
3. commits or allows to be committed any sex offense against such child;
4. commits or allows to be committed an act or acts of torture upon such child;
5. inflicts excessive corporal punishment; or
6. commits or allows to be committed against the child certain criminal offenses, including, but not limited to, offenses involving the sale, distribution, or transfer of controlled substances.

C. "Neglected child" means any child who (1) is not receiving the proper or necessary nourishment or medically indicated treatment; or (2) otherwise is not receiving the proper or necessary support or medical or other remedial care recognized as necessary for a child's well-being, including adequate food, clothing and shelter; or (3) who is abandoned by his or her parents or other person responsible for the child's welfare without a proper plan of care. A child shall not be considered neglected solely because the child's parent or other person responsible for his or her welfare depends upon spiritual means through prayer alone for the treatment or cure of disease or remedial care. A child shall not be considered neglected or abused solely because the child is not attending school in accordance with the requirements of *The School Code.*

III. Procedures to Be Followed by School Personnel Who Suspect That a Student Is a Victim of Abuse or Neglect

A. School personnel who have reasonable cause to believe that a student may be a victim of abuse or neglect must immediately initiate a verbal report to DCFS. The oral report must be made to DCFS on their Hotline or to the nearest DCFS office. A written confirmation report must be made to DCFS within forty-eight (48) hours of the oral report.
B. School personnel making an oral report to DCFS of abuse or neglect regarding a child shall also orally notify the building principal or superintendent immediately upon notifying DCFS. School personnel shall also direct to the building principal or superintendent a copy of their written report to DCFS.
C. The building principal or other individual designated by the superintendent shall be responsible for coordinating the involvement, if necessary, of other school personnel, including, but not limited to, a school social worker or psychologist in responding to the alleged abuse or neglect.
D. The building principal or other designated individual shall serve as the contact person between the school district and DCFS throughout the investigation of any case. All contacts with DCFS, except for the initial oral report and written confirmation, shall be made by the building principal or designated individual.
E. Prior to making a report, any person may consult with the building principal or superintendent regarding a suspected case of child abuse or neglect. The building principal and superintendent how ever, shall not exercise any control or restraint over or otherwise modify or change a report to be forwarded to DCFS under any circumstances.
F. No employee shall be discharged, demoted or suspended, or threatened with such, for making a good faith oral or written report of suspected child abuse or neglect or acting as a witness in any proceeding concerning such a report.

IV. Training of Employees

A. For all persons hired by the School District who have the obligation to report claims of abuse or neglect under the Act, the building principal shall conduct appropriate building-based training and provide necessary information so that all such employees shall have knowledge and understanding of their reporting requirements. Such training shall occur, and information be provided, prior to the commencement of the employees' duties with the school district.
B. Prior to the commencement of employment, all newly hired employees shall execute a statement that the employee has knowledge and understanding of the reporting obligations.

C. The executed copy of the statement shall be retained in the employee's personnel file.

V. Professional Privilege Overridden

The duty to report suspected child abuse and neglect overrides any professional privilege that would otherwise attach to a communication between a professional person and a client (e.g., psychologist-patient privilege and social worker-patient privilege).

Do you think these rules and regulations fully reflect the legal and practical requirements of child abuse and neglect reporting? What changes, if any, would you suggest?

Suppose District No. 10's child psychologist has been treating third-grade student Jane for more than a year. The psychologist has become concerned because Jane has suffered from severe flu-like symptoms for long periods of time. Jane never misses school during her bouts with illness. When the school psychologist asked Jane about whether she is receiving medical treatment, Jane responded that "her parents do not care if she ever gets well, and do nothing to help." When the school psychologist tried to schedule a meeting with Jane's parents, the parents refused. Should the psychologist "report" Jane's case as a suspected incident of child abuse or neglect?

Suppose Jane's parents, upon discovering that they have been reported as suspected "abusers," become enraged and write the school board a letter that states: "we are outraged that one of your employees would report us to the state. Our deeply-held religious beliefs preclude us from providing medical care to our sick children. How dare you defame our name and violate our religious beliefs. You can expect civil action for damages for defamation and for your violation of our constitutional rights." Your school board client is understandably concerned and wants you to discuss the merits of any claims brought by Jane's parents. What advice would you provide?

In researching the issues presented by the letter, you discover that nearly every state, including yours, has a statute that provides that a "child who does not receive specific medical treatment by reason of the legitimate practice of the religious belief of said child's parents . . . shall not be considered an abused or neglected child." *See* Fischer, at 100, citing Mo. Rev. Stat. §210.115(3) (Supp. 1979). How does the existence of such a statute alter your view of the merits of the potential claims brought by Jane's parents? Should such a statute affect the language of District No. 10's policy and procedures governing child abuse and neglect?

School District No. 10's regulations require school personnel to report to the state's department of family services, when they have "reasonable cause to believe" that a child is an "abused or neglected child." What should the district do if the state's department refuses to investigate the report? Do cultural differences or parenting styles influence the definition of "abuse"? Suppose the parents of a suspected victim of "excessive corporal punishment" respond to the claim of abuse by declaring that "in our family, we spank our kids when they do not behave—and that's the way we've done it for generations"?

D. CORPORAL PUNISHMENT AND CONSTITUTIONAL TORTS

Four kinds of intentional torts are particularly relevant to issues of corporal punishment and excessive discipline in the school setting: (1) battery; (2) assault; (3) false imprisonment, and (4) intentional infliction of emotional distress. The tort of battery is the intentional act of offensive touching that causes injury. *See* Keeton et al., *Prosser and Keeton on Torts* 39 (5th ed. 1984). Assault occurs when the defendant intends to create in a victim the reasonable apprehension of imminent physical harm. *Id.* at 43. False imprisonment is the intentional act of unlawfully restraining the physical liberty of another without the other's consent. *Id.* at 47. Finally, intentional infliction of emotional distress involves purposeful conduct that results in such emotional distress as to create physical harm. *Id.* at 54.

These tort claims are more difficult to establish than strict liability or negligence claims because the victim must prove that the perpetrator acted with the requisite state of mind. If proven, however, these claims tend to allow recovery against school districts and even board members, because the principles of immunity typically do not extend to intentional wrongdoing. Moreover, these claims allow for the recovery of punitive damages when the tortious conduct has been particularly outrageous.

The specter of each of these torts appears when educators engage in excessive forms of student discipline, particularly corporal punishment. In a recent school year, at least 342,038 students in American public schools were subjected to corporal punishment. *See U.S. Department of Education, Office for Civil Rights, 2000 Elementary and Secondary School Civil Rights Compliance Report* (hereinafter *2000 OCR Compliance Report).* "Corporal punishment" is the infliction of bodily pain as a penalty for unsatisfactory behavior. *Daily v. Board of Education of Morrill County School District No. 62-0063,* 588 N.W.2d 813 (Neb. 1999). In order to constitute "corporal punishment," the act must be "corporal" such that it inflicts pain on the body of the victim, and it must be "punishment" such that the intent of the actor is punitive. *Id.*

A teacher or administrator who strikes a student as an act of "corporal punishment" arguably engages in an act of battery. Similarly, a teacher or administrator may assault a student by creating in that student the reasonable fear of being struck. The tort of false imprisonment is arguably implicated whenever a student is required to stay after school in a closed "detention" room as a form of punishment. When a teacher intentionally causes physical harm to a student, that conduct also may implicate the tort of intentional infliction of emotional distress. Finally, acts of excessive punishment administered by public school officials may in extreme cases give rise to constitutional tort claims.

1. Common Law Torts and the Evolving State Law Perspectives on Corporal Punishment

In addressing the merits of each of these intentional tort claims, the courts traditionally have afforded schools and their administrators wide latitude in disciplining their students. In *Ingraham v. Wright,* 430 U.S. 651

(1977), the Supreme Court held that corporal punishment, including the act of paddling students, did not on its face constitute "cruel and unusual punishment" in violation of the Eighth Amendment to the Constitution. In reaching its constitutional decision, the Supreme Court in *Ingraham* relied heavily on the common law tradition of corporal punishment: "at common law a single principle has governed the use of corporal punishment since before the American Revolution: teachers may impose reasonable, but not excessive force to discipline a child."

The traditional common law recognition of the propriety of corporal punishment at least in some situations has allowed conduct which would otherwise constitute assault, battery, false imprisonment or intentional infliction of emotional distress to escape tort liability. So long as the conduct does not go beyond what the educator reasonably believes is necessary to discipline a student, the courts are unlikely to find that conduct to be tortious. *Compare Wexell v. Scott,* 2 Ill. App. 3d 646, 276 N.E.2d 735 (Ill. Ct. App. 1971) (teacher who scolded student not liable for intentional infliction of emotional distress) *with Frank v. Orleans Parish School Board,* 195 So. 2d 451 (La. Ct. App. 1967) (teacher liable for lifting and shaking student). Since educators are responsible for discipline in school, the courts generally have permitted educators to make physical contact with students for that purpose. *Sims v. Board of Education of Independent School District No. 22,* 329 F. Supp. 678 (D.N.M. 1971); *People v. Ball,* 58 Ill. 2d 36, 317 N.E.2d 54 (Ill. 1974); *Carr v. Wright,* 423 S.W.2d 521 (Ky. Ct. App. 1968); *Marlar v. Bill,* 181 Tenn. 100, 178 S.W.2d 634 (Tenn. 1944). While teachers are granted discretionary authority to use corporal punishment on their pupils, however, the punishment must be reasonable. *See, e.g., People v. Ball,* 58 Ill. 2d 36, 317 N.E.2d 54 (Ill. 1974); *Tinkham v. Kole,* 252 Iowa 1303, 110 N.W.2d 258 (Iowa 1961).

No precise common law rule defines what is unreasonable punishment. *See, e.g., Suits v. Glover,* 260 Ala. 449, 71 So. 2d 49 (Ala. 1954); *Tinkham v. Kole,* 252 Iowa 1303, 110 N.W.2d 258 (Iowa 1961); *Carr v. Wright,* 423 S.W.2d 521 (Ky. Ct. App. 1968). Whether a particular punishment administered is reasonable is a question of fact to be determined by the jury. *Calway v. Williamson,* 130 Conn. 575, 36 A.2d 377 (Conn. 1944); *Christman v. Hickman,* 225 Mo. App. 828, 37 S.W.2d 672 (Mo. Ct. App. 1931); *Harris v. Galilley,* 125 Pa. Super. 505, 189 A. 779 (Pa. Super. Ct. 1937). The reasonableness of a teacher's conduct in administering corporal punishment is assessed by weighing factors such as the nature and severity of the student's misconduct, the students' attitude and past behavior, the severity of the punishment, the availability of less severe but equally effective means of discipline, the teacher's motive in discipline and the student's age and physical condition. *LeBoyd v. Jenkins,* 381 So. 2d 1290 (La. Ct. App. 1980). *Compare State v. Cortner,* 602 N.E.2d 779 (Ohio Ct. App. 1992) (a teacher's action did not create liability when the teacher held the arm of a student behind his back, in order to prevent him from injuring other students) *with Chrysinger v. Decatur,* 445 N.E.2d 260 (Ohio Ct. App. 1982) (trial court erred in granting summary judgment to high school principal in battery action brought by student victim of corporal punishment, when the affidavits indicated that student suffered serious bruises from a paddling and could not rest on his back for one week following the incident). The courts do agree that, as a rule, educators may not use physical violence against a child merely because the child is unable to perform academically, even if the teacher considers such violence to be a part of instruction and encouragement. *Spacek v. Charles,* 928 S.W.2d 88 (Tex. Ct. App. 1996).

Although the common law of torts continues to protect teachers from liability for the reasonable use of disciplinary force, educational psychologists are now virtually unanimous in opposition to the use of such force. In 2000, the American Academy of Pediatrics officially issued a recommendation that "corporal punishment be abolished in all states by law. . . ." *American Academy of Pediatrics Policy Statement,* 106 Pediatrics 343 (Aug. 2000). In a comprehensive empirical and statistical study, John Guthrow recently concluded: "Clearly, those states which have banned paddling altogether and which employ more positive disciplinary measures in the classroom achieve far greater educational success and have created far more functional societies than those states which still use the paddle. That fact is simply irrefutable." Guthrow discovered an "undesirable" relationship between "paddling and pathology" such that schools in states which still allow corporal punishment produce students with "relatively lower test scores, higher drop-out rates, higher poverty rates, and lower-quality health care." *See* J. Guthrow, *Correlation Between High Rates of Corporal Punishment in Public Schools and Social Pathologies* (2002).

The National Association of School Psychologists also recently reaffirmed its formal policy opposing corporal punishment in schools because "[e]vidence indicates that corporal punishment negatively effects the social, psychological and educational development of students. . . ." *See National Association of School Psychologists Position Statement on Corporal Punishment in Schools* (Oct. 2003).

As educational experts began to question the effectiveness of aggressive forms of punishment, state legislatures became increasingly convinced that corporal punishment disserved the goals of education. The majority of states (27 and the District of Columbia) now have passed statutes that specifically make corporal punishment illegal. Of the states that have not yet passed statutes criminalizing corporal punishment, Texas reports the highest number of students (73,994) struck per school year, such that 22 percent of all corporal punishment in the nation is administered in Texas. In Mississippi, however, the highest *percentage* of students receive such punishment. Data released in February 2003, reveals that 9.8 percent of the students in Mississippi, or 48,627 children, received corporal punishment in the 1999-2000 school year. *See 2000 OCR Compliance Report.*

2. Federalizing Tort Law in Schools: Constitutional Violations and Corporal Punishment

Victims of aggressive school discipline also began to seek redress under 42 U.S.C. §1983, claiming that such punishment violated their constitutional rights. Students who are detained against their will, for instance, may have been "seized" unreasonably in violation of their Fourth Amendment rights. In addition, corporal punishment may in some situations constitute "cruel and unusual punishment," violating Eighth Amendment rights. Such forms of discipline also may deprive students of their "liberty" without substantive or procedural due process, in violation of the Fourteenth Amendment.

Since *Ingraham v. Wright,* 430 U.S. 651 (1977), the lower federal courts have recognized that punishment of students which is "so brutal, demeaning, and harmful as literally to shock the conscience" could give rise to a claim that the public school has deprived the student of a protected liberty interest in violation of substantive due process. *See, e.g., Hall v. Tawney,* 621 F.2d 607 (4th Cir. 1980); *Garcia v. Miera,* 817 F.2d 650 (10th Cir. 1987). *But see Cunningham v. Beavers,* 858 F.2d 269 (5th Cir. 1988).

While corporal punishment by school officials implicates a constitutionally protected liberty interest under the Fourteenth Amendment, however, it is not per se unconstitutional. *Wallace by Wallace v. Batavia School District 101,* 870 F. Supp. 222 (N.D. Ill. 1994). An act of corporal punishment does not deny a student substantive due process of law when the punishment administered is not excessive, follows multiple warnings that the student's misconduct will not be tolerated, and is not inflicted maliciously and sadistically for the purpose of causing harm. *Wise v. Pea Ridge School District No. 109,* 675 F. Supp. 1524 (W.D. Ark. 1987). The Eighth Circuit has reaffirmed that even paddling a student so as to create bruises does not constitute a violation of substantive due process. *Wise v. Pea Ridge School District,* 855 F.2d 560 (8th Cir. 1988). That court also held that a struggle between teacher and student, in which the student "slammed" the teacher against a table and the teacher banged the student's head against a metal pole, was insufficient to violate the student's substantive due process rights. *London v. Directors of the DeWitt Public Schools,* 194 F.3d 873 (8th Cir. 1999). On the other hand, when a high school principal slapped, punched and choked three students, he used excessive force in violation of the students' due process rights. *P.B. v. Koch,* 96 F.3d 1298 (9th Cir. 1996).

Similarly, the device of punishing students by "detention," if reasonable, does not violate their substantive due process rights. In a case where sixth grade students were taken on a field trip to a jail, for instance, a disrespectful student was punished by being placed in a cell for 50 minutes. The parents claimed a violation of the student's rights under the Fourth, Eighth and Fourteenth Amendments. The Fifth Circuit, however, concluded that no constitutional claims could be asserted. *Hassan v. Lubbock Independent School District,* 55 F.3d 1075 (5th Cir. 1995). *See also Harris v. County of Forsyth,* 921 F. Supp. 325 (M.D.N.C. 1996).

The freedom that the courts have traditionally offered educators to discipline children raises again the issue of the proper role of education in shaping character. Who is responsible for the discipline of a child: the school, the family or both? Do you agree with the court's answer in *Baker:* "the state has a countervailing interest in the maintenance of order in the school sufficient to sustain the right of teachers and school officials to administer reasonable corporal punishment" even over a parent's objections? *Baker v. Owen,* 395 F. Supp. 294 (M.D.N.C. 1975), *aff'd without opinion,* 423 U.S. 907 (1975).

As these cases indicate, the courts are not particularly receptive to finding that isolated acts of punishment in a school setting rise to the level of a deprivation of constitutional rights.

Bisignano v. Harrison Central School District

113 F. Supp. 2d 591 (S.D.N.Y. 2000)

Opinion and Order

William C. Conner, District Judge.

Plaintiffs Victoria and Anthony Bisignano bring the instant action on behalf of their minor daughter Amanda Bisignano against defendants Harrison Central School District (the "District") and teacher Vincent Nicita. Plaintiffs claim that defendants falsely imprisoned Amanda, subjected her to excessive force, and deprived her of her property in violation of the Fourth and Fourteenth Amendments, the Civil Rights Act of 1871, 42 U.S.C. §1983, and New York State law. Plaintiffs also assert claims against defendants for negligence and intentional infliction of emotional distress. . . .

Background

At the time of the events underlying the instant lawsuit, Amanda Bisignano was thirteen years old and an eighth-grade student at Louis M. Klein Middle School in Harrison, New York. Amanda took a gym class taught by defendant Nicita every other day. Nicita began working as a coach in the District in 1983, and as a physical education teacher in 1991.

On November 5, 1998, Amanda found a twenty-dollar bill on the floor of the gymnasium. It was not money that she had dropped or lost. Amanda testified that she asked other students in class whether they had dropped the bill. Within seconds after she found the money, Nicita told her it was his. Nicita told Amanda that if she gave him the money, he would buy her lunch. When Amanda failed to hand over the money, Nicita said "something like then get in the closet or something. He said like you're going to have to like stay in the closet until you give me back my money." Amanda said she did not give Nicita the money because she thought he was joking when he said that it was his. Nicita stated that he had a twenty-dollar bill in his pocket in the morning, but when he checked his pocket after he saw Amanda pick up the money from the floor, he realized his pocket was empty.

Amanda said that after Nicita dismissed the class, she ran out of the gymnasium laughing and Nicita ran after her. Amanda testified that Nicita told her she could not leave until she returned the twenty-dollar bill to him and then he gave her "a little push" into an equipment closet. Nicita testified during his deposition that he did not push Amanda into the closet, but that she ran into the closet herself.

Amanda testified that the doors to the closet were completely closed and there was no light inside the closet. Nicita said he believed the lights were on. Amanda said she remained in the closet for slightly more than thirty seconds while Nicita held the doors shut from the other side. Amanda said she demanded to be released from the closet, but Nicita told her he would not release her until she gave him the money. According to Amanda, Nicita, who was laughing, then opened the door about a foot, and Amanda slipped out. Nicita remembered the incident differently. He testified that he pushed the door closed, then walked away from it. He said Amanda then exited the closet.

Amanda testified that after she exited the closet, Nicita grabbed and twisted her left wrist, and yelled at her to give him back his twenty dollars. She said she screamed for help. Then, when she reached into her pocket to retrieve the bill, Nicita grabbed her upper right arm. Amanda said she threw the bill, which glanced off Nicita's chest and fell to the ground. Nicita told her to pick up the bill and hand it to him "like a human being." Nicita testified that when Amanda left the closet, she was holding the bill in her hand. He said he "just held her hand as it was there," and that he held her hand "[t]ight enough so that she couldn't get away, but not that tight." Nicita said Amanda threw the bill on the floor, and he told her to pick it up and hand it to him. Amanda said she ran out of the room and went into the girls' locker room where she showed her friends the red marks on her arms. She was crying. She then went to the nurse's office, where the nurse put ice packs on her arms. Ann Doniger, a health assistant, testified that Amanda's arm was "slightly red" near her wrist.

Nicita came to the nurse's office and asked Amanda to take a walk with him. Amanda said they went to Nicita's office and Nicita apologized and told her that he did not mean to hurt her. Rosemary Brooke, the principal of the middle school, said that when Amanda came to her office following the incident, Amanda had marks on her upper arm and wrist. Brooke described Amanda's injuries as "slight." Brooke telephoned Amanda's parents and Amanda chose to spend the rest of the day in school rather than go home. Brooke testified that she reported the incident to the District superintendent. Subsequently, the principal and superintendent met with plaintiffs and Nicita.

Amanda states she had "many" sessions with a psychologist following the incident. Amanda complained of frequent stomachaches and headaches, although Amanda testified she had suffered from migraine headaches prior to the incident.

In her deposition, Amanda testified that during the spring 1998 softball season, Nicita, who was her coach, told her that "we should do the batting order by my I.Q. and instead of playing I should bring a pillow so I can sit on it."

Brooke testified that other students had incidents with Nicita. Brooke said that a memorandum in her correspondence file reported that Nicita, "in correcting an incident in the locker room[,] . . . said to [a student] you were a little faggot, I should lock you in the room to have someone beat your ass." Brooke said she did not speak with Nicita about the incident and did not report the incident to the District superintendent. Brooke also testified that a May 1997 document made "reference to a youngster who reported to the nurse that he had a sore arm," and that "Mr. Nicita twisted his arm to take candy from him, area slightly red, ice applied." In a 1992 memorandum from Brooke to Nicita, Brooke reprimanded Nicita for telling a student, "You turn me on."

Brooke testified that during her tenure as principal, the District provided teachers with a handbook and at times invited speakers to discuss "being sensitive to the kids" with faculty, but did not offer training focused on disciplining students or interpersonal skills.

Discussion

II. Plaintiffs' Claims Against Nicita

. . . Not every state law tort becomes an actionable constitutional tort under section 1983 simply because it was committed by a state actor. Thus, our initial inquiry is whether the alleged actions, if taken as true, deprived Amanda Bisignano of a constitutional right.

A. Plaintiffs' Fourth Amendment Claim

Plaintiffs claim that Nicita violated Amanda's Fourth Amendment rights, as applied to the states by the Fourteenth Amendment, by forcibly confining her in the storage closet. The Fourth Amendment guarantees citizens the right "to be secure in their persons . . . against unreasonable . . . seizures" of the person.

In a case in which two Florida junior high school students complained of being paddled by their teachers—one to the point of suffering a hematoma requiring medical attention, and the other paddled on the arm so that he lost use of it for a week—the Supreme Court noted in dictum that "the principal concern of [the Fourth] Amendment's prohibition against unreasonable searches and seizures is with intrusions on privacy in the course of criminal investigations." *Ingraham v. Wright,* 430 U.S. 651, 674 (1977). However, in a later case, the Court addressed the issue of whether a school administrator violated a student's Fourth Amendment rights when he searched her purse and found evidence that led to the student's adjudication of delinquency. *New Jersey v. T.L.O.* The Court determined that the Fourth Amendment applies to searches conducted by school authorities, but stated that the determination of the standard of reasonableness "depends on the context within which a search takes place," . . .

The *T.L.O.* reasonableness test reflects a balancing of the need to guard against arbitrary invasions of a student's privacy and security with "the value of preserving the informality of the student-teacher relationship" and the necessity of maintaining order in our schools. In applying that test to the facts of this case, we must first consider whether Nicita's alleged actions were "justified at [their] inception," and second, whether his actions were "reasonably related in scope to the circumstances which justified the interference in the first place." Looking at the facts in the light most favorable to Amanda, as we must on a motion for summary judgment, we find that material issues of fact exist which preclude a grant of summary judgment for Nicita on this claim.

Both parties agree that Nicita's actions took place after class was dismissed. Certainly, a teacher may elect to discipline a student after class to minimize the disruption to other students. Furthermore, a teacher may be justified in demanding the return of money he lost if he reasonably believed it was his. However, a reasonable jury could find that the loss of a twenty-dollar bill did not justify pushing a thirteen-year-old girl into an unlit closet and holding the doors closed from the other side, even if, as Amanda admitted in her deposition, she was running from the teacher at the time. Likewise, a reasonable jury could conclude that Nicita's alleged actions were not "reasonably related in scope to the circumstances" under which the incident arose.

We certainly hesitate to allow "a federal case" to be made of an incident that lasted only a few moments. We appreciate the benefits of a certain level of familiarity between students and teachers and the daunting task teachers have in maintaining discipline in the classroom. However, a teacher who uses the power of his authority to pursue his financial interest gains abuses the trust placed in him by his charges, their parents and the state. Defendant Nicita's motion for summary judgment as to plaintiffs' Fourth Amendment claim is denied.

B. Plaintiffs' Substantive Due Process Claims

Plaintiffs claim that Nicita's conduct toward Amanda violated her right to substantive due process. This claim must be dismissed.

As an initial matter, we note that the Supreme Court has held: Where a particular Amendment "provides an explicit textual source of constitutional protection" against a particular sort of government behavior, "that Amendment, not the more generalized notion of 'substantive due process,' must be the guide for analyzing these claims." *Albright,* 510 U.S. at 273, 114 S. Ct. at 813 (plurality opinion of Rehnquist, C.J.) (quoting *Graham v. Connor,* 490 U.S. 386, 395, 109 S. Ct. 1865, 1871, 104 L. Ed. 2d 443 (1989). . . .

The Supreme Court has stated that not all constitutional claims relating to physically abusive conduct arise under either the Fourth or Eighth Amendments, but "if a constitutional claim is covered by a specific constitutional provision, such as the Fourth or Eighth Amendment, the claim must be analyzed under the standard appropriate to that specific provision, not under the rubric of substantive due process." *United States v. Lanier,* 520 U.S. 259, 272 (1997).

At least one other district court found, in the wake of *T.L.O.,* that the momentary use of force by a teacher against a student should be judged not pursuant to the Fourth Amendment reasonableness standard, but as a potential violation of substantive due process. *Kurilla v. Callahan,* 68 F. Supp. 2d 556 (M.D.Pa.1999).

There, a student got into a fight with another student. A teacher called both students to his desk and asked them what happened. One of the students interrupted the other to explain his side of the story and the teacher told the student to "[s]hut up or I will lay you out on the floor." When the student persisted with telling his side of the story, the teacher grabbed the student's shirt with clenched fists and pulled the student hard, causing the student's chest to come into contact with his fists. The court held that the teacher's actions did not effect a "seizure" of the student under the Fourth Amendment. Instead, the court applied the "shocks the conscience" standard used to determine whether a student's substantive due process rights were violated.

However, the *Kurilla* case is distinguishable from the one at bar. Here, Amanda claims that she was forcibly detained in a closet, while *Kurilla* was a simple case of a teacher's use of force. In fact, the *Kurilla* court acknowledged that, with the exception of the Seventh Circuit's decision in *Wallace* in which a teacher grabbed a student by the elbow and wrist, most of the cases in which courts applied the Fourth Amendment in the school discipline context "involved factual scenarios more closely aligned with Fourth Amendment protection." *Kurilla,* 68 F. Supp. 2d at 562.

To the extent that plaintiffs could bring a separate claim regarding Nicita's alleged use of force against Amanda, i.e., grabbing and twisting her wrist and, considering the possibility that we have erred in our conclusion that the instant case arises under the Fourth Amendment, we will examine the facts alleged in the context of substantive due process.

In *Ingraham,* the Supreme Court held that corporal punishment in public schools implicates a constitutionally protected liberty interest where "school authorities, acting under color of state law, deliberately decide to punish a child for misconduct by restraining the child and inflicting appreciable physical pain." De minimis impositions do not implicate the Fourteenth Amendment.

The Court left open the question whether the infliction of severe corporal punishment on schoolchildren violates substantive due process. *Ingraham,* 430 U.S. at 659, n.12. Examining the issue of whether corporal punishment violates a student's right to procedural due process, the Court held that "traditional common law remedies are fully adequate to afford due process." 430 U.S. at 672.

In the wake of *Ingraham,* some federal courts have held that claims of substantive due process violations resulting from the exercise of corporal punishment are foreclosed where the state affords the student adequate post-punishment remedies. *See, e.g., Harris v. Tate County Sch. Dist.,* 882 F. Supp. 90 (N.D. Miss. 1995); *Carestio v. Sch. Bd. of Broward County, 79* F. Supp. 2d 1347, 1349 (S.D. Fla. 1999). Other courts have found that a student who has been subjected to corporal punishment may make out a claim for a violation of her substantive due process rights regardless of the availability of state law remedies. *See, e.g., Hall v. Tawney,* 621 F.2d 607, 613 (4th Cir. 1980); *Meyer by Wyrick v. Litwiller,* 749 F. Supp. 981 (W.D. Mo. 1990). These courts apply the test articulated by the Second Circuit in *Johnson v. Glick,* 481 F.2d 1028 (2d Cir. 1973), overruled on other grounds by *Graham,* or a version thereof, to determine whether a school official's actions "shock the conscience." The "shocks the conscience" standard has been adhered to as the benchmark for cognizable abuse of official power since it was first articulated by the Supreme Court in *Rochin v. California,* 342 U.S. 165, 172, 72 S. Ct. 205, 209, 96 L. Ed. 183 (1952). *See Sacramento v. Lewis,* 523 U.S. 833, 846-47, 118 S. Ct. 1708, 1717, 140 L. Ed. 2d 1043 (1998).

The *Johnson* test provides that a court must look to such factors as: the need for the application of force, the relationship between the need and the amount of force that was used, the extent of injury inflicted, and whether force was applied in a good faith effort to maintain or restore discipline or maliciously and sadistically for the very purpose of causing harm. 481 F.2d at 1033. *See also Hall,* 621 F.2d at 613 ("[T]he substantive due process inquiry in school corporal punishment cases must be whether the force applied caused injury so severe, was so disproportionate to the need presented, and was so inspired by malice or sadism rather than a careless or unwise exercise of zeal that it amounted to a brutal and inhumane abuse of official power literally shocking to the conscience."); *Meyer,* 749 F. Supp. at 985 (student plaintiff may recover for constitutional violations if plaintiff's evidence permits fact-finder to conclude force applied by teacher was so disproportionate to need for discipline and so inspired by malice that teacher's behavior shocked the conscience); *Webb,* 828 F.2d at 1158 (school principal who, during a school trip, broke down the locked door to a hotel bathroom, hitting a student who had locked herself inside, and who then threw that student against a wall and slapped her may have violated the student's substantive Fourteenth Amendment due process rights).

Here, even if we assume that the facts alleged by plaintiffs are true, Nicita's actions do not "shock the conscience" of the Court. Amanda did not suffer the kind of "appreciable physical pain" which implicates the Fourteenth Amendment. *See Ingraham,* 430 U.S. at 674, 97 S. Ct. at 1414. At most, her physical injuries amounted to red marks on her arms, stomach upset and headaches. Although we can appreciate how such an altercation with a teacher could cause substantial embarrassment to Amanda and Amanda testified to having seen a psychologist several times following the incident, these injuries were not "so severe" that substantive due process rights were implicated. *Webb,* 828 F.2d at 1158.

Defendant Nicita's motion for summary judgment as to plaintiffs' substantive due process claim is granted. . . .

III. Plaintiffs' Claims Against the District

Section 1983 applies to municipalities and other local government units. *Monell v. Department of Soc. Servs. of the City of New York,* 436 U.S. 658, 690, (1978). However, section 1983 will not support a cause of action based upon respondeat superior liability. . . . A municipality will be liable for a violation of section 1983 only where the municipality itself was the "moving force" behind the plaintiff's deprivation of federal rights. *Board of the County Comm'rs of Bryan County, Okl. v. Brown,* 520 U.S. 397, 400 (1997). A municipality will not be held liable solely because it employs a tortfeasor. . . . The plaintiff must show that her injuries were a result of a municipal "policy" or "custom."

"A single incident alleged in a complaint, especially if it involved only actors below the policymaking level, generally will not suffice to raise an inference of the existence of a custom or policy." *Dwares v. City of New York,* 985 F.2d 94, 100 (2d Cir. 1993). In cases in which a plaintiff does not claim that a municipality directly inflicted an injury, but nonetheless caused an employee to do so, "rigorous standards of culpability and causation must be applied to ensure that the municipality is not held liable solely for the actions of its employee." . . . The Supreme Court has held that a municipality will be liable for inadequate training or supervision of its employees "only where the failure to train amounts to deliberate indifference to the rights" of those with whom municipal employees will come into contact. *City of Canton, Ohio v. Harris,* 489 U.S. 378, 388 (1989).

Plaintiffs allege that the District, "aware of Nicita's violent and aggressive behavior, has deliberately and/or recklessly taken no remedial and/or no effective remedial action as a result of which Nicita's said propensities have been encouraged, condoned and/or ratified by the District." In their brief in opposition to defendants' motions, plaintiffs claim that the District had a custom or policy of failing to take remedial action "with respect to reports of physically abusive behavior by Nicita towards students at the District's Middle School," and that the District failed to train its employees and supervisors regarding appropriate conduct toward and discipline of students.

The Second Circuit set forth the following three-part test for determining when a municipality's failure to train or supervise rises to the level of "deliberate indifference": First, the plaintiff must show that a policymaker knows "to a moral certainty" that her employees will confront a given situation. . . . Thus, a policymaker does not exhibit deliberate indifference by failing to train employees for rare or unforeseen events. Second, the plaintiff must show that the situation either presents the employee with a difficult choice of the sort that training or supervision will make less difficult or that there is a history of employees mishandling the situation. . . . [Third], the plaintiff must show that the wrong choice by the city employee will frequently cause the deprivation of a citizen's constitutional rights. *Walker v. City of New York,* 974 F.2d 293, 297 (2d Cir. 1992).

In the instant case, plaintiffs have offered three documented incidents other than that at bar in which Nicita behaved inappropriately with a student: one case in which Nicita called a student "a little faggot" and told him "I should lock you in the room to have someone beat your ass;" another in which Nicita twisted a student's arm to take candy from him, causing the student's arm to turn "slightly red;" and a third in which Nicita told a student "You turn me on." Plaintiffs also offered evidence that the District did not provide teachers and staff training specifically targeted to disciplinary procedures and interpersonal skills.

This evidence is insufficient to impose liability, vicariously or directly, upon the District for any constitutional deprivation. There is no evidence the District condoned the activity of which Nicita is accused, nor is there any evidence that the District specifically directed, supervised, participated, authorized, or even knowingly acquiesced in the incident upon which the claim for relief is based. Plaintiffs have not demonstrated that the District knew "to a moral certainty" that the alleged incident was likely to take place. Defendant Nicita might have demonstrated questionable judgment on several occasions, but failure to address those events in a more comprehensive fashion does not lead us to conclude that the District was deliberately indifferent to the constitutional rights of Nicita's students. Accordingly, summary judgment is granted to defendant District as to plaintiffs' federal law claims against it. . . .

IV. Qualified Immunity

None of the parties disputes that Nicita, as a state actor, possesses qualified immunity. Qualified immunity shields state actors from personal liability "insofar as their conduct does not violate clearly established statutory or constitutional rights of which a reasonable person would have known," *Harlow v. Fitzgerald,* 457 U.S. 800, 818 (1982), "or insofar as it was objectively reasonable for them to believe that their acts did not violate those rights." *Brown v. D'Amico,* 35 F.3d 97, 99 (2d Cir. 1994); *see also Walker v. McClellan,* 126 F.3d 127, 129 (2d Cir. 1997); *Davidson v. Scully,* 114 F.3d 12, 14 (2d Cir. 1997); *Gardiner v. Incorporated Village of Endicott,* 50 F.3d 151, 156 (2d Cir. 1995).

A court evaluating a claim of qualified immunity "must first determine whether the plaintiff has alleged the deprivation of an actual constitutional right at all, and if so, proceed to determine whether that right was clearly established at the time of the alleged violation." *Wilson v. Layne,* 526 U.S. 603, 609 (1999).

"Clearly established" for purposes of qualified immunity means that "[t]he contours of the right must be sufficiently clear that a reasonable official would understand that what he is doing violates that right. This is not to say that an official action is protected by qualified immunity unless the very action in question has previously been held unlawful, . . . but it is to say that in the light of pre-existing law the unlawfulness must be apparent." *Anderson v. Creighton,* 483 U.S. 635, 640 (1987).

It is well settled that children do not "shed their constitutional rights . . . at the schoolhouse gate." *Tinker v. Des Moines Indep. Community Sch. Dist.,* 393 U.S. 503, 506 (1969), although "the nature of those rights is what is appropriate for children in school." *Vernonia Sch. Dist. 47J v. Acton,* 515 U.S. 646, 656 (1995). . . . The issue at this stage of the analysis is the more specific, "objective inquiry" of whether a reasonable public school teacher could have believed that confining a student in an unlit storage closet during an encounter after class had ended "was lawful, in light of clearly established law and the information [the teacher] possessed." *Wilson,* 526 U.S. at 615.

We hold that material issues of fact preclude a grant of summary judgment to defendant Nicita on the issue of qualified immunity. No reasonable school official could have believed that the conduct Amanda described was lawful. The dearth of Supreme Court and Second Circuit decisions squarely on point with the facts of this case is likely a function of the aberrational quality of the alleged acts, and cannot serve to shield a teacher from the consequences of confining a student in a closet. *See Wilson,* 526 U.S. at 621, (Stevens, J., concurring in part and dissenting in part) ("The absence of judicial opinions expressly holding that police violate the Fourth Amendment if they bring media representatives into private homes provides scant support for the conclusion that in 1992 a competent officer could reasonably believe that it would be lawful to do so."). Accordingly, we deny defendant Nicita summary judgment on the issue of qualified immunity. . . .

NOTES AND QUESTIONS

1. In the *Bisignano* case, the court concludes that the teacher's act of pushing a student into a closet and keeping the door closed creates a genuine issue of material fact as to whether the act was an unreasonable seizure in violation of the Fourth Amendment. How would you resolve that fact issue?

2. The court finds that the teacher's conduct may be an unreasonable seizure, but it does not "shock the conscience." How can those conclusions be reconciled?

3. In *Bisignano,* the court also finds that the school district cannot be liable absent a showing that it was "deliberately indifferent" to the student's rights. At the same time, however, the court concludes that the teacher

cannot necessarily establish his "qualified immunity" defense because, "[n]o reasonable school official could have believed that the conduct" at issue was lawful. How can those two conclusions be reconciled?

4. The Supreme Court of Mississippi has held that a school board policy or administrative rule that makes punishment mandatory is valid. The court explained: "As a matter of state substantive due process, a school board's disciplinary rule or scheme is enforceable when fairly viewed it furthers a substantial legitimate interest of the school. Mandatory school disciplinary rules are not unconstitutional simply because they are mandatory. The fact that a school rule may be worded in mandatory language does not deprive school boards and their subordinates of the authority to administer the rule with flexibility and leniency." *Clinton Municipal Separate School District v. Byrd, 477* So. 2d 237 (Miss. 1985). Recall that corporal punishment is still legal in Mississippi. Could a school district in that state adopt a mandatory corporal punishment policy? Would such a policy survive constitutional challenge? Would the policy "shock the conscience"?

5. In those states in which corporal punishment is not illegal, the most recent available evidence indicates that African-American students are struck by educators at a rate that is more than two times their makeup in the population. These students comprise 17 percent of the student population in public schools throughout the United States, and receive 39 percent of the acts of corporal punishment. White students in these same schools comprise 62 percent of all students, but receive only 53 percent of the incidents of corporal punishment. In fact, the percentage of white children who are struck by educators has declined from 65 percent in 1976 to 53 percent in 2000, while the percentage of non-white children who are hit has increased from 29 percent in 1976 to 39 percent in 2000. *See 2000 OCR Compliance Report* (data reported in February 2003 for 1999-2000 school year). How should this racial component to corporal punishment influence the legal, political and philosophical arguments about its continued use?

6. The *Bisignano* court refers to the *Kurilla* case as an example of a thorough analysis of whether disciplinary conduct in the school setting is so severe as to "shock the conscience" in violation of a student's due process rights. As you read the *Kurilla* opinion, consider whether it is possible to define the "shock the conscience" test.

KURILLA V. CALLAHAN

68 F. Supp. 2d 556 (M.D. Pa. 1999)

VANASKIE, Chief Judge.

This is a civil rights action under 42 U.S.C. §1983 set in the factual context of use of force by a school teacher, Kevin Callahan, against a student, Robert Kurilla. . . . Having carefully considered the issues de novo, I find that the momentary use of force by a schoolteacher is to be judged by the shocks the conscience standard. I also find that Callahan's conduct, which consisted of striking a blow to Kurilla's chest that resulted in bruising but otherwise did not require medical care, was not so " 'brutal' and 'offensive to human dignity' " as to shock the judicial conscience.

While Callahan's conduct did not violate substantive due [process] standards, Mid-Valley School District may nonetheless be held accountable for having established a policy or custom that caused the injury allegedly sustained by Kurilla. Because I find that Kurilla has presented sufficient evidence to warrant a trial on the question of the existence of a policy or custom to tolerate use of excessive force by a teacher, the School District's summary judgment motion will be denied.

Although so-called reasonable acts of corporal punishment may not give rise to tort liability, most school districts have enacted policies which limit or bar the practice. The districts which have enacted these policies have come to believe that acts of corporal punishment or verbal abuse do not serve any legitimate educational purpose.

I. Background

On October 3, 1995, Kurilla was an eighth grade student at Mid Valley Secondary Center. According to Kurilla, on that date, he was attending a study hall supervised by Defendant Kevin Callahan ("Callahan"), where Kurilla got into a fight with another student. Callahan called both Kurilla and the other student to his desk, and asked the other student what happened. Kurilla interrupted and began explaining his side of the story, to which Callahan responded by telling Kurilla to "Shut up or I will lay you out on the floor." Kurilla attempted again to tell his side of the story when Callahan grabbed him by the shirt with clenched hands and proceeded to pull Kurilla very hard, causing Kurilla's chest to strike Callahan's closed fists. Kurilla claims that Callahan's action, which allegedly had the identical effect as if Callahan punched him, resulted in bruising on Kurilla's chest.

The bruise was on Kurilla's right side, above the nipple. In addition to the bruise on his chest, Kurilla alleges that he had a red mark on the back of his neck and on the left side of his chest. . . .

The threshold inquiry in addressing Kurilla's §1983 excessive force claim involves "identifying the specific constitutional right allegedly infringed. . . ." Identification of the specific constitutional right allegedly infringed is essential because the standard against which the defendant's conduct is to be assessed depends upon the right that is purportedly violated. Kurilla argues that the Fourth Amendment "reasonableness" standard should be applied in this case. The premise of this argument is that he was subjected to a "seizure" when Callahan grabbed his shirt and punched him in the chest.

. . . In this case, the question is whether the momentary use of force by a teacher against a student who refuses to be quiet despite having been admonished not to interrupt another student's account of an in-classroom altercation is "covered by" the Fourth Amendment prohibition against unreasonable seizures. In making this determination, it is important to bear in mind the "unique constitutional position" of public school students. *Wallace by Wallace v. Batavia School District 101,* 68 F.3d 1010, 1013 (7th Cir. 1995). "Once under the control of the school, students' movement and location are subject to the ordering and direction of teachers and administrators." *Id.* at 1013. Public school children are subject to the state's authority in a way that has been described as "custodial and tutelary, permitting a degree of supervision and control that could not be exercised over free adults." *Vernonia School District 47 J. v. Acton,* 515 U.S. 646, 655 (1995). . . .

The only case cited by Kurilla that applied Fourth Amendment principles to a claim of excessive force by a teacher was *Wallace.* In *Wallace,* a teacher, in an effort to break up a fight between two students, grabbed one of the students by her wrist and elbow to move her out of the classroom. While finding that the Fourth Amendment "covered" this scenario, the Seventh Circuit also noted that there is "little parallel . . . between the school and law enforcement situations when there is a seizure of the person." Explaining that "[t]he basic purpose for the deprivation of a student's personal liberty by a teacher is education, while the basic purpose for the deprivation of liberty of a criminal suspect by a police officer is investigation or apprehension," the court held that "application of the Fourth Amendment is necessarily different" in the school context. *Id.* The court elaborated:

> The reasonableness of a Fourth Amendment seizure of a public school student by a teacher must be evaluated in the context of the school environment, where restricting the liberty of students is a sine qua non of the educational process. Deprivations of liberty in schools serve the end of compulsory education and do not inherently pose constitutional problems.
>
> The premise of a general constitutionally permissible liberty restriction is, of course, not the case in the law enforcement context. Seizures of individuals by police are premised on society's need to apprehend and punish violators of the law. As such, they inherently threaten the individual's liberty to live free of the criminal justice process. There is no analogous liberty for students to live free of the educational process.

The court went on to apply an objective reasonableness standard that purports to take into account the "special needs" of the school environment. Under the test applied by the Seventh Circuit, the court does not concern itself with the teacher's intentions, but instead with whether the alleged seizure "was objectively unreasonable."

Wallace recognized that the school environment is qualitatively different than the law enforcement environment. Public school students' liberty interests are necessarily restrained in a manner that is not present outside the school setting. Some official conduct that would not be tolerated outside school must be allowed in the school. "[A] proper educational environment requires close supervision of school children, as well as the enforcement of rules against conduct that would be perfectly permissible if undertaken by an adult." *T.L.O.,* 469 U.S. at 339. *Wallace* accommodates this distinctive environment by qualifying the "objective reasonableness" inquiry. But *Wallace* suggests no meaningful standard by which this accommodation is to be effected. While the "shocks the conscience" test has been justly criticized as "amorphous and imprecise," standards have been established for its application. More importantly, substantive due process has been the basis for considering claims of governmental abuse of power where the conduct in question does not implicate a specific constitutional protection. The momentary application of force by a teacher in reaction to a disruptive student is a scenario to which the Fourth Amendment does not textually or historically apply. I thus decline to follow *Wallace.*

In short, the momentary use of physical force by a teacher in reaction to a disruptive or unruly student does not effect a "seizure" of the student under the Fourth Amendment. Because Kurilla's claim is not governed by the Fourth Amendment, substantive due process principles will be applied to determine whether there is a triable excessive force claim here. . . .

Substantive due process has been described as "the right to be free from state intrusions into realms of personal privacy and bodily security through means so brutal, demeaning and harmful as literally to 'shock the conscience' of the court." *Lillard v. Shelby County Board of Education,* 76 F.3d 716, 725 (6th Cir. 1996). The threshold for establishing a constitutional tort for excessive use of force is set so high in light of Supreme Court admonitions "against an overly generous interpretation of the substantive component of the Due Process Clause." The conduct in question "must do more than 'offend some fastidious squeamishness or private sentimentalism. . . .' " "[T]he constitutional concept of conscience-shocking duplicates no traditional category of common-law fault. . . ." The pertinent inquiry is " 'whether the force applied caused injuries so severe, was so disproportionate to the need presented, and was so inspired by malice or sadism rather than a merely careless or unwise excess of zeal that it amounted to a brutal and inhumane abuse of official power literally shocking to the conscience.' "

In this case, Callahan's punching of Kurilla in the chest caused a bruise and some red marks. While Kurilla sought medical care, there is no evidence that medical attention was reasonably necessary. Kurilla's injuries did not even warrant x-ray examination or prescription of any medication. Thus, Kurilla's injuries could hardly be described as "severe."

Callahan's striking of a blow to Kurilla's chest is akin to the slap across the student's face considered in *Lillard v. Shelby County Board of Education.* In that case, the court held: "[I]t is simply inconceivable that a single slap could shock the conscience. We do not quarrel with the suggestion that [the teacher's] actions were careless and unwise; but they fall short of 'brutal,' or 'inhumane,' or any of the other adjectives employed to describe an act so vicious as to constitute a violation of substantive due process. In contrast to *Webb* the blow inflicted here was neither severe in force nor administered repeatedly. Moreover, the slap did not result in any physical injury to Lillard. While we do not mean to suggest that school systems should tolerate a teacher who slaps a student in anger, neither do we conclude that one slap, even if made for no legitimate purpose, rises to the level of a constitutional violation. While [the teacher] should reasonably expect to face serious consequences for his treatment of Lillard, those consequences should not be found in a federal court through the mechanism of a section 1983 action."

This rationale applies with equal force here. Callahan was reacting to a disruptive student. While Callahan's reaction could be categorized as overzealous, and may be actionable under state tort law, it does not amount " 'to a brutal and inhumane abuse of official power literally shocking to the conscience.' "

"To say that due process is not offended by [Callahan's] conduct described here is not, of course, to imply anything about its appropriate treatment under state law." *County of Sacramento v. Lewis,* 118 S. Ct. at 1721 n. 14. But "[d]ecisions about civil liability standards that 'involve a host of policy choices . . . must be made by locally elected representatives [or by courts enforcing the common law of torts], rather than federal judges interpreting the basic charter of Government for the entire country." *Id.,* quoting *Collins v. Harker Heights,* 503 U.S. 115, 129, 112 S. Ct. 1061, 117 L. Ed. 2d 261 (1992). Kurilla has asserted common law tort claims of assault, battery, and intentional infliction of emotional distress. The viability of those claims is unaffected by the decision here. Moreover, the state criminal process was employed here and Kurilla could petition the school board for redress. That Kurilla is without a civil rights claim for Callahan's conduct thus does not leave him without effective means to redress the alleged wrong.

In summary, while Callahan's conduct violated state laws that balance the justification for use of force against a teacher's right to use force to maintain discipline, and may be actionable under tort law, it was not so brutal or inhumane as to shock the conscience. Accordingly, Callahan's summary judgment motion will be granted and Kurilla's summary judgment motion will be denied. . . .

As noted above, application of force by a teacher implicates liberty interests protected by the Fourteenth Amendment. Consistent with the reasoning of [our prior cases], Mid-Valley School District may be held liable if it had a custom or policy condoning use of excessive force by teachers that evidenced a deliberate indifference to the student's constitutional rights in bodily integrity protected by the Due Process Clause of the Fourteenth Amendment. . . .

Thus, to establish liability on the part of the School District under §1983, Kurilla must establish that officials at a policymaking or supervisory level 1) had actual or constructive knowledge that Callahan had violent propensities and was a threat to students; 2) followed a policy or custom of tolerating or ignoring the risk Callahan or other violent teachers posed; and 3) exhibited indifference to the safety of students who were likely to be harmed by violent teachers.

Kurilla claims that "[t]he School District had a policy or custom of permitting Callahan to assault students without fear of action being taken against him. This policy or custom also extended to attempting to appease the parents of assaulted students in order to assure that Callahan's assaults would not be made public. The policy or custom also included creating a paper record of willingness to supervise or train Callahan, but in reality refusing to do so." . . .

In this case, there were three (3) incidents involving Callahan in less than one year. There is no evidence of any independent investigation by the School District of any of these incidents. No disciplinary action was taken against Callahan. Even following Callahan's convictions of the summary offense of harassment in connection with his physical abuse of students, no disciplinary action was taken against Callahan. While Callahan's assault on Kurilla was preceded by only one incident, the failure to take any disciplinary action against Callahan following the three incidents in the span of less than one year is probative of the question of whether the School District had a policy or custom to tolerate or be deliberately indifferent to excessive use of force by teachers. . . .

[T]he existence of a custom or policy that condoned or was deliberately indifferent to excessive use of force by teachers in the Mid-Valley School District is a triable issue. Accordingly, Mid-Valley School District's motion for summary judgment will be denied.

NOTES AND QUESTIONS

1. In concluding that Kurilla's injuries were not "severe," the Court distinguishes those situations in which courts have found excessive force. For example, in *Hall v. Tawney,* 621 F.2d 607 (4th Cir. 1980), a student had been beaten with a paddle to such a degree that hospitalization for a period of ten days was required. In *Garcia v. Miera,* 817 F.2d 650 (10th Cir. 1987), *cert. denied,* 485 U.S. 959 (1988), a student had been hit multiple times with a split board causing bleeding and a permanent scar.

2. The *Kurilla* court found a genuine issue of material fact as to whether the school district had a custom or policy condoning excessive force by teachers, or was deliberately indifferent to the use of such force. What steps should a school district take to protect its students from the excessive use of force by teachers?

3. ***Corporal Punishment Practicum.*** Consider the following school district policy regarding student discipline:

   > Corporal punishment shall not be used. Corporal punishment is defined as slapping, paddling, or prolonged maintenance of students in physically painful positions, or intentional infliction of bodily harm. Corporal punishment does not include reasonable force as needed to maintain safety for other students, school personnel, or persons, or for the purpose of self-defense or the defense of property.

   Does this language insulate a school district from §1983 liability?

4. ***Disciplinary Policy Practicum.*** In light of the common law and constitutional law issues raised in the preceding materials, draft a school district policy regarding the district's use, if any, of student "isolation" or "time out" as disciplinary devices.

E. DEFAMATION

The tort of defamation occurs when school officials or employees intentionally make false statements to third parties that damage the plaintiff's professional (not personal) reputation. *See* Keeton et al., *Prosser and Keeton on Torts* 771-848 (5th ed. 1984).

Libel consists of publishing defamatory material by written or printed words or by any other *physical* visual form of communication such as e-mail or television that has the potentially harmful qualities of written or printed words. Slander, by contrast, involves defamatory auditory communications such as speech. *See* Restatement (Second) of Torts §568 at 177-178 (1977), Keeton et. al., *Prosser and Keeton on Torts* 773 (5th ed. 1984).

The defamatory torts of libel and slander arise in two contexts within the education arena. First, the school district may be accused of defaming its own teachers or other educational professionals. Second, the school district through its agents may be accused of defaming students. In both contexts, the common law generally immunizes school administrators and teachers who make communications in good faith, without malice and in the performance of their responsibilities. *See, e.g., Hett v. Ploetz,* 20 Wis. 2d 55, 121 N.W.2d 270 (Wis. 1963) (superintendent's allegedly defamatory letter about former teacher was entitled to conditional privilege because it was made without malice and was "reasonably calculated to accomplish the privileged purpose"); *Chapman v. Furlough,* 334 So. 2d 293 (Fla. Ct. App. 1976) (conditional privilege attaches to communication by teacher to parents regarding students' drug use, and no liability results absent actual malice).

1. Defamation of Educators

As a result of the conditional privilege which school district administrators enjoy, they also are generally able to make nonmalicious communications about a teacher's performance where doing so is part of their administrative responsibilities. As a rule, negative evaluations of teachers and negative letters of recommendation will not give rise to claims for libel or slander unless they were made with actual malice. *See, e.g., Ginwright v. Unified School District,* 756 F. Supp. 1458 (D. Kan. 1991) (no liability for communications to prospective employer about teacher's alleged child abuse).

Nonetheless, when administrators and officials go beyond what is necessary to meet their responsibilities and make malicious, defamatory comments about faculty members, they will be liable for those comments. For instance, school board members who make gratuitous comments about a teacher's incompetence or drinking habits outside of any necessary evaluation or recommendation process have been held liable for those comments. *See, e.g., Ford v. Jeane,* 106 So. 558 (La. 1925) ("He is no good as a teacher"); *Larive v. Willitt,* 315 P.2d 732 (Cal. Ct. App. 1957) (teacher was "intoxicated" in public). In addition, negative comments about a teacher in a phone conversation with a prospective employer that do not match the teacher's record or written evaluations could properly be found to have been made with reckless disregard for the truth and give rise to liability for defamation. *True v. Ladner,* 513 A.2d 257 (Me. 1986).

Cases such as *Ladner* caution school administration against making disparaging statements about school personnel that are not recorded in evaluations. So long as the negative statements are in keeping with a record of performance, however, school administrators are generally able to make truthful, critical comments about personnel as part of their employment responsibilities.

School board members often discuss difficult, and potentially defamatory, personnel or personnel-related matters both in executive session and publicly. Accordingly, statements made by board members in executive session are generally privileged from tort claims. *See, e.g., Brubaker v. Board of Education, School District 149,* 502 F.2d 973 (7th Cir. 1974). Board action taken in public resulting from closed-session conversations about negative qualities of a staff member are also privileged from defamation claims.

What if parents make defamatory comments about a teacher? Do the school district's officials have a responsibility to prevent such comments? Clearly parents have the ability to complain about a teacher's performance to the school board in letters or in public comments, so long as their complaints are not maliciously untruthful. In *Desselle v. Guillory,* 407 So. 2d 79 (La. Ct. App. 1981), the Louisiana Court of Appeals confirmed that parents who convey potentially defamatory material to school officials about a teacher enjoy a qualified privilege in doing so. There, a parent complained to a school principal about allegations that certain teachers had molested female students. The court concluded that, even if the communications were false, the parent was protected from liability for the communications because they were made to school officials sharing an "interest or duty" in student protection and were made "without malice." If parents make public statements to school board members, those members and their administrators also are able to respond in good faith to any inquiry about a teacher's competence. *Williams v. School District of Springfield,* 447 S.W.2d 256 (Mo. 1969).

Suppose, however, that a group of parents signs up to speak at a school board meeting about the "incompetence" of a currently employed teacher. As part of the public comments section of the meeting, one of the parents begins to launch into a tirade about the teacher's lack of professional integrity and morality. The board members are aware of no evidence supporting the accusations. How should the board proceed? Should the board cut off the speaker, respond by rejecting the comments, state that the comments do not represent the district's views, ignore the comments, or adjourn the meeting to return to "executive session"?

2. Defamation of Students

The other situation in which claims for defamation may arise in the school setting involves an educational professional's communications about a student. Teachers may be sued for libelous statements made about a student which are published or placed in the student's "permanent record." *Dawkins v. Billingsley,* 172 P. 69 (Okla. 1918) (false claims about student's substance abuse placed in school records). Where teachers make nonmalicious comments about students in the student's records or send student recommendations that are truthful or reflect the teacher's professional judgment about the student, however, no liability for libel or slander will result. *See Walter v. Davidson,* 104 S.E.2d 113 (Ga. 1958). *See also Morrison v. Mobile County Board of Education,* 495 So. 2d 1086 (Ala. 1986) (school officials who referred to evidence of students' substance abuse not liable for slander); *Chapman v. Furlough,* 334 So. 2d 293 (Fla. Ct. App. 1976) (statements by teachers and principal regarding students' suspected drug use as part of investigation do not give rise to defamation claims).

In *Davidson,* the court specifically relied on the principle of *in loco parentis* to support its conclusion that educators, like parents, should have wide latitude in matters of evaluating and disciplining students: "Any legal restraint of either parent or faculty in the reasonable discharge of duty, not only would not be beneficial to the child or student, but might well be disastrous to them." 104 S.E.2d at 115.

Despite the reluctance by courts like *Davidson* to impose liability for defamation, the case law does provide insight into measures that should be taken by educational institutions and their personnel to avoid the risk of any such liability. Information about students should never be conveyed by a school district or its employees for any reason other than a legitimate, professional educational purpose. No information should be conveyed that has not been specifically requested by the educational institution as part of a records policy, by prospective employers or by the state or federal government. School district personnel should avoid gossip about students, or any other forms of unsolicited views about students. Finally, where information is conveyed pursuant to a legitimate professional obligation, that information should be accurate and truthful.

As discussed more fully in Chapter 12, these common law protections against defamatory student records have been supplemented by the federal Family Educational Rights and Privacy Act of 1974 (FERPA), 20 U.S.C. §1232(g). Under that Act, schools receiving federal funds must adhere to a pupil records policy that guarantees that formal education records (not a teacher's personal notes) of individual students containing "personally identifiable information" must be kept confidential, and generally may not be released absent the written consent of the students' guardian, or of the student upon reaching 18 years of age. The Act also guarantees that the student or guardian will be allowed to inspect any records about the student. The FERPA thus allows teachers to send student recommendation letters without showing the letters to the student, only if the student waives the access and consent rights otherwise afforded by the Act. Yet, although the FERPA creates a framework for the proper use of student records, it does not insulate school district personnel from the common law liability associated with defamatory statements in those records.

3. Defamation of Public Educational Figures

If the subject of a defamatory statement is a public figure, the communicator must have made the false statement with knowledge of its falsity or with reckless disregard for its truthfulness. In *New York Times v. Sullivan,* 376 U.S. 254 (1964), the Supreme Court held that the First Amendment's protection of freedom of speech requires that any claims for libel or slander brought by public officials cannot succeed without a showing that the defamatory statements were made with "actual malice." *See also Milkovich v. Lorain Journal Co.,* 497 U.S. 1 (1990).

School board members, superintendents and principals generally have been found to be "public figures." *See, e.g., Cabin v. Community Newspapers, Inc.,* 270 N.Y.S.2d 913 (N.Y. 1966) (elected official); *Johnson v. Robbinsdale*

Independent School District, 827 F. Supp. 1439 (D. Minn. 1993) (principal). On the other hand, teachers typically are not considered to be public figures. *See, e.g., Johnson v. Southwestern Newspapers Corp.,* 855 S.W.2d 182 (Tex. Ct. App. 1993); *Richmond Newspapers, Inc. v. Lipscomb,* 274 Va. 277, 362 S.E.2d 32 (Va. 1987).

F. TORTS IN THE EDUCATIONAL ENVIRONMENT PRACTICUM

Fifth-graders Bobbie and Dominic were always causing trouble in class and were constantly having to stay after school and write on the chalkboard, "I promise to behave in class and I am sorry Ms. Saddler for not listening." Their latest craze was to catch spiders and snakes during recess and hide them under their shirts when they walked into the classroom and then surprise the girls with them. The other classmates' screams were so loud and disruptive that the neighboring classes were interrupted as well. The principal and custodians always had to be called in to catch the little critters so classes could start up again. This new entertainment had been going on for a week and detentions and writing on the chalkboard did not seem to deter Bobbie and Dominic from misbehaving during recess. Ms. Saddler was beside herself and decided that Bobbie and Dominic would have to miss recess for the next month so she could actually get some teaching done during class. Bobbie and Dominic were devastated to miss recess with all their friends. Bobbie and Dominic became increasingly upset about not being able to go outside and play during recess. On one particular sunny afternoon, their tempers flared. When Ms. Saddler went in the hallway to escort the other classmates inside from recess, the boys' mischievous nature turned to frustration and they both picked up the glass jars from the back science table that contained the latest experiment and threw them against the chalkboard, glass shattering everywhere. Sadly, Debbie, a classmate just walking in from recess, suffered lacerations from the shattered glass on her face, neck and right arm. The school immediately rushed Debbie to the hospital to attend to her cuts.

A week later, Debbie's parents filed a number of tort claims against Ms. Saddler and the school district. Consider the merits of every conceivable tort claim that Debbie's parents could pursue in this matter.

Consider again the tort of educational malpractice in the context of bullying. Assume that Bobbie and Dominic frequently enjoyed bullying other students in the class, particularly Debbie. When Ms. Saddler left the classroom, the boys often taunted Debbie about her physical appearance, her academic abilities and her family situation. Debbie became physically ill as a result of the boys' conduct. Does any civil liability result?

Finally, suppose Ms. Saddler, in an effort to protect Debbie from being picked on by the boys in the class, tells Debbie in front of several of her friends: "Debbie, I realize that you are only in fifth grade, but you should watch how you act. If you act and dress like a prostitute, you will be treated like one." Discuss all of the liability issues associated with Ms. Saddler's comments.

SECTION VI

THE RIGHTS AND RESPONSIBILITIES OF TEACHERS

In many areas of education law, courts and legislatures have recognized that a school is a unique legal environment. We have already seen how the custodial responsibility school districts and professional educators have over students has led judges and policy-makers to defer to their professional judgments. At the same time, we have observed that students retain many of the constitutional rights afforded adults, and that the law generally recognizes the value of student expression and autonomy in achieving the fundamental goals of education. Is the uniqueness of the educational environment also evidenced in the judicial and legislative treatment of the rights and responsibilities of teachers?

In this section, teachers are recognized as both employees and as communicators of ideas. As employees, teachers have constitutionally protected interests in continued employment and in maintaining their reputations. They also are protected from employment discrimination by state and federal statutes. Teachers generally have the right to form unions and to bargain collectively over the terms and conditions of their employment.

Yet, as custodians of the community's children, teachers also are subjected to intense public scrutiny. They must satisfy state-imposed education, certification and tenure requirements. Moreover, their position as role models for impressionable students has led some courts and legislatures to impose exceptional limitations on their expression and even lifestyle. As you analyze the materials in this section, consider whether the law should treat teachers differently from other employees and other purveyors of ideas.

CHAPTER 17

THE CONSTITUTIONAL AND STATUTORY RIGHTS OF TEACHERS

A. THE CONSTITUTIONAL DUE PROCESS RIGHTS OF TEACHERS

The terms and conditions of a teacher's employment are heavily regulated by state law. The legislatures in every state have defined the process by which a teacher is hired, evaluated, retained, tenured and even dismissed. In some situations, teachers may acquire a "property" interest in their continued employment as soon as they are hired. Teachers also acquire a "liberty" interest in retaining their good name and reputation in order to have the opportunity to attain future employment. These property and liberty interests are created by state law.

Once these property or liberty interests are created, however, the Fourteenth Amendment to the United States Constitution prohibits a state through its public school districts from taking these interests away without "due process of law." In this context, the "due process" clause requires school districts to afford teachers procedural protections, such as an impartial hearing prior to any deprivation of the teacher's liberty or property. As the *Roth* and *Perry* cases indicate, there are situations in which the "due process" clause requires school districts to provide such process protections even for probationary teachers.

BOARD OF REGENTS OF STATE COLLEGES v. ROTH

408 U.S. 564 (1972)

Mr. Justice STEWART delivered the opinion of the Court.

In 1968 the respondent, David Roth, was hired for his first teaching job as assistant professor of political science at Wisconsin State University-Oshkosh. He was hired for a fixed term of one academic year. The notice of his faculty appointment specified that his employment would begin on September 1,

1968, and would end on June 30, 1969.[1] The respondent completed that term. But he was informed that he would not be rehired for the next academic year.

The respondent had no tenure rights to continued employment. Under Wisconsin statutory law a state university teacher can acquire tenure as a "permanent" employee only after four years of year-to-year employment. Having acquired tenure, a teacher is entitled to continued employment "during efficiency and good behavior." A relatively new teacher without tenure, however, is under Wisconsin law entitled to nothing beyond his one-year appointment. There are no statutory or administrative standards defining eligibility for re-employment. State law thus clearly leaves the decision whether to rehire a nontenured teacher for another year to the unfettered discretion of university officials.

The procedural protection afforded a Wisconsin State University teacher before he is separated from the University corresponds to his job security. As a matter of statutory law, a tenured teacher cannot be "discharged except for cause upon written charges" and pursuant to certain procedures. A nontenured teacher, similarly, is protected to some extent *during* his one-year term. Rules promulgated by the Board of Regents provide that a nontenured teacher "dismissed" before the end of the year may have some opportunity for review of the "dismissal." But the Rules provide no real protection for a nontenured teacher who simply is not re-employed for the next year. He must be informed by February 1 "concerning retention or non-retention for the ensuing year." But "no reason for non-retention need be given. No review or appeal is provided in such case."

In conformance with these Rules, the President of Wisconsin State University-Oshkosh informed the respondent before February 1, 1969, that he would not be rehired for the 1969-1970 academic year. He gave the respondent no reason for the decision and no opportunity to challenge it at any sort of hearing.

The respondent then brought this action in Federal District Court alleging that the decision not to rehire him for the next year infringed his Fourteenth Amendment rights. . . . The only question presented to us at this stage in the case is whether the respondent had a constitutional right to a statement of reasons and a hearing on the University's decision not to rehire him for another year. We hold that he did not.

I

The requirements of procedural due process apply only to the deprivation of interests encompassed by the Fourteenth Amendment's protection of liberty and property. When protected interests are implicated, the right to some kind of prior hearing is paramount. But the range of interests protected by procedural due process is not infinite.

. . . We must look to see if the interest is within the Fourteenth Amendment's protection of liberty and property.

---

[1] The respondent had no contract of employment. Rather, his formal notice of appointment was the equivalent of an employment contract.

"Liberty" and "property" are broad and majestic terms. They are among the "great [constitutional] concepts . . . purposely left to gather meaning from experience. . . . They relate to the whole domain of social and economic fact, and the statesmen who founded this Nation knew too well that only a stagnant society remains unchanged." *National Ins. Co. v. Tidewater Co.,* 337 U.S. 582, 646 (Frankfurter, J., dissenting). For that reason, the Court has fully and finally rejected the wooden distinction between "rights" and "privileges" that once seemed to govern the applicability of procedural due process rights. The Court has also made clear that the property interests protected by procedural due process extend well beyond actual ownership of real estate, chattels, or money. By the same token, the Court has required due process protection for deprivations of liberty beyond the sort of formal constraints imposed by the criminal process.

Yet, while the Court has eschewed rigid or formalistic limitations on the protection of procedural due process, it has at the same time observed certain boundaries. For the words "liberty" and "property" in the Due Process Clause of the Fourteenth Amendment must be given some meaning.

II

"While this Court has not attempted to define with exactness the liberty . . . guaranteed [by the Fourteenth Amendment], the term has received much consideration and some of the included things have been definitely stated. Without doubt, it denotes not merely freedom from bodily restraint but also the right of the individual to contract, to engage in any of the common occupations of life, to acquire useful knowledge, to marry, establish a home and bring up children, to worship God according to the dictates of his own conscience, and generally to enjoy those privileges long recognized . . . as essential to the orderly pursuit of happiness by free men." *Meyer v. Nebraska,* 262 U.S. 390, 399. In a Constitution for a free people, there can be no doubt that the meaning of "liberty" must be broad indeed.

There might be cases in which a State refused to reemploy a person under such circumstances that interests in liberty would be implicated. But this is not such a case.

The State, in declining to rehire the respondent, did not make any charge against him that might seriously damage his standing and associations in his community. It did not base the nonrenewal of his contract on a charge, for example, that he had been guilty of dishonesty, or immorality. Had it done so, this would be a different case. For "where a person's good name, reputation, honor, or integrity is at stake because of what the government is doing to him, notice and an opportunity to be heard are essential. . . ." In such a case, due process would accord an opportunity to refute the charge before University officials. In the present case, however, there is no suggestion whatever that the respondent's "good name, reputation, honor, or integrity is at stake."

Similarly, there is no suggestion that the State, in declining to re-employ the respondent, imposed on him a stigma or other disability that foreclosed his freedom to take advantage of other employment opportunities. The State, for example, did not invoke any regulations to bar the respondent from all other public employment in state universities. Had it done so, this, again, would be a different case. For "to be deprived not only of present government employment but of future opportunity for it certainly is no small injury. . . ." . . . The Court has held, for example, that a State, in regulating eligibility for a type of professional employment, cannot foreclose a range of opportunities "in a manner . . . that contravene[s] . . . Due Process," and, specifically, in a manner that denies the right to a full prior hearing. . . . In the present case, however, this principle does not come into play.

To be sure, the respondent has alleged that the nonrenewal of his contract was based on his exercise of his right to freedom of speech. But this allegation is not now before us. The District Court stayed proceedings on this issue, and the respondent has yet to prove that the decision not to rehire him was, in fact, based on his free speech activities.[14]

Hence, on the record before us, all that clearly appears is that the respondent was not rehired for one year at one university. It stretches the concept too far to suggest that a person is deprived of "liberty" when he simply is not rehired in one job but remains as free as before to seek another.

III

The Fourteenth Amendment's procedural protection of property is a safeguard of the security of interests that a person has already acquired in specific benefits. These interests — property interests — may take many forms.

Thus, the Court has held that a person receiving welfare benefits under statutory and administrative standards defining eligibility for them has an interest in continued receipt of those benefits that is safeguarded by procedural due process. . . . Similarly, in the area of public employment, the Court has held that a public college professor dismissed from an office held under tenure provisions, *Slochower v. Board of Education,* 350 U.S. 551, and college professors and staff members dismissed during the terms of their contracts, *Wieman v. Updegraff,* 344 U.S. 183, have interests in continued employment that are safeguarded by due process. Only last year, the Court held that this principle "proscribing summary dismissal from public employment without hearing or inquiry required by due process" also applied to a teacher recently hired without tenure or a formal contract, but nonetheless with a clearly implied promise of continued employment. *Connell v. Higginbotham,* 403 U.S. 207, 208.

Certain attributes of "property" interests protected by procedural due process emerge from these decisions. To have a property interest in a benefit, a person clearly must have more than an abstract need or desire for it. He must have more than a unilateral expectation of it. He must, instead, have a legitimate claim of entitlement to it. It is a purpose of the ancient institution of property to protect those claims upon which people rely in their daily lives, reliance that must not be arbitrarily undermined. It is a purpose of the constitutional right to a hearing to provide an opportunity for a person to vindicate those claims.

---

[14] . . . Whatever may be a teacher's rights of free speech, the interest in holding a teaching job at a state university, *simpliciter,* is not itself a free speech interest.

Property interests, of course, are not created by the Constitution. Rather, they are created and their dimensions are defined by existing rules or understandings that stem from an independent source such as state law—rules or understandings that secure certain benefits and that support claims of entitlement to those benefits. . . .

Just as the welfare recipients' "property" interest in welfare payments was created and defined by statutory terms, so the respondent's "property" interest in employment at Wisconsin State University-Oshkosh was created and defined by the terms of his appointment. Those terms secured his interest in employment up to June 30, 1969. But the important fact in this case is that they specifically provided that the respondent's employment was to terminate on June 30. They did not provide for contract renewal absent "sufficient cause." Indeed, they made no provision for renewal whatsoever.

Thus, the terms of the respondent's appointment secured absolutely no interest in re-employment for the next year. They supported absolutely no possible claim of entitlement to re-employment. Nor, significantly, was there any state statute or University rule or policy that secured his interest in re-employment or that created any legitimate claim to it. In these circumstances, the respondent surely had an abstract concern in being rehired, but he did not have a *property* interest sufficient to require the University authorities to give him a hearing when they declined to renew his contract of employment.

IV

Our analysis of the respondent's constitutional rights in this case in no way indicates a view that an opportunity for a hearing or a statement of reasons for nonretention would, or would not, be appropriate or wise in public colleges and universities. For it is a written Constitution that we apply. Our role is confined to interpretation of that Constitution.

We must conclude that the summary judgment for the respondent should not have been granted, since the respondent has not shown that he was deprived of liberty or property protected by the Fourteenth Amendment. The judgment of the Court of Appeals, accordingly, is reversed and the case is remanded for further proceedings consistent with this opinion.

NOTES AND QUESTIONS

1. Although the *Roth* Court makes clear that the Fourteenth Amendment's due process clause generally does not require a hearing before the nonrenewal of a nontenured teacher's contract with a state educational institution, the Court also clearly indicates that an interest in continued employment could become a "property" right protected by the due process clause, and the opportunity to pursue future employment could become a "liberty" interest protected by that clause. Certainly a tenured teacher and a teacher under a contract has a protected interest. Under what circumstances would a nontenured teacher acquire a property or a liberty interest in retention protected by the Fourteenth Amendment?

2. If the nontenured teacher has acquired a protectable property or liberty interest in the context of a nonretention decision, what procedural protections must be afforded? The Court states that due process would require that the teacher have "an opportunity to refute" any charge that would affect the teacher's reputation. What form would that opportunity take?
3. Roth argued that the decision not retain him was motivated by the college's dislike for his expressed political ideas, in violation of his First Amendment rights. That issue did not reach the Supreme Court because the district court stayed litigation on that question. Nonetheless, the Court declared: "Whatever may be a teacher's rights of free speech, the interest in holding a teaching job at a state university, *simpliciter,* is not itself a free speech interest." 408 U.S. at 575, n.14. If, however, the university were to "directly" impinge upon a teacher's interest in free speech or free press in a way comparable to the seizure of books or the preclusion of rallies or public meetings, then a First Amendment interest might be implicated. If such an interest were implicated, notice and the opportunity for a "fair adversary hearing" must precede any adverse action taken. *Id.* In *Valter v. Orchard Farm School,* 541 S.W.2d 550 (Mo. 1976), the Missouri Supreme Court declared that the minimal due process hearing protections include the opportunity to be heard, to present evidence, to present witnesses, to cross-examine witnesses and to be represented by counsel. Notice of the hearing in advance presumes as well that the teacher be afforded access to evidence against him or her sufficiently in advance of the hearing to be able to meet any charges on the merits.
4. Does due process preclude a school board, school board member or school board designee from being a hearing examiner in a teacher's hearing? Recall that in *Hortonville Joint School District No. 1 v. Hortonville Education Ass'n,* 426 U.S. 482 (1976), the Supreme Court held that as public servants, the members of a board of education who do not have any personal or financial interest in the issues being heard are qualified to be neutral examiners in an impartial hearing.
5. In *Perry v. Sindermann,* 408 U.S. 593 (1972), which was decided together with *Roth,* the Supreme Court found a property interest in an untenured junior college teacher's expectation of continued employment based on the following language in the college's faculty handbook: the college "wishes" that a nontenured teacher who performs satisfactorily will "feel that he has permanent tenure." That language created an objective, legitimate expectation in retention that subjected any contrary decision to due process requirements.
6. In *Bishop v. Wood,* 426 U.S. 341 (1976), the Supreme Court refused to find a liberty interest in otherwise stigmatizing negative comments made about a probationary policeman because those comments and the reasons for the officer's nonrenewal were not publicly communicated. The public comments about a teacher's racial prejudices, stability and competence have all been found to be sufficiently stigmatizing to implicate a "liberty" interest in opportunities for future employment. *See, e.g., Wellner v. Minnesota,* 487 F.2d 153 (8th Cir. 1973); *Stewart v. Pearce,* 484 F.2d 1031 (9th Cir. 1973).

B. THE RIGHTS OF TEACHERS TO FREEDOM OF EXPRESSION AND ACADEMIC FREEDOM

Teachers are unique in the eyes of the law. They are entrusted by parents and by the government with the care and tutelage of children. As such, teachers historically have been limited in their ability to express their personal viewpoints in the educational setting. *See Wieman v. Updegraff,* 344 U.S. 183 (1952) (Frankfurter, J., concurring) (teachers are "priests of our democracy"). Yet, as "priests" of a uniquely democratic education, teachers also are expected to participate in a free and robust exchange of ideas in the classroom.

Are teachers private citizens or public trustees? Perhaps their constitutional rights to freedom of expression should be protected to a greater degree than those of non-teachers because of their role as educators—as interlocutors in the marketplace of ideas. These constitutional rights in fact may afford teachers the "academic freedom" to experiment with novel points of view and instructional materials. On the other hand, perhaps a teacher's right to freedom of expression and academic freedom should be carefully circumscribed because of the arguably compelling interests that the state has in controlling the education of its youth.

1. Freedom of Expression

In *Pickering v. Board of Education,* 391 U.S. 563 (1968), the Court, for the first time, fully recognized a teacher's First Amendment right to freedom of expression, and held that "a teacher's exercise of his right to speak on issues of public importance may not furnish the basis for his dismissal from public employment." Pickering was dismissed after sending a letter to the local newspaper extremely critical of the board of education's proposal to increase taxes through a referendum-supported bond issuance. The teacher's letter argued that the board would "stop at nothing" to "push tax-supported athletics down our throats."

In rejecting the district's dismissal of the teacher, the Supreme Court acknowledges that a school district has an interest in regulating a teacher's speech that is different from the state's interest in regulating the speech of other citizens, but concluded that the interest must be balanced against the "interests of the teacher, as a citizen, in commenting upon matters of public concern. . . ."

Pickering v. Board of Education of Township High School District 205, Will County

391 U.S. 563 (1968)

Mr. Justice Marshall delivered the opinion of the Court.

Appellant Marvin L. Pickering, a teacher in Township High School District 205, Will County, Illinois, was dismissed from his position by the appellee Board of Education for sending a letter to a local newspaper in connection with a recently proposed tax increase that was critical of the way in which the Board and the district superintendent of schools had handled past proposals to raise new revenue for the schools. Appellant's dismissal resulted from a determination by the Board, after a full hearing, that the publication of the letter was "detrimental to the efficient operation and administration of the schools of the district" and hence, under the relevant Illinois statute, Ill. Rev. Stat., c. 122, §10-22.4 (1963), that "interests of the school require[d] [his dismissal]."

Appellant's claim that his writing of the letter was protected by the First and Fourteenth Amendments was rejected. Appellant then sought review of the Board's action in the Circuit Court of Will County, which affirmed his dismissal on the ground that the determination that appellant's letter was detrimental to the interests of the school system was supported by substantial evidence and that the interests of the schools overrode appellant's First Amendment rights. On appeal, the Supreme Court of Illinois, two Justices dissenting, affirmed the judgment of the Circuit Court. We noted probable jurisdiction of appellant's claim that the Illinois statute permitting his dismissal on the facts of this case was unconstitutional as applied under the First and Fourteenth Amendments. For the reasons detailed below we agree that appellant's rights to freedom of speech were violated and we reverse.

I

In February of 1961 the appellee Board of Education asked the voters of the school district to approve a bond issue to raise $4,875,000 to erect two new schools. The proposal was defeated. Then, in December of 1961, the Board submitted another bond proposal to the voters which called for the raising of $5,500,000 to build two new schools. This second proposal passed and the schools were built with the money raised by the bond sales. In May of 1964 a proposed increase in the tax rate to be used for educational purposes was submitted to the voters by the Board and was defeated. Finally, on September 19, 1964, a second proposal to increase the tax rate was submitted by the Board and was likewise defeated. It was in connection with this last proposal of the School Board that appellant wrote the letter to the editor (which we reproduce in an Appendix to this opinion) that resulted in his dismissal.

Prior to the vote on the second tax increase proposal a variety of articles attributed to the District 205 Teachers' Organization appeared in the local paper. These articles urged passage of the tax increase and stated that failure to pass the increase would result in a decline in the quality of education afforded children in the district's schools. A letter from the superintendent of schools making the same point was published in the paper two days before the election and submitted to the voters in mimeographed form the following day. It was in response to the foregoing material, together with the failure of the tax increase to pass, that appellant submitted the letter in question to the editor of the local paper.

The letter constituted, basically, an attack on the School Board's handling of the 1961 bond issue proposals and its subsequent allocation of financial resources between the schools' educational and athletic programs. It also charged the superintendent of schools with attempting to prevent teachers in the district from opposing or criticizing the proposed bond issue.

The Board dismissed Pickering for writing and publishing the letter. Pursuant to Illinois law, the Board was then required to hold a hearing on the dismissal. At the hearing the Board charged that numerous statements in the letter were false and that the publication of the statements unjustifiably impugned the "motives, honesty, integrity, truthfulness, responsibility and competence" of both the Board and the school administration. The Board also charged that the false statements damaged the professional reputations of its members and of the school administrators, would be disruptive of faculty discipline, and would tend to foment "controversy, conflict and dissension" among teachers, administrators, the Board of Education, and the residents of the district. Testimony was introduced from a variety of witnesses on the truth or falsity of the particular statements in the letter with which the Board took issue. The Board found the statements to be false as charged. No evidence was introduced at any point in the proceedings as to the effect of the publication of the letter on the community as a whole or on the administration of the school system in particular, and no specific findings along these lines were made.

The Illinois courts reviewed the proceedings solely to determine whether the Board's findings were supported by substantial evidence and whether, on the facts as found, the Board could reasonably conclude that appellant's publication of the letter was "detrimental to the best interests of the schools." Pickering's claim that his letter was protected by the First Amendment was rejected on the ground that his acceptance of a teaching position in the public schools obliged him to refrain from making statements about the operation of the schools "which in the absence of such position he would have an undoubted right to engage in." . . .

II

To the extent that the Illinois Supreme Court's opinion may be read to suggest that teachers may constitutionally be compelled to relinquish the First Amendment rights they would otherwise enjoy as citizens to comment on matters of public interest in connection with the operation of the public schools in which they work, it proceeds on a premise that has been unequivocally rejected in numerous prior decisions of this Court. *E.g., Wieman v. Updegraff,* 344 U.S. 183 (1952); *Shelton v. Tucker,* 364 U.S. 479 (1960); *Keyishian v. Board of Regents,* 385 U.S. 589 (1967). "The theory that public employment which may be denied altogether may be subjected to any conditions, regardless of how unreasonable, has been uniformly rejected." *Keyishian v. Board of Regents.* At the same time it cannot be gainsaid that the State has interests as an employer in regulating the speech of its employees that differ significantly from those it possesses in connection with regulation of the speech of the citizenry in general. The problem in any case is to arrive at a balance between the interests of the teacher, as a citizen, in commenting upon matters of public concern and the interest of the State, as an employer, in promoting the efficiency of the public services it performs through its employees.

III

The Board contends that "the teacher by virtue of his public employment has a duty of loyalty to support his superiors in attaining the generally accepted goals of education and that, if he must speak out publicly, he should do so factually and accurately, commensurate with his education and experience." Appellant, on the other hand, argues that the test applicable to defamatory statements directed against public officials by persons having no occupational relationship with them, namely, that statements to be legally actionable must be made "with knowledge that [they were] . . . false or with reckless disregard of whether [they were] . . . false or not," *New York Times Co. v. Sullivan,* 376 U.S. 254, 280 (1964), should also be applied to public statements made by teachers. Because of the enormous variety of fact situations in which critical statements by teachers and other public employees may be thought by their superiors, against whom the statements are directed, to furnish grounds for dismissal, we do not deem it either appropriate or feasible to attempt to lay down a general standard against which all such statements may be judged. However, in the course of evaluating the conflicting claims of First Amendment protection and the need for orderly school administration in the context of this case, we shall indicate some of the general lines along which an analysis of the controlling interests should run.

An examination of the statements in appellant's letter objected to by the Board reveals that they, like the letter as a whole, consist essentially of criticism of the Board's allocation of school funds between educational and athletic programs, and of both the Board's and the superintendent's methods of informing, or preventing the informing of, the district's taxpayers of the real reasons why additional tax revenues were being sought for the schools. The statements are in no way directed towards any person with whom appellant would normally be in contact in the course of his daily work as a teacher. Thus no question of maintaining either discipline by immediate superiors or harmony among coworkers is presented here. Appellant's employment relationships with the Board and, to a somewhat lesser extent, with the superintendent are not the kind of close working relationships for which it can persuasively be claimed that personal loyalty and confidence are necessary to their proper functioning. Accordingly, to the extent that the Board's position here can be taken to suggest that even comments on matters of public concern that are substantially correct, may furnish grounds for dismissal if they are sufficiently critical in tone, we unequivocally reject it.

We next consider the statements in appellant's letter which we agree to be false. The Board's original charges included allegations that the publication of the letter damaged the professional reputations of the Board and the superintendent and would foment controversy and conflict among the Board, teachers, administrators, and the residents of the district. However, no evidence to support these allegations was introduced at the hearing. So far as the record reveals, Pickering's letter was greeted by everyone but its main target, the Board, with massive apathy and total disbelief. The Board must, therefore, have decided, perhaps by analogy with the law of libel, that the statements *were per se* harmful to the operation of the schools.

However, the only way in which the Board could conclude, absent any evidence of the actual effect of the letter, that the statements contained therein were *per se* detrimental to the interest of the schools was to equate the Board members' own interests with that of the schools. Certainly an accusation that too much money is being spent on athletics by the administrators of the school system (which is precisely the import of that portion of appellant's letter containing the statements that we have found to be false) cannot reasonably be regarded as *per se* detrimental to the district's schools. Such an accusation reflects rather a difference of opinion between Pickering and the Board as to the preferable manner of operating the school system, a difference of opinion that clearly concerns an issue of general public interest.

In addition, the fact that particular illustrations of the Board's claimed undesirable emphasis on athletic programs are false would not normally have any necessary impact on the actual operation of the schools, beyond its tendency to anger the Board. For example, Pickering's letter was written after the defeat at the polls of the second proposed tax increase. It could, therefore, have had no effect on the ability of the school district to raise necessary revenue, since there was no showing that there was any proposal to increase taxes pending when the letter was written.

More importantly, the question whether a school system requires additional funds is a matter of legitimate public concern on which the judgment of the school administration, including the School Board, cannot, in a society that leaves such questions to popular vote, be taken as conclusive. On such a question free and open debate is vital to informed decision-making by the electorate. Teachers are, as a class, the members of a community most likely to have informed and definite opinions as to how funds allotted to the operation of the schools should be spent. Accordingly, it is essential that they be able to speak out freely on such questions without fear of retaliatory dismissal.

In addition, the amounts expended on athletics which Pickering reported erroneously were matters of public record on which his position as a teacher in the district did not qualify him to speak with any greater authority than any other taxpayer. The Board could easily have rebutted appellant's errors by publishing the accurate figures itself, either via a letter to the same newspaper or otherwise. We are thus not presented with a situation in which a teacher has carelessly made false statements about matters so closely related to the day-to-day operations of the schools that any harmful impact on the public would be difficult to counter because of the teacher's presumed greater access to the real facts. Accordingly, we have no occasion to consider at this time whether under such circumstances a school board could reasonably require that a teacher make substantial efforts to verify the accuracy of his charges before publishing them.

What we do have before us is a case in which a teacher has made erroneous public statements upon issues then currently the subject of public attention, which are critical of his ultimate employer but which are neither shown nor can be presumed to have in any way either impeded the teacher's proper performance of his daily duties in the classroom or to have interfered with the regular operation of the schools generally. In these circumstances we conclude that the interest of the school administration in limiting teachers' opportunities to contribute to public debate is not significantly greater than its interest in limiting a similar contribution by any member of the general public.

IV

The public interest in having free and unhindered debate on matters of public importance—the core value of the Free Speech Clause of the First Amendment—is so great that it has been held that a State cannot authorize the recovery of damages by a public official for defamatory statements directed at him except when such statements are shown to have been made either with knowledge of their falsity or with reckless disregard for their truth or falsity. . . . The same test has been applied to suits for invasion of privacy based on false statements where a "matter of public interest" is involved. *Time, Inc. v. Hill,* 385 U.S. 374 (1967). It is therefore perfectly clear that, were appellant a member of the general public, the State's power to afford the appellee Board of Education or its members any legal right to sue him for writing the letter at issue here would be limited by the requirement that the letter be judged by the standard laid down in *New York Times.*

This Court has also indicated, in more general terms, that statements by public officials on matters of public concern must be accorded First Amendment protection despite the fact that the statements are directed at their nominal superiors. . . .

While criminal sanctions and damage awards have a somewhat different impact on the exercise of the right to freedom of speech from dismissal from employment, it is apparent that the threat of dismissal from public employment is nonetheless a potent means of inhibiting speech. We have already noted our disinclination to make an across-the-board equation of dismissal from public employment for remarks critical of superiors with awarding damages in a libel suit by a public official for similar criticism. However, in a case such as the present one, in which the fact of employment is only tangentially and insubstantially involved in the subject matter of the public communication made by a teacher, we conclude that it is necessary to regard the teacher as the member of the general public he seeks to be.

In sum, we hold that, in a case such as this, absent proof of false statements knowingly or recklessly made by him, a teacher's exercise of his right to speak on issues of public importance may not furnish the basis for his dismissal from public employment. Since no such showing has been made in this case regarding appellant's letter . . . his dismissal for writing it cannot be upheld and the judgment of the Illinois Supreme Court must, accordingly, be reversed and the case remanded for further proceedings not inconsistent with this opinion.

NOTES AND QUESTIONS

1. In its Appendix, the majority in *Pickering* sets forth the entire contents of Pickering's letter, and determines, after a line-by-line analysis, that it was not knowingly or recklessly false. Accordingly, the teacher's expression was protected by the First Amendment. If the Court had determined that Pickering's letter was not protected by the First Amendment, would the school district's termination have been legitimate?
2. The *Pickering* Court distinguishes the teacher's expression in the case from statements that are "directed towards any person with whom [the teacher]

would normally be in contact with as part of daily work as a teacher." The Court suggests that teachers generally do not have daily working relationships with school board members or superintendents. Suppose Pickering's letter had been critical of the school's principal or a group of co-teachers supportive of the referendum. Would the outcome of the case have been different? *See, e.g., Kinsey v. Salado Independent School District,* 950 F.2d 988 (5th Cir. 1992) (school board's termination of superintendent who was critical of board members did not violate superintendent's First Amendment rights).

3. The *Pickering* Court also had "no occasion" to reach the question of whether a school district may require a teacher to "verify the accuracy" of charges which would adversely affect the daily operation of a school before publishing them. Does the Court's reasoning allow a school district to do so? What policy language could be drafted to insure that the school district properly requires its educators to verify the accuracy of public statements regarding school operations before publishing them?

In *Mt. Healthy City Board of Education v. Doyle,* 429 U.S. 274 (1977), the Supreme Court imposed additional First Amendment limitations upon the discretion of a school district in deciding whether to rehire a nontenured teacher. The Supreme Court concluded that public employees establish a prime facie case of a constitutional violation by showing that they were engaged in an activity protected by the First Amendment and that such an activity was a substantial or motivating factor in the decision to alter their employment status. The state may then defend its action by showing by a preponderance of the evidence that its action would have been taken even in the absence of the exercise of the constitutionally protected right.

Mt. Healthy City Board of Education v. Doyle

429 U.S. 274 (1977)

Mr. Justice Rehnquist delivered the opinion of the Court.

Respondent Doyle sued petitioner Mt. Healthy Board of Education in the United States District Court for the Southern District of Ohio. Doyle claimed that the Board's refusal to renew his contract in 1971 violated his rights under the First and Fourteenth Amendments to the United States Constitution. After a bench trial the District Court held that Doyle was entitled to reinstatement with backpay. The Court of Appeals for the Sixth Circuit affirmed the judgment, and we granted the Board's petition for certiorari, to consider an admixture of jurisdictional and constitutional claims. . . .

I

Having concluded that respondent's complaint sufficiently pleaded jurisdiction under 28 U.S.C. §1331, that the Board has failed to preserve the issue whether that complaint stated a claim upon which relief could be granted against the Board, and that the Board is not immune from suit under the Eleventh Amendment, we now proceed to consider the merits of respondent's claim under the First and Fourteenth Amendments.

Doyle was first employed by the Board in 1966. He worked under one-year contracts for the first three years, and under a two-year contract from 1969 to 1971. In 1969 he was elected president of the Teachers' Association, in which position he worked to expand the subjects of direct negotiation between the Association and the Board of Education. During Doyle's one-year term as president of the Association, and during the succeeding year when he served on its executive committee, there was apparently some tension in relations between the Board and the Association.

Beginning early in 1970, Doyle was involved in several incidents not directly connected with his role in the Teachers' Association. In one instance, he engaged in an argument with another teacher which culminated in the other teacher's slapping him. Doyle subsequently refused to accept an apology and insisted upon some punishment for the other teacher. His persistence in the matter resulted in the suspension of both teachers for one day, which was followed by a walkout by a number of other teachers, which in turn resulted in the lifting of the suspensions.

On other occasions, Doyle got into an argument with employees of the school cafeteria over the amount of spaghetti which had been served him; referred to students, in connection with a disciplinary complaint, as "sons of bitches"; and made an obscene gesture to two girls in connection with their failure to obey commands made in his capacity as cafeteria supervisor. Chronologically the last in the series of incidents which respondent was involved in during his employment by the Board was a telephone call by him to a local radio station. It was the Board's consideration of this incident which the court below found to be a violation of the First and Fourteenth Amendments.

In February 1971, the principal circulated to various teachers a memorandum relating to teacher dress and appearance, which was apparently prompted by the view of some in the administration that there was a relationship between teacher appearance and public support for bond issues. Doyle's response to the receipt of the memorandum—on a subject which he apparently understood was to be settled by joint teacher-administration action—was to convey the substance of the memorandum to a disc jockey at WSAI, a Cincinnati radio station, who promptly announced the adoption of the dress code as a news item. Doyle subsequently apologized to the principal, conceding that he should have made some prior communication of his criticism to the school administration.

Approximately one month later the superintendent made his customary annual recommendations to the Board as to the rehiring of nontenured teachers. He recommended that Doyle not be rehired. The same recommendation was made with respect to nine other teachers in the district, and in all instances, including Doyle's, the recommendation was adopted by the Board. Shortly after being notified of this decision, respondent requested a statement of reasons for the Board's actions. He received a statement citing "a notable lack of tact in handling professional matters which leaves much doubt as to your sincerity in establishing good school relationships." That general statement was followed by references to the radio station incident and to the obscene-gesture incident.

The District Court found that all of these incidents had in fact occurred. It concluded that respondent Doyle's telephone call to the radio station was "clearly protected by the First Amendment," and that because it had played a "substantial part" in the decision of the Board not to renew Doyle's employment, he was entitled to reinstatement with backpay. The District Court did not expressly state what test it was applying in determining that the incident in question involved conduct protected by the First Amendment, but simply held that the communication to the radio station was such conduct. The Court of Appeals affirmed in a brief *per curiam* opinion.

Doyle's claims under the First and Fourteenth Amendments are not defeated by the fact that he did not have tenure. Even though he could have been discharged for no reason whatever, and had no constitutional right to a hearing prior to the decision not to rehire him, *Board of Regents v. Roth,* 408 U.S. 564 (1972), he may nonetheless establish a claim to reinstatement if the decision not to rehire him was made by reason of his exercise of constitutionally protected First Amendment freedoms. *Perry v. Sindermann,* 408 U.S. 593 (1972).

That question of whether speech of a government employee is constitutionally protected expression necessarily entails striking "a balance between the interests of the teacher, as a citizen, in commenting upon matters of public concern and the interest of the State, as an employer, in promoting the efficiency of the public services it performs through its employees." *Pickering v. Board of Education,* 391 U.S. 563, 568 (1968). There is no suggestion by the Board that Doyle violated any established policy, or that its reaction to his communication to the radio station was anything more than an ad hoc response to Doyle's action in making the memorandum public. We therefore accept the District Court's finding that the communication was protected by the First and Fourteenth Amendments. We are not, however, entirely in agreement with that court's manner of reasoning from this finding to the conclusion that Doyle is entitled to reinstatement with backpay. . . .

Since respondent Doyle had no tenure, and there was therefore not even a state-law requirement of "cause" or "reason" before a decision could be made not to renew his employment, . . . the board legally could have dismissed respondent had the radio station incident never come to its attention. . . . We are thus brought to the issue whether, even if [the district would have decided not to rehire Doyle had the constitutionally-protected incident never occurred], the fact that the protected conduct played a "substantial part" in the actual decision not to renew would necessarily amount to a constitutional violation justifying remedial action. We think that it would not.

A rule of causation which focuses solely on whether protected conduct played a part, "substantial" or otherwise, in a decision not to rehire, could place an employee in a better position as a result of the exercise of constitutionally protected conduct than he would have occupied had he done nothing. The difficulty with the rule enunciated by the District Court is that it would require reinstatement in cases where a dramatic and perhaps abrasive incident is inevitably on the minds of those responsible for the decision to rehire, and does indeed play a part in that decision—even if the same decision would have been reached had the incident not occurred.

The constitutional principle at stake is sufficiently vindicated if such an employee is placed in no worse a position than if he had not engaged in the conduct. A borderline or marginal candidate should not have the employment question resolved against him because of constitutionally protected conduct. But that same candidate ought not to be able, by engaging in such conduct, to prevent his employer from assessing his performance record and reaching a decision not to rehire on the basis of that record, simply because the protected conduct makes the employer more certain of the correctness of its decision.

This is especially true where, as the District Court observed was the case here, the current decision to rehire will accord "tenure." The long-term consequences of an award of tenure are of great moment both to the employee and to the employer. They are too significant for us to hold that the Board in this case would be precluded, because it considered constitutionally protected conduct in deciding not to rehire Doyle, from attempting to prove to a trier of fact that quite apart from such conduct Doyle's record was such that he would not have been rehired in any event.

In other areas of constitutional law, this Court has found it necessary to formulate a test of causation which distinguishes between a result caused by a constitutional violation and one not so caused. We think those are instructive in formulating the test to be applied here. . . .

Initially, in this case, the burden was properly placed upon respondent to show that his conduct was constitutionally protected, and that this conduct was a "substantial factor"—or, to put it in other words, that it was a "motivating factor" in the Board's decision not to rehire him. Respondent having carried that burden, however, the District Court should have gone on to determine whether the Board had shown by a preponderance of the evidence that it would have reached the same decision as to respondent's re-employment even in the absence of the protected conduct.

We cannot tell from the District Court opinion and conclusions, nor from the opinion of the Court of Appeals affirming the judgment of the District Court, what conclusion those courts would have reached had they applied this test. The judgment of the Court of Appeals is therefore vacated, and the case remanded for further proceedings consistent with this opinion.

So *ordered.*

NOTES AND QUESTIONS

1. The Supreme Court accepts the district court's finding that Doyle's communication to the radio station regarding the principal's memorandum instituting a "dress code" for teachers was a matter of public concern protected by the First Amendment. Do you agree? Was Doyle's speech about the issue of dress codes generally, or about his private employment relations?
2. The *Mt. Healthy* Court supports its rule of causation by arguing that it is "especially" appropriate where the school district's employment decision involves tenure because the "long-term consequences of an award of

tenure are of great moment both to the employee and to the employer." In other words, the district should not be forced to grant tenure to an otherwise unqualified teacher merely because the teacher engaged in protected speech. Should a school district be given *less* discretion in its decision to rehire an untenured teacher because of that teacher's protected speech than it has when deciding to grant tenure or retain a tenured teacher?

3. In *Connick v. Myers,* 461 U.S. 138 (1983), the Supreme Court made explicit *Pickering's* implicit distinction between speech regarding private matters and speech involving matters of public concern. The Court declared that if an employee's speech "cannot be fairly considered as relating to any matter of political, social, or other concern to the community," the state (and school district) must have "wide latitude" in making employment judgments without First Amendment impediments. If, however, the teacher's expression does involve a matter of public concern, any decision adversely affecting the teacher's employment must be justified by compelling, counterbalancing interests. In *Connick,* an attorney reacted to her transfer by distributing to her co-workers a questionnaire seeking input on issues of employee morale. The Court found the attorney's communications to be of personal concern such that the evidence of their disruptive impact on the daily operations of the office justified dismissal.
4. In *Givhan v. Western Line Consolidated School District,* 439 U.S. 410 (1979), the Supreme Court made clear that a teacher's private communications with the school principal regarding the teacher's belief that the school's employment policies are racially discriminatory constituted constitutionally protected speech on matters of public concern. *See also Piver v. Pender County Board of Education,* 835 F.2d 1076 (4th Cir. 1987) (private criticism of employer's discriminatory policies can be a matter of public concern); *Wren v. Spurlock,* 798 F.2d 1313 (10th Cir. 1986), *cert. denied.,* 479 U.S. 1085 (1987) (teacher's filing a formal grievance against school principal is a matter of public concern). *But see Ferrara v. Mills,* 781 F.2d 1508 (11th Cir. 1986) (commentary about high school registration procedures not public concern).
5. The Supreme Court's opinions in *Pickering, Mt. Healthy, Connick* and *Givhan* provide the foundation for any analysis of whether a school district's decision to discipline an educational professional violates that professional's First Amendment right to freedom of expression. In *Pickering,* the teacher's protected expression was about a matter of "public concern" rather than private employment relations. The teacher's letter did not criticize an immediate supervisor or co-worker; it did not have an adverse impact on the actual "day-to-day" operations of the district's schools, and it did not falsely criticize an employer in such a way as to interfere with the teacher's daily performance or the regular operation of the schools. In *Mt. Healthy,* the Court establishes a burden-shifting analysis for decisions by a school district that arguably implicate protected speech. The teacher has the initial burden of showing that his or her conduct was constitutionally protected and was a "substantial factor" in a school district's adverse employment decision. Once the teacher makes this initial showing, the

burden then shifts to the school district to prove by a preponderance of the evidence that it would have reached the same decision even in the absence of the teacher's protected activity. In *Connick,* the Court reaffirms the *Pickering* distinction between matters of public interest and private concern, while in *Givhan* the Court makes clear that even some private communications can constitute protected speech.

6. If asked by your client, the school board, to create a template for the legal analysis of its decisions implicating teacher speech, what would your template be? Is it possible to create from the seminal Supreme Court decisions a consistent template for the analysis of any school district decision that arguably implicates a teacher's protected speech? The lower federal courts have attempted to do so. In *Roberts v. Van Buren Public Schools,* 773 F.2d 949 (8th Cir. 1985), the Eighth Circuit created a three-step analysis: (1) the teacher must demonstrate that the conduct was constitutionally protected because it addresses a matter of public concern; (2) the teacher must show that the protected conduct was a substantial factor in the school district's adverse employment decision; and (3) the school district may prove by a preponderance of the evidence that its employment decision would have been the same absent the protected conduct. *See also Daniels v. Quinn,* 801 F.2d 687 (4th Cir. 1986). *Roberts* further suggested that *Pickering* and its progeny created a balancing test that requires a court to weigh the degree of public concern involved in the teacher's conduct against the degree of disruption to the everyday operations of the school and the classroom generated by that conduct. *See also Stronman v. Colleton County School District,* 981 F.2d 152 (4th Cir. 1992) (even if a teacher's personal grievance about pay touched on a matter of public concern, any protected interest is outweighed by the district's interest in teacher morale and adherence to policies). Do you agree that the Supreme Court's cases establish such a balancing test?
7. ***Educational Professionals and Protected Speech Practicum.*** Superintendent Anderson of School District 10 in North Dakota has operated successfully in the district for three years. She supports the current seven-member board of education and has enjoyed a productive working relationship with them. Accordingly, the superintendent decided to help campaign for the reelection of the four incumbent board members whose terms are expiring. (The remaining three board members' terms expire two years later, as the district has created staggered board terms.) Superintendent Anderson makes public speeches supporting the incumbent board members and writes letters to parents and teachers regarding their abilities. Nonetheless, none of the four incumbents is reelected. Immediately after the four newly elected board members assume their responsibilities, they decide that Superintendent Anderson should be removed. As is typical, Superintendent Anderson is an untenured administrator whose long-term contract allows the Board to terminate her for any "lawful cause." The Board ultimately votes 4-3 to terminate Anderson, and votes 4-3 to hire a new superintendent, with the four new board members providing the majority.

Superintendent Andersen now seeks legal advice. What are the merits of the various legal claims she might file in connection with her nonrenewal? What defenses might the board offer in response to any such claims? For one court's view, *see Kinsey v. Salado Independent School District,* 950 F.2d 988 (5th Cir. 1992).

2. Academic Freedom

The United States Supreme Court and the lower courts have defined "academic freedom" broadly as the right of an educational professional to deliver instruction to students without fear of unwarranted governmental control. *See, e.g., Keyishian v. Board of Regents,* 385 U.S. 589 (1967). As broadly defined, academic freedom has been supported by three different types of arguments.

First, as the Supreme Court has recognized, the courts are "particularly ill-equipped to evaluate" the judgments made by an "individual professor" regarding the delivery of instruction to students and the student evaluation process. *Board of Curators of the University of Missouri v. Horowitz,* 435 U.S. 78 (1978).

Second, academic freedom has been justified as an aspect of an individual teacher's liberty to express himself or herself in a public setting. *See, e.g., Keyishian,* 385 U.S. at 603. *See also Meyer v. Nebraska,* 262 U.S. 390 (1923) (a teacher's "right thus to teach" in accordance with professional judgment is a "liberty" interest protected by the Fourteenth Amendment from undue state interference).

Finally, the Supreme Court also has declared that academic freedom is vital to the American democratic regime and to the acquisition of knowledge. *See Meyer,* 262 U.S. at 399. In *Keyishian v. Board of Regents,* the Supreme Court reaffirmed that, "[o]ur nation is deeply committed to safeguarding academic freedom, which is of transcendent value to all of us and not merely to teachers concerned." 385 U.S. at 603. The Court found academic freedom to be a "special concern of the First Amendment, which does not tolerate laws that cast a pall of orthodoxy over the classroom." *Id. See also* Byrne, *Academic Freedom: A Special Concern of the First Amendment,* 99 Yale L.J. 251 (1989). The educational environment best suited to the American liberal democracy is one in which students experience "wide exposure to that robust exchange of ideas that discovers truth 'out of a multitude of tongues' [and not] through any kind of authoritative selection." *Keyishian,* 385 U.S. at 603, citing *United States v. Associated Press,* 52 F. Supp. 362, 372 (S.D.N.Y. 1943), *aff'd,* 326 U.S. 1 (1945). If public education is to serve the ends of the American democracy, "[t]eachers and students must always remain free to inquire, to study and to evaluate. . . ." *Sweezy v. New Hampshire,* 354 U.S. 234 (1957). The Supreme Court has made clear that the state may not "chill that free play of the spirit which all teachers ought especially to cultivate and practice." 354 U.S. at 250.

The teacher's First Amendment right to freedom in the delivery of instruction is strong, but it is not unlimited. That right must be balanced against the state's legitimate interest, through its local educational agencies, in regulating the content of the curriculum delivered to students.

KEEFE V. GEANAKOS

418 F.2d 359 (1st Cir. 1969)

ALDRICH, Chief Judge.

. . . The plaintiff is the head of the English department and coordinator for grades 7 through 12 for the Ipswich (Massachusetts) Public School System, with part-time duties as a teacher of English. He has tenure, pursuant to Mass. G.L. c. 71, §41. The defendants are the members of the Ipswich School Committee. Briefly, after some preliminaries, five charges were furnished the plaintiff as grounds for dismissal, and a hearing was scheduled thereon, which plaintiff seeks to enjoin as violating his civil rights. 42 U.S.C. §1983. . . .

Reduced to fundamentals, the substance of plaintiff's position is that as a matter of law his conduct which forms the basis of the charge did not warrant discipline. Accordingly, he argues, there is no ground for any hearing. He divides this position into two parts. The principal one is that his conduct was within his competence as a teacher, as a matter of academic freedom, whether the defendants approved of it or not. The second is that he had been given inadequate prior warning by such regulations as were in force, particularly in the light of the totality of the circumstances known to him, that his actions would be considered improper, so that an ex post facto ruling would, itself, unsettle academic freedom. The defendants, essentially, deny plaintiff's contentions. They accept the existence of a principle of academic freedom to teach, but state that it is limited to proper classroom materials as reasonably determined by the school committee in the light of pertinent conditions, of which they cite in particular the age of the students. Asked by the court whether a teacher has a right to say to the school committee that it is wrong if, in fact, its decision was arbitrary, counsel candidly and commendably (and correctly) responded in the affirmative. This we consider to be the present issue. . . .

On the opening day of school in September 1969 the plaintiff gave to each member of his senior English class a copy of the September 1969 Atlantic Monthly magazine, a publication of high reputation, and stated that the reading assignment for that night was the first article [written by Robert Lifton] therein. September was the educational number, so-called, of the Atlantic, and some 75 copies had been supplied by the school department. Plaintiff discussed the article, and a particular word that was used therein, and explained the word's origin and context, and the reasons the author had included it. The word, admittedly highly offensive, is a vulgar term for an incestuous son. Plaintiff stated that any student who felt the assignment personally distasteful could have an alternative one.

The next evening the plaintiff was called to a meeting of the school committee and asked to defend his use of the offending word. Following his explanation, a majority of the members of the committee asked him informally if he would agree not to use it again in the classroom. Plaintiff replied that he could not, in good conscience, agree. His counsel states, however, without contradiction, that in point of fact plaintiff has not used it again. No formal action was taken at this meeting. Thereafter plaintiff was suspended, as a matter of discipline, and it is now proposed that he should be discharged.

The Lifton article, which we have read in its entirety, has been described as a valuable discussion of "dissent, protest, radicalism and revolt." It is in no sense pornographic. We need no supporting affidavits to find it scholarly, thoughtful and thought-provoking. The single offending word, although repeated a number of times, is not artificially introduced, but, on the contrary, is important to the development of the thesis and the conclusions of the author. Indeed, we would find it difficult to disagree with plaintiff's assertion that no proper study of the article could avoid consideration of this word. It is not possible to read the article, either in whole or in part, as an incitement to libidinous conduct, or even thoughts. If it raised the concept of incest, it was not to suggest it, but to condemn it; the word was used, by the persons described, as a superlative of opprobrium. We believe not only that the article negatived any other concept, but that an understanding of it would reject, rather than suggest, the word's use.

With regard to the word itself, we cannot think that it is unknown to many students in the last year of high school, and we might well take judicial notice of its use by young radicals and protesters from coast to coast.[7] No doubt its use genuinely offends the parents of some of the students — therein, in part, lay its relevancy to the article.

Hence the question in this case is whether a teacher may, for demonstrated educational purposes, quote a "dirty" word currently used in order to give special offense, or whether the shock is too great for high school seniors to stand. If the answer were that the students must be protected from such exposure, we would fear for their future. We do not question the good faith of the defendants in believing that some parents have been offended.[8] With the greatest of respect to such parents, their sensibilities are not the full measure of what is proper education.

We of course agree with defendants that what is to be said or read to students is not to be determined by obscenity standards for adult consumption. *Ginsberg v. New York,* 390 U.S. 629 (1968). At the same time, the issue must be one of degree. A high school senior is not devoid of all discrimination or resistance. Furthermore, as in all other instances, the offensiveness of language and the particular propriety or impropriety is dependent on the circumstances of the utterance.

Apart from cases discussing academic freedom in the large, not surprisingly we find no decisions closely in point. . . . We accept the conclusion of the court below that "some measure of public regulation of classroom speech is inherent in every provision of public education." But when we consider the facts at bar as we have elaborated them, we find it difficult not to think that its application to the present case demeans any proper concept of education.

---

[7] *E.g.,* "Up against the wall, m*therf*cker."

[8] It is appropriate in this connection to consider what, exactly, is the charge with which plaintiff is presently faced.

> 3. Use of offensive material in the classroom on September 3, 1969, and subsequently, which use would undermine public confidence and react unfavorably upon the public school system of Ipswich. . . .

The general chilling effect of permitting such rigorous censorship is even more serious.

We believe it equally probable that the plaintiff will prevail on the issue of lack of any notice that a discussion of this article with the senior class was forbidden conduct. . . . In the present case, however, the circumstances would have disclosed that no less than five books, by as many authors, containing the word in question were to be found in the school library. It is hard to think that any student could walk into the library and receive a book, but that his teacher could not subject the content to serious discussion in class.

Such inconsistency on the part of the school has been regarded as fatal. . . . We, too, would probably so regard it. At the same time, we prefer not to place our decision on this ground alone, lest our doing so diminish our principal holding, or lead to a bowdlerization of the school library.

Finally, we are not persuaded by the district court's conclusion that no irreparable injury is involved because the plaintiff, if successful, may recover money damages. Academic freedom is not preserved by compulsory retirement, even at full pay. . . .

NOTES AND QUESTIONS

1. What are the precise contours of the concept of "academic freedom"? Does that concept originate in a teacher's constitutional right to freedom of expression, or does it originate in a student's right to be exposed to an idea? What value does it serve? Do teachers have greater constitutional protection for freedom of expression than nonteachers? Should they? Recall the Supreme Court's partial reliance on academic freedom in its recent affirmative action cases to validate the state's interest in a diverse student body. How is academic freedom relevant to affirmative action?
2. One strong rationale for academic freedom stems from John Stuart Mill's conception that a marketplace of ideas is a vital means toward the end of the attainment of truth. In Chapter II of *On Liberty,* entitled, "Of the Liberty of Thought and Discussion," Mill declares: "the peculiar evil of silencing the expression of an opinion is, that it is robbing the human race. . . . If the opinion is right, they are deprived of the opportunity for exchanging error for truth; if wrong, they lose . . . the clearer perception and livelier perception of truth, produced by its collision with error." *See* Mill, *On Liberty,* ch. II, "Of the Liberty of Thought and Discussion" (Penguin Classics 1982). Recall that the educational philosophy of John Dewey likewise suggests that the free interchange of competing ideas in the classroom is central to a democratic education. What does the principle of academic freedom suggest about the way in which students learn? How is that kind of learning arguably unique to a democracy?
3. There must, of course, be limits on a teacher's right to freedom of expression, limits set not only by the community's standards of decency, but also by a school district's curricular goals. Where does a school district's interest in insuring that all of its students receive a consistent education end, and a teacher's right to freedom in the classroom begin? Suppose the school district's curricular goals require each teacher to instruct third-grade

students on test-taking strategies so that students may succeed on the battery of state-mandated standardized tests. Several teachers refuse to do so, arguing that such instruction is not beneficial to the students. May the district discipline the teachers, or do the teachers have "academic freedom" to select their own instructional practices?

4. In *Palmer v. Board of Education of the City of Chicago,* 603 F.2d 1271 (7th Cir. 1979), the Seventh Circuit addressed the issue of whether a public school teacher is free to disregard the prescribed curriculum concerning patriotic matters. Palmer, a member of the Jehovah's Witnesses, was a probationary kindergarten teacher in the Chicago public schools. After her appointment, Palmer informed her principal that because of her religion she would be unable to teach any subjects having to do with love of country, the flag or other patriotic matters in the curriculum. In rejecting Palmer's claim that she was terminated because of her religious beliefs, the Court observed:

   > . . . Plaintiff in seeking to conduct herself in accordance with her religious beliefs neglects to consider the impact on her students who are not members of her faith. Because of her religious beliefs, plaintiff would deprive her students of an elementary knowledge and appreciation of our national heritage. She considers it to be promoting idolatry, it was explained during oral argument, to teach, for instance, about President Lincoln and why we observe his birthday. However, it would apparently not offend her religious views to teach about some of our past leaders less proudly regarded. There would only be provided a distorted and unbalanced view of our country's history. Parents have a vital interest in what their children are taught. Their representatives have in general prescribed a curriculum. There is a compelling state interest in the choice and adherence to a suitable curriculum for the benefit of our young citizens and society. It cannot be left to individual teachers to teach what they please. Plaintiff's right to her own religious views and practices remains unfettered, but she has no constitutional right to require others to submit to her views and to forego a portion of their education they would otherwise be entitled to enjoy. In this unsettled world, although we hope it will not come to pass, some of the students may be called upon in some way to defend and protect our democratic system and Constitutional rights, including plaintiff's religious freedom. That will demand a bit of patriotism.

   Although the teacher's refusal to adhere to the curriculum was based on her religious objections, the court's reasoning extends to any personal objection a teacher might have to prescribed instructional practices. Do teachers have the "academic freedom" to decline to teach "patriotism" to their students?

5. Is there a meaningful distinction between a teacher's role in the classroom during instructional time and the teacher's role outside the classroom during noninstructional time? *See Fowler v. Board of Education of Lincoln County Ky.,* 819 F.2d 657 (6th Cir.), *cert. denied,* 484 U.S. 986 (1987) (finding that a teacher's decision to allow students to see an R-rated movie on a "noninstructional" day was not a protected First Amendment interest in

academic freedom or expression, and therefore did not preclude her resulting dismissal).

6. When untenured teachers are not rehired "because of" the exercise of their academic freedom, is the analysis identical to the situation in which such teachers are not rehired "because of" the exercise of their First Amendment rights of expression? *See, e.g., Mt. Healthy City Board of Education v. Doyle,* 429 U.S. 274 (1977). As the *Cockrel* case suggests, academic freedom often may be difficult to distinguish from freedom of expression. Is there a meaningful legal distinction?

Cockrel v. Shelby County School District

270 F.3d 1036 (6th Cir. 2001)

Karen Nelson Moore, Circuit Judge. Plaintiff Donna Cockrel ("Cockrel") appeals the district court's decision granting the Shelby County Public School District ("School District" or "District"), Superintendent Leon Mooneyhan, and Principal Bruce Slate's (collectively referred to as "defendants") motion for summary judgment with respect to Cockrel's First Amendment retaliation claim, which she brought pursuant to 42 U.S.C. §1983. We REVERSE and REMAND the case to the district court for further proceedings consistent with this opinion.

I. Background

Plaintiff Donna Cockrel, a tenured fifth-grade teacher at Simpsonville Elementary School in the Shelby County, Kentucky School District was terminated on July 15, 1997 by the District's superintendent, Dr. Leon Mooneyhan. The School District's proffered grounds for Cockrel's termination were insubordination, conduct unbecoming a teacher, inefficiency, incompetency, and neglect of duty. As the basis for these charges, the School District detailed seventeen specific instances of misconduct engaged in by Cockrel, including: failing to teach and disparaging the school's "Just Think" curriculum; calling Principal Harry Slate names in front of staff members and students; and failing to cooperate with the Title I program and the Title I aides in her class, as well as with other faculty members and staff of Simpsonville Elementary School.

While the School District alleged numerous reasons for its decision to terminate Cockrel, she claims that the District fired her due to her decision to invite Woody Harrelson, the television and film actor most famous for his role as "Woody" on the network television show "Cheers," and others to her classroom to give presentations on the environmental benefits of industrial hemp. Hemp, an illegal substance in Kentucky, is a plant from which both marijuana and a valuable fiber can be harvested. There are two varieties of the hemp plant. One is the marijuana plant itself, with approximately four to seven percent of its weight comprised of tetrahydrocannabinol ("THC"), the active chemical in the marijuana drug; the other is industrial hemp, a plant which grows in stalks and from which fibers can be taken to make various goods such as paper and clothes. Unlike marijuana, the industrial hemp plant is only comprised of between 0.1 and 0.4 percent THC, an insufficient amount to have any narcotic effect. Nevertheless, Kentucky law prohibits possession of both varieties of the hemp plant, including "its seeds or resin or any compound, mixture, or preparation which contains any quantity of these substances."

Cockrel claims that on at least three occasions during her seven-year tenure at Simpsonville Elementary she organized outside speakers to come to her class to speak about industrial hemp. Cockrel further claims that both Principal Slate and Superintendent Mooneyhan knew that she organized industrial hemp presentations. While Principal Slate alleges that he never knew industrial hemp was being discussed in Cockrel's class, he does admit that Cockrel's lesson plans, on at least one occasion, specifically mentioned that hemp was to be discussed.

On or about April 9, 1996, following Cockrel's decision to end the 1995-96 school year with a project entitled "Saving the Trees," in which the use of industrial hemp fibers as a possible alternative to wood pulp was to be discussed, Cockrel was contacted by a representative of the Cable News Network ("CNN") and asked if she would permit CNN's cameras to film her class presentation for use in a larger program on tree conservation. Cockrel claims that she then immediately informed Slate of CNN's potential visit to their school, though Slate does not recall this conversation.

In early May 1996, Joe Hickey, president of the Kentucky Hemp Growers Association, informed Cockrel that Woody Harrelson might visit Kentucky with CNN, and that Harrelson might also visit her classroom. Cockrel claims that she was given no specific information as to when Harrelson might visit her classroom, and that it was not until the morning of May 30, 1996, the last day of the school year, that she was notified that Harrelson would be visiting Simpsonville Elementary School that day. Cockrel informed Principal Slate of the impending visit, and he agreed to allow it, though Slate claims that he was only told that the presentation to be given was about agriculture.

Harrelson arrived at the school later that morning with an "entourage, including representatives of the Kentucky Hemp Museum and Kentucky Hemp Growers Cooperative Association, several hemp growers from foreign countries, CNN, and various Kentucky news media representatives." As stated in Cockrel's complaint, Harrelson spoke with the children about his opposition to marijuana use, yet he distinguished marijuana from industrial hemp and advocated the use of industrial hemp as an alternative to increased logging efforts. As part of the presentation, products made from hemp were shown to the children, as were hemp seeds, a banned substance in the state of Kentucky. Harrelson's visit received both local and national media attention. One student who did not have parental permission to be videotaped or photographed by the news media was included by the press in a class photograph with Harrelson.

Following Harrelson's visit and the media attention it garnered, parents and teachers wrote numerous letters to members of the Shelby County School District voicing their concern and dismay regarding the industrial hemp presentation. Several of the letters noted the mixed message the school was sending on drug use as Harrelson's presentation occurred on the same day that many Simpsonville Elementary School students were graduating from the Drug Abuse Resistance Education ("D.A.R.E.") program offered in the school.

Based on the complaints expressed in the letters, Superintendent Mooneyhan decided to initiate an investigation into Cockrel's conduct. Following the investigation, Mooneyhan advised the Kentucky Education Professional Standards Board ("EPSB") that Cockrel had allowed hemp seeds, an illegal substance, to be passed around to students in her class during Harrelson's class visit. The Standards Board, after investigating the matter, ultimately dismissed Mooneyhan's complaint without prejudice, stating that there was an "insufficient basis to warrant [a] certificate revocation action."

In the months following Harrelson's visit, Simpsonville Elementary School adopted a new visitors policy for "controversial" topics that required advance approval by school administration and written consent by students' parents. This policy was put to use when, during the next school year, Cockrel informed Slate that Harrelson would be making a second visit to her classroom to discuss industrial hemp. Cockrel met all of the requirements of the new visitors policy, including providing the requisite advance notice to Principal Slate and obtaining permission from the parents of her students for their children to attend the presentation. Slate did not attempt to discourage Cockrel from having another class presentation on industrial hemp, nor did he tell her that Harrelson should not be invited back to the school. According to Cockrel, however, Superintendent Mooneyhan did tell her earlier in the school year that it would not be in her best interests if Harrelson made any more visits to her class. While Harrelson was unable to attend on the day of his scheduled visit, a small group of parents, unaware that Harrelson was not coming, went to the school and "loudly voiced their objections" to Slate about his permitting Harrelson to visit the school a second time.

Harrelson rescheduled the visit for the following week, January 29, 1997, and Cockrel again fully complied with the school's visitors policy. Principal Slate again approved Harrelson's visit. This time Harrelson did make an appearance. Harrelson was met by a group of parents outside the school who were protesting his visit. Due to school scheduling problems, Harrelson was only able to speak to the students for a few minutes before the students had to leave for lunch. Harrelson's visit again garnered national media attention from CNN. Principal Slate, who had been asked by CNN for an interview regarding Cockrel's presentations on industrial hemp, chose to issue a written statement instead. In his statement, Slate said the following:

> The media has reported that Ms. Cockrel has experienced problems with Shelby County school officials, including me, regarding her teaching about industrial hemp. I admit that we have had problems, however, not all our concerns are about Ms. Cockrel's teaching about hemp. I have also received complaints about her conduct in other areas. The Shelby County school officials and I do not disapprove of Ms. Cockrel teaching about hemp, per se, which we admit has educational value as to its historical and current uses and its potential as an alternative crop. Rather, we have been concerned about the methods Ms. Cockrel has used to present issues regarding hemp to her students.

Slate's statement then went on to criticize Cockrel's permitting hemp seeds to be passed around to the students at the first presentation, as well as her failure to inform him promptly of Harrelson's first visit, which occurred on the same day as the D.A.R.E. graduation.

In the months following Harrelson's initial visit, and shortly after his second visit in January 1997, Slate sat in on Cockrel's class for purposes of conducting evaluations. That school year, Cockrel was the only tenured teacher at Simpsonville Elementary to be reviewed after two years, whereas tenured teachers in the School District are typically reviewed only once every three years. Slate stated in his deposition that the reason for Cockrel's early review was his perception that things had been "going downhill" between the two of them for the previous two years. Slate further explained that Cockrel was neither communicating nor cooperating with him and the rest of the staff and faculty of Simpsonville Elementary, nor was she adequately following the school's curriculum and policies.

Citing examples of this downward trend in Cockrel's attitude and performance, Slate testified that Cockrel did not want Deputy Yeager, the police officer in charge of the D.A.R.E. program at Simpsonville who had spoken out against the Harrelson visits, in her classroom instructing her students. She asked Slate to find someone else to teach the D.A.R.E. program. Slate further stated that two teachers had approached him to let him know that Cockrel was calling him names outside his presence. In addition, a parent notified Slate that her child had heard Cockrel call Slate a name in class. Slate also noted that there were many times when Cockrel simply refused to speak with him or failed to attend meetings.

In the 1996-97 school year, during and after the news that Harrelson would be visiting her class once again, five students, at their parents' request, were transferred out of Cockrel's class. Each time Slate attempted to inform Cockrel of a student's transfer, Cockrel would refuse to talk with him, sometimes walking right past him when he tried to speak with her, or turning her back to him, or refusing to meet with him in his office when he so requested.

On February 20, 1997, in the wake of Cockrel's decision to continue discussing the benefits of industrial hemp with outside speakers, the Simpsonville Parent Teachers Association ("PTA") adopted a "position statement," which stated, in part:

> In our opinion, Mrs. Cockrel's behavior over the past few months has been inappropriate for a teacher and role model for our children. We feel she violated the professional code of ethics for KY. [sic] school personnel. In our opinion, she can no longer be an effective educator in our system and our children's education would be better served by another teacher.

A little more than a month later, Principal Slate issued a "summative evaluation" of Cockrel's performance, stating that Cockrel did not meet the requisite level of performance in five of the forty-three categories of evaluation. Deficient performance was noted in the following areas: communication with parents regarding student performance and teacher expectations; documentation of lesson plans; showing "consistent sensitivity to individual academic, physical, social, and cultural differences and responding to all students in a caring manner"; ability to build positive relationships within the school and between the school and community; and acting in accordance with laws and with school regulations and procedures. Attached to the evaluation were several letters from parents complaining about Cockrel's discussion of hemp in class, as well as documentation of other alleged misconduct. Based on this evaluation, Slate recommended to Superintendent Mooneyhan that Cockrel be terminated. Cockrel was terminated by Mooneyhan on July 15, 1997.

The termination letter informing Cockrel of her discharge detailed numerous instances of misconduct, all of which allegedly served as the basis for her discharge. Several of these charges detailed misconduct that occurred well before Harrelson made his initial visit to Simpsonville Elementary. There is no evidence in the record, however, that Cockrel had been reprimanded for such activity prior to Harrelson's visits to her classroom.

As is her right under Kentucky law, Cockrel initially decided to appeal the Superintendent's decision to terminate her. Shortly thereafter, however, she withdrew her appeal.

Pursuant to Ky. Rev. Stat. §161.120, Superintendent Mooneyhan forwarded on to the EPSB the proffered reasons for terminating Cockrel in case the Board wished to revoke Cockrel's teaching certificate. Following review by the EPSB, Cockrel entered into a written agreement whereby her teaching certificate was surrendered for two years . . . and suspended for two years. . . .

. . . On June 4, 1998, Cockrel filed suit in the United States District Court for the Eastern District of Kentucky. Cockrel brought a claim pursuant to 42 U.S.C. §1983 in which she alleged that she was terminated in retaliation for exercising her First Amendment right of free speech when discussing the potential environmental benefits of industrial hemp. Cockrel also included a state law breach of contract claim. Following limited discovery, the defendants moved for [and obtained] summary judgment on Cockrel's §1983 claim. . . .

II. Analysis . . .

C. Cockrel's First Amendment Retaliation Claim . . .

1. The Elements of a First Amendment Retaliation Claim

. . . Donna Cockrel, a teacher in the Shelby County Public School District, is a public employee. For a public employee to establish a claim of First Amendment retaliation, this court has held that she must demonstrate:

> (1) that [she] was engaged in a constitutionally protected activity; (2) that the defendant's adverse action caused [her] to suffer an injury that would likely chill a person of ordinary firmness from continuing to engage in that activity; and (3) that the adverse action was motivated at least in part as a response to the exercise of [her] constitutional rights.

Leary v. Daeschner, 228 F.3d 729, 737 (6th Cir. 2000). To demonstrate that she was engaging in constitutionally protected speech, Cockrel must show that her speech touched on matters of public concern, and that her "interest in commenting upon matters of public concern . . . outweighs the interest of the State, as an employer, in promoting the efficiency of the public services it performs through its employees." . . . If the plaintiff can establish the three elements of her First Amendment retaliation claim, the burden of persuasion then shifts to the defendants, who must show, by a preponderance of the evidence, that they "would have taken the same action even in the absence of the protected conduct." . . .

a. Was This Speech?

Before deciding whether Cockrel's speech was constitutionally protected, this court must first address the question of whether Cockrel's activity can be considered speech at all. . . .

[T]he district court erred in holding Cockrel's conduct not to be speech. First, to the extent the district court was persuaded that Cockrel's actions did not constitute speech because Woody Harrelson, rather than Cockrel, was doing the speaking, this was error. As the Supreme Court stated in *Hurley v. Irish-American Gay, Lesbian & Bisexual Group,* 515 U.S. 557, 570 [(1995)], to receive First Amendment protection, a speaker does not have "to generate, as an original matter, each item featured in the communication." For example, cable operators, even though they only broadcast material written, spoken, and produced by others, are still considered to be engaged in protected speech. The same First Amendment protections exist for newspapers, which in their opinion pages simply collect and present the speech of others. *Hurley,* 515 U.S. at 570. We see no reason, nor have the defendants explained to this court, why a teacher's selection of a speaker for an in-class presentation is less a form of speech than a cable operator's decision as to which programs it chooses to present to its viewing audience.

To the extent that the district court relied on the argument that Cockrel's conduct was not speech because she had no advocative purpose when bringing industrial hemp enthusiasts to her class, this was also error. The Supreme Court has held that films, radio programs, and live entertainment are all protected by the First Amendment. *Schad v. Borough of Mount Ephraim,* 452 U.S. 61, 65 (1981). Moreover, to have constitutional protection, those who choose to show the film or stage the play need not show that they intended to convey a particularized message in doing so, nor that they approved or disapproved of its content, for such activities are inherently expressive and entitled to constitutional protection. . . .

Thus, while we believe that Cockrel had an advocative purpose in bringing in speakers who presented her students with information on the environmental benefits of industrial hemp, even if Cockrel did not have such a purpose when organizing these presentations, her decision to present these speakers to her class still constitutes speech.

b. Is Cockrel's Speech Constitutionally Protected?

Given our determination that Cockrel's decision to bring industrial hemp advocates into her class is speech, the next question we must ask is whether that speech is constitutionally protected. As stated earlier, speech of a public employee is protected by the First Amendment only if it touches on matters of public concern, and only if "the employee's interest in commenting upon matters of public concern . . . outweighs the interest of the State, as an employer, in promoting the efficiency of the public services it performs through its employees." If Cockrel's speech cannot meet both of these standards, then her First Amendment retaliation claim cannot go forward.

i. Does Cockrel's Speech Touch on a Matter of Public Concern?

In determining whether Cockrel's speech touched on a matter of public concern, we turn to *Connick v. Myers,* 461 U.S. 138, (1983), the Supreme Court's most instructive case on this issue. In *Connick,* the Court stated that matters of public concern are those that can "be fairly considered as relating to any matter of political, social, or other concern to the community[.]" There is no question that the issue of industrial hemp is a matter of great political and social concern to many citizens of Kentucky, and we believe that Cockrel's presentations clearly come within the Supreme Court's understanding of speech touching on matters of public concern.

In support of this conclusion, we first turn to the district court's opinion, which unequivocally stated "that the issue of industrial hemp is politically charged and of great concern to certain citizens." Second, in the past year alone, industrial hemp advocacy in Kentucky has made news on several occasions, revealing the significant extent to which industrial hemp has become an important and publicly debated issue in the State. . . .

While discussion of industrial hemp plainly meets the broad concept of "public concern" as defined by the Supreme Court, some courts have focused on other portions of the Supreme Court's *Connick* decision in concluding that a teacher's classroom speech does not touch on matters of public concern. *See Boring v. Buncombe County Bd. of Educ.,* 136 F.3d 364, 368-69 (4th Cir.) (en banc), *cert. denied,* 525 U.S. 813, 142 L. Ed. 2d 36, 119 S. Ct. 47 (1998); *Kirkland v. Northside Indep. Sch. Dist.,* 890 F.2d 794, 797-99 (5th Cir. 1989), *cert. denied,* 496 U.S. 926, 110 L. Ed. 2d 641, 110 S. Ct. 2620 (1990). These cases pay particular attention to the following portion of the *Connick* Court's holding:

> When a public employee speaks not as a citizen upon matters of public concern, but instead as an employee upon matters only of personal interest, absent the most unusual circumstances, a federal court is not the appropriate forum in which to review the wisdom of a personnel decision taken by a public agency allegedly in reaction to the employee's behavior.

Connick, 461 U.S. at 147. Based upon this language, the Fourth and Fifth Circuits have determined that a teacher, in choosing what he will teach his students, is not speaking as a citizen, but rather as an employee on matters of private interest. *Boring,* 136 F.3d at 368-69; *Kirkland,* 890 F.2d at 800.

We believe that the Fourth and Fifth Circuits have extended the holding of *Connick* beyond what the Supreme Court intended. Under the courts' analyses in *Boring* and *Kirkland,* a teacher, regardless of what he decides to include in his curriculum, is speaking as an employee on a private matter. *Boring,* 136 F.3d at 368-69; *Kirkland,* 890 F.2d at 800. This essentially gives a teacher no right to freedom of speech when teaching students in a classroom, for the very act of teaching is what the employee is paid to do. Thus, when teaching, even if about an upcoming presidential election or the importance of our Bill of Rights, the Fourth and Fifth Circuits' reasoning would leave such speech without constitutional protection, for the teacher is speaking as an employee, and not as a citizen.

The facts in *Connick* indicate that the Fourth and Fifth Circuits have read the Supreme Court's language too broadly. In *Connick,* an assistant district attorney, following a disagreement with a supervisor, prepared a questionnaire seeking the opinions of her co-workers on issues such as "office transfer policy, office morale, the need for a grievance committee, the level of confidence in supervisors, and whether employees felt pressured to work in political campaigns." *Connick,* 461 U.S. at 141. Connick was later fired for circulating the questionnaire on the grounds of insubordination. *Id.* The Court held that, while many of the questions simply reflected the plaintiff's efforts to gather information to use against her supervisors in her private employment dispute, Myers's question regarding the pressure to work on political campaigns did touch on a matter of public concern. 461 U.S. at 149. Thus, the Court held that, even though Myers was speaking as an employee out of her private interest in combating her supervisors' decision to transfer her, the fact that one of her questions dealt with the fundamental constitutional right not to be coerced into campaigning for a political candidate was enough to make this particular issue touch on a matter of public concern. *Id.*

If the Fourth and Fifth Circuits' interpretation of *Connick* were correct, then any time a public employee was speaking as an employee, like Myers was when she asked her question about employees being pressured to campaign, the speech at issue would not be protected. As the Supreme Court made clear in its analysis, however, the key question is not whether a person is speaking in his role as an employee or a citizen, but whether the employee's speech in fact touches on matters of public concern. 461 U.S. at 148-49. Thus, even if a public employee were acting out of a private motive with no intent to air her speech publicly, as was the case with Myers, so long as the speech relates to matters of "political, social, or other concern to the community," as opposed to matters "only of personal interest," it shall be considered as touching upon matters of public concern. 461 U.S. at 146-49.

In Cockrel's case, although she was speaking in her role as an employee when presenting information on the environmental benefits of industrial hemp, the content of her speech, as discussed *supra,* most certainly involved matters related to the political and social concern of the community, as opposed to mere matters of private interest. Thus, contrary to the analyses in *Boring* and *Kirkland,* we hold that Cockrel's speech does touch on matters of public concern.

ii. *Pickering* Balancing

Having held that Cockrel's speech touches on matters of public concern, we must now weigh the employee's interest in speaking against the employer's interest in regulating the speech to determine if the speech is constitutionally protected. In *Pickering v. Board of Education,* 391 U.S. 563 (1968), the Supreme Court endeavored to strike a balance between a public employee's speech rights on matters of public interest (in that case a public school teacher's speech outside of school) and the State's interest as an employer in maintaining a productive workplace. In accordance with the balancing test created in *Pickering,* public employee speech, even if touching on matters of public concern, will not be constitutionally protected unless the employee's interest in speaking on these issues "outweighs 'the interest of the State, as an employer, in promoting the efficiency of the public services it performs through its employees.' " In striking the balance between the State's and the employee's respective interests, this court has stated that it will "consider whether an employee's comments meaningfully interfere with the performance of her duties, undermine a legitimate goal or mission of the employer, create disharmony among co-workers, impair discipline by superiors, or destroy the relationship of loyalty and trust required of confidential employees." *Williams v. Kentucky,* 24 F.3d 1526, 1536 (6th Cir.), *cert. denied,* 513 U.S. 947 (1994) (citing *Rankin v. McPherson,* 483 U.S. 378, 388, 97 L. Ed. 2d 315, 107 S. Ct. 2891 (1987)).

Before engaging in a "particularized balancing" of the competing interests at stake in this case, *Connick,* 461 U.S. at 150, it is important to note that "if an employee's speech substantially involves matters of public concern, an employer may be required to make a particularly strong showing that the employee's speech interfered with workplace functioning before taking action." *Leary,* 228 F.3d at 737-38 (quotation omitted). In this case, it is clear that Cockrel's speech did substantially involve matters of public concern, and thus the defendants will have to make a stronger showing that their interests in regulating plaintiff's speech outweighed Cockrel's interests in speaking.

Weighing in plaintiff's favor in this analysis is the fact that her speech substantially involved matters of significant public concern in Kentucky. Defendants claim, however, that their "interest in maintaining loyalty, efficient operation of the schools, and workplace harmony" outweighs the plaintiff's interest in speaking about industrial hemp. We first note that the defendants do not claim that Cockrel's presentations on industrial hemp meaningfully interfered with the performance of her teaching duties. Defendants would have a difficult time making this argument, however, considering they openly acknowledged in a public statement to CNN that there was "educational value" in teaching students about industrial hemp as an alternative crop. We further note that defendants' purported interest in "maintaining loyalty" is inapposite in this case. While this circuit has stated that it would consider in its balancing whether employee speech operated to "destroy the relationship of loyalty and trust required of confidential employees[,]" *Williams,* 24 F.3d at 1536, a public school teacher, we believe, is hardly the type of confidential employee the court had in mind. Thus, any loyalty concerns that the defendants may have will not be taken into consideration in our weighing of the competing interests at stake.

Turning to the defendants' proffered interests in an efficient operation of the school and a harmonious work environment, there is evidence that plaintiff's speech has led to problems in both of these areas. . . .

Although this evidence of a contentious and periodically disrupted work environment weighs in favor of the defendants, the amount of weight we should give this evidence is an entirely different question. We are troubled by the fact that, whereas school officials gave plaintiff prior approval to host all three of the industrial hemp presentations at issue in this case, defendants now forward concerns of school efficiency and harmony as reasons supporting their decision to discharge Cockrel. . . . We do not believe that defendants can use the outcry within the school community protesting Cockrel's speech, speech that was approved by school officials in advance, as a shield for their decision to discharge her. While ordinarily we would give substantial weight to the government employer's concerns of workplace efficiency, harmony, and discipline in conducting our balancing of the employee's and employer's competing interests, we cannot allow these concerns to tilt the *Pickering* scale in favor of the government, absent other evidence, when the disruptive consequences of the employee speech can be traced back to the government's express decision permitting the employee to engage in that speech.

Accordingly, we hold that, on balance, the defendants' interests in an efficient operation of the school and a harmonious workplace do not outweigh the plaintiff's interests in speaking about the benefits of industrial hemp, an issue of substantial political and economic concern in Kentucky. Thus, because Cockrel's speech touches on matters of public concern and because the balancing of interests under *Pickering* weighs in her favor, her speech is constitutionally protected. We now proceed with an examination of the remainder of the elements of plaintiff's First Amendment retaliation claim.

c. Did the Plaintiff Suffer an Injury as a Result of Her Speech That Would Chill an Ordinary Person From Continuing to Engage in Such Speech?

For the next element of Cockrel's retaliation claim, she must show "that the defendant[s'] adverse action caused [her] to suffer an injury that would likely chill a person of ordinary firmness from continuing to engage in that activity[.]" *Leary,* 228 F.3d at 737. There is no question that, by being terminated, Cockrel has suffered an injury that would chill an ordinary person from continuing to engage in speech on the environmental benefits of industrial hemp.

d. Was the Decision to Terminate Cockrel Motivated, at Least in Part, by Plaintiff's Decision to Speak About Industrial Hemp?

The final element of Cockrel's First Amendment retaliation claim requires her to show that defendants' decision to discharge her was motivated, at least in part, by the exercise of her free speech rights. . . . In other words, to survive defendants' motion for summary judgment, Cockrel must present sufficient evidence to allow a reasonable fact finder to conclude, by a preponderance of the evidence, that her speech, at least in part, motivated the defendants to discharge her. . . .

After examining this evidence, we conclude that a jury could find, by a preponderance of the evidence, that the defendants' decision to discharge Cockrel was motivated, at least in part, by her decision to teach her students about industrial hemp. The temporal proximity between the Harrelson visits and Cockrel's series of unscheduled evaluations, as well as the influence the parent and teacher complaints appeared to have on the defendants in the wake of the Harrelson visits, constitute sufficient evidence for Cockrel to establish the causation element of her First Amendment retaliation claim.

2. Rebutting the Plaintiff's First Amendment Retaliation Claim

Because Cockrel has successfully established for purposes of the summary judgment stage the three elements of her First Amendment retaliation claim, the burden of persuasion shifts to the defendants. As stated earlier, to defeat the plaintiff's claim at trial, the defendants must show by a preponderance of the evidence that they would have terminated Cockrel even had she not engaged in constitutionally protected activity. *Leary,* 228 F.3d at 737. . . .

In the July 15, 1997 termination letter sent by Superintendent Mooneyhan to Cockrel, seventeen reasons were given as the basis for the school district's decision to discharge her. Among the litany of reasons offered by the defendants for Cockrel's discharge were: her calling Principal Slate names in front of staff members and students; her failure to teach the school's mandatory "Just Think" curriculum; her persistent failure to follow the school's Title I program; her inappropriate language and displays of anger in class; and her general failure to cooperate with other members of the Simpsonville school community, a point which we have already discussed in detail. There is no question that Cockrel's conduct, if it did in fact occur as the defendants allege, was completely inappropriate. Furthermore, we have no doubt that conduct of this nature can serve as adequate grounds for an employee's termination. Despite this, however, after viewing all the evidence in the record in the light most favorable to Cockrel, we do not believe that the defendants have met their significant burden of showing that every reasonable juror would conclude that, even had Cockrel not spoken to her students about industrial hemp, she would have been terminated in any event. . . .

In this case, although Mooneyhan cited seventeen charges constituting the basis for Cockrel's termination, several of the proffered reasons provide a less than compelling basis for termination. For example, Mooneyhan cited Cockrel's frequent use of the school's telephone for non-school-related business, her failure to prepare adequate lesson plans for substitute teachers, and her failure to follow the school's visitors policy for the first Harrelson visit. For each of these charges, there is no evidence in the record that Cockrel had ever been disciplined or reprimanded in any way for these violations prior to their inclusion as bases for her termination. Furthermore, while many of the more serious allegations detailed in the termination letter *(i.e.,* calling Principal Slate names and inappropriate displays of anger in class) occurred well before Harrelson came to Simpsonville to speak on industrial hemp, there is no evidence that this misconduct was ever acted upon by any school administrator until after Harrelson made his initial visit. Based on this evidence, we do not believe that the defendants have met their burden at the summary judgment stage of showing that their decision to discharge Cockrel would have been made regardless of her decision to engage in constitutionally protected speech.

We are well aware that Cockrel's decision to speak cannot immunize her from an adverse employment decision arising out of inappropriate workplace behavior unrelated to her protected speech. Similarly, an employer is not immunized from its decision to terminate an employee based on her speech simply because that employee has engaged in other conduct that could have constituted legitimate grounds for discharge. Rather, on review of a defendant's motion for summary judgment, if the plaintiff has made out the elements of her First Amendment retaliation claim, we must be confident that the defendant's decision to terminate the plaintiff was not based in part upon the plaintiff's decision to speak. In this case, the defendants have not met this burden, and we believe that a genuine issue of material facts exists from which a reasonable jury could conclude that Cockrel would not have been terminated had she not engaged in constitutionally protected activity. Thus, this matter should be resolved at trial rather than at the summary judgment stage. . . .

NOTES AND QUESTIONS

1. In footnote 7, the *Cockrel* court observed:

> Rather than apply *Pickering,* several circuits have chosen to apply the Supreme Court's analysis of students' in-class speech rights in *Hazelwood School District v. Kuhlmeier,* 484 U.S. 260 (1988), to cases in which teachers' in-class speech rights are at issue. *See Ward v. Hickey,* 996 F.2d 448, 453 (1st Cir. 1993); *Silano v. Sag Harbor Union Free Sch. Dist. Bd. of Educ.,* 42 F.3d 719, 723 (2d Cir. 1994), *cert. denied,* 515 U.S. 1160 (1995); *Miles v. Denver Pub. Schs.,* 944 F.2d 773, *777* (10th Cir. 1991); *Bishop v. Aronov,* 926 F.2d 1066, 1074 (11th Cir. 1991), *cert. denied,* 505 U.S. 1218 (1992). The *Pickering* balancing analysis has been consistently applied to cases of teacher speech in this circuit. . . . We see no reason to part from *Pickering* when deciding cases involving a teacher's in-class speech, nor have either of the parties in this case argued that *Pickering* should not apply.

   Recall that in *Hazelwood* the Supreme Court held that, "educators do not offend the First Amendment by exercising editorial control over the style and content of student speech in school-sponsored expressive activities so long on their actions are reasonably related to legitimate pedagogical concerns." How would that analysis apply in cases involving academic freedom? How would such an analysis be different from the *Pickering* approach? Finally, which analysis *(Pickering* or *Hazelwood)* is more appropriate in the specific context of instructional practices?
2. The court in *Cockrel* finds that the teacher's "decision to present these speakers to the class" itself constitutes an act of speech or expression. The court ultimately rejects Judge Milburn's analysis in *Fowler v. Board of Education,* 819 F.2d 657 (6th Cir.), *cert. denied,* 484 U.S. 986 (1987). Judge Milburn wrote that a teacher's decision to present materials to a class cannot be considered expression unless the teacher intended to convey a particular message. The *Cockrel* court, however, concludes that a teacher's very decision to present materials to a class constitutes protected "speech" even if the teacher has no "advocative purpose" in so doing. Who has the better argument, the court in *Cockrel* or Judge Milburn? Does every choice a teacher makes regarding the presentation of materials to a classroom constitute speech?
3. The *Cockrel* court employs its own *Pickering* and *Connick* template, and purports to weigh the teacher's interest in speaking on matters of public concern against the school's interest as an "employer, in promoting the efficiency of the public services it performs through its employees." How does a district's decision to curtail speech promote the efficiency of its public services? Does the school district *as employer* have an interest in

curtailing the speech of its teachers as *employees* that is stronger than the school district's interest in curtailing the speech of its students? Is a public school district a different kind of employer than other public employers such as police departments, sanitation authorities or hospitals?

4. The Sixth Circuit in *Cockrel* relies on *Connick* in rejecting the distinction made by the Fourth and Fifth Circuits between the teacher's private decision as an employee to select materials to present to a class, and the teacher's public speech as a citizen on matters of public concern. According to the Sixth Circuit, *Connick* indicates that any expression by a teacher that touches on matters of "public concern" must be protected, even if that expression were made in the context of the private motives of an employee. Do you agree with the Sixth Circuit's focus on the content of the speech itself rather than on the context in which it was uttered?
5. ***Teacher Expression Practicum.*** Suppose a teacher is disciplined for the following remarks delivered in a meeting of a faculty committee dedicated to improving the school's services for children identified as "gifted and talented": "We will never be able to deliver adequate services to our gifted and talented students unless we have more staff; I cannot continue to maintain even my current caseload." Is the teacher's speech a matter of public concern or private employment? Should the legitimacy of the district's disciplinary action depend upon the distinction?
6. After recognizing that an employer's interest in "maintaining loyalty" could, in some work environments, outweigh an employee's speech on matters of public concern, the *Cockrel* court concluded that there is no such significant "loyalty" interest with respect to a "public school teacher." Do you agree?
7. In *Urofsky v. Gilmore,* 216 F.3d 401 (4th Cir. 2000), the Fourth Circuit upheld the constitutionality of a Virginia statute restricting the ability of professors employed by public colleges and universities to access sexually explicit material on state-owned computers. The statute was challenged by six professors who claimed that it denied them their First Amendment rights to use the material as part of their academic work. The court concluded, however, that "[b]ecause Plaintiffs assert only an infringement on the manner in which they perform their work as state employees, they cannot demonstrate that the speech to which they claim entitlement would be made in their capacity as citizens speaking on matters of public concern." Does the court's reasoning allow a public university to regulate the research and expressions of its professors because that research and expression is invariably part of the employment responsibilities of a professor? *See also Boring v. Buncombe County Board of Education,* 136 F.3d 364, 368-69 (4th Cir. 1998) (en banc) (discharge of high school drama teacher because of her selection of school play not unconstitutional because the choice was made by teacher in her capacity as a school employee).
8. The issue of "academic freedom" raises particularly difficult questions when a teacher's expression or instructional practices arguably discriminates against students based on their race or gender. In Chapter 12, the issue of antiharassment policies was addressed in the context of a student's right to freedom of expression. Do such policies improperly

interfere with a *teacher's* academic freedom? In *Only Words,* at 55 (1993), Catharine MacKinnon observes that university policies prohibiting sexual or racial harassment on campus or in the classroom "have been denounced in and out of court as intolerable restrictions on academic inquiry and violations of freedom of speech." MacKinnon rejects the notion that a teacher's discriminatory remarks about race or gender in the classroom, or a teacher's willingness to allow students to make such comments, can be justified as freedom of expression or a protected dialogue in the grand marketplace of ideas. *Only Words,* at 52-53. MacKinnon believes that protections for such expression in the educational environment are illegitimate because they ignore the lack of actual equality among students in the classroom. She writes that the, "law of equality and the law of freedom are on a collision course in this country." In her view, forms of expression that harm women or minorities in the classroom are improperly legitimated because they purportedly serve the goals of academic freedom. MacKinnon would reaffirm the power of the state or a school district to protect female and minority students in the classroom by subjecting a teacher's academic freedom to a code that prohibits discriminatory speech. Do you agree?

C. THE RIGHTS OF TEACHERS AND EMPLOYMENT DISCRIMINATION

Teachers are protected from employment discrimination in two primary ways. The equal protection clause of the United States Constitution prohibits public school districts from intentional acts of prohibited discrimination against teachers. Moreover, federal and state statutes, including Title VII of the Civil Rights Act of 1964, 42 U.S.C. §2000e-2, prohibit school employers from conduct which has the purpose or effect of discriminating against teachers based upon protected classifications such as race and gender.

As demonstrated in Chapter 11, the Supreme Court, in its equal protection decisions, has developed an analysis of governmental conduct that requires three different levels of scrutiny. We have seen that classifications that affect a fundamental constitutional right or a discrete and insular minority must undergo "strict scrutiny." That scrutiny requires the government to establish that its actions are narrowly tailored to achieve a compelling governmental interest. *See City of Richmond v. J.A. Croson Company,* 488 U.S. 469, 492 (1989). We also have observed that state action that discriminates based on gender has received intermediate scrutiny, such that a public school must provide an exceedingly persuasive justification for its different treatment of men and women. Finally, all other governmental classifications will be upheld so long as they have a "rational basis." This same three-tiered approach governs employment discrimination claims by teachers against public educational institutions under the equal protection clause.

As also discussed in the context of school desegregation cases and the constitutional rights of students, the equal protection clause generally prohibits only *intentional* discrimination by the *state*. *See Washington v. Davis,* 426

U.S. 229 (1976). The Supreme Court recently made clear that "state" action includes conduct by a statewide athletic association organized to regulate competition among member public schools because of the "persuasive entwinement" of state school officials in the structure of the association. *Brentwood Academy v. Tennessee Secondary School Athletic Ass'n,* 531 U.S. 288 (2001). This definition of state or governmental action clearly is broad enough to include local educational agencies, state and local school districts and any interdistrict educational association.

Where a public school district, therefore, purposefully discriminates against its employees, the equal protection clause may prohibit employment discrimination. In each case, the school district can attempt to defend its practices by demonstrating that its actions are justified by a countervailing state interest. As the *Ambach* and *South Carolina* cases suggest, however, the state may have interests in screening its teachers that are different from those of other employers. *Ambach* involves an equal protection clause challenge to a state's citizenship requirement for public school teachers. The *South Carolina* case involves both equal protection and Title VII challenges to the state's use of teacher certification tests that allegedly have the purpose and effect of discriminating against potential teachers based on race.

1. Teacher Citizenship Requirements and Equal Protection

AMBACH, COMMISSIONER OF EDUCATION OF THE STATE OF NEW YORK v. NORWICK

441 U.S. 68 (1979)

Mr. Justice POWELL delivered the opinion of the Court.

This case presents the question whether a State, consistently with the Equal Protection Clause of the Fourteenth Amendment, may refuse to employ as elementary and secondary school teachers aliens who are eligible for United States citizenship but who refuse to seek naturalization.

I

New York Education Law §3001 (3) forbids certification as a public school teacher of any person who is not a citizen of the United States, unless that person has manifested an intention to apply for citizenship. The Commissioner of Education is authorized to create exemptions from this prohibition, and has done so with respect to aliens who are not yet eligible for citizenship. Unless a teacher obtains certification, he may not work in a public elementary or secondary school in New York.

Appellee Norwick was born in Scotland and is a subject of Great Britain. She has resided in this country since 1965 and is married to a United States citizen. Appellee Dachinger is a Finnish subject who came to this country in 1966 and also is married to a United States citizen. Both Norwick and Dachinger currently meet all of the educational requirements New York has set for certification as a public school teacher, but they consistently have refused to seek citizenship in spite of their eligibility to do so. Norwick applied in 1973 for a teaching certificate covering nursery school through sixth grade, and Dachinger sought a certificate covering the same grades in 1975. Both applications were denied because of appellees' failure to meet the requirements of §3001 (3). Norwick then filed this suit seeking to enjoin the enforcement of §3001 (3), and Dachinger obtained leave to intervene as a plaintiff. . . .

II

A

The decisions of this Court regarding the permissibility of statutory classifications involving aliens have not formed an unwavering line over the years. State regulation of the employment of aliens long has been subject to constitutional constraints. In *Yick Wo v. Hopkins,* 118 U.S. 356 (1886), the Court struck down an ordinance which was applied to prevent aliens from running laundries, and in *Truax v. Raich,* 239 U.S. 33 (1915), a law requiring at least 80% of the employees of certain businesses to be citizens was held to be an unconstitutional infringement of an alien's "right to work for a living in the common occupations of the community. . . ." At the same time, however, the Court also has recognized a greater degree of latitude for the States when aliens were sought to be excluded from public employment. . . .

Although our more recent decisions have departed substantially from the public-interest doctrine of *Truax's* day, they have not abandoned the general principle that some state functions are so bound up with the operation of the State as a governmental entity as to permit the exclusion from those functions of all persons who have not become part of the process of self-government. In *Sugarman v. Dougall,* 413 U.S. 634 (1993), we recognized that a State could, "in an appropriately defined class of positions, require citizenship as a qualification for office." We went on to observe:

> Such power inheres in the State by virtue of its obligation, already noted above, "to preserve the basic conception of a political community." . . . And this power and responsibility of the State applies, not only to the qualifications of voters, but also to persons holding state elective or important nonelective executive, legislative, and judicial positions, for officers who participate directly in the formulation, execution, or review of broad public policy perform functions that go to the heart of representative government. 413 U.S., at 647 (citation omitted).

The exclusion of aliens from such governmental positions would not invite as demanding scrutiny from this Court. . . .

Applying the rational-basis standard, we held last Term that New York could exclude aliens from the ranks of its police force. *Foley v. Connelie,* 435 U.S. 291 (1978). Because the police function fulfilled "a most fundamental obligation of government to its constituency" and by necessity cloaked policemen with substantial discretionary powers, we viewed the police force as being one of those appropriately defined classes of positions for which a citizenship requirement could be imposed. Accordingly, the State was required to justify its classification only "by a showing of some rational relationship between the interest sought to be protected and the limiting classification."

The rule for governmental functions, which is an exception to the general standard applicable to classifications based on alienage, rests on important principles inherent in the Constitution. The distinction between citizens and aliens, though ordinarily irrelevant to private activity, is fundamental to the definition and government of a State. The Constitution itself refers to the distinction no less than 11 times, . . . indicating that the status of citizenship was meant to have significance in the structure of our government. The assumption of that status, whether by birth or naturalization, denotes an association with the policy which, in a democratic republic, exercises the powers of governance. The form of this association is important: an oath of allegiance or similar ceremony cannot substitute for the unequivocal legal bond citizenship represents. It is because of this special significance of citizenship that governmental entities, when exercising the functions of government, have wider latitude in limiting the participation of noncitizens.

B

In determining whether, for purposes of equal protection analysis, teaching in public schools constitutes a governmental function, we look to the role of public education and to the degree of responsibility and discretion teachers possess in fulfilling that role. Each of these considerations supports the conclusion that public school teachers may be regarded as performing a task "that [goes] to the heart of representative government." *Sugarman v. Dougal.*

Public education, like the police function, "fulfills a most fundamental obligation of government to its constituency." *Foley.* The importance of public schools in the preparation of individuals for participation as citizens, and in the preservation of the values on which our society rests, long has been recognized by our decisions:

> Today, education is perhaps the most important function of state and local governments. Compulsory school attendance laws and the great expenditures for education both demonstrate our recognition of the importance of education to our democratic society. It is required in the performance of our most basic public responsibilities, even service in the armed forces. It is the very foundation of good citizenship. Today it is a principal instrument in awakening the child to cultural values, in preparing him for later professional training, and in helping him to adjust normally to his environment. *Brown v. Board of Education,* 347 U.S. 483, 493 (1954). . . .

Other authorities have perceived public schools as an "assimilative force" by which diverse and conflicting elements in our society are brought together on a broad but common ground. *See, e.g.,* J. Dewey, *Democracy and Education* 26 (1929); N. Edwards & H. Richey, *The School in the American Social Order* 623-624 (2d ed. 1963). These perceptions of the public schools as inculcating fundamental values necessary to the maintenance of a democratic political system have been confirmed by the observations of social scientists. *See* R. Dawson & K. Prewitt, *Political Socialization* 146-167 (1969); R. Hess & J. Torney, *The Development of Political Attitudes in Children* 114, 158-171, 217-220 (1967); V. Key, *Public Opinion and American Democracy* 323-343 (1961).

Within the public school system, teachers play a critical part in developing students' attitude toward government and understanding of the role of citizens in our society. Alone among employees of the system, teachers are in direct, day-to-day contact with students both in the classrooms and in the other varied activities of a modern school. In shaping the students' experience to achieve educational goals, teachers by necessity have wide discretion over the way the course material is communicated to students. They are responsible for presenting and explaining the subject matter in a way that is both comprehensible and inspiring. No amount of standardization of teaching materials or lesson plans can eliminate the personal qualities a teacher brings to bear in achieving these goals. Further, a teacher serves as a role model for his students, exerting a subtle but important influence over their perceptions and values. Thus, through both the presentation of course materials and the example he sets, a teacher has an opportunity to influence the attitudes of students toward government, the political process, and a citizen's social responsibilities. This influence is crucial to the continued good health of a democracy.

Furthermore, it is clear that all public school teachers, and not just those responsible for teaching the courses most directly related to government, history, and civic duties, should help fulfill the broader function of the public school system. Teachers, regardless of their specialty, may be called upon to teach other subjects, including those expressly dedicated to political and social subjects. More importantly, a State properly may regard all teachers as having an obligation to promote civic virtues and understanding in their classes, regardless of the subject taught. Certainly a State also may take account of a teacher's function as an example for students, which exists independently of particular classroom subjects. In light of the foregoing considerations, we think it clear that public school teachers come well within the "governmental function" principle recognized in *Sugarman* and *Foley*. Accordingly, the Constitution requires only that a citizenship requirement applicable to teaching in the public schools bear a rational relationship to a legitimate state interest. *See Massachusetts Board of Retirement v. Murgia,* 427 U.S. 307, 314 (1976).

III

As the legitimacy of the State's interest in furthering the educational goals outlined above is undoubted, it remains only to consider whether §3001 (3) bears a rational relationship to this interest. The restriction is carefully framed to serve its purpose, as it bars from teaching only those aliens who have demonstrated their unwillingness to obtain United States citizenship. Appellees, and aliens similarly situated, in effect have chosen to classify themselves. They prefer to retain citizenship in a foreign country with the obligations it entails of primary duty and loyalty. They have rejected the open invitation extended to qualify for eligibility to teach by applying for citizenship in this country. The people of New York, acting through their elected representatives, have made a judgment that citizenship should be a qualification for teaching the young of the State in the public schools, and §3001 (3) furthers that judgment.

Reversed.

NOTES AND QUESTIONS

1. The *Ambach* Court emphasizes that public school teachers perform an important governmental function which justifies New York's citizenship requirement. How does the Court define that governmental function?
2. In footnote 6, the Court declares:

> The dissenting opinion of Mr. Justice Blackmun, in reaching an opposite conclusion, appears to apply a different analysis from that employed in our prior decisions. Rather than considering whether public school teachers perform a significant government function, the inquiry mandated by *Foley v. Connelie,* 435 U.S. 291 (1978), and *Sugarman v. Dougall,* the dissent focuses instead on the general societal importance of primary and secondary school teachers both public and private. Thus, the dissent on the one hand depreciates the importance of New York's citizenship requirement because it is not applied to private school teachers, and on the other hand argues that the role teachers perform in our society is no more significant than that filled by attorneys. This misses the point of *Foley* and *Sugarman.* New York's citizenship requirement is limited to a governmental function because it applies only to teachers employed by and acting as agents of the State. The Connecticut statute held unconstitutional in *In re Griffiths,* 413 U.S. 717 (1973), by contrast, applied to all attorneys, most of whom do not work for the government. The exclusion of aliens from access to the bar implicated the right to pursue a chosen occupation, not access to public employment. . . . The distinction between a private occupation and a government function was noted expressly in *Griffiths:*
>
>> Lawyers do indeed occupy professional positions of responsibility and influence that impose on them duties correlative with their vital right of access to the courts. Moreover, by virtue of their professional aptitudes and natural interests, lawyers have been leaders in government throughout the history of our country. Yet, they are not officials of government by virtue of being lawyers.

   Do you accept the majority's distinction between private attorneys and public school teachers? In footnote 15, the Court also found a rational basis for New York's exclusion of aliens from teaching while allowing them to serve on school boards, arguing that "board members teach no classes, and rarely if ever are known or identified by students." Do you agree that teachers serve a different public function than school board officials?
3. In footnote 7, the *Ambach* Court also declares:

> As *San Antonio Independent School Dist. v. Rodriguez* recognized, there is no inconsistency between our recognition of the vital significance of public education and our holding that access to education is not guaranteed by the Constitution. . . . Although private schools also are bound by most of these requirements, the State has a stronger interest in ensuring that the schools it most directly controls, and for which it bears the cost, are as effective as possible in teaching these courses.

   Is there any inconsistency in the *Ambach* Court's particular approval of a citizenship requirement for teachers based on the overriding governmental interest in public education and the absence of a fundamental right to education?

4. The Court, in footnote 9, stresses the power of educators:

> although the findings of scholars who have written on the subject are not conclusive, they generally reinforce the common-sense judgment, and the experience of most of us, that a teacher exerts considerable influence over the development of fundamental social attitudes in students, including those attitudes which in the broadest sense of the term may be viewed as political. *See, e.g.,* R. Dawson & K. Prewitt, *Political Socialization* 158-167 (1969); R. Hess & J. Torney, *The Development of Political Attitudes in Children* 162-163, 217-218 (1967). *Cf.* Note, *Aliens' Right to Teach: Political Socialization and the Public Schools,* 85 Yale L.J. 90, 99-104 (1975).

Yet, in its next footnote, the *Ambach* Court also rejects an appeal to "academic freedom":

> Appellees contend that restriction of an alien's freedom to teach in public schools is contrary to principles of diversity of thought and academic freedom embodied in the First Amendment. We think that the attempt to draw an analogy between choice of citizenship and political expression or freedom of association is wide of the mark, as the argument would bar any effort by the State to promote particular values and attitudes toward government. Section 3001 (3) does not inhibit appellees from expressing freely their political or social views or from associating with whomever they please. Cf. *Givhan v. Western Line Consol. School Dist.,* 439 U.S. 410, 415-416 (1979); *Mt. Healthy City Board of Education v. Doyle,* 429 U.S. 274 (1977); *Pickering v. Board of Education,* 391 U.S. 563 (1968). Nor are appellees discouraged from joining with others to advance particular political ends. Cf. *Shelton v. Tucker,* 364 U.S. 479 (1960). The only asserted liberty of appellees withheld by the New York statute is the opportunity to teach in the State's schools so long as they elect not to become citizens of this country. This is not a liberty that is accorded constitutional protection.

How can the Court's limitations on academic freedom be reconciled with the Court's acceptance of the value of an individual teacher?

2. Racial Discrimination in Teacher Certification and Composition

Title VII of the Civil Rights Act of 1964, 42 U.S.C. §2000e-2, prohibits public school districts from discriminating against any individual with respect to "compensation, terms, conditions, or privileges of employment because of that individual's race. . . ." In establishing a claim that a school district violated Title VII, the employee need not provide direct evidence of intentional discrimination. Rather, the employee may establish a prime facie case of unlawful discrimination by showing: (1) membership in a racial minority; (2) application for a job; (3) rejection, despite qualifications, and (4) after rejection, the position was filled by a nonminority applicant, or was left open. *McDonnell Douglas Corp. v. Green,* 411 U.S. 792 (1973). Once this prime facie case is established, the burden shifts to the school district to "articulate some legitimate, nondiscriminatory reason for the employee's rejection." *Green,* 411 U.S. at 802. *See also Furnco Construction Corp. v. Waters,* 438 U.S. 567 (1978). The articulation of the nondiscriminatory reason for the action may take the form of establishing a "business necessity" for the action or that the action was "related to job performance." *See Griggs v. Duke Power Co.,* 401 U.S. 424 (1971) (rejecting testing of job applicants as a justification for disparate racial impact, unless the tests are "demonstrably a reasonable measure of job performance"). In the Civil Rights Act of 1991, 42 U.S.C. §2000a-z, Congress expressly codified the "business necessity" and job relatedness concepts enunciated in *Griggs*. In that statute, Congress also reaffirmed that Title VII provides private remedies for victims of intentional acts of employment discrimination and for victims of an employer's conduct that has a disparate impact on a protected class of employees. By these standards, a state that uses a teacher examination to qualify and compensate its teachers must attempt to justify any disparate racial impact of that exam by demonstrating that the exam is a "business necessity" or is legitimately related to a teacher's job performance. *See United States v. South Carolina,* 445 F. Supp. 1094 (D.S.C. 1977), *aff'd, NEA v. South Carolina,* 434 U.S. 1026 (1978).

United States v. South Carolina

445 F. Supp. 1094 (D.S.C. 1977)

Judges:

Haynsworth, Chief Circuit Judge, Russell, Circuit Judge and Simons, District Judge.

Opinion:

. . . The United States brought this action on September 15, 1975, against the State of South Carolina, the South Carolina State Board of Education, the South Carolina State Retirement System, the South Carolina Budget and Control Board, and three local school boards in their individual capacities and as representatives of a defendant class of all local school boards in the State. The defendants are charged with violations of the Fourteenth Amendment to the Constitution of the United States and Title VII of the Civil Rights Act of 1964, as amended, 42 U.S.C. §2000e, *et seq.* (1970), through the use of minimum score requirements on the National Teacher Examinations (hereinafter "NTE") to certify and determine the pay levels of teachers within the State. . . .

For over thirty years the State of South Carolina and its agencies have used scores on the NTE to make decisions with respect to the certification of teachers and the amount of state aid payable to local school districts. Local school boards within the State use scores on the NTE for selection and compensation of teachers. From 1969 to 1976, a minimum score of 975 was required by the State for its certification and state aid decisions. In June, 1976, after an exhaustive validation study by Educational Testing Service (ETS), and, after a critical review and evaluation of this study by the Board of Education's Committee on Teacher Recruitment, Training and Compensation and the Department Staff, the State established new certification requirements involving different minimum scores in various areas of teaching specialization that range from 940 to 1198. . . .

The local boards are required by the State to hire only certified teachers . . . , but there are no uniform standards with respect to test scores used by the local school boards in selecting from among the pool of certified applicants.

Plaintiffs challenge each of the uses of the NTE. They contend that more blacks than whites historically have failed to achieve the required minimum score, and that this result creates a racial classification in violation of the constitutional and statutory provisions cited in their complaints. Each complaint seeks declaratory and injunctive relief with respect to the use of the minimum score requirement in certifying and determining the pay levels of teachers, injunctive relief to upgrade the certification levels of teachers adversely affected by the minimum score requirement, and monetary relief for alleged financial losses of teachers, together with costs. . . .

I. Constitutional Issues

We first consider whether the use by the State and its Board of Education of a minimum score requirement on the NTE violates the equal protection clause of the Fourteenth Amendment. . . . Plaintiffs allege that the disparate racial impact of defendants' certification and compensation systems creates a racial classification in violation of the Fourteenth Amendment. In order to sustain that allegation, the Supreme Court's decision in *Washington v. Davis,* 426 U.S. 229 (1976), requires plaintiffs to prove that the State intended to create and use a racial classification. If plaintiffs fail to prove intent (or defendants adequately rebut that proof), then we must evaluate this classification under the rational relationship standard required by the Fourteenth Amendment as to all such classifications.

A. Discriminatory Intent

Because of its paramount importance under *Washington v. Davis,* we look first at whether the plaintiffs have proved that any of the challenged decisions of defendants were motivated by an intent to discriminate. The purpose or intent that we must assess is the purpose or intent that underlies the particular act or acts under review. In its decision in *Village of Arlington Heights v. Metropolitan Housing Development Corp.,* 429 U.S. 252 (1977), the Supreme Court suggested that evidence as to several factors might have probative value in proving intent: historical background, the sequence of events leading up to the challenged decision (including substantive and procedural departures from the norm), legislative history, and testimony from officials. With these factors in mind, we look separately at the defendants' actions with respect to the use of the NTE for certification purposes and those relating to its use for state aid purposes.

1. Certification

South Carolina requires persons who teach in the public schools to hold a certificate issued by the State Board of Education. S.C. Code §21-354. From 1945 to the present the State has had four certification systems, each requiring prospective teachers to take the NTE. Candidates are able to take the NTE an unlimited number of times. (The tests are given by the State three or four times each year.)

The record before us indicates that during this period, the racial composition of the South Carolina teacher force has closely paralleled the racial composition of the State's population. The 1950 census estimated that 61.1% of the population was white and 38.8% was black. In 1953-54, the State employed a teacher force that was 58% white and 42% black. The 1960 census showed a population that was 65.1% white and 34.9% black. In 1966-67, the teacher force was 65.6% white and 34.4% black. The 1970 census showed a population that was 69.5% white and 30.5% black. In 1975-76, the teacher force was 70.1% white and 29.3% black.

From 1945 through 1968, the State issued four grades of certificates: A, B, C and D. From 1945 through 1956, candidates were awarded certificates based on their relative standing with respect to test scores of all candidates in the State for the year: *A* certificates went to the top 25%; *B* certificates to the middle 50%; C certificates to the next 15%; and *D* certificates to the bottom 10%. Under this system, every candidate who met the other requirements was licensed.

In 1957, a new system of absolute, rather than relative, requirements was instituted. Under this system, a score of 500 or more on the Common Examinations portion of the NTE was required for an *A* certificate; a score of 425 to 499 for a *B* certificate; a score of 375 to 424 for a C certificate; and a score of 332 to 374 for a *D* certificate. Those with scores below 332 were not licensed. During the academic year 1967-68, that restriction eliminated less than 1% of the candidates from predominantly white colleges and approximately 3% of the candidates from predominantly black colleges. The reason for these low percentages is that the 332 minimum score, when placed on the NTE score scale of 300 to 900 points, is very near the lowest attainable score.

In 1969, the certification system was further revised by replacing the four-tiered system with two types of certificates: the professional certificate and the warrant. The minimum score requirement was set at 975 for the professional certificate, including a score of at least 450 on the Common Examinations and at least 450 on the applicable Area Examination; and 850 for the warrant, including a score of at least 400 on the Common Examinations and 400 on the applicable Area Examination. Those who attained scores below 400 were not licensed. In the academic year 1969-70, the maximum score requirement of 400 on the Common Examinations eliminated approximately 41% of the graduates of predominantly black colleges and less than 1% of the graduates of predominantly white colleges. Similar results were obtained in succeeding years, despite the fact that a score of 400 is usually below the 11th percentile nationally, and almost 90% of the candidates who take these tests get a higher score.

In 1976, the certification system was again revised, the two-tiered system being replaced with a single certificate with separate minimum score requirements in each of the 18 fields of teaching specialty replacing the single minimum score requirement. These combined scores on both Common Examinations and Area Examinations ranged from 940 in Agriculture to 1178 in Library and Media Specialties; and are set forth in detail hereinafter. There are no statistics in the record indicating the impact of the new score requirements because they will be applied first to the class of 1977; however, plaintiffs predict that, under these requirements, the disparate impact may be even greater.

Plaintiffs have asserted four acts by the State indicating discriminatory intent: (1) The decision in 1945 to institute an NTE requirement; (2) The decision in 1956, effective in 1957, to institute an absolute rather than relative score requirement; (3) The decision in 1969 to revise the absolute score requirement to include the Area Examinations as well as the Common Examinations and raising the previous required scores; and (4) The decision in 1976 to change the single composite score requirement to separate composite score requirements for each teaching field, and in all but one case raising the required scores again. We conclude for the following reasons that such actions by the State were not motivated by an intent to discriminate because of race.

The 1945 decision: In 1941, a committee was appointed by the General Assembly to review the certification and compensation of teachers. The committee recommended that a thorough study of the certification system be made and suggested that the use of an NTE score requirement be explored because of the great variation in teacher training institutions. The State Board undertook a two-year study that resulted in a four-volume report, made available in 1944.

That report recommended four different teacher credentials based on relative NTE scores. On the basis of the report, the State Board adopted the four-tiered system described above under which no candidate was denied licensing. At that time, South Carolina maintained a dual public school system with segregated student bodies and faculties. After the decision to institute the new certification system, but before its effective date, the State Board tested 50% of the teachers in the State, which revealed that 90% of the white teachers, and only 27% of the black teachers, would qualify for *A or B* certificates (the two top grades). The remaining candidates—10% of the whites and 73% of the blacks—would receive C and *D* certificates. After receiving these data, the State Board did not rescind its decision to institute the new certification system.

We are unable to find any discriminatory intent from these facts. Although the historical background of segregated schools might provide some basis for the inference urged by plaintiffs, any such inference has been rebutted. The committee based its recommendation concerning the NTE in part on its conclusion that the tests "can be scored objectively and impartially and their use would not be subject to the accusation that they are used for purposes of discrimination." The Board's extensive study is viewed as an earnest effort in its time, and provided reasonable support for its decision to institute an NTE requirement. The Board's knowledge of differential impact, without more, does not support a finding of discriminatory intent.

The 1956 decision: From 1945 through 1956, the State Board received from ETS statistical summaries of the test scores of South Carolina candidates showing that blacks as a group had lower average scores than whites as a group. In 1954 and 1955, the Supreme Court handed down its historic decisions in *Brown v. Board of Education,* 347 U.S. 483 (1954), 349 U.S. 294 (1955), which announced the end of the "separate but equal" rationale for segregated school systems. South Carolina did not thereafter integrate its schools, but instead adopted policies which maintained its dual school system until well into the 1960's. In 1956, the School Board adopted the absolute score system without a professional study relating the scores to effective teaching or academic achievement in the teacher preparation program.

Again, we find nothing in the record to support a finding of discriminatory intent. Plaintiffs have not persuaded the court that the State's reluctance to integrate its schools infected its decisions on teacher certification. The minimum score requirement of 332 was so low as to preclude us from presuming or even inferring that this was the case. Only 3% of the candidates from black colleges (and 1% of the candidates from white colleges) were denied certificates under this system during the last year it was in effect; and its effect in earlier years was not substantially different. The State Board did not move to change the system when it discovered that very few blacks were excluded, and significantly, this system was maintained for over 11 years.

The 1969 decision: From 1957 through 1969, the State Board continued to receive from ETS statistical data indicating disparate impact by race. During this period, the State continued to maintain its essentially dual school system through a variety of administrative measures. In 1968, the State Board received a report from a committee formed in 1967 to study the certification system. The committee included black and white members who were educators, teachers, state administrators and others. The committee had before it, *inter alia,* two documents, one which was critical of the NTE as a predictor of performance in student teaching, and the other which set out the ETS position that the test scores should not be used as a sole criterion for certification if other measures were available. The committee reviewed the academic programs and admission requirements at the State's 25 teacher training institutions and determined that not all had the same resources and strengths. The committee recommended that the minimum score levels be raised to 975 for professional certificates and 850 for warrants. From the data supplied by ETS, the committee would have been able to predict the impact of its recommendations on black teacher candidates as a group and on white candidates as a group (although it is unclear that such a prediction was ever made). The State Board adopted the committee's recommendations.

We are unable to find any intent to discriminate with respect to this decision. Plaintiffs offer no direct evidence of such an intent, even though one obvious source, the black members of the committee, was apparently available to them. The State's authority to re-define minimal competence from time to time cannot reasonably be questioned.

The 1976 decision: ETS urged that the State validate its cut-off score adopted in 1969. In 1971, ETS issued Guidelines that made its position clear. In the absence of any affirmative response by the State, in 1974 ETS announced its intention to cease the reporting of scores to South Carolina. In 1975, a three-judge court issued an interim decision in the case styled *United States v. North Carolina,* 400 F. Supp. 343, 11 FEP Cases 257 (E.D.N.C. 1975), vacated 425 F. Supp. 789, 14 FEP Cases 971 (E.D.N.C. 1977) which required objective proof by the State of a rational relationship between the minimum score requirement on the NTE and the State's objective of certifying only minimally competent teachers. Shortly thereafter, the State Board authorized an extensive validity study which was conducted by ETS over a period of three months. The results of the study are set out in a two-volume, 300-page report, which was delivered to the State Board in January, 1976. The Board adopted the study report's recommendation that there be separate minimum score requirements by teaching field, and set new higher score levels based on the data produced by the study.

. . . Plaintiffs offer no additional proof with respect to the defendants' alleged intent to discriminate in establishing the new certification requirements in 1976. They apparently rely on the cumulative historical background and the imminence of litigation with regard to the prior system. Even if we had found intent to discriminate with respect to one of the State's earlier decisions, this cumulative history would be without probative value as to the 1976 decision.

While historical circumstances may illuminate the purpose of a particular State action, recent events are far more probative than distant events. With the exception of the 1969 adoption of minimum cutoff scores, the "history" relied on by plaintiffs occurred over 20 years ago. Plaintiffs' elaborate web of historical circumstances, from which the court is being asked to infer discriminatory purpose, is noticeably silent about recent events. Significantly, the cases relied on by the Supreme Court in *Village of Arlington Heights v. Metropolitan Housing Development Corp., supra,* and by plaintiffs in this case (for the proposition that historical circumstances do bear upon invidious purpose) involved events occurring within four years of the state act or decision under review.

With respect to the constitutional challenge to South Carolina's use of the NTE for certification purposes, we conclude that the plaintiffs have not demonstrated the required discriminatory intent with respect to any of the specific decisions setting certification standards based on NTE scores. This is especially true in connection with the State's 1976 change in requirements where there is no indication whatsoever that the State and its officers were motivated by anything more than a desire to use an accepted and racially neutral standardized test to evaluate the teacher applicants competing for relatively few jobs in South Carolina.

The NTE are developed and administered by ETS, an independent nonprofit organization of recognized professional reputation. ETS recommends that minimum score requirements not be used as a sole determinant of certification decisions where other appropriate information or criteria are available.

In this case, the plaintiffs have come forth with no other reasonably appropriate criteria upon which certification may be properly based.

Neither have plaintiffs been able to establish any defect in the NTE indicating that the examinations themselves discriminate on the basis of race. The choices as to subject matter and question format are reasonable and well-documented on the record, and although other subject matters or other examination forms might be possible or even preferable, there is no proof of any inherent discrimination. The inference that plaintiffs would have us draw from the statistics which indicate that blacks as a group have lower average scores than whites is rebutted by the evidence with respect to the construction of the tests and their content validity. Since we find that the NTE create classifications only on permissible bases (presence or absence of knowledge or skill and ability in applying knowledge), and that they are not used pursuant to any intent to discriminate, their use in making certification decisions by the State is proper and legal.

2. Pay Scales

Plaintiffs raise a separate constitutional challenge to South Carolina's use of the NTE as a partial determinant of the salaries paid to public school teachers. The use of the NTE for salary purposes is distinct from, and, in significant ways, unrelated to the use of the NTE for certification purposes. Accordingly, we must again examine plaintiffs' proof with respect to intent.

Public school teachers are hired and paid by local school boards in each of the 92 school districts within the State. Each year since 1942 the Legislature has provided state funds for use by the local school districts in paying teacher salaries. This state aid is provided in accordance with a schedule, enacted into law annually. The schedule is the formula by which the amount of state aid for each school district is calculated. In some districts, teachers are paid only the amount available through state aid. In most districts there is a local supplement. The formula for state aid with respect to each teacher's salary takes into account the number of years of college or post-graduate training, the number of years of teaching experience, and the type of teaching credential held (professional certificate, warrant, or *A, B,* C, or *D* graded certificate).

Plaintiffs challenge the state-aid formula insofar as it uses as one criterion the type of teaching credential and thus, indirectly, NTE scores. Plaintiffs claim that the formula creates a racial classification and was so intended by the State.

In this instance we have approximately 34 separate annual decisions by the Legislature to enact the state aid schedule and to appropriate funds pursuant to that schedule. However, there are two turning points with respect to our inquiry into intent: the decision in 1945 to relate eligibility for state aid to certification requirements and thereby incorporate NTE scores into salary decisions; and the decision in 1969 to retain as a basis for the state aid formula the four-tiered certification system with its built-in NTE score requirements. With respect to each of these decisions, we find as follows:

The 1945 decision . . . We are unable to find a discriminatory intent from these facts, even though the historical background of a dual pay system and a delay in implementing a unitary system after the Fourth Circuit struck down a similar system in another state provide some support for such an inference. Such inference is adequately rebutted by the evidence with respect to what the Legislature actually did. The unitary pay system was based in part on the amount of educational training and years of teaching experience possessed by each teacher. Plaintiffs make no claim that the use of either of these factors was motivated by discriminatory intent, and it is evident that the monetary rewards available through these avenues alone, without regard to the grade of certificate, were significant. The link between the new unitary pay system and the new certification system is not without a reasoned basis. It was important to the State to use its limited resources to improve the quality of the teacher force and to put whatever monetary incentives were available in the salary schedule to that task. As before stated, we have found that no discriminatory intent has been established with respect to the decision in 1945 to adopt a certification system based in part on NTE scores; and, therefore, without independent proof, there is no associated discriminatory intent in linking the certification and salary systems.

The only independent proof offered by plaintiffs is the availability of statistics provided by ETS showing differential performance by race and the presumption that the Legislature knew of this impact when it enacted the salary system. Statistics indicating differential impact are without independent constitutional significance, *Washington v. Davis,* 426 U.S. 229, 242, 12 FEP Cases 1415, 1420, 48 L. Ed. 2d 597, 96 S. Ct. 2040 (1976), therefore knowledge of such statistics is similarly unpersuasive.

The 1969 decision: In July 1969, the State Board replaced the old *A-B-C-D* certificates (prospectively only) with a professional certificate and a warrant. At the same time the Legislature retained the state-aid formula based on the *A-B-C-D* classifications. Holders of professional certificates and warrants were paid at the rates applicable to holders of *A* certificates. Some changes tinkering with the system had been made over the years and was reflected in the system retained in 1969.

From 1945 through 1969, statistical data was made available indicating that the percentage distribution of teachers among the four categories of teaching credentials was not uniform by race. Significant numbers of blacks qualified each year for *A* and *B* certificates, but a relatively higher percentage of blacks were in the C and *D* categories. Similarly, although it could be predicted that significant numbers of blacks would achieve professional certificates, a relatively higher percentage of blacks would hold warrants.

Plaintiffs urge that the Legislature was motivated by an intent to discriminate because the state aid schedule provided fewer benefits and incentives for two classifications of teachers in which there were relatively more blacks than whites; the classifications continued to be based, if only in part, on examination scores; and the developer of the tests was later opposed to their use for this purpose. In the absence of any competent or persuasive direct evidence of intent, plaintiffs would have us draw an inference from the facts that are available. But such an inference can stand only if there is no equally persuasive explanation consistent with a legitimate intent. Here the reordering of priorities with respect to the limited resources available for teacher salaries appears entirely consistent with an intent to obtain the maximum incentive for improvement that could be accomplished with a fixed number of dollars. We are unable to find an intent to discriminate.

B. Application of Rational Relationship Standard

In the absence of discriminatory intent, the classifications of teachers for both certification and pay purposes may be assessed under the "rational relationship" standard required by the Fourteenth Amendment of all classifications. The Supreme Court has defined this standard in the following terms:

> Although no precise formula has been developed, the Court has held that the Fourteenth Amendment permits the States a wide scope of discretion in enacting laws which affect some groups of citizens differently than others. The constitutional safeguard is offended only if the classification rests on grounds wholly irrelevant to the achievement of the State's objective. State legislatures are presumed to have acted within their constitutional power despite the fact that, in practice, their laws result in some inequality. A statutory discrimination will not be set aside if any state of facts reasonably may be conceived to justify it.

We conclude that the State's use of the NTE for both certification and pay purposes meets the "rational relationship" standard . . . and consequently does not violate the equal protection clause of the Fourteenth Amendment. No more rigorous constitutional standard need be applied to a case which does not involve express differentiation by race or other "suspect" classification, and does not involve discriminatory intent. We find however, that were an intermediate standard applied, the defendants' use of the NTE bears a "fair and substantial relationship to the achievement of an important and constitutionally permissible governmental objective." . . .

Nevertheless, we find that the defendants have offered a legitimate and important governmental objective for their use of the NTE. The State has the right to adopt academic requirements and to use written achievement tests designed and validated to disclose the minimum amount of knowledge necessary to effective teaching. . . . The evidence in the record supports a finding that South Carolina officials were concerned with improving the quality of public school teaching, certifying only those applicants possessed of the minimum knowledge necessary to teach effectively, utilizing an objective measure of applicants coming from widely disparate teacher training programs, and providing appropriate financial incentives for teachers to improve their academic qualifications and thereby their ability to teach. We conclude that these are entirely legitimate and clearly important governmental objectives.

In considering whether defendants' use of the NTE bears a fair and substantial relationship to these governmental objectives, we conclude that it does.

The record supports the conclusion that the NTE are professionally and carefully prepared to measure the critical mass of knowledge in academic subject matter. The NTE do not measure teaching skills, but do measure the content of the academic preparation of prospective teachers. . . . Like the test at issue in *Washington v. Davis, supra,* the NTE program "is neutral on its face and rationally may be said to serve a purpose the Government is constitutionally empowered to pursue." Plaintiffs have not contended nor proved that the NTE are racially biased or otherwise deficient when measured against the applicable professional and legal standards.

Furthermore, there is ample evidence in the record of the content validity of the NTE. The NTE have been demonstrated to provide a useful measure of the extent to which prospective teachers have mastered the content of their teacher training programs. In a similar challenge to a bar examination the Fourth Circuit has held that proof of such content validity is persuasive evidence that the equal protection clause has not been violated. *Richardson v. McFadden,* 540 F.2d 744 (4th Cir. 1976). The Supreme Court has held that a substantial relationship between a test and a training program—such as is found here—is sufficient to withstand challenge on constitutional grounds. *Washington v. Davis,* 426 U.S. at 248-52, 12 FEP Cases at 1422-1424. State officials surely have the right to require graduation from approved teacher training programs as a prerequisite to being certified to teach in South Carolina. Plaintiffs have acknowledged the substantial relationship between the academic training program and the job of teaching by advocating that a requirement of graduation from an approved program *alone* is sufficient to protect the public interest. . . .

We also conclude that defendants' use of the NTE for salary purposes bears the necessary relationship to South Carolina's objectives with respect to its public school teaching force. Although the NTE were not designed to evaluate experienced teachers, the State could reasonably conclude that the NTE provided a reliable and economical means for measuring one element of effective teaching—the degree of knowledge possessed by the teacher. Having so concluded, defendants could properly design a classification system relying on NTE scores for compensating teachers and providing incentives for teachers to improve their knowledge in the areas that they teach. . . .

II. Title VII Issues

We turn now to the question whether defendants' uses of the NTE violate Title VII, 42 U.S.C. §2000e, *et seq.* (1970). . . .

In *Washington v. Davis,* 426 U.S. 229 (1976), the Supreme Court summarized the order of proof:

> Under Title VII, Congress provided that when hiring and promotion practices disqualifying substantially disproportionate numbers of blacks are challenged, discriminatory purpose need not be proved, and that it is an insufficient response to demonstrate some rational basis for the challenged practices. It is necessary, in addition, that they be "validated" in terms of job performance in any one of several ways, perhaps by ascertaining the minimum skill, ability or potential necessary for the position at issue and determining whether the qualifying tests are appropriate for the selection of qualified applicants for the job in question.

Thus, it was held not sufficient for the governmental entity to prove that the classification resulting from the test scores had a rational basis, that is, that it differentiated between persons who did and did not have some minimum verbal and communication skill. It was necessary, in addition, for the governmental entity to demonstrate that the minimum verbal and communication skill, in turn, had some rational relationship to the legitimate employment objectives of the employer. And *Washington v. Davis* left intact the holding in *Griggs v. Duke Power Co.,* 401 U.S. 424 (1971), that the employment practice must be a "business necessity."

A. Certification

Plaintiffs have proved that the use of NTE scores by the State in its certification decisions disqualifies substantially disproportionate numbers of blacks. The burden of proof was thereby shifted to the defendants, and in an effort to meet this burden the State commissioned an extensive validity study by ETS. The design of this study is novel, but consistent with the basic requirements enunciated by the Supreme Court, and we accordingly hold such study sufficient to meet the burden placed on defendants under Title VII.

The study seeks to demonstrate content validity by measuring the degree to which the content of the tests matches the content of the teacher training programs in South Carolina. It also seeks to establish a minimum score requirement by estimating the amount of knowledge (measured by the ability to answer correctly test questions that have been content validated) that a minimally qualified teacher candidate in South Carolina would have. . . .

The design of the validity study is adequate for Title VII purposes. The Supreme Court made clear once again in *Washington v. Davis* that a content validity study that satisfies professional standards also satisfies Title VII. . . .

We find that the results of the validity study are sufficiently trustworthy to sustain defendants' burden under Title VII. First, the possible error rate was not high. Second, the key question is not whether some of the panel members failed to understand the instructions or for other reasons failed to follow the instructions, but whether they would have reached any different result if they had understood and followed the instructions. Plaintiffs misconceive their burden once defendants have made a reasonable showing that the study was executed in a responsible, professional manner designed to produce trustworthy results. In order to rebut the presumption that trustworthy results were indeed produced, plaintiffs must not only show that the study was not executed as intended, but also that the results were adversely affected. . . .

In any decision-making process that relies on a standardized test, there is some risk of error. The risk of excluding a truly qualified candidate whose low test score does not reflect his or her real ability can be decreased by lowering the minimum score requirement. That also increases the risk of including an unqualified candidate whose low test score does reflect his or her real ability. The State must weigh many facets of the public interest in making such a decision. If there is a teacher shortage, a relatively high minimum score requirement may mean that some classrooms will be without teachers, and it may be better to provide a less than fully competent teacher than no teacher at all. But to the extent that children are exposed to incompetent teachers, education suffers. It may be that education suffers less than would be the case if classrooms were overcrowded due to lack of teachers. We think it is within the prerogative of the State to accept some unqualified teachers under circumstances where that is judged by the State to be on balance in the public interest, and that such an action by the State is not a violation of Title VII.

There remains, however, the question whether the State has satisfied the "business necessity" requirement set out in *Griggs v. Duke Power Co.*, 401 U.S. 424 (1971). This "business necessity" doctrine appears neither in the explicit language nor the legislative history of Title VII. The Court in *Griggs* and subsequent Title VII cases did not establish judicial standards for determining whether a particular practice is a business necessity. The EEOC Guidelines are of little assistance because they were published before *Griggs* and have not been updated since that time. . . .

It is our view that the Supreme Court intended an examination of the alternatives available with respect to the legitimate employment objective identified by the employer to determine whether there is available to the employer an alternative practice that would achieve his business purpose equally well but with a lesser disparate impact by race. In examining alternatives, the risk and cost to the employer are relevant.

Here, plaintiffs have suggested only one alternative to the use of the NTE for certification purposes. Plaintiffs contend that mere graduation from an approved program should be sufficient and would have a lesser disparate impact on blacks. We cannot find that this alternative will achieve the State's purpose in certifying minimally competent persons equally well as the use of a content-validated standardized test. The record amply demonstrates that there are variations in admissions requirements, academic standards and grading practices at the various teacher training institutions within the State. The approval that the State gives to the teacher training program is to general subject matter areas covered by the program, not to the actual course content of the program, and not to the means used within the program to measure whether individual students have actually mastered the course content to which they have been exposed. The standardized test scores do reflect individual achievement with respect to specific subject matter content, which is directly relevant to (although not sufficient in itself to assure) competence to teach, and thus the use of these scores for certification purposes survives the business necessity test under Title VII.

B. Pay Scales

There remains, finally, the question whether the uses of the NTE for salary purposes are a violation of Title VII. Where the salary system was linked to the certification system, some salary benefits were available only by improving the grade of the certificate; and that, in turn, could be done only by achieving certain minimum NTE scores. That system continued in effect after March 24, 1972, when Title VII was made applicable to states, and in 1976, the distribution of teachers within the four grades of the pay scale system showed a substantial disparate impact by race. A higher proportion of whites (98%) were classified in the two higher grades *(A* and *B)* and a higher proportion of blacks (51%) were classified in the lower grades (C and *D)*. By such showing plaintiffs have satisfied their burden of proof under Title VII to shift the burden of proof to the defendants to show a rational relationship to a legitimate employment objective and to show business necessity. The State identifies its legitimate employment objective as providing an incentive for improvement, so that teachers without adequate knowledge to teach effectively will upgrade their capability; and the State offers the same evidence of a rational relationship between its pay scales and this objective as it did with respect to the constitutional challenges. We think that evidence is sufficient to establish the relationship.

We believe that a distinction for pay purposes between those who are qualified as well as between those who are not qualified survives the business necessity test. There appears to be no alternative available to the State, within reasonable limits of risk and cost, for providing the incentive necessary to motivate thousands of persons to acquire, generally on their own time and at their own expense, the necessary additional academic training so that they will be minimally competent teachers. Having made the investment of four years in an undergraduate education, it seems reasonable to try to upgrade the talent of unqualified teachers where possible, rather than rejecting them altogether.

In accordance with the foregoing findings and conclusions, we conclude that plaintiff and plaintiff-intervenors have failed to establish their right to any of the relief sought in their respective complaints. It is, therefore, ORDERED that judgment be entered in favor of the defendants.

NOTES AND QUESTIONS

1. The *South Carolina* decision demonstrates a critical distinction between equal protection analysis and Title VII analysis. Under the equal protection clause, the plaintiffs had the burden of proving that the state *intentionally* employed its testing regime to exclude or disadvantage teachers based on their race. Under Title VII, by contrast, plaintiffs were able to meet their initial evidentiary burden by demonstrating that the state's testing regime had the *effect* of excluding or disadvantaging teachers based on their race. In justifying the disparate impact of its testing and wage policies, however, the state was able to show a legitimate interest in assessing the "degree of knowledge possessed by the teacher" served by the tests. Under what circumstances would a standardized test used to measure teacher competence not be rationally related to the state's interest in maintaining a competent teaching staff?
2. The courts also have been reluctant to invalidate standardized tests of *students* on the ground that such tests discriminate on the basis of race. In *Debra P. v. Turlington,* 644 F.2d 397 (5th Cir. 1981), the Fifth Circuit indicated that Florida's requirement that high school students pass the state's literacy test in order to obtain their diploma would violate the equal protection clause unless the state could establish: (1) the instructional validity of the test, and (2) that the test does not perpetuate the effects of past racial discrimination in education. On remand, the state was able to make both showings. First, the state demonstrated the validity of the test by showing that it was a "fair" measure of what was actually taught in the public schools. Second, the state convinced the court that the test could be used as a diagnostic tool to identify those students who need additional instruction and to help remove the vestiges of racial discrimination. *Debra P. v. Turlington,* 564 F. Supp. 177 (M.D. Fla. 1983). Although the state ultimately prevailed, the *Debra P.* litigation indicates that schools which use tests to measure student or teacher competence must be prepared to defend the validity of those tests. Recall the critique of standardized testing by Alfie Kohn and others set forth in Chapter 2 and Chapter 9. Does that critique apply to a state's use of such tests to screen teachers?

3. As *South Carolina* suggests, proof that a school district has discriminated against its current or prospective teachers based on race may take the form of complex statistical comparisons. In *Hazelwood School District v. United States,* 433 U.S. 299 (1977), the United States government claimed that Hazelwood School District in St. Louis, Missouri was engaged in a "pattern or practice" of employment discrimination in violation of Title VII. The government mounted its "pattern or practice" attack by adducing evidence of: (1) a history of alleged racially discriminatory practices, (2) statistical disparities in hiring, (3) standardless and largely subjective hiring procedures, and (4) specific instances of alleged discrimination against 55 unsuccessful African-American applicants for teaching jobs. In particular, the government demonstrated a statistical disparity between the number of African-American teachers in Hazelwood and the number of African-American teachers in the relevant labor market area. Selecting St. Louis County and St. Louis City as the relevant area, the government showed that 15.4 percent of teachers in that area were African-American while only 1.4 percent of Hazelwood's teachers were African-American. On review, the Supreme Court first made clear that statistical evidence could form the basis of a Title VII claim:

> This Court's recent consideration in *Teamsters v. United States,* 431 U.S. 324 (1977), of the role of statistics in pattern-or-practice suits under Title VII provides substantial guidance in evaluating the arguments advanced by the petitioners. In that case we stated that it is the Government's burden to "establish by a preponderance of the evidence that racial discrimination was the [employer's] standard operating procedure—the regular rather than the unusual practice." We also noted that statistics can be an important source of proof in employment discrimination cases, since "absent explanation, it is ordinarily to be expected that nondiscriminatory hiring practices will in time result in a work force more or less representative of the racial and ethnic composition of the population in the community from which employees are hired. Evidence of long lasting and gross disparity between the composition of a work force and that of the general population thus may be significant even though . . . Title VII imposes no requirement that a work force mirror the general population." . . . Where gross statistical disparities can be shown, they alone may in a proper case constitute prima facie proof of a pattern or practice of discrimination. . . .

Nonetheless, in remanding the action for further factual findings, the Supreme Court in *Hazelwood* also rejected the relevance of any statistical comparison between the racial composition of a teaching staff and the racial composition of the student population. Furthermore, the Court directed the district court to determine the "relevant labor market area" before making any valid statistical findings comparing the racial composition of the applicant pool with the racial composition of the teaching staff. Why does a gross disparity between the racial composition of the student population and the racial composition of the teaching staff not provide strong evidence of racial discrimination in the hiring and retention of teachers?

4. In *Wygant v. Board of Education,* 476 U.S. 267 (1986), the Supreme Court declared unconstitutional a school district's attempt to provide role models

for minority students and to alleviate the effects of societal discrimination by implementing a collective bargaining agreement provision that gave preferential layoff protection to minority teachers over more senior nonminority teachers. The Court concluded that the interest in providing minority teachers as role models for minority students could not justify the racial classification, and thus violated the equal protection clause. The Court distinguished *Hazelwood* on the ground that *Hazelwood* involved a proper comparison between the racial composition of the district's teachers with the applicant pool, while *Wygant* involved an improper comparison between the racial composition of the district's teachers and its students. Do you agree with *Wygant's* apparent rejection of a district's interest in matching the percentage of minority teachers with the percentage of minority students in order to create effective role models?

5. Although *Wygant* involved the equal protection clause, the Third Circuit in *Taxman v. Board of Education of Piscataway,* 91 F.3d 1547 (3d Cir. 1996) reached a similar result under Title VII. In that case, the school district decided to lay off a nonminority teacher rather than a minority teacher of equal seniority in order to maintain its racially balanced work force. The district's purpose in retaining the minority teacher was not to remedy the effects of prior employment discrimination; rather its "sole purpose" was to obtain the "educational benefit which it believed would result from a racially diverse faculty." The court held that the district's actions violated Title VII because its racial classification was not intended to remedy past discrimination or a manifest imbalance in its minority employment. *See also Britton v. South Bend Community School,* 819 F.2d 766 (7th Cir. 1987) (striking down collective bargaining agreement provision giving minority teachers preference over nonminorities in any reduction in force because it was not justified by goal of remedying past discrimination).
6. What do *Hazelwood, Wygant* and *Ambach* suggest about the value of a diverse teaching staff? *Ambach* stresses that teachers perform a governmental function that is different from ordinary employees. Yet *Wygant* and *Hazelwood* seem to focus entirely on teachers as employees, not as key role models or participants in a diverse marketplace of ideas. If the state may control the composition of its teaching staff and preclude noncitizens in order to insure that its students receive the value of democratic citizenship, why should the state not also be permitted to control the composition of its teaching staff and achieve racial diversity to insure that its students receive the value of diversity in a democracy?

3. Discrimination Against Teachers Based on Age and Disability

(a) Age

In *Ambach,* the Supreme Court relied upon *Massachusetts Board of Retirement v. Murgia,* 427 U.S. 307 (1976), which held that a Massachusetts law providing that a state police officer "shall be retired . . . upon his attaining age fifty," does not deny the police officer equal protection. After finding that the law should not be given strict judicial scrutiny because it neither denied officers a fundamental right nor involved a "discrete and insular group in need of extraordinary protection from the majoritarian political process," citing *United States v. Carolene Products Co.,* 304 U.S. 144, 152-153 n.4 (1938), the Court proceeded to find that the Massachusetts statute clearly meets the requirements of the equal protection clause:

> The State's classification rationally furthers the purpose identified by the State: through mandatory retirement at age 50, the legislature seeks to protect the public by assuring physical preparedness of its uniformed police. Since physical ability generally declines with age, mandatory retirement at 50 serves to remove from police service those whose fitness for uniformed work presumptively has diminished with age. This clearly is rationally related to the State's objective. . . .
>
> That the state chooses not to determine fitness more precisely through individualized testing after age 50 is not to say that the objective of assuring physical fitness is not rationally furthered by a maximum-age limitation. It is only to say that with regard to the interest of all concerned, the state perhaps has not chosen the best means to accomplish this purpose. But where rationality is the test, a state "does not violate the Equal Protection Clause merely because the classifications made by its laws are imperfect." *See also Vance v. Bradley,* 440 U.S. 93 (1979) (mandatory retirement age of 60 for foreign service workers upheld as rationally related to interests in high performance, promotion opportunities).

In its Age Discrimination in Employment Act, 29 U.S.C. §621 *et seq.,* Congress prohibits employers from adverse job action against individuals who are at least 40 years of age "because of . . . age." Claims of age discrimination are analyzed in accordance with the burden-shifting construct established in *McDonnell Douglas Corp. v. Green,* 411 U.S. 792 (1973), but the plaintiff need not show that he or she was replaced by someone younger than 40 so long as the new employee is "sufficiently younger" to establish an inference of age discrimination. *O'Connor v. Consolidated Coin Caterers Corp.,* 517 U.S. 308 (1996). The Act also provides that employers may defend any claim of age discrimination in employment by showing that, "age is a bone fide occupational qualification reasonably necessary to the essential operations of the particular job or business," or that the employer has a "factual basis" for believing that age is an indicator of the ability to perform a job safely. *See Western Airlines, Inc. v. Criswell,* 472 U.S. 400 (1985); *Coupe v. Federal Express Corp., 121* F.3d 1022 (6th Cir. 1997). Accordingly, where a school district provides a factual basis for believing that employees over a certain age are generally unable to perform safely, and that it would be impractical to test each such employee individually, the district may be able to justify a categorical age restriction. *Id.* A school district may not impose such a blanket age rule, however, if the district is able to engage in an individual evaluation of each employee without an undue burden. *See, e.g., Tullis v. Lear School, Inc.,* 874 F.2d 1489 (11th Cir. 1989). Moreover, a school may be liable for age discrimination if it engages in a "reduction in force" that results in the replacement of employees over 40 years of age with "younger" employees. *See, e.g., Showalter v. University of Pittsburgh,* 190 F.3d 231, 234 (3d Cir. 1999) (indicating that replacing older employees with employees who are eight years younger could support claim for age discrimination).

Based on *Murgia,* or the Age Discrimination Act, could a school district terminate all teachers over 40 years of age, arguing that its differentiation is not based on age, but on its financial interest in hiring *cheaper* teachers (who happen to be less senior) to take their place? Suppose the district were to create a retirement incentive for its teachers over the age of 40 that had the purpose and effect of inducing a large percentage of such teachers to elect retirement? Again, the district would attempt to justify its retirement package by the cost savings that would result by replacing the higher paid senior teachers with lower paid junior teachers. How would the courts analyze a claim that such a retirement program discriminates based on age? The courts seem to be willing to uphold such retirement incentives where they provide employees with a *real* choice in deciding whether to elect retirement. *See, e.g., Shager v. Upjohn Co.,* 913 F.2d 398 (7th Cir. 1990); *Christopher v. Mobil Oil Corp.,* 950 F.2d 1209 (5th Cir. 1992).

(b) Disability

As discussed in the context of student rights, Congress has passed two central provisions that protect individuals from discrimination based on an actual or perceived disability. First, section 504 of the Vocational Rehabilitation Act of 1973 prohibits employers who receive federal funds from denying to "otherwise qualified handicapped individuals" employment or employment benefits "solely by reason of handicap." Case law interpreting this provision indicates that a school district or university that receives federal funds may not discriminate against any of its employees because of their "handicap" where those employees are able with reasonable (i.e., without an undue administrative or financial burden) accommodation to perform the essential functions of the position. *See, e.g., School Board of Nassau County v. Arline,* 480 U.S. 273 (1987) (teacher with tuberculosis was "handicapped" employee protected by §504 so long as employee can perform essential job functions with reasonable accommodation); *Wood v. Omaha School District,* 25 F.3d 667 (8th Cir. 1994) (diabetic school bus driver could not be reasonably accommodated in existing job without undue financial burden); *Chalk v. United States District Court,* 840 F.2d 701 (9th Cir. 1988) (school district cannot justify its removal of a teacher with AIDS based on the fear of parents).

Second, Congress has enacted the Americans with Disabilities Act of 1990, 42 U.S.C. §12101 *et seq.* (the ADA), which prohibits all public and private educational institutions with at least 15 employees from discriminating against any employee because of that employee's disability. The ADA defines "disability" to include any "physical or mental impairment that substantially limits one or more of the major life activities." 42 U.S.C. §12102(2)(A). The Supreme Court has suggested that a qualifying impairment under the ADA is one that alters the employee's nonworkplace life tasks such as mobility, vision and hearing. *Toyota Motor Manufacturing, Inc. v. Williams,* 534 U.S. 184 (2002) (although employee with "carpal tunnel syndrome" may be impaired in performing job functions, that impairment does not necessarily alter major life functions). By analogy to the judicial interpretations of §504, the ADA thus prohibits educational institutions from refusing to make reasonable accommodation for their employees who suffer from an impairment that substantially limits a major life function.

In *Pandazides v. Virginia Board of Education,* 946 F.2d 345 (4th Cir. 1991), for example, the court reached the question of whether federal law requires a state board of education to accommodate a teacher with a learning disability. In that case, Pandazides, who suffers from "several learning disabilities," sued the state board alleging handicap discrimination under §504. Pandazides was an applicant for a professional teacher certification in Virginia. Virginia requires that prospective teachers pass the National Teachers' Examination ("NTE") Core Battery test and any appropriate specialty area test of the NTE. The core test at issue contains three components: general knowledge, professional knowledge, and communication skills. Pandazides took and failed the communications skills portion of the NTE six times. She adduced evidence that she suffers from three types of "learning disabilities" which prevented her from passing the test.

In concluding that the trial court erred in rejecting Pandazides' §504 claim, the Fourth Circuit reasoned:

> The trial court held, in effect, that because Pandazides was unable to pass the test that she was not otherwise qualified. . . . [D]efendants cannot merely mechanically invoke any set of requirements and pronounce the handicapped applicant or prospective employee not otherwise qualified. The district court must look behind the qualifications. To do otherwise reduces the term "otherwise qualified" and any arbitrary set of requirements to a tautology. . . . As a consequence, a determination of whether Pandazides is otherwise qualified involves two factual determinations: first, whether she can perform the "essential functions" of a school teacher; and second, whether the requirements actually measure those functions. Even if the trial court were to determine that she could not perform her duties, it would also have to determine whether or not modifications could be made to allow Pandazides to teach. . . . A review of the district court opinion reveals that in the wake of its conclusion that Pandazides was not otherwise qualified, no factual determinations were made as to whether the NTE requirements represented the essential functions of the job, whether she could perform the essential functions of the position, and whether a test waiver was a reasonable accommodation. Consequently, there are many material facts in dispute and unaddressed by the opinion.

On remand, how would Pandazides demonstrate that she is otherwise "qualified" to teach despite her learning disabilities? How would the board of education demonstrate that her disabilities prevented her from performing the essential functions of teaching, and that such disabilities could not be reasonably accommodated?

4. Gender Discrimination and Sexual Harassment

Chapter 12 addressed the issue of gender discrimination and sexual harassment of students. In this section, these issues reappear in the specific context of school district *employment* decisions that treat educational professionals differently because of their gender. In this employment context, the constitution's equal protection clause prohibits public school districts from intentional discrimination against, or harassment of, teachers because of their gender. *See, e.g., Bohen v. City of East Chicago, 799* F.2d 1180 (7th Cir. 1986) (intentional acts of sexual harassment against women in the workplace because of their gender violates the equal protection clause); *Trautvetter v. Quick,* 916 F.2d 1140 (7th Cir. 1990) (intentional discrimination, including harassment against teachers because of their gender, could be actionable under the equal protection clause).

The equal protection clause's prohibitions against intentional gender discrimination in public employment are supplemented by federal statutory prohibitions. The Equal Pay Act, 29 U.S.C. §206(d)(1), for instance, prohibits employers, including school districts, from paying female employees less wages than male employees for work requiring equal skill, effort and responsibility under similar working conditions. *See, e.g., Buntin v. Breathitt County Board of Education,* 134 F.3d 796 (6th Cir. 1998). The Act, however, permits school districts to pay different wages for reasons other than gender, including merit and seniority. 29 U.S.C. §206(d)(1). *See also* 42 U.S.C. §2000e-2(h) (Title VII of the Civil Rights Act of 1964 now incorporates the Equal Pay Act provisions); *Corning Glass Works v. Brennan,* 417 U.S. 188 (1974); *Stanley v. University of Southern Calif.,* 13 F.3d 1313 (9th Cir. 1994).

The prohibitions of Title IX of the Education Amendments of 1972, 20 U.S.C. §1681, against discrimination based on sex in any educational program or activity also apply to employment discrimination. *See North Haven Board of Education v. Bell,* 456 U.S. 512 (1982) ("employment discrimination comes within the prohibition of Title IX"). Under Title IX, a teacher victimized by employment discrimination based on gender may bring a private right of action for damages. *Franklin v. Gwinnett County Public Schools,* 503 U.S. 60 (1992). In order to prevail, however, the teacher must establish that the school district had actual knowledge of the discriminatory conduct and evidenced a "deliberate indifference" to that conduct. *Gebser v. Lago Vista Independent School District,* 524 U.S. 274 (1998). Although the federal courts have held that Title IX does not create a private right of action against a school for retaliating against employees who complain about gender discrimination, the Supreme Court has indicated its intent to consider that issue. *See Jackson v. Birmingham Board of Education,* 309 F.3d 1333 (11th Cir. 2002), *cert. granted,* 124. S. Ct. 2834 (2004).

Perhaps the most significant source of protection for teachers from gender discrimination and sexual harassment in employment, however, remains Title VII of the Civil Rights Act of 1964, 42 U.S.C. §2000e-2(h), and the regulations promulgated by the Equal Employment Opportunity Commission (EEOC) pursuant to its authority under Title VII. The statute makes it unlawful for a school district employer "to discriminate against any individual . . . because of such individual's . . . sex. . . ." Under *McDonnell Douglas Corp. v. Green,* 411 U.S. 792, 802 (1973), the Title VII plaintiff must first show that he or she: (1) is a member of a protected class; (2) applied, and was qualified for, a position; (3) was rejected despite being qualified, and (4) the position remained open.

Once the plaintiff makes this prime facie showing, the burden of proof then shifts to the school district to establish a legitimate, nondiscriminatory reason for its conduct. *See, e.g., Spears v. Board of Education of Pike County, Ky.,* 843 F.2d 882 (6th Cir. 1988). Ultimately, the burden of proof remains with the teacher to establish that the district's employment decision was made "because of" the teacher's "sex." Yet, the teacher need not prove the "precise causal role" played by illegitimate motives in any employment decision. Rather, the teacher may prevail by proving that the district relied on *any* "sex based consideration in coming to its decision," including impermissible stereotypes. *Price Waterhouse v. Hopkins,* 490 U.S. 228 (1989).

Because Title VII precludes employers from relying on any "sex based considerations," school districts and universities may not offer better or cheaper health, disability, pension or retirement benefits to men because of any real or perceived differences between men and women. *Los Angeles Dept. of Water & Power v. Manhart,* 435 U.S. 702 (1978). Nor may such employers discriminate against woman because of any condition related to pregnancy, childbirth or abortion. *See* 42 U.S.C. §2000e(k); *Turic v. Holland Hospitality, Inc.,* 85 F.3d 1211 (6th Cir. 1996).

Title VII and the EEOC regulations also prohibit sexual harassment in employment as an aspect of discrimination "on the basis of sex." 29 C.F.R §1604.11(a). The EEOC regulations expressly define prohibited sexual harassment as: "[u]nwelcome sexual advances, requests for sexual favors, and other verbal *or* physical conduct of a sexual nature," *when* (1) submission to such conduct is made explicitly or implicitly a term or condition of an individual's employment; (2) submission to or rejection of such conduct by an individual is used as a basis for employment decisions affecting such individual; or (3) such conduct has the purpose or effect of unreasonably interfering with an individual's work performance or creating an intimidating, hostile or offensive working environment. 29 C.F.R. §1604.11(a).

In *Meritor Savings Bank v. Vinson,* 477 U.S. 57 (1986), the Supreme Court interpreted these guidelines to prohibit two different types of sexual harassment. First, Title VII prohibits employers with power and control over a subordinate from inducing that subordinate to engage in sexual activity in return for employment benefits. As *Meritor* makes clear, however, Title VII not only prohibits this so-called *quid pro quo* discrimination, it also prohibits an employer's conduct, through its supervisors and agents, that has the purpose or effect of creating a "hostile" working environment. *See* 29 U.S.C. §1604.11(c). A work environment will be found to be "hostile" where that environment is reasonably "perceived" to be hostile based on factors such as the severity of the conduct, the pervasive nature of the conduct and the interference with working conditions. *See Pennsylvania State Police v. Suders,* 124 S. Ct. 2342 (2004). An environment may be "hostile" even if no employee has been injured (economically or psychologically) by any specific conduct by the employer or its agents. *Harris v. Forklift Systems,* 510 U.S. 17 (1993).

In the companion cases of *Burlington Industries, Inc. v. Ellerth,* 524 U.S. 742 (1998), and *Faragher v. City of Boca Raton,* 524 U.S. 775 (1998), the Supreme Court reviewed the law governing sexual harassment in the workplace. The Court makes clear that an employee who refuses a supervisor's unwelcome and threatening sexual advance, but suffers no tangible job consequence, may nonetheless establish a violation of Title VII. The Court reaffirms that an employer may be strictly liable for the harassment of its supervisor that "culminates in a tangible employment action, such as discharge, demotion, or undesirable reassignment." *Ellerth,* 524 U.S. at 765. Yet, the Court also held that an employer may be liable for the conduct of its subordinate in creating a hostile work environment, even where no tangible employment action is taken. These cases, however, also create an affirmative defense in hostile environment cases. That defense allows an employer such as a university to escape liability by proving by a preponderance of the evidence that the employer used reasonable care to prevent and correct sexual harassment in the work environment, and that the plaintiff unreasonably failed to take advantage of any preventive or corrective opportunities provided by the employer.

Burlington Industries, Inc. v. Ellerth

524 U.S. 742 (1998)

Justice Kennedy delivered the opinion of the Court.

We decide whether, under Title VII of the Civil Rights Act of 1964, 78 Stat. 253, as amended, 42 U.S.C. §2000e et seq., an employee who refuses the unwelcome and threatening sexual advances of a supervisor, yet suffers no adverse, tangible job consequences, can recover against the employer without showing the employer is negligent or otherwise at fault for the supervisor's actions.

I

Summary judgment was granted for the employer, so we must take the facts alleged by the employee to be true. The employer is Burlington Industries, the petitioner. The employee is Kimberly Ellerth, the respondent. From March 1993 until May 1994, Ellerth worked as a salesperson in one of Burlington's divisions in Chicago, Illinois. During her employment, she alleges, she was subjected to constant sexual harassment by her supervisor, one Ted Slowik.

In the hierarchy of Burlington's management structure, Slowik was a mid-level manager. Burlington has eight divisions, employing more than 22,000 people in some 50 plants around the United States. Slowik was a vice president in one of five business units within one of the divisions. He had authority to make hiring and promotion decisions subject to the approval of his supervisor, who signed the paperwork. According to Slowik's supervisor, his position was "not considered an upper-level management position," and he was "not amongst the decision-making or policy-making hierarchy." *Ibid.* Slowik was not Ellerth's immediate supervisor. Ellerth worked in a two-person office in Chicago, and she answered to her office colleague, who in turn answered to Slowik in New York.

Against a background of repeated boorish and offensive remarks and gestures which Slowik allegedly made, Ellerth places particular emphasis on three alleged incidents where Slowik's comments could be construed as threats to deny her tangible job benefits. In the summer of 1993, while on a business trip, Slowik invited Ellerth to the hotel lounge, an invitation Ellerth felt compelled to accept because Slowik was her boss. When Ellerth gave no encouragement to remarks Slowik made about her breasts, he told her to "loosen up" and warned, "you know, Kim, I could make your life very hard or very easy at Burlington."

In March 1994, when Ellerth was being considered for a promotion, Slowik expressed reservations during the promotion interview because she was not "loose enough." The comment was followed by his reaching over and rubbing her knee. Ellerth did receive the promotion; but when Slowik called to announce it, he told Ellerth, "you're gonna be out there with men who work in factories, and they certainly like women with pretty butts/legs."

In May 1994, Ellerth called Slowik, asking permission to insert a customer's logo into a fabric sample. Slowik responded, "I don't have time for you right now, Kim—unless you want to tell me what you're wearing." Ellerth told Slowik she had to go and ended the call. A day or two later, Ellerth called Slowik to ask permission again. This time he denied her request, but added something along the lines of, "are you wearing shorter skirts yet, Kim, because it would make your job a whole heck of a lot easier."

A short time later, Ellerth's immediate supervisor cautioned her about returning telephone calls to customers in a prompt fashion. In response, Ellerth quit. She faxed a letter giving reasons unrelated to the alleged sexual harassment we have described. About three weeks later, however, she sent a letter explaining she quit because of Slowik's behavior.

During her tenure at Burlington, Ellerth did not inform anyone in authority about Slowik's conduct, despite knowing Burlington had a policy against sexual harassment. *Ibid.* In fact, she chose not to inform her immediate supervisor (not Slowik) because "it would be his duty as my supervisor to report any incidents of sexual harassment." On one occasion, she told Slowik a comment he made was inappropriate. *Ibid.*

In October 1994, after receiving a right-to-sue letter from the Equal Employment Opportunity Commission (EEOC), Ellerth filed suit in the United States District Court for the Northern District of Illinois, alleging Burlington engaged in sexual harassment and forced her constructive discharge, in violation of Title VII. . . .

II

At the outset, we assume an important proposition yet to be established before a trier of fact. It is a premise assumed as well, in explicit or implicit terms, in the various opinions by the judges of the Court of Appeals. The premise is: a trier of fact could find in Slowik's remarks numerous threats to retaliate against Ellerth if she denied some sexual liberties. The threats, however, were not carried out or fulfilled. Cases based on threats which are carried out are referred to often as *quid pro quo* cases, as distinct from bothersome attentions or sexual remarks that are sufficiently severe or pervasive to create a hostile work environment. The terms *quid pro quo* and hostile work environment are helpful, perhaps, in making a rough demarcation between cases in which threats are carried out and those where they are not or are absent altogether, but beyond this are of limited utility.

Section 703(a) of Title VII forbids "an employer—" (1) to fail or refuse to hire or to discharge any individual, or otherwise to discriminate against any individual with respect to his compensation, terms, conditions or privileges of employment, because of such individual's . . . sex." 42 U.S.C. §2000e-2(a)(1).

"Quid pro quo" and "hostile work environment" do not appear in the statutory text. The terms appeared first in the academic literature, *see* C. MacKinnon, *Sexual Harassment of Working Women* (1979); found their way into decisions of the Courts of Appeals, *see, e.g., Henson v. Dundee,* 682 F.2d 897, 909 (CA11 1982); and were mentioned in this Court's decision in *Meritor Savings Bank, FSB v. Vinson, 477* U.S. 57, 91 L. Ed. 2d 49, 106 S. Ct. 2399 (1986). *See generally* E. Scalia, *The Strange Career* of Quid Pro Quo *Sexual Harassment,* 21 Harv. J. L. & Pub. Policy 307 (1998).

In *Meritor,* the terms served a specific and limited purpose. There we considered whether the conduct in question constituted discrimination in the terms or conditions of employment in violation of Title VII. We assumed, and with adequate reason, that if an employer demanded sexual favors from an employee in return for a job benefit, discrimination with respect to terms or conditions of employment was explicit. Less obvious was whether an employer's sexually demeaning behavior altered terms or conditions of employment in violation of Title VII. We distinguished between *quid pro quo* claims and hostile environment claims, and said both were cognizable under Title VII, though the latter requires harassment that is severe or pervasive. The principal significance of the distinction is to instruct that Title VII is violated by either explicit or constructive alterations in the terms or conditions of employment and to explain the latter must be severe or pervasive. The distinction was not discussed for its bearing upon an employer's liability for an employee's discrimination. On this question *Meritor* held, with no further specifics, that agency principles controlled. . . .

We do not suggest the terms *quid pro quo* and hostile work environment are irrelevant to Title VII litigation. To the extent they illustrate the distinction between cases involving a threat which is carried out and offensive conduct in general, the terms are relevant when there is a threshold question whether a plaintiff can prove discrimination in violation of Title VII. When a plaintiff proves that a tangible employment action resulted from a refusal to submit to a supervisor's sexual demands, he or she establishes that the employment decision itself constitutes a change in the terms and conditions of employment that is actionable under Title VII. For any sexual harassment preceding the employment decision to be actionable, however, the conduct must be severe or pervasive. Because Ellerth's claim involves only unfulfilled threats, it should be categorized as a hostile work environment claim which requires a showing of severe or pervasive conduct. . . . [W]e accept the District Court's finding that the alleged conduct was severe or pervasive. The case before us involves numerous alleged threats, and we express no opinion as to whether a single unfulfilled threat is sufficient to constitute discrimination in the terms or conditions of employment.

When we assume discrimination can be proved, however, the factors we discuss below, and not the categories *quid pro quo* and hostile work environment, will be controlling on the issue of vicarious liability. That is the question we must resolve.

III

We must decide, then, whether an employer has vicarious liability when a supervisor creates a hostile work environment by making explicit threats to alter a subordinate's terms or conditions of employment, based on sex, but does not fulfill the threat. We turn to principles of agency law, for the term "employer" is defined under Title VII to include "agents." 42 U.S.C. §2000e(b). In express terms, Congress has directed federal courts to interpret Title VII based on agency principles. Given such an explicit instruction, we conclude a uniform and predictable standard must be established as a matter of federal law. . . .

Although *Meritor* suggested the limitation on employer liability stemmed from agency principles, the Court acknowledged other considerations might be relevant as well. *See,* 477 U.S. at 72 ("common-law principles may not be transferable in all their particulars to Title VII"). For example, Title VII is designed to encourage the creation of antiharassment policies and effective grievance mechanisms. . . . To the extent limiting employer liability could encourage employees to report harassing conduct before it becomes severe or pervasive, it would also serve Title VII's deterrent purpose. As we have observed, Title VII borrows from tort law the avoidable consequences doctrine, and the considerations which animate that doctrine would also support the limitation of employer liability in certain circumstances.

In order to accommodate the agency principles of vicarious liability for harm caused by misuse of supervisory authority, as well as Title VII's equally basic policies of encouraging forethought by employers and saving action by objecting employees, we adopt the following holding in this case and in *Faragher v. Boca Raton,* also decided today. An employer is subject to vicarious liability to a victimized employee for an actionable hostile environment created by a supervisor with immediate (or successively higher) authority over the employee. When no tangible employment action is taken, a defending employer may raise an affirmative defense to liability or damages, subject to proof by a preponderance of the evidence, *see* Fed. Rule Civ. Proc. 8(c). The defense comprises two necessary elements: (a) that the employer exercised reasonable care to prevent and correct promptly any sexually harassing behavior, and (b) that the plaintiff employee unreasonably failed to take advantage of any preventive or corrective opportunities provided by the employer or to avoid harm otherwise. While proof that an employer had promulgated an anti-harassment policy with complaint procedure is not necessary in every instance as a matter of law, the need for a stated policy suitable to the employment circumstances may appropriately be addressed in any case when litigating the first element of the defense. And while proof that an employee failed to fulfill the corresponding obligation of reasonable care to avoid harm is not limited to showing any unreasonable failure to use any complaint procedure provided by the employer, a demonstration of such failure will normally suffice to satisfy the employer's burden under the second element of the defense. No affirmative defense is available, however, when the supervisor's harassment culminates in a tangible employment action, such as discharge, demotion, or undesirable reassignment.

IV

Relying on existing case law which held out the promise of vicarious liability for all *quid pro quo* claims, Ellerth focused all her attention in the Court of Appeals on proving her claim fit within that category. Given our explanation that the labels *quid pro quo* and hostile work environment are not controlling for purposes of establishing employer liability, Ellerth should have an adequate opportunity to prove she has a claim for which Burlington is liable.

Although Ellerth has not alleged she suffered a tangible employment action at the hands of Slowik, which would deprive Burlington of the availability of the affirmative defense, this is not dispositive. In light of our decision, Burlington is still subject to vicarious liability for Slowik's activity, but Burlington should have an opportunity to assert and prove the affirmative defense to liability. . . .

It is so ordered.

Faragher v. City of Boca Raton

524 U.S. 775 (1998)

Justice Souter delivered the opinion of the Court.

This case calls for identification of the circumstances under which an employer may be held liable under Title VII of the Civil Rights Act of 1964, 78 Stat. 253, as amended, 42 U.S.C. §2000e et seq., for the acts of a supervisory employee whose sexual harassment of subordinates has created a hostile work environment amounting to employment discrimination. We hold that an employer is vicariously liable for actionable discrimination caused by a supervisor, but subject to an affirmative defense looking to the reasonableness of the employer's conduct as well as that of a plaintiff victim.

I

Between 1985 and 1990, while attending college, petitioner Beth Ann Faragher worked part time and during the summers as an ocean lifeguard for the Marine Safety Section of the Parks and Recreation Department of respondent, the City of Boca Raton, Florida (City). During this period, Faragher's immediate supervisors were Bill Terry, David Silverman, and Robert Gordon. In June 1990, Faragher resigned.

In 1992, Faragher brought an action against Terry, Silverman, and the City, asserting claims under Title VII, 42 U.S.C. §1983, and Florida law. So far as it concerns the Title VII claim, the complaint alleged that Terry and Silverman created a "sexually hostile atmosphere" at the beach by repeatedly subjecting Faragher and other female lifeguards to "uninvited and offensive touching," by making lewd remarks, and by speaking of women in offensive terms. The complaint contained specific allegations that Terry once said that he would never promote a woman to the rank of lieutenant, and that

Silverman had said to Faragher, "Date me or clean the toilets for a year." Asserting that Terry and Silverman were agents of the City, and that their conduct amounted to discrimination in the "terms, conditions, and privileges" of her employment, 42 U.S.C. §2000e-2(a)(1), Faragher sought a judgment against the City for nominal damages, costs, and attorney's fees. . . .

II

A

Under Title VII of the Civil Rights Act of 1964, "it shall be an unlawful employment practice for an employer . . . to fail or refuse to hire or to discharge any individual, or otherwise to discriminate against any individual with respect to his compensation, terms, conditions, or privileges of employment, because of such individual's race, color, religion, sex, or national origin." 42 U.S.C. §2000e-2(a)(1). We have repeatedly made clear that although the statute mentions specific employment decisions with immediate consequences, the scope of the prohibition " 'is not limited to "economic" or "tangible" discrimination,' " *Harris v. Forklift Systems, Inc.,* 510 U.S. 17, 21 (1993) (quoting *Meritor Savings Bank, FSB v. Vinson),* and that it covers more than " 'terms' and 'conditions' in the narrow contractual sense." *Oncale v. Sundowner Offshore Services, Inc.,* 523 U.S. 75 (1998). Thus, in *Meritor* we held that sexual harassment so "severe or pervasive" as to "alter the conditions of [the victim's] employment and create an abusive working environment" violates Title VII.

In thus holding that environmental claims are covered by the statute, we drew upon earlier cases recognizing liability for discriminatory harassment based on race and national origin, just as we have also followed the lead of such cases in attempting to define the severity of the offensive conditions necessary to constitute actionable sex discrimination under the statute. . . .

So, in *Harris,* we explained that in order to be actionable under the statute, a sexually objectionable environment must be both objectively and subjectively offensive, one that a reasonable person would find hostile or abusive, and one that the victim in fact did perceive to be so. 510 U.S. at 21-22. We directed courts to determine whether an environment is sufficiently hostile or abusive by " 'looking at all the circumstances,' including the 'frequency of the discriminatory conduct; its severity; whether it is physically threatening or humiliating, or a mere offensive utterance; and whether it unreasonably interferes with an employee's work performance.' " 510 U.S. at 23. Most recently, we explained that Title VII does not prohibit "genuine but innocuous differences in the ways men and women routinely interact with members of the same sex and of the opposite sex." *Oncale,* 523 U.S. at 81. A recurring point in these opinions is that "simple teasing," *id.,* at 82, offhand comments, and isolated incidents (unless extremely serious) will not amount to discriminatory changes in the "terms and conditions of employment."

These standards for judging hostility are sufficiently demanding to ensure that Title VII does not become a "general civility code." Properly applied, they will filter out complaints attacking "the ordinary tribulations of the workplace, such as the sporadic use of abusive language, gender-related jokes, and occasional teasing." We have made it clear that conduct must be extreme to amount to a change in the terms and conditions of employment, and the Courts of Appeals have heeded this view.

While indicating the substantive contours of the hostile environments forbidden by Title VII, our cases have established few definite rules for determining when an employer will be liable for a discriminatory environment that is otherwise actionably abusive.

. . . In order to accommodate the principle of vicarious liability for harm caused by misuse of supervisory authority, as well as Title VII's equally basic policies of encouraging forethought by employers and saving action by objecting employees, we adopt the following holding in this case and in *Burlington Industries, Inc. v. Ellerth,* also decided today. An employer is subject to vicarious liability to a victimized employee for an actionable hostile environment created by a supervisor with immediate (or successively higher) authority over the employee. When no tangible employment action is taken, a defending employer may raise an affirmative defense to liability or damages, subject to proof by a preponderance of the evidence, *see* Fed. Rule. Civ. Proc. 8(c). The defense comprises two necessary elements: (a) that the employer exercised reasonable care to prevent and correct promptly any sexually harassing behavior, and (b) that the plaintiff employee unreasonably failed to take advantage of any preventive or corrective opportunities provided by the employer or to avoid harm otherwise. While proof that an employer had promulgated an anti-harassment policy with complaint procedure is not necessary in every instance as a matter of law, the need for a stated policy suitable to the employment circumstances may appropriately be addressed in any case when litigating the first element of the defense. And while proof that an employee failed to fulfill the corresponding obligation of reasonable care to avoid harm is not limited to showing an unreasonable failure to use any complaint procedure provided by the employer, a demonstration of such failure will normally suffice to satisfy the employer's burden under the second element of the defense. No affirmative defense is available, however, when the supervisor's harassment culminates in a tangible employment action, such as discharge, demotion, or undesirable reassignment.

NOTES AND QUESTIONS

1. In the companion cases *of Ellerth* and *Faragher,* the Supreme Court assumes that acts of sexual harassment had in fact taken place. The Court reviews the characteristics of both "*quid pro quo*" and "hostile environment" gender-based discrimination. What is the difference? How should a school district, in its policies, define a hostile environment?
2. In *Pennsylvania State Police v. Suders,* 124 S. Ct. 2342 (2004), the Supreme Court reaffirmed its *Ellerth* and *Faragher* constructs, and extended them to a case in which the employee alleges that an abusive working environment becomes so intolerable that resignation constitutes a "constructive discharge."
3. Based on the blueprint for avoiding liability provided by the Court in *Ellerth* and *Faragher,* what policy language should school district attorneys

insist that their clients adopt? Can a policy be drafted that insures that a school district will be able to meet its affirmative defense to *any* claim of sexual discrimination or harassment in the educational workplace?

4. Consider the application of the *Ellerth* and *Faragher* defense in the following case.

MASSON V. THE SCHOOL BOARD OF DADE COUNTY, FLORIDA

36 F. Supp. 2d 1354 (S.D. Fla. 1999)

Background

Plaintiff Carmen Masson ("Masson") filed a two-count amended complaint alleging hostile work environment (count I) and failure to promote (and demoting) (count II), both in violation of Title VII of the Civil Rights Act of 1964, as amended. Defendant Dade County School Board (the "School Board") has answered the complaint and now files this motion for partial summary judgment as to Masson's claim for hostile work environment.

Facts

The undisputed facts as taken from Masson's amended complaint and the record are as follows: Masson was hired by the School Board in 1983 as a culinary arts teacher at Lindsey Hopkins Technical Education Center and served there until July 1997. Since 1992, Masson alleges she was subjected to a hostile work environment based upon the actions and explicit sexual remarks of John Leyva ("Leyva"), the school principal since 1991 and Masson's supervisor. The following are allegations made by Masson and undisputed by the School Board concerning Leyva's conduct:

(1) She was offended when she heard Leyva said she was good-looking in addition to being the most competent employee in the kitchen;
(2) At a grievance hearing, Leyva stated "he wouldn't kiss [Masson's] face but would kiss [Masson's] ass for all the work she had done at Lindsey Hopkins to put it on the map;"
(3) Leyva and two female staff members engaged in an inappropriate conversation in Leyva's office concerning sexual portraits, lingerie and sex toys. Masson excused herself from the conversation and left the office;
(4) Leyva was always making remarks about Masson's hair and clothing. In one incident, Leyva said "Your hair looks great. You look like a lion" and he started to approach Masson but stopped and said "I forgot you're married;"
(5) Masson saw Leyva kissing a secretary at school;
(6) In a meeting, after Masson was able to help Leyva obtain additional seating at a school event, Leyva leaned over and kissed Masson on the cheek or jaw; and
(7) An assistant principal said that he would be administering the cafeteria like "ladilla" which Masson took to mean he would be all over the place, like crabs.

Masson also alleges Leyva has a pattern and practice of sexually harassing his other subordinate female employees.

Discussion . . .

II. Hostile Work Environment Sexual Harassment under Title VII

The burden of proof in a Title VII action is set out in *McDonnell Douglas Corp. v. Green,* 411 U.S. 792, and its progeny . . . Initially, the plaintiff must establish a prima facie case of hostile work environment.

A. Prima Facie Case

Hostile work environment sexual harassment occurs when "an employer's conduct has the purpose or effect of unreasonably interfering with an individual's work performance or creating an intimidating, hostile or offensive environment." *Steele v. Offshore Shipbuilding, Inc.,* 867 F.2d 1311, 1315 (11th Cir. 1989). To establish a prima facie case for hostile work environment sexual harassment, Masson must show the following: (1) she belonged to a protected group; (2) she was subjected to unwelcome sexual harassment; (3) the harassment complained of was based upon sex; (4) the harassment complained of affected a term, condition or privilege of employment; and (5) the School Board knew or should have known of the harassment and failed to take prompt remedial action. *Henson v. City of Dundee,* 682 F.2d 897, 903-05 (11th Cir. 1982). The Supreme Court has instructed that for such an allegation to be actionable, "a sexually objectionable environment must be both objectively and subjectively offensive, one that a reasonable person would find hostile or abusive, and one that the victim in fact did perceive to be so." *Faragher v. City of Boca Raton,* 524 U.S. 775 (1998). Thus, a court should determine whether an environment is sufficiently hostile or abusive by looking at all the circumstances, including the frequency of the conduct, its severity and whether it unreasonably interferes with an employee's work performance or is mere offensive utterance. *Id.* This inquiry prevents Title VII from becoming a "general civility code" and filters out "the ordinary tribulations of the workplace, such as the sporadic use of abusive language, gender-related jokes, and occasional teasing."

The School Board initially argues Masson cannot prove a prima facie case for hostile work environment sexual harassment. The Court disagrees.

Not surprisingly, the School Board dismisses Masson's allegations as nonactionable, mere offensive speech. This Court certainly has addressed allegations far more outrageous and demeaning than those alleged by Masson. And while Masson's allegations are, in the Court's view, borderline, the Court believes they were severe and pervasive enough to constitute sexual harassment. There is no question Masson subjectively felt the comments were sexually objectionable and the Court believes a reasonable person would see them that way.[3] Accordingly, the Court finds Masson has established a prima facie case of hostile work environment sexual harassment.

---

[3] The Court is somewhat bothered that the School Board, in arguing that Masson was not sexually harassed, is so cavalier about Masson's allegations. For instance, the School Board argues that "the fact that her supervisor said she was good looking in addition to being the most competent employee in the kitchen should be considered a compliment and certainly not inappropriate, let alone sexual harassment." And with respect to Masson's allegations that Leyva

B. Employer Liability

The Supreme Court in *Faragher* recently addressed the issue of an employer's liability for a hostile work environment created by an employee's supervisor. The Court stated that "an employer is subject to vicarious liability to a victimized employee for an actionable hostile work environment created by a supervisor with immediate (or successively higher) authority over the employee." *Faragher,* 524 U.S. 775; *see also Burlington Industries v. Ellerth,* 524 U.S. 742 (1998). The Court, however, created an affirmative defense for employers where, as here, no tangible employment action was taken against the employee. To take advantage of the defense, the School Board must show (1) "that [the School Board] exercised reasonable care to prevent and correct promptly any sexually harassing behavior," and (2) "that [Masson] unreasonably failed to take advantage of any preventive opportunities provided by the employer or to avoid harm otherwise." *Faragher,* 118 S. Ct. at 2293. The School Board argues it has met its burden under both prongs of the Faragher defense in that the School Board exercised reasonable care to prevent harassment and Masson never took advantage of the School Board's antiharassment policy.

With respect to the first prong of the defense, the Supreme Court has stated the following:

> While proof that an employer had promulgated an antiharassment policy with complaint procedure is not necessary in every instance as a matter of law, the need for a stated policy suitable to the employment circumstances may appropriately be addressed in any case when litigating the first element of the defense.

Faragher, 118 S. Ct. at 2293. Here, it is undisputed the School Board has an officially promulgated, nondiscrimination/harassment policy and complaint procedure. In support of its argument, the School Board submits the affidavit of Rafael Urrutia, the Director for the School Board's Office of Equal Educational and Employment Opportunity. In his affidavit, Urrutia states that he conducts workshops and training sessions for supervisors concerning compliance with federal and state statutes and School Board rules that prohibit sexual harassment. Urrutia further states the School Board's policy is widely disseminated to employees and that the policy provides a comprehensive procedure for processing harassment complaints. In response, Masson argues the School Board has "failed to develop a comprehensive anti-harassment policy" and in fact did not provide harassment training to supervisors. Masson, however, does not provide factual support for her argument and essentially rests on conclusory allegations about the deficiencies in the School

---

kissed her, the School Board argues that "it seems clear that in this County, if every individual who was kissed on the cheek took offense, there would be a lot of offended residents." Were these comments isolated, the Court may view the School Board's statements simply as argumentative rhetoric. However, it is well known—and acknowledged by the School Board—that the School Board has in the past experienced problems with other supervisors concerning allegations of sexual harassment. Thus, while the School Board is entitled to present its arguments in any form it chooses, it appears to this Court that the School Board, rather than so flippant, should be extra sensitive to the types of allegations made by Masson.

Board's policy. Thus, because Masson does not provide factual evidence to counter Urrutia's statements concerning the School Board's policy, Urrutia's affidavit is essentially undisputed. *See Matsushita,* 475 U.S. at 586 (the nonmovant "must do more than simply show that there is some metaphysical doubt as to the material facts."). Thus, the Court finds the School Board has satisfied the first prong of the Faragher defense by showing it has exercised reasonable care to prevent sexual harassment by creating and implementing an antiharassment policy and complaint procedure.

With respect to the second prong of the defense, the Supreme Court has stated:

> And while proof that an employee failed to fulfill the corresponding obligation of reasonable care to avoid harm is not limited to showing an unreasonable failure to use any complaint procedure provided by the employer, a demonstration of such failure will normally suffice to satisfy the employer's burden under the second element of the defense.

Faragher, 118 S. Ct. at 2293. The School Board argues Masson failed to reasonably avail herself of the avenues created by the School Board's policy to put the School Board on notice of the ongoing harassment. Masson states she complained to Roger Cuevas, the Assistant Superintendent, about being replaced by Tom Saslgiver (a male chef) and that Cuevas "understood my claim to be gender discrimination." Masson further states she complained about the same incident (being replaced) to David Schleiden, the Vocational Supervisor, and also filed six grievances with her union. Finally, Masson claims she faxed a memorandum of understanding to Nelson Diaz, the Superintendent of Management and Labor Relations.

It appears the focus of Masson's communication with these individuals concerned her job reassignment rather than Mr. Leyva's alleged inappropriate conduct. That Masson believes Cuevas understood her claim to be gender discrimination cannot, by itself, support Masson's argument that she complained to others about Leyva's alleged sexual harassment. More importantly, it is undisputed that Masson never took advantage of the School Board policy and never filed a complaint with Urrutia. Masson never argues she was unaware of the policy and does not assert any reason why she chose not to follow its procedures.

While recognizing the "enormous difficulties" involved in lodging complaints about sexual harassment in the workplace, the Eleventh Circuit recently noted:

> Federal law has now attempted to correct the problem of workplace discrimination, but it cannot be done without the cooperation of the victims, notwithstanding that it may be difficult for them to make such efforts. When an employer has taken steps, such as promulgating a considered sexual harassment policy, to prevent sexual harassment in the workplace, an employee must provide adequate notice that the employer's directives have been breached so that the employer has the opportunity to correct the problem.

Coates v. Sundor Brands, Inc., 164 F.3d 1361, 1999 WL 12822, at *5 (11th Cir. 1999). Thus, while the School Board's hands may not be clean, the Court cannot in every instance hold it liable for actions about which it is unaware—especially when the complainant does not follow the procedures provided for in the School Board's policies. *Id.* Accordingly, the Court finds the School Board has met its burden under the second prong of the *Faragher* defense by showing that Masson unreasonably failed to take advantage of any preventive or corrective opportunities provided by the School Board.

Because the School Board has satisfied its burden under *Faragher,* the Court finds there is no genuine issue of material fact that exists to support a finding either (1) that the School Board did not exercise reasonable care in preventing the harassment or (2) that Masson herself acted reasonably to put the School Board on notice of a problem. As a result, summary judgment in favor of the School Board as to count I of the amended complaint is appropriate.

5. Religious Discrimination

As we have seen, the First Amendment's establishment and free exercise clauses prohibit public schools from advancing or inhibiting religion, and from precluding students or teachers from the free exercise of their religious beliefs. The First Amendment is violated when a public school district requires a teacher to perform an act which violates that teacher's religious beliefs, or treats the teacher differently because of those beliefs. *See e.g., Hobbie v. Unemployment Appeals Comm. of Florida,* 480 U.S. 136 (1987). Where a public school, as an agent of the state, has violated the First Amendment by engaging in such acts of religious discrimination, the teacher may bring an action for damages under 42 U.S.C. §1983. *See e.g., Monnell v. New York City Dept. of Social Services,* 436 U.S. 658 (1978).

More specifically, Title VII expressly prohibits virtually all public and private educational institutions from discriminating against educators in employment "because of their religion." The term "religion" encompasses all aspects of religious observance, practice and belief, and is not limited to organized religious groups. 42 U.S.C. §2000e. Any "moral or ethical beliefs as to what is right and wrong which are sincerely held with the strength of traditional religious views" are protected by Title VII from employment discrimination. *Frazee v. Ill. Dept. of Employment Sec.,* 489 U.S. 829 (1989). Indeed, even discrimination because of the *absence* of religious belief is prohibited by Title VII. *EEOC v. Townley Engineering & Manufacturing Co.,* 859 F.2d 610 (9th Cir. 1988). *See also Cowan v. Strafford R-VI School Dist.,* 140 F.3d 1153 (8th Cir. 1998) (school board's decision not to renew teacher's contract because fundamentalist group objected to teacher's instructional practice of encouraging students to rub a "magic rock" violated Title VII).

The 1972 Amendments to Title VII, however, allow an employer to defend a claim of religious discrimination by proving that it cannot reasonably accommodate the religion of an employee or applicant without suffering an "undue hardship." In *Trans World Airlines v. Hardison,* 432 U.S. 63 (1977), the Supreme Court suggested that an employee would suffer an "undue hardship" if it were required to create "special exemptions" from its work schedule to allow an employee to observe the Sabbath. Yet, where a teacher's decision to participate in religious holidays or observances can be accommodated with *de minimus* burden on the school district, the school district must make a reasonable effort to accommodate the teacher's request. *Compare Ansonia Bd. of Ed. v. Philbrook,* 479 U.S. 60 (1986) (school district satisfied its duty of reasonable accommodation by presenting a plan to accommodate a teacher's request for additional paid leave to attend religious meetings) *with Wangsness v. Watertown School Dist.,* 541 F. Supp. 332 (D.S.D. 1982) (school violated Title VII by dismissing teacher for absence to attend religious gathering where absence was easily accommodated by provision of substitute teachers).

Pinsker v. Joint District Number 28J of Adams and Arapahoe Counties

735 F.2d 388 (10th Cir. 1984)

Logan, Circuit Judge.

Plaintiffs Gerald Pinsker and the Aurora Education Association[1] appeal from the district court's dismissal of their claim under Title VII of the 1964 Civil Rights Act, 42 U.S.C. §§2000e to 2000e-17, and from the district court's finding that they had not shown a violation, cognizable under 42 U.S.C. §1983, of the right to free exercise of religion guaranteed by the First and Fourteenth Amendments.

Pinsker is a teacher in the Aurora, Colorado, public schools. He claims that the defendant school district's school schedule and leave policy discriminate against him and other Jewish teachers on the basis of religion and unconstitutionally burden his right to free exercise of religion. The basis of his claim is that the school year in the district is arranged so that Christmas is not a school day, and in most school years there has been no school on Good Friday or Good Friday afternoon; thus, Christian teachers need not use their personal leave time or take unpaid leave to observe religious holidays. Pinsker does not work on three Jewish holidays: one day for Yom Kippur and two days for Rosh Hashanah. In some years all three of those holidays fall on school days.

The leave policy in the defendant district is a product of collective bargaining. A teacher has a pool of twelve days of paid leave, all of which the teacher may use for sick leave and parts of which the teacher may use for other specified purposes. A teacher may use a maximum of two days from the pool for "special leave." Teachers have been allowed to use special leave to observe Jewish holidays. Only twenty teachers may take special leave on any one day.

During the six years before he brought suit Pinsker took a total of three days of unpaid leave to celebrate Jewish holidays. In 1981, for example, Yom Kippur and both days of Rosh Hashanah fell on school days, so Pinsker used his two days of special leave and took one day of unpaid leave to celebrate those holidays. Apparently defendant did not actually dock Pinsker's pay for that day of "unpaid" leave. Also, although twenty teachers had already signed

---

[1] Aurora Education Association, the collective bargaining agent for teachers in the defendant school district, intervened on the side of Pinsker in this action. The parties stipulated that any relief provided Pinsker would be provided to other teachers of his religion.

up for special leave on one of the Jewish holidays in 1981, Pinsker was allowed to take special leave on that day.

I

Under Title VII it is an unlawful employment practice for an employer "to fail or refuse to hire or to discharge any individual, or otherwise to discriminate against any individual with respect to his compensation, terms, conditions, or privileges of employment, because of such individual's race, color, religion, sex, or national origin." 42 U.S.C. §2000e-2(a)(1). Pinsker still works for defendant, and the terms and conditions of his employment are identical to those of other teachers similarly situated. However, 42 U.S.C. §2000e(j) provides:

> The term "religion" includes all aspects of religious observance and practice, as well as belief, unless an employer demonstrates that he is unable to reasonably accommodate to an employee's or prospective employee's religious observance or practice without undue hardship on the conduct of the employer's business.

The Supreme Court has held that the intent and effect of this definition of "religion" is to make it a violation of §2000e-2(a)(1) for an employer not to make reasonable accommodations, short of undue hardship, for the religious practices of employees and prospective employees. *Trans World Airlines, Inc. v. Hardison,* 432 U.S. 63, 74 (1977). Simply put, Title VII requires reasonable accommodation or a showing that reasonable accommodation would be an undue hardship on the employer. In this case Pinsker essentially contends that his employer failed to reasonably accommodate his religious practices.

Pinsker does not suggest that he should receive more paid leave or other special treatment. Rather, he argues that Title VII requires the defendant to institute a generally applicable policy that is less burdensome to his religious practices than its present policy. At trial plaintiffs showed that other school districts have leave policies under which Pinsker would not have to take unpaid leave in a year when Yom Kippur and both days of Rosh Hashanah fell on school days. For example, one district allows three days of religious leave. Another district allows teachers to make up religious leave by doing extracurricular work.

Title VII requires reasonable accommodation. It does not require employers to accommodate the religious practices of an employee in exactly the way the employee would like to be accommodated. Nor does Title VII require employers to accommodate an employee's religious practices in a way that spares the employee any cost whatsoever. Defendant's policy and practices jeopardized neither Pinsker's job nor his observation of religious holidays. Because teachers are likely to have not only different religions but also different degrees of devotion to their religions, a school district cannot be expected to negotiate leave policies broad enough to suit every employee's religious needs perfectly. Defendant's policy, although it may require teachers to take occasional unpaid leave, is not an unreasonable accommodation of teachers' religious practices. Thus, the trial court correctly determined that plaintiff did not make a prima facie showing of discrimination.

II

Plaintiffs also claim that defendant's leave policy unconstitutionally burdens Pinsker's First Amendment right to free exercise of religion. The trial court correctly characterized the issue as whether the economic impact of losing a day's wages in order to attend a religious service is a denial of freedom of religion.

In *Thomas v. Review Board of the Indiana Employment Security Division,* 450 U.S. 707, 67 L. Ed. 2d 624, 101 S. Ct. 1425 (1981), the Supreme Court considered whether the First Amendment permits a state to deny unemployment benefits to a man who quit his job because it required him to engage in behavior that violated his religious beliefs. The Court set out the following standard:

> Where the state conditions receipt of an important benefit upon conduct proscribed by a religious faith, or where it denies such a benefit because of conduct mandated by religious belief, thereby putting substantial pressure on an adherent to modify his behavior and to violate his beliefs, a burden upon religion exists.

Id. at 717-18. Loss of a day's pay for time not worked does not constitute substantial pressure on a teacher to modify his or her behavior. *Cf. Braunfeld v. Brown,* 366 U.S. 599, 6 L. Ed. 2d 563, 81 S. Ct. 1144 (1961) (Sunday closing laws do not deny free exercise of religion even though they work to the economic disadvantage of Orthodox Jewish merchants whose religion requires them to close on Saturday as well).

NOTES AND QUESTIONS

1. Consider *Pinsker* together with the academic freedom and religious freedom cases. Is there a consistent approach to protecting a teacher's interest in religious freedom? Or, does that interest mean one thing in the class room and something else in the workforce?
2. The Court makes clear that Title VII and its regulations require school districts to make reasonable accommodations for their teacher's religious beliefs, unless doing so would produce an "undue hardship." What accommodations could have been made in this case that were not made? Would they have produced an undue hardship? This case raises the issue of what constitutes an "undue hardship." Is that concept merely economic? How should a school lawyer define that principle for a client? *Pinsker* pointed out that other school districts allow their teachers to take a certain number of days for "religious leave." What are the advantages and disadvantages of such a policy?
3. A school or university also may defend a Title VII claim of religious discrimination by demonstrating that religion is a bona fide occupational qualification. For what kind of teaching jobs, would "religion" be a bona fide occupational qualification? May a Catholic grade school, for instance, refuse to hire non-Catholic teachers? Is Catholicism a bona fide occupational qualification for teaching at a Catholic university or law school? *See, e.g., Pime v. Loyola University of Chicago,* 803 F.2d 351 (7th Cir. 1986).

6. Family Leave

In 1993, Congress enacted the Family and Medical Leave Act (FMLA), 29 U.S.C. §2612 *et seq.* The FMLA grants to employees of any public "local educational agency" and to employees of "any private elementary and secondary school," the right to request leave for care-taking purposes, including the birth or adoption of a child, and the care of an ill child, parent or spouse. The employee must have worked for at least one year consisting of at least 1,250 hours prior to the leave to be eligible. The employee is entitled to receive as much as 12 weeks of unpaid leave within any single year. The leave generally can be for sporadic periods of time. When a school employee who acts "principally in an instructional capacity" can foresee a planned leave based on medical treatment that will result in more than a 20 percent reduction in services, however, the employer may direct the duration and timing of the leave.

In *Nevada Dept. of Human Resources v. Hibbs,* 538 U.S. 721 (2003), the Supreme Court held that state workers, including public school teachers, have a private right of action for damages against their state employers for the denial of their rights under the FMLA. Justice Rehnquist, who authored the opinion, stressed the FMLA's purposes of allowing both men and women to balance the needs of family with those of the workplace, thereby eradicating the practice of stereotyping women as caregivers. According to the Court, Congress's intent in protecting employees is consistent with allowing these employees to sue even a public, state educational institution if leave is improperly denied.

CHAPTER 18

THE PROFESSIONAL AND CONTRACTUAL RESPONSIBILITIES AND RIGHTS OF TEACHERS

A. THE PROFESSIONAL AND CONTRACTUAL RESPONSIBILITIES OF TEACHERS

1. General Education Requirements

Every state requires that certified teachers have earned, at minimum, a bachelor's degree. Beyond this basic requirement, the states also have enacted general education and teacher education requirements. *See, e.g.,* Elizabeth A. Kaye, ed., *Requirements for Certification of Teachers, Counselors, Librarians, and Administrators for Elementary and Secondary Schools* (2002). Typically, the states require course work in subjects including humanities, social studies, natural science, math, and English or communication. Moreover, every state requires additional course work in particularized areas. For example, New York requires the study of a foreign language. Arizona and California require teachers to pass a U.S. Constitution test or to complete course work regarding the Constitution. Arizona also requires teachers to pass a state constitution test or course. In Oregon, candidates for certification must demonstrate knowledge of the laws prohibiting discrimination, including Title VI of the Civil Rights Act of 1964 and Title IX of the Education Amendments of 1972. Many states require that secondary teachers who specialize in one subject complete a subject matter major rather than an education major.

2. Teacher Education Requirements

Most states also require course work in education. Some states specify that completion of a program approved by a national college accrediting agency such as the National Council for Accreditation of Teacher Education Standards (NCATE) meets the education requirement for certification. NCATE is an accrediting organization for teacher preparation programs, and establishes performance based standards for such programs. For example, elementary school teacher training programs must provide courses and experiences in five categories: (1) child development, learning and motivation, (2) curriculum, (3) instruction, (4) assessment, and (5) professionalism. The states that have adopted such accrediting standards have delegated to the accrediting agency the review and sanctioning of teacher education programs. Other states have established their own requirements, which are similar to the NCATE requirements. States that have adopted their own certificate requirements for teachers retain the ability to conduct their own review of educational training programs.

Some states have enacted additional instructional practice requirements. For example, 16 states require course work in teaching reading or phonics. Ohio, South Dakota and Texas require a course on integrating technology into instruction. Many states require course work in recognizing and addressing the needs of exceptional students, including the learning disabled and gifted. In their continued attempt to address the needs of diverse school populations, some states have established even more specific requirements. Illinois and Texas require the study of multiculturalism. Kansas, Nebraska, South Dakota and Texas require a course in human relations. Minnesota requires completion of a human relations program, including instruction on racial, cultural, and economic groups and interpersonal relations. Alaska requires courses in Alaska studies and cross-cultural communication. Similarly, South Dakota requires a course in Native-American studies. Washington requires courses in child abuse recognition, while New York requires training in violence intervention and prevention.

3. Testing Requirements

Every state now requires its teachers to pass standardized teacher certification and competency tests. These tests are designed to measure both teaching skills and knowledge of subject matter. Some states have generated their own tests, such as the California Basic Educational Skills Test (CBEST), the New York State Teacher Certification Exam (NYSTE) and the Examination for the Certification of Educators in Texas (ExCET). Most of the states, however, have adopted a national examination. The National Teacher Exam (NTE), formerly used by many states, has been effectively replaced by a battery of three tests known as the "Praxis Series." The national, standardized Praxis tests are designed to assess academic skills (Praxis I), competence in specific subject areas (Praxis II) and classroom performance (Praxis III). Additional subject matter tests generally are required of secondary teachers seeking specializations. As we have seen, in *NEA v. South Carolina,* 434 U.S. 1026 (1978), the Supreme Court upheld the legitimacy of the NTE exam against a challenge that its results disproportionately burdened minority teachers.

4. Background/Fingerprint Checks

Twelve states, including Florida, Pennsylvania and New York, require fingerprinting and a background check before they grant certification. States that do not have this requirement at the state level may still require a background check at the local school district level. Other states, including Massachusetts, Nebraska, Ohio and West Virginia, require evidence of sound moral character.

5. Citizenship and Residency

Recall that in *Foley v. Connelie,* 435 U.S. 291 (1978), *and Ambach v. Norwick,* 441 U.S. 68 (1979), the U.S. Supreme Court upheld laws requiring the denial of teacher certification to any applicant who is not an American citizen or who did not express an intent to attempt to become one. The Court found that New York had a legitimate state interest in requiring its teachers to be either American citizens or to be in the process of becoming American citizens. For similar reasons, school district policies requiring teachers to be residents of the school district have been upheld as advancing legitimate educational purposes. *See, e.g., Wardwell v. Board of Education,* 529 F.2d 625 (6th Cir. 1976). What are those purposes?

6. Changing Requirements for Certification and Recertification

Many states have recently changed their certification requirements, and others are in the process of doing so. Many of these states now have multistep certification regimes. For example, new requirements went into effect on July 1, 2003 in Illinois. The Illinois regime begins with an Initial Certificate. After four years of teaching and after fulfilling one of six continuing education options, a certificate holder may apply for and obtain a Standard Certificate. In six states, including Arkansas and Kentucky, beginning teachers must take part in a mentoring program before applying for the next level of teaching certificate. Many states now require continuing education at the graduate level for recertification. Some states also have developed alternative certification programs to encourage career changes.

7. Insubordination, Incompetence and Immorality

A school district may decide not to renew a nontenured teacher's contract for any reason at all, so long as the reason is not an unlawful one, such as the constitutionally protected activity of the teacher. School districts, however, have no such unbridled discretion in their decision to dismiss a tenured teacher. Virtually every state has a statutory regime by which teachers may obtain tenure or an equivalent long-term contract. The statutes typically provide that a teacher with tenure may not be dismissed absent a showing of good cause or "just cause." By statute and interpretive case law, the standard of "just cause" has come to require evidence of a teacher's insubordination, incompetence or immorality.

(a) Insubordination

Insubordination is defined as the "constant or continuing intentional refusal to obey a direct or implied order, reasonable in nature, and given by and with proper authority." *See In re Proposed Termination of James E. Johnson's Teaching Contract,* 451 N.W.2d 343 (Minn. Ct. App. 1990). When a teacher repeatedly violates an administrator's directive or a school policy, the evidence of insubordination is ample to justify a district's dismissal decision. *See, e.g., Gaylord v. Board of Education,* 14 Kan. App. 2d 462, 794 P.2d 307 (Kan. Ct. App. 1990). Even if the teacher disobeys a single, reasonable directive, however, that single act of insubordination can justify dismissal. In *Christopherson v. Spring Valley Elementary School,* 90 Ill. App. 3d 460, 413 N.E.2d 199, 45 Ill. Dec. 866 (Ill. Ct. App. 1980), the court validated the school board's decision to terminate a senior, tenured teacher for insubordination where the teacher disobeyed the board's decision to refuse the teacher's request for five-days leave to attend a workshop on strategies for teaching students how to read.

Similarly, in *Board of Education of Jefferson County School District v. Wilder,* 960 P.2d 695 (Colo. 1998), the Colorado Supreme Court upheld the school board's dismissal of a tenured teacher for insubordination because the teacher failed to follow the school's policy requiring the teacher to provide the principal with prior written notice of the teacher's decision to use any controversial teaching materials. In *Wilder,* the teacher showed an R-rated film to his class, but the court determined that the dismissal was not based on the content of the instructional materials. Rather, the dismissal was because of the teacher's failure to comply with the school's procedures for using such material.

As *Wilder* suggests, issues of insubordination may touch upon the teacher's right to academic freedom and to freedom of expression. Yet, the key ingredient of insubordination is the teacher's refusal to follow an administrator's directive. Accordingly, teachers who refrain from doing a prohibited activity after being instructed not to do so cannot be properly dismissed for insubordination. *See, e.g., Thompson v. Wake County Board of Education,* 292 N.C. 406, 233 S.E.2d 538 (1977).

(b) Incompetence

The minimal standards of teacher competence are defined by state statutes imposing certification, recertification and continuing education requirements. A teacher who has met the state law statutory standards is presumed to be competent, and that presumption can be rebutted by a school district only through affirmative evidence of incompetence. *See, e.g., Blunt v. Marion County School Board,* 515 F.2d 951 (5th Cir. 1975) (teacher competence is to be judged by educational authorities and not generally by the courts). In proving incompetence, however, the school district may submit evidence that a teacher lacks the substantive knowledge required for teaching a subject. *See, e.g., Jennings v. Caddo Parish School Board,* 276 So. 2d 386 (La. Ct. App. 1973). More frequently, incompetence is found when a teacher's lack of teaching skills results in a perceived lack of control or discipline in the classroom. *See, e.g., Board of Directors of Sioux City Community School District v. Mroz,* 295 N.W.2d 447 (Iowa 1980); *Mims v. West Baton Rouge Parish School Board,* 315 So. 2d 349 (La. Ct. App. 1975); *McWhirter v. Cherokee County School District No. 1,* 274 S.C. 66, 261 S.E.2d 157 (S.C. 1979). At the same time, evidence of a teacher's lack of *appropriate* discipline has led courts to uphold a district's claim of incompetence. *See, e.g., Rolando v. School Directors of District No. 125,* 44 Ill. App. 658, 358 N.E.2d 945, 3 Ill. Dec. 402 (Ill. Ct. App. 1976) (sixth-grade teacher using cattle prod for discipline was properly discharged).

In each case in which "incompetence" was properly found, however, the school district had amassed a compelling record of irremedial performance problems or extremely unacceptable, even outrageous, conduct. In the absence of such a record, the courts are reluctant to uphold even the judgment of a local school district to dismiss a tenured teacher. *See, e.g., Collins v. Faith School District No. 46-2,* 574 N.W.2d 889 (S.D. 1998) (overturning school board's decision to dismiss teacher despite teacher's single inappropriate incident involving graphic description of homosexual sex in the classroom because that single incident was not of such a magnitude to outweigh nearly 30 years of good teaching); *Missoula County School District No. 1 v. Anderson, 232* Mont. 501, 757 P.2d 1315 (Mont. 1988) (teacher who performed poorly in substantive interview could not be dismissed for incompetence after more than a dozen years of satisfactory teaching).

(c) Immorality

The position of teacher as "role model" or "exemplar" for children has led legislatures and courts to endorse the dismissal of teachers for conduct defined as immoral, indecent, unprofessional or unfit. *See Horosko v. Mt. Pleasant Township School District,* 335 Pa. 369, 6 A.2d 866 (Pa. 1939) (defining immorality as a "course of conduct as offends the morals of the community and is a bad example to the youth whose ideals a teacher is supposed to foster and elevate"). Dismissals for "immorality," no matter how defined, fall into two categories: (1) conduct that is so criminally reprehensible that dismissal is per se appropriate even when the conduct has no effect in the classroom; and (2) other arguably improper conduct that does interfere with the teaching function.

There is no doubt that a teacher may be properly terminated for conduct that amounts to serious criminal behavior involving violence, deceit, illegal drugs, intoxication while driving or specific harm to children. *See, e.g., In re Thomas,* 926 S.W.2d 163 (Mo. Ct. App. 1996); *Board of Directors of Lawton-Bronson v. Davies,* 489 N.W.2d 19 (Iowa 1992); *Chicago Board of Education v. Payne,* 430 N.E.2d 310 (Ill. Ct. App. 1981); *Zelno v. Lincoln Inter. Unit No. 12,* 786 A.2d 1022 (Pa. 2001). So, too, the courts consistently have upheld the dismissal of a teacher for inappropriate sexual contact between the teacher and a young student. *Weissman v. Board of Education,* 190 Colo. 414, 547 P.2d 1267 (Colo. 1976); *Lombardo v. Board of Education,* 100 Ill. App. 2d 108, 241 N.E.2d 495 (Ill. Ct. App. 1968); *Fadler v. Illinois State Board of Education,* 153 Ill. App. 3d 1024, 506 N.E.2d 640, 106 Ill. Dec. 840 (Ill. Ct. App. 1987).

In addition, school districts have been found to have properly terminated teachers for lesser forms of improper conduct, so long as there is a direct relationship between that conduct and the teacher's ability to educate students in the classroom. In *Adams v. State Professional Practices Council,* 406 So. 2d 1170 (Fla. Ct. App. 1981), for example, the court upheld the decertification of teachers who grew marijuana plants in a greenhouse, reasoning that the teachers' failure to maintain a high moral standard in the community significantly interfered with their effectiveness as teachers. Similarly, in *Board of Directors of Lawton-Bronson v. Davies,* 489 N.W.2d 19 (Iowa 1992), the Iowa Supreme Court upheld the school's termination of a tenured teacher for "just cause" when the teacher's effectiveness had been irreparably damaged by the fact that the community was aware that she had been charged with shoplifting.

The issue of whether a teacher's allegedly "immoral" conduct interferes with the teacher's ability to teach so as to constitute "just cause" for termination arises often in cases involving a teacher's sexual activities. When a teacher engages in any inappropriate physical contact of a sexual nature with minor students, the courts have found the teacher's conduct to constitute just cause for termination on its face. *See, e.g., Weissman v. Board of Education,* 190 Colo. 414, 547 P.2d 1267 (Colo. 1976) (tenured teacher who touched female students, rested on a motel bed with a female student on a field trip and frequently made sexual comments to female students was properly dismissed for immoral conduct that made him unfit to teach); *Fadler v. Illinois State Board of Education,* 153 Ill. App. 3d 1024, 506 N.E.2d 640, 106 Ill. Dec. 840 (Ill. Ct. App. 1987) (teacher who fondled student dismissed for immoral conduct rendering him unfit to teach). In these cases, a teacher's sexual contact with a minor student renders the teacher unfit as a matter of law.

In cases involving a teacher's sexual conduct with nonstudents, however, dismissals have been upheld only upon a more precise showing that the conduct interferes with teaching ability. In situations involving a teacher's public displays of sexual activity deemed inappropriate by the community, decisions to dismiss that teacher based on a lack of effectiveness in the classroom within that same community have generally been upheld. *See, e.g., Wishart v. McDonald,* 500 F.2d 1110 (1st Cir. 1974) (tenured teacher who made sexually suggestive gestures to a mannequin in public properly dismissed because damage to his professional reputation would render him ineffective); *In re Grossman,* 127 N.J. Super. 13, 316 A.2d 39 (N.J. 1974) (students' knowledge that teacher was a transsexual rendered teacher incapable of performing teaching duties in that particular district); *Ross v. Springfield School District,* 300 Or. 507, 716 P.2d 724 (Or. 1986) (teacher who engaged in sexual intercourse in public properly dismissed).

Can a teacher be removed from the classroom, however, if the teacher engages in private sexual conduct which the "community" later discovers and deems immoral? In *Morrison v. State Board of Education,* 82 Cal. Rptr. 175, 461 P.2d 375 (Cal. 1969), the court held that a teacher's private homosexual activity could not support the decision by the state's board of education to revoke a teacher's certification because no evidence could be presented demonstrating a connection between the private activity (which occurred three years earlier) and the teacher's ability to deliver instruction. Similarly, the courts have held that unmarried teachers who become pregnant cannot be terminated for "immorality" in the absence of compelling evidence that the teacher's private conduct adversely affected the teacher's ability to educate students. *See, e.g., Drake v. Covington County Board of Education,* 371 F. Supp. 974 (M.D. Ala. 1974); *Avery v. Homewood City Board of Education,* 674 F.2d 337 F.2d (5th Cir. 1982).

On the other hand, in *Gaylord v. Tacoma School District No. 10,* 88 Wash. 2d 286, 559 P.2d 1340 (Wash. 1977), the Washington Supreme Court upheld the school district's discharge of a teacher where the district established that the teacher became ineffective after it became known that the teacher was a homosexual. The evidence on which the district relied for its claim that the teacher became ineffective consisted of the objections raised by one student and three co-teachers to the teacher's sexual preference.

In a community in which a few teachers, students or parents dislike the sexual preference of a teacher, does that teacher thereby become ineffective to teach in the community? In *Gaylord,* the teacher's sexual preference was made known by the school itself; the teacher endeavored to maintain privacy. If a teacher's private sexual behavior is discovered and disclosed by community members, does that behavior become "public" and therefore justify dismissal based on a claim that the teacher's perceived immorality renders the teacher ineffective in the classroom? If so, what is left of the realm of privacy in a teacher's life?

B. THE PROFESSIONAL AND CONTRACTUAL RIGHTS OF TEACHERS: TENURE AND THE COLLECTIVE BARGAINING PROCESS

Within the parameters established by federal and state law, a teacher's employment relationship with a school district is in the nature of a contract. The traditional elements of contract formation and enforcement apply to teacher contracts as well. Contracts may be either expressed in writing or implied by conduct. Whether written, oral, expressed or implied, however, an enforceable contract requires that the teacher and the district both: (1) have the capacity to enter into an agreement, (2) have evidenced mutual assent through the acceptance of an offer on sufficiently definitive terms, and (3) have exchanged valid consideration.

These elements of an enforceable contract, however, are influenced by the statutory law governing education. For example, state law may prohibit a contractual arrangement between a teacher and a district that delegates too much administrative power to teachers, or authorizes them to do tasks for which they are not certified. *See, e.g., Board of Education v. Round Valley Teachers Assn.,* 52 Cal. Rptr. 115, 914 P.2d 193 (Cal. 1996). Similarly, although each teacher within a district must enter into his or her own individual contract with the district, that contract cannot be inconsistent with the terms of a collective bargaining agreement between the district and the teacher's bargaining unit. Individual contracts that violate state law or a collective bargaining agreement will be unenforceable, as a violation of public policy.

State law also bears on the issue of contractual capacity. Most states delegate the authority to execute a school district's contract only to the president of the board of education, acting under the authority of the board pursuant to action taken at a properly conducted board meeting. *See, e.g., Board of Education of D.C. v. Wilson,* 290 A.2d 400 (D.C. Ct. App. 1972). Accordingly, if a principal or superintendent enters into a contract with a teacher, that contract generally cannot be enforced against the district.

Where a teacher seeks employment in a district without unionized employees, that teacher must personally negotiate his or her contract. In such situations, each contract could theoretically have different terms. As a practical matter, however, even nonunionized teachers tend to have similar employment contracts. For efficiency, morale and equity reasons, school districts without unionized teachers tend to use the same contractual framework for all of their teachers.

1. Tenure

State law or "custom" confers the unique benefit of tenure on qualified members of the education profession. *See Perry v. Sindermann,* 408 U.S. 593 (1972). Virtually every state has a statutory regime that confers on its teachers tenure or an equivalent long-term renewable contract. All such statutes allow a school district or local education agency to grant tenure to teachers after a delineated period of probation and evaluation. In Virginia, for example, the probationary period is three years. In Illinois, the period was recently increased from two to four years, although there is pending legislation that would reinstate a shorter time frame.

Once tenure has been granted, a tenured teacher may only be removed for good or just "cause." A showing of "cause" sufficient to justify the removal of a tenured teacher is extremely difficult. Typically "cause" does not include general incompetence or the mere failure to meet the standards of performance established by the district or the state. Instead, as we have seen, "cause" requires an act of insubordination, extreme incompetence or moral turpitude specifically related to the teaching function. Absent such extraordinary circumstances, it is difficult for a school district to terminate a teacher, even if it believes the teacher to be unsatisfactory. Tenured teachers, however, may generally be dismissed as part of a bona fide school district response to a material change in financial condition.

Barton v. Independent School District No. 1-99 of Custer County, Oklahoma, a/k/a Clinton Public Schools,

914 P.2d 1041 (Okla. Sup. 1996)

. . . Facts

The appellant, Jim R. Barton (Barton/teacher) is certified by the State of Oklahoma to teach general industrial arts, wood and metal technology, zoology, biology and driver/safety education in the public school system. The appellee, the Independent School District No. I-99 of Custer County (school district/board) hired him to teach driver's education in Clinton, Oklahoma. After he taught driver's education for the school district for 19 years, the school superintendent determined that a reduction-in-force was necessary to reduce the 1992-93 school year budget expenditures by approximately $120,000.00.

On March 24, 1992, the superintendent informed the school board that it needed to eliminate at least four teaching positions for the 1992-93 school year to reduce the school budget by approximately $120,000.00. Although the superintendent was of the opinion that normal attrition would remedy some of the budgeting problems, he recommended that the board eliminate the driver's education program and nonrenew Barton's teaching contract. On March 26, 1992, the school board notified the teacher of the superintendent's recommendations and set a hearing on the recommendations for May 4, 1992.

On May 5, 1992, almost a month after *Babb v. Independent School Dist. I-5 of Rogers Co., Okla.*, 829 P.2d 973 (Okla. 1992) was promulgated, the board wrote Barton advising him that the driver's education program would be eliminated, and that his teaching contract would not be renewed. Thereafter, the school district employed eight more certified teachers for the 1992-1993 school year than it had employed the previous year, and it increased expenditures by approximately $600,000.00 over the previous year's budget.

On May 17, 1993, Barton filed a lawsuit against the school district, alleging that: 1) the school district breached his employment contract and acted in bad faith when it decided not to renew his teaching contract; and 2) it violated the Oklahoma Open Meeting Act, 25 O.S. 1991 §301 et seq., when it met to consider whether to renew Barton's employment contract. The school district denied the allegations and moved for summary judgment. On February 3, 1995, the trial court granted summary judgment to the school district. The teacher appealed, and the Court of Appeals affirmed. We granted certiorari. . . .

The teacher asserts that the trial court erred in granting summary judgment because material fact questions exist concerning: 1) whether another teaching position existed for the 1992-1993 school year for which he was qualified to teach and which was occupied by either a nontenured or a probationary teacher; and 2) whether the school board acted in good faith in implementing its reduction-in-force plan. The school district contends that pursuant to the terms of its 1990-91 collective bargaining agreement, it was not required to offer the teacher another assignment. Nor, notwithstanding the terms of the collective bargaining agreement, does Oklahoma law require it to reassign him to another teaching position occupied by either a nontenured or a probationary teacher which he was qualified to teach. We disagree. . . .

Our decision in *Babb v. Independent School Dist. No. I-5 of Rogers Co., Okla.*, 829 P.2d 973 (Okla. 1992) is dispositive of the question of whether the entry of summary judgment was erroneous. Babb involved the issue of whether a tenured teacher who was certified to teach the same subject taught by a nontenured teacher has priority for contract renewal over the nontenured teacher when a reduction-in-force plan is implemented. In Babb, a tenured classroom teacher was reassigned to the position of elementary librarian. The following school year, the superintendent recommended to the school board that a reduction-in-force plan be implemented for the next school year. The board met and voted not to renew the contracts of fifteen nontenured teachers. At the board's next meeting, it voted not to renew the tenured teacher's contract and it voted to reemploy the fifteen nontenured teachers. The tenured teacher brought suit in district court, seeking reinstatement of tenure status. The school board asserted that the tenured teacher's contract was nonrenewed pursuant to its reduction-in-force plan, and that the RIF plan had been implemented in good faith.

The Babb Court said:

> Teacher tenure law is intended to give job security to competent and qualified teachers and to protect them from dismissal or nonrenewal for political, personal, arbitrary or discriminatory reasons. Tenure status, which is statutorily conferred upon teachers who have been in employment of the school district the required number of years, demonstrates legislative intent to grant teachers substantive rights in their continued position, which are not possessed by those in a temporary or probationary status. Under this regime, teacher contracts are automatically renewed on a continuing basis unless a school board or a teacher acts to prevent the employment's renewal. *Once attained, tenure status cannot be lost except on the grounds sanctioned by law.*
>
> While the Code does not specifically address a school board's authority not to reemploy teachers when implementing its RIF plan, that power clearly is implicit in the statutory scheme which allows local school boards to formulate a complete education program for the students in the district and to determine the number of personnel necessary to implement the plan within the existing funding limits.
>
> When declining enrollment requires a reduction-in-force, a school board must balance a district's needs against available resources and take appropriate action to curtain personnel. While a school board may exercise wide latitude and autonomy in choosing a method for reducing the teaching force, its RIF policy must nonetheless conform to the commands of tenure law. Tenured faculty have a claim to preferential status over nontenured faculty in implementation of a reduction-in-force plan. To hold otherwise would emasculate the statutory tenure policy and let school boards do indirectly what they cannot do directly. Tenure rights must be protected and school boards afforded the necessary discretion to so shape quality education programs as to make them meet the available financial resources.
>
> In sum, a school board is always free to adjust its teachers' roll to meet economic necessity, but it cannot invoke unsanctioned grounds to subvert the statutorily mandated security-from-termination protection for tenured teachers. (Emphasis in original.) (Citations omitted.)

The school district's RIF policy is contained in its 1990-91 collective bargaining agreement. The agreement provides that when a reduction-in-force is implemented and the school board has determined that a teaching position or positions will be eliminated, the position eliminated will be the determining factor, not the teachers occupying those positions. If a position is eliminated, licensed teachers are released first, followed by probationary teachers and career teachers [those who have completed at least three consecutive school years in the district] are the last to be released. The collective bargaining agreement also provides that a career teacher may involuntarily be transferred to another teaching position if the enrollment or the class size changes. Under this scheme, a career teacher who occupies a teaching position, must be renewed before other nontenured teachers or probationary teachers are assigned to teaching positions which the career teacher may be qualified to teach. This scheme prevents the involuntary transfer of a career teacher to a position which may then be eliminated. Otherwise, a tenured teacher could be prevented from receiving priority consideration for renewal over a nontenured or probationary teacher. Regardless of whether a school district acts in good faith or bad faith, failure to provide preference to career teachers could manipulate job assignments thereby defeating the rights of tenured teachers and circumventing the purpose and spirit of the tenure law. When a reduction-in-force plan is implemented, tenured teachers have priority for contract renewal over nontenured teachers. A school board's RIF plan may not give priority for contract renewal to nontenured teachers over qualified tenured teachers.

The teacher is certified by the State of Oklahoma to teach general industrial arts, wood and metal technology, zoology, biology and driver/safety education in the public school system. He presented evidentiary materials alleging that the school district could have made reasonable accommodations with minimal effort to renew his contract by rearranging the schedules of two other teachers and by not renewing a probationary teacher's contract - resulting in preservation of his career status over a nontenured teacher. Accordingly, we find that a controversy exists on the material issues of whether the teacher could have been retained by a reasonable reassignment of classes among other teachers and that failure to do so, whether in good faith or bad faith, was a form of manipulation of job assignments which failed to protect his tenure status. Summary judgment was improper.

As the *Barton* Court recognizes, tenure is the creation of state statutes and therefore generally can be eliminated by state law. Where a state statute creates a contractual right to tenure, that contractual right cannot be "impaired" by subsequent legislation without violating article I, section 10 of the Constitution. *Indiana ex rel. Anderson v. Brand,* 303 U.S. 95 (1938). This impediment to statutory revocation of tenure has been overcome, however, by language in state statutes that simply allows school districts to grant tenure rights that are not contractual, or to grant contractual rights that are always subject to a change in law.

If the tenure process hampers school districts from removing an unsatisfactory teacher or from responding flexibly to a change in economic circumstances, then what justifies the tenure institution? In *Smith v. School District of Darby,* 388 Pa. 301, 130 A.2d 661 (Pa. 1957), the Pennsylvania Supreme Court declared that tenure's purpose is to secure "the maintenance of an adequate and competent teaching staff, free from political or arbitrary interference, whereby capable and competent teachers might feel secure, and more efficiently perform their duty of instruction." Within this general statement of tenure's objectives appear the following distinct justifications: (1) tenure provides a job benefit that attracts qualified teachers; (2) tenure encourages qualified teachers to keep teaching; (3) tenure helps develop and maintain a consistent number of experienced professionals who teach; (4) tenure frees teachers from the time constraints of job status issues and allows them more time to teach; (5) tenure protects good teachers from arbitrary terminations; and (6) tenure protects teachers from being removed for freely expressing unpopular ideas in the classroom, and thereby is vital to academic freedom and to the creation of a marketplace of ideas.

Each of these arguments favoring tenure, of course, raises countervailing questions. Is each argument separately or together sufficient to overcome the disadvantages of the tenure system? Even if each argument expresses a vital concern, can that concern be addressed by means other than tenure? For instance, what does tenure add if teachers already have the right to be free from adverse job actions because of the content of their political expression?

Recall that "tenure" is a property interest created by state law that can only be taken from a teacher if the district follows the steps mandated by the Constitution's due process clause. Yet, "tenure" is not always necessary for the creation of a protectable property interest. A legitimate expectation in continued employment is also a property right protected from deprivation under the due process clause. How might a state provide teachers with a protected property interest in their continued employment (and hence due process protections) without a tenure system?

2. Collective Bargaining

In the vast majority of school districts, teacher contracts are developed through a process of collective bargaining between the teacher's union and the school district. Teachers have a First Amendment constitutional right to association that extends to the right to join a union. *See McLaughlin v. Tilendis*, 398 F.2d 287 (7th Cir. 1968). In addition, 34 states have enacted legislation that expressly grants to teachers the right to unionize and to engage in collective bargaining.

(a) The Legal Landscape of Bargaining

State laws generally give to the representatives of public educational institutions and to the representatives of teachers' unions the exclusive authority and duty to bargain. Most states expressly grant to teachers the right to bargain collectively over all issues involving wages, hours and working conditions, but not over matters of managerial policy.

In *Central State University v. American Ass'n of University Professors*, 526 U.S. 124 (1999), the Supreme Court upheld the constitutionality of an Ohio statute requiring state universities to develop "instructional workload" standards for faculty that would be exempt from the "collective bargaining" process. Faculty members challenged the law on the grounds that the prohibition on their right to engage in collective bargaining over the issue of faculty teaching loads constituted a denial of equal protection of the laws. In rejecting that argument, however, the Supreme Court found that Ohio's law was rationally related to the legitimate state interest in increasing the time faculty spent in the classroom. That interest justified the state's decision to exempt the issue of faculty workloads from the collective bargaining process.

In keeping with the Supreme Court's suggestion in *Central State,* the states also have legitimately exercised their power over the collective bargaining process by establishing certain mandatory terms in any negotiated agreement. For example, most states require that collectively negotiated contracts contain specific grievance procedures. Further, state statutes frequently prohibit strikes or any work stoppages during the term of the agreement. Many states also have created educational labor relations boards that are empowered to regulate all matters involving labor relations in the education field.

State labor laws also define and sanction unfair labor practices, such as refusing to bargain in good faith to impasse, interfering with the formation or existence of a collective bargaining agreement and otherwise violating the agreement itself. Although impasse results whenever the parties after good faith efforts cannot reach agreement, state law tends to define impasse by time period. For instance, impasse may be defined as the inability to reach an agreement after 60 days of beginning good faith bargaining.

State laws also generally impose a structure of dispute resolution. That structure may require the parties to undergo arbitration or mediation. In most states, teachers are permitted to strike only after that dispute resolution process has failed. These limitations on the power of teachers to strike are based on an effort to balance the teacher's right to strike where bargaining has reached an impasse against the strong public policy favoring the education of students without disruption. That balance is sometimes litigated in the midst of a threatened strike or of an attempt to enjoin a threatened strike. The *Timberlane* case presents an excellent example of the collective bargaining process, the typical sticking points in negotiations and the ultimate judicial balancing of the labor rights of teachers against the educational rights of students.

Timberlane Regional School District v. Timberlane

114 N.H. 245, 317 A.2d 555 (N.H. 1974)

Kenison, CJ. delivered the Opinion. The major issue in this case is whether the presiding justice properly denied the plaintiff's petition to enjoin the defendants from engaging in or aiding and abetting a strike. . . . The Timberlane Regional Education Association (hereinafter TREA) is the collective bargaining agent for some, if not all, of the teachers in the Timberlane Regional School District and is affiliated with the New Hampshire Education Association, whose membership consists of school teachers employed throughout the State. The TREA and the Timberlane Regional School Board (hereinafter board) agreed to meet during the spring and summer of 1973 for the purpose of negotiating a contract for the 1974-75 school year.

The board proceeded to hire a professional negotiator and delayed meeting with the TREA until July 31, 1973. The parties met throughout the fall and early winter and, by January 14, 1974, had reached a tentative agreement on approximately one-quarter of the items submitted for negotiation by the TREA.

The majority of the remaining items, which included salary schedules, sick and emergency leave, teacher rights and responsibilities, teacher evaluation, academic freedom and grievance procedures, had been declared non-negotiable by the board. It became apparent that an impasse was developing in regard to these items, and the members of the TREA voted to submit their differences with board to a mediator for resolution. The TREA contacted the Federal Mediation Service which agreed to undertake mediation if both parties so requested. The board, however, declined to accept this offer, and several other attempts to find a mutually agreeable mediator came to naught.

The parties resumed negotiations on February 15, 1974, and met again on February 18, 20 and 23. These meetings resulted in a tentative agreement on several of the remaining items, but their differences with respect to a great majority of these items were unresolved. During the course of negotiations on February 23, 1974, the TREA discovered for the first time that on February 16, 1974, the board had submitted salary proposals to the budget committee, despite the fact that an agreement had not been worked out between the parties on this matter. The board then stated at the end of this session that it would go no further and declined to negotiate on the evening of February 23, or at any time on February 24, and 25, 1974.

The members of the TREA met on February 25, 1974, and voted to call for mediation because of an impasse in negotiations and to refuse to teach until mediation began. Last minute efforts to achieve compromise between the positions of the parties came to no avail, and the strike commenced on February 26, 1974. Approximately two-thirds of the teaching staff in the district did not report to work, and pickets were set up in the vicinity of the schools. The board was initially able to keep all of the schools in the district open by hiring substitute teachers, and student attendance did not drop appreciably. The board, however, was ultimately forced to shut down the Timberlane Regional High and Junior High Schools.

"[P]ublic employer collective bargaining is now an established fact at the federal level and in the majority of state and local governments. The transition from uniform disapproval to majority acceptance of public employer collective bargaining began in 1955, when New Hampshire adopted legislation authorizing town governments to engage in collective bargaining with public employee unions." Blais, *State Legislative Control over the Conditions of Public Employment: Defining the Scope of Collective Bargaining for State and Municipal Employees,* 26 Vand. L. Rev. 1, 2 (1973). Nevertheless, in most jurisdictions a strike by public employees is prohibited either by statute or by judicial decision. New Hampshire is no exception to this rule, for this court held . . . that such strikes are illegal under the common law of this State and characterized this prohibition as a matter of public policy solely within the province of the legislature. *See* N. Edwards, *The Courts and the Public Schools* 682 (1971).

We are aware of the general dissatisfaction with the effect of this prohibition on labor negotiations between government and public employees. *See, e.g.,* Anderson, *The Impact of Public Sector Bargaining,* 1973 Wis. L. Rev. 986, 1023-25 (1973); Burton & Krider, *The Role and Consequences of Strikes by Public Employees,* 79 Yale L.J. 418, 437-40 (1970); Edwards, *The Emerging Duty to*

Bargain in the Public Sector, 71 Mich. L. Rev. 885, 891-93 (1973); Foegen, *A Qualified Right to Strike—in the Public Interest,* 18 Lab. L.J. 90, 98-99 (1967); Kheel, *Strikes and Public Employment,* 67 Mich. L. Rev. 931 (1969); Wellington & Winter, *Structuring Collective Bargaining in Public Employment,* 79 Yale L.J. 805, 822-25 (1970). In the private sector, the right to strike is viewed as an integral part of the collective bargaining process. Anderson, *Strikes and Impasse Resolution in Public Employment,* 67 Mich. L. Rev. 943, 957 (1969). In the public sector, however, the denial of the right to strike has the effect of heavily weighing the collective bargaining process in favor of the government. Without legislation providing alternative methods for resolving impasses in negotiation, there is no ultimate sanction available to the public employees for compelling the good faith of the government, and as a consequence, the only recourse available to them, if they are being treated unfairly, is to terminate their employment or to engage in an illegal strike. Bernstein, *Alternatives to the Strike in Public Labor Relations,* 85 Harv. L. Rev. 459, 464-66 (1971); Lev, *Strikes by Government Employees: Problems and Solutions,* 57 A.B.A.J. 771 (1971); Note, *Striking a Balance in Bargaining with Public School Teachers,* 56 Iowa L. Rev. 598, 599-601 (1971); Note, *Teacher's Strikes—ANew Militancy,* 43 Notre Dame Lawyer 367 (1968).

It is not a proper judicial function to make policy judgments as to the merits of providing public employees with the right to strike or of developing alternative processes such as compulsory mediation or arbitration to resolve government labor disputes. For an excellent discussion of such policy matters, *see* Anderson, *The Impact of Public Sector Bargaining,* 1973 Wis. L. Rev. 986 (1973); Wellington & Winter, *Structuring Collective Bargaining in Public Employment,* 79 Yale L.J. 805 (1970). This decision must be made [by] the legislature. RSA ch. 98-C (Supp. 1973) (prohibiting strikes by state employee organizations where an agreement has been entered into with the State providing mediation and arbitration procedures for impasse resolution); RSA ch. 105-B (Supp. 1973) (prohibiting strikes by police organizations, but providing mediation and arbitration procedures for impasse resolution); *see* N.H. House bill 889 (1973 session; vetoed) (prohibiting public employee strikes but requiring the employer to bargain in good faith and providing procedure for impasse resolution); *see, e.g.,* Alaska Stat. §23.40.200 (1972) (granting right to strike to certain public employees, including teachers, if not detrimental to public health, safety and welfare); Hawaii Rev. Stat. §89-12 (Supp. 1973) (authorizing strikes by public employees if there is no danger to public health and safety); Pa. Stat. Ann. tit. 43, §1101.1003 (Supp. 1973) (permitting strikes by public employees if collective bargaining process is exhausted and no clear or present danger to public health, safety and welfare); Vt. Stat. Ann. tit. 16 §2010 (Supp. 1973) (allowing strikes by teachers unless clear and present danger to a sound program of school education). *See also* Alderfer, *Follow-up on the Pennsylvania Public School Strikes,* 25 Lab. L.J. 161 (1974); Note, *Teacher Negotiations in Illinois: Statutes and Proposed Reforms,* 1973 U. Ill. L.F. 307 (1973).

However, in the absence of legislation, the courts are necessarily compelled to consider the problems inherent in labor relations between the government and public employees when called upon to issue an injunction to prevent an illegal strike. The injunction is an extraordinary remedy which is only granted under circumstances where a plaintiff has no adequate remedy at law and is likely to suffer irreparable harm unless the conduct of the defendant is enjoined. The availability of injunctive relief is a matter within the sound discretion of the court exercised on a consideration of all the circumstances of each case and controlled by established principles of equity. . . .

In view of the nature of this remedy, a growing number of jurisdictions have applied equitable principles to deny the government the use of an injunction against illegal strikes by teachers unless there is a showing of irreparable harm to the public. One of the first cases in formulating this new approach was *School Dist. for Holland v. Holland Education Association,* 380 Mich. 314, 157 N.W.2d 206 (1968), in which the Michigan Supreme Court indicated that the refusal of the government to bargain in good faith would be a factor of importance in the determination of whether or not to issue an injunction. *Id.* at 327, 157 N.W.2d at 211. This position was embraced by the Rhode Island Supreme Court in *School Committee of Westerly v. Westerly Teachers Association,* 299 A.2d 441, 445 (R.I. 1973), which held that an injunction would not issue "unless it clearly appears from specific facts . . . that irreparable harm will result. . . ." *See* C. Nolte, *Law and the School Superintendent §7.14* (2d ed. 1971).

We are persuaded by these recent developments that it would be detrimental to the smooth operation of the collective bargaining process to declare that an injunction should automatically issue where public teachers have gone on strike. Note, *Ohio Public Sector Labor Relations Law: A Time for Reevaluation and Reform,* 42 U. Cinn. L. Rev. 679, 702-07 (1973); *see NEA Report on Strikes in 1972-73 School Year,* 541 BNA Gov't Employ. Rel. Rep. D-1 thru D-3 (Feb. 11, 1974). The essence of the collective bargaining process is that the employer and the employees should work together in resolving problems relating to the employment. The courts should intervene in this process only where it is evident the parties are incapable of settling their disputes by negotiation or by alternative methods such as arbitration and mediation. . . . Judicial interference at any earlier stage could make the courts "an unwitting third party at the bargaining table and a potential coercive force in the collective bargaining processes." *School Committee v. Westerly Teachers Ass'n,* 299 A.2d 441, 446 (R.I. 1973). Accordingly, it is our view that in deciding to withhold an injunction the trial court may properly consider among other factors whether recognized methods of settlement have failed, whether negotiations have been conducted in good faith, and whether the public health, safety and welfare will be substantially harmed if the strike is allowed to continue. *See Levitt v. Maynard,* 105 N.H. 447, 450, 202 A.2d 478, 480 (1964); Gosseen, *Labor Relations Law,* 1972/73 Annual Survey of American Law, 445, 460 n.108 (1973).

We have reviewed the master's report and the record and are satisfied that the trial court took these matters into account in denying the injunction for the present. We agree with the master's opinion that the parties had not yet exhausted the possibilities of finding compromise in the collective bargaining process at the time the injunction was refused.

Plaintiff's exception overruled.

(b) The Political Landscape of Bargaining

At the heart of an excellent educational environment is a healthy relationship between teachers and administrators. That relationship often is forged on a collective basis in the context of collective bargaining. The way in which the various stakeholders in a district approach bargaining often sets the tone for the district itself, and even for the delivery of services to students. School boards that approach collective bargaining as a "private sector" arm's length, adversarial relationship tend to find themselves overseeing a district of disgruntled employees with little organizational growth. Conversely, school boards who try to appease teachers at the expense of legitimate administrative concerns and sincere fiscal constraints find themselves overseeing a district that is either bankrupt or rudderless. The key is establishing a relationship between teachers, administrators and board members that is based on honesty, communication, respect and trust. Based on that relationship, the stakeholders in the bargaining process can begin to invest in negotiations that are different from the traditional adversarial model.

The collective bargaining process is a complex dynamic involving many stakeholders. The traditional model provides that a "management" team made up of representatives of the school board and the administration negotiate "against" a team of "labor" made up of teacher and union representatives. This form of bargaining is often characterized as "position bargaining," because each "side" begins by staking out an adverse position and then reaches a settlement, if at all, by trading back and forth. The approach is a competitive one, very much like an arm's length agreement, in which the parties do not strive to understand each other's perspective, but simply trade competing contractual terms. The approach also usually involves the active, sometimes adversarial, presence of attorneys throughout the process.

Another approach, which is used in some districts, is often termed "expedited bargaining" because an artificial time constraint is placed on the process. The idea of expedited bargaining is that if the parties (often without attorneys) were placed in a room for a short period, and "forced" to reach a deal, they would find a way to get it done quickly. The approach, however, often fails to accomplish its objective of avoiding a prolonged negotiation period because the parties frequently find it difficult to reach a deal in the time allotted. Even where a deal is reached, that deal is often the product of stress, rather than sincere understanding. Accordingly, the terms reached in such a process may have unforeseen, negative consequences.

A third bargaining mode can be characterized as "interest-based bargaining." By this approach, the parties begin the process by producing a joint list of issues to be addressed by both teams together. Dialogue occurs with respect to issues, not positions. Together, the bargaining representatives work to "problem-solve" and to resolve each of the issues. The process is collaborative and conversational. Yet, the parties still insure that their perspectives on an issue are weighed and addressed. The outcome is an agreement based on mutual understanding of each other's perspective.

Although this "interest-based" bargaining approach has great advantages, the reality is that most complex bargaining experiences travel a path that employs all three methods of bargaining. At some point, as time and patience grow short, the process becomes "expedited" in the sense that all parties simply want to get it done to avoid labor strife. At that point, the trading of positions may replace genuine dialogue about issues and interests. Nonetheless, there is little doubt that an approach to bargaining that encourages the school district and the teachers to listen carefully to the other's viewpoint on issues affecting children and to resolve those issues in ways that take into consideration the other's viewpoint is extremely beneficial to intradistrict relations and ultimately to the students.

C. COLLECTIVE BARGAINING PRACTICUM

Attorneys for school districts spend a large portion of their time in collective bargaining negotiations. Assume that the Lakewood School District has enjoyed relatively cooperative relations with its unionized teachers, and would like to keep it that way. The teacher's contract expires in six months, and the district's board has indicated that it would like to get going on the process of negotiating a new contract. The board believes that the teachers are generally excellent and should be compensated fairly for their efforts. The board also faces tremendous fiscal pressure to maintain a balanced budget in all funds, and a balanced education fund budget as well. Like all school districts, about 80 percent of its education fund budget involves teacher's benefits and salaries. Moreover, over 90 percent of its revenue is derived from local property taxes, and the remainder derives from a shrinking pool of federal and state dollars. The teachers have traditionally enjoyed annual salaries and benefits that are competitive with other teachers in the area. As such, those terms have included annual increases in salary in excess of the Consumer Price Index, which is only about 3 percent. What advice should the district's lawyer give to the district regarding its approach to collective bargaining this time around?

Assume that the board decides to engage in "interest-based" bargaining, and that the parties have compiled the following list of issues: (1) fair increases in salary for each level of seniority; (2) reasonable insurance benefits for employees and their families; (3) retirement incentives; (4) the proper length of the teacher's day and the teacher's year; (5) the appropriate amount of planning time allotted to teachers during the school day and its uses; (6) family and religious leave; (7) sick days and personal days; (8) continuing professional education and reimbursement for its expense; (9) job sharing; (10) class size limits; (11) stipends for extracurricular supervision; and (12) compensation for district committee representation.

Which of these issues are proper subjects of bargaining as opposed to inherent managerial matters? For example, is the issue of "class size" a mandatory subject of bargaining because it involves a teacher's workload, or is it a prohibited subject of bargaining because it involves managerial issues?

Assuming that all of the issues will be bargained, what are the likely interests of the teachers with respect to these issues? Do all teachers in a district have a common interest with respect to all of these issues? Finally, assuming that the district's interests are not compatible—operationally and fiscally—with those of the teachers, what compromises can be reached to achieve a fair settlement?

Appendices

APPENDIX A

THE UNITED STATES CONSTITUTION

Article I

Section 1. All legislative Powers herein granted shall be vested in a Congress of the United States. . . .

Section 8. The Congress shall have the Power to lay and collect Taxes, Duties, Imports and Excises to pay the Debts and provide for the common Defense and general Welfare of the United States . . . To regulate Commerce . . . among the several States. . . .

Section 10. No State shall . . . pass any . . . law impairing the obligation of contracts. . . .

Article III

Section 1. The judicial Power of the United States shall be vested in one Supreme Court and in such inferior Courts as the Congress may from time to time ordain and establish.

First Amendment

Congress shall make no law respecting an establishment of religion, or prohibiting the free exercise thereof; or abridging the freedom of speech, or of the press; or the right of the people peaceably to assemble, and to petition the Government for a redress of grievances.

Fourth Amendment

The right of the people to be secure in their persons, houses, papers, and effects, against unreasonable searches and seizures, shall not be violated, and no warrants shall issue, but upon probable cause, supported by oath or affirmation, and particularly describing the place to be searched, and the persons or things to be seized.

Fifth Amendment

No person . . . shall be compelled in any criminal case to be a witness against himself, nor be deprived of life, liberty, or property, without due process of law; nor shall private property be taken for public use, without just compensation.

Eighth Amendment

Excessive bail shall not be required, nor excessive fines imposed, nor cruel and unusual punishments inflicted.

Tenth Amendment

The powers not delegated to the United States by the Constitution, nor prohibited by it to the States, are reserved to the States respectively, or to the people.

Eleventh Amendment

The judicial power of the United States shall not be construed to extend to any suit in law or equity, commenced or prosecuted against one of the United States by citizens of another State, or by citizens or subjects of any foreign State.

Fourteenth Amendment

Section 1. All persons born or naturalized in the United States, and subject to the jurisdiction thereof, are citizens of the United States and of the State wherein they reside. No State shall make or enforce any law which shall abridge the privileges or immunities of citizens of the United States; nor shall any State deprive any person of life, liberty, or property, without due process of law; nor deny to any person within its jurisdiction the equal protection of the laws.

APPENDIX B

FEDERAL STATUTES GOVERNING EDUCATION

Section 1983 of the Civil Rights Act of 1871

42 U.S.C.A. §1983

Every person who, under color of any statute, ordinance, regulation, custom, or usage, of any State or Territory, subjects, or causes to be subjected, any citizen of the United States or other person within the jurisdiction thereof to the deprivation of any rights, privileges, or immunities secured by the Constitution and laws, shall be liable to the party injured in an action at law, suit in equity, or other proper proceeding for redress.

Title VI of Civil Rights Act of 1964

42 U.S.C.A. §2000d

No person in the United States shall, on the ground of race, color or national origin, be excluded from participation in, be denied the benefits of, or be subjected to discrimination under any program or activity receiving Federal financial assistance.

Title VII of Civil Rights Act of 1964

42 U.S.C.A. §2000e-2(a)

It shall be an unlawful employment practice for an employer (1) to fail or refuse to hire or to discharge any individual, or otherwise to discriminate against any individual with respect to his compensation, terms, conditions, or privileges of employment, because of such individual's race, color, religion, sex, or national origin; or (2) to limit, segregate, or classify his employees or applicants for employment in any way which would deprive or tend to deprive any individual of employment opportunities or otherwise adversely affect his status as an employee, because of such individual's race, color, religion, sex, or national origin.

Title IX of Education Amendments of 1972

20 U.S.C.A. §1681

(a) Prohibition against discrimination; exceptions. No person in the United States shall, on the basis of sex, be excluded from participation in, be denied the benefits of, or be subjected to discrimination under any education program or activity receiving Federal financial assistance, except that:

(1) Classes of educational institutions subject to prohibition in regard to admissions to educational institutions. This section shall apply only to institutions of vocational education, professional education, and graduate higher education, and to public institutions of undergraduate higher education;

(2) Educational institutions commencing planned change in admissions in regard to admissions to educational institutions. This section shall not apply (A) for one year from June 23, 1972, nor for six years after June 23, 1972, in the case of an educational institution which has begun the process of changing from being an institution which admits only students of one sex to being an institution which admits students of both sexes, but only if it is carrying out a plan for such a change which is approved by the Secretary of Education or (B) for seven years from the date an educational institution begins the process of changing from being an institution which admits only students of only one sex to being an institution which admits students of both sexes, but only if it is carrying out a plan for such a change which is approved by the Secretary of Education, whichever is the later;

(3) Educational institutions of religious organizations with contrary religious tenets. This section shall not apply to an educational institution which is controlled by a religious organization if the application of this subsection would not be consistent with the religious tenets of such organization;

(4) Educational institutions training individuals for military services or merchant marine. This section shall not apply to an educational institution whose primary purpose is the training of individuals for the military services of the United States, or the merchant marine;

(5) Public educational institutions with traditional and continuing admissions policy in regard to admissions. This section shall not apply to any public institution of undergraduate higher education which is an institution that traditionally and continually from its establishment has had a policy of admitting only students of one sex;

(6) Social fraternities or sororities; voluntary youth service organizations. This section shall not apply to membership practices—

(A) of a social fraternity or social sorority which is exempt from taxation under section 501 (a) of Title 26, the active membership of which consists primarily of students in attendance at an institution of higher education, or

(B) of the Young Men's Christian Association, Young Women's Christian Association, Girl Scouts, Boy Scouts, Camp Fire Girls, and voluntary youth service organizations which are so exempt, the membership of which has traditionally been limited to persons of one sex and principally to persons of less than nineteen years of age;

(7) Boy or Girl conferences. This section shall not apply to—

(A) any program or activity of the American Legion undertaken in connection with the organization or operation of any Boys State conference, Boys Nation conference, Girls State conference, or Girls Nation conference; or

(B) any program or activity of any secondary school or educational institution specifically for—

(i) the promotion of any Boys State conference, Boys Nation conference, Girls State conference, or Girls Nation conference; or

(ii) the selection of students to attend any such conference;

(8) Father-son or mother-daughter activities at educational institutions. This section shall not preclude father-son or mother-daughter activities at an educational institution, but if such activities are provided for students of one sex, opportunities for reasonably comparable activities shall be provided for students of the other sex; and

(9) Institution of higher education scholarship awards in "beauty" pageants. This section shall not apply with respect to any scholarship or other financial assistance awarded by an institution of higher education to any individual because such individual has received such award in any pageant in which the attainment of such award is based upon a combination of factors related to the personal appearance, poise, and talent of such individual and in which participation is limited to individuals of one sex only, so long as such pageant is in compliance with other nondiscrimination provisions of Federal law.

(b) Preferential or disparate treatment because of imbalance in participation or receipt of Federal benefits; statistical evidence of imbalance.

Nothing contained in subsection (a) of this section shall be interpreted to require any educational institution to grant preferential or disparate treatment to the members of one sex on account of an imbalance which may exist with respect to the total number or percentage of persons of that sex participating in or receiving the benefits of any federally supported program or activity, in comparison with the total number or percentage of persons of that sex in any community, State, section, or other area: Provided, That this subsection shall not be construed to prevent the consideration in any hearing or proceeding under this chapter of statistical evidence tending to show that such an imbalance exists with respect to the participation in, or receipt of the benefits of, any such program or activity by the members of one sex.

(c) "Educational institution" defined.

For purposes of this chapter an educational institution means any public or private preschool, elementary, or secondary school, or any institution of vocational, professional, or higher education, except that in the case of an educational institution composed of more than one school, college, or department which are administratively separate units, such term means each such school, college, or department.

Equal Pay Act

U.S.C.A. §206(d)(1)

No employer . . . shall discriminate . . . between employees on the basis of sex by paying wages to employees . . . at a rate less than the rate at which he pays wages to employees of the opposite sex . . . for equal work on jobs the performance of which requires equal skill, effort and responsibility, and which are performed under similar working conditions, except where such payment is made pursuant to (i) a seniority system; (ii) a merit system; (iii) a system which measures earnings by quantity or quality of production; or (iv) a differential based on any other factor other than sex. . . .

Age Discrimination in Employment Act

29 U.S.C.A. §623

§623. Prohibition of Age Discrimination

(a) Employer practices

It shall be unlawful for an employer—

(1) to fail or refuse to hire or to discharge any individual or otherwise discriminate against any individual with respect to his compensation, terms, conditions, or privileges of employment, because of such individual's age;

(2) to limit, segregate, or classify his employees in any way which would deprive or tend to deprive any individual of employment opportunities or otherwise adversely affect his status as an employee, because of such individual's age; or

(3) to reduce the wage rate of any employee in order to comply with this chapter.

Civil Rights Restoration Act of 1987

20 U.S.C.A. §1687

For the purposes of this chapter, the term "program or activity" and "program" mean all of the operations of

(1)(A) a department, agency, special purpose district, or other instrumentality of a State or of a local government; or

(B) the entity of such State or local government that distributes such assistance and each such department or agency (and each other State or local government entity) to which the assistance is extended, in the case of assistance to a State or local government;

(2)(A) a college, university, or other postsecondary institution, or a public system of higher education; or

(B) a local educational agency (as defined in section 7801 of this title), system of vocational education, or other school system;

(3)(A) an entire corporation, partnership, or other private organization, or an entire sole proprietorship—

(i) if assistance is extended to such corporation, partnership, private organization, or sole proprietorship as a whole; or

(ii) which is principally engaged in the business of providing education, health care, housing, social services, or parks and recreation; or

(B) the entire plant or other comparable, geographically separate facility to which Federal financial assistance is extended, in the case of any other corporation, partnership, private organization, or sole proprietorship; or

(4) any other entity which is established by two or more of the entities described in paragraph (1), (2), or (3);

any part of which is extended Federal financial assistance, except that such term does not include any operation of an entity which is controlled by a religious organization if the application of section 1681 of this title to such operation would not be consistent with the religious tenets of such organiztion.

Section 504 of Rehabilitation Act of 1973

29 U.S.C.A. §794

(a) Promulgation of rules and regulations

No otherwise qualified individual with a disability in the United States, as defined in section 705(20) of this title, shall, solely by reason of her or his disability, be excluded from the participation in, be denied the benefits of, or be subjected to discrimination under any program or activity receiving Federal financial assistance. . . .

The Americans with Disabilities Act and 2009 Amendments

42 U.S.C.A. §12112

No covered entity shall discriminate against a qualified individual on the basis of disability of such individual in regard to job application procedures, the hiring, advancement, or discharge of employees, employee compensation, job training, and other terms, conditions and privileges of employment.

42 U.S.C.A. §12111(8)

The term "qualified individual with a disability" means an individual with a disability who, with or without reasonable accommodation, can perform the essential functions of the employment position that such individual holds or desires.

42 U.S.C.A. §12102

The term "disability" means . . .

(A) a physical or mental impairment that substantially limits one or more of the major life activities of such individual;

(B) a record of such an impairment; or

(C) being regarded as having such an impairment.

42 U.S.C.A. §12111(9)(A)(B)

The term "reasonable accommodation" may include—(A) making existing facilities . . . readily accessible; and (B) job-restructuring . . . acquisition or modification of equipment or devices, appropriate adjustment or modifications of examinations, training materials or policies, the provisions of qualified readers or interpreters, and other, similar accommodations. . . .

42 U.S.C.A. §12111 (10)(A)(B)

The term "undue hardship" means an action requiring significant difficulty or expense.

Equal Access Act

20 U.S.C.A. §4071

§4071. Denial of Equal Access Prohibited

(a) Restriction of limited open forum on basis of religious, political, philosophical, or other speech content prohibited

It shall be unlawful for any public secondary school which receives Federal financial assistance and which has a limited open forum to deny equal access or a fair opportunity to, or discriminate against, any students who wish to conduct a meeting within that limited open forum on the basis of the religious, political, philosophical, or other content of the speech at such meetings.

(b) "Limited open forum" defined

A public secondary school has a limited open forum whenever such school grants an offering to or opportunity for one or more non-curriculum related student groups to meet on school premises during non-instructional time.

(c) Fair opportunity criteria

Schools shall be deemed to offer a fair opportunity to students who wish to conduct a meeting within its limited open forum if such school uniformly provides that—

(1) the meeting is voluntary and student-initiated;

(2) there is no sponsorship of the meeting by the school, the government, or its agents or employees;

(3) employees or agents of the school or government are present at religious meetings only in a non-participatory capacity;

(4) the meeting does not materially and substantially interfere with the orderly conduct of educational activities within the school; and

(5) non-school persons may not direct, conduct, control, or regularly attend activities of student groups.

(d) Construction of subchapter with respect to certain rights

Nothing in this subchapter shall be construed to authorize the United States or any State or political subdivision thereof—

(1) to influence the form or content of any prayer or other religious activity;

(2) to require any person to participate in prayer or other religious activity;

(3) to expend public funds beyond the incidental cost of providing the space for student-initiated meetings;

(4) to compel any school agent or employee to attend a school meeting if the content of the speech at the meeting is contrary to the beliefs of the agent or employee;

(5) to sanction meetings that are otherwise unlawful;

(6) to limit the rights of groups of students which are not of a specified numerical size; or

(7) to abridge the constitutional rights of any person.

(e) Federal financial assistance to schools unaffected

Notwithstanding the availability of any other remedy under the Constitution or the laws of the United States, nothing in this sub-chapter shall be construed to authorize the United States to deny or withhold Federal financial assistance to any school.

(f) Authority of schools with respect to order, discipline, well-being, and attendance concerns

Nothing in this subchapter shall be construed to limit the authority of the school, its agents or employees, to maintain order and discipline on school premises, to protect the well-being of students and faculty, and to assure that attendance of students at meetings is voluntary.

Family Educational Rights and Privacy Act

---

20 U.S.C.A. §1232g

§1232g. Family Educational and Privacy Rights

(a) Conditions for availability of funds to educational agencies or institutions; inspection and review of education records; specific information to be made available; procedure for access to education records; reasonableness of time for such access; hearings; written explanations by parents; definitions

(1)(A) No funds shall be made available under any applicable program to any educational agency or institution which has a policy of denying, or which effectively prevents, the parents of students who are or have been in attendance at a school of such agency or at such institution, as the case may be, the right to inspect and review the education records of their children. If any material or document in the education record of a student includes information on more than one student, the parents of one of such students shall have the right to inspect and review only such part of such material or document as relates to such student or to be informed of the specific information contained in such part of such material. Each educational agency or institution shall establish appropriate procedures for the granting of a request by parents for access to the education records of their children within a reasonable period of time, but in no case more than forty-five days after the request has been made.

(B) No funds under any applicable program shall be made available to any State educational agency (whether or not that agency is an educational agency or institution under this section)

that has a policy of denying, or effectively prevents, the parents of students the right to inspect and review the education records maintained by the State educational agency on their children who are or have been in attendance at any school of an educational agency or institution that is subject to the provisions of this section.

(C) The first sentence of subparagraph (A) shall not operate to make available to students in institutions of postsecondary education the following materials:

(i) financial records of the parents of the student or any information contained therein;

(ii) confidential letters and statements of recommendation, which were placed in the education records prior to January 1, 1975, if such letters or statements are not used for purposes other than those for which they were specifically intended;

(iii) if the student has signed a waiver of the student's right of access under this subsection in accordance with subparagraph (D), confidential recommendations—

(I) respecting admission to any educational agency or institution,

(II) respecting an application for employment, and

(III) respecting the receipt of an honor or honorary recognition.

(D) A student or a person applying for admission may waive his right of access to confidential statements described in clause (iii) of subparagraph (C), except that such waiver shall apply to recommendations only if (i) the student is, upon request, notified of the names of all persons making confidential recommendations and (ii) such recommendations are used solely for the purpose for which they were specifically intended. Such waivers may not be required as a condition for admission to, receipt of financial aid from, or receipt of any other services or benefits from such agency or institution.

(2) No funds shall be made available under any applicable program to any educational agency or institution unless the parents of students who are or have been in attendance at a school of such agency or at such institution are provided an opportunity for a hearing by such agency or institution, in accordance with regulations of the Secretary, to challenge the content of such student's education records, in order to insure that the records are not inaccurate, misleading, or otherwise in violation of the privacy rights of students, and to provide an opportunity for the correction or deletion of any such inaccurate, misleading or otherwise inappropriate data contained therein and to insert into such records a written explanation of the parents respecting the content of such records.

(3) For the purposes of this section the term "educational agency or institution" means any public or private agency or institution which is the recipient of funds under any applicable program.

(4)(A) For the purposes of this section, the term "education records" means, except as may be provided otherwise in subparagraph (B), those records, files, documents, and other materials which—

(i) contain information directly related to a student; and (ii) are maintained by an educational agency or institution or by a person acting for such agency or institution.

(B) The term "education records" does not include—

(i) records of instructional, supervisory, and administrative personnel and educational personnel ancillary thereto which are in the sole possession of the maker thereof and which are not accessible or revealed to any other person except a substitute;

(ii) records maintained by a law enforcement unit of the educational agency or institution that were created by that law enforcement unit for the purpose of law enforcement;

(iii) in the case of persons who are employed by an educational agency or institution but who are not in attendance at such agency or institution, records made and maintained in the normal course of business which relate exclusively to such person in that person's capacity as an employee and are not available for use for any other purpose; or

(iv) records on a student who is eighteen years of age or older, or is attending an institution of postsecondary education, which are made or maintained by a physician, psychiatrist, psychologist, or other recognized professional or paraprofessional acting in his professional or paraprofessional capacity, or assisting in that capacity, and which are made, maintained, or used only in connection with the provision of treatment to the student, and are not available to anyone other than persons providing such treatment, except that such records can be personally reviewed by a physician or other appropriate professional of the student's choice.

(5)(A) For the purposes of this section the term "directory information" relating to a student includes the following: the student's name, address, telephone listing, date and place of birth, major field of study, participation in officially recognized activities and sports, weight and height of members of athletic teams, dates of attendance, degrees and awards received, and the most recent previous educational agency or institution attended by the student.

(B) Any educational agency or institution making public directory information shall give public notice of the categories of information which it has designated as such information with respect to each student attending the institution or agency and shall allow a reasonable period of time after such notice has been given for a parent to inform the institution or agency that any or all of the information designated should not be released without the parent's prior consent.

(6) For the purposes of this section, the term "student" includes any person with respect to whom an educational agency or institution maintains education records or personally identifiable information, but does not include a person who has not been in attendance at such agency or institution.

(b) Release of education records; parental consent requirement; exceptions; compliance with judicial orders and subpoenas; audit and evaluation of federally-supported education programs; recordkeeping

(1) No funds shall be made available under any applicable program to any educational agency or institution which has a policy or practice of permitting the release of education records (or personally identifiable information contained therein other than directory information, as defined in paragraph (5) of subsection (a) of this section) of students without the written consent of their parents to any individual, agency, or organization, other than to the following—

(A) other school officials, including teachers within the educational institution or local educational agency, who have been determined by such agency or institution to have legitimate educational interests, including the educational interests of the child for whom consent would otherwise be required;

(B) officials of other schools or school systems in which the student seeks or intends to enroll, upon condition that the student's parents be notified of the transfer, receive a copy of the record if desired, and have an opportunity for a hearing to challenge the content of the record;

(C)(i) authorized representatives of (I) the Comptroller General of the United States, (II) the Secretary, or (III) State educational authorities, under the conditions set forth in paragraph (3), or (ii) authorized representatives of the Attorney General for law enforcement purposes under the same conditions as apply to the Secretary under paragraph (3);

(D) in connection with a student's application for, or receipt of, financial aid;

(E) State and local officials or authorities to whom such information is specifically allowed to be reported or disclosed pursuant to State statute adopted—

(i) before November 19, 1974, if the allowed reporting or disclosure concerns the juvenile justice system and such system's ability to effectively serve the student whose records are released, or

(ii) after November 19, 1974, if—

(I) the allowed reporting or disclosure concerns the juvenile justice system and such system's ability to effectively serve, prior to adjudication, the student whose records are released; and

(II) the officials and authorities to whom such information is disclosed certify in writing to the educational agency or institution that the information will not be disclosed to any other party except as provided under State law without the prior written consent of the parent of the student.

(F) organizations conducting studies for, or on behalf of, educational agencies or institutions for the purpose of developing, validating, or administering predictive tests, administering student aid programs, and improving instruction, if such studies are conducted in such a manner as will not permit the personal identification of students and their parents by persons other than representatives of such organizations and such information will be destroyed when no longer needed for the purpose for which it is conducted;

(G) accrediting organizations in order to carry out their accrediting functions;

(H) parents of a dependent student of such parents, as defined in section 152 of Title 26;

(I) subject to regulations of the Secretary, in connection with an emergency, appropriate persons if the knowledge of such information is necessary to protect the health or safety of the student or other persons; and

(J)(i) the entity or persons designated in a Federal grand jury subpoena, in which case the court shall order, for good cause shown, the educational agency or institution (and any officer, director, employee, agent, or attorney for such agency or institution) on which the subpoena is served, to not disclose to any person the existence or contents of the subpoena or any information furnished to the grand jury in response to the subpoena; and

(ii) the entity or persons designated in any other subpoena issued for a law enforcement purpose, in which case the court or other issuing agency may order, for good cause shown, the educational agency or institution (and any officer, director, employee, agent, or attorney for such agency or institution) on which the subpoena is served, to not disclose to any person the existence or contents of the subpoena or any information furnished in response to the subpoena. . . .

Individuals with Disabilities in Education Act

20 U.S.C. §§1400 *et seq.*

§1401. Definitions

(3) Child with a disability—

(A) In general

The term "child with a disability" means a child—

(i) with mental retardation, hearing impairments (including deafness), speech or language impairments, visual impairments (including blindness), serious emotional disturbance (hereinafter referred to as "emotional disturbance"), orthopedic impairments, autism, traumatic brain injury, other health impairments, or specific learning disabilities; and

(ii) who, by reason thereof, needs special education and related services.

(B) Child aged 3 through 9

The term "child with a disability" for a child aged 3 through 9 may, at the discretion of the State and the local educational agency, include a child—

(i) experiencing developmental delays, as defined by the State and as measured by appropriate diagnostic instruments and procedures, in one or more of the following areas: physical development, cognitive development, communication development, social or emotional development, or adaptive development; and

(ii) who, by reason thereof, needs special education and related services.

(8) Free appropriate public education—

The term "free appropriate public education" means special education and related services that—

(A) have been provided at public expense, under public supervision and direction, and without charge;

(B) meet the standards of the State educational agency;

(C) include an appropriate preschool, elementary, or secondary school education in the State involved; and

(D) are provided in conformity with the individualized education program required under section 1414(d) of this title.

(11) Individualized education program

The term "individualized education program" or "IEP" means a written statement for each child with a disability that is developed, reviewed, and revised in accordance with section 1414(d) of this title.

(12) Individualized family service plan

The term "individualized family service plan" has the meaning given such term in section 1436 of this title.

(15) Local educational agency—

(A) The term "local educational agency" means a public board of education or other public authority legally constituted within a State for either administrative control or direction of, or to perform a service function for, public elementary or secondary schools in a city, county, township, school district, or other political subdivision of a State, or for such combination of school districts or counties as are recognized in a State as an administrative agency for its public elementary or secondary schools.

(B) The term includes—

(i) an educational service agency, as defined in paragraph (4); and

(ii) any other public institution or agency having administrative control and direction of a public elementary or secondary school.

(C) The term includes an elementary or secondary school funded by the Bureau of Indian Affairs, but only to the extent that such inclusion makes the school eligible for programs for which specific eligibility is not provided to the school in another provision of law and the school does not have a student population that is smaller than the student population of the local educational agency receiving assistance under this chapter with the smallest student population, except that the school shall not be subject to the jurisdiction of any State educational agency other than the Bureau of Indian Affairs.

(19) Parent

The term "parent"—

(A) includes a legal guardian; and

(B) except as used in sections 1415(b)(2) and 1439(a)(5) of this title, includes an individual assigned under either of those sections to be a surrogate parent.

(22) Related services

The term "related services" means transportation, and such developmental, corrective, and other supportive services (including speech-language pathology and audiology services, psychological services, physical and occupational therapy, recreation, including therapeutic recreation, social work services, counseling services, including rehabilitation counseling, orientation and mobility services, and medical services, except that such medical services shall be for diagnostic and evaluation purposes only) as may be required to assist a child with a disability to benefit from special education, and includes the early identification and assessment of disabling conditions in children.

(25) Special education

The term "special education" means specially designed instruction, at no cost to parents, to meet the unique needs of a child with a disability, including—

(A) instruction conducted in the classroom, in the home, in hospitals and institutions, and in other settings; and

(B) instruction in physical education.

(28) State educational agency

The term "State educational agency" means the State board of education or other agency or officer primarily responsible for the State supervision of public elementary and secondary schools, or, if there is no such officer or agency, an officer or agency designated by the Governor or by State law.

The No Child Left Behind Act of 2001

20 U.S.C.A. *§6301 et seq.*

Title I—Improving the Academic Achievement of the Disadvantaged

20 USC §§6323, 6369, 6369a, 6369b, 6370.

Sec. 101. Improving the Academic Achievement of the Disadvantaged Title I of the Elementary and Secondary Education Act of 1965 (20 U.S.C. §6301 et seq.) is amended to read as follows:

Title I—Improving the Academic Achievement of the Disadvantaged

SEC. 1001. Statement of Purpose.

The purpose of this title is to ensure that all children have a fair, equal, and significant opportunity to obtain a high-quality education and reach, at a minimum, proficiency on challenging State academic achievement standards and state academic assessments. This purpose can be accomplished by—

(1) ensuring that high-quality academic assessments, accountability systems, teacher preparation and training, curriculum, and instructional

materials are aligned with challenging State academic standards so that students, teachers, parents, and administrators can measure progress against common expectations for student academic achievement;

(2) meeting the educational needs of low-achieving children in our Nation's highest-poverty schools, limited English proficient children, migratory children, children with disabilities, Indian children, neglected or delinquent children, and young children in need of reading assistance;

(3) closing the achievement gap between high- and low-performing children, especially the achievement gaps between minority and nonminority students, and between disadvantaged children and their more advantaged peers;

(4) holding schools, local educational agencies, and States accountable for improving the academic achievement of all students, and identifying and turning around low-performing schools that have failed to provide a high-quality education to their students, while providing alternatives to students in such schools to enable the students to receive a high-quality education;

(5) distributing and targeting resources sufficiently to make a difference to local educational agencies and schools where needs are greatest;

(6) improving, and strengthening accountability, teaching, and learning by using State assessment systems designed to ensure that students are meeting challenging State academic achievement and content standards and increasing achievement overall, but especially for the disadvantaged;

(7) providing greater decision-making authority and flexibility to schools and teachers in exchange for greater responsibility for student performance;

(8) providing children an enriched and accelerated educational program, including the use of schoolwide programs or additional services that increase the amount and quality of instructional time;

(9) promoting schoolwide reform and ensuring the access of children to effective, scientifically based instructional strategies and challenging academic content;

(10) significantly elevating the quality of instruction by providing staff in participating schools with substantial opportunities for professional development;

(11) coordinating services under all parts of this title with each other, with other educational services, and, to the extent feasible, with other agencies providing services to youth, children, and families; and

(12) affording parents substantial and meaningful opportunities to participate in the education of their children. . . .

(b) ACADEMIC STANDARDS, ACADEMIC ASSESSMENTS, AND ACCOUNTABILITY—

(1) CHALLENGING ACADEMIC STANDARDS—

(A) IN GENERAL—Each State plan shall demonstrate that the State has adopted challenging academic content standards and challenging student academic achievement standards that will be used by the State, its local educational agencies, and its schools to carry out this part, except that a State shall not be required to submit such standards to the Secretary.

(B) SAME STANDARDS—The academic standards required by subparagraph (A) shall be the same academic standards that the State applies to all schools and children in the State.

(C) SUBJECTS—The State shall have such academic standards for all public elementary school and secondary school children, including children served under this part, in subjects determined by the State, but including at least mathematics, reading or language arts, and (beginning in the 2005-2006 school year) science, which shall include the same knowledge, skills, and levels of achievement expected of all children.

(D) CHALLENGING ACADEMIC STANDARDS—Standards under this paragraph shall include—

(i) challenging academic content standards in academic subjects that—

(I) specify what children are expected to know and be able to do;

(II) contain coherent and rigorous content; and

(III) encourage the teaching of advanced skills; and

(ii) challenging student academic achievement standards that—

(I) are aligned with the State's academic content standards;

(II) describe two levels of high achievement (proficient and advanced) that determine how well children are mastering the material in the State academic content standards; and

(III) describe a third level of achievement (basic) to provide complete information about the progress of the lower-achieving children toward mastering the proficient and advanced levels of achievement.

(E) INFORMATION—For the subjects in which students will be served under this part, but for which a State is not required by subparagraphs (A), (B), and (C) to develop, and has not otherwise developed, such academic standards, the State plan shall describe a strategy for ensuring that

(F) EXISTING STANDARDS.—Nothing in this part shall prohibit a State from revising, consistent with this section, any standard adopted under this part before or after the date of enactment of the No Child Left Behind Act of 2001.

(2) ACCOUNTABILITY—

(A) IN GENERAL—Each State plan shall demonstrate that the State has developed and is implementing a single, statewide State accountability system that will be effective in ensuring that all local educational agencies, public elementary schools, and public secondary schools make adequate yearly progress as defined under this paragraph. Each State accountability system shall—

(i) be based on the academic standards and academic assessments adopted under paragraphs (1) and (3), and other academic indicators consistent with subparagraph (C)(vi) and (vii), and shall take into account the achievement of all public elementary school and secondary school students;

(ii) be the same accountability system the State uses for all public elementary schools and secondary schools or all local educational agencies in the State, except that public elementary schools, secondary schools, and local educational agencies not participating under this part are not subject to the requirements of section 1116; and

(iii) include sanctions and rewards, such as bonuses and recognition, the State will use to hold local educational agencies and public elementary schools and secondary schools accountable for student achievement and for ensuring that they make adequate yearly progress in accordance with the State's definition under subparagraphs (B) and (C).

(B) ADEQUATE YEARLY PROGRESS—Each State plan shall demonstrate, based on academic assessments described in paragraph (3), and in accordance with this paragraph, what constitutes adequate yearly progress of the State, and of all public elementary schools, secondary schools, and local educational agencies in the State, toward enabling all public elementary school and secondary school students to meet the State's student academic achievement standards, while working toward the goal of narrowing the achievement gaps in the State, local educational agencies, and schools.

(C) DEFINITION—"Adequate yearly progress" shall be defined by the State in a manner that—

(i) applies the same high standards of academic achievement to all public elementary school and secondary school students in the State;

(ii) is statistically valid and reliable;

(iii) results in continuous and substantial academic improvement for all students;

(iv) measures the progress of public elementary schools, secondary schools and local educational agencies and the State based primarily on the academic assessments described in paragraph (3);

(v) includes separate measurable annual objectives for continuous and substantial improvement for each of the following:

(I) The achievement of all public elementary school and secondary school students.

(II) The achievement of—

(aa) economically disadvantaged students;

(bb) students from major racial and ethnic groups;

(cc) students with disabilities; and

(dd) students with limited English proficiency; except that disaggregation of data under subclause (II) shall not be required in a case in which the number of students in a category is insufficient to yield statistically reliable information or the results would reveal personally identifiable information about an individual student;

(vi) in accordance with subparagraph (D), includes graduation rates for public secondary school students (defined as the percentage of students who graduate from secondary school with a regular diploma in the standard number of years) and at least one other academic indicator, as determined by the State for all public elementary school students; and

(vii) in accordance with subparagraph (D), at the State's discretion, may also include other academic indicators, as determined by the State for all public school students, measured separately for each group described in clause (v), such as achievement on additional State or locally administered assessments, decreases in grade-to-grade retention rates, attendance rates, and changes in the percentages of students completing gifted and talented, advanced placement, and college preparatory courses.

APPENDIX C

REPRESENTATIVE STATE CONSTITUTIONAL PROVISIONS GOVERNING EDUCATION

A. THE PROVISION OF FREE PUBLIC SCHOOLS FOR ALL

All of the states have constitutional language like Oklahoma's that either directly or indirectly requires the establishment and maintenance of public schools:

> The Legislation shall establish and maintain a system of free public schools wherein all the children of the State may be educated. . . . 1907 Const. of Oklahoma, art. XIII.

In addition to Oklahoma, the following 16 states have constitutional language explicitly requiring that public schools be "free": Arizona, Connecticut, Florida, Georgia, Illinois, Indiana, Maine, Maryland, Missouri, Montana, Nebraska, New York, South Carolina, South Dakota, Tennessee and Virginia.

B. THE PROVISION OF PUBLIC EDUCATION FOR DEFINED AGES

The following 11 states have constitutional language requiring public education for students of a defined age or grade level: Alabama, Arizona, Colorado, Connecticut, Georgia, Illinois, Missouri, Montana, Nebraska, New Jersey and Wisconsin. For instance, New Jersey requires the Legislature to provide:

> free public schools for the instruction of all the children in the State between the ages of five and eighteen years. New Jersey Const. (1947), art. VIII, sec. IV.

C. DECLARATIONS OF THE VALUE OF PUBLIC EDUCATION

The following 20 states have constitutional language expressing the value of public education to the state (i.e., the importance of a "general diffusion of knowledge" or the "fundamental goal" of providing education to all citizens): Arkansas, California, Florida, Idaho, Illinois, Indiana, Maine, Massachusetts, Michigan, Minnesota, Missouri, Montana, New Hampshire, North Carolina, North Dakota, Rhode Island, South Dakota, Tennessee, Texas, and Vermont. For example, Texas' Constitution declares:

> A general diffusion of knowledge being essential to the preservation of the liberties and rights of the people, it shall be the duty of the Legislature of the State to establish and make suitable provision for the support and maintenance of an efficient system of public free schools. Texas Const., art. VII, sec. 1.

Moreover, Florida affirmatively declares in its Constitution that, "[t]he education of children is a fundamental value of the people in the State. . . . " Florida Const. (1968), art. IX, sec. 1. *See also* Illinois Const. (1970), art. X, sec. 1 (declaring the "educational development of all persons to the limits of their capacities" to be a "fundamental goal").

D. THE PROVISION OF AN EFFICIENT EDUCATIONAL SYSTEM

The following 12 states have constitutional language requiring an "efficient" educational system: Arkansas, Delaware, Florida, Illinois, Kentucky, Maryland, Minnesota, New Jersey, Ohio, Pennsylvania, Texas and West Virginia.

E. THE PROVISION OF A THOROUGH OR UNIFORM SYSTEM OF EDUCATION

The following 16 states require a "thorough" or "uniform" educational system: Colorado, Florida, Idaho, Indiana, Minnesota, Nevada, New Jersey, New Mexico, Ohio, Oregon, Pennsylvania, South Dakota, Washington, West Virginia, Wisconsin and Wyoming.

APPENDIX D

REPRESENTATIVE STATE TEACHER CERTIFICATION AND TENURE REQUIREMENTS

A. CERTIFICATION

New York's recently revised teacher certification and professional development requirements provide in pertinent part:

§80-3.3 Requirements for the initial certificate.

(a) General requirements:

(1) Duration. The initial certificate shall be valid for three years from its effective date. A candidate may be granted an extension of the time validity of the initial certificate for a period not to exceed one additional year for the purpose of completing a master's or higher degree program needed to fulfill the education requirement for a professional certificate, pursuant to Section 80-3.4 of this Subpart, provided that the candidate completes at least 24 semester hours of such study by the end of the three-year period of the initial certificate. The application for the one-year extension of the validity of the initial certificate shall be accompanied by documentation satisfactory to the commissioner demonstrating the candidate's progress to date in the graduate program and the compelling need for additional time to complete such program. At the expiration of the additional one-year period, the time validity of an initial certificate shall not be extended again for the same purpose.

(2) A candidate with a baccalaureate or higher degree who holds a certificate issued by the National Board for Professional Teaching Standards in a title which the department has determined to be equivalent to the title of the initial certificate sought shall be deemed to have met the requirements for such initial certificate prescribed in subdivision (b) or (c) of this section.

(3) Additional requirements for certain candidates.

(i) A candidate who has not applied for the initial certificate within two years of completing his or her program for such certificate, meeting all educational requirements for the initial certificate, shall be required to demonstrate successful completion of the requirements set forth in subparagraphs (ii) and (iii) of this paragraph, which shall be additional to that prescribed in subdivision (b) or (c) of this section, as applicable.

(ii) The candidate shall successfully complete acceptable professional development, prorated at a rate of one and one-half clock hours per month, beginning two years after completing the program for the initial certificate and ending on the date the candidate submits his or her application to the department for the initial certificate, up to a maximum of 75 clock hours. The professional development shall be completed in any month during such computation period, except that in the case of a candidate required to complete 75 clock hours of professional development, 45 of such clock hours shall be completed within one year prior to the candidate's applying to the department for the initial certificate. The definition of acceptable professional development and the measurement of professional development study shall be that prescribed in Section 80-3.6 of this Subpart.

(iii) The candidate shall submit evidence of having achieved a satisfactory level of performance on the New York State Teacher Certification Examination liberal arts and sciences test, written assessment of teaching skills, and content specialty test(s) in the area of the certificate, which shall be taken within one year prior to the candidate's applying to the department for the initial certificate.

§80-3.4 Requirements for the professional certificate.

(a) General requirements.

(1) Validity of certificate. The professional certificate shall be continuously valid, provided that the professional development requirement prescribed in Section 80-3.6 of this Subpart is met by the professional certificate holder. The professional certificate holder shall be required to meet such professional development requirement to maintain the continued validity of the professional certificate.

(2) The candidate shall meet the requirements for the initial certificate for the certificate title sought or the requirements for the transitional certificate for career changers and others holding a graduate degree or professional degree, as prescribed in Section 80-3.5(a) of this Subpart, for the certificate title sought.

(b) Requirements for professional certificates in all titles in classroom teaching service, except in a specific career and technical subject within the field of agriculture, business and marketing, family and consumer sciences, health, a technical area, or a trade (grades 7 through 12). The candidate shall meet the requirements in each of the following paragraphs.

(1) Education. The candidate shall meet the education requirement by successfully completing:

(i) a program registered pursuant to Section 52.21 of this Title or its equivalent;

(ii) a master's or higher degree program in the content core of the initial certificate or in a related content area; or

(iii) a master's or higher degree program in any field, provided that the candidate has completed at least 12 semester hours of graduate study in the content core of the initial certificate or in a related content area.

(2) Teaching experience. The candidate shall successfully complete three school years of teaching experience, or its equivalent. The candidate who completes this requirement in total or part through teaching in New York public schools shall be required to participate in a mentored program in the first year of employment, as prescribed in Part 100 of this Title, unless the candidate has successfully completed two years of teaching experience prior to such teaching in the public schools.

§80-3.6 Professional development requirement.

(a) Definitions. As used in this section:

(1) Regularly employed by an applicable school in New York means employed 90 days or more in a professional development year by a single applicable school in New York in a position requiring certification pursuant to this Part. For the purposes of this definition, a day of employment shall include a day actually worked in whole or in part, or a day not actually worked but a day paid. In addition, the City School District of the City of New York and any of its components, including but not limited to community school districts, high school divisions, special education divisions, and the Chancellor's district, shall be considered together a single applicable school in New York.

(2) Professional development period means the five-year period commencing on July 1st after the effective date of the triggering certificate, and each subsequent five-year period thereafter.

(3) Professional development year shall mean each year of the five-year professional development period, beginning on July 1st and ending the following June 30th.

(4) Applicable school in New York means a school district or board of cooperative educational services located in New York State. For purposes of this definition, the City School District of the City of New York and any of its components shall be considered together a single school district.

(5) Triggering certificate means the earliest issued certificate which requires the holder to take professional development, pursuant to subdivision (b) of this section.

(b) Mandatory requirement:

(1) Requirements.

(i) Requirement for holders of professional certificates in the classroom teaching service. The holder of a professional certificate in the classroom teaching service shall be required to successfully complete 175 clock hours of acceptable professional development during the professional development period.

(ii) Requirement for holders of level III teaching assistant certificates. The holder of a level III teaching assistant certificate shall be required to successfully complete 75 clock hours of acceptable professional development during the professional development period.

(2) The professional development requirement prescribed in paragraph (1) of this subdivision shall be reduced by 10 percent for each professional development year the certificate holder is not regularly employed by an applicable school in New York.

(3) The professional development requirement prescribed in this subdivision may be completed at any time during the five-year professional development period.

(4) Notwithstanding the requirements of paragraph (1) of this subdivision, a holder of a certificate who achieves certification from the National Board for Professional Teaching Standards shall be deemed to have met the professional development requirement, prescribed in this subdivision, for the five-year professional development period in which such national board certification is achieved.

B. TENURE

California's statutory requirements governing teacher tenure (permanent employment) provide:

> 44929.20 Every certificated employee of a school district of any type or class having an average daily attendance of less than 250, and every certificated employee of any school district in a position requiring a supervision or administration credential, may be offered a continuing contract to cover a period longer than one year but not to exceed four years.
>
> 44929.21 (a) Every employee of a school district of any type or class having an average daily attendance of 250 or more who, after having been employed by the district for three complete consecutive school years in a position or positions requiring certification qualifications, is reelected for the next succeeding school year to a position requiring certification qualifications shall, at the commencement of the succeeding school year be classified as and become a permanent employee of the district.
>
> This subdivision shall apply only to probationary employees whose probationary period commenced prior to the 1983-84 fiscal year.
>
> (b) Every employee of a school district of any type or class having an average daily attendance of 250 or more who, after having been employed by the district for three complete consecutive school years in a position or positions requiring certification qualifications, is reelected for the next succeeding school year to a position requiring certification qualifications shall, at the commencement of the succeeding school year be classified as and become a permanent employee of the district.
>
> The governing board shall notify the employee, on or before March 15 of the employee's second complete consecutive school year of employment by the district in a position or positions requiring certification qualifications of the decision to reelect or not reelect the employee for the next succeeding school year to the position. In the event that the governing board does not give notice pursuant to this section on or before March 15, the employee shall be deemed reelected for the next succeeding school year.

This subdivision shall apply only to probationary employees whose probationary period commenced during the 1983-84 fiscal year or any fiscal year thereafter.

44929.23. (a) The governing board of a school district of any type or class having an average daily attendance of less than 250 pupils may classify as a permanent employee of the district any employee, who, after having been employed by the school district for three complete school years in a position or positions requiring certification qualifications, is reelected for the next succeeding school year to a position requiring certification qualifications. If that classification is not made, the employee shall not attain permanent status and may be reelected from year to year thereafter without becoming a permanent employee until a change in classification is made.

(b) Notwithstanding subdivision (a), Section 44929.1 shall apply to certificated employees employed by a school district, if the governing board elects to dismiss probationary employees pursuant to Section 44948.2. If that election is made by the governing board of the school district thereafter shall classify as a permanent employee of the district any probationary employee, who, after being employed for two complete consecutive school years in a position or positions requiring certification qualifications, is reelected for the next succeeding school year to a position requiring certification qualifications as required by Section 44929.21. Any probationary employee who has been employed by the district for two or more consecutive years on the date of that election in a position or positions requiring certification qualifications shall be classified as a permanent employee of the district.

(c) If the classification is not made pursuant to subdivision (a) or (b) the employee shall not attain permanent status and may be reelected from year to year thereafter without becoming a permanent employee until the classification is made.

APPENDIX E

EDUCATION RESOURCES AND WEBSITES

A. EARLY CHILDHOOD EDUCATION

Developmentally Appropriate Practice in Early Childhood Education
http://www.ed.psu.edu/k-12/edpgs/su96/ece/dap1.html

Early Child Development
http://www.worldbank.org/children/

Early Childhood Care and Development
http://www.ecdgroup.com/

Early Childhood Education
http://www.edpsych.com/

Early Childhood Education Online
http://www.ume.maine.edu/ECEOL-L/

Early Childhood Today
http://place.scholastic.com/ect

National Academy of Child Development
http://www.nacd.org

National Association for the Education of Young Children
http://www.naeyc.org/

National Association of Early Childhood Specialists in State Departments of Education
http://www.ericps.crc.uicuc.edu/naecs/

National Head Start Association
http://www.nhsa.org/

National Network for Child Care—Child Development
http://www.nncc.org

Zero to Three
http://www.zerotothree.org/

B. SPECIAL EDUCATION

Americans with Disabilities Act Document Center
http://www.jan.wvu.edu/links/adalinks.htm

Behavioral Interventions and Support
http://www.pbis.org

Classroom Discipline
http://7-12educators.miningco.com/msub49.htm

Classroom Management and Special Education
http://www.pacificnet.net/~mandel/SpecialEducation.html

IDEA 97
http://www.ed.gov/offices/OSERS/IDEA

Individualized Education Program: The Progress
http://www.ldonline.org/ld_indepth/iep/iep_process.html

School and Classroom Discipline
http://www.nwrel.org/scpd/sirs/5/cu9.html

Seven Habits of Highly Effective IEP Teams
http://www.ldonline.org/ld_indepth/iep/seven_habits.html

Tips on Classroom Management for ADD
http://www.enteract.com/~peregrin/add/50clas.html

Writing Individualized Education Programs for Success
http://www.ldonline.org/ld_indepth/iep/success _ieps.html

Your Child's IEP—Practice and Legal Guidance for Parents
http://www.ldonline.org/ld_indepth/iep/iep_guidance.html

C. DIVERSITY

Center for Multilingual and Multicultural Research
http://www.usc.edu/dept/education/CMMR/

Center for Research on Educational, Diversity & Excellence
http://www.crede.ucsc.edu

Consortium for Equity in Standards and Testing
http://www.Csteep.bc.edu/ctest

Diversity in the Classroom
http://www.princeton.edu/~djbutler/ditclink.htm

Equity and Cultural Diversity
http://eric-Web.tc.columbia.edu/equity

Multicultural/Bilingual Education
http://departments.weber.edu/mbe/htmls/mbe.html

National Association for Bilingual Education
http://www.nabe.org

Tolerance
http://www.splcenter.org/teachingtolerance/tt-index.html

D. EDUCATIONAL STANDARDS

Content Knowledge and Standards
http://www.mcrel.org/standards-benchmarks/

Developing Educational Standards
http://edstandards.org/Standards.html

Home School Advisor
http://www.hsadvisor.com/

National Center for Research on Evaluation, Standards and Student Testing
http://cresst96.cse.ucla.edu

National Center on Educational Outcomes
http://www.coled.umn.edu.NCEO/

National Education Goals
http://www.negp.gov

National Science Education Standards
http://www.nap.edu/readingroom/books/nses/html/contents.html

National Standards for Art Education
http://www.artteacherconnection.com/pages/standards/htm

National Standards for Foreign Language Education
http://www.sscnet.ucla.edu/nchs/standards.html

E. EDUCATION LAW

Cornell Law School
http://www.law.cornell.edu/topics/education.html

Department of Education
http://www.ed.gov

Ed.Net.Briefs
http://www.edbriefs.com

Education Law
http://www.edlaw.net

Education Law Association
http://www.educationlaw.org/

Education Law Center
http://www.edlawcenter.org/

Education Library
http://www.library.stmarytx.edu/acadlib/doc/electronic/dbeduc.htm

Education Review
http://www.ed.asu.edu/edrev

Educator's Reference Desk
http://www.eduref.org/

Legal Database
http://www.legal-database.com/educationlaw.htm

No Child Left Behind
http://www.nclb.esc.org/nclb

No Child Left Behind—Government
http://www.ed.gov/nclb/landing.jhtml?src=In

Thomas—Legislative Information on the Internet
http://thomas.loc.gov

Wrightslaw—Special Education Law & Advocacy
http://www.wrightslaw.com/

F. EDUCATIONAL DATA SOURCES

Environmental Protection Agency
http://www.epa.gov

Fedstats
http://www.fedstats.gov

First Government
http://www.firstgov.gov

House of Representatives
http://www.house.gov

Library of Congress
http://marvel.loc.gov/

National Archives and Records Administration
http://www.archives.gov/

National Science Foundation
http://www.nsf.gov

Office of Elementary and Secondary Education Programs
http://www.ed.gov/offices/OESE/

Office of Postsecondary Education Programs
http://www.ed.gov/offices/OPE/

Senate
http://www.senate.gov

U.S. Department of Education Funding Opportunities
http://www.ed.gov/topics/topics.jsp?&top=Grants+%26+Contracts

U.S. Department of Education Grants and Contracts Information
http://www.ed.gov.GrantApps/

White House
http://www.whitehouse.gov/WH/Welcome.html

G. STATE EDUCATION DEPARTMENTS

Yahoo! State Governments
http://dir.yahoo.com/Government/U_S_Government/State_Government/

Alabama
http://www.alsde.edu

Alaska
http://www.educ.state.ak.us

Arizona
http://www.ade.state.az.us

Arkansas
http://arkedu.sk12.ar.us

California
http://goldmine.cde.ca.gov

Colorado
http://www.cde.state.co.us

Connecticut
http://www.state.ct.us/sde

Delaware
http://www.doe.state.de.us

District of Columbia
http://www.k12.dc.us

Florida
http://www.firn.edu/doe

Georgia
http://www.doe.k12ga.us

Hawaii
http://www.k12.hi.us

Idaho
http://www.state.id.us

Illinois
http://www.isbe.state.il.us

Indiana
http://www.doe.state.in.us

Iowa
http://www.state.ia.us/educate

Kansas
http://www.ksbe.state.ks.us

Kentucky
http://www.kde.state.ky.us

Louisiana
http://www.doe.state.la.us

Maine
http://janus.state.me.us/education/homepage.htm

Maryland
http://www.msde.state.md.us

Massachusetts
http://info.doe.mass.edu

Michigan
http://www.mde.state.mi.us

Minnesota
http://www.educ.state.mn.us

Mississippi
http://www.mde.k12.ms.us

Missouri
http://services.dese.state.mo.us

Montana
http://www.metnet.state.mt.us

Nebraska
http://www.nde.state.ne.us

Nevada
http://www.nsn.k12.nv.us/nvdoe

New Hampshire
http://www.ed.state.nh.us

New Jersey
http://www.state.nj.us.education

New Mexico
http://sde.state.nm.us

New York
http://www.nysed.gov

North Carolina
http://www.dpi.state.nc.us

North Dakota
http://www.dpi.state.nd.us

Ohio
http://www.ode.state.oh.us

Oklahoma
http://sde.state.ok.us

Oregon
http://www.ode.state.or.us

Pennsylvania
http://www.pde.psu.edu

Rhode Island
http://www.ridoe.net/

South Carolina
http://www.sde.state.sc.us

South Dakota
http://www.state.sd.us/state/executive.deca

Tennessee
http://www.state.tn.us/education

Texas
http://www.tea.state.tx.us

Utah
http://www.usoe.k12.ut.us

Vermont
http://www.state.vt.us/educ

Virginia
http://www.pen.k12.va.us

Washington
http://www.k12.wa.us

West Virginia
http://wvde.state.wv.us

Wisconsin
http://www.dpi.state.wi.us

Wyoming
http://www.k12.wy.us

H. EDUCATIONAL ADMINISTRATION

American Association of School Administrators
http://www.aasa.org

American Council on Education
http://www.acenet.edu

American Educational Research Association
http://www.aera.net

American Federation of Teachers
http://www.aft.org

Association of American Universities
http://www.tulane.edu-/~aau

National Association of Elementary School Principals
http://www.naesp.org/naesp.htm

National Association of Secondary School Principals
http://www.nassp.org

National Association of State Boards of Education
http://www.nasbe.org

National Center for Research on Teacher Learning
http://ncrtl.msu.edu

National Education Association (NEA)
http://www.nea.org

National Middle School Association
http://www.nmsa.org

National School Board Association
http://www.nsba.org

Parent Teacher Association
http://www.pta.org

Public Education Network
http://www.publiceducation.org

I. EDUCATION REFORM

Association of Effective Schools
http://www.mes.org

Center for Educational Innovation
http://www.ceiintl.org.

Center for Educational Reform
http://www.edreform.com

Chronicle of Higher Education
http://www.chronicle.merit.edu

Institute for Research on Learning
http://www.irl.org

National Assessment of Educational Progress
http://www.nces.ed.gov/nationsreportcard

National Association for Gifted Children
http://www.nagc.org

National Association of Independent Schools
http://www.nais.org

National Center for Education and the Economy
http://www.ncee.org

National Institute for Literacy
http://www.novel.nifl.gov

Rethinking Schools
http://www.rethinkingschools.org

Smithsonian Institute
http://www.si.edu

Teach for America
http://www.teachforamerica.org

U.S. Charter Schools
http://www.uscharterschools.org

Table of Cases

Principal cases are denoted by italics.

Index